THE AMERICAN CHALLENGE:
A New History of the United States, Vol II
Second Edition

THE AMERICAN CHALLENGE:
A New History of the United States, Vol II
Second Edition

John Moretta
Houston Community College System
Houston, Texas

Michael Phillips
Collin College
Plano, Texas

Keith J. Volanto
Collin College
Plano, Texas

Edited by
Keith J. Volanto
Michael Phillips

Abigail Press   Wheaton, IL 60189

Design and Production: Abigail Press
Typesetting: Abigail Press
Typeface: AGaramond
Cover Art: Sam Tolia

THE AMERICAN CHALLENGE:
A New History of the United States, Vol. II

Second Edition, 2013
Printed in the United States of America
Translation rights reserved by the authors
ISBN 1-890919-77-2 ISBN 978-1-890919-77-1

Copyright @ by Abigail Press Inc., 2050 Middleton Dr., Wheaton, IL 60189

All rights reserved. No part of the material protected by the copyright notice may be reproduced or utilized in any form or by any means, electronic or mechanical, including photocopy, recording, or any information storage and retrieval system, without permission in writing from the publisher.

Contents in Brief

Chapter Seventeen
    RECONSTRUCTION: The Turning Point That Never Turned   470

Chapter Eighteen
    THE RISE OF INDUSTRIAL AMERICA & THE POLITICS OF THE NEW ORDER   512

Chapter Nineteen
    INDIAN EXPULSION AND WHITE SETTLEMENT IN THE TRANS-MISSOURI WEST   552

Chapter Twenty
    THE IMPERIAL REPUBLIC   582

Chapter Twenty-one
    THE PROGRESSIVE REFORMATION OF INDUSTRIAL AMERICA   612

Chapter Twenty-two
    THE "GREAT" WAR: World War I   644

Chapter Twenty-three
    THE CONTENTIOUS TWENTIES   678

Chapter Twenty-four
    THE GREAT DEPRESSION AND THE NEW DEAL   708

Chapter Twenty-five
    DEMOCRACY, FASCISM, AND COMMUNISM AT WAR, 1921-1945   744

Chapter Twenty-six
    THE ORIGINS OF THE COLD WAR   794

Chapter Twenty-seven
    AMERICAN CULTURE FROM 1945-1960   836

Chapter Twenty-eight
    REFORM AND BACKLASH UNDER KENNEDY AND JOHNSON   874

Chapter Twenty-nine
    ROLLING THUNDER: The Vietnam War Under Kennedy and Johnson   914

Chapter Thirty
    THE NIGHTMARE YEAR, 1968   948

Chapter Thirty-one
    AMERICAN FRUSTRATION AND DECLINE IN THE 1970s   982

Chapter Thirty-two
    AMERICAN CULTURE AND THE COUNTERCULTURE OF THE 1960s and 1970s   1022

Chapter Thirty-three
    THE RISE OF CONSERVATISM: Ronald Reagan to George H.W. Bush   1058

Chapter Thirty-four
    A DIVIDED AMERICA: Bill Clinton to George W. Bush   1090

Chapter Thirty-five
    BARACK OBAMA: A Milestone in United States History   1136

APPENDIX
    A. Declaration of Independence   1156
    B. Constitution of the United States   1158
    C. Presidential Elections   1171
    D. Supreme Court Justices   1175
    E. Admission of States to the Union   1178
    F. Population Growth   1179

GLOSSARY   1180

INDEX   1210

Contents

CHAPTER SEVENTEEN
RECONSTRUCTION: The Turning Point That Never Turned 470
   Confederacy's Defeat 472
   Reconstruction's Overarching Issues 474
   Wartime/Presidential Reconstruction 475
      Abraham Lincoln 475
      Radical Republicans and Reconstruction 477
   Andrew Johnson and Reconstruction 478
      Johnson's Reconstruction Policy 480
      The Black Suffrage Issue in the North 480
      Southern Defiance 480
      The Black Codes 481
   Land and Labor in the Postwar South 481
      The Freedmen's Bureau 482
      The Issue of Land for the Landless 484
   The Origins of Radical Reconstruction 484
      The Fourteenth Amendment 485
      The 1866 Congressional Elections 486
      The Reconstruction Acts of 1867 487
      The White Backlash During Presidential Reconstruction: The 1866 Race Riots in
      Memphis and New Orleans 488
   The Impeachment of Andrew Johnson 490
   The Southern Response to the Reconstruction Acts 492
   The Completion of Formal Reconstruction 493
   The First Grant Administration 494
      The Election of 1868 494
      The Fifteenth Amendment 496
      Grant in the White House 497
      Civil Service Reform 499
      Foreign Policy Issues 499
   The White Backlash Continues 502
      The 1872 Presidential Election 503
      The Panic of 1873 504
   Retreat From Reconstruction 505
      The 1876 Presidential Election 507
   Chronology 509
   Review Questions 510
   Glossary of Important People and Concepts 510
   Suggested Readings 511

CHAPTER EIGHTEEN
THE RISE OF INDUSTRIAL AMERICA & THE POLITICS OF THE NEW ORDER 512
   The Railroads: The United States' First Big Business 516
      Andrew Carnegie 518
      John D. Rockefeller, Standard Oil and the Trust 520
      American Inventors and the Plutocracy 521
      The Emergence of Mass Marketing 523

The Flush Toilet: Technology Changes Daily American Life...524
From Competition to Consolidation: The Rise of the Corporation..................................525
   J. P. Morgan and Finance Capitalism..526
Social Darwinism and the Gospel of Wealth...527
Internal Migration and European Immigration..529
   Why They Came..529
   Immigrant Labor...530
   From the Farm to the City...531
The New South..533
Laissez Faire in Theory and Practice...534
   Labor Strife...534
   The Great Railroad Strike of 1877...535
   Haymarket Square...536
   Henry George and Edward Bellamy...537
   The Homestead Lockout..538
   The Pullman Strike...538
Gilded Age Politics..539
   The Political Culture of the Gilded Age...539
   Patronage Politics in the States..540
   The Shadow Presidents..541
1884: The Democrats Finally Win the Big One..543
   Grover Cleveland in the White House...543
   Tariffs and Pensions..543
The 1888 Election..545
The Railroads, the Trusts, and the Federal Government..545
   The Fight for Free Silver..546
   The Depression of 1893-1897...547
Changing World...548
Chronology..549
Review Questions..550
Glossary of Important People and Concepts...550
Suggested Readings...551

CHAPTER NINETEEN
INDIAN EXPULSION AND WHITE SETTLEMENT IN THE TRANS-MISSOURI WEST........552

Western Indians Before the Civil War...554
   Conflicting Pressures...555
Massacres and Detention During the Civil War..556
Conquest by the Railroad..557
   The Homestead Act..558
The Western Economy, Environmental Destruction, and Crime..559
   Billy the Kid...561
   Outlaw Chic...563
Women in the West..564
   Abortion Restriction in the West...566
Chinese Workers..567
Mexican Labor...568
Buffalo Soldiers...568
African Americans and the Western Labor Movement...569
   Black Colonies in Oklahoma...570
The Reservation Era..570

    The Buffalo Massacre 571
    Little Big Horn 571
Geronimo and the Twilight of Indian Resistance 573
    The Dawes Severalty Act 574
The Populist Uprising... 574
    Forming the People's Party 575
    The 1896 Presidential Election... 576
    The Collapse of Populism 577
The Real and Mythic West.. 577
    Joseph, Chief of the Nez Percé.. 578
Chronology.. 579
Review Questions... 580
Glossary of Important People and Concepts 580
Suggested Readings.. 581

CHAPTER TWENTY
THE IMPERIAL REPUBLIC 582
    America's Quest for Empire: 1880-1900 584
        Voices for Expansion 584
        The Imperialists 585
        Admiral Alfred Thayer Mahan and the Rise of American Militarism 586
    The Spanish-American War 588
        "A Splendid Little War" 590
    The United States Becomes a World Power 592
        Critics of Empire: The Anti-Imperialists.. 594
    Guerrilla War in the Philippines, 1898-1902 595
        Controlling Cuban and Puerto Rico.. 596
    The United States and China: The Open Door Policy 597
        The Boxer Rebellion 598
    Theodore Roosevelt and the Foundation of American Foreign Policy 598
        The Roosevelt Corollary.. 600
        The Panama Canal 600
        Political Cartoons and American Imperialism 606
    William Howard Taft and Dollar Diplomacy 607
    United States Expansion 608
    Chronology 609
    Review Questions... 610
    Glossary of Important People and Concepts 610
    Suggested Readings.. 611

CHAPTER TWENTY-ONE
THE PROGRESSIVE REFORMATION OF INDUSTRIAL AMERICA 612
    The Nature of Progressivism... 614
    Influences Upon Progressivism 615
    The Strands of Progressivism 615
    The Muckrakers... 616
    Local Urban Reforms.. 616
    State-Level Reforms.. 618
        Labor Reforms 618
        Prohibition 621

Woman Suffrage... 621
Political Reforms 622
Robert La Follette and the "Wisconsin Idea".. 623
Washington and Du Bois 624
Jack Johnson (1878-1946) 625
National Reform Under Roosevelt 626
The Rise of Theodore Roosevelt 626
Roosevelt Takes Command 627
The Northern Securities Company Case 628
The Anthracite Coal Strike 628
Roosevelt's Reelection... 629
Railroad Regulation 629
Regulation of the Nation's Food and Medicine.. 630
The First Environmental President.. 631
Roosevelt Chooses a Successor 632
The Taft Presidency... 632
The Election of 1912 634
National Reform Under Wilson 636
Wilson's Background... 636
Wilson's Economic Reforms... 637
The Pinnacle of National Progressivism—Wilson's Acceptance of Social Reform.......... 639
The Election of 1916 639
The Legacy of Progressivism 640
Chronology 641
Review Questions.. 642
Glossary of Important People and Concepts 642
Suggested Readings... 643

CHAPTER TWENTY-TWO
THE "GREAT" WAR: World War I 644
Wilsonian "Missionary Diplomacy" 646
The Outbreak of the Great War 648
Causes for the War 648
American Neutrality.. 650
Naval and Submarine Warfare 652
Declaration of War 655
Propaganda and Hysteria.. 655
Women and the War 656
The Great War and U.S. Government Propaganda 657
Dissenters and the Suppression of Civil Liberties... 658
African Americans in the Military 659
The American "Doughboys" 662
The AEF in France 663
The Home Front.. 665
Wartime Diplomacy.. 667
The End of the War and the Search for Peace 668
The Fight for the League 670
Postwar Racism and the Red Scare 672
Postwar Normalcy 674
Chronology 675
Review Questions.. 676

Glossary of Important People and Concepts 676
Suggested Readings 677

CHAPTER TWENTY-THREE
THE CONTENTIOUS TWENTIES 678
ABr The "Spanish Flue" Pandemic" 679
Postwar Economic Problems 680
Postwar Economic Boom 680
The Myth of the "Roaring 20s" 682
"Ballyhoo" and Record-Breaking 683
    The Black Sox Scandal 685
The "New Woman" 686
The Misappropriation of Freud 688
The Impact of the Great Black Migration 688
Cultural Reaction/Defenders of Tradition 689
    Restrictions on Dress, Dancing, and Movies 690
    Prohibition 691
    Nativism and Immigration Restriction 692
    Fundamentalism 693
    The Second Ku Klux Klan 696
Resurgent Political Conservatism 697
    Election of 1920 698
    The Failed Harding Presidency 699
    Keeping Cool With Coolidge 701
    "The Business of America" 702
The Election of Hoover and The Great Crash 703
Chronology 705
Review Questions 706
Glossary of Important People and Concepts 706
Suggested Readings 707

CHAPTER TWENTY-FOUR
THE GREAT DEPRESSION AND THE NEW DEAL 708
The Great Depression 710
Herbert Hoover 710
    The Technocrat as President 710
    The Deepening Depression 712
    The Bonus Army March 712
The Lord of the Manor: FDR 714
    Roosevelt Liberalism 715
    President Roosevelt 716
    The "Hundred Days" 717
Saving the People 718
    The NRA and AAA 719
Rebuilding the Nation 722
    The Tennessee Valley Authority 723
Populist Opposition to the New Deal 725
    The Rise of the Demagogues: Huey Long and Father Charles Coughlin 725
The "Second Deal" 727
    Labor Resurgent 729

The Depression, the New Deal, and a Change in Values 731
    The Rise of the Radical Third Parties 731
    The Election of 1936 733
    Forgotten Americans 734
    The New Dealers 736
        1930s Film 738
    Stalemate, 1937-1940 739
    The "Court Packing" Debacle 739
The Recession of 1937-1938 740
New Deal Legacy 741
Chronology 741
Review Questions 742
Glossary of Important People and Concepts 742
Suggested Readings 743

CHAPTER TWENTY-FIVE
DEMOCRACY, FASCISM, AND COMMUNISM AT WAR, 1921-1945 744
The World Drifts to War 745
America and the World During the 1920s 746
    Stabilizing the European Economy 746
    Toward the Good Neighbor Policy 746
    Active Global Diplomacy 747
The Rise of Totalitarianism in Asia and Europe 748
    Japanese Militarism and the Takeover of Manchuria 749
    The Rise of Mussolini and the Invasion of Ethiopia 749
    The Rise of the Nazis 750
    The Spanish Civil War 751
American Isolationism 751
    The Neutrality Acts 752
The Coming of World War II 752
    The Japanese Invasion of China 752
    The High Water Mark of Appeasement: Austria and Czechoslovakia 753
    The Nazi-Soviet Partition of Poland 754
World War II Begins in Europe 754
    Neutrality Revision 755
    The Fall of France 755
The American Reaction to War 755
    Roosevelt vs. Lindbergh 756
    The Election of 1940 756
    Lend-Lease 757
    The Undeclared Naval War vs. Germany in the Atlantic 757
    Worsening Relations with Japan 758
    The Road to Pearl Harbor 758
Halting the Axis, 1941-1942 761
    The Fall of the Philippines 761
    The Battles of Coral Sea and Midway 762
    Allied Victories in Egypt and Russia 763
    The Battle of the Atlantic 764
The American Home Front 764
    Industrial Mobilization 765
    Manpower Mobilization 766

    Financing the War... 767
    Civilian Sacrifice 768
    Women during World War II 768
    The African American Experience 770
    Hispanics and the War 772
    Native American Contributions 772
    The Internment of Japanese Americans 773
       Frank Fujita, Jr.—A Japanese Texan Prisoner of the Empire of the Rising Sun 774
Victory in Europe, 1943-1945 775
    The Debate Over Strategy in Europe 775
    Operation Torch 776
    The Allied Invasions of Sicily and Southern Italy 777
    Strategic Bombing 778
    The Tehran Conference 780
    D-Day 780
    The Yalta Conference 781
    End of the War in Europe 782
Victory in the Pacific, 1943-1945 783
    The South Pacific Campaign 784
    The Central Pacific Campaign 784
    The Fight for the Philippines 785
    The Bloody Fight for Iwo Jima and Okinawa 786
    The New President 787
    Naval Blockade and Fire Bombing of Japan 787
    The Defeat of Japan 789
Chronology 791
Review Questions 792
Glossary of Important People and Concepts 792
Suggested Readings 793

CHAPTER TWENTY-SIX
THE ORIGINS OF THE COLD WAR 794
    The Emerging Cold War 795
    The Truman Doctrine and Containment 797
        The Marshall Plan 799
        The Berlin Crisis 800
        The 1948 Election 801
        Harry Truman and the Fair Deal 803
        The Formation of NATO 805
    The Fall of China 806
    The Creation of the "Cold War Mentality" 807
        The Politics of Anticommunism 808
        The Spy Trials 809
        McCarthyism 810
           Chills and Fever during the Cold War 812
    The Korean War 814
    The Eisenhower Era and the Cold War 818
        The 1952 Election 818
        Eisenhower and the End of the Korean War 820
        The Eisenhower Cold War Frame of Reference 821
    John Foster Dulles and the "New Look" 821

- Critics of the New Look and Massive Retaliation 823
- Ike and the Soviets 824
- The Hungary Crisis 824
- The U-2 Incident 825

The Emergence of the Third World 826
- The Cold War in the Third World 826

The Suez Crisis 827

Eisenhower and Vietnam 829

Sputnik 831

Chronology 833

Review Questions 834

Glossary of Important People and Concepts 834

Suggested Readings 835

CHAPTER TWENTY-SEVEN
AMERICAN CULTURE FROM 1945-1960 836

American Racism Before World War II 838
- Immigration Restriction Before World War II 839
- Race Before and After World War II 840

The Cold War and Race Relations 841

President Truman and Racial Politics 841

Black Political Activism 843
- School Desegregation 843
- The *Brown* Decision 844

"Massive Resistance" 845
- The Murder of Emmett Till 846
- Rosa Parks and the Montgomery Bus Boycott 847
- The Little Rock Crisis 848

Mexican-American Activism 850

Rosie the Riveter After the War 854
- Women in 1950s Popular Culture 854

Family Life and the Baby Boom 855
- Family Troubles 855

The Double Standard 856

Porn in the U.S.A. 856
- The Cost of Sexual Hypocrisy 857

Oppression and the Birth of the Gay Rights Movement 857

On the Road 859

TV Nation 860
- Television and Professional Sports 861

Subterranean Rebels 863

"Seduction of the Innocent": The Comic Book Wars 864

Rock 'n' Roll 865
- *The Comics Code* 866

The Lasting Influence of the 1950s 870

Chronology 871

Review Questions 872

Glossary of Important People and Concepts 872

Suggested Readings 873

CHAPTER TWENTY-EIGHT
REFORM AND BACKLASH UNDER KENNEDY AND JOHNSON 874

- The Sit-In Movement 875
- The 1960 Presidential Election 877
  - Democratic Primaries 878
  - Civil Rights and the 1960 Campaign 879
  - The Catholic Issue Returns 880
  - Television and the Kennedy-Nixon Debates 880
- The Reasons for Kennedy's Victory 881
- The "New Frontier" 882
  - The Bay of Pigs Fiasco 883
  - The Kennedy-Khrushchev Clash 883
  - The Cuban Missile Crisis 884
- The Space Race 885
- The Warren Court 887
- Freedom Riders 888
  - Sheriff "Bull" Connor and Police Violence 888
  - On To Montgomery 889
  - Negotiations Behind the Scene 890
- Integrating "Ole Miss" 890
- "Bombingham" and the University of Alabama 891
- Racial Tensions and the Final Months 892
  - The March on Washington 893
  - Four Little Girls 894
- The Kennedy Assassination and Its Impact 894
  - *Where were you when President Kennedy was shot?* 896
- LBJ: Unlikely Civil Rights Ally 896
  - A Political Force of Nature 898
- Johnson as President 899
  - The 1964 Civil Rights Act 900
- Freedom Summer 900
  - The Schwerner, Chaney, and Goodman Murders 901
- The Mississippi Freedom Democratic Party 902
- Bloody Sunday 903
- Voting Rights Act 904
- "By Any Means Necessary" 905
  - Long Hot Summers 907
  - An Undeclared Civil War 907
- Two Nations 907
- Black is Beautiful 908
  - White Backlash 908
- 1960-1967: The Best of Times 909
- 1960-1967: The Worst of Times 910
- Chronology 911
- Review Questions 912
- Glossary of Important People and Concepts 912
- Suggested Readings 913

CHAPTER TWENTY-NINE
ROLLING THUNDER: The Vietnam War Under Kennedy and Johnson 914
Bearing Any Burden 916
The Diem Regime 916
Cautious Engagement 917
Quarantine 918
"A Buddist Barbecue Show" 919
"A Promising Coup D'etat" 921
"The Prospects Now Are For a Shorter War" 921
"Extremism in the Defense of Liberty" 923
"Not a Ship, Nor the Outline of a Ship . . ." 923
Into the Stone Age 925
Gulf of Tonkin Resolution 925
Soldiers' Stories 926
Bad Chemistry 927
"Killing is the Easiest Part" 928
Search and Destroy 928
"Feasting on the Body" 930
Race Matters 932
The Hanoi Hilton 932
The "Television War" 934
"Our Worst Enemy" 935
Class Warfare 935
Dodging the Draft, Elite Style 936
The Whole Thing is a Mess 936
Problems Troubling and Unresolved 937
The Burning of Norman Morrison 940
"No Vietcong Ever Called Me Nigger" 940
Armies in the Night 941
Apologies and Forgiveness 942
Chronology 945
Review Questions 946
Glossary of Important People and Concepts 946
Suggested Readings 947

CHAPTER THIRTY
THE NIGHTMARE YEAR, 1968 948
Revolutions & Student Unrest on College Campuses 950
Up Against the Wall 950
The Occupation 951
The Taking of the *Pueblo* 951
A Drastically Different Kind of War 952
One of the Great Pictures of the Vietnam War 953
Losing the Most Trusted Man in America 955
The Banality of Evil: A Massacre at My Lai 956
Uncommon Valor 958
A Dark Night of the Soul 958
Last Crusades 960
Clean For Gene: An Upset in New Hampshire 961
The Wise Old Men 962
Martin Luther King, Jr., and Black Power 964

  The FBI War on MLK 965
  "The Day of Violence is Here" 966
  "I've Been to the Mountaintop" 967
 Aftermath of a Killing 968
  Robert Kennedy on the Death of Martin Luther King 969
 "If You Do Not Do This, Who Will Do This?" 970
  "On to Chicago" 970
 "Poor Richard" 971
  In Exile 972
  "Pointy-headed Bureaucrats" 973
  Last Man Standing 973
  "The Whole World is Watching" 974
 "If You Mean It, We're With You" 975
 Branding Nixon 976
 1968: The "What-Ifs" 977
 Chronology 979
 Review Questions 980
 Glossary of Important People and Concepts 980
 Suggested Readings 981

CHAPTER THIRTY-ONE
AMERICAN FRUSTRATION AND DECLINE IN THE 1970s 982
 The Southern Strategy 984
  Affirmative Action 985
 Nixonomics 985
  Acid, Amnesty, and Abortion 986
  Stagflation 988
 The First Energy Crisis 988
 The "Nixon Doctrine" 989
  A Coup in Chile 990
  Cracks in the Communist World 991
  "Peace With Honor" 993
  Operation Menu 994
  The Moratorium 994
  "An Age of Anarchy" 995
  Four Dead in Ohio 995
  "Collapsing in the Field" 996
 The Pentagon Papers 997
 The Christmas Bombing 998
 "Nothing More To Say After That": Aftermath of the Vietnam War 999
 The Killing Fields 1000
 A Cancer Close to the Presidency: The Watergate Scandal 1001
  Third-rate Burglary 1002
  "Stonewall It" 1003
  "The Saturday Night Massacre" 1003
 A Ford, Not a Lincoln 1005
  "A Full, Free, and Absolute Pardon" 1005
 The Reform Congress 1006
  "Whole Dollars and Seemingly All at Once" 1007
  Welfare Queen 1007
 "Establishing Justice in a Sinful World" 1008

"No Soviet Domination of Eastern Europe" 1009
Power Failure 1010
"The Great Inflation" 1011
Human Rights 1011
"Just Waiting for the Proper Invitation" 1012
"The Peacock Throne" 1013
"Malaise" 1014
America Held Hostage 1015
The Moral Majority 1015
"There You Go Again": The Election of Ronald Reagan 1016
Americans Get Angry 1017
Chronology 1019
Review Questions 1020
Glossary of Important People and Concepts 1020
Suggested Readings 1021

CHAPTER THIRTY-TWO
AMERICAN CULTURE AND THE COUNTERCULTURE OF THE 1960s and 1970s 1022

Organization Men: The Suburbs and the Birth of the 1960s Counterculture 1024
"What Are You Rebelling Against?": The Childhood of 1960s Radicals 1025
"The Order is Rapidly Changin'": Bob Dylan and 1960s Protest Music 1026
"Tuning in and Dropping Out": The Hippie Culture 1028
"Listen to the Colors of Your Dreams": Hippies and Psychedelic Drugs 1028
"Black Power" 1029
"Tomism" 1030
"Black is Beautiful" 1031
Roots 1033
Latino Protests 1033
César Chávez and the United Farm Workers 1034
Chicanismo 1034
Back to Wounded Knee: The American Indian Movement 1035
Days of Rage 1036
Silent Spring 1037
Mercy, Mercy Me: The American Environmental Movement 1038
"The Problem With No Name" 1039
"The Bunny Law" 1039
Glass Ceilings 1040
The Failure of the Equal Rights Amendment 1041
"Back Alley Abortions" 1043
Roe v. Wade 1044
Roe v. Wade, 410 U.S. 113 (1973) 1045
The Birth of the Anti-Abortion Movement 1045
Stonewall 1046
"A Civilization Without Insanity": Religious Experimentation in the 1960s 1048
"Revolutionary Suicide" 1049
"A God in Your Universe" 1050
The Promise and the Disappointment of American Culture, 1960-1980 1050
Chronology 1055
Review Questions 1056
Glossary of Important People and Concepts 1056
Suggested Readings 1057

CHAPTER THIRTY-THREE
THE RISE OF CONSERVATISM: Ronald Reagan to George H.W. Bush 1058
- A Perspective on Ronald Reagan's 1980 Election Victory 1060
  - Ronald Reagan and the "Moral Majority" 1062
- **The Reagan Years** 1063
  - *That Old Time Religion: American Evangelism in Historical Perspective* 1064
    - Domestic Policy Agendas 1067
    - Deregulation 1067
    - Reaganomics 1068
- **Reagan Confronts the World** 1072
  - The Soviet Union, and Crises in the Middle East and Central America 1072
- **The Election of 1984** 1075
  - Falling Apart 1077
  - The Iran Contra Affair and Other Scandals 1078
  - Reaching New Heights 1079
- **The Reagan Legacy: George H. W. Bush** 1081
- **The George H.W. Bush Presidency** 1082
  - The Cold War Ends 1083
  - Operation Desert Storm 1083
  - The Politics of Frustration 1085
- **Domestic Upheaval** 1086
- **Chronology** 1087
- **Review Questions** 1088
- **Glossary of Important People and Concepts** 1088
- **Suggested Readings** 1089

CHAPTER THIRTY-FOUR
A DIVIDED AMERICA: Bill Clinton to George W. Bush 1090
- **The 1992 Election: Bill Clinton and the Triumph of Neo-Liberalism** 1092
- **The Clinton Years** 1095
  - "Don't Ask, Don't Tell" 1096
  - Health-care Reform 1097
- **The 1994 Republican Counter Revolution** 1098
  - The Right's Momentary Triumph 1098
  - *The Multiculturalism Debate* 1100
- **The 1996 Election: Clintonian Liberalism Vindicated and Triumphant** 1103
- **Bill Clinton and the World: Clintonian Foreign Policy** 1104
  - Clinton Doctrine and The People's Republic of China 1105
  - Middle East 1105
  - Africa 1106
  - Other Crises 1107
  - Trade Agreements 1108
- **The Clinton Economy** 1109
- **The Lewinsky Debacle and the Clinton Presidency** 1109
- **The 2000 Election** 1110
  - The 2000 Post-Election Debacle 1111
  - A Challenged Democracy 1113
- **American Exceptionalism** 1113
- **The Bush Agenda** 1114
  - Bush and Foreign Policy Pre-September 11 1115
  - September 11, 2001 1116

    The Price Paid for "Freedom" 1120
The United States Counterattacks 1122
The Iraq War 1124
    The 2004 Election 1125
The Bush Second Term 1125
    The Unraveling of the Bush Presidency 1126
    Hurricane Katrina 1126
Republicans Divided and Defeated 1128
A Wired Nation and Mass Culture Trends 1128
    Health Care and AIDS 1128
    Entertainment 1130
    Personal Computer 1131
Chronology 1133
Review Questions 1134
Glossary of Important People and Concepts 1134
Suggested Readings 1135

CHAPTER THIRTY-FIVE
BARACK OBAMA: A Milestone in United States History 1136
The 2008 Election 1138
    Race in America in the 21st Century 1139
Barack Obama: New Deal Liberal or Neo-liberal Centrist? 1140
    The Financial Crisis 1140
    The Health-Care Debate 1142
    The Tea Party Movement 1143
The 2010 Congressional Elections 1144
The Obama Administration and the World 1147
    The Club of Rome, The Environmental Movement, and the Issue of Global Warming .. 1148
    Narrowing the Struggle 1149
The End of Osama bin Laden and Arab Spring 1150
The 2012 Presidential Election 1151
Chronology 1153
Review Questions 1154
Glossary of Important People and Concepts 1154
Suggested Readings 1155

APPENDIX
    A. Declaration of Independence 1156
    B. Constitution of the United States 1158
    C. Presidential Elections 1171
    D. Supreme Court Justices 1175
    E. Admission of States to the Union 1178
    F. Population Growth 1179

GLOSSARY 1180

INDEX 1210

MAPS

CHAPTER 17
- Map 17.1 Reconstruction Districts
- Map 17.2 The Election of 1868
- Map 17.3 The Election of 1876

CHAPTER 18
- Map 18.1 Railroad Expansion, 1870-1890.
- Map 18.2 The Great Railroad Strike of 1877
- Map 18.3 The Election of 1884
- Map 18.4 The Election of 1892

CHAPTER 19
- Map 19.1 Major Indian Battles
- Map 19.2 Western Trails
- Map 19.3 Cattle and Railroads
- Map 19.4 The Election of 1896

CHAPTER 20
- Map 20.1 Spanish-American War in the Philippines
- Map 20.2 Major Battles in Cuba
- Map 20.3 American Empire, 1900
- Map 20.4 The Panama Canal Zone and the Panama Canal

CHAPTER 21
- Map 21.1 The Election of 1912
- Map 21.2 The Election of 1916

CHAPTER 22
- Map 22.1 European Alliances (1915)
- Map 22.2 Western Front, 1918
- Map 22.3 Europe After World War I

CHAPTER 23
- Map 23.1 The Election of 1920
- Map 23.2 The Election of 1928

CHAPTER 24
- Map 24.1 The Election of 1932

CHAPTER 25
- Map 25.1 World War II in the Pacific
- Map 25.2 World War II in Europe
- Map 25.3 Prescribed zones for a divided Berlin

CHAPTER 26
- Map 26.1 Europe after 1945
- Map 26.2 The Election of 1948
- Map 26.3 The Korean War
- Map 26.4 The Geneva Accords

CHAPTER 27
- Map 27.1 The Interstate Highway and Defense System Act of 1956

CHAPTER 28
- Map 28.1 The Election of 1960

CHAPTER 29
- Map 29.1 Vietnam War

CHAPTER 30
- Map 30.1 The Election of 1968

CHAPTER 31
- Map 31.1 Israel, Six Day War 1967
- Map 31.2 The Middle East 1948-1989
- Map 31.3 The Election of 1976
- Map 31.4 The Election of 1980

CHAPTER 33
- Map 33.1 El Salvador and Nicaragua

CHAPTER 34
- Map 34.1 The Election of 1992
- Map 34.2 Breakup of Yugoslavia
- Map 34.3 The Election of 2000
- Map 34.4 Afghanistan
- Map 34.5 The Middle East 1989-2007

CHAPTER 35
- Map 35.1 The Election of 2008

Preface

Every nation encounters challenges during its existence. Some are common to all countries, some are quite unique. How a people rise to overcome these challenges, or fail in their attempts to address them adequately, engenders much of that country's history. Americans experienced a series of internal and external challenges over the past 500 years even before the creation of the United States: exploration of unknown lands, intense military conflicts, demanding technological problems, divisive political battles, and epic social upheavals, just to name a few. This textbook is an attempt to relay how Americans have risen to their own set of challenges and either prevailed over them or continue to deal with those not yet overcome.

The work's subtitle—"A New History of the United States"—refers to the effort by the authors to synthesize the latest historical scholarship (and borrow, when pertinent, from other disciplines) to provide a fresh account of this country's national story. Unlike many older textbooks originally produced during the Cold War era and simply updated with token changes, the authors of *The American Challenge* have written their chapters entirely from the perspective of the early twenty-first century. At the conclusion of each chapter, the authors have included a list of suggested readings consisting of a few classic works and numerous recent publications that influenced their interpretation of a particular period. These books can also provide an important starting point for students interested in delving deeper into the introduced topics.

Every textbook contains a tremendous amount of information. To guide the retention of material, the authors of *The American Challenge* have emboldened key terms to aid readers in distinguishing the most important persons, events, and concepts appearing in each chapter. A glossary at the end of the book serves as a compilation of all bold terms, providing informative descriptions. To further help digest the information, each chapter also contains a chronology to act as a quick-guide for those wishing to keep track of key events over time, and a set of five summary review questions that students should feel comfortable answering before moving on to the next chapter. To enhance the overall learning experience, all chapters include helpful maps, interesting photographs of noteworthy people and everyday scenes, and other enlightening illustrations relevant to a particular period.

Supplements from Abigail Press are also available for each volume of *The American Challenge*. *Historical Perspectives: A Reader and Study Guide* offers primary source documents and introductory comments designed to help develop an interest in America's past and appreciate the relevance of the course material. Selections cover all periods of United States history, including the Discovery of America, Colonization, the American Revolution, the Civil War, Reconstruction, Westward Expansion, World Wars, the Depression, Cold War, and the Modern Period. *Imperial Presidents: The Rise of Executive Power from Roosevelt to Obama* provides an additional supplement for Volume Two. Transcending the partisan tone of current American debate, authors John Moretta, Michael Phillips, and Carl Luna present a balanced evaluation of the modern presidents. Each essay consists of a biographical portrait of each president, followed by a positive and negative assessment of each man's tenure in office (endeavoring to be as even-handed as possible in their conclusions), and a section devoted to the dramatic expansion of the federal government and the growth of the Executive Branch.

I am very proud to be associated with the fine group of scholars who authored *The American Challenge*. Each professor channeled their broad experiences as academics and classroom educators to produce a book that not only reflects the latest historical scholarship, but also written in a compelling manner which will resonate with today's college students. John A. Moretta earned his Ph.D. in History from Rice University and is currently a Professor of History at Central College, Houston Community College System in Houston, Texas where he has taught for over thirty years. John is currently servings as department chair for the social sciences and humanities for the new Community College of Qatar, which is located on the Arabian Gulf. John has broad historical interests as reflected in his published biographies of William Penn and the Texas statesman William Pitt Ballinger and his numerous contributions to both volumes of *The American Challenge*. John has just finished a book on the Hippies for Oxford University Press, with an anticipated publication date of early fall of 2012. My colleague at Collin College, Michael Phillips, earned his Ph.D. in History from the University of Texas at Austin. His teaching and books on race in Dallas and Texas House Speakers demonstrate his strong interest and expertise in American government as well as race, class, and gender issues. Doug Cantrell holds the rank of Professor of History and chairs the History Department at the Elizabethtown Community and Technical College where he has taught for the past 25 years. Professor Cantrell studied at the University of Kentucky and has authored numerous articles and book reviews in academic journals and encyclopedias in the field of immigration and ethnic history. Norwood Andrews is currently a Visiting Professor of History at University of Dallas. He earned his doctorate at the University of Texas at Austin and specializes in American criminal justice history. Austin Allen received his Ph.D. from the University of Houston and is an Associate Professor of History at the University of Houston-Downtown where he has taught since 2002. A specialist in the legal history of the antebellum United States, Austin has written a book detailing the origins of the Dred Scott Case and is presently working on a book about the Fugitive Slave Law. Finally, I received my Ph.D. in American history from Texas A&M University and currently teach history and serve as Chair of the History Department at Collin College in Plano, Texas. I have taught American and Texas history for the past 15 years and published a book and several articles reflecting my interests in 20th century American politics and race relations. The authors hope you enjoy this effort and welcome feedback from our readers.

Keith J. Volanto

Chapter Seventeen

RECONSTRUCTION: The Turning Point That Never Turned

In April 1864, one year before Abraham Lincoln's assassination, wealthy South Carolina slave owner and rice planter Robert Allston died of pneumonia. His daughter, Elizabeth, was bereft of "terrible desolation and sorrow." As the Civil War raged on around her, Elizabeth and her mother tried to maintain their many rice plantations. With Yankee troops ravaging their way through coastal South Carolina in the late winter of 1864-65, Elizabeth's grieving for the loss of her father turned to "terror" for she was certain that the Union soldiers would ransack her plantation and inflict "all manner of mischief and unspeakable behavior" upon her and her mother and even their slaves. Union soldiers did indeed pillage their home, looking for liquor and hidden valuables as well as encouraging the slaves to have their way with the Allston's furniture and other household goods. Some slaves did take such items from the "Big House" to their slave cabins, but after the soldiers had left, returned them to the Allston house. However, before they left, the Yankee soldiers did give the keys to crop barns to the semi-free slaves.

When the war was over, the widow Adele Allston took an oath of allegiance to the United States and secured a written order from the local Union general in command for her former slaves to give back the keys. She and Elizabeth made plans to return in the early summer of 1864 to begin anew the family plantation, thereby reestablishing white authority of their black labor force, which although now free was supposed to continue to work for the Allston family per the orders of the Union army of occupation. Mrs. Allston was assured that although their former slaves were free and could even now possess firearms as a "means to a livelihood, no outrage has been committed against whites except in the matter of property." To the Allstons, property was the key issue, and the possession of the keys to the barns, Elizabeth wrote, would be the "test case" of whether former slaves or their former masters would control land, labor and its fruits, and even subtle aspects of interpersonal relations.

No doubt the Allston women returned to their estate, Nightingale Hall, with much trepidation, not knowing how they would be greeted by their former slaves. To their surprise and relief, a pleasant reunion took place, for many of the slaves had always liked the women and had remained loyal to the family throughout slavery and the war. The Allston women knew all of their slaves' names, greeted them accordingly, inquired after their children, and caught up on the affairs with whom they had lived closely for many years. To their further delight, a trusted foreman handed over the keys to the barns. Such an interesting scene of harmony and the display of good will of blacks towards whites and vice versa was more common than not in the South in the war's and emancipation's immediate aftermath.

However, not every black-white encounter was "sunshine and roses" at the Allstons' plantations in the South Carolina Low Country. At Guendalos, a plantation owned by a son absent during the war fighting with the Confederacy, the Allston women encountered a very different scene. Apparently the son was not nearly as kind to his slaves, who resented their master intensely for his often cruel treatment and were now ready to ventilate their rage on the Allston women. As their carriage arrived and moved toward the crop barns, an armed group of angry former slaves menaced the women's buggy as it slowly drove toward the barns. The women politely asked for the keys to the barns from a former black driver, Uncle Jacob, but as he was about to hand the women the keys, the other freedmen shouted "Ef yu gie up de key, blood'll flow." Uncle Jacob slipped the keys back into his pocket. The other freedmen "would be damned" if they would relinquish barns full of rice and corn put there by black labor. The Allston women then proceeded to the Big House, where they locked themselves in as best they could. Through the night freedmen who had threatened the Allston women sang freedom songs and danced while waving hoes, pitchforks, and guns to discourage anyone from going into town for help. Two "loyal" freedmen, however, managed to escape the celebration and made it to town to find some Union soldiers who they convinced to come to the plantation and rescue the Allston women. The two freedmen returned and told their fellows that the Yankee soldiers were on their way and that they would be most upset with what had taken place. Early the next morning, the women were awakened by a knock at the front door. Adele slowly opened the door, and there stood Uncle Jacob. Without a word, he gave her the keys.

The story of the keys reveals many of the human ingredients of the Reconstruction era. Despite defeat and surrender, southern whites were determined to regain control of both their land and labor—their former slaves. Despite sporadic, half-hearted attempts by federal officials to redistribute wealth in the South by destroying the prewar landed elite and giving their land to the freedmen, throughout Reconstruction, law, property titles, and federal enforcement remained on the side of the former "slaveocracy." The Allston women were friendly, even solicitous of their slaves in a very maternalistic way, insisting on the restoration of the deferential relationship that had existed before the war. In short, both Adele and Elizabeth both feared and cared about their slaves' well-being particularly as it affected their own future. The freedmen likewise revealed mixed feelings toward their former masters. At different plantations they demonstrated a variety of emotions: anger, loyalty, love, resentment, and pride. Even at Guendalos, respect was paid to the person of the Allstons but not to their property and crops. The freedmen's actions indicated that what they wanted was not revenge for generations of bondage but economic independence and freedom.

In this encounter between former slaves and their mistresses, the role of northern officials, particularly that of the United States Army, is also revealing. The Union soldiers literally and symbolically gave the keys of freedom to the blacks but did not stay around long enough to guarantee that freedom, and such would be the case throughout most of Reconstruction relative to the freedmen protection of both his person and economic and civil rights. Although encouraging the freedmen to plunder the Allston's estate and take possession of the crops, they then disappeared, leaving the ultimate decision to engage in such activity up to the freedmen. The soldiers' retreat demonstrated to freedmen that in the end, they would be on their own to find a way through a very changed existence. Indeed, Uncle Jacob appeared to grasp the limits of northern help, handing the keys to land and liberty back into the hands of whom he prophetically or instinctually knew his future fate in the South would ultimately lie. The Guendalos freedmen knew that if they wanted to ensure their freedom, they had to do it themselves.

A major theme of the immediate postwar years is the story of what happened to the conflicting goals and dreams of three groups as they sought to form new social, economic, and political relationships during the Reconstruction era. Amid devastation and divisions of class and race, white Southerners sought to put their lives back together again while black Southerners attempted to establish themselves as a respected free people. Meanwhile, northern whites, with varying degrees of motivation, commitment, humanity, and success, tried to help the freedmen achieve a life of social and economic independence as well as a respect for their rights as human beings and citizens. The interplay of these three groups guaranteed that the Reconstruction era would be divisive, leaving a mixed legacy of human gains and losses.

THE CONFEDERACY'S DEFEAT

The Civil War presents one of the greatest paradoxes in United States history. For forty years (1820-1860), white Americans debated slavery, sometimes violently and never without acrimony. Yet, rarely if ever, did their arguments reflect any genuine humanitarian concern for the plight of the millions of African Americans in bondage. Even many abolitionists worried more about the sin and stigma of slavery upon the nation's image than about the institution's barbarity. White Americans were divided not on the morality of slavery but on the institution's political and economic ramifications. Such little regard for the slaves' condition reflected an inherent and prevailing racism among the majority of northern whites, including a good number of even the most zealous of abolitionists.

Five generations lived on Smith's Plantation, Beaufort, South Carolina, 1862.

Although condemning slavery on moral and religious grounds and recognizing and valuing African Americans as human beings, many abolitionists nonetheless believed blacks to be innately inferior to whites. Such underlying racist sentiments among even abolitionists helped to reinforce the ghettoization and marginalization of the thousands of free blacks already living in the North in 1860. For the majority of them, daily life was not that much better than it had been in bondage; the only appreciable difference was that at least one was "free" and no longer chattel. Thus, when pushed by other northern whites on the issue of post-emancipation assimilation of the freedmen, abolitionists either dodged the issue or advocated a deportation/colonization agenda. Such a position by those who were supposedly the African Americans' greatest champions for manumission were at the same time opposed to integration and equality for black Americans as their more overtly racist counterparts. Such northern white racism towards African Americans shaped the course of Reconstruction.

Since the nation's official beginning in 1787 with the enactment of the Constitution and over the course of the next seventy-three years, the political elite avoided confrontation and the potential disruption of the Union by promulgating a series of compromises on the slavery expansion issue. However, by the late 1850s, the political leadership at that time proved incapable of finding common ground to forge another compromise. By 1860, southern whites, led by the "slaveocracy," concluded that their inalienable right to "property" (their slaves) was no longer secure in the Union and thus seceded, declaring that the Union that had been created in 1787 had been subverted by a "black Republican" Party determined not only to abolish slavery but also to abrogate states' rights, which to southern slave owners meant the right to own slaves and to take their property anywhere they deemed essential for their "pursuit of happiness." Therein lies part of the paradox of the Civil War: a conflict caused by slavery yet became the nation's greatest bloodbath ignited by secession. In the end, the United States convulsed in bloody conflict, not to end the blight of human bondage but to preserve the Union—for an abstract entity rather than for the liberation of human beings.

Reinforcing this theme was the fact that the majority of northern whites were as racist in their attitudes and treatment of the free blacks in their communities as their white southern counterparts. Indeed, by 1860, significant numbers of northern whites had come to despise the "Black Republicans" for their position on slavery while denying civil rights to the black people in their own states. Secession, however, united northern whites. In the northern white mind, secession and slavery were mutually exclusive issues: the former tied to the sanctity of nationhood, with the latter associated with a race of inferior people, not worth a blood sacrifice. Nonetheless, an interesting coalition formed in the North during the war years that helped to guarantee a Union triumph. Unionists and antislavery men put aside their differences and joined forces, for both knew they could not obtain their respective objectives without the other. Both opposed secession and agreed that the Union must be preserved. Unionists, however, did not see the abolition of slavery and the preservation of the Union as symbiotic. Yet, the Unionists knew they could not defeat the secessionists without antislavery support, and abolitionists knew they would not see the end of slavery without Unionist support, nor without defeating the Confederacy. Thus an uneasy alliance formed between the two groups. The Union victory put an end to the coalition, for the two allies no longer needed one another. Most importantly, the Confederacy's defeat transformed the issue of union into a question of race, and the freedmen (ex-slaves) had few northern supporters and thus were doomed almost from the beginning of Reconstruction to a life of continued servility, oppression, poverty, illiteracy, terror, and, all too frequently, an early death. Whenever a successful coalition dissolves after a war because of dissension among the victors, the vanquished, if shrewd and united, almost always find an opportunity to reassert or reclaim their power, often in a greater, more dominating form than before the conflict. That was precisely what the white South was able to accomplish by the end of Reconstruction.

RECONSTRUCTION'S OVERARCHING ISSUES

Without question, the emancipation of four million African Americans from bondage presented both white and black Americans with Reconstruction's most pressing issue. There was simply no consensus among whites, and even among some blacks, about the possible place of freed people in a reconstructed United States. Both black and white leaders, including Abraham Lincoln, wondered, if not doubted, whether different races could ever peacefully co-exist, let alone be willing to accept each other as equal citizens. Also vexing, especially for white Northerners, was the question of how southern whites, particularly those who had aided and encouraged the slaveholders' rebellion, were to be treated. Should they be punished—executed or imprisoned, permanently disenfranchised or their property confiscated? On what terms should the Confederate or rebellious states return to the Union? And finally, what would be the powers of the states and of the national government in a reconstructed Union?

The Civil War cost $6.5 billion, not including the pensions for wounded and elderly soldiers and widows and orphans of the conflict (by 1890 such payments represented 40 percent of the federal budget). That amount of money would have been more than enough in 1861 for the Lincoln administration to buy the freedom of all four million southern slaves from their masters, which, after all, was what Lincoln had advocated all along—"emancipation with compensation." Moreover, there would have been enough money left over to give each African-American family 40 acres and a mule and some cash. The breaking up of rebel plantation estates and parceling out that land to freedmen in 40-acre allotments was the Radical Republican's initial vision and agenda for the South's economic reconstruction. However, the plan was never implemented.

Although Reconstruction would affect every aspect of southern life, its most dramatic and enduring impact was social—the daily working out by black and white, male and female, and rich and poor of how they were to treat each other in these changed times. In some instances these social dramas reflected old ties sundered or renewed, as when former slaves drifted back to the plantation after having enjoyed freedom for a few weeks, looking for work or someone to provide for them as "old massa" had for years. Sometimes the bonds were reversed: a freedmen bringing food to a former master who was now steeped in poverty, a white man being hauled before a black judge, African Americans defending their homes with rifles, a black militia instead of a white slave patrol, or interracial crowds of Union League supporters celebrating Independence Day. Other transformations were smaller: freedmen driving newly bought buggies or poor black and white children attending school together. Of such seemingly insignificant changes revolutions are made; against such dread reordering, the forces of reaction launch their strongest battalions. So it would be in the Reconstruction of the South.

Reconstruction unleashed unforeseen conflicts that propelled events along a startling revolutionary path. The dialectic between conservatism and revolution, along with the desire for order and for freedom, defined Reconstruction in terms of its successes and failures. In the beginning, only one certainty prevailed: thousands of black

Abraham Lincoln

Southerners eagerly awaited its advent while thousands of their white counterparts dreaded its inaugural.

WARTIME AND PRESIDENTIAL RECONSTRUCTION

Abraham Lincoln

No history of **Reconstruction** would be complete, or accurate, without a discussion of **Abraham Lincoln**'s views and policies, no matter how ambiguous, conflicting, inconsistent, and half-hearted they might have been. Although Lincoln is considered to be the nation's greatest president because he successfully held the country together through its most perilous ordeal, he nonetheless had flaws, especially when it came to the issue of race, which became Reconstruction's most critical dynamic. Perhaps the first question that must be asked regarding Lincoln and his racial views is: Was Lincoln a racist himself? The answer is a qualified "yes." As he declared during the 1858 Illinois Senate race in one of his debates with Stephen Douglas, "I am not, nor ever have been in favor of bringing about in any way the social and political equality of the white and black races; that I am not, nor ever have been in favor of making voters or jurors of Negroes, nor of qualifying them to hold office, nor to intermarry with white people . . . . there is a physical difference between the white and black races, which I believe will forever forbid the two races living together on terms of social and political equality. And inasmuch as they cannot so live, while they do remain together there must be the position of superior and inferior, and I as much as any other man am in favor of having the superior position assigned to the white man."

If the above statement is taken at face value, then Lincoln was indeed a "white supremacist," holding the same racial attitudes at that time as the majority of his fellow white citizens. But was Lincoln's racism simply "political"; that is, was he expressing such views in order to win votes? Four years earlier a different Lincoln is revealed, one who recognized that color prejudice was a totally irrational basis for determining race relations. "If A can prove conclusively that he may of right enslave B—why may not B snatch the same argument, and prove equally, that he may enslave A? You say A is white and B is black. It is *color* then; the lighter having the right to enslave the darker? Take care. By this rule, you are to be the slave to the first man you meet with a fairer skin than your own. You do not mean *color* exactly? You mean the whites are *intellectually* the superiors of the blacks, and therefore you have the right to enslave them? Take care again. By this rule, you are to be slave to the first man you meet with an intellect superior to your own. But you say, it is a question of *interest*; and if you make it your interest, you have the right to enslave others. Very well. And if he can make it his interest, he has the right to enslave you."

Unfortunately for posterity, Lincoln never publicly stated this lean and muscular bit of reasoning. Had he done so, the racist label would have been expunged, especially when coupled with his public declaration that both he and his party (the Republicans) considered slavery as "a wrong . . . a moral, social, and political wrong." Thus, at best, Lincoln, like many of his white contemporaries, was ambiguous about race in America. Lincoln, without question, believed blacks to be people, human beings, albeit "inferior" but nonetheless members of the human race entitled to their freedom. To enslave them and strip them of their humanity and reduce them to property was, as he publicly announced, morally, socially, and politically wrong, particularly in a country that proclaimed to the world in 1776 that "all men are created equal." To Lincoln, this included "men of color" as well.

Although publicly condemning human bondage and acknowledging the slaves' humanity, Lincoln was not willing to engage in a clash of arms to rid the nation of chattel slavery. From the moment that the first salvos were fired, Lincoln believed that the Civil War was unequivocally about preserving the Union, and thus the slavery issue became of much lesser importance. He made this point very clear in a letter to newspaper publisher Horace Greeley in August 1862. "My paramount objective is to save the Union, and is not either to save or destroy slavery. If I could save the Union without freeing any slave, I would do it; and if I could save it by freeing all the slaves, I would do it; and if I could save it by freeing some and leaving others alone, I would also do that. What I do about slavery and the colored race, I do because I believe it helps to save this Union." Interestingly, the Emancipation Proclamation, though at this point unannounced, was already in his desk, the result of his conclusion that such an act would help the Union cause by giving Yankee soldiers and northern whites hopefully something more tangible to fight for than an abstraction—the Union—while simultaneously crippling the Confederate war effort by depriving it of valuable labor. Thus for reasons political and strategic, Lincoln "freed the slaves" in the states still in rebellion against the United States on January 1, 1863.

As the man who issued the Emancipation Proclamation and as the key leader in securing congressional adoption of the **Thirteenth Amendment**, Lincoln could certainly be called the "Emancipator," albeit a reluctant one. No sooner did the Emancipation Proclamation go into effect than Lincoln initiated "phase two" of his manumission agenda—the colonization of freedmen outside the United States in Haiti, in Panama, or elsewhere in the Western Hemisphere in which could be found countries with all-black populations. Could such an initiative be further proof of Lincoln's inherent racism? Perhaps, for it appears that Lincoln had thought about this idea for quite some time as part of his overall emancipation plan. He tested black receptivity to his scheme in August 1862 when he invited to the Oval Office a group of already free African Americans, some of whom had been interested in colonization, to confer with him about such a prospect. Usually a man with great sensitivity to others' feelings, Lincoln on this occasion seemed hard-hearted and insensitive. Observing that whites and blacks were of different races, he said further, "your race suffers greatly and we of the white race suffer from your presence. Even when you cease to be slaves, you are yet far removed from being on an equality with the white race. On this broad continent, not a single man of your race is made the equal of a single man of ours. I cannot alter it if I could. It is a fact. It is better for us both to be separated." He then proceeded to describe to them the attractions of an area in Colombia (the future country of Panama) made available for such purposes by the Colombian government, which at the time needed to populate the isthmus. Lincoln urged them to emigrate there as soon as possible.

Again, if Lincoln's words are taken at face value, then he most definitely was a racist. However, Lincoln's racist rhetoric and callousness could also be interpreted as an awkward attempt at humanitarianism. By painting such a bleak and cruel picture of post-emancipation for freedmen, perhaps Lincoln was trying to impress upon African Americans a harsh reality few could envision. In effect, what Lincoln was trying to say to his black audience was that America was for whites only and that the overwhelming majority of white Americans, including himself, subscribed to that racist premise and thus a post-Civil War United States would be anything but a safe haven for freedmen. By encouraging emigration, Lincoln hoped to save blacks from the oppression, violence, and anguish that would become part and parcel of their everyday life in the South for the next 100 years.

Entirely separate from the harshness of telling African Americans that they were to pursue their new life as a free people in some place other than the land of their birth, Lincoln's plan was completely unrealistic: the United States had neither the facilities to colonize four million human beings nor a place to which it could send them. At the existing procreation rate, no less than five hundred black Americans were being born in the United States every day, it would thus be logistically impossible to "colonize" (deport) the African-American population as rapidly as it was increasing. Moreover, increasing numbers of black leaders, abolitionists, and many Republicans objected to Lincoln's policy, rightly arguing that such action would punish the victims of racial prejudice rather than its perpetrators. Blacks were Americans. Why should they not have the rights of American citizens instead of being urged to leave the country?

Nonetheless, Lincoln actually got a colonization experiment into operation in April 1863, when a group of 453 freedmen settled on Cow Island (Île à Vache), off Haiti. Predictably, they suffered and died from smallpox, malaria, and poisonous insects. They were unable to sustain themselves because of infertile soil, and in March 1864, a Navy transport arrived and took 368 survivors back to the United States. Despite the dismal failure of the Cow Island experiment, Lincoln, to his death, continued to believe that African-American emigration was the solution to the "Negro issue" if the nation hoped to avoid generations of bitter, vicious, and tragic race relations. Lincoln's dream of colonization prevented any significant public discussion about the hard question of the position of former slaves in American society.

Although addressing the freedmen issue, Lincoln made the re-assimilation of southern *whites* his priority, especially those white Southerners whose loyalty to the Confederacy had been lukewarm. He believed these people would become the foundation for his overall objective for a rapid restoration of the Union. Lincoln's desire for leniency for southern whites became a divisive issue not only within the Republican Party but also among northern whites, many of whom believed *all* southern whites were guilty of secession and should be punished accordingly. For the moment, however, Lincoln prevailed on this issue with the promulgation of his Proclamation of Amnesty, which offered a presidential pardon to all southern whites (excluding Confederate government officials and high-ranking military officers) who took an oath of allegiance to the United States and accepted the abolition of slavery. More importantly, in any state where the number of white males aged 21 or older who took this oath equaled 10 percent of the number of 1860 voters, that group could establish a state government, which Lincoln promised he would recognize as legitimate, and that state could reenter the Union, as if it had never left.

Lincoln's so-called Ten Percent Plan outraged many Republicans, who rightly claimed that Lincoln's amnesty policy favored former Confederates at the freedmen's expense. To this opposition, Lincoln's plan smacked of betrayal and hypocrisy, for it rewarded "traitors" to the country with a complete restoration of their political rights while denying such rights to black men who had fought *for* the Union. Further incensing these Republicans was Lincoln's Proclamation of Reconstruction, which allowed ex-Confederate landowners and former slaveholders to establish labor regulations and other measures to control the freedmen's labor, so long as they recognized manumission and made minimal provisions for their ex-slaves' education.

The freedmen issue was not the only source of conflict between Lincoln and some Republicans. The question of which branch of government—executive or legislative—should have authority and control over the Reconstruction process also caused rancor. In Lincoln's mind, it should be the president. Lincoln based this prerogative on his belief that he had been engaged for four years in suppressing an insurrection, which according to Lincoln's interpretation of the Constitution was clearly an executive, not legislative, responsibility. Moreover, Lincoln never asked Congress for a "declaration of war," only the right to use force to suppress an internal rebellion, the exact term he used in April 1861 when he called for 75,000 volunteers to join the United States Army for six months. Thus, in Lincoln's mind, no state of war existed between North and South because a war can only be fought between two "legitimate" nations. In Lincoln's view, the Confederate States of America never existed as a legitimate nation because no state has the Constitutional right to secede from the Union. Based on such an interpretation of his executive powers, Lincoln assumed the right to reorganize the South and guide it back into the Union largely on his own authority as commander-in-chief.

Many congressional Republicans thought otherwise. They interpreted Lincoln's call for volunteers to suppress rebellion not to be an executive order but a declaration of war, which only Congress can approve. By sanctioning Lincoln's call for troops, Congress believed a state of war existed between the United States of America and another political entity, the Confederate States of America. If that were the case, then the legislative branch, not the executive branch, should have authority over Reconstruction, for only Congress can declare war, not the president; he can only ask for such a proclamation. Disturbing these Republicans most was Lincoln's apparent states' rights disposition. By insisting that secession was illegal, that the southern states had never actually left the Union, Lincoln appeared to be asserting that the southern states thus maintained their right to govern their own affairs. Such a rendering was completely unacceptable to hardline Republicans who rejected any notion that the rebellious states had the right to immediately reclaim their **Antebellum** status without retribution for their treason. Congressional Republicans believed that the only way to avoid such an insult to the Union dead was to challenge Lincoln's interpretation of the crisis by defining the Civil War as a war rather than a rebellion. If that conception prevailed, they, not the president, would have the Constitutional right of jurisdiction over Reconstruction, thus guaranteeing punishment of Confederates for their treasonous acts. This controversy coupled with the debate over the status of the freedmen destined the two branches of government for a showdown for power. Such a confrontation, however, would not occur until the ascendancy of Andrew Johnson to the presidency.

Radical Republicans and Reconstruction

Those within the party who opposed Lincoln's agenda became known as the "**Radicals Republicans.**" Contrary to Lincoln, these men, led by Charles Sumner of Massachusetts in the Senate and Thaddeus Stevens of Pennsylvania in the House, believed not only that the white South must be punished for secession and rebellion but for the sin of slavery as well. To the Radicals, it was quite obvious and simple what should be done in the South in the war's aftermath: all white Southerners, regardless of status, should be punished for their treason, either by their property confiscated or disfranchisement, or both. Appropriated rebel land should then be given to freedmen to help them to establish themselves. The Radicals feared that Lincoln's lenient policies would result in the old ruling class being restored to power. To prevent that possibility, Radicals Republicans proposed that freedmen be given the right to vote, which, they

John Wilkes Booth

believed, would ensure a genuine nucleus of loyal supporters in the South.

The Radicals countered with their own plan, the **Wade-Davis Bill** (named for Senator Benjamin Wade of Ohio and Representative Henry Winter Davis of Maryland), which required white Southerners to take a much more stringent loyalty oath (the "**iron clad oath**") as well as requiring 50 percent rather than Lincoln's 10 percent of the population to swear allegiance to the Union. Surprisingly, the Wade-Davis Bill made no provision for black enfranchisement, the result of the Radicals being a minority within the Republican Party at that time (1864). The majority of congressional Republicans were moderates and conservatives, cool to the idea of black voting rights and thus were more inclined to support Lincoln's agenda rather than that of the Radicals. With such a coalition behind him, Lincoln killed the Wade-Davis Bill with a pocket veto (whereby a bill passed at the end of a congressional session fails to become law if it is not signed by the president).

Although upset with Lincoln, the Radicals were loyal Republicans and thus united with their more moderate comrades to ensure Lincoln's and their party's victory and control of both the White House and Congress. By the spring of 1865, the Confederacy's collapse was only a matter of weeks, setting the stage for a compromise between Lincoln and Congress on a policy for the postwar South. Two days after Lee's surrender to Ulysses S. Grant at Appomattox, Lincoln promised that he would soon announce a more thorough Reconstruction agenda, which he intimated would include provisions for black enfranchisement and stronger guarantees to protect their civil rights.

Tragically for the entire nation, no one will ever know what Lincoln had in store for the South or for four million African Americans. On April 14, 1865, as Lincoln and his wife watched a play at Ford's Theater in Washington, a rebel fanatic actor named John Wilkes Booth shot Lincoln at close range in the back of the head, leaped to the stage, and escaped. Lincoln never recovered consciousness, dying early the next morning.

Booth was part of a larger conspiracy of rebel zealots, which almost succeeded in beheading the national executive branch in one, coordinated fatal blow. While Booth murdered Lincoln, his two compatriots, Lewis Powell and George Atzerodt, were supposed to kill Secretary of State William Seward (Powell's target) and Vice President Andrew Johnson (Atzerodt's assigned victim). Atzerdodt got drunk and backed down. Powell came close to succeeding with his knife, but a heavily-wounded Seward fought off his attacker enough to survive. Powell was later hanged with the other conspirators. After a long and frantic search, Booth was captured and killed in a Virginia barn. The assassin's bullet lost a hero for the North, a potential ally for fair and equal opportunity for African Americans, and a leader who called for "charity toward all" and "malice toward none" for southern whites.

ANDREW JOHNSON AND RECONSTRUCTION

Between 1865 and 1868, the United States confronted one of the greatest political crises of its history—the battle between President Andrew Johnson and Congress over Reconstruction. The struggle resulted in profound changes in the nature of citizenship, the structure of constitutional authority, and the meaning of American freedom.

Booth's bullet elevated to the presidency a man who still thought himself a Democrat and a Southerner: Andrew Johnson of Tennessee. Originally from North Carolina of poor white heritage, Johnson rose to power in Tennessee politics as a Jacksonian populist, championing the cause of the small, non-slaveholding farmers, shopkeepers, and artisans of East Tennessee against the planter elite of the state's central and western regions who controlled Tennessee politically. True to his Jacksonian core, Johnson was equally suspicious and hostile toward banks, corporations, bondholders, and New Englanders. He fervidly opposed the Whig/Republican policy of government participation in, and promotion of, the

Andrew Johnson, 1866.

nation's economic development. Johnson's enemies list included not only the plantation aristocracy but also the "bloated, corrupt aristocracy" of the commercial-industrial economy emerging in the Northeast. A devoted Unionist, Johnson was the only senator from a seceding state not to support the Confederacy. For his loyalty, the Republicans in 1864 rewarded him with their party's vice-presidential nomination, hoping that his presence on the ticket would attract the votes of northern pro-war Democrats and Upper South yeoman Unionists.

Although many Radicals believed that Johnson would be too "soft" on his white southern brethren, such concerns faded quickly as the new president displayed an enmity toward "the stuck up [slaveholding] aristocrats" that shocked at times even the most passionate of Radicals. In Johnson's mind it was clear from the start that it was the South's slaveholding elite who had been responsible for secession and war. Thus the time had come to punish these "traitors. Traitors must be impoverished; they must not only be punished, but their social power must be destroyed."

The Radical Republicans delighted in Johnson's harsh rhetoric. His rantings against the slaveocracy seemed to convey that he was in agreement with the Radicals on the type of reconstruction policy to be pursued—one that would disenfranchise former Confederates but would enfranchise the freedmen. With Johnson's support, the Radicals envisioned the creation of a coalition between the freedmen and the small minority of southern white Unionists. Together they would become the basis for a new southern political order; naturally they would become Republicans, the party of Union and emancipation. Once such a coalition took power in the southern states, they would pass laws to provide civil rights and economic opportunity for African Americans. Not incidentally, these new Republicans would also strengthen the party nationally by ending the Democrats' domination over the southern states.

Much to the Radicals' and even some moderate Republicans' dismay, Johnson proved hostile to the party's vision of the freedmen's place in society. Although earlier proclaiming to be black Tennesseans "Moses," leading them out of bondage, Johnson never embraced the liberal tenets of the antislavery ideology. Indeed, Johnson had once owned slaves himself. To Johnson, the Civil War concerned combating secession and destroying the power of those responsible—the planter elite; it was never a crusade to end slavery. In 1866, a black delegation led by Frederick Douglass visited with Johnson to urge the president to include provisions for black suffrage in his reconstruction agenda. Johnson parried their arguments and afterwards remarked to his secretary: "Those damned sons of bitches thought they had me in a trap! I know that damned Douglass; he is just like any other nigger, and he would sooner cut a white man's throat than not."

Johnson clearly was a racist, sharing with his white brethren, North and South, a firm belief in white supremacy. Johnson and other non-slaveholding white Southerners may have despised the slaveocracy, but it was not because they owned slaves. It had been their possession of disproportionate political power that had caused such dislike.

This ideology even took hold in the North, which saw the Democratic Party aggressively champion white supremacy, resulting in the party's ability to attract the Irish, southern Midwest "Butternuts" (white Southerners who migrated to the southern areas of free states such as Indiana, Illinois, and Ohio), and unskilled laborers to its camp. These people believed blacks to be inferior, and no matter how poor they might be, these white people were still better than blacks. Like their southern non-slaveholding counterparts, they feared emancipation because it would render their whiteness meaningless.

To many Republicans' further consternation, Johnson, like Lincoln, believed Reconstruction (which he preferred to call "restoration") to be primarily an executive function. He also believed in Lincoln's theory of "indestructible states"—that the rebellion had been one of individuals, not states, and although the individuals might be punished, the states retained all their constitutional rights. Given such conflicting views about who should control the reconstruction agenda and what the priorities were to be, it would only be a matter of time before the inevitable occurred: a nasty showdown between the president and a Republican-dominated Congress.

Johnson's Reconstruction Policy

In May 1865, Johnson fired the opening salvo in his war with congressional Republicans when he issued two proclamations on his own initiative. The first provided for a blanket amnesty and restitution of property (except slaves, of course) to all who would take an oath of allegiance. Excluded from Johnson's general pardon were Confederate civil and diplomatic officials, army officers above the rank of colonel, state governors, and all persons owning taxable property valued at $20,000 or more. Johnson was true to his word that he would punish those most responsible for having caused the war—the stuck-up aristocrats. In his second edict, beginning with North Carolina, Johnson personally appointed provisional governors for the former Confederate states, directing them to call elections for delegates to draft new state constitutions. Only those white men who had received amnesty and had taken the oath of allegiance could vote. The state conventions were to draft constitutions that abolished slavery, nullified secession, and repudiated all debts incurred by the state while it was a member of the Confederacy (on the grounds that, secession being illegal, all indebtedness acquired in its behalf was null and void). Johnson's policy was clear. He excluded both the freedmen and upper-class whites from the Reconstruction process. The new political foundation for the "restored South" would be those white yeomen and artisans who had remained loyal Unionists in alliance with those who now proclaimed their fidelity.

Johnson outraged the Radical Republicans by his complete disregard for the freedmen and by his blatant slight of Congress. It appeared that Johnson was not only a dedicated white supremacist but also intent on usurping power to the executive branch by arrogating taking complete control of Reconstruction. In hopes of rallying northern opinion to their side, the Radicals bombarded voters with speeches, pamphlets, and editorials, all declaring that the president's policies would inevitably lead to the restoration of the old power structure in the South, minus only slavery.

None of the southern conventions made any provision for black suffrage in their new constitutions. Johnson made no more gestures in the direction of black enfranchisement. He stated that voting qualifications were a state matter and that it was beyond his constitutional right to interfere. Johnson's refusal to push any further for even a limited black suffrage not only alienated moderate Republicans but encouraged southern defiance on other issues as well.

The Black Suffrage Issue in the North

The Radical cause for black enfranchisement in the South received a devastating blow in the fall of 1865 when Connecticut, Minnesota, and Wisconsin held referendums on whether to amend their respective constitutions to allow the right to vote to the few black men in their states. Everyone knew that in some measure the referendums' outcomes would reveal much about northern white racial attitudes. The Democrats in these states engaged in their usual race-mongering and black-baiting with the result that the amendments were defeated in all three states. Republicans in those states voted overwhelmingly for allowing black men the right to vote. Most contemporaries interpreted the election outcomes as a northern white mandate against black suffrage. Southern whites were delighted with the results, for in their mind the amendments' defeat was confirmation that their northern white brethren were just as determined to keep the United States "a white man's country." Perhaps more importantly, the defeat of black suffrage in the North only further emboldened southern whites to flagrantly defy Johnson's Reconstruction mandates.

Southern Defiance

Not only did the southern state constitutional conventions reject black enfranchisement in any capacity, but some even balked at ratifying the Thirteenth Amendment and at repudiating the Confederate debt. Once again, throughout the South could be heard disparaging anti-Northern rhetoric and deprecating and mocking of all things "Yankee." It sounded and felt like 1861 all over again. White, neo-Confederate paramilitary units appeared, terrorizing blacks and their white sympathizers. Johnson seemed to encourage such activities by his own rhetoric and refusal to address such reprisals.

Compounding Johnson's troubles with white violence perpetrated on freedmen was the issue of presidential pardons. This particular matter caused more immediate acrimony between the president and congressional Republicans than any other controversy. After all his bluster about punishing southern traitors, Johnson had reversed himself by the fall of 1865, issuing special pardons to 13,500 ex-Confederates and restoring all property and political rights to them. The majority of these individuals were the stuck-up aristocrats who he had vowed he would impoverish and destroy only a few months earlier. What had caused this transformation in Johnson's attitude and behavior, from one who spoke menacingly about the crime of treason to one who now spoke of forgiveness? Johnson was a Southerner and had no more liking for the Radical Yankee ethos than the majority of his southern brethren. Moreover, his exchanges and encounters with the Radicals during the summer and fall of 1865 convinced him that his real friends were his southern white compatriots, including the very individuals that he once personally despised and publicly lambasted. They praised his policies and flattered his ego, while the Radicals chastised him openly and moderates expressed their concerns in private. Reveling in his power over these once-haughty aristocrats who had deprecated him as a humble tailor, Johnson waxed eloquent on his "love, respect, and confidence" toward southern whites for whom he now felt "forbearing and forgiving." Perhaps more important was the outpouring of support by northern Democrats, many of whom disingenuously whispered in his ear that he would be their party's choice in the 1868 election if he could manage to reconstruct the South in such a way that would maintain the Democratic majority there.

To the Republicans' further dismay, under the new state constitutions established by Johnson's policy, southern voters elected hundreds of former Confederates to state offices. Northerners were even more outraged by the election to Congress of nine ex-Confederate congressmen, seven former Confederate state officials, four generals, four colonels, and the selection of Confederate Vice President Alexander H. Stephens to the U.S. Senate by the new Georgia legislature. For Republicans, it appeared that the rebels, unable to capture Washington in war, were about to do so in peacetime.

The Black Codes

As many Radicals feared, no sooner did southern whites reclaim their governments than they passed the infamous "**black codes**," reflecting not only devotion to white supremacy but a determination as well to reduce the freedmen to a condition of virtual re-enslavement. The freedmen were excluded from juries and voting and could not testify against whites in court. Also forbidden was interracial marriage, and blacks suffered much harsher punishment than whites for certain crimes. Most states passed vagrancy laws, subjecting to forced labor on a plantation any unemployed freedmen. Blacks could not lease land and any black youth whose parents could not adequately provide for his or her care was apprenticed to a white man.

The black codes outraged Republicans who could not believe this latest manifestation of southern white arrogance and brazenness. For many Republicans the codes were the last straw in their war with Andrew Johnson, whom they held responsible for this latest insult to the Union dead.

LAND AND LABOR IN THE POSTWAR SOUTH

Although blatantly racist and oppressive, the black codes were designed to address a legitimate problem. Emancipation plunged black-white relations into a world of uncertainty, fear, and hostility with whites especially bitter toward their former slaves. In much of the South, the Yankee army had physically destroyed the southern landscape and antebellum economy. Burned-out plantations, fields gone to seed, railroads without tracks or bridges, and rolling stock marked the effects of total war visited upon the South by the invading Federal armies. Over half of the South's livestock was gone as well as much of its sustainable land, compounding already serious food shortages; possible starvation loomed for both white and black Southerners. Lawlessness was also rampant with roaming bands of hungry ex-rebel soldiers and black vagabonds looking for food and shelter often engaging acts of violent crime to survive. The war ended early enough in the spring to allow the planting of at least some crops but who would plant and cultivate them? The South had lost one-quarter of its white farmers in war, and the slaves had been freed.

Despite such struggles, life went on. Soldiers' widows and their children plowed and planted; masters without slaves and their wives calloused their hands for the first time. Former slave owners now had to ask their former chattels if they would be willing to work the land for wages or shares of the crop, and many freedmen readily agreed to such a changed capital-labor relationship. Plantation life and economy was all they had known for generations. Many freedmen, however, wanted nothing to do with their former masters, choosing instead to get as far away from the old plantation as possible. Thousands migrated to the nearest city or town in search of work rather than return to the painful memory of bondage. Some wandered aimlessly, simply enjoying freedom as long as they could until getting hungry or "disciplined" by roaming white vigilante groups. Nonetheless, for the majority of freedmen, true emancipation meant never returning to the plantation. As a black preacher told his congregation, "You ain't, none of you, gwinter feel rale free till you shakes de dus' ob de ole plantashun offen yore fee an an' goes ter a new place why you kin live out o'sight o' de gret house." (dialect in original source).

The Freedmen's Bureau by A.R. Waud.
A man representing the Freedmen's Bureau stands between armed groups of white Americans and African Americans. 1868.

The Freedmen's Bureau

Attempting to bring a semblance of order and stability to the South was the United States Army and the **Freedmen's Bureau**. Tens of thousands of United States troops remained in the South as an occupation force, establishing martial law in the ex-Confederate states until civil government could be restored. Perhaps more important to the history of Reconstruction was the Freedmen's Bureau (the agency's official name was the Bureau of Refugees, Freedmen, and Abandoned Lands) created by Congress in March 1865. This particular federal initiative marked the first time in the history of the Republic that the national government established an agency to protect and promote the socio-economic welfare of its citizens. Although the Bureau's primary purpose was to safeguard the freedmen from white reprisals, whether legal, physical, or from whatever form such retaliation might take, white Southerners too benefited from this program. The Bureau issued food rations to 150,000 people daily in 1865, one-third of them to whites.

The Bureau's commissioner, General Oliver O. Howard, established his headquarters in Washington. In each former slave state, an army general was assigned as assistant commissioner and directed his field operatives from the state's capital or largest city. The majority of the Bureau's 550 local agents were junior officers from middle-class northern backgrounds. Some took genuine interest in their charges' well-being, displaying a sincere belief in equality, while others were simply marking time until something better in the civilian world came along. Sadly, the officers of the latter disposition often displayed toward the freedmen the same racist attitudes and general disdain for blacks as their southern white counterparts. The Bureau also appointed some civilian agents, including a few African Americans. Although the number of agents was too few to reach every corner of the South, these agents—backed by the army's occupation troops—nevertheless had considerable potential power to transform postwar southern labor relations.

Once it became clear that the federal government intended no massive land redistribution for the freedmen's benefit, the Bureau then focused its energies on trying to forge a new relationship between planters and freedmen. The agents' main objective was to encourage (or require) planters and laborers to sign written contracts that specified the amount and kind of work to be done, the wages to be paid, and other conditions of employment. Wages

RECONSTRUCTION: *The Turning Point That Never Turned* / **483**

This print depicts African Americans gathered outside the Freedmen's Bureau in Richmond, Virginia. The Bureau is issuing rations to the old and sick. 1866.

agreed upon ranged from eight to fifteen dollars a month, plus room and board, and sometimes work clothes and equipment and even medical care. Freedmen were paid either in cash or a share of the crop. Because of a shortage of money, planters preferred to pay laborers with a percentage of the crop, which would not be paid until after harvest. Such a contract ensured worker loyalty by creating a relationship in which both planter and freedmen had a vested interest in getting the crops out of the ground. Thus, one of the Bureau's principal tasks was to protect freedmen from potential exploitation as its agents adjudicated thousands of complaints registered by black workers against their employers not only for abuse but for violation of contracts as well. Because southern state courts would never give freedmen a fair hearing, General Howard urged Congress to revise the original bill to empower the Bureau to establish special courts to function as military tribunals until Congress declared the rebellious states restored to the Union. Johnson vetoed the new mandate, but the Radicals in Congress would not be deterred and worked to override the president's rejection. With usually only one agent acting as judge and jury, these "special courts" remained in existence until 1868.

Southern whites, particularly the antebellum elite, came to despise the Bureau, denouncing it as a "curse," a "ridiculous folly," and a "vicious institution." Interestingly, such remarks reflected not so much a hatred of the Bureau for what it did but, rather, for what it symbolized—conquest and emancipation. Planters insisted they could "make the nigger work" if meddling Bureau agents would only leave them alone. In reality, such complaints and denunciations were unfounded. More often than not, the Bureau proved to be more of a planter ally than a manifestation of emancipation and alleged white degradation. Agents got idle freedmen back to work by enforcing contracts whose terms favored employers rather than workers. Reflecting sensitivity to criticism in both the northern and southern press that the Bureau was promoting a welfare ethic among freedmen, many Bureau officers would cut off rations to able-bodied blacks to force them to work. While publicly vilifying the Bureau, privately planters admitted that without it the postwar labor situation would have been even more chaotic. Indeed, in late 1865, the Bureau helped to suppress a possible insurrection among freedmen when they learned that they were not going to receive their anticipated "**forty acres and a mule**." In response to the news, thousands of freedmen throughout the South refused to sign contracts for the next year. To the Bureau fell the unhappy task of disabusing the freedmen about land redistribution and compelling them to sign contracts. In 1867, a Bureau official assessed the contract system: "It has succeeded in making the Freedman work and in rendering labor secure & stable—but it has failed to secure the Freedman his just dues or compensation."

The Issue of Land for the Landless

Naturally, freedmen wanted land for themselves rather than having to work for former masters or other whites. The majority of freedmen believed that only ownership of their own land would make them truly free. For most former slaves, however, purchasing land was impossible. Few had money, and if they had, even the most destitute whites often refused to sell or even rent land to them for fear of having African Americans being anything other than subservient and dependent. Thus, freedmen looked to the federal government to help gain true independence from continued white control. The hope for "forty acres and a mule" was no delusion of ignorant minds. By June 1865, the Freedmen's Bureau had appropriated almost 500,000 acres of plantation lands along the Georgia and South Carolina coastal areas and had settled in those areas nearly 10,000 black families. General William T. Sherman also gave freedmen captured horses and mules so they could work the land. Elsewhere in the South, Freedmen's Bureau agents took it upon themselves to reallocate to freedmen nearly a million acres of abandoned or confiscated land in their respective areas.

Such initiatives by Union generals and Bureau agents raised expectations throughout the South that all freedmen would soon be given their own land by a massive confiscation and redistribution plan being formulated in Washington. Such was precisely the agenda envisioned by Thaddeus Stevens of Pennsylvania and other Radical Republicans who advocated the appropriation of land owned by wealthy former Confederates and allocating forty acres of this land to each adult freedman. The remainder was to be sold to finance war pensions and repay the war debt.

Unfortunately, Andrew Johnson and Congress dashed such hopes. Johnson's amnesty and pardon proclamation restored all property to their original owners, and Congress failed to pass effective legislation that would have allowed for even abandoned land to be turned over to freedmen. Commissioner Howard, however, refused to comply with Johnson's edicts. Howard considered the amnesty proclamation inapplicable to abandoned or confiscated property, which he interpreted as being "set apart [for use] by refugees and freedmen." Johnson believed otherwise, ordering Howard to restore property to all pardoned Confederates, but Howard ordered his agents to stall and delay as long as possible property restoration to rebels, hoping to retain as much land as possible until Congress met in December. Howard hoped Congress would challenge the president on this issue and allow for the freedmen's possession of at least some of the land under Bureau control.

In February 1866, Congress passed an addendum to the Freedmen's Bureau Bill that allowed for those freedmen given land along the Georgia and South Carolina coastal areas to keep the land for three years. But Johnson vetoed the bill, and Congress failed to pass it over the veto. In July 1866, Republicans finally managed to pass a revised bill over the president's veto, but the new law called for the displacement of freedmen from Georgia and South Carolina proper to those states' respective offshore islands. Worse, the dispossessed freedmen now had to purchase the government-held land on those islands, albeit at a price below market value. Only 2,000 displaced black families were able to purchase the offshore land. The new policy marked a sad ending to the high hopes of 1865. By the end of 1866, nearly all the arable land once controlled by the Freedmen's Bureau had been returned to its ex-Confederate owners.

Perhaps to atone for such betrayal, Congress passed the Southern Homestead Act soon after its earlier measure had displaced Georgia and South Carolina freedmen. Similar in design and purpose to the 1862 **Homestead Act** for the Great Plains area (the former "Great American Desert"), this law set aside 44 million acres of public land in five southern states (Alabama, Arkansas, Florida, Louisiana, and Mississippi) to be parceled out in 80-acre allotments to black settlers. If they improved the land over a five-year period, then, as stipulated in the 1862 act, it was theirs for the keeping, free of charge. In order to ensure that the land designated in these states went to freedmen and white Unionist, the law forbade anyone who had supported the Confederacy from settling in the specified areas. Generous in conception, the Southern Homestead Act was largely a failure in practice. Typically, most of the remaining public land in these states was marginal at best, and few freedmen possessed enough money to purchase seed, tools, livestock, and building materials to improve the land. Consequently, fewer than 7,000 freedmen relocated to these states, and only 1,000 of these homesteaders were able to fulfill the requirements for final ownership. Thus, meaningful land reform did not become part of Reconstruction, and with such a failure came the inevitable return of the majority of freedmen to a status of quasi-bondage (debt peonage) in the form of sharecropping and tenant farming.

THE ORIGINS OF RADICAL RECONSTRUCTION

It was only a matter of time before the growing schism between Andrew Johnson and the Republican-dominated 39th Congress would escalate into an outright power struggle over who should control the Reconstruction process. However, not until the Radicals gained dominance within the party did a full-fledged assault on the president become a certainty. As long as Republicans were divided along Radical, moderate, and conservative alignments, Johnson's Reconstruction policies would prevail. However, once Republicans put aside their differences and united in a determination to oppose Johnson and agree on the course Reconstruction should take, then the president's days as an effective leader would indeed be numbered.

What goodwill existed between Republicans and the president began to evaporate when Johnson vetoed two bills to protect the freedmen. The first extended the life of the Freedmen's Bureau, expanded its legal powers, and authorized the agency to build and support schools. The second bill defined the freedmen's civil rights and gave federal courts appellate jurisdiction in cases concerning these rights.

Johnson knew his veto would alienate the moderates and move him toward an alliance with the Democrats, who held mass rallies in support of the president's veto. After one such gathering, the celebrants marched to the White House where Johnson feted the crowd with one of the most remarkable presidential speeches ever delivered. Johnson denounced the Radicals as traitors who did not want the Union restored. He also told the crowd that the Radicals were plotting his assassination, comparing them to Judas and himself to Christ. "If my blood is to be shed because I vindicate the Union and the preservation of this government in its original purity and character, let it be shed; let an altar to the Union be erected, and then if it is necessary, take me and lay me upon it, and the blood that now warms and animates my existence shall be poured out as a fit libation to the Union."

The president's behavior mortified many Americans. "Was he drunk?" they asked. Radicals could now declare to their moderate colleagues "I told you so!" The final straw for moderate and Radical Republicans came with Johnson's veto in March 1866 of a civil rights bill for freedmen, initiated by the moderate leader Lyman Trumbull of Illinois. The measure defined freedmen as United States citizens and guaranteed their rights to own or rent property, to make and enforce contracts, and to have access to the courts as parties and as witnesses. Interestingly, Trumbull's initiative did not call for black enfranchisement, or mandate that African Americans sit on juries, or require integrated schools and public accommodations. Republicans therefore expected Johnson to sign this moderate bill despite his states' rights convictions. Even his cabinet was unanimous in urging the president to sign the measure.

Like his earlier veto, this one also provoked Democratic euphoria and Republican condemnation. Democratic editors rejoiced that Johnson did not believe "in compounding our race with niggers, gipsies [sic], and baboons." If Johnson's objective with his vetoes had been to isolate the Radicals while forging a moderate/conservative coalition in support of his policy, he had badly miscalculated just how far moderates were willing to go to obtain at least a modicum of rights for the freedmen.

The Fourteenth Amendment

Johnson had thrown down the gauntlet with his veto of the Freedmen's Bureau and Civil Rights bills. Congressional Republicans, led by the Radicals, did not hesitate to pick it up, pushing through Congress in June 1866 the **Fourteenth Amendment** to the Constitution. (It would take an additional two years before the requisite two-thirds of the states ratified the amendment). The measure defined all native-born and naturalized persons, including African Americans, as American citizens and prohibited the states from denying any such individual from the "privileges and immunities" of citizenship and from depriving "any person of life, liberty, or property without due process of law." The initiative further mandated that states enfranchise black males or they would forfeit a proportionate number of congressional seats and electoral votes. Another section barred a significant number of ex-Confederates from holding federal or state offices while repudiating the Confederate debt. All of the bill's stipulations were to be enforced by Congress by "appropriate legislation."

White Southerners and Democrats naturally denounced the bill as one more manifestation of Radical vengeance on men who had already suffered enough for their sins. Radical Republicans countered by declaring the measure did not go far enough to punish traitors and prevent their political resurgence. Radicals and abolitionists also decried the bill for not making fiat in all states black enfranchisement. The bill penalized southern states from denying black suffrage but allowed northern states to do so with impunity because their black population was too small to make a difference in the basis of representation. Abolitionists condemned the bill as a "swindle," a "wanton betrayal of justice and humanity."

For the moment, the Radical Republicans accepted the amendment as the best they could get while hoping that future events would move the country toward universal African-American male suffrage. Despite Radical and abolitionist lamentations, the Fourteenth Amendment had far-reaching consequences—the initiative became the most important constitutional provision for defining and enforcing civil rights in the nation. Unlike the first ten amendments (the Bill of Rights), which imposed restrictions on federal power, the Fourteenth Amendment greatly expanded federal authority to prevent state violations of civil rights. To the joy of the Radicals, the bill also greatly expanded African-American rights (at least on paper), while curtailing ex-Confederates' political power. That is why Johnson and his Democratic supporters, with their states' rights, proslavery mentality, opposed it.

The 1866 Congressional Elections

In many ways the 1866 congressional elections were a referendum on the Fourteenth Amendment, which the Republicans made the centerpiece of their party's platform. Since moderates still held sway in the party, they offered Southerners a carrot: any ex-Confederate state that ratified the amendment would be declared "reconstructed," and its representatives and senators could then take their respective congressional seats. Tennessee accepted this overture, ratified the amendment, and seated its representatives and senators. Johnson, believing he could still stem the congressional Republican tide against him by rallying southern and northern Democrats to his position, unwisely counseled other southern legislatures to reject the amendment, and they did so. Johnson then prepared for an all-out campaign to gain a pro-administration northern majority in the congressional elections by cobbling together a coalition of a few conservative Republicans, border-state Unionists, and Democrats. The new alliance called itself the **National Union Party**. No sooner was the coalition formed than the Democratic tail soon began to wag the National Union dog, thus dooming from the outset the party's chances of victory at the polls. Northern voters remained suspicious of Democrats, many of whom still believed the party had betrayed the country by opposing the war. Also, adversely affecting Johnson and his coalition was the ongoing violence against freedmen, which resulted in vicious race riots in New Orleans and Memphis, where white mobs rampaged against freedmen and their white allies, killing 80 blacks, among them several former Union soldiers. The endemic violence against African Americans only served to confirm the Republican contention that without greater federal protection and intervention in the South, African Americans were doomed to a life of perpetual fear, proscription, and terror.

Perhaps the National Union Party's greatest liability was Andrew Johnson, who in a speech in St. Louis soon after the melees in New Orleans and Memphis, blamed Republicans for provoking the white mobs while expressing no regret for the victims. In a whistle-stop tour of the North, Johnson engaged in shouting contests with hecklers and traded insults with hostile crowds. The substance of his speeches never varied: the South was loyal; the real traitors were the Radicals, who were bent on revenge, further polarizing the nation. Furthermore, he, Andrew Johnson, was willing to give his life if necessary for the salvation of the Union and the Constitution. In virtually every speech, Johnson closed by comparing himself to Jesus and his Republican adversaries to Judas. The National Union Party was embarrassingly routed at the polls, with the Republicans sweeping the election and gaining a 3-to-1 majority in the next Congress. Southern intransigence and the condoning of the wanton, often violent, persecution of the freedmen coupled with Johnson's tacit, if not blatant, approval of both actions accomplished what the Radicals alone could not achieve: the conversion of moderates to black suffrage and the congressional takeover of the Reconstruction process.

Above, a satirical cartoon by Thomas Nast that blames the Democratic Party for anti-black violence in the South. Nast mocks what he sees as the three wings of the Democratic Party. From the left, Nast depicts an Irish immigrant, a Confederate soldier and a greedy Wall Street investor. The three stand on a dead African-American soldier from the Union Army. In the background, black schools and orphanages are in flames. This illustration appeared in an 1868 edition of *Harper's Magazine*.

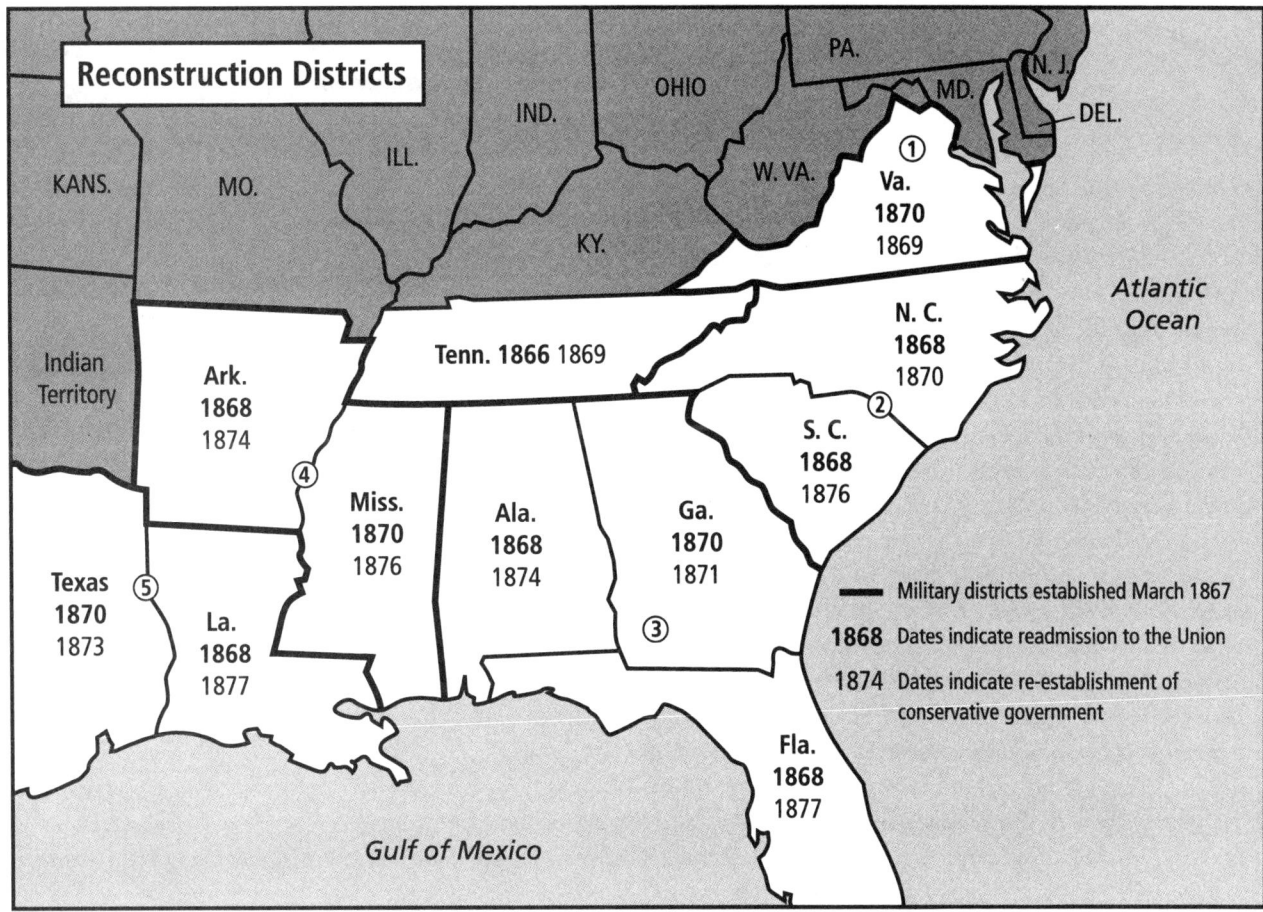

Map 17.1 Reconstruction Districts

The Reconstruction Acts of 1867

No sooner did the Republicans gain control of Congress with the Radicals in the ascendancy, than the history of the post-war South took yet another turn, one that many southern whites to this day would come to despise. As far as the Radicals and many of their once-moderate allies were concerned, the South had yet to be properly reconstructed; nor had southern whites sufficiently atoned for their sins of slavery and secession—treason. Until that reformation occurred, the South would have to be placed under martial law, for not only the freedmen's protection but for those white Southerners who had remained loyal to the Union. Thus, the **Reconstruction Acts of 1867** divided the ten southern states into five military districts under the authority of a Union general and whose sub-commanders in the states in his district were to register voters for the election of delegates to new constitutional conventions. *All* adult males over the age of 21 were to be enfranchised to vote in those elections. However, the act disenfranchised (for these elections only) those former Confederates who were disqualified from holding office under the not-yet-ratified Fourteenth Amendment, which translated to fewer than 10 percent of all eligible white male voters. The act further stipulated that all new state constitutions had to ratify the Fourteenth Amendment as well as guarantee equal civil and political rights to all citizens, regardless of race. Until that occurred, the state's congressional representatives would not be seated.

The Radical Republicans believed that the reduction of ex-Confederate states to the status of "conquered territories" would bode well for their larger vision and agenda for southern Reconstruction. They hoped that such a condition would allow time for the Freedmen's Bureau, freedmen's aid societies, northern soldiers and settlers, and northern money to flow into the South to help elevate and educate the freedmen and protect them from white reprisals. The Radicals believed that until the southern rebels felt the heavy hand of national power and presence, they would continue to resist all attempts at reformation.

The 1867 Reconstruction Acts reflected a true revolution—"the maddest, most infamous revolution in history," according to many southern whites. Just a few years earlier white Southerners had been masters of four million slaves and leaders of an independent Confederate nation. Now they had been stripped of political power and their former slaves not only freed but politically

The White Backlash During Presidential Reconstruction:
The 1866 Race Riots in Memphis and New Orleans

Throughout the Reconstruction era the majority of white Southerners refused to accept any notions of treating freedmen with any degree of dignity and respect for their person, let alone entertain any possibility of accepting them as equals, either before the law or in any social context. Indeed, white Southerners during the decade after the Civil War repeatedly engaged in violent reprisals against any attempts by freedmen to assert the political and civil rights guaranteed them by the federal government. A few weeks after Congress passed the 1866 Civil Rights Act, white citizens in the cities of Memphis and New Orleans made it clear that they would not accept the federally-mandated decree by unleashing a several-days-long reign of violent terror on those cities' respective black residents.

In Memphis, the black population had multiplied four times since the end of the war, as former slaves left the Tennessee countryside in hopes of better opportunities in the city. As the black population in Memphis increased, so did white fears and hostility. "Would to God they were back in Africa, or some other seaport town," declared the Memphis Argus, "anywhere but here." Interestingly, Andrew Johnson's proscriptive policies toward the old Tennessee elite succeeded in their ousting from power in Memphis, but their replacements, aggressive parvenu Irish politicians, proved to be just as racist and as oppressive of blacks as the old guard. Not surprisingly, the city's new political leaders turned blind as tensions between white and blacks escalated, resulting in numerous incidents of physical assaults by whites (by both Irish and WASP residents) on the freedmen. It was only a matter of time before such conflicts would produce the incident that would spark a full-scale riot. On May 1, 1866, two hack drivers—one white and one black—had a traffic accident, and when the police arrived, they, of course, arrested the black driver, even though the run-in was not his fault. A group of black veterans tried to prevent the arrest, which attracted white bystanders who proceeded to attack the veterans. The former soldiers fought back, and within minutes the "Memphis Riots" had begun. Over the course of the next three days, rampaging whites burned hundreds of black homes, churches, and schools. Five black women were raped, and nearly fifty people, all but two of them black, were killed.

Three months later, the same racial violence occurred in New Orleans. As was happening throughout the South during Presidential Reconstruction, both state and municipal governments were coming under the control of ex-Confederates, who were not about to protect the freedmen from white reprisals. However, the New Orleans massacre had more explicitly political dimensions. For decades, the city had a well-established free black population. By 1866, they had not only become the most vociferous advocates for black political and civil rights, but for all those disillusioned with the presidential reconstruction agenda, which by that year had completely abandoned any civil rights initiatives for freedmen. A group of white and black Radicals issued a call to bring the state's 1864 constitutional convention back into session in hopes of bringing the issue of black political and civil rights to the forefront of the state's reconstruction program. This black-white radical alliance called for enfranchising the freedmen while disenfranchising all "rebels," as well as for turning out the members of the current state government regime of ex-Confederates and establishing an entirely new state government composed of the free black elite in conjunction with the white Radicals. The convention was scheduled to meet on July 30, 1866.

However, as the delegates convened, white mobs set out to stop them. Led by the city's police and firemen, consisting mostly of ex-Confederates, they first attacked a parade of about two hundred blacks who were marching to the Mechanic's Institute to support the delegates. When the mob reached the convention hall, deadly violence ensued. They assaulted the building, busting through its doors, shooting and killing delegates as they tried to escape through the windows. The slaughter continued, even though many attendees raised the white flag of surrender. As one Union veteran who witnessed the massacre reported, "the wholesale slaughter and the little regard paid to human life" were worse than anything he had seen in battle. When the mob finally dispersed, thirty-four blacks and three white supporters had been killed, and another hundred had been injured.

News of the Memphis and New Orleans melees quickly filtered north, becoming explosive political issues, which the Radicals exploited to further discredit Andrew Johnson and his reconstruction policies. Johnson, not known for his political savvy, played into the Radicals' hands. In late August 1866, Johnson undertook an unprecedented political campaign tour designed to generate voter hostility toward Congress, particularly the Radicals, whom he blamed for the calamities in New Orleans and Memphis. At one point during one of his tirades, he suggested that Radical Congressman Thaddeus Stevens should be hanged. Republicans charged in turn that Johnson's own policies had been responsible for the massacres—his blatant racist attitudes toward blacks and his lack of concern for their well-being encouraged the vicious attacks. His obvious disdain for the freedmen had revived both white racism and white rebelliousness, both of which were unleashed upon the black citizens of New Orleans and Memphis.

*The 1866 congressional elections thus became a referendum on competing visions of what American democracy should mean. For Andrew Johnson, "democracy" meant government by local majorities, which meant white supremacy. For African Americans and a growing number of Republicans, genuine democracy could only be constructed on a firm foundation of equal civil and political rights. Northern voters overwhelmingly rejected the president's notion of democracy, and as the **New York Times** declared, the results "clearly, unmistakably, decisively" reflected "Congress and its policy." The 1866 congressional elections also brought an overwhelmingly Republican majority to both houses of Congress, giving the party a veto-proof hold on both the House and Senate, and perhaps even more damaging to Johnson, the incidents in Memphis and New Orleans, radicalizing many former moderate Republicans, convincing them that Andrew Johnson and his policies were making a mockery of both democracy and of the Union dead. Radical Reconstruction was about to begin.*

empowered as well. The "Old South" was (temporarily) vanquished, and the Radicals could not have been more delighted, for as they argued correctly, the revolution that began in 1863 with emancipation would never be realized as long as the old master class retained economic and social preeminence.

Despite Radical hopes that all would go smoothly with the presence of federal troops, southern whites continued to breathe defiance and refused to cooperate. Although white reprisals on the freedmen somewhat abated, thousands of white Southerners who were eligible to vote refused to do so, hoping that their non-participation would delay the process long enough for northern voters (the majority of whom were as racist as their southern brethren) to come to their senses and elect Democrats to Congress to reverse this "mad revolution."

Literate freedmen, white southern unionists, and northern white emigrants organized Union leagues to inform and mobilize new black voters into the Republican Party. Southern Democrats contemptuously labeled southern white Republicans as "**scalawags**" and northern migrants as "**carpetbaggers**." It was obvious to the southern "loyalists" (to the Lost Cause) that the Radicals intended to use the new black registrants and their white allies to gain control of the upcoming constitutional conventions. Since white Republicans were a minority in the South, the key to establishing such regimes in the southern states was the black vote. Thus, to prevent blacks from registering and voting, whites engaged in all manner of terrorist activities against freedmen, officially sanctioning such reprisals with the organization of the **Ku Klux Klan** in Pulaski, Tennessee in 1867. Although the Klan's terrorizing of blacks and whites who supported the Radical agenda would not become a serious problem until the early 1870s, the fact that such an organization emerged rather early in Reconstruction reflected white determination to resist any changes in the socio-political order that the war had brought.

With their huge majority, congressional Republicans were confident that could stymie the president's capacity to thwart the enactment of the new Reconstruction mandates. However, as commander in chief of the army and as head of the branch of government charged with executing the laws, Johnson still retained great power to frustrate the implementation of Congress's stipulations. Johnson made clear his intention to do so. Indeed, the president did all he could to try to stop the Radical momentum, encouraging southern whites to obstruct and delay voter registration and the election of convention delegates. Never in the history of the Republic had these two branches been more bitterly at odds.

Johnson's plan in obstructing the congressional agenda was to retard the process until 1868, in the hope that northern voters would repudiate the Radicals' program and elect him president on a Democratic ticket. Encouraging Johnson in this direction were the off-year state elections, held in the fall of 1867, which saw Republicans take a beating at the polls in several northern states, especially where they endorsed referendum measures to enfranchise black males. After the elections results, however, such Democratic euphoria was destined to be short-lived. There was no way the Radical Republicans would allow Johnson to prevail on these crucial issues. Many were willing to go to any extreme necessary to defeat the president, even if it meant removing him from office. Increasing numbers of Radicals concluded that the South's proper Reconstruction would never come about as long as Andrew Johnson was President of the United States. They thus put forth a concerted effort to impeach the president and remove him from office, hoping to replace him with the Radical Republican President pro tempore of the Senate, Benjamin Wade of Ohio.

The Senate court of impeachment for the trial of Andrew Johnson. 1868.

THE IMPEACHMENT OF ANDREW JOHNSON

The Radicals' drive to rid themselves of the "Johnson nuisance" began with the passage of the 1867 **Tenure of Office Act**, which required Senate approval of the president's removal of any cabinet members. Johnson naturally vetoed the bill, rightly declaring it to be unconstitutional. In Johnson's view, the act violated presidential authority and prerogative: the right of presidential appointment of cabinet members. Although all such individuals selected by the president had to be approved by the Senate, once confirmed, the president could remove them at his discretion.

Adding to the sensitivity of this particular showdown was the fact that through the course of the war, Lincoln had greatly expanded presidential power, ranging from the unprecedented issuance of executive orders to the suspension of the writ of *habeas corpus*, all in the name of national security and crisis. Indeed, Lincoln perhaps became the most notorious executive violator of civil liberties and other usurpations of constitutional authority. As a result, during Lincoln's presidency, Congress increasingly found itself becoming subservient to the executive branch. In the eyes of many Radicals, Johnson's obstructionism provided the perfect opportunity (or excuse) to reverse such an imbalance in national power, which they contended Johnson (not Lincoln) had so egregiously upset. In reality, however, the Radical Republicans simply used such arguments to mask their own personal antipathy toward Johnson's "copperheadedness" and obvious pro-southern and anti-freedmen sentiments. Although Johnson brought upon himself much of the Radicals' scorn and opposition with his arrogance and self-righteousness, nonetheless, he did not warrant impeachment; constitutionally none of his actions could be considered "Treason, Bribery, or other high Crimes and Misdemeanors." The Radicals, however, asserted that impeachment was not a criminal proceeding but rather a means of punishing a public official for "grave misuse of his powers, or any mischievous nonuse of them—for any conduct which harms the public or perils its welfare." In the Radical view, Johnson's obstructionist policies and his consorting with rebels to oppress the freedmen and restore the political status quo antebellum had most definitely harmed the public welfare. To substantiate their position, Radicals pointed to Johnson's wholesale pardons of ex-rebels, his open defiance of Congress, his intimation that Congress was an illegal body, his disgraceful public speeches, and his complicity by inaction in the New Orleans and Memphis riots.

The Radical Republicans believed Johnson had demonstrated no intention of enforcing the law in good faith and thus wanted to begin impeachment proceedings immediately. Moderates, however, feared that impeachment might make Johnson a martyr. Unfortunately for Johnson, he allowed his petulance and arrogance to get the better of him, and to the Radicals' delight, he took their "bait" (the Tenure of Office Act) and fired the last member of his cabinet, Secretary of War Edwin Stanton, who supported congressional Reconstruction. To try to stave off a full-fledged Radical assault on his administration, Johnson attempted to mollify Republicans with the appointment of General Ulysses S. Grant as interim Secretary of War. Grant was the most popular man in the North, and, despite a personal aversion to politics, Republicans were determined to make him their standard-bearer in 1868. However, some Radicals worried that Grant's acceptance of the position reflected his support for the president's policies. To their great relief, it did not. Indeed, Grant had urged Johnson not to remove Stanton, and he only accepted the position so he could serve as a buffer between Johnson and the army to prevent Johnson from doing more mischief. Grant, for example, refused Johnson's request to replace the more zealous, "Radically-inclined" commanders of the military districts, such as Grant's best friend, General William T. Sherman, of the Louisiana-Texas district, with more willing individuals. Grant refused and eventually resigned from the office, turning the reigns of power back to Stanton. In the meantime, Johnson took the initiative to replace Sheridan and other generals with men of a more moderate disposition, especially toward southern whites. As predicted, these moves outraged the Radicals, for Johnson's actions further encouraged the growing southern resistance to Reconstruction. By February 1868, both moderates and Radical Republicans had had enough; the House voted to impeach Johnson by a vote of 126-47. All 47 opposition votes were Democratic. The official reason for impeachment was Johnson's violation of the Tenure of Office Act. The real reason was Johnson's stubborn defiance of three-quarters of Congress on the most important issue before the nation—Reconstruction.

Under the Constitution, impeachment by the House does not remove an official from office. The process is more like a grand jury indictment that must be tried by a petit jury—the Senate, which sat as a court to try Johnson on the impeachment charges brought by the House. If convicted by a two-thirds majority of the Senate, Johnson would be removed from office, and president pro tempore of the Senate, Benjamin Wade, a Radical, would become president.

Tension filled the Senate chambers as Johnson's impeachment trial began on March 4, 1868. The trial proved to be long and complicated, which boded well for Johnson by allowing passions to cool. A plus for Johnson was also his defense counsel, which included some of the best lawyers in the country: Henry Stanbery, the attorney general; William M. Evarts, a future secretary of state; and Benjamin R. Curtis, a former Supreme Court justice, who had written the principal dissenting opinion in the *Dred Scott* case. During the trial these men demonstrated greater legal acumen than their opponents. These counselors

"Farewell, a long farewell, to all my greatest."
The caricature shows Andrew Johnson dressed as a king crying. 1869.

argued that a government official can be impeached only for criminal offenses that would be indictable in ordinary courts—Johnson had committed no crime by seeking to test the constitutionality of the Tenure of Office Act. In short, they exposed the act's technical ambiguities that raised doubts about whether Johnson had actually violated it.

To counter these assertions, the prosecution argued that to allow a president to disobey a law in order to test it in court would set a dangerous precedent. Regardless of whether Johnson was guilty of any crime, the impeachment trial was a political maneuver. To the Radicals and their supporters, Johnson had been impeached and was now on trial for two years of relentless opposition to the Republican reconstruction vision and agenda. Perhaps most important, Johnson's impeachment reflected the culmination of the long power struggle between the legislative and the executive branches, which as alluded earlier, began with the Lincoln administration. In many ways, Congress, not Johnson, had become the abusers and usurpers of power. Many moderates and the American public feared the creation of a precedent by which a two-thirds majority of Congress could remove any president who happened to disagree with them. In short, despite public and partisan disgust with Johnson, neither moderate Republicans nor the American people wanted to emasculate or disgrace the executive branch.

Behind the scenes moderates and other anti-impeachment coalitions worked to get Johnson to concede on some of the key Reconstruction issues that had caused the crisis. Apparently, the president understood the gravity of his predicament and responded positively to such overtures. He conducted himself with dignity and restraint during the trial. He gave no more self-righteous, emotionally-charged, irrational speeches or interviews. Most importantly, he promised to enforce the Reconstruction Acts. As a further sign of conciliation (even capitulation), Johnson appointed General John M. Schofield as Secretary of War, an individual acceptable to all factions. Johnson's willingness to reach such accords with Congress portended well for his acquittal. However, such a prospect remained in doubt until the very end. The final roll call took on the dimensions of high drama; not until West Virginia's Senator Peter G. Van Winkle, near the end of the alphabet, voted nay did it become clear that Johnson had been acquitted by one vote short of the necessary two-thirds majority. The final tally was 35-19. Had Van Winkle voted yes, Andrew Johnson would have become the first president in United States history to have been removed from office. Johnson remained on his best behavior for the rest of his term. Congressional (Radical) Reconstruction proceeded without any further presidential hindrance. A crisis that had shaken the constitutional system to its foundation ended without any fundamental alteration of that system.

THE SOUTHERN RESPONSE TO THE RECONSTRUCTION ACTS

Much to the surprise and disappointment of many Radicals, prominent ex-Confederates advised their white compatriots to accept the inevitable—defeat and the end of slavery—and comply with the laws. The thinking of such members of the antebellum elite was that cooperation with the congressional mandates would allow them to influence the process in a moderate direction, especially when it came to the freedmen issue. Many of these individuals still possessed their sense of pre-war paternalism and saw themselves as the freedmen's natural protectors and benefactors who knew what was best for their people. They certainly believed they knew their "negroes" better than any alien Yankee intruders, whom they believed (somewhat correctly) were only using the freedmen as political pawns to remake the South into a Republican majority. The old elite thus organized interracial political meetings and barbecues at which they urged the freedmen to vote Democratic with their fellow white Southerners in order to keep out the Yankees.

This convergence approach became known as the **New Departure**, and it became part of a persistent effort in postwar southern politics led mainly by former Whigs to create a moderate third force independent of both Democrats and Republicans. These New Departure advocates believed in enfranchising the freedmen as well as guaranteeing them their full civil rights. That is not to suggest such individuals believed in equality. They were all committed racists, but, nonetheless, they believed that it was wrong to wage aggressive war on the freedman, strip him of his basic constitutional rights, ostracize him, humiliate him, and rob him of elemental human dignity. To the proponents of convergence, African-American degradation was not a necessary corollary of white supremacy. As prominent antebellum attorney William Pitt Ballinger of Texas told a friend, although freedmen were "in our power," whites, particularly those of Ballinger's class, were their "custodians. We should extend to them as far as possible, all civil rights that will help them to be decent and self-respecting, law-abiding, and intelligent citizens. If we do not help elevate them they will surely bring us down." As far as Ballinger (and other New Departure proponents) was concerned, it was time for white Southerners "to bury the past and move forward." Southern whites had to accept "the fact of the negro's right to vote," and thus white reprisals of "intimidation and violence" toward freedmen must end. By downplaying the race issue, Ballinger and his compatriots hoped convergence would attract black votes, for African Americans would realize that their true guardians were patricians, like himself, and not the Radicals. The New Departure movement also hoped to win the support of moderate and conservative white Republicans once they became convinced that the postwar South's true leaders had accepted the accomplished facts of the war.

Unfortunately, Ballinger's and others' pleas for moderation and accommodation went unheard. The majority of white Southerners rejected the legitimacy of Reconstruction or the permanence of black suffrage. Even among many of its supporters, the New Departure was less of a genuine commitment to the democratic revolution manifested in Reconstruction than a strategy for mollifying Northerners about the southern Democratic Party's intentions. Most northern whites knew that in their hearts few of their southern brethren accepted black civil and political equality.

Assisting Republicans in mobilizing black voters was the Freedmen's Bureau and the Union League, which together were capable of overwhelming any efforts by the convergers to draw black voters away from the Republican Party. Some Bureau agents served simultaneously as Union League officials and, in their military capacity, as supervisors of voter registration under the Reconstruction Acts. These partisan activities gave white Southerners another reason to condemn the Bureau—not only did it intervene in their labor relations with the freedmen but now it was helping to rally these workers into an alien political party. As Republican success in wooing black voters to the Grand Old Party became clear, many southern whites, including some convergers, began to change their tune about accommodation. Yet, many remained sanguine that somehow or other Andrew Johnson or the northern Democrats could reverse the process and overthrow the Radicals. All such hopes, however, were dashed with Johnson's impeachment proceedings, which turned Johnson into one of the lamest of duck presidents in the Republic's history. The way was now clear for the final implementation of congressional Reconstruction.

THE COMPLETION OF FORMAL RECONSTRUCTION

Under the mandates established by the Reconstruction Acts of 1867, the southern states held their constitutional conventions during the winter and spring of 1867-68. Hostile whites, especially those who had been disenfranchised by the **iron-clad oath**, derisively referred to the gatherings as the "Bones and Banjoes Conventions" and the Republican delegates, many of whom were black, as "ragamuffins and jailbirds, baboons, monkeys, and mules." In a typical denunciation, Louisiana conservatives labeled the new charter written by the state convention as a "base conspiracy against human nature. It is the work of ignorant negroes cooperating with a gang of white adventurers." No doubt the Republican Party dominated the assemblages, comprising 75 percent of the delegates attending the ten state conventions. About one-quarter of those Republicans were relocated northern whites ("Carpetbaggers"), 45 percent were native southern whites ("Scalawags"), and about 30 percent were African Americans. Only in South Carolina were blacks in the majority. In Louisiana 50 percent of the attendees were African Americans, while in Texas only 10 percent of the delegates were freedmen. Regardless of their number, the black delegates constituted the elite of their race. At least half of them had been free before the war, and most of those who had been slaves belonged to the upper strata of the slave community. About four-fifths of all the black delegates were literate. Their predominant occupations were clergymen, teachers, artisans, and independent yeoman farmers. Contrary to white backlash propaganda, very few were former field hands or unskilled, illiterate laborers.

Much to the consternation of the **white backlash**, the delegates produced some of the most progressive state constitutions in the nation. In all ten states of the former Confederacy, universal male suffrage was enacted, putting the South ahead of most northern states in this most controversial issue. Some of the constitutions disfranchised certain classes of ex-Confederates for several more years, but by 1872, all such restrictions had been lifted. Ironically, the removal of such disqualifications allowed for southern whites by the early 1870s to redeem their states, that is, a return to white supremacy and political control by the antebellum elite. For the first time in southern history a mandated public school system was established for both races. Though the constitutions permitted segregated schools, formal education of any kind for African Americans represented a great step forward. Most of the constitutions expanded the state's responsibility for social welfare beyond anything previously known in the South. Some constitutions established state boards of public charities, and several of them enacted badly needed prison reforms and reduced the number of capital crimes. Such welfare expansion naturally had to be paid for, and thus property taxes increased significantly. Alleged exorbitant taxation became the initial rallying cry of the "Redeemers."

Despite the increases, most states provided homestead exemptions that assisted small landowners by exempting from taxation real and personal property up to $2,000 or $3,000 from attachment for debts. Although some of the Radical attendees urged confiscating the land of disfranchised ex-Confederates, no convention promulgated such a decree. Only the South Carolina convention made any gesture in this direction, authorizing the state land commission to buy abandoned property at market value and resell it in small tracts (mostly to freedmen) on liberal terms.

Reactionary whites opposed these new charters and worked assiduously to defeat ratification. Most southern whites could not believe that their northern brethren would abandon them at this crucial hour, allowing the Radicals to impose "Negro rule" on the South. So determined were southern whites to defeat ratification that they resorted to violent intimidation and terrorizing of black voters, whom they believed were the key to Republican ascendancy. Naturally leading this crusade was the KKK, which made it first serious appearance and forays during these elections. However, the main conservative tactic was to boycott the polls. If enough whites could be persuaded or coerced to stay home, the vote in favor of ratification might fall short of a majority of registered voters. In some states, such as Alabama, such a ploy initially worked. By the close of 1868, seven ex-Confederate states had ratified their constitutions and elected new legislatures that also ratified the Fourteenth Amendment, which became part of the Constitution the following summer. The newly elected representatives and senators from those seven states took their seats in the House and Senate.

Despite having neutralized Andrew Johnson and establishing (at least for the moment) Republican rule in the South, many party members were reluctant to take the final step of readmission. Causing them the greatest uneasiness was the reduction of federal troops, which would result as soon as self-government had been restored. Moreover, it would only be a matter of time before disfranchised whites regained the ballot, and, once they had, the days of Republican control would end soon thereafter. Moreover, the various Republican coalitions that had written the state constitutions, and subsequently took control, were fragile at best. During the ratification process, the vulnerability of its black constituents to intimidation became apparent. With troop presence on the decline, what would prevent a Democratic resurgence in the South and the certain dismantling of the new constitutions, black suffrage, and all the other reforms established? But political necessities and realities dictated readmission, and, whether the Radicals liked it or not, those southern states which had complied with all congressional mandates had to be readmitted to the Union. Northern voters wanted an end to the contention, for the majority no longer wanted to think about nor cared about the Negro problem. In the minds of most northern whites, Reconstruction appeared to be completed. Events, however, would soon demonstrate that it had barely begun.

THE FIRST GRANT ADMINISTRATION

The Election of 1868

Just as the 1864 presidential election had been a referendum on Republican war policies, so the 1868 contest reflected yet another mandate on Reconstruction. Initially however, it appeared that the financial question might supersede Reconstruction as the central campaign issue. The origins of this issue went back to the wartime legislation promoted by Lincoln, which made legal tender paper money called "**greenbacks**," while simultaneously creating a host of national banks through which this currency flowed throughout the northern economy. The flood of greenbacks into the economy resulted in inflation, causing an 80 percent cost of living increase in the North from 1861-1865. Such an acceleration fell gradually but steadily after the war was over. With the suspension of specie payments and the adoption of greenbacks in 1862, the United States went off the gold standard, though it still used gold for international trade.

After the war, Secretary of the Treasury Hugh McCulloch, a "hard-money" advocate (a believer in specie/gold as the only legitimate currency for a nation to circulate), pursued a policy of returning the nation's monetary system to the gold standard by slowly retiring greenbacks while bringing the remainder in circulation to par with gold. By 1867, McCulloch had reduced the value of greenbacks in circulation to $319 million and the gold premium stood at 140 ($140 greenbacks were required to buy $100 in gold). McCulloch's policies, however, caused deflation and a postwar recession, and those economic sectors hurt by the secretary's agenda blamed the contraction of greenbacks for their plight. Alarmed, Congress forbade further greenback reduction in 1868. The issue created a

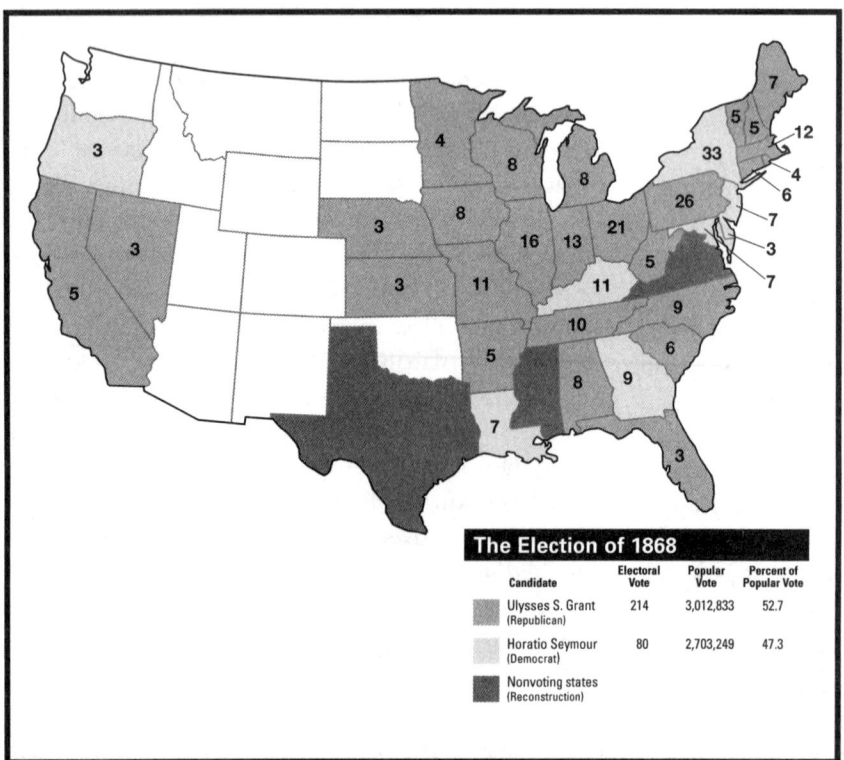

Map 17.2   The Election of 1868

new sectional alignment: East against West (the West was still an overwhelmingly rural and agrarian region) as both western Democrats and Republicans opposed contraction, which hit the Western states' economy harder than the Northeast, whereby bankers, financiers, and industrialists all favored contraction and the return to the gold standard. Western farmers and other debtors favored soft money, for they would be repaying debts with depreciated currency if the greenbacks continued in circulation. Moreover, such individuals favored greenbacks as legal tender because it was cheap money that inflated prices for farm goods. A return to a strict gold standard would negate such a boon for farmers and other debtors.

Led by Ohio party leader Senator George H. Pendleton, western Democrats attempted to make the monetary question a major campaign issue. Pendleton, a leading candidate for his party's presidential nomination, favored making greenbacks the nation's legal tender, replacing gold but keeping the new currency on a gold standard. The Pendleton Plan found its way into the Democratic platform, but when the party turned to New Yorker Horatio Seymour, a "**gold bug**," as its standard bearer, this plank became a dead letter as Reconstruction and the candidates' war records took center stage. The monetary debate was not dead. Indeed, once Reconstruction had ended, this particular issue reignited, rivaling at times in intensity and partisanship the North-South slavery debate of the antebellum period.

As the 1868 election neared, the Republican nominee became a foregone conclusion: General-in-Chief of the Army and Union war hero, **Ulysses S. Grant**. Only one issue continued to mar Republican unanimity: the problem of black suffrage in the northern states. Radicals insisted it must be a central feature of the party's platform while moderates believed it essential to downplay the crusade, fearing of alienating northern white voters, the majority of whom had made it clear in various state elections that they adamantly opposed black enfranchisement. In the end, the moderates agreed to impose black suffrage on the ex-Confederate states while allowing the "question of suffrage in all the loyal [northern] States to properly belong to the people of those States." This hypocrisy outraged abolitionists and Radicals, who denounced this "mean-spirited, foolish, and contemptible" plank.

The Democrats initially had an abundance of candidates, including Andrew Johnson, whom, it was quickly realized, possessed too many political liabilities to become a viable contender. The other possibilities—George Pendleton of Ohio, Thomas Hendricks of Indiana, and General Winfield Scott Hancock—all had supporters, but as the convention progressed and ballot after ballot had been cast, one by one they all fell by the wayside, ultimately leaving the "dark horse," Horatio Seymour of New York, as the last man standing, whom party officials had to hustle out of the hall to prevent him from declining the nomination. In the end, Seymour reluctantly accepted his party's dubious honor of running against Grant.

The Democratic platform naturally condemned the Reconstruction Acts as "a flagrant usurpation of power, unconstitutional, revolutionary and void." The platform also demanded "the abolition of the Freedmen's Bureau, and all political instrumentalities designed to secure negro supremacy." It was clear the Democrats hoped to win by engaging in **race-baiting**, negrophobia, and the promotion of white solidarity and supremacy with its southern colleagues. In this approach, vice-presidential candidate Frank Blair of Missouri became the party's mouthpiece. In his famous Brodhead Letter, Blair set his party's campaign agenda. "There is but one way to restore the Government and the Constitution, and that is for the President-elect to declare these [Reconstruction] acts null and void, compel the army to undo its usurpations at the South, disperse the Carpet-bag governments, and allow white people to reorganize their own governments." Implicitly Blair and his party were calling for a counterrevolutionary movement to overthrow the southern Republican governments, and the only way to achieve such a goal was to terrorize and suppress southern Republican voters. The Klan naturally heard Blair's and the Democrats' call to arms, and during the election, the Klan and similar white backlash terrorist organizations unleashed upon both white and black pro-Republican supporters and voters violent mischief and murder. In Louisiana alone between April and November 1868, more than a 1,000 persons, mostly blacks, were killed. Such intimidation by the Klan and other white paramilitary organizations did help the Democrats carry Louisiana and Georgia, but their activities hurt the party in the North by lending substance to Republican charges that Rebels (ex-Confederates) and Copperheads (white Northerners, mostly Democrats, who had sympathized with the South before and during the war) were trying to achieve by terrorism what they had failed to accomplish by war.

In the end, Grant won handily, receiving 55 percent of the northern vote, virtually the same proportion as Lincoln had in 1864. Seymour carried only three northern states, Oregon, New Jersey, and New York, as well as three border/former slave states, Delaware, Maryland, and Kentucky, and two of the eight reconstructed ex-Confederate states, Georgia and Louisiana, giving him 80 electoral votes to Grant's 214.

The Fifteenth Amendment

During the year after Grant's election, Congress focused on the unfinished task of Reconstruction by working assiduously on a constitutional amendment to enfranchise African-American males in every state, not just southern freedmen. Without such an amendment, the future of black suffrage would become a farce, especially in the southern states where the Democrats were destined to regain control. Moreover, the inequity of mandating black suffrage in the South while allowing northern states the option disturbed many Republicans, for their party's lassitude on the issue smacked of racism and hypocrisy.

With such sentiments motivating their efforts, the Republican-dominated Congress passed the **Fifteenth Amendment** on February 26, 1869, marking the highpoint of Reconstruction's constitutional achievements. The amendment prohibited states from denying the right to vote on grounds of race, color, or previous condition of servitude. Its purpose was not only to prevent any future revocation of black suffrage by the reconstructed states but also to extend equal suffrage to the border states and to the North. Within four months of congressional passage, seventeen Republican legislatures then in session ratified the amendment, and the four Democratic counterparts in session predictably rejected it. It remained uncertain where enough votes could be won among the eleven more states when their respective legislatures met in the fall. Fortunately, the Republicans had an opportunity to mitigate the chances of defeat by mandating in the still unreconstructed states of Virginia, Mississippi, and Texas that if they hoped to be readmitted, their legislatures had to ratify both the Fourteenth and Fifteenth Amendments. All three states complied and were restored to the Union in 1870. Georgia remained the lone ex-Confederate state still unreconstructed. However, after several months of interesting maneuvers and behind-the-scenes deals, Georgia rejoined the Union and ratified the Fifteenth Amendment, giving the two-thirds majority required. With Georgia's ratification the Fifteenth Amendment became part of the Constitution on March 30, 1870. Many Republicans believed the amendment represented the last great point that remained to be settled on the issues of the war. Now the nation could focus on the other issues long neglected because of preoccupation with sectional strife. Even since Texas's annexation a quarter-century earlier, the Republic had scarcely a moment's respite from this tension. "Let us have done with Reconstruction," pleaded the *New York Tribune* in

First African American Senator and Representatives in the 41st and 42nd Congress of the United States, by Currier and Ives, 1872.
(Left to right) Senator Hiram Revels of Mississippi, Representatives Benjamin Turner of Alabama, Robert DeLarge of South Carolina, Josiah Walls of Florida, Jefferson Long of Georgia, Joseph Rainey and Robert B. Elliot of South Carolina.

April 1870. "The Country is tired and sick of it. LET US HAVE PEACE."

Another motivating factor for many politicians to support the Fifteenth Amendment was to silence the outcry among northern white women, the "suffragettes," who had been lobbying for the right to vote for decades. Congress never anticipated the suffragette outrage when the Fourteenth Amendment passed, not only making citizens of ex-slaves but also automatically giving them the right to vote at age 21. Even black females allegedly had this right for the amendment made no specific mention of gender. Such legislation incensed the suffragettes, for not only were they white (a good number of these women were racists) but also had never been property (chattel) in the same sense as the freedmen. To give an ex-slave such privileges while white women continued to languish as non-citizens in this capacity was simply unacceptable to the suffragettes. Thus, in many ways the Fifteenth Amendment was a sort of "throw-away" piece of legislation, designed to clarify who was specifically eligible to now vote in this country: all adult *males*, 21 years or older, regardless of *race, color*, or *previous condition of servitude*. Since *gender* was not mentioned, it was to be naturally *assumed* that women, regardless of color, were to be excluded from the franchise. No doubt suffragettes felt duped and betrayed, especially by the Radicals whose talk of supposed equality for all smacked of hypocrisy and political opportunism, especially at the expense of white women. Thus the promulgation of the Fifteenth Amendment reflected that when it came to the extension of full-fledged citizenship to white women, few, if any, white males were ready to go that far. Even in the most revolutionary of times, American white male chauvinism continued unabated.

Grant in the White House

Few presidents in American history entered the White House with more prestige and goodwill than Ulysses S. Grant. Now that Reconstruction was supposedly over, Republican supporters were eager to focus on other pressing issues such as the currency and related financial problems, civil service reform, and foreign policy, an area that had been particularly neglected because of sectional strife and civil war. Unfortunately, rather than solving or ameliorating these problems, Grant's inexperience and errors in judgment coupled with the venality of some of his associates not only worsened many of these issues but created a whole new set of troubles for the president as well. Compounding these domestic difficulties was the ongoing insolvable problems of Reconstruction, all of which ultimately dashed the hopes of many Americans that the hero of the War of the Rebellion would be the nation's messiah. In short, the Grant years were plagued by scandals, corruption, and graft that seemed to pervade his administration from top to bottom from the moment he took office.

Within months of his first term, Grant had to deal with an attempt by two of the Gilded Age's most notorious Wall Street buccaneers, Jay Gould and Jim Fisk, to corner the gold market. Prompting Gould and Fisk to try such shenanigans was Congress's passing of the **Public Credit Act**, which allowed for the redemption of all government bonds in gold or its equivalent and the pledging to bring greenbacks to par with gold at the earliest practicable period. In the meantime, the price of gold fluctuated, creating the perfect opportunity for speculators such as Gould and Fisk, both of whom had previously made a killing among capitalist titans (Gould and Fisk against Cornelius Vanderbilt) for control of one of the nation's most important railroad lines, the Erie. With their profits from this venture, Gould and Fisk hoped to corner the gold market by buying as much gold as possible when the market price reached its lowest point, which they were certain it would soon because of the uncertain, fluctuating nature of the nation's overall financial system.

Much to their chagrin, the government (the Treasury) sold only specified amounts monthly, which greatly limited the amount of the bullion Gould and Fisk could buy at one time. Not to be deterred, the corsairs found an ally in the White House in Abel R. Corbin, the president's brother-in-law, who introduced Grant to Gould and Fisk, who convinced the president to suspend the monthly sales allotment and simply let as much gold be sold on the open market as possible. Gould told the president that such a free-wheeling policy of allowing the price of gold to rise would benefit the nation, especially the farmers by lowering the dollar price of wheat in European markets, thereby increasing exports. Grant was noncommittal, but his brother-in-law assured Gould that the government would suspend restricted gold sales. No sooner did the Treasury lift the limitations on gold sales than Gould and Fisk began buying every ounce of gold in sight, driving up the premium to 144. By late September 1869, the price of gold had risen to 162. Grant saw that he had been hoodwinked by Gould and Fisk and immediately ordered the Treasury to stop gold sales and then only sell $4 million each month thereafter. Grant's action caused a quick tumble in the gold market, which settled at 133, leaving scores of brokers and speculators ruined. Gould avoided disaster by selling at the top of the market, and his sidekick Fisk simply repudiated several of his contracts. Although acting promptly upon learning the truth of Gould's schemes, the gold fiasco nonetheless tainted Grant's image as being an individual susceptible to nepotism and cronyism.

Sadly for Grant, the Gould-Fisk escapade was only the beginning of a wave of scandals and corruption that sullied his White House years. The president's private secretary, Orville Babcock, became involved in the infamous "**Whiskey Ring**," a network of distillers and revenue agents that bilked the government of millions of excise tax dollars on whiskey while amassing fortunes. In one scandal, it was proved that Grant's Secretary of War William Belknap (who was subsequently impeached) had been accepting bribes from men whom he had appointed as agents on Indian reservations—in effect selling government posts at a price that the agent would recover by cheating the Indians.

Although honest himself, Grant appeared to have an indiscriminate reverence for wealth, and he seemed quite blind to the effect of having the president associate with rich, unscrupulous looters and market manipulators such as Jay Gould and Jim Fisk. Grant was also too trusting of subordinates. He appointed many former members of his military family, as well as several of his wife's relatives, to offices for which they were scarcely qualified. However, not all of the era's scandals emanated from the White House; this was an era notorious for corruption at all levels of government with the infamous **Tammany Hall** "Ring" of Democratic "Boss" William Marcy Tweed of New York City leading the way. Tweed and his associates may have stolen more money from New York City taxpayers than all the federal agencies combined, and the New York legislature was famous for the buying and selling of votes. The Tweed Ring used the simple device of taking whatever funds they wanted from the municipal treasury on the pretext of paying for goods and services that were never ordered and never received. In one day they helped themselves to $14 million by this uncomplicated method.

Perhaps the most notorious and widely publicized scandal of the era was the **Crédit Mobilier Affair**, which much to Grant's relief involved Congress and not members of his administration. This particular debacle pertained to the building of the Union Pacific Railroad. When the railroad company was organized, it did not manage the construction of its own road; rather, it farmed out the line's building to a construction company named somewhat fancifully and pretentiously the Credit Mobilier of America. Although such an arrangement was not unusual, quite legitimate in fact, what made this particular deal suspect was the fact that the railroad company's directors had organized the construction company. Then in their capacity as railroad directors they awarded themselves, as contractors, the contracts to build a cheaply constructed road at exorbitant prices. In this way they could easily siphon off government grants, leaving the railroad company almost bankrupt but themselves wealthy. Now all these rascals had to do was avoid any government inquiry into their shenanigans, which they did by distributing shares of construction company stock to targeted, susceptible, influential members of the House of Representatives, including its Speaker, soon-to-be vice president, Schuyler Colfax, to keep them from becoming too vigilant. The influence-peddling was eventually exposed and became the first clear illustration that the public received of what can happen when a group of insiders gains control of a wealthy enterprise that they do not own. The separation of ownership and control marked a new trend in American capitalist development and became over the next several decades an unfortunate hallmark of Gilded Age politics and economics.

What accounted for this explosion of corruption in the postwar decade, which one historian has called "The Era of Good Stealings"? The expansion of government

A cartoon depicts President Ulysses S. Grant as a circus acrobat being pulled down by several figures in his administration implicated in the "Whiskey Ring" scandal. Multiple scandals marred Grant's presidency. Illustration from an 1880 edition of *Puck* magazine.

contracts and the bureaucracy during the war created new opportunities for the unscrupulous, compounded by a general relaxation of tensions and standards following the intense sacrifices of the war years. In other words, for four long, bloody years, white Americans (especially those in the North) seemed to have adhered to a comparatively rigid moral and ethical code, one that placed a premium on the virtues of self-sacrifice, frugality, and altruism, all for the good of a greater cause. Now that the cause had ended, with the Union preserved and slavery abolished, so ended four years of pent-up emotional and material self-deprivation. Americans were now eager to embrace the new industrial order the war had wrought, especially in the North, and with such change came opportunities for one to not only enjoy a life of material abundance but in the process become rich as well. Enterprises such as railroad construction became the consummate symbolic example of the get-rich-quick mentality and greed that took hold of many post-war Americans, satirized by Mark Twain and Charles Dudley Warner in their 1873 novel *The Gilded Age*, which gave its name to the era. In many ways, post-Civil War American culture produced attitudes, behaviors, and values not unfamiliar to Americans of the late twentieth and early twenty-first centuries: an ethos of crass materialism, hedonistic self-indulgence, and a passion to accumulate monetary wealth regardless of how ethical the endeavor or how detrimental the affects on others.

Civil Service Reform

As a result of the endemic corruption, a civil service reform movement emerged to try to cleanse an inefficient government bureaucracy that had become rife with malfeasance, cronyism, and nepotism—in many ways the inevitable result of decades of the spoils system initiated by Andrew Jackson's administration of the late 1820s. Beginning with Jackson and through Grant, the victorious party in an election rewarded party loyalists with federal appointments, usually at the lower bureaucratic level such as postmasters, customs collectors, and the like. Even when a party was out of power, the possibility of appointment helped to maintain the party faithful. The spoils system politicized the bureaucracy and staffed it with unqualified personnel who spent more time working for their party than for the government. Such were the realities and conditions on which reformers focused a harsh light—into the dark corners of corruption previously obscured by the sectional conflict, war, and reconstruction. Although much of the corruption may have been exaggerated by reformers for publicity purposes, plenty was nonetheless there to warrant serious investigation and rectification.

Reformers were mainly well-educated northeastern professionals, and many came from some of the nation's most pedigreed families. Most of them were Republicans, cut from the old Conscience Whig cloth of the party. They admired the incorruptible efficiency of the British civil service and wanted to emulate that system. Professional politicians on both sides of the aisle, however, looked askance at such notions. To them, patronage was the lifeblood of democracy and had been since the days of the "Jacksonian revolution." They accused the reformers of being elitists and ridiculed them as dilettantes trying to play at the serious business of nitty-gritty American politics.

Civil service reformers wanted to separate the bureaucracy from politics by mandating competitive examinations for the appointment of civil servants. This movement gained momentum during the 1870s and finally achieved success in 1883 with the passage of the **Pendleton Act**, which established the modern structure, system, and procedure for positions within the civil service. When Grant took office, he appeared to share the sentiments of the civil service reformers. Several of his cabinet officials—Secretary of the Treasury George Boutwell, Secretary of the Interior Samuel D. Cox, and Attorney General Rockwood Hoar—inaugurated examinations for certain appointments and promotions in their respective departments. Grant also named a civil service commission headed by the editor of *Harper's Weekly* and a leading reformer, George William Curtis. Unfortunately too many of Grant's contemporaries opposed reform. They simply found the spoils system too personally beneficial to do away with. Patronage was the grease of the political machines that kept them in office and all too often enriched them and their political chums. They managed to subvert reform, sometimes using Grant as an unwitting ally and turning many reformers against the president. Thus, much to the disappointment of the reformers, a thoroughgoing reform of the spoils system was not achieved in the 1870s.

Foreign Policy Issues

Although the Grant administration's focus was domestic rather than foreign, there were significant foreign policy developments and issues during these years, some of which added to Grant's woes. One such setback was the **Santo Domingo Affair**, an attempt by the Grant White House to annex the island nation of Santo Domingo (present-day Dominican Republic). Such a move by the administration reflected a resurgent American nationalism and the concomitant momentary revival of Manifest Destiny, led ironically by post-war Republicans, not Democrats, as had been the case in the past. Leading the rejuvenated expansionist spirit was Secretary of State William Seward, the individual most responsible for the U.S. purchase of Alaska from Russia in 1867. Seward had also earlier attempted to purchase the Virgin Islands from Denmark, for the Civil War had demonstrated the need for a U.S. naval base in the Caribbean. The Senate killed this treaty but not the idea of U.S. expansion into the Caribbean.

To the surprise of many and to the dismay of many others, President Grant was as keen on American expansion as his secretary of state. Grant too was interested in promoting a U.S. presence in the Caribbean and thus when approached by wily Dominican dictator, Bonaventura Baez, who wanted the United States to acquire his country as a means to bolster his power against insurgent movements, Grant jumped at the opportunity to acquire the island nation. So too were unsavory land speculators, commercial developers, mercenaries, promoters of fabulous gold and silver mines, and naval officers who wanted a Caribbean base and dreamed of a canal built across modern-day Panama. For Grant the acquisition of the Dominican Republic represented the opportunity for the United States to bring peace and stability to a country of chronic revolutions, develop its rich resources, open the gateway for the extension of beneficent American influence throughout the region, and initiate the Isthmian canal project. Grant hoped to make the annexation the showpiece foreign policy achievement of his administration.

Grant let his enthusiasm for the scheme get the better of him, as he committed one political blunder and diplomatic faux pas after another throughout the negotiation process, beginning with his peremptory ordering of the purchase without first lining up key political support among his cabinet and Congress. Without consulting either group, Grant sent his private secretary, Orville Babcock, to the island nation in July 1869 to open negotiations. The overzealous Babcock did more than discuss the possibilities of acquisition. He brought back a treaty of annexation. After the irregularities of the procedure had been pointed out by Cabinet members, Grant, determined to have Santo Domingo, regardless of having violated a multitude of diplomatic protocols, sent Babcock back to Santo Domingo with State Department authorization to renegotiate the agreement properly. Baez agreed to the terms, and Babcock returned with a treaty that made Santo Domingo a U.S. territory and declared her 120,000 people to be American citizens, all at a bargain price of $1.5 million. Santo Domingans unanimously approved annexation. In January 1870, Grant proudly submitted the treaty for Senate ratification. In effect, he handed the Senate an unwelcomed, distasteful *fait accompli*, which incensed Senate leaders of both parties.

Leading the anti-annexation movement in the Senate were Charles Sumner of Massachusetts and Carl Schurz of Missouri. Along with other senators from both sides of the aisle, Schurz and Sumner castigated the corrupt promoters who had bought up land in expectation of windfall profits from annexation. Schurz and Sumner invoked the traditional Whig/Republican hostility to expansion with Schurz questioning the wisdom of incorporating a new mixed-blood Catholic people into an American population that already had more than enough trouble with racial issues. "These islands by climate, occupation, and destiny belong to the colored people," Sumner declared. "We should not take them away. No greed of land should prevail against the rights of this race."

Outraged by Sumner's and Schurz's opposition as well as their criticism of his high-handedness, Grant went on a personal rampage, dismissing or sending out to political pasture as many of Sumner's and Schurz's allies as fast as he possibly could. Grant's counterattack yielded little favorable results except to alienate a growing number of Republicans from the administration. On June 30, 1870, the Senate defeated the treaty by a tie vote of 28-28, with nineteen Republicans joining nine Democrats in opposition. Open warfare now erupted between Grant and Sumner, becoming increasingly savage as the months wore on.

The Santo Domingo affair seriously divided the Republican Party. Both the president and senators had demonstrated traits of petty vindictiveness. Sumner's vain ego and righteous moralism seemed to grow more excessive with age. To the senator's friends, however, Grant's vendetta seemed to be an attack on the idealism that had made the Republican Party great. They feared that the party, under Grant's lack of leadership and general personal fortitude, was fast falling into the hands of spoilsmen and opportunists. By 1871, a new noun, "**Grantism**," had entered Washingtonian verbiage. It became a catch-all term for all the things the old Republicans believed were wrong with postwar America: spoilsmanship and corruption in government; crude, vulgar taste and anti-intellectualism in culture; dishonesty in business; and a boundless materialism and a get-rich-quick acquisitiveness that was becoming more and more to define a new American creed. This breach between old and new Republicans would split the party in the 1872 election, giving rise to the Liberal Republican movement.

The Grant administration also had to reckon with Great Britain and Mexico over events that were in a sense unfinished business from the war itself. One involved the French-supported empire of Austrian archduke Maximilian in Mexico. The other concerned the United States's claims against Great Britain for having permitted the construction and outfitting, as well as a safe haven, for the Confederate commerce raider, the *Alabama*, which ravaged the U.S. merchant marine during the war.

At the beginning of the U.S. Civil War, the Mexican government had defaulted on its debts to Britain, Spain, and France. All three nations agreed to use force if necessary to collect what they were owed, but they also agreed that none would attempt to gain peculiar advantage from the situation. The French emperor, Napoleon III, however, had no intention of fulfilling his pledge, for he saw a grand opportunity to begin the resurrection of his uncle's empire (Napoleon I), which he believed he was destined to achieve. In secret negotiations with the ruling Habsburgs of the Austro-Hungarian empire, Napoleon III arranged for the archduke Maximilian to become emperor of Mexico with French support. Great Britain and Spain knew nothing of this deal. In 1862, the creditor nations invaded Mexico, driving into exile into the northern Mexican mountains and deserts its president, Benito Juarez. By 1863 England and Spain had grown weary of the whole affair and withdrew their troops, leaving France in charge of future operations. Napoleon could not have asked for a more perfect scenario to implement his scheme. French armies occupied Mexico City a month before the Battle of Gettysburg, and, shortly afterward, a hand-picked group of wealthy, conservative, anti-Juarez Mexican landowners, Catholic clergy, and military officers offered Maximilian the throne as Emperor of their country, which the Austrian accepted in 1864. In reality, Maximilian was barely the emperor of Mexico City, for all around him were the Juarista republican insurgents.

The Lincoln administration was greatly upset by this blatant violation of the Monroe Doctrine, and Congress responded by voting angry resolutions. But there was little the United States could do at the moment, embroiled as Secretary of State William Seward stated, "in a struggle for our own life." Both Lincoln and Seward knew, however, that the French invasion portended ill for national security. Indeed, the French invasion, occupation, and the establishing of an empire represented the most serious direct threat to American security since the War of 1812. Both Lincoln and Seward were biding their time. After Lee's surrender, and with Lincoln's death, the job of getting the French out of Mexico fell to Seward, who began to pressure Napoleon, gently at first, to leave Mexico. When such nudging failed, Seward became more aggressive and bellicose, demanding in February 1866 that France set a date to get out of Mexico or U.S. troops would be sent into Mexico to drive them out. Napoleon knew Seward was serious. Moreover, all of Europe knew that the Union Army had fought itself into being one of the best armies in the world and could have easily crushed the French forces in Mexico, which would have become a most humiliating defeat for a supposed great European power. Thus, in April 1867, Napoleon agreed to begin the withdrawal process. Aside from U.S. pressure, by that time Napoleon had found his venture more costly and unpopular than he had anticipated.

Maximilian remained in Mexico, regarding himself as a Mexican and a legitimate ruler. For such a delusion, he paid with his life at the hands of a Mexican firing squad in June 1867. Apparently the Mexicans did not see Maximilian in the same light as he saw himself. During all these developments, Seward never invoked the Monroe Doctrine, but Napoleon's withdrawal from Mexico was perhaps the most important victory it ever scored.

The second piece of war-related unfinished business was the damage claims against Britain for losses caused by the C.S.S. *Alabama* and other Confederate commerce raiders (the *Florida* and the *Shenandoah*) built in British shipyards. This particular issue should have been settled quickly, for the British were in a conciliatory mood, admitting that the building of such ships had violated the principles of neutrality. The British also feared the possibility of American retaliation—that the United States might allow an enemy of England to build commerce raiding ships in American ports that would attack Brit-

Charles Sumner of Massachusetts - great senator and statesman, a champion of civil and political equality.

ish merchant marines. Complicating negotiations were a cluster of other issues as well: a dispute about possession of the San Juan Islands off Vancouver; questions about Canadian-American fishing rights; Irish-American aid to Irish revolutionists; and, most of all, a lingering American desire for the United States to annex all or part of Canada. Because of these issues, negotiations did not begin until 1869.

No sooner did talks begin than Senator Charles Sumner blasted the negotiations, declaring Britain financially accountable not only for destroyed American merchant ships but also for prolonging the war by two years, for according to Sumner (and some others), after Gettysburg and Vicksburg, it was only British support that enabled the Confederacy to continue fighting. He proposed astronomical damages—far greater, in fact, than Germany would soon impose on France at the end of the Franco-Prussian War. Sumner's tirade caused negotiations to break off, and for two years strained relations existed between the U.S. and Great Britain. Newspapers on both sides of the Atlantic traded bellicose threats.

Thanks to the skillful handling by Secretary of State Hamilton Fish, the impasse was finally broken when the Grant administration agreed to the Treaty of Washington (1871), which called for submitting the dispute to an international arbitration commission comprised of the United States, Britain, Switzerland, Italy, and Brazil. By a 4-1 vote (Britain dissenting) the arbitrators declared that the British government had failed to exercise due diligence to prevent the building and arming of the Confederate raiders and awarded the United States $15.5 million for the damages done by these ships.

The events leading to the Treaty of Washington also resolved another long-festering issue affecting relations between Britain and the United States: the status of Canada. The seven separate British North American colonies were especially vulnerable to U.S. desires for annexation. Indeed, so angered were many Northerners toward Britain for the Confederate raiders' depredations, that they demanded that England relinquish her Canadian provinces as payment for these damages. Such bellicosity strengthened Canadians' loyalty to Britain as a counterweight to American aggression. In 1867, Parliament passed the British North American Act, which united most of the Canadian colonies into a new and largely self-governing Dominion of Canada.

Further strengthening Pro-British Canadian nationalism were the actions of the Irish American Fenian Brotherhood, a secret society organized during the Civil War dedicated to the overthrow of British rule in Ireland. The Fenians believed that a U.S. invasion and acquisition of Canada would go far toward achieving an independent Ireland. Three times from 1866 to 1871, Fenians, composed mainly of Irish American ex-Union army veterans, crossed the U.S.-Canadian border, only to be driven back after light skirmishes. The Fenian invasions intensified Canadian anti-Americanism, complicating the negotiations leading to the 1871 Washington Treaty. However, the successful conclusion of that treaty cooled American-Canadian tensions, leading to resolutions of disputes over American commercial fishing in Canadian waters. U.S. troops prevented further Fenian raids, and American demands for annexation of Canada also dissipated as well. The easing of these tensions helped to usher in a prolonged period of peaceful relations between the U.S. and Canada, who share a 3,500-mile border with the United States that remains the longest unfortified frontier in the world.

The purchase of Alaska from Russia, the result of Secretary of State William Seward's astuteness, taking advantage of a financially hard-pressed Russian government that had overextended itself in the far Pacific Northwest, was not recognized as a major event. Through diplomatic back-channels, Seward found out that Russia would be interested in selling Alaska to the United States and jumped at the possibility, settling on the negotiated price of $7.2 million. For Seward, the Alaska purchase represented a grand opportunity to increase U.S. ports on the Pacific, which would further facilitate the nation's trade possibilities with the Far East, even potentially with Russia. To the commercial-minded Seward, Russia's present backwardness made it a perfect market for America's burgeoning manufacturing enterprises to dump their surplus goods. When the public found out about "Seward's Folly," the secretary was chastised in the press and in government circles for having purchased this frozen wasteland. Some congressmen even had to be bribed to vote for the appropriation. Despite the criticism, Seward persevered, certain that some day his folly would be worth far more than the purchase price to the United States. The treaty was ratified in 1867, the payment voted in 1868, and then Alaska was put away and forgotten, unexplored and unknown, until the 1897 Klondike Gold Rush, which turned out to be the greatest in American history, yielding more gold than all other such finds combined.

THE WHITE BACKLASH CONTINUES

No sooner did Republican regimes come to power in the South than southern whites were determined to bring them down. Always ready to help in such crusades was the Ku Klux Klan, whose terrorist acts reached a crescendo in 1870 and 1871. Although keeping freedmen subjugated was the Klan's priority, members also believed it their mission to destroy the Republican Party by terrorizing its voters and, if necessary, murdering its leaders. No one knows the number of politically motivated killings that occurred in the South during Reconstruction, but it was certainly in the hundreds, if not in the thousands, with African Americans easily comprising the lion's share of victims. In one notorious incident, the "Colfax Massacre" in Louisiana (April 18, 1873), a confrontation between black militia and armed whites left three whites and nearly one hundred blacks dead, with the majority of the latter shot down in cold blood after they had surrendered. In some states, most notably Arkansas and Tennessee, Republicans formed state militias to protect themselves and successfully suppressed Klan raids and other terrorist activities. But in most of the southern states the militias were outgunned and outmaneuvered by ex-Confederate veterans who had joined the Klan. Some Republican governors were reluctant to use black militia against white guerrillas, fearing that such an encounter could spark a racial bloodbath as happened at Colfax.

No matter what the Republican governments did, they appeared to be losing the battle with the Klan, whose popularity among white Southerners seemed to be increasing daily. It was time to seek federal help. In 1870 and 1871, Congress enacted three laws intended to enforce the Fourteenth and Fifteenth Amendments with federal marshals and troops if necessary. Interference with voting rights became a federal offense, and any attempts to deprive another person of civil or political rights became a felony. The third law, popularly called the Ku Klux Klan Act, gave the president the power to suspend the writ of *habeas corpus* and send in federal troops to suppress armed resistance to federal law.

Although virtually handed by Congress carte blanche to deal with the Klan as forcefully as warranted, Grant showed restraint, sensitive to charges of being a military despot. He suspended the writ of *habeas corpus* in only nine South Carolina counties. Nevertheless, there and elsewhere federal marshals backed by troops arrested thousands of suspected Klansmen. Federal grand juries indicted more than three thousand, and several hundred defendants pleaded guilty in return for suspended sentences. To clear congested court dockets so that the worst offenders could be tried quickly, the Justice Department dropped charges against nearly two thousand others. About six hundred Klansmen were convicted. Most received fines or light jail sentences, but sixty-five went to a federal penitentiary for terms of up to five years.

The 1872 Presidential Election

The crackdown on the Klan helped to bolster Grant's image, especially among the Radicals and even among a still strongly supportive northern white majority, many of whom remained in a vindictive mood toward white Southerners. However, within the GOP a dissident group had emerged to challenge Grant's reelection.

President Grant (left) signs the "Ku Klux Klan" or "Force Act," which breaks the back of the southern terrorist group. April 20, 1871.

Disillusioned with his record on civil service reform, disgusted with the scandals and corruption that seemed to have infected his White House, and disturbed with his consorting with Robber Barons such as Jim Fisk and Jay Gould served to alienate the more high-minded, righteous purists within the party. These disgruntled Republicans broke with the party and organized a splinter group, calling themselves the Liberal Republicans, who believed that in alliance with the Democrats they could defeat Grant. Their slogan became "Anything to beat Grant." With Democratic approval and support, this fusion party nominated Horace Greeley, the famous editor of the *New York Tribune*, who, ironically, had been a Democratic nemesis for decades. The Liberal Republican-Democratic coalition called for a new policy of conciliation toward southern whites rather than continued military intervention as the only way to achieve peace in the region. The party's platform thus denounced Grant's supposed "bayonet rule" in the South, and Greeley urged fellow Northerners to put the issues of the Civil War behind them and to "clasp hands across the bloody chasm which has too long divided" North and South.

Much to the party's chagrin, most northern voters were still not prepared to trust either Democrats or southern whites. Powerful anti-Greeley lampoons by political cartoonist Thomas Nast showed Greeley shaking the hand of a Klansman dripping with blood of a murdered black Republican. Nast's most famous cartoon portrayed Greeley as a pirate captain bringing his craft alongside the ship of state while ex-Confederate leaders, armed to the teeth, hid below waiting to board it. To no one's surprise, Grant swamped Greeley by over a million popular votes. Republicans carried every northern state and ten of the sixteen southern and border states. In the Electoral College, Grant received 286 votes to Greeley's 66. Southern blacks enjoyed more freedom in voting than they would enjoy again for a century. But this apparent triumph of Republicanism and Reconstruction proved to be short-lived.

The Panic of 1873

President Grant had but one year to bask in the rays of his resounding victory over Horace Greeley. The following September, the worst economic decline in the Republic's history to date rocked both the Grant administration and the American people, ushering in close to a decade of hard times for millions of Americans. Most importantly, the panic proved to be the death knell for Reconstruction. Northern whites, now distracted and consumed by a more pressing economic crisis, simply lost what little interest or passion they had left for Reconstruction and turned away from the cause, wanting an end to issues and concerns that had never really affected their daily lives in the first place. Economic survival now became the order of the day for the majority of northern whites, and with such preoccupation came the abrupt end for sustaining either the freedmen's rights or for the Republican regimes established to defend those rights and reform the South.

The U.S. economy had grown at an unprecedented rate since recovering in 1867 from a mild postwar recession. As many miles of new railroad track (35,000) were laid down in eight years as in the preceding thirty-five. The first transcontinental railroad had been completed on May 10, 1869, when a golden spike was driven at Promontory Point, Utah Territory, linking the Union Pacific and Central Pacific. But it was the construction of a second transcontinental line, the Northern Pacific, that precipitated a Wall Street panic in 1873 and plunged the economy into a five-year depression and a ten-year general downturn.

Ironically, the hero of Civil War finance, Jay Cooke, was the main culprit. Cooke's banking firm, fresh from its triumphant marketing of Union war bonds, took over the Northern Pacific in 1869. Despite government land grants and loans, the company had not yet laid a single mile of track. Cooke pyramided every imaginable kind of equity and loan financing to raise money to begin laying rails west from Duluth, Minnesota. Other investment firms did the same as a fever of speculative financing swept the country. In September 1873, the pyramid of paper collapsed. Cooke's firm was the first to go under.

Horace Greeley, c. 1872.

The swearing-in of President Ulysses S. Grant for his second term, March 4, 1873.

Like dominoes, hundreds of banks and businesses also collapsed. By 1875, over 18,000 railroad related enterprises had failed. Northern unemployment rose to 14 percent, and hard times set in across the region.

RETREAT FROM RECONSTRUCTION

It is almost a given in American politics that the party responsible or blamed for economic hard times will most certainly lose and usually big in the forthcoming election. That axiom proved true in the 1870s as the Democrats made large gains in the 1874 congressional elections, winning a majority of House seats for the first time in eighteen years. Compounding Republican woes, the Panic of 1873 caused northern public opinion to turn against Republican policies in the South, believing continued support for the Republican governments to be a waste of valuable money and effort that could be put to better use trying to ameliorate the northern economic crisis. When the Liberal Republican-Democratic coalition in 1872 clamored against bayonet rule and carpetbag corruption in the South, their braying at the time fell mostly on deaf ears. However, by 1874, those charges found increasingly receptive northern audiences. Intraparty battles among southern Republicans enabled Democratic Redeemers (along with the use of terror and violence) to regain control of several southern state governments, which became an almost inevitable outcome once southern whites regained their right to vote. No sooner did that occur than they simply voted the scalawags, carpetbaggers, and freedmen out of office, and if they resisted, they would be visited by the Klan or one of the many other white backlash organizations that had emerged to overthrow "negro rule" and restore white supremacy.

Well-publicized corruption scandals, especially in Louisiana, also discredited Republican leaders. Although malfeasance was probably no worse in southern states than in many parts of the North, southern postwar poverty made waste and extravagance seem worse and gave the reform impulse an extra impetus. Southern white Democrats pointed to the corruption as confirmation of the Negroes alleged inherent depravity, incompetence, and ignorance—their complete unfitness to participate in political life. The only reason they had gained political office was because they had been placed there by the scalawags and carpetbaggers who, in reality, had only used them for their own political aggrandizement.

Northerners grew increasingly weary of what seemed the endless turmoil of southern politics. From the beginning of Reconstruction, most northern whites had never had a very strong commitment to racial equality, and they were increasingly willing to let white supremacy restore

A Thomas Nast cartoon, "Worse than Slavery" from *Harper's Weekly* in 1874, portrays the sinister alliance of violent terror organizations—the so-called "White League" and the Ku Klux Klan—that bullied and murdered African Americans in the South during Reconstruction. Armed with guns and knives, the two groups shake hands above a frightened family of freedman. A lynched African American looms in the background. Such organizations sought to frighten away African Americans from seeking an education or exercising their just-won right to vote.

itself in the South. Also motivating many northern whites was the fact that beginning in the 1870s, and over the course of the next four decades, the North would be inundated with millions of southern and eastern European immigrants. About 30 million such individuals came to the United States from 1870-1910. Never before had so many from Europe come to the United States, and, more importantly, they had not come from those regions of Europe. The United States had always been for White Anglo-Saxon Protestants, and now WASP America was about to be overwhelmed by Italians, Poles, Czechs, Slovaks, Greeks, and a whole host of swarthy individuals whom white Americans believed to be ethnically, if not racially, inferior to them and thus a threat to the American way of life. Moreover, these new immigrants not only represented an ethnic and racial menace but a religious problem as well, for the majority were Catholic, or Orthodox, or, horror of all horrors, many were Jews. Not only was the United States a white man's country, but it was Christian as well. To most Anglo-Saxon Americans that meant Protestant. As a result of immigration, a peculiar bond of white solidarity began to take shape between northern and southern whites with the former now declaring they understood southern whites' negro problem, for now Northerners had a similar immigrant problem. In the minds of many northern whites, they could not in good conscience continue to force black equality upon their southern brethren if they were unwilling to accept immigrant equality. Thus, by the mid-1870s, as northern whites became increasingly obsessed with their immigrant issue, they were no longer willing to support Republican governments in the South that forced negro rule on their poor, beleaguered white comrades. As immigrants flooded northeastern cities, Anglo-Saxon Northerners found the Fifteenth Amendment's ambiguous wording a very effective tool to disenfranchise the immigrants, whom they feared would become the unsuspecting pawns of big city bosses and their local henchmen and lackeys. Interestingly, the Republicans, more than the Democrats, used the amendment for such purposes, thus becoming the party of an often vicious nativism.

With the loss of northern white support, it was no surprise that by 1875 only four southern states remained under Republican control: South Carolina, Florida, Mississippi, and Louisiana. In those states white Democrats had revived paramilitary organizations under various names: White Leagues (Louisiana), Rifle Clubs (Mississippi), and Red Shirts (South Carolina). Unlike the Klan, these terrorist squads operated openly. In Louisiana they fought pitched battles with Republican militias in which scores were killed. When Grant sent troops to Louisiana to quell the violence, both northern and southern whites cried out against military rule. The protest grew even louder when soldiers marched into the Louisiana legislature in January 1875 to expel several Democratic legislators after a contested election in which voter fraud was committed along with the terrorizing of black voters away from the polls. Liberal Republicans, such as Carl Schurz, delighted in such events, for such Republican reprisals only helped fuel the fires of northern discontent with Republican rule in the South, which Schurz and others wanted to end.

Southern resistance leaders were quick to sense that the tide was turning in their favor. By 1874, the Redeemers had regained control of Texas, Arkansas, and Alabama, leaving Radical control of only four states—Florida, Louisiana, South Carolina, and Mississippi. Only the first three had black majorities, which allowed the Republican regimes to hang on by a thread for a few more years. In Mississippi, however, whites did not hesitate to institute a reign of terror on African Americans to regain power. That violence became a key to their return to control of the state, for even with all whites voting Democratic, the party could still be defeated by the 55 percent black majority. Economic coercion against black sharecroppers kept some freedmen away from the polls, but overt violence became the most effective means. Democratic rifle clubs (code for terrorist paramilitary groups) showed up at Republican rallies, attended mostly by black voters, provoked riots and then shot down in cold blood as many freedmen as possible in the ensuing melees.

The Grant administration had washed its hands of Reconstruction. It had finally succumbed to the antifederal intervention sentiment of the majority of northern whites, thus dooming one of the last Republican regimes in the South to being violently overthrown. All Mississippi Redeemers had to do now was persuade the 10 to 15 percent of white voters still calling themselves Republicans to switch to the Democrats. The Mississippi Plan worked like a charm. In five of the state's counties with large black majorities, the Republicans polled 12, 7, 4, 2, and 0 votes, respectively. When the Democratic legislature met the following January 1875, the Democrats took complete control of the state.

The 1876 Presidential Election

The various scandals of the Grant administration, along with those occurring in northern cities and states as well as in many southern states under Republican rule, ensured that reform would be the leading issue in the year's presidential race. In this centennial year of the nation's birth, Americans wanted to present their nation as the beacon of virtue, justice, righteousness, and morality for all to behold. Although the reality of the last two decades could not have been further from the truth, Americans nonetheless believed they could find their way back to such an image if they chose the right president to lead them in the right direction. Thus, both major parties gave their presidential nomination to governors who had earned reform reputations in their respective states: Democrat Samuel J. Tilden of New York and Republican Rutherford B. Hayes of Ohio.

Democrats entered the campaign as the favorites for the first time in two decades. They based their optimism on the belief that they could put together an electoral majority of solid South Democrats, disaffected northern Republicans (Liberal Republicans) and by carrying New York and two or three other big northern states, hopefully Ohio and Indiana or Illinois, where Grantism and Radical Reconstruction had caused Republican Party splits. So desperate for victory, the Democrats even openly supported the Mississippi Plan in the South, encouraging their southern white counterparts to continue their violent rampages against blacks and the use of other terrorist tactics to keep freedmen from the polls and voting Republican.

When the returns were in, Tilden had won the popular vote by 252,000 but had lost in the Electoral College by one vote, 185-184. The result, screamed the Democrats,

Rutherford B. Hayes

was fraudulent "Negro-Carpetbag-Scalawag" voting in the three unredeemed southern states of Florida, Louisiana, and South Carolina. Tilden had carried all the rest of the southern states, including all the border states, as well as West Virginia. In the North, he captured New York, New Jersey, Indiana, and Connecticut. Unfortunately for the Republicans, the Democratic accusations of fraud were more than likely correct. Obvious voter irregularities popped up in several Louisiana parishes and in other districts in both Florida and South Carolina where two years earlier many of those same districts and parishes had returned sizeable Democratic majorities and now they had miraculously gone Republican. The opposite also had occurred: in 1874, a Louisiana parish had recorded 1,688 Republican votes, but in 1876, Republicans only tallied one brave vote, the result of obvious voter intimidation by whites of both black and white Republicans. The Democrats refused to yield, continuing to shout fraud and even threatened an armed march on Washington. The country now faced a serious constitutional crisis because the document offered no clear guidance on how to deal with such a scenario. The only point of clarity was that a concurrence of both houses of Congress was required to count the electoral votes of the states, but with a Democratic-controlled House and a Republican-dominated Senate an impasse would surely be the result. To break the deadlock, Congress created a special electoral commission consisting of five House members, five senators, and five Supreme Court justices split evenly between the two parties.

The commission discovered that even in three disputed southern states, Tilden had won a majority, but an estimated 250,000 southern Republicans had been terrorized away from the polls. In a genuinely fair and free election, the Republicans might have carried Mississippi and North Carolina, as well as the three disputed states. After three months of wrangling, threats, and outright nastiness among partisans of both parties, the electoral commission issued its ruling. By a strict party vote of 8-7, the commission awarded all the disputed states to Hayes, but the Democrats refused to accept the decision and began a House filibuster to delay the final electoral count beyond the inauguration date of March 4. Such a move would throw the election into the House, an eventuality that threatened to bring anarchy. To avoid such a cataclysm, behind the scenes less-partisan Democrats and Republicans negotiated a compromise. To these individuals, preventing another North-South showdown was essential so the country could proceed with the business of economic recovery and development. Thus,

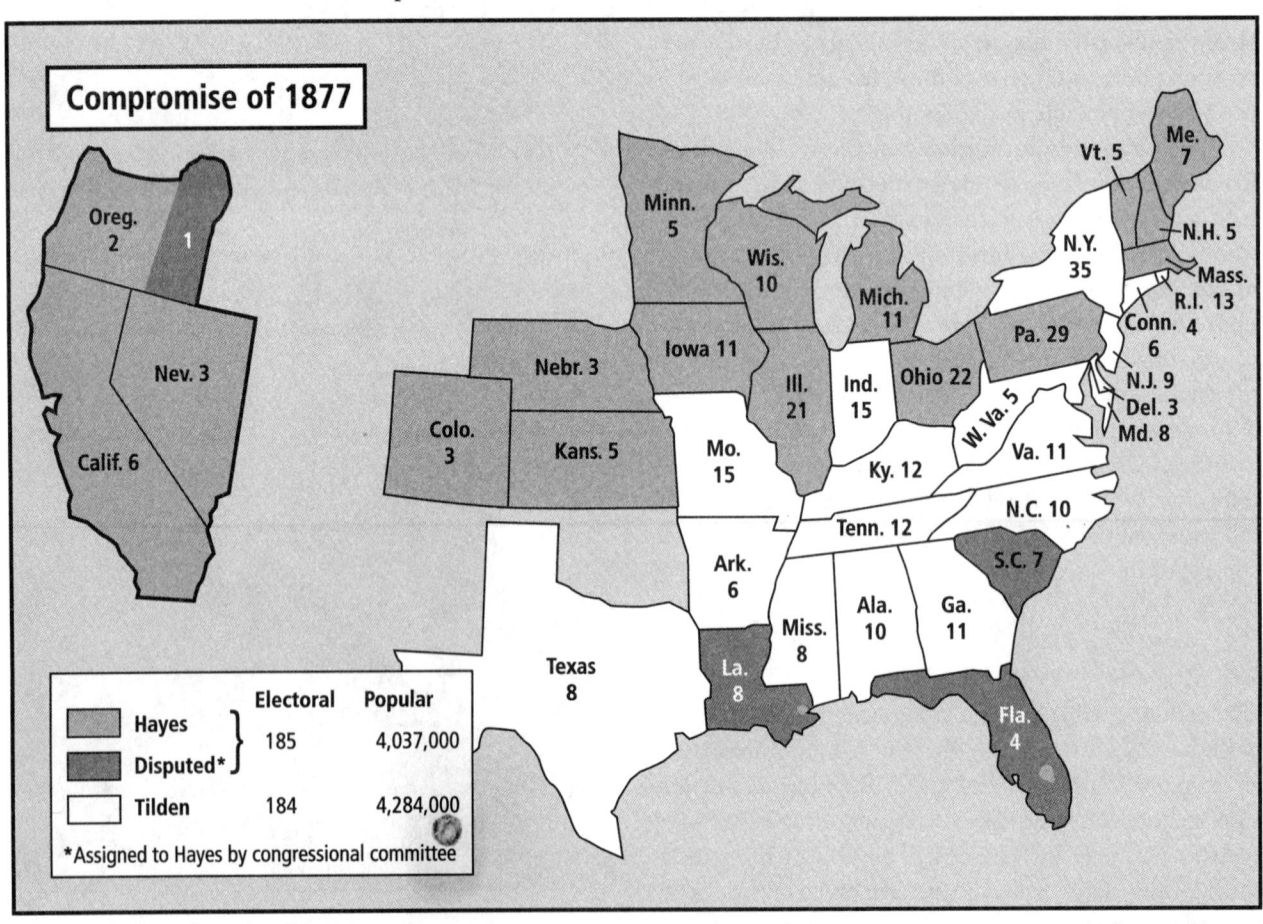

Map 17.3 The Election of 1876

Hayes promised his support for federal appropriations to rebuild war-destroyed levees on the lower Mississippi River and federal aid for a southern transcontinental railroad. Hayes' lieutenants also hinted at the appointment of a Southerner as Postmaster General, who would have a considerable amount of patronage at his disposal. Most important, Hayes signaled that he fully supported the end of bayonet rule, which meant he would withdraw from South Carolina, Florida, and Louisiana, and anywhere else in the South federal troops still resided, allowing a return of complete power to southern whites. In return for his pledge, Hayes asked for and received promises from white Southerners and their respective Democratic state government officials that freedmen would receive fair treatment and respect for their constitutional rights. Such promises were easier to make than to keep, as future years would reveal.

As a result of the backroom negotiations, the Democratic filibuster collapsed, and Hayes was inaugurated on March 4, 1877. No sooner did he take office than ex-Confederate David Key of Tennessee became Postmaster General. The South received more federal money in 1878 for improving its infrastructure than it had ever received before, and federal troops left the capitals of South Carolina and Louisiana. Old abolitionists and Radical Republican warhorses denounced Hayes as a traitor to his party, as well as having sold out the freedmen.

Chronology

1863 Lincoln issues Proclamation of Amnesty and Reconstruction.
Lincoln proposes his Ten Percent Plan

1864 Congress passes stringent Wade-Davis Bill.

1865 Freedmen's Bureau established.
Civil War ends.
Lincoln assassinated (April 14).
Andrew Johnson succeeds to the presidency.
Black Codes enacted by southern legislatures.
Thirteenth Amendment.

1866 Fourteenth Amendment.
Congress passes Civil Rights Act and Freedmen's Bureau Act over Johnson's veto.
Ku Klux Klan founded.
Republicans triumph in congressional elections despite Johnson's efforts.
Southern Homestead Act.

1867 Congressional Reconstruction Act.
U. S. purchases Alaska from Russia.
Congress passes Military Reconstruction Acts, Tenure of Office Act.

1868 President Johnson is impeached but acquitted.
Fourteenth Amendment ratified.
Ulysses S. Grant elected president.

1869 Ratification of the Fifteenth Amendment.

1870 Last four southern states admitted to the Union.
Enforcement Act.

1871 Ku Klux Klan Act.

1872 Grant re-elected president.

1873 Financial panic leads to five-year depression.

1875 Whiskey Ring scandal further discredits Grant administration.
Civil Rights Act.

1876 Disputed presidential election of Hayes vs. Tilden.

1877 Electoral commission awards presidency to Rutherford B. Hayes.

Review Questions

1. Describe Lincoln's Reconstruction plan. What were Lincoln's views on race?

2. How did the Radicals' plan differ from Lincoln's? Who were the "Radicals," and how did they perceive the defeated white South? What was their view of how the freedmen should be treated?

3. Describe the white South "backlash" led by the KKK and other white terrorist organizations against Radical Reconstruction.

4. As a result of the collapse of the Radical regimes, what happened to the freedmen in the aftermath of the Radicals' downfall?

5. What led to Andrew Johnson's impeachment ordeal? Why and how did Johnson alienate the Radicals as well as northern whites?

Glossary of Important People and Concepts

Black Codes
"carpetbaggers"
Crédit Mobilier Affair
Fifteenth Amendment
"Forty Acres and a Mule"
Fourteenth Amendment
Freedmen's Bureau
"Gold Bug"
Ulysses S. Grant
"Grantism"
"Greenbacks"
Homestead Act of 1862
"Iron-clad oath"
Ku Klux Klan
Abraham Lincoln
National Union Party
New Departure
Pendleton Act
Pendleton Plan
Presidential Reconstruction
Public Credit Act
Race-baiting
Radicals Republicans
Reconstruction Acts of 1867
Santo Domingo Affair
"scalawags"
Tammany Hall
Tenure of Office Act of 1867
Thirteenth Amendment
Wade-Davis Bill
"Whiskey Ring"
White backlash

SUGGESTED READINGS

Edward L. Ayers, *The Promise of the New South: Life After Reconstruction* (1992).
Dan T. Carter, *When the War Was Over: The Failure of Presidential Reconstruction in the South, 1865-1867 (1985)*.
LaWanda Cox, *Lincoln and Black Freedom* (1981).
Richard Nelson Current, *Those Terrible Carpetbaggers* (1988).
W.E. B. DuBois, *Black Reconstruction in America* (1935).
Laura Edwards, *Gendered Strife and Confusion: The Political Culture of Reconstruction* (1997).
Barbara J. Fields, *Slavery and Freedom on the Middle Ground: Maryland During the 19th Century* (1985).
Eric Foner, *Reconstruction: America's Unfinished Revolution, 1863-1877* (1988).
___, *A Short History of Reconstruction* (1990).
George Frederickson, *The Black Image in the White Mind* (1971).
William Gillette, *Retreat From Reconstruction, 1869-1879* (1980).
Herbert Gutman, *The Black Family in Slavery and Freedom, 1750-1925* (1976).
Steven Hahn, *A Nation Under Our Feet: Black Political Struggles in the Rural South From Slavery to the Great Migration* (2003).
William Hesseltine, *Lincoln's Plan of Reconstruction* (1960).
Harold Hyman, *A More Perfect Union: The Impact of the Civil War and Reconstruction on the Constitution* (1973).
Jacqueline Jones, *Labor of Love, Labor of Sorrow: Black Women, Work, and the Family from Slavery to the Present* (1985).
Leon Litwack, *Been in the Storm So Long: The Aftermath of Slavery* (1979).
William S. McFeely, *Grant: A Biography* (1981).
___, *Frederick Douglass* (1990).
Eric McKitrick, *Andrew Johnson and Reconstruction* (1960).
James McPherson, *Ordeal by Fire* (1992).
Michael Perman, *Emancipation and Reconstruction, 1862-1879* (1987).
Benjamin Quarles, *Lincoln and the Negro* (1962).
George C. Rable, *There Was No Peace: The Role of Violence in the Politics of Reconstruction* (1984).
Roger L. Ransom and Richard Sutch, *One Kind of Freedom: The Economic Consequences of Freedom* (1977).
Heather C. Richardson, *Greatest Nation of the Earth: Republican Economic Policies During the Civil War.* (1997).
___, *The Death of Reconstruction: Race, Labor, and Politics in the Post-Civil War North* (2001).
John C. Rodrigue, *Reconstruction in the Cane Fields: From Slavery to Free Labor in Louisiana's Sugar Parishes, 1862-1880* (2001).
Willie Lee Rose, *Rehearsal for Reconstruction: The Port Royal Experiment* (1964).
Theodore Rosengarten, *All God's Dangers: The Life of Nate Shaw* (1974).
Mark W. Summers, *Railroads, Reconstruction, and the Gospel of Prosperity: Aid Under the Radical Republicans* (1984).
Hans L. Trefousse, *Andrew Johnson* (1989).
___, *The Radical Republicans: Lincoln's Vanguard for Justice* (1969).
Joel Williamson, *The Crucible of Race* (1984).
C. Vann Woodward, *Origins of the New South, 1877-1913* (1951).
___, *The Strange Career of Jim Crow* (1974).

ELLIS ISLAND

Chapter Eighteen

THE RISE OF INDUSTRIAL AMERICA & THE POLITICS OF THE NEW ORDER

It was a cool, clear crisp October morning in the Italian Alpine town of Piantedo—population 650—when fourteen-year-old Aurelia Rossotti awoke at 6 a.m. to catch the train to Milano, which left at 7 a.m. The year was 1903. Aurelia was the third oldest child in a family of ten children—six girls and four boys. Her older brother Pietro and older sister Lena had left for America two years earlier. Now it was her turn to leave for the "Promised Land" of the United States. Her siblings had sent her the money for her trip over on a steamer—the same way they had come—that left once a month out of the port city of Genoa. It had taken "Pep"—that is now what Pietro called himself because it was easier for Anglo-Americans to pronounce and sounded less foreign—and Lena six months each of work to save enough money to send to their sister, Aurelia. Pep had gotten a job in a lumber mill in northern California, earning about a dollar a day for 12 hours of work. Lena worked as a "domestic" for the mill's owner, a man named Pierce, whose Anglo-American family had been in California since the Gold Rush days of the early 1850s. Indeed, the Pierce family was not only the richest in the area, owning several businesses, including the Eureka Hotel, and thousands of acres of prime land, but also controlled the city government—a Pierce was mayor and another relative was Chief of Police. At the time, the most lucrative enterprise was timber, and the Pierce family owned several mills worth millions of dollars. At first, the Pierces used cheap Chinese labor in their mills, but white California nativism raised its ugly head and drove the Chinese out of the area decades earlier. Filling that labor void would be the "new" immigrants, who, beginning in the 1880s on, were primarily from southern and eastern Europe, like Pep Rossotti. Pep was just one of several of these new immigrants working in the mill. Working alongside him as he fed raw timber into the cutting saws were other immigrants—a "Bohunk" (the generic WASP pejorative for a Slav or Hungarian) and a Russian, whom the WASP bosses simply called Ivan, even though that was not his real name. Since these three men did not speak a word of each other's languages, if they wished to communicate with each other, they all had to learn English. None of the Rossotti children had much formal education—the equivalent of the sixth or seventh grade in the United States—so learning a language as difficult as English was not easy. But they all did and were quite proud of that accomplishment until the day they died.

A the time of Aurelia's emigration, a one-way ticket to America cost around $200 (which would be well over $1,000 in present U.S. value) and that was for space in "steerage"—the bottom of the ship. This was not a luxury liner or cruise ship—no sun decks, no swimming pools, no all-you-can-eat buffets, no exotic shore-leaves, and no shuffleboard. This was a ship built for simply packing into its cargo hold as many human beings as possible and transporting them across the Atlantic to the New World, that strange and distant land discovered some five hundred years earlier by another Italian hoping to find fame and fortune. Living conditions on these immigrant steamers were at best barely tolerable and most of the time deplorable. Quarters were cramped with no privacy, rats roamed freely, and the food was usually not worth eating, and so many of the immigrants brought their own familiar fare with them in their packs—salami, cheese, bread, and fruit from the homeland. Despite the rather wretched conditions on board, hundreds of immigrants believed it was worth enduring for the opportunity to have a new and better life in America. This was what Aurelia hoped for. Aurelia was also somewhat of a rarity; she was one of only a relative handful of northern Italians on board. The steamer, after picking up Aurelia and some others at Genoa, then steamed south to Naples and then to the island of Sicily, where the majority of the "cargo" got on board. Why were the majority of Italian immigrants who came to America from southern Italy? The answer was simple: southern Italy was by far the poorest region in the country, especially so for the inhabitants of the island of Sicily. Southern Italy was (and still is) overwhelmingly agricultural and rural, its farmers dependent on the cultivation of olives, some wheat, livestock, and that's about it. Land is not that fertile, especially that of Sicily, which is essentially an island of rocks, whose soil and terrain is only conducive to the growing of olives and the making of olive oil. Today, such commodities, especially in the United States, are considered to be healthy foods. A hundred years ago, few, if any, WASP Americans even knew what olive oil was. Sicily was also a very violent place, run by very powerful warlord-type families who were constantly feuding with each other for control of the island. Violence was endemic, part of daily life, which saw murder and assassination become commonplace as gun-battles between the families raged in broad daylight, fought with "luparas"—shotguns used for the killing of wolves, which once roamed the island. All too frequently, innocent bystanders were killed for just being in the wrong place at the wrong time. Thus, one can easily understand why someone would want to leave such a place.

After about two weeks of travel, Aurelia's steamer entered New York City's harbor, where it unloaded its passengers at the newly built processing facility at Ellis Island. There, Aurelia and hundreds, if not thousands, of immigrants were put through a battery of different questions, physical examinations, baggage checks, in short, as thorough of a screening as was possible to determine whether the individual was physically and mentally healthy enough to enter the United States. Aurelia was. However, her only problem was her first name—none of the Irish or Welsh processors could pronounce it correctly. Finally, as her papers were approved and had stamped on them "WOP"—which meant "without passport" but has since come to be one of the pejoratives for Italians—a Welsh immigration official looked at Aurelia, noticed her red hair and rosey-red cheeks, and decided that henceforth her new American name would be Rosie. From that moment on, Aurelia Rossotti became Rosie Rossotti.

After spending a few days in New York City in an Italian-owned boarding house, Rosie boarded the train at Penn Station in NYC and headed west for California to join her brother and sister. It only took about seven days for the train to reach San Francisco, as it stopped only twice along the way to take on more passengers. To travel 3,000 miles in that short of time was remarkable testimony to the speed and facility of the American railway system, which had only finished its transcontinental lines a decade and a half earlier. When Aurelia arrived at the station in San Francisco, her brother and sister were there to meet her. She was so excited and relieved to see them, especially since she could "speak" again. Ever since she left Italy, Aurelia had spoken hardly at all for there were very few people with whom she could converse! Even on board the steamer with fellow Italians, Aurelia had difficulty speaking with them because of their different dialects. Aurelia spoke Lombardia, a northern Italian dialect very different from the Italian spoken by a Siciliano, Napolitano, or Calabrese. There was no official Italian language yet; the Italian government was still trying to create one when Aurelia left Italy. She spoke not a word of English but did speak surprisingly a little German, which she had been taught in school. The region of Italy, Lombardia, where Aurelia was from had once been part of the Austro-Hungarian empire and while under Habsburg rule, all Italians were forced to learn German. Along the way to California, Aurelia met some "tdeschi"—the Italian word for Germans—and had brief but pleasant conversations with them. She was amazed by how quickly they were able to switch from German to English and English to German. She someday wanted to be able to do that as well.

After spending the day in San Francisco with her siblings and other Italians (many of whom were also from Lombardia and other areas of northern Italy, with whom she very much enjoyed the company of, especially their cooking!) in the North Beach area of that city, the Rossottis boarded a train for Eureka, arriving there late the next day. No sooner was Rosie in her new home, a flat that Lena and Pep rented near the town's hospital, than Aurelia got a job at the hospital as a cleaning woman for about 80 cents a day. It obviously was very little money for such hard work, but it helped Lena and Pep pay the rent. Aurelia stayed with her brother and sister for two years, all the while working in the hospital. One day a local lumberjack came in with a badly cut hand. His name was Amadeo Acquistapace, was also from Piantedo, and whom Aurelia knew by name only. The Acquistapaces were legendary in the area for their passionate support of socialism. They were outspoken critics of the constitutional monarchy that ruled Italy at the time and vociferously urged its overthrow by revolutionary means, if necessary. Such public advocacy got young Amadeo into trouble with the law, and thus to escape possible imprisonment, he fled to the

United States in 1900. By the time Aurelia met him, he was known as Andy and spoke perfect English, at least according to Aurelia. He was twenty-six when they met; Aurelia was sixteen. They married in 1906 and went to San Francisco for their honeymoon, which turned into the most frightful event of their lives. The young couple experienced one of the worst natural disasters in United States history: the 1906 San Francisco earthquake. The quake itself did not destroy the city. It was the ensuing fires that did the most damage to life and property. The newlyweds escaped the calamity, returning to Eureka as soon as they could get out of the city. Andy and Rosie remained in Eureka until 1931. In those years, they worked hard, saved their money, and in 1920, they bought the Eureka Hotel from the Pierce family. They prospered as hotel owners. During the 1920s Californians discovered the "north Coast" of the state—coming there to vacation. Also, beginning in that decade, Italians began buying land in the area to start vineyards, and today, as a result of Italian entrepreneurship, many California wines are recognized as some of the best in the world.

Andy and Rosie had six children—four girls and two boys. In 1931, as a result of the Great Depression, Andy and Rosie were forced to sell their hotel. The tourists weren't coming anymore—they had no money to spend on vacations and other amenities—and so for many small business owners like Andy and Rosie, dependent on tourism for survival, the depression meant the end of their dream. They swept up their children and moved to Auburn, California, a small town of about 2,000 people, nestled in the foothills of the Sierra Nevada Mountains. Andy and Rosie moved there because it reminded them of Piantedo. They briefly thought about going back to Italy but quickly dismissed that idea for Andy was still a hardcore socialist. The fascist Mussolini had been in power since 1922, and since that time, had declared "open season" on all opposition, especially targeting socialists and communists for his reign of terror. Moreover, they were Americans now—proud of their citizenship, which they both attained in 1914. Rosie was proud of her English, though spoken with a noticeable accent. Rosie got a job in the post office, "the lady who gave you your stamps," while Andy opened a hardware store. They made it even through the darkest days of the Great Depression. All six of their children became "one hundred percent American"—that is, they refused to speak Italian, especially in public, refused to eat or cook Italian food, went to public schools, and some even married non-Italians. However, I am proud of my "one hundred percent Italian heritage," for I am one of Andy's and Rosie's ten grandchildren. My mother is Anna Acquistapace, who married an "Italian boy," John Anthony Moretta, from Brooklyn, New York in 1946. John and Anna named one of their five sons, John Anthony Moretta, Jr., co-author of **The American Challenge: A New History of the United States.**

In the decades following the Civil War, the United States underwent one of the most rapid and profound economic transformations of any nation in world history. Slavery and sectionalism, the two dominant forces of antebellum America, gave way to industry and the various social and political issues that were associated with it. Although industrial development began in the Northeast before the Civil War, it sped to a fever pitch from 1865-1890. By the end of the nineteenth century the United States led the world in manufacturing, far surpassing Great Britain, the undisputed leader in production throughout most of the nineteenth century. In the years between 1865 and the 1890s, the country was transformed from an overwhelming agrarian and rural society to a nation of factories and cities. Industrial progress, however, caused unprecedented socioeconomic and political upheaval, as cycles of boom and bust dominated the economic landscape. Panics, sharp economic downturns usually precipitated by stock market crashes and accompanied by bank failures and unemployment, occurred more often than not and caused two major depressions, one following the Panic of 1873 and a deeper depression after the Panic of 1893. Industrialization was an exclusively Northeastern phenomenon, while the South and the West remained predominantly rural and agricultural. Outside of the Northeast, only the cities and states bordering the Great Lakes, such as Chicago, Illinois, or Cleveland, Ohio, experienced industrial expansion. In those places busy ports witnessed an influx of cheap labor and a correspondingly impressive outflow of American industrial, finished, or processed goods.

Post-Civil War industrialization created a new class in the United States, men whose wealth and concomitant political power were derived from the new industrial order. These "**plutocrat**s" as they came to be called, represented only a handful of individuals, but their dominance of the economy and politics of the Gilded Age was so complete that they have had few rivals since. Their names are legendary still: Andrew Carnegie, Jay Gould, John D. Rockefeller, and J. P. Morgan were larger-than-life figures who controlled not only the economy and politics but the popular imagination as the heroes and villains in the high drama of industrialization.

Bound closer by a network of railroads and telegraphs, with the fate of small towns linked as never before to the fortunes of big cities, the United States was finally becoming the vision of Alexander Hamilton and Henry Clay: an integrated, national, self-sufficient economy, a nation united in fact as well as in name. Perhaps ideologically as important as the realization of the Hamiltonian vision or of Henry Clay's American System was the fact that industrialization meant the end of Jeffersonian agrarianism as the nation's ethos. By the 1890s, the businessman had replaced the yeoman farmer as the new symbol of America.

THE RAILROADS: THE UNITED STATES' FIRST BIG BUSINESS

Without question the most important and dominant post-war industry was the railroad. From the end of the Civil War to 1900, the United States embarked on building a massive railroad network. In the process, the railroad builders also created the nation's first big business. The Republic's first transcontinental rail system was completed in 1869 when the Union Pacific and Central Pacific lines met at Promontory Point, Utah and drove the famous golden spike into the ground commemorating the occasion. Over the course of the next thirty years, the amount of track laid quadrupled, totaling over 193,000 miles by 1900. That total was greater than the entire track laid in all of Europe and Russia combined. The impressive amount of track belied the fact that most of the nation's system was haphazard at best with poor organization and very few integrated networks. Most of the early lines, except for the first transcontinental, did not connect with one another and trains ran on tracks of varying gauges. During the 1870s, more than one thousand roads appeared, often built for financial speculation rather than for viable transportation. Speculation in railroad stock became notorious and an easy way to make fortunes (or lose them as the case was more often than not) by "watering stock"—that is stock issued in excess of the actual assets of the railroads. Buyers could be found for the overvalued stock, and a handful of individuals turned huge profits.

Jay Gould, one of the nation's most legendary plutocrats and railroad developers came from a wealthy family. Gould bought his first railroad line at age 25. He purchased a dilapidated track less than a hundred miles long from a nearly bankrupt company, made minimal improvements, and sold it to another group of investors just two years later at a tidy profit of $130,000. Thus started the career of one of the era's most notorious "Robber Barons" and the beginning of a truly national railway network.

Gould never claimed expertise about railroads but he nonetheless "wrote the book" on the concept of corporate expansion and arose as the architect of the vast, haphazard railroad system that developed in the 1870s. His ruthlessness knew no bounds, and he knew his wealth translated into vast power. Gould bought railroads not to provide a service, but to gain short-term profit. He swam through the business seas like a shark looking for bleeding prey, swallowing financially vulnerable rail lines and destroying his competition by keeping the price of his services artificially low.

Immigrants from eastern Europe on the deck of the S. S. Amsterdam. 1899.

The ease with which Gould was able to manipulate railroad stock and control lines illustrates the reckless nature of the early rail industry. The federal government was partly responsible, which was so anxious to develop the West in the post-war years that it gave vast amounts of the public domain to the railroad builders for free. The railroads not only received land for rights-of-way but were granted liberal sections on alternating sides of the track (sometimes up to twenty square miles) to do with as they pleased, most often to sell to settlers who followed the lines westward. Between 1870 and 1900, the federal government granted the lines a total of 180 million acres, an area larger than the state of Texas. But the lion's share of the capital for the roads came from private investors, a good portion of whom were foreigners, mostly Englishmen.

During the 1870s, the railroads competed fiercely for business on the eastern seaboard. A manufacturer who needed to ship goods to market and who was fortunate enough to be in an area inundated by competing lines could get a greatly reduced shipping rate in return for promising to use that particular road exclusively. This type of cutthroat competition between the lines caused many to lose money and go under. Those that survived realized that such competition was ruinous to all and thus set up agreements or "pools" to divide up territory more equitably and set uniform rates. But these informal combinations invariable failed because they were never legally formalized and because Gould was determined to destroy all competitors by undercutting whatever rates they offered their customers.

In the 1880s, Gould attempted to put together a second transcontinental system to compete with the Union and Central Pacific. His decision meant that other railroads had no choice but to defend their interests by adopting his strategy of expansion and consolidation. Beginning in that decade and stretching into the next, the other railroad titans went to war with Gould, resulting ultimately in his defeat, but in the process, by the 1890s, the lines west of the Mississippi had been consolidated into three major roads that controlled all rail travel—the Southern Pacific, the Northern Pacific, and the Atchison, Topeka, and Santa Fe.

One of the most important by-products of the emerging railroad industry was the introduction of new, more efficient business practices, such as new cost accounting methods and new business structures that enabled the railroads to run at a profit and gave new meaning to the term big business. In the antebellum period, even the largest northern textile mill employed only 800 workers, most often working in one town or even one factory. By 1874, the Pennsylvania Railroad, the largest line in the East, and for awhile in the country, employed more than 55,000 workers and managers and controlled more than 6,000 miles of track spanning half of the nation. Capitalized at over $400 million, the Pennsylvania could boast that it was the largest private enterprise in the world. The Pennsylvania could rightly be called one of the nation's first corporations, and its organization, size, and profitability pointed the way toward the future for all other businesses wanting to become as powerful and profitable. Consolidation became the key to such status, and thus the transformation began from small partnerships to huge incorporated entities.

An equally important revolution in communications coincided with the growth of the railroads. In the 1840s Samuel F. B. Morse developed a code to send messages across electrical wire. Morse's intricate series of dots and dashes, tapped out on a single key, allowed telegraphers to send messages instantaneously over the wires, thus giving the country its first national communication system. The telegraph marched across the continent with the railroads, on rights-of-way furnished by the lines themselves. The telegraph system became the nerve center for the railroads, providing the companies with the instantaneous communication they needed to control their rail empires. Again, Gould played a crucial role. In 1878, through stock manipulation, the robber baron gained control of Western Union, the company that monopolized the telegraph industry. With control of Western Union, Gould dictated to the other roads the price they had to pay for such services. Needless to say, Gould's acquisition of Western Union only made him that much more powerful and that much more hated by his competitors.

Not all of the early railroad magnates were as ruthless as Gould. James J. Hill, owner of the Great Northern (Minneapolis, Minnesota to Seattle, Washington), built his line well and without the benefit of federal largesse. Hill had to plan carefully and calculate which areas would best be served by the line to maximize returns to his investors. As a result, the Great Northern was one of the few major roads able to remain solvent and running during the 1890s, when depression hit the country. In contrast, speculators like Daniel Drew and Jim Fisk, Gould's partners at the Erie Railroad, could more accurately be described as wreckers than as builders. They ruined the Erie, one of the East's most important early lines, by gambling with its stock to line their own pockets. In the West, the Big Four railroad moguls—Collis P. Huntington, Richard Crocker, Leland Stanford, and Mark Hopkins—became so powerful that critics claimed the Southern Pacific held California in the grip of an "octopus."

The public's increasing alarm at the railroad tycoons' control of the economy provided a barometer of attitudes

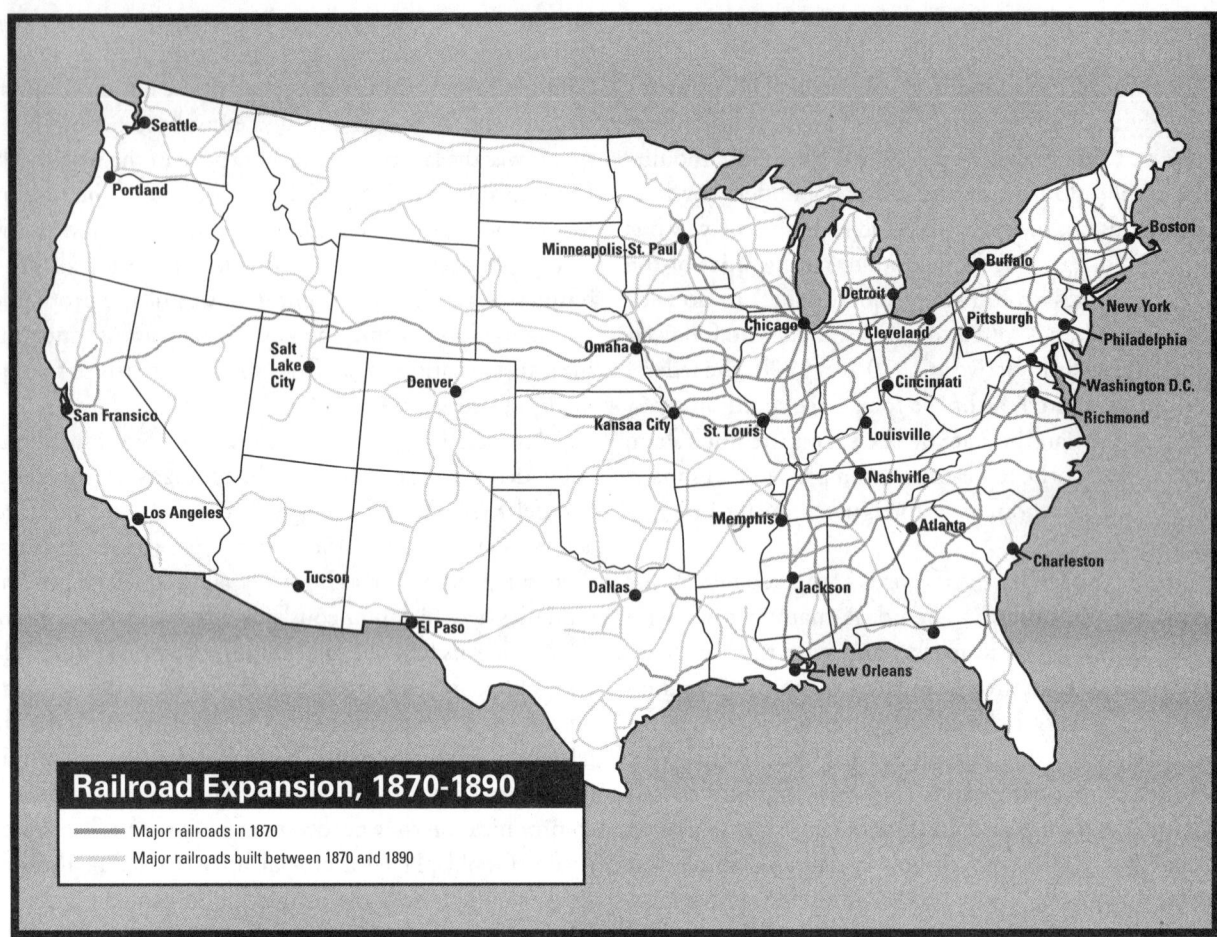

Map 18.1 Railroad Expansion, 1870-1890.

toward big business itself. When Jay Gould died in 1892, the press described him as "the world's richest man," estimating his fortune at over $100 million. His competitor for that title, the Commodore Cornelius Vanderbilt, who built the New York Central Railroad, judged Gould "the smartest man in America." But to the public, he was, as he himself admitted shortly before his death, "the most hated man in America." Why? Many remembered Gould's attempt to corner the gold market in 1869. Also, anti-Semitism was a factor since many mistakenly believed Gould to be Jewish. Finally, many Americans had long hated men who earned great wealth by shuffling paper and speculation with other people's money rather than by their own physical exertions or producing goods. Since Gould did neither, his image was further tarnished. However, by the time of his death, more than 150,000 miles of track stretched across the country, and no one could claim to have had a greater hand in its building than Jay Gould.

Andrew Carnegie

The rise of the railroads spawned the birth of another major American industry: steel. Even though steel was stronger and more flexible, it was too expensive prior to the mid-nineteenth century. Railroad companies relied on fragile iron tracks that cracked easily, posing a danger to travelers and requiring frequent, expensive repairs. In the 1840s and 1850s, Henry Bessemer in England and William Kelly in the United States independently developed less costly ways to develop steel from pig iron. Around the same time vast deposits of pig iron were discovered near the Great Lakes. Transporting this vital material became cheaper, thanks in large part to the railroad. With such an abundance of iron ore, the Bessemer process found its most enthusiastic employers among American steel manufacturers. **Andrew Carnegie** was one of the first steel producers to use the Bessemer process and the first champion of the new "King Steel." Within a decade, Carnegie monopolized the steel industry.

Unlike Jay Gould, who by the time of his death was despised, almost from the beginning of his rise to industrial preeminence, Andrew Carnegie became an American icon. The hatred toward Gould and the affection for Carnegie testified to the country's divided reaction to industrialism. Carnegie, a barely literate Scots immigrant, came to personify the American dream (or myth) of rags-to-riches. He rose from a job in a textile factory cleaning bobbins at age twelve for a $1.20 a week to become one of the richest men in America. Before he died, he gave away more than $300 million of his fortune, most notably to the formation of public libraries. His generosity or philanthropy, combined with his own rise from poverty, went far to promote a popular image with the public. In reality, Carnegie was a shrewd, often ruthless, manipulative businessman, in many respects no different than Gould. He simply atoned for his callousness and greed in his twilight years by becoming a philanthropist.

Carnegie's swift rise coincided with the propagation of the popular myth promoted by the writer Horatio Alger, whose novels, such as *Ragged Dick, Mark the Matchboy, and Pluck and Luck,* filled Americans' heads with the notion that if one just worked hard, led a clean, sober life, like Carnegie allegedly did, they too could become millionaires. To a certain degree, such was possible in the immediate aftermath of the Civil War. In many ways, Carnegie was in the right place at the right time. After he left the textile factory, while still a teenager, he got a job as a telegraph operator for the Pennsylvania Railroad. Under the auspices of Tom Scott, the line's superintendent, Carnegie rose through the ranks, all the while maintaining Scott's friendship. It was Scott who loaned Carnegie the money for his first investments in the stock market that netted him enough money to plunge into the steel business. Carnegie's twelve years with the railroad also provided him with a great education in business management that he put to good use when he struck out on his own to reshape the iron and steel industries.

In 1872, Carnegie applied the lessons of cost accounting and efficiency he had learned at the Pennsylvania Railroad, turning steel into the nation's first manufacturing big business. In the town of Braddock, on the outskirts of Pittsburgh, he built the most modern Bessemer steel plant in the world and began turning out steel at an unprecedented rate. By the 1890s, Carnegie's blast furnaces poured out an incredible ten thousand tons of steel a week. Using railroad accounting methods, he cut the cost of making rails in half, from $58 to $25 a ton. Carnegie's formula for success was simple: "Cut the prices, scoop the market, run the mills full; watch the costs and profits will take care of themselves." Indeed, by 1900, Carnegie Steel earned more than $40 million in a single year. But at what human costs? Cut the prices meant, like for Gould, you simply destroy all competitors by having lower prices than anyone else. Lower prices meant lowering the costs of production, which meant cutting potentially the most expensive production cost—labor. Carnegie's workers were grossly overworked and underpaid. Workers toiled at least twelve hours a day in most of his plants, and when the shift changed every other week, they worked twenty-four hours at a stretch in the hazardous steel mills. Carnegie held a majority of the stock in his company and rarely paid dividends to his shareholders. Instead, he poured the profits back into new plants and new machinery—not into higher wages, safer working conditions, nor shorter hours for his workers.

Carnegie's steel monopoly was the result of a system of business organization or incorporation called **vertical integration**, whereby all facets of a given manufacturing enterprise, from the procuring of essential raw materials to the finished product, including transportation, are under the control of one business or ownership. In Carnegie's case, as one contemporary observer noted, "from the moment these crude stuffs were dug out of the earth until they flowed in a stream of liquid steel in the ladles, there was never a price, profit, or royalty paid to any outsider." Between 1875 and 1900, Carnegie sought to control every aspect of the steel making process, from the mining of iron ore on the Great Lakes to its transport to his mills, to the production of crude steel and rails.

Andrew Carnegie dominated the steel industry for three decades, building Carnegie Steel into an industrial giant, the largest steel producer in the world. Carnegie's steel built the nation's first skyscraper, formed the skeleton of the Washington Monument, supported the elevated

Andrew Carnegie

trains in Chicago and New York, and provided the superstructure for the Brooklyn Bridge. By 1900, Andrew Carnegie was world famous, and steel had replaced iron as the most important heavy construction material.

John D. Rockefeller, Standard Oil and the Trust

Edwin Drake's oil discovery in Pennsylvania in 1859 sent thousands rushing to that state's oil fields searching for black gold. In the days before electricity, the automobile, and gasoline, crude oil was refined for lubrication oil for machinery and kerosene for lamps to light homes and streets. Observing the difference between the price of crude oil gushing from wells at fifty cents a barrel (forty-two gallons) and the kerosene sold in the East at fifty cents a gallon, smart entrepreneurs turned to oil refining as the key to making a potential fortune from this particular resource. The amount of capital required to buy or build an oil refinery in the 1860s and 1870s was relatively low, about $25,000, the cost of laying one mile of railroad track. Since the investment cost was low, the story of the new petroleum industry was one of riotous, cutthroat competition among small refineries. One man, John D. Rockefeller, came to dominate oil refining through the use of yet another new business organizational strategy called the **trust**. By the 1890s, Rockefeller controlled nine-tenths of the oil refining business through his Standard Oil Company.

John D. Rockefeller, the son of a shrewd Yankee doctor who peddled quack cures for cancer, learned early some of the more invidious skills that would help him establish his oil empire. "I cheat my boys every time I get a chance," Bill Rockefeller boasted. "I want to make'em sharp." Rockefeller started out rather humbly, a bookkeeper in Cleveland, but owned his own business by the time he was twenty-one. One of the secrets of his success lay in his ability to obtain loans. He borrowed constantly to build up his profits, making other people's money work for him. Rockefeller, like Gould and Carnegie, hired a substitute to fight for him during the Civil War, so he could remain on the home front, profiting from the war. Rockefeller became wealthy during the war years. At the end of the Civil War, he borrowed money, bought out his business partner, and assumed control of the largest oil refinery in Cleveland. Thus, in 1870, he incorporated his oil business, founding the Standard Oil Company, the precursor of today's Exxon-Mobil Corporation.

As the largest refiner in Cleveland, Rockefeller demanded rebates or kickbacks from the railroads, which they gave. His volume of shipping was so great that the railroads not only gave him the rebates on his fares but also slipped him under the table a portion of the fares paid by his competitors. Such wheeling and dealing allowed Rockefeller to undercut his competitors. He not only could ship his oil at a dollar a barrel cheaper but he also received a dollar a barrel "rake-off" on every barrel his competitors shipped. Using this kind of leverage, Rockefeller soon pressured competing refiners to sell out to him or face ruin. By 1871 Standard Oil had cornered the petroleum business in Cleveland, and now Rockefeller set his sights on the national market.

The cities of Cleveland, Pittsburgh, Philadelphia, and New York City competed to become the center of the nation's petroleum business. By combining railroad rebates with efficient production, Standard Oil strengthened its position. Major refiners began to sell out. In a series of secret mergers, or combinations, they received stock in Rockefeller's company and continued to run their refineries as before under their own names. Stubborn independents who refused to capitulate to Rockefeller's often menacing demands to sell, either unwittingly sold to companies that were secretly controlled by Standard Oil or somehow mysteriously blew up. Rockefeller was infamous for doing whatever it took to eliminate his competition. Not until 1879, when a New York legislative committee investigated railroad practices did the American people learn the extent of Standard Oil's hidden empire.

Rockefeller's clandestine activities were necessary because such combinations were illegal. Laws forbade one corporation from controlling another. Rockefeller, however, circumvented the laws by shrewdly developing yet another new organizational structure that came to be called a trust. Such an entity was a form of **horizontal integration**, which differed from Carnegie's vertical approach in steel. In a trust, several trustees hold stock in the various companies doing the same business in trust for the parent company's stockholders. In the case of Standard Oil, trustees held stock in the various refineries "in trust" for Standard's stockholders. Initially, Rockefeller did not attempt to control every facet of the oil business from crude oil at the well to the final product. Rather, he opted to move horizontally to control only the refining process by taking over all the refineries he could. He used the trust to increase profits by controlling output, thus raising prices consumers had to pay. Because Standard Oil monopolized the market and controlled the output of an essential commodity—heating oil, used for lighting for homes, schools, hospitals, businesses, and street lights, the public soon cried out against the company, accusing it of conspiring against the public for private profit. When the federal government threatened to outlaw the trust as a violation of free trade, Rockefeller simply changed his tactics and organized Standard Oil into a

THE RISE OF INDUSTRIAL AMERICA | 521

John D. Rockefeller

holding company, which operated in much the same way as a trust but was legal. Instead of competing companies agreeing to set prices and determine territories, such as the railroads did for awhile, the holding company simply combined competing companies under one central administration. The state of New Jersey helped to promote this new form of consolidation and monopoly by passing laws that allowed state-chartered corporations to hold stock in out-of-state enterprises. Quickly conglomerates such as Standard Oil company and a host of other large combinations transferred their company headquarters to New Jersey, which by the end of the century was home to some of the nation's largest corporations.

As Rockefeller's empire grew, central control became essential. Rockefeller personally did not move to New Jersey but to neighboring New York City, where he began to vertically integrate á la Carnegie steel, Standard Oil. In reality, Standard Oil became unique: it was both horizontally and vertically integrated, allowing it to ultimately control the entire petroleum industry from crude oil sources in the ground (which at this time were exclusively located east of the Mississippi in the states of Pennsylvania, Ohio, and parts of West Virginia) to home and business delivery of the final product.

Rockefeller enjoyed unprecedented business success. Before he died in 1937 at the age of ninety-eight, he had become the nation's first billionaire. Despite his mod-

est, pious Baptist habits, and his many philanthropic acts, the American people never embraced him the way they had Carnegie. The individual most responsible for Rockefeller's negative public image was journalist and muckraker Ida M. Tarbell, whose classic magazine expose, *The History of the Standard Oil Company*, published in *McClure's Magazine* beginning in 1902, revealed to the American people that Rockefeller was ruthless and callous. Tarbell's devastatingly thorough history showed an individual so determined in his business pursuit that he willingly and unashamedly used whatever tactics—threats, assassination, sabotage—that would bring the desired result: complete control of the petroleum industry of the United States. By the time Tarbell finished her story, Rockefeller had become such a demon in the public's eye that he literally slept with a loaded revolver by his bed to defend himself against possible assassins.

Even though Andrew Carnegie could be at times as cold and ruthless, it was Rockefeller who aroused the people's fear of industrial concentration. Americans vilified him because they feared the vast power of one company to so completely control the production and supply of so vital a resource such as oil. At any time, Standard Oil could shut the nation down if its unscrupulous, greedy owner thought he could make more money by doing so. However, plutocrats such as Rockefeller, despite having their own personal fears for their safety, were secure for years to come from any laws being passed by the federal government curtailing their power, regardless of the harm done to the public welfare.

American Inventors and the Plutocracy

At the turn of the century, Alexander Graham Bell and Thomas Alva Edison had become folk heroes. Regardless of how profound or revolutionary the invention, the inventor and his creation ultimately came under the plutocrats' control. Such was the case for two of the most important innovations in technological history—the telephone and electricity—both of which were the brain child of American genius.

Alexander Graham Bell, like Carnegie, a Scots immigrant, developed a way to transmit voice over wires—the telephone. Bell formed his own company, American Bell, with himself as owner. But he was an inventor, not a businessman, and thus wisely deferred such matters to his brilliant professional manager, Theodore N. Vail, who over the course of two decades built Bell America and its subsidiary, American Telephone and Telegraph (AT&T) into one of the nation's largest communications corporations. In 1900, AT&T became the parent company of the entire "Bell system." Taking a page from Rockefeller's

Alexander Graham Bell, 1904.

book, Vail organized Bell America first then AT&T, both vertically and horizontally, which meant that AT&T had a complete monopoly over the new telephone industry and would remain in control of it until the late twentieth century. Via Western Electric, which AT&T also owned, the company manufactured and installed its own equipment as well as controlling long-distance telephone service. The arrival of AT&T meant that Americans could communicate not only locally in their towns and cities but across the country. Unlike a telegraph message, which had to be written out and taken to a telegraph office, sent over the wire, and then delivered by hand to the recipient, the telephone connected both parties immediately and privately. Bell's invention proved a boon to business, contributing greatly to speed and efficiency.

Since AT&T monopolized this new communication industry, the company dictated supply, service, and prices. If one wanted phone service, then it would be provided, but at AT&T's convenience and price. Many rural folk, for example, would not have a telephone in their homes for decades after it became a household item for most urban dwellers because it simply was not profitable for AT&T to supply service to people living in the countryside. However, if one lived in the rural areas and wanted to be connected, rates would be exorbitant compared to those paid by city folk. Thus, ironically, the telephone, which could have brought Americans closer together (which it did for urban residents), only served to further separate country folk from city folk.

In the eyes of Americans, **Thomas Edison** came to personify the virtues of rugged individualism and Yankee ingenuity, working twenty hours a day in his laboratory in Menlo Park, New Jersey, vowing to turn out "a minor invention every ten days and a big thing every six months or so." Edison almost fulfilled his pledge. At the height of his career, he averaged a patent every eleven days and invented such devices as the phonograph, the motion picture camera, and the electric light bulb. No industry that developed in the post-Civil War period faced more obstacles than electric light and power. Edison's invention of a filament for the electric light bulb in 1879 ushered in the age of electricity. But perplexing Edison was the way to sell this most important product. Before he could begin marketing electric light and power, he had to develop an integrated system of conductors, power stations, generators, lamps, and electrical machines. Because electricity was so technically complex and so potentially dangerous, it demanded an entirely new system of marketing, one that relied on skilled engineers. Initially, the new industry depended on private generators. Financier J.P. Morgan had electricity installed in his New York City mansion on Madison Avenue in 1882, making it the first private home in the country with electric lighting. An engineer visited the house daily to start the generator. When the lamp in Morgan's library short-circuited and set fire to his desk, the engineer promptly fixed the problem and restored Morgan's faith in electricity, so much so that he invested heavily in the Edison General Electric Company.

Edison worked diligently to build power stations and provide electric current. But his system had one serious

Thomas Alva Edison, standing in his laboratory. East Orange, New Jersey, c1901

drawback: it relied on direct current (DC), which for technical reasons limited its effective power distribution to only two miles from a generating power plant. George Westinghouse, already known for inventing the compressed air brake for trains, solved the problem by developing a workable alternating current (AC) system by which electricity could be transmitted over long distances with minimal losses compared to direct current. Westinghouse saw the potential for great profits and created his own company to compete with Edison General Electric. Both companies created large, complex, vertically integrated enterprises to meet their unique marketing and distribution needs. They staffed sales offices with technicians trained to advise consumers, safely install and operate equipment, and provide repair services. Westinghouse eventually won this "War of the Currents," and his superior alternating current system became the accepted standard for electric power distribution. Contributing greatly to this victory was Croatian immigrant scientist Nikola Tesla's successful development of the first AC motor, which converted the transmitted AC electricity to a wide range of mechanical uses.

By 1900 electricity had become, like the telephone, part of American urban life. It powered trolley cars, subways, and factory machinery. It lighted homes, apartments, factories, and office buildings. As late as the 1930s, only 10 percent of rural America enjoyed or had access to this most important product. As was the case with the telephone, those who controlled the electrical power business, like Westinghouse and others, hoped to personally profit and thus only provided to markets where money could be made—the cities. Poor farmers and other rural folk could not afford the rates charged because to provide such a population with electricity would have cost too much for the electric companies to profit. Thus, rural Americans would have to wait until the New Deal to have what had become a necessity of life for urban Americans some forty years earlier.

While Americans thrilled to the new electric cities, the day of the inventor quietly yielded to the heyday of the corporation. In 1892, J.P. Morgan consolidated the electric industry, selling Edison General Electric, of which he had become its major investor and shareholder, out from under its inventor and dropping Edison's name from the corporate title. The new General Electric Company, which was four times the size of its closest competitor, Westinghouse, soon dominated the market.

The Emergence of Mass Marketing

By the 1880s, a national mass market emerged for producers of consumer goods. Indeed, the United States was one of the first industrial nations to produce simultaneously **capital and consumer goods**, the latter often in greater quantities than the former. Manufacturers of consumer goods integrated methods of mass production with those of mass distribution via the railroads to establish some of the first major consumer-oriented enterprises in America, such as the meatpacking and food processing industries.

What Carnegie did for steel, Gustavus Swift did for meatpacking. Until well after the Civil War, cattle were transported out of the West (mainly Texas until the 1880s) on the hoof (actual live steers) to be slaughtered by local butchers. To feed an expanding Northeastern population, Texas cowboys would drive large herds to the closest railheads, and then from there the live steers would be shipped to the meatpacking plants where they would be slaughtered. The problem was that the cattle lost weight from the long cattle drives and were not good quality once they reached the packing house. Swift believed it would be more efficient and produce a better quality of beef if the cattle were slaughtered in the Midwest, such as in cities like Kansas City, Missouri, and then transported North or East in refrigerated railcars while still fresh. To accomplish this, Swift created a vertically integrated meatpacking business headquartered in Chicago that controlled the entire process—from the purchase of cattle for slaughter to the mass distribution of initially fresh then processed meat to retailers and consumers. Swift was the first to use the refrigerated railcars, and through high quality, low prices, and effective advertising, he won over consumers who worried about buying meat not butchered locally. Swift's success led the older meatpackers, such as Philip Armour, to build similarly integrated businesses to compete with Swift. Armour, for example, was able to initially corner the market on processed meat in the form of bologna and hot dogs. Thanks to Swift and Armour, by the 1890s, the city of Chicago had become the center of the nation's meatpacking industry. From the Windy City, all manner of fresh and processed meat found its way into homes all across the nation. Though the quality of processed and even fresh meat was often questionable, the innovative ideas of Swift and Armour provided American consumers with a quantity and variety of food that was envied by the rest of the world.

Just as Swift combined mass production with mass distribution to revolutionize meatpacking, Henry John Heinz transformed the processed food industry. For several years, Heinz had produced pickles, sauces, and condiments for the local Pittsburgh market. After recovering from the Panic of 1873, Heinz decided to go national with his products by adopting new, more efficient methods of canning and bottling while building a network of sales offices to advertise his fifty-seven varieties of condiments

The Flush Toilet: Technology Changes Daily American Life

Today it is difficult for Americans to realize that not that long ago the "bathroom" was an outdoor facility called an "outhouse" or an indoor "device" called a "chamber pot," used mostly to relieve oneself during the night. The problem with chamber pots was the disposal of their refuse, which many urban Americans simply poured out the window, often on unsuspecting passersbys. For rural folk elimination of waste was less of a problem. Country residents just found a convenient spot outdoors when they had to relieve themselves. But in crowded places or in the cold of winter, privies (outhouses) and chambers pots did the job. On farms, outhouses were located as close to the main house as possible. In the cities, they were placed in one's backyard. Regardless of location, a "privy's" principal purpose was to provide a place for human waste as material passed directly into a pit (which could overflow and seep into the yard), or even into a nearby body of water. The most sanitary of such devices were those that channeled the waste into a special container that could be periodically emptied.

In urban homes, the chamber pot for night use was often enclosed in a wooden box called a commode, hence the name some people use today for their in-house "bathroom." The commode was very convenient for night usage and was emptied by a housewife or servant at daytime. Such a chore for either individual was not, to say the least, very pleasant. In 1849, Harriet Beecher (soon to be Harriet Beecher Stowe, author of **Uncle Tom's Cabin**), *already known for a series of widely read domestic advice books, urged her audience to install "earth closets" in their homes. In such "closets" people dumped dirt on their refuse, allowing their waste to decompose naturally. Although the dirt eventually had to be hauled away, the earth closet idea had merit: no water required for disposal thus saving homeowners the expense of having to install an appropriate plumbing system.*

As technological breakthroughs proliferated, it became more economical and practical to install a water system to deal with the disposal of human waste: hence the development of the "water closet." Although initially requiring a reliable water supply, adequate plumbing, and municipal investment in sewage systems and related disposable facilities, the water closet offered the quickest and cleanest way to dispose of human waste. Flush toilets drew upon technological innovations in steam power in the mid-18th century. The toilet also stimulated the plumbing trade, as increasing numbers of urban homes installed toilets. Until cities constructed adequate water and sewer systems, real improvements in American sanitary waste development and disposal would be slow. By 1875, most of the nation's larger metropolitan areas provided municipal water to most of their neighborhoods and a few years later began building sewer systems. By 1900, innovations and manufacturing of the essential "plumbing" components were common.

The flush toilet went through several different iterations before attaining a physical appearance modern Americans would readily recognize. The first apparatuses, the "pan closet," featured an earthenware bowl sitting on top of a copper pan holding several inches of water. When the user pushed a lever, the copper pan dumped the refuse into a cast iron container connected to the drainage system. Developed by John Randall Mann in 1870, the "siphonic closet" used water from three pipes. One pipe provided water for the basin's flushing rim, another deposited water into the basin to start the action, while the third brought in new water after the flush. Many other inventors made refinements to the siphonic closet. Twentieth-century toilet innovators offered improvements like placing the thank on top of the bowl, the arrangement we are familiar with today. Gradually, first in more affluent homes and then in middle-class residents, the bathtub, sink, and toilet came to be placed in one room, hence the "bathroom."

and sell them across the nation. To ensure the necessary and continuous flow of vegetables and other foodstuffs into his factories, he created a large buying and storing organization to contract with local farmers. By 1888 Heinz had become one of Pittsburgh's wealthiest citizens, and ketchup had become a household staple. Using similar methods, the owners of other processed food companies, such as Quaker Oats, Campbell Soup, and Borden Condensed Milk, coordinated mass production with mass distribution to produce inexpensive, canned, and easily prepared foods for a national market. Companies producing other commodities such as tobacco, grain, matches, and soap also integrated manufacturing and distribution to dominate their respective markets. American Tobacco, Procter & Gamble, and Pillsbury Flour all started during the Gilded Age, becoming giants in that time and still flourishing today.

To boost and sustain sales, businesses realized the importance of advertising. Just as the railroads made possible a national market, newspapers made possible advertising on a national scale. Gilded Age advertising bore little resemblance to the slick, sophisticated industry of today.

THE RISE OF INDUSTRIAL AMERICA

fession of quacks and phony medicines, prohibited its members from plying their trade in print. By the turn of the century, however, advertising and attitudes toward it began to change. As companies pursued a larger share of the national market, they turned to advertising to boost sales by extolling the virtues of their products. Ivory Soap—"99.44% pure—so pure it floats;" Quaker Oats—"the easy food;" and Coca Cola—"The ideal brain tonic"—cashed in on the growing trend toward national advertising. As companies competed for the national market, advertising became more professionalized, as ad agents began increasingly to not just place ads but actually write them as well. By the end of the century full-service advertising agencies started appearing in the larger urban areas such as New York City, soon to become the home to the burgeoning advertising industry.

FROM COMPETITION TO CONSOLIDATION: THE RISE OF THE CORPORATION

Even as Rockefeller and Carnegie built their empires, their days of independent ownership and autonomy

Drink Coca-Cola 5 Cents
An advertisement of a well dressed young woman holding up a glass of Coca-Cola. On the table is a paper giving the location of the home office. 1890

Nineteenth-century advertising agents neither wrote the copy nor selected the illustrative materials. All of that was done by the advertiser, the client or business wishing to display its products, primarily in newspapers and later in magazines. What the agent did do was buy and sell space in the newspapers and magazines. With more than 8,000 papers printed in the United States by 1876, few business owners could afford the time away from their companies to learn the names and locations of the papers, let alone check the circulation figures and bargain for advertising space. That became the agent's job, taking the client's prepared copy and placing it in specified papers. The ad agent earned his livelihood by being paid a commission, not by the advertiser, but the newspaper publishers.

Gilded Age advertising was tainted by its frequent association with all manner of questionable products, ranging from quack medicine cure-alls to rotten canned or processed meats. Products like Lydia Pinkham's Vegetable Compound, a "sure cure for female complaints," pioneered early advertising and made Lydia Pinkham a household name. Reputable firms eschewed advertising because of its dubious, unethical practices. Organizations like the American Medical Association, which emerged in the late Gilded Age to try to purge the medical pro-

An advertisement of a pioneer washing with Ivory soap at his campsite. Procter & Gamble, c1898

were numbered as once privately-owned and operated companies were selling out to impersonal, anonymous entities called corporations, which by the beginning of the twentieth century became the dominant form of American business organization. Soon corporations, managed by faceless boards of directors—supposedly educated, professional business experts—replaced the great business titans of the previous decades. Already by the end of the nineteenth century, the corporation had begun to eclipse the partnership and sole proprietorship as the major business enterprise. Corporations had the advantage of limited liability, which protected investors from losing their own assets should the company go under. A corporation could outlive its owners and was not susceptible to the vagaries that frequently destroyed family businesses, as one generation could ruin a company painstakingly created by its predecessors. Corporations also separated ownership and management, placing the company's daily operations in the hands of professional managers. Since the corporation could raise money by issuing stocks and bonds, the owners in most instances were individual investors, a consortium of the majority stockholders, who were more than glad to leave management to elected or chosen boards of directors and the daily operations to trained experts. Since the law—the Fourteenth Amendment—recognized the corporation as a person and granted it protection under that legislation's due process clause, it was difficult to regulate or redress corporate abuse through legislation. Finally, corporations could buy out and control other corporate entities, and it was this power that came to dominate in the early twentieth century as businesses consolidated into ever larger corporate giants.

Banks and financiers played a key role in this consolidation process. No one better defined this role than J.P. Morgan, the great New York banker, who single-handedly reshaped American business at the turn of the century, consolidating several major industries, including the railroads and steel, into large corporate entities. During these years, a new social philosophy, based on Darwinian theory, helped to justify consolidation and to prevent state or federal intervention to regulate or control the excesses or corporate capitalism. The Supreme Court, a bastion of conservatism during this time, further promoted consolidation by strictly interpreting the Constitution and declaring unconstitutional legislation designed to regulate railroad rates and to outlaw trusts and monopolies.

J. P. Morgan and Finance Capitalism

The new consolidationists loathed competition and whenever possible pursued a policy of incorporation and central control. No one was a more zealous promoter of incorporation than **J. Pierpont Morgan**. Morgan was one of the most dominant Wall Street financiers of all time. The son of a successful banker, J.P. Morgan inherited along with his wealth the stern business code of the old-fashioned merchant bankers, men who valued character and reputation. From his own age, Morgan embraced the new business ethos and believed that investment banking could play a decisive role in reorganizing business and transforming the stock market.

Morgan acted as a power broker in the reorganization of the railroads and in the creation of corporations like General Electric and United States Steel. When depression engulfed the nation in the early 1890s, the railroad industry was hit hard. Morgan, with his passion for order and his access to capital, decided it was time to restructure the entire industry, consolidating as many of the lines as possible to prevent the industry's future collapse. He had already restructured the Baltimore and Ohio, the Reading, and the Chesapeake and Ohio Railroads in the 1880s. After the panic of 1893, he added the Santa Fe, the Erie, and the Northern Pacific and Southern Railroads to his list. In 1901, Morgan's railroad empire reached its zenith when he created the **Northern Securities Company**, a supersystem designed to bring peace between the feuding Great Northern and Northern Pacific Railroads. The Northern Securities Company established a community of interest among the new entities managers, men Morgan handpicked. Often, Morgan partners sat on the boards of competing firms, forming **interlocking directorates**. By the time Morgan was finished reorganizing the railroad industry, seven major groups, all under his auspices, controlled two-thirds of the nation's rail lines.

Banker-control of the railroads rationalized or coordinated the industry, but behind the scenes Morgan's machinations proved to be as self-serving and ruthless as those of Jay Gould as he blatantly overcapitalized the companies by watering their stocks, which saddled them with enormous debts. Equally detrimental was the management style of the Morgan directors, who were not railroad men but essentially cost analysts whose background was banking and accounting. Their conservative policies discouraged the continued technological and organizational innovation necessary to run the line effectively.

In 1898 Morgan believed it was time to consolidate the steel industry. The story of his acquisition of Carnegie Steel is not only legendary, but symbolic of the passing of an old era and the coming of a new one. The heyday of the individual entrepreneur was ending by the late nineteenth century, and in its wake came the rise of the corporation. Carnegie represented the old order—Morgan, the new. As he began to challenge Carnegie's empire, Morgan

THE RISE OF INDUSTRIAL AMERICA / 527

J. P. Morgan

wisely merged all the smaller steel companies first, thus eliminating the last remnant of competition in the steel industry. In the process, Morgan also vertically integrated his new cartel by having his companies move from the manufacture of finished steel products into actual steel production. Carnegie, who had monopolized crude steel production for decades, countered this obvious move by creating a new plant for the manufacturing of finished steel products such as tubing, nails, wire, and hoops.

The press covered the impending war between the feisty Scot and the arrogant Wall Street broker as if it were a major sporting event, but the battle of the titans proved in the end to be little more than the wily maneuvering of two shrewd businessmen so adept that even today it is hard to discern who won. The sixty-six-year-old Carnegie, for all his obstinacy, longed to retire and may well have invited Morgan's bid for power. Surely, Carnegie knew that Morgan was probably the only individual who had enough money to buy him out. When an intermediary sought Carnegie out on the golf course and asked him to name his price, Carnegie scrawled a number on his score card, and the go-between scurried back to Morgan's office and handed him the card. Morgan, who disdained haggling, accepted the price; he agreed to pay $480 million for Carnegie Steel. Carnegie's personal take was more than $250 million. According to legend, when Carnegie later teased Morgan that he should have asked for a $100 million more, Morgan had the last laugh, telling the Scotsman, "You would have got it if you had."

Morgan quickly merged Carnegie Steel with his other steel companies, forming one of the largest conglomerates in United States history and in the world at the time: United States Steel. Created in March 1901, U.S. Steel became the country's first billion dollar corporation. Yet despite its monolithic size and despite Morgan's attempt to gain a monopoly on steel production, he could not. There remained enough smaller, independent producers, such as Bethlehem Steel, to create a competitive system know as oligopoly, in which several large combinations, not one alone, controlled production. Other industries, such as meatpacking and electricity, were also oligopolies. Businesses in this new arrangement did not compete with each other by cutting prices; rather they simply followed the lead of giants like U.S. Steel in setting prices and dividing the market so that each business held a comfortable, profitable share. Although oligopoly did not eliminate competition all together, it definitely limited the competitors to a handful of companies.

Morgan was driven by the pursuit of personal power and order, which he believed consolidation of businesses into corporations would achieve. Morgan's imprint on the Gilded Age, and even today, was far greater than that of either Carnegie or Rockefeller. When the country faced bankruptcy in 1895, it was Morgan to whom the president turned. And as the reorganizer of American's railroads and the creator of U.S. Steel, General Electric, and other large combinations, Morgan ushered in the era of oligopoly that has continued to be an integral feature of the nation's business scene to the present.

SOCIAL DARWINISM AND THE GOSPEL OF WEALTH

Many plutocrats worried how they would be publicly perceived. Would the people embrace them as the epitome of rugged individualism, the realization of the American dream that hard work and a clean, sober life brings material success and rewards? Or, would they be viewed as ruthless, self-serving scoundrels who made their money by callously exploiting others? Even those who cared less about their public image, nonetheless, believed it essential to find justification or rationalization for how and why they made it while the majority of people suffered in miserable poverty, despair, and hopelessness. The road to wealth and power taken by these robber barons was strewn with ruined competitors and brutally exploited labor. Such ruthlessness not only seemed to become increasingly necessary for personal aggrandizement, it was also transformed into a virtue by the twin ideologies of **Social Darwinism** and the "**Gospel of Wealth**."

For men like Andrew Carnegie, the writings of Social Darwinists Herbert Spencer and William Graham Sumner helped expiate feelings of personal guilt. "I remember that light came as in a flood and all was clear," Carnegie remarked after reading Spencer's work. Spencer and his disciples believed that the same natural forces or laws that determined evolution and survival in the animal world applied to the human condition as well. As in the animal world, Darwin's concept of natural selection meant that in human society, the fittest individuals survived and flourished in the marketplace while those less endowed were destined or predetermined to be swept away by obviously superior individuals. Survival of the fittest supposedly enriched not only the winners but also society as a whole. Human evolution would produce what Spencer called "the ultimate and inevitable development of the ideal man" through a culling process of eliminating supposedly weaker, inferior human beings.

According to the Social Darwinists, poverty and slums were as inevitable as the concentration of wealth. Spencer argued that "there should not be a forcible burdening of the superior for the support of the inferior." Sumner, asserted "If we do not like the survival of the fittest, we have only one possible alternative, and that is the survival of the unfittest." Both men believed that government or charitable intervention to improve the conditions of the poor interfered with the functioning of supposed natural law and prolonged the life of defective gene pools to the detriment of society as a whole. Social Darwinists propagated a perverted Darwinism designed to justify the plutocrats' ruthless rise to power and wealth. Overt racism and ethnocentrism defined much of the Social Darwinist theory, for the fit or superior individuals were clearly Anglo-Saxon or white Northern Europeans (excluding the degenerate Irish, of course), while the unfit or inferior were the rest of humanity who were not of that stock and were thus to be either subordinate at all times to the superior race or ultimately extinguished. Social Darwinism became very popular among the nation's **WASP** (White, Anglo-Saxon Protestants) elite, especially from the 1890s on because of the massive influx of Southern and Eastern European immigrants whom they regarded as the unfit.

Plutocrats like Carnegie and Rockefeller enthusiastically embraced this theory. Rockefeller told his Baptist Sunday school class, "The growth of large business is merely the survival of the fittest. This is not an evil tendency in Business. It is merely the working out of nature and a law of God." Some who found the callousness of Social Darwinism unpalatable sought religious justification instead. Since colonial times, the Protestant work ethic had informed the American creed, denouncing idleness and viewing material success as evidence of being among the "elect"—God's chosen people for whom salvation was a certainty. Expanding on this assumption, the more religiously affected plutocrats constructed the gospel of wealth.

In this context, some were simple and direct in their certainty, like Rockefeller, that their rise to industrial preeminence and wealth was ordained by God: "God gave my riches," Rockefeller sanctimoniously declared as a reward for having led a most clean, sober, diligent and righteous life. Carnegie produced a written, logically argued rationale for his success: "Not evil but good, has come to the race," he wrote, "from the accumulation of wealth by those who have the ability and energy that produces it." To justify his exploitation of labor, Carnegie was certain that the masses would waste any extra income "on the indulgence of appetite." "Wealth, passing through the hands of the few," Carnegie wrote, "can be a much more potent force for the elevation of our race than if it had been distributed in small sums to the people themselves," whom the steel magnate was convinced would only spend it on the pleasures derived from vice and dissipation. In short, Carnegie believed that individuals like himself who have clearly demonstrated their fitness, or superiority, should decide what other people needed. In Carnegie's case, he took that responsibility seriously, distributing over $300 million to such philanthropic causes as the founding of libraries and the Carnegie Foundation.

Among the most effective apologists for the wealthy were religious leaders such as the Episcopal Bishop William Lawrence, who proclaimed that "Godliness is in league with riches." Not only did the elite deserve their wealth, but the poor were responsible for their low status because of their obvious personal flaws and defectiveness. God was punishing them for their alleged sins of depravity and laziness. The eminent preacher Henry Ward Beecher reaffirmed this belief when he announced that "no man suffers from poverty unless it be more than his fault—unless it be his sin."

Thus, according to supposed scientific and religious thought, the maldistribution of wealth was not only inevitable but desirable, for it ultimately would cleanse society of all the unfit and leave only those worthy of continued existence. Probably more important was the support and propagation of such perversion by popular culture. *McGuffey Readers* stressed the virtue of hard work and its inevitable rewards. Popular literature reinforced the idea that success always came to those who deserved it in America, the land of opportunity.

INTERNAL MIGRATION AND EUROPEAN IMMIGRATION

The appeal of Social Darwinism among WASP America intensified during the last decade of the nineteenth century and into the early twentieth century because of unprecedented European immigration. Never before or since had so many human beings come to the United States seeking a new and better life. Indeed, between 1880 and 1920, some 23 million people arrived in the United States, mainly from Europe but from Canada, Mexico and Latin America, and Japan as well. Europe, however, provided over 80 percent of the total, and after 1880 and until 1914, the majority of immigrants came from southern and eastern Europe. Among them were 4 million Italians, 2 million Russian and Polish Jews, 2 million Hungarians, 4 million Slavs, and 1 million from Lithuania, Greece, and Portugal. Hundreds of thousands came as well from Turkey, Armenia, Lebanon, Syria, and other Near Eastern lands abutting the European continent.

It was this particular phase of immigration that resurrected the nativism, prejudice, and discrimination WASP America had previously displayed in the antebellum period toward the Irish and Germans. The same fears WASP America had about the Irish and Germans they now simply transferred to the Italians, Hungarians, eastern European Jews, Turks, Armenians, Poles, Russians, and other Slavic peoples. Not only did WASP America fear the Catholicism and supposed ethnic and racial inferiority of the new arrivals, but many of the new people weren't even Christian. They were Jewish or Muslim, two faiths the majority of white Americans had no understanding or knowledge of and had always viewed with suspicion, contempt, and hostility. Up to this time, except for the momentary fear the influx of Irish and Germans created in the 1840s, WASP America's supremacy was unchallenged. That was about to change with the massive invasion of Europe's unwanted and unfittest. Indeed, as the popular journal *Public Opinion* editorialized, "they are the very scum and offal of Europe." Though a very high percentage of these immigrant groups were indeed illiterate peasants from some of the most impoverished areas of southern and eastern Europe who were coming to America to escape such despair, they were nonetheless all castigated for being uneducated, backward, and outlandish in appearance. Terence Powdrly, head of the labor organization the **Knights of Labor**, complained—with a degree of accuracy because they were discriminated against and segregated into the city's most wretched areas—that the newcomers "herded together like animals and lived like beasts."

Old-stock WASP elites like Henry Cabot Lodge of Massachusetts, formed an unlikely alliance with organized labor (which was also at this time WASP-dominated and feared that the influx of unskilled labor, which the immigrants represented, would adversely affect their jobs and status) to press for immigration restriction. A precedent for keeping out undesirables had been established in 1882, when labor agitation and racism in California led to passage of the Chinese Exclusion Act, which stopped the legal immigration of Chinese nationals. On the east coast Lodge and his nativist followers championed a literacy test, designed to limit immigration from Italy and eastern Europe by requiring immigrants to demonstrate the ability to read and write in their own language. Since the vast majority of Italian and Slavic peasants had little to no formal education, it was assumed few would be able to pass the test. In 1897, Congress approved a literacy test for immigrants, but President Grover Cleveland promptly vetoed it. "It is said," the president reminded Congress, "that the quality of recent immigration is undesirable. The time is quite within recent memory when the same thing was said of immigrants, who, with their descendants, are now numbered among our best citizens."

Why They Came

The new wave of immigration that brought southern and eastern Europeans to the United States beginning in the 1880s resulted from a number of factors. Improved economic conditions in northwestern Europe, as well as immigration to Australia, Canada, and Argentina, curtailed the flow of old immigrants to the United States. Prior to the 1880s, the overwhelming majority of new arrivals came from Germany, Ireland, Great Britain, Scandinavia, the Low Countries, and France. At the same time, a protracted economic depression in southern Italy, the religious persecution of Jews in eastern Europe, especially in Russia, and a general desire to avoid conscription into the Russian army (which affected both Slavs and Poles) led many in southern and eastern Europe to come to the United States.

Economic factors in the United States also played a role, the most important of which was American industries' insatiable demand for cheap, unskilled labor, especially during good times. So important was immigrant labor in the rise of American industrial preeminence that without it the United States would not have become the leading industrial power in the world, at least not as rapidly. Had the millions of Europeans remained in their respective homelands or migrated instead to Germany, England, or France, then it was possible that one of those nations, not the United States, would have been the greatest industrial power by 1900. Nor would the plutocrats' profits and wealth been as great or as legendary had it not been for such cheap labor costs.

Though socioeconomic factors played a key role in European migration, in the final analysis, the decision whether to leave the Old Country and come to the United States remained an individual or family choice. Immigration fever affected whole villages, as the entire population of a rural hamlet in southern Italy or in the Balkans would collectively decide to come to America or at least pool resources and send its most able-bodied. As historian John Higham wrote in his masterpiece, *Strangers in the Land: Patterns of American Nativism, 1860-1925*, factory and mine owners and railway companies set up offices in Europe to encourage immigration, with *padronse* (recruiters) who traveled to remote villages with promises of the cheap land available across the Atlantic. Some immigrants heard fabulous tales of prosperity and how easy it was to become rich in America. The immigrants themselves fueled such fantasies in letters from relatives and friends who had already reached the United States and who either wanted the company of loved ones or didn't want to make their friends and families believe they had failed in the new land. Most immigrants suffered cruel disappointment when they arrived. "I came to America because I heard the streets were paved with gold," one Italian immigrant said. "When I got here, I found out three things: First, the streets weren't paved with gold; second, they weren't paved at all: and third, I was expected to pave them."

By the beginning of the twentieth century, almost 70 percent of the new immigrants had settled in cities, mostly in the Northeast. Added together, immigrants and their first-generation American children made up substantial majorities in several American cities, including 75 percent in Chicago and around 80 percent in New York City.

One particular group—dubbed "birds of passage" by immigration officials—became particularly vulnerable to exploitation, overwork, low wages, and racist, anti-immigrant backlash. Approximately 8 million young men, primarily impoverished rural peasants from Sicily and elsewhere in southern Europe, would travel to the United States to earn money for their families back home, returning to the homeland as soon as economically feasible. Their lives resembled those of modern migrant farm workers from Latin America. They faced similar resentments from native whites who saw these low-salaried temporary laborers as undercutting the struggle of unions to improve wages. Only when some of these migrants realized that they weren't going back home again did they join the union cause and they often became leaders.

Jews from eastern Europe most often came as family units and came to stay. In the 1880s, a wave of violent

Street peddlers' carts on Elizabeth Street, looking north from Hester Street, New York City. c. 1902.

persecutions, or pogroms, in the Russian empire led to the departure of more than a million Jews in the next two decades. They settled mostly in the port cities of the East coast. New York City's Lower East Side replicated the Jewish ghettoes of eastern Europe, teeming with street peddlers and push carts. Hester Street, at the heart of New York's Jewish section, rang with the calls of vendors hawking their wares from pickles to feather beds. Jews were not the only immigrants to have their own neighborhoods. Virtually all the immigrant groups were segregated into their own enclaves by a WASP America fearful of their possible mixing or integration. Springing up in New York City or Boston were the "Little Italys," or "Little Polands." In such enclaves the immigrants would remain (some forever) for several generations. As their numbers swelled and their affect on the city landscape became more pronounced, WASP America realized that the new Americans were here to stay. Once old-stock Americans accepted this reality, they wisely realized that if the immigrants intended to make the United States their permanent home, then the best policy to pursue was the newcomers' acculturation and assimilation. Such a new attitude proved successful in transforming the once unwanted into acceptable citizens.

Immigrant Labor

How important were the immigrants to the industrial work force? In the first decade of the twentieth century, immigrant men and their sons constituted 70 percent of the workforce in 15 of the 19 leading U.S. industries.

Their concentration was highest in industries where the work was most exploitative and dangerous: railroad construction and tunnels; in the coal, iron ore, and other mineral mines; in the steel mills; and in the putrid, disease-infested meatpacking houses. Certain ethnic groups predominated. For example, after 1900, Slovaks and Poles overwhelmingly worked the coal mines and steel mills of western Pennsylvania, Buffalo, and Cleveland, while Poles, Lithuanians, and Italians were the rank and file in the meatpacking and food processing industries. Italians also exceeded all other groups in the heavy construction business, such as the building of New York City's subway system. In the lighter but no less arduous work of garment manufacturing, Jews and Italians predominated. Most egregious, however, was the preponderance of immigrant children in the garment industry sweat shops. Hunched over sewing machines, twelve to fourteen hours a day, with tiny, nimble fingers often getting torn to shreds by the rapidly-moving needles, could be found young immigrant women and boys and girls as young as ten years of age, earning pennies per piece of clothing. Not only did these sweat shops callously exploit immigrant youth, they also were physically some of the most deplorable, hazardous, and sometimes fatal workplaces.

Immigrant labor workweeks averaged 60 hours—10 hours per day except Sunday. Workers who were granted Saturday afternoons off—thus reducing their workweek to 55 hours—considered themselves fortunate. Steel workers were not so lucky. They labored from 72 to 89 hours a week and were required to work one 24-hour shift every two weeks. Immigrants were forced to work long hours just to barely make ends meet. In 1900 the annual earnings of American industrial workers averaged between $400 and $500 a year, although there were substantial variations from region to region and level of skill. Southern workers only earned on average $300 annually, while their northern counterparts earned $460. The better paying jobs by the late nineteenth century went to the older immigrants—Yankees, Germans, Irish, and Welsh. Through their unions, workers of Northern European extraction also controlled access to new jobs that opened up and usually managed to fill them with a son, a relative, or fellow countrymen. Consequently, relatively few of the new immigrants rose into the prosperous ranks of skilled labor. Though old immigrant skilled workers earned more than the recent arrivals, as the nineteenth century progressed, the old immigrants found themselves increasingly unemployed as the captains of industry replaced them with machines, easily operated by the unskilled new immigrants.

From the Farm to the City

Not all of urban America's newcomers were foreign-born immigrants. In fact, until the 1880s, the majority of the new urban inhabitants arrived from the country's rural areas as hundreds of thousands of farm boys and girls looked for jobs in the burgeoning industrial centers. The lure of the bright lights and the promise of wages, coupled with the theaters, the dance halls, the great amusement parks like Coney Island in New York City, and the cultural and educational advantages, the likes of which they never dreamed existed, all served as a powerful magnet for many young people.

For at least one group of Americans, the city promised something more. African Americans began to migrate northward, not just for employment but also to escape limited economic opportunities, oppression, and violence. In the countryside, broad new vagrancy laws reinforced planters' control over their labor force. These codes per-

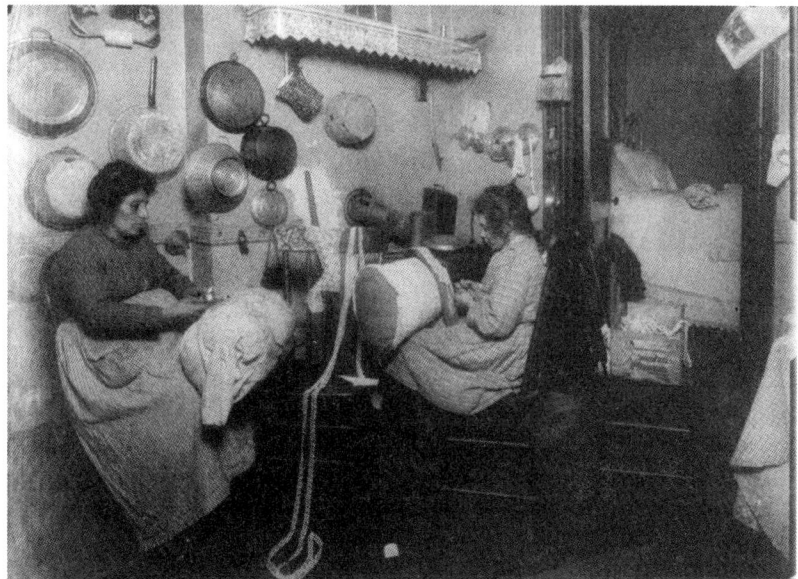

A mother and her daughter are working on fancy lace perhaps for a pillow. They are both illiterate and working in the dirty kitchen of their tenement house. Women and children earned additional income in the home by doing "piece work." Employers paid for each finished item. December 1911.

National Child Labor Committee, No. 92. Main entrance Gary, W. Va. Mine. Miners will be in the mine over 10 hours from 7AM to 5:30 PM. In this photo a boy is beginning his career as a picker. Working in the underground mine shafts was extremely dangerous. Poor working conditions also caused illnesses, such as black lung disease. Explosions and cave-ins were a constant danger. September 1908.

mitted the arrest of any unemployed person and made it a crime to leave a job before the expiration of a contract. Criminal laws increased the penalty for even the pettiest offenses. A convict-lease system expanded to permit the hiring-out of most prisoners. Mines, railroads, lumber companies, and planters vied for these new forced laborers, most of whom were blacks convicted of minor transgressions.

Sharecropping, the primary agricultural system to replace slavery in the plantation belts of the ex-Confederate states, perpetuated black economic dependence upon whites. Under the sharecropping system, planters retained ownership of their land, but subdivided the plantation into separate plots to be worked for wages by individual families. Because planters only paid the laborers with a half-share of their crop at harvest time, the laborers had to borrow from the landowner, at high rates of interest, against their wages for their necessities. Inevitably, due to low crop prices, the high rates of interest, and (if they had an unscrupulous boss as many did) questionable arithmetic by the plantation store manager who provisioned the croppers, they became enmeshed in a web of debt from which financial escape was virtually impossible. Increasingly, physical escape from a local area, or the South entirely, became the only option for many wanting a better life.

Another impetus for outmigration from the South proved to be the increased marginalization of African Americans by means of legal segregation. Southern customs had long separated the races, but beginning in the 1880s a series of Jim Crow laws made segregation into a rigid system. The term, derived from a popular minstrel show character, denoted a code for racial segregation in all areas of public interaction -- schools, residences, transportation, and entertainment. In 1896, the Supreme Court ruled in the *Plessy v. Ferguson* case that a Louisiana law mandating distinct railroad cars for blacks and whites did not violate equal protection guaranteed by the Fourteenth Amendment as long as "separate but equal" facilities were available. In an impassioned dissent, Justice John Harlan, a Southerner who formerly owned slaves, famously declared in opposition that "The Constitution is colorblind." Later decisions, however, extended this "separate but equal" doctrine to other public facilities, particularly schools. Of course, accommodations were never really equal, and Jim Crow became central to the southern way of life.

With such an endorsement by the highest court in the land, white Southerners felt free to use whatever intimidation and violence necessary to keep the African Americans in their place. A dramatic increase in white violence took place during the 1890s, designed to keep blacks more firmly in their place. The decade averaged 187 lynchings per year. The overwhelming majority of the victims were black. Some were well-planned public events, attracting large audiences and family outings. Some victims were accused of crimes, but the crime of many of the victims was uppityness. Others supposedly made sexual advances to white women. The fear that white women might be attracted to black sexuality became a further underpinning for rigid segregation.

These indignities combined with the lack of economic choices impelled many southern blacks to leave their homes and seek a safer and materially better life in the

North. "To die from the bite of frost is far more glorious than at the hands of a mob," proclaimed the *Defender*, Chicago's largest African-American newspaper. By the 1890s, many southern blacks agreed. By the early 1880s, disillusionment with the end of Reconstruction had already led more than fifty thousand African Americans to leave the South in order to seek opportunities in Kansas. These "Exodusters" represented only a small percentage of those who would have migrated if more opportunities in the North existed. With industrialization underway in the 1890s, Southern black migrants now headed to northern cities in increased numbers. They usually found jobs at the bottom of the occupational ladder, as janitors, cooks, common unskilled laborers, or domestic servants. Unfortunately, racism in the North was as commonplace as in the South, though often not as overt, keeping them a segregated, subordinate class. Nevertheless, the urban North continued to attract African Americans. By 1900, New York, Philadelphia, and Chicago had become home to the largest African-American communities in America. Although the greatest black exodus out of the South would occur during and after World War I (over 90 percent of black Americans in 1900 continued to live in the South), over 185,000 African Americans had already moved to the North by 1890. The Great Migration was underway.

THE "NEW SOUTH"

The American economy leaped forward at an astonishing pace during the 1880s, with the South sharing the buoyant mood sweeping the country. The collapse of the last few Republican state governments led to the domination of southern politics by a new class of men—merchants, bankers, railroad promoters, and even some industrialists—who allied with the old planter class, which despite a decline of its prewar power, retained considerable influence in rural areas. Calling themselves Redeemers because of their claim that they had "redeemed" the South from corrupt and extravagant Republican rule, they proclaimed the beginning of a "New South" devoted to economic modernization and frugal government.

Henry Grady, editor of the *Atlanta Constitution*, became the foremost exponent of the expansive New South ideology. Announcing there would be a new stress on the "gospel of work as the South's great need," he assured Northerners that the South had learned its lesson in its defeat and was now willing to embrace northern economic and social standards. In a famous 1886 speech, Grady promised that the New South understood "that her emancipation came because through the inscrutable wisdom of God her honest purpose was crossed, and her brave armies beaten." Southerners, he declared, were glad that "the American Union was saved from the wreck of war."

Despite the widespread publicity given to the ideas of the New South's advocates, the problem with the image they sought to build was its general inaccuracy. Far from admitting that the Confederate cause had been wrong, most Southerners believed it had always been right. They were defenders of the "Lost Cause" and slavery. Every Confederate Memorial Day, they paraded Confederate battle flags down the main streets of small towns and cities.

A more important difficulty with the New South conception involved the continuing backwardness of the southern economic and social system. The new state governments set out to reduce government spending and property taxes. In doing so, they retreated from Reconstruction commitments to state responsibility for the welfare of its citizens. Florida abandoned a nearly completed college, leaving the state without any institution of higher learning. Alabama closed public hospitals. Public schools were the principal victims of the cutbacks. Louisiana spent so little on its system that the percentage of literate whites actually declined between 1880 and 1900. Above all, black schools, so laboriously built and maintained, were hit the hardest as the gap between spending for black and white schools invariably widened.

Many New South crusaders concentrated on a campaign to develop industry. They achieved success in the expansion of southern textile mills, which by 1900 surpassed the output of New England's linen factories. The new fad of cigarette smoking led to tremendous growth in the tobacco industry. Leading the way was James Buchanan "Buck" Duke, who had perfected the mass production of cigarettes. In 1890, he combined with his competitors to form the American Tobacco Company. Investing heavily in advertising, the conglomerate soon controlled 90 percent of the domestic market. Railroad construction also continued at a rapid pace. Southern lines were integrated into the national railroad network under the control of northern capitalists. Despite these advances in industrialization, fueled by promises of low taxes, special concessions, and a docile labor force, the South remained overwhelmingly agricultural. In fact, even by 1900, the New South accounted for a smaller percentage of the nation's industry than the Old South had in 1860.

While the new upper class continued to prosper, most Southerners, white and black, fell into even deeper poverty. Publicists touted the cotton mills as the salvation of poor whites. But when the poor white farmers gave up their struggle with the land and went to work in the mills, they replaced one life of destitution with another. Men earned wages of about 50 cents a day, and women and children supplemented family income at even lower wages. Companies controlled all aspects of life in company towns and the poor white worker found that, "I owe my soul to the company store." These mill villages remained all-white and consciousness of racial superiority grew in importance as the century ended.

LAISSEZ-FAIRE IN THEORY AND PRACTICE

Prevailing economic theory also bolstered greed, exploitation, and opposition to any government or private intervention to alter the natural laws of the free marketplace and the forces of unbridled capitalism. Adam Smith's theory, usually adhered by many, asserted that the market was directed and controlled by an "invisible hand" composed of a multitude of individual choices. If government did not meddle, competition would naturally lead to the production of desired goods and services at reasonable prices—the natural laws of supply and demand. Smith believed that since all humanity was motivated by self-interest, no individual or group of individuals would willingly succumb to greed, for to do so would only hurt their realization of personal—material—happiness. Individuals must be left alone to act according to self-interest and in the process, the resulting economy would be best suited to meet society's demands.

Acceptance of Smith's theory led to a policy called **laissez-faire**. Government was to leave the economy alone and not disrupt the operation of these natural forces. Business leaders naturally endorsed the theory's rejection of governmental intervention and regulation, yet they saw no contradiction in asking government for aid and subsidies to further promote industrialization and modernization. To a large extent, Gilded Age capitalists got what they wanted: a laissez-faire policy that left them alone to pursue their objectives, free from all government interference, and government assistance whenever they asked to further expand and protect their enterprises, regardless of the harm their pursuit of self-interest had on people and the environment.

Unfettered industrial capitalism boggles the modern mind. Yet, such a possibility did not occur until the Progressive period, and really not until the 1930s and the New Deal. Until then, no laws protected the consumer from adulterated foods, spurious claims for ineffective or even dangerous patent medicines, the sale of stock in non-existent companies, any sort of regulation of the stock market, no laws abolishing child labor or establishing a forty-hour work week, or unsafe and overpriced transportation services. No national regulating agency of any kind existed before the establishment of the Interstate Commerce Commission in 1887.

While denying support and protection to consumers and workers, government at all levels willingly aided the plutocrats. Alexander Hamilton's vision of an industrializing nation promoted and protected by government participation had never entirely died. It was resurrected by the Republican Party by 1860. In that year, the party pledged to enact higher tariffs to protect domestic northern industry, to subsidize the completion of a transcontinental railroad, and to establish a stable national banking system—all Hamiltonian ideas first introduced in the 1790s. The Republican victory in that year and for the next several decades undoubtedly boded well for the emerging business and industrial elite, as the party evolved into the strongest supporter and promoter of big business and their interests.

Big business not only found a strong ally in the Republican Party but in the U.S. Supreme Court as well. During the 1880s and 1890s, the Court increasingly reinterpreted the Constitution to protect business from taxation, regulation, labor organization, and antitrust legislation. In a series of landmark decisions, the Court used the Fourteenth Amendment, originally intended to protect freed slaves from state laws violating their rights, to protect corporations. The Fourteenth Amendment declares that no state can "deprive any person of life, liberty, or property, without due process of law." By defining corporations as persons under the law, the Court determined that legislation designed to regulate corporations deprived them of due process. Using this rationale, the Court struck down state laws regulating railroad rates, declared income tax unconstitutional, and judged labor unions as a "conspiracy in restraint of trade."

Labor Strife

With such attitudes shared by the government and plutocrats toward the working class, it was inevitable that sooner than later, the nation's working classes would rise up in protest against the plutocracy's exploitation and oppression. Perhaps the violent confrontations between labor and the industrial capitalists could have been avoided had the government been more concerned with the workers' plight. Since it was not, workers, finding no redress of their grievances through either the established political or legal system, decided to take matters into their own hands and through their own efforts, try to win the rights and respect they were entitled to as citizens.

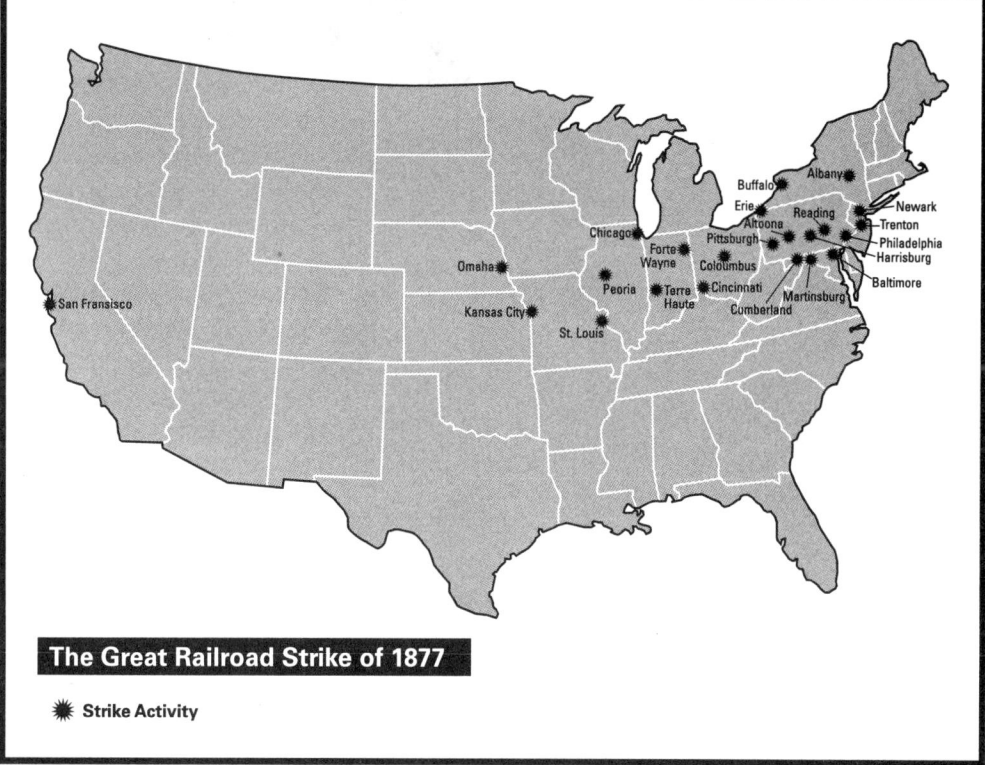

Map 18.2 The Great Railroad Strike of 1877 brought rail traffic to a standstill. The strike was the beginning of working-class and trade union negotiations.

Several factors drove workers toward protest and organizing and joining unions. Workplace safety, for example, was one such cause. The drive for greater speed and productivity on railroads and in factories gave the United States the unfortunate distinction of having the world's highest rate of industrial accidents. Another factor was the erosion of worker autonomy in factories, as increasingly machinery replaced skilled workers and managers made operational decisions about pace and procedure rather than the workers. As the Gilded Age progressed, once proud, skilled craftsmen became commodities to be bought for wages rather than a mastery whereby the worker sold the product of his labor rather than the labor itself. For skilled artisans this was an alarming trend. Their efforts to preserve or recapture independence from bosses and robber barons fired much of the era's labor unrest, which often escalated into violent, bloody confrontations between workers and owners.

The Great Railroad Strike of 1877

Because railroads were the nation's first, most important, industrial corporations, it would only be natural that they became the focal points of early labor strife. Citing declining revenues during the depression of the 1870s, several railroads cut wages by as much as 35 percent between 1874 and 1877. When the Baltimore and Ohio Railroad announced its third 10 percent cut on July 16, 1877, workers struck and prevented the line's trains from running. The strike spread rapidly to other roads, and within weeks all rail traffic from St. Louis to the East coast was brought to a standstill. Ten states called out their militias to try to force strikers back to work, but workers would not succumb to such intimidation and fought back, not only firing on the troops but setting fire to rolling stock and roundhouses as well. By the time federal troops restored order in the first week of August, at least one hundred railroad workers, militia, and bystanders had been killed, and hundreds more injured, as well as millions of dollars of railroad property razed. It was the worst episode of labor violence in U.S. history to that time; the specter of class conflict frightened many upper and middle-class Americans who believed that the nation was headed for social revolution.

As a result of the **Great Railroad Strike**, many workers hoped that through better organization they could win a redress of grievances without having to resort to striking, which they just witnessed would be brutally suppressed by the plutocrats and the government. Thus emerged the Knights of Labor, initially a secret fraternal society founded in 1869 in Philadelphia. However, in 1879, under the leadership of Terence Powderly, a skilled machinist by trade, the Knights declared themselves a federation of unions, or assemblies, as they were officially known. Powderly organized the Knights' assemblies by industry rather than by craft, giving many unskilled and semiskilled workers union representation for the first time. Some assemblies admitted women and black workers as

The Haymarket Square bombing in Chicago.

A bomb exploded during a mass labor rally in 1886 calling for the eight-hour work day and protesting police violence against striking workers at the nearby McCormick plant.

well, but despite this inclusiveness, tendencies toward exclusivity of craft, gender, and race divided and weakened many assemblies.

The goal of most of the union's members was to improve their situation within the system through higher wages, shorter hours, better working conditions, and job security—the nuts and bolts objectives of working class Americans from this time forward. This meant collective bargaining with employers; it also meant striking if such concessions were not granted. The assemblies won some strikes and lost some. Powderly and the Knights' leadership, however, discouraged the calls for strikes for they believed that in the end strikes only weakened assemblies because workers, more often than not, lost to management who replaced the striking workers with strikebreakers or scabs, if not breaking the strike all together with the use of force. Powderly also opposed strikes for ideological reasons. Powderly was a closet socialist, who believed that strikes constituted a tacit recognition of the legitimacy of the wage system, which siphoned off to capital a part of the wealth created by labor. Powderly believed capitalism would ultimately give way to workers' cooperatives, which would own the means of production. But if workers continued to strike and alienate especially the middle class, which he believed would become sympathetic to the workers' plight and support them, then there was no hope for workers to someday through cooperatives to own and operate mines, factories, and railroads to the benefit of all Americans. Despite Powderly's pleas for workers to avoid strikes, the Knights gained their greatest triumphs by striking. In 1884 and 1885, successful Knight-led strikes against the Union Pacific and Missouri Pacific railroads won enormous prestige and a rush of new members, which by 1886 totaled 700,000. But defeat in a second strike against the lines in 1886 was a serious blow. Then came the Haymarket bombing in Chicago.

Haymarket Square

Since the late 1870s, Chicago had become the center of labor radicalism, home to not only the Socialist Labor Party but to anarchism as well. The majority of anarchists were foreign-born, mostly Germans, and by 1886, they had gained significant influence within the Windy City's Socialist Party. The anarchists called for the violent destruction of the capitalist system so that a new socialist order could be built on its ashes. Anarchist had also infiltrated some of the city's unions, and from such bases of operation they led the call for a general strike on May 1, 1886, to achieve the eight-hour workday. Compounding an already nervous environment was the fact that Chicago police were notoriously hostile to labor organizers and strikers, so the scene was ripe for an inevitable violent confrontation between workers and police.

The object of the strike was the McCormick farm machinery plant in Chicago. A fight broke out between striking workers and scabs, which resulted in a police attack on the strikers in which four people were killed. Anarchist used the incident to call for a massive protest rally at **Haymarket Square** on May 4. Toward the end of the meeting, as the rain-soaked crowd dispersed, the police suddenly arrived in force. When someone threw a bomb into their midst, the police opened fire indiscriminately. When the melee was over, 50 people lay wounded and 10 dead, 6 of them policemen.

The alleged riot unleashed a wave of anti-labor hysteria throughout the city and even the nation. Chicago police rounded up hundreds of labor leaders, including eight German-born anarchists they believed responsible for the bombing incident. They were tried for conspiracy to commit murder, though not a shred of evidence ever surfaced to prove that any of them had thrown the bomb. Nonetheless, all eight were convicted, and seven were sentenced to be hanged, of which only four ended up swinging from the gallows. One committed suicide and two others' sentences were commuted to life imprisonment. The affair became a cause célèbre that bitterly divided the country. Some Americans believed it a blatant act of repression of civil rights and judicial murder; others, the majority of citizens, applauded the court's actions and hoped it would send a warning signal to labor radicals that their ideas and actions faced zero tolerance.

In the aftermath of the Haymarket affair, the Knights of Labor soon dissolved. However, a new national labor organization emerged to take its place: the American Federation of Labor founded in 1886 by immigrant cigar-maker Samuel Gompers. Gompers organized the new union not by industry, as Powderly had done, but by trade or craft, which in effect made the new union for skilled workers only. Under Gompers's leadership the AFL shunned radical crusades, accepted capitalism and the wage system, and worked for better conditions, higher wages, shorter hours, and job security—"pure and simple unionism" as Gompers called his organization's agenda. The AFL's endorsing of the capitalist order, his condemning of militancy and radicalism, and its not too outlandish demands for workers' rights allowed the AFL not only to survive but to prosper in a difficult climate. In short, Gompers's call for working within the system did not alienate or arouse the hostility of the capitalist plutocrats. As a result, the union's membership grew from 140,000 in 1886 to nearly one million by 1900. Though Gompers was able to calm the fears of capitalists and the anxieties of Americans that labor was not going to plunge the nation into social revolution if its demands were not met, labor militancy did not die. Two best-selling books helped to keep it alive, especially the call for a more egalitarian social order, and affected the millions who read them.

Henry George and Edward Bellamy

Progress and Poverty, by Henry George and *Looking Backward* by Edward Bellamy seemed unlikely books at the time for best-seller status, for both works blatantly attacked late nineteenth century corporate capitalism excesses and the self-serving, materialistic culture it had bred. Appalling both authors was the extremes of wealth and poverty industrial capitalism had spawned in the United States. To George, the cause of such a chasm was the control of land and resources by the few at the expense of the majority of citizens. His solution was 100 percent taxation on the unearned increment in the value of land—on the difference between the initial purchase price and the eventual market value (minus improvements), or what today we would call capital gains. Such gains were created by society, he insisted, and thus should be confiscated by taxation for the benefit of society. This would eliminate the need for all other taxes, George argued, and help narrow the gap between rich and poor by either giving all the unused land to the landless or using the money to provide work for all. Although not an easy book to read, by 1905, *Progress and Poverty* had sold over 2 million copies and had been translated into several languages. The book's real impact came from George's descriptions of grinding, abject poverty and despair in the midst of plenty. George became a hero to labor. He joined the Knights, moved to New York City, and ran for mayor in 1886 and narrowly lost. His campaign dramatized labors' grievances and alerted the major parties to the power of that constituency.

The other Gilded Age work, *Looking Backward,* was a utopian romance that took place in the year 2000 and contrasted the America of that year with the America of Bellamy's time of 1887. In 2000, all industry is controlled by the government; everyone works for equal pay; there are no rich and no poor, no strikes, and no class conflict. *Looking Backward* had obviously a socialist leaning, even though Bellamy preferred to call his collectivist order nationalism, not socialism. He definitely was not a Marxist socialist for he condemned the idea of class conflict as the only means to achieve the cooperative state. His vision of a world without social strife appealed to many middle-class Americans, who bought 500,000 copies of his book every year for several years in the early 1890s. Inspired by Bellamy's work, Nationalist clubs sprang up throughout the nation, advocating government ownership if not of all industries at least public utilities—gas and water socialism.

An offshoot of Bellamy's Nationalist movement and inspired by his work was the Social Gospel movement that emerged in the 1890s in American cities, and significantly affected mainstream Protestantism and many Catholic leaders as well. Appalled by the poverty and overcrowding in the sprawling tenement districts of urban America, clergymen and laypeople associated with the movement embraced a new theology of social activism: helping to ameliorate the plight of the poor was just as important, or should be, to religious leaders as saving souls. They were willing to go into the bowels of the immigrant tenement slums and not only help save the inhabitants from engaging in sinful activities but help to deliver them as well from poverty. Social Gospelites pressed for legislation to curb the immigrant worker exploitation and provide them with opportunities for betterment.

The Homestead Lockout

By the 1890s, there was plenty of evidence to feed the fears of many middle-class Americans that the nation was unraveling. Strikes occurred with a frequency and fierceness. The most dramatic confrontation took place in 1892 at the Homestead plant of the Carnegie Steel Company. Carnegie and his plant manager, Henry Clay Frick, were determined to break the power of the country's strongest union, the Amalgamated Association of Iron, Steel, and Tin Workers. Frick used a dispute over wages and work rules as his opening salvo in his war with the union. He staged a lockout to reopen the plant with nonunion workers. The union laborers, however, refused to abide by the new terms and surrounded the plant in a desperate effort to implement the new policy with the employment of imported nonunion "scab workers." To secure control of the factory, Frick called in 300 guards from the Pinkerton detective agency—a company specializing in union busting. When the private guards arrived in the early morning hours of July 6, a gun battle erupted at the entrance to the plant leaving nine workers and seven detectives dead with scores wounded. Convinced that more violent confrontations would ensue and that a more forceful show of arms was needed to break the strike, the Pennsylvania governor ordered 8,000 militiamen to the Homestead plant. The militia's presence proved effective as the plant reopened. Public sympathy, much of it pro-union at first, shifted when an anarchist tried to murder Frick in his office. Frick was severely wounded but lived. The result, however, was the turning of the public against the union, which allowed the militia to crush the union and the strike with popular support.

The Pullman Strike

Even more alarming than the Homestead strike was the Pullman Strike of 1894, which had national repercussions. In 1880 George Pullman, manufacturer of elegant dining, parlor, and sleeping cars for the nation's railroads, constructed a factory town, called Pullman, ten miles south of Chicago. The planned community provided solid brick homes for workers, beautiful parks and playgrounds, and even its own sewage-treatment plant. Pullman also closely watched his workers' activities, outlawing saloons, and insisting that his properties turn a profit. When the 1893 depression hit, Pullman slashed his workers' wages without reducing rents. In response, thousands of workers joined the newly formed American Railway Union, led by the fiery young organizer Eugene V. Debs. The union called for a strike, which Pullman's workers willingly joined. Union members working for the nation's largest railroads refused to switch Pullman cars, paralyzing rail traffic in and out of Chicago, one of the nation's most important rail hubs. In response, the General Manager's Association, an organization of top railroad executives, decided to break the union. The managers imported jobless scabs from the East coast and asked U.S. Attorney General Richard Olney, a former railroad attorney, for a federal injunction (court order) against the strikers for allegedly refusing to move railroad cars carrying U.S. mail. In truth, the strikers volunteered to switch mail cars onto any trains not pulling Pullman cars, and it was the railroad's managers who were delaying the mail by refusing to send their trains without the full complement of cars. Nevertheless, Olney, bolstered by President Cleveland and citing the **Sherman Antitrust Act,** secured an injunction against the union's leaders for restraint of commerce. Despite the government's crackdown, union leaders refused to back down and return to work. But the government was determined to break the union. Debs was arrested, and federal troops were sent to Pullman to crush the strike, which they eventually did but not after the loss of thirteen lives, fifty-three wounded and the burning of seven hundred freight cars. By exploiting and fabricating middle-class fears that strikers and unions were hotbeds of labor radicalism, crafty corporate leaders persuaded state and federal officials to help them squash organized labor's desire to negotiate with business for basic worker rights. When the Supreme Court in the 1895 case, *In re Debs,* upheld Debs's prison sentence and legalized the use of injunctions against labor unions, the judicial system made its blatant support of big business clear and that in the future, the plutocrats could count on that body to help preserve the status quo and their hegemony over it. By the beginning of the new century, it was painfully clear that the United States and its middle-class citizenry had no intention of embracing unions or even the idea that its industrial workers were entitled to basic rights. Working-class America was viewed with suspicion and hostility, and even its slightest attempt at a redress of grievances was regarded as radical. The Pullman strike made it clear that from this point on, federal and state officials would side with the plutocrats against its working class citizenry. Ineffective in the political arena, blocked by state officials, and frustrated by court decisions, American unions failed to expand their base of support. Post-Civil War labor turmoil had drained the vitality of organized labor and given it a negative public image that it would not shed until the 1930s, when a change in middle-class values and attitudes would find common cause with that of the working classes.

GILDED AGE POLITICS

The most interesting and dramatic individuals of the era were not politicians but the businessmen-entrepreneurs and financiers who so dominated the time period. Political leadership, especially at the national level, was marked by some of the most uninspiring, complacent, and outright lackluster men ever to sit in the Oval Office. While men like Carnegie, Rockefeller, and Morgan jump vividly from the pages of the past, the presidents lie pallid on those same pages. Though many Americans today complain about the lack of strong, vibrant, and purposeful presidential leadership, if they had lived in the Gilded Age with those same expectations and hopes, they would feel even more depressed and disassociated. The weakness of the presidency and the federal government in the years between Abraham Lincoln (1861-65) and Theodore Roosevelt (1901-1909) was one of the most pronounced and prolonged periods in the nation's history. Beginning with Reconstruction and the tumultuous presidency of Andrew Johnson, presidential leadership seemed to plummet to an all-time low. The lack of quality men in the White House allowed Congress to gain ascendancy, and it was that body the plutocrats that manipulated and controlled to ensure that there would be no governmental interference in their affairs. During the Gilded Age, a good portion of both the House and Senate membership were on the plutocrat's payroll. This waning of federal power, especially in the executive branch, became a persistent pattern in American government interrupted only by the activism of the progressive movement under the leadership of Theodore Roosevelt, and, later, during the Great Depression of the 1930s, when Franklin Roosevelt assumed the Oval Office.

The presidents from Rutherford B. Hayes (1877-1881) to Grover Cleveland (1885-1889, 1893-97), are indeed forgotten men, sad but understandable because so little was expected of these presidents and the federal government in general. Until the 1890s, when the excesses of industrial capitalism became apparent, few Americans believed that the president or the national government should have any role in addressing the problems accompanying the industrial transformation. The dominant creed of laissez-faire coupled with the tenets of Social Darwinism warned government to leave business alone; intervention to ameliorate even the most vile effects of industrialization would only retard the natural evolutionary progress allegedly taking place in the United States, led by those best fit to do so—the plutocrats. This belief in non-government intervention in the economy and society reduced the role of the federal government to something of a sideshow. The real energy and action took place elsewhere—in party politics on the local and state levels and in the centers of business and industry. Nevertheless, important changes transformed American political life in the decades following the Civil War, as industrialism replaced sectionalism as the driving force in national politics. The corruption and abuses associated with party politics produced civil service reform. By the 1880s, important economic issues such as the protective tariff, the currency, and federal regulation of the trusts and railroads moved to the forefront.

The Political Culture of the Gilded Age

Looking back on Gilded Age politics, there is some irony in the fact that voters of that time turned out in record numbers to elect those lackluster presidents—averaged a hefty 80 percent, compared with a turnout of only 51 percent in 2000. Since the Jacksonian Era, political parties had used patronage or the spoils system to reward party loyalists for their support. Such individuals owed their livelihood to party bosses—the local party leader or hack responsible for sustaining the spoils system. Often these local politicians were involved in graft and corruption in order to maintain party loyalty and control of local politics. During the Gilded Age, machine politics, particularly at the municipal level, became the order of the day. Machine politics meant the control of every level of city government by either of the dominant parties, Republican or Democrat, depending upon the city involved. Under the guiding hand and sharp eye of the boss, political power was organized vertically within the machine in a hierarchical system of patrons and clients. Gilded Age bosses were a rough-hewn bunch who cultivated a very personalized style of politics. Their stock and trade was jobs and appointments, transit franchises, paving contracts, public construction bids, licenses, permits, and hundreds of other saleable items needed to conduct city business.

The impulse motivating the city boss was essentially conservative: the need to bring a semblance of order to his district. From at least mid-century, bosses like New York City's William Marcy Tweed and Philadelphia's James McManes had watched the aimless spreading of their cities and understood the problem of managing them. Tweed frankly admitted that New York's population was "too

William Marcy "Boss" Tweed

hopelessly split into races and factions to govern under universal suffrage, except by bribery of patronage and corruption."

Bosses seldom achieved the efficiency they sought. In the 1890s the bosses' failings in efficiency and accountability would give progressive reformers much ammunition in attacking the urban machines. However, the bosses did provide a minimum of order and services. It also must be remembered that the bosses and their machines provided one of the chief forms of entertainment for voters and nonvoters alike in an age before mass recreation and amusement. The local machine sponsored parades, rallies, speeches, picnics, torchlight processions, and Fourth of July fireworks, attracting thousands of city dwellers, all for the purpose of ensuring machine support and keeping machine candidates elected.

Patronage Politics in the States

In the 1870s such state bosses as Roscoe Conkling in New York and James G. Blaine, the "Plumed Knight" from Maine, were highly visible, colorful characters. By the 1880s, however, a new generation was taking over, achieving political control in many states and building loyal machines. The new bosses of the 1880s were quieter, behind-the-scenes operators who were much cleverer and more cautious than their more raucous predecessors. They were determined to avoid the constant feuding among placemen, which helped to contribute to their forerunner's demise. Matt Quay in Pennsylvania, Tom Platt in New York, Nelson Aldrich in Maine, William Vilas in Wisconsin, and George Hearst in California were typical of a new breed of party chieftains who conducted national business in Washington while keeping a vigilant eye on their cronies back home, solving patronage quarrels, settling factional disputes, and smoothing discontent.

The key device for harmonizing party interests at the state level was the caucus, where local bosses, county chairmen, and state legislators gathered to approve the state's boss choice of candidates for various offices. Here was the real power-base of the men mentioned above, and their ability to force subordinates to accept their men" kept them in power. Naturally, the process involved bribery, even extortion if necessary. Democratic Party bosses won control over their states more slowly than Republicans and, particularly in the one-party South, kept a looser grip on the party reins. Yet, southern Democratic, or "Bourbon," conservatism, soon became the model for long-time Democrats who continued to invoke the name of Jefferson in deploring the "spirit of centralization" while quietly employing just that concept in staffing and strengthening their organizations. In both parties, as in the business world after 1880, consolidation was the order of the day.

Increasingly in the 1890s, politics became limited to white males only. Although black men voted during Reconstruction, the abandonment by the Republican Party of southern blacks after the Compromise of 1877, greatly affected black voting thereafter. One of the main goals of the Redeemers was to wrest political power from the freedmen and that was accomplished by the 1890s. Through the use of terror and intimidation, white Southerners denied black men their right to vote, and those who attempted or asserted their right usually ended up swinging from a tree at the end of a rope. White supremacy and rule was entrenched by the 1890s and so was one-party rule—the Democrats. From the end of Reconstruction and for the next seventy years, the old Confederate South voted Democratic in every election. Labeling the Republican Party the agent of Negro rule, white southern Democrats engaged in race baiting to keep southern voters (white, of course) voting straight Democrat—the party of white supremacy.

Opposing the Solid South was the Republican Northeast, with nearly enough electoral votes to guarantee its control of the White House. To preserve Republican ascendancy at the national level, the party had to carry key states such as Ohio, Indiana, and New York and had to prevent an alliance from developing between the agricultural South and the West. Northern Republican politicians, like their southern Democratic counterparts, continued to fan the flames of sectionalism with emotional appeals to the Civil War, a tactic known as "waving the bloody shirt," which was used effectively by the party in the 1868 election to get U.S. Grant into the Oval Office. Strong Unionist states in the Midwest responded by voting consistently Republican. "Iowa will go Democratic," one observer joked, "when Hell goes Methodist." Veterans of the **Grand Army of the Republic** formed an important base of Republican Party support, which rewarded their loyalty with generous pensions. By 1886, an astounding one-quarter of the federal budget went to pensions, not a penny of that to ex-Confederates.

Despite being left out of pension benefits and being labeled as traitors, ex-Confederates and southern whites, in general, were fine with Republican hegemony at the national level. This was true because as long as the Republicans did not interfere with their "Negro problem" and allowed southern whites to oppress blacks, then the trade-off was more than acceptable. Southern white priority was not seeing one of their own in the White House but control of the region's black majority. As long as the Republicans turned a blind eye toward Jim Crow and other forms of southern segregation, then southern whites willingly accepted Republican hegemony at the national level, including the White House.

Religion and ethnicity also played a significant role in politics. In the North, Protestants, from the old-line denominations, were drawn to the Republican Party, which championed a series of moral reforms such as temperance. The Democratic Party courted immigrants and attracted Catholic and Jewish voters by consistently opposing laws to close taverns and other businesses on Sunday and by charging that crusades against liquor only masked the real intention of temperance crusaders: a blatant, ethnocentric attack on immigrant culture.

The power of the two major parties remained about equally divided throughout the 1870s and 1880s and into the 1890s. Although the Republicans dominated the White House, they rarely controlled Congress. The Democrats, noted more for their local control and appeal than for their national unity, for the most part, dominated the House of Representatives. Not until the Seventeenth Amendment was passed were senators directly elected by voters. Until then, (1912), the state legislatures selected senators. In an era legendary for its tolerance of all but the most flagrant bribery and corruption, state legislatures rather easily and all too frequently came under the control of the powerful capitalist-industrialist interests. In *Wealth Against Commonwealth* (1894), his book on the Standard Oil Company, journalist Henry Demarest Lloyd wrote, "The Standard has done everything with the Pennsylvania legislature except to refine it." Senators were often closely allied with business interests, as in the case of Nelson Aldrich, the powerful Republican from Rhode Island, whose daughter married John D. Rockefeller, Jr. and who didn't mind being called "the senator from Standard Oil."

The Shadow Presidents

President Rutherford B. Hayes, whose disputed 1876 election marked the end of Reconstruction, proved to be a hard-working, well-informed executive who wanted peace, prosperity, and an end to party strife. Although ridiculed by the Democratic press as "Rutherfraud," and "His Fraudulency," Hayes was a man of integrity and honesty, who seemed well-suited for his role as a national leader. But Hayes faced a formidable task in attempting to end party strife, which greatly handicapped his implementation of any national agenda or vision he might have had. Unfortunately for Hayes and his Republican successors, his party remained wracked by internal factionalism and was controlled by party bosses who boasted that they could make or break a president.

The three Republican factions bore the colorful names **Stalwarts**, **Half-Breeds**, and **Mugwumps**. The Stalwarts, led by New Yorker Roscoe Conkling, were Grant supporters and thus were associated with the scandals of his administration. Opposing them were the Half-Breeds, led by Senator James G. Blaine of Maine, a group that was only slightly less corrupt than Conkling's bunch. Against both factions was a small but noteworthy group of liberal Republican reformers, mostly from Massachusetts and New York, whose critics dubbed them the Mugwumps, the name of an Algonquian Indian chief, but used by the faction's opponents who asserted that the Mugwumps were fence-straddlers when it came to the most important issue of party loyalty. The Mugwumps were determined to purge the Republican Party of all those who had so tarnished its image as the party of the Union and the Grand Army of the Republic. They were determined to institute badly needed governmental reforms to ensure that competent, honest men were in control. They evaded the complex and divisive economics issues, such as tariff reform and monopolies, and instead focused on civil service reforms designed to set standards for office holders and put an end to the spoils system.

Party bosses like Blaine and Conkling easily overpowered and destroyed Hayes' modest though sincere attempts at party reform. Fiery, dynamic, shrewd, manipulative, petty, and vindictive, as well as tied to corporate interests, Blaine and Conkling dominated national politics at this time. Conkling had nothing but contempt for the Mugwumps. He lambasted "snivel service" reform. His archri-

JAMES A. GARFIELD — REPUBLICAN CANDIDATE FOR PRESIDENT
CHESTER A. ARTHUR — REPUBLICAN CANDIDATE FOR VICE PRESIDENT

val, James G. Blaine, was a charismatic Irish-American with a devoted following so fanatical in their support that they were dubbed "Blaniacs." Blaine condemned blatant Stalwart corruption but was himself tarnished by questionable dealings in railroad bonds. More careless than criminal in his business relations, Blaine drew no fine distinction between public service and private gain. Indeed they were symbiotic to men of Blaine and Conkling. Yet, Blaine's shady dealings caused enough public disaffection to cost him the Republican nomination in 1880 and the presidency four years later.

In 1880, the Mugwumps had just enough influence to block a Stalwart attempt to bring U.S. Grant out of retirement and run again for the presidency. Blaine, too, was passed over, and instead a dark-horse candidate, Representative James A. Garfield of Ohio, a virtual nobody, was nominated. Conkling insisted that Chester Alan Arthur, a fellow Stalwart from New York, be put on the ticket as vice president. The Democrats, still trying to unite a sectionalized party, nominated ex-Union general (the Republicans had had great success with such nominees—Grant, Hayes, and now Garfield), Winfield S. Hancock. But such a choice was not going to endear southern Democrats even though the Solid South voted for Hancock over Garfield. Although the popular vote was close, Garfield won 214 electoral votes to Hancock's 155.

"My God," Garfield cried out after only a few months in the Oval Office, "what is there in this place that a man should ever want to get into?" Garfield, like Hayes, confronted the difficult task of remaining independent while attempting to placate the screaming bosses for jobs and the howling reformers for a massive overhaul of the federal bureaucracy. To an indecisive and easily overwhelmed man like Garfield, the presidency was a nightmare. He found the job of dispensing federal patronage grueling and distasteful, especially as he was forced to award positions to individuals whom he knew were not only completely unqualified for the job but venal and corrupt as well. More than 140,000 federal civil service jobs needed filling. Thousands of office seekers swarmed into Washington, each clamoring for a place. In an era before constant Secret Service protection for the president was established, the White House door was literally wide open. Garfield took a fatalistic view: "Assassination," he told a friend, "can no more be guarded against than death by lightning, and it is best not to worry about either."

On July 2, 1881, less than four months after taking office, Garfield was indeed assassinated, waiting for a train at a Washington, D.C. railroad station. His assassin, Charles Guiteau, though clearly insane, was a disgruntled office seeker who claimed to be motivated by political partisanship. He told the police officer who arrested him, "I did it; I will go to jail for it; Arthur is president, and I am a Stalwart. Garfield did not die instantly or in a few days; he lingered on through the summer, finally succumbing in September 1881. The press was outraged, holding the Stalwarts responsible for the president's tragic, violent death. Even though the Stalwarts were not responsible for Guiteau's actions, they nonetheless helped to create the hostile political environment that produced such individuals and violence. Stalwart leader Roscoe Conkling, who came under heavy attack for his partisanship in the wake of the assassination, had to give up his presidential ambitions and retire from politics and assumed a career as a corporate lawyer. Assaults on the spoils system increased, as did public demand for civil service reform. Though Garfield's death galvanized support for civil service reform, the ensuing congressional, as well as public, debate was long and hard. Those opposing reform cried out that it was class and ethnically biased. When Mugwumps spoke of government run by the best men, they meant men of their own class and ethnic stock—WASPs. Reform would be particularly detrimental to Irish-Americans, who by this time were attaining increasing numbers of positions of political power in Northeastern cities. They would not want to see government once again in the hands of an educated Yankee elite. At a time when few men had more than an elementary school level of education, office seekers would not want to take a written civil service examination. One opponent argued, "George Washington would not have passed examination for a clerkship," noting that "in his will written by his own hand, he spells clothes, cloathes."

Despite acrimonious debate, civil service reform at the national level was instituted with the passage of the Pendleton Act in 1883. Both parties claimed credit for the act, which established a permanent Civil Service Commission of three members, appointed by the president. Some 14,000 jobs were placed under a merit system that required examinations for office and made it impossible to remove individuals for political reasons. Half of the postal jobs and most of the customhouse jobs—long two of the most rewarded jobs under the spoils system—passed to the control of the Civil Service Commission. The new law prohibited federal officeholders from contributing to political campaigns, thus helping to dissolve a major portion of the party bosses' revenue. Soon business interests replaced officeholders as the nation's chief political fund-raisers. Ironically, civil service reform thus gave the plutocracy an even greater influence in political life than it already had.

"Chet Arthur, president of the United States! Good God!" exclaimed many Americans upon hearing of Garfield's death. Such foreboding was not unwarranted, for there was little in Arthur's background that qualified him for the highest office in the land. Only four years earlier he had been dismissed from his customhouse position in New York on charges of corruption. But a sort of metamorphosis took place as Arthur, now free of Conkling's grasp, quickly dispelled the nation's fears and acted independently signing the Pendleton Act that his fellow Stalwarts had so long opposed. Arthur himself had little faith in reform but was politically savvy enough not to stand in the path of public sentiment. Beyond signing the Pendleton Act, Arthur's presidency was one of the most lackluster in history, doing nothing else of consequence. As election year 1884 approached, Republicans were excited that their most charismatic standard bearer, James G. Blaine, would breathe new, more exciting life into the party and carry them to victory once again.

1884: THE DEMOCRATS FINALLY WIN THE BIG ONE

Grover Cleveland in the White House

At their tumultuous Chicago convention, the Republicans, as predicted, turned to James G. Blaine to lead them to victory in 1884. Blaine represented the younger, more dynamic wing of the Republican Party that was now eager to shed the taint of Grantism with Conkling out of the way. Blaine and his supporters also promoted continued economic development and a more assertive foreign policy. Unfortunately for Blaine, however, his charisma could not overcome the stigma of being involved in the tawdry politics of the Gilded Age. It was leaked that in 1876, while serving as Speaker of the House, Blaine had offered political favors to a railroad company in exchange for stock. Blaine also supported the spoils system, though

not as rabidly as Conkling. Nonetheless, in the eyes of staunch Mugwumps like E. L. Godkin, editor of the respected magazine, *The Nation,* Blaine "wallowed in spoils like a rhinoceros in an African pool."

The Democrats chose an individual who politically represented a sharp contrast to Blaine: Grover Cleveland of New York. Cleveland's rather meteoric rise from reform mayor of Buffalo to governor was noteworthy because along the way he fought the bosses and spoilsmen and won. He was short, rotund, and resembled a bull dog, but he was his own man. But Cleveland was not without liabilities, the most notorious of which was his admission that he had fathered an illegitimate child as a young man. The Republicans naturally exploited this, jeering at rallies, "Ma, Ma, where's my pa?" Cleveland also had to overcome the powerful influence of New York City's Tammany Hall who hated Cleveland for his attempts while governor to destroy their machine. Tammany still controlled the immigrant vote of the city, which was increasingly more important as that population grew. If immigrant voters stayed home come election day, Cleveland could lose his own state. But in October a rabid Protestant Republican clergyman denounced the Democrats as the party of "Rum, Romanism, and Rebellion." Blaine failed to immediately repudiate the remark, which allowed Cleveland's supporters to claim that such a statement only showed that the Republicans were anti-Catholic, anti-drink, and were insulting patriotic Democrats tired of the "bloody shirt." This blunder and the Mugwumps' defection allowed Cleveland to carry New York state by 1200 votes and with it the election. Cleveland won the popular vote by only 25, 685 votes and in the Electoral College the margin of victory was 37 votes.

Tariffs and Pensions

Though he had established himself as his own man when it came to dealing with machine politicians, Cleveland showed no such boldness or courage when it came to

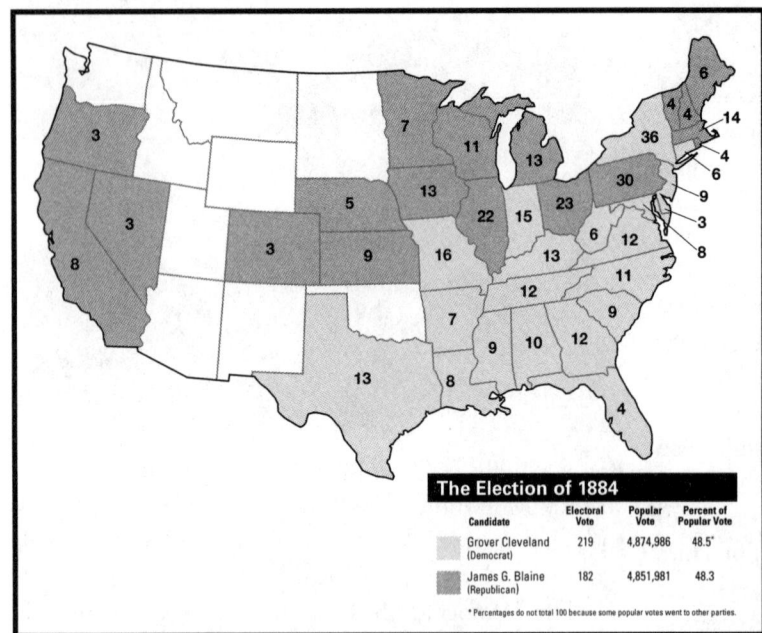

Map 18.3 The Election of 1884

challenging the business elite. In most respects Cleveland embraced the belief that government must not meddle in the economy. By the 1880s the plutocrat's rallying cry was against any form of government intervention in their affairs. Approving of this ethos, Cleveland asserted presidential power mostly through his vetoes and displayed a limited understanding of industrialization's impact. For example, he vetoed a bill that would have provided seeds to drought-stricken Texas farmers, admonishing that people should not expect the government to solve their problems.

One public issue did arouse Cleveland: the tariff, a matter involving a tangle of conflicting economic and political interests. Tariff duties were a major source of federal revenue in the era before the income tax, so the tariff was really a form of taxation. The producers of such commodities as coal, hides, timber, and wool demanded tariff protection against foreign competition, and industries that prospered behind tariff walls—iron and steel, textiles, machine tools—wanted protection to continue. Workers in these industries agreed, convinced that protection meant higher wages and secure jobs. Other manufacturers, however, while seeking protection for their finished goods wanted low tariffs on the raw materials they required but had to import. Massachusetts shoe makers, for example, urged high duties on imported shoes but low duties on imported hides. Most farmers, by contrast, hated the protective tariff, charging that it inflated farm-equipment prices (because large farm machinery companies such as John Deere and International Harvester had monopolies because tariffs had locked out foreign farm equipment makers) and by impeding trade, made it hard to sell American farm products abroad.

Cleveland's call for the lowering of tariffs arose initially from the fact that in the 1880s the high tariff, generating millions of dollars in federal revenue, was feeding a growing budget surplus. Since government expenditures were negligible during this time, a huge surplus of money had accrued in the treasury, largely from tariff and land sales revenue. This surplus tempted many legislators, especially those from the low-income and undeveloped South and West, to demand that the money be distributed in the form of veterans' pensions or expensive public works projects in their home districts. Cleveland viewed the budget surplus as a corrupting influence. In his annual congressional message in 1887, Cleveland argued that lower tariffs would not only cut the federal surplus but would also reduce prices and slow down mergers and consolidations by introducing a degree of competition (foreign) in many markets. Cleveland's talk of lowering the tariff alienated many once-supportive plutocrats.

Cleveland stirred up another hornet's nest when he took on the Grand Army of the Republic. Veterans' disability pensions cost the government millions of dollars annually. No one opposed pensions for the deserving, but by the 1880s fraudulent claims had become a public scandal. Unlike his predecessors—who were all Republicans and who did not want to lose this most important voting bloc—Cleveland investigated these claims and rejected many of them. In 1887 he vetoed a bill that would have pensioned the disabled veterans (even if their disability had nothing to do with military service) and their dependents. The pension list should be an honor roll, he declared, not a boondoggle.

THE 1888 ELECTION

By 1888, many disaffected Democrats, and even Republicans who had defected, concluded that Cleveland must go. Blaine, bowed out of seeking the Republican nomination. Party chieftains, especially those tied to the plutocracy, believed it necessary to find someone who could win but whom they could control. They turned to Benjamin Harrison of Indiana, the grandson of old "Tip," former president William Henry Harrison. A corporation lawyer and former senator, Harrison was so void of personality and aloof that some ridiculed him as the human iceberg.

The issues quickly distilled down to two: the tariff and veterans' pensions, which Harrison hit hard. Cleveland was falsely accused of free trade—the elimination of all tariffs. Harrison asserted that the high protective tariff ensured prosperity, decent wages for industrial workers, and a healthy home market for farmers. Thanks to donations from big business, the Republicans amassed a campaign chest of $4 million. Such a war chest went far, not only for posters and buttons but also votes. Despite Republican chicanery, Cleveland beat Harrison in the popular vote by over 100,000 but Harrison triumphed in the Electoral College by winning 233 votes to Cleveland's 167. The Republicans held the Senate and regained the House.

Harrison quickly rewarded his supporters via the spoils system, handing out hundreds of jobs to individuals whom the Republican power brokers recommended. Pensions ballooned from 676,000 to nearly a million. This massive pension system, coupled with medical care in a network of veterans' hospitals, became the nation's first large-scale public welfare program. In 1890, the triumphant Republicans also enacted the McKinley Tariff, which raised the rates on many imported manufactured goods to an all-time high of over 40 percent *ad valorem*. This new tariff drew a storm of protest. The people had elected Harrison to preserve protection not to enact a higher tariff. The McKinley Tariff helped deplete the surplus by raising duties so high that many foreign producers simply stopped selling their goods in the United States. Democrats naturally seized on the unpopularity of the tariff, labeling the Republican Congress that passed it as "The Billion Dollar Congress," as it unleashed an unprecedented spending frenzy of the entire surplus. Most of the money was spent on pork-barrel programs, legislation passed for no real benefit other than to bring federal largesse to a congressman's or senator's favorite constituents. So upset were voters with such programs and spending that in the off-year election of 1890, they swept the hapless Republicans, including McKinley, out of office. Two years later, in a rather remarkable come back, Cleveland defeated Harrison for the presidency, promising to lower the tariff.

THE RAILROADS, THE TRUSTS, AND THE FEDERAL GOVERNMENT

American voters may have disagreed on the tariff, but increasingly they concurred on the need for federal regulation of the railroads and federal legislation against the trusts. As early as the 1870s, farmers organized to combat the railroads and their exploitive, discriminatory policies. One of the first such organizations was the **Grange**, founded in 1867, initially as a social and educational association for farmers. However, by the 1870s, the Grange became politicized because of railroad abuse and launched an independent political party for a redress of their grievances against the railroads. At the local and state level, the Grangers elected a number of officials, making it possible for several Midwestern states to pass laws regulating the railroads. At first, the Supreme Court upheld their right to do so. In *Munn v. Illinois* (1877), the Court ruled in favor of regulation. But in 1886, the Supreme Court reversed itself in the **Wabash case** (*Wabash, St. Louis, and Pacific Railway Co. v. Illinois*) and ruled that because railroads crossed state lines, they fell outside state jurisdiction. With more than three-fourths of railroads crossing state lines, the Supreme Court's decision effectively stopped regulation.

Public outcry was so great over the Court's ruling that the first Cleveland administration passed the first federal law to regulate the railroads, the **Interstate Commerce Act of 1887**. The act established the nation's first federal regulatory agency, the Interstate Commerce Commission, which was charged with the power to investigate and oversee railroad activities. In its early years, the ICC was never strong enough or sure enough of its role to pose a serious threat to the railroads' continued monopolistic practices. In the end, the act and the commission proved more important as a precedent than as an effective watchdog.

Concern over the growing power of the trusts led the federal government during the Harrison administration to pass the Sherman Antitrust Act in 1890. The Sherman Act allowed for corporations but struck at the trusts. Businesses could no longer enter into agreements to restrict competition. The law outlawed pools and trusts but did nothing to prohibit huge holding companies like Standard Oil, since a holding company, no matter how big, was one entity and not an agreement among separate businesses to set prices or restrict trade.

The Sherman Act proved to be a weaker, more feeble attempt at government regulation than the Interstate Commerce Act. In the decade after the passage of the Sherman Act, the government successfully mandated the break up of only six trusts. However, the law was used four times against labor by outlawing unions as a conspiracy in restraint of trade. In 1895, the Supreme Court dealt the law a crippling blow in the *E.C. Knight* case. The Court drastically narrowed the law by allowing the American Sugar Refining Company, which controlled 98 percent of the nation's sugar production, to continue its monopoly on the grounds that manufacture did not constitute trade. Both the Sherman Act and the Interstate Commerce Act testified to the nation's growing concern about the excesses of corporate capitalism and an increasing willingness to turn to the federal government as a source of redress for such abuses. Not until the twentieth century would more reform-minded activist presidents be willing to engage the corporations and use the full power of the federal government to protect the public welfare.

The Fight for Free Silver

In the 1870s, supporters of cheap money (paper) organized a third-party movement, the **Greenback Labor Party**, whose platform argued that the nation needed an expanding monetary system to keep up with population growth and commercial expansion. Greenbackers insisted the paper money was "the people's currency, elastic, cheap, and exportable, based on the entire wealth of the country." But in 1879, Congress voted to resume the gold standard, thus siding with creditors as opposed to debtors by tying the nation's currency to its gold reserves. Greenbackers responded by running General James B. Weaver for president in 1880. Despite the appeal of inflation among Southerners and Westerners, especially the farmers of those regions, voters below the Mason-Dixon line could not bring themselves to cast their ballot for a former Union general, and the party soon dissolved after the election. Despite Congress's resolve with the gold standard, the currency issue would not go away. As a result of the return to the gold standard, money became even tighter. By the 1890s, the call for easier money and credit reappeared, with debtors calling not for the reissuing of greenbacks but for backing the dollar with silver.

The silver controversy stirred passions like no other issue of the day. On one side stood the gold bugs—mainly northeastern creditors who believed that gold constituted the only honest money and who did not want to be paid in devalued dollars, which they asserted silver would do. On the opposite side, stood the silverites—led by the western silver mining interests, whose stake in the battle was obvious. In the 1860s and 1870s, the West exploded in a silver bonanza, producing far more silver than gold. However, there was so much silver on the market that the price of silver plummeted. Mining states like Colorado and Nevada wanted the government to buy silver and mint silver dollars to help raise the price. Allied with the silver mining companies for very different reasons were southern and western farmers who had fallen on hard times during the 1870s and 1880s and who saw in silver a panacea for their problems. A grinding cycle of debt and deflation had left farmers in those regions in need of relief. Farmers hoped that increasing the money supply—inflation—with silver dollars would give them some relief.

Silverites pointed out that until 1873, the country had enjoyed a system of bimetallism, with both silver and gold coins minted. In that year, Congress demonetized (stopped buying and minting) silver, an act bimetallists denounced as the "**Crime of '73**." They accused the demonetizers of a conspiracy to limit the money in circulation and place the West and the South at the mercy of northeastern financiers. In 1878 Congress took steps to appease the silverites by passing the **Bland-Allison Act** over Hayes's veto. The measure required the government to buy silver and issue silver certificates. The act also helped mine owners, who now had a buyer for their ore, but it had little inflationary impact. Pressure for inflation continued, but the silverites were unable to make any progress until 1890, when in return for their support of the McKinley Tariff, Congress passed the Sherman Silver Purchase Act, increasing the amount of silver the government bought. Once again, the measure fell far short of generating inflation, and advocates began to call for the free and unlimited coinage of silver, a plan whereby virtually all the silver that was mined would be minted into silver coins and circulated at the rate of sixteen ounces of silver to one ounce of gold.

The silver issue crossed party lines, but the Democrats hoped to use it to achieve an alliance between western and southern voters. Though the Democrats recaptured the White House in 1892 with Grover Cleveland's second administration, the president was still as economically conservative as he was during his first term. Cleveland supported the gold standard unequivocally; so much so that in 1893 he called a special session of Congress and browbeat that body into repealing the Sherman Silver Purchase Act. Repeal only further divided the country, making the Mississippi River for a time as potent a political boundary as the Mason Dixon line. Angry farmers warned Cleveland not to travel west of the river if he valued his life.

THE RISE OF INDUSTRIAL AMERICA / 547

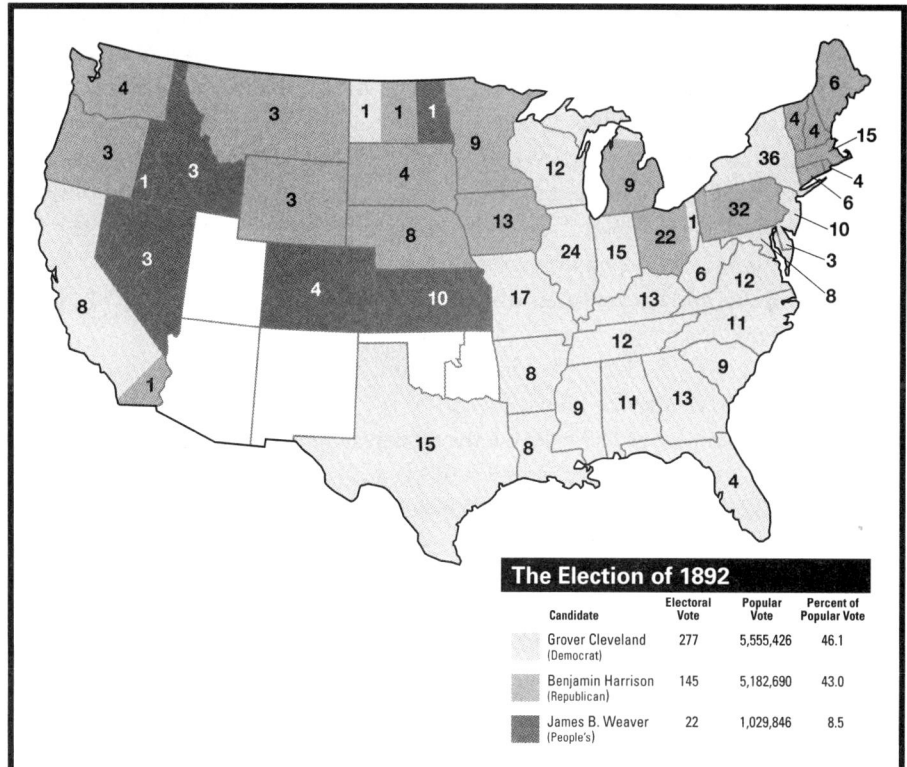

Map 18.4 The Election of 1892

Compounding the silver controversy was the Panic of 1893, which the silver-gold issue helped to cause. As was the case in the Panic of 1873, the railroad industry once again was responsible for initiating this most recent downturn. Investment in the railroad boom of the 1880s triggered speculation among investors. Railroad companies issued more stock (and enticing investors with higher dividends) than the soundness of the line warranted. Weakened by agricultural stagnation, railroad expansion halted in the early 1890s, affecting many related industries, including iron and steel.

The first hint that this most vital industry was faltering came with the failure of one of the East's most important roads, the Philadelphia and Reading Railroad. The line's failure occurred at the same time as the silver-gold controversy was intensifying, especially as the public's confidence in the gold standard waned. This diminished faith had several sources. First, when a leading London investment bank collapsed in 1890, hard-pressed British investors sold millions of dollars worth of stock in American railroads and other corporations and converted their dollars to gold, draining U.S. gold reserves. Second, the Harrison administration's lavish pork-barreling and veteran payouts drained government resources at a time when tariff revenue was declining because of the high McKinley Tariff. Third, the 1890 Sherman Silver Purchase Act further strained the gold reserve by requiring the government to pay for its monthly silver purchases with treasury certificates redeemable in either gold or silver; naturally certificate holders chose gold over silver. When Cleveland took office, the gold reserve had plummeted. This decline alarmed those who viewed the gold standard as the only sure evidence of the government's solvency.

Fear fed on itself as scared investors converted their stock holdings into gold. Stock prices plunged in May and June 1893; gold reserves sank; seventy-four railroads had gone under as well as more than 15,000 commercial institutions, including 600 banks. After the Panic of 1893 came four years of depression.

The Depression of 1893-1897

By 1897, about a third of the nation's railroads were in bankruptcy. The Depression of 1893 took a heavy human toll. Industrial unemployment soared to almost 25 percent, leaving millions of factory workers with no money to feed their families and heat their homes. Recent immigrants faced disaster. Jobless men tramped the streets and rode freight trains from city to city, region to region, looking for work.

Rural America, already hard-hit by declining agricultural prices, faced ruin. Farm prices dropped by more than 20 percent between 1890 and 1896. Corn plummeted from fifty cents to twenty-one cents a bushel and wheat from eighty-four cents to fifty-one cents. Cotton sold for five cents a pound in 1894. In Massillon, Ohio, a self-taught monetary expert, **Jacob Coxey**, proposed as a solution to unemployment a $500 million public-works program funded with paper money not backed by gold or silver, simply designated legal tender (just as it is today). A man of action as well as ideas, Coxey organized the first serious "march on Washington," to lobby for his scheme. Thousands joined him en route, and several hundred actually reached the Capital in late April 1894. Police arrested Coxey and other leaders when they attempted to enter the Capitol grounds, and the marchers disbanded. Although some considered Coxey an eccentric, his proposal closely resembled programs the New Deal implemented during the 1930s to help relieve the unemployed.

In the harsh winter of 1894-95, Cleveland aggravated an already highly charged political climate by his deal with J.P. Morgan, having the financier lend the government $62 million in exchange for U.S. bonds at a special discount. With this loan, the government purchased enough gold to replenish its reserve. Naturally, Morgan and his partner, August Belmont, resold the bonds for a substantial profit. Cleveland saved the gold standard but at a high price. His dealings with Morgan and Belmont only underscored many people's suspicions of an unholy alliance between Washington and Wall Street. Cleveland's policies split the Democratic Party. Farm leaders and silver Democrats condemned his repeal of the Sherman Silver Purchase Act.

South Carolina's Ben Tilman, running for the Senate in 1894, announced that Cleveland was a scoundrel and an "old bag of beef and I am going to Washington with a pitch-fork and prod him in his fat old ribs." This split in Democratic ranks affected the 1894 and 1896 elections and reshaped politics as the century ended.

CHANGING WORLD

The 1893 depression changed social thought. Middle-class charitable workers and reformers, long convinced that individual character flaws caused poverty, now realized that even sober, hardworking people could succumb to economic forces beyond their control. As the social work profession developed in the early-twentieth century, its disciples spent less time preaching to the poor and more time investigating the social and environmental sources of poverty. Many Americans also began to question the sanctity and validity of the laissez-faire ethos as many depression-worn citizens began embracing the idea of government intervention on behalf of the public welfare. In the early twentieth century, this new view would energize powerful political forces. The depression, in short, not only brought suffering; it also taught lessons.

Chronology

1869 Completion of first transcontinental railroad.
Knights of Labor founded.

1870 John D. Rockefeller incorporates Standard Oil Company.

1871 Chicago's Great Fire.

1873 "Crime of 1873" demonetizes silver.
Panic on Wall Street leads to depression.

1876 Alexander Graham Bell demonstrates telephone.

1877 Rutherford B. Hayes sworn in as president.
Great Railroad Strike.
Munn v. Illinois.

1878 Bland-Allison Act to remonetize silver passed over Hayes' veto.

1879 Henry George publishes *Progress and Poverty*.
Congress votes to resume gold standard.
Thomas Alva Edison perfects lightbulb.

1880s Jay Gould attempts to build a second transcontinental railway system.
Gustavus Swift revolutionizes meatpacking with refrigerated rail cars.
H.J. Heinz pioneers mass production and distribution of his fifty-seven varieties of condiments.
James A. Garfield elected president.

1881 Garfield assassinated by Charles Guiteau.
Vice President Chester A. Arthur becomes president.

1882 John D. Rockefetter develops the trust.
Chinese Exclusion Act.

1883 Railroads establish four standard time zones.
Pendleton Civil Service Act.
Brooklyn Bridge opens.

1884 Grover Cleveland elected president.
Mark Twain's *Huckleberry Finn* published.

1886 Haymarket bombing.
American Federation of Labor founded.
Wabash v. Illinois

1887 Edward Bellamy publishes *Looking Backward*
Interstate Commerce Act.

1888 Benjamin Harrison elected president.

1889 Standard Oil reorganizes into a holding company.

1890 McKinley Tariff.
Sherman Antitrust Act.
Jacob Riis publishes *How the Other Half Lives*.

1892 Grover Cleveland elected to second term as president.
J.P. Morgan consolidates creating the General Electric Company.
Homestead lockout.

1893 Financial panic begins economic depression.
Congress repeals Sherman Silver Purchase Act

1894 Coxey's Army marches on Washington.
Pullman strike.

1895 J.P. Morgan bails out U.S. Treasury.

1896 Grover Cleveland vetoes immigrant literacy test.

1900 Ellis Island opens.

1901 U.S. Steel incorporated.

Review Questions

1. Why were the railroads considered to be the first important, major industry in the United States from the post-Civil War era through the 1920s? Discuss the various dynamics about the industry that made it the most preeminent.

2. Discuss the rise of the plutocracy and what allowed such individuals to obtain such economic and political power if not domination in both arenas in the aftermath of the Civil War.

3. As a result of consolidation of the modern corporation during the Gilded Age, what effect did such conglomerates have on competition, small businesses, consumers, and workers?

4. Why did over 30 million primarily eastern and southern Europeans come to the United States in the decades following the Civil War up to the eve of World War I?

5. Assess the causes of the various labor strikes that occurred during the Gilded Age, which became some of the most bloodiest and destructive of property in American history.

Glossary of Important People and Concepts

American Federation of Labor
Bessemer process
Bland-Allison Act 1878
Capital goods
Consumer goods
"Crime of '73"
Gospel of Wealth
Grand Army of the Republic
Grange
Great Railroad Strike of 1877
Greenback Labor Party
Half-Breeds
Haymarket Square
Horizontal integration
Interlocking directorates
Interstate Commerce Act 1887
Jacob Coxey and Coxey's Army
Knights of Labor
Laissez faire
Mugwumps
Munn v. Illinois
Northern Securities Company
Plutocrat
Sherman Antitrust Act 1890
Social Darwinism
Stalwarts
Trust
Vertical Integration
Wabash Case
WASP

SUGGESTED READINGS

Paul Avrich, *The Haymarket Tragedy* (1984).
David H. Bain, *Empire Express: Building the First Transcontinental Railroad* (1999).
Robert V. Bruce, *Alexander Graham Bell and the Conquest of Solitude* (1973).
Sean Dennis Cashman, *America in the Gilded Age* (1984).
Alfred D. Chandler, *The Visible Hand: The Managerial Revolution in American Business* (1977).
___, *The Railroads: The Nation's First Big Business* (1965).
___, *Scale and Scope: The Dynamics Of Industrial Capitalism* (1990).
Dino Cinel, *From Italy to San Francisco: The Immigrant Experience* (1982).
Peter Collier and David Horowitz, *The Rockefellers: An American Dynasty* (1976).
Vincent P. DeSantis, *The Shaping of Modern America, 1877-1920* (2nd. Ed., 1989).
Melvyn Dubofsky, *Industrialism and the American Worker, 1865-1920* (1975).
Richard Ellis, *American Political Cultures* (1993).
Saul Engelbourg, *Power and Morality: American Business Ethics, 1840-1914* (1980).
Philip S. Foner, *The Great Labor Uprising of 1877* (1977).
Donna Gabaccia, *From the Other Side: Women, Gender, and Immigrant Life in the U.S., 1820-1990* (1994).
John A. Garraty, *The New Commonwealth, 1877-1890* (1968).
Ray Ginger, *Age of Excess* (1963).
Julius Grodinsky, *Jay Gould, 1867-1892* (1957).
Herbert C. Gutman, *Work, Culture, and Society in Industrializing America: Essays in American Working-Class and History* (1976).
Robert Higgs, *The Transformation of the American Economy, 1865-1914* (1971).
John Higham, *Strangers in the Land* (1955).
Richard Hofstadter, *The Age of Reform* (1955).
Ari Hoogenboom, *Outlawing the Spoils: The Civil Service Reform Movement, 1865-1883* (1961).
___, *The Presidency of Rutherford B. Hayes* (1988).

Irving Howe, *World of Our Fathers* (1976).
Jacqueline Jones, *The Dispossessed: America's Underclass from the Civil War to the Present* (1992).
Matthew Josephson, *The Robber Barons: The Great American Capitalists, 1861-1901* (1934).
Thomas Kessner, *The Golden Door: Italian and Jewish Mobility in New York City, 1880-1915* (1977).
Maury Klein, *The Life & Legend of Jay Gould* (1987).
Sidney Lens, *The Labor War: From the Molly Maguires to the Sitdowns* (1974).
Andre Millard, *Edison and the Business of Innovation* (1990).
Gwendolyn Mink, *Old Labor and New Immigrants in American Political Development* (1986).
David Montgomery, *The Fall of the House of Labor: The Workplace, the State, and American Labor Activism, 1865-1925* (1987).
Humbert Nelli, *Italians of Chicago, 1880-1920* (1970).
James D. Norris, *Advertising and the Transformation of American Society, 1865-1920* (1990).
Nell Irvin Painter, *Standing at Armageddon: the United States, 1877-1919* (1987).
Glen Porter, *The Rise of Big Business, 1860-1910* (1973).
Andrew Sinclair, *Corsair: The Life of J. Pierpont Morgan* (1980).
John Sproat, *The Best Men: Liberal Reformers in the Gilded Age* (1968).
David J. Rothman, *Politics and Power: The United States Senate, 1869-1901* (1966).
Ronald Takaki, *Stringers From A Different Shore: A History of Asian Americans* (1989).
George R. Taylor and Irene D. Neu, *The American Railroad Network, 1861-1890* (1956).
Peter Temin, *Iron and Steel in Nineteenth-Century America* (1964).
Irwin Unger, *The Greenback Era: A Social and Political History of American Finance* (1964).
James A. Ward, *Railroads and the Character of America, 1820-1887* (1986).
Allen Weinstein, *Prelude to Populism: Origins of the Silver Issue, 1867-1878* (1970).
Robert H. Wiebe, *The Search for Order, 1877-1920* (1967).
Virginia Yans-McLaughlin, *Family and Community: Italian Immigrants in Buffalo, 1880-1930* (1977).

Joseph, Chief of Nez Percé

Chapter Nineteen

INDIAN EXPULSION AND WHITE SETTLEMENT IN THE TRANS-MISSOURI WEST

By the 1880s, starvation, disease, warfare with the United States Army, and the mass slaughter of buffalo and other big game had devastated the Native American population. Less than 300,000 Indians remained in North America, compared to a native population of approximately 2.5 million at the time of Christopher Columbus. Many Plains Indians sought relief from suffering and fear through religion, according to Dee Brown in his classic work **Bury My Heart at Wounded Knee: An Indian History of the American West**. In 1870, Tavibo, a Paiute shaman in Western Nevada, proclaimed that while meditating he received a vision from "The Great Holy Force Above" that promised Native Americans salvation from hunger, want, and the persecution of whites. A world-shaking earthquake, Tavibo promised, would soon swallow American soldiers, missionaries, railroad builders, ranchers and all others who had tried to destroy Indian civilization. Native Americans alone would survive, and their old way of life would return.

Initially met with scorn from other Native Americans, Tavibo began to preach that the Great Holy Force Above allowed Native Americans to suffer and die because they had abandoned their religious traditions, lost respect for virtue, and imitated the ways of the white man. Both whites and unbelieving Indians would perish soon in a great earthquake, Tavibo prophesized, and endure eternal punishment in the afterlife.

This message finally resonated with a wider audience, and Tavibo gained followers among not just the Paiutes but also the Shoshone, Ute, and Bannock peoples. When Tavibo suddenly died, the prophetic mantle fell upon his son Wovoka, who received his own revelations beginning in 1889. Wovoka, called "Jack Wilson" by whites, said that spirits had visited him. He told his audience that he had suffered a fever as a solar eclipse unfolded in the heavens. The spirits showed him a coming paradise in which Indian warriors slain in battle and their women would return to life, grass would spring abundantly from the plains, and buffalo would once again roam the land unimpeded.

Wovoka said that God had turned against white men because they had killed Him when He came to Earth as Jesus Christ. Wovoka told his audiences that he was the Second Coming of Jesus and that he would lead the native people to salvation. Wovoka's followers began meditating, praying, chanting, and performing "Ghost Dances" in rituals lasting five consecutive days. Although the dance varied some by tribe and by location, all involved dancing in a circle. Dancers often went into a hypnotic trance; some dropped from sheer exhaustion.

The Ghost Dance religion, with its promise of future redemption, lifted Indians out of despair. Ghost dances were organized in Idaho, Montana, Utah, Wyoming, Colorado, Nebraska, Kansas, the Dakotas and the Oklahoma Territory by tribes as diverse as the Arapaho, Cheyenne, and Pawnee. Ghost Dances generally were non-violent, with the faithful waiting for the intervention of the Great Spirit to end white oppression. Among the Sioux, however, especially the Oglala, Blackfeet, and Hunkpapa, the dances had a more militant tone. Sioux disciples of the movement taught that wearing

Ghost Dance of the Sioux Indians in North America, 1891.

white ghost shirts would make Indians immune to the bullets of white soldiers.

One Sioux, Tatanka Yotanka (called Sitting Bull by whites) emerged as political leader among the Plains Indians as the Ghost Dance swept the Plains. Nearing his sixties, the charismatic Sitting Bull helped destroy General George Custer's forces at the famous Battle of Little Big Horn in 1876. Held prisoner by the United States Army for two years, he was a featured attraction for a brief time in Buffalo Bill Cody's circus-like "Wild West" show as it toured the Eastern United States. Cody dressed his Native American performers in brightly colored war bonnets and face paint, with men like Sitting Bull mounted on horses and acting out frontier battles. Feeling humiliated by the experience, Sitting Bull became a bitter critic of white society. "The love of possessions is a disease with them," he bitterly observed. "They take tithes from the poor and weak to support the rich who rule. They claim this mother of ours, the earth, for their own and fence their neighbors away."

As the Ghost Dances spread, terror gripped whites living in the Plains. James McLaughlin, an Indian agent, refused to acknowledge how much the new Native faith derived from Christianity. "A more pernicious system of religion could not have been offered to a people who stood on the threshold of civilization," McLaughlin said with disgust. "Our religion seems foolish to you, but so does yours to me," Sitting Bull retorted.

Army personnel became alarmed that the movement might lead to an uprising and that the Ghost Dance rituals whipped the Indians into a bloodthirsty frenzy. "Indians are dancing in the snow and are wild and crazy," a Bureau of Indian Affairs agent at the Pine Ridge Reservation in South Dakota wrote frantically to President Benjamin Harrison in 1889. Several thousand federal troops were dispatched to the Sioux reservations to crush any rebellion.

In December 1889 when **Sitting Bull** sought permission to go on the Pine Ridge Reservation to meet with Wovoka, the local Indian agent set a trap for him, and soldiers fatally shot the Sioux leader. Sitting Bull's entourage fled the scene, only to be apprehended near **Wounded Knee Creek**, South Dakota, by the Seventh Cavalry, Custer's old regiment. The Indians laid down their arms on December 29, 1890. Indians surrendered, but after a rifle accidentally discharged, nervous soldiers opened fire. In the following battle, Indian warriors killed 30 soldiers, but they were badly outgunned. Indian men, women and children were mowed down in minutes by the army's new Hotchkiss machine guns. More than 200 Sioux lay dead or dying in the snow. Even nursing babies numbered among the victims.

Jules Sandoz, a settler, inspected the scene the day after the massacre. "Here in ten minutes an entire community was as the buffalo that bleached on the plains," he later wrote. "There was something loose that hated joy and happiness as it hated brightness and color, reducing everything to drab agony and gray." Some of the wounded Indians were carried to a church at nearby Pine Ridge. As they were carried, they passed under a Christmas banner that read, "PEACE ON EARTH. GOOD WILL TOWARDS MEN."

WESTERN INDIANS BEFORE THE CIVIL WAR

Before European colonists reached the Western Hemisphere, the native peoples of the Great Plains, the Southwest, and the Far West had occupied the land for more than 20,000 years. Hundreds of Indian nations cultivated corn, foraged for wild plants, hunted and fished, and built cities of several thousand inhabitants. The invasion of their territories by Spanish and other European invaders brought disease, missionaries and new trading patterns, but relative geographic isolation gave the Western tribes a margin of survival unknown in the East.

Prior to European contact, Indians in the North American West combined hunting and gathering with settled agriculture and the raising of domestic animals. Some peoples, such as the Anasazi in the modern Four Corners region of Arizona, New Mexico, Utah and Colorado, built elaborate cities of terraced cliff dwellings. Although wide diversity existed among the different native cultures, in general Indian societies rested upon extended kinship networks and valued cooperation and mutual responsibility as opposed to the extreme individualism and competition that came to dominate American culture. Different Indian societies designated certain hunting grounds or lakes or rivers as especially sacred to the group, but typically land was seen as a shared resource, whereas Anglos viewed land as a commodity to be bought, traded and fenced in.

The arrival of the Europeans and their American successors, however, forever altered the Indian civilizations in the West even before the mass white invasion of the Trans-Missouri region in the late 1800s. Spanish conquerors realized the huge advantage they enjoyed due to their monopoly on horses and tried to keep their herds out of Native hands. However, Spanish military raids and their kidnapping of Indians fated for slavery provoked a violent and acquisitive Indian response. Nomadic bands like the Apaches began punitive raids on Spanish settlements. Obtaining horses for transportation, hunting, and warfare became a major goal of these expeditions.

Acquiring not just horses but also firearms, Western Indians developed a new equestrian culture. Transformed into highly mobile hunters who followed buffalo herds with greater efficiency than before, Plains Indians enjoyed vastly expanded hunting grounds. Competing for resources over a broader terrain, Indian nations in the West soon used the new technology in an increasing number of wars against each other. For all their mobility, however, these Native Americans could not avoid a fatal collision with white America.

Conflicting Pressures

During the Civil War, American Indians faced a dangerous choice in deciding whether the United States Army or the Confederate forces presented the greater danger. Whites did not allow Native Americans living near the borders of the Union and the Confederacy the option of neutrality. The Confederate government expected that, as owners of African-American slaves, the so-called Five Civilized Tribes (the Cherokee, Chickasaw, Choctaw, Creek, and Seminole peoples) would side with the South. Living in the Indian Territory (modern-day Oklahoma), the tribes shared a border with the Confederacy and felt great pressure from their southern neighbors. John Ross, an elderly Cherokee and a survivor of Andrew Jackson's Indian "removal" policies in the 1830s, begged the Confederate government to leave Native Americans alone. "[W]e do not wish to be brought into the feuds between yourselves and your Northern Brethren," Ross wrote to one supporter of the Rebel cause. "Our wish is for peace. Peace at home and Peace among you."

Caught in the crossfire, and facing pressure from both North and South to choose sides, many native peoples reflected on their long-term victimization by the federal government in Washington, D.C., and placed their bets on the Confederacy. The Wichita, Caddo, Osage, Shawnee, Delaware, and Quapaw nations, in and near the Indian Territory, allied with the South and fought Northern troops as warriors or served as scouts and spies. The Comanche and Kiowa Indians in particular provided military aid to the Confederate cause, conducting raids in Union territory in Kansas. Comanche and the Kiowa raiders regularly attacked mule-driven caravans carrying provisions, ammunition and other equipment from Fort Leavenworth in Kansas to Union troops in New Mexico.

Some Indian nations, such as Cherokees, mirrored the larger conflict. The Cherokees split into supporters of the federal government and backers of Dixie. The war gave Union commanders an excuse to encroach on the Indian Territory as pro-Confederate Cherokees battled Union troops. By the end of the Civil War, the Cherokees lost land, political unity, and a quarter of their population.

Although Abraham Lincoln never committed Northern society to total war, the Civil War thoroughly militarized Northern society, with devastating effect on Native Americans. Volunteer American army regiments were raised in every Western state. When the Confederate threat passed, these Western volunteers turned their guns on Indians. Moreover, the development of mines, the expansion of the railroads, and federal legislation in Washington drew thousands of Anglos to seize Indian land west of the Mississippi. Mining exploration expanded in Colorado, New Mexico and Arizona, precipitating wars between Indians and whites that led Washington to seek a final solution to the Indian problem.

MASSACRES AND DETENTION DURING THE CIVIL WAR

Whites often responded to Indian defense of their land with extreme violence. One of the most important white-Indian incidents in the West broke out in Colorado. There, in 1861, Cheyenne and Arapaho had been forced onto a reservation in the southeastern part of Colorado, a "dry and desolate" region called the Sand Creek Reserve. Mines, white settlements, and the fencing of white-owned farmlands had disrupted buffalo migratory routes. Food became scarce. The Cheyenne and Arapaho began staging raids along the Platte River, attacking trains in search of food and other supplies.

The territorial governor, John Evans, warned the Cheyenne and Arapaho that unless they remained confined to the reservation they would "suffer the consequences." With Evans's encouragement, the civilian Colorado Volunteers launched attacks on Cheyenne campgrounds. Chief Black Kettle sought protection for 800 Cheyenne and returned his people to Sand Creek, after getting reassurances about his people's safety. Black Kettle sent his men out to hunt while the elderly, women and children stayed at the camp. Spotting a vulnerable target, the Colorado Volunteers attacked on the morning of November 29, 1864. Desperately hoping that the Volunteers would stop their assault on an unarmed Indian community, Black Kettle flew an American flag and a white truce banner, but to no avail. Many of the 700 Volunteers were drunk as the attack began. The Volunteers massacred 200 Cheyenne men, women and children, desecrating the corpses and collecting scalps for trophies. One eyewitness, a Cheyenne woman named Iron Teeth, later testified about seeing a woman "crawling on the ground, shot, scalped, crazy, but not yet dead." The local commissioner of Indian affairs would condemn the Volunteers for butchering the villagers "in cold blood." Over the next several months, the **Sand Creek Massacre** (also known as the Chivington Massacre) provoked retaliations from Cheyennes, Sioux and Arapahos who attacked civilian outposts and killed entire families.

Some of the most brutal fighting between whites and Indians during the Civil War took place in the New Mexico and Arizona territories. A Confederate expeditionary force sought to occupy these territories and repeatedly attacked the Apaches and Navajos in the region. The Navajos and Apaches responded with numerous raids on white settlements. All-out war broke out between Texas troops and Apaches, with the Texans faring poorly. In a single month, August 1862, Mescalero Apache forces killed 46 whites, seized large herds of horses, cattle and other valuable livestock and kidnapped dozens of white

These prisoners traveling through the snow from Black Kettle's camp were captured by General Custer. 1868

children. Mescalero Apaches reoccupied the territories by October 1862. General James H. Carleton, commander of the First California Regiment, ordered an offensive against the Mescaleros. Desiring to teach the Natives a "wholesome lesson," Carleton issued harsh orders to his men, insisting that there would be no negotiations with the enemy. "The men are to be slain whenever and wherever they are found," Carleton said. "Their women and children may be taken prisoner."

By the winter of 1862-63 constant military pressure forced the Mescaleros to abandon their traditional lands. General Carleton directed that a forty-square-mile area along the Pecos River be set aside as a military reservation, Fort Sumner, and an internment camp for Indian prisoners. With the Mescaleros placed in a concentration camp, Carleton turned his attention to Navajo warriors, who had battled with gold and silver miners in eastern Arizona and western New Mexico. Carleton had defeated the Navajo and forcibly relocated them to the Fort Sumner reservation by 1864. By this time, the camp was home to 10,000 Indian prisoners.

The Indians were expected to support themselves by raising their food from garden plots and fields, but the hot sun and repeated droughts withered the corn and other food crops. The prisoners suffered from the heat, malnutrition, and disease. They faced starvation but were delivered from the brink by occasional government rations of low-grade flour, corn, salt, pork and beef. Stagnant water standing in the riverbed provided a perfect breeding environment for mosquitoes, resulting in an outbreak of malaria. The unclean water also promoted the spread of dysentery. Troops at Fort Sumner infected many of the Indian women with syphilis and gonorrhea, which spread throughout the Indian community. About 25 percent of the Indians at Fort Sumner had died by 1868 when the survivors were finally freed to return to their traditional homelands.

CONQUEST BY THE RAILROAD

The Mescalero War replayed with deadly regularity in the next three decades, with increasing numbers of white settlers drawn into Indian territory with the promise of gold, silver, or Indian land that whites regarded as free and theirs by racial right. Indians responded with armed resistance, provoking a massive military response from the U.S. government. This led to Indian slaughter and their expulsion to ever-smaller reservations.

The railroad served as a harbinger of Indian doom. In the last 35 years of the nineteenth century, the white population west of the 95th meridian (a line from Galveston to Kansas City to Minnesota) climbed 400 percent, increasing to more than 8,628,000. This population increase exceeded the rate in the remainder of the United States by a factor of five. Much of this white migration west resulted from Republican Party legislation passed during the Civil War and Reconstruction. The Civil War had been fought, by the end of the conflict, to free African-American slaves, but the chief immediate results were the wildly increased wealth of white northern capitalists and the elimination of Indian independence.

Abraham Lincoln won election as president in 1860 on a Republican platform that called for federal support for constructing a railroad to the Pacific coast. With the Democratic opposition largely absent from the Congress from 1861 to 1874, the Republicans passed much of their pro-business economic agenda. Protective tariffs (taxes on foreign-produced goods) raised needed revenues for the army but also gave a competitive edge to Northern manufacturers who were now able to sell goods at a lower price than their European competitors.

One of the chief beneficiaries of Republican political dominance proved to be the railroad industry. Before the Civil War, congressional Democrats fiercely opposed spending federal money on infrastructure such as railroads and canals. By the 1850s congressional Democrats finally agreed on the desirability of a transcontinental railroad line that would link the country from the Atlantic to the Pacific Ocean, but those dreams would be deferred until the Civil War.

Once the war started, however, money flowed to the railroads not just from stock speculators, but also from generous state legislatures and the federal government, which granted huge direct subsidies, land grants, and tax breaks to railroad companies. The railroads received public land from the federal government. Railroad companies received land not just for the right-of-way but also huge chunks of real estate on alternating sides of the track to dispose of as they pleased. Most often, railroads sold this land to settlers who followed the tracks west. Over the years, the federal government distributed to already wealthy railroad company executives over 180 million square acres, an area larger than Texas. Towns realized the economic benefits of becoming a stop on the railroad line. Towns engaged in cutthroat competition with their neighbors, offering rich cash incentives to persuade rail executives to route the railroad through their boundaries.

Early American railroads offered dangerous and uncomfortable rides in rickety cars that alternated between being too hot in the summer and too cold in the winter. Customers suffered an appallingly high injury and fatality rate. Summer travel subjected passengers to "the heat, the

558 / CHAPTER NINETEEN

Map 19.1 Major Indian Battles

glare, the dust, the cinders [from the train's engine], and the rattle, plus the flies," according to historian Stephen Ambrose. Nevertheless, technological improvements in the manufacture of steel and the national political dominance of Republicans during and after the Civil War led to an exponential spread of the American railway network. In turn, the construction of more than 72,000 miles of railroad track west of the Mississippi spurred the rise of Western cities like Reno, Cheyenne, Kansas City, and Omaha, which in turn encouraged more white immigration to the West.

The settlers in these new towns came from all over the world. As historian Sarah Deutsch argues, "The railroad, linking city to city, coast to coast, countryside to market . . . revolutionized the demography and altered the pattern of opportunity in the West . . . [B]lacks and Europeans searching for a better life, and Mexican and Chinese laborers responding to the higher wages of the West, could do so in unprecedented numbers and reach the farthest corners of the region. The plains were no longer remote."

Technological advances rapidly improved the safety and comfort of railroad travel and sped the laying of track across what once had been known as the Great American Desert. Technicians invented the swiveling truck, which allowed trains to negotiate the sharpest curves. Other innovations kept trains on the track over the roughest patches of land and allowed them to climb ever-steeper angles through mountain passages. Thousands of African American, Mexican and Mexican American, Chinese, Irish, German, English, African and South American workers served in work crews that toiled through Indian attacks, high altitudes, bad food, lack of water, scorching heat, blizzards, and disease epidemics. Workers transported dirt dug from construction sites with carts, used drills and sledgehammers to start tunnels, eventually blasted through mountain passages with dynamite, laid the rail ties, and drove in the spikes that held the rails in place.

The Homestead Act

The West became a multi-racial region, but an Anglo majority ruled it. Besides bills directly supporting the railroad companies, other Republican legislation encouraged white immigration and contributed to the Anglo conquest of the West. In 1862, Congress passed the **Homestead Act**. Fearing that it would lead to the

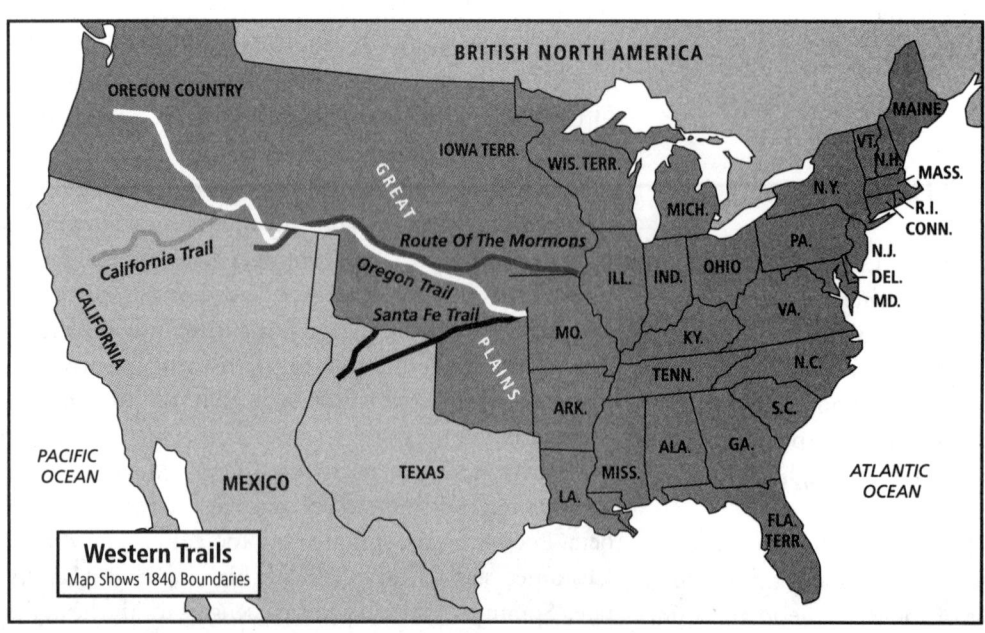

Map 19.2 Western Trails

admission of more free states to the Union, Southern legislators blocked passage of this legislation before the Civil War. After the Southern states seceded, the new law allowed farmers to obtain 160 acres out of the public domain for free, provided they cultivated it for five years. Farmers also could buy the land for $1.25 an acre if they cultivated it for six months. Meant to provide financial independence for family farmers, the bill allowed northeastern land speculators to hire proxies to purchase much of the land, which then went on the market at greatly inflated prices.

Along with the Morrill Act (a law also passed in 1862 that gave states land that was then sold to endow the construction of "agricultural and mechanical colleges"), these Republican-sponsored laws fueled a mass movement of white farmers who rode the rapidly expanding railway networks west to claim their homesteads. In the last three decades of the nineteenth century, the number of American farms more than doubled, from 2.5 million to 6 million, and the production of corn, wheat and oats nearly tripled. Farmers poured into Texas, Kansas, Nebraska, and the Dakota Territory. Mass immigration resulted in the admission of nine new states into the Union between 1867 and 1896.

THE WESTERN ECONOMY, ENVIRONMENTAL DESTRUCTION, AND CRIME

Cattle ranching became an engine of the Western economy. Before the 1860s, profit margins from cattle suffered due to the lack of rail connections. Ranchers had few customers in the low-population West and could not deliver meat to the vast Eastern market. The Civil War changed that. The federal government became the largest customer for beef needed to feed Union troops. Prices climbed to a record $40 a head. The railroads built during and after the war closed the distance to Eastern and California markets, boosting the profitability of cattle ranching. Some rail lines existed in Texas but crossed such great distances that their use greatly reduced profit margins. As a result, as early as 1866, the year after the Civil War ended, cowboys led the first great cattle drives from Texas to Missouri, where the livestock were put on trains bound for the Eastern markets. Cattle drives became the industry norm by the following year, aided in large part by the construction of the Kansas-Pacific Line in Abilene, Kansas. Previously forced to march cattle across Missouri to the nearest depot, cowboys could

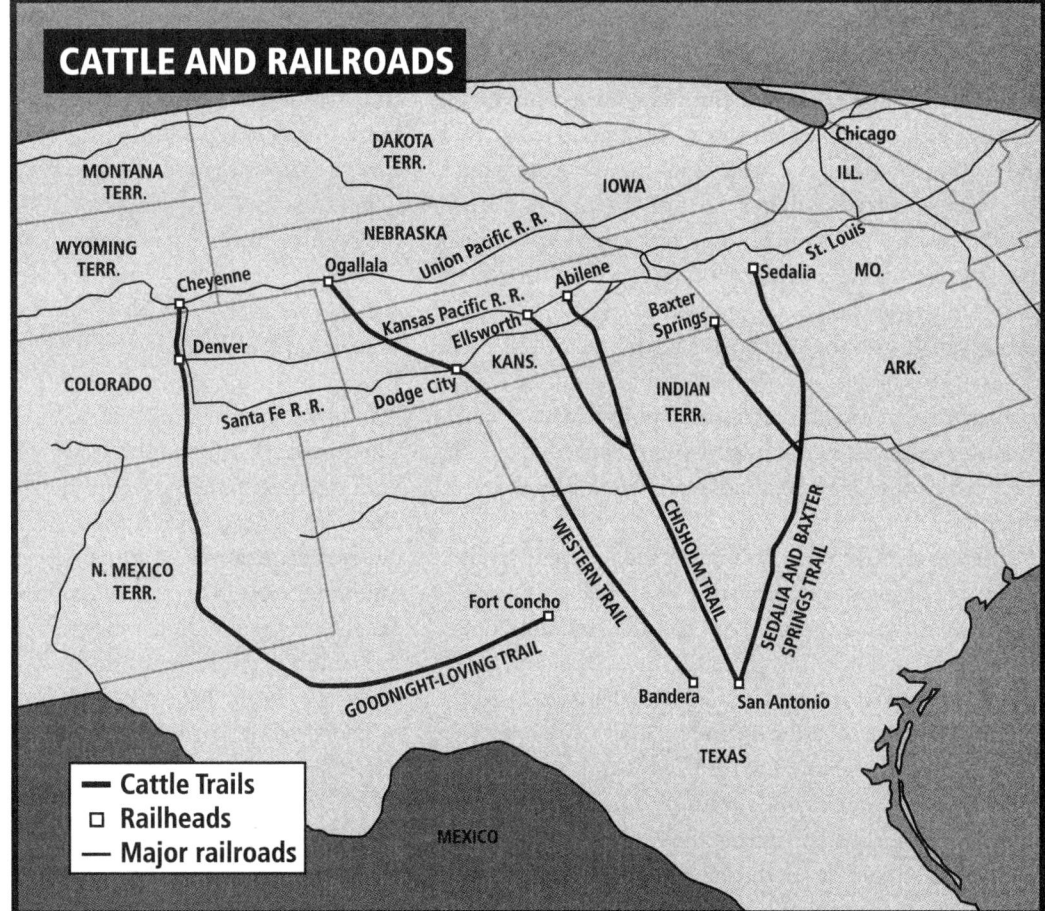

Map 19.3 Cattle and Railroads

now simply cross the Indian Territory to the new railway station, which was 150 miles closer to the vast ranches in Texas. The invention of the refrigerated railcar in the 1870s turned Chicago into the famed cattle and "hog butcher of the world," allowing trains to pick up beef and pork processed in the Windy City and ship the goods to the four corners of the country.

High profits in ranching, however, carried a heavy price. "The introduction of cattle, sheep, and goats was, in many regions, a shock to the ecological system from which it never quite recovered," observed historian Patricia Nelson Limerick. Overgrazing and the repeated planting of the same grasses to feed livestock led to depletion of nutrients in Western soils, the erosion of topsoil, the removal of trees needed to anchor topsoil, and other factors that would create the devastating Dust Bowl in the Plains states in the 1930s.

Large ranchers would soon graze their cattle on millions of acres of free, unfenced public land, cutting into the grazing land left for the buffalo that the Plains Indians depended on for food and clothing. These moves increased Indian poverty and hunger. Meanwhile, needing wide-open spaces to feed their growing herds, cattle ranchers also fought "range wars" with farmers and sheep ranchers. In the 1880s, ranchers in the Plains suffered through record cold weather; thousands of cattle froze to death. In the 1890s an oversupply of beef caused prices to spiral downward. Ranchers abandoned the cattle trails, cut the size of their herds, and started buying or renting land, using barbed wire to fence in their livestock and feeding them hay or other feed stored for the winter. These barb-wired ranches further disrupted buffalo migratory patterns, contributing to their disappearance from the Plains. Ranchers also began breeding Angus and Hereford cattle that were significantly meatier than the leaner longhorns the cowboys had driven in the cattle drives. The increased volume of meat produced more than made up for the increased shipping costs ranchers encountered after the abandonment of cattle drives. The brief age of the cowboy disappeared as rapidly as it had arisen.

Before the Civil War, mining served as a major engine of the West's economic growth. The 1858 discovery of gold in the Pikes Peak region of Colorado, and subsequent finds near modern-day Denver and Boulder, drew 100,000 prospectors into the area. Residents declared the birth of the state of Jefferson and applied to Congress for admission to the Union, but the Civil War delayed action, with Colorado not made a territory until 1861 or state until 1871. At the same time as the Colorado strikes, gold discoveries in Nevada sparked rapid population growth in that area as well, so that by 1864, just six years after the mines opened in Carson City and Virginia City, Nevada became the newest state.

Scientific discoveries in the Northeast also added impetus to Western migration. Profitable copper mines opened in Montana and Arizona partly as a result of several late nineteenth century inventions including Alexander Graham Bell's telephone in 1876 and Thomas Edison's light bulb in 1879. These inventions created a demand for thousands of tons of copper wire. Mining towns sprang up across the western frontier.

Western bloodshed joined with violence against nature. Tombstone, Arizona's unexpected economic boom turned quickly to bust, and the aftermath left ugly ruins. Searching for ever-deeper veins of silver, miners in 1881 hit an underground river, forcing mining companies to purchase expensive pumps in order to keep the mines from flooding. By the end of the 1880s, a glut in the silver market drove prices for the precious metal rapidly downward, and the busy buzz of Tombstone's boomtown days gave way to an eerie quiet. Mining companies left behind burned-out mills, waterlogged mines and abandoned homes, the townspeople migrating in search of the next rich strike.

The hydraulic mining used at the **Comstock Lode**, a rich source of silver found in California in 1859, poisoned salmon streams and filled the soil with toxic metals. To fuel metal smelting, loggers stripped forests near Virginia City, Nevada. Mercury mining poisoned San Francisco Bay. Elsewhere, hydraulic mining of copper created huge heaps of tailings, poisoning the soil and leaving an often barren, strip-mined landscape, with mountains reduced to ugly streams of muddy ooze.

Mining camps drew diverse populations, with Anglos from across the country joining Civil War draft dodgers and deserters from the North, migrant Mexican workers from the New Mexico territory, eastern and southern European immigrants, and imported Chinese labor. Mining towns often became anarchic centers of violence. The discovery of precious metals and ores often spurred both rapid economic development and lawlessness. The discovery of nearby silver in 1878 led to the breathtaking industrialization of Tombstone, which lay fifty miles south of the Southern Pacific Railroad line. In spite of its distance from a main travel artery, prospectors swamped the region even as quartz mills dotted the surrounding landscape. From 1881 to 1882, Tombstone's population exploded from just below 1,000 to perhaps as many as 14,000.

As housing, saloons, and the other infrastructure of frontier towns rapidly rose in the desert landscape, new residents denuded the surrounding countryside in search of lumber for buildings and cordwood for cooking and warming hearths. Population growth attracted livestock ranchers, and a one-time isolated blip on the arid landscape gave birth to a vibrant livestock industry, which further stressed the local environment. Such breathtaking growth outstripped the development of local civic institutions. Crude economic competition, racial tensions, a lack of faith in the local justice system, and the notion of popular sovereignty also encouraged widespread western violence.

The presence of silver and livestock attracted bands of robbers and cattle thieves organized into criminal gangs, such as the Clanton family and the McLaury brothers, that often preyed on the local Mexican population. Mostly Anglo men from Texas, these outlaws, often called by locals the "cowboys," held "feelings towards Mexicans [that were] so bitter that they had no compunction about stealing from them or shooting and robbing them," as one resident observed. The cowboys crisscrossed the Arizona-Mexico border, stealing cattle in Sonora in North Mexico and selling it in the United States, or vice-versa. These raids often resulted in murder, such as the mass killing of eight Mexicans in Skeleton Canyon in July 1881.

Mining regions often sought to improvise a legal system, well ahead of the establishment of a territorial or state government. In Jacksonville, Wyoming, for instance, miners elected a magistrate and a sheriff. The prospectors and miners served on improvised juries in criminal and civil cases. Any murderer, horse or mule thief, and anyone who stole gold dust from a miner's tent, or any items valued at more than $100 (around $1,300 today) faced a possible hanging. Thieves taking less than $100 faced having their heads and eyebrows shaved and expulsion from the mining camp. Many criminals, however, escaped these fates. As the historian Frederick Merck noted, "When crimes were detected, punishment was uncertain. A miner's camp meeting was prone to gusts of feeling, rage in some cases, maudlin sympathy in others. Since crime was not effectively dealt with, vigilante committees had to be set up . . ."

Vigilante justice, however, remained part of western life even after formal courts and government institutions had been established. According to western historian Michael J. Pfeifer, twenty-three lynch mobs killed thirty-six persons in Wyoming between 1878 and 1918. Whites accounted for most of the victims, twenty-five, while mobs murdered four blacks, four Indians, and one Hispanic victim. In California from 1875 and 1947, forty-two lynch mobs murdered thirty-four whites, fourteen Hispanics, eight Indians, three Chinese immigrants, and two African Americans. Complex social currents sparked western lynchings, Pfeifer argues. "Collective killings were sometimes performed by groups of working class white men suddenly aroused by news of a crime that seemed to offend wageworkers' sense of social order," Pfeifer wrote. "Racial, ethnic, and gender ideologies had particular effect in transient settings where mobile, exploited workers often did not know each other well. Laborers such as miners, loggers, and railroad men relied instead on informal, hastily constructed reputations predicated upon personal friendship, and on the reflexive comfort of racial and ethnic solidarities amid temporary social crisis. Working class men might respond with nearly spontaneous lethal violence to alleged violations of sexual and gender etiquette, especially those tinged with racial and ethnic overtones."

Outside of mining and logging camps, robberies and vengeance killings became part of the West's daily routine. One murder per night is estimated to have taken place at Gibson Station in the Indian Territory. The Indian Territory became known as the "Robber's Roost" and a local proverb proclaimed, "There is no Sunday west of St. Louis—no God west of Fort Smith."

Billy the Kid

In western communities that lacked deeply established social institutions, outlaws often became admired anti-heroes who would enjoy a second life as counterculture icons in the twentieth century. In Lincoln County, in the New Mexico Territory, a teenager named Henry Antrim (who already went by the alias Billy Bonney) was well on his way to becoming both famous and infamous as **Billy the Kid**. A drifter and horse thief, Billy became a "soldier" in the so-called Lincoln County War, a bloody battle between two rival criminal rings that sought monopoly control of trade and political dominance in South Central New Mexico.

As historian and Billy the Kid biographer Robert Utley notes, this region "excelled in habits of violence. The combination of whiskey and guns so prevalent in the West seemed particularly volatile in Lincoln County." Racist tensions simmered between Anglos and the local Mexican population and pitted white residents against "nigger soldiers" stationed at the Fort Stanton army base, even as all these groups feared and hated the native population at the nearby Apache reservation. "Casual law enforcement and ineffective courts imposed the weakest of formal restraints on the drunken killings and maimings that had grown routine," Utley noted.

One gang led by Lawrence J. Murphy, called "The House" because it operated out of a store that resembled a home, dominated local commerce and held a lucrative contract providing beef for the United States Army obtained when gang members, called "the Boys," stole local livestock. The Boys also ruthlessly enforced contracts and terrorized opponents of The House. A wealthy Englishman, John Henry Tunstall, challenged the power of The House, and won backing by the powerful cattle baron John Simpson Chisum, who had tired of The House's cattle rustling.

Tunstall opened a bank and a store to compete with The House's businesses, finding customers among small ranchers and farmers in the area and winning a monopoly of his own on all livestock feed grown in Lincoln County. He then secured agreements with local landowners that won him near-total control of local water rights. At the instigation of The House, a sheriff's posse, while attaching cattle as part of a lawsuit between the two rival gangs, shot Tunstall to death on February 18, 1878. One of Tunstall's henchmen, Alexander McSween, gathered an army of local outlaws to retaliate, a force called "the Regulators," that would include the 18-year-old Billy the Kid. The Regulators hunted down men they blamed for the Tunstall killing and eventually assassinated Sheriff William Brady, thought to be a puppet of The House.

Billy Bonney would be implicated not only in the death of Brady but also the killings of two of his deputies. Eventually Bonney would be blamed for more than twenty murders, though he likely killed no more than four men. Just a teenager, Bonney already displayed a charismatic personality and physical courage that impressed his partners in crime. "The Kid was as active and graceful as a cat," Utley quotes one of his sidekicks as later remembering. "At Seven Rivers he practiced continually with a pistol or rifle, often riding at a run and dodging behind the side of his mount to fire, as the Apaches did. He was very proud of his ability to pick up a handkerchief or other object from the ground while riding at a run."

In mid-July, a sheriff's posse eventually trapped several of The Regulators in McSween's house, starting a siege known locally as the Five Day Battle that ended on July 19 when the building was set on fire, and five members of the Regulators attempted to escape. McSween died in a blaze of gunfire, but Billy the Kid and other members of the gang successfully slipped away. With McSween's death, the Lincoln County War basically ended. In an attempt to dampen further violence, newly appointed Territorial Gov. Lew Wallace proclaimed a general amnesty for anyone involved in the Lincoln County War who was not already under indictment.

Bonney fled to Texas, where he assumed the alias Henry McCarty. Under indictment for murder, he wrote to Gov. Wallace requesting amnesty in return for his testimony on a Lincoln County War-related trial. The two met in Lincoln County, where Bonney greeted the governor holding a rifle in one hand and a revolver in the other. Nevertheless, a deal was struck, and Bonney was granted amnesty in return for his court appearance. As part of the deal, Bonney was supposed to be held in the local jail for a short time and released, but District Attorney John Dolan (affiliated with The House) reneged, forcing Bonney to escape with the help of friends. Bonney later allegedly killed a man named Joe Grant while playing cards in a Fort Sumner, New Mexico saloon. Newspaper coverage by this point already had elevated Bonney to national celebrity status.

Pat Garrett won election as Lincoln County sheriff in November 1880, running on a law-and-order platform. He quickly formed a posse to pursue Bonney, who was captured near Fort Sumner on December 24. On April 9, 1881, a jury found Bonney guilty of murdering Sheriff Brady. A judge sentenced the 21-year-old to be hanged. Transferred to Lincoln for his May 13 execution date, Bonney escaped with help from local friends, hiding out in the vicinity of Fort Sumner. The daring escape again captured headlines nationwide and added to the Kid's mystique. Garrett and two deputies were interrogating a local resident, Pedro Maxwell, about the Kid's whereabouts when Bonney unexpectedly showed up at the residence. Witnesses and friends of Garrett and Bonney later told different stories about the encounter, but Garrett shot Bonney just above the heart, killing the outlaw at age 21.

Five wildly inaccurate and florid biographies of Billy the Kid reached readers within a year of his death, but the legend of this outlaw received its biggest boost with the publication of Pat Garrett's book (co-written with M.A. "Ash" Upson), *The Authentic Life of Billy the Kid*, which appeared in 1882. This book, also consisting of many fabrications about Billy's early life, established the two main features of the outlaw's legend. As biographer Utley puts it, Garrett and Upson portrayed Billy Bonney as a divided soul, "happy, likeable youth who was also a merciless killer." During another period of flamboyant gangsters and seemingly unchecked crime, the 1920s, newspaperman Walter Noble Burns' bestseller, *The Saga of Billy the Kid*, permanently fixed the gunman's image in popular culture as a latter-day Robin Hood, a good-hearted thief motivated to commit his crimes by his frontier sense of justice and fair play. In a society that sanctioned mass murder against Native Americans and the lynching of African Americans, and in which corrupt politicians and infamously greedy business tycoons seemed to rob the public with impunity, such poor and working class outlaws hardly stood out as villains. Instead, they seemed glamorously rebellious and comparatively honest not just to nineteenth century reading audiences but to twentieth century book buyers and fans of radio, television and movie Westerns.

Jesse James

Outlaw Chic

Billy the Kid hardly represented the only celebrity gun-slinging lawbreaker and lawman of the late-nineteenth-century West. Jesse Woodson James became such a media-savvy robber of banks and trains that once, after he and other members of the Cole-Younger criminal gang robbed $22,000 in gold and currency (more than $350,000 in today's dollars) from a train in Gadshill, Missouri in January 1874, he startled the engineer by throwing him a stick that was wrapped with a press release James had written. Headlined, "THE MOST DARING TRAIN ROBBERY ON RECORD," the press release read in part, "The robbers were all large men, all being slightly under six feet. After robbing the train they started in a southerly direction. They were all mounted on handsome horses. P.S. They are a hell of an excitement in this part of the country."

The brutal career of Jesse James reveals why such outlaws attracted so much attention and even admiration among contemporaries and have figured so largely in later Wild West mythology. During the Civil War, Missouri natives Jesse and Frank James rode with the murderous William Clarke Quantrill and his band of Confederate guerillas. "Quantrill's Raiders" in 1864 looted and burned Centralia, Kansas, before coldly executing seventy-five Union prisoners of war. James killed at least three Union soldiers in hot pursuit of the gang, launching his bloodletting career.

As the Civil War ended in 1865, a general amnesty was offered guerilla fighters, but probably because of James' role in the infamous Centralia Massacre, when he rode to Lexington, Missouri, along with his brother Frank and his future partner in crime Cole Younger, Union soldiers ambushed the band. Riding lead, Jesse James rode into the soldiers' crosshairs, and a bullet knocked him off his horse and pierced his lung. He crawled to safety and escaped to Nebraska, where his mother nursed him to health. The James Brothers suffered in their transition to civilian life, according to Western historian Jay Robert Nash. "The James boys had tasted battle and blood and adventure," Nash observed. "They had survived the worst carnage ever seen in the country, and either out of boredom or an ambition that went beyond the dull chores of their farm, they, like many others in that turbulent era, buckled gun belts, mounted horses, and rode into small towns to rob banks." The James Brothers gave voice to the regional and class resentments of the era, blaming "Yankee bankers and railroad magnates" for their financial troubles, sentiments widely shared by the general public that would elevate these violent criminals to heroic status.

The next year, the James Brothers and their cousin Cole Younger formed a criminal gang and launched their career as bank robbers, carrying off more than $60,000 in gold and money (worth more than $682,000 in today's currency) from the Clay County Savings Bank. The gang murdered an innocent bystander, William "Jolly" Wymore, passing by the scene of the crime on his way to classes at William Jewell College, who stared too long at one robber who feared he had been recognized.

Yet, no matter how ruthless the tactics of the **James-Younger Gang**, their perceived resistance to Northern "invaders" and the unprincipled actions of law enforcement continued to win the gang admiration and sympathy. James and his associates had murdered several employees of the Pinkerton Detective Agency, well known in the nineteenth century known for its violent tactics against labor unions. Bearing a grudge, Pinkertons surrounded the farm of the James Brothers' remarried mother Zerelda Samuels when James and Frank paid her a visit on the evening of January 26, 1875. The detectives shouted out to the James Brothers, demanding their surrender as a bomb was thrown through the farmhouse window. The blast severed Samuels' arm and killed Frank and Jesse James' eight-year-old half-brother Peyton Samuel, who suffered for an hour before his death. The Pinkerton attack, labeled an "inexcusable and cowardly deed" by contemporary newspapers, disgraced the Pinkerton agency, which never fully recovered its reputation.

The gang's end came the next year with a daring but unsuccessful robbery in Northfield, Minnesota. While part of the gang entered the First National Bank, armed lookouts waited outside and were spotted by townspeople, who responded by arming themselves and taking concealed positions as they fired at the robbers. Locals fatally shot gang members Clell Miller and Bill Chadwell, while bullets struck Cole, Bob and Jim Younger and Charlie Pitts. The surviving members of the gang made it out of town, but the wounded James Brothers split off from the Youngers and Pitts. Authorities trapped the latter group near a swamp in Madelia, Minnesota and in a shootout killed Pitts. The Youngers surrendered and were later sentenced to life imprisonment. Having killed a cashier and others in the misadventure, the James Brothers were now seen by many as mere murderers. They now drew hundreds of pursuers who searched for the outlaws in vain across the Midwest.

The Brothers formed a second gang in Missouri, but their infamy made life dangerous, especially after a robbery on the Chicago, Rock Island and Pacific train in Winton in July 1881 resulted in the slaying of a train engineer. Missouri Gov. Thomas Crittendon offered a $10,000 reward (worth more than $176,000 today) for the capture and conviction of Frank and Jesse James. The earlier James gang had been built on family kinship, but the reward money proved too tempting for the James's newer, less familiar associates. Jesse James would murder one gang member, Ed Miller, when he suspected the latter planned to turn himself in and inform on the brothers. A dispute over money stolen during a robbery at Blue Cut, Missouri led to the killing of another gang member. In return for the reward, on April 3, 1882, gang member Robert Ford shot Jesse James in the head as the notorious gunman stood on a chair to straighten a picture at his home.

Fearing that Frank James would seek vengeance, Robert Ford's brother Charlie, also a member of the gang, suffered nightmares and eventually committed suicide. The public generally saw Robert Ford as a traitor and a coward. Ford used his reward money to open several saloons but ended up drifting from town to town before being murdered himself at the age of 30 in Creede, Colorado, June 8, 1892. By then, the public again transfigured Jesse James into a folk hero, a Robin Hood who resisted unjust authority, robbing from the rich and helping the poor. This image shines through a folk song, later performed by twentieth-century folk singer and protestor Pete Seeger, which proclaimed:

> Jesse was a man, a friend to the poor …
> Talking with his family brave.
> Robert Ford came along like a thief in the night
> And laid poor Jesse in his grave.

Romanticized in dime novels, plays, and "true detective" magazines, the Western outlaw provided nineteenth-century urban readers with fantasies of adventure in the wide-open spaces and vengeance against the wealthy and powerful. In the end, many Americans saw Billy the Kid, Jesse James, and other gunslingers as less lawless, sinister and greedy than "robber barons" like the Rockefellers, the Astors, and the rest of the callous rich whose gaudy wealth stood in shocking contrast to the appalling poverty seen in America's spreading urban landscape.

WOMEN IN THE WEST

The outlaw culture of the West crossed gender boundaries. Myra Belle Shirley, who later assumed the alias "Belle Starr," won fame as a stagecoach robber, cattle rustler, and horse thief in the 1870s and 1880s. In addition to those criminal activities, she fenced stolen goods and became know for successfully harboring wanted criminals. Working as a card dealer at a Dallas, Texas, saloon in the late 1860s, she gave birth to a daughter fathered by one legendary gunman (Jesse James' crime partner Cole Younger) and married outlaw Jim Reed, the couple fleeing to California after a warrant was issued for their arrest.

The couple returned to Texas, and Shirley again dealt cards and worked as a prostitute until Reed was killed in 1874. Shirley entered into a series of volatile relationships with six common-law husbands, all of them criminals. Living in the Indian Territory, she died mysteriously from several shotgun blasts in 1889, shortly before her 41st birthday. Though no one was ever arrested for her murder, two of her sons figured as prominent suspects.

Martha Jane Burke, a sometimes prostitute who became famous as "**Calamity Jane**," earned fame by dressing as a man at age 23 and joining an otherwise all-male geological exploration of the Black Hills in South Dakota. Then, in 1876, again in disguise, she volunteered for service with a 1,300-man force commanded by Gen. George Crook in a war expedition against the Sioux and Northern Cheyenne peoples. She served an important role, rapidly traveling 90 miles, including a swim across the Platte River at one point to transmit secret military dispatches. Burke later made dubious claims that she had married and borne a child with another "Wild West" celebrity, gunman James Butler "Wild Bill" Hickok and that she also was a friend of General George Armstrong Custer, famous then for his defeat and death at the **Battle of Little Big Horn**. Burke performed in William "**Buffalo Bill**" Cody's "Wild West Show" in 1893, entertaining crowds as an expert horse rider and trick gun shooter. Sadly, alcoholism destroyed her entertainment career and hastened an early death at age 51 from pneumonia.

The West, however, offered much less excitement and drama for many women, some of whom endured lives of isolation. Elite women, in particular, chafed against the lack of culture and community. A doctor's wife, A.K. Clappe, complained bitterly in letters of life near the California gold mines, sharing with her sisters the emptiness of life with "no newspapers, no churches, no lectures, concerts or theaters; no fresh books, no shopping, calling nor gossiping little tea-drinkings; no parties, no balls, no picnics, no tableaus, no charades, no latest fashions, no daily mail . . . no promenades, no rides or drives; no vegetables but potatoes and onions, no milk, no eggs, no nothing."

Such cultural niceties did not concern working-class women who faced exhausting work but also missed the extended family networks that they left behind in the East. Women constituted only about 20 percent of the adults in Western mining communities. As historian Elliott West has observed, women seeking social bonds in such communities faced two major obstacles. First, "there were few women with whom to form new relationships, especially in the early years of a town's life. Second, the mining camps were among the most unstable and transient gatherings in the history of the unsettled young republic." About 90 of every 100 residents moved elsewhere within a decade, making it difficult to form communities or create lasting friendships. As one Denver prospector's wife put it in her diary in an 1863 passage, "I never was so lonely and homesick in all my life. My sweet sweet home! Why did I ever leave you in the stranger's land to dwell?"

Men and women struggled side-by-side to survive in the West, whether they lived in one of the new frontier cities, in mining camps, in the desert, or in farming communities. The family farm depended on hard work from both the men and the women, with women assigned not only the endless chores of feeding the chickens and other poultry, planting seeds, watering the crops, and helping with the harvest, but also cooking, caring for the young, doing the laundry, hauling water to the house from the well, making and repairing clothes, and acting as a physician when someone in the household fell ill. Women milked cows, churned butter, and gave birth to large families.

In mining towns, women often earned incomes as domestic servants. Some women contributed to the family income by taking in renters, and cooking or doing laundry for other families. In many cases, family structures were informal. In several Central Arizona mining communities in the 1860s and 1870s, almost half the adult women were not married to the men with whom they lived. These couples were often mixed race, with white men cohabitating with Hispanic women. Such women dealt with a sexual double standard in which the community looked the other way when men had sex outside of marriage but defined a woman as being immoral for engaging in the same behavior.

In spite of the more loosely structured gender roles in the West, however, in mining camps, more than 90 percent of women "kept house," according to late nineteenth-century censuses. Marriage became more common as frontier towns became more settled. Recent studies suggest that spousal abuse, marital rape, and violence against children were commonplace in the late-nineteenth century West.

Mining camps in particular posed hazards for mothers raising young children. "The fouled water, streets strewn

Martha Jane Burke, "Calamity Jane," on horseback, c1901

with garbage and offal, and the crowded living conditions encouraged the spread of cholera, diphtheria, influenza, measles, and other child killers," wrote Elliott West. Childhood mortality became a cruel commonplace for these mothers, including one who lost three children in four days in Caribou, Colorado in 1879. The landscape posed another lethal hazard. Young ones were liable to accidentally tumble into mine shafts, be exposed to lethal amounts of mercury, swallow lye or wander into the paths of fast-charging horses or heavy wagons. "This is an awful place for children and nervous mothers would 'die daily,'" as one woman wrote in Rich Bar, California.

Women lived public as well as private lives. Women married to or living with miners on strike brought food to their husbands on the picket line and threw projectiles at soldiers and Pinkerton Guards sent to quash the uprising. Women campaigned publicly for the right to vote and sometimes lobbied influential husbands to vote for suffrage. The Grange and other farmers' organizations allowed women not only to join but also to hold offices within the organization, and women took the leadership role in the campaign for the federal and state prohibition of alcohol.

Women won the right to vote in the West before any other region. In the 1876 Colorado state constitution, women won the right to vote in school elections and to hold seats on local school boards. By the 1890s, Wyoming, Utah, Colorado, and Idaho had approved women's suffrage. By 1914, they were joined by California, Washington, Oregon, Arizona, Kansas, Nebraska, and Montana. Many historians have argued that the central role women played in the family economy in the West persuaded men to accept full citizenship rights for women. Such men also wanted increased female migration to the West to increase the congressional representation for the region and thus expand the West's political clout. Others note that in states like Colorado, women used the years before winning full statewide suffrage to form organizations such as local chapters of the Women's Christian Temperance Union.

Prohibition emerged as a feminist cause for many reasons. Women argued that alcohol led to spousal and child abuse, was a factor in workplace injuries suffered by wage-earning husbands, that money spent on spirits could be better invested in the home economy, and that much alcohol consumption took place in male-intense environments like saloons where men solicited services from prostitutes, often contracted social diseases, and later infected their wives.

Women also formed church groups, literary clubs, and organizations that sought to improve city sanitation, hospitals, and schools. These groups often attacked issues considered part of the "domestic sphere," for instance addressing the needs of children and preserving the safety and sanctity of the family. Nevertheless, woman gained vital political experience in these groups. As historian Elizabeth Jameson argues, ". . . [T]heir participation in rural reform movements, organized labor, and partisan politics contributed to suffrage victories."

Abortion Restriction in the West

In one realm of their lives, Western women steadily lost autonomy as the nineteenth century progressed: reproduction. As in the East, fear of the nation's changing racial and ethnic demographics and increased male domination over women's medical care led to the outlawing of abortion in several states. The criminalization of abortion did not begin until the second third of the nineteenth century. Early on, **abortion laws** did not focus on the morality of the issue but instead were aimed at outlawing specific abortion methods said to threaten a mother's health. Several early laws, for instance, outlawed the use of poisons to perform abortions. By 1840, only eight states had enacted laws restricting abortion.

The struggle of the American Medical Association, founded in 1847, to ban abortions overlapped with the campaign by male doctors to "professionalize" the medical field and eliminate competition from female midwives who provided most health care to women. Before the mid-nineteenth century, most women, if they sought help in childbirth outside of friends and family, consulted midwives, who also provided information on natural methods of birth control, abortion and women's health and nutrition. To many male doctors, midwives represented a loss of income.

The AMA successfully lobbied states across the Union to require medical licenses for practitioners. Since medical schools of the era did not admit women, this legislation effectively eliminated women as health-care providers. Deaths and injuries occurring at the hands of midwives and other female medical providers during abortions provided major sensational evidence for male doctors in their arguments for excluding women from the profession and for outlawing abortion. Abortions at the time had a 30 percent mortality rate for women, as opposed to 3 percent mortality in live births.

Rivalry between male and female medical providers and concern about women's safety did not alone account for the new interest in abortion. Between 1800 and 1900, the rate of fertility—the average number of children born to each woman—dropped for white women by almost 50 percent, from seven children per woman to 3.56. This occurred even as an unprecedented number of "new immigrants" from Eastern and Southern Europe arrived at the East Coast and from Japan and China on the West Coast from the 1870s to the 1900s. Anglos expressed a fear of "**race suicide**" instigated by the failure of white Protestants to have enough children to keep up with the birth rates of Catholic, Jewish and East Asian immigrants and African Americans. An 1865 tract by anti-abortion physician Horatio Storer, for example, warned that abortion was "infinitely more frequent among Protestant women than Catholic." Other doctors inveighed against abortions sought by women of "high repute." Another physician complained that "our most intelligent communities," meaning wealthy white Protestants, sought to limit family size through abortion and contraception while people of color, Catholics and other outsiders gave birth to increasingly large families.

In the West, with its proximity to Mexico, its importation of Chinese railroad workers, the increasing immigration of African Americans and the still large presence of the Native American population, such demographic warnings no doubt frightened Anglo elites. The West helped lead the national trend toward abortion abolition. While anti-abortion activism in the North and South paused during the Civil War, the West was less affected by the conflict and responded more quickly to the AMA's anti-abortion lobbying. Politicians in five western territories in the West drew up anti-abortion clauses in the region's new legal codes. Performing an abortion "on a woman then being with child" became a criminal offense in the Colorado and Nevada Territory in 1861, and in the Arizona, Idaho, and Montana territories by 1864. Part of this emphasis stemmed from the federal control of the western territories at a time when the Republican Party dominated national politics. Ideologically, the Republican Party more willingly embraced the power of the state to "systematize and professionalize public policy" than Democrats. Republicans also were, as abortion historian James C. Mohr noted, "very open to the influence and the advice of professionals and experts."

Farther west, legislators moved from restrictions on procedures that physically harmed women to outright bans on abortion itself. In 1864 in Oregon, the state legislature eliminated allowances of abortion before the "quickening," when the fetus begins moving in the uterus, and defined the aborting of any "child" in utero as manslaughter, whether or not the mother suffered injury from the procedure. By 1869 in Nevada, the legislature outlawed even the dissemination of information on abortifacient drugs and abortion procedures. By the 1880s, states had passed 40 different anti-abortion statutes, laws that generally provided an exception only when abortion was necessary to save the life of a mother.

Men saw women as a reproductive weapon in the conquest of the West and had enacted laws to make sure Anglos remained a demographic majority in the region.

CHINESE WORKERS

Perhaps no group inspired greater nativist panic within the Anglo community in the West than Chinese immigrants. Dangerous railroad construction depended heavily on low-wage Chinese workers, buffeted on one side by the resentment of Anglo workers and on the other side by the exploitation of bosses who kept their wages low with the threat of deportation. The West Coast in particular experienced an explosion in Chinese immigration that, though small in numbers in comparison to the total United States population, made a major impact on the California economy. In the years between 1850 and 1880, the Chinese population in the United States skyrocketed from 7,520 to 105,465, with the Chinese comprising almost 9 percent of California's total population and about 25 percent of the state's total workforce.

Only 5 percent of Chinese immigrants were women. Railroad companies at times purchased Chinese women who were used as prostitutes servicing the male workers. Chinese labor built the particularly difficult Sierra Nevada portion of the first transcontinental line, a project that resulted in thousands of workers' deaths. Toward the end of the nineteenth century, Chinese men worked not only in railroad construction but also as domestic servants in textile and shoe manufacturing and in cigar factories.

Companies hiring the Chinese happily played a game of divide and conquer with Anglo workers and their Asian peers. The press published stories accusing Chinese men of forcing white women into prostitution and cheating white customers at Chinese-owned businesses. Workers simmered with anger at the use of Chinese immigrants as replacement workers, which allowed employers to stymie white-run unions' demands for higher wages. Adding fuel to the anti-Chinese fire, popular magazines and newspapers printed stories accusing Chinese men of being sexual predators. "No matter how good a Chinaman may be, ladies never leave your children with them, especially little girls," *Scribner's Monthly* warned. Not surprisingly in this atmosphere, violence against the Chinese became pandemic in California and other western states.

Whites savagely beat Chinese residents in Eureka, Truckee, and other California towns. In 1871 in Los Angeles, Anglo mobs murdered twenty-one Chinese immigrants, while in 1885 whites in Rock Springs, Wyoming, killed twenty-eight and wounded fifteen in a Chinese neighborhood. White workers battled to end

Chinese immigration to the United States. Cigars made by whites in California bore a "union label" signifying that no Chinese worker had been involved in the manufacture of the product. In San Francisco, the home of the nation's largest Chinese population, an Irish immigrant named Denis Kearney formed the Workingman's Party in 1878, its platform proclaiming, "Treason is better than to labor beside a Chinese slave." In spite of worker unrest, crews completed five transcontinental rail lines between 1869 and 1893.

MEXICAN LABOR

Pressure from labor unions, and elites worried about the arrival of "racial undesirables" on American shores, led to passage of the Chinese Exclusion Act in 1882, which banned the further immigration of Chinese people to the United States. Wealthy whites found other cheap labor sources, from Japan, Korea, and the Philippines. An emerging source of labor came with Mexicans and Mexican Americans, who drew Anglo hostility that often matched that shown the Chinese. In the white mind, Mexicans descended from three "inferior" racial groups: Indians, blacks, and the Spanish. The Protestant majority also disdained the Mexicans' Catholicism.

Most Mexicans within the United States were poor, working their own small farms or serving as migratory agricultural labor. Before the Mexican American War, wealthy Mexicans in California owned about 15 million acres. Anglos poured in following the 1848 conclusion of the war and the subsequent annexation of California. One-time Mexican elites found themselves surrounded by land-hungry newcomers. Wealthy *Mexicanos* held land titles issued by the Mexican government. Anglo judges repeatedly invalidated these land claims. Whites often supplemented lawsuits with petty harassment or even violence.

White merchants, bankers, and lawyers in New Mexico conspired to raise property taxes to force Mexican landowners to sell. By 1854, Anglos had seized all but one Mexican land grant in Texas. The **Texas Rangers**, a state law enforcement agency, initiated a campaign of terror against Mexicans within the state, murdering as many as 5,000 in the nineteenth century. The seized land would then be distributed to whites, who subsequently made fortunes as ranchers and farmers.

Formerly rich Mexicans declined into poverty and depended on low wages paid by the now-dominant whites. The poverty of the former landowners was then taken as evidence of Mexicano cultural and racial inferiority. Author Richard Dana expressed a typical Anglo attitude, describing Mexicans as "an idle, thriftless people." Another author, Lansford Hastings, complained that a Mexican "always pursues that method of doing things, which requires the least physical or mental exorcise [sic] unless it involves some danger, in which case, he always adopts some other method."

Mexicans worked as migrant farm labor or as low-wage workers in urban barrios (ghettoes). As irrigation methods became more sophisticated, improved technology brought more acreage into cultivation, and the spreading railroads expanded the marketplace for western farmers, a wave of Mexicans poured into the United States. The biggest surge of Mexican immigration would await the bloody Mexican Revolution of 1910-1920.

The level of discrimination faced by Mexicans and Mexican Americans depended on how large their population was in a given area, the presence of whites or African Americans seeking similar employment, and whether the immigrants were perceived as transient or as seeking permanent residence. Mexicans faced particularly harsh discrimination in many parts of Texas.

No law mandated segregation of Mexican and Mexican-American students in any Texas school system, but administrators assigned Anglo and Hispanic children to different schools as a matter of custom. Where there were few Mexican children, no segregation occurred. In farm communities, however, separate quarters for Mexicans and Anglos were established early on. In 1902, Seguin, in South Texas, became the first school system to segregate Mexican children but the practice spread until, by 1930, 90 percent of heavily Mexican South Texas schools provided separate facilities for Anglo and Mexican children. Restaurants in Texas and other Southwestern states often would not serve Mexican customers or would require them to wait outside for food. Park and public pool managers frequently excluded Hispanics.

BUFFALO SOLDIERS

Partly in grudging acknowledgment of the brave service provided by 200,000 black soldiers in the Union Army during the Civil War, in 1866 the federal government created the first all-black infantry and cavalry regiments to serve in the Western United States. Even "Radical" Republicans were not fully immune from the white supremacist ideas of the era, and the law establishing these segregated units required them to be led by white officers. These units primarily served in the American West where, as historian Monroe Lee Billington notes, "they guarded wagon trains, stagecoaches, and railroads taking Americans to the frontier. They aided local law enforcement officers to round up cattle rustlers and other outlaws. In addition, they built roads, strung telegraph wire and performed other perfunctory duties that aided the movement of the nation westward..." While African Americans in the South and the East suffered confinement to the lowest rung in the nation's racial hierarchy, in the West they formed part of a conquering army that suppressed Native American resistance and paved the way for white and black seizure of Indian lands.

With African Americans composing 10 percent of soldiers serving from the end of the Civil War to the Spanish American War in 1898, black fighters played a highly visible role in the "Indian Wars." Native Americans reportedly dubbed these men "**Buffalo Soldiers**," perhaps because Indians reportedly thought the hair and skin color of African Americans resembled that of buffalo, or because many of the soldiers wore buffalo skin robes in the wintertime, or because of their respect for both the buffalo and for African Americans as fighters. Most black soldiers served in Texas and Kansas, as well as in the Oklahoma, Arizona and New Mexico territories. The African American Ninth Cavalry played a key role in defeating the forces of Chief Victorio, a Warm Springs, New Mexico, Apache leader, in a war that lasted from 1876 to 1880.

African-American troops often suffered as the U.S. Army placed them in the uncomfortable role of restraining white settlers intent on illegally taking Indian land and serving as strikebreakers. After its victory over Apache leaders Victorio and Nana in New Mexico, commanders dispatched the Ninth Cavalry for the job of restraining white "boomers" from crossing the Kansas border and taking land illegally in Oklahoma, action that often resulted in violence between black soldiers and would-be settlers. In more than fifty cases, beginning in the late 1870s and continuing until the start of the twentieth century, railroad and mine owners and other powerful western business owners exploited black soldiers to replace striking white workers. The army also dispatched black military units to quell violence in the previously mentioned Lincoln County War in New Mexico.

Sadly for the black servicemen in the West, an antimilitary mood gripped the country after the Civil War and soldiers in the late nineteenth century did not enjoy the respect accorded their wartime predecessors, a problem intensified by racism, according to Monroe Billington. " ... [T]his postwar army was composed primarily of lower-class urban workers, European immigrants, and African Americans—people for whom other Americans often expressed contempt," Billington wrote.

African Americans frequently endured hostility from the whites they encountered. When whites murdered black soldiers, as often as not authorities looked the other way. Meanwhile, local law enforcement often harassed black soldiers, arresting them on trumped-up charges, beating and killing them, or sentencing them to lengthy sentences for the most minimum of offenses.

Meanwhile, the Army discriminated against black men. In spite of their often-acknowledged bravery, black soldiers received only 4 percent of the Medals of Honor awarded in the period between the end of the Civil War and the Spanish American War. The Army promoted no African American enlisted man to the rank of officer in that time period, though no military rules prohibited such an action. Only 22 African Americans received appointments to the West Point military academy in the late nineteenth century, and only three could overcome the racism at that institution and graduate. Military records also note repeated instances of black soldiers denigrated by their officers with racial slurs.

AFRICAN AMERICANS AND THE WESTERN LABOR MOVEMENT

Black soldiers were not alone in being used as strikebreakers by ruthless businessmen west of the Missouri. In 1891 in Washington state, African-American civilians, excluded from unions and needing decent-paying jobs, arrived under the protection of Pinkerton guards in Newcastle, near Seattle, to serve as replacement workers at coal mines owned by the Oregon Improvement Company (OIC). White workers had gone on strike against the OIC, which subjected its employees to long hours in unsafe conditions and housed them in "company towns" where the OIC served as landlord. Miners received wages not in cash but in company "scrip" redeemable only in OIC-owned stores. White workers attempted to affiliate with the Knights of Labor, an effort that led the company to bring in African-American replacement workers from Iowa, Illinois, Indiana and Missouri.

One group of white workers assembled in Pierce County near Seattle and resolved that "we will no longer submit to the introduction of the negro race among us, and that we cannot and will not recognize the negro as worthy of association with us; neither will we submit to any association with them in any manner whatsoever." Some white labor leaders believed that black workers were naïve dupes of the mining company and expressed the hope that once they realized how bad conditions were at the OIC mines they would leave. In fact, leaving was almost impossible for most of the imported miners who were too poor to return home and who, in any case, were closely monitored by OIC guards told to prevent their escape.

Regardless, most black replacement workers had rational reasons for staying. "Part of the reason was economic self interest," labor historian Robert A. Campbell wrote. "They were trying to earn a living, support their families and live a respectable life in a society that did its best to perpetuate their former status as slaves. Their opportunities were limited and they had to take advantage of those that were available." If white workers demanded class solidarity from their marginalized black peers, they proved incapable of maintaining it themselves. White miners started returning to their jobs by late June. In any case, the Knights' virulent racism had fatally undermined their cause and allowed the OIC to split the work force along racial lines.

Black Colonies in Oklahoma

In 1889, when the United States government opened up much of the Indian Territory in present-day Oklahoma to non-Native American settlers, thousands of African Americans participated in the land rush. For a time the federal government split the future state into separate Oklahoma and Indian territories, and a land rush commenced in both sections. These colonists joined blacks who had once been or were descended from slaves brought to the territory by the "Five Civilized Tribes"—slave-owning Indians forced to migrate West from Georgia and nearby states in the 1830s. African Americans frequently merged their land claims and created all-black towns. Nearly 40,000 African Americans lived in the Indian Territory by 1900. Once there, African Americans built churches, school systems, businesses, and local governments.

African-American "boosters" promoted many of these colonies. E.P. McCabe, an African-American Republican politician from Kansas, founded the town of Langston and used his newspaper, the *Langston Herald*, to promote black migration from the former Confederacy to the Indian Territory, which he portrayed as a black promised land. "What will you be if you stay in the South?" he asked in one editorial. "Slaves liable to be killed at any time and never treated right; but if you come to Oklahoma you have equal chances with the white man, free and independent. Why do southern whites always run down Oklahoma and try to keep the Negroes from coming here? Because they want to keep them there and live off their labor. White people are coming here every day."

Rumors spread that McCabe planned on creating an all-black territory and hoped he would be appointed its governor. McCabe also supposedly planned for Oklahoma to become the first all-black state. Panicked whites and Native Americans warned of the dangers that would be posed by such "Negro supremacy." Ultimately, President Benjamin Harrison decided not to appoint McCabe territorial governor. Black immigration to the territory slowed dramatically because the financial hardships of relocation proved too steep for most African-American families. McCabe focused then on the economic development of the Twin Territories' all-black towns.

Gary O. Carney, a chronicler of these communities, said various motives spurred immigrants to settle in the all-black towns. "Some blacks wanted to live with people of their own race, which gave them a sense of security in a new homeland," he wrote. "Others saw the black towns as an opportunity to control their own destiny, politically and economically, without interference from whites. Many viewed the towns as a safe haven from groups such as the Ku Klux Klan." These communities quickly declined after Oklahoma statehood in 1907. McCabe departed Oklahoma the following year and resettled in Chicago, living the rest of his life, as Carney observes, in obscurity. As of the 1990 census, thirteen of these towns still existed.

THE RESERVATION ERA

As white, Chinese, Mexican, and African-American men and women followed the railroads and staked a new life in the West, those immigrant-bearing trains brought death and destruction to the Native Americans living along the path. Sensing the danger that railroads presented to their future, Sioux and Cheyenne warriors attacked rail line workers and tore up track laid by the Union Pacific line in the late 1860s. Indians were expelled from their remaining homelands and herded onto reservations. The snake-like expansion of white-owned railroads, mines, farms, and cattle herds in the West also meant less land and less freedom for Native Americans who moved to cramped, inadequate reservations.

Many whites doubted if Indians could ever be incorporated into white society and concluded that they represented an obstacle to Anglo wealth and progress. Some white newspapers and politicians openly called for Indian extermination. Civil War General Philip Sheridan famously declared that the "only good Indian was a dead Indian." Sheridan was hardly alone in his sentiments. The *New York Herald* declared that for the Indian the drawing of blood was "as much of a passion as it is to the tiger, or the shark, who has no possibilities of civilization, and whose fate must be extermination . . ." Even as the *Herald* declared the Indian doomed, however, the newspaper preferred the more passive approach of penning Native Americans in overcrowded, disease-ravaged reservations, hoping that nature would provide a "final solution" to the Indian problem.

Toward this end, the **Medicine Lodge Treaty of 1867** assigned reservations in the Dakota Territory to Arapaho, Cheyennes, Comanches, Apaches, and Kiowas, squeezing these peoples together with already imprisoned Bannocks, Navajos, Shoshones, and Sioux. Eventually more than 100,000 people scrabbled for existence on bleak, shrinking lands. These different Indian nations battled over dwindling resources. At the same time, corrupt **Bureau of Indian Affairs** officials routinely stole government aid meant for the Indians. This embezzlement reduced Indian food supplies, thus promoting malnutrition, disease, and widespread depression on the reservations.

The so-called "reservation period" of Anglo-Indian relations lasted roughly from 1867 to 1887. Well-meaning liberals, ignoring the diversity and complexity of Indian culture, hoped that the reservations would provide an atmosphere in which "primitive" migratory Indians could be converted into stationary, law-abiding wards of a white republic. Helen Hunt Jackson wrote a heartbreaking 1881 bestseller, *A Century of Dishonor*, that detailed white brutality toward the Native population, and inspired many readers to call for reform in Indian policy. Reformers hoped that Indians would win acceptance by whites and would rise from poverty if they could be induced to surrender their language, culture, religion, and traditions and accept white cultural norms. Reformers saw reservations as training grounds for Indian citizenship.

Tragically, for many Indians, the reservations more closely resembled a concentration camp. The Indian population, about 2.5 million at the time of first European contact in 1492, had dropped to 250,000 by 1890. This appalling death rate only accelerated at the end of the nineteenth century, a situation attributable to the food shortages and poor sanitation that prevailed in overcrowded reservations. Indians entered the reservations with their minds reeling from the loss of their homes, the pain of battling for a lost cause, the pressure of white reformers who wanted to strip away their traditions and faith, and the fear of being under constant surveillance of corrupt and abusive federal agents.

The Buffalo Massacre

The Lakota, or Sioux, in particular resisted the white invasion of the West. With the arrival of the horse, the Lakota adopted an itinerant culture of following and hunting buffalo herds. In the late nineteenth century, however, whites launched a mass slaughter of buffalo, threatening the survival of the Lakota people.

In the early nineteenth century, eyewitnesses reported that the ground literally shook when massive buffalo herds charged across the landscape. Between 30 million and 60 million buffalo roamed the land from Canada in the north to the Mexican border in the south, and east to west from Pennsylvania to California. Buffalo rapidly vanished, however, when railroad companies paid hunters armed with rifles to kill buffalo to provide meat for rail construction crews. Others sought the buffalo for their hides. After skinning the animals, they would leave the rest of the carcasses to rot in the sun. Railroad executives and mining camp managers viewed the buffalo as a nuisance, since herds sometimes charged across the tracks in front of incoming trains, knocked over telegraph poles, or wrecked storage buildings or other structures.

Railroad companies provided rifles for passengers, encouraging them to fire at the herds purely for sport, leaving the dead animals behind as the train chugged on. The newest rifles, such as the .50 caliber sharpshooters, were accurate within a range of 600 feet. Thus armed, sportsmen devastated buffalo herds. Western showman William "Buffalo Bill" Cody bragged that he had killed 4,000 buffalo in 18 months. One hunter said, "I saw buffaloes lying dead on the prairies so thick that one could hardly see the ground. A man could have walked for twenty miles upon their carcasses."

The United States Army saw the buffalo massacre as a tactic in the war against Native Americans. The army referred to the animals as the "Indian commissary." Indians ate buffalo meat, clothed themselves in buffalo hides, made their tents from buffalo skin, and used buffalo fat to make candles. Military commanders reasoned that the extermination of the buffalo would force Plains Indians to abandon their nomadic ways and accept confinement on reservations. If Indians starved to death along the way, many Army officers thought that was all for the better. "Kill every buffalo you can," one officer said. "Every buffalo dead is an Indian gone."

The Lakota and other hunting nomads began to experience hunger and had to travel over broader swaths of land in search of prey. In the 1870s, Anglo hunters killed as many as 200,000 buffalo a year. An 1883 scientific expedition found only find 200 buffalo in the Western United States. Their access to their chief food source gone, Lakotas, Oglalas, and other Plains Indians concluded the only options left to them were waging war against whites or accepting their own extinction.

Little Big Horn

One of the fiercest Indian wars pitted the United States Army against the Oglala Sioux. In 1851, the Oglala

572 / CHAPTER NINETEEN

The last scene of the last act of the Sioux War.
This print shows a Native warrior laid to rest on a scaffold with a Native seated and a horse lying on the ground beneath. To the right, in the background, wolves or coyotes have gathered.

surrendered vast lands to the United States government. Oglala leaders underestimated the number of white miners who would swamp their territory. They also did not anticipate that the U.S. Army would construct a chain of forts in the middle of their most important buffalo range along the Bozeman Trail in Wyoming. Oglala Chief Red Cloud temporarily halted the white advance, battling to an impasse with the U.S. Army in the Great Sioux War of 1865-1867. Unable to suppress Oglala resistance, the government abandoned Fort Reno, Fort Phil Kearny and Fort C.F. Smith. The Oglala burned these forts to the ground.

Under the 1868 Treaty of Fort Laramie, the federal government created the Great Sioux Reservation, located within the present state of South Dakota west of the Missouri River, but territorial disputes remained unsettled. The northern tribes pledged to allow the peaceful passage of railroads near the territory. Unfortunately, construction in the area, and the railway companies' policy of buffalo eradication, disturbed the buffalo herds that ranged farther away from the Oglala settlements. This forced the Oglala to hunt over larger territories, which brought them into conflict not just with other whites but with other Indian groups as well. Numerous small battles broke out between the Sioux and Cheyenne warriors and the Army between 1868 and 1876.

The Treaty of Fort Laramie guaranteed the Sioux the right to live and hunt within the Black Hills for "as long as the grass shall grow." That promise became unimportant to the U.S. government and white prospectors when they realized that the Black Hills contained rich gold

Sitting Bull c1881

deposits. Prospectors intruded on Sioux land, and Colonel George Armstrong Custer directed his troops to conduct a surveying mission during the summer of 1874. Custer reported to Congress that the Black Hills contained abundant veins of ore and recommended that the U.S. expel the Sioux living there. Suspicious of white activities in the area, Oglala Sioux, Cheyennes, and Arapahos formed an alliance and prepared for battle.

Federal agents commanded the Indians to return to their reservations by February 1, 1876, or face an army assault. By this point Red Cloud had stepped down as the Oglala military leader because he believed resistance was futile. Crazy Horse now led the Oglala, who fought alongside Hunkpapa Sioux under the command of Sitting Bull. Four columns of American troops arrived and the soldiers engaged in several skirmishes with local Indians and destroyed 100 Indian lodges. Army scouts detected a major Sioux encampment in a valley at a site known to white soldiers as Little Big Horn and to the Oglala as Greasy Grass.

Custer decided to divide his column into four groups and positioned three of them to prevent Indians from retreating from their settlement. He then led 225 men in a charge along the Little Big Horn River into the valley on June 25, 1876. Between 2,000 and 4,000 Cheyenne and Sioux warriors closed in on the American forces and slaughtered Custer and all his men. In militarily defeating Custer, the Oglala and their allies unintentionally handed the American government a propaganda tool that whipped up anti-Indian frenzy in white society. Reportedly upon hearing of Custer's death, **Chief Sitting Bull** remarked, "Now they will never let us rest." Custer's "Last Stand" became the battle most frequently depicted in American art. Paintings, art prints, and newspapers depicted the cavalrymen bravely fighting off an overwhelming force of near-naked savages. Custer's defeat became a public symbol of the American resolve to fight on for a just cause to the last drop of blood. The *New York Herald* quoted the commissioner of Indian Affairs as responding to the massacre with the remark, "A white man's life is worth more than an Indian's" and that, "It is not too much to say that the prevailing feeling among the public favors the policy of extermination." The U.S. Army pursued warring Indian nations until, by 1877, the Sioux leadership of Indian resistance in the Plains ended.

GERONIMO AND THE TWILIGHT OF INDIAN RESISTANCE

The western Apaches would be the last Indian peoples to surrender. Federal authorities attempted to pin Apaches down on one reservation in New Mexico and three in Arizona. In the 1870s and 1880s, Apache warrior bands rejected confinement, gained control over previously white-ruled territory, and raided ranches for cattle and other livestock. Meanwhile, a loose confederation of Cheyenne, Kiowa, Kataka and Comanche warriors joined the Arapaho in one of the bloodiest conflicts in the West, facing off against troops led by Gen. William T. Sherman in the Red River War of 1874-1875.

Years of pursuit by the American Army in the difficult desert climate, added to high casualties, eventually depleted Native American morale. Nevertheless, a decade-long series of small battles followed, with **Geronimo** leading Apache attacks on small white settlements across the hot and dry Arizona terrain. Geronimo resisted until only thirty of his once powerful warrior band survived. In September 1886, Geronimo finally capitulated, thus concluding two decades of intense warfare in the American Southwest.

Humiliation awaited Geronimo in his final years. Stripped of his right to hunt freely and needing to make a living, he became a chief attraction at the St. Louis Exposition in 1904 where he sold pictures of himself for 25 cents apiece. He also accepted an invitation to ride in President Theodore Roosevelt's 1905 inaugural parade. Depressed, Geronimo said in a newspaper interview that, "I want to go back to my old home before I die . . . Want

Geronimo, the great Apache chieftain, stands still erect and proud at the age of 70, at the St. Louis World's Fair, 1904.

574 / CHAPTER NINETEEN

to go back to the mountains again. I asked the Great White Father to allow me to go back, but he said no." The federal government had banned Apaches from returning to their traditional lands in Arizona. Instead, when Geronimo died in 1909, his remains were interred in Oklahoma.

The Dawes Severalty Act

Having stripped Indians of their land, the federal government now sought to shatter their ethnic identities. In 1887 Congress passed the **Dawes Severalty Act**, which authorized the president to distribute land to individual Indians provided they broke all ties to their tribes. The stated intent of the law was to turn hunting, nomadic Indians into small farmers and to bring them into the American economic mainstream. Nevertheless, greed played a big part in the drafting of legislation. Knowing that Plains Indians were unfamiliar with farming, white currency, and Anglo courts, and that the land they were given was poorly irrigated, sponsors of the bill realized that many of the Indian "farmers" would soon be forced to sell to speculators what had once been tribal land. The already small amount of land controlled by Indians shrank even further. In 1881, Indians controlled about 155 million acres. Just nineteen years later, in 1900, the land under Indian control had shrunk to 78 million acres.

By 1892, the Indian struggle for survival limped to an end in the Wounded Knee Massacre. Resulting from a white misunderstanding of a native religious movement with no apparent warlike intentions, the killings summed up four centuries of dishonor that began when Columbus encountered Native Americans for the first time in the Caribbean in 1492. The Indian population hit an all-time low by 1900, dropping to 237,000, but eventually recovered. About 1.9 million Indians were counted in the 1990 census. The Indian way of life, however, had been destroyed. Reservations would become pockets of poverty, bad health, and inadequate education throughout the twentieth century and serve as symbols of infinite broken promises made by the United States government to the original inhabitants of North America.

THE POPULIST UPRISING

By the last twenty years of the nineteenth century, it had become clear that Anglos, not Indians, would dominate the politics and culture of the West. As more Anglo-owned farms sprang up in the Plains and in the Western U.S., however, droughts, freezes, hail storms, and waves of locusts battered the newcomers. Nevertheless, American farm production increased 135 percent between 1870 and 1900. These bountiful harvests backfired, however, sinking the prices farmers could expect for their crops. Farm prices steadily declined for a decade, a situation aggravated by the productivity of foreign competitors. Wheat and cotton prices dropped about 60 percent between the 1870s and 1890s.

Government policies made the farming crisis worse. During the Civil War, the federal government faced unprecedented budgetary demands. Straining to pay for the expenses of the Civil War, the federal government temporarily inflated the currency, but when so-called

Slaughtered frozen bodies of the Sioux at Wounded Knee were piled like cordwood.

"greenbacks" were withdrawn from currency after the war, farmers suffered a sharp reduction in income. During the 1880s, tens of thousands of farmers formed "alliances," cooperative efforts at mutual aid and lobbying for political reform. As the movement grew, the farmers consolidated into two regional alliances, the Northwestern Farmers Alliance, which included the old Grange states of the Midwest and the Plains states and the far more radical Southern Farmers Alliance, which began in Texas but spread as far east as the Carolinas. By 1887, the Southern Alliance claimed more than 200,000 members, and just three years later it could count more than 3 million adherents. The Southern Alliance even reached across the color line, according to historian Lawrence Goodwyn, and sponsored a separate National Colored Alliance that enrolled another quarter million members.

Borrowing an idea from the Grange, the Alliance established farmers' cooperatives. Farmers sold commodities as a group instead of competing with each other in the hope that they could command higher prices. The Alliance also established country stores, which became sources of low-interest credit for Alliance members. Alliance stores and other businesses quickly opened in a dozen states, but floundered when Alliance members could not obtain credit and supplies from merchants, wholesalers, bankers and manufacturers. The Texas Exchange, an effort to create a statewide cooperative, survived only one season. After this failure, farmers concluded that reform could succeed only through political reform of the American money and credit systems.

Alliance members met in Cleburne, Texas in 1886 to draft a set of demands that called for state legislatures and the Congress to regulate railroads, outlaw land speculation, ease access to credit for farmers, and issue paper and silver currency to expand the money supply. These reforms languished, however, stymied by Democratic and Republican politicians dependent on the campaign contributions and even bribes paid by big businesses. Alliance leaders began to consider formation of a third political party as the only means to get these demands met.

Forming the People's Party

Advocates of a third party carried the day at an 1892 convention of workers and farmers in St. Louis. Forming the People's Party, candidates under this banner called for creation of the so-called **subtreasury**, which would act as a combination of government warehouse and creditor. Farmers could store nonperishable crops in government facilities until commodity prices allowed them to sell at a reasonable profit. In the meantime, farmers would receive credits from the federal government based on the amount of crops they stored, which would allow them to maximize their earnings and "get by" until the next growing season. Mainstream newspapers and powerful Republican and Democratic politicians denounced the idea as farfetched and communistic.

Populists also called for excessive land bought for speculative purposes by foreign investors and railroad companies to be seized by the government and redistributed to poor farmers. Other demands called for government ownership of the railroads and telegraph lines as a way to end overcharging. Addressing the tight money supply, the party called for the coining of silver and the printing of greenbacks. Wishing to expand their appeal beyond the farm belt, Populists also supported the eight-hour workday and the abolition of convict labor. Finally, the platform advocated laws requiring the secret ballot, the direct election of senators, and the right of referendum and recall of elected officials.

The People's Party did well for a third party, capturing more than a million votes in the 1892 presidential election, about 8.5 percent, and twenty-two votes in the Electoral College. A tragedy prevented the party from even better results. The most popular leader of the Populists, Leonidas K. Polk of the Southern Alliance, had won the party's presidential nomination but died before he could begin his campaign. A veteran of the Confederate Army, Polk had worked extensively to build the Northwestern Alliance and was well liked across regional lines. His replacement, James B. Weaver of Iowa, carried the baggage of being a former Union commander, which hurt him in the South (though the party chose a Confederate general, James G. Field of Virginia, for vice president in an attempt at regional balance). Southern Democrats also claimed that Populists would split the white vote and if they succeeded, the supposed "negro rule" of Reconstruction would return. Populists stood accused of being race traitors and of insulting the memory of the Confederate dead by supporting a Yankee officer for president. In the North, Republicans also played on regional passions, bashing Populists for voting side-by-side with former Confederates. This political exploitation of unresolved bitterness from the Civil War came to be known as "**waving the bloody shirt**." The tactic proved effective in many communities.

But what inspired more fear and rage among Southern Democrats was the willingness of Populists to form alliances with black farmers. Tom Watson, a leading Georgia Populist, argued that Democrats had kept all farmers economically powerless by playing a game of racial "divide and conquer." He promised that the Populists would "wipe out the color line." When angry white Democrats in Georgia threatened to lynch a black Populist preacher, Watson gathered 2,000 gun-toting white Populists to form a protective ring around the preacher's house.

Republicans and Democrats alike brutally oppressed the movement. In the North, Republicans turned to vote fraud, bribery and intimidation. In the South these methods were supplemented with violence, up to and including the murder of Populist leaders and supporters. Nevertheless, Populism grew even stronger as a result of a national depression that began in 1893. Both farmers and factory workers were devastated by this depression, which lasted for four years and, at its low point, left three million people, or 20 percent of the country's workforce, out of work. Hunger and suicide became rampant in parts of the country as hard times dragged on.

The 1896 Presidential Election

The People's Party fared well in the 1894 congressional elections. Populists won a half-million more voters than in 1892. With discontent turning to despair, voters seemed eager for an alternative to the Republican and Democratic parties, and the Populists looked like a serious threat in the 1896 presidential race. The tight money supply grew worse as established politicians insisted on the gold standard. The coinage of silver became a particularly popular political stand in western states where silver mines had opened. Farmers in the South and West hoped that an inflation of the money supply would ease access to credit and improve the prices farmers received for their crops. Populists pinned their hopes of victory on being the only political party advocating the coinage of silver. These hopes grew when the Republicans ignored public discontent with the status quo, nominating a rock-ribbed conservative, Ohio Senator William McKinley, for president in 1896. Throughout the campaign, McKinley remained a solid supporter of the gold standard.

Southern and western Democrats rebelled against the incumbent Democratic president, Grover Cleveland, whose economic policies were indistinguishable from McKinley's. Instead, the party nominated former Congressman **William Jennings Bryan** of Nebraska, who attracted a national following by focusing on the miseries of the farm belt and by blasting the greed of bankers and big business. In his acceptance speech at the 1896 Democratic National Convention, Bryan loudly declared his support for coining silver, telling a rapturous audience, "Having behind us the producing masses of this nation and the world, supported by the commercial interests, the laboring interests and the toilers everywhere, we will answer their demand for a gold standard by saying to them: You shall not press down upon the brow of labor this crown of thorns, you shall not crucify mankind upon a cross of gold." Bryan aimed his speech not just at the Democrats at the Chicago convention, but at the millions of Populists he hoped would join a common front with the Democrats against a still solidly pro-business Republican Party.

Even though ten Populist governors had been elected and forty-five party candidates won seats in the U.S. Congress during a four-year period, the Populist leadership grew impatient with the third-party strategy and concluded that they should back Bryan's campaign. As a result, the People's Party also nominated Bryan for president, although they replaced Bryan's Democratic

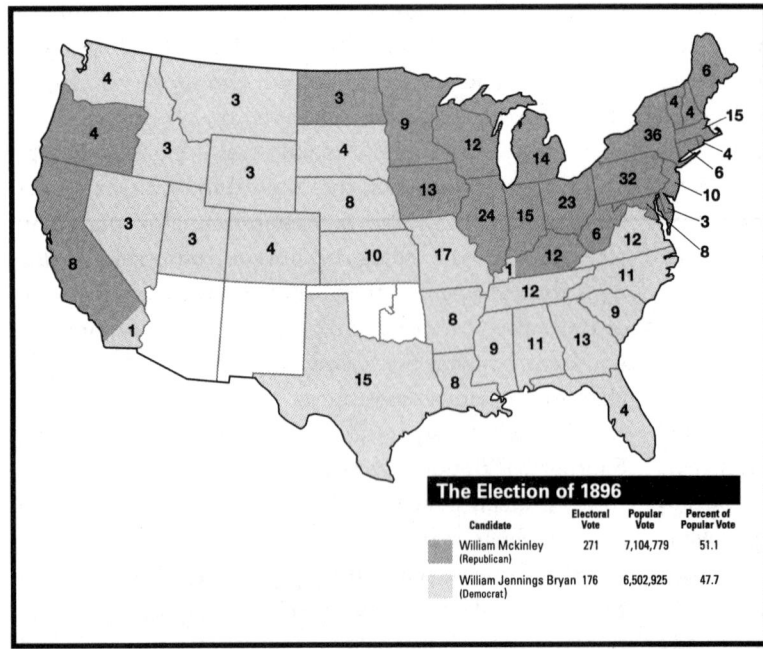

Map 19.4 The Election of 1896

running mate, economic conservative Arthur Sewell, with former Congressman Tom Watson, as the vice presidential candidate. In spite of this support, Bryan's policies, however, represented pseudo-Populism at best. He embraced only the least significant part of the Populist program, the coining of silver. More substantial reforms called for by the Populists, such as access to government credit for farmers, establishment of cooperative warehouses, and government ownership of the railroads and telegraph lines, were ignored by the Democratic nominee.

Ultimately, the nomination of Bryan undermined Populism. Many southern Populists could not swallow supporting the Democratic presidential candidate when so many had been the target of Democratic fraud and violence in the 1892 and 1894 elections. Support for the **Populist Party** dropped sharply in the South. Nevertheless, even though McKinley raised an unprecedented $4 million in campaign contributions from corporate interests (more than twice the amount raised by any previous presidential candidate), the election proved to be surprisingly close.

For his part, Bryan had only his eloquence and his tirelessness as he crisscrossed the country, delivering more than 600 speeches that reached 5 million voters in the three months after the convention. In spite of their reservations, many Southerners backed Bryan, and the Nebraskan did well in the silver-rich West. The heavily populated Northeast backed McKinley. In numerous states, the winner claimed victory by 1,000 votes or less. Several factors hampered Bryan. An improvement in the economy just before the election made many voters reluctant to back a candidate widely perceived as radical and, as in past elections, Republicans north of the Mason Dixon line padded their vote total through deceit. Southern voters supportive of the Democrats also suffered confusion since Bryan's name appeared on the ballot twice, once as a Democrat and once as a Populist, and he was paired with two different running mates. In the end, McKinley carried twenty-three states to Bryan's twenty-two, even though the Electoral College gave the Republican a comfortable 271-176 margin.

The Collapse of Populism

"**Fusion**"—joining forces with the Democrats—proved a disaster for the People's Party, which won less than 300,000 votes nationwide, more than a million less than they polled in the 1894 off-year elections. In their clamor to support the Democrat Bryan, Populists had lost their separate identity. With an improved economy, Southern whites returned to the party of their fathers, the Democrats. The People's Party straggled on for years, a shell of its former self. The party withered and with it the agrarian revolt that had dominated politics in the 1880s and 1890s.

Although forward-looking ideas animated much of Populism, the movement featured an unpleasant underside. The agrarian rebels rigorously maintained segregation in their movement even though black support was critical to southern populism. The racial cooperation that white Populists sought was, with few exceptions, self-centered and based on claims that, as farmers, whites and blacks faced the same hardships. Populists never directly addressed the difficulties that uniquely faced black farmers, such as segregation, racism, and the constant threat of racial violence. Yet, even the limited white-black cooperation in the southern Populist movement, whether it was opportunistic or idealistic, threatened white elites. In Populism's aftermath the politically powerful would incite lynch mobs to kill hundreds of African Americans. State constitutions were rewritten to take the vote away from not only blacks, but also poor whites who might become African Americans' political allies.

THE REAL AND MYTHIC WEST

Even before a more realistic view of the West faded from public discussion, a mythical West filled the American imagination. The violent business of forcing Native Americans into reservations, the environmental disaster of Western mining, and the corruption and greed that spurred the development of the railroads gave way to more inspiring legends. The West that captured first American and then worldwide audiences starred lonely cowboys wistfully following cattle trails, brave cavalrymen battling villainous Indians, sheriffs in white hats hunting down bad men wearing black, and bad men with hearts of gold putting the greedy and politically corrupt rich in their place. Such stories became a mainstay of the dime novel, the forerunner of the 20th century's mass-market paperback. These widely read books turned Billy the Kid, Wild Bill Hickok, Butch Cassidy and the Sundance Kid, and Calamity Jane into household names and fed urban children and adults with dreams of life in the wide-open spaces.

Immortalized as well in the paintings of Frederic Remington, the mythic West became flesh and blood in the late 19th century with William F. "Buffalo Bill" Cody's "Wild West" shows. Cody first starred in the dime novels written by Edward Judson (under the pen name of "Ned Buntline") in which Buffalo Bill saved damsels in distress, and beat bad men and Indians with his quick draw and flawless aim. Cody's shows starred famous Native Americans like Sitting Bull, rope twirlers

Joseph, Chief of the Nez Percé

Hin-mah-too-yah-lat-kekt, which means "Thunder Rolling Down the Mountain"

The Nez Percé Indians were a small tribe living peacefully in the beautiful Wallowa Valley of Oregon, a fertile area of mountain forests, meadows, winding rivers, and a pure blue lake. Earlier in their history, when the half-starved and illness-weakened Lewis and Clark expedition entered their territory, they had welcomed the whites, supplied them with food, and looked after their horses. In seventy years of contact, they had never killed a white settler. In the 1850s, the Christian, "progressive" branch of the tribe agreed to turn over large tracts of mineral-rich land to the federal government. They accepted the white man's offer to live on a large reservation set aside for them in Idaho. In 1863, the discovery of gold greatly diminished this reservation. But the larger group under its leader, the dignified and statesman-like Chief Joseph, refused to sign any treaty giving up more land. Joseph reflected the views of most Native Americans when he declared: "The earth was created by the assistance of the sun, and it should be left as it was....The country was made without lines of demarcation, and it is no man's business to divide it." While most whites saw the land and its resources as there to be exploited, Native Americans believed that people were a part of nature, not its master. Chief Joseph affirmed, "The earth and myself are of one mind. The measure of the land and the measure of our bodies are the same." Like other Indians, he felt that land could be used but could no more be owned than the air all people breathed.

An advocate of peaceful coexistence with whites, Joseph and his tribe were able to survive on their little piece of paradise until the 1870s. White settlers began to covet this prime area. They pressured the government into forcing the rest of the Nez Percé onto the Idaho reservation in 1877. With a heavy heart, Joseph convinced his people that resistance was futile, and they began their long journey from the land they loved to the reservation. On the way, however, some of the younger hot-heads in the tribe, fortified by alcohol and angry at their plight, killed four white settlers.

Joseph understood that retribution would be swift and terrible. He persuaded his people to flee with him, hoping to gain sanctuary in Canada where many Sioux Indians had received refuge. At the battle of White Bird Canyon, he was able to drive off the pursuing American troops. Then the Nez Percé scattered in many directions. Joseph led the largest group of 200 men and 350 women, children, and old people. A remarkable chase followed through Idaho and Montana. The Nez Percé traveled east through Yellowstone Park where they frightened some of the astonished tourists and almost encountered General Sherman fishing in the area. Then they headed north. The weary band of Indians covered 1,321 miles in 75 days, hunted by some 5,000 embarrassed government troops. Fascinated readers of Eastern newspapers, uniformly sympathetic to the underdog Indians, eagerly followed each day's story. (Native Americans had long since been eliminated there, so Easterners could far more easily feel tolerance toward the Indian.) The embarrassed generals explained their ineptitude by dubbing Joseph, "the red Napoleon."

The army regiments finally caught up with the Nez Percé within sight of the Canadian border. Some bands of resolute warriors were able to slip across the border where Sitting Bull in his Sioux Canadian village welcomed them. But Joseph and most of his tribe surrendered, exhausted, freezing, and broken hearted. Of the four hundred Nez Percé left, only eighty-seven were fighting men. General Nelson Miles, who greatly admired Joseph's efforts for his people, agreed to allow the band to return to the Idaho reservation. After meeting with the general, Joseph declared, "Hear me, my chiefs. I am tired; my heart is sick and sad. From where the sun now stands, I will fight no more forever." Then, the chief swept his blanket across his face as a symbol of mourning and surrendered. It had cost almost $2 million to vanquish Joseph and his followers.

The American government reneged on the promise General Miles had made to the Nez Percé. Rather than sending them to the Idaho reservation, it moved them from one desolate place to another, finally settling them in a flatlands reservation in Oklahoma. Many died from malnutrition and disease, including Joseph's six children. In 1885, the government transferred the survivors to a reservation near Spokane, Washington, where their descendants remain to this day. Chief Joseph puzzled Buffalo Bill Cody when he joined the "Wild West" shows. The chief was willing to repeat his famous speeches, but he always refused to don war paint and re-enact the end of his people's quest. He died in 1904. The Indian agency physician listed the cause of death as "a broken heart."

and trick shooters such as Annie Oakley (Phoebe Butler), who could shoot a small coin out of her husband's hand at a distance. Cody's show crisscrossed America and Europe for three decades, bringing the thrill of the Imaginary West to generations. Beginning in the early 20th century, city slickers who wanted a more "real" experience than sitting in the audience for a stage show began traveling West for vacations at "dude ranches" where they could enjoyed a simulated life as a cowboy.

The invention of the motion picture camera came in the 1890s just as the western frontier was declared "closed" by the federal government. "Westerns," set in the late 19th century, were the most popular American movie genre from the first decade of the 20th century until the 1950s, beginning with *The Great Train Robbery*, produced by inventor Thomas Edison in 1903.

In the coming decades, cowboy serials starring actors like Tom Mix, and musicals featuring singing cowboys like Roy Rogers, filled theaters. Westerns became the most popular radio and TV dramas of the 1950s and 1960s, including *Bonanza*, and encompassed one of the longest-running television programs in history, *Gunsmoke*. The imaginary West depicted in popular books, movies, and radio and TV dramas did not include African Americans, Mexicans, or Chinese workers, and women were passive audiences as courageous men stood off evil, challenging villains to gun duels. A handful of Indian characters, like Tonto in the popular *Lone Ranger* radio and TV programs, were portrayed positively, though in a subservient, patronizing light, but Indians usually served as the enemies of white progress in these cowboy melodramas.

American audiences easily confused myth with reality. American soldiers fighting in the Philippines in the late 19th and early 20th centuries, or against the Japanese in World War II, or against communist forces in Vietnam in the 1960s and 1970s, imagined themselves as the U.S. cavalry leading the charge against the "redskins." The so-called "frontier" West became a racist fantasy, a metaphor for American invincibility and of white modernity overcoming dark savagery.

Chronology

1862	Homestead Act
	Sioux War erupts in Minnesota
1864	Sand Creek massacre of Cheyennes
1867	The Grangers founded—first national farmers' organization
	Joseph McCoy organizes cattle drives to Abilene, Kansas
	Treaty of Medicine Lodge
1869	First transcontinental railroad completed
1872	Yellowstone National Park established
1873	Giant silver strike discovered at Nevada's Comstock Lode
1874	Gold found in Black Hills of South Dakota
	Barbed wire invented
1876	Custer and his troops annihilated at Little Big Horn
	Colorado admitted to the Union
1877	Chief Joseph surrenders
1881	Helen Hunt Jackson writes *A Century of Dishonor*
1880s	Buffalo herds decimated
1882	Chinese Exclusion Act
1883	Buffalo Bill Cody introduces his Wild West show
1886	Droughts and blizzards on the Plains devastate cattle ranching and wheat farming
1886	Geronimo surrenders
1887	Dawes Act passed
1889	Indian territory in Oklahoma opened to settlement
	Rise of Ghost Dance religion
1890	Massacre of Sioux at Wounded Knee, South Dakota
	Sitting Bull killed
1892	Populist Party formed
1893	Frederick Jackson Turner, "The Significance of the Frontier in American History"
	Major economic depression begins
1896	McKinley defeats Bryan

Review Questions

1. How did the Civil War affect Native Americans?

2. What were the ecological consequences of economic development in the West?

3. What economic role did women and immigrants play in the West?

4. What impact did federal government policies like the Dawes Severalty Act, the creation of Indian reservations, and the slaughter of buffalo have on Native Americans?

5. What factors led to the rise and fall of the Populist Movement?

Glossary of Important People and Concepts

Abortion laws
"Billy the Kid"
"Boomers" and "Sooners"
William Jennings Bryan
Buffalo Soldiers
Bureau of Indian Affairs
"Calamity Jane"
"Buffalo Bill"
Comstock Lode
Dawes Severalty Act
Fusion
Geronimo
The Homestead Act
James-Younger Gang
Little Big Horn
Medicine Lodge Treaty of 1867
Populist Party
"Race Suicide"
Sand Creek Massacre
Sitting Bull
Subtreasury
Texas Rangers
"Waving the bloody shirt"
Wounded Knee Creek Massacre

SUGGESTED READINGS

Stephen Ambrose, *Nothing Like it in the World: The Men Who Built the Transcontinental Railroad* (2000).

Susan Armitage and Elizabeth Jameson, eds., *The Woman's West* (1987).

Monroe Lee Billington and Roger D. Hardaway. *African Americans on the Western Frontier* 1998.

Dee Brown, *Bury My Heart At Wounded Knee: An Indian History of the American West* (1970).

Willard Wesley Cochrane. *The Development of American Agriculture* 1993.

William Cronon, et. al., eds, *Under the Open Sky: Rethinking America's Western Past* (1992).

Arrell Morgan Gibson. *The American Indian: Prehistory to the Present* (1980).

Lawrence Goodwyn. *The Populist Moment: A Short History of the Agrarian Revolt in America* (1978).

William F. Holmes, *American Populism* (1994).

Reginald Horsman. *Race and Manifest Destiny: The Origins of American Racial Anglo-Saxonism* (1981).

Andrew C. Isenberg. *The Destruction of the Bison: An Environmental History, 1750-1920* (2000).

Patricia Nelson Limerick, *The Legacy of Conquest: The Unbroken Past of the American West* (1987).

Frederick Merck. *History of the Westward Movement* (1978)

James C. Mohr. *Abortion in America: The Origins and Evolution of National Policy, 1800-1900* (1978).

David Montejano. *Anglos and Mexicans in the Making of Texas, 1836-1986* (1987).

Joane Nagel. *American Indian Ethnic Renewal: Red Power and the Resurgence of Identity and Culture* (1997).

Jay Robert Nash. *Encyclopedia of Western Lawmen and Outlaws* (1992).

Michael J. Pfeiffer. "Race and Lynching in the American West in the Early Twentieth Century" (2001).

Robert J. Rosenbaum. *Mexicano Resistance in the Southwest: "The Sacred Right of Self-Preservation"* (1981).

Richard Slotkin. *The Fatal Environment: The Myth of the Frontier in the Age of Industrialization, 1800-1890* (1985).

Ronald Takaki. *The Indispensable Enemy: Labor and the Anti-Chinese Movement in California* (1971).

___, *Iron Cages: Race and Culture in American Culture* (1978).

Samuel Truett. *Fugitive Landscapes: The Forgotten History of the U.S.-Mexican Borderlands* (2006).

Robert M. Utley. *Billy the Kid: A Short and Violent Life* (1989).

James Diego Vigil. *From Indians to Chicanos: the Dynamics of Mexican American Culture* (1980).

James Wilson. *The Earth Shall Weep: A History of Native America* (1998).

Ronald Wright. *Stolen Continents: 500 Years of Conquest and Resistance in the Americas* (1992).

THEODORE ROOSEVELT

Chapter Twenty

THE IMPERIAL REPUBLIC

In January 1899, the United States Senate was locked in an intense debate over whether to ratify the Treaty of Paris, officially ending the recent war with Spain, allegedly fought for the liberation of Cuba. While the politicians argued, thousands of United States soldiers, half-way around the world, were engaged in a vicious, brutal guerrilla war against Filipino rebels, wanting the same thing their Cuban counterparts had longed for—independence. Unfortunately for both groups, neither would receive their independence for decades to come. Both countries became the victims of eventual U.S. colonialism. Ironically, only a few weeks before, Americans and Filipinos had been allies, together defeating the Spanish to liberate the Philippines. The American fleet under Admiral George Dewey had destroyed the Spanish naval squadron in Manila Bay on May 1, 1898. Three weeks later, a U.S. warship brought from exile the Filipino insurrectionary Emilio Aguinaldo to lead rebel forces on land while the United States' gunboats patrolled the seas.

At first, the Filipinos believed the Americans to be their liberators. Although U.S. intentions were never clear, Aguinaldo believed, like his Cuban counterparts, that the Americans had no imperial ambitions; their purpose was pure and altruistic—to help liberate an oppressed people. They would simply drive the Spanish out and then leave the Philippines to the self-determination of the Filipino people. In June, Aguinaldo declared Philippine independence and began setting up a constitutional government. U.S. officials completely discounted the independence ceremonies. When an armistice ended the war in August, American troops denied Aguinaldo's Filipino soldiers an opportunity to liberate their own capital city and shunted them off to the suburbs. The armistice agreement recognized American rights to the "harbor, city, and bay of manila," while the proposed Treaty of Paris gave the United States the entire Philippine Islands archipelago.

When news of the U.S. "acquisition" of the islands reached Filipinos, they protested in the streets of Manila and elsewhere. This was not what they believed would happen. They now viewed Americans, especially the troops stationed there, as an army of occupation, which, in effect, it was. Tensions between American and Filipino soldiers escalated to the point that the streets of Manila became a war zone as both sides dug trenches spanning 14 miles through the city. Taunts, obscenities, and racial epithets were shouted across the neutral zone. Barroom skirmishes and knife fights between the soldiers became "normal" occurrences. American soldiers wantonly searched houses without warrants and looted stores. Their behavior was completely unjustified and deplorable.

On the night of February 4, 1899, Privates William Grayson and William Miller of Company B, 1st Nebraska Volunteers were on patrol in Santa Mesa, a Manila suburb surrounded on three sides by insurgent trenches. The Americans had orders to shoot any Filipino soldiers who were in the neutral area. As the two Americans cautiously worked their way to a bridge over the San Juan River, they heard a Filipino signal whistle, answered by another. Then a red lantern flashed from a nearby blockhouse. The two froze as four Filipinos emerged from the darkness on the road ahead. "Halt!" Grayson shouted. The native lieutenant in charge answered "Halto!"— either mockingly or because he had similar orders. Standing less than fifteen feet apart, the two men repeated their commands. After a moment's hesitation, Grayson fired, killing his Filipino "ally" with one bullet. As the other Filipinos jumped out at them, Grayson and Miller "opened up" and shot two more. As they fired at the Filipinos, Grayson exulted that he shot *"my first nigger."* While three Filipino soldiers laid dying in the streets of their own city, killed by men supposedly their friends and comrades-in-arms, Grayson and Miller ran back to their own lines shouting warnings of attack. Within minutes of Grayson's and Miller's return, the Filipinos retaliated, launching a full-scale attack in revenge for the murder of their cohorts.

The next day, Commodore Dewey cabled Washington that the "insurgents have inaugurated general engagement" and promised a quick and decisive suppression of the insurrection. The outbreak of hostilities ended the Senate debates, which had up to this point favored the rejection of the treaty for its obvious imperialist ramifications. But now, with the beginning of a full-fledged revolt against U.S. subjugations, those senators who were wavering voted to support the treaty for they could not vote against it while American soldiers were so engaged. On February 6, 1899, the Senate ratified the Treaty of Paris, thus formally annexing the Philippines and sparking a war between the United States and Aguinaldo's Filipino revolutionaries who represented a small percentage of the population.

Filipino nationalists attempted to undermine the American will through hit-and-run tactics. American soldiers, meanwhile, remained in heavily garrisoned cities and undertook search-and-destroy missions to root out rebels and pacify the countryside. The Filipino-American War lasted until 1902, three years longer than the Spanish-American War that caused it and involved far more troops, casualties, and monetary and moral costs. The United States won its first encounter with a nationalist uprising fought by guerrillas.

AMERICA'S QUEST FOR EMPIRE 1880-1900

The United States had been an expansionist nation since its inception. At the heart of this impulse was an exuberant faith in the democratic creed: Anglo-Americans were a chosen race, and their appointed mission was to extend the area of "freedom." Late-nineteenth-century imperialists resurrected Manifest Destiny and applied its basic tenets to justify the United States' need to expand beyond the confines of the North American continent in pursuit of an empire. By the end of the century, American hegemony was established in the Western Hemisphere, as well as in the Pacific Rim. Motivating many Americans to engage in an aggressive, acquisitive foreign policy was the desire to see the United States take its rightful place among the world's great powers, many of whom were themselves intensely involved in drives for empire (most notably England, France, Germany, and Japan) to either expand their existing dominions or, as in the case of Germany and the United States, to "join the imperialist club." By the end of the century, the drive for empire among the great powers, which will include the United States, brought much of the underdeveloped world under the control of the Western industrial nations.

Voices for Expansion

Several different groups helped to promote American imperialism. One of the earliest and most vociferous were Protestant missionaries. Integration of the world economy made evangelical Protestants, like most Americans, more conscious of the diversity of the world's peoples. Overseas missionary activity intensified between 1870 and 1900, most of it directed toward China, which saw increasing numbers of Western, including American missionaries, penetrate that nation in an attempt to convert the Chinese to Christianity. Convinced of their superiority, Anglo-Saxon Americans and Englishmen considered it their Christian duty to teach the Gospel to the "ignorant" Asian masses and save their souls. Missionaries also believed that their proselytizing would help to "civilize" and "uplift" an inferior people, who resembled the immigrant masses at home whom they were also trying to "redeem." Thus, American imperialism—as well England's—imbued a sense of righteous duty incumbent upon civilized Christian nations to bring "enlightenment" and "freedom" to the "heathen" and supposedly save them from themselves.

American industrial capitalists and investors also played key roles in promoting overseas expansion, hoping to increase business profits and their personal fortunes in foreign lands. The Asian market was especially alluring to such men, who believed that China, with its 400 million people, was a potential "gold mine" of opportunity. By the late 1880s, James B. Duke, head of American Tobacco, was selling one billion cigarettes a year in East Asian markets. Looking for ways to fill boxcars for his Northern Pacific Railroad, heading west from Minnesota to Tacoma, Washington, J. J. Hill wanted to load them with wheat and steel destined for China and Japan. He actually published and distributed wheat cookbooks throughout East Asia, trying to convince the people there to change their diets and eat less rice and more bread, which he believed would make them healthier. Although export trade with East Asia during this period never fulfilled Hill's or others' expectations, their promotion of Asia as a source of great potential markets for the United States convinced many politicians and imperialists that this part of the world was important to the national well-being.

The economic crises of the 1890s also intensified the clamor for foreign markets. The capitalists' agitation for material expansion was reinforced ideologically by one of the most important historical theories ever promulgated within the confines of American academic and intellectual circles: Frederick Jackson **Turner's "frontier thesis."** By 1890, that year's census revealed the United States had completed the task of internal westward movement. In 1893, Turner, an assistant professor of history at the University of Wisconsin, published his seminal essay, "The Significance of the Frontier in American History," that articulated what many of Turner's fellow citizens feared: that the frontier had been essential to the nation's economic growth and to the cultivation of democracy. It had provided (white) Americans, filled with wanderlust, an opportunity to own land, which was once in abundance. The fact that land was in such plentiful supply helped to relieve the nation of potential social unrest born of class tensions created by economic inequities. Simply put, as long as there was the frontier, Americans could escape the congested cities and wretched factories and start anew somewhere in the West on their own land. It was in the wilderness, Turner argued, that the American identity was born because that environment forced Europeans coming to the New World to transform themselves into different human beings if they hoped to survive and "make it." As they adapted to the wilderness, the Europeans slowly but steadily shed all their Old World customs, habits, and beliefs and over the decades acquired uniquely American characteristics—rugged individualism, egalitarianism, and a democratic faith. Now that the frontier was allegedly "closed," Turner and others wondered if the United States could continue to prosper and provide its citizens with the stability and security that had long been the hallmarks of its historical development?

In recent years, historians of the American West have disavowed Turner's thesis, arguing that the very idea of the frontier as uninhabited wilderness negates the fact that Native Americans had lived in the West for thousands of years. They also asserted that today and even in Turner's time much of what Americans believed about the West had been highly romanticized and distorted: more myth than reality. Contrary to what Turner claimed, the West was still a very undeveloped region by the 1890s and thus provided Americans with ample opportunity to exploit for their own aggrandizement. It was not until the 1930s and after World War II that Western resources were fully exploited and the region developed.

Even though modern historians' assessments of Western development are accurate, Turner's contemporaries expressed a fear concern about the disappearing frontier and a concern that the increasingly urbanized and industrialized nation had lost its way. Turner's essay appeared just as the country was entering the deepest, longest, and most conflict-ridden depression and decade in its history. What could the republic do to regain its economic prosperity and political stability? Where would it find its new frontiers that would save the nation from upheaval and renew the people's faith in the great democratic republican experiment? One answer to these questions came from the proponents of overseas expansion. As Senator Albert J. Beveridge of Indiana declared in 1899: "We are raising more than we can consume....We are making more than we can use. Therefore, we must find new markets for our produce, we must find new occupation for our capital, new work for our labor."

Much of the impetus for overseas expansion in the last third of the nineteenth century was mental. Old political ideas like the Monroe Doctrine were imbued with more expansionist overtones, and newer ones like manifest destiny offered spiritual sustenance for aggressive behavior. Proliferating theories of racial superiority, buttressed by science or pseudoscience, became accepted "wisdom." Regardless of class or education, the majority of WASP Americans believed their country had a special mission, sanctified by geography and race, to lead and dominate the unfit and the uncivilized peoples of the world.

The Imperialists

Eager to assist the expansionist capitalists who believed that the acquisition of overseas markets would be the panacea for the nation's economic woes were a group of politicians, intellectuals, and military strategists who viewed such expansion (the acquisition of territory) as essential for great power status. They wanted the nation to take its place alongside Britain, France, Germany, and Russia as a great imperial nation. They believed that the United States should join the intensifying competition among the major European powers for colonies; it should build a strong navy, solidify a **sphere of influence** in the Caribbean, and extend markets into Asia, just as the Europeans were doing, not only in that region of the world but in Africa and the Middle East as well. By the late nineteenth century, only two independent countries existed in Africa—Liberia on the west coast and Ethiopia in the east. The rest of the continent had been carved up by the European powers. Even tiny Belgium had a "piece of the action," controlling the resource-rich present-day nation, the Congo, while France possessed geographically the largest empire in Africa, even though most of it was desert. Watching the European superpowers carve up the world were the envious American imperialists who began agitating for the United States to get into the race for empire while "the gittin' was still good."

The imperialists resurrected the rhetoric of manifest destiny that now became consonant with imperialism. Indeed, they were now one-in-the-same. John Fiske, noted American anthropologist and imperialist, as well as a popular lecturer, toured the country giving a presentation entitled "Manifest Destiny." Fiske asserted that "The work the English race began when it colonized North America is destined to go on until every land on the earth's surface that is not already the seat of an old civilization shall become English in its language, in its religion, in its political habits and traditions, and to a predominant extent in the blood of its people."

Darwinian theory was distorted to reinforce the cult of capitalism, allowing plutocrats like Rockefeller and Carnegie a way to justify their ruthless acquisitiveness and their brutal exploitation of their workers. The imperialists also found ideological assistance from Social Darwinism to bolster their expansionist assertions. Implicit in Social Darwinism was the claim of Anglo-Saxon racial superiority. The imperialists were overwhelmingly of such ethnic and racial stock. They quickly incorporated Darwinism into their new approach to imperialism. Fiske argued that Anglo-Saxon expansion justified any conquest.

The most popular supporter of Anglo-Saxon imperialism was the Protestant evangelical, Josiah Strong, whose tribute to Anglo-Saxonism, *Our Country*, was a national best-seller in the late 1880s. In his book, Strong asserted that "the wonderful progress of the United States as well as the character of its people, are the results of natural selection." For Strong and his disciples, the Anglo-Saxon people represented civil liberty and "pure spiritual Christianity." North America was to be "the great home of the Anglo-Saxon, the principal seat of his power, the center of his life and influence." With its obvious genetic and biological superiority, the Anglo-Saxon people "will spread itself over the earth" to Mexico, to Central and South America, and "out upon the islands of the sea" to Africa and beyond.

Strong's sanctimonious boosterism and racism would be easy to dismiss as rubbish if it had not been so popular with the nation's increasingly anxious (because of immigration) Anglo-Saxon masses or if his rantings had not been embraced and articulated in the classrooms and lecture halls of some of the nation's best universities. Late nineteenth-century American academic institutions lacked today's student diversity, and those sitting in the classrooms were overwhelming young WASP males, who wholeheartedly concurred with their professors who preached white, Anglo-Saxon supremacy and the need to dominate all others to prevent the "mongrelization" of humanity. Darwin, to his chagrin, set scholars scrambling to determine racial superiority by measuring facial angles, skull size, brain weight, and even human hair. There was hardly a major university in the United States that did not include racially-based courses in its core curriculum. To the imperialists and Social Darwinists, success in international competition and conquest reflected the laws of nature. America's destiny required that it prove itself the military equal of the strongest European nations and the master of the "lesser" peoples of the world.

As the nineteenth century came to a close, the United States was a restless and racist society. Those who believed the myth of Anglo-Saxonism could ascribe inferiority to masses of people at home and abroad: African Americans, Native Americans, workers, immigrants, and most foreigners. Such a cultural atmosphere was extremely conducive to imperialist initiatives, because imperialism—like Anglo-Saxonism, Social Darwinism, and manifest destiny—was also based on the principle of racial inequality.

Admiral Alfred Thayer Mahan and the Rise of American Militarism

Perhaps the most influential imperialist was Admiral **Alfred Thayer Mahan**, whose seminal work, *The Influence of Sea Power on History, 1660-1783* (1890), laid out the blue-print for the nation's first, most significant peacetime military buildup. In his book, Mahan argued that all the world's great empires, beginning with Rome, sustained their hegemony by controlling the seas. If the United States hoped to attain great power status, it was imperative that it embark immediately on an aggressive expansion and modernization of its navy, with enough ships and fire-power to make its presence felt everywhere in the world. Ironically, during the Civil War, the United States possessed one of the world's largest navies; by the 1880s the United States ranked twelfth behind sleeping China, decrepit Turkey, and tiny Chile. To be effective, that global fleet would require a canal across Central America through which U.S. warships could pass swiftly from the Atlantic to the Pacific Oceans. It would also demand a string of service bases from the Caribbean to the southwestern Pacific. Mahan thus urged the United States government to take possession of Hawaii and other strategically located Pacific islands with superior harbor facilities.

Presidents William McKinley and Theodore Roosevelt would eventually make almost all of Mahan's vision a reality. In the early 1890s, however, Mahan believed his ideas and exhortations were falling on deaf ears, for he was certain that few Americans were willing to bear

The inauguration of President McKinley, March 4, 1901.

the costs and responsibilities of empire. Although the imperialists counted in their ranks prominent individuals like Theodore Roosevelt and Senator Henry Cabot Lodge of Massachusetts, there were still too many Americans who insisted that the United States should not aspire to world power by emulating the Europeans by using military might and force to acquire bases and colonies. Such an approach, they believed, would not only degrade the United States, putting the nation on the same level as the Europeans, but tarnish, as well, the revered image of a country whose people were known for their sense of justice, decency, and humanity.

Mahan's skepticism quickly dissipated as the government's alarm over the Europeans' expansionist policies moved both Congress and the presidents to action. Every administration from the 1880s on committed itself to a big navy policy. By 1898, the U.S. navy had moved from twelfth to fifth in the world; by 1900 it ranked third, behind only England and Germany. Already in 1878, under the farsighted auspices of James G. Blaine, who was serving as Secretary of State for Rutherford B. Hayes, the United States secured rights to Pago Pago, a superb deepwater harbor in Samoa (a collection of islands in the southwest Pacific inhabited by Polynesians).

These attempts to project U.S. power overseas had already deepened the government's involvement in the affairs of foreign lands. For example, in 1889, four years after securing harbor rights to Pago Pago, the United States established a **protectorate** (the uniquely American term for colony) over part of Samoa, a move intended to block German and British attempts to weaken American presence and influence on the islands.

In the early 1890s, Grover Cleveland was increasingly drawn into Hawaiian affairs, as tensions between American sugar planters and native Hawaiians upset the islands' economic and political stability. By that decade, a small but powerful coterie of American sugar planters had gained economic and political control of the islands, relegating the native population to an underclass of subservients. Tensions between native Hawaiians and whites began as early as the 1820s when American missionaries arrived to try to convert the islanders to Christianity. In the process they began buying up huge parcels of land and to subvert the existing feudal system of landholding. They simultaneously encouraged American businesses to buy into sugar plantations, and by 1875, U.S. corporations dominated the sugar trade. American capitalists, in effect, turned the islands into one vast sugar-producing economy, which they completely controlled. By this time Hawaii appeared in James G. Blaine's opinion to be "an outlying district of the state of California," and he began to push for annexation. In 1887, a new treaty allowed the United States to build a naval base at Pearl Harbor on the island of Oahu. Now, together with Pago Pago, the United States had two Pacific fueling stations for its growing naval fleet.

Emboldened by the Pearl Harbor Treaty, American sugar planters took a step further toward hopeful annexation by pressuring a weak king, Kalakaua, to sign a constitution that deprived a majority of native Hawaiians their voting rights, stripped the monarchy of numerous executive powers, and greatly increased the influence of the planter-dominated Hawaiian legislature. After Kalakaua's death in 1891, his strong-willed sister, Liliuokalani, assumed the throne. Determined not to be subservient to the planters, Queen "Lili" tried to assert her independence by drafting a new constitution that would give the monarchy veto power over the legislature and restore voting rights to disenfranchised native Hawaiians.

Wishing to maintain their dominance over the islands, the planters under the leadership of Sanford B. Dole and aided by a cadre of U.S. marines based at Pearl Harbor overthrew the queen in 1893. The planters then asked the U.S. government to formally annex the islands. In the United States, Republican congressional leaders and President Benjamin Harrison both supported annexation, but Harrison had recently been defeated in his reelection bid by Democrat Grover Cleveland and the Republicans lost control of the Senate and House of Representatives. Before assuming office, President-elect Cleveland successfully convinced Senate Democrats during the lame-duck session to stall on a proposed annexation treaty before they formally took over control of that house of Congress in the next session. After an investigation revealed the role of U.S. marines in the insurrection and that most native Hawaiians preferred the return of Queen Lili, Cleveland refused to pursue annexation any further, telling the planters to restore the queen to her throne. The planters balked at the notion, instead declaring the independence of the "Republic of Hawaii" under the presidency of Sanford Dole. In 1900, however, two years after the Spanish-American War, during Republican William McKinley's presidency, a new Senate voted to ratify a treaty annexing the islands.

By this time, imperialist sentiment in Congress and throughout the nation was being energized by "**jingoism.**" Jingoists—the word was originally coined in Great Britain in the 1870s and quickly entered American foreign policy discussion—were supernationalists (hardcore Social Darwinists as well) who believed that an aggressive, arrogant foreign policy with a willingness to go to war would enhance the nation's glory. They were constantly on the alert for insults to their country's honor and prestige and swift to call for military retaliation if so affronted. This predatory brand of nationalism emerged not only in Britain and in the United States but in France, Germany, and Japan as well. The anti-imperialist editor, E.L. Godkin, of *The Nation* exclaimed in 1894, "The number of men and officials in this country who are now mad to fight somebody is appalling." Spain's behavior in Cuba in the 1890s gave the imperialists the war they sought. The imperialists had grown up in a period of weak presidents, an exploding economy, escalating military power, rising expectations, and disappointing performance. Now the time for action was fast approaching, and they would seize it.

THE SPANISH-AMERICAN WAR

By the 1890s the islands of Cuba and Puerto Rico were virtually all that remained of Spain's once vast New World empire. Ever since the late 1860s the Cubans had been in a constant state of revolt against Spanish rule. Though ultimately suppressing the early uprisings, by the late 1890s, the Spanish were finding it increasingly more difficult to subdue the Cuban rebels, whose numbers were growing each year. Helping to ignite the 1895 insurrection was a tariff passed by the United States a year earlier that made sugar, Cuba's main export, too expensive for the U.S. market. The tariff caused economic contraction, which in turn only intensified Cubans' resentment toward their Spanish rulers, even though they had not caused the depression. The fighting between Spanish soldiers and Cuban rebels was brutal, as both sides often committed unspeakable atrocities. The rebels razed large areas of the island, not only destroying tobacco and sugar crops but making it uninhabitable as well. The Spanish army retaliated, responding in kind on the orders of General Valeriano Weyler, who rounded up thousands of Cubans and relocated them into concentration camps where they were horribly mistreated, causing thousands to die. Indeed, an estimated 200,000 Cubans—one-eighth of the island's population—died of starvation and disease.

Such reprisals, especially those attributed to "Butcher" Weyler (as he was now being labeled in the U.S. press), inflamed American public opinion. Many Americans sympathized with the Cubans, whom they believed were fighting the same anticolonial war they themselves had waged over 100 years earlier. The American public was kept well-apprised of events in Cuba, especially in the newspapers published by either William Randolph Hearst or Joseph Pulitzer, who together owned the majority of the nation's largest dailies. Pulitzer and Hearst were revolutionizing American journalism in the late nineteenth century by creating a new kind of newspaper, which catered openly to a readership of lower socioeconomic status than those citizens who read the more traditional press. They created the first tabloids, which today can be seen in every supermarket check-out stand around the nation. Like today's *National Enquirer*, Hearst's and Pulitzer's papers specialized in lurid, sensational news; when such news did not exist, editors were not above making it up. All such presentation was designed to boost circulation, which meant more money for Hearst and Pulitzer. By the 1890s, both men were engaged in a ruthless circulation war, and they saw the struggle in Cuba as a great opportunity. Both sent hordes of reporters and illustrators to the island with orders to provide accounts of Spanish atrocities committed on innocent Cubans. All too frequently Hearst and Pulitzer reporters greatly exaggerated or distorted what was actually taking place in Cuba, if not blatantly fabricating stories to please their greedy publishers. They were accused by the legitimate press of engaging in "**yellow journalism**"—embellishing stories with titillating details when the true reports did not seem dramatic enough. "You furnish the pictures," Hearst supposedly told an overly scrupulous artist, "and I'll furnish the war."

Helping the jingoists and interventionists agitate the American public were the thousands of Cuban émigrés in the United States living primarily in the cities of Miami, Philadelphia, New York, and Trenton, New Jersey. These Cubans Americans gave extensive support to the Cuban Revolutionary Party, headquartered in New York, and helped to make its slain leader, Jose Marti, a "freedom-fighting" hero and martyr in the eyes of many sympathetic but duped Americans. With the financial backing of prominent American capitalists, Cuban Americans formed other clubs and associations to support the cause of *Cuba Libre*. In some areas of the country, the émigrés' activities and solicitations were more important in garnering popular support for U.S. intervention in Cuba than the falsehoods circulated by the yellow journalists.

The increasing public outcry against alleged Spanish brutality and imperialist agitation for U.S. intervention in Cuba failed to move President Grover Cleveland to action. He proclaimed American neutrality and urged New York City officials to muzzle Cuban émigrés there who were trying to rally New Yorkers to the cause of Cuban independence. Cleveland's Republican successor, William McKinley, elected in 1896, appeared more amenable to the jingoists' and imperialists' cries for intervention in Cuba. Soon after taking office, McKinley formally protested Spain's uncivilized and inhuman behavior, causing the Spanish government (which was growing more fearful of American intervention) to recall Weyler, significantly modify its relocation policy, and grant Cubans limited autonomy. At the end of 1897, because of the concessions granted by the Spanish, the insurrection abated and for the moment it seemed that U.S. intervention might be averted. The jingoists and imperialists naturally believed that it was their "saber rattling" that had caused Spain to capitulate and modify their Cuban policy. To a degree they were correct; the Spanish government wanted to avoid a war with the United States at all costs—a war Spain knew it could not win.

Unfortunately, the events of February 1898 mitigated the chances for a peaceful settlement. The first crisis occurred with the publication in American papers of the **de Lôme letter**, a communiqué written by the Spanish minister in Washington, Enrique Dupuy de Lôme, that had been stolen by a Cuban agent in Havana and found its way into U. S. dailies. In this private correspondence, de Lôme described McKinley as a weak man and "a bidder for the admiration of the crowd." Interestingly, many Americans felt the same way about the president, including Assistant Secretary of the Navy Theodore Roosevelt, who privately declared that McKinley had "no more backbone than a chocolate éclair." Americans accepted as part of partisan politics the right of citizens to openly criticize their president. But no foreigner was allowed such freedom, and if one had the audacity to do so, they would quickly incur the wrath of the American public. Such was the situation for Enrique de Lôme, who promptly resigned after reading his comments in American newspapers.

While anger over the de Lôme letter was still high, the U.S. battleship *Maine* blew up in Havana harbor, causing the death of 260 sailors. McKinley had recently sent the *Maine* to Cuba to protect American citizens and property after a riot by Spanish soldiers engulfed Havana. Upon hearing that General Weyler had been removed by Spanish authorities seeking to appease critics of the military's reconcentration policy, troops loyal to the commander undertook a rampage that killed and hurt many Cubans, destroyed Cuban property, and threatened many Americans living in the city. No sooner did the *Maine* explode than the jingoists and imperialists screamed for revenge and retribution, certain that the Spanish had sunk the warship. Helping their view, a rushed U.S. Navy inquiry board declared (inaccurately) that an external explosion, probably caused by a mine, had caused the disaster. Later evidence has shown that the incident occurred as a result of an accidental explosion in the gunpowder magazine, probably triggered by an undetected fire in the coal bunker. By poor ship design, the bunker was situated too

The battleship *Maine* in Havana Harbor, February 1898.

closely to the magazine, only separated by a bulkhead that did not prevent enough heat from transferring to the magazine and igniting the gunpowder." Regardless of the true cause, at the time, sufficient numbers of Americans were convinced it was the dastardly act of the evil Spanish, and thus war hysteria swept the land and Congress, responding to the public clamor for retaliation, unanimously appropriated $50 million for military preparations. "Remember the *Maine*" became the new Anglo-American mantra for revenge against the Spanish.

McKinley still hoped to avoid a conflict; others in his administration, including Theodore Roosevelt, clamored for war. In March 1898, the president notified the Spanish government of his conditions for avoiding war: Spain would pay an indemnity for the *Maine,* abandon its concentration camp policy, end the fighting with the rebels, and commit itself to Cuban independence. On April 9, Spain agreed to all the demands but one—Cuban independence. Though McKinley was inclined to accept Spain's bid for peace, the jingoist and imperialist pressures from within his own administration, as well as from the general public, proved too great for him to withstand. Jingoist and imperialist propaganda had been successful in whipping the American public into a war frenzy; nothing short of a violent display of new American power would satisfy the American people. Moreover, the nation's new war machines, especially the navy, had been modernized at great expense, and now the opportunity presented itself to see whether it was sufficient enough to earn the United States the respect it deserved as a great power. In short, the imperialists believed it was essential for the U.S. to go to war. If Spain simply acquiesced to American demands then the nation would not have the opportunity to demonstrate its awesome military power. There was no better way to show the other great powers that the United States had arrived militarily and economically than to unleash upon another country its new war machines and in a brief, decisive war earn an empire. Thus, on April 11, 1898, McKinley asked Congress for authority to go to war. Three days later Congress approved a war resolution, which included a declaration (spelled out in the **Teller Amendment**) that the United States would not use the war as an opportunity to acquire Cuba. On April 24, Spain responded with a formal declaration of war against the United States.

"A Splendid Little War"

Secretary of State John Hay called the Spanish-American conflict "a splendid little war," a view most Americans—with the exception of the actual combatants—seemed to share. Declared in April 1898, it was over by August of that year. The war was brief largely because the Cuban rebels, after years of fighting, had significantly weakened Spanish forces on the island, thus making U.S. intervention in many respects nothing more than a "mopping up" operation. Out of the one million men who volunteered to fight, only 460 were killed in battle or died from wounds. However, 5,200 others perished from such diseases as malaria, dysentery, and typhoid. Casualties among the Cuban rebel forces who continued to bear the brunt of the fighting were much higher.

Another factor contributing to the relatively easy American victory was U.S. naval superiority. In the war's first major battle, a naval engagement in Manila harbor on May 1, 1898, in the Philippines, Spain's strategic Pacific possession, an American fleet commanded by Commodore George Dewey, destroyed an entire Spanish fleet while losing only a sailor to heat stroke. In mid-August, U.S. troops occupied the capital, Manila.

On land the story was different, as the nation went to war with a standing army of only 26,000 troops, which were scattered throughout the western United States, whose only combat experience had been skirmishing with Indians and chasing down bandits and other desperadoes. The army was ill-equipped and ill-prepared to fight an all-out war. Even though Spain was not a great power, it nevertheless was going to fight to keep the last vestiges of its once vast empire. Thus an 80,000-man strong Spanish army greeted American forces on Cuba. Congress immediately increased the army to 62,000 and called for an additional 125,000 volunteers. The response to this call was astounding but outfitting, training, and transporting the new recruits overwhelmed the army's capacities. U.S. soldiers endured serious supply problems: a shortage

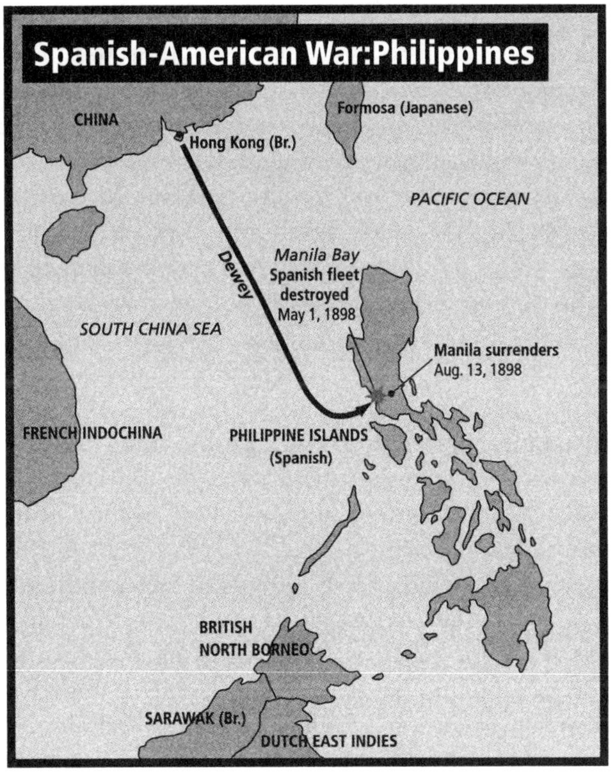

THE IMPERIAL REPUBLIC / 591

Map 20.1 Spanish-American War in the Philippines

of modern rifles and ammunition, having to wear blue flannel uniforms, totally inappropriate attire for the hot, humid Caribbean weather, inadequate medical services, and food rations so bad that many soldiers died from food poisoning. It took more than five days in June to ship an invasion force of 16,000 men the short distance from Tampa, Florida to Daiquiri, Cuba.

There were also racial conflicts. A significant number of the combatants, whether they were volunteers or regular army, were African Americans. In the regular army there were black regiments who had been stationed in the West to defend white settlements from Indian raids and were now transferred east to fight in Cuba. As the "**Buffalo Soldiers**" traveled through the South toward the training camps, they resented the rigid segregation and name-calling they were subjected to and occasionally fought back. Black soldiers in Georgia deliberately camped out in a "whites-only" park; in Florida, they beat a white soda-fountain worker who refused to serve them; in Tampa, attempted white intimidations provoked a black retaliation that resulted in a nightlong black-white confrontation that left thirty white civilians wounded.

An interesting and ironic racist taint to the war was the fact that the majority of the Cuban guerrilla fighters were black. This shocked U.S. forces because they believed the Cuban "freedom-fighters, fully nine-tenths of them," were white because American newspaper reports had described them as "intelligent, civilized, and democratic, possessing an Anglo-Saxon tenacity of purpose." The Spanish oppressors, by contrast, were portrayed as dark complexioned—"dark, cruel eyes, dark swaggering men," is how the writer Sherwood Anderson depicted them—and possessing the characteristics of their "dark race": barbarism, cruelty, and indolence. The U.S. troops' first encounters with Cuban and Spanish forces dispelled these myths. Their Cuban allies appeared poorly outfitted, rough in their manners, and primarily dark-skinned. By contrast, the Spanish soldiers were light-complexioned, appeared well-disciplined, and tougher in battle than was expected. The Cuban rebels were actually skilled guerrilla fighters, but racial prejudice prevented American soldiers and reporters from crediting their contributions to eventual victory. Instead, they judged the Cubans harshly, asserting that they were primitive, savage, and incapable of self-control or self-government. Such ascriptions went far in helping the imperialists persuade the American people that Cuba must become a U.S. protectorate, if for no other reason than to save the Cubans from themselves. During the actual fighting, the majority of the white American troops refused to associate with their black Cuban allies. They refused to fight alongside the Cubans, and increasingly they denied their allies information about Spanish movements and other strategy.

Despite the U.S. Army's ineptitude and racial prejudice, its soldiers were filled with the appropriate martial spirit, as all of them—both black and white—were eager for combat. No one was more excited about that prospect than Theodore Roosevelt, who, along with Colonel Leonard Wood, led a volunteer cavalry unit comprised of an interesting and somewhat motley crew of Ivy League gentlemen (Roosevelt's Harvard cronies), western cowboys, sheriffs, prospectors, Indians, and small numbers of Hispanics and ethnic European Americans. Roosevelt's "**Rough Riders**," as the battalion came to be known, landed with the invasion force and played an active role in the three battles fought in the hills surrounding Santiago de Cuba, the main theater of action on the island's southeastern coast. Their most famous action, the one on which TR (as Roosevelt's friends called him) would build his lifeline reputation as a warrior and hero, was a furious charge on foot, not on horse, up Kettle Hill into the heart of the Spanish defenses. Roosevelt's bravery was remarkable though his judgment was faulty. Nearly 100 men were killed or wounded in the charge. Accounts of TR's bravery overshadowed the equally, if not more courageous, performance of other troops, most notably the 9th and 10th Negro Cavalries, which played a key role in clearing away Spanish fortifications on Kettle Hill and allowing Roosevelt's Rough Riders to make the charge. One of TR's men commented: "If it had not been for the Negro cavalry, the Rough Riders would have been exterminated." Another added, "I am a Southerner by birth, and I never thought much of the colored man. But I never saw such fighting as those Tenth Cavalry men did. They didn't seem to know what fear was, and their battle hymn was 'There'll be a hot time in the old town tonight.'" The 24th and 25th Negro Infantry Regiments performed equally important tasks in the U.S. Army's taking of the adjacent San Juan Hill.

Despite prejudice, discrimination, and segregation, African-American soldiers risked their lives in proving their patriotism and courage. At the time, Roosevelt and others publicly lauded their contributions to ultimate victory. He praised his black comrades-in-arms as "an excellent breed of Yankee," and declared that no "Rough Rider will ever forget the tie that binds us to the Ninth and Tenth Cavalry." But soon after returning home, he began diminishing their role, even to the point of calling their behavior cowardly. Like most white American officers and enlisted men of the time, TR had difficulty believing blacks could fight well. By the time of U.S. entry into the Great War in 1917, the U.S. military had adopted a policy of excluding black troops from combat roles altogether. Moreover, it must be remembered that if African-American soldiers' bravery and contributions to victory were too exalted by white America, such acclaim could go far toward helping African Americans achieve equality at home—something few white Americans were ready to embrace.

By mid-July 1898, American troops were short of food, ammunition, and medical facilities. Their ranks were so decimated by malaria, typhoid, and dysentery that Roosevelt despaired, "We are within measurable distance of a terrible military disaster." Fortunately, the Spanish had lost the will to fight, realizing that to do so would cause even greater humiliation and death. As Spain's Atlantic fleet tried to retreat from Santiago harbor, the U.S. navy raked and sank their archaic fleet, killing 474 Spanish sailors. The Spanish army in Santiago surrendered on July 16. Two days later, the Spanish government asked for peace. While Spanish and U.S. officials negotiated an armistice, American forces took Puerto Rico. On August 12, the U.S. and Spanish government agreed to an armistice, but before the news reached the Philippines, the U.S. captured Manila and took 13,000 Spanish soldiers prisoner. In the ensuing formal peace settlement, finalized in the Treaty of Paris in December 1898, Spain recognized Cuban independence, ceded Puerto Rico and the Pacific island of Guam to the United States, and after receiving a payment of $20 million, the Spanish agreed to give the Philippines, as well, to the victorious United States. Americans now possessed an island empire stretching from the Caribbean to the Pacific.

THE UNITED STATES BECOMES A WORLD POWER

The United States' acquisition of the Philippines, Guam, and Puerto Rico had little, if anything, to do with the reasons the nation had gone to war. Initially, the U.S.

Future President Teddy Roosevelt leading his "Rough Riders" in Cuba during the Spanish American War in 1898.

THE IMPERIAL REPUBLIC / 593

Colonel Theodore Roosevelt of the "Rough Riders" after his return from Cuba. November 14, 1898

proclaimed to the world and to its own citizens that the Republic was going to war to help liberate the Cuban people from their brutal Spanish oppressors, and in that context, the country would be upholding its democratic creed of self-determination. For the imperialists such rhetoric was simply a ruse to disguise their real intention, which was to incorporate Cuba into a new American empire. Naïve anti-imperialists, who supported the war, believed it was to liberate the Cubans from the last decadent "remnant" of the Old World, Spain. Naturally the imperialists delighted in the Treaty of Paris, which ceded to the U.S. Guam, Puerto Rico, and the Philippines, the last viewed as essential for the projection of U.S. power in the Pacific and Asia. In the end, President McKinley was just as much an imperialist as the men who surrounded him and who were the architects of the expansionist policy and the war. McKinley annexed Hawaii, giving the U.S. permanent control of its first-rate deep-water port at Pearl Harbor. Then, he set his sights on setting up a naval base at Manila. Never before had the United States pursued such a large military presence outside the Western Hemisphere.

In a departure of even greater significance and future ramifications, the McKinley administration announced that the newly acquired territories would be regarded as colonies and governed as such. Virtually all the territory previously acquired by the United States had been settled by Americans, who eventually petitioned for statehood and were admitted to the Union with the same rights as existing states. In the case of the new possessions, only Hawaii would be allowed to follow the traditional path toward statehood, occurring largely because of the influence of the powerful American sugar planters who controlled the island and believed it best for their economic interests if Hawaii was made a territory in the traditional sense so that it could someday become a state. In 1900, Congress obliged the sugar planters by passing an act extending U.S. citizenship to all Hawaiian residents and putting the islands on the road to statehood in 1959. The story of the Philippines was quite different. There was no residing powerful American clique who desired eventual statehood status. The U.S. had little interest in the Philippines beyond controlling Manila harbor. The decision to make the whole country an American colony was proclaimed to prevent other powers, such as Japan and Germany, from gaining a foothold somewhere in

Map 20.2 Major Battles in Cuba

the 400-island archipelago and launching attacks on the American naval base at Manila.

The McKinley administration might have taken a different approach toward the Philippines had it not been for the racism that dominated much of American imperialist policy and attitudes at this time. Helping U.S. forces to defeat the Spanish in the Philippines was a broad-based indigenous rebel movement led by Emilio Aguinaldo, who, like his Cuban counterparts, looked to the United States as the liberator of his country. However, much to Aguinaldo's eventual disappointment and betrayal, the U.S. never had any intention of granting the islands their independence, which they could have done by simply brokering a deal with Aguinaldo, giving the Philippines independence in exchange for a naval base at Manila. An American fleet stationed there would have protected the islands from other aggressive imperialists, such as Japan or Germany, serving the larger interests of both the U.S. and Filipinos. Outright annexation was also an alternative, granting the Filipinos the same status as the Hawaiians and putting them on the road toward statehood. However, McKinley chose none of these possibilities. He believed, like most other imperialists, that the Filipinos were an inferior people incapable of self-government and the right of self-determination. McKinley believed that American rule would enormously benefit the Filipinos, whom he called "our little brown brothers." A devout Methodist, he explained that America's mission was "to educate the Filipinos and to uplift and civilize and Christianize them, and by God's grace do the very best we could by them." The majority of Filipinos were already Christianized, Catholic in fact, a legacy of centuries of Spanish rule. Indeed, a substantial percentage of the islanders not only had assumed Spanish names but were bilingual as well, able to speak both Spanish and their native tongue. They were hardly a people bereft of civilization. Nonetheless, the U.S. would undertake a solemn mission to civilize the Filipinos and help to prepare them for independence. Until the U.S. deemed they were sufficiently civilized, the island would be ruled by American governors appointed by the president. The Filipinos believed they were civilized enough and ready for their independence and if it was not given freely, then they would take it from the United States by fighting a second war of national liberation.

Critics of Empire: The Anti-Imperialists

Even before the ink was dry on the Treaty of Paris, strong voices of opposition to empire had emerged, led by the recently organized Anti-Imperialist League. The association's membership was an impressive list of noted Americans, ranging from former president Grover Cleveland to

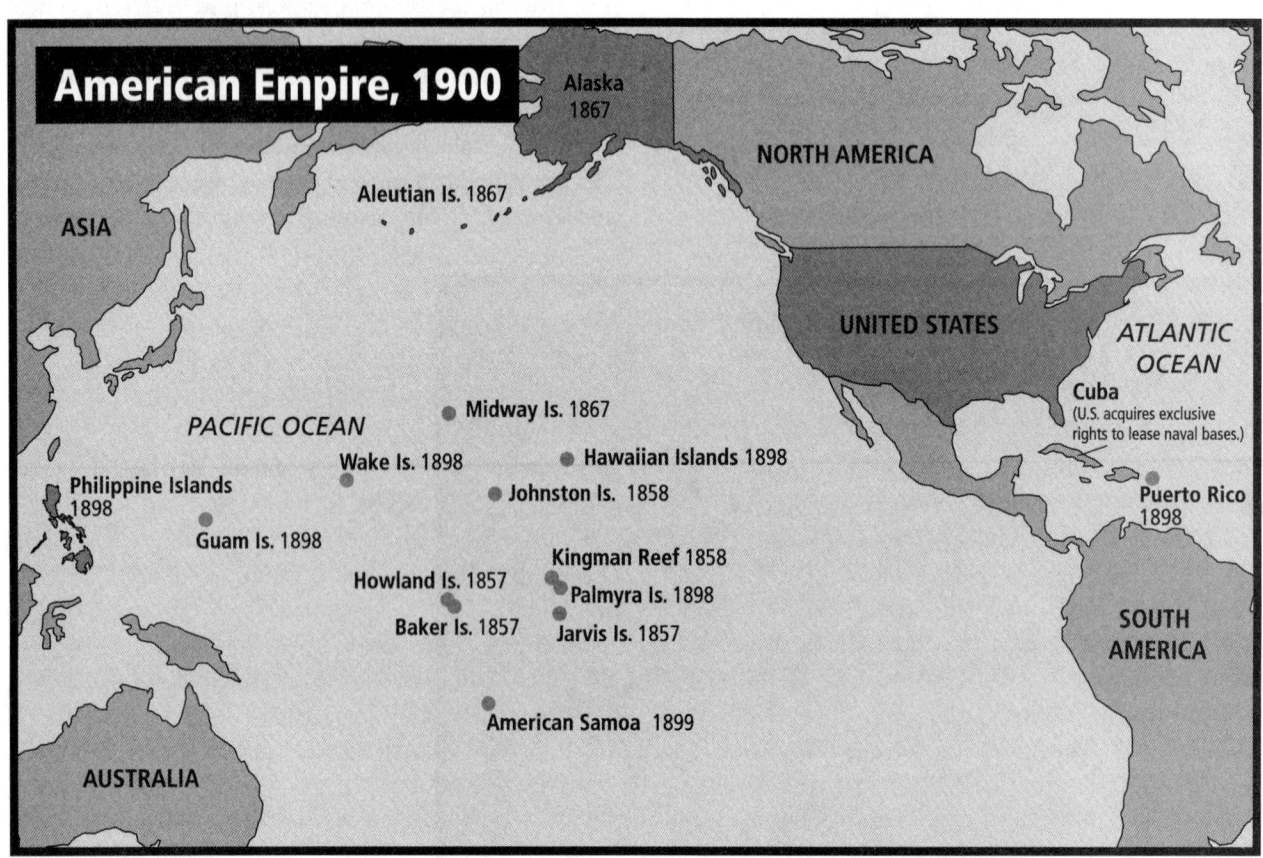

Map 20.3 American Empire, 1900

Andrew Carnegie, to the labor leader Samuel Gompers, and to some of the nation's foremost men of letters and intellectuals such as Mark Twain, William James, and William Dean Howells. They believed that the acquisition of the Philippines was a blatant contradiction and violation of the nation's most precious principle: the right of all people to independence and self-government. Moreover, they feared that the large military and diplomatic establishment that would be required to administer the colony would threaten political liberties at home. Though capitalists like Carnegie could be found among the more righteous and altruistic anti-imperialists, the majority of Carnegie's cohorts joined the cause out of self-interest. U.S. sugar producers feared competition from Filipino producers. Trade unionists, like Gompers, worried that cheap Filipino labor would stream across the Pacific and flood the American labor market and reduce wage rates. Some businessmen warned that the cost of maintaining an "imperial" outpost in the Philippines would far exceed any economic benefits the colony could provide to the nation. Many Democratic anti-imperialists typically used the acquisition of the islands for partisan purposes, as an entrée to criticize Republican foreign policy in general. Finally, many anti-imperialists were hardcore social Darwinists who already were anxious about the massive influx of southern and eastern Europeans and their "breeding" potential for mongrelization. They now feared the contaminating effects of contact with inferior Asian races.

In February 1899, the anti-imperialist coalition in the Senate failed by one vote to prevent that body's ratification of the expansionist Treaty of Paris. Helping to deliver the imperialist victory was the news on the eve of the vote that the Filipinos had risen in revolt against the U.S. army of occupation. With another war looming and the lives of American soldiers imperiled, a few senators who had been reluctant to vote for the treaty may have felt obligated to support the president. McKinley's overwhelming reelection victory in 1900 and the defeat of the expansionist critic William Jennings Bryan eroded the anti-imperialist cause. Nevertheless, at a time of jingoistic rhetoric and militaristic posturing, many of them had upheld an older and finer vision of the United States.

GUERRILLA WAR IN THE PHILIPPINES, 1898-1902

Unfortunately for both Americans and Filipinos, "uplifting" the latter embroiled the United States in a bloody struggle that lasted for nearly five years and cost the lives of over 4,000 American soldiers and as many as 20,000 Filipino resistance fighters. By the time the fighting ended in the summer of 1902, more than 120,000 U.S. soldiers had served in the Philippines. The conflict cost $160 million, or eight times what the U.S. paid Spain for the archipelago. The war brought Americans face-to-face with a disturbing reality: American actions on the islands were all too often no different than those of the Spanish on Cuba. Like Spain, the United States refused to recognize a people's desire for self-rule. Like "Butcher" Weyler, American generals turned a blind eye as their soldiers used savage tactics to search and destroy rebel encampments, units, and any civilian hamlets believed to be harboring rebels or their supplies. Whole communities suspected of supporting the rebels were relocated into concentration camps, while their entire village was razed. American soldiers executed so many insurrectionists (whom they called "**goo-goos**") that the ratio of Filipino dead to wounded reached 15 to 1, a statistic that made the U.S. Civil War, in which one soldier had died for every five wounded, seem relatively humane. One New Yorker wrote home that his unit had killed 1,000 Filipinos—men, women, and children—in retaliation for the killing of a single American soldier. Reflecting the racist attitude of most Americans, whether civilian or military, toward the Filipinos, the infantryman wrote home that "I am in my glory when I can sight my gun on some dark skin and pull the trigger." Estimates of total Filipino deaths from American bullets, starvation, and disease range from 50,000 to 200,000.

The United States finally gained the upper hand after General Arthur MacArthur (father of World War II General Douglas MacArthur), was appointed commander of the islands in 1900. MacArthur did not seek an immediate peace settlement. Indeed, the fighting's ferocity continued unabated. He realized, however, that peace could not be won by guns alone and thus initiated an amnesty program for all Filipino rebels who laid down their arms. He also cultivated close relations with the island's wealthy elites. McKinley supported this effort to build a Filipino constituency accepting of U.S. presence. To that end, he sent William Howard Taft (a federal judge from Ohio and future president) to the islands in 1900 to establish a civilian government. A year later, Taft became the colony's first "governor-general" and declared that he intended to prepare the Filipinos for independence. Taking a page from British imperialism, Taft and subsequent American governor-generals, created the façade that the colonists were governing themselves, ruled through puppet local elites. Everyone knew, however, that the United States still controlled the islands and that whatever autonomy had been granted was the result of American self-interest. Nonetheless, many governmental functions were transferred to Filipino control, and Taft initiated a vigorous program of public works (roads, bridges, schools) that would give the Philippines the infrastructure necessary for economic development and political independence. Naturally, few such projects were undertaken without an eye toward usefulness to the United States as well. After all, it was an American colony from which benefits were expected. By 1902, the combination of ruthless suppression and concessions ended the revolt. Though sporadic fighting continued until 1913, American control of the Philippines was secure. In 1946, nearly half a century after Admiral Dewey's guns had boomed in Manila Bay, independence finally came to the Philippines.

Controlling Cuba and Puerto Rico

Helping the Cubans free themselves from Spanish oppression and then allowing for their independence had allegedly been the main purpose for war against Spain. However, as in the case of the Philippines, American altruism quickly changed as the McKinley administration made it clear that the United States was not about to relinquish control of the island. At the president's urging, Congress attached the **Platt Amendment** to a 1901 army appropriations bill that abolished the earlier Teller Amendment, which had disavowed any American intention of acquiring Cuba. Despite its confusing verbiage, the Platt Amendment made Cuba another American colony, stipulating that the island country would not be permitted to make treaties with foreign powers; that the United States would have broad authority to intervene in Cuban political and economic affairs; and that the island's government would sell or lease land to the United States for naval stations. Cuban nationalists felt betrayed and outraged by the Americans but, unlike the Filipinos, did not rise in revolt. The dependence of Cuba's vital sugar industry on the American market and the presence of a substantial U.S. army of occupation rendered resistance futile.

The Cubans had no choice but to write the Platt Amendment into their constitution. Economic dependence on the United States allowed for their constant political subjugation. Between 1889 and 1914, American trade with Cuba increased more than tenfold—from $27 million to $300 million—while investments more than quadrupled—from $50 million to $220 million. The United States intervened in the island's political affairs five times between 1906 and 1921 to protect its capitalist interests. As in the Philippines, the United States ruled through a pro-U.S. business elite that remained in power until 1959, when Cuban rebels, led by Fidel Castro, overthrew the last of such puppet regimes. Until then, the Cubans endured a half century of internal suppression and external exploitation of their country. The economic, military, and political control the United States imposed on Cuba would fuel anti-American sentiment for years to come and help prepare the way for Castro's victory.

Puerto Rico received somewhat different treatment. The United States was not going to grant the Puerto Ricans independence, even though ironically under Spanish rule the islanders enjoyed a large measure of political autonomy. Nor did the United States impose Puerto Rico any sort of Platt Amendment that made the island a colony like its Caribbean neighbor, Cuba. Instead, the U.S. annexed the island outright via the **Foraker Act** (1900). This act was unprecedented in U.S. history for unlike all previous annexations, this measure made no provision for making the inhabitants citizens of the United States. Puerto Rico was designated an "unincorporated" territory, which meant that Congress would dictate the island's government and specify its inhabitants' rights. With the Foraker Act, Congress had invented a new imperial mechanism for ensuring sovereignty over lands deemed vital to U.S. economic and military security. Though in effect another U.S. colony, Puerto Rico fared better than allegedly "independent" Cuba. Puerto Ricans were granted U.S. citizenship in 1917 and won the right to elect their own governor in 1947. Still, Puerto Ricans did not have the same rights as other Americans in the 48 states. Moreover, as "citizens," their standard of living was still far below that of the mainlanders. As late as 1998, one-fourth of Puerto Rican households subsisted on $1,000 or less annually, a figure far below the official United States poverty line of $16,530 for a family of two adults and two children. In its skewed distribution of wealth and its lack of industrial development, Puerto Rico resembled the poorly developed nations of Central and South America more than it did the affluent country that took over its government in 1900.

Unlike the Philippines, very few Americans were disturbed by the subjugation of Cuba and the annexation of Puerto Rico. Since the 1823 Monroe Doctrine, the United States had, in effect, claimed the Western Hemisphere as its sphere of influence. Many Americans believed the United States possessed the right to act unilaterally to protect its interests from foreign interlopers and aggressors. Before 1900, most U.S. international actions (with the exception of the Mexican War) focused on keeping the European powers out of the hemisphere—Britain, France, Russia, and Spain. After 1900, however, the U.S. assumed a more aggressive role, seizing land, overturning governments not "favorably disposed" to American interests and exploitation, forcing its economic and political policies on weaker neighbors to turn the Caribbean Sea into what policymakers called an "American Mediterranean."

THE UNITED STATES AND CHINA: THE OPEN DOOR POLICY

In the aftermath of the Philippines debacle, the imperialists wisely made no further attempts to subjugate other Asian territory, which might well have precipitated a conflict with the other great powers already established in the region. Moreover, the American public, weary of the bloodshed and cost of suppressing the Filipino rebellion, rejected any further, overly-ambitious and financially burdensome engagements in the area. Much to the disappointment of some of the more bellicose imperialists within the McKinley administration, diplomacy rather than militarism prevailed when it came to achieving other foreign policy initiatives relative to Asia. Of the greatest interest and concern for policy makers was the nation's relationship with China, a country representing vast commercial potential for American capitalists and, for the geopolitical imperialists, a prospective ally and countervailing force against rival powers, most notably the Russians, Japanese, British, French, and Germans, all who were seeking to increase their hegemony over China. By 1900, these powers had succeeded in carving China into "spheres of influence," seizing by force large chunks of Chinese territory, which they then occupied and exploited for their own economic aggrandizement.

In effect, via their respective spheres of influence, these nations dominated China, either by exacting economic and territorial concessions from the weak Chinese government or by taking outright the land and trading privileges they desired. Once in control of such areas, the foreign powers closed off all outside access to their sphere of influence, especially forbidding trade relations with other countries. Much to the dismay of American capitalists and their imperialist allies, the United States was shut out of the lucrative China market.

Leading the effort to get the other powers to open up their spheres of influence to outside trade was McKinley's Secretary of State and noted imperialist, John Hay, whose objective was twofold: to prevent China's further division if not dissolution, while simultaneously gaining American commercial access to the whole of China. For this purpose, Hay sent "**Open Door**" notes to the major powers, asking each of the nations with spheres of influence in China to open their respective territories to the trade of other countries. Hay also asked for reasonable harbor fees, railroad rates, and, most important, for the other powers to respect Chinese sovereignty by enforcing tariff duties and to cease any further designs they may have on increasing their spheres at China's expense.

This last stipulation reflected the desire of Hay and imperialists within Congress and the McKinley administration to begin cultivating China as a potential U.S. ally by championing Chinese sovereignty and independence from foreign power. If the United States could present itself as a protector and savior from foreign intervention, then, once China had liberated itself from the other imperial powers, it would look favorably upon the United States for having supported their independence movement. In appreciation, China undoubtedly would grant the United States increased trade and other concessions and privileges. This is what Hay and other American imperialists hoped would be the long-term effect of the Open Door initiative. By the 1920s Hay's vision came to fruition as the United States had become China's most important Western protector and benefactor while American goods flooded the China market.

Although impressed by Hay's diplomacy (or audacity), the secretary's Open Door overture engendered little enthusiasm among the other powers. Hay should have expected at best a lukewarm response or acceptance, for there was absolutely nothing for the other powers to gain by supporting Hay's proposal other than not wanting to irritate the United States, an emerging world power but not yet really tested. Crushing a hapless country like Spain in six weeks might have been a great ego boost for American imperialists and militarists, but the U.S. victory hardly impressed the great European powers. For the major powers, Hay's attempt to persuade them to relinquish valuable territory because their stranglehold on Chinese resources and trade was "unfair" seemed pretentious, if not ridiculous, coming from a nation that had just recently modernized its armed forces. To the Europeans, hardened by centuries of warfare, only the prospect of a clash of arms would motivate them to seriously ponder the Hay proposal. Knowing neither the American people nor their government representatives would be willing to militarily engage them over China, the great powers did not have to fear a military reprisal from the United States if they did not agree to Hay's mandates. Doing what was decent or moral to promote goodwill had little stock in the competitive, self-interested world by which the European powers operated.

Interestingly, Hay, not wanting the United States to appear weak by being unable to convince others to heed its requests, declared to the American public that China's occupiers had agreed to observe his Open Door principles and that he regarded their "assent" as a "final and definitive" acceptance of his initiative. A naïve American people, flushed with nationalist pride after displaying their supposed military and moral superiority over a corrupt and decadent European nation (Spain), bought Hay's pretentious bragging. Suffice it to say, the other powers were taken aback by Hay's effrontery.

The Boxer Rebellion

No sooner was the Open Door Policy allegedly proclaimed than it was challenged, not by the Europeans but by Chinese nationalists, who naively misinterpreted the initiative, believing its real intent was to protect Chinese sovereignty as well as a declaration of U.S. assistance when the Chinese attempted to liberate themselves from foreign occupation. Such a scenario occurred in May 1900, when a nationalist movement, known as the "Boxers," rose in armed rebellion in order to "cleanse" China of all "foreign devils" and influences. The Boxers, who considered themselves the protectors of traditional Chinese culture and society, rightly claimed that European occupation had destroyed centuries of security and stability, leaving China divided. The Boxers killed hundreds of European "devils" as well as many Chinese men and women who had converted to Christianity. The insurrection caught the foreign community by surprise, and thus the Boxers initially appeared to be winning their war for national liberation.

For fifty-five days the Boxers laid siege to the foreign legations in Beijing, cutting off communication between the city and the outside world. In order to raise the siege, the imperial powers momentarily put aside their own rivalries and formed a coalition force to rescue the diplomats and punish the rebels. At this juncture the United States found itself in a dilemma: although sympathetic to the Chinese nationalist movement, which if successful could economically benefit the United States, if they did not join the coalition they would alienate the very powers they were attempting to woo into accepting the Open Door initiative. In the end, the U.S. opted to side with the other imperialist powers. After all, they were all members (except the Japanese) of the allegedly same superior white race, and in the name of white (although not Anglo-Saxon) solidarity, the United States joined the coalition to help put down the "mongrel" uprising. The McKinley administration ordered 5,000 troops to be rushed from the Philippines to help the other powers break the Beijing siege and crush the Boxer insurrection, which was accomplished by October 1900.

Hay feared the **Boxer Rebellion** spelled the end of any hope his Open Door policy might have had, for he believed the uprising would prompt the other major powers to demand even greater power over China. Hay, however, was not to be deterred. He sent out another round of circulars, in which he not only reiterated his original Open Door proposal but also warned the other powers that it had been their refusal to respect China's political independence and territorial integrity that had provided the impetus for the Boxers to rally their countrymen to their cause. Hay believed that the only way to prevent future insurrections was for the other powers to accept his Open Door agenda. Impressed by America's show of military prowess in helping to suppress the Boxers, and worried that the Chinese rebels might strike again, the key imperialist rivals—Great Britain, France, and Germany—endorsed Hay's policy outright. With such powerful support behind him, Hay was able to check the designs on Chinese territory of the Russians and Japanese, who eventually capitulated to the Open Door as well once they saw the forces arrayed against them. When the powers demanded that the Chinese government pay them reparations for the damages done by the Boxers to their property and personnel, Hay convinced them to accept cash payments rather than taking more Chinese territory as compensation. Thanks to Hay, what remained of China was kept intact, and for the time being, open to free trade. The United States had achieved, largely by Hay's persistent diplomacy, a major foreign policy victory. Perhaps most important for the future, Americans began to see themselves as China's savior and protector.

THEODORE ROOSEVELT AND THE FOUNDATION OF AMERICAN FOREIGN POLICY

Rarely in the history of the United States has one individual left as indelible a mark on both domestic and foreign

Rebels against foreign domination of their country— called "Boxers"—are held by the United States 6th Cavalry in Tientsin, China, c. 1901.

These Boxers were put on trial before the High Court, China. c. 1919

policy as Theodore Roosevelt, whose legacy is perhaps more significant in the area of foreign policy. During his presidency, and mostly because of his personal initiatives, the United States became the respected (and feared) world power that Roosevelt and other imperialists envisioned during the 1890s. It was during that decade that Roosevelt emerged as one of the most outspoken champions of utilizing the nation's industrial might into making the United States one of the world's great powers—a destiny, he believed, ordained by God and the superiority of the Anglo-American character. Roosevelt and his imperialist cohorts had worked assiduously, both publicly and privately and often clandestinely, to convince their fellow Americans to embrace their vision for the nation. Roosevelt believed that the chains of isolationism had to be forever broken and that the United States must muster all its resources, both human and material, for the purpose of realizing its destiny as a great power. In that status also laid true greatness, for to Teddy Roosevelt it was incumbent on the United States to exercise its power for the preservation of peace while simultaneously serving as an example to the world the virtues of a democratic republican government. Only by playing an active role in world affairs could the United States realize its ultimate responsibility to humanity, which was to lead the rest of the world down the righteous and glorious path toward democracy and freedom.

Roosevelt's conception of the United States' role in world affairs not only resonated with many of his contemporaries but, perhaps more significantly, with future presidents and foreign policy makers as well. In many ways, Roosevelt laid the essential foundations of modern American foreign policy upon which his successors added new dimensions in order to deal with exigencies that did not exist in his time. Roosevelt established this fundamental premise, captured in his quip, "**Speak softly but carry a big stick.**" In effect, Teddy Roosevelt wanted to project to the world an image of the United States that was dedicated to world peace, stability and freedom, yet not afraid to unleash its awesome military and economic power upon an adversary if provoked. It has been this image of American power and presence first articulated by Roosevelt that still defines the essence of United States foreign policy.

For all his exuberance, bluster, and arrogance, Roosevelt understood the dynamics of practical politics; he never for a second assumed that because of Americans' supposed ethnic/racial (Anglo-Saxon) superiority and righteousness that the other nations of the world would simply acquiesce to United States' dictums. A nation, like an individual, had to strive for and earn respect and greatness. It had to demand of its citizens physical and mental toughness, the essential components of military preparedness, for in the history of all great nations war was an unfortunate but inextricable part of a country's rise to preeminence. TR believed that the United States must train and develop a skilled and dedicated warrior class capable of not only defending the nation but of projecting American power abroad as well. Potential adversaries must live in fear that if provoked, the United States possessed the armed forces—army and navy—capable of annihilating enemies as well as protecting American interests and citizens around the globe.

Teddy Roosevelt's passion for the good fight caused many to worry about the ascension of this "cowboy" to the White House after McKinley's assassination in 1901. However, Roosevelt was no saber-rattling war monger. He understood the complexities, machinations, and historical imperatives of international relations and power politics. As much as he craved power for himself and the nation, he knew the United States could not dominate every portion of the globe through military or economic means. Consequently, he pursued a policy of bringing about a balance of power among the great industrial nations through negotiation rather than war. Since all the great powers had mutual interests and concerns—that of maintaining their preeminence—then all should be willing to peacefully resolve tensions among them and pursue an agenda of collective security in order to preserve their status. Such a rapprochement would enable each imperial power to safeguard its key interests while helping to maintain world peace and progress.

Unfortunately, absent from the president's thinking was concern for the world's lesser nations and their peoples. Reflecting not only his own inherent racism and ethnocentrism but that of the great powers as well, Roosevelt turned a deaf ear to the cries of sovereignty and human rights coming from small countries, whose people TR believed weak and inferior. In his eyes, Latin Americans, Asians (except the Japanese), and Africans fell into the Social Darwinian category of inferior humans, incapable of self-government and material progress without being under the "tutelage and care" (subservience) of the superior Anglo-Saxon and peoples of Europe and the United States. Roosevelt wholeheartedly embraced the "white man's burden" rhetoric of his time.

The Roosevelt Corollary

Perhaps no initiative better reflected Roosevelt's mentality and his desire to establish American hegemony in a vital region of the world than his 1904 "**corollary**" to the Monroe Doctrine. The original 1823 Doctrine's purpose had been to promote a degree of hemispheric solidarity against any further European intrusions in New World affairs. Most important, the United States declared itself the hemisphere's spokesman and guardian by asserting its right to use force if necessary to keep the European powers from meddling in the hemisphere's business, especially in matters relating to Latin America. However, at the time, the United States lacked the military might to prevent European intervention, and thus throughout most of the nineteenth century the European powers violated the doctrine with impunity.

By the time of Roosevelt's presidency, the economic and military condition of the United States had changed dramatically. America was no longer a second-rate power. Quite the opposite, the United States possessed the third largest navy in the world, fully capable of defending the hemisphere from European encroachment. In his corollary the president declared that the United States had the right to intervene in the domestic affairs of hemispheric nations to quell disorder and prevent European intrusion. In many ways, Roosevelt's "addendum" simply formalized the United States' previous military occupation of a "troubled" Cuba and Puerto Rico in 1900 and 1901. However, it was events in Venezuela and the Dominican Republic that hardened TR's resolve to establish intervention as a necessary component of United States hemispheric policy. To Roosevelt, his corollary not only helped to preserve hemispheric stability but also reflected his determination to establish in the eyes of the European powers that the New World, particularly the Caribbean and Central America, was under United States control.

Helping TR to further justify U.S. intervention was the fact that both the governments of Venezuela and the Dominican Republic were controlled by corrupt, brutal dictators who had defaulted on loans owed to German and British banking houses. Their reneging prompted a German-led European naval blockade and bombardment of Caracas, Venezuela in 1902 and a potential invasion of the Dominican Republic by Italy and France in 1903. In response, TR issued a statement to Germany threatening military action if they did not withdraw from the Venezuelan coast, which they did in 1903. In the Dominican Republic, after an insurrection overthrew the dictator, the U.S. assumed control of the nation's customs collections in 1905 and refinanced the Dominican national debt through U.S. financiers.

Unfortunately for the Latin American people of the Caribbean and Central America, the first several decades of the twentieth century saw the coming to power of corrupt, dictatorial regimes and the willingness of European bankers to loan these governments money. Within a few years, such relationships ended in bankruptcy, social unrest and, ultimately, to foreign intervention. To prevent further European invasion and occupation of Latin American countries, Roosevelt now made it clear that henceforth the United States would assume the responsibility of policing the hemisphere and that all future issues between the Europeans and Latin American nations would be arbitrated by the United States. In effect, TR declared American hegemony over the entire hemisphere and that any attempt by the European powers to ignore or violate such sovereignty would be met by a military reprisal.

As far as the Latin Americans suffering under such endemic oppression and violence were concerned, TR dismissed their plight as simply confirmation of their inferiority—their inherent incapacity for democratic government and socioeconomic progress. Roosevelt's only interest was maintaining hemispheric order and, in the process, asserting and sustaining U.S. hegemony. Thus, when the Cubans revolted in 1906 in an attempt to liberate themselves from a repressive U.S.-backed puppet government, Roosevelt sent in the Marines to crush the uprising and maintain the status quo. American troops remained in Cuba for three years to ensure there would be no further populist insurrections against the American capitalist-supported-regime.

The Panama Canal

Without question the acquisition and construction of the Panama Canal marked the high point of Roosevelt's agenda in establishing the United States as a recognized world power. Roosevelt, influenced by his reading of

Alfred T. Mahan's seminal works on sea power, believed more passionately than ever that since the United States had become a naval power, it needed a way of moving its ships swiftly from the Pacific Ocean to the Atlantic Ocean. The United States could no longer afford to traverse the great oceans by going around the tip of South America. Such a journey of several months could result in the nation not being able to protect its far-flung possessions. Thus, Roosevelt concluded that for reasons of national security, the United States must find a way to reduce the travel time within its empire; the Imperial Republic needed a canal, and the logical place to build one was across Central America at its narrowest width: the Colombian province of Panama. In the 1880s, a French company had attempted such an undertaking. However, technological difficulties and the financial costs of literally moving mountains stymied their effort. Moreover, French doctors could not control the spread of malaria and yellow fever, which incapacitated or caused the death of hundreds of workers. By the time Roosevelt became president, the French Panama Company had gone under.

Roosevelt was not deterred by the French failure. He was as confident as ever that superior American ingenuity, skills, and perseverance could overcome any natural obstacle and build a canal across Central America. However, before he could move boldly ahead, TR did have to overcome a few, minor diplomatic niceties. First, he had to get the British to approve the United States building a canal on its own; since 1850, the two nations had agreed that any canal project in the region would be a joint undertaking. The 1901 **Hay-Pauncefote Treaty** with Great Britain released the United States from such an arrangement. Although initially intending to build the canal across Nicaragua, TR changed his mind when he realized that the Panamanian route was shorter and that the canal begun by the French was 40 percent complete. However, the French company, Compagnie Universelle du Canal Interoceanique, initially wanted $109 million for a "buy out," but after some tough bargaining by Hay, the company was willing to accept $40 million, which Congress readily approved. Not to lose momentum, Hay then quickly negotiated an agreement with the Colombian charge d'affaires in Washington, Tomás Herrán, (**Hay-Herrán Treaty**), which gave the United States the right to build a canal along a six mile wide strip across the province of Panama. For this privilege, the United States was to pay Colombia a one-time payment of $10 million and annual rent of $250,000.

Much to TR's subsequent chagrin and rage, the Colombian legislature reneged on the arrangement, demanding instead a onetime payment of $20 million and a share of the $40 million paid to the French government. The Colombians hoped to stall negotiations until 1904 when the French company's contract expired. When that occurred, the Colombian government not only would regain the right to the canal zone but to the $40 million sale price promised as well to the French. Roosevelt felt deceived by the Colombians even though they were acting within their rights as a sovereign nation. Infuriated by such a betrayal, TR decided that he would use military action to get what he believed was a deal between the French company and the United States government. Behind closed doors, TR, in conjunction with Philippe Bunau-Varilla, the director of the French company, and Panamanian "freedom fighters" (for 25 years the Panamanians had sought independence, rebelling several times against the Colombian government), planned another uprising. Roosevelt promised the Panamanians that they would succeed in securing their independence this time because he would offer assistance—the United States navy and troops. With such an assurance, the Panamanians revolted in 1903, and true to his word, TR sent the *U.S.S. Nashville* to prevent Colombian troops from entering Panama. U.S. Marines then came ashore to help the new nation retain its freedom. The United States formally recognized the sovereign state of Panama only two days after the revolt against Colombia began.

Further questionable arrangements followed between the United States and Panama, reflecting TR's determination to build and own a canal regardless of his actions' legitimacy. Bunau-Varilla declared himself Panama's diplomatic representative, even though he was a French citizen and member of a Wall Street law firm and had not been in the country for fifteen years. Roosevelt accepted Bunau-Varilla as Panama's bona fide ambassador and ordered Hay to quickly sign a treaty with him that would give the United States its desired objective. Thus in 1903, the **Hay-Bunau-Varilla Treaty** formalized the United States' right to a ten-mile wide canal zone in return for the package Colombia had rejected—$10 million down and $250,000 annually. Thus, by rather dubious means the United States (Theodore Roosevelt) secured its canal. When the legitimate Panamanian delegation arrived in Washington to discuss and negotiate a treaty, the United States handed the officials a *fait accompli*, which infuriated the Panamanians, but there was nothing they could do to change the conditions. Nonetheless, one member of the delegation, upon seeing Bunau-Varilla, became so enraged that he knocked the Frenchman out cold. Despite such a betrayal, Panama was stuck with the treaty. If it refused to acknowledge the arrangement, the U.S. might withdraw its troops, leaving Panama vulnerable to a Colombian invasion force and loss of

Panama Canal Construction. c. 1913.

independence. The treaty, which no Panamanian signed, embittered relations between Panama and the United States for the rest of the twentieth century.

Roosevelt's high-handedness infuriated many Americans, including the one-time imperialist, William Randolph Hearst, whose newspapers labeled the Panama foray as "nefarious" and "a quite unexampled instance of foul play in American politics." Typically, President Roosevelt was not intimated nor worried by such criticism of his actions. Moreover, TR had his cabinet's full support, as reflected in a comment by Elihu Root, his new Secretary of State, after a meeting with the president. Root told TR that, "You have shown that you were accused of seduction and you have conclusively proved that you were guilty of rape." With his customary bravado, TR later gloated, "I took the Canal Zone and let Congress debate!"

Roosevelt turned the building of the canal into a showcase of superior American technology, ingenuity, and perseverance. Engineers overcame every physical or natural obstacle; doctors developed drugs to combat malaria and yellow fever; and some 30,000 West Indian "coolie" workers labored for a 10-year period, for 10 hours a day, for six days a week, for ten cents an hour, making "the dirt fly." Roosevelt visited his project in 1906, the first American president to travel outside the United States while in office.

When the canal opened with great fanfare in 1914, the British ambassador to the United States, James Bryce, described the waterway as "the greatest liberty Man has ever taken with Nature." The canal shortened the voyage from the West Coast to the East Coast by some 8,000 miles, and the undertaking greatly enhanced the United States' international prestige. From the beginning, driving TR to acquire the territory on which to build the canal was his obsession to demonstrate to the great powers that the United States possessed all the essential material, technological, and human will power to engage in such an enterprise. Prior to the construction of the Panama Canal, the only other nation to have performed such an engineering feat and human endeavor was Great Britain

Gatun Locks - Panama Canal

with the construction of the Suez Canal and its completion in 1869. Roosevelt believed it imperative for the United States to build and own a waterway as important to the world and the United States as the Suez was to Great Britain. The Panama Canal became the perfect venue for TR to impress the great powers (especially England) that the United States had not only "arrived" industrially and technologically but that the American people possessed as well the moral and physical character essential to accomplish such an undertaking. Roosevelt was not about to let any nation outdo the United States, no matter what the adventure or struggle. Finally, the canal's strategic location further bolstered TR's corollary, making the sending of U.S. troops for intervention or occupation purposes to Central America or the Caribbean that much easier.

In 1921 the United States paid the Colombian government $25 million as compensation (atonement) for having, in effect, stolen Panama. However, sincere restitution was made over 70 years later when President Jimmy Carter signed a treaty with Panama in 1977 for turning the Canal Zone over to Panamanian sovereignty and the transfer of the canal itself to Panama by the year 2000. With some minor "modifications," the Bill Clinton administration honored the Carter accord.

President Roosevelt's aggressive policy of asserting United States hegemony with military force in the Caribbean and Latin America abated in his Asian initiatives. No doubt, a more militaristic and bellicose posture would not "fly" with the great powers heavily involved in the region—Russia, Japan, and the United Kingdom—affected Roosevelt's attitude. Thus, TR pursued a policy of maintaining acceptance of the Open Door Policy relative to China and of playing the balance of power game relative to the rest of the area. However, the thwarting of particularly Russian and Japanese aggression in China proved more difficult than initially reckoned. Both nations coveted Manchuria and Korea. For Russia having a warm water port on the Pacific was necessary, and Japan, in the

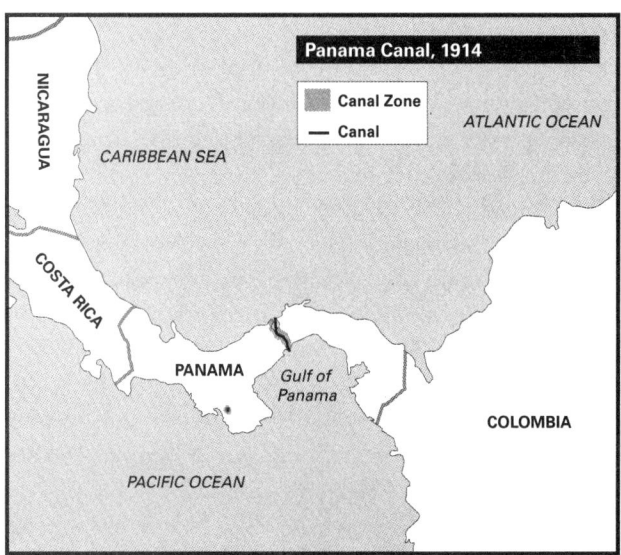

Map 20.4 The Panama Canal Zone and the Panama Canal

throes of industrialization, desired access, if not complete control, of the rich ore deposits of Manchuria. For Japan, Korea had no value other than giving Japan a foothold on the Asian continent from which it could launch a future invasion of China proper.

Competition for the territory escalated into a full-blown war between Russia and Japan in 1904. Much to the surprise of the European powers, who still regarded the Japanese as an "inferior yellow people" incapable of defeating a great, white European power such as Russia, the Japanese routed the Russians on both land and sea with superior naval and land forces. The conflict quickly became a war Russia should never had engaged. Much to the shock of the other great powers, the conflict revealed that Russia was still essentially an industrially backward nineteenth century country, incapable of fighting, let alone winning, a modern (industrial) war. Moreover, the **Russo-Japanese War** unleashed the 1905 Russian revolution, as the Russian people, particularly those in urban areas, suffered from all manner of exploitation and deprivation, much of it caused by the demands of war. Popular uprisings, street demonstrations, and strikes by workers and leftist groups opposed to czarist autocracy and the war began in earnest on Easter Sunday 1905 in St. Petersburg after government troops opened fire on peaceful marchers, slaughtering hundreds who had come to plead with Nicholas II for relief. Although ultimately put down by the czarist regime, the 1905 Revolution marked the beginning of the end of the Russian Empire, ruled for 300 years by the tyrannical Romanov family.

A Russian defeat in Asia would end Russian presence in the region, thus ending the precarious Asian balance of power, allowing the Japanese to gain ascendancy, especially in China, over the other great powers. Sensing such an outcome, Roosevelt entered into secret negotiations with both belligerents, seeking to end the war before Russian annihilation became complete. If that occurred, Japanese preeminence would prevail in the area, establishing Japan as a potential threat to United States' interests in Asia and the Pacific.

President Roosevelt invited to the United States (**Portsmouth**, New Hampshire) representatives from both countries, hoping to secure a negotiated compromise that would preserve the balance of power. Despite all of Roosevelt's cajoling, brow-beating, and admonishing, the Japanese came out "winners," refusing to relinquish the territory its forces had won on the battlefields and sea. Korea became a Japanese protectorate while the southern part of Sakhalin Island, Port Arthur (China), and the South Manchurian Railroad also came under Japanese control. However, thanks to TR's intercession, Russia did not have to pay Japan a huge indemnity, and it retained

Portraits of the envoys at the Portsmouth Peace Conference, Baron Komura and Kogoro Takahira (left) M. Witte and Baron Rosen (right) and President Theodore Roosevelt (center). At the bottom of the card was written "We are fighters for peace." c. 1905

Siberia (a "wasteland" in Japanese eyes), thus preserving its image (albeit a significantly diminished one) as an East Asian power. TR's only coup at Portsmouth was his persuading of both Russia and Japan to leave Manchuria, thus maintaining China's territorial integrity and simultaneously the United State's Open Door agenda. For his peace initiative, Roosevelt became the first American to win the Nobel Peace Prize in 1906.

Typically, TR had little interest in protecting or upholding the sovereignty of smaller, weaker Asian nations. Roosevelt's main objectives were simple and straightforward: to preserve the Asian balance of power among the great powers while simultaneously securing respect for American interests in the region. Such a priority was reflected in the secretly negotiated **Taft-Katsura Agreement** of 1905, whereby the United States recognized Japanese suzerainty over the Korean peninsula in exchange for a Japanese promise to respect U.S. hegemony over the Philippines and never attempt to take by force the U.S. possession. In the 1908 **Root-Takahira Agreement**, the

U.S. reversed its earlier stand on the inviolability of Chinese sovereignty by allowing the Japanese to expand into southern Manchuria. Roosevelt recognized that Japan's power was on the rise in Asia, and that in the future Japan, not China or Korea, or any other Asian country, would dictate Asia's future. Although allegedly not possessing the qualities of superiority ascribed to the Anglo-Saxons, TR nonetheless respected and admired Japanese industrial and military might. Indeed, he viewed Japanese imperialism and expansion into East Asia as the assertion of a naturally superior people's dominion over supposedly inferior humans—the Chinese and other East Asians. Based on this perception, Roosevelt even promoted the idea of allowing Japan the right to create spheres of influence throughout all of East Asia, similar to what the U.S. had established in Central America. Hopefully, such recognition of Japan as an equal power with the United States and the Europeans would establish peaceful relations between the United States and Japan.

Implementing such an accord with Japan was a delicate diplomatic task, requiring TR's utmost skills in international relations, especially when simultaneously in California another outbreak of anti-Japanese hysteria engulfed the state. White Californians had long resented Asians in their state, and for several decades the federal government capitulated to such nativism. In 1882 Congress passed the Chinese Exclusion Act, which ended most Chinese immigration to the United States. By the early twentieth century Japanese immigration had replaced the Chinese influx; by 1906, the Japanese population in California had reached 24,000. Reflecting a blatant racism, in that year the San Francisco school board ordered the removal of all Asian schoolchildren from the city's public school system so they would not "contaminate" the white children. In 1907 the California legislature seriously considered passing a law that would stop all future Japanese immigration into the state. Violent anti-Asian riots erupted in San Francisco and Los Angeles. Most of the outbreaks were caused by the press, whose editorials about the **"Yellow Peril"** whipped white Californians into such a frenzy.

The Japanese government was outraged by the treatment of its citizens. Japanese militarists began talking about a possible war with the United States. Roosevelt, putting his own racism aside, assured the Japanese government that he too was appalled by white Californians' behavior. In 1907, TR reached a "gentleman's agreement" with Japanese officials by which the Japanese government agreed to halt the further immigration of Japanese adult male laborers to the United States in return for Roosevelt's pledge to bring an end to anti-Japanese discrimination in California. TR upheld his word; he forced the San Francisco school board to retract its segregation ordinance. However, de facto segregation of Japanese citizens, both children and adults, continued, as did violent assaults on the Japanese people and their property.

Not wanting to appear weak to the other major powers or to Japan for acquiescing to Japan's demands that he protect its citizens from white reprisals, TR ordered 16 battleships of the United States fleet to embark on a 45,000 mile world tour with stops at every major port-of-call, including Tokyo Bay. Without doubt, TR wanted to display to the world (particularly Japan) U.S. military and industrial might, and at this time, there was no better way of showing off such prowess than for a large navy made of steel ships, with guns that could shoot for miles, to steam around the world and visit all the major powers. TR was criticized for such bravado, as many congressmen not only deplored the cost of the tour but worried as well that such a display of U.S. power, especially in a Japanese port, would provoke the Japanese into a military response. Typically, TR ignored his critics, and true to his prediction, the Japanese were not provoked; rather, they were impressed by America's industrial and military strength embodied

In spite of embracing the use of military power, President Theodore Roosevelt won the Nobel Peace Prize in 1906. In this contemporary cartoon by Charles Lewis Bartholomew, Roosevelt receives the peace prize in a Christmas stocking with symbols of the president's aggressive foreign policy—a sword, a rifle and a "big stick"—in the background.

Political Cartoons and American Imperialism

One of the most revealing, poignant, and entertaining ways of recovering past attitudes and values is through political cartoons. Ralph Waldo Emerson once said, "Caricatures are often the truest history of the times." A deft drawing of a popular or unpopular politician can freeze ideas and events in time, conveying more effectively than columns of words the central issues of the day and creating an immediate viewer response. It is this freshness that makes caricatures such a valuable source when attempting to understand the past. Cartoonists are often at their best when they are critical, exaggerating a physical feature of a political figure or capturing anti-government sentiment.

The emergence of the United States as a world power and the rise of Theodore Roosevelt both as president and main architect of U.S. foreign policy in the early twentieth century gave cartoonists plenty to draw about. The proliferation of cheap newspapers at the turn of the century, most notably those of publishing magnates William Randolph Hearst and Joseph Pulitzer, provided cartoonists with ample space for their caricatures. When the Spanish-American War broke out, the Hearst and Pulitzer papers whipped up public sentiment by having artists draw pictures of "lustful" Spaniards stripping American women at sea and encouraging cartoonists to depict the Spanish as "brutes." Hearst, in particular, used such cartoon portrayals of the Spanish to increase his papers' daily circulation to one million copies. However, by the time of the Philippines debate, to the imperialists' dismay, many previously supportive cartoonists had reversed their attitude toward this particular manifestation of American colonialism, and used their creative talents to criticize the government's Philippine policy. One such rendition had "Liberty" stopping "American Butchery in the Philippines" (1899). A year earlier, cartoonists supported the war against Spain, and thus released such classics as "The Spanish Brute Adds Mutilation to Butchery." Both cartoons condemned the "butchery" of native populations, but by 1899, Uncle Sam had become the killer, although in his depiction, he was not nearly as menacing as the Spaniard as an ugly gorilla. However, both cartoons shared a similarity of stance: blood-covered swords with a trail of bodies behind.

Only a handful of U.S. presidents have provided cartoonists with as rich a potential for caricature as Theodore Roosevelt. His physical appearance and personality made him instant fodder for the cartoonists' pens. His broad grin, eye-glasses, and walrus moustache were the kind of features that fueled the cartoonist's imagination. A man of boundless energy, TR's style was as distinctive as his look. Other factors, such as the "Rough Rider" nickname, the symbol of the "big stick," and policies like "gunboat diplomacy" made Teddy the perfect subject.

in the showcasing of the "**Great White Fleet**." In many ways TR's various negotiations with Japan marked the highpoint of his foreign policy initiatives. Unlike most Americans, he did not allow his racist attitudes to dictate his agenda. He knew when to make concessions and when to stand firm. His policies lessened the prospect of war with Japan (at least for the time being) while preserving a strong U.S. presence in East Asia.

Although TR pursued a conciliatory policy toward Japan, especially on the issue of accepting Japanese imperialism, one nonetheless cannot help but wonder if the seeds of future tensions between the U.S. and Japan were not sown by Roosevelt, particularly by such initiatives as the "**Gentlemen's Agreement**," an obvious sop to white racism. By condoning Japan's right to assert its hegemony over the rest of Asia, TR confirmed the growing belief among Japanese militarists that it was Japan's destiny to dominate all of Asia because of Japanese superiority. By the 1920s and certainly by the early 1930s, this mindset came to dictate Japanese foreign policy, and it would be only a matter of time before the delicate balance of power in East Asia would become completely imbalanced by Japanese aggression.

WILLIAM HOWARD TAFT AND DOLLAR DIPLOMACY

Roosevelt's hand-picked successor, the three-hundred pound, jovial William Howard Taft, brought valuable foreign policy experience to the presidency. He was the first governor-general of the Philippines, and as Roosevelt's Secretary of War, he served as chief negotiator of the delicate 1905 Taft-Katsura Agreement. Under TR's auspices, Taft learned a great deal about international politics and how to deal with the United States' imperialist rivals. Yet, although an educated, intelligent man, Taft lacked Roosevelt's understanding in the area of balance-of-power politics and the charisma for leadership in foreign affairs. Moreover, Taft proved to be much less personally involved and interested in foreign policy. He preferred instead to delegate authority to supposed experts, such as his Secretary of State, Philander C. Knox, the one-time corporate lawyer from Pittsburgh, Pa. Unfortunately, Knox's grasp of the often complex dynamics of international power politics was at times wholly lacking. Philander C. Knox proved to be no John Hay or Elihu Root when it came to formulating and implementing American imperialist policies. Indeed, Knox's grasp of the often complex dynamics and exigencies of the international power politics scene was at times wholly lacking. Reflecting his years of defend-

President William Taft (left) and City College President Dr. John Finley (right) 1912.

ing the excesses of American corporate capitalism and the plutocracy responsible for such wantonness, Knox believed that at this point in American foreign policy, the main focus should be on expanding American corporate investment abroad—a disposition that prompted critics to deride his agenda as "**Dollar Diplomacy**."

Taft and Knox, however, were not deterred by such carping. Both men believed that U.S. investments would not only reap great rewards for the U.S. economy but offer a more peaceful, less bellicose and coercive way of winning new international friends for the United States while simultaneously maintaining order and stability, especially in the Western Hemisphere without the use of military action. Chiding TR's "big stick policy," Taft announced that in his view, "modern diplomacy is commercial."

Taft's and Knox's inabilities to grasp the complexities of power politics led to diplomatic reversals in East Asia, upsetting the delicate balance of power TR had established with Japan. Knox, prodded by his Wall Street friends, sought to expand American investment in China, even into Manchuria, an area Roosevelt had previously declared to be a Japanese sphere of influence. In 1911, Knox put together a consortium of European bankers to buy the South Manchuria Railway (then under Japanese control) for the purpose of opening up North China to international trade. The Japanese naturally viewed Knox's scheme as a U.S. attempt to deprive them of a sphere of influence that Roosevelt had recognized.

In response, the Japanese signed a friendship treaty with their former adversary, Russia, allowing that country's goods into Manchurian markets while preventing the penetration of American, French, and British products into the region. The Japanese knew they could not stand alone against such a powerful Western power. They were thus willing to engage in détente with Russia, which desperately needed markets for its industrializing economy. If Russia joined with Japan in such an arrangement, perhaps the Western powers would back off, for they would not want to alienate future potential allies, as tensions between Britain/France and Germany/Austro-Hungarian empire mounted. As a result of the Russo-Japanese cordial relations, Knox's syndicate idea collapsed, dealing America's Open Door Policy a serious blow in the process. Most important, in 1912, the foreign-controlled puppet government of China fell, precipitating ten years of revolution and civil war, resulting in the loss of millions of U.S. investment dollars. It appeared that Taft's and Knox's over zealous devotion to the value of the U.S. dollar in determining foreign policy initiatives had backfired.

Dollar diplomacy fared somewhat better in the Caribbean and Central America. Knox thus encouraged American investment in the hemisphere, both to provide corporations with opportunities for profit and to supplant the European investors already there or to beat them to the punch in acquiring new ventures. During the Taft administration, over half of all U.S. dollars invested abroad were found in various Latin American enterprises, ranging from oil to public utilities to railroads and agriculture. Most important, U.S. conglomerates became such powerful economic entities in these host countries, especially in the more vulnerable countries of Central America, that they not only controlled the country's economy but politics as well. Such was the power of the United Fruit Company of Boston, Massachusetts, founded by Minor Keith. By controlling the majority of the banana plantations of Costa Rica and Honduras, (bananas were the main export crop of both countries), the company virtually owned both nations. So driven by their devotion to dollar diplomacy were Taft and Knox that they assured U.S. corporations that if at any time their enterprises were threatened by political opposition or turmoil in the countries they had such a presence, the U.S. would simply send troops to protect their interests.

Such a provocation occurred in 1910 when the Nicaraguan dictator, Jose Santos Zelaya, allegedly began negotiating with a European country to build a second trans-Isthmian canal. Upon hearing of such supposed double-dealing, Taft sent a force of U.S. Marines to overthrow his regime. Marines landed again in 1912 when Zelaya's successor, Adolfo Diaz, a U.S. puppet, alienated his own people by his pro-American policies. Nicaraguans rose in rebellion against Diaz, but Taft sent Marines to keep the Diaz government in power. Except for a brief period in 1925, U.S. troops would remain in Nicaragua continuously from 1912 to 1933. Interestingly, in his willingness to send troops to safeguard his dollar diplomacy approach, Taft engaged in the same militarism his predecessor readily employed in order to sustain puppet governments friendly to the United States and maintain order in Latin America.

UNITED STATES EXPANSION

America's rise to a global power by the eve of World War I can be assessed from two perspectives: either in relation to the imperialist agendas of the great powers or in the context of the fulfillment or realization of the American mission to export to the world its democratic ideals. America's emergence in a relatively short time to great power status is impressive, for the nation achieved its major objectives: the U.S. established its undisputed hegemony over the Western Hemisphere and projected its military and economic power into Asia. Such was accomplished with minimal loss of American lives while muffling the jingoistic impulse for more aggressive military adventure and conquest. The U.S. added only 125,000 square miles to its empire in the years 1870-1914, while Great Britain, France, and Germany enlarged their respective dominions by 4.7, 3.5, and 1.0 million square miles. Comparatively few foreigners were subjected to American colonial rule. By contrast, in 1900, the British empire extended over 12 million square miles and embraced one-fourth of the world's population.

Nonetheless, American suzerainty could be harsh; witness the brutal suppression of the Filipino insurrection of soldiers and civilians alike. Yet, on the whole, American dominion was no more severe than British rule and significantly less oppressive than that of the French, German, Belgian, or Japanese imperialists. Perhaps most important, until 1917, America's imperialist presidents—McKinley, Roosevelt, and Taft—all placed limits on American expansion and worked assiduously to prevent becoming so entangled in international power politics that war would be the end result.

If American foreign policy is assessed in the context of the nation's own democratic ideals, then U.S. initiatives must be judged more harshly. American policy was racist, exploitive, and militaristic, in many ways not any different in attitude and behavior than the European imperialists to whom we proclaimed we were different. The Cubans, Puerto Ricans, Filipinos, and Nicaraguans would beg to differ, for American subjugation, whether economic or military, of those peoples' countries confirmed that the U.S. was similar in every capacity. Like their European counterparts, American imperialists regarded the peoples they subjugated as inferior, primitive, and barbaric, and thus not "worthy" of self-government. In the eyes of Latin Americans, Filipinos, Hawaiians, and Asians, Americans were hypocrites, declaring to value liberty more than power. The Open Door Policy, the Platt Amendment, the Roosevelt Corollary, the Panama Canal, the Gentlemen's Agreement, and Dollar Diplomacy substantiated the belief held by many that the United States had become a full-fledged member of the European imperialist club.

Many Americans of the time judged their nation by both standards and thus faced a dilemma that would affect the nation throughout the twentieth century. On the one hand, they agreed with President Roosevelt that the size, economic strength, and honor of the United States required the nation to accept its destiny as a world power and policeman, whose most important mandate, bequeathed by Providence, was to use its superior power and character to preserve world peace. On the other hand, many Americans believed that the principal mission of United States presence in world affairs was to spread the values of 1776 to the farthest reaches of the earth. We are still debating these same issues today; we are still trying to decide what should be America's principal role in world affairs.

Chronology

1875	U.S. agrees to allow Hawaii to export sugar to America duty-free.
1878	U.S. gains treaty rights for base at Pago Pago in Samoa.
1887	U. S. gains treaty rights for base at Pearl Harbor in Hawaii.
1889	First Pan-American Congress.
1890	Alfred Thayer Mahan publishes *The Influence of Sea Power on History*. U.S. ends favored status of Hawaii in sugar trade.
1893	U.S. sugar planters in Hawaii foment rebellion against weak native king. Cleveland rejects attempt to annex Hawaii.
1894	Wilson-Gorman tariff on Cuban sugar.
1895	President Cleveland defends Monroe Doctrine in border dispute between Venezuela and Guiana.
1896	William McKinley elected president.
1898	William Randolph Hearst, publishes de Lôme letter. U.S. battleship *Maine* explodes in Havana harbor. Congress declares war on Spain. Dewey destroys Spanish fleet in the Philippines. U.S. troops defeat Spanish forces in Cuba. Treaty of Paris ends war with Spain and cedes Puerto Rico, Philippines, and Guam to theU.S. United States annexes Hawaii. Anti-Imperialist League formed.
1898-1902	Philippines revolt against American rule.
1899	Senate ratifies Treaty of Paris. Hay releases "Open Door notes" on China.
1900	Foraker Act establishes civil government in Puerto Rico. Hawaii granted territorial status. Boxer rebellion breaks out in China. McKinley reelected president.
1901	American forces capture Filipino rebel leader Emilio Aguinaldo. U.S. establishes civil government in Philippines. Platt Amendment.

Review Questions

1. Discuss the various arguments used by the imperialists that ultimately led the United States to becoming a major world power in possession of an empire.

2. Discuss the arguments against the United States engaging in such an aggressive policy of foreign territorial expansion.

3. Assess the causes and consequences of the 1898 Spanish-American War.

4. Part of the imperialists "grand plan" called for a strong American presence in both the Pacific and Asia. Why were the imperialist so interested in Asia, in China specifically, and what were the short-term and long-term consequences of the United States' attempts to establish spheres of influence in that particular region?

5. What foreign policy legacy did Theodore Roosevelt leave for his successors to uphold or to subsequently change?

Glossary of Important People and Concepts

Boxer Rebellion
Buffalo Soldiers
de Lôme Letter
"Dollar Diplomacy"
Foraker Act 1900
Gentlemen's Agreement
"Goo-goos"
Great White Fleet
Hay-Bunau-Varilla Treaty
Hay-Herrán Treaty
Hay-Pauncefote Treaty
"jingoism"
Alfred Thayer Mahan
Open Door Policy
Platt Amendment
Protectorate
Roosevelt Corollary
Root-Takahira Agreement
"Rough Riders"
Russo-Japanese War
"Speak softly but carry a big stick"
Sphere of Influence
Taft-Katsura Agreement
Teller Amendment
Treaty of Portsmouth
Turner's "frontier thesis"
Yellow journalism
"Yellow Peril"

SUGGESTED READINGS

Robert L. Beisner, *From the Old Diplomacy to the New, 1865-1900.* (1986).

—, *Twelve Against Empire: The Anti-Imperialists, 1898-1900* (1968).

James E. Bradford, *Crucible of Empire: The Spanish American War and Its Aftermath* (1993).

Michael Blow, *A Ship to Remember: The Maine and the Spanish-American War.*

Paul Carano and Pedro Sanchez, *A Complete History of Guam* (1964).

Raymond Carr, *Puerto Rico: A Colonial Experiment* (1984).

Warren J. Cohen, *America's Response to China* (1971).

Graham A. Cosmas, *An Army for Empire: The United States Army in the Spanish-American War* (1971).

John Dobson, *America's Ascent: The United States Becomes a Great Power, 1880-1914* (1978).

Philip S. Foner, *The Spanish-Cuban-American War and the Birth of American Imperialism,* 2 volumes (1972).

William B. Gatewood Jr., *"Smoked Yankees; Letters From Negro Soldiers 1898-1902* (1971).

David F. Healy, *U.S. Expansionism: Imperialist Urge in the 1890s.* (1970).

Walter R. Herrick, *The American Naval Revolution* (1966).

James H. Hitchman, *Leonard Wood and Cuban Independence, 1898-1902* (1971).

Paul M. Kennedy, *The Samoan Tangle* (1974).

Walter LaFeber, *The Cambridge History of Foreign Relations: The Search for Opportunity, 1865-1913* (1993).

Patricia Nelson Limerick, *The Legacy of Conquest: The Unbroken Past of the American West* (1987).

Gerald F. Linderman, *The Mirror of War: American Society and the Spanish-American War* (1974).

William E. Livezey, *Mahan on Sea Power* (1981).

Thomas J. McCormick, *China Market: America's Quest for Informal Empire, 1890-1915* (1971).

Ernest R. May, *Imperial Democracy: The Emergence of America as a Great Power* (1961).

Stuart Creighton Miller, *"Benevolent Assimilation:" The American Conquest of the Philippines, 1899-1903* (1982).

Joyce Milton, *The Yellow Journalists* (1989).

H. Wayne Morgan, *America's Road to Empire* (1965).

Edmund Morris, *The Rise of Theodore Roosevelt* (1979).

Louis A. Perez, *Cuba Under the Platt Amendment, 1902-1934* (1986).

Julius W. Pratt, *Expansionists of 1898* (1936).

—, *America's Colonial Empire* (1950).

Emily Rosenberg, *Spreading the American Dream: American Economic and Cultural Expansion, 18909-1945* (1982).

William A. Russ Jr., *The Hawaiian Republic, 1894-1898 and Its Struggle to Win Annexation* (1961).

Daniel B. Schirmer, *Republic or Empire? American Resistance to the Philippine War* (1972).

Peter Stanley, *A Nation in the Making: The Philippines and the United States, 1899-1921* (1974).

Merze Tate, *The United States and the Hawaiian Kingdom* (1965).

E. Berkeley Tomkins, *Anti-Imperialism in the United States, 1890-1920: The Great Debate* (1970).

David F. Trask, *The War With Spain,* (1981).

Richard E. Welch, Jr. *Response to Imperialism: The United States and the Philippine War, 1899-1902* (1979).

William Appleman Williams, *The Tragedy of American Diplomacy*

Marilyn B. Young, *The Rhetoric of Empire: American China Policy, 1895-1901* (1968).

Horse-drawn fire engines in the street on their way to the Triangle Shirtwaist Company fire, New York City. March 25, 1911

Chapter Twenty-one

The Progressive Reformation of Industrial America

On March 25, 1911, New York City experienced a horrific industrial fire at the Triangle Shirtwaist Company, a manufacturer of popular ladies' blouses. Beginning late on a Saturday afternoon among one of the many piles of discarded fabric clippings, the inferno spread rapidly across the upper floors of the ten-story Asch Building where the factory was located in the heart of Manhattan's Garment District. Workers on the eighth and tenth floors were able to escape, but those on the ninth floor found themselves trapped. Though the floor had many exits, only a few lucky ones were able to catch an elevator while it was still in operation in order to reach the ground floor. A few others used a stairway to reach the roof. Flames prevented large numbers of workers from using another stairway while the main exit was useless because its doors had been illegally locked by guards who were told to screen employees from walking off their jobs to prevent them from stealing cloth. Increasingly desperate, many ran to the single fire escape, which was poorly maintained and thus quickly collapsed from the overload of weight, dropping victims over a hundred feet to the pavement below. Fire engines soon arrived on the scene, but their ladders reached no higher than the sixth floor. Eventually, in an action to be replicated ninety years later at the World Trade Center on 9/11, sixty-two desperate women horrified onlookers as they jumped to the street below. None of them survived. As one reporter later related the details of the terrible scene that he witnessed:

... [A] young man helped a girl to the windowsill on the ninth floor. Then he held her deliberately away from the building, and let her drop. He held out a second girl the same way and let her drop. He held out a third girl who did not resist. They were all as unresisting as if he were helping them into a street car instead of into eternity. He saw that a terrible death awaited them in the flames and his was only a terrible chivalry. He brought around another girl to the window—I saw her put her arms around him and kiss him. Then he held her into space—and dropped her. Quick as a flash he was on the windowsill himself. His coat fluttered upwards—the air filled his trouser legs as he came down. I could see he wore tan shoes.

In all, 146 victims, most of them young Jewish and Italian immigrant women, had perished in the city's worst workplace disaster.

The incident and subsequent outpouring of emotion, which included a Fifth Avenue procession of grief in which over 100,000 took part and another 400,000 witnessed, led to demands for a full investigation. The state legislature responded by creating a Factory Investigating Commission, which completed a broad survey of factory safety and health that included recommendations to improve the protection of workers. Thirteen bills based on the Commission's suggestions

Triangle Shirtwaist Co., New York City, March 26, 1911 Crowd outside of the pier morgue.

became law, leading to improvements in fire safety, factory ventilation, sanitation, machine guarding, and other special measures for specific industries.

The fire reinforced arguments made by many reformers during the Progressive Era—that business could not go on as usual. In the early days of the Industrial Revolution, many Americans were reluctant to embrace a wide range of intrusions on corporations lest the industrialization process be hindered, but opinions of a majority of Americans had changed by the turn of the twentieth century. Reformers argued that the processes of industrialization and urbanization could be greatly improved and made more efficient if the country would adopt a more ordered approach. As America entered a new century, an increasing number of citizens began to listen to those who professed that the means existed to maintain the benefits of industrialization without the sometimes appalling human cost such as occurred that terrible day in 1911.

THE NATURE OF PROGRESSIVISM

Contemporaries and later historians have used the term "**progressivism**" to describe the reform impulse that surged in American political and social life at the turn of the twentieth century. A significant response to the tremendous changes that marked America's transition to an urban-industrial nation, the effort marked the end of unbridled laissez-faire capitalism. Progressive activists did not desire to dismantle big business or the rise of large metropolises by "turning back the clock" to a simpler time, but, rather, sought to bring rational order to a significantly altered society. They wished to keep the more positive benefits brought about by industrialization while seeking to limit its least desirable aspects.

Diversity remains one of the Progressives' salient characteristics. Though particularly strong among the urban middle class of the Northeast, reformers came from all walks of life (as did their opponents). Progressives not only could be found among the recently emerging middle class but also among the old-money elite, some wealthy businessmen, members of the industrial working class, and residents of small towns and rural areas. Progressivism crossed party lines—there were Republican reformers, Democratic reformers, and even some Socialists who supported progressive causes. Though its nature changed with geography, reform leaders and their supporters showed strength across the country—in the Northeast, the Midwest, the Far West, and the South.

Progressives were united in their desire for constructive changes in response to the new realities of twentieth-century life. They also tended to share common approaches to problems, believing strongly in the tools of science, the value of mass publicity, and the powers of government to investigate problems, educate the public, and provide solutions through legislation. Certainly no Progressive supported all the proposals being offered during the period. Many definitely vehemently opposed some suggestions. Perhaps the best way to understand the nature of Progressivism is through the concept of "shifting coalitions." Diverse groups and individuals such as doctors, women's activists, certain religious organizations, and businessmen, for example, might come together for different motivations to strongly support the prohibition of alcohol, yet when it came to factory regulation proposals, the businessmen might balk at the notion and refuse to ally themselves further with the previous coalition because they might perceive the proposal as working against their interests. These types of revolving alliances appeared frequently during the era.

INFLUENCES UPON PROGRESSIVISM

Progressive Era reformers responded to numerous influences that guided their thoughts and actions, some having more impact than others depending on the individual. The legacy of late-nineteenth century political reform efforts, for example, continued to stimulate thought and provoke action. Protests against laissez-faire capitalism levied by Socialists provided a vigorous critique of the status quo. Memories of the "Mugwump" political reformers kept alive the ideal of a government run by honest public servants. Populist demands for more active government involvement to solve the nation's problems became more accepted dogma.

New stimuli from religious organizations reacting to the pronounced changes brought about by the Industrial Revolution also influenced reformers across the country. Initially arising in evangelical Protestant churches (but eventually seeping into many Catholic churches and Jewish synagogues), a reform spirit soon to be labeled the "Social Gospel" began to take hold as religious leaders such as Walter Rauschenbush and their followers sought to better the lives of their fellow men on Earth and rid the world of the evils produced by industrialization. Hearkening back to the antebellum religious reform tradition that sought, for example, to end alcohol consumption and slavery, evangelical Progressives believed it was their Christian duty to fight for the downtrodden and to better society through reform.

Historians have also noted the impact of new scientific thought on reformers. By the turn of the century, colleges and universities produced many new professionals who often sought to apply the latest developments in their fields to the problems of society. Whether they were trained in the natural or social sciences, this slew of new educators, economists, sociologists, social workers, medical doctors, city planners, and civil engineers believed that the scientific approach provided the best means to bring order to the nation. Problems needed to be investigated with accurate data obtained, proposals for reform initiated (often through the passage of new laws), and solutions implemented to eradicate the problems.

THE STRANDS OF PROGRESSIVISM

As Progressivism became a reality at the local, state, and national levels, the reforms reflected the great variety of the individuals and groups who had supported them. Seemingly contradictory actions by different groups of reformers often occurred. For example, while some social Progressives sought to aid foreign immigrants in American cities, other reformers with an equal claim to the Progressive mantle lobbied to bar immigrants from entering the country altogether. While the variance of progressivism was pronounced, historians often group the types of reforms produced during the Progressive Era into three main categories, or strands, based upon the reformers' varying motivations.

The demand for social justice comprised one major strand of Progressivism. Large numbers of men and women supported a wide range of reforms designed to improve the lives of urban residents and industrial workers. Whether referring to an outraged middle-class parent appalled by the notion of nine-year old children toiling in a factory somewhere, or a sociologist convinced that long working hours by women had a detrimental effect on families, or a social worker endeavoring to provide a decent home life for urban residents, social progressives fought for a wide range of municipal and labor reforms they hoped would improve the living and working environment of the urban masses.

Equally progressive were the efforts by many reformers to constrain various individuals through numerous social controls. Many advocates believed that ethnic minorities possessed traits needing to be mitigated. Thus, among the most well-known reform efforts coming from the period that bore this strain–prohibition of alcohol, foreign immigration restrictions, and southern laws enforcing segregation and disenfranchisement of African Americans–were efforts to employ social coercion in order to "improve" society. In their endeavors on behalf of these and related causes, reformers also used the classic Progressive formula of investigation, data collection, the use of moralistic rhetoric to persuade others, and a call for increased government action to alleviate the problems.

One last strand of Progressivism involved the efforts of efficiency experts in numerous fields who sought to apply scientific methods taught by their profession to solve a host of local, regional, and national problems. City planners seeking a more orderly environment through the application of zoning laws or a more efficient urban layout reflected this strand of reform. Engineers seeking more efficient production methods, doctors resolving to end quackery in their profession, and even trained foresters seeking to limit wanton waste of the nation's timberlands though scientific conservation methods would also fit into this broad category.

THE MUCKRAKERS

The efforts of determined investigative journalists greatly helped to spread awareness of problems and proposed solutions across the country. A true phenomenon of the age, new ten-cent national magazines such as *Collier's*, *McClure's*, and *Cosmopolitan* regularly carried exposés (often later published as books) designed to elevate subscription sales while also arousing the public on a variety of issues. Some writers, such as Lincoln Steffens in his *McClure's* series "The Shame of the Cities," described the power of urban political machines. Others focused on corporate power and influence, such as Ida Tarbell, whose damning *McClure's* articles on John D. Rockefeller's ascent to power by crushing honest competitors through immoral and illegal actions and use of special privileges were later published as *The History of the Standard Oil Company*. Some reporters used the power of photography to illustrate their findings, such as newspaperman Jacob Riis who used photographic images to clearly display the misery of New York City slum life in *How the Other Half Lives*. Many writers also used fiction to dramatize a real-life issue. In Frank Norris's novel *The Octopus*, the author used drama based on fact to demonstrate the power of the Southern Pacific Railroad over the citizens of California, especially its farmers.

Ida M. Tarbell, c. 1922

While the work of the investigative reporters received a wide audience, not everyone was pleased with the constant tone of confrontation that often coincided with the latest revelations. In a 1906 speech designed to please many Washington politicians whose support he needed for aspects of his domestic program, **President Theodore Roosevelt** coined the term **"muckrakers"** to characterize the era's investigative reporters. Referring to a character in John Bunyan's *Pilgrim's Progress* who was so focused on his job of raking up the muck that he did not look up to see the beauty and goodness there was in the world, Roosevelt decried those individuals who solely focused on the negative aspects of American life, or spread untruths in an effort to promote the greater good, while acknowledging that there were many evils in the world that needed to be exposed and eradicated, concluding: "I hail as a benefactor every writer or speaker, every man who, on the platform, or in book, magazine, or newspaper, with merciless severity makes such attack, provided always that he in his turn remembers that the attack is of use only if it is absolutely truthful. . . . The soul of every scoundrel is gladdened whenever an honest man is assailed, or even when a scoundrel is untruthfully assailed."

LOCAL URBAN REFORMS

Energetic urban reform during the Progressive Era emanated from those active "in the streets," endeavoring to solve everyday problems produced by modern urban-industrial life. Publicity surrounding the labors of the nation's first generation of social workers focused increased attention on the myriad of problems produced by the

Lincoln Steffens, April 1914

sprawling industrial cities. Inspired by British students from Oxford University who founded Toynbee Hall in a London slum during the mid-1880s, some Americans similarly sought to establish so-called "settlement houses" to live and work amongst the immigrant poor. Often but not always consisting of college-educated middle- and upper-class women wishing to do useful work beyond the limits of acceptable roles dictated by traditional society, settlement house workers sought to reduce class antagonisms through the establishment of close personal contact with neighborhood residents—seeking to earn their trust through the sponsorship of a variety of educational, cultural, and social activities designed to improve their living environment. Stanton Coit first brought the settlement idea to the United States in 1889 when he and several friends from several women's colleges helped to establish the College Settlement in a tenement area of New York City's Lower East Side. Later that same year, Rockford College classmates Jane Addams and Ellen Gates Starr established the most famous settlement house—Chicago's Hull House. From their South Halsted Street base, Addams, Starr, and their fellow social workers sponsored lectures, exhibits, and festivals designed to reinforce pride in the immigrants' cultural heritage. Simultaneously, they taught classes ranging from homemaking to American history while establishing nurseries, day care centers, kindergartens, and playgrounds for urban youth. They also investigated social conditions, lobbied for changes with local government authorities, joined municipal reform campaigns, and did much to educate the general public about the need for concrete changes in numerous aspects of American city life. By 1910, hundreds of young men and women had followed their lead, operating approximately 400 **settlement houses** across the country.

The club movement offered another avenue for middle- and upper-class women to engage in urban reform efforts. Though unable to vote or hold public office in most regions of the country, many women during the Progressive Era influenced local political battles by using their social clubs to lobby for a host of reforms designed to improve city life. Ever mindful of societal limits regarding what was deemed women's proper place, these women often characterized themselves as "municipal housekeepers" to overcome these gender expectations by asserting that their activism reinforced their role as protector of family and home. In this manner, progressive women claimed that their campaigns strengthened families by producing a healthier and safer environment through such efforts as city beautification projects, library and hospital construction, and establishment of juvenile courts for youth offenders.

Jane Addams, a progressive who led the "settlement house" movement, c. 1912.

A cadre of reform-minded mayors also contributed to important urban changes often emulated elsewhere in the country. Elected the Mayor of Detroit, Michigan in 1890, Republican Hazen S. Pingree, sponsored efforts to create municipally owned competitors to the electric and gas company monopolies that existed in an effort to drive down utility prices. During the Depression of 1893, he aggressively expanded public welfare programs through the creation of public works programs for the unemployed and opening up city-owned land for use by the poor to grow food crops. During his tenure as mayor of Toledo, Ohio from 1897 to 1905, Democrat Samuel L. "Golden Rule" Jones also made a name for himself nationally by pressing for city control over utilities and arranged for funds to be allocated for the construction of recreational facilities and places for the city's homeless to live.

Nonpartisan efforts to provide "honest, effective, businesslike government" to root out corruption and the perceived inefficiency of urban political machines also occurred across the nation. After being elected mayor on a reform platform supported Republicans and anti-Tammany Hall Democrats in 1894, Republican merchant William L. Strong reorganized many city departments, established a Board of Education, created a series of municipal parks, and appointed Theodore Roosevelt as Police Commissioner who energetically transformed the

New York Police Department into a modern urban force through a series of reforms much emulated across the country—new disciplinary rules, creation of a mobile bicycle squad, direct communication among all precinct headquarters via telephones, standardized use of pistols by officers with requisite firearms training, annual physical exams, establishment of meritorious service medals, and appointment of new recruits based on their physical and mental qualification rather than political affiliation.

In other cities, reformers sought additional means to correct "structural defects" in the organization of municipal governments. After a devastating hurricane destroyed Galveston, Texas, for example, residents approved a massive overhaul of the city government to speed up rebuilding efforts. The Texas state legislature allowed Galveston to cast aside its mayor-city council form of local government in favor of a rule by a five-member commission. Each commission member undertook personal responsibility for one of the key departments of city governance such as police, fire, housing, and utilities. As the town slowly recovered, the appeal of the "Galveston Plan" rose across the country. Other cities sought to bring about changes in their localities without the interference of partisan political rancor and self-interest. Des Moines, Iowa adopted a **commission-style government** in 1908, followed by hundreds of other middle-sized cities over the next decade.

The inherent challenges presented by the emerging urban-industrial order offered numerous opportunities for many professionals eager to apply their training in an effort to solve them. While social workers involved themselves in settlement work, city planners began to ply their trade in many cities across the country. Not an entirely new concept, city planning began to be taught as a field of intense study in the nation's universities during the Progressive Era, producing recent graduates wishing to reorganize American city life. Zoning became the primary means of accomplishing their task. By advocating the segregation of various city districts by function, planners hoped to create a much safer and efficient urban environment. Whereas previously the cities had grown in an unrestrained and unregulated manner, planners sought the passage of laws that would limit the use of land in a given area. Junkyards and industrial plants, for example, would now be kept some distance away from parks and schools. Residential areas would now be located away from heavy commercial districts. Medical doctors also sought to improve the health of the nation's cities and rural areas. Physicians actively supported political campaigns and education drives that championed sanitation reforms, creation of local health boards, construction of hospitals, the eradication of diseases, and improvement in medical school standards through which the nation's doctors were produced.

STATE-LEVEL REFORMS

Labor Reforms

Even before the Progressive Era, many state governments in the Northeast during the first decades of the Industrial Revolution succumbed to strong pressure from organized labor and were already investigating working conditions in factories and mines, publishing findings through annual reports of state bureaus of labor statistics. The information gathered, often highlighting the number and nature of industrial accidents, led labor groups to further push for the passage of factory inspection legislation modeled after the pioneering laws in this field implemented in England.

Progressives worked aggressively to strengthen these safety laws and their enforcement as well as to secure additional labor reforms that they felt were necessary to humanize the Industrial Revolution. Ending child labor, for example, became the passionate calling for many social progressives who viewed the practice as a resident evil in need of eradication. Historically, American children, as youths elsewhere in the world, were an important part of the pre-industrial work force. Children performed a variety of tasks on family farms plus many were apprenticed at a young age to learn a trade. The expansion of industry after 1880 led to a tremendous increase in native-born children working in Appalachian coal mines and southern textile mills. (In 1899, 25 percent of all workers in southern cotton mills were under the age of 15.) In addition, the huge influx of immigrants from southern and eastern Europe led to a large number of children working in the cities of the Northeast and Midwest as factory workers, shoe shiners, newspaper sellers, and product peddlers on the streets. Statistics from the 1900 Census, which underestimate the extent of the problem, show that at the very least, 1.75 million children aged 10-15 (26 percent of boys, 10 percent of girls, and 18 percent total) were employed.

The large number of children working in factories, mines, farms, or on the streets alarmed many progressives, as did the often rough working conditions for the youths. After 1900, progressives began to organize efforts to regulate or end child labor. Settlement house workers, women's clubs, and local reform groups led the way by forming state child labor committees. In 1904, the National Child Labor Committee was established to arouse public indignation and target state legislatures

Group of mill girls, Dallas Cotton Mill, Dallas, Texas. October 1913.

for effective changes. Utilizing expert investigators to gather data, effective use of photography to document and publicize the plight of child workers, mass mailings of pamphlets and leaflets to alert the public, and a heavy dose of political lobbying, the Committee successfully convinced two thirds of the states to enact some form of child labor legislation by 1907 such as minimum wages, maximum hours, and the prohibition of children working in certain occupations, though many loopholes remained in terms of excluded trades and lax enforcement procedures. Acknowledgement of these limitations led many child labor advocates to seek federal remedies.

Social progressives also sought to regulate the wages and hours of working women at the state level. Florence Kelley, the daughter of a Pennsylvania Quaker businessman and congressman, led the crusade. After graduating from Cornell University and studying for a time in Europe, Kelley arrived in Chicago in 1891 to work at Hull House and pursue a law degree at Northwestern University. After Kelley persuaded the Illinois legislature in 1893 to pass a factory labor law that limited women to eight-hour work days and banned the use of children under the age of fourteen (overturned by the state supreme court two years later), Governor John P. Altgeld named her to be the state's chief factory inspector. Kelley remained at Hull House working alongside Jane Addams for the remainder of the decade until she moved to New York City's Henry Street Settlement where she tirelessly collected data and published articles on the ill effects of long hours on the health and safety of female workers. In 1899, Kelley became the general secretary for the National Consumers' League, an organization which coordinated the efforts of local groups seeking to educate the public about women's and children's working conditions and to organize consumer boycotts of goods produced by employers who exploited their workers.

As a result of a mobilized electorate, many states began to pass laws limiting the working hours of women in certain occupations. Opposition from employers often led to legal challenges, none as significant as ***Muller v. Oregon*** argued before the Supreme Court in 1908. In 1903, Oregon passed a law restricting women to work no more than ten hours per day. Portland laundry owner Curt Muller refused to obey the law and was fined ten dollars. The businessman appealed to the state supreme court, but the tribunal upheld his conviction. The U.S. Supreme Court agreed to hear Muller's federal appeal during which his lawyers brought up the high court's ruling in *Lochner v. New York* (1905) whereby a New York general labor statute limiting working hours under such terms was thrown out as a violation of the right to contract between employer and employee. Defenders of the Oregon law retained the services of constitutional lawyer Louis D. Brandeis whose famous "Brandeis Brief" (with data assembled by **Florence Kelley** and actually written by her friend Josephine Goldmark) used sociological, medical, and other scientific evidence to document the point that women's "physical structure and the performance of her maternal functions" placed them at such a disadvantage that their physical well-being became an object of public interest. Brandeis proved to the Court's satisfaction that long working hours were harmful to the well-being of women and affirmed the overall principle that governmental interest in public welfare outweighed any absolute freedom of contract. Progressives generally cheered the ruling, though many feminists voiced displeasure that the basis of the ruling relied heavily upon the separation of the sexes into stereotyped gender roles. Nevertheless, in the decade following the decision, most states began to pass laws limiting the working hours of women.

Passage of the nation's first **workers' compensation** laws by several states marked another advance for laborers. By 1900 numerous industrializing countries in Western Europe had already established insurance systems to compensate those injured or killed on the job. However, in the United States, where industrial accidents numbered in the hundreds of thousands per year, the only recourse for workers and their families was to sue in court—an often long, drawn-out, and expensive process (for workers and companies alike) that seldom produced adequate compensation. Using the standard progressive tools of data acquisition and publicity, reformers gathered statistical evidence and published reports showing the toll that industrial accidents took on the nation's workforce as well as business productivity. Crystal Eastman was one such progressive. Published in 1910, her book *Work Accidents and the Law* was based on painstakingly studying over a thousand cases of worker accidents in Pittsburgh, noting the nature of each incident and the economic effects of the resulting injuries and deaths on the workers' families. She found that, contrary to the arguments of employers, worker carelessness caused only a minority of the accidents. Workers and their families also bore the brunt of the economic cost of those mishaps. She calculated that a majority of families who had workers killed on the job received less than $100. Of those injured on the job, most employers paid hospital costs but only a third received any subsequent payment.

Continued agitation by progressive reformers, along with improvements in technology and plant design and a growing realization by companies that reducing accidents made business sense, provided an impetus to greatly improve factory and mine safety. Workers' compensation began to be accepted increasingly not only as a means to aid victims of industrial accidents but also as a strong preventative device. Crystal Eastman had argued in her book that if employers had an economic incentive to reduce hazards in the workplace they would implement such improvements. The workers' compensation systems passed during the Progressive Era were rather conservative in nature and thus favored by the business community. When accidents occurred, claimants did not go to the employer but, rather, sought compensation from a state pool, funded by businesses or their insurance companies, according to a set pay schedule determined by law and based on the nature of the disability (or death). In this manner, employers found it cheaper and more manageable to operate with predictable costs into the state fund rather than having to deal with the unpredictable nature of variable numbers of accidents and legal costs to cover litigation, not to mention the protection now provided from the occasional large court award from a judge or jury. Reliance on the state fund for compensation also shifted the emphasis of the debate in that the system lent credence to the notion that frequent accidents were a normal part of factory or mine work in the industrial era. Organized labor initially opposed the establishment of such compensation systems but increasingly came to see them as a better means to reduce accidents since the amount of employer payments and their accident insurance premiums were based upon their individual safety ratings. Overall, these first systems produced a slightly better process for laborers to receive something for injuries and deaths. By 1921, 46 states had workers' compensation laws in effect and the entire concept would later be expanded to the national level during the 1930s when the idea was written into the Social Security Act.

Improving general occupational health marked another important concern of progressives. Not just limiting their efforts to reducing industrial accidents, many reformers also concentrated on common health dangers in the workplace. In 1909, a team of researchers led by Alice Hamilton for the Illinois Occupational Disease Commission produced a pioneering report on the subject, highlighting the detrimental effects upon workers of exposure to toxic chemicals. The most significant section of the report publicized the dangers of lead poisoning in numerous trades. Another campaign led by John B. Andrews sought to outlaw the use of white phosphorous in matches because repeated exposure to the chemical by workers led many of them to develop phosphorous necrosis or "phossy jaw," a disfiguring disease that eroded the teeth and jaw bones of laborers in the match factories. Already banned in many European countries, Congress finally acted in 1912 when it placed a large tax on white phosphorous matches. Meanwhile, the Diamond Match

The Anti-Saloon League at the White House, January 16, 1924.

Company waived its patent on a harmless substitute for white phosphorous that allowed competitors to begin using them in the manufacture of matches. The efforts of progressives such as Hamilton and Andrews focused national attention on the issue of occupational safety and led to an entirely new field of study for social scientists and members of the American medical science profession.

Prohibition

Efforts to curb or eliminate alcohol from American life had existed since colonial days. In 1851, Maine became the first state to prohibit alcohol within its borders. During the 1870s, women's groups, most notably the Woman's Christian Temperance Union, actively sought to close down saloons and promote individual moral reform. By the turn of the twentieth century, efforts to prohibit alcohol had become a reform supported by a large number of progressives who viewed the availability of cheap mass-produced alcohol as a societal danger in need of removal. Alcohol was viewed by women's groups as a family-wrecking evil, by doctors as the source of countless health problems, by businessmen as a factor contributing to inefficiency, and by urban political reformers as a lifeblood of saloons that functioned as centers of moral degeneracy promoting drunkenness, violent crime, prostitution, and police corruption. (Many progressives also opposed Prohibition efforts for a variety of reasons.)

By the mid-1890s, the **Anti-Saloon League (ASL)** emerged as a major special interest group promoting Prohibition at the state level. Enlisting the support of many Protestant congregations, ASL members pledged only to support "dry" Democratic or Republican candidates for public office. The ASL pressured legislators for community "local option" laws and statewide prohibition statutes. In states that allowed referendums, the ASL succeeded in placing proposed Prohibition measures before local and statewide voters. Some of these efforts failed (such as in Texas where referendums held in 1908 and 1911 barely failed to pass), while many others proved successful. By 1917, 21 states had banned saloons entirely and three fourths of Americans lived in a legally dry county. While achieving many state-level successes, prohibitionists still desired passage of a proposed federal constitutional amendment to outlaw liquor and would pursue that goal vigorously after the outbreak of World War I.

Woman Suffrage

Similar to Prohibition, the woman suffrage movement had its origins in the antebellum era but evolved into a Progressive era crusade. Organized efforts to promote female voting in America had existed since the 1840s, with a main line of argument being that men were denying civil rights to women. While that approach continued into the twentieth century, many pragmatic suffragists in the early 1900s began to gain crucial support by persuading reformers that their endeavors to end child labor, prohibit alcohol, and even limit the voting strength of immigrants would be greatly bolstered with the addition of qualified

Woman Suffrage Headquarters in Cleveland, Ohio. 1912

women voters. (In the South, some feminist groups argued openly that adding women to the voter rolls would increase white voting power over African Americans due to their larger numbers.)

After the Civil War, the suffrage movement experienced internal divisions over tactics and priorities, leading to a factional split. In 1890, a major reconciliation among suffragists led to the formation of the **National American Woman Suffrage Association (NAWSA)**, which revitalized the movement. The organization sponsored state-level educational activities, well-financed referenda drives, and brisk lobbying of legislators. In its first six years of operation, NAWSA's work bore some fruit with the admission of Wyoming and Utah into the Union with woman suffrage written into their state constitutions and voters in Colorado and Idaho granting unrestricted female voting by referendums. The next fourteen years, however, proved disappointing. Despite the launching of 480 separate petition campaigns to give women the vote in states across the country, only a few succeeded in getting the measures on the ballot, and none passed. Starting in 1910, former NAWSA President Carrie Chapman Catt's renewed efforts to organize effective state-level campaigns began to pay off. Seven western states granted unlimited female suffrage by 1914, with Oklahoma and South Dakota following suit by 1918. Nevertheless, the failure to gain the franchise in most central and eastern states (except for the allowance in some states to participate in local or presidential elections only) led not only to a wave of congressional petitions to introduce a proposed federal constitutional amendment but also to an increase in deliberately abrasive tactics by so-called militant suffragists to use more aggressive tactics employed by British suffragists to bring about the desired change at the national level.

Political Reforms

The arguments of woman suffragists to allow female voter participation worked well among Progressives who concerned themselves with reforming politics and government. Motivated by a desire to reduce corruption and improve the efficiency of government, reforms that they adopted democratized the political process for many common citizens while other changes actually restricted access to participation for members of certain groups. Nevertheless, the perceived need to adapt to changed times unified them to seek alterations in the nation's political system.

By the 1890s, most states had moved to the so-called Australian ballot system, whereby voters cast their votes in secret on publicly printed ballots (in English) with all candidates listed available only at official polling places. Other states went further to limit potential corruption by outlawing vote-buying and corporate donations while limiting acceptable uses of campaign funds. Though many hailed these and other reforms, they often contributed to a decline in excitement at election time and decreased voter turnout.

Most Progressives did not mind an overall reduction in voter participation—their goals were often to "improve" the quality of the electorate rather than to expand its numbers. Such thinking guided more open disfranchisement efforts in the North and South at the turn of the century. In the South, Democrats alarmed by the Populist challenge of the 1890s sought to greatly reduce black and poor white involvement in elections through a variety of devices including poll taxes, literacy tests, "civics" exams, and other restrictions. Meanwhile, Republicans in the North and West used similar devices to reduce the influence of potential voters from recent immigrant groups. While these efforts disregarded the spirit of the Fifteenth Amendment, they did not violate the letter of the amendment, which stated only that a citizen could not be denied the right to vote on grounds of race or color.

The **direct primary** became a quintessential Progressive reform. Activists often found their efforts stymied by conservative political bosses and their corporate allies in both major political parties who arranged for the nomination of candidates who usually held anti-reform views at state conventions. In an effort to break down these barriers, Progressives across the country sought to take the power of nominations away from the party bosses and place them in the hands of responsible citizens. Over a dozen states allowed for the direct primary by the 1912 presidential election. Most states had the device by 1920. Riding on the heels of the direct primary's popularity, three-quarters of the states ratified the Seventeenth Amendment to the U.S. Constitution in 1913, which allowed for the direct election of U.S. senators by popular vote rather than state legislatures.

Further efforts to limit the power of conservative Democratic and Republican party bosses under the sway of corporate influence involved the inclusion of eligible citizens in the legislative process. Among these "direct democracy" provisions adopted by a growing number of states by 1920, the referendum also allowed voters to express their opinion and advise the legislature how to act on a controversial issue. Meanwhile, the initiative allowed activists to gather signatures to qualify legislation for approval by the voters. If passed, the proposition would become law without approval needed by the state legislature. Some states adopted the recall, allowing disgruntled citizens to gather enough signatures on a petition to call for a special election to seek the removal of certain officeholders.

Robert LaFollette and the "Wisconsin Idea"

Under its vibrant governor **Robert M. LaFollette,** Wisconsin proved to be a leader in state-level progressive innovation. A former Republican congressman who broke with his party's establishment because of his belief that they were in the pockets of corporate business interests, LaFollette spent much of the 1890s building up a coalition of rank-and-file members in an effort to seize the gubernatorial nomination. He finally succeeded in 1900 and won in the general election. For the next six years, "Battlin' Bob" worked tirelessly to reform his party and his state. He successfully campaigned for state legislature candidates who supported his call for the direct primary (his main proposal for achieving government accountability and corporate regulation) and other key elements of his reform agenda, including workers' compensation, creation of a state railroad regulation, a comprehensive civil service law, and a state income tax on the wealthy, which were eventually adopted.

Before leaving the governorship in 1906 to fill a vacant U.S. Senate seat, LaFollette worked closely with faculty members of the University of Wisconsin (his alma mater) to craft legislation geared toward addressing public policy issues. Soon to be known as the "Wisconsin Idea," LaFollette relied on these collegiate experts to examine specific problems in society and government, gather evidence, and propose legislative solutions. To aid the state government in this endeavor, the legislature created the Legislative Research Library to provide an agency with state funds to aid in the development of new laws. Often called the "laboratory of democracy," Wisconsin during the Progressive Era produced many pioneering reforms that influenced the way states across the country reacted to similar concerns.

Robert M. LaFollette, July 5, 1924

Washington and Du Bois

Despite the end of Reconstruction leading to the establishment of second-class status for African Americans in southern society, black voting had not been entirely eliminated. With their economic clout, conservative members of the new upper class felt that they could effectively manage the black vote. In the late 1880s and early 1890s, however, growing agricultural unrest led to the formation of the Populist Party which, for a while, seemed capable of merging oppressed black and marginal white farmers into an effective coalition to challenge conservative rule. Southern Democratic politicians responded by reviving racist propaganda and returning to warnings about "Negro domination" and "revival of black Reconstruction" to discredit the Populists. After successfully maintaining their power, these leaders soon undertook a major effort to disfranchise black and poor white voters in the name of "good government." Rather than expanding the electorate, "election reform" advocates argued that reducing the number of eligible voters to those "better qualified" to participate in the process would improve the overall quality of government and reduce corruption. Between 1890 and 1910, the southern states imposed poll taxes, literacy requirements, and other creative means to suppress the vote. Four states even instituted "grandfather clauses" into their voting laws, allowing men to vote only if their ancestors had voted before 1867 (when blacks had been first granted the vote). The Supreme Court eventually overturned this obvious violation of the Fifteenth Amendment, but not until 1915. Combined, these measures succeeded in an almost total elimination of black voting in the South. As late as 1896, over 130,000 blacks continued to vote in Louisiana. By 1904, only 1,342 were able to do so. Although loopholes and lax enforcement permitted whites to vote far more often than blacks, poll taxes and literacy laws did reduce the number of poor illiterate white voters in many southern localities.

African Americans responded to the imposition of segregation and disfranchisement, along with the threat of violence to sustain the system, in a variety of ways. Large numbers accepted the accommodationist philosophy of Booker T. Washington—the principal of Alabama's Tuskegee Institute who, by the turn of the twentieth century, had emerged as the most well-known black leader in the nation. Educated at Virginia's Hampton Institute, one of many new black colleges founded by sympathetic white Northerners after the Civil War, Washington brought Hampton's emphasis on manual training for teachers to the Alabama Black Belt when he founded Tuskegee in 1881. His students did not receive an advanced education in subjects deemed "impractical" in the current environment. Instead, they learned the basic skills necessary to return to their communities and teach others how to become a better farmer or tradesman.

In political matters, Washington refused to agitate for change. Though publicly expressing his hope many times that segregation and disfranchisement would eventually end, Washington refused to protest openly for change, choosing to accept the status quo rather than threaten a white backlash that he believed would only lead to violence and the closing of his school. Instead, he often commented on his belief that whites would ultimately accept blacks in southern society and grant them equal rights. Washington most famously expressed his public views in his 1895 Cotton States and International Exposition Address in Atlanta before a large predominately white audience. Calling for interracial cooperation, he asked whites to aid industrious African Americans by giving them gainful employment. Meanwhile, he reminded blacks that the chance "to earn a dollar in a factory just now is worth infinitely more than the opportunity to spend a dollar in an opera house." He then bowed to Jim Crow segregation by using a famous metaphor: "In all things that are purely social we can be as separate as the fingers, yet one as the hand in all things essential to mutual progress." Such public positions made Washington acceptable to southern leaders while allowing the educator to channel money from northern and southern philanthropists to simultaneously build up Tuskegee and his personal reputation. Privately, however, Washington worked behind the scenes to subvert the system by funding legal challenges to segregation and supporting campaigns to thwart the implementation of the grandfather clause in Louisiana. While this covert activity has led some modern critics to label Washington a hypocrite, the "Wizard of Tuskegee" viewed himself as a pragmatist—a practical realist who sought tangible benefits within a harsh environment.

A growing number of black intellectuals strongly disagreed with Washington's public approach. In Boston, William Monroe Trotter began publishing *The Guardian*, a newspaper dedicated to constant agitation for complete acceptance of African Americans as equals, laying vicious criticism not only on Jim Crow and disfranchisement, but also on Booker T. Washington for his appeasement of white supremacy. Initially supportive of the educator and his accomplishments, W.E.B. Du Bois, the first African American to receive a Ph.D. from Harvard University, came to reject Washington's narrow focus on material well-being at the expense of equality. In education, Du Bois argued for increased opportunities for African Americans beyond manual training. A classical education would foster the emergence of qualified black leaders—the "talented tenth"–while expanding curiosity and intellectual

JACK JOHNSON (1878-1946)

Boxing legend Jack Johnson, the first African American to win the world heavyweight boxing championship, was born in Galveston on March 31, 1878. He left school in the fifth grade to help support his parents, both former slaves, and their nine children. He swept out a barbershop, worked as a porter in a gambling house, and later labored as a dockworker. Johnson began his boxing career as a sparring partner and participant in "battle royals," where several black youths would fight each other at the same time with the winner receiving money thrown to him from the white spectators. He started fighting in private clubs in the Galveston area, finally becoming a professional prizefighter in 1897.

Johnson left Galveston in 1899 and did not return. He spent his time traveling the country, fighting, and gaining increasing recognition. By 1902 he won over 50 fights against white and black opponents. In 1903 he won the Negro heavyweight championship, but the reigning white heavyweight champion, Jim Jeffries, refused the challenge to fight him. Johnson had to wait until after Jeffries's retirement for his opportunity. In 1908, he defeated the Canadian world champion Tommy Burns in Australia. The boxing community did not recognize Johnson as the actual champion until 1910 when Jim Jeffries came out of retirement to fight Johnson in Reno, Nevada, but was soundly defeated. Race riots broke out in many parts of the country, including Texas, as a result of Johnson's triumph.

Jim Jeffries was the first of many recruited "great white hopes" charged with the task of defeating Johnson, who infuriated the majority of whites because of his color, his taunting and trash-talking of opponents, and his non-conformist behavior, especially scandalous public relationships with white women. He was easily the most famous (and in many circles the most hated) African American in the country. Johnson's propensity for white women (usually, but not always prostitutes) made him a constant target for authorities. In 1913 he fled a conviction for violation of the Mann Act, a federal law designed to combat prostitution by forbidding the transportation of women across interstate lines for "immoral purposes." In practice, authorities during the Progressive Era often used the law as a weapon to prosecute individuals engaging in premarital, extramarital, or (as in the case with Johnson) interracial relationships. Facing a fine and prison time if he remained in the country, Johnson left the United States for an extended tour in Europe, Mexico, and Canada.

Johnson finally lost the heavyweight championship to a white man, Jess Willard, in Havana, Cuba in 1915. Despite his age (he was 37 by then) and the extreme tropical heat, he was not knocked out until the 26th round. In 1920, Johnson returned to the United States and was arrested for his Mann Act conviction and served over a year in Leavenworth Prison. Upon his release, he returned to boxing, but he was well past his prime. He gave up professional fighting in 1938. During the last decade of his life he promoted fights, refereed bouts, and occasionally managed and trained boxers. Johnson's raucous life ended the way he lived it—in a high-speed car crash near Raleigh, North Carolina in 1946.

development for African Americans with a desire to learn more about the world. "Is not life more than meat?" Du Bois asked in his 1903 seminal work *The Souls of Black Folk.*

Du Bois also looked with disgust at Booker T. Washington's contention that African Americans should wait for their rights to be bestowed by whites. Mocking Washington's 1895 Cotton Exposition Speech as the "Atlanta Compromise," he believed that blacks should settle for nothing less than immediate social and political equality. Before 1906, Du Bois generally limited his complaints to writings and his lectures at Atlanta University, but after a bloody race riot that year claimed dozens of black lives, the professor became radicalized, determined to become a proactive force for change. Along with William Trotter and 27 other black leaders, Du Bois convened a conference in Niagara Falls, Canada (hotels in nearby Buffalo, New York barred blacks) to formally renounce Washington's accommodationism and form a new organization—the "Niagara Movement"—to promote their goals. Three years later, they merged with white allies (including Florence Kelley and Oswald Garrison Villard, a grandson of abolitionist William Lloyd Garrison) to form the National Association for the Advancement of Colored People (NAACP). Eschewing grass-roots protesting, the early NAACP pursued a strategy of legal challenges to Jim Crow statutes while educating the public and generating publicity through its journal *The Crisis* (edited by Du Bois). Though decades would pass before these efforts produced results, Du Bois and his devotees had accepted the challenge of overturning centuries of entrenched racial prejudice in America.

NATIONAL REFORM UNDER ROOSEVELT

The Rise of Theodore Roosevelt

The death of William McKinley by an anarchist's bullet at the 1901 Pan American Exposition in Buffalo, New York elevated Theodore Roosevelt to the presidency, culminating a remarkable political rise. Born on October 27, 1858, into a New York "old money" family, young Teddy received encouragement from his father to overcome his childhood bouts with asthma by building up his body through rigorous physical activity. While engaging in athletics and other outdoor activities, he also exercised his mind through voracious reading, especially books on history, politics, and natural science. Roosevelt's application of this life philosophy, which he called the pursuit of the "strenuous life," came to dominate his personality. While attending Harvard, he met and married his first wife, Alice Hathaway Lee. After graduation in 1880, Roosevelt studied law while writing a naval history of the War of 1812, the first of many books that he authored in his lifetime.

Unlike others within his social class, Roosevelt desired to formally enter the political arena, and in 1881 he won election as a Republican to the New York Assembly. With his youthful energy and idealism, Roosevelt won over many of his colleagues and earned the position of minority leader before resigning the post when, on the same day in 1884, his young wife Alice died after giving birth to the couple's only child, followed by his mother who succumbed to typhoid fever. Leaving his young child temporarily with family members, he journeyed

President Theodore Roosevelt, his wife Edith, and their children, c. 1903. Roosevelt earlier married Alice Hathaway Lee of Massachusetts, but the woman died at an early age from kidney failure two days after their infant Alice was born. Later, Roosevelt married Edith Kermit Crow, with whom he had five more children.

to the Badlands of the Dakota Territory to oversee two cattle ventures and to forget his personal troubles by immersing himself in the western lifestyle that he had read so much about. Though he lost heavily on his monetary investment, the experience boosted his physical and mental condition while adding to the life narrative that benefited his subsequent political career. Upon his return from the frontier in 1886, Roosevelt remarried and made a failed run for mayor of New York. As he started a new family life with his wife and new children, Roosevelt gained his first federal government post when President Benjamin Harrison appointed him to the Civil Service Commission. After six years, he returned to New York City to serve a two-year term as president of the police commission.

With the city's police force modernized in numerous ways that proved to be influential on municipalities across the country, Roosevelt returned to Washington, D.C. to serve as Assistant Secretary of the Navy under President William McKinley. Always interested in naval history and possessing a strong belief that the country needed a large, modern navy, Roosevelt enjoyed promoting his ideas in the years leading up to the Spanish-American War. When the conflict arrived, he convinced himself he could not just support the war from the sidelines—to be true to his principles, he had to volunteer to fight. Growing up enamored with books that touted the supposed gallantry of military struggle, Roosevelt also wanted to experience combat personally. After organizing a volunteer regiment that trained outside of San Antonio, Texas, "Roosevelt's Rough Riders" saw extensive fighting in the heights surrounding Santiago, Cuba. Colonel Roosevelt emerged from battle alive and, thanks to his journalist friends in the press corps, a war hero.

In 1898, Roosevelt gained the Republican nomination for the governorship of New York and narrowly defeated his Democratic opponent. For the next two years, he earned the reputation of an able administrator who would frequently rankle leaders within his party by openly differing with them on political appointments, regulation of corporations, and other public policies. After the death of McKinley's first vice president, public pressure grew (encouraged by many Republican Party leaders in New York who wanted Roosevelt out of the state) for the governor to join the ticket with McKinley as the vice presidential nominee in the upcoming election of 1900. Given the weakness of the vice presidency and temperamentally opposed to taking the back seat to anybody, Roosevelt preferred to remain as governor and seek the presidency in 1904. Nevertheless, not wishing to disappoint party members who might feel snubbed if he turned down the popular clamor for his candidacy, Roosevelt accepted the honor. Though conservative Senator Mark Hanna prophetically chided his colleagues by exclaiming, "Don't any of you realize that there's only one life between that madman and the presidency?", the McKinley-Roosevelt team proved unstoppable in 1900, handily defeating the Democratic nominee William Jennings Bryan.

Roosevelt Takes Command

Upon McKinley's death from an assassin's bullet, 42-year-old Theodore Roosevelt became the youngest president in U.S. history. His youthful energy, leadership style, and precedent-setting actions reinvigorated the executive branch, paving the way for the transformation of the presidency to its modern empowered position in the federal government relative to its declining status during the Gilded Age. Understanding the power of publicity since his days as New York City police commissioner and governor of New York, President Roosevelt created a strong bond with the national press corps. While making himself accessible to reporters in an unprecedented fashion, he also used the media to channel his message by purposefully leaking stories with selected information, issuing press releases and giving press conference timed for maximum exposure, and punishing reporters who criticized him or betrayed his confidence by releasing information he wished to remain out of public view. Roosevelt also endeared himself to the national media because he could always be relied upon for a good story, such as occurred when the president, though an avid sportsman with the rifle, refused to kill a small bear while on a hunting trip in Mississippi. The resulting news coverage of the incident led executives at a toy company to start issuing the first stuffed "Teddy Bears." The new president's independent streak also became readily apparent, perhaps with no better example than his October 1901 dinner invitation to the African American leader Booker T. Washington. While members of the southern press lambasted the president for committing in their minds an outrageous inherent acceptance of racial equality, Roosevelt never apologized (though he never repeated the gesture).

More than a recognizable change in style, Roosevelt's presidency marked a considerable change in substance. During his first term, he overcame the lack of a mandate due to his elevation to the presidency through non-electoral means by positioning himself on the popular side of many key progressive issues. He also avoided potential clashes with conservative opposition in Congress by often pursuing foreign and domestic policy agendas that did not necessitate congressional involvement.

The Northern Securities Company Case

The question of how the nation should respond to the rise of large dominant corporations, or "trusts," that controlled numerous sectors of the national economy became the primary domestic issue of Roosevelt's presidency. As a result of the unprecedented growth and size of big business, many Americans felt threatened by the notion of corporations wielding unaccountable economic and political power. On this matter, Roosevelt's ideas were clear: the people, through the power of the federal government, should establish its supremacy by passing and enforcing laws that established proper rules of conduct and regulated corporate behavior. Initially, the young president sought to use publicity to praise corporations who acted properly while lambasting those that acted in a socially irresponsible manner. In the bill creating the Department of Commerce that Roosevelt signed into law in early 1903, the president reveled in an amendment attached to the measure that created a Bureau of Corporations empowered to assemble data on national businesses for the purposes of allowing the president to make recommendations to Congress, which also gave him the power to selectively release such information to the public.

Roosevelt's main effort to assert the power of the federal government over corporations came with his administration's suit in federal court against the **Northern Securities Company**, a recently established railroad monopoly that had the potential to dominate the nation's railroad traffic from Chicago to the West Coast. Created to settle a potentially bitter competitive dispute among railroads controlled by magnates James J. Hill, E. H. Harriman, and J.P. Morgan, the Northern Securities Company was a holding company possessing the stock of the Great Northern and Northern Pacific Railroads whose appearance greatly alarmed farmers, businessmen, newspaper editors, and politicians across the Northwest. Sensing the popular mood, and strongly against the combination personally, Roosevelt asked his attorney general, Philander C. Knox, to seek the breakup of the monopoly for violation of a section of the 1890 Sherman Antitrust Act, which outlawed monopolies determined to have used their dominant market position to restrain trade. In March 1904, the Supreme Court laid down a landmark 5-4 decision in favor of the Justice Department's position that the Northern Securities Company violated the Sherman Act and must be dismantled—the first business entity to be broken up by a federal court order. As the decision reverberated throughout the corporate world, Roosevelt would continue to dissolve other perceived illegal combinations. But while the president often received the title of "The Trust Buster" in the national press, Roosevelt did not seek to dissolve every monopoly in the country. He did not believe that the size of a company mattered as much as its behavior. Roosevelt left other monopolies alone, such as J.P. Morgan's U.S. Steel Company, and more often sought to cajole the trusts into proper legal and moral behavior with the combination of information gathered by the Bureau of Corporations and the threat of a lawsuit from the Justice Department. It was an uneven and unpredictable approach but perhaps the best Roosevelt could do with the tools available under existing statutes.

The Anthracite Coal Strike

The 1902 **Anthracite Coal Strike** presented another opportunity for Theodore Roosevelt to seize upon a popular issue while also seeking to expand the powers and responsibilities of the presidency. In May 1902, over 100,000 Pennsylvania coal miners walked off the job to protest low pay, poor working conditions, and the non-acceptance of their union by management. By late September, many began to fear the onset of a nationwide coal shortage as the winter months approached. Instances of hoarding commenced, and coal prices doubled.

Roosevelt responded by inviting mine owners and the president of the United Mine Workers Union, John Mitchell, to a tense White House meeting. The president left the conference believing the owners acted unreasonably, preferring that the administration stay out of the affair if federal troops would not be sent to handle the strikers. Roosevelt soon unveiled a plan calling for the mine owners and workers to accept the rulings of a special presidential arbitration commission that would hear both sides of the case and seek a settlement. To pressure the mine operators to accept the offer, the president let it be known to them that he had drawn up plans to declare a national emergency and was preparing to send federal troops into the mining areas to extract the coal without profit for the mining companies. While doubting the courts would ever sanction such an action, the mine owners believed Roosevelt to be serious and knew that favorable public opinion bolstered his resolve, so they eventually submitted to the creation of the commission. In the meantime, the striking laborers agreed to go back to work and await the commission's findings.

Ultimately, the commission determined that the coal miners should receive a 10 percent pay increase, a 9-hour working day, and the establishment of an arbitration system to resolve work-related disputes. The mine owners, however, benefited from the commission's avoidance of other worker complaints, most importantly, the non-recognition of the workers' union as the members' legitimate bargaining agent. While the results were mixed for the dueling parties, the resolution of the coal strike clearly benefited Theodore Roosevelt and his efforts to elevate the power and prestige of the presidency. Unlike previous chief executives, Roosevelt injected the White House directly into a major labor dispute in a way other than sending in troops to break a strike. The president resolved the potential economic crisis by employing the arbitration principle—though a commonly used device today, the move was an unprecedented action at the time. In the process, Roosevelt bolstered the labor movement in the country by elevating the representatives of labor to an equal basis with business executives. Rather than assuming a pro-union stance, Roosevelt believed he acted out of fairness for the workers (providing them a "Square Deal," as he came to call his domestic agenda) while seeking to end the crisis for the good of the country as a whole.

Roosevelt's Reelection

Despite misgivings among conservatives in his party, Roosevelt experienced little difficulty securing the Republican Party nomination in 1904. After pleasing them by accepting one of their own, Senator Charles W. Fairbanks of Indiana as the vice-presidential nominee, Roosevelt enjoyed unanimous renomination at the Republican National Convention and awaited his Democratic opponent. After William Jennings Bryan's defeat in 1900, conservative Democrats regained power within the party and achieved the nomination of New York state judge Alton B. Parker. Given the party's hold on the southern states, Democrats believed Parker could triumph by carrying his sizeable home state (which also happened to be Roosevelt's home state), and then picking up a few modest-sized northern and border states. They portrayed him as a candidate with a calm, judicious, conservative mind to be contrasted against Roosevelt's alleged brash, reformist tendencies. The strategy backfired. By presenting themselves as the more conservative party, Democrats miscalculated the temper of the times. By trying to make Roosevelt's personality a major campaign issue, they gave the popular president a political gift. In comparison, Parker seemed dull, aloof, and uncharismatic. Though worried about his reelection chances to the very end, Roosevelt achieved an overwhelming victory over Parker who was only able to carry the southern states. Roosevelt's 336-140 win in the Electoral College and almost 20-percentage point margin in the popular vote (56.4 percent to 37.6 percent) provided him with a strong affirmation of his foreign and domestic policies and convinced him that he had received a mandate to press for further progressive reforms.

On election night, Roosevelt issued a statement thanking the nation and informing the citizenry that he would only serve one full term before retirement. Though some believed that he acted out of impulse in appreciation for the incredible endorsement that he had just received from the public, Roosevelt had pondered the issue and truly believed at the time that even though he had not been elected the first time, he had filled out most of William McKinley's term and no person should serve for more than two terms (term limits for presidents did not come until the 1950s by constitutional amendment). While a noble gesture that he did not have to make, the pledge worked to undermine Roosevelt's ability to govern during his second term. Instead of keeping everyone guessing about whether he would run again, and thus using that uncertainty as a source of political capital, the anti-third-term-pledge instantly made him a "lame duck" president. Though still able to achieve some solid accomplishments during his second term, his power with respect to Congress eroded and limited his ability to achieve many items on his agenda.

Railroad Regulation

Regulation of the nation's railroads became a major priority for Roosevelt early in his second term. Two years earlier, the president had supported the Elkins Act, which had banned the practice of railroads giving rebates to shipping businesses. That legislation, however, was not controversial—few members in either house of Congress opposed the bill. In fact, the railroad companies largely

welcomed the law because it eliminated a practice used by many large shippers to apply pressure in order to receive preferential rates.

During his second term, Roosevelt threw his weight behind the growing movement in the country to regulate the rates that railroad companies charged for the shipment of goods. For years, many citizens had called for federal government oversight of railroad rates, preferably by the Interstate Commerce Commission (ICC), as a means of curbing inflated charges and eliminating price discrimination. Roosevelt did not create the movement for railroad rate regulation—he joined an already popular effort and fought for its success by his typical means of generating publicity and actively working with members of Congress to enact the best bill possible. Eschewing an alternative that would have empowered the ICC to set specific rates, Roosevelt endorsed a bill sponsored by Representative William Hepburn of Iowa that called for the ICC to have the authority to set maximum rates that a railroad could charge. When Senate resistance stiffened, the president backed an amendment supported by many conservatives (and opposed by many progressives including Robert LaFollette who had been elected to the Senate in 1905) that allowed for federal courts to review and overturn ICC rate decisions, though the burden of proof would rest with the carriers rather than the shippers or the ICC to supply evidence to challenge those rate determinations. With that legislative addition, further opposition crumbled. Shepherding the **Hepburn Act** through Congress was one of Roosevelt's signature achievements. The new law not only empowered the ICC to fix maximum railroad rates, subject to court review, but also vastly improved government oversight of the railroad industry by prescribing uniform bookkeeping procedures of company records and allowing ICC officials to review these company records in order to better render its decisions. The law would have lasting significance, not only for railroad regulation but also for government supervision of the national economy as a whole. The Hepburn Act marked the first time that a federal law authorized inspection of any national business's financial records and marked the first time the rates and prices of a company would be subject to federal government review—it would not be the last.

Regulation of the Nation's Food and Medicine

Soon after passage of the Hepburn Act, Roosevelt quickly joined another growing regulatory cause, this time, the desire for supervision of the food processing and medicine-producing industries. For years, muckrakers had been delivering a steady drumbeat of revelations detailing ways in which food manufacturers altered spoiled products to make them palatable or added harmful ingredients to preserve them longer. Pharmaceutical companies frequently made claims about the curative powers of their medicines without the science to back them up, often including compounds in their products that were far more harmful than beneficial to a patient's health. Published in 1906, Upton Sinclair's novel on the Chicago meatpacking industry, ***The Jungle***, became the most powerful work of this genre. A journalist with strong socialist beliefs, Sinclair wrote the exposé after spending weeks working undercover in meatpacking plants and interviewing laborers. Though Sinclair's main purposes were to publicize the lives and working conditions of the immigrants while promoting socialism as an alternative to capitalism, the novel's sections detailing the unsanitary processing of meat resonated far more with the public and President Roosevelt than the portions highlighting the harshness of life in the slums or the exploitation of workers. Sinclair's descriptions of how meatpackers employed such practices as incorporating the meat of cows suffering from tuberculosis, added chemicals to spoiled meat to alter their appearance, and tried to contain rats by laying out poisoned bread amongst unguarded meat, just to name a few, struck a powerful chord with consumers who demanded action. Roosevelt responded to the growing public pressure by sending investigators to Chicago who verified Sinclair's descriptions of abysmal processing conditions at the plants in a damning two-part report. When recalcitrant lawmakers continued to drag their feet, Roosevelt released the first part of the report to the public and threatened to reveal its entire contents. By this time, the large meatpacking firms had already determined that regulation was in their best interest, not just because of the public clamor in the United States but also due to threatened boycotts of American meat products by the governments of many European nations. The new rules would actually place the larger firms at a competitive advantage in relation to their competition—these large companies could now afford the additional expense of maintaining sanitary conditions if their smaller competitors were forced to do the same. Meanwhile, the reputation of the quality of American meat exports would be bolstered. When the industry secured a provision, with Roosevelt's approval, calling for the federal government to cover the cost of inspections, opposition soon dissipated. The subsequent **Meat Inspection Act** empowered the U.S. Department of Agriculture to establish regulations for the sanitary processing of meat products and to provide for regular inspections of meat processing facilities. While the president and much of the nation greeted the reform law with satisfaction, Upton Sinclair displayed indifference to the measure. In noting how the nation fixated on the meat processing aspects of his book rather than the plight of industrial workers or the message of the Socialist Party of America, Sinclair wryly reminisced: "I aimed at the public's heart, and by accident I hit it in the stomach."

Passed into law on the same day as the Meat Inspection Act, the **Pure Food and Drug Act** addressed the safety of other foods intended for human consumption as well as medicines. This law created a new federal government agency, the Food and Drug Administration, to test and approve drugs before being allowed for sale on the market. The bill also banned, for the first time in the nation's history, certain items from being included in a food or drug. For years, cocaine had been used as a stimulant in products, including Coca-Cola. Heroin had been sold over-the-counter as a mood relaxer. Crude petroleum was sometimes used in laxatives. These and other ingredients found to have no medicinal value, too addictive, or better served by an otherwise safer alternative could no longer be legally sold in the country. The law also targeted untruthful labeling by manufacturers. For the first time, labels had to specify if certain ingredients on a government-approved list were included in the product, and it was now unlawful to state that an ingredient was included in a product when, in fact, it was not. Together with the Hepburn Act, passage of the Meat Inspection Act and the Pure Food and Drug Act marked the apex of Roosevelt's regulatory agenda seeking to bring the nation's corporations under federal supervision.

The First Environmental President

Of all his endeavors as president, Theodore Roosevelt took most pride in his conservation efforts. Already possessing a strong affinity with the outdoors, Roosevelt shared the views of many who were outraged that existing federal land policy sanctioned wasteful practices that despoiled the landscape and threatened to deplete the nation's resources. He believed that uncontrolled development of federal lands during the late-nineteenth century led to exploitation of forests, mineral resources, and public grazing lands, potentially leaving little for future generations of Americans to use. Though many progressive reformers agreed on the problem, they characteristically disagreed on proposed solutions. Two general reform camps emerged by the early twentieth century. The preservationists led by Sierra Club founder John Muir represented the most radical supporters of a new direction in land management. They sought to keep as much pristine wilderness away from development as possible to preserve the natural landscape. Though a close friend of Muir, Theodore Roosevelt typically sided with U.S. Chief Forester **Gifford Pinchot** and other so-called conservationists who favored resource development guided by federal regulation based upon scientific management. In their opinion, trees on public lands could and should be cut down, for example, but the amount should be strictly regulated and supplemented with increased plantings to ensure that the nation had ample supplies of lumber. While many citizens sympathized with these early environmentalists, tough opposition frequently had to be overcome from many Westerners who generally resented eastern meddling in their affairs and believed federal limitations hindered economic development, as well as smaller stockmen and lumber companies who felt that government regulations worked against their interests (Larger cattle and timber businesses operators, by contrast, tended to support rational land use as the best policy for the long-term stability of their industries).

Roosevelt made government supervision of federal land use his own personal crusade. In the process, he became the first president to make conservation of the nation's resources a national priority. Early in his first term, the new president supported the National Reclamation Act sponsored by Nevada Senator Francis G. Newlands, which allocated money from the sale of public lands to build dams, reservoirs, and irrigation canals to aid in reclaiming desert lands in the West for agricultural use. On his watch, Roosevelt also initiated a system of licenses

President Theodore Roosevelt and Chief Forester Gifford Pinchot on a trip down the Mississippi River in October 1907.

and fees for those wishing to use the public domain for the grazing of cattle and sheep or the extraction of mineral resources.

Chief Forester Gifford Pinchot proved to be Roosevelt's closest advisor and primary advocate on conservation issues. Similar to the president, Pinchot came from a wealthy old-money New York family and believed strongly in the great outdoors. Educated at Yale, he pursued his interest in forestry by studying in Germany before returning to the United States to lead the U.S. Forest Bureau under President McKinley. In 1905, Roosevelt arranged for Congress to transfer jurisdiction over the nation's forest reserves from the Interior Department to Pinchot's agency (which would be renamed the United States Forest Service) in the Agriculture Department. Pinchot recruited a new force of agents he labeled Forest Rangers, designed their distinctive badges and green uniforms, and provided the charismatic force that motivated the agency's employees to perform their best while managing the reserves. Together, Roosevelt and Pinchot worked to regulate, but not eliminate, use of the nation's publicly-held timberlands. While Roosevelt tripled the size of national forest reserves to be excluded from public use to over 170 million acres (including a single 16 million-acre designation in 1907 just before a congressional deadline), the federal government during Roosevelt's presidency regularly collected large sums for timber use fees. From 1905 to 1906 alone, the government received $800,000, equal to the entire congressional appropriation for the Forest Service. A much-publicized quarrel between Pinchot and the preservationists took place over the chief forester's support for San Francisco, California's plans to damn the beautiful secluded Hetch Hetchy Valley, located adjacent to the popular Yosemite Valley, for the purpose of building a reservoir to act as the city's water supply after a devastating 1906 earthquake. While Roosevelt stayed out of the fracas, Muir threw himself into a desperate publicity campaign to arouse the nation's conscience. In the end, Muir succeeded only in delaying the valley's flooding. Construction of the reservoir finally commenced in 1913 during the Woodrow Wilson administration.

Though Roosevelt more often sided with Pinchot's views than Muir's, the president nevertheless performed many acts that elated the preservationists. Besides authorizing the creation of five new national parks, 150 national forests, and over 50 wildlife refuges, Roosevelt also established the nation's first national monuments, including the Grand Canyon, under power granted by the 1906 Antiquities Act, designed to preserve areas of important historical and archeological significance from economic development.

Roosevelt Chooses a Successor

At fifty years of age in 1908, Theodore Roosevelt prepared to become the youngest former president in American history—not a moment too soon for many conservatives in his own party who often displayed a façade of unity while privately disdaining his positions. Still energetic after seven and a half years in the White House, Roosevelt nevertheless honored his election night pledge and prepared to step aside but actively sought to choose a successor who would continue his policies and fight for what had not yet been achieved. Immediately ruling out Vice President Charles Fairbanks and other conservatives, Roosevelt also found most of the leading Republican progressives, such as Wisconsin's Robert LaFollette, to be unpalatable because of personal differences or the belief that they were simply too radical in their views. His two favorite choices, Massachusetts Senator Henry Cabot Lodge and Secretary of State Elihu Root, took themselves out of the running. Ultimately, Roosevelt settled on his good friend William Howard Taft. A former federal judge and U.S. Solicitor General from a prominent Ohio family, Taft served as governor of the Philippines before Roosevelt appointed him to be Secretary of War in 1904. The two men had known each other since the early 1890s and enjoyed a warm relationship. Though Roosevelt believed that they held similar views, he would later find Taft's progressivism to be more limited.

Roosevelt secured the Republican presidential nomination for Taft and campaigned hard for his friend in the general election against the Democratic nominee, William Jennings Bryan, making his third attempt to win the presidency. Taft needed the help. While a likeable man with a large six-foot, 300-pound frame who exuded confidence, the presidency was the first public office that Taft ever sought. He leaned heavily on Roosevelt's campaign experience, and it paid off. Despite Bryan's superior energy and oratorical talents along with a Democratic Party platform that mirrored many of Roosevelt's positions on the major issues of the day, Taft won 29 states (sweeping the Northeast, Midwest, and much of the West) with 321 electoral votes compared to Bryan's 17 states (mostly in the Solid South) with 162 electoral votes. The popular vote tally matched McKinley's victory over Bryan in 1900, with Taft securing 52 percent of the roughly 14 million votes cast.

THE TAFT PRESIDENCY

William Howard Taft experienced a rough time as president. Any individual following Theodore Roosevelt would have found themselves under incredible scrutiny and relentless comparison, but Taft bore the additional burden of being Roosevelt's chosen successor. He found it very difficult to emerge from Roosevelt's shadow positively in the eyes of the former president's rabid supporters who wished he had run for a third term. While personally affable, Taft lacked Roosevelt's dynamism and political skills. Truly disdaining the everyday give-and-take of politics, his main aspiration in life was never to be president but to be Chief Justice of the U.S. Supreme Court (a goal finally achieved when President Warren Harding appointed him to the post in 1921). Further complicating his tenure, Taft's primary advisor and confidante, his wife Helen, suffered a debilitating stroke two months after becoming First Lady thus limiting her ability to aid her husband.

Though the new president agreed with Roosevelt on many progressive issues, Taft differed philosophically on the proper role of the president in the legislative process. While Roosevelt never cowered from the prospect of wrestling with members of Congress over issues, Taft believed the president should propose items for consideration rather than guide legislation through each house. He also believed in restrained presidential power as opposed to Roosevelt's broad assertions of executive authority. Whereas Roosevelt often asked: "Is there a specific law that would keep the president from performing this action?" Taft would often ask: "What law authorizes the president to do this?"

Progressive congressmen in Taft's own party made life difficult for him even before he took office when they opened a controversy over limiting the power of conservative Republican House Speaker Joseph G. Cannon of Illinois. Angered by his seemingly autocratic rule, insurgent Republicans such as George W. Norris of Nebraska sought to restrict Cannon's authority over committee appointments and parliamentary procedures. Taft initially expressed sympathy for the cause but then quickly backed away after Cannon and other conservatives threatened to thwart all of the president's legislative proposals. The speaker later returned the favor by supporting Taft's call for tariff reform. Though only a few imported products received a direct reduction in tariff rates, Taft found satisfaction with a provision he supported that allowed the president to reduce rates further if a reciprocity agreement could be reach with individual countries that agreed to reduce their tariff rates on American exports. Flustered when the president retracted his public support for their efforts, progressive Republicans and Democrats continued to push for further tariff reductions and to reduce Speaker Cannon's power. Ultimately they got nowhere on additional tariff changes during Taft's presidency, but they succeeded in adopting new rules that expanded House Rules Committee membership from five to fifteen members, made membership elective rather than appointed by the Speaker, and excluded the Speaker himself as a member. The newly formed committee then created new house rules that made all committees elective.

Another rift between Taft and the progressives took place over conservation policy and the so-called **Ballinger-Pinchot Affair.** The root of the conflict involved Chief Forester Gifford Pinchot's strong dislike for Taft's choice of Richard Ballinger as Secretary of the Interior. A former mayor of Seattle, Washington and U.S. land commissioner, Ballinger favored western economic development and during his tenure would open more than a million acres of public land for commercial use. Pinchot soon opened a campaign against the secretary using speeches and other publicity-generating techniques that Roosevelt often employed to place doubts in conservationists' minds about Ballinger. When Ballinger came under suspicion of corruption while serving as Roosevelt's land commissioner, Pinchot leaked information to the press about the subsequent congressional investigation. Believing Ballinger to be innocent of the charges, Taft ordered Pinchot to desist from the attacks, but the forester only increased them when he became aware of a private deal arranged with the secretary's approval for a group of Ballinger's Seattle business associates and New York banker J.P. Morgan to develop previously-reserved Alaskan coal lands. Taft then fired Pinchot for insubordination, raising the ire of many progressives.

These political blunders obscured a series of progressive achievements during the Taft presidency. In four years, Taft oversaw the withdrawal of more public land for forest and oil reserves than Roosevelt had done in almost twice the time. He also accelerated the pace of antitrust prosecutions under the Sherman Act, most notably against the John D. Rockefeller's Standard Oil Company and James Buchanan Duke's American Tobacco Company, which were both ordered to be broken up and reorganized into smaller independent operations. In all, Taft's Justice Department instigated 90 such cases versus 57 during the Roosevelt presidency. Taft's support of the Mann-Elkins Act enabled its passage, which strengthened the ICC by allowing it to initiate freight rate changes and gave the agency regulatory jurisdiction over telephone and telegraph companies. The president also succeeded in getting congressional approval for an eight-hour work day for federal employees, the first mine safety standards, and creation of a federal Children's Bureau empowered to investigate and publicize upon all matters pertaining to the welfare of children but in practice specialized in highlighting child labor issues.

Though Taft viewed his accomplishments with satisfaction, he found himself constantly embroiled in inter-party divisions that were imploding the Republican Party. Whenever he made moves favorable to reform-minded Republicans, he alienated members of his party's Old Guard. When he pleased conservative Republicans, progressive Republicans inevitably cast him as a tool of the conservative establishment. Viewing it all from the sidelines was Theodore Roosevelt. Though he had left the country for an extended tourist jaunt through Europe capped by a hunting safari in Africa, the former president kept tabs on current events back home (and received constant updates from Gifford Pinchot and others who complained often of Taft's quiet progressivism when they believed that the times called for Roosevelt-style exuberance and action). After Roosevelt's lively return to America in June 1910 capped by a New York City ticker-tape parade, he largely kept quiet in order to promote party unity. The mid-term elections in 1910, however, proved to be disastrous for the Republicans. In primary elections, Taft made the decision to side with conservatives he favored over reformers that he disliked, but in most cases the voters supported the progressives. Democrats took advantage of the rift, adding 12 Senate seats and gaining 58 seats in the House of Representatives to seize solid control of that body.

Even before the mid-term elections concluded, Roosevelt began delivering a series of speeches calling for the acceptance of further reforms promoting social justice and direct democracy. He argued that his advocacy for change was not radicalism but meant to avert significantly radical ideas from gaining traction in the country. Privately, he tried to coax Taft to be more assertive with progressive causes that irked the president who began to resent his friend's meddling in his administration's affairs. The final breaking point between the two men occurred when Taft's Justice Department announced the filing of an anti-trust suit against J.P. Morgan's United States Steel Corporation, specifically citing its 1907 takeover of the Tennessee Coal and Iron Company. In fact, Roosevelt had personally allowed Morgan to merge the two companies without any trouble from his Justice Department as a means of helping to avert a growing crisis on Wall Street. At the time, a major brokerage firm, which had invested heavily in the stock of the Tennessee Iron and Coal, found itself on the brink of bankruptcy. In an early twentieth century example of a corporation being deemed by the government to be "too big to fail," Roosevelt allowed Morgan to swallow up Tennessee Iron and Coal to preserve the brokerage house, helping to alleviate the panic. While a subsequent congressional investigation provided much impetus for the creation of the Federal Reserve System in 1913 to enable the federal government to have greater control over the nation's credit so such deals would not have to be made in the future, the immediate impact of the lawsuit (which U.S. Steel ultimately won) was to irritate Roosevelt and end his friendship with Taft. For the first time, Roosevelt publicly criticized Taft for excessively filing anti-trust measures. Rather than seeking to break up monopolies, the best approach in his mind was for the federal government to strictly monitor corporate behavior and use the threat of dissolution to guarantee proper moral and legal behavior. By early 1912 the estrangement between Roosevelt and Taft was complete. The two men by then were no longer on speaking terms, and Roosevelt finally announced in February that he would seek the Republican Party nomination for an unprecedented third term as president.

The Election of 1912

The 1912 presidential election was a monumental affair in American politics presenting multiple candidates delivering impassioned but disparate messages to the voters regarding their visions of the proper direction for the country. Theodore Roosevelt campaigned hard to win 9 of the 12 states that held Republican Party primaries (Robert LaFollette won two states and Taft won only one), but the thirty-six remaining states had yet to adopt the primary. Thus, a majority of delegates to the Republican national convention held during June in Chicago were selected at state conventions directed by leaders loyal to the president. As a result, Taft secured enough delegates to take the nomination. Roosevelt and his supporters responded by bolting the convention with plans of forming a third party based on reform principles that they hoped would transform American politics. Knowing he would probably not be reelected, Taft only gave a few speeches in the coming campaign and remained in the contest largely to ensure Roosevelt's defeat. His main support derived from Republican Party loyalists, mostly conservatives. All hope for Roosevelt's success depended upon who won the Democratic nomination. If they selected a conservative or a candidate without national appeal, Roosevelt would have had a significant chance by appealing to progressives across party lines.

Three Democratic candidates dominated the presidential field—House Majority Leader Oscar Underwood of Alabama, Speaker of the House Champ Clark of Missouri, and New Jersey Governor Woodrow Wilson. The fact that the party held onto its archaic rule requiring two-thirds of the assembled delegates to agree upon a candidate promised a raucous meeting at the party's national convention in Baltimore. Speaker Clark held the lead in delegates entering the convention, but, after days of effort,

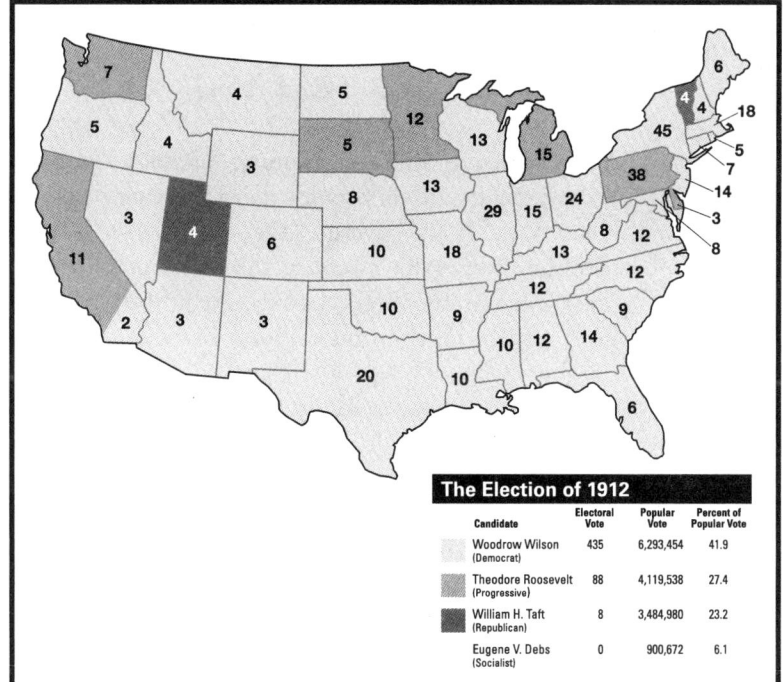

Map 21.1 The Election of 1912

his supporters failed to control the requisite number for the nomination. Eventually, the work of Wilson's convention floor managers and the endorsement of William Jennings Bryan produced victory for the governor on the forty-sixth ballot, much to Roosevelt's chagrin. Though generally acceptable to conservative Democrats, Wilson made a name for himself by supporting numerous state-level progressive measures while governor of the Garden State. His call for major national economic reforms promised to keep enough progressive Democrats within the party as they sought to win the White House for the first time since Grover Cleveland's victory in 1892.

Wilson's selection dismayed Roosevelt but did not deter him or his supporters from organizing their third party. In August, they reconvened in Chicago to host a national convention and launch their "**Progressive Party**." After Roosevelt told a reporter that he felt "fit as a bull moose" for the coming fight, the Bull Moose soon became the party's symbol. Ever since, most Americans have usually referred to the Progressive Party as the "Bull Moose Party" rather than the organization's official name.

Yet a fourth candidate vying for the presidency gave voters an additional choice. Eugene Debs, a former Democratic state legislator and national labor leader from Indiana, accepted his third bid as the nominee of the Socialist Party of America. A dynamic orator, the Socialists had no better messenger to spread their alternative to both laissez-faire capitalism and corporate regulation. Seeing the major problems of the Industrial Revolution caused by capitalism, not industrialization itself, Debs and the Socialists sought to awaken Americans to a path they believed would end the exploitation of labor and consumer price gouging; namely, government ownership of major banks, industries, and utilities managed on a non-profit basis in the public interest.

Ultimately, the race boiled down to a contest between Roosevelt and Wilson. The Bull Moose Party platform endorsed most of the major, social justice, direct democracy, and campaign reforms championed by progressives that exist today but had yet to be enacted. In addition to calls for active government regulation and supervision of big business, the Progressive Party platform also included demands for social insurance for the elderly, unemployed, and the disabled, minimum wages and maximum weekly hours for workers, compensation for work-related injuries, an end to child labor, a constitutional amendment to allow the collection of income taxes, woman suffrage, direct election of U.S. senators, primary elections for all state and national offices, acceptance of the initiative and referendum, the recall of elected officials, and limits to campaign contributions. Throughout the race, Roosevelt used the label "New Nationalism" (borrowed from a book by supporter Herbert Croly) to tout the party's message, which he believed was a "corrective to socialism and an anecdote for anarchy."

For his part, Wilson endeavored to maintain Democratic Party unity while proposing many reforms of his own. Though the Democratic platform included calls for a workers' compensation law, extension of the presidential primary system, and a constitutional amendment providing for a federal income tax, Wilson's "New Freedom" agenda concentrated on national economic reforms designed to restore competition in the marketplace. Believing that high protective tariffs contributed to the high cost of living, he desired a lower, revenue-only tariff. Wilson agreed with those who believed that the time had come for an overhaul of the nation's banking system to free up credit and overturn the national economy's reliance on New York bankers. Finally, the governor favored strong antitrust legislation, stating that, unlike Roosevelt who preferred regulating behavior, he wished to limit the actual size of corporations. By establishing thresholds in the marketplace that a corporation could not legally exceed, Wilson hoped that monopolies would dissipate and other companies would fill the void, thus returning competition to the American economy for the benefit of all.

The election received a severe jolt on October 12 when a deranged man with a pistol shot Roosevelt in the chest as he left a Milwaukee, Wisconsin hotel to deliver a speech. Seriously wounded from the bullet that tore through his heavy coat, eyeglass case, and speech notes, he nevertheless assessed that vital organs were missed and demanded to be taken to his engagement. Upon his arrival, Roosevelt explained that he had just been shot but that it would take "more than that to kill a Bull Moose." Though he stated that given the circumstances he would not be talking long, he spoke for over an hour and a half to the concerned but adoring crowd about the principles for which he was fighting. After the speech, Roosevelt spent the next nine days in the hospital as the other candidates suspended their campaigns until doctors released him for the final two weeks of the race.

As most everyone expected, Wilson took full advantage of the Republican split to triumph on election night. Receiving almost 6.3 million popular votes, he carried 40 states with 435 electoral votes. Roosevelt finished second with 4.2 million popular votes, winning six states with 88 electoral votes. Taft became the only president seeking reelection to finish in third place, tallying only 3.5 million popular votes and winning only two small states with eight electoral votes. **Eugene Debs** collected no electoral votes, but garnered over 900,000 popular votes—the high water mark for the Socialist Party in any presidential election. Wilson and the Democrats were elated. Not only had their party won the White House after a twenty-year drought, they also picked up enough seats to gain a majority in the Senate, giving them complete control of Congress.

NATIONAL REFORM UNDER WILSON

Wilson's Background

A government professor by training, **Thomas Woodrow Wilson** spend much of his adult life in academia before his meteoric rise to the governorship of New Jersey in 1910 followed soon by his ascent to the presidency in 1912. Born in Staunton, Virginia on the eve of the Civil War, Wilson spent much of his early life in Georgia and the Carolinas. Though a deeply religious man whose father served as a Presbyterian minister and seminary professor, he decided against a life in the ministry. Instead, Wilson attended Princeton University in New Jersey before studying law for a year at the University of Virginia. After withdrawing due to health reasons, he continued his studies at home, passed the Georgia bar exam, and briefly practiced law in Atlanta. Bored with the law and realizing that it was not aiding his growing interest in politics, Wilson attended graduate school at Johns Hopkins University in Baltimore, eventually earning a PhD in history and political science. Hoping to become a force in politics as an observer and known author, the young professor began to make a name for himself in the scholastic world through his publications, public lectures, and holding political science professorships, eventually landing a tenured position at Princeton. After his election to the presidency of his alma mater in 1902, Wilson soon became a nationally known university leader through his expansion of campus facilities, recruitment of noteworthy individuals for the faculty, and especially for a highly-publicized but failed effort to transform campus culture by seeking to abolish the school's exclusive social clubs.

As Wilson failed in other ways to reform social life at Princeton, he prepared to resign his post when New Jersey Democratic Party bosses presented him with the opportunity of a lifetime. Viewing the college president as a political conservative with name recognition who might help them resist the efforts of progressives in the state legislature from enacting various reforms, the bosses approached Wilson about the possibility of accepting their party's nomination for governor. In the past, Wilson had written essays critical of Theodore Roosevelt and William Jennings Bryan while touting a traditional, Jeffersonian states' rights and limited government viewpoint that was consistent with his southern upbringing. However, by 1910 Wilson knew which way the political winds were blowing. After securing the nomination, he quickly pivoted to a pro-reform stance during the campaign, a move that the bosses interpreted as mere grandstanding. But, after Wilson's victory in the general election, they soon discovered their miscalculation. The new governor not only failed to become the naïve political rookie dependent upon the bosses' advice to perform his duties, he also linked up with progressive-minded Democrats and Republicans in the legislature to enact a broad reform agenda that included the establishment of primary elections, enactment of campaign spending limits, a workers' compensation system, and the regulation of public utilities. Wilson's moves garnered national attention and propelled him to the short list of potential Democratic Party presidential candidates. Just two years later, he would enter the White House.

Wilson's Economic Reforms

Viewing himself as a party leader as well as president, Wilson assumed a primary role in mapping out the Democratic Party's legislative agenda. Moving quickly, he called a special session of Congress to enact his measures. In a major break from tradition, Wilson became the first president to appear before a joint session of Congress since John Adams. Theodore Roosevelt recognized the maneuver as a masterful political stroke designed to dramatize the moment and generate publicity while showing members of Congress that the president wished to work directly with them on the important issues of the day. (Roosevelt wondered openly why he had never thought of performing such a perfect act of political theatrics.) Thus began the regular Wilsonian practice of appearing personally at the Capitol to deliver State of the Union addresses and other speeches in which the president desired that Congress act decisively on important issues. By the end of his presidency, he would appear before Congress more times than any other chief executive before or since.

Wilson's first congressional appearance dealt with the subject of tariff reform. Since the Democrats historically opposed high tariffs, their newfound majority status seemed to dictate that downward revisions would soon become a reality. On the House floor, Majority Leader Oscar Underwood easily produced the votes needed for passage. Trouble occurred in the Senate, however, when industry lobbyists and their senatorial allies slowed down the process and attempted to dilute the effort through a serious of crippling amendments. Wilson directly interjected himself into the fray when he publicly criticized the obstructionist senators while shining the spotlight on the power of the countless lobbyists engulfing the capital, at one point complaining that a brick couldn't be thrown in Washington without hitting one of them. In the Senate, Robert LaFollette also turned up the heat when he denounced the lobbyists and began a public investigation of their influence on legislation. Ultimately, the president and pro-reform forces in the Senate prevailed.

The resulting **Underwood-Simmons Tariff Act** became law, leading to a 25 percent average reduction of tariff rates on almost a thousand imported items while adding 100 items (including important consumer goods and raw materials such as sugar, wool, cement, coal, and iron ore) to the free-entry list. To offset the loss of government revenue due to the reduced import duties, the law levied the first income taxes since passage of the Sixteenth Amendment, which authorized their collection. Mainly impacting wealthy Americans, the tax started at a rate of 1 percent for individuals earning at least $3,000 annually then increased on a graduated scale (2 percent for citizens making at least $20,000 per year up to a maximum of 7 percent for annual incomes over $500,000).

Wilson next sought to work with Congress on enacting the first banking and currency reforms since the Civil War. While all the major industrializing nations of Europe had some form of central banking system, the United States lacked such an institution. Many Americans saw the positive benefits of a national banking structure, but great disagreement existed on its proper configuration, especially if it should be a centralized or decentralized organization and whether control should lay with private bankers or government bureaucrats. After allowing the matter to stalemate in Congress, Wilson delivered his second address before the body to dramatize the issue and lay down the general principles he wished the legislation should possess, including his endorsement of public control. The resulting **Federal Reserve Act** ultimately bore the characteristic marks of compromise. The law established Federal Reserve Banks in twelve regions of the country to be owned by member banks within their districts but under the general supervision of a Federal Reserve Board appointed by the president. The member banks allocated a portion of their capital to the district banks, which could then loan money to other banks within their regions. Despite this decentralized structure, the federal government now possessed an important tool to promote economic stability. The new system enabled the Board to influence the national money supply through various mechanisms at its disposal, including the ability to impact interest rates that banks charged, as well as setting the percentage of capital that banks were required to keep in reserve. In times of low business activity, the Board could stimulate the economy by pursuing policies that freed more capital and credit into the marketplace. In times of high inflation, the Board's policies could also tighten credit to slow the pace of economic activity in order to reign in prices. Though the new system could not guarantee prosperity, the national dependence upon the decisions and actions of New York bankers for economic growth and stability

One hundred and fifty National Geographic Society employees marched in the Preparedness Parade on Flag Day, June 14, 1916. With World War I underway in Europe and increasing tensions along the Mexican border, President Woodrow Wilson led the parade alongside 60,000 participants, just one event of many around the country intended to rededicate the American people to the ideals of the nation and to demonstration the country's preparedness. The president marched holding the American flag.

began to lessen as financial power in the country shifted from Wall Street to Washington.

As Wilson tackled the antitrust portion of his agenda, the president deviated for the first time from positions that he articulated during the campaign. Upon determining that his proposal for limiting the size of corporations held only lukewarm support in Congress, Wilson embraced Theodore Roosevelt's idea of a potentially powerful government agency to regulate corporations by resolutely enforcing the antitrust laws. He also favored new legislation that would more specifically define what constituted "restraint of trade" and "unfair competition" under the law. In the fall of 1914, Congress passed the **Federal Trade Commission** Act, which replaced the Bureau of Corporations with a five-member Federal Trade Commission (FTC) appointed by the president. The new agency had the power to initiate investigations of corporations suspected of violating the nation's antitrust and unfair competition laws. Upon determining the existence of unlawful behavior, the FTC could issue "cease-and-desist" orders, though much to the chagrin of progressives, Wilson allowed conservative legislators to attach an amendment providing corporations with the ability to appeal the Commission's orders in federal court. Also in the fall, Congress approved the Clayton Antitrust Act, which improved the Sherman Act by detailing numerous prohibited practices including price discrimination (companies charging different prices for goods and services), exclusive dealings (corporations preventing companies from dealing with their competitors as a condition of doing business), interlocking directorates (members of board of directors forbidden to serve on the board of a competitor), the formation of cartels to control markets, and companies buying the stock of competitors. The new law also aided organized labor by specifically stating that labor unions were not an unlawful combination in restraint of trade subject to court injunctions (the Supreme Court had ruled to the contrary in a 1894 case involving the Sherman Act).

In his first 18 months in office, Wilson displayed fine leadership in guiding significant national economic reforms through Congress. Nevertheless, on the social justice front, his record left much to be desired. Though distracted by the death of his wife, Ellen, in August 1914 (within a year Wilson became the only president to remarry while in the White House), his latent belief in states' rights on social reform matters explains much of his disinterest. In other instances, Wilson's racist beliefs inculcated by his upbringing in the postbellum South, account for his terrible record on civil rights issues. (Earlier he had praised the Ku Klux Klan in a history of the United States he authored. While president, he enthusiastically endorsed D.W. Griffith's epic film *The Birth of a Nation*, which presents an openly racist and decidedly pro-Confederate view of the Civil War and Reconstruction-Era South). He supported passage of the Smith-Lever Act of 1914, which created the Federal Extension Service to provide vital services to aid farmers with their agricultural operations and home life but also consented to the establishment of a separate Negro Division, which offered inadequate assistance to southern black farm families (due to the unequal allocation of resources, not the energetic efforts of its black county agents.) This decision paralleled Wilson's acquiescence to southern members of his cabinet who established strict segregation within their departments. Not concerned with racial issues, however, most social progressives began to show disfavor with the president because of his obvious disinterest in their reform efforts. He made no effort to endorse the movement for a federal woman suffrage amendment or to support the call for a restriction of child labor, believing both to be under the purview of the states. With the next presidential election looming, social progressives began to communicate their displeasure to Wilson in order to spur him into action, threatening to withhold support for him or to cast their lots with his opponent.

The Pinnacle of National Progressivism—Wilson's Acceptance of Social Reform

The 1914 mid-term elections gave Wilson reason to take stock of the political landscape. Across the country, Republican conservative candidates defeated many noteworthy insurgents during party primaries followed by victories against Democrats and Bull Moosers in the November general elections. While Democrats maintained a slim majority in Congress, Theodore Roosevelt appeared as a wild card, reading the results and contemplating a return to the Republican Party. The former president's displeasure with Wilson's desire to remain neutral since the outbreak of World War I in 1914 (Roosevelt favored U.S. intervention on the Allied side) guided his thinking along with a growing belief that many who had joined the Progressive Party were too radical for his liking.

Wilson sought to openly convert these progressives in 1916 as he set aside his previous objections to federally-sponsored social reforms for the sake of political expediency in order to keep himself and his party in power. To the delight of social progressives, Wilson signed the **Keating-Owen Child Labor Act**, which prohibited the interstate shipment of goods produced in whole, or in part, by children younger than 14 years of age. Though the Supreme Court ruled against its constitutionality three years later, Wilson probably gained a few hundred thousand votes in the coming election from the moment that he signed the bill into law. By signing the **Adamson Act**, which established an eight-hour workday for railroad laborers, he approved the first federal legislation setting maximum hours for workers of private companies. Wilson accepted creation of a workers' compensation system covering all workers performing work under a federal government contract. To aid rural areas, Wilson signed the Federal Farm Loan Act, which extended federal credit to farmers for the first time, the Warehouse Act allowing growers to store their crops and use them as loan collateral, and the Federal Highways Act, which provided funds to the states for road construction, helping to diminish the degree of rural isolation. In addition to these and other tangible actions, Wilson also made a significant symbolic gesture designed to garner political support of social progressives. When a vacancy on the Supreme Court appeared, Wilson nominated social justice champion Louis Brandeis for the post and actively lobbied for his eventual acceptance by the Senate. A major advisor to Wilson during the campaign and throughout his first term, Brandeis became the first Jewish person to serve on the High Court.

The Election of 1916

President Wilson's endorsement of key social reforms greatly aided his reelection, as did his acceptance of a notable increase in the size of the nation's military forces. In an effort to blunt the criticism of Theodore Roosevelt and others on the "preparedness" issue, Wilson called for, and received from Congress, a tripling in the number of active army personnel to increase to almost 250,000 men and a large naval expansion program. To pay for this expansion that they opposed, progressive congressmen enacted the Revenue Act of 1916, which increased taxes on the wealthy and munitions makers by increasing the top income tax rate on those earning over $2 million annually to 15 percent, added a 10 percent estate (inheritance) tax on large fortunes, and establishing a 12.5 percent levy on the income of defense industries.

At their national convention, the Democrats excitedly renominated Wilson for the presidency by affirmation. In the process, the keynote speaker, former New York governor Martin Glynn, unintentionally developed a major campaign theme when he detailed Wilson's steps toward maintaining American neutrality in the bloody conflict raging in Europe at the time, culminating with the cry: "We didn't go to war!" The peace message from the speech resonated so well with the delegates that other speakers worked it into their addresses until it became the major theme of the meeting and the subsequent campaign. After the conclave ended, party activists molded Glynn's yell into the slogan: "Vote for Wilson. He kept us out of war!"

For their part, the Republicans hoped they could rebound from the previous election by nominating a candidate acceptable to members of the sagging Bull Moose Party, eventually selecting Charles Evans Hughes—a former progressive governor of New York from 1907 to 1910 until being nominated to serve on the Supreme Court. As the Progressive Party officially disbanded, Roosevelt returned to the Republican fold and brought some prominent Bull Moosers with him (though many more flocked to Wilson). On foreign affairs, Hughes tried a difficult balancing act, sometimes criticizing Wilson for not being tough enough with the Allies, but, not wanting to appear pro-German, he refused to accept the endorsement of

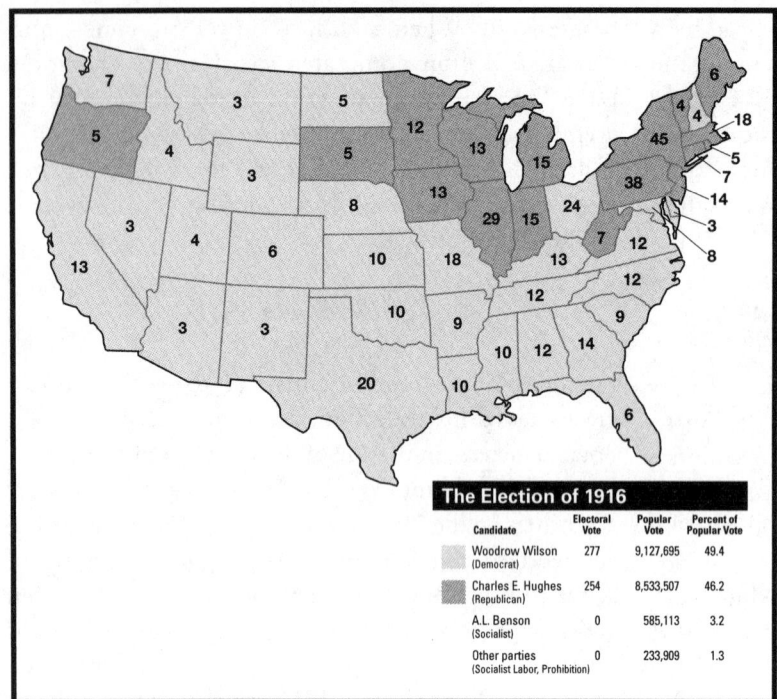

Map 21.2   The Election of 1916

German-American organizations and Irish nationalist groups with strong anti-British views, nor did he criticize Roosevelt when the ex-president made strong public statements mocking the Kaiser, Germany's leader. Though a lackluster campaigner, Hughes tried his best to hammer Wilson on two main domestic matters, the Revenue Act and the Adamson Act. The increased income and estate taxes led wealthy conservatives to solidly back Hughes, but they would have supported the Republican candidate anyway. Hughes's assault on the Adamson Act was more promising, as he shaped his argument to convince voters that the law was a sell-out by Wilson to organized labor. Though Hughes made headway with some voters with such attacks, Wilson support for union exemption from antitrust prosecution in the **Clayton Act** and passage of the Adamson Act guaranteed solid support from organized labor. Ultimately, the election may actually have all turned on a highly-publicized snubbing of California's Bull Moose governor Hiram Johnson (Roosevelt's running mate in the 1912 contest) by the Hughes campaign. Though Hughes and Johnson were in the same town, the Hughes campaign made no effort to arrange a meeting, and Hughes's opponents made the most of the rebuff—a costly gaffe given the eventual closeness of the election.

Both candidates went to bed on election night not knowing who had won. After sweeping the Northeast and Midwest, Hughes held the upper hand, needing only California's 13 electoral votes to win. Over the next couple of days, however, revised tallies culminated with Wilson being certified the winner in the Golden State by less than 4,000 votes. With the president's solid showing in the South and most of the western states, Wilson eked out a 277-254 victory in the Electoral College (with 9.1 million popular votes versus 8.5 million votes for Hughes).

The supreme irony of the 1916 campaign, of course, is that Wilson's triumph meant that the candidate whose primary slogan was "He Kept Us Out of War!" would be asking Congress for a declaration of war just one month after being inaugurated. For his part, Wilson disliked the mantra, though he did nothing to stop his people from using it. As he once prophetically stated concerning the possible sinking of American ships on the high seas by German submarines (the eventual cause of U.S. entry into the First World War): "I can't keep this country out of war. Some damned little German lieutenant can plunge this nation into war through a calculated outrage."

THE LEGACY OF PROGRESSIVISM

Reform efforts reached their pinnacle by the end of Wilson's first term. With U.S. entry into World War I in 1917, progressivism began to wane but never disappeared from American life. The nature of progressivism would evolve over time as fresh generations of reformers emerged to tackle new issues. The battles between these reformers and conservatives would characterize much of the country's political story for the remainder of the century and beyond.

Americans living today may recognize certain reforms that originated during the Progressive Era while also noting their limitations. Regulatory laws, for example, like all other laws, are only as potent as they are enforced. Political scientists often take note of the phenomenon of "agency capture," whereby a government regulatory agency acts more in the interest of the industry that it is supposed to be monitoring rather than the public interest due to the particular philosophies of the regulators or the possibility of a lucrative private sector job within the industry when their public service tenure ends. The inability of the Federal Reserve Board to enact policies providing a quick economic recovery following the arrival of the "Great Recession" that began in 2008 at the end of the George W. Bush administration also displays the limits of that important reform (while reinforcing the notion that the federal government does not have complete control over the American economy). Primary elections may have made the political process more democratic but still have not negated the power of money in elections.

Taken as a whole, however, the reforms enacted during the Progressive Era impacted a majority of Americans for the better. By the 1930s when the United States entered a new phase of reform with Franklin Roosevelt's New Deal, the nation had state and national laws in place that improved the political process, provided some important protections for workers and consumers, aided farmers and organized labor, brought more orderly business operations, and even focused attention on the environment. To be sure, not all benefited immediately from these efforts, especially African Americans. Those who objected to limits placed on individual freedoms by such progressive measures as the prohibition of alcohol could find much fault with the goals of certain reformers. Nevertheless, there can be no doubt, that the aspirations of the progressives provided an important corrective to the direction of the country at the turn of the twentieth century as they pushed for the realization of what progressive author Herbert Croly dubbed "The Promise of American Life."

Chronology

1900	Robert LaFollette elected governor of Wisconsin
1901	William McKinley assassinated Theodore Roosevelt becomes the 26th U.S. President
1902	Anthracite Coal Strike
1903	Bureau of Corporations created; Elkins Act
1904	Northern Securities Company dissolved Theodore Roosevelt reelected president
1905	U.S. Forest Service created under Gifford Pinchot
1906	Hepburn Act; *The Jungle* published Meat Inspection Act Pure Food and Drug Act Antiquities Act
1908	*Muller vs. Oregon* decision William Howard Tat elected the 27th U.S. president
1909	Ballinger-Pinchot Affair
1910	Gifford Pinchot fired by President Taft Woodrow Wilson elected governor of New Jersey
1911	Triangle Shirtwaist Fire Standard Oil dissolved
1912	Woodrow Wilson elected the 28th U.S. president
1913	16th Amendment (income tax) ratified 17th Amendment (direct election of U.S. senators) ratified Underwood-Simmons Tariff Act Federal Reserve Act
1914	Federal Trade Commission Act Clayton Antitrust Act World War I begins (Wilson declares U.S. neutrality)
1916	Adamson Act Keating-Owen Act Federal Farm Loan Act Wilson reelected
1917	U.S. entry into World War I
1918	World War I ends
1919	18th Amendment (Prohibition) ratified
1920	19th Amendment (Woman suffrage) ratified

Review Questions

1. Describe the many similarities and differences among Progressive Era reformers.

2. Describe the ways in which progressivism impacted the cities and states before the advent of national-level reform.

3. What did you believe was Theodore Roosevelt's most significant domestic achievement as president? Why?

4. Describe the achievements and failures of William Howard Taft as president.

5. What did you believe was Woodrow Wilson's most significant domestic achievement as president? Why?

Glossary of Important People and Concepts

Adamson Act
Anthracite Coal Strike
Anti-Saloon League (ASL)
Ballinger-Pinchot Affair
"Bull Moose" (Progressive) Party
Clayton Act
Commission-style government
Eugene Debs
Direct Primary
Federal Reserve Act
Federal Trade Commission
Hepburn Act
The Jungle
Keating-Owen Child Labor Act
Florence Kelley
Robert LaFollette
Meat Inspection Act
"Muckrakers"
Muller v. Oregon
National American Woman Suffrage Association (NAWSA)
Northern Securities Company
Gifford Pinchot
progressivism
Pure Food and Drug Act
Theodore Roosevelt
settlement houses
William Howard Taft
Underwood-Simmons Tariff Act
Woodrow Wilson
workers' compensation

SUGGESTED READINGS

H.W. Brands, *TR: The Last Romantic* (1997).
Douglas Brinkley, *The Wilderness Warrior: Theodore Roosevelt and the Crusade for America*, (2009).
John D. Buenker, *Urban Liberalism and Progressive Reform* (1973).
Kendrick A. Clements, *The Presidency of Woodrow Wilson*, (1992).
Paolo E. Coletta, *The Presidency of William Howard Taft*, (1973).
John Milton Cooper, Jr., *Pivotal Decades: The United States, 1900-1920*, (1990).
___, *The Warrior and the Priest: Woodrow Wilson and Theodore Roosevelt* (1983).
Allen F. Davis, *American Heroine: The Life and Legend of Jane Addams* (1973).
___, *Spearheads for Reform: The Social Settlements and the Progressive Movement, 1890-1914*, 1967.
Lewis L. Gould, *The Presidency of Theodore Roosevelt*, (1991).
Samuel P. Hays, *Conservation and the Gospel of Efficiency: The Progressive Conservation Movement, 1890-1920*, (1975).
Gabriel Kolko, *The Triumph of Conservatism: A Reinterpretation of American History, 1900-1916*, (1967).
Aileen S. Kraditor, *The Ideas of the Woman Suffrage Movement, 1890-1920*, (1981).
Arthur S. Link and Richard L. McCormick, *Progressivism*, (1983).
Judith N. McArthur, *Creating the New Woman: The Rise of Southern Women's Progressive Culture in Texas, 1893-1918* (1998).
Edmund Morris, *The Rise of Theodore Roosevelt*, (1979).
Thomas R. Pegram, *Battling Demon Rum: The Struggle for a Dry America, 1800-1933*, (1998).
Jacob Riis, *How the Other Half Lives* (1997).
Patricia A. Schechter, *Ida B. Wells-Barnett and American Reform, 1880-1930* (2001).
Upton Sinclair, *The Jungle*, (1906).
James H. Timberlake, *Prohibition and the Progressive Movement, 1900-1920* (1970).
Robert Von Drehle, *Triangle: The Fire That Changed America*, (2003).
Robert H. Wiebe, *Businessmen and Reform: A Study of the Progressive Movement* (1962).
___, *The Search for Order, 1877-1920*, (1967).

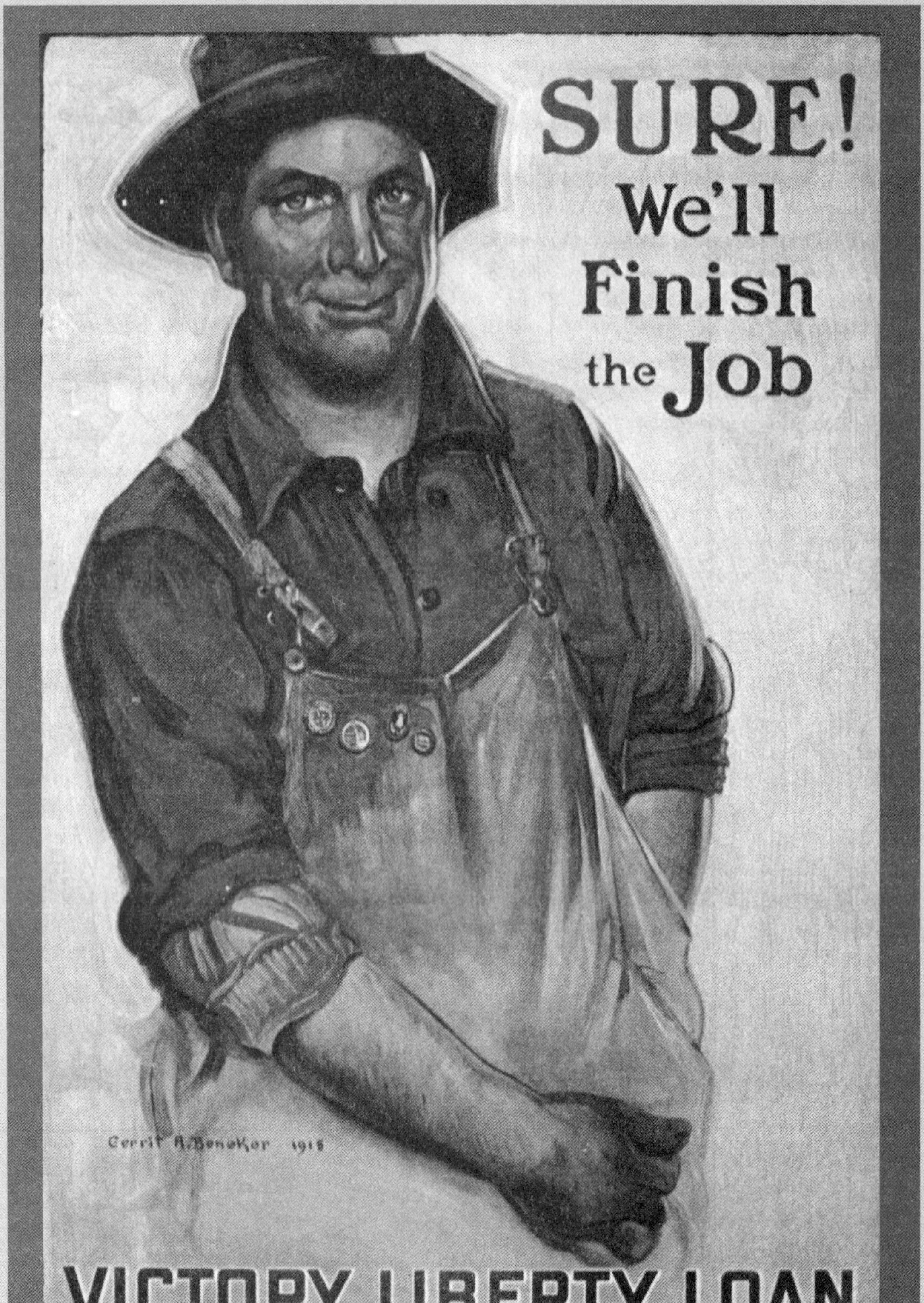
SURE!
We'll
Finish
the Job
VICTORY LIBERTY LOAN

Chapter Twenty-Two

THE "GREAT" WAR: World War I

The war years and their immediate aftermath witnessed some of the most brutally violent and destructive moments of racial tension and discrimination in this nation's history. Only a handful of the riots occurred in the South; rather it was in northern cities such as Chicago and St. Louis where the most serious outrages took place. In the summer of 1919 both cities exploded into what became the two worse episodes of racial violence in the United States until the 1960s. As this letter from an African American caught in the middle of the terror in East St. Louis, Illinois confirms, the rage exhibited by whites toward black citizens bordered on the psychopathic. Over the course of several days, rabid white mobs attacked African Americans, many of whom, to the surprise of their attackers, did not hide or flee their homes. Instead, they fought back. When the smoke cleared, 39 African Americans had been killed, most of whom were unarmed, innocent bystanders who simply found themselves in the path of the white fury. Prompting such rage among primarily working class whites was their fear of losing their jobs to African-American migrants in the war industries. In many ways the plutocrats who owned the factories were initially responsible for the outbursts. They willingly employed (and exploited) in their plants the cheaper African-American workers at the expense and anger of their more costly white counterparts. Wartime profiteering took precedent over maintaining racial harmony in many northern urban/industrial centers.

Dearest Louise:
Was very glad to hear from you. Your letter was forwarded from what used to be my house. Louise, it was awful. I hardly know where to begin telling you about it. First, I will say we lost everything but what we had on and that was very little.

It started early in the afternoon. We kept receiving calls over the phone to pack our trunks and leave, because it was going to be awful. We did not heed the calls but sent grandma & the baby on to St. Louis & said we would stick no matter what happened. At first, when they first started, we stood on Broadway & watched it. As they [the white mob] neared our house, we went in & went to the basement. It was too late to run then. They shot & yelled something awful, finally they reached our house. At first they did not bother us (we watched from the basement window), they remarked that "white people live in that house, this is not a nigger house." Later someone must have tipped them that it was a "nigger" house, because, after leaving us for about 20 minutes, they returned & yelling like mad, "kill the niggers, burn that house."

It seemed the whole house was falling in on us. Then someone said, they must not be there, if they are they are certainly dead. Then someone shouted, "they are in the basement. Surround them and burn it down." Then they ran down our steps. Only prayer saved us, we under tubs & anything we could find praying and keeping as quiet as possible because if they had seen one face, we would have been shot or burned to death. When they were about to surround *the house and burn it, we heard an awful noise & thought they were dynamiting the house. (The Broadway Theater fell in we learned later.) Sister tipped the door to see if the house was on fire. She saw the reflection of a soldier on the front door—pulled it open quickly & called for help. All of us ran out then & was taken to the city hall for the night—just as we were. The next morning we were sent on to St. Louis. Had to walk across the bridge with a line of soldiers on each side in the hot sun, no hats & scarcely no clothing.*

On Tuesday evening our house was burned with two soldiers on guard. We were told that the crowd looted the house before burning it.

WILSONIAN "MISSIONARY DIPLOMACY"

Historians often contrast the diplomatic philosophy of Franklin Delano Roosevelt (president during World War II) and Woodrow Wilson (president during World War I). Roosevelt was a realist, seeing the world as it was, not as he wished it to be. Wilson, however, was an idealist, seeing the world as it should be, not as it was. He believed that the United States had a special destiny to spread democracy, capitalism, and American religious (Protestant) tenets all over the globe. For Wilson, foreign policy was missionary work.

Wilson generally upheld the idea that people should be ultimately responsible for creating and maintaining the governments of their choosing, or to what he called the right of every nation to self-determination. Wilson, however, did not have such regard for non-Western peoples. He believed, similar to Theodore Roosevelt and other imperialists, that the more advanced, civilized (white) nations should assume the role of mentor to the non-Western (non-white) nations or people of Africa, the Middle East, and Asia. Wilson also believed that people's rights, liberties, and freedoms were best guaranteed when promulgated in written constitutions. Ironically, when non-Western people tried to gain his support in writing their constitutions, such as in the case of a young Vietnamese nationalist named Ho Chi Minh, Wilson refused to help. Instead, he supported continued French occupation until the Vietnamese people were deemed ready by their French tutors to embrace democratic ideals.

Wilson also believed in universal disarmament—without a prevalence of advanced arms and weapons among the great powers the chance of future wars would dwindle. Finally, he viewed the United States as a redeemer nation, believing that God had mandated America to spread enlightened, humanitarian, and democratic blessings throughout the whole world. Initially, Wilson believed this particular role could best be accomplished by the United States remaining neutral throughout the European war. In the early spring of 1917, however, he had changed his mind, believing that the U.S. could only help fix the world's ills by joining the crusade to make the Great War "the war to end all wars." Interestingly, prior to the outbreak of war in Europe in the summer of 1914, Wilsonian idealism was tested repeatedly in the nation's own backyard.

Despite having campaigned on a non-interventionist platform, Woodrow Wilson became as intimately involved in Latin American affairs as his predecessors. Prior to becoming president, Wilson had lambasted the administrations of Roosevelt and Taft for their heavy-handed-imperialism and interventionist policies in the Western Hemisphere and pledged he would eschew such an approach. Within months of his inauguration, Wilson sent Marines into Nicaragua, ostensibly to protect American interests. Such a move reflected a policy no different than Taft's Dollar Diplomacy or TR's interventionist pursuits. In fact, Wilson invoked the Roosevelt Corollary to justify U.S. occupation of Nicaragua. The Marines remained in Nicaragua until President Franklin Roosevelt ordered their removal in 1933.

Wilson sent William Jennings Bryan to negotiate a treaty with that nation's most powerful controlling family, Chamorro, led by General (and future dictator) Emiliano Chamorro. The Bryan-Chamorro Treaty gave the U.S. sole right to build and maintain a canal through Nicaragua. The Senate passed the Nicaraguan Canal Treaty in 1916. It appeared that when it came to canal building Wilson wanted to leave a legacy equal to that of his rival Theodore Roosevelt.

Wilson also sent Marines into Haiti in 1915 and the following year into the Dominican Republic. In both instances, the president believed American military forces were necessary to bring stability to the hemisphere by ending the civil war and violence that seemed to plague both of those countries. Naturally, he hoped that with U.S. assistance both Haiti and the Dominican Republic would be transformed into pro-U.S. democratic governments. American policies failed in both countries as Haitians and Dominicans lived under corrupt and brutally oppressive dictatorships, suffering through decades of constant civil war. The United States has rarely succeeded in creating democratic-capitalist pro-U.S. regimes as a result of military intervention and occupation.

Throughout most of its history, the United States traditionally expanded its frontiers and spread its political and economic values through territorial acquisition by purchase or negotiation: the Louisiana Purchase (1803); Florida (1819), Oregon country (1846), southern Arizona and New Mexico through the Gadsden Purchase (1853), Alaska (1867), and Guam (1899), to name a few. Thus, in 1917 Wilson, with the consent of Congress, purchased the Virgin Islands from Denmark.

Closer to home, and much more problematic for Wilson, was the issue of the Mexican Revolution, which erupted in 1910 when lawfully elected presidential candidate Francisco Madero triumphed at the polls over one of Mexico's longest-standing dictators, Porfirio Diaz. Although Diaz had agreed to the election and had promised to step down if defeated, he reneged, largely because he succumbed to foreign capitalist pressure led by the United States to remain in power. Foreign investors were wary of Madero, who had pledged during the campaign that he would nationalize all foreign-owned enterprises, which by 1910 controlled most of Mexico's most important industries—railroads, telegraph, telephone, mining, and oil. Foreigners also controlled either directly or indirectly the bulk of Mexico's land. American newspaper magnate, William Randolph Hearst, owned ten million acres in the northern state of Chihuahua. As a result of Diaz's close ties with foreign capitalists, if Madero wanted to become Mexico's president, he unfortunately had to take office by force. Thus began the Mexican Revolution, a ten-year-long bloodbath in which thousands of Mexicans died or fled across the Rio Grande to the United States for safety.

Rallying to Madero were other anti-Diaz and anti-*gringo* leaders, whose names have become legendary on both sides of the Rio Grande: Pancho Villa, Emiliano Zapata, Alvaro Obregon, Plutarco Calles, and Venustiano Carranza. Although many of these **caudillos** joined with Madero for personal reasons and frequently engaged in outright banditry and murder in the name of the Revolution, they nonetheless were united in their cause to drive both Diaz, who they regarded as a *gringo* lackey, and all foreigners out of Mexico. In 1911, Madero, with the help of such individuals, defeated Diaz's forces and the former president fled to Cuba and eventually to Spain, where he lived the remainder of his life.

No sooner did Madero take office than counterrevolutionary, right-wing military leaders in collusion with foreign capitalists conspired to overthrow his government. In 1913 General Victoriano Huerta succeeded in toppling the Madero regime via a *coup d'etat*. Madero was held prisoner for a few days then along with his entire family and cabinet brutally executed by Huerta henchmen. Madero's murder had the full-fledged support of the foreign capitalists. With Huerta in power, European and American businesses could now continue their exploitation of Mexico's resources and industries and its people for their own private profit. Despite the backing of United States and European capitalists, Huerta could not quell the fires of revolution. Villa, Zapata, and the other pro-Madero chieftains formed uneasy alliances to overthrow the Huerta regime.

Much to the chagrin of American and foreign capitalists, Wilson considered Huerta a brute, and allowed American arms to flow across the Rio Grande to Huerta's principal rivals, Carranza and Villa. It was only a matter of time before a showdown would occur between the Huerta regime and the Wilson administration. The volcano erupted at the Gulf of Mexico seaport city of Tampico, when Mexican authorities arrested a small group of American sailors for disorderly conduct. The sailors were indeed unruly, engaging in unprovoked fisticuffs and barroom brawling and assaulting innocent Mexicans. Local police, realizing that their action could cause further rancor between the U.S. and Mexico, promptly released the seamen and apologized to the American legation. They refused, however, to comply with the U.S. admiral's demand for a twenty-one-gun salute as an act of contrition. Wilson unwisely and precipitously used this insult as an excuse to eliminate Huerta, asking Congress for authority to use force against Mexico. Before Congress could act Wilson retaliated, ordering the navy to seize the Mexican port of Veracruz until Huerta formally apologized for insulting the United States. The American navy bombarded the city and when the smoked cleared, the Marines assaulted and declared Veracruz under United States occupation. Much to Wilson's surprise, the Mexican people and even Carranza and Villa rallied to the Huerta regime in defiance of this high-handed Yankee maneuver. Critics in the United States, Europe, and Latin America branded the capture of Veracruz a reckless act that could escalate to a general war between the United States and Mexico at a most inopportune time. Fortunately, a shooting conflict was avoided when Argentina, Brazil, and Chile interceded, offering to mediate the dispute.

The situation defused when the Huerta government collapsed in July 1914, the result from pressure from the very European powers that had helped him come to power in the first place. Apparently they no longer considered him to be as reliable a puppet as they had previously thought. Seizing power in the wake of Huerta's collapse was Venustiano Carranza, who Wilson officially recognized as Mexico's legitimate president.

By the time Carranza assumed power, he and Villa had become estranged. Carranza no longer considered Villa to be a fellow revolutionary but a brigand out for personal plunder. For Carranza, the revolution was over, confirmed by Wilson's de facto recognition of his seizure of power. Thus, all opposition to the new Mexican president's legitimacy was to be crushed. Wilson's support for Carranza resulted in Villa launching attacks against U.S.

U.S. Marines stand ready near railroad tracks in Veracruz near the Hotel Terminal during Venustiano Carranza's revolt against the Mexican government of President Victoriano Huerta, May 16, 1914.

interests on the Mexican side of the U.S.-Mexican border. In January 1916, Villa's men hauled 16 young American mining engineers off a train traveling in northern Mexico and executed them. Villa, who had now come to despise Carranza as a *gringo* sell-out, hoped to provoke a war between Wilson and "el presidente." In March 1916, Villa with five hundred men blazed across the border and raided Columbus, New Mexico, killing another twenty innocent Americans. In retaliation, Wilson ordered a U.S. Army expeditionary force to invade Mexico.

Under the leadership of the grim-faced, ramrod-erect General John "Black Jack" Pershing, a veteran of the Cuban and Philippine campaigns, the U.S. contingent of 15,000 troops sought to find Villa, bring the outlaw to justice, and destroy his bandit army. Pershing's troops penetrated deep into the rugged terrain of the northern Mexican state of Chihuahua, Villa's home. They engaged both Carranza's and Villa's forces, defeating them handily in all encounters but failed to locate and apprehend Villa. In retrospect, Wilson should have known there was no way Pershing would ever find Villa, for no Chihuahuan would have ever cooperated with the *gringos* in the seizure of their region's most celebrated revolutionaries. After a year of aimlessly wandering the mountains and deserts of northern Mexico, searching in vain for Villa, Wilson in January 1917 recalled Pershing and his army. Tensions with Germany had reached the breaking point and Wilson realized that potential war with that country represented a more urgent crisis than having the United States Army senselessly roaming northern Mexico.

THE OUTBREAK OF THE GREAT WAR

To the majority of Americans, the European powers had been engaged in constant warfare for centuries, and thus when the Great War began in the summer of 1914, few were surprised that they were at it again. George Washington and Thomas Jefferson, in their respective farewell addresses, had warned fellow citizens to remain as detached from European affairs as was possible and to maintain a policy of isolationism to prevent from becoming entangled in European politics, which invariably led to conflict among the great powers. Although by 1914 the majority of Americans took great pride in their nation's world power status, they nonetheless remained committed to avoiding involvement in any capacity in a general European conflagration. Americans still embraced a semi-isolationist mentality, and thus when war erupted in Europe in 1914, they were determined to have the United States maintain a neutral position.

Causes for the War

Although several long-standing issues ultimately caused Europe to convulse in war in 1914, four in particular seemed to have had the most significant impact: militarism (arms race), nationalism, secret alliances, and imperialism. Since the 1880s and the Second Industrial Revolution in Europe, France, Great Britain, and Germany had become embroiled in an intensely competitive and potentially dangerous arms race. The rivalry between Great Britain and Germany had become especially keen in the race for empire and in the building of war ships. They increasingly used their technology and resources to produce the most advanced war machines their respective military-industrial complexes could deliver. The impetus for such militarism had been the United States' Civil War, which the great powers found fascinating, not only for the conflict's brutality and carnage but also by the new and impressive weaponry the Americans unleashed upon each other.

Many of the weapons the Europeans would use to kill each other to the tune of 9 million soldiers dead, made their first appearance in the Civil War. From the Gatling gun (which the British transformed into the machine gun), to the repeating rifle, hand grenade, and to even the submarine, the Europeans would develop these weapons into even more precise killing apparatuses. Of all the modern weaponry first introduced during the American Civil War, it was perhaps the submarine that proved to be the most devastating. The Confederacy developed a crude but fairly effective version of this particularly important device (and one the Germans would perfect and use with deadly precision on Allied shipping in the Atlantic) to try to break the Union blockade of its seaports. It was the issue of submarine warfare that ultimately led Woodrow Wilson to declare war on the German Empire in April 1917.

Imperial rivalry also caused tension among Europe's great powers, and again this particular problem became most serious between Great Britain and Germany. Since its unification in 1870, Germany aspired to become the most powerful country in Europe. English leaders believed their nation was the only country powerful enough to block such pretensions. Those German leaders believed one of the prerequisites for supremacy was the possession of a colonial empire, which the British had proven over the centuries to have been the key to their prolonged wealth, power, and global hegemony. Beginning in the 1880s and over the course of the next several decades, Germany embarked on one of the most aggressive territorial acquisition campaigns in European history, gobbling up as many colonies and spheres of influence in Africa, Asia, and the Pacific as it possibly could. Since Germany (and the United States) joined the race for empire late in the game, the Germans often found their ambitions stymied, especially by the British, who certainly did not welcome such a challenge to their suzerainty.

Compounding the Anglo-German imperial rivalry was the Franco-German tension over the same issue, and frequently this led to France and Great Britain allying against Germany in certain areas of the world to block German expansionism. Germany did not take kindly to such obstruction to its quest for power, and consequently the German, French, and British governments found themselves often perilously close to war wherever they competed for colonies.

Without question, the greatest "tinderbox" in Europe was the Balkan states, which for decades witnessed constant unrest and fighting as the Slavic Christian majorities engaged in wars of national liberation from the Muslim Ottoman Empire. No sooner did these Slavic peoples free themselves from the Turks than they found a new potential oppressor in the form of the Austro-Hungarian Empire, whose Habsburg rulers had long wanted to expand the empire into southeastern Europe but for centuries had been blocked by the Ottomans. Now the Habsburgs believed the Serbs, Bosnians, and Montenegrans would be easy prey for their imperial ambitions. The Slavic peoples of those countries were acutely aware of Habsburg designs and for protection turned to Russia, a fellow Slavic country. The Romanovs were more than willing to offer the Balkan Slavs security, for the Romanovs were just as territorially ambitious in this region as their rival the Habsburgs. Thus, by 1914, the tensions between the Habsburg and Russian empires in this most volatile part of Europe had reached the point where both sides anticipated a showdown. They were simply waiting for a crisis to occur.

Finally, and perhaps what in retrospect was one of the more absurd causes for the Great War, was the long list of countries who promised to mobilize their forces in support of other allies if they found themselves at war with another coalition. By 1914, in an effort to establish a basic balance of power on the continent, the major powers had divided into two binding alliance systems: the Triple Entente of Russia, Great Britain, France, and the Central Powers, consisting of Germany, Austria-Hungary, Turkey and Italy, which wisely opted to remain neutral when the war began in 1914. However, the Italians' sagacity was momentary; in 1915 they joined with the Triple Entente, believing that their affiliation with the members of that alliance would prove more beneficial in the war's aftermath. As will be seen, they were sorely disappointed.

Compounding this senseless obligatory military union was the interesting relationship among three of the major powers' heads of state: Alexandra, the Czarina of Russia, Kaiser Wilhelm II of Germany, and King George V of England were first-cousins, a kinship arranged in the nineteenth century by the matriarch of Europe, Queen Victoria of Great Britain. Victoria believed she could ensure peace in Europe for generations to come by uniting via marriage the major ruling households of Europe by blood, then they would never go to war, for to behave in such a manner would upset "Grand-Mama" Victoria. As long as Victoria reigned in England, her grandchildren did indeed comport themselves according to Her Majesty's wishes. No sooner did Victoria die than the arrangement quickly dissipated. "Cousin Willie" of Germany in particular had been waiting for the old lady to pass, for he never had any intention of restraining himself in the name of family and European peace. Within a few years of Victoria's death, a war among the cousins became a certainty. All that was needed was an episode that would give them the excuse.

The incident that lit the fuse of the powder keg on which the major powers had been sitting on for several years was the assassination of the Archduke Franz Ferdinand of Austria, nephew of Emperor Franz Josef II of the Austro-Hungarian Empire and heir to the throne, and his wife Sophia in late June 1914 by a Serbian nationalist (Gavrilo Princip) who was the young member of a terrorist group with ties to radical anti-Austrian members of Serbia's government. The murder prompted an ultimatum from Austria-Hungary to Serbia, stating that non-compliance with its terms would mean war between the two countries. Austrian leaders, however, were already determined to go to war with Serbia in order to avenge the assassination and also eliminate Serb meddling in its Balkan affairs once and for all. With Germany as a key Austrian ally, Serbia's defeat would be assured and Serbia would be absorbed into the Austro-Hungarian Empire. Thus, the terms of Austria's ultimatum were deliberately made to force Serbia's refusal to comply. Keenly aware of Austrian intentions, the Serb government turned to their protector, Russia, who vowed to come to Serbia's aid. While the clock ticked, Germany mobilized its forces in preparation for war against Serbia.

Meanwhile, the Russians mobilized their army in preparation for war against Austria but not Germany. "Cousin Niki" (Czar Nicholas II of Russia) pledged that although he was preparing his forces for a possible conflict with Austria, he was not about to declare war on his "Cousin Willie"—Kaiser Wilhelm II of Germany. Much to Nicholas' chagrin, the Kaiser declared war on Russia. That shock precipitated a French declaration of war on Germany due to French obligations to come to Russia's aid if war erupted between Russia and any member of the Central Power alliance. Before the French could mobilize, the Germans implemented the **Schlieffen Plan**, which called for a quick knock-out of the French before the British could come to their rescue. For the strategy to be effective, the Germans had to reach Paris as quickly as possible and that meant invading through neutral Belgium, which they did. Much to the Germans' surprise, the Belgians resisted, allowing time for the French to mobilize and for the English to come to their assistance. The invasion of Belgium was the official reason that Britain entered the conflict, but the British worried that a German victory would upset the balance of power on the continent and thus threaten Great Britain itself.

All diplomatic attempts to stop the madness failed, and war came, again, to the Europeans in the summer of 1914. Unlike previous wars, this one proved to be horrific in the sheer number of causalities. For example, at the conclusion of the First Battle of the Marne (September 1914) over 500,000 German, French, and British had been killed. Europe would eventually lose an entire generation of young men before the guns fell silent on the eleventh hour, of the eleventh day, of the eleventh month of 1918.

American Neutrality

No sooner did "the Guns of August" begin to fire, than Woodrow Wilson asked his fellow citizens to remain neutral. The president had multiple reasons for such an approach. First, Wilson worried that a protracted European conflict could negatively impact the American economy. To prevent such a possibility, Wilson believed that Americans should be allowed to trade with all combatants provided that the U.S. was not a belligerent itself.

Second, on the home front, WASP nativism re-emerged toward German Americans, whom many feared would manipulate the United States into the war on the Fatherland's side. German populations were especially significant in the states of Wisconsin, Illinois, Michigan, Minnesota, and South and North Dakota, where WASP xenophobia and anti-German nativism was most evident, with Anglo-Americans wondering if their German neighbors would support their newly-adopted land or their homeland.

Also suspect were Irish-Americans. Because of their strong Catholicism and equally passionate support for Irish independence, which saw many Irish-Americans donate money to such ultra-nationalist and quasi-terrorist organizations as the Irish Republican Army and Sinn Fein, many Anglo-Americans still disdained the Irish and questioned their loyalty to the United States. To a certain degree, Anglo-American leeriness was somewhat justified. For many Irish-Americans, the liberation of their homeland from centuries of English oppression and exploitation became their principal motivation in their support for U.S. neutrality. They were confident that if America refrained from participation, a German victory would be the result and with such a triumph would come the end of British rule, for in the war's aftermath a humiliated and

Map 22.1 European Alliances (1915)

indebted English government would no longer want or be able to sustain such a rebellious colony. Moreover, U.S. neutrality and British preoccupation on the continent would create the perfect scenario for a massive Irish uprising during the war, which, it was hoped, would lead to Irish independence at that time. Such a prospect occurred on Easter Sunday, 1916, but unfortunately for the Irish rebels, the British had enough force already stationed in Ireland to put down the insurrection, thus crushing Irish (and Irish-American) hopes for independent Ireland during the war.

For many Irish-Americans, the key to their homeland's liberation was American neutrality. Thus, during the Great War, and especially after the United States entered the conflict, Irish-Americans became some of the Wilson administration's most vociferous critics for having abandoned neutrality in favor of war on the Allied side. Much to the outrage of the Irish-American community and other progressive civil libertarians, many of their fellow citizens were charged with sedition and incarcerated for speaking out against Wilson's wartime policies. Such harsh reprisals, especially against Irish-Americans, reflected the Wilson administration's desire to not offend in any way its British allies.

Third, why should the United States pick a side? There was no reason to believe that this war would be any different from other European conflicts. Regardless if it was the Balkan War, Franco-Prussian War, or the Crimean War, the U.S. had sat on the sidelines, the best and safest seat in the house to watch the Europeans engage in senseless slaughter. Thus to Wilson and to the majority of Americans there was no good, tangible, beneficial reason to join this latest European madness.

Finally, Woodrow Wilson dreamed about creating what he called the "New World Order," and this could only come about if the United States remained dispassionately objective regarding both the war's causes and its outcome. Only by remaining neutral would the U.S. be in the best position (economically, militarily, politically, and diplomatically) to remake the world (in a Wilsonian image) in the war's aftermath. All that would be required for establishing a lasting peace would be for all the belligerents, whether they ended up on the winning or losing side, to construct a postwar peace based on his impartial "Fourteen Point" assessment, which Wilson had drafted months before the United States entered the war on the Allied side. In fact, Wilson had been formulating in his postwar agenda in his mind almost from the war's outset.

Initially, he had hoped to implement his vision without the United States having to enter the conflict. Unfortunately, the Germans left him no choice but to fight if he hoped to see his New World Order come to fruition.

Naval and Submarine Warfare

Wilson ultimately used German submarine warfare to justify, on moral grounds, U.S. entry into the conflict. In speeches denouncing the German employment of such a weapon, Wilson referred to submarine attacks on Allied shipping as a "cruel and unmanly business." Although Wilson ultimately declared war on Germany because of its policy of unrestricted submarine warfare, which saw the killing of hundreds of American citizens traveling on belligerent luxury liners, at the war's outset the United Kingdom and France were the more egregious violators of American neutral trading rights. For example, the Royal Navy threw up an undeclared blockade and mined the North Sea. Both actions flew in the face of international agreements, such as those mandated at the 1899 and 1907 Hague Conventions. In addition, the United Kingdom armed merchant ships. Through World War I, ships were either designated as military or for civilian use. The latter had special protections and were defined as civilian, in large measure because they were prohibited from being armed. Military ships did have the right to stop and search civilian ships for contraband. However, military ships did so without fear of being attacked, such as when German submarines would surface in order to board English merchant ships. When those submarines, which Germany called *Unterseeboot*, or **U-boat**, surfaced, they lacked the ability to launch torpedoes, thus making themselves proverbial sitting ducks. The armed British merchant ships then opened fire on the German military ships, contravening international agreements.

The United Kingdom unilaterally expanded products it considered to be contraband, stopped American ships, and confiscated property that appeared on its list of items that they would not allow to be sold or traded during war. Great Britain blacklisted American companies that engaged in commerce with neutral countries suspected of trading with Germany or its allies. England routinely stopped U.S. mail ships, confiscated letters and packages, opened the mail, and then censured or destroyed what the United Kingdom decided jeopardized their war efforts.

Finally, English ships flew an array of flags of neutral countries, hoping to confuse the German U-boats lying in wait in the Atlantic ready to torpedo British ships carrying munitions and other war materiel from countries such as the United States. British merchant ships often flew the American flag, hoping to scare Germany into steering clear, or else risk unleashing the full force of the U.S. war effort if Germany dared to attack an American ship.

Compared to Great Britain's actions, Germany was restrained. They did have a public relations problem, especially when it came to German naval attacks in the Atlantic. After numerous English violations of international agreements, Germany declared that they would alter their tactics to include firing on suspected merchant ships that were armed or British ships trying to evade attack by flying the flags of neutral countries. Ultimately, Germany warned all ships flying neutral flags to stay away from English waters. Shortly thereafter, President Wilson gave his first speech on the issue of torpedoes on the high seas:

> If the commanders of German vessels of war should act upon the presumption that the flag of the United States was not being used in good faith and should destroy on the high seas an American vessel or the lives of American citizens, it would be difficult for the Government of the United States to view the act in any other light than as an indefensible violation of neutral rights, which it would be very hard, indeed, to reconcile with the friendly relations now happily subsisting between the two governments.

This piece of diplomatic ambiguity was intended as a thinly-veiled threat to Germany yet one that would not propel the U.S. into a war that Wilson believed the nation was unprepared to fully fight. Wilson's first threat would be tested on the war's first anniversary. In August of 1915, a German U-boat attacked a British ship and when a nearby merchant ship (the *Arabic*) flying the English flag came to rescue the survivors, that vessel was torpedoed as well. The dead included two Americans. The German government quickly apologized, promising that their nation's U-boats would never fire on passenger ships without offering sufficient warnings and only after securing the safety of non-combatants. Within a month, the German government issued a report to Secretary of State Robert Lansing. According to their investigation, the German U-boat commander fired on the *Arabic* because he feared that the ship was going to ram his submarine, a tactic often employed by English merchant ships after they surrendered to a surfaced U-boat. In 1916 German officials authorized their naval commanders to attack armed merchant ships but not passenger ships. A French passenger ferry, the *Sussex*, was torpedoed by a German U-boat, resulting in the deaths of many French but no American citizens. Wilson once again waved his diplomatic finger in the face of the German government, demanding that they cease these attacks. Despite Wilson's constant public proclamations that his administration remained committed to neutrality, the Germans believed that it was only a matter of time before the United States would enter the war on the Allied side. Thus, to forestall the inevitable as long as possible, the German government issued the "**Sussex Pledge**," in which they declared that their U-boats would no longer attack any civilian ship without first securing the safety of its non-combatants.

These attacks, promises, threats, and pledges all followed on the heels of the greatest loss of civilian life on the high seas. In the early spring of 1915, carrying nearly 2,000 passengers from the U.S. to England, the British luxury liner **Lusitania** was hit by a single torpedo from a German submarine. The ship sunk in less than twenty minutes with the loss of nearly 1200 of its passengers, including 128 Americans.

Prompting the German U-boat to sink the *Lusitania* was the Germans' long-held suspicion that American arms manufacturers were secretly loading war materiel on Allied passenger liners. Such an assertion was true because the *Lusitania* was carrying contraband. De-classified government documents confirmed that this clandestine activity did indeed occur on a regular basis. Moreover, from the moment the war began, American munitions manufacturers were keenly aware of the immense profit to be made selling their wares to the belligerents. Initially they played no favorites, but as the war dragged on, it became apparent that the Allies were in greater need of weapons than the Germans. By 1915, U.S. arms makers were almost exclusively selling their products to the Allies, and it became clear that the U.S. was no longer impartial. The Germans doubted the sincerity of Wilson's repeated assurances that his administration and his fellow citizens were faithful to neutrality in both sentiment and action. Consequently, they no longer felt morally obligated to respect U.S. neutrality if American capitalists had no intention of honoring that position. The German government thus ordered its U-boats to sink all Allied ships regardless of the cargo they were carrying.

Historians still debate what knowledge of this activity Wilson had, and if he was aware of the activity, why did he not publicly and formally condemn such underhanded behavior. Some believe that by 1915 Wilson personally was ready for war against Germany but needed to convince the American public of the moral imperative of becoming involved against such an immoral country as Germany—a nation that did not hesitate to kill innocent civilians. Despite Wilson's outrage and condemnation of the Germans, the sinking of the largest, fastest, luxury ship in the world did not propel the U.S. to officially enter the war. Wilson would have to wait until there was a direct threat to American sovereignty.

By the beginning of 1917, the tide of war had shifted in Germany's favor. In February of that year the Russian Revolution began, largely as a result of the Russian army's devastating defeats at the hands of the Germans on the Eastern Front. The Germans were hopeful that it would only be a matter of time before Russia would be defeated and out of the war. If that became reality, the Germans could then transfer men and materiel from the East to the Western Front and launch a massive offensive that

A German U-boat in New York. Photo credit: Library of Congress

would overwhelm and defeat the Allies before the U.S. could enter the war. In order for such a plan to work, the Germans had to prevent the Allies from getting American military hardware. Despite Wilson's repeated warnings that a declaration of unrestricted submarine warfare would have dire consequences relative to U.S.-German relations, the Germans announced in early 1917 that their U-boats would sink *all* Allied ships, regardless of type, crossing the Atlantic.

German leaders knew their manifesto would more than likely be the final straw for Wilson and that the United States would soon thereafter enter the war on the Allied side. Thus, they decided that if U.S. entry was inevitable, then they needed to find a way to prevent the Americans from coming to Britain's and France's aid before they could launch their massive spring offensives. In short, the Germans needed to keep the Americans pinned down in their own backyard long enough for them to finish off the Allies. To put their plan into operation they needed to find a potential New World ally willing to go to war against "the colossus of the North." The Germans concluded that Mexico was the logical choice for a new comrade-in-arms.

Why Mexico? The Germans were aware of how strained U.S.-Mexican relations had become during Wilson's tenure. They were confident they could entice the Mexican government with a generous alliance proposal, which included helping Mexico get back territory lost to the *gringos* during the Mexican-American War of 1846. Although there was certainly no great love lost between the U.S. and Mexico, the Germans underestimated the wily and opportunistic Mexican President Carranza, whose regime Wilson had recognized over a year earlier as legitimate. Carranza knew any German alliance proposal would not only be disingenuous but absurd as well. Carranza had long reconciled that the Southwest was U.S. territory and that any attempt to retake the region whether by invasion or by negotiation was lunacy. The German promise of money and troops was equally preposterous; how could they afford to spread themselves so thin when their objective was to knock-out the Allies. Moreover, whether he liked it or not, Carranza knew he had to live with the *gringos*; the two countries shared a two-thousand-mile border and the Mexican economy remained dependent on U.S. investment. Carranza thus concluded that the Germans' offer was all "gas," and that if he helped to expose this latest German conspiracy to violate United States sovereignty, such a gesture would go far toward currying even greater favor with the Wilson administration. Thus, the German attempt to prevent U.S. entry into the war failed.

Arthur Zimmermann, German Foreign Secretary, sent an encoded telegram to Heinrich von Eckardt, German Ambassador to Mexico in January of 1917. The telegram

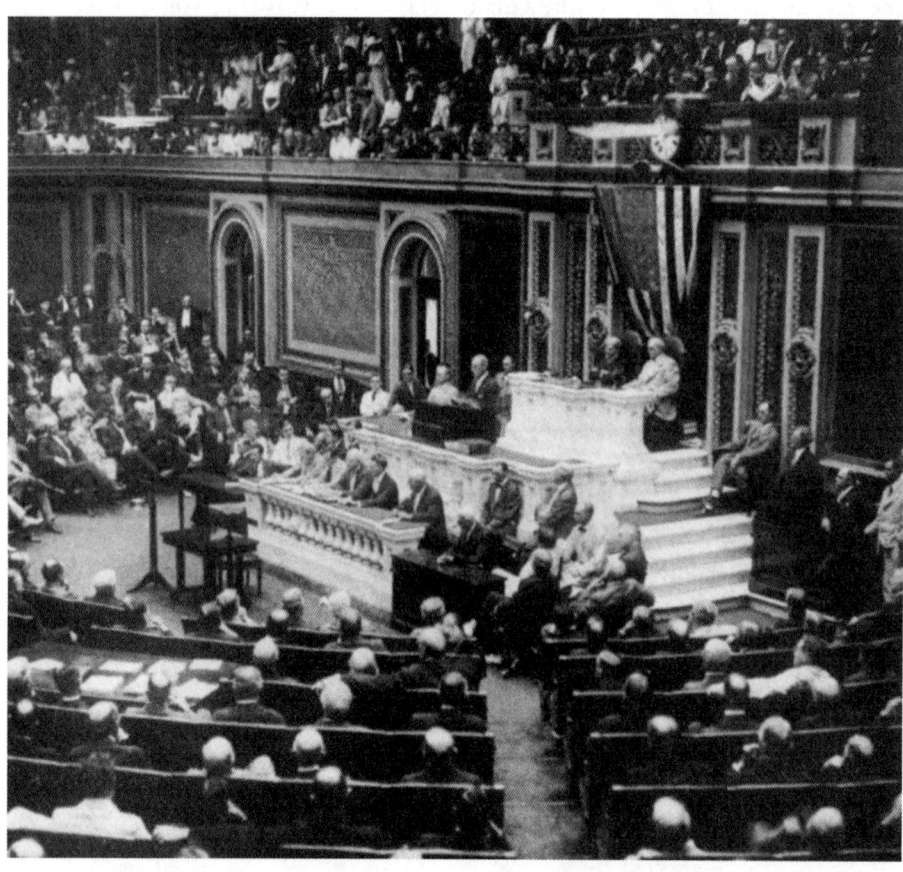

President Woodrow Wilson addressed Congress on April 2, 1917, asking Congress to declare war on Germany.

was intercepted by British intelligence on Galveston Island (located about 30 miles south of Houston, Texas), decoded, and handed over to President Wilson a month later:

> We intend to begin on the 1st of February unrestricted submarine warfare. We shall endeavor in spite of this to keep the United States of America neutral. In the event of this not succeeding, we make Mexico a proposal of alliance on the following basis: make war together, make peace together, generous financial support and an understanding on our part that Mexico is to reconquer the lost territory in Texas, New Mexico and Arizona."

Although the **Zimmermann Telegram** was widely published in American newspapers beginning on March 1, 1917, over a month's time passed before Wilson asked Congress for a declaration of war. In the intercession, Wilson gave his second inaugural address. He talked about the economic soundness of the country and only in the most cursory, oblique way did he touch upon the storm clouds on the horizon. He called for peace and for everyone who loved liberty and justice to continue to be impartial in thought and action relative to the European conflict. Wilson debated with himself, his friends, and his cabinet over what the U.S. should do next. He did not choose the path to war lightly, because, as Wilson confided to the editor of *The World*, Frank Cobb, "Once lead these people into war . . . they'll forget there ever was such a thing as tolerance . . . the spirit of ruthless brutality will enter into the very fiber of our national life . . . every man who refused to conform would have to pay the penalty." In other words, Wilson feared that American entry into the war would forever change this nation. He was correct.

DECLARATION OF WAR

On April 2, 1917, Wilson asked, and two days later received, a declaration of war against Germany—not Austria, the Ottoman Empire, or any of the other several countries aligned with the German Empire. The Senate voted 82 to 6 to declare war on April 4, 1917; the House concurred on April 6 by a vote of 373 to 50. Jeannette Rankin of Montana, the first woman to serve in the House of Representatives, was among those who voted against the war.

Over fifty members of the House agreed with Rankin, including the Chairman of the House Ways and Means Committee, Claude Kitchin (D-NC). Kitchin rejected the decision for war, believing that those who will be called to fight and die will not be the ones who declared the war to begin with: "Let me once remind the House that it takes neither moral nor physical courage to declare a war for others to fight."

General Leonard Wood, the one-time U.S. military commander and governor of Cuba, was Wilson's Chief of Staff until 1914. Wilson and Wood disagreed on their interpretations of how prepared the nation was for war. Wilson feared that preparing for war would necessarily lead to war, while Wood believed that creating and maintaining a ready standing army should be a matter of general policy. No matter how one interpreted the situation, the United States was undeniably woefully unprepared for war. Much of the Navy's front-line ships had not been updated since Teddy Roosevelt had sent the fleet on its round-the-world tour. Not only was the U.S. Navy unprepared to transport American soldiers and equipment to Europe, but most of this country's military was engaged in the Mexican civil war. Relative to military equipment, where was the United States going to get all the guns, bullets, and other war material? What about food and fuel? Did the U.S. grow and produce enough food and fuel for the needs of its citizens as well as for U.S. troops fighting abroad?

Propaganda and Hysteria

Once committed to war, Wilson made a priority the boosting of American morale on the home front. To accomplish that objective, Wilson created the **Committee on Public Information (CPI)**, headed by George Creel. Creel's and his agency's main task was to affirm to our allies, our enemies, and to the American people that the nation's citizens favored U.S. intervention on the Allied side as well as supporting a possible protracted conflict.

The CPI found Hollywood to be a most useful medium through which to promote the theme of a united America, determined to "make the world safe for Democracy." CPI had Hollywood produce a series of patriotic movies depicting clear and explicit differences between the liberty-loving Americans and the German animals, such as "The Claws of the Hun" and "The Kaiser: The Beast of Berlin."

Creel created a special pool of amateur speakers whose main audience was to be those immigrant communities that he and the Wilson administration believed could be wavering in their support for the U.S. war effort because of possible lingering sentimental attachment to the homeland. Wilson and Creel were determined to convey to the Allies that when the United States goes to war, *all Americans,* regardless of place of origin, whether native born or naturalized, wholeheartedly embraced the cause and that the virtues and qualities of American life had transformed all into one-hundred percent Americans. The speakers were to deliver their propaganda message in no more than four minutes. In homage to the American Revolution and to further promote patriotism, Creel named these on-call orators the "Four-Minute Men." According to Creel, over 75,000 individuals gave an estimated 7.5 million speeches. Major ethnic groups such as Jews, Germans, and even Native Americans were targeted to ensure their support for the war. Rabbi A.G. Robinson of New York reported that Jewish speakers reached "about 25,000 people per week. We expect soon to have every Jewish audience in a motion-picture house or a Jewish playhouse addressed by a Jewish speaker."

German-American communities were asked to take "The Pledge" (an oath in support of the U.S. war effort against the Huns). Progressive era groups, such as the American Protective Association, focused on homes with German sounding names to ensure that there were no pictures of the Kaiser on their walls. American flags blossomed all over the country, like tulips and daffodils in the spring. A new group, the Boy Scouts of America, sold war bonds and collected money, rubber, and tin in support of the war effort. German groups and clubs were banned, closed, and at times burned by those liberty and justice-loving Americans willing to use whatever means necessary to promote one-hundred percent Americanism. Such violent reprisals against suspect groups such as the Germans were, of course, all for the purpose of national security.

Robert Prager, a German-born American refused to sign the Pledge. One evening members of the local "Council of Defense" (a self-appointed ultrapatriotic group charged with routing out all anti-Americanism as they defined anti-Americanism) knocked on Prager's front door. They gave him one final chance to sign the Pledge. When Prager refused, someone in the crowd shouted, "Get the rope!" According to Prager, "The first I knew was when the rope was about my neck and around my body under my arms." Fortunately, he was not lynched as some members of the Council believed that by giving him a good scare he would now take the Pledge, which Prager promptly did on the spot. Although Prager barely escaped with his life, many other German-Americans and other suspect ethnics did not.

Women and the War

Women also joined in the preparation efforts. Women took jobs in U.S. weapons factories (a precursor of things to come in the 1940s). They sold Liberty Bonds at church, school, and social functions and they led clothing drives for soldiers and immigrants, ran canteens for American service men in England, and over 10,000 American women volunteered as Red Cross nurses in France. Women's organizations put their work on the back burner in order to help in the total war effort. For example, the National American Woman Suffrage Association (NAWSA) sponsored mobile field hospitals in France and England and urged their female workers and supporters to go to other western European nations affected by the war and help to staff those hospitals as well. Some NAWSA leaders were concerned that Jeannette Rankin's "no vote" would taint their organization. Rankin had been one of the movement's stalwarts for years. Much to NAWSA's relief, their efforts assuaged any reservations other citizens may have had about the association's devotion to the war effort. Even Rankin participated in some of the more humanitarian programs sponsored by NAWSA.

The first meaningful step undertaken by the federal government after declaring war was to create a capable military and in order to make that a reality Congress believed it necessary to pass the **Selective Service Act** on May 15, 1917. The "draft" as the act became popularly called soon after its passage, required all men between the ages of 18 and 30 to register with the federal government for possible conscription into the nation's armed services. Ten months later, and fearing that the U.S. military had not secured a sufficient amount of men to fight in the war, the Senate debated a bill that would have created mandatory and universal military training for all male citizens

THE "GREAT" WAR: World War I / 657

> ### The Great War and U.S. Government Propaganda
>
> *All governments produce propaganda, especially during times of war, as they try to convince citizens in the righteousness, morality, and justness of the war's cause, that individual and collective sacrifice is required by all if the nation is to prevail, even survive the supposed threat to its way of life. Even before the United States entered the Great War, both Germany and Great Britain attempted to sway American public opinion to their respective sides. Both nations planted stories, photographs, and other messages in American newspapers hoping to convince Americans that their side was the right side in this conflict. The British were particularly shameless at times in this tactic, releasing propaganda messages, both written and visual, that depicted the Germans as barbaric Huns, brutes and beasts, who killed little boys and Catholic nuns. The British hoped such stories would rally the American people to the righteousness" of the Allied cause.*
>
> *No sooner did the United States enter the Great War, than the Wilson administration created its own special propaganda committee headed by George Creel to instill in the American heart and mind that the struggle against Germany represented a crusade against evil, and thus Creel and his office bombarded the American public with graphic images of German soldiers, even the Kaiser, as the personification of demonic brutes. The committee organized a national network of "four-minute men," rabid pro-war local citizens whose job it was to whip a crowd into a patriotic frenzy of not support for the American effort but hatred for all things and people German. The Creel Committee also produced written propaganda material all with the same theme and purpose: fear and hatred of Germany and thus the righteousness of the American cause. One pamphlet,* **Why America Fights Germany***, described in lurid detail a possible German invasion of the United States. The committee found especially effective in spreading propaganda the emerging motion picture industry, whose technology could help disseminate the message to thousands at a time. Indeed, the government fully grasped the power of the new medium and adopted it to train soldiers, instill patriotism, and help the troops avoid the temptations of alcohol and sex.*
>
> *One such film,* **Fit to Fight***, shown to all servicemen, was an hour-long drama that followed the careers of five young recruits, four of whom succumbed to the dissipated life, catching venereal disease, which the movie grotesquely and graphically showed the different forms of the disease the men had contracted. The movie also glorified athletics, especially football and boxing, promoted as great "substitutes" for sex.* **Fit to Fight** *emphasized the importance of patriotism and purity for America's fighting force. In one scene, Bill Hale, the only soldier in the film to remain "pure," breaks up an anti-war peace rally by pummeling the speaker. "It serves you right," the pacifist's sister announces, "I'm glad Bill punched you."*
>
> **Fit to Fight** *was so successful that the government commissioned another picture,* **The End of the Road***, the story of two young women (Mary and Vera) who lived near military bases, which was the film's overarching message to young women exposed to soldiers in such proximity. The film also retained a progressive quality through the character of Mary. Vera's strict mother tells her daughter that sex is dirty, leaving Vera to discover on her own, through distorted and obscene information, sex on the street. She has sex with the first man who comes along and contracts a venereal disease. Mary, by contrast, has an enlightened mother who explains where babies come from, and as a result, matures into a secure, confident, capable young professional woman, a nurse. In the end, she falls in love with a doctor and gets married.* **The End of the Road** *has a number of subplots and many disturbing scenes of syphilitic sores, along with several illustrations showing the danger of indiscriminate sex. Among other things the film preached the importance of science and sex education and the need for self-control.*

between 19 and 21. The Senate defeated the measure by a vote of 36 to 26. Approximately 24 million men registered for the draft and nearly three million American males were inducted into military service by the end of the Great War.

The federal government also blitzed the public with one of the most overwhelming advertising campaigns in American history in an effort to "sell" the war. Posters became the most important medium used; radio was in its infant stages of development and television was nonexistent. Many of the posters simply tried to remind Americans of their duty to support the war by purchasing war bonds. One poster showed a grandmother figure with out-stretched arms standing in front of a U.S. flag. Peaking from behind the flag one could see bodies, sinking boats amidst tumultuous waves with a caption that read "Women! Help America's Sons Win the War! Buy U.S. Government Bonds!"

The Wilson administration readily turned to Hollywood to make propaganda movies designed to not only

658 / CHAPTER TWENTY-TWO

Poster showing the *Lusitania* in flames and sinking with people in the water and lifeboats in the foreground.

boost American morale but to promote the righteousness and moral necessity of the United States' involvement. Of course, historical parallels with past heroic Americans at war became a major theme. One motion picture that conveyed such a message was *The Spirit of '76*. Set during the American Revolution, the idea behind the movie was that the colonists were unprepared to battle, let alone win in a war, against the largest, best military in the world: Great Britain. Of course, the unprepared and outmatched but relentlessly determined and virtuous Americans triumphed, which was the movie's message. If American patriots could overcome their unpreparedness for battle in 1776, surely the Americans of 1917 could do the same. The director of the movie, Robert Goldstein (a Jewish American of German descent), portrayed the British in the movie as not only the enemy (which they were) but also as brutes who inflicted all manner of cruelties on the Americans. Goldstein's presentation of the British in such a light proved to have been a rather foolish act, for when the movie came out (1917) the British were American allies and thus they did not take too kindly to being portrayed in American cinema as barbarians. The British and American press lambasted Goldstein, who eventually was arrested and found guilty of violating the 1918 Sedition Act for having shown the two war-time allies (Great Britain and the U.S.) fighting against one another. Wilson, however, understood Goldstein's intent with his picture and reduced Goldstein's sentence from ten years to eighteen months in prison.

Dissenters and the Suppression of Civil Liberties

One of the first victims of nearly every U.S. war is the First Amendment, and World War I proved no exception. The Espionage Act temporarily trumped Americans' rights to religious freedom, to speak freely, to publish freely, and to freely petition their government. The **Espionage Act** of 1917 made it a crime to interfere with U.S. military operations, including the promotion of insubordination in the military or interference with military recruitment. Eugene Debs, the noted labor leader and perennial Socialist Party presidential candidate, was arrested for delivering a speech in which he encouraged Americans to avoid the draft. Tried under the Espionage Act, Debs was convicted and sentenced to a ten-year prison term. To shore up the Espionage Act, Congress passed the **Sedition Act** in 1918, expressly prohibiting anyone from using "disloyal, profane, scurrilous, or abusive language" about the United States government, the American flag, or the U.S. armed forces.

The Attorney General, Thomas Gregory, wanted to do more and thus instructed the Postmaster General, Albert Burleson, to censure and if necessary discontinue delivering any anti-American or pro-German mail (letters, magazines, and newspapers). Gregory also enthusiastically supported the work of the **American Protective League (APL)**. The APL curbed dissent at home by compelling German-Americans to sign a pledge of allegiance. The APL also conducted extra-governmental surveillance on pro-German activities and organizations (such as unions). Created by the native-born Chicago millionaire, A.M. Briggs, the APL's real purpose was to end all union activities in the country, which of course plutocrats like Briggs believed handicapped the war effort. The most targeted union on the APL's list was the radical **Industrial Workers of the World** (IWW or "Wobblies"), formed in 1905 in an attempt by more left-leaning labor leaders to bring together in one organization socialists, communists, anarchists, and all other leftist groups who opposed the anti-strike position of the American Federation of Labor.

Gregory and Burleson targeted thousands of suspected enemies of the state including such prominent Socialists as Eugene Debs, Mary Harris Jones (aka "Mother Jones"),

Emma Goldman, and Max Eastman because of their use of the U.S. mail to distribute what Gregory and Burleson considered to be un-American literature. Besides Socialist newspapers such as *The Call*, Burleson prohibited the delivery of what he considered to be anti-British publications such as *The Irish World* and *The Gaelic American*.

Anti-German fervor during the Great War at times bordered on the ridiculous and the extreme, resulting even in the renaming of German (or German-sounding) food. Sauerkraut became "liberty cabbage," frankfurters became "hot dogs," and Salisbury steak transformed into meat loaf. Extralegal organizations, such as the Wisconsin Loyalty League, sought to control their relatively large German population as well as their own elected officials who questioned the war. Wisconsin Senator Robert La Follette, a Progressive Republican, decried American entry into the war on the basis that the U.S. had indeed been breaking international law by shipping explosives on civilian ships (such as the *Lusitania*) and thus going to war to protect neutral rights was absurd to the Wisconsin. Former president Teddy Roosevelt called La Follette a "shadow Hun" and "the most sinister enemy of democracy in the United States." The senator was certainly no traitor nor enemy of the state, and Wisconsin voters rallied to their popular senator, reelecting him every time he ran for the Senate until his death. Wisconsinites also sent to the House of Representatives this nation's first Socialist Party member, Victor Berger (1910-1912, 1918-1920, and 1922-1928).

In its 1919, **Schenck v. United States** decision, the U.S. Supreme Court upheld the constitutionality of the Espionage and Sedition Acts. Just the year before, Charles Schenck, a leader of the Socialist Party who oversaw his organization's anti-draft pamphleteering campaign, was charged with sedition, found guilty, and imprisoned. In a unanimous decision, thrice-wounded Civil War veteran Chief Justice Oliver Wendell Holmes, Jr. stated "[w]hen a nation is at war many things that might be said in time of peace are such a hindrance to its effort that their utterance will not be endured so long as men fight, and that no Court could regard them as protected by any constitutional right." In other words, in Holmes's opinion, the needs of the state, especially in times of crises, superseded those of the individual, and thus dissent of any stripe or form was illegal.

African Americans in the Military

For the second time since the end of slavery, African Americans served this country during a time of foreign war not only for traditional patriotic reasons but also to prove to white Americans that black folk were as intelligent, honorable, dedicated, courageous, and as loyal to the Republic as their fellow white citizens. Although slavery had long since been abolished, a de facto apartheid existed in the South, popularly known as Jim Crow. Creating a completely segregated black and white America was deemed not only appropriate by the majority of white

Eugene Debs, leader of the Socialist Party of America, was convicted of sedition for opposing U.S. involvement in World War I and sentenced in 1918 to 10 years imprisonment under the Wilson administration, but President Warren Harding commuted his sentence to time served December 23, 1921. Here he is leaving the White House three days after his release. Photo credit: Library of Congress.

Americans but constitutional as well, evidenced by the 1896 Supreme Court decision in *Plessy v. Ferguson*.

Despite their oppression, over 400,000 African-American males entered the ranks of the U.S. military during World War I. Most African Americans in the armed services had been drafted, and the number of black draftees accounted for 13 percent of all American males conscripted. Yet, they represented only 10.7 percent of the total U.S. population in 1910 and 9.9 percent in 1920. Only a small percentage of African-American soldiers saw combat. The overwhelming majority worked mainly as mess-boys (mealtime aides), laborers, and stevedores (ship cargo handlers). Although relegated to often menial tasks, some jobs such as that of a stevedore, proved indispensable to the war effort. Sometimes working 24 hours non-stop, black stevedores unloaded vital supply ships with incredible speed and efficiency. Surprisingly, especially to their white counterparts, black AEF soldiers, regardless of assignment or task, were welcomed by the French military and people and treated with respect—as equal human beings. Such displays of humanity initially shocked African-American troops, but as they interacted with the French people, they came to realize that not all white societies were like that of the United States. There were predominantly white countries in which they could live free from prejudice and discrimination. It was no surprise that after the war hundreds of black veterans chose to remain in France for the rest of their lives, enjoying a quality of life as an expatriate that they sadly could only dream about having back home in the United States.

The American military at the time of the Great War reflected the segregated nature of American society. All branches of the armed services were separated into all-white and all-black units, with white officers in charge of African-American enlistees and draftees. The relegation of the majority of black soldiers and sailors to menial, often demeaning, work reflected the white military establishment's belief that African-American men were incapable of holding up in combat, certain they would run at the first sign of a fight or danger because of their supposed inherent character defects such as cowardice. Although we know today that such an assessment of African Americans in combat is ridiculous, at the time such beliefs were widespread among white officers and their superiors in the chain of command. When given the opportunity to fight, however, black soldiers distinguished themselves. Such was true of the famous and highly decorated all-black 369th Infantry known as the "Harlem Hell Fighters," the 803rd Pioneer Infantry Band, No. 16, and the 370th Regiment, Illinois National Guard, to name a few. The Harlem Hell Fighters, under the command of Colonel William Hayward, became one of the most decorated U.S. military units of the war. They were the first U.S. outfit to be awarded the French Croix de Guerre. The commander of the American Expeditionary Force, General John "Blackjack" Pershing, "loaned" the 369th to France and this nearly-all-black (save for the officers), brigade saw some of the war's most vicious and brutal fighting long before any other American soldiers, such as that witnessed at **Chateau-Thierry** and **Belleau Wood**, where nearly 10,000 Allied troops were killed or wounded. The Hell Fighters spent 191 days in the trenches (longer than any unit from either side), and they were the first Allied contingent to cross the Rhine.

The federal government created a new officer training school in Iowa where over 1,000 African-American men received commissions as officers for the war. Only a handful, however, ever commanded fellow black soldiers. Even the country's first black graduate of the U.S. Military Academy at West Point, Charles Young, who saw combat in Cuba, the Philippines, Haiti, and Mexico, was not allowed to command troops in Europe.

Many prominent African Americans joined the service, including Spotswood Poles (a popular and talented centerfielder for the New York Lincoln Giants of the Negro Leagues) and James Reese Europe, probably the most nationally-known African American to serve in the military. As a famous Harlem bandleader, he was probably the most popular song writer of the early twentieth century. His music inspired new dance steps, led to the creation of new, dance-oriented night clubs, and in the process, helped to transform dancing into one of the most popular forms of entertainment among young people. In 1914, Europe's orchestra (usually known as Europe's Society Orchestra) became the first black band to record commercially in the United States. Assigned to the 369th as a lieutenant (the highest ranking black soldier in the unit), Europe led the unit's renowned band. After the war, Europe began writing and recording popular songs that capitalized on his wartime experiences. Songs such as "On Patrol in No Man's Land" evoked feelings of patriotism while under fire from a German mortar barrage and "All of No Man's Land Is Ours" is a love song in which a returning combat veteran calls his fiancé upon arriving back in the U.S. He did not live long enough to profit from his postwar fame. During a live performance in Boston in early May 1919, a heated argument developed between Europe and one of his drummers, Herbert Wright, who whipped out a knife and killed Europe by stabbing him in the neck. He died en route to the hospital. Newspapers reported the loss with the banner "Jazz King is Dead." James Reese Europe was buried in Arlington National Cemetery.

German soldiers on horseback are viewing an abandoned British trench, which was captured by the Germans. Between 1914 and 1918

Given the nature of African-American oppression at home, why any black men, let alone someone of Reese's stature, would enlist in the New York National Guard. Perhaps motivating Reese and others was a true patriotism, which even for a moment more militant black leaders such as W.E.B. Du Bois promoted as well. Du Bois believed that despite their oppression, African Americans had a duty to serve in the military as a way of demonstrating their intelligence, bravery, and loyalty to country and to white Americans. Du Bois publicly called upon his brothers to enlist, to fight and, if necessary, to lay down their lives for the United States. "If this is our country," declared Du Bois "then this is our war. We must fight it with every ounce of blood and treasure." Like many black leaders before him, Du Bois hoped that the patriotism and courage demonstrated by black soldiers in battle would prove yet again that African Americans deserved to sit as full participants at the table of equality. However, such was not to be the case for either returning African-American soldiers or for the larger black community at home. Life for the majority of African Americans in the war's aftermath remained tragically as oppressive and brutal as it was before the Great War.

Despite the existing prejudice, African Americans supported the war effort either by enlisting or as civilian activists for the cause at home. One such home front booster was Emmett J. Scott. Scott spent most of his career working for the NAACP, which included eighteen years as Booker T. Washington's private secretary. When the U.S. declared war on Germany, President Wilson wanted a spokesman for black troops in the War Department and Scott became a special assistant to Newton Baker, the Secretary of War, overseeing the recruitment, training, and overall morale of Africa-American troops.

No amount of African-American displays of patriotism could mitigate the brutality of Jim Crow. Without question one of the most infamous episodes of white resistance and shame occurred in Houston, Texas, in the summer of 1917, the now legendary "**Camp Logan Riots.**" The incident involved African-American troops from California and Wyoming sent to Houston for training at a camp set up just outside the city for such purposes, Camp Logan, which today is the site of the city of Houston's premier recreational park, Memorial Park. Like their counterparts throughout the South, white Houstonians were not terribly happy to see the influx of black people, especially potentially "uppity" black soldiers.

Although more progressive than most southern cities in black-white race relations, Houston nonetheless had its own version of Jim Crow—just as restricting, just as blatantly discriminatory and just as harsh in enforcement as elsewhere in the South. Black folk could not ride on certain trolleys, eat at certain restaurants, or congregate in groups of more than five people in most public places. Houston's all-white law enforcement establishment was especially leery of having such a large contingent of black soldiers on the city's outskirts, fearing that when they came to town on leave there could be trouble, which they were ready to suppress at the slightest provocation and with the harshest reprisals.

One hot, sticky August day, a young African-American recruit tried to stop a Houston policeman's beating of an African-American woman for resisting arrest after allegedly calling the officer vile names. The cop, Lee Sparks, turned his club against the young soldier, who overcame Sparks, but to no avail as several fellow officers came to Sparks' rescue. Wielding their night-sticks furiously at him, they beat the recruit unconscious and literally dragged him to jail. Upon hearing the news of the arrest of one of his men, non-commissioned officer Corporal Charles Baltimore went to Houston to inquire about what had happened. No sooner did he arrive at the police station than he was arrested as well. When the news of Baltimore's incarceration reached Camp Logan, the rest of the outfit became enraged, determined to not only set their comrades free but to resist with force any further insult or degradation. They marched with their weapons to the police station and demanded their brothers' release, which initially the police refused to do. That proved to be the final straw. The soldiers attacked in full fury those police at the station. In the ensuing melee, which lasted for several hours and saw the city's white and black civilian population become involved, fifteen people died, including five policemen and six blacks, four of whom were African-American soldiers.

The brawl would officially be called "The Camp Logan Riots." In the ensuing investigation by United States Army officials, sixty-three African-American troops would be arrested and charged with mutiny. At the first of several courts martial, thirteen African-American soldiers were found guilty and sentenced to death, including Corporal Baltimore. Seven more troops would be executed at the close of the second trial, and dozens imprisoned with sentences raging from 24 months to life at the final court martial proceedings.

Although few and far between, there were instances where black folk successfully resisted and triumphed over Jim Crow oppression. Such occurred in Rocky Mount, North Carolina, where black female workers in a textile factory walked off their jobs to protest the verbal abuse of their white floor manager. According to the *Norfolk Journal and Guide*, "when the superintendent learned of the trouble later in the day he immediately began to visit the homes of the operatives asking them to return to work. The offending white manager was discharged and the girls returned to their work with no loss of time." Apparently, the last thing the Wilson administration needed was a strike at an important wartime industry such as textiles, for any stoppage in production could adversely affect the overall war effort. After all, soldiers needed uniforms on a regular basis.

Perhaps most important, the war years saw the first major emigration of African Americans out of the South to the North. Prompting many black Southerners to move North during the war years was the potential for jobs in northern industrial cities, many of whose factories were intimately involved in wartime production. As a result of this internal exodus, between 1910 and 1920, the African-American population of manufacturing cities such as Gary, Indiana and Detroit, Michigan witnessed an increase of 1300 percent and 611 percent respectively. New York, which already had a well-established African-American community (over 90,000 in 1910), saw its black population increase by 66 percent (to over 150,000 by 1920). Many of these black migrants became the first members of their family since the end of slavery to not only have left the South but to have earned a livelihood other than as a sharecropper or agricultural laborer. Equally significant for the future demographics of post-Great War America, the majority of these mostly young men would not return to the South after the war. Life in the urban North was more exciting, less circumscribed, less emotionally and psychologically oppressing, and potentially more materially rewarding. Thanks to the money earned during the war years, a legitimate and viable black middle class emerged and flourished during the 1920s in many northern cities.

The American "Doughboys"

In 1918, a Yankee of Irish roots named George M. Cohan, penned what became one of the most popular, patriotic ditties ever written in the history of war-time America, **Over There**. It was as if Woodrow Wilson had Cohan's song in mind when he asked young men to drop their plowshears, leave their factory jobs or the universities, and enter the ranks of the military to prevent Germany from running roughshod over Europe. So inspirational was Cohan's song for the nation's warriors and the home front, that on the eve of the U.S. entry into World War II, Congress presented Cohan with a Congressional Medal of

Honor in recognition of his prolific patriotic song-writing career as well as for his having written what became the unofficial U.S. anthem during the Great War, *Over There*.

In the end, neither uplifting lyrics nor impassioned calls to arms could alleviate the emotional and psychological distress experienced by thousands of American soldiers after witnessing the greatest human slaughter in the history of mankind.

No sooner did the United States enter the Great War than Wilson appointed as commander of American troops General John "Black Jack" Pershing, whom he had recently recalled from Mexico. Pershing, a career soldier and combat veteran, was well aware of the army's lack of preparedness, especially for the type of warfare American soldiers would be called upon to fight. Pershing knew that if not trained properly, American soldiers would be invited to the slaughter, for they would be encountering on the Western Front a battle-hardened German soldier supported by one of the most advanced war machines the world had seen. Realizing the horrible reality of modern warfare American lads were about to confront, Pershing insisted that his troops undergo at least six months of rigorous training, with basic preparation in the United States and with more focused, intense, combat-readiness training upon arrival in Europe. Despite Pershing's pleas for such preparedness, the Wilson administration buckled to the Allies' insistence that the Americans forego training in the United States and get to Europe as quickly as possible before it was too late. Thus, by the time of their first engagement, relatively few "**doughboys**" had been properly trained for modern, total warfare.

The AEF in France

The first U.S. troops arrived in France in October 1917. Eventually, about 2 million American soldiers served in France as members of the **American Expeditionary Force (AEF)**. Although arriving in the fall of 1917, American troops did not see combat until the spring of 1918 when in March of that year, Germany launched a major offensive along the Somme. A few American battalions (about 3,000 soldiers) participated in the fighting around Amiens and Armentieres, helping to stem the German advance. In May 1918, the Germans launched their second assault along the Aisne River, driving the Allies back to the Marne, giving the Germans a nearly open road to Paris, fifty miles away. As the French government prepared to evacuate the "City of Lights," American forces arrived in strength, with parts of three Army divisions (about 27,000 men) and a Marine brigade (about 4,000 soldiers), helping to stop the Germans at the town of Chateau-Thierry and nearby Belleau Wood.

These two German offensives had punched deep holes (salients) in the Allied line. A German drive intended to capture the cathedral city of Rheims between these two salients was stopped with the help of 85,000 American troops. Allied victories at Chateau-Thierry and Belleau Wood proved to be the war's turning point. From that point on, the Germans would be on the defensive. They would be desperately trying to stave off defeat, which now appeared imminent with the presence of tens of thousands of fresh American troops and plentiful amounts of U.S. military hardware and money at the Allies' disposal. Contributing to the Germans' failed offensives as well as to their ultimate defeat was the fact that many of their soldiers, already weakened by battle fatigue and poor diet, fell victim to influenza, an infectious disease that would soon emerge as a deadly worldwide pandemic.

Some 270,000 American soldiers fought in the last Allied offensive to push the Germans back from the Marne. The counterattack, the Second Battle of the Marne, began on a rainy July 18, 1918 and lasted until August 6, 1918. The rain turned the roads into bogs, making it difficult for the Americans to transport men and supplies. The Americans persevered, and by August they and the British could claim another Allied victory, having driven the Germans almost back to the Belgian frontier. Thanks to the Americans, Parisians no longer worried about having to evacuate their beloved city, for by the fall of 1918, the Germans were pushed back over 100 miles east of Paris.

Pershing's first fully independent command came in September 1918, when Supreme Allied Commander Marshal Ferdinand Foch, authorized an AEF campaign to close a German salient around the town of St. Mihiel on the Meuse River, about 150 miles east of Paris. Pershing assembled over 500,000 American and 100,000 French soldiers for his massive offensive. Shelling of German positions began at 1:00 a.m. on September 11, and as an American recorded in his diary, "In one instant the entire front was a sheet of flame, while the heavy artillery made the earth quake." Within four days the salient was closed, in part because some German units had already withdrawn. Even so, St. Mihiel cost 7,000 U.S. casualties.

The war's last battle, part of the Meuse-Argonne Forest campaign, began on September 26 and lasted until November 1918. The assault represented the most protracted period that American soldiers were involved in combat and the first time they had to endure the filth, vermin, and dysentery that had become part and parcel of the trench warfare their Allied and German counterparts had suffered for four years. The stench of poison gas (first used by the Germans in 1915) hung in the air, and bloated rats scurried in the mud, gorging on human remains. Few of the American doughboys who fought in this particular

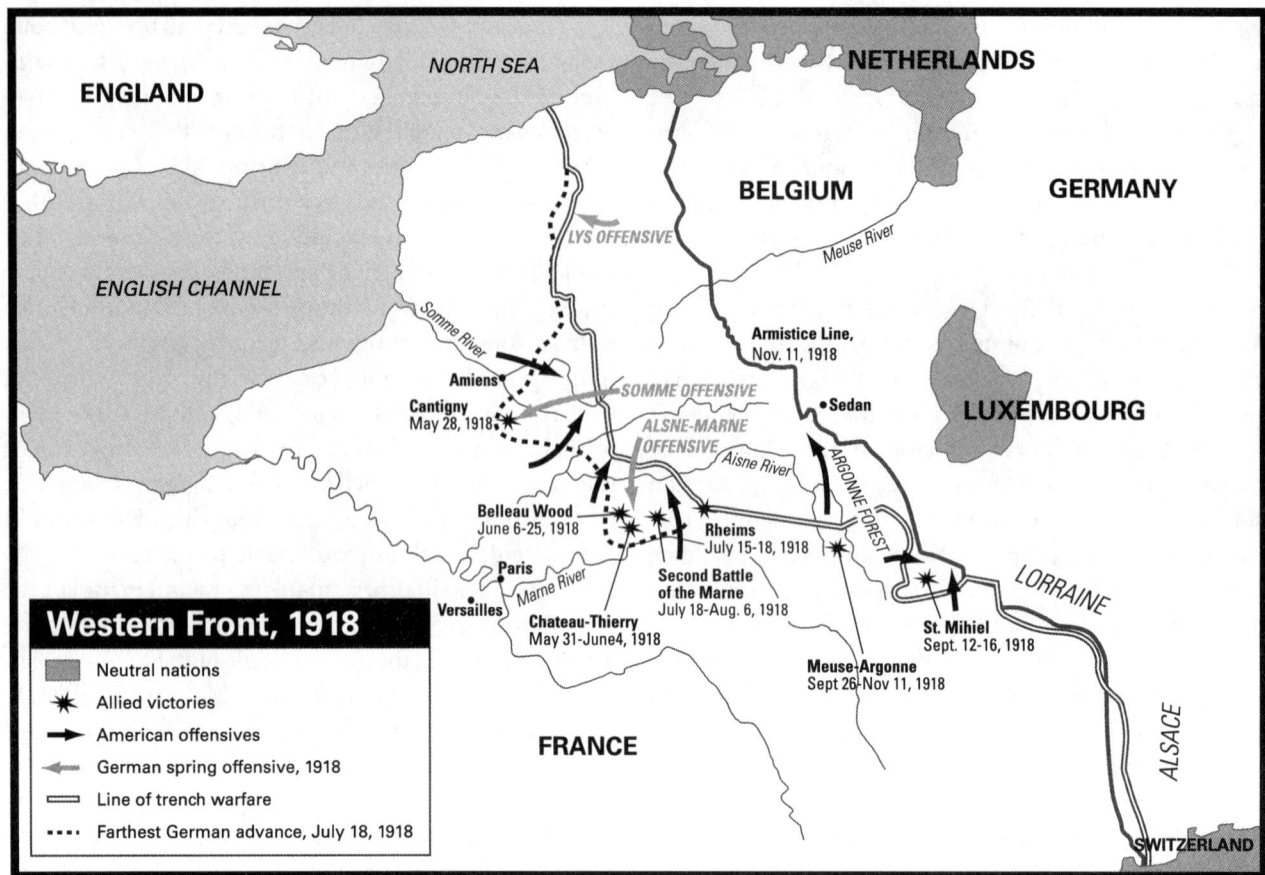

Map 22.2 Western Front, 1918

offensive would forget what they experienced for several months in the fall of 1918. As shells streaked over head at night, one American recalled, "We simply lay and trembled from sheer nervous tension." Many welcomed injuries, even inflicting them upon themselves as a ticket out of the trenches. Others collapsed emotionally and were hospitalized for "shell shock." The fighting for the Americans was particularly ferocious in the Argonne Forest, which saw many instances of vicious hand-to-hand combat between German and American soldiers. "We are not men anymore, just savage beasts," wrote a young American after three days of such fighting along three long, heavily fortified German trenches called Stellungen. Even the hardened Pershing could not hold back emotion after witnessing such slaughter. One day as he rode in his staff car past the site of a particularly gruesome scene where dead German and American soldiers were still entangled from having engaged and killed one another in hand-to-hand combat, Pershing buried his head in his hands and moaned his dead wife's name: "Frankie, Frankie, my God, sometimes I don't know how I can go on with this madness." But the AEF prevailed, overrunning the dreaded German trenches and pushing the Germans ever deeper into Belgium and Alsace-Lorraine by early November 1918. By that date it had become apparent to the German High Command that with the American presence, which they had hoped to prevent, the Allies were poised for victory. If an invasion of Germany proper was to be avoided then it was time to surrender before such a calamity could unfold.

The war came to an end on November 11, 1918 at 11 a.m. Although over 200,000 Americans had been wounded and 113,000 troops died (around 52,000 in battle and 60,000 from non-combat causes such as disease), the comparatively short presence of the United States in the war saved American soldiers from experiencing the horrors of trench warfare and the massive loss of lives which were the reality for the Russian, German, French, and English people. Military and civilian deaths for Great Britain topped one million, 1.7 million for France, 2.3 million for Russia, and 2.5 million for Germany. About 500,000 combatants alone were killed or wounded during the First Battle of Marne (1914), 230,000 at the Battle of Ypres (1914), and 700,000 at Verdun (1916). Compared to the loss of life and property suffered by the Europeans after four years of slaughter, Americans escaped the madness relatively *physically* unscathed. The psychological and emotional impact, however, on both the American people and the nation's warriors was surprisingly deep and profound. There laid the greatest scars and most searing memories of the war's awfulness, and it would be the trauma and anguish suffered at that level that would prove to be some of the most important factors in defeating Woodrow Wilson's postwar vision for the United States and the world.

THE HOME FRONT

Once the U.S. openly joined the war, Congress worked to ensure that Americans at home and the soldiers fighting in Europe had sufficient resources with which to sustain such an unprecedented human and material effort. Congress adopted the Fuel and Food Control Act in 1917. The Fuel Administration controlled the production, distribution, and price of the nation's main fuel sources, such as oil, gas, and coal. Directing the agency was Dr. Harry A. Garfield (son of assassinated President James B. Garfield) who did not believe the war effort demanded greater government control of the economy. At a meeting of the Academy of Political Scientists, he offered a justification for the Fuel Administration's existence as well as assurances that under his watch the agency would not nationalize the fuel industry. In his speech entitled "Task of the Fuel Administration," the gap between the fuel needs of a country at war compared to the needs of the U.S. in 1916 would be largely met through conservation, he argued, not a government takeover of the industry.

Food production and consumption also worried the Wilson administration, and the president issued Executive Order (2679A) creating the U.S. Food Administration. Headed by future president Herbert Hoover, Wilson charged the agency with assuring the supply, distribution, and conservation of food during the war, facilitating commodities transportation, preventing monopolies and hoarding, and maintaining governmental power over foods by using voluntary agreements and a licensing system.

In trying to get Americans to conserve what they had and to use less of what they grew or made, Hoover promoted "Meatless Mondays" and "Wheatless Wednesdays." Hoover also targeted the new immigrant populations, inundating their communities with all manner of visuals such as posters to remind them that they were in America now, and that one of the ways they could demonstrate their loyalty to their new homeland was to support the food conservation program. One such poster portrayed a well-lit, golden-colored, Oz-like New York in the far background with the Statue of Liberty in the near-background and a halo rainbow of red, white, and blue that seemed to hang in the sky as a physical divider between light and dark, new and old, progressive and regressive.

In the foreground you saw numerous immigrants dressed in Old World clothes including babushkas on the elderly women. "FOOD WILL WIN THE WAR," the poster proclaimed, "WHEAT is needed for the Allies—Waste Nothing. You came here seeking Freedom. You must now help to preserve it." Another Hoover slogan urged Americans to "Serve Beans by all Means," which suggested that people could find equally nutritious substitutes for those food commodities needed to feed the troops overseas. Even president Wilson did his part by pasturing a flock of sheep on the White House lawn.

The Food Administration asked Americans to grow their own vegetables (called "Victory Gardens") and to pledge to follow the call to preserve, consume less, and grow more in order to ensure that sufficient meat, wheat, fats, and sugars made it to the U.S. troops and American allies. The *Milwaukee Journal*, the largest daily in Wisconsin, proclaimed that 100 percent of their citizens took the pledge to eat less and conserve more. Wisconsin had more German immigrants than any other state as well as an active Socialist movement and it was important for the newspaper's publisher to ensure his readers locally and nationally, that *all* Wisconsinites, regardless of ethnicity or ideology, were one hundred percent behind the "war to

end all wars." The publishers of *Good Housekeeping* urged its readers to support the government efforts believing that:

> its large circle of earnest, patriotic women readers will respond gladly to a call to service at home. It is a tremendous task—this one of conservation and elimination of waste. Every woman is urged to do her part. It can best be done through close cooperation with the government. Enlist now and pledge yourself to do your share.

Finally, the War Industries Board (WIB), created in mid-summer of 1917, was another federal bureau tasked with ensuring that Americans at home and abroad had access to acceptably priced merchandise and equipment. Wilson appointed Wall Street financier Bernard Baruch to head this particular agency. As part of Wilson's "War Cabinet," he worked closely with Hoover. While Hoover's emphasis was on agriculture, Baruch focused on transforming American industry into an efficient, prolific producer of every essential for a country at war. He wanted U.S. soldiers to not only have the best weaponry that American manufacturers could produce but all other supplies as well, from boots to uniforms, to blankets, to medical supplies, and in conjunction with Hoover's agency, more than adequate nourishment.

The WIB's main purpose was to ensure that all of the nation's key productive industries were producing at maximum output for the war. It was thus vital that the nation's raw materials were not squandered on superfluous products or were withheld for the purpose of profiteering. Thus the WIB set production quotas for war-related industries and oversaw the allocation of raw resources. The WIB controlled all aspects of war procurement and production, from the distribution of raw resources to the placing of price controls on finished goods, which included chemical, steel, textile, rubber, and leather products. The standardization of bicycle manufacturing, for example, saved tons of steel. Perhaps most important, the establishment of the WIB marked the first time in U.S. history that the federal government participated in such a capacity in the private sector.

These two agencies represented the tip of the regulatory iceberg. Nearly 5,000 government-created agencies supervised home front activities. Some others of note were the Shipping Board, which regulated the transport of goods by water; the National War Labor Board, which worked assiduously to resolve labor-management disputes that if not ameliorated, could have led to striking workers that would have jeopardized production; and the Railroad Administration, headed by treasury secretary William McAdoo. When lines refused to allow their competitors to use their tracks to transport goods, a stoppage occurred in the flow of supplies to Europe in the winter of 1917-1918. McAdoo's agency intervened and soon transformed (consolidated) the thousands of miles of track owned by the competing companies into an efficient national rail system under his board's direction (control). McAdoo (with Wilson's and Congress' approval) "semi-nationalized" the nation's rail system by bringing all major carriers under direct government regulation for the war's duration. Although tightly monitoring the railroads' shipments of goods, the federal government did not take the revenue for such services. Significant profits from such enterprise continued to flow into the coffers of the railroad magnates. The railroad remained the king of mass transportation, and the lines' owners became some of the most notorious robber barons of the early twentieth century.

American businesses, much maligned by Progressives before the conflict, saw the war emergency as an opportunity to revamp their public image. Corporate executives such as Baruch ran regulatory agencies; factory owners distributed pro-war propaganda to workers; and trade associations coordinated war production. Unfortunately much of the patriotic ballyhoo was disingenuous, a plutocratic ruse to get the federal government and reformers out of their businesses, not only during the war but also more importantly after the conflict was over. By presenting a more solicitous, public-spirited face during the war, both the American populace and the federal government would look kindlier upon them, thanking them for their significant wartime contributions by allowing them to once again reign supreme.

Even before the war ended and government restraints removed, big business was on the march as witnessed by the ongoing process of corporate consolidation and economic integration. Wilson's track record of progressive trust-busting before the war was at best mediocre. During the war his administration stopped all such endeavors and instead encouraged private sector cooperation in the name of the war effort. Businesses cooperated all right, seizing a rare, government-sanctioned opportunity to further consolidate their enterprises. As a result, the number of corporate mergers jumped sharply. Commenting on the epidemic of "mergeritis," the Progressive magazine, *Harper's Weekly* observed, "The war has accelerated a tendency that was already irresistible. Instead of punishing companies for acting in concert, the government is now in some cases forcing them to unite. If this trend continues, the years after this war are over could come to represent some of the worst abuses of the commonweal by the corporations. The war has opened a Pandora's Box of business consolidation, the likes of which the country has not seen in years. It may be impossible to put these companies back into the box after the war."

The nineteen months in which the United States participated in the Great War was good for American businesses. Despite added business taxes imposed by Congress, wartime profits soared. After-tax profits in the copper industry, for example, jumped from 12 percent in 1913 to 24 percent in 1917.

Wartime Diplomacy

Woodrow Wilson envisioned a quick war, and to that end, Wilson believed it essential that the Allies coordinate as expeditiously as possible through a Supreme War Council, all food production, equipment needs, and communication to produce victory. Representing the United States on the council was Army Chief of Staff Tasker H. Bliss. The council focused on mobilizing resources and securing an Allied military victory, but as triumphed neared, the Council turned its attention to the equally pressing issue of the postwar peace settlement.

To Wilson, if the Great War just concluded was to be "the war to end all wars," then it was imperative that the United States not only participate fully in the peace process but also provide the blueprint as well for an end to international conflict. Thus, in a speech given on January 8, 1918, Wilson outlined his goals—a "fourteen-point" program for not only how the war should end but a vision as well that he believed would ensure lasting peace for the postwar world.

Many of the ideas that Wilson expressed before Congress were the initiatives of an assemblage of academics that the president had called together soon after the United States entered the conflict in 1917. Nicknamed the "Inquiry," these members of the nation's intelligentsia met in secret at the offices of the American Geographic Society in New York City. Wilson charged the group to develop proposals, based on their knowledge and research of European and world history, which he could then formulate into an agenda and present to the European belligerents as the basis for a just and permanent peace settlement. Wilson had great confidence in the Inquiry's ability to provide him with the right ideas, for as the 28-year old Harvard graduate, Walter Lippmann, who recruited the scholars and managed the Inquiry in its formative phase, declared, "We are skimming the cream of the younger and more imaginative scholars. What we are on the lookout for is genius—sheer, startling genius, and nothing else will do." Wilson formalized the Inquiry's genius into The **Fourteen Points**, which the president unveiled in his January speech before Congress.

In his address, Wilson reminded the joint session of Congress that the U.S. entered the Great War not only to protect American liberties at home but also to propagate the nation's ideals throughout the world. Wilson envisioned a world "made fit and safe to live in and particularly that it be made safe for every peace-loving nation, which, like our own, wishes to live its own life, determine its own institutions, and be assured of justice and fair dealing by other peoples of the world as against force and selfish aggression." Among the points that the president called for were international trade unrestricted by law or tariffs, an end to secret treaties and military alliances, and an end to colonialism. To Wilson, none of the first thirteen points could be established and enforced without the creation of a vigilant world organization for international cooperation. He described such a body in the final of his fourteen points, "A general association of nations must be formed under specific covenants for the purpose of affording mutual guarantees of political independence and territorial integrity to great and small states alike."

Much to Wilson's surprise, American and European leaders accused the president of wanting to remake the postwar world in an American image. Wilson quickly dismissed such allegations, reassuring his listeners that "the United States has no desire to interfere in European affairs or to act as arbiter in European territorial disputes." In other words, Wilson wanted to convey to the European belligerents that his January 8 speech was not any sort of plan to rebuild the world along American dictates.

England and France were the most wary of Wilson's Fourteen Points agenda, for of all the allies (excluding Russia, now the Soviet Union) they had fought the longest and sacrificed the most in both material and human lives. They did not greet Wilson's ideas for a new world order with open arms. Arthur Balfour, the British Foreign Secretary and one-time Prime Minister, seemed to be uninterested in any sort of negotiated settlement, instead calling for Germany to provide England and France with "unconditional restoration and reparation" of all taken, plundered, and destroyed lands. Neither did the Belgian Prime Minister accept Wilson's extensive plan. Baron Charles de Broqueville demanded "reparation for damages and guarantees against repetition of the aggression." Earlier, Wilson had called for "peace without victory," which meant that the Allies did not need to crush and then humiliate Germany with unrealistically harsh reparations and demands. However, that was precisely the Anglo-French position and thus the Inquiry and Wilson underestimated the Allies' desire to punish Germany not only as the vanquished but for having allegedly caused the war as well. To the British and French, the old cliché was still relevant: "to the victor(s) go the spoils of war." Sensing hostility to his proposals and determined to see his ideas prevail, Wilson believed it essential that he go to Paris, France, in order to secure future peace.

THE END OF THE WAR AND THE SEARCH FOR PEACE

Thirty-six nations gathered from January to June 1919 at the famous Versailles Palace just outside Paris. Excluded from the gathering were both Bolshevik Russia and Germany. Wilson was as anti-Bolshevik as his English and French counterparts, who prodded him in August 1918, even before the Great War had ended, to send 15,000 American troops into Russia to help defeat the **Bolsheviks**, who at the time were engaged in a bloody civil war against various Russian anti-Bolshevik factions, known collectively as the "**Whites**."

The second phase of the Russian Revolution had begun in November 1917 when the Marxist Bolshevik Party overthrew via *coup d'etat* the quasi-democratic/parliamentary Provisional Government headed by **Alexander Kerensky**, who came to power during the revolution's first phase in February 1917. It was Kerensky and his followers who had forced Czar Nicholas II to abdicate. From the moment that Kerensky and his tenuous coalition of anti-Bolshevik socialists (Mensheviks), Kadets, SR's (Social Revolutionaries), constitutional monarchists, and an assortment of other ideologically disparate factions seized power, their tenure was destined to be short-lived. Although Kerensky's government faced a multitude of domestic issues and crises, it was his government's refusal to withdraw Russia from the war and to fight on instead that ultimately toppled his regime. By the time Kerensky became *defacto* executive of the Provisional Government, the Russian people, especially the nation's soldiers, had grown sick of the war. The conflict had brought them nothing but untold miseries, ranging from starvation to never-ending strikes, to the slaughter of hundreds of thousands of poorly-clad and equipped peasant conscripts on the battle fronts. By succumbing to the Allies' relentless pressure to have Russia remain in the war (largely for the Allies' own selfish reasons), Kerensky sealed the fate of the country's brief experiment in parliamentary government.

When the Bolshevik Party, led by the ruthless V. I. Lenin, proclaimed that his party offered "peace, land, and bread," Kerensky's days were numbered. No sooner did Lenin seize control of Russia, then he quickly initiated peace talks with Germany (who had helped to smuggle him back into Russia so he could overthrow the Provisional Government) while urging workers in Europe and the United States to rise in revolt against the "capitalist-imperialist war," for which they had become lackeys and fodder. To further discredit the supposed righteousness of the Allied cause, Lenin published secret treaties that the Allies had made among themselves to carve up the territories and colonies of the Central Powers at war's end. Such revelations were especially embarrassing for Woodrow Wilson's claims that the United States had entered the conflict to help establish the right of all people to self-determination. Finally, the Bolsheviks' calls for a revolution that would bring about far-reaching social transformations, ending the corrupt and bankrupt notions of bourgeois-capitalist liberalism, had great appeal among the downtrodden around the world. For some, the fiery revolutionary Lenin, not the intellectual reformist Wilson, seemed the towering figure of the age.

Although supporting liberal-capitalist reform movements throughout the world, Wilson opposed anti-capitalist revolutions, not only in Russia but in China and Mexico as well. He wanted to reform capitalism; the Bolshevik leader Lenin wanted to destroy it. The Wilson administration used a variety of means—diplomatic, economic, and military—to isolate and hopefully destroy Lenin and the Bolsheviks. Despite massive aid, all of Wilson's as well as the other Allies' (including Japan) efforts failed. By 1920 the Red Army, under the brilliant leadership of Leon Trotsky, had crushed the Whites and with their defeat, all foreign imperialist mercenaries left the country. The Bolshevik Revolution (and Terror) could not proceed without the fear of being externally overthrown.

Despite Wilson's insistence in his Fourteen Points address that nations should engage in "open covenants, openly arrived at," all major discussions and decisions at Versailles were made not only behind closed doors but became the handiwork of essentially the four individuals representing the victorious Allies: Woodrow Wilson of the United States; David Lloyd George, prime minister of Great Britain; Vittorio Orlando, prime minister of Italy, and "Le Tigre," Georges Clemenceau, president of France, who proved to be the most insistent in demanding revenge and security for France.

Accompanying Wilson to France were nearly all of the members of the Inquiry as well as his closest friend and unofficial adviser, Edmund M. House. Wilson's entourage of perceived diplomatic novices and neophytes not only irritated the State Department's sense of protocol but insulted many of its members' professionalism, expertise, and years of experience. Although greeted everywhere in Europe Wilson went—France, England, and Italy—with the greatest fanfare, close to two million Frenchmen lined the Boulevard des Champs-Elysees and screamed his name while throwing flowers in his path, not all diplomats shared in the popular adulation. Not even remotely impressed was the bitter and vindictive Clemenceau, who complained that "Wilson thinks he is another Jesus Christ come upon earth to reform men." In the end, however, it would not be Clemenceau's vengeful obstructionism to Wilson's agenda but rather the president's own arrogance, high-mindedness, and inattention to other developments at home that made it a certainty the American people would reject the Versailles Treaty. Before leaving, Wilson did not engage public or congressional opinion. Perhaps most damaging, he failed to build bipartisan support for his program: his handpicked delegation included only one Republican of marginal influence. The wise choice would have been the powerful Senate Foreign Relations Committee chairman, Henry Cabot Lodge. Wilson's snubbing of such stalwarts as Lodge was especially remiss considering that the 1918 off-year congressional elections saw the Republicans sweep to majority control of both houses of Congress.

Despite Wilson's shunning of diplomatic niceties and shortsightedness in picking the right entourage, his overarching problem at Versailles was his allies. France and England had no interest in discussing anything but how they were going to dismantle the German empire, both in Europe and in those areas around the world where Germany had colonies. Despite vehement opposition to such a policy by Wilson, the Allies successfully carved up the German empire. The Rhineland, one of Germany's most vital natural resource areas, was demilitarized and designated a French protectorate for fifteen years. The treaty also allowed the French to occupy the coal-rich Saar region for a similar period. The treaty also returned to France the province of Alsace-Lorraine taken by Germany in 1871 at the conclusion of the Franco-Prussian War, which saw Prussia defeat France in six weeks time and then humiliate France by dictating the peace terms at Versailles. It was now France's turn to humble a defeated Germany. To add further insult to injury, the treaty cut eastern Germany into two parts by giving the newly independent Poland access to the Baltic by way of the east Prussian city of Danzig, which now became a Polish city where close to one million Germans would live. Another 500,000 Germans of the Sudetenland became Czech citizens. In the end, the treaty stripped Germany of one-eighth of its territory, one-tenth of its population, and all of its colonies and saddled the nation with a reparations bill of $33 billion to be paid to France and Great Britain. The treaty humiliated and enraged the Germans without crushing them and fueled their desire for revenge. To his credit Wilson tried to prevent such reprisals, all the while warning the British and French that if they imposed such a harsh and dishonorable settlement upon the Germans they would be sealing their own future fate, that of ensuring another European conflagration of retribution. In 1939, Woodrow Wilson's prediction came true.

Wilson could not prevent the Allies from grabbing territory they had promised each other in secret treaties mentioned above. For example, for abandoning neutrality and joining the Allies in 1915, Italy received the promised seaport on the Adriatic (Trieste) and the South Tyrol from Austria. The Ottoman empire was also dismembered, with Great Britain acquiring Palestine, Jordan, and most importantly oil-rich Mesopotamia (present-day Iraq). Great Britain also received all of Germany's African colonies. From the Ottomans France received Syria and Lebanon. Japan obtained all of Germany's islands in the Pacific and its sphere of influence in China, Shantung province. Also ignored by the Allies was Wilson's call for freedom of the seas and tariff reductions. The president did not push for these points because he feared that if he did, Clemenceau would have used the mandates as negotiating points to impose an even harsher treaty on Germany, one that would have made the Rhineland, for example, permanently French.

Not all of Wilson's entreaties fell on deaf ears. The Allies accepted and implemented Wilson's call for self-determination, especially for Eastern Europe, by creating an independent Poland and recognizing as sovereign nations the Baltic states of Estonia, Latvia, and Lithuania (territories Germany had seized from Bolshevik Russia in 1918 at the treaty of Brest-Litovsk). Also created by the concept of self-determination were the nations of Czechoslovakia and Yugoslavia, the latter a uniting of the various Slavic peoples of the previously independent entities of Serbia, Bosnia, Herzegovina, and Montenegro. As noted earlier, although the Czechs and Slovaks received a shared homeland, Czechoslovakia, the Allies also foolishly placed hundreds of thousands of Germans living in the mountainous Sudetenland under Czechoslovak control in an effort to protect the young country's western border from German attack. The move would lead to dire consequences for European peace within two decades.

It should also be noted that Poland's creation reflected the Allies ulterior motives when it came to their supposed embracing of the Wilsonian idea of self-determination. Poland not only served as a zone of occupation for about a million east Germans (the city of Danzig) but also as a buffer between the West and the Soviet Union, which the Allies perceived as the greatest threat to their present security. They hoped that by creating a large Polish state, the Poles could serve as a bulwark against the spread of Bolshevism. In the Great War's aftermath, the Allies

Map 22.3 Europe After World War I

wanted to put the greatest distance between them and the Bolsheviks, and a large Polish state would go far toward that end.

Although in the end forced to accept Allied dictates, especially when it came to Germany, Wilson hoped such shortsightedness would be ameliorated through the work of the **League of Nations**. Wilson insisted the League be made part of the peace treaty. The covenant for the new international organization called for a small but powerful executive council to be comprised of the alleged "superpower" nations of the moment: France, Italy, Great Britain, Japan, and the United States. In reality, only three could claim any legitimate superpower status: the United States, Great Britain, and Japan. The League would have a large assembly in which every independent nation in the world would be represented and have one vote. The League's headquarters would be Geneva, Switzerland. The most important component of the League's charter was Article 10, which established the concept of collective security, whereby each member nation would pledge to respect and preserve each other's independence and territorial integrity against aggressors, and to use whatever means appropriate or necessary—economic or military sanctions—to stop the invader and restore peace. In an attempt to avoid future wars, members agreed to submit for arbitration all disputes that created tensions between countries that could lead to war. They also agreed to address the arms race issue and to create a permanent court of international justice, popularly known as the World Court.

Wilson believed that all the shortcomings of the Versailles Treaty would ultimately be rectified by the League of Nations, led by the moral persuasion and strong presence of the United States. To Wilson, the League with the United States as its most active participant was the world's best hope for peace and security. As Wilson exclaimed to the Senate when he presented the treaty in July 1919 for ratification, "The stage is set, the destiny disclosed. It has come about by no plan of our conceiving, but by the hand of God who led us this way. We cannot turn back. America shall in truth show the way."

The Fight for the League

The president's vision of a liberal, harmonious, and peaceful world order would soon lie in ruins. Even before

Railroad car in which the Armistice was signed, November 11, 1918.

Wilson returned from Europe with the treaty, opposition to the document had emerged, led by the powerful isolationist Republican senator from Massachusetts, Henry Cabot Lodge. Instigated by Lodge, thirty-nine Republican senators sent a letter to Wilson in February 1919 rejecting the League in its present form. Irritating the senators most was Article 10, the collective security clause, which was interpreted as an obligation by the United States to enter into every peace-keeping endeavor (war) that involved an act of aggression upon one of the League's member nations. To many of these legislators, the Senate's authority under Article I, Section VIII of the U.S. Constitution to "To declare war, grant letters of marque and reprisal, and make rules concerning captures on land and water" would be trumped by any tyrant, king, or madman who invaded a member state. Although Lodge and many of his Republican cohorts took exception with Article 10, they did not reject the whole treaty, and thus Lodge and his followers, which included Democrats such as William Jennings Bryan, became known as the "**Reservationists**." They accepted the treaty but wanted to amend the United States' role relative to the League of Nations and until Wilson agreed to such a modification, Lodge kept the treaty bottled up in the Foreign Relations Committee after Wilson had sent the document to the Senate for ratification in July 1919.

Lodge and his contingent were the least of Wilson's political worries. An even more powerful group of Republican senators led by William Borah of Idaho were determined to torpedo both the treaty and the League of Nations and have the United States return to the security of isolationism. Much to Wilson's surprise and eventual dismay, senators rejected U.S. membership in the League and called instead for a return to isolationism because they feared that the League of Nations would be a body controlled by Europe's imperial powers. They worried that the League would be exploited by nations like Britain and France to promote further colonialism around the world. These senators became known as the "**Irreconcilables**." Together, both groups presented Wilson with an unanticipated battle for ratification. Furious at both Lodge and Borah for their obstructionism and convinced that he could rally public support for the treaty, Wilson left Washington on September 3, 1919 on a barnstorming western speaking tour. Speaking before large and enthusiastic crowds in every western state he visited, Wilson covered 9,000 miles by train and gave 37 speeches in 22 days arguing for the necessity for the United States to join the League of Nations. People wept as the president graphically described his visits to American war cemeteries in France and cheered his vision of a new world order to be led by the United States.

Wilson appeared on the brink of victory of rallying public support for the League when tragedy befell him. While speaking in Colorado on September 25, Wilson collapsed from exhaustion. His train sped back to Washington where the president suffered a devastating stroke on October 2. For a time he lay near death. Despite a partial recovery, Wilson spent the rest of his term a reclusive invalid, his fragile emotions fluctuating between vindictive actions and tearful outbursts. He broke with close advisers, refused to see foreign ambassadors, and dismissed his Secretary of State, Robert Lansing, for "disloyalty." In January 1920, his physician advised him to resign, but Wilson refused and since the Twenty-fifth Amendment, dealing with issues of presidential disability, was not adopted until 1967, Wilson, despite his debilitations, could legally remain in office.

Stepping into the leadership void was Wilson's imperious second wife, Edith Galt, whom he married in 1915. Edith fiercely guarded her husband's incapacity. Mrs. Wilson hid her husband's condition from the public, controlled his access to information, and decided who could see him. Regardless of their stature—Cabinet members, foreign diplomats, congressional leaders, even the vice-president—all were screened first by Mrs. Wilson for she wanted no one or no issue to upset her husband. As she told one political leader who desperately needed to talk to the president, she did not care about "the welfare of the country. I am not thinking of the country now, I am thinking about my husband." Although Mrs. Wilson's single-minded devotion to her husband's well-being could be lauded, politically her actions proved disastrous, for they doomed to defeat what her husband most cherished: ratification of the **Treaty of Versailles** and U.S. membership in the League of Nations.

With Wilson "out of the way," the treaty's defeat was almost a certainty. Led by Borah, Hiram Johnson of California, and Robert La Follette of Wisconsin, the isolationist Irreconcilables had a field day carving up the treaty, claiming that every one of Wilson's Fourteen Points would somehow lead the country into another world calamity in which the United States would get nothing in return but debt, thousands of dead fellow citizens, and the violation of many Americans' civil liberties. Despite the Irreconcilables' persuasive hyperbole, there was still a chance for a Wilsonian victory if president been willing to compromise by embracing some of the Lodge-led Reservationists' amendments to U.S. membership in the League. Indeed, the consensus among historians of this time period is that if Wilson had accepted accommodation, the Senate would probably have ratified the treaty, bringing the United States into the League of Nations. Wilson's illness, however, exacerbated his already non-conciliatory nature. From his isolation in the White House, he instructed Senate Democrats to vote against even the slightest modification of the treaty as it stood. To Wilson, any altering of the document and any weakening of U.S. participation in the League represented "a knife thrust into the heart of the treaty."

The treaty's death knell came in many ways from the American people, who despite giving Wilson enthusiastic receptions on his speaking tour did not rally behind the League. Two factors contributed to the peoples' rejection of the treaty and League. First, by 1919, the full, terrible impact of the war had reached the American public as they watched the "doughboys" return from Europe, either in coffins, or maimed and scarred for life, both physically and emotionally. Many Americans felt ashamed, guilty, for having sent overseas so many young men to die or come home missing limbs, or with bodies scarred or flesh burned, in order to "make the world safe for democracy." To the postwar American public, the price had been too high and not worth the sacrifice of so many. Many Americans thus felt duped and betrayed by Wilson and vowed to those who had died and to those who had returned that they were not only sorry for having supported such an ignoble war but that they would never call upon another generation of young Americans to make such a worthless sacrifice. The Irreconcilables found much public support for their position and with such popular endorsement felt confident they could defeat the treaty in the Senate.

The second factor that contributed to the treaty's defeat was the Wilson administration's reactionary and proscriptive policies during the war years, especially toward the conflict's opponents. Wilson's desire to create the image of an American people one-hundred percent committed to the war effort witnessed some of the most egregious violations of many citizens' civil liberties in the history of the United States. Wilson's actions were now coming back to haunt him. As the editor of the liberal *The Nation* magazine opined, "If Wilson loses his great fight for humanity, it be because he was deliberately silent when freedom of speech and the right of conscience were struck down in America." With such distaste and opposition arrayed against Wilson, few Americans were surprised that the Senate rejected the Treaty of Versailles and United States' membership in the League of Nations. A president elected amid grand expectations in 1912, hailed when he called for war in 1917, and adulated when he arrived in Europe in 1918 lay isolated and debilitated, his leadership repudiated.

Postwar Racism and the Red Scare

With the fighting in Europe over and the issue of U.S. membership in the League finally put to rest, white Americans returned to a more familiar type of fighting: against other races and against foreign ideas. The war left a bitter aftertaste, especially when it came to black-white relations. The years 1919-1920 saw new racial violence. Violence toward African Americans, especially in northern cities, was particularly violent and appalling. White mobs in various parts of the country lynched seventy-six blacks in 1919, the worst toll in fifteen years. The victims included ten veterans, several still in uniform. Some of these killings were incredibly brutal, such as the episode in Omaha, Nebraska, where a mob shot a black prisoner more than a thousand times, mutilated him, and hung his body in a busy intersection as a warning to other African Americans that the war had changed nothing relative to race relations.

The city of Chicago witnessed the most devastating race riot of the immediate postwar years. Other cities exploded such as Washington, D.C. and Tulsa, Oklahoma. Why such white hostility toward African Americans in the postwar years? According to the NAACP it appeared that many whites perceived the "New Negro" as potential radical subversives in which somehow black folk during the war years had become "infected" with communism and other radical un-American ideas. To many whites, postwar African-American demands for equality reflected not the simple desire to be treated fairly and decently but rather the influence of subversive radicals and the propagation among the black community of their ideas, which allegedly got normally docile "Negroes all agitated and uppity." Many whites believed there was a supposed conspiracy among African Americans and radical groups such as the Wobblies (members of the labor union, the International Workers of the World, which did allow both African American and female membership) and other "reds" to overthrow the established order of white supremacy. Many white Americans believed that the Negro must be kept in his place and a similar repression must be put into effect against all radical organizations. Thus, a postwar **Red Scare** crested as Anglo-Americans in particular went after all whom they considered a threat "to the American way of life," which meant adherence to White, Anglo-Saxon, and Protestant values, ideals, and beliefs. Anything else was to be considered "un-American."

Fears of bolshevism intensified when a rash of strikes broke out in 1919. Anti-union sentiment had always been strong in the United States, largely because of unionism's collective nature, which many Americans believed to be anti-thetical to one of the nation's most cherished notions: rugged individualism. The majority of Americans had disdained unions since their inception in the latter part of the nineteenth-century. Unions seemed unnecessary because of the supposed inherent quality of unfettered American capitalism to ensure all citizens a decent standard of living by allowing workers to individually negotiate with their employers for wages and benefits free from the artificial restraints and dictates of unions. To the laissez-faire free-marketeers of the postwar era, the booming prosperity the war brought made unions not only unwarranted but impediments as well to an individual's right, via personal initiative, to gain for himself his supposed fair share of prosperity and security. Such an interpretation of American capitalism at the beginning of the decade of the 1920s could not have been more inaccurate. It was all propaganda designed to justify, with government assistance if necessary, the crushing of unions as dangerous, subversive, and self-serving entities determined to overthrow American capitalism. When labor leaders in Seattle, Washington in February 1919 united in a general strike for higher wages, the politically ambitious conservative mayor of the city, Ole Hanson, contrary to all evidence, immediately colored the striking workers "red," ensuring that he would have universal support in crushing the strike, because it "duplicated the anarchy of Russia." The mayor had no problem requesting federal troops to maintain public order, even though there was no need for such heavy-handedness. The striking workers had created a General Strike Committee, which had set up milk delivery for children and laundry service for hospitals and organized some five hundred uniformed war veterans to patrol the streets.

In Boston, even the police struck, walking off their beats when the police commissioner suspended nineteen officers for attempting to establish a patrolmen's union affiliated with the AFL. Unfortunately for the striking officers, a wave of rowdyism, theft, and violence hit the city, which in turn enraged Massachusetts governor Calvin Coolidge, who denounced the policemen for their dereliction of duty and declared that none of the strikers would be rehired. To restore law and order in Boston, Coolidge mobilized state troopers while he recruited unemployed veterans for an entirely new police force. Mayors, governors, and the general public applauded Coolidge's stand.

Anxiety engulfed Washington, D.C. when various public officials received packages containing bombs. One blew off the hands of a senator's maid. Another damaged the home of Attorney General A. Mitchell Palmer. When 350,000 steel workers went on strike in September 1919, they virtually shut down the industry in ten states. The steel owners responded with a reign of terror on the striking workers and their supporters as company goons beat, arrested, shot, and drove out of steel towns the troublemakers. In Clairton and Glassport, Pennsylvania, club-wielding state troopers wantonly attacked peaceful worker gatherings. If violent reprisals failed to get the workers off strike, company owners then resorted to splitting the strikers along ethnic and racial lines by bringing in African-American and Mexican-American strikebreakers. Throughout the walkout's duration, newspapers and company propaganda constantly labeled the strike a Bolshevik plot engineered by "Red agitators." Unfortunately, the fact that the majority of the striking workers were of immigrant backgrounds (primarily eastern Europeans with a smattering of Italians) helped to further the public's fear that the conflict was an attempted revolution by foreign-born radicals. With such overwhelming forces arrayed against the walkout, the workers' resolve weakened. In January 1920, the unions threw in the towel and workers returned to the mills. The immigrant steelworkers had demonstrated a capacity for sustained militancy and discipline but because the steel barons had overwhelming government and popular support, they were able to crush even the most massive of walkouts.

The strikes gave the federal government and state governments the excuse to politicize the anti-radical paranoia. In November, the House of Representatives refused to seat the legally elected Socialist Victor Berger of Wisconsin because of his earlier indictment under the Espionage Act. The New York legislature expelled several socialist members, and the federal government via the Justice Department ordered the arrest of hundreds of suspected communists and radicals. In December 1919, the government deported 249 Russian-born aliens, including the radical Emma Goldman, a leader of the birth-control movement. The government's anti-radical crusade won enthusiastic support from the American Legion, a newly founded veteran's organization as well as from the National Association of Manufacturers. The worst however was yet to come.

In January 1920, in one of the most intense dragnets ever initiated by the federal government in conjunction with local police, Attorney General A. Mitchell Palmer authorized the Justice Department to raid the homes of suspected radicals in thirty-three cities without search or arrest warrants. Law enforcement officials took more than 5,000 persons into custody, with some 550 eventually deported. Many of the apprehended were humiliated as police paraded them through the streets handcuffed or in chains and then confined them in crowded and unsanitary cells with hardened criminals without formal charges or the right to post bail. The individual most responsible for these egregious wartime violations of thousands of Americans' civil liberties during the war was a Quaker, someone whose religion supports pacifism.

A report prepared by a group of distinguished lawyers questioned the legality of Palmer's highhanded tactics. The Attorney General's popularity had waned by the spring of 1920, when it became clear to most Americans that his earlier forecast that revolutionary uprisings were imminent were wildly exaggerated. Nonetheless, the Red Scare left an ugly legacy—wholesale violations of thousands of citizens' civil liberties, deportations of hundreds of innocent people, and fuel for the fires of nativism and intolerance. Organizations such as the National Association of Manufacturers found "red-baiting" to be a most effective postwar tool in squashing unionization in their factories. In many ways, the Red Scare of 1919 helped to pave the way for that future dark moment called "McCarthyism."

In reaction to these attacks on Americans' civil rights, progressive reformers such as Helen Gurley Flynn helped to organize the **American Civil Liberties Union (ACLU)**, which would come to the future assistance of those Americans finding their constitutional rights being violated by federal, state, or other public (and eventually even private) agencies and institutions. As the nation entered the new decade of the Roaring Twenties, the majority of Americans wanted to put the war years behind them and thus the country's first "Red Scare" faded away.

POSTWAR NORMALCY

Compared to the casualties and socio-political upheavals that swept across Europe in the aftermath of the Great War, the United States largely escaped such trauma and dislocation. Upon closer scrutiny, it is readily apparent that the war years unleashed powerful socio-economic and political forces that reshaped much of American life long after Armistice Day. Republican administrations during the next decade would resurrect the pre-Progressive Era alliance between big business and the government. The postwar plutocracy became even more powerful and entrenched, as their ethos came to define the United States in so many capacities during the 1920s. It was the progressive Wilson administration that opened this Pandora's Box, the result of wartime production needs, which big business was more than glad to supply, but at a future cost.

The war years undermined the best aspects of the progressive reform impulse—its openness to new ideas, its commitment to social justice, and its humanitarian concern for the downtrodden and oppressed. Government war propaganda fostered an intolerance of dissent, ideological conformity, and a fear of radicalism. The climate of reaction intensified in 1919-1920, as the nation repudiated Wilsonian idealism. The nation that celebrated the armistice in November 1918 was very different from the one that Woodrow Wilson had solemnly taken into battle only nineteen months earlier.

The wartime measure of national prohibition evolved into one of the most contentious social issues in United

States history. Sophisticated sales techniques, psychology, and propaganda used to promote the war effort at home transformed into the new mega-industries of advertising and public relations, both of which made millions by telling Americans forever more what they should buy, eat, wear, and even who and what they needed to see. The growing visibility of immigrants and African Americans in the nation's burgeoning cities provoked a xenophobic and racist backlash in the decade's politics. More than anything else, the desire for "normalcy" reflected the deep anxieties evoked by the United States' wartime experience.

Chronology

1914	U.S. troops occupy Veracruz, Mexico. Archduke Franz Ferdinand assassinated. World War I begins in Europe. Wilson declares American neutrality.
1915	U.S. marines occupy Haiti and the Dominican Republic. *Lusitania* sunk. Women's Peace Party formed. Wilson begins preparedness program. Italy joins Allies.
1916	After sinking the *Sussex*, Germany promises to cease unannounced U-boat attacks. General Pershing pursues Pancho Villa.
1917	Wilson reelected. Germany resumes unrestricted submarine warfare. Zimmermann telegram intercepted. United State declares war on Germany (April 6). Selective Service Act. War Industries Board and Committee on Public Information. Espionage Act. Sedition Act.
1918	Wilson outlines his Fourteen Points, Jan. 8. Armistice ends World War I (Nov. 11). Worldwide influenza epidemic claims more than 20 million lives.
1919	Paris Peace conference begins. Treaty of Versailles signed. Wilson launches speaking tour.. Wave of labor strikes hit nation.
1920	Justice Department launches Palmer Raids. "Red Scare" hits nation. Nineteenth Amendment (Women's Suffrage) ratified. Senate rejects Treaty of Versailles. Warren G. Harding elected president.
1924	Woodrow Wilson dies.

Review Questions

1. Discuss President Woodrow Wilson's foreign policy views and how Wilson's beliefs affected his conduct of foreign policy relative to the Mexican Revolution and the war in Europe.

2. Assess the fundamental causes of the Great War.

3. Discuss the impact of America's entry into the war on the home front. Once Wilson committed the US to war, what were his war aims and how did they affect the American public?

4. Assess the Versailles Treaty. In what ways did this document help to cause World War II?

5. The war's aftermath unleashed not only the nation's first "Red Scare" but also some of the worst race riots and labor unrest in the nation's history. How did the war years contribute to the outbreak of these events?

Glossary of Important People and Concepts

American Civil Liberties Union (ACLU)
American Expeditionary Force (AEF)
American Protective League (APL)
Battles of Chateau-Thierry and Belleau Woods
Bolsheviks
Camp Logan Riots
Caudillo
Committee on Public Information (CPI)
Doughboys
Espionage Act
Fourteen Points
Gringo
Industrial Workers of the World (IWW)
Irreconcilables
Alexander Kerensky
League of Nations
Lusitania
Over There
Red Scare
Reservationists
Schenck v. United States
Schlieffen Plan
Selective Service Act
Sussex Pledge
Treaty of Versailles
U-Boat
the Whites
Zimmermann Telegram

SUGGESTED READINGS

Arthur E. Barbeau and Florette Henri, *The Unknown Soldiers: Black American Troops in World War I* (1947).

Lisa Budreau, *Bodies of War: World War I and the Politics of Commemoration, 1919-1933* (2011).

Richard D. Camp, *The Devil Dogs at Belleau Wood: The U.S. Marines in World War I* (2008).

Edward Coffman, *The War to End All Wars: The American Military Experience in World War I* (1998).

Justus D. Doenecke, *Nothing Less Than War: A New History of America's Entry into World War I* (2011).

Robert H. Ferrell, *Woodrow Wilson and World War I, 1917-1921* (1983).

Thomas Fleming, *The Illusion of Victory: America in World War I* (2003).

Philip S. Foner, *History of the Labor Movement in the United States: Labor and World War I, 1914-1918* (1987).

Ernest Freeberg, *Democracy's Prisoner: Eugene V. Debs, The Great War, and the Right to Dissent* (2008).

Frank Freidel, *Over There* (1964).

Lettie Gavin, *American Women in World War: They Also Served* (2006).

Martin Gilbert, *The First World War: A Complete History* (1994).

Maurine W. Greenwald, *Women, War and Work* (1980).

Ellis W. Hawley, *The Great War and the Search for a Modern Order: A History of the American People and Their Institutions* (1992).

Jennifer Keene, *World War I: The American Soldier Experience* (2011).

David M. Kennedy, *Over Here: The First World War and American Society* (1980).

Celia Malone Kingsbury, *For Home and Country: World War I Propaganda on the Homefront* (2010).

Arthur S. Link, *Woodrow Wilson: Revolution, War, and Peace* (1979).

Carole Marks, *Farewell—We're Good and Gone: The Great Black Migration* (1989).

Daniel Malloy Smith, *The Great Departure: The United States and World War I, 1914-1920* (1965).

William H. Thomas, Jr., *Unsafe for Democracy: World War I and the Justice Department's Covert Campaign to Suppress Dissent* (2008).

Barbara Tuchman, *The Guns of August* (1962).

William Tuttle Jr., *Race Riot: Chicago and the Red Summer of 1919* (1970).

Chad Louis Williams, *Torchbearers of Democracy: African American Soldiers in the World War I Era* (2010).

Robert H. Zieger, *America's Great War: World War I and the American Experience* (2001).

1921 MODEL T

Chapter Twenty-three

THE CONTENTIOUS TWENTIES

Perhaps no American had a more profound impact on the decade following the First World War than Henry Ford. Though he did not invent the automobile, Ford's contribution lay with improving the assembly-line technique of manufacturing cars by utilizing moving conveyor belts. This innovation led to the mass production of the vehicles, reducing their price to affordable levels for millions of middle-class families. By the 1920s, the automobile not only gave the country expanded transportation opportunities, but also transformed many elements of American social life. In the opinion of Ford and other Americans, however, these changes were not always desirable.

In many ways, Ford retained the mentality of a rural mechanic born on a small Michigan farm during the Victorian Age who only had eight years of formal schooling. He often railed against many aspects of the modernizing world of which the automobile had become an integral part. While he hoped that citizens would frequently use the automobile to escape urban areas in order to experience the beauty of nature, cars also led to pollution, suburban sprawl, and the withering away of many formerly pristine rural areas across the country. In the media, Ford extolled many of his personal views, such as his strong opposition to cigarettes, alcohol, jazz music, wild dancing, and looser sexual morals. Yet, the automobile provided an easier means for many to avoid Prohibition laws by attending secret "speakeasies" where smoking, drinking, and wild dancing took place, not to mention the greater ease that autos allowed individuals to sneak away to engage in sexual escapades.

*Still, Henry Ford continued to promote the dominant values of an earlier time. His sense of nostalgia sometimes served noble purposes, such as spending large sums of money to build re-creations of small eighteenth- and nineteenth-century towns. Other times, his lack of education and worldliness showed a dark side, such as when he evoked his blatantly anti-Semitic views in his **Dearborn Independent** newspaper, blaming Jews for everything from labor unrest to the spread of communism. (Ford also sponsored the publication of 500,000 copies of the **Protocols of the Elders of Zion**—a fraudulent work originating in Russia that purported to reveal a secret Jewish plan to dominate the world—thus greatly increasing its visibility and further inciting anti-Semitic views domestically and internationally.) In many ways, these internal divisions within Ford symbolized the new era of American history. Like the nation itself, Ford kept one foot in the old world and one foot in the new.*

THE "SPANISH FLU" PANDEMIC

America experienced a tumultuous social and economic transition period following the First World War. Even before the conflict ended, the nation weathered a biological calamity in the form of an influenza pandemic that ultimately killed five times as many Americans as the number of soldiers lost during the Great War. Grossly mislabeled the "**Spanish flu**" because Spanish King Alfonso XIII became an early celebrity affected by the sickness, the pandemic actually began in the Southern Plains of the United States. In the spring of 1918, the first reported cases of the illness (caused by a virus probably spread from birds to swine and then to humans) were noted at Fort Riley, Kansas. This particular strain of flu virus attacked the body by forcing the immune system to turn against itself, producing pneumonia. This process explains why most victims were otherwise young healthy individuals rather than infants or the elderly, as is often the case with influenza. Close soldiers' quarters led to the spread of the disease among American military personnel and, by the fall of 1918, to the civilian population.

Troop movements spread the flu quickly from Middle America to the Atlantic coast, then to Europe and beyond. Current estimates suggest that the pandemic killed perhaps 50 million people across the globe with few populated areas being spared. Confusion and fear of the unknown reigned across the country as it would again thirty years later when the polio outbreak occurred. Ordinary residents wearing surgical masks became a common sight in towns and cities across the country. Public places such as dance halls, theaters, and even churches closed as citizens and their governments desperately tried to limit the epidemic even though its exact cause was unknown at the time. By the summer of 1920, when the disease ran its course, over 500,000 American citizens had died.

POSTWAR ECONOMIC PROBLEMS

The cessation of wartime government contracts, the removal of price controls and minimum pay requirements, and the passage of anti-strike legislation led to a period of high inflation and widespread labor unrest (discussed in the previous chapter) as well as a severe postwar recession. While the overall economic situation improved greatly by mid-1920s, certain sectors of the economy—agriculture and the so-called "**sick industries**"—continued to languish throughout the decade. When the Great Depression arrived, the downturn merely made worse what these producers had already been experiencing for several years.

Coal mining, textile manufacturing, and railroads were among the most notable "sick industries" plagued by excessive productive capacity with declining demand and labor conflict. Competition from rival industries—electricity for the coal producers, synthetic rayon for cotton mills, and motor trucks for the railroads—caused further problems resulting in low financial returns and high unemployment. The passage of the Prohibition Amendment also hurt the nation's breweries during the 1920s, leading most to close and others to weather the storm through diversification. As a result, the nation saw the former producers of Budweiser, Schlitz, Miller, and Pabst turn to the manufacturing of near beers, root beers, colas, and malt extract (syrup) in an effort to stay in business.

American agriculture, which had been booming during wartime, went into a sharp decline following the end of hostilities. Many farmers borrowed heavily to buy additional land and equipment as they took advantage of increased wartime prices. On average, farm prices rose 82 percent from 1913 to 1917, leading to a 150 percent net increase in farm income. Once the war ended, however, the termination of government purchases and the revival of European agriculture led to a sharp decline in domestic prices and income. Wheat prices dropped from $2.50 per bushel to less than $1. Wool prices fell from 60 cents per pound to 19 cents. Similar declines took place across the board, affecting the nation's cotton, tobacco, beef, and dairy producers especially hard. The collective response to the burst price bubble, however, was not decreased production. To the contrary, as farmers received less for their crops, many tried to make up the difference by raising more. Along with increased efficiency created by more widespread use of mechanization, fertilizers, high-quality seeds, and improved farming techniques, the maintenance of high production levels contributed to further price declines and income stagnation. By the end of the decade, average per capita income for American farmers was only 25 percent the level for urban dwellers, leading many rural residents to leave the land to seek better employment opportunities.

POSTWAR ECONOMIC BOOM

The postwar revival in the American economy began to take place in 1922. Corporate profits rose and unemployment began to drop as many old and new industries saw a marked uptick in demand and more efficient production. In terms of aggregate profits and high employment, the American economy during the 1920s enjoyed its best performance to date. Average corporate profits rose 62 percent from 1923 to 1929 while the national unemployment rate never topped 3.7 percent. Workers' incomes rose 30 percent during the decade while inflation remained low (the annual average increase in prices never topped 1 percent.) This increase in purchasing power (along with the inauguration of installment buying that allowed consumers to make extensive purchases on credit) helped to fuel a vast consumer spending binge that lasted until 1929.

During this unprecedented economic boom, **Henry Ford** led the way by transforming the automobile industry from a maker of luxury vehicles for the rich into an economic sector that manufactured affordable transportation for millions of middle-class families. Ford began production of his "Model T" in 1909, producing over 1,700 cars for $950 each. His greatest contribution to the industry would be his modification of Ransom Olds's use of the assembly line by introducing moving conveyor belts in 1914. With workers specialized in performing one or two specific operations of the total of forty-five needed, the vehicle began to take shape more quickly and efficiently. A Model T could be produced every 90 minutes and sold profitably for less than $500. By 1920, 1.25 million rolled off the assembly line as one car could be produced every 60 seconds and sold for as low as $350. Fifty-seven percent of all cars in America were Fords by 1923, making the company owner a billionaire.

Despite relatively high pay compared to other industrial jobs (many line workers could earn as much as 5 dollars per day), work on a Ford assembly line could be quite dehumanizing. Employee tasks involved much repetitive motion throughout each working hour. In addition, Ford demanded that his employees remain so focused on their assigned task that he forbade talking, singing, and even whistling on the job. Ford's behavioral edicts also extended to his workers' personal lives. Any employee found to have used tobacco or consumed alcohol (on or off the job) would be immediately terminated. Because Ford did not hire any workers who belonged to a labor union, there was no avenue for appeal. Indeed, one major reason why Ford paid higher wages was to undercut potential union activity in his factories. Ford also hired company spies to monitor his employees, especially looking for signs of union organizing.

Though Ford controlled a majority of the industry's market share in the early 1920s, he did not completely dominate the market. His major rivals—General Motors, Chrysler, Studebaker, Packard, and Hudson – continued to eat away at Ford's market share through creative innovations. In 1925, General Motors introduced the K Model Chevrolet, which included among its features a convertible roof, wider leg room, and a windshield with automatic wipers. Hudson began producing its closed-roof Essex coach, which offered consumers a car with a sturdier frame and a sportier look than the Model T. When Ford's market share dropped below 50 percent, he decided to shut down his massive River Rouge plant in Detroit for an entire year to revamp his entire operations in order to begin production of his new car—the Model A, which incorporated many features begun by Ford's competitors: a sleeker look, availability in multiple colors (the Model T had only been available in black), and installment buying for the first time. By 1929, Ford once gain produced a majority of cars in the American market.

The impact of Ford and his rivals on the American economy went far beyond the benefits to the auto companies, their workers (during the 1920s, 7 percent of all industrial workers labored in automobile factories), the economies of the towns and cities where automobile plants were located, or the financing and marketing apparatuses behind the sale of the vehicles. The American automobile industry was simply the largest driver of the national prosperity during the decade as the demand for cars greatly stimulated other sectors of the economy. The providers of raw materials for automobile manufacturing benefited tremendously as massive orders came in from the auto companies for steel, glass, rubber, and paint, not to mention the huge demand for gasoline that the cars' internal combustion engines required. The need for repair and maintenance services provided many new jobs for mechanics and repair specialists. The necessity for various forms of assistance to the increased number of road travelers offered an untold number of employment opportunities for service station attendants, motel employees, workers in the booming tourist industry, and road construction laborers.

While the automobile industry was king during the 1920s, many other sectors of the economy also performed well. In addition to cars, large numbers of upper- and middle-class Americans purchased a host of new electrical household appliances including washing machines, dishwashers, refrigerators, vacuum cleaners, flat irons, and toasters that promised to relieve many (usually female) home dwellers from the toils of domestic upkeep. Americans began mass consuming copious amounts of other new products that have become commonplace in homes today, everything from new food items such as freeze-dried vegetables, candy bars, and frozen popsicles to new sundries in the form of disposable handkerchiefs (Kleenex), disposable razors, and Listerine mouthwash.

Among the many additions to American homes during the 1920s, perhaps the most significant was the radio. In 1920, KDKA in Pittsburgh became the first station in the country to broadcast regularly scheduled programming as it transmitted popular music, news bulletins, and sporting events. Over 3 million radios were in use by 1923 when Americans could tune in to over 500 stations nationwide. By the middle of the decade, the National Broadcasting Company (NBC) and the Columbia Broadcasting System (CBS) emerged as the leading networks of affiliated stations. Money derived from commercial advertisements sent over the airwaves soon became the major revenue stream for broadcasters.

While the availability of jobs and increase in average workers' incomes provided the fuel for the economic recovery, the extensive advertising efforts by the first generation of modern corporate marketers often determined the direction in which consumer money would flow. Companies paid marketers billions of dollars to lure consumers to their products over the radio, in movie houses, and the traditional print media. Under the weight of saturation advertising, consumers were bombarded with messages that often conflicted with more traditional values of thrift and savings. Indulgence was celebrated: the Eastman Kodak Company in 1928 began to sell its "Vanity Kodak," a handheld camera directly marketed to women. Not only were the cameras available in five different colors—"Sea Gull" (gray), "Cockatoo" (green), "Redbreast" (red), "Bluebird" (blue), and "Jenny Wren" (brown)—the implication in the company's ad was that women should own all five versions of the camera in order to limit the possibility of the device's color clashing with their wardrobes. Advertisers often emphasized the notion that buyers needed to be current with the latest styles: "Was your present watch in style when Uncle Tom's Cabin came to town?" asked one ad from 1927 for the Elgin Watch Company. Other ads directly played on consumers' insecurities, such as the famous advertisement for Listerine that depicted a sad, lonely woman with the caption: "Often a bridesmaid, but never a bride." Her problem being that she had chronic "halitosis"—a phrase invented by a New York marketing firm to describe bad breath.

In addition to the power of advertising, companies lured new buyers to their products through increased use of installment buying. Though increasing sales by expanding consumer purchasing power, installment buying led many irresponsible consumers to overextend themselves with large amounts of personal debt. A contemporary study made during the mid-1920s found that 25 percent of jewelry, 50 percent of sewing machines, radios, and electric refrigerators, 65 percent of vacuum cleaners, 75 percent of washing machines, 75 percent of automobiles, 80 percent of phonographs, and 90 percent of furniture purchases were made on credit. These numbers portended dire consequences for the economy if consumer spending could not be maintained at levels necessary to sustain prosperity.

THE MYTH OF THE "ROARING 20s"

An enduring myth about social life during the 1920s is the notion that most Americans broke away from their traditional values and celebrated the end of the war and postwar economic prosperity by partaking in a binge of hedonistic excess characterized by attending wild parties, consuming copious amounts of alcohol, gyrating to the latest wild dance crazes, obsessing over relatively superficial events making headlines, discarding the old time religion, and generally loosening their moral standards. A majority of women presumably basked in the achievement of suffrage and enjoyed the liberation provided by new modern household appliances by going out and having fun while dressed in the new provocative styles touted by New York City fashion designers.

This image of the decade as the "**Roaring Twenties**," however, is only a caricature based on the activities of some Americans. Serious historians now discard such stereotypical depictions of the 1920s as a means of describing what a majority of Americans were thinking and doing at the time, arguing that the activities of these individuals recounted in the media at the time, and since,

"**Where there's smoke there's fire**" This 1920s illustration captures the style of a fashionably dressed "flapper," with a cigarette indifferently hanging from one hand, leaving a seductive, curving line of smoke. Flappers represented the sexual rebellion of the so-called "New Woman" in the post-war decade.

have been blown out of proportion. The Roaring Twenties stereotype has two main origins. First, there were, in fact, some individuals during the 1920s who did partake in rowdy behavior deemed unacceptable by traditional standards. After the First World War, a minority of largely middle- and upper-class urban youth who had the time, money, and inclination to pursue these new behaviors, modes of dress, and popular fads adopted a more carefree lifestyle in an effort to put the negativity of the war behind them, take advantage of new freedoms provided by technological advances such as the widespread availability of the automobile, and follow the latest trends publicized in mainstream magazines and movies. Second, during the 1920s, and since, popularizers of the Roaring Twenties myth have crafted enduring depictions of the era in books and film. Writing in the early 1930s, journalist Frederick Lewis Allen produced a best-selling reflection of the just-concluded decade entitled *Only Yesterday: An Informal History of the 1920s*, in which he devoted much attention to the new modes of dress, the fads and crazes that made the news, and examples of individuals who discarded old thoughts and beliefs to further the notion that these activities were the norm for most people living during these times. Allen's book, along with F. Scott Fitzgerald's popular novels *The Great Gatsby* and *This Side of Paradise*, not to mention many Hollywood films have done much to solidify the view that wildness and excitement dominated the years between World War I and the Great Depression. Allen and the others have erred, however, by taking the new behaviors exhibited by a minority of the population and applying them to explain the mentality and lifestyle of the majority. Nevertheless, many important modernizing influences crept into American life during the 1920s, foreshadowing much of what would later become commonplace. Though a growing number of Americans embraced certain aspects of this social and economic change, others were rabidly determined to contain and reverse these trends, lest the traditional way of life that they understood and provided them with comfort be lost to an age of uncertainty and moral confusion.

"BALLYHOO" AND RECORD-BREAKING

One of Frederick Lewis Allen's major themes in *Only Yesterday* was the misplaced notion that most Americans did not care about "important issues" during the 1920s. As evidence, he cited the country's apparent obsession with various crazes, fads, stunts, record-breaking, and publicity-grabbing incidents that continuously made headlines in the print media of the day. While Allen overemphasized the importance of such sources in determining the national mood (he was, after all, editor of *Harper's Magazine*), there is no doubt that many Americans became interested in such **Ballyhoo** phenomenon that has been strongly linked to the 1920s ever since.

A stunt actor named Alvin "Shipwreck" Kelly inaugurated the decade's flagpole sitting fad. Though his initial foray lasted half a day, Kelly continuously pushed the boundaries as others got into the act. In 1927 he spent an entire week on a stool affixed to a 50-foot pole atop the

Marathon dancers, April 20, 1923

St. Francis Hotel in Newark, New Jersey, living off milk, broth, coffee, and cigarettes hoisted to him. For this effort he received national fame along with $1000 promised to him by a promoter plus extra money that the "Flagpole Rooster" received for holding up advertisement banners. His crowning achievement occurred in 1929 when he spent a record 49 days on a pole at a pier in Atlantic City, New Jersey.

While flagpole sitting events made the news because they were unknown in the United States before the 1920s, such stunts served more as publicity-generating devices rather than elements of a craze that lured huge numbers of active participants. The same could not be said for marathon dancing, however, which attracted many more devotees. Originally beginning as fun competitions for individuals or couples to win small prizes and gain some local notoriety, the phenomenon of dance marathons soon evolved into commercial ventures pushed by promoters across the country as a way to make money. Formal contests began to charge admission to spectators, pay a growing number of professional marathon dancers who traveled the country to compete, and doled out cash prizes to the winners. Established rules were developed for each contest, dictating how long the participants could take breaks and governing such behavior as eating, napping, bathing, and using restrooms. Though organizers occasionally instructed contestants to perform such popular dances as the Charleston and the Fox Trot, they were never graded on technical ability—what mattered was endurance, to be the last dancer standing with their feet still moving. As some competitions continued into days and weeks, the physical and emotional exhaustion among the remaining dancers entered an element of drama that promoters often exploited for effect. This early example of a "reality show" involving normal people entertaining an audience by their dancing as well as their struggles to stay in the competition remained popular well into the 1930s as contestants sought prize money in the midst of the Great Depression. Though dance marathons continue to take place, usually as fundraisers for charity, the modern versions are a pale comparison to the exploitive spectacles from which they evolved.

During the 1920s, the American media also fixated on individual feats of athletic prowess. Baseball fans marveled at the exploits of Babe Ruth who popularized the home run by producing record numbers of them, helping to revive baseball's popularity after the 1919 "Black Sox Scandal" in which some Chicago White Sox players accepted money from gamblers in return for throwing the World Series. Football fans cheered Harold "Red" Grange—the "Galloping Ghost"—as the elusive University of Illinois and Chicago Bears running back

George Herman "Babe" Ruth, started his professional baseball career with the Boston Red Sox but was traded to the New York Yankees in time for the 1920 season. Ruth established himself as one of the game's all-time homerun kings.

broke countless records at the collegiate and professional level. Champions in boxing (Jack Dempsey), tennis (Bill Tilden), golf (Bobby Jones), and many other sportsmen also garnered tremendous notoriety and public attention. While male athletes predominated among these celebrated sports personalities, Gertrude Ederle, the daughter of German immigrants and a 1924 Olympic gold medal winner, captured the headlines in 1926 by becoming the first woman to swim across the English Channel, completing the accomplishment in fourteen and a half hours—almost two hours quicker than the previous record held by a man (only five men before her had ever been able to swim through the strong currents, rough winds, and frigid water). When Ederle returned home to New York City, a massive crowd recognized her exploit by giving her a ticker-tape parade down Broadway—the first in honor of an individual woman.

Then there were the pilots who gained tremendous publicity for themselves and the fledgling aircraft industry.

The Black Sox Scandal

During the early twentieth century, professional baseball players joined factory laborers as an exploited group, often mistreated by unscrupulous employers desiring to squeeze production out of their workforce. This case was certainly true for the 1919 Chicago White Sox, a talented assortment of ballplayers on a team controlled by parsimonious owner Charles Comiskey. An ex-professional player himself, Comiskey garnered the hatred of his players for such practices as underpaying them, sitting players near the end of the season to deprive them of achieving performance bonuses based on their yearly statistics, and even deducting the cost of laundering their uniforms from their paychecks. Upset with their treatment and lured by greed, some White Sox players became enticed to purposely lose the 1919 World Series against the underdog Cincinnati Reds in exchange for payoffs equal to many times their annual salaries and, of course, the ability to place bets against their own team.

After the Series loss, rumors circulated that the White Sox had thrown the Series—eventually corroborated with evidence gathered by an energetic sportswriter. A Chicago grand jury indicted eight White Sox players for active participation in the conspiracy, or knowing about the scheme but failing to report the malfeasance. Though convicted in the national "court of public opinion," the local jury in Chicago acquitted all eight players of wrongdoing. Still, baseball owners knew that the "Black Sox Scandal" could potentially threaten the integrity of their business. In response, Major League Baseball created the office of Commissioner of Baseball to police the sport, appointing respected federal judge Kenesaw Mountain Landis to the post. Landis' first action was to ban the eight White Sox players for life, citing his granted power to act in the best interest of baseball.

The commissioner's move did much in the short term to address the issue of corruption in baseball, but the game's return to prominence during the spectator-sport-crazy decade of the 1920s coincided with the excitement generated by George Herman "Babe" Ruth, who revolutionized the game with his ability to hit long and frequent home runs. In 1919, the same year that the White Sox won the American League pennant and earned the right to play in the World Series, Ruth set a new major league record by swatting 29 home runs for the Boston Red Sox (the previous record of 27 had been set in 1884). During the off season, not wishing to accede to Ruth's pay demands, the Red Sox owner infamously sold Ruth's contract to the New York Yankees. Ruth rewarded his new team by slugging an astounding 54 home runs. The following year, he clubbed 59 round-trippers—a feat thought never to be broken until he hit 60 home runs in 1927 as part of the Yankees' famous "Murderers' Row" lineup that included future Hall of Famers Lou Gehrig, Tony Lazzeri, and Earle Combs. In that year alone, Ruth's epic performances helped Major League Baseball draw over 20 million people—a definite sign that for most sports fans, the Black Sox scandal had already faded into distant memory.

Many were former World War I aviators who sought to make a living after the war while honing their flying skills. The term "barnstormer" began to be applied to those pilots who flew from place to place around the country to thrill crowds with daredevil flying demonstrations and to charge passengers for rides. By the latter end of the 1920s, aviators tended to operate from just one airfield (so-called "fixed-base operations") while they continued to make a living by performing stunts and charging for rides, in addition to training new pilots and occasionally flying advertisement banners over local areas.

Those pilots who sought to gain fame and wealth by setting or breaking records gathered the most attention. By far the most popular aviator of the era was **Charles A. Lindbergh**. The son of a Swedish immigrant who became a Minnesota congressman, Lindbergh dropped out of the mechanical engineering program at the University of Wisconsin in 1920 to pursue his interest in flying. After completing his initial flight school, he barnstormed for a while to gain flying experience and earn money before beginning a year of flight training with the United States Army Air Service. Upon his graduation in 1925, Lindbergh served as an Army reserve officer while returning to civilian aviation as an air mail pilot covering the route between Chicago and St. Louis. In 1927, though only 25 years old and a trained pilot for only five years, Lindbergh sought to claim the elusive Raymond Orteig Prize offered up by a French hotelier for the first person to pilot a non-stop solo transatlantic flight between New York and Paris. In pursuit of this prize and the accompanying notoriety, six aviators had already died and three injured (including Richard Byrd, who claimed to be the first to fly across the North Pole in 1926 though that assertion has been doubted by many critics).

Financed by loans from St. Louis businessmen and his personal savings, Lindbergh oversaw the construction of a custom-built single-engine, single-seat monoplane dubbed *The Spirit of St. Louis*. To boost fuel efficiency with an improved center of gravity, the plane's large fuel tank was placed in the forward section of the fuselage. This design, however, dictated that there would be no windshield in front of the pilot. Besides a small retractable periscope, his visibility would be limited to side windows only. To maximize space, Lindbergh had to sit in a cramped cockpit so small he could not stretch his legs and only carried with him a map, his passport, four sandwiches and a couple of canteens of drinking water.

Taking off from Long Island's Roosevelt Field in a morning rainstorm on May 20, 1927, Lindbergh stayed airborne, sometimes at 10,000 feet, sometimes just above the ocean's waves, for the next thirty-three and a half hours. Along the way he battled poor visibility caused by icing and fog. He also combated his own body's resistance. Fatigue caused him to hallucinate, fall asleep, and occasionally lose track of his bearings (what pilots today refer to as "spatial disorientation"). Adrenaline kicked in twenty-six hours after take-off, however, when the aviator spotted a small group of fishing boats indicating that he was nearing land (the Irish coast). Adjusting his course, Lindy reached France as darkness fell for the second time during his epic flight. He landed at Paris's Le Bourget Airport at 10:22 p.m. on May 21. A crowd of over 100,000 enthusiastic spectators charged the airfield and triumphantly carried Lindbergh on their shoulders while souvenir hunters tore at the *Spirit's* fabric-covered fuselage. Lindbergh's flight made him an instant celebrity, gave further publicity to the budding aviation industry, and revived the belief of many Americans and others throughout the world in the ability of mankind to push the boundaries of achievement in the spirit of past pioneers. While other pilots over the next couple of decades would catch the public's attention, including Amelia Earhart who became the first woman to duplicate "Lucky Lindy's" accomplishment the very next year, Charles Lindbergh's feat was the most celebrated by the era's pilots and came to symbolize the adventurous energetic spirit so synonymous with the Roaring Twenties image.

THE "NEW WOMAN"

The beginning of the 1920s witnessed a tremendous advance for women in the form of the ratification of the **Nineteenth Amendment** to the U.S. Constitution barring the denial of voting rights for citizens on the basis of gender. Though states could still restrict the vote by means of poll taxes, literacy tests, and other means that continued to deny large numbers of African Americans from voting in the South, the Nineteenth Amendment nevertheless retained large symbolic importance while marking a huge practical gain for middle- and upper-class white women. Passage of the Nineteenth Amendment resulted from the determined efforts of multiple generations of woman suffragists, culminating with successful agitation by female and male activists during the Progressive Era. While some turn-of-the century reformers continued to lobby for suffrage on the basis of simple justice and ending the denial of basic civil rights, many began to utilize more innovative lines of reasoning to promote their cause. Among the most powerful new arguments in favor of woman suffrage was the notion of "municipal housekeeping," which suffragists used to overcome gender expectations by reinforcing the traditional ideals of domesticity and maternalism. In this manner, they justified activism for the vote by emphasizing the need for women to participate within the political process. Thus, suffrage would not destroy the traditional family but, rather, would strengthen the institution by helping civic-minded women better protect their homes by voting for proper candidates and supporting essential reforms. Some suffragists also reflected the racial biases of their times by claiming the vote was necessary in order to allow Anglo women to better protect their families by negating the negative influences of foreign-born radicals and black males.

While an important achievement, passage of the woman suffrage amendment did not completely satisfy the most outspoken radical feminists. Led by **Alice Paul**, activists within the National Woman's Party (NWP)—an offshoot of the National American Woman Suffrage Association (NAWSA)—had been among the most vociferous of the suffragists, employing aggressive publicity-generating tactics learned from the British suffrage movement. Though often described as "militant suffragists" because of their vociferous activism, Paul and other members of the NWP used only nonviolent means to garner attention, such as picketing the White House (some chained themselves to the gates), allowing themselves to be arrested for disturbing the peace, and undertaking hunger strikes (where they were often force-fed by authorities) while incarcerated. After passage of the Nineteenth Amendment, Paul sought acceptance of a new constitutional amendment that would end gender discrimination by eliminating all legal distinctions between men and women: "Men and women shall have equal rights throughout the United States and every place subject to its jurisdiction." Many female Progressive leaders such as Florence Kelley and Jane Addams balked at Paul's proposal, arguing correctly that the Equal Rights Amendment (ERA) would result in the end of protective legislation for women. Kelley and Addams had been working for such laws for most of their adult lives and believed that they were not only important reforms for women but also served (along with their efforts to end child labor) as a vital starting point in an extended campaign to win protections for all workers. Paul, however, countered that laws such as limiting work hours or preventing women from working at night or in certain occupations stigmatized women and reduced their economic opportunities, not to mention the separate status they assigned for women in the workplace and society in general. While the infighting in the women's movement raged, members of Congress introduced Paul's ERA for debate in 1923. The merits and drawbacks of the ERA would continue to divide feminists and the major political parties alike for the next 50 years. In 1972, an amendment based on Paul's initial proposal ("Equality of rights under the law shall not be denied or abridged by the United States or by any State on account of sex") passed both houses of Congress but ultimately fell short of ratification by the required three-quarters of the states.

While Paul and the NWP sparred with old progressives and members of the new League of Women Voters (formerly NAWSA) over many issues, they tended to fall into agreement that many young women of the postwar generation were squandering their hard-fought achievements through self-indulgent actions and behavior that simply fed into prevailing stereotypes of women as non-intellectuals who were overly concerned with physical appearances, reliant upon men for stability and happiness, and obsessed with obtaining the latest highly-desired consumer goods. In their minds, the only worse notion than women seeking satisfaction through finding a husband, raising a large family, and living in material comfort were those young women increasingly referred to as "flappers" who sauntered around as gadflies flaunting social convention by their outrageous dress and behavior before settling down. While the origin of the term flapper is in dispute (some believe it derived from the movement of unfastened galoshes that were popular at the time, while others point to much earlier uses in England referring to young birds who furiously beat their wings as they learn to fly), the appearance of these young women who wore short skirts, bobbed their hair, listened to jazz, danced to the latest popular wild dances, drank alcohol, smoked in public, drove automobiles, treated sex in a more casual manner, and generally displayed disdain for accepted social standards regarding acceptable female public behavior caused quite a stir among those raised in Victorian America. While condemned by many preachers on Sunday mornings, the flapper image was popularized in national magazines, newspapers, novels, and many Hollywood films as the most vibrant manifestation of the "new woman" who was not beholden to past societal norms. In the ensuing decades, the iconic flapper image endured whenever Americans thought of the 1920s. Though certainly a new phenomenon worth noting, in reality only a minority of young middle- and upper-class women adopted such a lifestyle.

In addition to the flappers, **Margaret Sanger** radically challenged traditional ideas concerning women by launching the modern birth control movement. Sanger witnessed firsthand how large families could wear down women even before she began working as a nurse to the poor in the Lower East Side slums of Manhattan. Born the sixth of eleven children to a mother who also had seven miscarriages, Sanger was greatly affected by her mother's early death (at the age of 48) and the struggle to help her parents raise her siblings. After her nursing training, she met and married an architect, gave birth to three children, and started promoting the use of contraceptives among the immigrant poor in violation of state and federal laws. To Sanger, birth control was not only a means to relieve the burdens of unwanted pregnancies and prevent amateur abortions, which could maim or kill poor women, but also a representation of freedom and equal rights. "No woman can call herself free," she wrote, "until she can choose conscientiously whether she will or will not be a mother."

Many religious groups, as well as some immigrant groups, opposed Sanger's activities on moral grounds, believing contraceptives to be against their religious beliefs or simply inviting women to be more promiscuous without ramifications. New York State authorities jailed Sanger in 1916 for operating a birth control clinic in Brooklyn where she distributed information about diaphragms and other contraceptive techniques. Though found guilty and sentenced to a thirty-day sentence, an appeals court later ruled that while Sanger was duly convicted, it would be legal for licensed physicians to prescribe contraceptives as a means to prevent the spread of diseases. As a result, she organized the American Birth Control League in 1921 to educate the public about "the dangers of uncontrolled procreation" and to operate family planning clinics where doctors could give women reliable methods of birth control.

Sanger's support for some aspects of the pseudo-scientific eugenics movement led to dissension with many birth control advocates. Running counter to the viewpoint of a majority of old Progressives who believed that one's environment served as the major factor in determining human behavior, the supporters of eugenics argued that heredity factors predominated, thus society would benefit from selective breeding. While Sanger never advocated euthanasia of those determined to be unfit (often defined as the mentally retarded, those determined to be insane, and repeat criminals), she publicly supported their sterilization as a way to prevent children with the supposedly inherited defective traits from being born. Many states passed legislation authorizing compulsory sterilization of certain classes of criminals and the mentally incompetent, a practice affirmed by a 1927 U.S. Supreme Court decision.

Though she resigned the presidency of the American Birth Control League in 1928 over differences with members due to her support of eugenics and her management style, Sanger continued to advocate for women's fertility rights for the next 40 years and helped to change perceptions about birth control in the nation. The American Birth Control League also continued under new directors. Renamed Planned Parenthood in 1942, the organization continues to dispense family planning information and remains a leader in protecting female reproductive rights in the modern era.

THE MISAPPROPRIATION OF FREUD

The theories of **Sigmund Freud,** often in perverted form, found a ready audience in the United States during the 1920s. The Austrian founder of psychoanalysis had pioneered the clinical approach of treatment through dialogue with patients. Among his most influential theories was the assertion that a person's sexual drives buried within the subconscious mind, rather than rational thought, environmental factors, or supernatural influences served as the driving force of human life. Only a small portion of a person's mind, what Freud dubbed the "ego," dealt with consciousness and rationality. A much larger part, which the psychologist labeled the "id," referred to the assortment of irrational passions and inner impulses that bore a strong influence on human behavior. At the core of the id, Freud posited, lay a person's sexual drive, or the "libido." Within every individual, Freud surmised, there is conflict between the ego and the id. Humans try to control the power of the id through reason or by channeling the id to more productive ends. Too much repression of one's subconscious drives, however, led to the many anxieties in the modern era, Freud believed, and the main goal of the psychoanalyst should be to help the patient use their ego to discipline the id while still allowing for means of meaningful expression for their inner desires.

Freud's ideas spread across the country by educated members of the middle class, often oversimplified by some looking for an easy justification of their Bohemian lifestyle. Taking the doctor's findings and arguments totally out of context, they justified their challenges to prevailing social conventions on the supposed scientific basis that sexual self-restraint was unnatural and unhealthy. Nevertheless, the popularity of Freud proved to be just a part of the broader postwar development of sexual topics being discussed more openly than in the past.

THE IMPACT OF THE GREAT BLACK MIGRATION

Begun during the First World War, the vast movement of African Americans from the rural South into northern industrial cities continued unabated during the 1920s. From 1920 to 1930, an estimated half-million blacks packed their bags to head north. Though not experiencing legal segregation as existed in the South, prevailing customs in the North led to *de facto* segregation in all-black neighborhoods. Despite these limitations, life in the northern urban enclaves proved to be generally less oppressive while being more emotionally and materially rewarding. As black enterprises catered to the public and cultural pride flourished, African Americans also became a growing political force as many took part in participatory democracy for the first time in their lives.

The growing popularity of **jazz** music among mainstream Americans (i.e., "when white Americans discovered jazz") during the 1920s is directly linked to the spreading of that unique blending of African and European musical styles from its native South by recent black migrants to northern cities where it was spread in nightclubs and broadcast over radio stations. Writers during the decade and since have described early jazz music, with its characteristic liveliness, syncopated rhythms, and often improvisational presentation, as synonymous with the mood of the 1920s. F. Scott Fitzgerald labeled the 1920s as the "Jazz Age" because of his connection of the art form's style to the wild behavior of the nation's youth that he often described in his novels. Though not an accurate description for the majority of Americans during the time, Fitzgerald's observation captured the spirit of the minority of youth, whose gyrating dancing to the Charleston, the Black Bottom, and the Fox Trot, not to mention their carefree lifestyle, upset the nation's moral guardians.

The profusion of jazz music into the public consciousness proved to be the most salient example of a great explosion in African-American culture and racial pride to appear during the 1920s. Though Chicago, Philadelphia, Detroit, St. Louis, and many other northern cities experiencing large black population gains displayed elements of the new profusion of music, literature, visual arts, theater, and intellectual works, the Harlem neighborhood of New York City's Upper West Side became the center of the phenomenon leading to the label "**Harlem Renaissance**" being applied to the entire movement that signaled a new era of thought and expression for African Americans. In Harlem, artists of various types attempted to create a new black identity so the country would be forced to no longer view all blacks as mere southern rural peasants incapable of displaying creativity and sophistication. Playwrights produced theater pieces in which the African-American characters displayed complex human emotions rather than stereotypical portrayals frequently appearing in vaudeville and minstrel shows. Poets and novelists such as Langston Hughes sought to create original written works that celebrated his race while often protesting existing social conditions. Musicians including Duke Ellington and Jelly Roll Morton and a large host of singers showcased their talents before crowds dancing excitedly to the artists' lively compositions. Within the pages of Harlem-published *Crisis* magazine, the official journal of the NAACP edited by W.E.B. Du Bois, enthusiastic readers found the nation's leading forum for exhibitions of African-American poetry, essays, novel excerpts, and works of art.

The most radical expression of black racial pride during the 1920s proved to be **Marcus Garvey**'s "Negro Nationalism" movement. A well-traveled and well-read Jamaican immigrant who traveled to America in 1916, Garvey applied his experience as a printer and editor to the promotion of his United Negro Improvement Association (UNIA), which he created to unite and uplift all individuals of African ancestry. Garvey's means of uplift entailed not only glorification of the race but also racial separation from whites in a manner that placed him directly at odds with Du Bois and other black leaders who were fighting for racial integration and acceptance by whites. Garvey exhorted African Americans to maintain racial purity by avoiding interracial contact and to build a strong economic base by only patronizing black-owned businesses, especially the grocery stores, laundries, and restaurants operated by UNIA, as well as the Black Star steamship line—the organization's main business effort designed to foster unity and trade between blacks in Africa and the Western Hemisphere. In exchange for monthly dues, UNIA members received health insurance and death benefits, the option to buy stock in the group's subsidiaries, and the emotional contentment derived from expressing racial solidarity in a common venture. At its height in the early 1920s, UNIA boasted over two million members in over 800 chapters in the U.S. and abroad.

While earning the wrath of Du Bois and other NAACP leaders for his separatist ideas (Du Bois once referred to Garvey as "the most dangerous enemy of the Negro race in America"), Garvey's activities garnered the attention of J. Edgar Hoover, the general intelligence division director of the Justice Department and future head of the Federal Bureau of Investigation, who came to believe Garvey was a potential fomenter of social unrest. With the encouragement of the NAACP, Hoover spent two years investigating UNIA's business dealings by paying spies to infiltrate the group and gather evidence. Prosecutors found little trouble in securing an indictment of Garvey on mail fraud charges (Black Star Line stock sales had taken place after the image of a ship appeared on a mailed brochure even though UNIA had not yet purchased the ship). A jury convicted Garvey, sentencing him to five years in a federal prison. Upon his release, he was deported to Jamaica thus ending the American branch of UNIA. Despite Garvey's removal, the notions of black nationalism and Pan-Africanism endured with the founding of the Nation of Islam in 1930 and experienced a more popular revival during the "Black Power" Movement of the 1960s.

CULTURAL REACTION/DEFENDERS OF TRADITION

As new modes of dress, behavior, and expression became acceptable to those who viewed such social changes as positive elements of modernization, large numbers of Americans during the 1920s, especially a majority of those reared in rural areas, clung to their familiar ways of life stronger than ever. In part, this attitude reflected the natural tendency to adhere to what is known in uncertain times, but it also represented a definite reaction to the Roaring Twenties lifestyles swirling about them. As a result, these Americans culturally retrenched and resisted change in a host of ways that belies the commonly-held

Marcus Garvey

Col. Sherrell, Supt. of Public Buildings and Grounds, issued an order that bathing suits at the Washington D.C. bathing beach must not be over six inches above the knee. Bill Norton, the bathing beach policeman, is measuring the distance between the knee and the bathing suit on a woman. 1922

notion that most wholeheartedly accepted the advent of a new modern America.

In his classic book on American thought covering the 1917-1930 period titled *The Nervous Generation*, historian Roderick Nash makes a vital point concerning the 1920s when he noted that most of the authors commonly associated with the decade in textbooks were largely avoided by the general public at the time. Later generations of Americans read F. Scott Fitzgerald and Ernest Hemingway rather than those living in the immediate years following World War I. The most popular contemporary author of the 1920s in terms of the number of books sold, in fact, was an Ohio dentist-turned-western writer named Zane Grey. From 1917 to 1924, Grey was never off national bestseller lists, writing novels that were often converted into full-length motion pictures, helping the writer become a millionaire and a major force in shaping many commonly-held myths about the Old West. While possessing only basic literary talent, Grey succeeded because his stories set in the Old West reaffirmed traditional values, striking a chord with millions of readers who much preferred to read books confirming their beliefs rather than challenging them.

Restrictions on Dress, Dancing, and Movies

Bathing suits became a hot topic of conversation during the 1920s when many areas of the country banned certain new styles from being worn in public. Until the turn of the twentieth century, most public beaches were segregated by gender (as well as by race). As authorities began to lift those limits, women began to intermingle with men along the shorelines but were still expected to wear cumbersome outfits with bloomers and heavy flowing skirts that resembled streetwear. Some women began to fight back against these regulations. During the summer of 1921, Louise Rosine, a Los Angeles resident visiting Atlantic City, New Jersey, was arrested for refusing to roll up her stockings above her knees. Other women caused similar uproars when they donned the new one-piece suits that many in the public found immoral or objectionable, considering them to be "men's suits." Countless similar episodes of protest by women can be found in contemporary newspapers, as well as the strong efforts to crack down on such new modes of dress, signifying how much of the country had not converted to the Roaring Twenties lifestyle.

Numerous government and church authorities made concerted efforts during the 1920s to clamp down on dancing, perceiving the activity as inherently immoral or leading to other forms of decadent behavior. In 1918, the Vatican prohibited Catholics from dancing the Tango, the Fox Trot, and other "modern dances." Baptists forbade dancing of any kind because of the "long train of attendant evil" that supposedly accompanied the practice. Most Methodist leaders agreed not only to a ban on dancing but also theater attendance and circus going. Newly elected governors Pat Neff of Texas and Jason Fields of Kentucky both cancelled inaugural balls because of their personal distaste for dancing.

Hollywood motion pictures also fell under intense scrutiny in many sections of the country during the 1920s. After a U.S. Supreme Court decision found that free speech guarantees did not apply to film, many states and localities began to institute censorship boards to oversee the content of movies shown in their jurisdictions. The large Hollywood studios also responded to the decision, naming **William H. Hays** to be the first president of the newly formed Motion Pictures Association of America (MPAA). Before heading the MPAA in 1922, Hays served as chairman of the Republican National Committee, Warren Harding's campaign manager in the 1920 presidential campaign, and Postmaster General in the Harding Administration. Studio executives chose Hays to lead the MPAA because he was an elder in the Presbyterian Church who could help Hollywood clean up its image with the public and avoid federal government regulation.

Hays endeavored to develop a standard voluntary code for filmmaking designed to produce films without objectionable material that would also save the studios money by not having to constantly edit their movies to comply with the desires of the myriad of local censors around the country. Hays began with a list of suggested "Don'ts and Be Carefuls"—a set of general rules based on the most frequent objections of local censorship boards. The 11 "Don'ts" to be avoided completely included profanity, nudity, miscegenation, acts of childbirth, ridicule of the clergy, and "any inference of sex perversion." The 26 "Be Carefuls" in which special care was to be exercised in the depiction of certain subjects included crime, violence, use of firearms, sympathy for criminals, seduction of females, drug use, and "excessive or lustful kissing." This list became the basis for the future Motion Picture Production Code (often referred to as the "Hays Code"), which began to be enforced by the motion picture industry's Production Code Administration (PCA). After 1934, all films had to be approved by the PCA before they could be released to the general public. (The Hays Code governed the content of Hollywood films for the next 35 years until replaced by the Movie Ratings System used in modified form today.) The MPAA's decision to hire Hays reflects the film industry's necessity to respect the prevailing national attitudes to avoid government regulation but also to curry favor with a public that did not completely adapt to the changing times. If the majority of the country had converted to the tenets of the Roaring Twenties, the Hays Code would certainly not have been necessary.

Prohibition

The prohibition of alcohol proved to be the most notable nationwide restriction to personal liberty during the 1920s while also providing the greatest challenge to the argument that the decade was a period in which the majority cast aside their previous inhibitions and undertook a radical change in their lifestyle and behavior. Advocates seeking to reduce alcohol consumption had existed in the country for over a hundred years, but at the turn of the twentieth century Prohibition turned into a Progressive social reform in response to the increased availability of cheaper alcohol provided by the processes of the Industrial Revolution as well as the conspicuous drinking of many foreign immigrants. Protestant organizations such as the Women's Christian Temperance Union and the Anti-Saloon League pushed for state and federal restrictions against alcohol, forging a coalition among those who believed that outlawing alcohol would "clean up society" in a myriad of ways: businessmen would have a more sober workforce, women would have less violent husbands who would not squander hard-earned money on drink, and doctors would witness the justification of research showing that the elimination of alcohol would lead to a healthier populace.

American entry into World War I aided Prohibition forces. By 1917, eighteen states, with nearly two-thirds of the country's population, had already banned the manufacture and sale of alcohol. As wartime need for grain plus vehement patriotism (many breweries were owned by German Americans) arose, reduced production and consumption of alcohol ensued. After the war's end, on January 16, 1919, the requisite number of states finally ratified the **Eighteenth Amendment** to the U.S. Constitution, outlawing the manufacture, sale, or transportation of intoxicating liquors. The amendment's enforcement legislation passed by Congress in October 1919, the Volstead Act, made it illegal to make, ship, or sell beverages with alcohol content greater than 0.5 percent beginning on January 16, 1920.

The most immediate effect of Prohibition was the closure of bars, saloons, and other public drinking establishments. While many estimates place the reduced consumption of alcohol at 50 percent (especially among urban ethnic groups who could not afford to consume as much illegal alcohol because of the higher prices), large numbers of Americans certainly did not stop drinking. Instead, the activity went underground. In cities across the country, secret "speakeasies" arose where patrons illegally consumed alcohol. The hip flask became a common item among those who ignored the law and wished to have a personal stash of their elixir of choice near them at all times. Those with access to alcohol took many trips into secluded rural areas, even caves, to drink.

The type of alcohol consumed during Prohibition varied between bottles of wine and hard liquor made before the law went into effect to more recently-made beverages, either smuggled from outside the country or domestically manufactured drinks from an assortment of stills and hidden manufacturing facilities (sometimes producing liquor with very harmful health effects). The reduced supply of alcoholic beverages led to increased prices for "bootleg liquor," luring many criminals to get in on the action. In the South, alcohol runners began to modify their vehicles to enable them to outrun law officials. (Some creators of these modified "stock cars" later started racing their vehicles in the 1930s, leading to the eventual formation of NASCAR). In the northern industrial cities, organized crime syndicates previously involved in gambling, prostitution, and narcotics (most famously, the empire led by Chicago's Al Capone) sought to dominate the illicit trade in booze. Gang violence became a more frequent occurrence as rival bands fought highly-publicized turf battles that led to many deaths and public calls for more resources dedicated to their suppression. Failing to receive adequate resources to deal with Prohibition-related issues, local, state, and federal officials constantly had their hands full trying to enforce the law. The increased focus on Prohibition crimes also diverted police attention away from other crime-related activities.

Though leading to a reduced consumption of alcohol, Prohibition failed in terms of the goal to eliminate drinking from American society and led to a whole slew of new problems unforeseen by its advocates. The failure of Prohibition, along with the arrival of the Great Depression, would lead to the eventual repeal of the Eighteenth Amendment (by ratification of the Twenty-first Amendment in 1933). Though often referred to as the "Noble Experiment," most of its supporters did not view Prohibition as a mere test. Instead, they doggedly held onto their belief that the effort to eliminate alcohol would improve society and caused more good than harm even after a majority of Americans determined otherwise.

Nativism and Immigration Restriction

Many old stock Americans during the 1920s felt threatened by the renewed influx of immigrants coming into the country after the conclusion of the First World War. After a four-year hiatus during the war when the flow of foreigners slowed to a trickle, starting in 1919 nearly a million new arrivals per year (two-thirds from Southern and Eastern Europe) entered the United States, renewing the belief of many that radical political ideas, not to mention Catholicism and Judaism, would spread unabated across the land. The popularity of this insular, anti-foreign viewpoint (often referred to as "nativism"), especially among rural folk and migrants from the countryside residing in the bustling cities, found expression in a new drive to restrict foreign immigration.

Congress responded to the public clamor in 1921 by passing the Emergency Quota Act of 1921, legislation that introduced numerical limits on the number of legal immigrants entering the country and use of a quota system for the first time. The law set the maximum number of legal immigrants at 350,000. Further, the number of new immigrants entering the country annually from any given country was limited to 3 percent of the number of each nationality residing in the United States in 1910, thus favoring immigrants from Northern and Western Europe. Whereas prior to 1921 the average number of Northern and Western Europe immigrants was 175,000 and those from other countries (primarily from Southern and Eastern Europe), reached 685,000, in 1921, 200,000 immigrants from Northern and Western Europe arrived but little more than 150,000 came from other countries. Three years later, Congress passed the **National Origins Act**, which further tightened the flow of legal immigration by reducing the cap level to 150,000 while altering the nationality quotas to 2 percent of the number of each nationality residing in the United States in 1890—a choice deliberately made to further drop the number of Southern and Eastern Europeans arriving because the majority of individuals from those groups had arrived after that base year. For the next four decades, the number of people legally entering the U.S. from Southern and Eastern European countries would be reduced to no more than 15 percent of the total immigration pool. In addition to addressing the concerns of Protestant Northeasterners and residents of the Midwest, these laws also showed the influence of political pressure applied by representatives of the western states. While the Emergency Quota Act and the National Origins Act placed complete bans on immigrants from Japan and other East Asian countries (with the notable exception of the U.S.-held Philippines), neither law placed limits on immigration from Latin American countries to continue to allow agribusinesses access to an ample supply of low-wage labor.

Beyond immigration restrictions, nativist prejudice during the 1920s manifested itself in other ways. Many western states prohibited Japanese residents from leasing or owning land. A majority of justices on the U.S. Supreme Court in 1922 ruled that Japanese *Issei*, or first-generation immigrants, as nonwhites, could never become naturalized citizens. Like other groups, Italian immigrants also suffered sporadic attacks, such as occurred in West Frankfort, Illinois in August 1920 when mobs terrorized Italian miners and their families for three days in an effort to drive them out before state troopers arrived to restore order.

No individual case revealed the deep divisions in society along nativist lines more than the saga of Italian immigrants **Nicola Sacco and Bartolomeo Vanzetti**. Arrested for a 1920 robbery of a shoe factory in South Braintree, Massachusetts that involved the murder of the company paymaster and a security guard, Sacco and Vanzetti gained the support of many inside and outside the United States who believed that the pair were being tried merely for being political radicals who followed Luigi Galleani, an Italian anarchist who advocated revolutionary violence against governments around the world. Historians who have intensely studied every aspect of the case have failed to reach a solid consensus about Sacco and Vanzetti's guilt. Though they had no prior criminal records, the men definitely had an association with Galleani's supporters and may have taken part in the robbery to amass funds for revolutionary activities. Still, plenty of grounds for reasonable doubt existed—the testimony of eyewitnesses proved to be inconclusive and there can be no doubt that the presiding judge, Webster Thayer, exhibited strongly biased behavior against the defense inside and outside of the courtroom. After a jury found them guilty of first-degree murder, Thayer sentenced Sacco and Vanzetti to death, leading to a highly-publicized six-year effort by radicals, intellectuals, Italian American groups, and other interested citizens to secure a stay of execution. After uncovering new evidence, including a confession for the murders by a convicted killer, the governor of Massachusetts appointed a three-man advisory panel to review the case. The board headed by Harvard University President Abbott Lowell (a member of the Immigration Restriction League), however, determined that the judge and jury had addressed the evidence fairly and saw no reason to overturn the conviction. The execution of Sacco and Vanzetti in the electric chair on August 23, 1927 led to a series of random protest bombings around the world by sympathetic anarchists and occasional explosions targeting the trial participants, including an attack on Judge Thayer's home that wounded his wife and demolished their residence.

Fundamentalism

The rise of religious **fundamentalism** proved to be another strong reaction to modernizing influences within American society. In the late nineteenth century, many scientists and intellectuals built upon scientific developments and new theories to present secular challenges to many aspects of organized religion. In response, some liberal theologians began applying historical and scientific methods to examine the Bible with a critical eye. Countless religious conservatives responded negatively to any updating of orthodox Christianity. Eventually, many evangelicals began to label themselves "Fundamentalists," with the name derived from the title of a noted series of essays—*The Fundamentals*—published from 1910 to 1915 by the Bible Institute of Los Angeles. Written by an assortment of conservative theologians and edited by evangelical pastor A. C. Dixon (the brother of Thomas Dixon, Jr. who wrote the novel *The Clansman*, which served as the inspiration for D.W. Griffith's film *The Birth of a Nation*, which glorified the Reconstruction-Era Ku Klux Klan), the authors stated their beliefs about the fundamentals of Christian faith (including the virgin birth, the resurrection of Jesus, and the Bible as the inspired word of God to be read literally) while attacking liberal theology, atheism, Catholicism, evolution and other modern scientific theories. Financed by California oil man Lyman Stewart, millions of copies of the essays were sent free to ministers and other active Christians, helping to spread the views presented in the *Fundamentals* and unifying like-minded believers.

In addition to being fueled by resentment toward secular challengers and liberal theologians, anti-Catholic and Jewish sentiment, fundamentalism also spread rapidly across the country during the first three decades of the twentieth century because of the dynamic efforts of many flamboyant and charismatic preachers who attracted multitudes to their campaigns. Among the myriad of evangelists to emerge, the most famous was **Billy Sunday**. An ex-major league baseball player from Iowa (whose father came from a family of German immigrants named Sonntag who anglicized their name to "Sunday" upon their arrival to America—a fortunate coincidence for the future preacher), Sunday began attending a Presbyterian church in Chicago in the middle of his career and became a convert. After his playing days ended, Sunday began working for the YMCA in Chicago where he became an assistant to J. Wilbur Chapman, a renowned Presbyterian minister who taught him the fine arts of preparing and delivering sermons while reinforcing the tenets of fundamentalism.

Starting in 1896, Sunday began his career as a minister of the old-time religion, taking advantage of his reputation as a baseball player to generate publicity. Preaching with a classic fear-of-damnation style across the country, he delivered his messages in a loud booming voice, often filling his sermons with animation as he would contort his face, flail his arms, run across the stage and dive as a ballplayer, and even smash chairs to assert his points. His message reflected all the tenets of fundamentalism, including the existence of a Devil, attacks on modernism, and an affirmation of a literal reading of the Bible.

From the Pentecostal strand of fundamentalism, **Aimee Semple McPherson** presented a fresh face during the Twenties. Born Aimee Elizabeth Kennedy on a Canadian farm, she spent much of her youth with her religious mother who worked for the Salvation Army. She met her first husband, a Pentecostal missionary from Ireland named Robert Semple, while attending a revival. Soon after getting married, the couple traveled to China to perform missionary work, but Robert died of malaria in 1910, forcing Aimee and her newborn daughter to return to the United States. She later married her second husband, a grocer named Harold McPherson, in 1912. The couple had a son the next year, but Aimee soon rebelled against the life of domesticity her traditional husband planned for her. With her children in tow, she left McPherson to become an itinerant Pentecostal minister, travelling in her "Gospel Car," a Packard touring car adorned with religious slogans written along the chassis. Though some were uncomfortable with a woman preaching the Gospel, McPherson attracted large crowds as she hosted revivals across the eastern United States. As she honed her oratorical skills, McPherson delivered deeply conservative messages that resonated with the crowds—constantly railing against numerous aspects of modernity and demanding that people remain true to the fundamentalist faith of the old time religion.

Seeking a permanent home for her family, McPherson moved in 1918 to Los Angeles, California—a city undergoing rapid population growth (from 575,000 in 1920 to over 1.2 million by 1930), with many of the newly arriving migrants coming from midwestern and southern rural areas holding strong fundamentalist beliefs. After establishing her new "International Church of the Foursquare Gospel," she made frequent trips across the country to raise money for construction of a large structure to house her growing congregation. On January 1, 1923, the nation's first "megachurch" opened when McPherson dedicated the new 5,300-seat Angelus Temple, which often filled to capacity. Besides the sense of community provided by the large crowds attending the Temple, devotees flocked to the church because of McPherson's personal charisma and her sense of dramatic flair. Arriving in grand fashion (often in a deluge of bright light surrounded by bouquets of roses; one time she entered on a motorcycle down the main aisle), she always produced immaculate stage presentations with orchestral accompaniment to drive home her messages and keep the audiences entertained. Unlike Billy Sunday and many other fundamentalist evangelists, McPherson preached optimism rather than fire and brimstone. Though tending to avoid using the Pentecostal label, she occasionally spoke in tongues and performed dramatic faith healing demonstrations in the Pentecostal tradition as part of her sermons. In addition to showing a gift for oratory and theatrics, McPherson also displayed a keen awareness of the potential of new media outlets to reach new potential converts. In 1924 she purchased a radio station and began preaching over the airwaves to the entire city.

McPherson's fame began to wane after a month-long disappearance from a Southern California beach in 1926 that ended when she was discovered alive in Douglas, Arizona claiming to have been drugged and held for ransom by Mexican kidnappers. Doubters were probably correct that the incident was designed to be part-publicity stunt and partly an effort to hide her affair with her married radio station manager. Nevertheless, her Foursquare Gospel Church endured the scandal, and McPherson continued preaching with less public fanfare until her death in the early 1940s.

Riding the success of a growing movement, fundamentalists during the 1920s sought to put their ideas into action to shape the direction of society. The largest bête noir for fundamentalists was the spreading of Charles Darwin's theory of evolution, especially in public education. For those who unquestioningly believed the story of creation of mankind presented in the Book of Genesis, Darwin's proposition that humans descended from primates was a blasphemous doctrine that had to be crushed. If the story of creation were to be disregarded, the entire Bible would then become disputed ground. Three-time former Democratic presidential nominee William Jennings Bryan, himself a devout fundamentalist, led the effort in the various states to pass laws removing the teaching of Darwinian theories from public education. A politician with strong reform credentials, Bryan believed that Darwin's views enhanced political conservatism by justifying a "survival of the fittest" mentality. He also believed that acceptance of evolution removed the consciousness of God's presence in people's daily lives, leading one to conclude that "no spiritual force has touched the life of man and shaped the destiny of nations."

Though a national effort, the anti-Darwin movement achieved its only successes in the South where several states banned textbooks with any mention of Darwin and made it a crime to teach evolution in public schools. In 1925, Tennessee fundamentalists, whipped into a frenzy by a recent Billy Sunday crusade, pressured members of their legislature to pass a law making it a misdemeanor "to teach any theory that denies the story of the Divine Creation of man as taught in the Bible, and to teach instead that man had descended from a lower order of animal." When some in the state decided to challenge the constitutionality of the new law, the stage was set for the biggest clash of the decade between secularists and fundamentalists.

The American Civil Liberties Union (ACLU), a free speech organization originally formed to defend those being punished for opposing American involvement in World War I, announced that it was willing to defend any teacher arrested for violating the Tennessee statue. Seeking a test case to appeal to the U.S. Supreme Court, ACLU lawyers found a group of collaborators in the form of some local leaders in the small town of Dayton, located midway between Knoxville and Chattanooga in eastern Tennessee. There, businessmen and attorneys concocted a plan to bring a show trial over evolution to Dayton to boost the town's sagging economy. Calling upon their high school's young and easygoing part-time general science instructor and football coach John T. Scopes to seek his participation in their scheme, the men got the 24-year old teacher's concurrence that biology could not be taught properly without addressing Darwin's theory of evolution and his consent to be arrested for violating the state's new antievolution statute.

The carnival-like atmosphere that would characterize the **Scopes "Monkey Trial"** developed quickly with the publicity being generated soon exceeding that for a Jack Dempsey boxing match. Though ACLU officials hoped for a simple, quiet test case to bring through the appellate courts, the Dayton leaders had other priorities. To increase the trial's notoriety, they invited William Jennings Bryan to take part in the court proceedings as an assisting prosecuting attorney. Upon hearing of Bryan's acceptance to participate, Chicago defense attorney **Clarence Darrow**—the most famous lawyer in the country and an evolution supporter – offered his services to aid the ACLU in defending Scopes. Though ACLU officials did not desire Darrow's help out of fear that his rabid agnosticism and gruff demeanor would present the wrong image to the public, Scopes wanted Darrow's counsel and retained him for his defense team. Dayton's residents, especially the town's merchants, welcomed the crush of out-of-town journalists, peddlers, hucksters, and curiosity-seekers who arrived to spend their time and money during the eleven-day trial. More than 200 newspaper reporters from across the country covered the trial and a live radio feed allowed Americans to listen to the first broadcasted trial in U.S. history from the comfort of their homes.

Inside the hot, poorly-ventilated courtroom, the opposing sides battled each other, not over the details of the case for the jury (Scopes freely admitted he was guilty of violating the law), but over the merits of the larger issues of evolution and acceptance of a literal interpretation of the Bible for the newspaper-reading and radio-listening national public. On the final full day of the trial, the judge moved the proceedings outdoors due to the stifling heat. Darrow then dramatically called Bryan to the witness stand. Over the lead prosecutor's objection, the judge allowed the questioning to proceed when Bryan stated that he wished to defend his beliefs as long as he would be allowed to question Darrow afterwards. In an effort to ridicule Bryan's views and to suggest that Bible stories were unscientific and therefore inadmissible in a science class, Darrow aggressively interrogated the aging politician about the veracity of numerous Bible passages, including God acceding to Joshua's request to make the sun stand still, Jonah being swallowed by a whale, the story of Adam and Eve, and the creation of the world in seven days. Bryan steadfastly stated that while he could not explain many contradicting passages in the Bible (such as where Cain found his wife and how there could have been a first, second, or third day if the sun was not created until the fourth day), he nevertheless believed it all unequivocally. At one point Bryan potentially upset many followers when he admitted under rigorous questioning to the possibility that the seven days of creation might refer to long epochs of time. Exhausted with the two-hour long exercise, the judge finally ended the session. On the next day he did not allow Bryan the opportunity for rebuttal and instead called for closing arguments. The jury then took only nine minutes to deliberate, finding Scopes guilty as the defense team expected, and hoped. The judge ordered Scopes to pay a $100 fine.

In the days that followed, Bryan died of a heart attack (becoming a martyr in the eyes of fundamentalists, though there was no direct link between the trial and his death), and ACLU lawyers filed their appeal. In 1927, members of the Tennessee state Supreme Court who feared that the U.S. Supreme Court would overturn the anti-evolution law, however, set aside Scopes's conviction on the technical grounds that under Tennessee law the jury should have decided such a high fine, not the trial judge. The prosecution refused to retry the case. Though the anti-evolution movement stalled after the Scopes Trial, evolution continued to remain separate from the scientific curriculum of numerous southern public education systems for decades until the U.S Supreme Court ruled in the 1968 *Epperson v. Arkansas* case that such bans stood in violation of the Establishment Clause of the First Amendment (Tennessee had repealed its anti-evolution statute the previous year.) Nevertheless, anti-evolution sentiment would remain within America's conservative Christian subculture, thriving in church-related education and home schooling.

Though much has been made over the years about how the Scopes Trial pitted "the two Americas" against each other, the majority of Americans during the 1920s were in between the two extremes of Darrow's rabid agnosticism and Bryan's devout fundamentalism. Nevertheless, the trial stands as one of the great symbolic experiences of the decade, clearly displaying that Americans were far from united in terms of their social and cultural views. Modernists (whether those with secular or liberal Christian viewpoints) viewed Bryan and his followers as backward, superstitious bumpkins out of tune with the discoveries of modern science. Fundamentalists, regardless of their denomination, believed that the supporters of Darwin were atheists or misguided Christians seeking to undermine the foundation of their religious beliefs. Such was the true America during the 1920s, and since.

The Second Ku Klux Klan

The **Ku Klux Klan** became the embodiment of the most extreme defenders of the old social order. Not only proclaiming to be the regulators of the color line, Klansmen during the 1920s set out to stem the tide of foreign immigration and stamp out the teaching of evolution while maintaining the sanctity of marriage, supporting Prohibition, and enforcing a proper Victorian Era code of public dress and conduct, by force if necessary.

In 1915, an unsuccessful former Methodist minister named William J. Simmons founded the Second Ku Klux Klan as a fraternal organization with membership limited to white, Protestant, native-born adults. Taking advantage of the popularity of the recently released film *Birth of a Nation*, which glorified the original Klan of Reconstruction days, Simmons borrowed the dress and many rituals from the hooded order to create a living memorial to the old group while focusing on new issues that were supposedly destroying American society. The Klan grew at a glacial pace over the next five years, largely reflecting Simmons's lack of organizational and promotional ability. By 1920 the group had only 5,000 members in Georgia and Alabama when Simmons entered into a business deal with Edward Clarke and Elizabeth Tyler—two Atlanta-area publicists with promotional and fundraising experience. Using corporate publicity techniques and a trained staff of one thousand recruiters (or "kleagles," as they were called by the Klan), Clarke and Tyler added greatly to Klan membership rolls by exploiting fear and prejudice against blacks, Mexicans, Catholics, Jews, and immigrants while championing support for Prohibition, patriotism, and traditional moral standards. They also got rich in the process. For every $10 "klectoken" (initiation fee) collected, Clarke and Tyler pocketed $4, the kleagle received $4, and the remainder went to Klan national headquarters in Atlanta. Kleagles received instructions to take a top-down approach when recruiting in a locality, first contacting local business, religious, and political leaders in order to gain prestige, then working down to the middle-class, and finishing by convincing those at society's bottom to join. These techniques proved to be very successful. By the end of 1922, the Ku Klux Klan boasted 700,000 members nationally.

No doubt some joined the Klan for simple business reasons, as Klan leaders preached a message of "vocational Klanishness" whereby members were expected to trade with each other at the expense of nonmembers. The vast majority joined the Klan, however, because the group seemed capable of providing a strong counterforce to all the negative aspects of life appearing in 1920s America. While providing a link to the glorified and mythologized past, the 1920s Klan attracted bewildered people, many of whom were bored or otherwise disgruntled with their mediocre lives, and promised to make them part of a cause greater than themselves. Others who disliked the Klan's many hate-filled statements and acts of violence nevertheless supported the order because they sympathized with its concerns, if not all of their deeds.

Regarding class membership of the Klan, a popular myth exists that this second manifestation of the Klan was primarily dominated by the "lower orders" of society. While the Klan did have lower-class members, research has shown that not only did the klaverns have modest numbers of upper-class individuals, the Klan's base consisted largely of middle-class membership. Though many middle-class Americans would have nothing to do with the Klan, the fact remains that men with such varied occupations as store owner, dentist, druggist, real-

KKK parade held in Washington D.C. on September 13, 1926.

tor, salesman, bookkeeper, clerk, skilled tradesman, and farm owner joined the group in large numbers. Another misconception about the 1920s Klan is that the order was primarily an anti-black organization. While many Klansmen held strong white supremacist views and some performed acts of violence against African Americans, other motivations accounted for the Klan's rise. Beyond fears of blacks crossing the color barrier, the majority of Klan members tended to view those issues as lesser aspects of the overall goal of controlling the rapidly modernizing world. Even more important to them were signs of moral decay and the breakdown of traditional societal norms represented by new "scandalous" forms of entertainment and dress, rampant lawlessness exhibited by evasion of the Prohibition laws, challenges to traditional Christianity, and decrepit moral behavior displayed by gamblers, prostitutes, and individuals who engaged in premarital and extramarital sex. In the end, devout Klansmen wanted to use their organization as a device to take the country back to an alleged time when these behaviors were rare. Many did not mind using violence and other extralegal means to enforce their models of social conformity. Many females also agreed with the Klan's efforts so strongly that they organized "Women of the Ku Klux Klan" auxiliaries in 36 states. Most were religious women who rejected the modernistic elements of the Roaring Twenties.

While the Klan provided a sense of community for its members through grand parades, dramatic initiation ceremonies, casual social events, and even occasional charity work, the hooded order became an outlet for others who wished to impose their desires through vigilantism. They spied on neighbors, issued threats to suspected wrongdoers, and took part in brutal acts of violence against their adversaries. Newspaper stories of Klan violence during the 1920s abound. Though many Klan attacks were directed against African Americans, large numbers of Klan victims were white. Klansmen escaped prosecution for these and other offenses because eyewitnesses were too afraid to testify, grand juries refused to indict offenders, and law enforcement officials (many of whom were Klansmen themselves) often looked the other way.

The Klan moved into the realm of politics starting in 1922 after a faction led by Hiram Wesley Evans, a Dallas dentist who had served as Cyclops of the Dallas klavern, gained control of the national organization. Unhappy with Simmons's leadership, Evans and his supporters supplanted the Klan's founders, eventually buying out Simmons and banishing Edward Clarke. Afterwards, Evans pushed for Klan entry into Democratic Party politics across the nation. He also sought to change the Klan's image as a violent organization (somewhat ironic since he led the group of Klansmen who brutally attacked and branded a Dallas bellhop accused of crossing the color line during the previous year). Klan-supported candidates achieved notable successes in many states, winning control of the legislatures of Texas, Oklahoma, Oregon and Indiana, and helping to elect six governors and three U.S. Senators, not to mention thousands of candidates for local offices.

Reaching its pinnacle of support by the mid-1920s (symbolized by thousands of Klansmen triumphantly marching down Washington, D.C.'s Pennsylvania Avenue in 1925), external and internal forces eventually overwhelmed the Klan. Judges and district attorneys began to press grand juries for indictments against Klansmen for violent acts. Major state newspapers and national magazines published anti-Klan editorials and articles detailing Klan violence (especially against whites) and accusations of political corruption. Many local chambers of commerce started to speak out against the Klan's lawlessness, and average citizens questioned the organization's growing political clout. Finally, many scandals involving prominent Klan leaders forever tarnished the group's image in the public's eyes. Some of the incidents involved financial impropriety while others involved personal failings or political corruption. The scandal that enveloped the Indiana Klan, however, included all these elements. After a jury convicted its leader, David Stephenson, of raping his secretary while in a drunken rage—an incident that eventually led to her suicide—the Klansman expected a pardon from the governor who he helped to get elected. When the anticipated clemency was not forthcoming, Stephenson released evidence of bribery and other illicit forms of corruption that disgraced the governor and many other state politicians. Demoralized as a result of such scandals and disillusioned with its growing number of electoral defeats, the Klan began a rapid descent. Continuous negative press about these events and ongoing citizen disgust with continuing acts of violence by renegade Klansmen delivered the final blows as prominent men began to depart from the organization. Eventually, the negative sentiment reached the point where the Klan began to become victims of violence themselves. In a sign of the changing times, unknown assailants detonated two bombs at the 4,000-seat klavern hall of Fort Worth (Texas) Klan No. 101, completely destroying the building.

RESURGENT POLITICAL CONSERVATISM

If as commonly portrayed, nontraditional and carefree attitudes characterized the 1920s, this reality would have been reflected in the successful election of countless unorthodox and even radical candidates for public office. Instead, the decade marked the resurgence of political conservatism and the waning of progressivism. To be sure, echoes of progressivism remained as indicated by efforts to enforce Prohibition, ratification of the woman suffrage amendment, creation of the Federal Extension Service to spread agricultural research and home economics information to the nation's farmers, and the passage of the Sheppard-Towner Maternity and Infancy Protection Act in 1921 providing federal funds to help states establish clinics providing instruction in pre-natal and infant health care (though Congress ended the program in 1929). Nevertheless, conservatism reigned, as reflected in Old Guard Republican control of Congress throughout the decade and three successive Republican presidents in the White House.

Election of 1920

With the infirmed Woodrow Wilson not seeking another term, both political parties sought to overcome internal divisions to select a winning candidate to succeed the president. The Democrats divided over three main candidates. William Gibbs McAdoo, a former Treasury Secretary and Wilson's son-in-law, enjoyed solid support from Prohibition supporters in the South and West. Opponents of Prohibition in the Northeast and Midwest supported two candidates—governors James M. Cox of Ohio and Al Smith of New York. After three days and 44 rounds of balloting at the Democratic National Convention in San Francisco, deals were struck to ensure Cox's nomination. Delegates then rallied behind Assistant Secretary of the Navy Franklin D. Roosevelt (a Wilson loyalist with the added benefit of being Theodore Roosevelt's cousin) for the vice president's slot.

The Republicans also were divided among three major candidates, though none of the contenders were able to win over the Republican National Convention to gain the nomination. General Leonard Wood, a former Army Chief of Staff who served as Teddy Roosevelt's superior officer in Cuba during the Spanish-American War, garnered support among those delegates who appreciated his bellicose stands on foreign policy and constant criticism of Woodrow Wilson. Frank Lowden, a popular governor from Illinois, enjoyed support from Midwestern states but not very popular away from his native region. California Senator Hiram Johnson, Teddy Roosevelt's Bull Moose running mate in the 1912 election, had the support of the party's progressive wing, but that faction was now definitely in the minority. Going into the convention Wood and Lowden each had the support of a third of the delegates, with Johnson lagging behind followed by lesser candidates from states who hoped that their man would rise from the crowded field as the convention's compromise choice. One of these favorite-son candidates, Senator **Warren G. Harding** from the key state of Ohio, followed this path to emerge victorious after ten rounds of balloting. For the vice presidential nomination, the delegates chose Governor Calvin Coolidge of Massachusetts, a politician probably more well-known to the nation than Harding because of his anti-union stance during the Boston police strike of 1919.

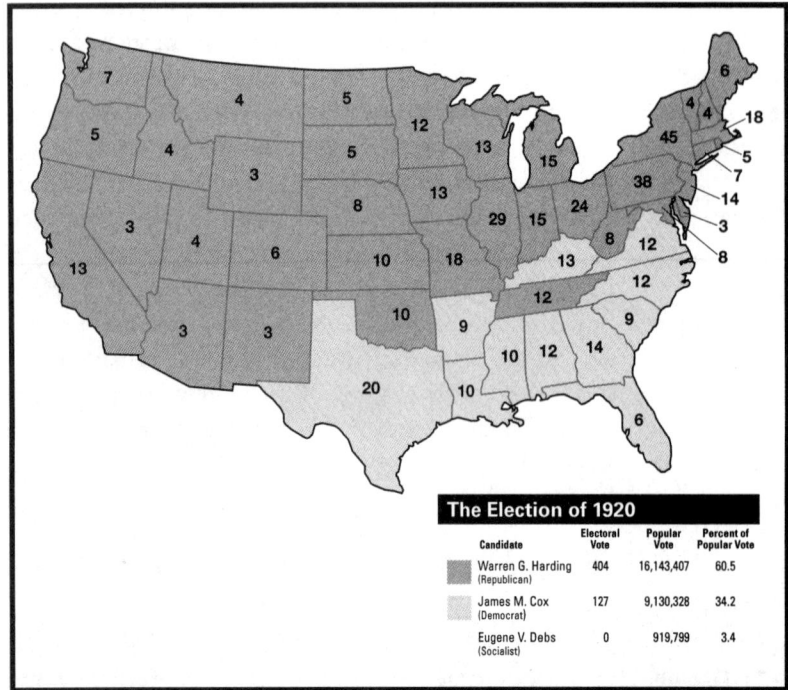

Map 23.1 The Election of 1920

Handsome and rather shallow, Harding did not have a hard time playing up to the part of a steady and modest Midwesterner running as an anti-Wilson candidate. Relying on his sizable advantage in funding, Harding spent most of the campaign in his hometown of Marion, Ohio, issuing press releases and giving occasional "front-porch talks," allowing him to control his message and avoid any slip-ups. The former small-town newspaper editor and his campaign manager, William Hays, correctly sensed that the nation after World War I wished to move away from grand idealistic crusades, both foreign and domestic. During a rare campaign appearance, Harding famously stated that the country's greatest need "was not nostrums but normalcy, not revolution but restoration"—Harding's way of calling for an end to reform and the return of calmer times at home as well as isolationism from troubles abroad. (He opposed the U.S. joining the League of Nations.) By contrast, Cox and Roosevelt, knowing that they were the underdogs, campaigned vigorously across the country making multiple speeches a day in an effort to out-hustle the Republicans. Despite the prevailing national mood, the Democratic nominees favored continued domestic reform efforts and joining the League. Ultimately, Harding and Coolidge routed their opponents, winning just over 16 million votes (60 percent of the total) and 37 states for 404 electoral votes. Cox and Roosevelt received only 9 million (34 percent) and 11 states, all in the South. Socialist Party candidate Eugene Debs (still in prison) picked up 920,000 votes, his party's highest vote tally ever, but the Socialists' percent share of the total electoral was less than half of its 1912 peak performance. The Republicans picked up 61 House seats to hold a solid majority, in addition to gaining 10 Senate seats allowing the party to have a 59-37 edge—the largest majority held by any party in that chamber in over 100 years.

The Failed Harding Presidency

Harding made reduced government spending and the curtailment of business regulation top priorities for his administration. He supported passage of the Budget and Accounting Act of 1921, which gave presidents authority over the federal budget. The law created the Bureau of the Budget whose director was responsible for working with the president to develop a yearly budget to be submitted to Congress. The act also established the General Accounting Office to oversee and audit budget expenditures. During the course of his three-year presidency, Harding approved budgets that reduced federal government spending by almost 50 percent. He also supported lax regulation of corporations by appointing conservative administrators to the Federal Trade Commission, the Interstate Commerce Commission, the Federal Reserve Board, and other important government agencies. Harding appointed four new Supreme Court justices friendly to business interests, including Chief Justice William Howard Taft—the only ex-president ever to serve on the High Court. The Taft Court invalidated federal child labor laws and a state minimum wage law for women, issued numerous injunctions against labor unions, and made many pro-business rulings. To fill his Cabinet positions, Harding made some choices

Warren G. Harding speaking in a session of the House of Representatives with Calvin Coolidge and Frederick Gillett seated behind the desk. c1921

that the contemporary press generally celebrated. In addition to selecting Charles Evans Hughes to handle foreign affairs as Secretary of State, the president made two notable appointments who forcefully guided economic policy.

Banker and businessman **Andrew W. Mellon**, then the third-wealthiest man in America, became Secretary of the Treasury and immediately made an imprint on administration monetary policy. While advocating reduced government expenditures, he famously called for marked reductions in corporate and high-income taxes. On Mellon's suggestion, Congress eliminated excess-profits taxes from the war, lowered the estate tax, and ended a federal gift tax. With the support of Harding (and Coolidge after he became president), Congress gradually reduced the maximum marginal income tax rates from 73 percent in 1921 to 25 percent by 1926. Mellon supported these tax reductions in the belief that more money in the hands of businesses and wealthy individuals would spur investment by corporations and members of the upper class, leading to employment that would benefit the middle- and lower classes. In the final analysis, while some sound investments occurred during the boom years of the mid-to-late 1920s, investors squandered much wealth on real estate booms, stock market speculation, and chasing elusive investment schemes, which contributed to financial instability by the end of the decade and helped spur the arrival of the Great Depression.

Commerce Secretary Herbert Hoover provided an element of business progressivism to the Harding Administration. A self-made millionaire who made his fortune as a mining engineer and consultant, Hoover served with distinction as Food Administrator and director of Belgian Relief during World War I before Harding asked him to lead the Commerce Department. Believing that unbridled laissez-faire capitalism led to inefficiency and waste, Hoover used his position to promote the idea of "associationalism," or cooperation between business and government via the establishment of trade associations. Through those private agencies, Hoover hoped that companies would standardize elements of their industries and share information on sales, production, and prices in an effort to set prices, reduce costs, and lessen the atmosphere of cutthroat competition. Hoover also sought to use the associations to spread information about business conditions and make recommendations on ways companies could produce more efficiently and pursue policies beneficial to the public interest. He hoped that government partnership with industry would help stabilize the American economy by ending boom-and-bust cycles. Overseeing the creation of hundreds of trade associations during the 1920s (he retained the Commerce post through Coolidge's administration), Hoover found himself often fighting efforts by businessmen to use the trade groups as a means of collusion to fix prices and allocate markets rather than the higher purposes that he sought.

Ultimately, most scholars view Harding's presidency negatively, one of the worse in history, and for good reasons. Though amiable and sympathetic to the plight of others (he freed Eugene Debs from prison, for example, supported anti-lynching legislation in Congress, spoke out against racial segregation, and signed the Sheppard-Towner Act into law), he possessed many flaws that have tarnished his legacy. Despite the Prohibition law, he drank heavily with friends at White House affairs. He also enjoyed many mistresses over the years—a practice that did not stop while president. In addition to these personal imperfections, his main trouble proved to be his intellectual limitations and his trusting nature. Harding was simply overwhelmed by the immensity of the job and heavily delegated responsibility to others. No harm was done when those he chose rose to the occasion and showed themselves to be exceptional administrators, such as Hughes, Mellon, and Hoover. Many other selections, however, proved to be selfish individuals who used their White House connections to engage in criminal activities that forever damaged his presidency. Harding did not condone or encourage such illegal activities, but he bears much responsibility for naively selecting many trusted cronies and associates for high office and for lax oversight of his people.

Harding showed pride when he signed the bill creating the Veteran's Bureau to aid returning soldiers from World War I. Charles Forbes, the friend who the president entrusted to direct the new agency, however, proved to be a crook worthy of the two-year jail sentence he eventually received. Forbes was a construction company executive who Harding named to head the bureau because of his war service and successful efforts to swing the Washington state delegation to Harding at the Republican National Convention. Soon after his appointment, Forbes began to disgracefully line his pockets at every opportunity—selling off medical supplies intended for veterans and pocketing the proceeds, receiving kickbacks from contractors for awarding them contracts to build veterans hospitals, and overbilling taxpayers for expensive jaunts across the country under the guise of hospital inspection trips. When he found out about the accusations, Harding demanded Forbes's resignation. The director obliged but not before bystanders had to pull Forbes away from Harding's choking grasp for embarrassing his administration.

One of Harding's closest associates, Harry Daugherty, also let the president down. The Ohio Republican Party operative received the post of Attorney General as a reward for managing Harding's efforts to receive the presidential nomination at the national convention. Along with his aide, Jesse Smith, Daugherty used his position to peddle influence for cash, receiving gifts and bribes in exchange for settling various government matters including pardons and disposing of confiscated German property from World War I. When rumors of investigations and indictments began to swirl, Smith shot himself. Daugherty remained at his post until fired by Calvin Coolidge. He twice avoided conviction at trials when juries failed to reach definitive verdicts, probably due to thoroughness in destroying evidence plus Smith no longer being alive to testify against him.

The Teapot Dome affair, the most famous of the Harding administration scandals, led to the first ever conviction and imprisonment of a cabinet member. Harding's choice for Secretary of the Interior, Senator Albert Fall of New Mexico, sought to profit directly from his position by receiving money ($100,000 cash plus $200,000 in war bonds) from two oil company executives. In return, Fall arranged for control of government-owned petroleum reserves at Elk Hills in California and Teapot Dome in Wyoming to be transferred from the U.S. Navy to his department, before leasing the lands to the oil companies. When rumors swirled that lavish improvements had been made to Fall's New Mexico ranch, Senator Burton Wheeler of Montana began to investigate and eventually uncovered evidence of bribery. A jury convicted the Secretary, sentencing him to a year in prison with a $100,000 fine.

Keeping Cool With Coolidge

In San Francisco while on an exhausting speaking tour of the West Coast during the summer of 1923, the 57-year old Harding suffered a heart attack and died just two and a half years into his term, before the full extent of the crimes committed by members of his administration became public knowledge. Much of the nation expressed shocked and grief at the sorrowful news. In the middle of the night, Vice President Calvin Coolidge heard the news while visiting his childhood home in Vermont. His father, a former state legislator, administered the oath of office under the light of a couple of kerosene lamps.

Early in his life, Coolidge had followed a political path similar to his father's before moving to higher office. Educated at Massachusetts' prestigious Amherst College, he studied law, serving in a series of local offices before being elected to the state legislature, the lieutenant governorship, and finally the governorship. Coolidge's sole claim to national fame occurred when he presented strong resistance to the Boston police strike of 1919, famously remarking: "There is no right to strike against the public safety by anybody, anywhere, any time." To the delight of conservatives across the country, he refused to rehire any of the policemen who picketed after the walkout ended. More than anything else he did as governor, his firm stand propelled his name for consideration for the vice presidency when Republicans convened for their 1920 national convention.

A staunch ideological conservative, Coolidge believed that the basic foundation of American social and political structure to be sound. In his mind, those who sought change were dangerous radicals who must be resisted. His belief that the role of government should be limited was unwavering, especially with regard to the regulation of business. Personally frugal and honest, he expected the same from government. He favored reduced expenditures and won over many in the public when he fired Harding's cronies from his administration while keeping respected members of the cabinet such as Mellon, Hoover, and Hughes.

Coolidge's removal of the tainted Harding personnel, the improvement of the American economy, and division among his opponents helped the new president in his bid to win a full term in 1924. Democrats divided between two of the major candidates from the 1920 campaign—William Gibbs McAdoo and Al Smith. After ten days of debate and 102 rounds of balloting, James Cox (the 1920 nominee) and other party leaders negotiated a settlement—the respected lawyer John W. Davis of West Virginia, Woodrow Wilson's solicitor general and a former ambassador to England, would receive the presidential nomination and Nebraska governor Charles W. Bryan (brother of William Jennings Bryan) would be the vice presidential nominee. Disgusted by the nomination of two pro-business conservatives by both major parties (Davis was a senior partner in a law firm whose most important client was J.P. Morgan and Company), progressive Wisconsin Senator Robert La Follette attempted to rally like-minded citizens into a grand campaign. Rather than creating a third party, which might hurt progressive Democrats and Republicans in congressional races, he entered the race as an independent candidate, hoping to attract progressives, old Populists, union members, and farmers through a program denouncing monopolies and corporate power, ending injunctions against labor unions, making the judiciary more responsive to public will through the election of federal judges, and government aid for the ailing agricultural sector of the economy. Coolidge easily won a term in his own right, with over 15 million popular votes and 382 electoral votes compared to Davis's 8 million popular votes and 136 electoral votes (all coming from the South.) La Follette's underfunded campaign finished a distant third, earning 4.8 million popular votes and only securing the electoral votes of his home state of Wisconsin. With the progressive spirit in check, the Republicans were ascendant, not only solidifying control of both houses of Congress but also continuing their state-level dominance of politics in states outside of the Old Confederacy.

"The Business of America"

For all his faults and limitations, Warren Harding had sought to educate himself on many issues and otherwise learn the ropes of being president. Calvin Coolidge, however, exuded a self-confidence that bordered on smugness and often strove to do as little as possible in the White House. Embodying this attitude, he prided himself on sleeping twelve hours every night as well as finding time to take an afternoon nap. Reiterating his philosophy in characteristically simple terms, Coolidge once stated that "The chief business of the American people is business." To that end, Coolidge scaled back executive actions, not only deferring to Congress but also to the large corporations who could now expect little trouble in the form of "burdensome government regulations."

In an effort to scuttle the advances of regulatory reform, Coolidge appointed anti-progressives to head numerous government agencies. To serve on the Federal Trade Commission (FTC), for example, the president appointed former congressman William E. Humphrey, a lumber industry attorney who had previously made numerous speeches attacking the FTC. On Humphrey's watch, FTC commissioners greatly reduced the degree of corporate oversight, promoting private settlements with business rather than issuing cease-and-desist orders against law violators. In other agencies, the Coolidge administration's budget cuts led to greatly reduced staff and fewer investigations of questionable corporate activities. This phenomenon of agencies empowered under the law to oversee business activities being led by advocates for the very industries they are supposed to regulate—known as agency "capture" by political scientists—continues to exist to the present day and displays the limits of the progressive faith in regulation as the primary means of checking corporate power.

Coolidge's defense of free market capitalism and his belief in limited government led naturally to his resistance to efforts by farm representatives to develop plans to aid agriculture, the weakest sector of the economy throughout the decade. Though the war increased demand for products across the agricultural spectrum, the boom ended by 1920. The return of world agricultural production and domestic overproduction led to a dramatic drop in farm prices. In Washington, congressmen from agricultural states formed the "farm bloc" to promote the interests of their constituents. Farm organizations and spokesmen lobbied tirelessly for many proposals to aid the nation's farmers and agribusinesses. The most dynamic agrarian advocate during the 1920s proved to be George N. Peek, president of Illinois's Moline Plow Company. For many years a Midwestern leader in the sale of plows and other farming implements, Peek's company collapsed after the war because of declining sales. Arguing "You can't sell a plow to a busted farmer," Peek developed a plan that proposed to help the nation's farmers improve their incomes. His scheme would be developed into legislative form in the proposed McNary-Haugen bills first introduced into Congress in 1924. Rather than encourage decreased production of farm commodities to lower domestic supply and boost prices, Peek proposed that the U.S. government use its financial resources to buy up crop surpluses in order to remove them from the domestic market. The government could then dump the surplus overseas into global markets for whatever prices they could receive. The difference between the price that the government paid and the price sold in world markets would be made up by charging farmers an "equalization fee" in order to prevent the government from having to incur any losses. Peek convinced many farmers and their representatives that growers would see substantial increases in their incomes to offset the surcharges.

Despite passing both houses of Congress in 1927 and 1928, the McNary-Haugen bills never became law, having been vetoed twice by Coolidge who believed the proposals expanded the role of government beyond its just limits and were probably unconstitutional. Many farmers resented Coolidge's rebukes, leading some northern and western producers to start rethinking their political allegiance to the Republican Party. Though they failed to become law, the effort to pass the McNary-Haugen bills became a strong catalyst to the formation of the farm bloc and its subsequent efforts to aid agriculture in the 1930s and beyond.

The money flowing to the country's corporations and upper classes as a result of the tax cuts advocated by Secretary Mellon spurred some sound investment by businesses and rich investors during the mid-to-late Twenties, but the flood of funds to the wealthy also led to wild speculation in real estate and the stock markets, eventually destabilizing the entire economy by the end of the decade. The greatest example of rampant real estate gambling took place in Florida, a state lightly populated before World War I (Miami had only 5400 residents in 1910). As investors spent billions developing areas of coastal Florida in the early 1920s and began publicizing the benefits of warm water and sunshine to chilled middle-class Midwesterners and residents living in the

Northeast, a flood of migrants arrived via the automobile. Land prices skyrocketed as Florida's population swelled from 968,000 in 1920 to 1.2 million in 1925 (with Miami growing to over 130,000). The boom led many to participate in the action without ever going to the state, choosing instead to gamble by purchasing residential and commercial lots from agents soliciting the sales as a sound investment with huge potential profits. In a practice to be replicated in the stock markets, many salesmen enticed buyers to place only a portion of the purchase price down with subsequent monthly installments and interest paid later. This so-called "margin buying" allowed more investors to participate in the mania, with the enlarged pool of available money leading to land prices being bid even higher. The bubble finally burst when the high level of funds necessary to maintain the speculation began to recede. Already declining, the coup de grace to the Florida land boom occurred in September 1926 when a powerful hurricane slammed into Miami, killing 400 people, leaving 50,000 homeless, and destroying in the public's mind the illusion that the Florida peninsula was a pristine paradise. Thousands of investors lost their fortunes as the number of tourists and investors dried up.

As the Florida economy declined in the late-Twenties, the New York Stock Exchange surged as stock prices reached record high levels. During the first two-thirds of the 1920s, stock prices displayed steady growth matching the rise in corporate profits. From 1928 through most of 1929, however, the massive gains did not reflect company performance and completely lost track of rational justification. Similar to the tremendous rise in Florida land prices, the sharp increase in stock prices mostly reflected the influx of funds into the market as investors simply bid up prices based on their belief that they would continue to rise, leading to amazing profits. Investors entered the fray with low margins, securing loans from brokers who charged them 20 percent interest and received commissions for each share bought or sold. (Buyers did not mind such charges if, for example, they bought Montgomery Ward stock at $117 per share in January 1928 and still held it in January 1929 when its value had risen to $440). Bankers poured billions into the stock markets, lending funds to brokers and purchasing stocks themselves. Though some began to call for more restraint, these pleas mostly fell on deaf ears. The consequences of Andrew Mellon's policies, heartily endorsed by Coolidge, would not become fully evident until the end of 1929 when the chickens came home to roost during the presidency of his successor, Herbert Hoover.

THE ELECTION OF HOOVER AND THE GREAT CRASH

Calvin Coolidge surprised many in 1927 when he announced that he would not seek another term as president. Rather than having foresight that the economy might start sinking and he wished to jump ship before that occurred, Coolidge simply believed he had led the country in the proper direction and wanted to enjoy life with his family. Commerce Secretary Herbert Hoover quickly emerged as the leading candidate for the Republican nomination. More progressive in his thought than Harding and Coolidge, many party leaders hoped another more conservative candidate would emerge, or perhaps Coolidge could be persuaded to run again. When neither occurred and Hoover clearly showed popularity with the voting public, most resistance to his candidacy evaporated. Hoover was nominated on the first ballot at the Republican national convention.

On the Democratic side, the urban Northeastern faction of the party finally succeeded in promoting their favorite candidate, New York's four-term governor Al Smith, to the presidential nomination at the party's national convention held in Houston, Texas. A New York City politician who opposed Prohibition, Smith's candidacy troubled the party's rural, southern, and western elements, but lacking a sound alternative they fell into line and elected him on the first ballot. Smith made history by becoming the first Catholic to win a major party's nomination. Arkansas Senator Joseph Robinson, a Prohibition supporter, balanced the ticket by securing the vice presidential slot.

Hoover's popularity drove the race. Benefiting from his reputation as a sound administrator and humanitarian through his direction of the Food Administration and aid to war refugees, his organization of relief for victims of the early-1920s Russian famine and Mississippi River Flood of 1927, and his supervision of the Commerce Department under Harding and Coolidge convinced a majority of Americans that he was simply the most qualified man for the job. Though known as a progressive who supported many state-level reforms while governor of New York, Smith chose to run a conservative campaign, wooing corporate donors by promising a more pro-business administration than Hoover would provide. With the regulation of business not an issue in the campaign, Smith's adversaries focused their fire on his Catholicism, opposition to Prohibition, and background as a Tammany Hall politician in New York City. Hoover ultimately prevailed handily, providing Republicans with their third consecutive presidential victory by securing 21 million popular votes and dominating the map with 444

electoral votes. Though the Republican brand name was still largely tarnished in the South, Hoover's reputation, when coupled with general prosperity plus the Prohibition and Catholic issues, helped him carry Texas, Florida, North Carolina, Virginia, and Tennessee. Smith did well in northern urban areas and among discontented western farmers but managed to only win 15 million popular votes, with his 87 electoral votes coming from the Deep South, Massachusetts, and Rhode Island.

Hoover enjoyed a nine-month honeymoon period as president before the bottom fell out of the economy. To be sure, warning signs were already evident even before the stock market crash of late-October 1929. By the summer of 1929, consumer spending declined to the point that economists noted the country was entering a recession. Producers of many items began to experience a condition known as "saturated markets," whereby the pool of potential buyers for products that had helped sustain prosperity during the boom period of the decade (such as cars, homes, household appliances, and radios) had begun to dry up, at least for levels necessary to sustain economic growth. Certainly not all Americans possessed these items, but those who had the funds and were inclined to buy them (even with installment buying plans in place) had already done so, pointing to an even larger structural problem with the American economy—the chronic mald-

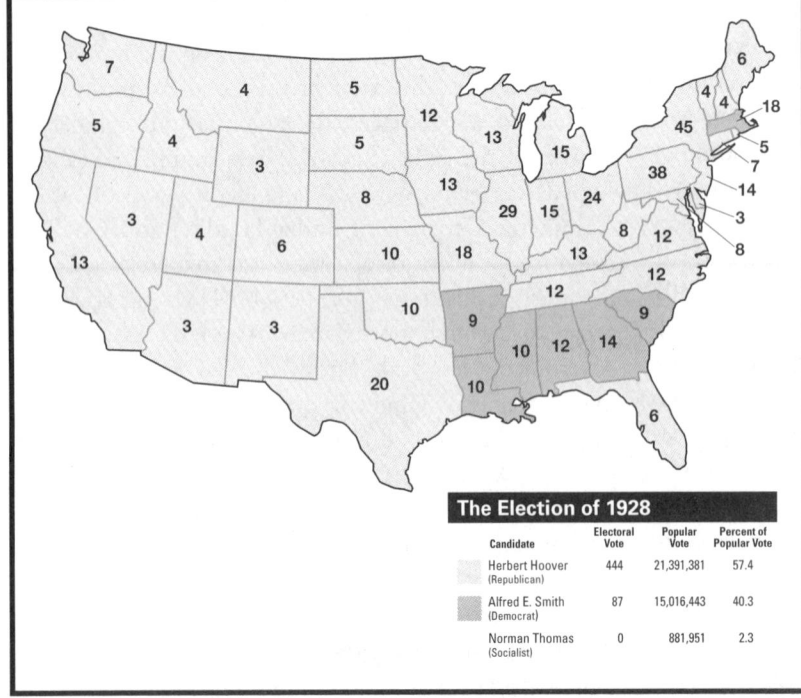

Map 23.2   The Election of 1928

istribution of wealth. Simply too much of the nation's wealth had accrued to the top and not enough reached the workers (who were also the consumers) to keep the economy going. With unsold inventories beginning to rise, companies began to lay off workers, adding to the severity of the situation. Meanwhile, average stock prices continued to set records for a few more months.

The Crash finally came in the last week of October, 1929. As more brokers began to place sell orders for their clients, the general consensus among dealers on the New York Stock Exchange was that speculators who had created the bubble were fearing it was about to burst and wanted to get out while they were still ahead. On October 24 —"Black Thursday"—sell orders rained down from the moment trading commenced, leading to plunging prices. By the closing bell, stockholders had lost $3 billion. Major banks and brokerages purchased several millions of dollars worth of stocks in an effort to instill confidence and quiet the panic, but the effort calmed the situation for only a few days. On "Black Tuesday," October 29, the bottom fell out as the torrent of selling continued, leading to a $10 billion loss for investors. Within three weeks, average stock prices had dropped 50 percent. The decline would continue unabated for the next four years—with average stock prices declining to one-fifth their pre-crash value by early 1933. Investors lost billions, many banks and corporations went out of business. As a crisis mentality soon overwhelmed the economy, those banks still solvent refused to lend funds to companies and individuals, adding to the strain. Businesses that had not gone bankrupt began to shut down production and lay off workers in an effort to stay afloat, contributing to the economy's downward spiral.

Though the stock market crash did not cause the Great Depression, the extreme market correction smashed confidence, ruined many institutions, and accelerated the downturn by exposing the severe fundamental flaws in the structure of the 1920s economy. In ordinary times, the nation would have benefited greatly from the diverse experiences and exceptional organizational skills of Herbert Hoover, who might have gone down in history as an above-average president with many noteworthy accomplishments. The Depression, however, defined his presidency. Though far from a supporter of laissez-faire (as Calvin Coolidge, who would have done nothing with his office to correct the economic decline), Hoover's reliance on the tenets of voluntary cooperation to combat the Depression instead of mobilizing the resources of the federal government would prove to be inadequate to the task. After four years of failure, the nation was ready for bolder efforts under the auspices of Franklin Roosevelt and the New Deal.

Chronology

1918 Spanish Flu epidemic begins.
World War I ends.

1919 18th Amendment (Prohibition) ratified.
Warren Harding elected president.
19th Amendment (Woman suffrage) ratified.
KDKA in Pittsburgh becomes the first U.S. radio station to broadcast regularly scheduled programming.

1921 American Birth Control League is organized.
Emergency Quota Act passes Congress.

1922 Sec of the Interior Albert Fall begins secretly leasing oil reserves at Teapot Dome, Wyoming.
William Hays begins his leadership of the Motion Picture Association of America.

1923 Aimee Semple McPherson opens the 5,300-seat Angelus Temple in Los Angeles, CA.
Equal Rights Amendment is proposed in Congress.
Marcus Garvey convicted of mail fraud.
Warren Harding dies.

1924 Calvin Coolidge elected to a full term as president.
National Origins Act passes Congress.

1925 The Scopes "Monkey Trial" takes place in Dayton, Tennessee.
Indiana Klan leader David Stephenson convicted of murdering his secretary.

1926 Gertrude Ederle becomes the first woman to swim across the English Channel.
Maximum federal income tax rate reduced to 26 percent.
Major hurricane hits Miami, Florida commencing the decline of the Florida land boom.

1927 Charles Lindbergh becomes the first pilot to fly solo across the Atlantic Ocean.
Marcus Garvey deported.
Sacco and Vanzetti executed.

1928 McNary-Haugen bill vetoed for a second time by Calvin Coolidge.
Herbert Hoover elected president.

1929 Shipwreck Kelly sits atop a flagpole in Atlantic City, New Jersey for a record 49 days.
Stock Market Crash.

Review Questions

1. Describe many aspects of the Roaring Twenties lifestyle. How widespread were these behaviors among Americans during the decade?

2. How did life change for American women during the 1920s and how did life remain the same when compared with the previous two decades?

3. Describe the impact of the Great Migration on African Americans and the United States.

4. Describe ways in which many Americans attempted to defend traditional values during the 1920s.

5. In what ways did Warren Harding and Calvin Coolidge promote business interests during the 1920s?

Glossary of Important People and Concepts

"Ballyhoo"
William Jennings Bryan
Calvin Coolidge
Clarence Darrow
Eighteenth Amendment
Henry Ford
Sigmund Freud
Fundamentalism
Marcus Garvey
Warren G. Harding
"Harlem Renaissance" William H. Hays
Herbert Hoover
Jazz
Ku Klux Klan
Charles A. Lindbergh
McNary-Haugen bills
Aimee Semple McPherson
Andrew W. Mellon
National Origins Act
Nineteenth Amendment
Alice Paul
"Roaring Twenties"
Sacco and Vanzetti
Margaret Sanger
Scopes "Monkey Trial"
"sick industries"
Billy Sunday
Spanish Flu
Teapot Dome Scandal

SUGGESTED READINGS

Charles C. Alexander, *The Ku Klux Klan in the Southwest* (1995).

Frederick Lewis Allen, *Only Yesterday: An Informal History of the 1920s,* (1931).

A. Scott Berg, *Lindbergh,* (1998).

David M. Chalmers, *Hooded Americanism: The First Century of the Ku Klux Klan: 1865 to the Present,* (1965).

Kendrick A. Clements, *The Life of Herbert Hoover: Imperfect Visionary, 1918-1928* (2010).

Edmund David Cronon, *Black Moses: The Story of Marcus Garvey and the Universal Negro Improvement Association,* (1955).

Paula S. Fass, *The Damned and the Beautiful: American Youth in the 1920s,* (1977).

John Kenneth Galbraith, *The Great Crash: 1929,* (1988).

John D. Hicks, *Republican Ascendency, 1921-1933* (1960).

Kenneth T. Jackson, *The Ku Klux Klan in the City, 1915-1930,* (1992).

David M. Kennedy, *Birth Control in America: The Career of Margaret Sanger* (1970).

Aileen S. Kraditor, *The Ideas of the Woman Suffrage Movement, 1890-1920,* (1981).

Edward J. Larson, *Summer for the Gods: The Scopes Trial and America's Continuing Debate over Science and Religion,* (1997).

David Levering Lewis, *When Harlem Was in Vogue,* (1989).

Nancy MacLean, *Behind the Mask of Chivalry: The Making of the Second Ku Klux Klan,* (1994).

Donald R. McCoy, *Calvin Coolidge: The Quiet President,* (1967).

Roderick Nash, *The Nervous Generation: American Thought, 1917-1930,* (1990).

Michael E. Parrish, *Anxious Decades: America in Prosperity and Depression, 1920-1941,* (1992).

Thomas R. Pegram, *Battling Demon Rum: The Struggle for a Dry America, 1800-1933,* (1998).

Andrew Sinclair, *Era of Excess: A Social History of the Prohibition Movement* (1964).

Chapter Twenty-four

THE GREAT DEPRESSION AND THE NEW DEAL

European immigrants eventually became assimilated, and once that process was complete, they quickly proved themselves to be worthy citizens, whose contributions were especially noteworthy in the nation's cultural and social life. One immigrant who gained such acclaim during the 1930s was motion picture director Frank Capra. Today, he is probably best remembered for his last successful picture, **It's a Wonderful Life,** *shown ever year at Christmas—sometimes in its new "colorized" version—to millions of American viewers. In the movie, George Bailey, a kind and compassionate small-town savings-and-loan officer (played by Jimmy Stewart, one of Capra's regular stars) is almost destroyed by a wealthy, greedy, and malicious banker. So distraught by his impending ruin, George was on the verge of committing suicide when he is visited by an angel who shows him what life would have been like in Bedford Falls—his town—had he never been born. Taking a page out of the Dickens's classic,* **A Christmas Carol,** *which was also made into a movie in the 1930s, Capra shows George, accompanied by his angelic guide, wandering through a coarse, corrupt, degraded town as he realizes that his life does indeed have value. He returns to the real Bedford Falls to find that his family, friends, and neighbors have rallied together to rescue him from his financial woes and affirm their value to each other.*

When **It's a Wonderful Life** *premiered, Frank Capra was already one of Hollywood's most popular and successful directors. Virtually every one of his 1930s films were commercial successes. Two movies won Academy Awards for Best Picture (and Capra himself won best director in 1934). Capra's artistic and creative talents were undoubtedly remarkable; equally impressive was his vision. His pictures were enthusiastically embraced by Depression-era Americans because Capra's personal social and political views resonated clearly with those of his fellow citizens as they struggled through a decade of unprecedented uncertainty and anguish.*

Capra, a Sicilian immigrant, came to the United States with his family in 1903. The Capras made their way to California where young Frank grew up. After working his way through college, Capra found a job in the still-young movie industry in his home state and eventually became a director of feature films. His great breakthrough came in 1934, with the romantic comedy, **It Happened One Night,** *which has since become a classic in that particularly film genre. The picture, starring Clark Gable and Claudette Colbert, won five Academy Awards, including best picture and best director. Over the next seven years, Capra built on that success by making a series of poignant sociopolitical commentary pictures, which helped to establish the director as a powerful voice of an old-fashioned vision of democracy and American life. Capra's pictures expressed his romantic notion of small town America and the virtuous and noble common man who came from such an environment, while simultaneously revealing his distaste for cities, his contempt for opportunistic politicians, and his condemnation of what he considered the amoral (often immoral) capitalist marketplace. In* **Mr. Deeds Goes to Town,** *(1936) a simple man from a small town inherits a large fortune, moves to the city, and—not liking the greed and dishonesty he finds there—gives the money away and moves back home. In* **Mr. Smith Goes to Washington,** *(1939), a decent man from a western state is elected to the*

U.S. Senate, refuses to join in the self-interested politics of Washington, and dramatically exposes the corruption and selfishness of his colleagues. The rugged Western's actor, Gary Cooper, played Mr. Deeds, while the epitome of small town innocence and virtue, Jimmy Stewart, played Mr. Smith. In 1941, as the United States was about to enter World War II, Capra made **Meet John Doe**, once again starring Gary Cooper. In the picture, Cooper plays an ordinary man manipulated by a fascist cartel to dupe the public on their behalf. He comes to his senses just in time and by threatening suicide, rallies ordinary people to turn against the evil plans of the fascists. He then disappears into the night.

Capra was conscious of the romantic populism that he brought to his pictures. "I would sing the songs of the working stiffs, of the short-changed Joes, the born poor, the afflicted," he once wrote, in an apparent allusion to one of his creative heroes, the great American chronicler through poetry of the common folk, Walt Whitman. "I would fight for their causes on the screens of the world." He was intensely patriotic, a characteristic of many successful immigrants, and he believed passionately that the United States stood for individual opportunity and was defined by the decency of ordinary people. He was not, he said (in an effort to distance himself from the communists) a "bleeding heart with an Olympian call to 'free the masses.'" Indeed, he loathed the term "the masses" and found it "insulting, degrading." He saw the people, rather, as a "collection of free individuals. . .each an island of human dignity."

When the United States entered World War II, Capra collaborated with the government (and the Walt Disney studios) to make a series of pictures designed to explain to new soldiers what the war was about—a series known as **Why We Fight**. Capra contrasted the individualistic democracy of the American small town with the dark collectivism of the Nazis and Fascists. He poured into them all his skills as a filmmaker and his romantic, patriotic images. *It's a Wonderful Life*, released a year after the war, continued his evocation of the decency of ordinary people. In the decades that followed, Capra, although still a relatively young man, ceased to be an important force in American cinema. The sentimental populism and comic optimism—the two central themes of his 1930s pictures—no longer appealed to postwar audiences. Filmmakers and their audiences now wanted harder, more realistic movies, and thus Capra faded into motion picture obscurity by the 1960s. A romantic to the end, Capra was never fully able to adjust to the vagaries of the postwar film industry. In a time of crisis, however, Capra had helped his viewers find solace in his romantic vision of the American past—in the warmth and goodness of small towns and the decency of common folk.

THE GREAT DEPRESSION

The soaring hopes of the 1920s abruptly vanished with the October 1929 stock market crash. The decade of the 1930s thus became one of the most traumatic and critically important eras in America's history. Many would conclude that after the Civil War, the Great Depression marked the second most pivotal crisis in the nation's history. Under the leadership of Franklin Delano Roosevelt (FDR) and his "New Dealers," the Republic met the crisis with unprecedented activism, changing the course of domestic history down to the present.

In the 1932 presidential election, a desperate and disillusioned electorate humiliatingly rejected Herbert Hoover, the personification of the 1920s pro-business spirit. Under Roosevelt, the national government implemented bold, innovative programs and policies, which offered material and emotional relief to millions of suffering and distraught citizens. Perhaps more important was the new president's determination to create a new relationship between the federal government and its citizens. Included in that new dynamic was also a reformation of the executive branch of government. In many ways, FDR, like his beloved cousin, Theodore Roosevelt, and like Abraham Lincoln and Andrew Jackson, significantly augmented the power, and expectations of that office. FDR inaugurated of the modern presidency, establishing during his four terms much of what we expect from our presidents down to the present.

In the end, the New Deal did not end the Great Depression; World War II ultimately did. Roosevelt's and the New Deal's importance, however, lies in the fact that from the 1930s on, the American people could turn to their government not only as the guarantor and protector of their liberties but as a source of assistance in time of need and provider of equal opportunities for all. The New Deal laid the foundation for postwar liberalism (the welfare state), replacing the laissez-faire business ethos (rugged individualism) that had dominated the American value system since the end of the Civil War.

HERBERT HOOVER

The Technocrat as President

At his 1929 inauguration, Herbert Hoover told the American public that, "We in America today are nearer to the final triumph over poverty than ever before in the history of any land. The poorhouse is vanishing among us." The nation had not yet reached that goal, he acknowledged, "but given a chance to go forward with the policies of the last eight years, we shall soon with the help of God be in sight of the day when poverty will be banished from this nation." Those words came back to haunt Hoover, for in eight short months after making that speech, the nation's economy began its declension, ultimately collapsing into the worse financial crisis in the nation's history. Hoover and his reputation were among the first casualties, along with the reverence for business that had been the hallmark of the New Era.

Herbert Hoover was inaugurated president only eight months before the nation's greatest economic calamity struck. Coming into office in March 1929, Hoover possessed all the credentials for a successful and popular tenure. He embodied the rags-to-riches ideal, having risen from poor orphaned beginnings to graduating from Stanford University with an engineering degree. By the age of thirty, Hoover had become one of the world's most successful mining engineers. Before the United States' entry into the Great War, he directed a private American relief agency that fed millions of civilian victims of a war-ravaged Europe. For his efforts, Hoover was acclaimed the "Great Humanitarian," and such status led Woodrow Wilson to name him head of the Food Administration once the United States entered the war. Under his directorship, the Food Administration was responsible for feeding and aiding hundreds of thousands of dispossessed postwar Europeans. As a reward for his achievements, Hoover was appointed Secretary of Commerce by the 1920 Republican victor, Warren G. Harding, and remained at that post until becoming president in 1928. In an era of lackluster presidents with mediocre cabinets, Herbert Hoover was a paragon of professionalism and competence.

Because he favored efficiency and growth, Hoover thought of himself as a progressive, but his reluctance to use the government as an agency of change and reform alienated him from prewar progressives. Having lived most of his adult life abroad, he had never even voted in a presidential election. Aware of his political limitations, Hoover confided to a friend: "I have no dread of the ordinary work of the presidency. What I do fear is the exaggerated idea that I am sort of superman, that no problem is beyond my capacity."

Hoover's initial responses to the depression were clear and firm. If the cooperative principles behind the modern economy were correct, as everyone seemed to embrace, Americans should then use them to stabilize the economy and then recover prosperity. "Progress is born of cooperation," the president reminded citizens. "The Government should assist and encourage these movements of collective self-help by itself cooperating with them." During the first two years of the crisis, Hoover turned to the principles he had followed as secretary of commerce,

President Herbert Hoover

with its emphasis on voluntary cooperation. For business, he sponsored meetings and forums, hoping to convince the heads of the major corporations that his idea was the best approach to recover the economy. Hoover made it clear to these individuals that they need not worry about the possibility of direct government intervention, nor was there a need for a massive overhaul or reform of the American industrial corporate system. He believed that the industrial chieftains were savvy enough to embrace his ideas, realizing that his proposal was the only way of not only eventually restoring employment and prosperity but of saving American capitalism as well. Hoover did, in fact, receive pledges from many industrialists that they would refrain from further layoffs and wage cuts. He also helped to organize a group of New York bankers to pool $500 million of their own money to aid smaller banks in distress. Unfortunately, the businessmen and bankers disappointed Hoover by failing to maintain their voluntary pledges as the economic climate deteriorated further. Their refusal to fully accept his ideas helped to plunge the economy ever deeper into depression.

For agriculture, the new Federal Farm Board issued large amounts of credit so that the commodity cooperatives could keep their products off the market and halt the decline in farm prices. For hard-pressed Americans everywhere, he made the president's office the coordinator (but not the provider) of private, voluntary relief. Between 1929 and 1932 donations for relief increased about eightfold, a remarkable accomplishment by any previous standard. Viewing the economy as a national system, Hoover was the first president in history to attack an economic depression systematically.

The Deepening Depression

As the economy itself, Hoover took a grim downturn in the middle of 1931. As his sense of control over affairs began to slip, he became more rigid, isolated, disillusioned, and frustrated by his inability to deal with the vast specter of oppressive forces. Particularly disturbing was big businesses' refusal to cooperate and enact his policies. Most only paid lip-service to the president's idea of cooperation, while others flat-out refused to acknowledge, let alone implement, any of his suggestions. As a consequence, unemployment in the industrial sector continued to rise as corporations continued to cut costs by laying off workers, something Hoover did not want to happen and believed would not if his advice had been heeded. So overwhelmed and despairing did Hoover become by 1932, that the White House became a funeral parlor. The president, never a charmer, looked, as one visitor remarked, as if a rose would wilt at his touch. In that mood, Hoover called together the villains of Wall Street who, in the president's view, had fed the Great Bull Market instead of facilitating legitimate business. When he demanded that they make massive new investments, they stalled. Finally, Hoover accepted the inevitable: the necessity of government intervention, as least as far as offering federal funds for credit. In January 1932, Hoover approved the establishment of the Reconstruction Finance Corporation (RFC), which provided $1.5 billion in low-interest government loans to ailing banks and corporations in order to prevent their collapse. The RFC was the biggest peacetime intervention in the economy to that point. The Home Loan Bank Board, set up that same year, offered funds to savings and loans, mortgage companies, and other financial institutions that lent money for home construction. Meanwhile, to ease the pressures on international finances, Hoover issued a moratorium on the payment of war debts owed to the United States by its former allies against Germany.

Hoover refused to offer the same generosity to suffering Americans. Still devoted to the concept of rugged individualism, Hoover detested the possibility of offering Americans in dire need direct federal relief. The idea of beginning the concept of a welfare state was an idea that never crossed Herbert Hoover's mind. Every citizen, he believed, must rely for survival on his or her own efforts. To give money to the poor, he insisted, would destroy their desire to work, undermine their sense of self-worth, and erode their capacity for citizenship. Critics pointed to the hypocrisy in such an attitude by reminding the president that in 1930 he refused a request of $25 million to help feed Arkansas farmers and their families but approved $45 million to feed the same farmers' livestock. And in 1932, shortly after rejecting an urgent request from Chicago for aid to help pay its teachers and municipal workers, Hoover approved a $90 million loan to rescue that city's Central Republic Bank. In the summer of 1932, Hoover reluctantly succumbed to political pressure and signed the Emergency Relief and Construction Act, providing $2 billion in federal emergency loans to the states for the creation of work relief projects. Viewing the law as a temporary measure to provide short-term relief, he remained firmly opposed to large-scale and permanent expenditures for government relief

By 1932 the president's policies lay in shambles. The exceptionally-high Hawley-Smoot Tariff, which Hoover had signed in 1930, was intensifying worldwide depression by cutting off the flow of international trade, virtually locking out of American markets foreign manufactured goods. Employers discarded their programs for spreading the work, and unemployment shot above 12 million. Local relief funds, both public and private, evaporated. As commodity prices fell, the Federal Farm Board simply ran out of credit. Farmers burned their crops or left them unpicked as with cotton because it no longer paid them to market the crop. In some Midwestern county seats, silent men with hunting rifles closed the courts so that their mortgages could not be foreclosed. It was no wonder that by the spring of 1932, there had emerged a groundswell of protest and resentment toward the president and his uncaring policies and attitude.

The Bonus Army March

In the spring of 1932, a group of World War I army veterans mounted an emotional challenge to the Hoover administration and its policies. In 1924, Congress had authorized a $1,000 bonus for Great War veterans in the form of compensation certificates that would mature in 1945. But now veterans were demanding the bonus immediately. Spearheaded by a group from Portland, Oregon, veterans decided to take action. Starting from that city and calling themselves the Bonus Expeditionary Force, they hopped onto empty boxcars of freight trains heading east, determined to stage a march on Washington. As the impoverished army veterans traveled eastward, many surviving on handouts from sympathetic citizens, their ranks swelled, reaching 20,000 vets, including wives and children. Upon their arrival in Washington, the **Bonus Army** encamped in the Anacostia Flats, southeast of the Capitol, and petitioned Congress for early payment of the promised bonus. The House of Representatives agreed to allocate the funds, but the Senate rejected the bill. Hoover supported the Senate, and, more importantly, refused to meet with any of the army's emissaries. To Hoover, the

The Bonus Expeditionary Force encamped in the Anacostia Flats, southeast of the Capitol, in Washington, D.C. 1932

gathering represented not a plea for help but a sign that potential revolution was on the horizon. By July 1932, after two months in Washington, the Bonus Army was becoming desperate for help. Hoover, however, was intransigent and secluded himself in the White House. After a group of veterans who had been staying in abandoned Washington apartments scuffled with police (who many claim were sympathetic to the veterans' plight), Hoover called on federal troops led by Army Chief of Staff Douglas MacArthur and 3rd Cavalry Commander George Patton to drive the veterans out. The troops attacked the veterans' Anacostia encampment, razed their tents and shacks, and dispersed with rather brutal force the veterans. In the process, more than fifty veterans were wounded, over one hundred arrested, and one infant died after inhaling tear gas.

News that impoverished veterans and their families had been attacked in the nation's capital intensified an already growing anti-Hoover sentiment. Those who suspected that the president never cared in the first place about the plight of the poor and dispossessed were now convinced that Hoover was a callous man, willing to use force to suppress cries for help. His days in the White House were numbered.

During the years 1921-29 relatively little was expected of the president as an individual. The modern political economy was, after all, a complex impersonal system, not the product of a particular administration, and it appeared to operate on its own momentum. But when the national economic system broke down, only the federal government had the resources and authority to repair it. Citizens began to look toward the executive branch for help, though throughout much of the nation's history, Congress actually dominated the national government because few presidents possessed either the willingness or the ideological inclination, or personal requisites, to assert executive authority and power. That was definitely true for both Warren G. Harding and Calvin Coolidge. Herbert Hoover certainly had the academic background to be an effective president, but he lacked both the personality and the willingness to use the full power of his office to address the crisis. The longer that the Depression persisted, the more inclined the American people were to turn to Hoover and not to Congress. Hoover was judged by new, demanding standards, and because he failed to deliver the people from the crisis, the popular verdict condemned him. By 1932, millions of people began to blame the president for their troubles in bitter, personal ways. A humane man with great administrative skills, Hoover lacked the flexibility, political instincts, and inspirational leadership required by the ordeal. Millions of Americans wanted desperately to believe that a brave new leader might transform the depression into prosperity. Thus, the American electorate turned completely against the Republicans and their president in the 1932 election. In that year, the Republicans were voted out of office after having ruled over national politics (excepting Woodrow Wilson's two terms) for 36 years. Hoover received only 39.6 percent of the popular vote and just 59 (of 531) electoral votes. The Democratic nominee, Governor Franklin D. Roosevelt of New York, won a resounding victory. His triumph, however, should not be viewed as a mandate for him or his New Deal. Americans were desperate for hope and change and were simply willing to give the man a chance, and if he proved to be as ineffective as his predecessor, then four years from now, they would turn to someone else.

Franklin D. Roosevelt and his running mate John Nance Garner of Texas in Peekskill, New York during the 1932 presidential campaign.

THE LORD OF THE MANOR: FDR

It is hard to believe today that Franklin Delano Roosevelt was a man of mystery to many Americans in 1932. Though no doubt name recognition helped his credibility—he was the distant cousin of Theodore Roosevelt, a strong leader and exceptional president—few Americans, outside of his native New York, knew much about his background and experience. Roosevelt was born in 1882 into a patrician Anglo-Dutch family whose pedigree on both sides dated back to the colonial period. By the time of his birth, the Hyde Park manor where he was raised had been in the family for over 200 years. He grew up among people who were convinced of their superiority in matters of ancestry, intelligence, and leadership. His education at Groton, Harvard College, and Columbia Law School was typical of the path followed by the sons of America's blue-blood elite. Though wealthy, the Roosevelt clan's holdings paled in comparison with that of some of their friends and neighbors, such as the Rockefellers, Carnegies, and Harrimans. The Roosevelts disdained the *nouveau riche* upstarts that made up many of the industrial elite.

Particularly galling to the old aristocratic families like the Roosevelts was the new elite's vulgar displays of wealth, their lack of taste and etiquette, their indifference to the natural environment, and their hostility toward those less fortunate than themselves. In short, the behavior and attitudes of the new-wealth industrial capitalists lacked that most important ingredient of quality rearing: a sense of *noblesse oblige*. In FDR's view, his cousin Theodore was the embodiment of this virtue and he wanted to emulate his career. In 1907, FDR began his ascent, following almost verbatim in the tracks of his beloved Uncle Teddy. Like Teddy Roosevelt, FDR envisioned first a seat in the New York State Assembly, then he would be appointed assistant secretary of the navy, and then he would become governor of New York, vice president and then President of the United States. Incredibly, this is almost exactly what happened (except that he became a state senator rather than an assemblyman, and he lost his 1920 bid for the vice presidency).

The governorship of New York and the presidency might have eluded him had he not been transformed by personal calamity. In 1921, at the age of 39, he was strick-

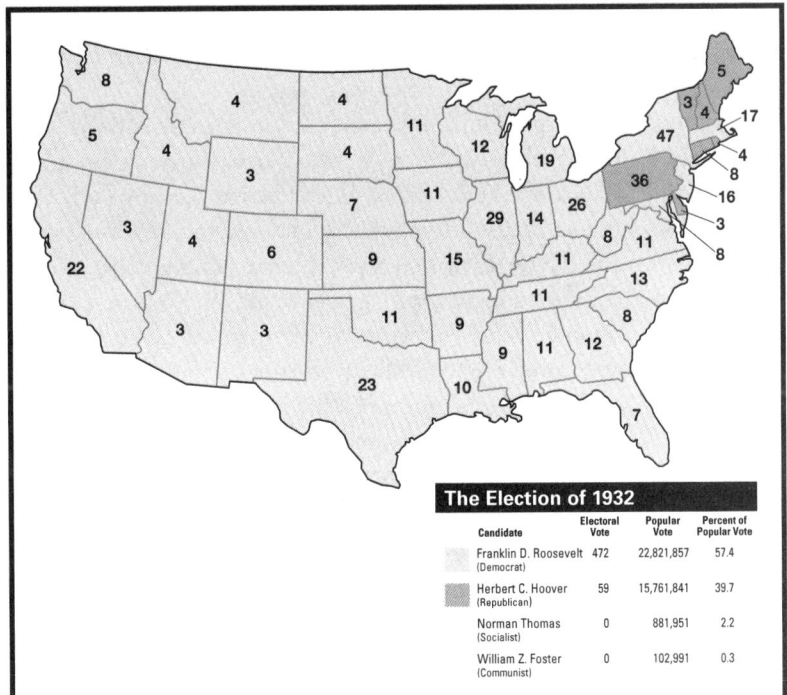

Map 24.1 The Election of 1932

en by polio, which luckily did not kill him but instead took away the use of his legs. Before becoming paralyzed, FDR's career, both professionally (the practice of law) and politically, was not that outstanding. He owed his political ascent more to his famous name. He was charming, gregarious, and popular among associates in the New York Democratic Party. He was quite the pleasure-seeker, a playboy in many ways, who devoted more time and energy to socializing and sailing, partying and womanizing, than he did developing a devotion to career and family. After his illness, he spent the next two years bedridden, and while confined to his bed, he seemed to experience a reformation of character and spirit, a desire to eschew his past life and forge a new one with a determination and seriousness of purpose conspicuously absent during his earlier years. He developed a sense of humility and compassion for those suffering misfortune that would later enable him to reach out to the millions caught in the Great Depression. FDR's physical debilitation also transformed his relationship with his wife, Eleanor. Her dedication to nursing FDR back to health forged a new bond between them. More conscious of his dependence on others, he now welcomed his wife as a partner in his career. Eleanor soon displayed a talent for political organization and public speaking, a gift that surprised those who knew her only as a shy, awkward woman. She would become an active, eloquent advisor, her husband's trusted ally and political confidante, and a key player in the formation of American liberalism. Indeed, many regard her as this nation's greatest First Lady.

Roosevelt Liberalism

During his four years as governor of New York, Roosevelt initiated various reform programs. Other programs,

Franklin D. Roosevelt and Herbert Hoover in a convertible automobile on their way to the U.S. Capitol for Roosevelt's inauguration. March 4, 1933.

however, seemed to embody a new reform impulse called liberalism, which called for government intervention in economic matters while maintaining libertarian views on questions of personal behavior. As the 1932 election approached, FDR appeared to be increasingly gravitating toward this new ideology. By the time of his nomination, he seemed wholly committed to implementing this new ethos after his election. In a rousing call to action, the future president told his supporters in his acceptance speech at the Chicago Democratic convention, "Ours must be the party of liberal thought, of planned action, of enlightened international outlook, and of the greatest good for the greatest number of citizens." He promised "a new deal for the American people." FDR made only two outright promises during the campaign: to repeal Prohibition and to balance the budget. Thus, the nation had to wait until March 4, 1933—the day FDR was sworn in as president—to learn what the New Deal would bring.

President Roosevelt

The reversal in presidential character and personality between Hoover and Roosevelt could not have been more striking. Hoover, one associate remarked, "didn't like the human element." Roosevelt reveled in it. Not only did he mix easily with all kinds of people, but he also made them feel that intuitively he sympathized with them. Hoover, taking no one's counsel, thought he knew what the nation wanted. Unlike Hoover, FDR welcomed the challenge of selling his programs to a demoralized nation. A master of popular phrasing, simple analogies, and, most important, the media, especially the radio, the president had a strong, warm voice that reached into millions of American homes through his famous "**Fireside Chats**," which began on the second Sunday after his inauguration. President Roosevelt projected the image of a kindly grandfather, gathering his children around him to read them a soothing bedtime story called the New Deal. He always spoke in a plain, friendly, reassuring voice that went far to calm the fears and anxieties of the forlorn and discouraged. In his first chat, he explained the banking crisis in simple terms but without condescension. "I want to take a few minutes to talk with the people of the United States about banking," he began. An estimated 20 million Americans listened. To hear the president speak warmly and conversationally—as though he were actually there in the living room—was riveting. An estimated 50,000 Americans wrote letters to FDR within days of his inaugural address. Millions more, many of them barely literate, would write to him and Eleanor over the next few years, thanking them for all they had done, or simply writing to them to air their troubles. Americans, regardless of party affiliation, began to hang portraits of FDR in their homes, often next to a picture of Jesus or the Madonna.

Urging bold experimentation for a devastated land, Roosevelt attracted a swarm of newcomers to Washington, a curiously mixed but effective group of advisers. For secretary of the treasury, he selected his close friend and Hyde Park neighbor, Henry Morgenthau, whose conscientiousness and loyalty made him indispensable to the president. For secretary of agriculture, the president appointed Henry Wallace, the son of Harding's secretary of agriculture. Another liberal Republican, Harold Ickes, became secretary of the interior and watched over his domain with a fierce jealousy and a scrupulous honesty. From his New York administration, FDR brought both the first woman to hold a cabinet post, Frances Perkins, to become secretary of labor, and the tough, dedicated administrator of relief, Harry Hopkins. All of these individuals served to the end of Roosevelt's presidency.

The administration also drew people who had never before influenced government policy: an obscure Montana professor named M.L. Wilson with a proposal for limiting agricultural production; Raymond Moley, Rexford G. Tugwell, and Adolf Berle of Columbia University, the "**Brain Trust**" of FDR's 1932 campaign, with ambitions to improve the economy's organization; and social workers with plans to aid the unemployed, disabled, and the aged. Together, this composition of human intelligence, vision, and a zeal for change composed the New Dealers. During Roosevelt's long tenure this term became part of the nation's everyday language—used with affection by some with hatred by others to express their strong feelings about FDR and his administration.

Behind the president's easy public style and gracious private manner lay a keen, calculating politically savvy mind that always sought to direct—control—people and events. He was never the benign father figure he made himself out to be. Behind closed doors, he could be arrogant, temperamental, and even harsh when dealing with individuals who dared question or criticize his ideas or policies. Always looking to expand the power of the presidency, as well as the Democratic Party, FDR often used the New Deal for those ends rather than for the nation's welfare. His public image was skillfully crafted. Compliant, if not intimidated, news photographers agreed not to show him in a wheelchair or struggling with the leg braces and cane he used to take even small steps.

The demands of his powerful office never ruffled Roosevelt. Reflecting his progressive background, FDR brought to the office a firm faith in the principles of his Uncle Teddy's New Nationalism. He wanted business to organize, industry by industry, and agriculture, set in motion tendencies that would long plague American politics: a shift in overwhelming power to the executive branch, and a steady expansion of the size and reach of federal bureaucracies.

The "Hundred Days"

Roosevelt's most pressing priority upon assuming office was to try to remedy the nation's banking system, which had collapsed by March 1933. By inauguration day several states already had closed their banks as accumulating panic spread from banks in the agrarian regions toward America's financial centers, principally in the cities of New York and Chicago. On March 4, 1933, Roosevelt's first action as president after taking the oath of office was to issue an executive order closing all remaining banks in the country for an indefinite period, declaring a national "Bank Holiday." Administration officials, congressmen, and representatives of the banking industry then met to quickly draft emergency legislation designed to help ailing financial institutions while bolstering public confidence in the banking system as a whole. Within 48 hours, the bank relief bill reached Congress, passed both houses, and

Harold Ickes was a serious-minded man with a reputation for absolute incorruptibility. Reporters dubbed him "Honest Harold."

commodity by commodity. He believed that an efficient labor, with rights protected by the federal government, not forced by unions, and private financial institutions working with industry and agriculture could restore prosperity. The government had only to assist them in regaining their strength and finding their proper places in the system. The new president selected equally orthodox or conservative men for the crucial administrative posts of the early New Deal: Hugh Johnson and Donald Richberg in business affairs; George Peek and Chester Davis in agriculture; Jesse Jones for the RFC; and Lewis Douglas for the Bureau of the Budget. All of these individuals were known conservatives. Some like Jones from Texas, notoriously so. Roosevelt never wanted to appear to be too far left, and thus with men like Jones in his cabinet, he was able to deflect much criticism from the right, which often accused him of trying to move the country toward socialism. FDR's conservative appointees' influence was more than checked by the imaginative, liberal appointees, among them Ben Cohen and Tom Corcoran, who set the long-term tone and direction of the New Deal.

To his credit, the president used his popularity and executive power to strengthen American democracy at a time when democracy was crumbling around the world. During his thirteen years in the White House, however, he

Harry Hopkins directed both the FERA and the WPA. He became so closely associated with FDR and the New Deal that reporters called him the "assistant president."

received the president's signature. Known as the Emergency Banking Act, the law authorized an extension of the bank holiday until expert teams of analysts investigated a particular bank's assets and liabilities. Those institutions found to be in sound financial shape received government approval to reopen immediately. Banks on the verge of collapse were closed forever, with any remaining assets used to pay off creditors. In this manner, the small, but significant number of institutions that had most damaged the reputation of the American banking system (and would soon be bankrupt anyway) were eliminated. A large number of banks that government agents considered stronger but savable became eligible for government aid in the form of low-interest loans from the RFC and government purchase of bank stock in order to quickly infuse the institutions with cash. Overall, the RFC initiated a transfusion of over a billion dollars into the banking system. Roosevelt then delivered over the radio the first of his Fireside Chats to the American public, in which he explained what the government was doing, why these actions were being undertaken, and to encourage citizens to return their money to the nation's banks where it would be safe and would aid the effort to generate national economic recovery. When banks reopened across the country, the reassured public returned money hidden in their mattresses to the banks, and as the level of deposits were greater than the amount of withdrawals, the panic subsided. It was an exemplary performance in the service of a free-enterprise system, and Wall Street joined Main Street in cheering the president. "In one week," journalist Walter Lippmann declared, "the nation, which had lost confidence in everything and everybody, has regained confidence in the government and itself."

Only after the financial crisis eased did President Roosevelt turn to the structural reform of banking. The Glass-Steagall Act (1933) separated commercial banking from investment banking. It also created the Federal Deposit Insurance Corporation (FDIC), which assured depositors that the government would guarantee up to $5,000 of their savings. The Securities Act (1933) and the Securities Exchange Act (1934) imposed long overdue regulation on the New York Stock Exchange, both by reining in buying on the margin (and other speculative practices) and by establishing the Securities and Exchange Commission to oversee the stock market's daily operation and enforce the new regulations and laws, as well as authority to investigate improprieties and punish the violators with fines, loss of licenses, and imprisonment if the infraction was especially egregious. The president wanted to ensure Americans that from this point on, the market would never crash again because of the activities of greedy speculators.

Roosevelt's treatment for the banking emergency and subsequent policies to regulate the stock market revealed the broad strategy of the New Deal's first months—**The Hundred Days**. Among the many popular prescriptions for halting an apparently endless economic decline, none appealed more to the president's spirit than a nationwide surge of activity that headed upward instead of downward. Mobilize confidence and synchronize energy, and prosperity would return because throughout the land people would suddenly behave as if it *were* returning. To a president who told Americans "that the only thing we have to fear is fear itself," that kind of grandiose bootstraps operation made perfect sense. As Roosevelt took office, he called Congress into special session, plied it with proposals, and during a whirlwind hundred days, guided through fifteen major laws, the greatest outburst of far-reaching legislative activity in United States history—and most of it emanating from the Oval Office, not Congress.

SAVING THE PEOPLE

Although a fiscal conservative at heart, Roosevelt understood the need to temper financial prudence with compassion. Congress responded swiftly in 1933 to the president's request to establish the **Federal Emergency Relief Administration (FERA)**, granting it $500 million for relief to the poor. To head it, he appointed a brash, young liberal reformer, Harry Hopkins, who disbursed $2 million during his first two hours on the job. True to his Roosevelt heritage, FDR was as much a conservationist as his beloved Uncle Teddy and was thus as interested in expanding the national park system and preserving the nation's natural beauty. The creation of the **Civilian Conservation Corps (CCC)** was a logical and natural compliment to this interest. FDR was also concerned about the rise in juvenile delinquency and crime, especially in the urban areas. What better way to do something about this problem than to transport the potential offenders hundreds if not thousands of miles (primarily to the Far West and Southwest) doing something not only constructive but also aesthetically pleasing and physically and spiritually fortifying. Functioning like an army boot camp, the program provided free room and board, as well as a paycheck. Enrollees received $30 per month, with $25 of the amount sent home to family members or deposited into a personal savings account. During its existence, the CCC employed 2.5 million young males, primarily in the 18-25 age bracket, planting trees, fighting forest fires, halting soil erosion, developing state and national parks, and otherwise improving and protecting the environment. The CCC became one of the most

Policemen reporting to depositors during a "run" in early 1933 that the bank was closed.

successful and popular of the New Deal work programs. African-American youth also benefited from the CCC, though racial prejudice impacted the agency's operations. Initially, the U.S. Army, which supervised the work camps, placed black enrollees in integrated camps throughout the country. When the director of the CCC, a Georgian named Robert Fechner, found out about the practice, however, he ordered the camps located in the South to be immediately segregated.

To help the unemployed survive the winter of 1933-34, FDR launched the **Civil Works Administration (CWA)**. This work program focused on providing jobs for working class or blue-collar Americans. For middle-class Americans threatened with the loss of their homes, he won congressional approval for the Home Owners' Loan Corporation to refinance mortgages. These direct subsidies to millions of jobless and home-owning Americans lent credibility to Roosevelt's claim that the New Deal would set the country on a new course.

The NRA and AAA

Two programs formed the heart of the early New Deal—the National Recovery Administration (NRA) and the Agricultural Adjustment Administration (AAA). During his first year in office, Roosevelt was confident that he could promote economic recovery, not from relief programs, but through industrial and agricultural cooperation. He regarded the **Agricultural Adjustment Act,** which created the Agricultural Adjustment Administration (AAA) in May 1933, and the **National Industrial Recovery Act (NIRA),** which created the National Recovery Administration (NRA) in June, to be the most important legislation of his Hundred Days. Both were based on the idea that curtailing production would trigger economic recovery. By creating scarcities in both agricultural and manufactured goods, Roosevelt's economists reasoned, they could restore the balance of normal market forces. FDR and his advisers believed that overproduction in both economic sectors had contributed to the depression. By artificially creating shortages, demand for goods would then exceed supply, prices would rise, and revenues from

These Civilian Conservation Corps boys are weeding pine seedlings at the Tennessee Valley Authority nursery, Wilson Dam, Alabama. The CCC planted over 80 million trees for soil conservation and flood control in the Tennessee Valley. June 1942

massive sales would climb. Farmers and industrialists, earning a profit once again, would increase their investment in new technology and hire more workers, and prosperity and full employment would be the final result.

The NIRA represented a continuation of Hoover-inspired government-sponsored business cooperation. Its most important provisions authorized each specialized segment of business to prepare a code of self-governance and established the NRA to supervise the process. FDR appointed the brash, loud World War I veteran, General Hugh Johnson, an experienced public affairs man, as director of the NRA, who immediately launched a campaign to enlist all Americans behind his program. Through parades—a massive one down New York City's Fifth Avenue—public rallies—staged an elaborate NRA celebration in Yankee Stadium— evangelical speeches, and assorted hoopla, Johnson made the Blue Eagle, the NRA's emblem of cooperation, synonymous with the New Deal itself. He counted on public opinion to make it correlative with Americanism. Blue eagles soon sprouted everywhere—on storefronts, at factory entrances, and on company stationery— usually accompanied by the slogan "We Do Our Part." Americans everywhere joined the campaign, and morale soared.

Johnson's first task was to persuade industrialists and businessmen, large and small, to raise employee wages to a minimum of 30 to 40 cents an hour and to limit employee hours to a maximum of 30 to 40 hours a week. The intent was to reduce the quantity of goods that any factory or business could produce. Next, Johnson brought together the largest producers in every manufacturing sector and asked them to prepare codes of fair competition. In the NRA's first four months, business groups wrote over seven hundred constitutions to govern their affairs. Where one or more large firms dominated an industry, the agency relied on them to prepare the codes; where no company controlled an industry, the NRA turned to a trade association. Although these blue codes varied from industry to industry, they usually included some agreement on prices, wages, and the acceptable limits of competition. The only integration among them was a common commitment to stabilization, a common freedom from antitrust prosecution, and a common dependence on the industrial groups themselves to regulate their own members. Johnson exalted the spirit of cooperation and swore at the slackers but never coerced businessmen into joining nor of having to adopt the blue codes. Johnson's policy of non-coercion was backed by his boss, FDR.

Section 7a of the NIRA authorized workers to organize and bargain in their own behalf, and some labor leaders, most notably John L. Lewis of the United Mine Workers, exulted that the government was now their sponsor. "THE PRESIDENT WANTS YOU TO JOIN THE UNION!" Although the NRA did not actually encourage an independent labor movement, it provided labor with other important benefits. It fostered a national pattern of maximum hours and minimum wages, and it eliminated child labor and the sweatshop.

In the summer and fall of 1933, the NRA codes drawn up for steel, textiles, coal mining, garment manufacture, rubber, and other industries seemed to be working. The economy picked up, and people began to hope that an end to the depression was near. However, in the winter and spring of 1934, economic indicators plunged downward once again, and manufacturers, blaming the NRA, began to evade the provisions of the codes. Also, contributing to the growing anti-NRA sentiment was the fact that from the program's beginning, small businesses felt left out of the grand plan and discriminated against because of their size. Moreover, small businesses could not adopt the minimum wage guarantees nor any of the other codes because they simply could not afford to do so. Their profit margins were already slight, and to have to pay a minimum wage to workers and other benefits, while simultaneously cutting back on production, was something they could not do without going out of business. Thus, by 1934, many small businessmen cried out against the NRA, asserting that it violated free enterprise and that the New Dealers responsible for it were conspiring to eliminate the small businessman altogether. Small businessmen believed that the real intent of the NRA was to consolidate industrial production, ensuring that in the future only a handful of major producers would supply the nation's manufactured goods. Though such was not the planned intent of the program, there was nonetheless sentiment in the White House among some New Dealers that the industrial sector would be better off if there was less competition.

Government committees set up to enforce the codes were powerless to punish violators. By the fall of 1934, it was clear that the NRA had failed. When the Supreme Court declared the agency's codes were unconstitutional in May 1935, FDR allowed the NRA to die. By then, New Dealers had given up on the idea that limiting production in the industrial sector would promote recovery.

The other cornerstone of the early New Deal was the Agricultural Adjustment Act. The fundamental objective of this program was to increase farm income by artificially creating shortages. By decreasing supply and increasing demand, it was hoped that farm income would rise to a level of parity, or equality, with the farmers' purchasing power just before World War I, the supposed golden years of farm production and income. The act was a grab bag of alternatives. It included provisions from almost every farm program proposed in the twentieth century: marketing agreements, commodity loans, export subsidies, government purchases, and even currency inflation. To these familiar devices, the government added the New Deal favorite of production restrictions, aimed at reducing agricultural surpluses at the source. During its first months of operation, the AAA used production cutbacks as a way of infusing emergency funds to the countryside. In the case of two agricultural commodities, desperate measures were employed. In mid-season, the government paid southern cotton farmers to plow under a portion of their already-growing crops. Meanwhile, government agents paid hog producers to slaughter six million baby pigs in order to boost pork prices by removing the piglets from the national market. Though this latter action provoked much criticism in a time of want, the government justified the move as a necessary expedient to remove the burdensome market glut. (Some of the meat eventually made it to canneries for distribution to aid families on relief.)

From the moment that the law was put into effect, the act aroused opposition from some farmers. Proud of their work ethic, many also did not readily believe that they would be compensated for producing fewer crops. Over time, however, the AAA garnered significant support from growers across the country, ultimately aiding millions of land owning family farmers and wealthy plantation owners. Nevertheless, the AAA made few provisions for southern sharecroppers, tenant farmers, and farm workers who were subsequently thrown out of work due to the reduced need for agricultural labor as a result of the agency's crop reduction policies. In the South, the victims were disproportionately black. A Georgia sharecropper wrote Harry Hopkins about his misery: "I have Bin farming all my life But the man I live with Has Turned me loose taking my mule [and] all my feed. . . . I can't get a Job so Some one said Rite you."

The AAA programs also proved inadequate to the plight of Great Plains farmers whose economic problems had been compounded by Mother Nature. Just as the depression rolled in, the rain stopped falling on the plains. The land, stripped of its native grasses by decades of excessive cultivation, dried up and turned to dust. And then the dust began to blow, sometimes traveling 1,000 miles across open prairie. Dust became a fixed feature of daily life on the plains, which soon became known as the **Dust Bowl**. The dust covered furniture, floors, and stoves, as well as penetrating people's hair and lungs. The worst dust storm occurred on April 14, 1935, when a great mass of dust, moving at speeds of 45 to 70 miles an hour, roared through Colorado, Kansas, and Oklahoma, blackening the sky, suffocating cattle, and dumping thousands of tons of topsoil and red clay on homes and streets. Despite government assistance via the Soil Conservation Service, which helped instruct Plains farmers with new cultivation techniques and subsidies, hundreds of thousands of dispossessed, desperate Plains farmers left the region, primarily migrating to California via the now famous Route 66. This exodus of humanity was the most significant and largest internal movement of citizens in the history of the nation. This "Okie" migration (They were called that because most, but not all, of these migrants came from Oklahoma.) made famous in John Steinbeck's *The*

Grapes of Wrath, disturbed many Americans, for whom the plight of these once-sturdy yeomen became a symbol of how much had gone wrong with the American dream.

The Supreme Court's ruling against the AAA forced the Roosevelt administration to work with Congress to find a quick replacement. Congress soon passed the Soil Conservation and Domestic Allotment Act (SCDAA). Under this law, signed by FDR on February 29, 1936, the government would continue to make payments to farmers (from the Federal Treasury rather than from processor taxes as the AAA had done), but for soil conservation practices rather than solely for production control. Growers would receive checks for diverting acreage formerly used to raise soil-depleting crops such as cotton to soil-building crops such as grasses and legumes, and for implementing approved soil conservation practices. The SCDAA proved to be an inadequate production control measure. In the case of cotton, drought conditions kept agricultural production low in 1936, but the return of good weather in 1937 coupled with the absence of planting restrictions led to a record southern cotton crop and the return of low prices. On February 16, 1938, Congress passed the Agricultural Adjustment Act of 1938. This law was the culmination of efforts undertaken to create a long-term price-support scheme for American farmers based on a combination of the administration's previous efforts: acreage restrictions, production quotas, conservation payments, and price-support loans. This system provided the basis for the federal government's agricultural programs for decades after World War II.

The use of subsidies, begun by the AAA, did eventually bring stability and prosperity to agriculture, but the costs were high. Agriculture became the most heavily subsidized sector of the nation's economy, and the Department of Agriculture grew into one of the government's largest bureaucracies. Rural poor, black and white, never received a fair share of federal benefits. Beginning in the 1940s and 1950s, they would be forced off the land and into the cities of the North and West.

REBUILDING THE NATION

In addition to establishing the NRA, the NIRA also launched the **Public Works Administration (PWA)**. The PWA was given a $3.3 billion budget to sponsor

Dust Storm approaching Spearman, Texas. April 14, 1935
Photo credit: FDR Presidential Library

internal improvements that would both refurbish and expand with new construction the nation's infrastructure of roads, bridges, sewage systems, hospitals, airports, and schools. The labor needed for these projects would shrink the relief rolls and reduce unemployment, especially among the industrial working class. The projects themselves could be justified in terms that conservatives approved: economic investment rather than short-term relief.

The PWA authorized the building of three major Western dams—The Grand Coulee, Boulder, and Bonneville—that opened up large stretches of Arizona, California, and Washington to industrial and agricultural development. It funded the construction of the Triborough Bridge in New York City and the 100-mile causeway linking Florida to Key West. PWA funds also paid for the construction of the Golden Gate Bridge in San Francisco."

The Tennessee Valley Authority

If there was one piece of legislation passed during the First New Deal that represented a strategy for economic recovery different from the one promoted by the NRA it was the **Tennessee Valley Authority Act** of 1933. Simply called the TVA, this particular approach called for the government—rather than private corporations—to directly foster economic development throughout the vast watershed area of the South known as the Tennessee Valley. This vast river basin winds through parts of six southern states and in the areas where these rivers flowed poverty was widespread because of the inhabitants' inability to control these rivers, especially during the rainy season. Flooding was endemic, and thus the towns and farms along the rivers were destroyed every year by the surging rivers. Thus the primary objective of the TVA was to control the flooding of the Tennessee River while simultaneously harnessing its water power to generate electricity, develop local industry (such as fertilizer production), improve river transportation, and, in the process, ease the poverty and isolation of the region's inhabitants. In some respects the TVA's mandate resembled that of the PWA, but the TVA had greater authority over economic development, which reflected the influence of New Dealers such as Rexford G. Tugwell, who were committed to statism: the creation of government-planned and government-operated enterprises. Although advisers such as Tugwell never publicly admitted so, they were drawn to certain socialist ideas such as public ownership of key industries and utilities.

The TVA's accomplishments were impressive. The program built, completed, or improved more than twenty dams, including the massive Wheeler Dam near Muscle Shoals in Alabama. Hydroelectric generators were also constructed at many of the dam sites, providing the region's population with electricity for the first time. The TVA became the nation's largest producer of electricity, and the low rates it provided consumers forced private utility companies to reduce their rates as well. The agency also constructed waterways to bypass unnavigable stretches of the river, reduced flooding, and taught farmers how to prevent soil erosion and use fertilizers. The project brought the Tennessee River Valley and its inhabitants into the twentieth century with a massive, government-planned and operated rural reclamation project.

Although the TVA was one of the New Deal's most touted successes and boldest experiments in government planning, it generated little enthusiasm for more ambitious programs in national planning. Only a handful of New Dealers wanted Roosevelt to nationalize established industries. Though it had never been done before, the TVA made it acceptable for the government to intervene to bring prosperity to an impoverished region. FDR, the majority of Congress, and the American people disapproved of any further extension of governmental power that such programs would necessitate. Contrary to what many conservative critics of the era asserted, and even after the depression was over, neither the president nor the New Deal embraced the idea of the federal government as a substitute for private enterprise. Nonetheless, when FDR wanted to sum up his proudest domestic achievement as president, he often cited the TVA. The significance of the TVA and similar projects can hardly be exaggerated. They were thought of as not mere public utility companies but as the pilot projects of a new and futuristic way of life. FDR and many of his supporters believed the TVA provided a model for a new kind of technological civilization superior to that of the early industrial era.

The region that underwent the most dramatic transformation thanks to New Deal development projects was the West. There, dam construction and other infrastructure ventures brought agrarian societies, which had been bypassed by the age of steam power, directly into the second industrial era of electricity and internal combustion engines in tractors, trucks, and cars. Between 1933 and 1939, per capital payments for public works projects, welfare, and federal loans in the Rocky Mountain and Pacific Coast states outstripped those of any other region. When Roosevelt assumed office, the United States, in many ways, was still two countries—an industrialized country, the Northeast, surrounded by a backward agrarian country in the South and West where there were hardly any factories and only a small urban, industrial working class. Roosevelt had to revive existing

The Public Works Administration funded the construction of more than 34,000 projects nationally, including this overseas highway in the Florida Keys.

industries in the Northeast and build them from nothing in the West and the South.

Central to Western development and inspired by the success of the TVA was the program of dam building that became one of the New Deal's most enduring legacies, especially in the West. For decades, Western land and agricultural capitalist developers wanted to dam the region's major rivers to provide water and electricity for urban and agricultural development. The costs, however, were prohibitive until the New Deal offered to help with federal dollars. Via the dispensing of funds through the Bureau of Reclamation, the bureau oversaw the building of the Boulder Dam (later renamed Hoover Dam), which brought drinking water for southern California, irrigation water for California's Imperial Valley, which eventually became the fruit and vegetable basket of the nation, and electricity for Los Angeles and southern Arizona. The greatest construction project of all was the Grand Coulee Dam on the Columbia River in Washington, which created a 150-mile long lake. Together with the Bonneville Dam (also on the Columbia), the Grand Coulee gave the Pacific Northwest the cheapest electricity in the nation and created the potential for significant economic and population growth. The Bonneville and Grand Coulee Dams made the state of Washington the largest per capita recipient of New Deal funds. The benefits of this dam building program, in terms of economic development and population growth, did not come to fruition until the post-World War II years. Dam building in the West was not seen as a threat to established capitalist businesses

President Franklin Roosevelt at the Grand Coulee Dam in Washington, October 2, 1937.
Photo credit: FDR Presidential Library.

because the government did not actually build the dams (as it did under the TVA) but rather hired private contractors to do the work, who became rich in the process. Western dam construction was meant to aid primarily agricultural development, and it was intended to aid private enterprise.

POPULIST OPPOSITION TO THE NEW DEAL

In their desire to rally popular support for such New Deal programs as the NRA, Roosevelt and the New Dealers unleashed new political forces that they would have to reckon with by 1935. Though opposition to the New Deal emerged from both the Right and the Left, initially it was a group of left-leaning dissidents who defied easy ideological classification, who posed the greatest threat to FDR and the New Dealers. The great fanfare created to boost popular support for key programs, such as the NRA, raised the people's expectations that recovery was on its way. Perhaps more important, it freed them from their torpor; the people now believed that if they came together en masse (which the NRA encouraged), they could effect significant changes, or at the very least their clamors for reform would be heard, and FDR and his Brain Trust would implement the desired policies. This politicized electorate also made it clear to the New Dealers that if they could not achieve economic recovery, in the name of *all* the people, then the people would turn to others who could. Early popular criticism of the New Deal was not directed at FDR but at his advisers and at the Democratic Congress. Still, the president worried that the breadth and depth of the insurgency threatened his political survival. However, once the president overcame his initial trepidation, his political instincts and shrewdness kicked in, and he was able to defeat these potential usurpers by embracing or co-opting many of their ideas. In the end, he had little to fear from these individuals, for the people, though attracted to these men's programs, were not going to forsake the man who already had delivered to them so much more than anyone in history had to date.

Some critics were disturbed not only by the New Deal's failure to bring recovery but also by what they perceived as the conservative orientation of many early New Deal programs. Banking reforms, the AAA, and the NRA, they asserted, all favored large economic interests, an assessment that was not unfounded or that inaccurate. In their opinion, FDR had failed in his promise to uplift the ordinary people, the "forgotten Americans," whom they claimed was their principal concern.

The Rise of the Demagogues: Huey Long and Father Charles Coughlin

Of the above individuals, the most alarming to the Roosevelt administration was the "Kingfish," Senator **Huey P. Long** of Louisiana. Long had risen to power in his home state by engaging in demagoguery: that is, by exploiting the fears, prejudices, and general feelings of alienation and hostility of middle and lower class Louisianans toward the conservative political oligarchy that controlled the state. This powerful coterie of bankers, oilmen, sugar planters, and utility company owners, primarily located in the southern part of the state, ruled Louisiana with an iron grip. Long's strident attacks on these interests won him the governorship in 1928, and from that office, he launched an all-out war on these individuals and their various enterprises. His purge of these men was so thorough and forceful that they were left with virtually no political power whatever. Many claimed that Long had become a dictator, which in effect, he had. He remained popular with the Louisiana electorate, however, in part because of his flamboyant, charismatic personality and captivating oratory, but also because he delivered the goods. He built roads, schools, and hospitals; revised the tax codes, distributed free textbooks; and lowered utility rates. To pay for his progressive programs, which he boasted were for the benefit of the common people, Long taxed wealthy Louisianans into the poor house. Barred by law from succeeding himself as governor, Long ran in 1930 for a seat in the United States Senate and won easily. He was now ready to take his ideas, first introduced in Louisiana, to Washington and to the American people in general.

U.S. Senator Huey Long was known as the political "Kingfish" of Louisiana.

Long supported Roosevelt for president in 1932, but broke with FDR within six months of the inauguration, believing that he broke his promise to deliver the American people from the plutocracy's continued abuse. In attacks on New Deal programs, Long alleged that "not a single dime of concentrated, bloated, pompous wealth, massed in the hands of a few people has been raked down to relieve the masses."

As an alternative to the New Deal, he advocated something he had introduced as governor: taxing the wealthy to force a redistribution of wealth "down to the people." He named his program the Share-Our-Wealth Plan. The government, he claimed, could end the depression easily by using the tax system to confiscate the surplus riches of the wealthiest men and women in the nation and distribute these surpluses to the rest of the population. That would, he claimed, allow the government to guarantee every family a minimum homestead of $5,000 and an annual income of $2,500. Long's mastery of the radio helped to create a membership in his Share-Our-Wealth Clubs of 10 million Americans, or so the senator claimed. Regardless of the accuracy of the number, Long's idea was popular with millions of unemployed, suffering, and disillusioned Americans, searching for a scapegoat for their woes. A majority of the clubs' rank and file came from middle-class people: independent proprietors who operated their own farms, businesses, and shops; self-employed doctors and lawyers; and plumbers, carpenters, electricians, and other contractors. Many members of these groups perceived the apparent big business favoritism of the New Deal programs as a direct threat to their future economic and social well-being. Substantial numbers of Share-Our-Wealth Club supporters also came from highly-skilled and white collar sections of the working class—railroad workers, bricklayers, postal workers, teachers, department store sales clerks, and others who aspired to a middle class income and status. By 1935, FDR considered the Kingfish to be the most likely challenger to his presidential reelection bid. Indeed, in the spring of 1935, a poll by the Democratic National Committee disclosed that Long's popularity might be enough to attract more than 10 percent of the vote if he ran as a third-party candidate, enough to tip a close election to the Republicans. But before that campaign began, Long was assassinated. In an act of revenge against Long on behalf of his wronged father-in-law (a judge redistricted out of a job), a young physician named Carl Weiss shot the governor on the night of September 8, 1935 as the governor left his office at the state capitol.

Meanwhile in the Midwest, **Father Charles Coughlin**, the "radio priest," delivered a message similar to Long's. At first a warm supporter of the president and the New Deal, which he called Christ's Deal, by 1934, Coughlin had become a harsh critic. In his weekly sermons broadcast nationally from his home parish in Royal Oak, Michigan, Coughlin proposed a series of monetary reforms—remonetization of silver, issuing of greenbacks, and nationalization of the banking system—that he insisted would restore prosperity and ensure economic justice. An estimated 30 to 40 million listened to his sermons. By late 1934, Coughlin had become disheartened by what the priest claimed was Roosevelt's failure to deal harshly with the money powers, which he contended were running the New Deal. Coughlin called for a strong government to set national priorities and force, if necessary, business, labor, agriculture, and even white-collar professionals to do its bidding to help recover the economy and usher in a more just capitalist system. In 1934, he founded the National Union of Social Justice (NUSJ) as a precursor to a political party that would challenge the Democrats in the 1936 election. By 1935, Coughlin began moving to the right, endorsing fascists like Benito Mussolini and his corporative state, as well as Il Duce's ruling by decree rather than by democratic consent, which he believed FDR should be doing as well "in the name of the people." As Coughlin's disillusionment with the New Deal intensified, his admiration for the fascist dictators grew more pronounced. Most disturbing and alarming was his increasing anti-Semitism, which permeated his radio talks. Reflecting his growing approval of Hitler and Mussolini, Coughlin claimed that Jewish bankers were the masterminds of a world conspiracy to suppress the toiling masses. Although Coughlin was a spellbinding speaker, he failed to build the NUSJ into a viable political entity. After the 1936 election, an embittered Coughlin moved further and further right, denouncing both Jews and democracy with incredible vehemence. His ravings became so extreme and vicious that many radio stations refused to air his program. Despite his fanaticism, millions of ordinary citizens continued to believe that the radio priest was their savior.

Another popular figure was **Francis Townsend**, an elderly California physician who claimed that the way to end the depression was to give every citizen over the age of sixty $200 a month, provided they retired (thus freeing jobs for younger, unemployed Americans) and spent the money in full (which would pump needed funds into the economy). By 1935, the Townsend Plan had attracted the support of more than 5 million older men and women. While the plan itself made little progress in Congress, the idea's popularity helped build support for the Social Security system, which Congress approved in 1935.

THE "SECOND DEAL"

The populist insurrections of 1934-35 forced a reluctant President Roosevelt to move to the left. Though personally and ideologically hesitant to move the New Deal down that path, the people had moved that way, and being the consummate politician, FDR knew that if he hoped to be reelected, he had to shift the New Deal in that direction as well. The president's rhetoric suddenly took on an anti-corporate tone. He called for the "abolition of evil holding companies," attacked the wealthy for their profligate and unpatriotic ways, and clamored for new programs to aid the poor and the downtrodden. He wanted to connect with the people and turn them away from radical solutions and, in the process, to win reelection. Thus, in the spring of 1935, Roosevelt launched the so-called Second New Deal.

The programs represented both a new focus and direction in New Deal policy. To help him develop programs reflecting this new direction, FDR turned to reform-minded businessmen, investment bankers, lawyers, economists, and labor leaders who embraced a new theory and advocated a new approach to hopefully ending the depression: underconsumptionism. Supporters of this idea believed that underconsumption, or an endemic weakness in consumer demand, had caused the Great Depression. Individual consumers simply had not had enough money during the twenties to buy what the nation's industries produced. Thus, the key to recovery was not to limit production as the First Deal had implemented but rather to increase Americans' purchasing power through a variety of government policies. These policies included government support for strong labor unions to force up wages; higher social welfare expenditures to put more money in the hands of the poor; and a significant increase in public works projects to increase the number of Americans working and thus earning and spending money. The underconsumptionists did not worry about a federal deficit that increased public works programs would create. The government could always borrow funds from private sources and, in fact, considered such an approach a crucial antidepression device. Those who received government assistance would have additional income to spend on consumer goods and producers would profit from increases in consumer spending. Government borrowing would increase the money supply or inflate a deflated economy and eventually would put an end to the depression.

This fiscal approach to economic downturns, which the depression in effect was, represented a reversal of traditional thinking that a government should always maintain a balanced budget. In the 1940s this new

Rural electrification in the San Joaquin Valley, California. November 1938

theory became known as Keynesianism, named after its originator, the British economist John Maynard Keynes. From 1935, the United States' economy became essentially Keynesian, that is, the government would henceforth do whatever was deemed necessary through various fiscal and monetary policies to revitalize a sluggish or depressed economy. Many politicians and economists rejected this new approach, believing that deficit spending would only create a debt-ridden government. FDR himself remained a fiscal conservative but was willing to give the new idea a try.

One of Roosevelt's first actions was his proposal to break up the great utility holding companies and spoke venomously of monopolistic control of their industry. At the time, thirteen utility companies controlled 75 percent of the nation's electric power. The Holding Company Act of 1935 was passed, but frantic lobbying by the utilities led to revisions that sharply limited its effects. A companion measure to the Holding Company Act was the law creating the **Rural Electrification Administration (REA)**, which oversaw the distribution of electricity at reasonable rates to hundreds of thousands of rural households. This New Deal agency was especially important to the South and West, largely rural regions where few inhabitants had electrical power. Indeed, the REA along with the Western dam projects were the cornerstones of Western modernization. Finally, Congress passed the Emergency Relief

NYA Project: Men working on metal bridge project in Texas, 1936
Photo credits: FDR Presidential Library

Appropriation Act, a $5 billion measure that dwarfed similar legislation passed during the first New Deal. FDR gave part of this sum to the PWA and CCC so those work-relief programs could continue while using another portion to create yet another work program, the National Youth Administration (NYA), which in Texas was directed by future president Lyndon Baines Johnson. The NYA had two main programs to offer American youth. The most well-known NYA program provided part-time jobs for high school and college students on their campuses, eventually employing two million young men and women to perform such jobs as landscape maintenance, library work, office work, and teacher assistance. The other, lesser-known NYA program, aided out-of-school youth through work programs that later served as the inspiration for the Job Corps (a Great Society program initiated during Johnson's presidency). Over two and a half million youths worked for wages and gained marketable skills learning a trade by training at established work centers and undertaking on-the-job training projects in the field.

FDR, however, directed most of the new relief money to a new agency, the **Works Progress Administration (WPA)**. This new work program was headed by the irrepressible Harry Hopkins, who was now referred to as "Minister of Relief." Though much of the WPA's money and focus continued or expanded infrastructure refurbishing and new construction, significant funds were funneled into an entirely new direction for the first time: the arts. Thanks largely to Eleanor Roosevelt, the WPA was largely responsible for not letting American cultural life die during the Great Depression. The agency funded a vast program of public art, supporting the work of thousands of painters, architects, writers, playwrights, actors, and intellectuals. Beyond extending relief to struggling artists, it fostered the creation of art that reflected and spoke of and to the values, customs, and lifestyles of ordinary Americans. All across the land, WPA artists adorned public buildings with colorful, story-telling murals, usually with a theme that showed how thanks to FDR and the New Deal, people were working and happy again. Photographers also traversed the nation, capturing with their cameras the suffering of hundreds of thousands of especially rural Americans. In many ways FDR used the WPA not only as a major work-relief program but also as a means of boosting morale. He also used the program to ensure, by the use of various artistic mediums, that future Americans would never forget how Depression-era Americans overcame the trauma of the second most severe crisis in the Republic's history, thanks largely to FDR and his New Deal. By the end of the 1930s, the WPA, in conjunction with an expanded RFC and the PWA, had brought about the building of 500,000 miles of roads, 100,000 bridges, 100,000 public buildings, and 600 airports. The New Deal transformed the nation's urban

and rural landscapes. Everywhere they turned, they found concrete examples of its accomplishments.

Equally alarming to the upper classes was the president's tax reform proposals, a program conservatives labeled as a soak-the-rich scheme, which, when compared to all previous taxation policies, it indeed did seem to discriminate against more affluent citizens. Politically, FDR's intention with his tax reform bill was to slow Huey Long's Share-Our-Wealth momentum, which it did by establishing the highest and most progressive peacetime tax rates in history. In retrospect, FDR's tax reform bill was put into effect not because he wanted to see a genuine redistribution of wealth, which he opposed, but rather for purely political reasons—he hoped to curtail the Kingfish's growing popularity by stealing his thunder. If Roosevelt could present to the people a more realistic and viable plan than Long, then, come 1936, the president could win back those wayward voters.

Without question, the most momentous piece of legislation to come out of the Second New Deal was the 1935 **Social Security Act**. From the beginning of the New Deal, important cabinet members such as Secretary of Labor, Frances Perkins, had been pressuring the president to create a system of federally sponsored social insurance for the elderly and the unemployed. FDR had consistently opposed such a measure until now. Like with his tax reform bill, he was responding politically rather than with any great conviction that such assistance was the right thing to do for such individuals. Regardless of his motivation, the Social Security Act laid the foundation of the modern welfare state. The legislation established several distinct programs. For the elderly, there were two types of assistance. Those who were presently destitute could receive up to $15 a month in federal aid. More important for the future, many Americans presently working were incorporated into a pension system, to which they and their employers would contribute by paying a payroll tax. This tax would provide them with an income upon retirement. Pension payments would not begin until 1942, and at that time, eligible persons would receive only $10 to $85 a month. Broad categories of workers (including domestic servants and agricultural laborers, occupations overwhelmingly dominated by African Americans and women) were excluded from the program. Nonetheless, the act was a crucial first step in building the nation's most important social net for the elderly.

Labor Resurgence

The emergence of a powerful trade union movement in the 1930s was one of the most important political and social developments of the decade. It occurred partly in response to government efforts to enhance the power of unions, but it was also a result of the increased militancy of American workers and their leaders. During the 1920s most workers rarely challenged their employers or demanded recognition of their unions. Moreover, shrewd employers such as Henry Ford, with their promotion of welfare capitalism in their industries, were able to greatly curtail the appeal of unionization among their workers. Also affecting unionization during the 1920s, especially among immigrant workers, was the trend toward Americanization at school, at work, and in popular entertainment, which not only made unions appear unnecessary but also anti-American at a time when working class ethnic Americans wanted to fit in and be accepted. The Depression, however, rapidly changed working class sentiment toward both unions and labor militancy, heightening the sense of awareness and shared experience among workers as few working-class families escaped the distress and despair of the early 1930s. The increased politicalization of the working class first became apparent in the 1932 election when many workers voted for Roosevelt. The NRA helped to transform their despair into hope. Moreover, clause 7(a) of the NIRA granted workers the right to join unions of their choosing and bound management to recognize unions and bargain with them in good faith. As a result, millions of workers, encouraged by such government promotion and protection, joined unions in 1933 and 1934.

Initially, union members' demands were quite modest. They wanted employers to observe the provisions of the NRA codes. They wanted to be treated fairly by their foremen, and they wanted management to recognize their unions. Few employers, however, were willing to give them any say in their working conditions. Most ignored the NRA's wage and hour guidelines. Workers appealed directly to FDR and Hugh Johnson for a redress of their grievances, but their pleas went unanswered. Workers decided to take matters into their own hands. In 1934, they staged 2,000 strikes across the country and in virtually every industry. Most of the walkouts attracted little attention and were peaceful. Some, however, were not, as they escalated into violent, bloody confrontations between workers and police. Such became the situation at the Electric Auto-Lite plant in Toledo, Ohio, in May 1934 when 10,000 surrounded the place and blocked all entrances and exits until the company agreed to shut down operations and negotiate a union contract. Management refused, called out the police to remove the striking workers, and the inevitable occurred. For seven bloody hours, a pitched battle raged between strikers and the police as the latter resorted to the use of fire hoses, tear gas, and gunfire to disperse the workers. Worker resistance, however, was more resilient than anticipated, forcing the governor to call out the National Guard, which succeeded in forcing the workers to disband but not until after more gunfire was exchanged and two workers lay dead. More violent and prolonged confrontations between police and striking workers occurred. From May through July 1934, National Guardsmen, police, and private security forces fought striking truck drivers and warehousemen in Minneapolis, leaving four dead and hundreds wounded. In San Francisco, striking longshoremen fought employers and police in street skirmishes throughout July, killing two and wounding scores of others. Employers there had hoped to break a two-month old strike with the use of force, but their attempt at intimidation only succeeded in gaining sympathy for the longshoremen, who were able to rally to their cause 100,000 additional workers in the transportation, construction, and service industries, who all walked off their jobs in a secondary supportive strike. As a result, for two weeks the city of San Francisco was virtually shut down. In the end, in both cities, politically astute municipal and state authorities intervened and eventually helped the workers win important concessions from employers.

These strikes and confrontations between workers and police paled in comparison to the largest and most violent strike of 1934, which began on September 1, 1934, when 400,000 textile laborers from Maine to Alabama, went on strike. Workers previously unwilling to unite because of ethnic and religious differences bonded together against a common foe: textile mill owners. New England Catholic Europeans joined with white Protestants from the Southeast to battle their respective employers. Both groups insisted that they were Americans first, bound together by class and national loyalties that transcended ethnic and religious identities. In the first two weeks of September, striking workers brought cotton production to a virtual standstill. Mill owners tried to bring in replacement workers and hired private security forces to protect them but that only caused greater anger among the workers and the result was violent confrontations between strikers and the police. In northern communities such as Saylesville and Woonsocket, Rhode Island, full-scale riots erupted, causing several deaths, hundreds of injuries, and millions of dollars in property damage. Similar encounters took place in the South, where local vigilante groups, claiming workers to be communists, sided with the police and National Guardsmen to beat up strikers, kill union organizers, and help to incarcerate hundreds of strikers in barbed wire camps.

The often brutal suppression of strikes and other labor protests made workers more determined than ever to organize and use such unity to combat management's obvious refusal to accept the right of their workers to join unions. For that purpose, in 1935, John L. Lewis of the United Mine Workers, Sidney Hillman of the Amalgamated Clothing workers, and the leaders of six other unions that had become alienated by the AFL's lack of support seceded from that organization and formed a new consortium called the Committee for Industrial Organization, later renamed the **Congress of Industrial Organizations (CIO)**. The new union's priority was to organize the millions of nonunion workers, regardless of skill level, gender, or race, into effective unions that would strengthen labor's political power. Hillman and Lewis made it clear that their new organization was pro-FDR and pro-New Deal and thus would vote *en masse* for the president and his party. Lewis and Hillman also pledged their union's financial support for FDR and pro-labor Democrats. Needless to say, Roosevelt was euphoric about such support, and by his next campaign labor had become part of the New Democratic coalition. The passage of the **Wagner Act** and the creation of the National Labor Relations Board (NLRB) in 1935 enhanced the labor movement's status and credibility. Because of the CIO's platform, labor union membership skyrocketed, and other union members began flexing their new muscles.

In late 1936, the United Auto Workers, a CIO affiliate, took on General Motors, considered by many the most powerful corporation in the world. Determined to improve wages and hours, as well as recognition of their union, workers in the Flint, Michigan plant took over the operation by employing a new tactic, the "sit-down strike," which saw workers simply, literally sit down at their job site and remain there until their grievances were redressed. For the first time in 50 years, a governor refused to call out the National Guard to end the strike. Frank Murphy, the governor of Michigan, wanted to avoid the violence and bloodshed he knew would ensue if he did and instead urged GM management to recognize the UAW and its right to collectively bargain on behalf of its workers. General Motors capitulated after a month of resistance. The CIO-UAW victory was followed up by another major triumph over a notorious anti-union corporation, United States Steel, which also announced that it too was ready to negotiate a contract with the CIO. The CIO successfully took on and won recognition and concessions from two of the most notorious anti-union corporations in the country.

As the CIO triumphed over big business, labor's stature in the nation grew along with its size. Many writers and artists, funded through the WPA, used their respective mediums to further popularize and establish the labor movement as America's first and best hope—the voice of the people and the embodiment of the nation's best and truest values—community, cooperation, and ethical individualism. Murals sprang up in post offices and other public buildings depicting blue-collar Americans at work, with faces reflecting a sense of pride and dignity as a result of their new status. Broadway's most celebrated play in 1935 was Clifford Odett's classic *Waiting For Lefty*, a raw drama about taxi drivers who confront their bosses and organize an honest union. Audiences were so inspired by the play that they often spontaneously joined in the final chorus of "Strike, Strike, Strike," the words that ended the play. *Pins and Needles*, a 1937 musical about the hopes and dreams of garment workers that was performed by actual members of the International Ladies Garment Workers Union (the play-within-the play, a new, Depression-era genre used by both Broadway and Hollywood during this time, especially in musical productions), became the longest-running play in Broadway history until *Oklahoma* broke its record of 1,108 performances in 1943.

Movies and novels also reflected the change of values brought forth by the labor movement. Both mediums celebrated the decency, honesty, and patriotism of ordinary Americans. In *Mr. Deeds Goes to Town* (1936) and *Mr. Smith Goes to Washington* (1939) director Frank Capra delighted audiences with stories of simple small-town heroes vanquishing the evil forces of wealth, corruption, decadence, and the abuse of power. Likewise, John Steinbeck's classic, *The Grapes of Wrath*, the best selling novel of 1939, told the story of an Oklahoma family's fortitude in surviving eviction from their land, migrating westward, and their exploitation in the promised land of California. In 1940, famed Hollywood westerns' director John Ford put Steinbeck's novel on the screen and made one of that year's most acclaimed pictures. Moviegoers found special meaning in the declaration of one of the story's main characters, Ma Joad: "We're the people, we go on." In themselves and in one another, Americans seemed to discover the resolve they needed to rebuild a culture that had surrendered its identity to corporations and businesses.

THE DEPRESSION, THE NEW DEAL, AND A CHANGE IN VALUES

Many New Deal liberals and intellectuals were harsh critics of what conservatives believed should dictate the marketplace—individualism, acquisitiveness, and egotistical behavior. These values informed the American political economy from the nation's founding through the 1920s. The Great Depression, however, destroyed much of the myth surrounding classical economic thought and its attendant values. As the 1930s progressed, Americans increasingly rejected those values and embraced instead the ideals of moral economics—the promotion of cooperation, justice, and compassion, especially a humanity inherent in a government's policies of protecting workers' rights and interests, as well as those of middle class consumers. Americans were torn by two opposing sets of values. Both were individualistic but one emphasized cooperation, the other competition. Worker organizations tended to promote cooperative individualism while businessmen were advocates of acquisitive individualism. Middle-class support of one or the other of these ideals was determined largely by historical and economic conditions. During times of relative prosperity, many in the middle class tried to emulate the upper classes and so adopted their values—the acquisitive ethic. During hard times, on the other hand, like the 1930s, many in the middle class identified with the working class cooperative ethos and looked to the government to rectify the economic and social inequities caused by the amoral marketplace—unfettered capitalism.

The Depression rapidly forced millions of Americans to rethink their devotion to traditional values, especially those associated with laissez-faire capitalism. The American Dream itself was questioned by many citizens. The economic collapse of the 1930s, at the very least, called for a readjustment in values. Searching for new values, some intellectuals found hope and inspiration in the idealization of peasant societies or regional agrarianism in the United States. More turned to the legacy of Marxist socialism or other manifestations of socialist thought. What 1930s intellectuals and common folk had in common was a search for a life of community and sharing as opposed to the acquisitive individualism of modern industrial capitalism.

The Rise of the Radical Third Parties

One of the most important repercussions of labor unrest was the emergence of left-leaning third party movements. In Wisconsin, for example, Philip La Follette, son of "Battling Bob" La Follette of Progressive-era fame, was elected governor in 1934 and 1936 as the candidate of the radical Wisconsin Progressive Party, which advocated, among other things, unemployment compensation and farm loans. Perhaps more disturbing to New Dealers was his anti-liberal rhetoric. La Follette publicly proclaimed in 1934 that "We [the Progressive party] are not liberal!" He further announced that "liberalism is nothing but a sort of milk-and-water tolerance.... I believe in a fundamental and basic change. I am a radical." La Follette believed there was "no alternative to conscious distribution of income," and thus in his opinion and that of his party, "this American principal of popular government, and the constitutions conceived to secure it, were not designed to sustain any particular economic system." Just what he had in mind as an alternative to capitalism, he never really articulated. Yet, his rhetoric found receptive ears in his home state as former Wisconsin Democrats and even some Republicans embraced La Follette's attack on New Deal liberalism and voted for his party rather than for Roosevelt's Democrats.

In Minnesota, the Farmer-Labor Party, a fusion of discontented farmers and urban laborers, rose to challenge and defeat Democratic New Dealers. Led by Governor Floyd Olson, who was elected in 1930, the party completely dominated state politics from that year until the end of the decade. The party's platform echoed that of Wisconsin's Progressive Party, with Olson using the same radical rhetoric of La Follette, declaring that capitalism was "on trial for its life," and that it was "steeped in the most dismal stupidity." Olson's relief agenda for his citizens far outstripped FDR's modest early approaches, with the governor threatening conservatives in the legislature that if they did not enact his relief bills he would declare martial law. Olson stated that those who opposed his measures "because they happen to possess considerable wealth will be brought in by the provost guard. They will be obliged to give up more than they are giving up now." He further announced that as long as he was governor there was "not going to be any misery in the state if I can humanly prevent it." "I hope," Olson told wildly cheering crowds, that "the present system of government goes right down to Hell." Like La Follette, Olson took great pride in being a radical, using that term constantly to describe his ideology and that of his party's. He proudly declared that he was a radical, not a liberal, because he wanted "definite change in the system. I am not satisfied with tinkering, I am not satisfied with hanging a laurel wreath upon burglars and thieves and pirates and calling them code authorities or something else." Olson went even so far as to intimate that he was a closet-socialist, when again, to a rousing ovation, he declared that "When the final clash comes between Americanism and fascism, we will find a so-called 'red' as the defender of democracy." As the rise to power of both La Follette and Olson indicated, the overwhelming majority of Minnesotans and Wisconsinites wanted more drastic change than the New Deal was producing.

The same message emanated from California in 1934-36. Instead of forming a third party, discontented Californians took over the Democratic Party. In the Golden State, former Socialist Party candidate and famous author Upton Sinclair led the anti-New Deal charge. In a book titled *I,* *Governor of California, And How I Ended Poverty: A True Story of the Future,* Sinclair outlined his plan. The novelist described how he would be nominated and elected, and how as governor he would create a production-for-use economy in the midst of capitalist California. Sinclair predicted that he would totally eliminate poverty in the state in less than four years. The central feature of Sinclair's End Poverty in California (EPIC) was the concept of production-for-use. The profit system, the writer argued, had produced itself into a depression. Under it, increased productivity was a curse because workers were not paid enough to buy what they made. This fact led to unemployment, idle factories and farms, and storehouses full of goods, especially food products people desperately needed but were destroyed while millions went hungry. To remedy this, Sinclair proposed that the state take over the idle land and factories and permit the unemployed to use the land and machines to provide for their needs. Sinclair also advocated the establishment of land colonies to produce food for the hungry and state-owned and operated factories to meet other needs. Sinclair's new socialism terrified California conservatives because it amounted to the old concept of a "moral economy of provision" as opposed to the political economy of the free market. Despite conservative opposition, which became vicious in its falsehoods and accusations labeling Sinclair an atheist (actually he was a Christian Democrat) and a free lover—he was a devoted husband—and of course a communist—the only thing Sinclair had in common with the communists was mutual animosity—his EPIC swept the Golden State like an old-fashioned Awakening. Come election time, the conservative coalition and its massive propaganda campaign against Sinclair, which included newsreels with Hollywood actors portraying **Okies** and people with putative Russian accents endorsing the novelist, was too much for EPIC to overcome. Sinclair was defeated by a closer-than-anticipated margin. Sinclair's defeat confirmed the leftward drift of American attitudes in another way. In order to win, the Republican Acting Governor, Frank Merriam, a borderline reactionary, felt constrained to speak favorably of the New Deal, calling for a thirty-hour workweek and endorsing the Townsend Revolving Pension Plan. Conservatives had to pose as progressives to have a chance of winning at this time. The American political structure as a whole had tilted definitely leftward.

Surprisingly, the American Communist Party (CP) at this time never became strong enough to pose a real political threat either in any of the states or nationally. In the early thirties, especially during Hoover's administration, the party had success in rallying to its platform homeless urban African Americans in the North, southern white and black sharecroppers, and Latino and Filipino agricultural workers in the West. The party mobilized those individuals into unions and unemployment leagues. The CP also played significant roles in the Minneapolis and San Francisco strikes. The party reached its zenith of membership (80,000 by 1938) when it stopped preaching world revolution in 1935 and, instead, began calling for a popular front of democratic forces against fascism. Despite its new popular front ideology, the party remained a dictatorial organization that took its orders from Moscow. Membership turnover was high, as many left the party after learning about its authoritarian character. Interestingly, the party's most important contribution to thirties politics was to channel popular discontent into unions and other political parties that, in turn, would force New Dealers to respond to the demands of the nation's dispossessed and forgotten.

The Election of 1936

Despite the thunder from the left and the anxiety it caused Roosevelt and the New Dealers, come election time, the president had little to fear from the populist insurgents. He was simply too shrewd a politician to allow an upstart, no matter how popular they or their rhetoric was, to unseat him. By moving the Second New Deal to the left, he not only silenced the populists, but also ensured both a victory for himself and his party. In his 1936 reelection campaign, he labeled the conservatives and corporate moguls and economic royalists who had "concentrated into their own hands an almost complete control over other people's property, other people's money, other people's labor—other people's lives." He called on citizens to strip the economic royalists of their power and "save a great and precious form of government for ourselves and the world." Voters responded by giving Roosevelt the greatest popular mandate in the history of American politics to that time. Roosevelt received 61 percent of the popular vote. His Republican challenger, Alf Landon of Kansas,—who even lost his own state—received only 36 percent. Only Maine and Vermont, with a combined total of 8 electoral votes, went for Landon.

Roosevelt's landslide represented not only overwhelming endorsement for the president and his New Deal but the beginning of Democratic/liberal ascendancy. From this moment forward, the Democratic Party became the party of reform and the party of the forgotten American. Perhaps more important for the Democratic Party's future, FDR began to assemble the various interest groups or coalition that would sustain the party and keep it the majority party for the next five decades. One of the party's key future blocs were African Americans, especially northern

Alf Landon, the Repubican nominee for the presidency in 1936, faces a battery of cameras when he arrived at the White House for a luncheon with President Roosevelt.

urban blacks who deserted the Republican Party en masse and voted Democrat. African Americans calculated that their interests would best be served by the "Party of the Common Man." Also, ethnic, working class Americans, especially those of Italian, Irish, and Jewish heritage, voted overwhelmingly Democratic. And finally, FDR did well among the Anglo-Saxon middle class, many of whom were grateful to him for pushing through the Social Security Act.

FDR's move to the left was politically motivated. Upon closer examination of the Second New Deal's legislation, many of the most important measures fell far short of their supposed intention of uplifting the downtrodden and the oppressed. For example, the Holding Company Act did little to break-up the big trusts, and Roosevelt's promise to deliver the nation's poor, like farm workers, were not covered by the Social Security Act or by the National Labor Relations Act. Consequently, thousands of southern black sharecroppers and Mexican-American farm workers in the Southwest were excluded from their protections and benefits.

Roosevelt's populist rhetoric also obscured the fact that many big business enterprises throughout the nation, but especially in the West, where corporations such as Kaiser of California and Brown and Root of Texas, enthusiastically supported the Second New Deal because it gave them such massive and lucrative infrastructure contracts to build dams and other projects. In the Midwest and East, FDR's corporate supporters included real estate developers, mass merchandisers (such as Bamberger's and Sears, Roebuck), and clothing manufacturers. All of these New Deal supporters were convinced that prosperity depended on high, stable levels of consumer spending and were thus willing to tolerate labor unions, welfare programs, and high levels of government spending. They had no intention, however, of surrendering either economic or political power. Though on the one hand the Democratic Party definitely became the party of the common people, on the other, it also became the party of big business. From one constituency came the votes; from the other came money to finance the campaigns.

Forgotten Americans

The New Deal was designed to ameliorate conditions for white middle and working class Americans. By the 1930s, this category included (because of their sheer numbers and potential political value) southern and eastern European ethnic groups—Italians, Slavs, Poles, and other previously discriminated groups from those European regions. By the 1930s, a very high percentage of individuals from these groups had been assimilated into mainstream WASP society, and, perhaps more important, they joined the Democratic Party. By the early 1930s, their potential political power was realized, especially in the urban North and West where no Democratic politician could afford to ignore them. FDR understood their importance, for he was a product of New York Democratic Party politics where such men as Al Smith and Robert Wagner had organized the ethnic vote even before 1920. Thus, after becoming president, he made sure that New Deal largesse—PWA and WPA infrastructure projects and other relief measures—found their way into the urban enclaves where these voters lived. As a result, Jewish Americans and Catholic Americans, especially those descended from southern and eastern European stock, voted for FDR in overwhelming numbers. Though Roosevelt and many of his WASP New Dealers were closet anti-Semites and anti-Catholic, they at least helped to promote the belief among these ethnic Americans that they were overcoming the stigma of their heritage and would someday soon no longer be considered second-class citizens.

More important to the rise in status and importance for southern and eastern Europeans was their strong working class presence. In many of the mass production industries in the Northeast, Midwest, and the West, they formed the majority of the workforce and made crucial contributions to the labor movement's rebirth, especially to the CIO's formation in 1935. FDR realized this early on in his presidency and accommodated their demands.

The New Deal, on the whole, paid little attention to the needs of African Americans and Mexican Americans. New Dealers believed that the issues of capitalism's viability, economic recovery, and the inequality of wealth and power in white society took precedence over the social problems of racial and ethnic discrimination. Few 1930s liberals were ready or willing to address these deep-seated social issues. Their priority remained saving American capitalism, and if along the way the quality and quantity of life for minorities could be improved then that was fine. Because they were disproportionately poor, most minority groups did not benefit from the populist and pro-labor New Deal reforms. In many ways, the New Deal did more to intensify racial discrimination than it did to ameliorate it. This was especially true for African Americans living in the South. Their northern counterparts, however, benefited somewhat from New Deal legislation, especially those blacks living in northern industrial centers. There, they joined unions, particularly the CIO, which welcomed them. Beginning in the 1936 presidential election, large numbers of northern blacks voted Democratic instead of Republican because they had received some attention from the New Deal. Yet, even in the North, in programs like the CWA, black workers received less pay than whites for doing the same work. In the South, blacks were barred from voting, often received few benefits from AAA programs, and denied federal protection from white reprisals when they tried to form their own farmer unions. Perhaps most unsettling was FDR's refusal to support anti-lynching legislation, a key objective of the decade's civil rights activists.

Not all New Dealers ignored the plight of African Americans. Particularly concerned for their welfare was the First Lady, who almost single-handedly did more to help blacks than any New Dealer, including her husband. Eleanor Roosevelt spoke out frequently against racial injustice. In 1939 she resigned from the Daughters of the American Revolution when the organization refused to allow black opera singer Marian Anderson to perform in its concert hall. With the support of another civil rights advocate, Secretary of the Interior Harold Ickes, Eleanor pressured her husband to sponsor the idea of permitting Anderson to sing from the steps of the Lincoln Memorial. On Easter Sunday, 1939, 75,000 people gathered at the memorial to hear Anderson sing while demonstrating their support for racial equality. FDR did not attend.

Though FDR succumbed to his wife's admonishments to appoint a few African Americans to second-level posts in his administration, he was never willing to make the fight for racial justice a priority—it was just too risky politically. He was not about to alienate white southern senators who controlled key congressional committees for the sake of even the most modest of civil rights proposals. Like the rest of his white cabinet, he believed that economic issues far outweighed in importance the racial ones. Roosevelt was the consummate politico who was always calculating potential political loss or gain. In his mind, support of civil rights legislation would be a definite political loss, not a gain, and thus only with the greatest of reservation would he expend any political capital on supporting even the most circumscribed civil rights bills. Unlike other groups, such as northern ethnics, African Americans at this time were not yet strong enough as an electoral constituency or as a reform movement to force the president to accede to their wishes.

Perhaps more adversely affected by the Depression years than African Americans were Mexicans and Mexican Americans. The plight of Hispanics was especially harsh in the Southwest, where at this time the majority lived. The most devastating manifestation of racial prejudice toward Mexican and Mexican Americans was repatriation, which actually began during the Hoover administration but was continued during the early New Deal years. Repatriation meant the returning of immigrants to their land of origin. As the depression worsened, and white Americans in certain regions looked for scapegoats for their woes, the Hoover administration in 1931 announced a plan for repatriating illegal aliens and giving their jobs to American (white) citizens. This policy focused on Mexican immigrants in the Southwest, especially those in California and Texas, the two western states with the largest Hispanic population at the time. Local governments in those two states were more than willing to enforce the law for they were eager to eliminate the minority poor from their relief rolls. Between 1929 and 1935, the federal government repatriated 82,000 Mexican immigrants in raids that occurred on businesses and homes. Those unable to prove his or her legal status with the necessary documentation were deported. California and Colorado authorities went even further than what was intended. Threatening to remove them from the relief rolls, California officials persuaded 12,000 unemployed Mexicans in the Los Angeles area to leave, offering them free railroad tickets to Mexico as a further inducement. Colorado authorities secured the departure of 20,000 Mexicans through similar techniques. Such a dragnet by federal, state, and local governments created a climate of fear within the Hispanic community and consequently 500,000 more returned to Mexico voluntarily. This total equaled the number of Mexicans who had come to the United States in the 1920s. Most revealing was the fact that in the ranks of the repatriated were a significant number of legal immigrants who were unable to produce their immigration papers, the American-born children of illegals, and, most egregious, thousands of Mexican Americans who had lived in the Southwest for generations.

Life grew more difficult for those immigrant Mexicans who stayed behind. Harassed by government officials, Mexicans everywhere sought to escape public attention and scrutiny. In Los Angeles, where their influence had been felt and accepted in the 1920s, they now retreated into the separate community of East Los Angeles. To many, they became the invisible minority. Mexican Americans did receive some benefit from the New Deal, especially from the program's pro-labor legislation. Those Chicanos living in urban areas and who worked in blue collar industries, such as in the cannery and garment sectors, joined CIO-affiliated unions in large numbers and won concessions from their employers. But most Chicanos lived in rural areas and thus were agricultural workers. The National Labor Relations Act did not protect their right to organize unions, while the Social Security Act excluded them from the new federal welfare system. The New Deal offered the rural Chicano majority virtually nothing.

The only group of truly forgotten Americans whose lives were significantly improved by New Deal liberalism were Native Americans. From the 1880s to the 1930s, the federal government had pursued a policy of removing Native Americans to reservations, and once they were confined there, they were neglected in hopes that they would all soon die off. By 1933 nearly half the Indians living on reservations whose land had been allotted were landless (They had been swindled out of their land by greedy white land speculators.) while those who still had their land were living in deserts or on land so marginal that no white person would want it. The shrinking land base in combination with a growing population intensified Native American power. Compounding this growing problem was the desire of assimilationists in the 1920s who put pressure on the Bureau of Indian Affairs (BIA) to outlaw all Indian religious ceremonies, to take Indian children from tribal communities and place them into federal boarding schools, and impose limits on the length of men's hair. This policy was finally redressed during FDR's presidency, especially by John Collier, whom the president appointed to run the BIA.

Collier was one of the few New Dealers who shared Eleanor Roosevelt's genuine humanitarianism. He was determined to improve the life of one of the nation's most forgotten citizens. No sooner was he in office than he pursued a policy of relentless pressuring of other New Deal agencies to include Native Americans. For example, a full Native American CCC was created, and Indians also were employed in numerous other agencies on projects

Indian Commissioner John Collier was determined to improve the lives of Native Americans. He pursued a policy of relentlessly pressuring other New Deal agencies to include Native Americans.

to improve reservation land, as well as to educate Native Americans in land conservation methods. Collier also exhorted Congress to pass the Pueblo Relief Act, which compensated the Pueblo Indians of Colorado for land taken from them in the 1920s. The 1934 Johnson-O'Malley Act was also passed, which gave federal money to states to provide for Indian health care, welfare, and education. Collier also pushed for the repeal of the once-mandatory federal boarding schools for Indian children and instead promoted their enrollment in local public schools. Perhaps one of his most important accomplishments was the allowing of Native Americans to once again practice their traditional religions. He also created the Indian Arts and Crafts Board, which promoted Indian artists and helped them to market their works.

The centerpiece of Collier's agenda was the **Indian Reorganization Act of 1934** (also known as the Wheeler-Howard Act). This act revoked the allotment provisions of the Dawes Act by restoring tribal lands and granting Indians the right to establish constitutions and bylaws for self-government. It also provided support for new tribal corporations that would regulate the use of communal lands and appropriate funds for the economic development of the reservation. This was a landmark act that ended the assimilationist policy pursued by previous administrations. The act recognized that Native American tribes possessed the right of self-determination and self-government, as well as the right to control their own cultural and economic well-being. It reflected Collier's commitment to what we would call today cultural pluralism, a doctrine which celebrates and accepts diversity in American society. Collier hoped that his policy of cultural pluralism would invigorate traditional Indian cultures and tribal societies and sustain both for generations. Cultural pluralism was not a popular idea in depression America, for too many white Americans believed it only caused greater division and the potential for racial or class warfare. Collier thus encountered opposition everywhere from Protestant missionaries and cultural conservatives who wanted to continue the assimilationist policy, from white farmers and businessmen who feared that the new legislation would protect Indian lands from their acquisition, and even from some Indian groups who had embraced assimilation.

One such tribe that believed the IRA was another white conspiracy against Native Americans was the Navajo, the nation's largest tribe, who voted to reject its terms. The Navajo and many other tribes rejected the IRA. Nevertheless, 181 tribes (nearly 70 percent of the total) supported Collier's agenda and organized new tribal arrangements under its auspices. Thanks to Collier and the BIA, many Native American tribes gained significant measures of freedom and autonomy. The New Deal, showed considerably more sensitivity to the needs and aspirations of Native Americans than had previous administrations. FDR's approval and support of Collier's reforms is interesting because there was no political gain to be had. Does that mean he was genuine in his concern and support for a truly neglected and oppressed people? Unlikely. Because Native Americans had been abused and oppressed for so long, and had become a truly invisible people, FDR probably saw little political harm if he came to their rescue. They would still remain a marginalized people, despite his help, and thus still forgotten.

The New Dealers

For the academics, policymakers, advisers, counselors, and bureaucrats who designed and administered the rapidly expanding programs and agencies of the New Deal, the years 1936-1938 were heady ones. Never before had the federal government employed so many individuals to carry forth its policies and programs. Fired by idealism and dedication, they were confident they could make the New Deal work. In the euphoria that set in after FDR's 1936 landslide victory, which the New Dealers interpreted as a popular mandate for their ideas, they devised countless schemes to expand the government's role especially in the nation's economic affairs. For example, the Farm Security Administration was created, an agency designed to help improve life for tenant farmers, sharecroppers, and farm laborers. In 1938, they drafted and got passed the Fair Labor Standards Act, which finally outlawed child labor, set minimum wages and maximum hours for adult workers, and put the federal government on its way to providing a home for all Americans by initiating low-cost housing projects in many urban areas.

Although the New Dealers proclaimed that all their efforts and ideas were for the people, in reality the New Dealers were members of a new technocratic elite that had little in common with the nation's plain folk. Few were genuine humanitarians determined like a Collier to uplift and protect the truly downtrodden and oppressed. Most were motivated by the prospect of building a strong state committed to prosperity and justice, but to order and stability. They delighted in the intellectual challenge and technical complexity of social policy. The majority of the New Dealers were well-educated, university graduates. Many were the progeny of some of the oldest, wealthiest, most prestigious families in America upon whom it had always been incumbent to serve the public. They were social conservatives at heart and by temperament, but they were willing to experiment with socioeconomic reform (or social engineering if such efforts could guarantee a more prosperous and stable society and economy).

Not all of the New Dealers had been raised among wealth and privilege. FDR was the first president since his cousin Teddy to welcome Jews and Catholics into his administration. Some became members of the president's inner circle of advisers, men such as Thomas "Tommy the Cork" Corcoran, Jim Farley, Ben Cohen, and Samuel Rosenman. These were men who had struggled from immigrant beginnings, but they were street smart, ambitious, politically savvy young men who brought to the Oval Office quick minds and mental toughness.

Though the New Deal offered opportunity to ethnics, a few blacks, Catholics, and Jews, such was not the case for women. The New Deal offered American females very little, especially when it came to the issues of greater economic opportunity, sexual freedom, and full equality. One reason why the issue of women's rights found few supporters was that the suffrage movement, after its 1920 triumph, had lost its momentum. Another was that prominent New Deal women, such as Frances Perkins, did not vigorously promote equal rights. They concentrated instead on protective legislation—laws that safeguarded female workers, who were thought to be more fragile than men. Those who insisted that women had special needs in the workplace could not easily argue that women were the equal of men. The most significant deterrent, however, to feminism was the general, pervasive male hostility that the depression only exacerbated. Men of all classes experienced a degree of emasculation during the Depression years because so many had lost their identity as the bread winner and provider for their families. For such men, being unemployed and then having to accept relief—the dole—unleashed feelings of inadequacy. The unemployment rates of men, especially among the ranks of blue-collar workers, tended to be higher than those of women, many of whom worked in white collar occupations, which were less vulnerable to job cutbacks. This fact only made unemployed men feel even more emasculated and useless. Resentment toward women, particularly those with jobs, intensified. The American male was not ready to accept the possibility that his wife or daughter could be a breadwinner.

This male anxiety had political and social consequences. Several states passed laws forbidding the hiring of married women. New Deal relief agencies were reluctant to authorize aid for unemployed women. The labor movement, even the CIO, made the protection of the male wage earner one of its principal goals. The Social Security pension system did not cover waitresses, domestic servants, and a host of other female-dominated occupations. Male fears of being emasculated and the venting of such anxiety became so intense during the 1930s that many artists, especially those involved in cartoon/comic strip production, started to project a strident masculinism in their work. Mighty Superman, the new comic-strip hero of 1938, reflected this male fretfulness. Superman was depicted as a working-class hero who, on several occasions, saved workers from mine explosions and other disasters caused by the greed and negligence of villainous capitalists. Superman's greatest vulnerability, besides kryptonite, was his fatal attraction to the sexy and aggressive working woman, Lois Lane. He was never able to resolve his dilemma by marrying Lois and making her a kept woman because the continuation of the comic strip demanded that Superman repeatedly be exposed to kryptonite and female danger. In other media, such as the movies, producers faced no such technical obstacles. Anxious men could go to the local motion picture theater and find comfort from the conclusions of such pictures as *Woman of the Year*, in which Spencer Tracy (in many ways the epitome of masculinity) persuades the ambitious Katherine Hepburn to exchange her successful newspaper career for the bliss of motherhood and domesticity. From a thousand different points, 1930s politics and culture made it clear that woman's proper place was in the home. Faced with such intense, sometimes virulent opposition to breaking the confines of domesticity, it is not surprising that female activists failed to make feminism a part of New Deal reform.

1930s Film

Just as some historians look at fiction to define a particular era's cultural history, others examine the movies to describe the "spirit of an age." Beginning with the silent motion picture era of the 1920s, the movies have visually reflected a variety of socio-cultural and political issues and topics, ranging from changing styles in clothing, habits, attitudes, and beliefs, as well as the expectations and the aspirations of the American people. We can even get some sense about ethnic and racial stereotypes and assumptions about gender and class via this most important medium of mass entertainment.

Motion pictures encompassed many varietal issues during the 1930s, a decade often considered to have been the "golden age of movies." During that time Hollywood cranked out on average about 500 motion pictures a year, ranging from films about gangster and cowboys to Marx Brothers and Laurel and Hardy comedies to historical romances to Busby Berkeley musical extravaganzas. The American public embraced them all, especially those movies that offered them a momentary escape from the misery and despair of the Great Depression. As one historian has asserted, "Not only did the movies amuse and entertain the nation through its most severe economic and social disorder, holding it together by their capacity to create unifying myths and dreams, but movie culture in the 1930s became a dominant culture for many Americans, providing new values and social ideals to replace shattered old traditions.

Many believe that the year 1934 marked the turning point for the movie industry. Like so many other businesses at that time, the movie industry suffered as well. By 1933, when the economy peaked at around 20 percent unemployment, which translated to about 25 percent of the American workforce out of a job, the effects of such a downturn reverberated throughout every form of mass entertainment. With little discretionary income in peoples' pockets, more than a third of the movie houses in the country shut down. Beginning in 1934, however, attendance began to rise, ushering in a revival that lasted until 1946. In 1934 the movie industry adopted its first manifestation of "self-censoring," agreeing to monitor what it revealed on the silver screen based on the "suggestions" of the Catholic Legion of Decency and other religious groups that had been lobbying Congress and pressuring Hollywood to forbid the production of movies that portrayed "sex perversion, interracial sex, abortion, incest, drugs and profanity." Even married couples could not be shown in the same bed. Although movies could depict immoral behavior, such "sin," of course, would be punished in the end. "Evil and good should never be confused," the code declared. Although modified from time to time, the code was not abandoned until 1966, when it was replaced by a rating system.

Prompting such a reaction and demand by 1930s moralists and their political supporters were the release of such controversial movies as the gangster classics **The Public Enemy** *(1931) and* **Scarface** *(1932), both of which for the time showed a considerable amount of violence. Musicals such as the* **Gold Diggers of 1933,** *which depicted scantily young women and pictures with main characters who were prostitutes, such as Jean Harlow in* **Red Dust** *(1932) and Marlene Dietrich in* **Blood Venus** *(1930), confronted the problems of real life in 1930s America. As the socio-economic climate improved with FDR and the New Deal, American movie-goers increasingly wanted to go to the theater and watch more positive, uplifting movies that promised a better tomorrow and in which good always triumphed over evil. Movie-goers also received a heavy dose of family moral values, patriotism, and the greatness of American democracy. Of course, sandwiched between the usual double-features were a cartoon or two, and a "newsreel" in which FDR and some sort of New Deal program was prominently depicted and praised. FDR and his Brain Trust knew full-well what a wonderful mode and source of propaganda Hollywood could provide for his presidency and his reform agenda.*

Two pictures in particular defined and articulated Hollywood's message to 1930s moviegoers: **It Happened One Night** *(1934), and* **Drums along the Mohawk** *(1939). Frank Capra, one of the decade's most prolific directors and propagators of many of the myths, master at entertaining without disturbing, directed* **It Happened One Night**, *starring two of the era's most popular actors, Clark Gable and Claudette Colbert. The picture was a comedy-romance in which a rich girl (played by Colbert) dives from her father's yacht off the coast of Florida, swims ashore, and takes a bus for New York. She meets a newspaper reporter (Gable), and together they have a series of madcap adventures and fall in love. But mix-ups and misunderstandings make it appear that she will marry her old boyfriend, a rich playboy. In the end, however, Gable and Colbert are reunited and marry in an elaborate outdoor ceremony. Of course, they live happily ever after. The movie is funny, clever, and witty in dialogue and entertaining. It also presented a variation on the poor-boy-marries-rich girl theme. Like so many movies of the time, this one suggested that a woman's life is not "fulfilled" until she finds the right man to marry.*

Stalemate, 1937-1940

By 1937-38, the New Deal began to lose momentum and popularity, especially among increasing numbers of middle-class Americans. Though initially supportive of the working class, labor's increasing militancy, exemplified by the CIO's rise to prominence, began alienating the middle class. After the UAW's victory over General Motors in 1937, other workers began imitating the successful tactics pioneered by the Flint, Michigan auto workers. The sit-down strike became widespread across the nation. Many middle-class Americans were becoming disturbed by labor's growing power and apparent radicalism. To many members of the middle class, Roosevelt had taken the New Deal too far to the left and they wanted him and the party to calm things down. This was the moment the right had been waiting for since 1936 to regain power. With the middle-class support waning for the New Deal, the right resurrected itself and began to aggressively assault both the president and his programs. Though the conservatives' criticisms found receptive ears, ultimately forcing FDR to move back to the center and curtail the more ambitious, left-leaning social reform programs of the New Deal, at really no time was the president ever in jeopardy of losing favor with the American people nor of being denied a third term.

The "Court Packing" Debacle

One year after receiving the greatest electoral landslide in American political history, the president committed one of the greatest political blunders of his career: his attempt to increase the size of the Supreme Court—"court packing," his critics derisively charged—by adding a new justice for each sitting justice who, having served at least ten years, did not resign or retire within six months after reaching the age of 70 (with a proviso that no more than six additional justices would be appointed). FDR's reason for his plan was that the current justices were too old and feeble to handle the large volume of cases coming before them. It became rapidly apparent to many Americans that it was not the justices who were feeble but that Roosevelt's excuse to expand the Court was feeble. In FDR's mind, for the New Deal to move forward, he had to find a way of removing the last obstacle to that end. He believed the most effective way was to propose the idea of simply adding more justices to the bench. Naturally, they would be liberals, and thus no further New Deal legislation would go the way of the NIRA, the Agricultural Adjustment Act, the Guffey Coal Act, and also some state laws—all shot down by a coalition of conservatives on the Court in 1935-36.

Much to Roosevelt's amazement, many Americans did not buy his arguments for judicial reform. Some perceived the move as a high-handed attempt to concentrate even greater power in the executive branch, removing the last check on the president's already immense control of the government. In the eyes of many Americans, Congress had become a rubber stamp for FDR's agenda. Members of the Senate, some of them quite old themselves, objected to the president bringing up the age issue. Southerners were especially aroused by the plan, for they read into it a conspiracy by Roosevelt and his Yankee New Deal liberals, led by "That Woman," Eleanor Roosevelt, to appoint liberal justices who would upset their region's racial order.

Throughout the nation, the Court packing crisis proved to be the beginning of the end of New Deal liberalism and the conservatives' ascendancy. The president's plan, conservatives maintained, proved that Roosevelt was dangerously power-hungry and that he aspired to be a dictator. The charges, though wildly exaggerated, resonated well with many Americans who were troubled by the advance of the European dictatorships.

FDR was stunned by the widespread opposition to his plan but kept fighting with a cadre of congressional supporters. Though Chief Justice Charles Evans Hughes had given congressional opponents some much-needed ammunition when he issued a letter refuting the president's reform claims, at the end of March 1937, Hughes and fellow conservative justice Owen Roberts broke away from the four reactionary justices on the Court to vote with three liberal justices to uphold a Washington state minimum wage law almost identical to a New York state minimum wage law that a majority had struck down as unconstitutional just six months earlier. Two weeks later, the same non-reactionary group produced a 5-4 majority to uphold the constitutionality of the Wagner Labor Relations Act.

This shocking course of events seemed to imply that Roosevelt's attempt at judicial reform had frightened Hughes and Roberts to switch their vote (famously referred to as the "switch in time that saved nine") in order to forestall the need for the president and his supporters to continue pressing FDR's scheme. Closer analysis, however, reveals a broader picture. Hughes and Roberts started to vote with the liberals in the minimum wage and Wagner Act cases is that while the decisions were not released to the general public until March and April 1937, the Court had actually voted on these cases in December 1936—a month after Roosevelt's landslide reelection and three months before the president surprised the Court, and the nation, with his court packing proposal. Thus, the extent of FDR's triumph, not reform proposal, jolted Hughes and Roberts into rethinking their opposition to the president's policies. As historian Michael Parrish has written: "Hughes and Roberts, both loyal Republicans who distrusted many of the New Deal's innovations, had played a high-stakes political game against the president in 1935-36. Voting with the Four Horsemen (as the Court's four reactionary, ultraconservative justices were often nicknamed) on crucial issues, they hoped to mobilize popular opposition against the administration by portraying it as dangerously radical, a threat to constitutional norms. When the voters rejected this interpretation and gave FDR an overwhelming mandate, the chief justice and Roberts had little choice but to temper their opposition, especially after February, when most observers predicted a quick presidential victory on the court-packing bill."

In the coming weeks, High Court approval of the Social Security Act (again, by a 5-4 majority) along with the retirement of reactionary justice Willis Van Devanter doomed the chances that the court-packing plan would survive. The final blow came when the bill's most energetic champion, Senator Robinson, suffered a heart attack and died. Nevertheless, while Roosevelt lost the political battle, most historians have concluded that he won the larger war. After 1937, the Hughes Court upheld the constitutionality of New Deal measures, and, as retirements occurred over the next six years, FDR would appoint nine vacancies to the Supreme Court.

FDR's once supposed passionate devotion to social welfare programs declined after 1937. This was not surprising when one remembers that he was never as committed to social reform or to championing organized labor. He was not a left-wing social Democrat. Pressured by leftists in his party and by populist demagogues like Huey Long, he reluctantly supported the 1935 Social Security Act on the condition that it be solvent and designed according to insurance principles. Nor was he as pro-union as his rhetoric led many to believe. He despised the dole for able-bodied citizens, preferring work programs like the CCC to welfare checks for non-workers. FDR was also a late convert to **Keynesian economic theory**, which only became the foundation of liberal political economy after his death. Most interesting, he resisted to the end leftist pressure to sponsor anti-lynching and civil rights laws, partly because he did not want to alienate southern white Democrats, but also because, unlike Eleanor, he shared the racial prejudices of most white Americans of his time—a fact illustrated by his support of Japanese-American internment during World War II.

THE RECESSION OF 1937-1938

Whatever hope Roosevelt may have had for a quick recovery from the court packing fiasco was dashed by a sharp recession that hit the country in late 1937 and 1938. Roosevelt had mostly himself to blame for the downturn. The expanded work program of the Second New Deal helped stimulate the economy to the degree that in 1937 production surpassed the highest level of 1929, and unemployment dropped to 14 percent. Confident the depression was easing, he made the mistake of cutting back on the federally sponsored work relief programs that sustained the supposed recovery. The Federal Reserve tightened credit, and new payroll taxes took $2 billion from wage earners' income to subsidize the Social Security pension fund. That withdrawal would not have hurt the economy had the money been returned to circulation as pensions for retirees. Instead, the money was held with no pensions scheduled to be paid until 1941. Once again, the economy lacked a sufficient money supply, and, once again, the stock market crashed. By October 1937, the market fell by almost 40 percent from its August high. By March 1938, the unemployment rate soared back to 20 percent.

The widespread distress resulting from the 1938 recession badly hurt Democrats in the 1938 mid-term elections. Republicans won a smashing victory, gaining 81 House seats and 8 seats in the Senate. The Congress that assembled in January 1939 was the most conservative of the New Deal years. Since all the Democratic losses had taken place in the North and West, particularly in such key states as Ohio and Pennsylvania, Southerners were now once again in a strong position, and they were in no mood to see any further extension of the welfare state. The House contained 169 non-southern Democrats, 93 southern Democrats, 169 Republicans, and 4 third-party Representatives. For the first time, the president could not form a majority without the help of Southerners and Republicans. Most observers agreed that the president could, at best, hope to consolidate but certainly not extend the New Deal.

By the end of 1938, it had become clear that any new ambitious goals faced an uncertain future. The New Deal had essentially come to an end as congressional opposition now made it difficult, if not impossible, for FDR to enact any major new programs. More important, perhaps, in ending the New Deal was the threat of world crisis, which hung heavy in the political atmosphere. Roosevelt was gradually growing more concerned with persuading a reluctant nation to prepare for war than with pursuing new avenues of reform. With such retrenchment at the national level, the way was now open for conservatives to mount an all-out attack on New Deal liberalism. Roosevelt would continue through the war years to say that the New Deal was not dead but on the back-burner. But everyone knew the New Deal had run its course.

NEW DEAL LEGACY

Elected in 1932, Franklin Roosevelt dominated the nation's history for the next thirteen years. He had few qualms about using the powers of the federal government to combat the Depression and reform society. Dire economic problems gave him unprecedented opportunities to redefine the federal government's relationship with the American people.

Americans' expectations created opportunities for FDR, but he faced serious constraints as well. Crisis or not, there were political and ideological limits on how much the president could change and how much he wanted to change. Many on the political left saw Roosevelt's election as a chance to reform society, to achieve social justice for all, and to restructure American capitalism to make it more human and responsive to the needs of the common people. But FDR had no intention of abandoning corporate capitalism or restructuring American society. Roosevelt's choices were thus shaped by public and political expectations and constraints as they intersected with the economic and social needs caused by the Depression. The result was the New Deal, a three-part barrage of legislation designed to bring about economic recovery, relief for Depression victims, and reforms to better regulate the economic sector. In the end, the New Deal did not end the Depression nor did it even provide adequate relief for the most destitute. The New Deal's legacy, however, saw the emergence of the federal government, especially the executive branch, as the most powerful and important level of government in the nation. Before the 1930s, people had looked to local, county, and state governments for help. After the New Deal, people looked to Washington for assistance, and government and politics were forever changed.

Thanks to the New Deal's extension of public relief to millions of Americans, we have come to accept the legitimacy of the welfare state. We recognize that many individuals in our society need such assistance to survive. In sharp contrast to progressivism, the reforms of the New Deal endured. Voters returned Roosevelt to office for an unprecedented third and fourth terms. And these same voters remained wedded for the next forty years to FDR's central idea: that a powerful state could enhance the pursuit of liberty and equality.

Chronology

1929 Herbert Hoover assumes the presidency.
Stock Market crashes on "Black Tuesday," October 29.

1930 Hawley-Smoot Tariff.

1931 2,000 U.S. banks fail.
Austrian bank failure triggers European depression.

1932 Unemployment rate reaches 25 percent.
Reconstruction Finance Corporation established.
Bonus Army marches on Washington.
Franklin D. Roosevelt defeats Hoover for presidency.

1933 Hundred Days legislation defines First New Deal.
Good Neighbor policy toward Latin America launched.
Reciprocal Trade Agreement lowers tariff.
"Bank Holiday."
Federal Emergency Relief Administration established.

1934 Charles Coughlin and Huey Long attack New Deal.
2,000 strikes staged across the nation.
Democrats overwhelm Republicans in off-year election.
Radical political movements emerge in Wisconsin, Minnesota, California, and Washington.
Indian Reorganization Act.

1935 Committee for Industrial Organization (CIO) founded.
Supreme Court declares NRA unconstitutional.
Second New Deal.
Social Security Act.
Wagner Act.
Holding Company Act.
Wealth Tax Act.
Emergency Relief Administration Act.
Rural Electrification Administration established.
Number of Mexican immigrants returning to Mexico reaches 500,000

1936 Franklin D. Roosevelt elected to a second term.
Supreme Court declares AAA unconstitutional.
Soil Conservation and Domestic Allotment Act.
Farm Security Administration established.

1937 United Auto Workers defeat General Motors in sit-down strike.
Roosevelt's court packing attempt defeated in the Senate.
Supreme Court upholds constitutionality of Social Security and National Labor Relations acts.
Economic recession slows recovery.

1938 Second Agricultural Adjustment Act.
Superman comic debuts.
Fair Labor Standards Act.
Administrative Reorganization Act.

1939 75,000 gather to hear black opera singer Marian Anderson perform at Lincoln Memorial.

1940 FDR reelected for unprecedented third term.

Review Questions

1. Assess the Hoover presidency and discuss why Hoover became a one-term president. What were Hoover's views regarding the government's role during a national economic crisis.

2. Describe Rooseveltian liberalism and how FDR's political and economic philosophy differed from that of Hoover, thus allowing FDR to more effectively deal with the Great Depression.

3. Discuss what you believe to be the most important New Deal programs and why.

4. As the New Deal unfolded and its various programs implemented, critics and opposition to such an unprecedented government intervention and assistance emerged. What were some of the opposition's arguments?

5. After the Great Depression and the New Deal, the relationship between the federal government and the American people would never be the same. Why?

Glossary of Important People and Concepts

Agricultural Adjustment Act
Bonus Army
"Brain Trust"
Civil Works Administration (CWA)
Civilian Conservation Corps (CCC)
Congress of Industrial Organizations (CIO)
Father Charles Coughlin
court packing plan
Dust Bowl
Federal Emergency Relief Administration (FERA)
"Fireside Chats"
The Hundred Days
Huey Long
Indian Reorganization Act of 1934
Keynesian economic theory
National Industrial Recovery Act (NIRA)
New Deal
"Okies"
Public Works Administration (PWA)
Rural Electrification Administration (REA)
Social Security Act (1935)
Tennessee Valley Authority (TVA)
Francis Townsend
Wagner Act
Works Progress Administration (WPA)

SUGGESTED READINGS

Anthony Badger, *The New Deal: The Depression Years* (1989).
Michael Bernstein, *The Great Depression: Delayed Recovery and Economic Change in America, 1929-1939*, (1987).
Alan Brinkley, *The End of Reform: New Deal Liberalism in Recession and War* (1995).
David Burner, *Herbert Hoover: A Public Life* (1979).
Lizabeth Cohen, *Making a New Deal: Industrial Workers in Chicago, 1919-1939* (1990).
Paul K. Conkin, *The New Deal* (1975).
Blanche Wiesen Cook, *Eleanor Roosevelt*, vol. 1 (1992).
Cletus E. Daniel, *Bitter Harvest: A History of California Farmworkers, 1870-1941* (1981).
Roger Daniels, *The Bonus March* (1971).
Michael Denning, *The Cultural Front: The Laboring of American Culture in the Twentieth Century* (1997).
Melvyn Dubofsky and Warren Van Tine, *John L. Lewis: A Biography* (1977).
Sidney Fine, *Sitdown: The General Motor's Strike of 1937-1937* (1967).
Steve Fraser and Gary Gerstle, eds. *The Rise and Fall of the New Deal Order, 1930-1980* (1989).
Frank Friedel, *Franklin D. Roosevelt: A Rendezvous With Destiny* (1990).
Colin Gordon, *New Deals: Business, Labor and Politics in America, 1920-1935* (1940).
Linda Gordon, *Pitted But Not Entitled: Single Mothers and the History of Welfare* (1994).
Ellis Hawley, *The New Deal and the Problem of Monopoly* (1967).
Dorothy Ray Healey and Maurice Isserman, *California Red: A Life in the American Communist Party* (1990).
Abraham Hoffman, *Unwanted Mexican Americans in the Great Depression: Repatriation Pressures, 1929-1939* (1974).
Herbert Hoover, *Memoirs: The Great Depression* (1952).
Irving Howe and Lewis Coser, *The American Communist Party, 1919-1957* (1957).
Barry D. Karl, *The Uneasy State, the United States from 1915-1945* (1983).
Lawrence C. Kelley, *The Assault on Assimilation:John Collier and the Origins of Indian Policy Reform* (1983).
Robin D.G. Kelley, *Hammer and Hoe: Alabama Communists During the Great Depression* 1990).
David Kennedy, *Freedom From Fear: The American People in Depression and War, 1929-1945*(1999).
Harvey Klehr, *The Heyday of American Communism: The Depression Decade* (1984).
Nelson Lichtenstein, *The Most Dangerous Man in Detroit: Walter Reuther and the Fate of American Labor* (1995).
Richard Lovitt, *The New Deal and the West* (1984).
William F. McDonald, *Federal Relief Administration and the Arts* (1968).
Robert S. McElvaine, *The Great Depression* (1984).
Barbara Melosh, *Engendering Culture: Manhood and Womanhood in New Deal Public Art and Theater* (1991).
Greg Mitchell, *The Campaign of the Century: Upton Sinclair's EPIC Race for Governor of California and the Birth of Media Politics* (1992).
Mark Naison, *Communists in Harlem During the Great Depression* (1990).
James T. Patterson, *The Struggle Against Poverty, 1900-1980* (1981).
Richard Pells, *Radical Visions and American Dreams: Culture and Social Thought in the Depression Years* (1973).
Albert V. Romasco, *The Poverty of Abundance: Hoover, the Nation, the Depression* (1965).
Vicki Ruiz, *Cannery Women/Cannery Lives: Mexican Women, Unionization, and the California Food Processing Industry, 1919-1950* (1987).
George J. Sanchez, *Becoming Mexican American: Ethnicity, Culture, and Identity in Chicano Los Angeles, 1900-1945* (1993).
Lois Scharf, *Eleanor Roosevelt: First Lady of American Liberalism* (1987).
Arthur M. Schlesinger Jr. *The Age of Roosevelt: The*
——— *Crisis of the Old Order* (1957).
———, *The Coming of the New Deal* (1958).
———, *The Politics of Upheaval* (1960).
Jordan Schwarz, *The New Dealers: Power Politics in the Age of Roosevelt*, (1993).
Harvard Sitkoff, *A New Deal for Blacks* (1978).
Graham D. Taylor, *The New Deal and American Indian Tribalism: The Administration of the Indian Reorganization Act, 1934-1935* (1980).
Studs Terkel, *Hard Times*.
Richard M. Vallely, *Radicalism in the States: The Minnesota Farmer Labor Party and the American Political Economy* (1989).
Geoffrey Ward, *Before the Trumpet: Young Franklin Roosevelt, 1882-1905* (1985).
Susan Ware, *Holding Their Own: American Women in the 1930s* (1982).
Harris G. Warren, *Herbert Hoover and the Great Depression* (1959).
T. H. Watkins, *The Great Depression: America in the 1930s* (1993).
Nancy J. Weiss, *Farewell to the Party of Lincoln: Black Politics in the Age of FDR* (1983).

USS ARIZONA

Chapter Twenty-five

Democracy, Fascism, and Communism at War, 1921-1945

Born into a large farm worker family in northern Mexico, three-year-old Macario García moved to Texas in 1923 with his parents and siblings. Together, they made a living by tending crops on a ranch near Houston. In late 1942, the U.S. Army drafted García, who became an infantryman in the Fourth Infantry Division. Wounded during the Normandy invasion, he recovered and rejoined his unit in time to participate in the final push against Germany. On November 27, 1944, he bravely distinguished himself in battle in western Germany when he singlehandedly assaulted two enemy machine-gun emplacements blocking his company's advance. Though wounded in the shoulder and foot, he crawled toward the machine-gun nests and destroyed the position with grenades, killing six German soldiers and capturing four others. President Harry S Truman personally awarded García the Medal of Honor at a White House ceremony on August 23, 1945. He also received the Purple Heart, the Bronze Star, and the Combat Infantryman's Badge. The government of Mexico later awarded García the Mérito Militar, the Mexican equivalent of the Medal of Honor. Receiving an honorable discharge from the army with the rank of sergeant, he returned to Texas with great fanfare as a war hero and was often asked to speak at meetings and banquets.

Despite his elevated status, García attracted media attention in September 1945 when the Anglo owner of a restaurant near Sugar Land, Texas outside of Houston refused to serve him because he was Hispanic. Upset with his treatment as a second-class citizen despite his military service, García quarreled with the proprietor. Local police arrested the veteran, who was subsequently charged with assault. García's case immediately became a symbolic rallying point for the Tejano community. Many groups, including the League of United Latin American Citizens, and individuals rallied to his aid by sponsoring fundraisers to pay for his defense. Well defended by two fine Tejano attorneys, García was acquitted by a local jury. In 1947, he became an American citizen.

Macario García's experiences were not uncommon for Hispanics and other minority groups before, during, and after World War II. Before the war, García worked hard despite his limited economic and social opportunities. The war provided an avenue for him to show loyalty to his adopted country and to contribute to America's ultimate victory. García's war experiences also changed the veteran, who became less tolerant of segregation and other indignities. As the United States emerged from World War II, the social forces unleashed by the conflict began to alter the country in significant ways.

THE WORLD DRIFTS TO WAR

The United States entered the years after the First World War inwardly confident but unsure of the future. During the 1920s the nation emerged as an active player on the world stage promoting global stability while expanding its economic reach. With the advent of the Great Depression and the rise of totalitarian regimes in Europe and Asia, however, the U.S. shied away from foreign diplomatic conflicts and focused on domestic matters in an effort to isolate itself from potential involvement in another great cataclysm. With the outbreak of renewed war, however, President Franklin Roosevelt led the United States into a fragile neutrality period that fell just short of open belligerency until the Japanese attack on Pearl Harbor in December 1941.

AMERICA AND THE WORLD DURING THE 1920S

Contrary to a commonly held perception, the United States did not stay aloof from international affairs during the first decade after World War I. In the 1920s, America became involved in foreign issues at an unprecedented level for peacetime. The nation flexed its economic muscles as it maintained a growing trading empire and worked with other countries to promote global stability, pursuing these efforts without military commitments or becoming involved in formal alliances. As historian Warren Cohen described American foreign policy during the decade, the nation's leaders sought to create an "empire without tears," benefiting from a predominant role in a stable postwar world without risking being drawn into another major conflict.

Emerging from the First World War as the world's wealthiest nation, American business and government leaders sought to leverage America's new economic power in an effort to supplant England's historic dominance over global investment and trade. Before World War I, the U.S. was a debtor nation, owing foreign investors close to $4 billion more than the amount lent by American investors abroad. By the war's end, however, reduced investment by foreign counties in the United States plus large loans by American banks to the Allied nations resulted in a reverse situation whereby the U.S. became a creditor nation with an almost $4 billion favorable balance. During the 1920s, Wall Street bankers greatly expanded financial investments to Europe, Canada, Latin America, Africa, and Asia. By 1929, the value of American exports tripled from pre-war levels, reaching over $7 billion.

Stabilizing the European Economy

European nations found it difficult to repay their American lenders after the war. The U.S. government's high tariffs on foreign goods, a consequence of legislation passed in 1922 and 1930 designed to reverse the previous reductions of the Wilson era, complicated Europe's financial problems. The victorious Allies sought to have much of their $10 billion debt to American bankers cancelled, but Woodrow Wilson refused to listen, as did the Republican presidents of the 1920s. Germany experienced great difficulty paying the burdensome war reparations dictated by the Versailles Treaty. After a German default in 1923, French and Belgian troops occupied the heavily industrial Ruhr region of western Germany to extract coal and steel resources while sending the message that non-payment was not an option. The Weimar Republic (Germany's new democratic government established after the war) responded by printing a vast amount of paper money, devaluing its currency, and producing a situation of grave hyper-inflation. The crisis stabilized only after the creation of an international commission headed by Chicago banker Charles G. Dawes, which formulated a plan calling for the flow of private capital (with a majority of the funds coming from American banks) to Germany in exchange for the removal of French and Belgian occupation forces and the resumption of German reparations payments. Approved by the Coolidge administration, the Dawes Plan established a system whereby American financiers made loans to Germany, which used the money to make reparations payments to the victorious Allies, who then began paying back their war loans to the United States (often to the same bankers making the original loans to Germany.) This triangular flow of capital brought financial stability but only as long as the Germans could secure American credit. In 1929, a new commission developed the Young Plan, calling for a sizeable reduction in reparations payments, but the Stock Market Crash and arrival of the Great Depression led American bankers to pull their loans to Germany with devastating economic and political consequences.

Toward the Good Neighbor Policy

The United States remained actively involved in Latin American affairs during the 1920s. While continuing to exert dominance in the region through the traditional means of trade, financial investment, and occasional military interventions, the U.S. also employed new efforts to extend good will. President Harding sought to improve relations with Latin America by recognizing the government of General Alvaro Obregón after the Mexican Revolution and encouraged the U.S. Senate to ratify a treaty authorizing a $25 million payment to Colombia as compensation for America's role in the Panamanian Revolution, which allowed the United States to receive the Panama Canal Zone. In 1924, President Coolidge withdrew marines from the Dominican Republic (under U.S. occupation since 1916), though American representatives remained to manage the revenues of the country and ensure payments of debts to U.S. banks. The American military also organized and trained Dominican forces to replace the departing American troops. (Their leader, General Rafael Trujillo, later overthrew the government and established a brutal thirty-year dictatorship). Coolidge also ordered the removal of American troops from Nicaragua in 1925, but he sent them back a year later when civil war broke out, and they remained until 1932. (The leader of U.S.-trained National Guard forces in Nicaragua, Anastasio Somoza, eventually centralized power under his control in 1936 and ruled by force for the next twenty years.)

President-elect Herbert Hoover signaled a further desire to seek a new relationship with the region when he embarked on a tour of ten Latin American nations in late-1928 and also reversed Woodrow Wilson's policy of not recognizing governments led by individuals who gained power by force. The U.S. government began to recognize any regime in control of its country as long as the new regime met its foreign debt obligations and promised to hold future elections. Hoover also approved public release of the Clark Memorandum, a policy statement written by an undersecretary of state that specifically repudiated the Roosevelt Corollary to the Monroe Doctrine, which had justified American military intervention in the Western Hemisphere.

Hoover's actions laid the groundwork for his successor, Franklin Delano Roosevelt (FDR), to pursue the more assertive **Good Neighbor Policy** during the 1930s. Seeking increased trade with Latin American nations in the midst of the Great Depression, as well as cooperation on mutual defense issues in light of the rise of totalitarian regimes in Europe and Asia, Roosevelt condemned America's past imperialist actions in Latin America. In 1933, Secretary of State Cordell Hull approved a resolution at the Pan-American Conference stating that no country had the right to intervene in the internal affairs of another. The next year, Hull signed an agreement with Cuba renouncing the Platt Amendment to Cuba's constitution, which had given the U.S. government the exclusive right to intervene in the island nation's affairs if its independence or internal order were threatened—a device by which America troops were twice sent to Cuba. In 1936, Roosevelt traveled to Buenos Aires, Argentina to open the Pan-American Conference with a speech reiterating his administration's desire to stay out of the internal affairs of Central and South American countries. By the end of that year, Roosevelt withdrew the last remaining U.S. troops from Latin American soil. The president's actions resulted in two major benefits to the United States by the end of the 1930s: a quadrupling of trade with Latin America and an increased desire by Western Hemispheric nations to join in a collective security alliance with the United States against potential aggression by Germany and Japan.

Active Global Diplomacy

After World War I, many Americans, including some influential members of Congress, became involved in a growing "peace movement," which sought proactive ways to prevent another horrendous modern war from befalling humanity. American leaders not participating in the movement also favored efforts to preserve global peace, believing that stability best served the interests of the country and its growing economic empire. The major manifestations of the 1920s peace movement were efforts to cooperate with the League of Nations, global armaments reduction, and the seeking of pledges from world governments to renounce war as an instrument of foreign policy.

Though American membership in the League of Nations was a dead issue after Warren Harding's election, the U.S. government still maintained contact with the League through correspondence and by sending diplomats to observe the global organization's meetings in Switzerland. American public opinion strongly supported United States membership in the World Court. Nevertheless, despite all three Republican presidents during the decade and a majority of Congress favoring American participation, the United States did not become a member of the World Court. Key opposition by Senators Henry Cabot Lodge and William Borah led to the Senate only approving the U.S. joining if the Court agreed to avoid addressing matters involving American interests. The Court's members refused the condition, and the United States never joined.

Through Secretary of State Charles Evans Hughes, the Harding administration took an active role in seeking to eliminate a postwar arms race, specifically focusing on the reduction of capital warships (battleships and carriers) held by the major world powers. A majority of Americans agreed with those in the peace movement who believed if nations had reduced armaments they would be less likely to engage in war. Hughes and other government leaders favored arms reductions for more nuanced reasons, specifically, cost savings from reduced defense budgets and significant limits on the naval growth of England and Japan. They also favored meeting with the world's powers to discuss ways to reduce ongoing tensions between them over China. Both Great Britain and Japan had been engaging in massive expenditures for naval construction and signaled a desire to engage in talks toward the goal of arms limitation if they could receive certain assurances that their security would still be protected.

In 1921, Harding invited eight powers to attend an arms limitation conference in the nation's capital. Secretary Hughes opened the **Washington Naval Conference** without obligatory diplomatic clichés expressing hope for success. Instead, he boldly expressed his desire to reach serious agreement on naval reductions and laid out a detailed plan calling for the destruction of specific ships currently in the navies of the invited nations. Over the course of the next several months, the conferees signed three major treaties. The first agreement, the Four-Power Treaty, accepted by the U.S., England, Japan, and France, allowed for a major arms reduction settlement by replacing the existing Anglo-Japanese defense alliance (greatly upsetting to American officials) with a pledge to respect each nation's island possessions in the Pacific. A Nine-Power Treaty, signed by delegates from the nations who agreed to the Four-Power Treaty plus Belgium, Italy, the Netherlands, Portugal, and China sought to reduce commercial rivalries in East Asia. Each nation agreed to adhere to the United States' coveted Open Door Policy in China, thus promising to respect China's territorial integrity while giving each foreign nation an equal opportunity for investment and trade rather than seeking to carve out monopoly privileges in certain regions of the country. The most important accord reached at the conference, however, was the Five-Power Treaty signed by the U.S., Great Britain, Japan, France, and Italy, which provided tonnage limits for each nation's battleships and aircraft carriers (at a ratio of 5:5:3:1.67:1.67 for the above nations, respectively) and a ten-year respite from further battleship construction. Though the agreement did not include smaller combat ships, such as cruisers, destroyers, and submarines, the deal temporarily slowed a growing arms race. Japan's government accepted a lower tonnage limit than England and the United States because it would remain the predominant naval force in the Western Pacific (the U.S. also sweetened the pot by agreeing not to build new Pacific bases or to further fortify Guam and the Philippines.) Meanwhile, the U.S. gained limits on England and Japan that ensured American predominance in Western Hemispheric waters and British leaders were satisfied that their navy would reign over the high seas everywhere else.

At the time, the Washington Conference seemed to be a significant achievement. Secretary Hughes and American diplomats had led the way to treaties that increased global security by reducing the size of fleets and came to agreement on divisive international issues such as the China trade. Despite the meeting's great promise, however, the deals all lacked tangible enforcement mechanisms beyond the goodwill of the participants. In the early 1930s, Japanese actions in East Asia soon led to the unraveling of all of the diplomats' hard work.

In the late 1920s, the United States also became a signatory of the **Kellogg-Briand Pact**, a diplomatic agreement seeking to outlaw war as an instrument of foreign policy. Salmon Levinson, a wealthy Chicago attorney with pacifist beliefs, first floated the notion of making the illegality of war a cornerstone of international law. Though the U.S. did not join the League of Nations, Levinson hoped that American involvement in a treaty with other countries pledging to resolve all differences through negotiations or arbitration might save the same purpose. Though Levinson's efforts were largely ignored by most who were not involved in the peace movement, French foreign minister Aristide Briand eventually seized upon the American lawyer's idea as a means to draw the United States within his country's security system. Extremely fearful of another conflict with Germany, Briand thought if he could sign a bilateral treaty with the United States renouncing war, the U.S. would be compelled to aid France if attacked by Germany in the future. In 1927, Briand announced his plans in a speech directed to the American public followed by a formal invitation to Calvin Coolidge's Secretary of State Frank Kellogg. Neither the president nor Kellogg was amused by Briand's tactics, which included coordinated help in generating publicity for the overture by scores of organizations associated with the peace movement. In the end, Briand's move backfired when Kellogg outmaneuvered him by calling on all nations of the world to sign a multilateral treaty renouncing war. Briand had no recourse but to accept the offer since the proposal was immensely popular with the peace groups. In August 1928, the United States, France, Great Britain, Japan, Italy, Belgium, Poland, and Czechoslovakia became the first nations to sign the pact outlawing war (with conditions allowing for self-defense), eventually followed by 54 other countries. Like the Washington Conference agreements, the Kellogg-Briand Pact lacked any enforcement provisions beyond the word of the signers and would eventually be ignored. Nevertheless, while providing a later moral and legal basis for resisting aggression in subsequent decades, the efforts on behalf of the Kellogg-Briand Pact demonstrate another example that the United States did not recede into isolationism during the 1920s.

THE RISE OF TOTALITARIANISM IN ASIA AND EUROPE

By the mid-1930s, the world witnessed the rise of dictatorships in Japan, Italy, and Germany—nations that held strong grievances after World War I whether they fought on the losing side (Germany) or contributed to the Central Powers' defeat (Japan and Italy). During the 1930s, the leaders of all three nations chose to pursue aggressive foreign policies with ultimately catastrophic results for their countries as they endeavored to undermine the efforts of the previous decade's peacemakers.

Japanese Militarism and the Takeover of Manchuria

By the turn of the twentieth century, Japan existed as the only industrializing nation in Asia. Its leaders, both civilian and military, sought access to the natural resources needed for industrialization that the island nation lacked, though they disagreed on how best to secure these resources. While both groups resented the continuing existence of American and European colonies in Asia, the military leaders who gained increasing control of the Japanese government throughout the 1920s and 1930s favored using force if necessary to acquire the materials that would enable Japan to become the dominant economic and military power in eastern Asia. The reduction of trade and high unemployment that followed the arrival of the Great Depression in Japan only further solidified the leaders' aggressive mindset.

In 1931, Japan became the first nation to abrogate the Nine-Power Treaty and the Kellogg-Briand Pact when its forces took over the loosely-governed Chinese province of **Manchuria**. Long invested commercially in the territory, Japan received half of its food and pig iron from Manchuria, which also served as an outlet for emigrants leaving their overpopulated home islands. Japanese leaders also viewed the region strategically as a vital buffer against Soviet expansion in eastern Asia. Increasingly concerned by Chinese Nationalist leader Chiang Kai-shek's assertion (Jiang Jièshí) of authority over the area, Japanese military leaders staged an incident to justify sending in troops to "restore order." Army units already stationed in the province to guard the Japanese-built South Manchuria Railway—a major thoroughfare from the resource-laden interior to ports on the southern coast—dynamited a section of the line then blamed renegade Chinese solders for the action. Japan soon converted Manchuria into a puppet state renamed "Manchukuo" under the control of Puyi, the last Manchu emperor of China who had been toppled after the Revolution of 1911. Though Secretary of State Henry Stimson strongly protested, President Herbert Hoover did not allow him to press American complaints beyond moral objections and a policy of non-recognition of the new regime, soon to be known as the "Stimson Doctrine." After members of the League of Nations followed suit, Japan formally withdrew from the global organization in 1933.

The Rise of Mussolini and the Invasion of Ethiopia

After World War I, Italy came under the domination of **Benito Mussolini**. A former Socialist Party editor and war veteran, Mussolini became the champion of the country's growing fascist movement—an extreme right-wing ideology characterized by ultra-nationalism, corporatism, militarism, rabid anticommunism, opposition to democracy, and submission to the state. He capitalized on the suffering postwar Italian economy and discontent with the relatively small amount of spoils that the country received from the Versailles Treaty. Demanding order and the restoration of Italian national pride, Mussolini led a march of tens of thousands of supporters on Rome in 1922 that turned into a political coup d'état when the king forced out the sitting prime minister and handed Mussolini the reins of power. Within a year, he received dictatorial powers by the national assembly and strengthened control over the country's economy, media outlets, and education system.

Mussolini advocated an expansionist foreign policy for Italy, seeking to create a modern Roman Empire. His initial efforts focused on East Africa where Italy already had a foothold in Somaliland and Eritrea on the eastern border of **Ethiopia** (which, with Liberia, was one of the last two African nations not under European control). In 1896, Italy had attempted to subjugate Ethiopia but suffered a humiliating military defeat at Adowa. Seeking to avenge that setback and finally bring Ethiopia under Italian control, Mussolini used a skirmish between Italian and Ethiopian forces along the Ethiopia-Somaliland border in late 1934 to justify an all-out attack in October 1935. When the emperor of Ethiopia, Haile Selassie, called for assistance from the League of Nations (of which Ethiopia was a member), he found Great Britain, France and the other major countries distracted by the global economic depression and unwilling to risk another major war. Instead, they filed official protests and enacted minor economic sanctions but fell short of embargoing oil shipments to Italy or taking further steps to force an Italian withdrawal. At one point, the British and French foreign ministers secretly proposed a partition of Ethiopia that was retracted after French journalists revealed the plan to the public. By mid-1936, Italian forces using planes, tanks, and chemical weapons completed their conquest against the outgunned Ethiopian resistance, forcing a dejected Selassie into exile. As historian Robert A. Divine has written: "Collective security, the Wilsonian formula for world peace, proved unworkable. No great power was willing to risk war to preserve peace."

Benito Mussolini

The Rise of the Nazis

In Germany, **Adolf Hitler** took notice of the League's impotence. An ethnic German born in Austria, the sociopathic Hitler became chancellor of Germany in 1933 after his fascist, anti-Semitic Nazi Party gained a plurality of seats in the Reichstag (the German Parliament). A small and insignificant fringe group for many years after World War I, the Nazis increasingly took advantage of popular discontent with the Weimar Republic's inability to stem the tide of massive unemployment and business failures caused by the Great Depression and fears generated by the growth of German communist groups. Like other German political parties, the Nazis gained adherents by denouncing the humiliating conditions of the Versailles Treaty, but their ideology and rhetoric went much further, espousing a sinister racism that guided much of their future actions. Touting the racial superiority of the German people, Hitler and other Nazi leaders demanded that all Germans in Europe reside under one government—a belief that justified annexing former German lands that had been taken away by the Versailles Treaty. Hitler also complained that postwar Germany was too small for its burgeoning population and needed to enlarge its borders, in order to survive. Thus, the Nazis justified expansion in the name of lebensraum, or "living space," for the German people, especially into the lands of Eastern Europe, which were currently held by racial inferiors. The Nazis also pushed a belief system that called for the elimination of all political and racial undesirables who might weaken their ideal German state. Hence, the later Nazi practice of establishing concentration camps and death camps for communists, Jews, and everyone else they despised. Their hatred of Jews, which was especially virulent, tapped into a longstanding prejudice in German society, making it easier for the Nazis to make scapegoats out of the Jewish people, blaming them for a myriad of problems in postwar Germany.

The Nazis gained more support as Hitler and other party leaders continually blamed the victorious Allied Powers from World War I, Jewish financiers, and communists for the country's ills and promised a restoration of national pride by establishing order, creating a bustling economy, and renouncing the Versailles Treaty. Within three years of assuming power, Hitler received dictatorial powers from the Reichstag, withdrew Germany from the League of Nations, began rebuilding the country's military, and sent troops into the demilitarized Rhineland along the border with France and Belgium with no ramifications.

Adolf Hitler

The Spanish Civil War

After the bloody three-year Spanish Civil War, Spain also witnessed the specter of fascism as right-wing rebels finally seized power in 1939. Eight years earlier, a combination of economic hardship caused by the Great Depression and ongoing popular resentment against a dictatorial general serving as prime minister led to the non-violent overthrow of King Alfonso XIII. A republic established to replace the monarchy brought to power many politicians whose liberal and anticlerical reforms appalled Spanish traditionalists. A new constitution called for the absence of religious involvement in government and educational affairs while allowing the possibility of the nationalization of many public services. Further, the new government allowed home rule for the province of Catalonia, upsetting those who believed that such action would lead to national disunity and the breakup of the Spanish state. In July 1936, after national elections won by left-leaning political parties were followed by a series of political assassinations and street fighting incidents conducted by extremists on both sides of the political spectrum, army units based in Spanish-held Morocco under the command of fascist General Francisco Franco revolted against the republican government. Though supported by monarchists, Catholic clergy and religious conservatives, large landowners, wealthy urban elites, and army troops based in several other regions of the country, Franco's move initially met with strong resistance from large segments of the population, especially the country's liberals, labor unions, socialists, and communists.

Both sides received foreign military aid. The rebels received generous support from Mussolini and Hitler who sought to test out new military equipment and tactics while currying favor with their ideological counterparts in Spain, possibly acquiring a valuable future ally if Franco could emerge victorious. The German "Condor Legion" consisting of air and ground forces directly aided Franco, beginning with twenty transport planes used to ferry Franco's forces from Morocco to southern Spain. German bombers also attacked Republican military positions and occasionally terrorized the civilian population (one such raid on a Spanish town inspired Pablo Picasso's famous painting *La Guernica*), as did Italian air forces based on the island of Majorca. For a time, Italian submarines sank Spanish loyalist ships in the Mediterranean Sea. Eventually over 50,000 Italian and 15,000 German troops entered Spain to equip, train and fight alongside the Spanish fascists. While the governments of England, France, the United States, and other major nations stood idly by in hopes of avoiding escalation into a major European war, the Soviet Union sent several hundred men and pilots along with money and military equipment to aid the Spanish loyalists. An additional 30,000 volunteers from other countries (including 3,000 Americans) formed various "international brigades" to fight for the republican cause.

Ultimately, the fascist forces gained the upper hand and drove the republicans from power. Though sympathetic to Germany and Italy, Franco never formally allied with Hitler or Mussolini, focusing instead on rebuilding the country and establishing a right-wing dictatorship that would control Spain until his death in 1975. Many conservatives hailed the general as the nation's savior who stamped out the forces of anti-clericalism, socialism, communism, and anarchism. For republicans and their allies outside of Spain, Franco's triumph was a victory for reactionary forces who favored the status quo that benefited the privileged classes at the expense of social reforms that would aid a broader spectrum of the population. For students of history, the Spanish Civil War represents a precursor of the much larger and bloodier European war yet to come.

AMERICAN ISOLATIONISM

During the 1930s, the United States turned inward and largely retreated from the global arena. Supporters of American **isolationism** believed that the rise of aggressive militarist regimes in Europe and Asia threatened world peace. Abstaining from involvement in the affairs of those continents might avert the United States being drawn into another bloody conflict matching or surpassing the carnage of the First World War. Not all Americans held this sentiment. Many internationalists believed it foolhardy to think that the U.S. had no stake in what took place in Europe or Asia, or that the nation could remain aloof from global affairs and be guaranteed that its security would not be endangered. Non-interventionists won the debates of the early-to-mid 1930s, however, because the Great Depression simply dominated the public's attention. As historian Robert Divine described the prevailing attitude: "Most Americans in the 1930s were neither isolationists nor internationalists. Rather than adhering to any dogmatic views of foreign policy, they simply ignored the world." Isolationist politicians in Congress tapped into this sentiment to drive American foreign policy during most of the 1930s until the outbreak of the Second World War caused many Americans to rethink their country's role as an innocent bystander.

The Neutrality Acts

Beyond the renewed threat of war, the 1930s spirit of noninvolvement had much to do with a reassessment of World War I. Popular novels such as Erich Maria Remarque's *All Quiet on the Western Front* fed into the public's growing repugnance to the glorification of war. Historians began to re-examine Woodrow Wilson's role in a negative light, blaming the president for policies that linked the United States inexorably closer to the Allies, making American involvement all but inevitable. Corporations also came under heavy fire for profiting heavily from the conflict. As calls rang out to investigate "the merchants of death," isolationists in Congress responded by probing the actions of businesses and their possible connection to U.S. entry into the war. Senator Gerald Nye of North Dakota headed a two-year special Senate committee investigation of armaments manufacturers, the shipbuilding industry, and investment bankers such as J.P. Morgan and Company. In addition to publicizing the huge profits reaped by bankers and munitions makers, the Nye Committee uncovered evidence of collusive bidding for government contracts and other nefarious practices but could never concretely substantiate the assertion that American businessmen used their power and influence to draw the country into the European war in order to garner huge profits.

The Nye Committee's findings led isolationist senators to sponsor neutrality legislation specifically designed to insulate the nation from repeating the steps that led the United States into the First World War. From 1935 to 1937, Congress passed three separate **Neutrality Acts** making the selling of arms or the issuance of loans to nations at war, regardless of circumstances, a criminal offense. American citizens could only legally trade non-military items to nations at war on a "cash and carry" basis, meaning without credit and only if the belligerents hauled away the items on non-American ships to avoid their potential sinking in a war zone leading to an international incident. Though President Franklin D. Roosevelt preferred language that would allow him to exercise discretion with regard to applying the legislation's terms, he reluctantly signed the Neutrality Acts into law. Understanding the prevailing political mood and needing the support of isolationist members of Congress to get key provisions of his New Deal program passed, FDR bowed to the pressure while reserving the idea of seeking revisions in the future. The president showed much more rigor in 1938 when he mobilized supporters in Congress to defeat the so-called Ludlow Amendment—a proposed constitutional amendment sponsored by an isolationist Indiana congressman that would have required a majority vote of the American people in a nationwide referendum before Congress could authorize U.S. involvement in any war.

THE COMING OF WORLD WAR II

Despite Roosevelt's dilemma of facing the threat to world peace posed by Germany, Italy, and Japan while isolationist sentiment remained strong in the United States, the president continued to speak out in an effort to influence public opinion. In October 1937, FDR gave his famous "Quarantine Speech" in Chicago in which he called on nations to rise up and contain the world's aggressors (which he refused to mention directly). Rather than issuing a specific plan of action, Roosevelt characteristically used a simple metaphor to make his point, describing war as a "contagion" and expressing his belief that the world must react to the "epidemic of world lawlessness" as the public would respond to a medical crisis: "When an epidemic of physical disease starts to spread, the community approves and joins in a quarantine of the patients in order to protect the health of the community against the spread of the disease." Though the isolationist press soundly criticized the address as unnecessarily provocative, a majority of editorials in American newspapers supported the president's stance and choice of words. Nevertheless, the western European democracies and the United States government continued to avoid taking a firm stand in the direct path of the aggressor nations.

The Japanese Invasion of China

In July 1937, the Japanese army took advantage of an ongoing civil war between Nationalist forces under Chiang Kai-shek and communist rebels led by Mao Zedong to commence an all-out invasion of China. Though civilian leaders in Japan had long sought to extract the wealth of China through diplomatic maneuverings and favorable trade deals, militarists within the government who assumed power by the mid-1930s determined to use force to exert their nation's dominance. The move into China culminated a series of recent actions by the Japanese government signaling the implementation of a more aggressive foreign policy. In the prior four years, Japanese leaders had withdrawn from the League of Nations, chose not to renew the Five-Power Treaty, and signed the Anti-Comintern Pact with Germany as a sign of mutual hostility against communism and to form the basis of a defensive alliance against the Soviet Union. Despite these moves, the American government was caught off guard as Japanese forces pressed deeply into northern China.

Upset at the unprovoked attack and believing that the neutrality legislation's provisions concerning arms and loan bans would favor Japan, President Roosevelt chose to use Japan's failure to formally declare war against China as a pretense for not applying the Neutrality Acts to the conflict.

As Japan's forces brutally dominated China's coastal regions and sacked its largest cities (killing an estimated 200,000 civilians in Nanking alone), Chiang and Mao declared a temporary cease fire and withdrew into the country's vast interior to wage a long fight against their common foe. Americans within China occasionally came under fire, most notably in December 1937 when overzealous Japanese pilots attacked the *Panay*, a U.S. Navy gunboat serving in a squadron stationed on the Yangtze River near Nanking to protect American nationals and oil tankers trading along the waterway. After a thirty-minute bombing and strafing run, the *Panay* and three nearby tankers sunk to the bottom of the Yangtze. The attack killed three American sailors and wounded forty-three others. Though U.S. State Department officials loudly protested, most Americans did not see the incident as the equivalent of the sinking of the *Maine* or the *Lusitania*. Many agreed with Senator William Borah's view that the incident was a regrettable consequence of the presence of Americans in a war zone. Japanese leaders quickly moved to resolve the matter by formally apologizing and agreeing to indemnify the United States government and families of the victims, though they continued to hold to the false assertion that the attack had been merely a case of mistaken identity. Though Americans soon forgot the *Panay* episode, they continued to sympathize with the Chinese as Japan solidified its hold over China. Nevertheless, the United States continued to supply Japan with oil, scrap iron, and other materials used for military purposes.

The High Water Mark of Appeasement: Austria and Czechoslovakia

In Europe, the people and governments of Great Britain and France feared the outbreak of another continent-wide war. Both countries assumed a defensive posture during the late-1930s by continuing a passive foreign policy while rearming their militaries. France spent considerably on its Maginot Line, a massive network of fixed fortifications along the French-German border stretching from Switzerland to Belgium, begun in 1930 as a deterrent to German aggression. In the two years since moving troops into the Rhineland, Adolf Hitler quietly rearmed the German war machine, aided Franco's forces in the Spanish Civil War, and formed an alliance with Italy (creating the Berlin-Rome "Axis") but did not make any belligerent moves for territory. This dormancy changed in early 1938 when Hitler began amassing troops on the Austrian border, demanding the union (or *anschluss*) of his homeland with Germany—something Austria's fascists (and some non-fascists) had been advocating for years. Not receiving support from England and France (or Italy, which had previously opposed Austro-German unification), Austrian chancellor Kurt Schuschnigg sought to avoid bloodshed by resigning and allowing the leader of the Austrian Nazis to replace him. Hitler soon received an invitation to send German troops into Austria. The next day, German storm troopers arrived, followed by Hitler himself who triumphantly returned to Vienna, the old Austrian capital where he lived as a young man before leaving to fight in the German army during World War I. Though forbidden by the Versailles Treaty, Germany soon formally annexed Austria with nary a protest from English and French leaders. The first phase of Hitler's expansionist agenda had succeeded.

Hitler soon made new territorial demands in Central Europe, this time upon the newly-formed nation of Czechoslovakia. In the Sudetenland, a mountainous region formerly part of Austria-Hungary that the Versailles agreement gave to the Czechs in order to create a militarily strong western border, the province's 3.5 million ethnic Germans (out of a total Sudeten population of 5 million) continually sought autonomy. Sudeten fascists went further, demanding annexation by Germany. Though Czech leaders reluctantly agreed to grant local autonomy, Hitler intervened and advocated the turnover of the entire province over to German control or face invasion. Shrouding himself under a veil of Wilsonian self-determination as a champion for the rights of a supposedly oppressed German minority, the dictator's real desire was to dismantle the rigid fortifications constructed in the mountain ranges along the border with Germany, which the large and well-equipped Czech army could use to severely hamper a potential attack.

Czech president Eduard Beneš appealed to France, which had a defense treaty with his country. The French government refused to act alone (nor did the Soviet Union, which had a conditional defense agreement with Czechoslovakia based on French action) but asked British Prime Minister Neville Chamberlain to intervene. In late-September 1938, Chamberlain traveled to Bavaria to meet personally with Hitler in order to resolve the crisis. Hitler continued to press for annexation of the Sudetenland, claiming its German majority were being grossly mistreated. Hoping to forestall war, Chamberlain accepted Hitler's demands in principle and informed the Czechs that they would eventually have to turn over the province to Germany as the price for peace. After Beneš reluctantly agreed to the conditions, Chamberlain relayed the Czech government's acceptance only to discover that Hitler now demanded the transfer of the Sudetenland to take place by October 1 or German troops would march.

French, British, and Czech public opinion bristled at Hitler's arrogance, while in the United States the mood soured as the specter of war appeared. Franklin Roosevelt then sent a message to Beneš, Hitler, Chamberlain, and President Edouard Daladier of France urging the leaders to meet and settle the matter peacefully. At no point, however, did Roosevelt suggest that he would personally take part in the proceedings. Hitler soon invited Chamberlain, Daladier, and Mussolini (but not Beneš) for a conference in Munich. When Roosevelt heard that Chamberlain accepted Hitler's invitation, the president sent a two word telegram to the prime minister: "Good man."

The **Munich Conference**, which took place from September 29-30, marked the high water mark for the failed efforts of the British and French governments to contain Hitler's ambitions through the policy of appeasement, or the continuous granting of concessions in the hope that violence would be averted. At Munich, Chamberlain agreed to German occupation of the Sudetenland by mid-October, but he truly believed that he scored a major diplomatic achievement in the form of a signed agreement by Hitler affirming that the dictator had no further territorial aspirations in Europe. Returning to London, the prime minister famously told a friendly crowd while holding the signed document that he had in his hand "peace in our time." Ultimately, the Munich Conference proved to be Hitler's greatest diplomatic victory because he had no intention of honoring the deal.

As German troops entered the Sudetenland, Hitler began to plan his next moves during the ensuing winter. On March 15, 1939, he largely expected to start the next major European war when he crassly ordered troops to invade Czechoslovakia. As German forces swept down from the Sudenland, the Czechs put up little resistance. The next day, Hitler proclaimed the creation of the Protectorates of Bohemia and Moravia out of the country's remaining Czech-majority western provinces. Fascists in the eastern Slovakian provinces soon proclaimed their independence and formed an alliance with Germany. To these actions, the shocked Chamberlain and Daladier filed formal diplomatic protests, ordered a quickened rearmament, and made pledges to Poland on Germany's eastern border regarding its territorial integrity—a German invasion of Poland would mean war with England and France.

The Nazi-Soviet Partition of Poland

Having basically torn up the Munich agreement with no ramifications, Hitler did not fear the British and French threats and prepared to attack Poland. The dictator did, however, feel unsure about the Soviet reaction to such a move. If England and France declared war against Germany, Hitler did not yet wish to become involved in a fight with the Russians (though he planned to attack the Soviet Union to acquire more lebensraum for Germany at a later date), so he sent diplomats to Moscow to negotiate an understanding over Polish territory. For his part, the Soviet leader Joseph Stalin wished to delay a war with Germany. Having seized power after the death of Vladimir Lenin, the ruthless Stalin spent much of the 1920s and 1930s creating a police state while expanding the country's industrial base and building up the Russian military. Ever fearful of being overthrown, the paranoid dictator added generals and other top army officers to his long list of real and imagined opponents that he ordered imprisoned or killed. Aware that his purge greatly weakened the leadership of his armed forces, Stalin proved willing to strike a deal with Hitler in order to buy more time. The announcement of the resulting **Nazi-Soviet Non-Aggression Pact** on August 20, 1939 shocked many throughout the world. The leaders of Fascist Germany and Communist Russia, two countries with polar opposite ideologies (though both controlled by dictators), publicly pledged mutual peace and promised neutrality if the other became engaged in a war with other nations. Privately, the two sides also agreed to divide Poland along stipulated boundaries—the Germans would occupy the western two-thirds of the country while the Russians would move into the eastern third.

WORLD WAR II BEGINS IN EUROPE

On September 1, 1939, German forces stormed into Poland. Though England and France could do nothing immediately to stop the onslaught, their governments carried out the threat to declare war on Germany. Stalin ordered Russian troops to occupy its prescribed zone, ostensibly to protect the western border of the Soviet Union. The valiant Polish resistance lasted three weeks. By the end of September, the Germans had captured the capital of Warsaw and dominated the western and central regions of the country. Meanwhile, Russian troops and secret police secured control of the eastern sector. Stalin ordered political leaders, army officers, and the Polish intelligentsia to be rounded up and imprisoned. The next year, he ordered over 20,000 to be executed, including

5,000 members of the officer corps in the Katyn Forest Massacre—an atrocity that the Nazis uncovered in 1943 and publicized for propaganda purposes.

Neutrality Revision

The outbreak of war in Europe led Franklin Roosevelt to immediately declare America's neutrality. Unlike Woodrow Wilson, Roosevelt did not ask the American people to be neutral in thought as well as action. In a fireside chat to the nation, the president stressed his desire to keep the United States at peace but stated clearly that neutrality did not necessarily mean impartiality. Seeking to aid the western allies and sensing public reaction shifting toward sympathy with England and France, the president soon called a special session of Congress to consider revision of the Neutrality Acts. The isolationists rallied in protest. While opposition congressmen organized a voting bloc, a flurry of celebrities from diverse backgrounds, such as the aviator **Charles Lindbergh**, Socialist Party leader Norman Thomas, and former President Herbert Hoover delivered mass appeals to pressure Congress to maintain the Neutrality Acts. Though still a potent force not to be ignored, the spirit of isolationism began to wane in the face of the Nazi juggernaut. Both houses of Congress passed a new Neutrality Act in early November 1939 that ended the arms embargo on nations at war provided that they adhered to the cash and carry system. Because the British navy could easily prevent any German merchant ships from traveling to the United States and returning with cargo, the revisions clearly benefited England and France.

The Fall of France

With the exception of the Soviet Union's costly but successful fight against neighboring Finland to secure territory around its vital port city of Leningrad, inactivity characterized the immediate winter months after the fall of Poland. This period of relative calm ceased in April 1940 when Germany began offensive operations in Western Europe by attacking Denmark and Norway. The following month, German ground troops supported by tanks and dive bombers employing new *blitzkrieg* ("lightning war") tactics emphasizing speed and concentrated power at the point of attack, sliced through the Netherlands and Belgium to press into northwestern France where they outflanked the Maginot Line defenders. Within a week, British forces sent to aid the French found themselves cut off and forced to retreat to the port city of Dunkirk along the English Channel. Miraculously, almost 340,000 British and French troops were able to evacuate via a combination of Royal Navy vessels and private craft, including fishing boats, yachts, and merchant ships. Italy entered the fight late by launching an attack on southern France in mid-June. Within six weeks, Nazi forces reached Paris—a goal that had eluded Germany in four years of fighting during World War I. The French government soon surrendered, leaving Germany in control of Western Europe. To conserve military resources, Hitler struck a deal with French leadership—German troops would occupy only the northern and western regions of the country while French fascist and reactionary collaborators led by 84-year old Philippe Pétain, the famed World War I marshal who defeated the Germans at Verdun, would establish a government in the south known as Vichy France (named after the city which served as its administrative center). The 100,000 exiled "Free French" forces based in England under the command of General Charles de Gaulle refused to recognize the legitimacy of Pétain's regime.

With his requests for a cease fire rebuffed by England's new Prime Minister, Winston Churchill, Hitler made plans for an invasion of the British Isles. The Royal Air Force and Royal Navy, however, stood in his way. The first phase of the attack, begun in mid-July 1940, involved an attempt to destroy England's air forces. To this end, German Luftwaffe (air force) commander Hermann Goering ordered daily sorties of bombers over England to hit military and industrial targets. This action would draw out British fighter planes, which he hoped to eliminate with escorting fighter squadrons. For the next four months, the **Battle of Britain** raged in the British skies. During the fight, German bombers struck airfields, port installations, and factories, but also deliberated targeted cities, especially London. While both sides suffered tremendous losses, the British began to seize the upper hand. Helped out by the new technology of radar, ground technicians tracked the arrival of raiding planes, allowing scrambling pilots to concentrate their defenses with maximum efficiency. Eventually, Hitler called off the air assault, not wishing to lose most of his air forces in a grinding battle of attrition. Confident that he neutralized England, the dictator chose to conserve his air forces for his planned invasion of the Soviet Union. That offensive, codenamed "Operation Barbarossa," would be Hitler's boldest move yet as he carried out the Nazi desire for lebensraum. The breaking of the Non-Aggression Pact with Stalin, however, also proved to be the beginning of his downfall.

THE AMERICAN REACTION TO WAR

The swiftness of France's defeat and the ferocity of Germany's subsequent air attacks on English cities during the Battle of Britain generated much fear and anxiety in the United States. Hitler's rapid victories meant that Americans could not simply rely on the latest round of European fighting to become the long grueling stalemate that occurred during World War I. Congress soon voted for a five-fold increase in the 1940 military budget (from $2 billion to over $10 billion), producing a tremendous increase in defense-related jobs that largely ended the Great Depression by early 1941. In September 1940, Congress approved FDR's request for the nation's first-ever peacetime draft. Noting the shift in American public opinion concerning the situation in Europe, Roosevelt became bolder in issuing executive decisions. Following a request for additional aid from Winston Churchill, the president authorized the transfer of fifty aging destroyers to England in order to be outfitted with modern equipment to help the British navy fight off German U-Boats. In exchange for these submarine hunters, the United States would take over British air and naval bases in the Western Hemisphere from Newfoundland to the West Indies. Though beneficial to American defense, the destroyers-for-bases deal was yet another move clearly designed to benefit Germany's enemies.

Roosevelt vs. Lindbergh

The president's actions led the nation's isolationists to launch a desperate counterattack. Through the America First Committee, anti-interventionists condemned Roosevelt and his supporters for policies they believed would needlessly draw the country into another European bloodbath. If the United States focused inwardly on national defense to create a "Fortress America" instead, committeemen argued, the U.S. would have nothing to fear from events occurring in Europe. Prominent internationalist opponents of the isolationist position formed the Committee to Defend America by Aiding the Allies under Kansas newspaperman William Allen White in order to influence public opinion toward all-out aid to England short of military intervention, believing such a policy would provide the best means to protect the United States from potential German aggression. By supplying the British with war material and other forms of vital aid, White's organization argued, the United States could contribute to Hitler's defeat without sending American soldiers to fight.

The famed aviator Charles Lindbergh emerged as America First's leading spokesman. Sharing the isolationist sentiments of his father (a Minnesota congressman who voted against U.S. entry into World War I), Lindbergh also feared that war would open the door for communist expansion in Europe. Unlike most isolationists, however,

Charles Lindbergh

the celebrity pilot publicly admired the Nazis for their technical prowess (especially with airplanes) and held blatantly anti-Semitic views. After Lindbergh began to make a series of highly publicized speeches promoting appeasement and openly criticizing Roosevelt, the administration hit back. The president accused Lindbergh of being no different than Clement Vallandigham, a northern Democratic "Copperhead" congressman who sympathized with the Confederacy during the Civil War. Secretary of the Interior Harold Ickes openly mocked Lindbergh as a "Knight of the German Eagle" because the pilot had once accepted a Nazi decoration during a 1938 visit to Germany. Angrily resigning his commission in the Army Air Corps in protest, Lindbergh continued to speak his mind. Refusing the requests of other isolationists to mix in condemnations of fascism and to express sympathy for Great Britain in his speeches, Lindbergh's criticism of his opponents' viewpoints only became more intense, culminating in a controversial speech at a September 11, 1941 American First rally held in Des Moines, Iowa. Titled "Who Are the War Agitators?" the pilot's address laid the blame for America inching toward war with Germany and Italy squarely at the foot of a conspiracy concocted by the British, the Roosevelt Administration, and Jewish interest groups. Widespread criticism followed, with some sharp venom coming from isolationist and anti-Roosevelt circles who believed the aviator had gone too far. Norman Thomas soon quit the organization, which became increasingly discredited in the public eye.

The Election of 1940

The war in Europe loomed heavily over the political landscape in the 1940 presidential race. Not wishing to hand the reins of government to a new leader in a time of global crisis (especially when that leader could have been a Republican), Franklin Roosevelt decided to seek an unprecedented third term. Isolationists who pinned their hopes on like-minded politicians such as Senator Robert Taft of Ohio or Senator Arthur Vandenberg of Michigan were gravely disappointed when Republicans nominated utility company executive Wendell Willkie of Indiana. Though an ardent opponent of New Deal business regulations, Willkie supported the president's policy of aiding England and endorsed both the destroyers-for-bases deal and the peacetime draft. Despite favoring aid to Britain, both Roosevelt and Willkie relentlessly sought to reassure voters that they favored staying militarily out of the European conflict. Near the end of the campaign, Willkie began to openly question Roosevelt's commitment to remain out of the war. The president responded in a speech delivered in Boston by famously declaring: "Your boys are not going to be sent into any foreign wars." When an adviser pointed out before the address that the statement might be misleading because it left out the possibility of America retaliating if directly attacked, Roosevelt replied: "Of course we'll fight if attacked. If somebody attacks us, then it isn't a foreign war is it?" Ultimately, with both candidates supporting aid to England while keeping American troops at home, a majority of voters chose the more popular and experienced leader, not wishing to change horses midstream. Though the energetic Willkie outperformed previous Roosevelt opponents, the president made American electoral history by securing his third term with a solid reaffirmation by the electorate, winning by a 27,307,819 (54.8 percent) to 22,321,018 (44.8 percent) popular vote margin and a 449-82 electoral vote tally.

Lend-Lease

A month after FDR's victory, Prime Minister Churchill penned a long letter to the president explaining Britain's dire financial condition. Due to run out of cash reserves within six months, England would no longer be able to purchase American war supplies. Churchill implored Roosevelt to find new ways to maintain the lifeline of supplies to help defeat Hitler. A few weeks later, the president explained the situation to a group of assembled reporters and announced his decision to ask Congress to authorize the leasing of American war material to Great Britain, likening the circumstances to loaning a garden hose to a neighbor whose house was on fire and then later taking back the hose free of charge. Isolationists who believed Roosevelt's proposal was both unnecessary and wasteful because war equipment loaned out for combat service would never be useful again preferred Senator Taft's analogy better, comparing the leasing of war supplies to lending out chewing gum—once used, "you don't want it back."

Despite isolationist opposition, FDR's opponents faced an uphill battle in their effort to stymie the president's plan and were soundly routed by large margins in both houses of Congress. Signed into law on March 11, 1941, the **Lend-Lease Act** authorized a $7 billion appropriation and empowered the president "to sell, transfer title to, exchange, lease, lend, or otherwise dispose of" any American defense articles to the government of any country whose defense the president deemed vital to the protection of the United States. The intention was clear: the United States government would no longer be merely allowing American manufactures to sell munitions to England. Though still expected to be hauled away on British naval vessels, weapons and other military equipment would now simply be purchased by the U.S. government (or taken directly from U.S. military stockpiles) and given to the British with no expectation of repayment. When Hitler finally broke the Non-Aggression Pact with Stalin and foolishly launched Operation Barbarossa against Russia in June 1941, Roosevelt authorized the extension of Lend-Lease aid to the Soviet Union.

The Undeclared Naval War vs. Germany in the Atlantic

Always desirous of establishing trust with those he worked with closely, Roosevelt invited Winston Churchill to attend a secret conference so the two leaders could converse about the latest war developments and form the basis of a personal friendship. For four days in early August, Roosevelt and Churchill convened onboard British and American warships off the coast of Newfoundland. After discussing ways to aid the Soviet Union and agreeing to give Japanese leaders a vague warning about the potential for war if their aggression in East Asia did not cease, Roosevelt and Churchill worked out a set of jointly held moral principles. Known as the Atlantic Charter, the joint statement announced that the two nations agreed to the principles of self-determination, equal access to raw materials, and freedom of the seas, while condemning Nazi tyranny and promoting a new system of international security. Though Churchill wished to have more definite commitments from Roosevelt, the prime minister understood the president's position. Until the American public signaled a willingness to enter the fight, he would have to be satisfied for the moment with Roosevelt's symbolic show of support.

After his meeting with Churchill, Roosevelt stepped up U.S. naval aid to the British. At the start of the war, the president had established a 300-mile neutrality belt in the western Atlantic. By the autumn of 1941, U.S. forces occupied Greenland and Iceland. Further, Roosevelt authorized U.S. naval ships to escort British convoys heading from America as far as Iceland's shores. The president also allowed American ships to assist British planes and ships in locating German submarines in the North Atlantic.

Provocative incidents were bound to occur. On September 4, 1941, a German U-Boat fired upon the *Greer*, an American destroyer that had been helping a British patrol plane track the submarine. After the plane dropped four depth charges, the U-Boat fired two torpedoes at the *Greer* (both missed) before escaping. Reporting the event to the American public before the details were completely known, Roosevelt deliberately whipped up public outrage in an effort to portray the incident as a completely unprovoked act of aggression by the German submarine, which he famously dubbed a "rattlesnake of the Atlantic." He then warned German and Italian ships that they entered the U.S. defense perimeter at their own peril. Hitler scoffed at Roosevelt's proclamations, but with the invasion of Russia still in doubt, he ordered German submarine commanders to avoid attacks on American vessels. Nevertheless, confrontations in the undeclared naval war continued to take place. On October 17, the U.S. destroyer *Kearney* responded to reports that several U-Boats were attacking a nearby Canadian convoy. Upon its arrival at the scene, the destroyer began dropping depth charges before being struck by a torpedo. The blast killed eleven sailors before the ship limped back to port in Iceland. Two weeks later, another U-Boat sunk the *Reuben James* while the U.S. destroyer escorted British merchant vessels. Though 115 sailors perished, only a quarter of Americans surveyed in a national poll favored war with Germany over the incident. In response to these hostilities, Congress (by a close vote in each house) revised the 1939 Neutrality Act by authorizing the arming of American merchant ships and allowing American merchant and naval vessels to enter war zones (thus ending cash-and-carry). Though the isolationists showed that their viewpoint could not be ignored, the internationalists once again retained the support of a majority of Americans and secured the necessary votes in Congress to continue their piecemeal stripping away of neutrality short of U.S. entry into the fight. At the time, most Americans believed that if their country entered the conflict it would result from a provocative act by Germany rather than Japan.

Worsening Relations with Japan

The outbreak of war in Europe presented opportunities for the Japanese in Southeast Asia. The region's French, English, and Dutch colonies stood virtually defenseless against any move by the Japanese military to secure control of their vital oil, rice, tin, and rubber resources. Only the United States stood in the way of these ambitions. Immediately after the fall of France, Japanese leaders made demands upon the Vichy French government to cut off an important aid route for Chiang Kai-shek's forces in southern China by shutting down a railroad link from North Vietnam. After the French acquiesced, England reluctantly gave in to Japanese demands to close the Burma Road being used to funnel supplies from British-held Burma into southern China.

Concerned about the possibility of a Japanese takeover of Southeast Asia, FDR implemented a series of cautious moves designed to send warnings to the Japanese leaders without unnecessarily provoking them into action. In May 1940, the president transferred the headquarters of the Pacific Fleet from California to Pearl Harbor in Hawaii. This relocation placed the nation's naval forces much closer to American possessions in the Western Pacific. Though justifiable as a defensive measure, the order sent a definite signal to Japan that Roosevelt was aware of the geopolitical situation and would not ignore further Japanese advances in Asia. He also began to advocate the use of limited economic sanctions against Japan. Though some of his advisers believed that trade embargoes would drive Japan to aggression, Roosevelt agreed with those who wished to see if economic pressure might persuade the Japanese leaders to alter their policies, beginning with aviation fuel and high-grade steel. When Japan demanded and received from Vichy France the right to place troops and airbases in the northern Vietnam portion of French Indochina in August 1940, Roosevelt banned all scrap iron and steel exports to Japan. Though Japan relied heavily on the United States for oil (90 percent of its imported petroleum came from America), the president chose to hold that card in his deck for the time being.

Chinese laborers working to reopen the Burma Road in southwest China, 1944

DEMOCRACY, FASCISM, AND COMMUNISM AT WAR, 1921-1945 / 759

In late-September 1940, Japanese leaders responded to the American embargoes by signing the Tripartite Pact with Germany and Italy. The treaty members pledged "to assist one another with all political, economic, and military means" if one of the nations were to be attacked "by a power at present not involved in the European War or in the Sino-Japan conflict." In case there was any doubt that the agreement was directly aimed at the United States, the treaty included a section specifically exempting the Soviet Union from its provisions. Thus, Japanese and German leaders hoped to dissuade the United States from military involvement against them by conjuring up the logistical nightmare of a two-front war to be fought on opposite ends of the globe. If Japanese leaders thought their action would allow them to pursue a free hand in Southeast Asia, however, they were mistaken. The Tripartite Pact irked Roosevelt and other American leaders, hardening their attitudes toward Japan. The treaty fed into the narrative that Japanese aggression in Asia had to be resisted not just because of the economic problems that a Japanese-dominated Asia would pose to American interests, but also because of the very real military threat that an empowered Japan in control of Asian resources and in league with the Berlin-Rome Axis would pose to American security.

Roosevelt responded to the announcement of the Tripartite Pact by adding pig iron, iron ore, and copper to the list of embargoed items while stepping up American aid to China. In addition to authorizing a $100 million loan to Chiang's government, the president allowed American military pilots to resign their commissions and volunteer to fight in China in squadrons under the command of Colonel Claire Chennault. Using American planes but flying Chinese Nationalist insignia, the "Flying Tigers" provided some semblance of a Chinese Air Force and helped to bog down sizeable numbers of troops and planes that the Japanese could have better utilized elsewhere.

The Road to Pearl Harbor

In an effort to warm relations, Japan sent a new ambassador to the United States in February 1941, the amiable Admiral Kichisaburo Nomura—a man with many prominent American friends who professed an honest desire to reach an understanding between the two countries. Nomura met over forty times throughout the year with Secretary of State Cordell Hull, but the talks eventually stalled. Japanese leaders would not settle for anything less than American acceptance of their country's dominance over eastern Asia while the United States continued to press for Japanese withdrawal from China and Indochina.

"Flying Tigers"

While negotiations continued, the Japanese government continued plans to expand into Southeast Asia. After Germany attacked the Soviet Union in June 1941, Japanese leaders felt secure about the northern flank of their empire. With the Russians preoccupied, they could now focus attention on the European colonies to the south of China. Hitler desired a Japanese attack on the Russians in eastern Siberia, but Japan refused—a clear sign that while Japan and Germany faced common enemies, they selfishly took advantage of each other's actions against their opponents without closely coordinating their moves. Ignoring Nomura's pleas to grant some concessions to the American position, Japanese leaders made plans to take over all of Indochina. This decision became quickly known to U.S. government officials because cryptographers with Naval Intelligence had recently broken the Japanese diplomatic codes. All messages sent to, and transmitted from, the Japanese embassy were routinely intercepted and deciphered. Before the Japanese invaded southern Indochina in late-July, Roosevelt had already prepared an executive order declaring an oil embargo plus a freeze of Japanese assets held in American banks, effectively severing all trade between the countries. Though the president realized his decision might provoke the Japanese to seize the Netherlands East Indies leading to war with the United States (a scenario he wished to avoid because of the perceived greater threat posed by

Germany), he refused to stand by idly while Japan continued its aggression with tacit American government approval. Determined to try one last round of economic coercion with the major commodity that Japan's industry and war machine truly relied upon, FDR placed the ball in Japan's court—if aggression continued, they would be the instigators and America would have no choice but to intervene in order to prevent all of East Asia falling under Japanese control.

Saddled with only a year's supply of oil in reserve and committed to expansion by force if necessary, Japan's leaders decided to seize the Dutch East Indies. Concluding that war with the United States was probably inevitable, they approved plans to get the upper hand in the coming fight by attacking the American Pacific fleet at **Pearl Harbor.** The strike would precede a larger series of moves designed to seize control of Southeast Asia and much of the Western Pacific. In mid-October, hardliners in the government forced the resignation of Prime Minister Prince Fumimaro Konoye (who had supported continued diplomacy with the United States) and installed General Hideki Tojo, a militant expansionist. After a final round of proposals and counterproposals led nowhere, a Japanese fleet headed for Pearl Harbor on November 26 under strict radio silence to carry out a mission that had been planned and practiced for several months. From intercepted diplomatic dispatches, American officials sensed the outbreak of hostilities at any moment but did not know where the Japanese would strike. Sightings of Japanese naval troop transports heading southward from the island of Formosa convinced many analysts that Japanese aggression would commence at one of the British or Dutch-held colonies in Southeast Asia. American forces in the western Pacific were placed on high alert. Hawaii also received such warnings, but a combination of complacency by local commanders and a lack of sufficient patrol resources limited the ability of the American fleet to provide ample protection for the fleet.

The Japanese attack on Pearl Harbor caught the American forces completely by surprise. In the early Sunday morning hours of December 7, 1941, two waves of over 350 fighters, bombers, and torpedo planes launched from six aircraft carriers assailed the docked American ships in the port as well as the American planes parked at adjacent airfields. The two-hour attack sunk three battleships, capsized a fourth, grounded another trying to leave the harbor, and damaged three others. Ten other ships, including cruisers and destroyers were sunk or damaged. Additionally, the Japanese destroyed 188 aircraft and damaged 155 planes. The human toll was heavy—more than 2,400 servicemen (and some civilians) killed and over 1,100 wounded.

Though devastating, a closer analysis reveals the Pearl Harbor raid's significant tactical shortcomings. Foremost, the attack failed to eliminate any of the American Pacific Fleet's three aircraft carriers—the ships that would become the true source of naval power in the Second World War. All three carriers were away from Pearl Harbor at the time of the attack (one was delivering combat planes to Midway Islands, another was returning from delivering a squadron to Wake Island, and a third was in San Diego, California being repaired.) The failure of the Japanese to destroy the U.S. Navy's oil storage tanks & repair docks at the port looms as another major deficiency. Had these facilities

USS Arizona **submerged off Ford Island, Pearl Harbor, Honolulu, HI**

been razed, Pearl Harbor would have been taken out of commission as an effective base for over a year. Japanese planners had made contingency for a third wave of planes whose purpose was to eliminate such vital support installations, but the plan left discretion for this phase of the attack to the fleet commander who decided against it due to the unknown whereabouts of the American aircraft carriers.

The decision to attack the United States also proved to be a monumental strategic mistake by Japanese leaders. Thinking that the assault would deal a crippling blow to the American military while subsequent attacks in the Western Pacific would allow the establishment of an extensive defense perimeter, the leaders underestimated the ability of the United States to quickly replace their losses and their own ability to maintain control of such a wide expanse of territory. America would soon replace the short-term loss of men, planes, and ships. (Two of the sunken battleships were actually raised and refitted for duty). Once reaching maximum capacity, the American industrial base produced thousands of ships and tens of thousands of aircraft. Tojo and the other Japanese militarists also blundered in believing that a crippling suckerpunch to the United States would smash the morale of the American public. In fact, the raid on American soil and subsequent attacks against American forces in the Pacific unified the country against Japan like nothing else.

Remaining isolationist sentiment was swept away in the national furor and demands for revenge. A shocked Franklin Roosevelt appeared before Congress the next day seeking a formal declaration of war against Japan. The Senate unanimously followed suit, while in the House, the first woman elected to the U.S. Congress, pacifist Representative Jeannette Rankin of Montana (who in 1917 voted against American entry into World War I) cast a lone, symbolic dissenting vote. The president and the American people did not immediately know what war against Japan would mean for the conflict in Europe. As a defensive treaty protecting members against attack from the United States, the terms of the Tripartite Pact did not apply. Nevertheless, on December 11, Germany and Italy announced declarations of war against the United States. Already irked by America's supplying of his enemies, Hitler predicted that the United States and Germany would fight each other eventually. Though he believed that the United States had the industrial might and superior racial makeup to defeat a smaller Asiatic country like Japan in a one-on-one fight, stretching American resources to support a two-front war with theaters of action separated half a world away would give both the Japanese and Germans their best chance of success. This failed gamble ranks as one of Hitler's biggest blunders, only outdone by his decision to attack the Soviet Union six months earlier.

HALTING THE AXIS, 1941-1942

A series of defeats at the hands of the Japanese created a pronounced sense of gloom in the United States during the first six months after the Pearl Harbor attack. Before May 1942, Japanese forces moved relatively unimpeded as they invaded American Pacific islands and European colonies in Southeast Asia to establish their defense perimeter, from the Thailand border with India in the west looping around the Dutch East Indies to the south and sweeping up through the islands of Micronesia to the east. On December 10, 1941, over 5,000 Japanese troops easily overran Guam's 500 defenders. At Wake Island, located over 2,000 miles west of Hawaii, the post's 500 defenders drove off an initial Japanese task force on December 7, but succumbed to a stronger second assault group two weeks later. Elsewhere, the Japanese moved into Thailand and defeated British forces in Burma, Hong Kong, and Singapore.

The Fall of the Philippines

American and Filipino forces on the main Philippine island of Luzon under the command of General Douglas MacArthur held out the longest despite the general's inadequate defense preparations. Though MacArthur received word of the Pearl Harbor raid as early as 3:30 a.m. local time, American planes remained parked in the open at Clark Field located 50 miles northwest of Manila when Japanese planes arrived at noon to bomb the base. The general lost half his aircraft in one strike, crippling his chances of defending the Philippines. Outflanked on the beaches by Japanese amphibious troops, MacArthur fell back to the Manila area, eventually settling his men on the jungle-infested Bataan Peninsula and nearby Corregidor Island, which guarded the mouth of the harbor. Short on food, medicine, and military supplies, the 15,000 American and 65,000 Filipino troops held out for several months against rampant malaria and frequent Japanese air and ground attacks. In the process, they temporarily denied the enemy use of Manila Bay and bought crucial time for Australia to beef up its defenses. In early March 1942, President Roosevelt ordered MacArthur and his family to leave the area. Sneaking out by torpedo boat before flying to Australia, the general famously proclaimed: "I shall return." Mindful of MacArthur's popularity with Republicans and knowing that the nation needed heroes at this desperate time, Roosevelt refused to reprimand the general for his many blunders and would soon accede to placing him in command of leading the counterattack against the Japanese in the South Pacific.

American and Filipino forces at Bataan finally surrendered on April 9, while those on Corregidor endured continuous bombardment until their surrender on May 6. During the subsequent Bataan Death March, Japanese soldiers drove their prisoners 65 miles northward to prison stockades, brutally murdering any who could not keep up because of wounds, starvation, disease, or exhaustion. Over 7,000 POWs died along the way to slave labor camps where almost half did not survive the war. The Japanese troops who committed these atrocities succumbed to the hateful preaching of their officers who constantly reinforced the notion that surrender was not an option, nor should any soldier who dishonored themselves by surrendering be treated with anything but repugnance. Often brutally beaten by their officers since their days in training camp, many Japanese soldiers internalized the violence and reflected their treatment back upon their prisoners. Similar incidents occurred wherever the Japanese military triumphed.

The Battles of Coral Sea and Midway

The Battle of the Coral Sea marked the first time that an American battle fleet stopped a Japanese offensive in the Pacific. Moving beyond simply consolidating their considerable gains in the six months following the Pearl Harbor attack, Japanese leaders succumbed to what many of them later described as "victory disease"—the prevailing belief that they were unstoppable. As a result of this arrogance, they began to make careless moves as they sought further glory. Seeking to capture Port Moresby in southeastern New Guinea (a large island twice the size of France located just to the north of Australia) as a preliminary move to controlling the air and sea lanes to Australia, a Japanese task force entered the Coral Sea only to be intercepted by an American flotilla led by two aircraft carriers. By that time, Naval Intelligence had broken the Japanese naval code, allowing the new Pacific Fleet commander, Admiral Chester Nimitz, to react quickly to thwart the offensive. The ensuing battle on May 7, 1942 became the first naval engagement in world history involving fleets not in sight of each other. The combat took the form of planes launched from aircraft carriers pounding away at their enemy's ships. Of its two carriers in the fight, the U.S. Navy lost the *Lexington* while the *Yorktown* suffered severe damage. Nevertheless, the Japanese were forced to turn back due to heavy damage to one carrier and another carrier losing most of its planes.

A month after the Battle of the Coral Sea, the Japanese launched another major offensive directed at the Midway Atoll, the westernmost of the Hawaiian Islands located 1000 miles from Pearl Harbor. In addition to providing the Japanese with an advanced base relatively close to the major Hawaiian Islands, the thrust would draw out the American Pacific Fleet for a grand showdown to eliminate the carriers not destroyed at Pearl Harbor. Once again, Naval Intelligence provided Nimitz with advanced knowledge of Japanese plans, allowing him to ignore a diversionary move against the Aleutian Islands in southern Alaska in order to concentrate on the main battle group led by four large Japanese aircraft carriers with experienced flight crews. Nimitz ordered the two American carriers then located at Pearl Harbor to head immediately towards Midway. When the damaged *Yorktown* finally arrived from the Coral Sea, Nimitz gave the ship's captain 72 hours to patch up the carrier, take on additional planes, and start heading for Midway. In the upcoming battle, Japanese planners expected at worst a 4-to-2 advantage in carriers. In addition to the early arrival of the *Enterprise* and the *Hornet*, the unexpected appearance of the *Yorktown* (only possible because of the Japanese failure to destroy Pearl Harbor's repair docks) added another element of surprise. Though the fighting began with Japanese planes pummeling Midway Island, the main battle took place in a similar manner to the Battle of the Coral Sea—both fleets dispatched scout planes over the horizon to locate the enemy fleet then sent scores of dive bombers and torpedo planes to eliminate the targets, focusing on enemy carriers. At the **Battle of Midway**, the Americans located the enemy first, and despite attacking in a haphazard and uncoordinated manner that resulted in the loss of entire squadrons of planes, the pilots eventually broke through enemy defenses to destroy all four Japanese carriers. (The Japanese were only able to sink the already heavily-damaged *Yorktown*.) The Battle of Midway proved to be a turning point of the war in the Pacific. Though the conflict was far from over, the Japanese were no longer capable of mounting major offensive naval operations.

Despite their defeat at Midway, many Japanese military leaders refused to give up the initiative, wishing to expand their perimeter of control and neutralize Australia as an American base of operations. Having failed to capture the vital air and naval base of Port Moresby in southern New Guinea because of the setback at the Battle of the Coral Sea, the Japanese attempted to seize the port by ordering troops overland from their holdings in northern New Guinea. The Japanese also landed troops at Guadalcanal, located at the southeastern tip of the Solomon Islands, in an attempt to set up an air base that would sever Allied supply lines to eastern Australia.

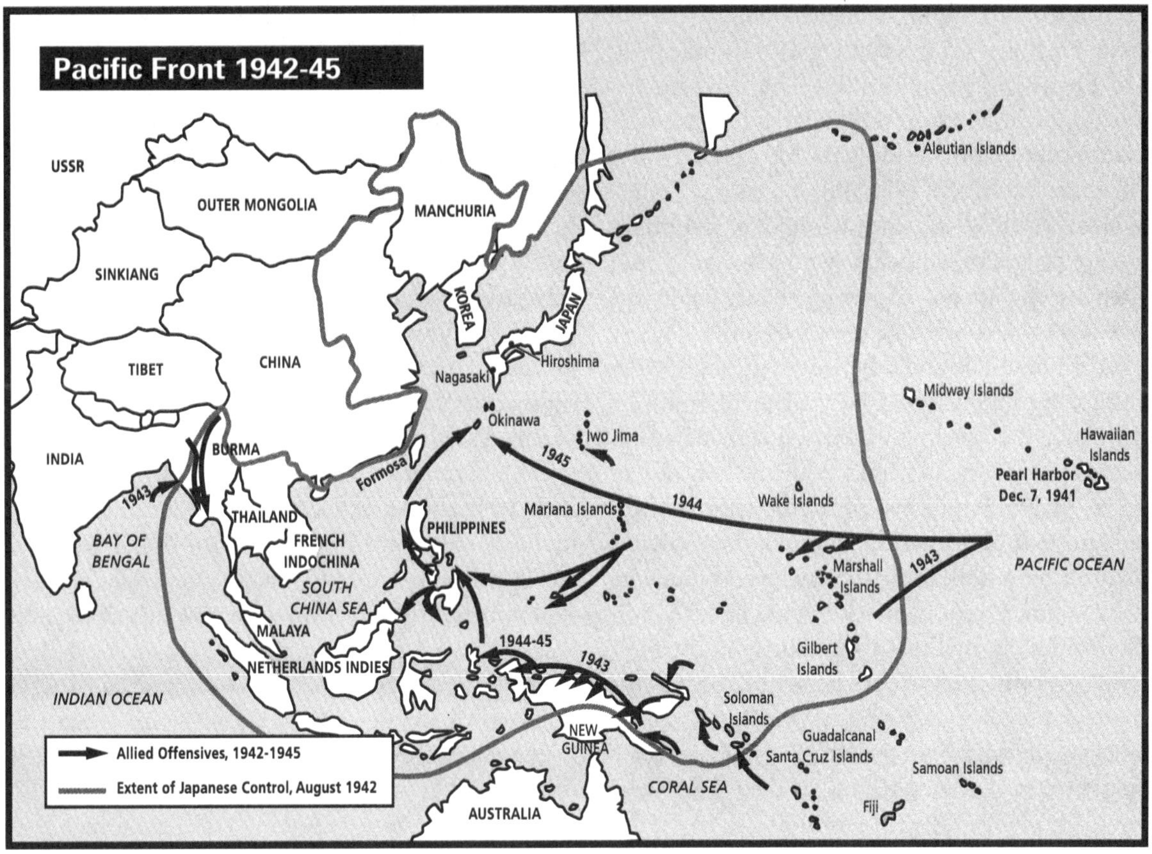

Map 25.1 World War II in the Pacific

Standing in the way of the Port Moresby attack force, however, was the imposing 10,000-foot Owen Stanley Mountains whose brutal conditions hampered supply lines and greatly weakened their numbers before determined Australian defenders finished them off. Meanwhile, the U.S. Navy reacted to the Japanese move on Guadalcanal by hastily landing marines who quickly seized the partially-constructed airfield but became embroiled in a six-month-long fight on the heavily wooded island. While the Navy fought five major engagements against the Japanese offshore, the undersupplied marines valiantly held on against the harsh environment and reinforced enemy troops until February 1943 when Japanese leaders admitted defeat and ordered a withdrawal. The twin defeats in southern New Guinea and at Guadalcanal ended Japanese offensive operations in the Pacific, forcing them to hunker down on the hundreds of islands under their control spread out over thousands of square miles, waiting to see if the Americans would risk the vast casualties necessary to dislodge them.

Allied Victories in Egypt and Russia

The Axis nations continued to make tremendous gains of territory in Europe throughout 1941 and most of 1942 before Allied forces finally stopped their momentum. An initial attempt by the Italians in the fall of 1940 to conquer Greece failed miserably, but after German forces quickly secured control of Yugoslavia in April 1941, Hitler invaded Greece and the nearby island of Crete. Both fell within a month. Meanwhile, in North Africa, an Italian thrust into Egypt launched from neighboring Libya in October 1940 was stymied by the British who then counterattacked. Once again, Hitler reluctantly sent reinforcements to bail out Mussolini, ordering General Erwin Rommel in February 1941 to create an *Afrika Korps* consisting of armored divisions to take over North African operations. Though perpetually short on supplies, Rommel eventually restored German and Italian control over eastern Libya before pressing forward into western Egypt. In early November 1942, however, British General Bernard Montgomery succeeded in smashing through Rommel's positions at El Alamein, just 150 miles to the west of the vital Suez Canal, forcing the Afrika Korps into headlong retreat back into Libya, never to regain the initiative. Coupled with the recent British capture of Ethiopia, Eritrea, and Somaliland from the Italians, the Allies held firm control over eastern Africa.

In Eastern Europe, the advance into the Soviet Union also began well for the Axis forces, only to be met with disaster by early 1943. In June 1941, over 3.5 million German troops, supplemented with another million fascist soldiers from Italy, Hungary, and Romania, attacked the Soviet Union and advanced along a 1000-mile front deep into Belorussia and Ukraine. The Russians fell back, moving civilians and even entire factories safely to relocation centers east of the Ural Mountains where war production resumed. The Axis forces threatened the capital of Moscow and the strategically important northern city of Leningrad before winter set in to shut down offensive operations. Expecting victory before the arrival of winter, the unprepared Germans suffered heavy losses in the extreme cold and experienced great difficulty maintaining long supply lines under frequent attack by partisans. After the grueling winter, Hitler ordered his forces to concentrate on Stalingrad along the Volga River in southern Russia, which served as the gateway into the petroleum-rich Caucasus. If captured, the Germans would deny the Soviets the use of their main oil-producing region. Stalin ordered his namesake city to be held at all costs. Both sides devoted massive resources in the fight for control of **Stalingrad**, which began in late-August 1942. Though greatly undersupplied, the Russians used their manpower advantage to great effect, albeit at tragic cost. Soviet troops without bullets in their rifles were often ordered to charge German positions and to use the ammunition of fallen comrades when it came available. After several months of brutal fighting, the Soviets began to turn the tide, surrounding German forces and cutting them off from supplies and reinforcements. Though Hitler ordered his forces to fight to the last man, Field Marshal Freidrich Paulus thought otherwise and surrendered on January 31, 1943. The Germans lost over 200,000 troops at Stalingrad, including 90,000 prisoners. Though victorious, the Russians suffered much higher casualties—close to half a million killed and over 600,000 wounded (more than the United States incurred during the entire war.) After Stalingrad, the Germans lost the initiative on the Eastern Front, forced to fall back, regroup, and assume a defensive posture for the remainder of the war.

The Battle of the Atlantic

In the Atlantic Ocean, U-Boats turned loose on American shipping exacted a heavy toll within a few weeks of U.S. entry in the war. With little preparation given by the American military to antisubmarine warfare, German submarines had a field day destroying merchant ships, especially oil tankers, off the eastern coast of the United States and the Gulf of Mexico. Many attacks, such as one taking place in June 1942 near Virginia Beach, Virginia, occurred in broad daylight. Though Admiral Karl Doenitz, commander of the U-Boat forces, only sent a dozen U-Boats to American waters, half of Allied shipping sunk in the early months of 1942 took place there. Coastal defenses eventually improved, however, as the country instituted mandatory seaside blackouts to prevent submarine crews from using the silhouettes of merchant ships against brightly-lighted shorelines and civilian-piloted Civil Air Patrol planes coordinated with military aircraft to monitor the nation's seaboards.

On the high seas of the North Atlantic, German submarines wreaked havoc on Allied shipping throughout 1942, threatening to sever the American supply line to Great Britain. Admiral Doenitz estimated that his submarines needed to sink an average of 700,000 tons of Allied shipping each month to weaken England effectively. German U-Boats reached Doenitz' threshold by June 1942, but effective Allied counter measures began to slowly reduce the damage. Allied aircraft began to use radar and high-intensity searchlights to locate surfaced submarines at night. American and British escort ships also began to utilize radio detectors to locate U-Boats by intercepting transmissions to their home bases.

Two major developments ultimately contributed to the eradication of the U-Boat menace in the North Atlantic. The first involved effective use of ULTRA, the designation for the breaking of the German military code (made possible by the British retrieval of a German deciphering machine from a captured U-Boat). ULTRA allowed the Allies to decode and analyze intercepted German military dispatches. In the **Battle of the Atlantic**, ULTRA intercepts allowed the Allies to anticipate U-Boat movements and to deliver telling blows upon their discovery. The other major boost to anti-submarine warfare proved to be the deployment of light escort carriers. Capable of carrying up to thirty planes, the carriers' pilots could patrol wide zones around convoys and undertake search-and-destroy missions against enemy subs. By mid-1943, U-Boats ceased to be a threat in the North Atlantic. The Germans sunk over 250,000 tons of shipping in April 1943, but two months later that figure plummeted to a mere 18,000 tons. Though U-Boats remained active away from the North Atlantic, German submarine crews found themselves in increasing peril. Of the 1,162 U-Boats deployed during the war, 941 were eventually sunk or captured. The Allied victory in the Battle of the Atlantic ranks alongside the great land battles of Stalingrad and the Normandy invasion in terms of overall contribution to the Axis defeat in Europe.

THE AMERICAN HOME FRONT

The Japanese attack on Pearl Harbor awoke a sleeping economic and military giant. Though it would take time for

Map 25.2 World War II in Europe

the groggy behemoth to become fully alert as the United States initially struggled to efficiently mobilize men and material, the Axis powers would soon bear the brunt of America's enormous industrial output and manpower resources. As the war raged, daily life became as profusely impacted by the conflict as by the Great Depression. Though wartime demands generated near-full employment, shortages of consumer goods and forced rationing disrupted everyday life. Despite these inconveniences, the war opened opportunities for women and minorities not only to demonstrate their loyalty to their country but also to showcase their abilities and value to the nation. Though the full social impact of World War II would not be seen until decades after the war's conclusion, the groundwork for the modern equal rights movements had been laid with these groups' wartime service.

Industrial Mobilization

During the American neutrality period, FDR addressed war preparation issues by creating a series of advisory boards to study and make recommendations about prioritizing production and manpower resources. These agencies lacked coercive powers, however, relying instead on seeking the voluntary cooperation of business leaders to emphasize future military needs over civilian desires for consumer goods. In early 1942, Roosevelt centralized these boards into one agency, the War Production Board (WPB), under the direction of former Sears Roebuck executive Donald Nelson. As the case with the previous boards, however, the WPB lacked any means of coercion, leading to its ineffectiveness as a means to provide central economic direction to the war effort. Since the WPB could only cajole businesses to direct production in certain directions, the agency would only be as assertive as its leader and Nelson proved to be far more conciliatory than aggressive. He often deferred to the purchasing bureaus of the separate military branches, allowing them to pursue their own needs rather than acting in the best interest of the nation as a whole. Ultimately, the president rectified the situation in May 1943 by creating the Office of War Mobilization (OWM) under former South Carolina senator and Supreme Court justice James Byrnes, granting him considerable authority to control and coordinate the mobilization effort and to serve as a court of final appeal to resolve any differences among defense industries or government agencies involving the allocation of defense-related materials or labor resources.

Though setting priorities (and finally enforcing them through the OWM), the Roosevelt administration and Congress never dictated to business what must be produced. Instead, the federal government lavished business with an incredible array of incentives to ensure that the military received what it needed to prosecute the war while still providing the necessities for the civilian population on the home front. As Secretary of War Henry Stimson recorded the administration's mindset in his diary: "If you are going to try to go to war, or to prepare for war, in a capitalist country, you have got to let business make money out of the process or business won't work." Companies enjoyed generous tax breaks and low-interest loans that covered the costs for defense-related plant expansion and equipment investments. The federal government also constructed many defense plants which it then leased to corporations, such as the Consolidated Vultee aircraft factory in Fort Worth, Texas and the Bell Aircraft facility in Marietta, Georgia. Most beneficial to business, the military negotiated contracts on a "cost-plus" basis whereby the price that companies charged the government guaranteed a profit. (Agricultural producers similarly benefited by a government guarantee of high prices at 110 percent of "parity," or the favorable price ratio of agricultural prices to industrial prices received by farmers during the prosperous 1909-1914 period. During the war, farm prices doubled.) For its part, the military gravitated toward the large corporations to fill out a large majority of its requisitions, a practice the Roosevelt administration did not challenge. The production levels that American industries eventually reached during the war were truly astounding: 300,000 planes, 100,000 tanks and armored vehicles, 80,000 landing craft, over 5,000 merchant ships, and 1,500 vessels for the U.S. Navy, not to mention the millions of small arms, tons of bombs, and the billions of rounds of ammunition manufactured as the national Gross Domestic Product doubled from 1939 to 1945.

The rapid development of wartime industry affected all geographic regions of the country, from the traditional manufacturing areas of the Northeast and Midwest to the agriculturally-dominated South and West. In Michigan, after the manufacture of new cars had been outlawed, Henry Ford constructed the massive Willow Run aircraft plant outside Detroit. The 67-acre complex with a mile-long assembly line eventually built over 9,000 B-24 Liberators and employed over 40,000 workers. To make up for the loss of access to natural rubber (Japanese-held Southeast Asia accounted for 90 percent of the U.S. prewar rubber supply), the federal government spent close to a billion dollars building fifty synthetic rubber factories, which it leased to private rubber companies. The largest facility in Institute, West Virginia operated jointly by U.S. Rubber encompassed 77 acres and produced 90,000 tons per year. From 1942 to 1944, American synthetic rubber production increased from 8,000 to over 750,000 tons, enough to meet national wartime needs. In the South, southern builders produced one quarter of American shipping, from torpedo boats and landing craft along the Gulf Coast to massive aircraft carriers at Newport News, Virginia. In Texas, oil producers stepped up production and the proliferation of military bases invigorated the state's economy. In the West, giant plants such as those operated by Boeing Aircraft in Seattle, Douglas Aviation in Los Angeles, and Consolidated Vultee in San Diego employed hundreds of thousands of workers and accounted for half of the country's wartime production of planes. At his Portland, Oregon and Richmond, California shipyards, Henry J. Kaiser used prefabricated materials and other mass-production techniques to vastly reduce the time necessary to construct the vital 10,000-ton transport vessels known as "Liberty Ships." In 1941 it took a full year to build a Liberty Ship, but within a year Kaiser reduced the production time down to less than two months. Two years later, his workers built a complete Liberty Ship in two weeks.

Manpower Mobilization

The mobilization of American armed forces began a year before the Pearl Harbor attack in September 1940 when Congress passed the Selective Training and Service Act creating the Selective Service System to implement the nation's first peacetime draft. The law authorized the initial conscription of 900,000 men between the ages of 21 and 27. Though isolationists railed against the measure, the draft did not become an election issue in 1940 because of Republican nominee Wendell Willkie's strong approval. After Pearl Harbor, the U.S. armed forces swelled as a result of the draft's expansion and citizen volunteering. Draft boards staffed by local leaders administered the system by overseeing registration, handling requests for exemptions or deferments, and listening to appeals of their decisions. Of the 50 million men that the Selective Service System registered, 10 million were drafted for active service. (Over six million serving in uniform volunteered.) About 10 million received an exemption or deferment from service on the basis of medical condition, family hardship, religious conscientious objection to war, or laboring at an "essential" industrial or agricultural occupation.

In addition to mobilizing manpower for the military, the federal government also oversaw the mobilization of the civilian workforce. Created in early 1942, the War Manpower Commission (WMC) became the main government agency involved in civilian workforce mobilization. The WMC recruited and trained male and female laborers for specific tasks, worked with the Selective Service System to classify occupations as essential and nonessential to the war effort, and coordinated the placement of workers into jobs that most optimized their skills. In an effort to prevent wartime strikes, Roosevelt brokered a no-strike pledge from the nation's leading labor unions and a no-lockout agreement with the country's leading corporations. The president also created the National War Labor Board to set wages and hours, promote collective bargaining, and negotiate labor disputes that might endanger production. Union membership soared during the war, rising from 9 million in 1939 to over 15 million by 1945.

Though Congress passed (over FDR's veto) the Smith-Connally War Labor Disputes Act making it a crime to advocate work stoppages and empowering the president to seize any factory or mine vital to the war effort if its workers engaged in a strike, hundreds of walkouts nevertheless occurred. Most of these protests were brief "wildcat" strikes unauthorized by union leaders, usually to highlight a particular grievance concerning workplace conditions. The largest exception was the series of United Mine Workers strikes in 1943 led by the flamboyant John L. Lewis. The actions embittered the public to the union and infuriated Roosevelt, who seized the mines and publicly threatened to draft the striking workers before eventually negotiating a deal that reopened the mines after granting Lewis's demands for higher wages to offset the dangerous but valuable work his union's members contributed to national defense.

The war brought about the end of many New Deal programs created during the Depression to provide work for the unemployed. With Americans pouring into the armed forces and defense plants, the national unemployment rate evaporated as work could now be readily found. During the 1942 midterm congressional elections, Republicans gained 46 House seats and 9 Senate seats. Forming a coalition with southern Democrats, they successfully dismantled the Works Progress Administration, Farm Security Administration, National Youth Administration, and the Civilian Conservation Corps.

Financing the War

Eventually costing over $300 billion, the Second World War was the largest expense for the federal government in American history. The Roosevelt administration worked with Congress to finance the war through a combination of increased taxation and deficit spending covered by war bonds. Taxes paid for almost half of wartime government outlays (compared to one-third for World War I), with terms largely laid out by the Revenue Act of 1942. This significant legislation greatly increased the number of citizens eligible to pay income taxes. In 1939, fewer than 4 million Americans earned the minimum income level of $1,500 necessary to file an income tax return. By 1943 that number had soared to over 40 million—a consequence of the increased revenues produced by wartime prosperity but also the lowering of the tax-exemption level to $624. Individual tax rates also increased, leading to the amount of revenue received by individual income taxes to rise from $1 billion in 1939 to over $19 billion in 1945, surpassing the level of corporate taxes for the first time. The Revenue Act also authorized the new withholding system whereby employers were required to deduct taxes from worker paychecks and collect the revenues on behalf of the government. Government borrowing financed approximately 55 percent of the war's cost, largely achieved through the sale of bonds. By including small-denominations to allow more citizens to participate, bond drives proved to be an effective means to boost patriotism and "sell the war" to the public. Nevertheless, three-quarters of the money raised through bond purchases came from banks and other financial institutions.

Though increased taxes and bond sales soaked up much consumer income during the war, the unprecedented levels of government spending energized the economy and largely legitimized the economic theories of British economist John Maynard Keynes who had long advocated national government spending programs and tax reductions during economic downturns to generate recovery by stimulating consumer demand. When the private sector lacks vigor and confidence to invest, preferring to sit on its wealth until the general economic climate improves, Keynes argued, a government should stimulate its country's economy by providing tax relief and bankrolling investments in infrastructure in an effort to put more money in consumers' hands. Their subsequent purchases would provide the fuel necessary to jumpstart a stalled economy. Though Roosevelt increased government spending to unprecedented levels during the Great Depression, his (and Congress') lack of total devotion to Keynesian principles meant that while the economic climate began to improve, general recovery had yet to be achieved by 1939. With the arrival of hostilities, however, FDR and Congress threw aside their aversions to budget deficits and spent lavishly to produce what was needed to win the war. The end result was not only victory on the battlefield, but nearly total employment and record-high profits for American business.

Civilian Sacrifice

While Americans on the home front saw the return of employment opportunities and substantially higher incomes than during the Depression, the military's insatiable demand for raw materials created huge shortages of consumer goods that risked inflation and profiteering. The government created the **Office of Price Administration (OPA)** to implement price controls, which in April 1942 capped most non-farm prices at the highest level reached by March 1. In July 1942, the National War Labor Board implemented a maximum 15 percent wage increase (based on average 1941 wages) to coincide with the 15 percent rise in prices over the same period. In April 1943, Roosevelt issued a "hold-the-line" order which froze all prices and wages at current levels for the duration of the war.

Beginning in 1942, the OPA also created a rationing system to guarantee equal distribution of several civilian items in short supply. Meat, sugar, coffee, butter, and shoes all made the OPA's list of rationed goods initially drawn up by the War Production Board (WPB). Gasoline found its way on the list, not due to a petroleum shortage, but as part of a greater effort to conserve rubber tires. Likewise, canned goods were rationed to reduce the use of tin. Shortages sometimes led to many items, especially meat, coffee, cigarettes, and canned goods, to become simply unavailable for significant lengths of time. Many nonessential civilian items disappeared completely, including refrigerators, silk stockings, tinfoil, cellophane, tennis balls, and bobby pins. The WPB also ordered restrictions on the "wasteful" use of materials found in numerous items, especially clothing. The agency impacted menswear by banning the manufacture of vests, cuffs, patch pockets, and extra pairs of pants with suits to save wool. Likewise, women's clothing saw the elimination of ruffles, pleats, and long skirts. Though some resorted to the black market for access to meat and other desired items, and many grumbled at the shortages of goods and the OPA's stamp books and changing point system to carry out its policies, the majority of citizens patriotically adhered to the agency's regulations.

Women during World War II

World War II greatly impacted the lives of American women. Whether raising a family at home or joining the workforce (or trying to do both), most women felt the strains and inconveniences of the war on a daily basis. Rationing, food shortages, and the absence of many common consumer goods complicated efforts to provide the basic comforts of home life. Many devoted valuable time volunteering as a nurse, participating in scrap drives, aiding government agencies in explaining civil defense programs, monitoring local grocery prices, and entertaining troops at the new United Service Organizations (USO) canteens created to maintain the morale of service men and women.

Some women actively served in the military during the war providing valuable support services for their country. About 200,000 American women served in the Women's Army Corps, or WACs, under the command of Colonel Oveta Culp Hobby (the wife of former Texas governor William Hobby). WACs performed 239 important support roles, ranging from secretarial duties to motor vehicle maintenance, freeing up men for other assignments including combat duty. Over 100,000 American women performed similar duty in the Navy as "Women Accepted for Volunteer Emergency Service," or WAVES. Close to 20,000 women served in the Marine Corps Women's Reserve while an additional 10,000 performed duties as members of the Coast Guard Women's Reserve (nicknamed SPARs after the motto Semper Paratus – "Always Ready").

Created to overcome the shortage of pilots and to free up more male pilots for combat duty, the **Women Airforce Service Pilots (WASPs)** provided another valuable contribution to the war effort. Commanded by aviator Jacqueline Cochran, the WASPs trained at Sweetwater, Texas's Avenger Field before its graduates transferred to flying assignments across the country. Though the federal government refused to grant the civilian WASPs any recognized military status (let alone use them in combat),

they played vital support roles throughout the war ferrying all types of military aircraft (including heavy bombers), providing instrument instruction and towing targets for male trainee pilots, testing damaged planes, and transporting cargo. Ultimately, over 25,000 women applied to be WASPs, 1,830 were accepted, 1,074 graduated, and 38 died while performing their duties.

The war altered the roles of women in American society in countless ways, but nowhere more than in the workplace. Before World War II, women were systematically excluded from many jobs, with 90 percent of the nation's 12 million working females laboring in ten categories. While working white women tended to gravitate to retail trade, teaching, and secretarial jobs, a majority of black and Hispanic women were relegated to domestic service. Following the prevailing custom, most working women were young and single (only 15 percent of married women worked). A 1936 Gallup poll revealed that 82 percent of men and 75 percent of women surveyed believed that wives with employed husbands should not work.

Defense industry leaders initially excluded women from factory employment, not having much faith in their ability to perform the required work in addition to naively believing that the male labor supply would not soon be depleted. From late 1942 on, however, female laborers were in peak demand. The War Manpower Commission and private corporations began to actively recruit women for war work. The response was overwhelming, with the number of employed increasing from 14.6 million in 1941 to almost 20 million (over a third of all adult American women) by 1944. The biggest change occurred among married women who outnumbered single women in the work force for the first time. Women poured into manufacturing jobs, especially defense-related employment, eventually making up a third of all war industry workers. Though many took clerical positions, large numbers also labored as welders, riveters, and steelworkers. While the male-dominated unions tended to be lukewarm about the presence of female workers, they doggedly fought to protect the principle of equal pay for equal work, if for no other reason than to prevent employers from undercutting the salaries of male workers.

For the most part, women welcomed their war work. Though some clearly wanted to prove they could do traditional "male work," most had more practical motivations than trying to make a social statement. Single and married women alike enjoyed the additional money they were able to earn for themselves and their families while often doing work that they would never have been allowed to perform during peacetime. Most married women especially enjoyed the challenge provided by their new jobs when compared to their domestic chores. Patriotism also played a role in deciding to work, especially in a defense industry, by allowing women the opportunity to show that they were "doing their part" to help the nation achieve victory. Large numbers had loved ones in uniform overseas and believed their work would help bring them home sooner.

Oveta (Culp) Hobby, ca. February 1953.

Answering the nation's need for womanpower, Mrs. Virginia Davis made arrangements for the care of her two children during the day and joined her husband at work in the Naval Air Base in Corpus Christi, Texas. Both were employed under Civil Service in the assembly and repair department. Mrs. Davis's training enabled her to take the place of her husband if he was called by the armed service. August 1942.

Even before the war ended, women in the war industries were gradually relieved of their duties. Employers, in tandem with the government, began to initiate campaigns preparing the country for women to return to their homes, allowing male war veterans to return to work in the factories. Women at the time expected this development and most complied without much protest, mostly being happy that the war would soon be over. Regardless, the war experience of women did help to produce a steady shift in attitudes among males and females about women's roles in the workplace and society in general. While most women of the war generation gladly returned to domesticity, many later raised their daughters to challenge the prevailing beliefs about a woman's proper station in society, establishing the basis for a growing women's movement during the postwar period.

The African American Experience

World War II allowed a record number of African Americans to serve in uniform and work in the industrial sector, though discrimination continued to limit opportunities. Before the war, fewer than 4,000 blacks served in the peacetime army of 230,000 soldiers, with only five African Americans holding officer rank (of which three were chaplains). All black soldiers served in segregated units under the command of white officers. The military completely excluded blacks from service in the Marine Corps and Army Air Corps. In the Navy, African Americans could only serve as cooks and mess men. Meanwhile, in the civilian workforce, very few of the 5 million employed blacks labored in the well-paying defense industry.

Glaring manpower needs, President Roosevelt's desire to gain African-American votes, and political pressure applied by black activists, however, began to effect noticeable changes. A month before the 1940 election, Eleanor Roosevelt urged FDR to meet with NAACP executive director Walter White and **A. Phillip Randolph**, the leader of the Brotherhood of Sleeping Car Porters (the largest African-American labor union in the country). After the meeting, Roosevelt arranged for the Army to add enough new black enrollees to reflect the African-American proportion of the total population (about 9 percent), the promotion of Colonel Benjamin O. Davis, Sr. to the rank of Brigadier General (making him the Army's first black general), and for the Marines and Army Air Corps to begin accepting African-American recruits. Black combat units, however, would remain segregated. After the election, Randolph began to organize a planned 10,000-man march on Washington to protest continued discrimination in the defense industry. Franklin and Eleanor Roosevelt both opposed the proposed march, fearing the protest would embarrass the administration and might lead to violence. Undaunted, Randolph continued with his plans, threatening to mobilize up to 100,000 to rally in Washington's Capitol Mall. After a personal meeting with Randolph in June 1941, Roosevelt capitulated. In return for Randolph calling off the march, FDR issued Executive Order 8802, which forbade discrimination by defense industry employers or government agencies based on race, color, creed, or national origin.

To investigate discrimination complaints, Roosevelt created the Fair Employment Practices Commission (FEPC), an agency which soon had its hands full trying to enforce Executive Order 8802. Discrimination persisted as the FEPC suffered from lack of sufficient funds and staff members. The agency was reactive, responding only to complaints rather than pursuing independent investigations. The FEPC did not have the power to coerce compliance if its agents found evidence of discriminatory practices, relying on publicity and moral suasion to produce a change in behavior. Despite its limitations, the FEPC alerted the country to the existence of various forms of discrimination and served as a precursor to future federal civil rights agencies.

Despite the persistence of discrimination by employers (as well as many unions), African-American employment in war production work greatly increased due to wartime necessity. The proportion of blacks employed in the defense industry rose from 3 percent in 1942 to 8.6 percent in 1945. More than 100,000 labored for the first time in iron factories and steel mills. Another 200,000 began to work in the federal civil service, close to half in good-paying clerical positions. Almost a half million black women moved away from domestic service positions to labor in industries for larger paychecks than they had ever received. Overall, average annual wages for African Americans increased from $500 to $2,000 (compared to an increase from $1000 to $2,600 for whites.)

The availability of industrial employment triggered the movement of one million African Americans from the rural South to urban areas across the country, especially in California, Illinois, Michigan, and New York. Over a third of the Deep South's young African Americans left for jobs in northern cities. Violent clashes with whites who were also flooding into high-employment urban areas occurred in all regions of the country. The largest racial clash during the war took place in Detroit where competition for housing and jobs, racial animosity, hot summer weather, and a steady increase of hostile incidents finally escalated to full-scale violence in June 1943. For two days, whites and blacks roamed the streets attacking and counterattacking each other before federal troops arrived to restore order. Nine whites and 25 blacks were killed with over 1,000 citizens injured.

As the case for industrial employment, Roosevelt's moves to boost African-American strength in the military resulted in noticeable changes, though limitations remained. Though the number of blacks serving in the U.S. Army increased from 100,000 in late 1941 to 700,000 by 1944, over half remained stationed in the United States due to the reluctance of Army commanders to use them overseas. At home or abroad, African-American soldiers were an underutilized resource, often performing support roles such as bridge building and road construction. Though the Navy began to organize black Marine units, a majority of blacks continued to serve as mess men, laundry hands, and dock workers. Nevertheless, some black combat units distinguished themselves when given the opportunity. Trained at Fort Hood, Texas, the all-black 761st Tank Battalion known as the "Black Panthers" served under General George Patton, earning distinction for its courageous fighting during the Battle of the Bulge in late 1944 and later helping to spearhead the final advance into Germany. The most famous African-American fighters of the war proved to be the **"Tuskegee Airmen"**—black military pilots who trained in Tuskegee, Alabama. Initially assigned outdated "hand-me-down" aircraft to perform ground support roles that prevented them from engaging in air-to-air combat, the African-American aviators for the 99th Pursuit (Fighter) Squadron were first deployed in the invasions of North Africa and Sicily before being assimilated into the 332nd Fighter Group based in southern Italy under the command of Colonel (later General) Benjamin O. Davis, Jr. The "Red Tails," as the pilots of the 332nd were known because of the distinctive red-painted tails on their P-47s and P-51s, achieved fame escorting B-29 Super Fortresses of the Fifteenth Air Force during strategic bombing raids on Germany and other enemy targets in Central Europe with minimal losses to the heavy bombers. Of the 1,000 pilots trained at Tuskegee, 445 were shipped overseas. One hundred and fifty died in combat or accidents while 32 were shot down and captured. By the war's end, the 99th and the 332nd earned three Distinguished Unit Citations, 150

Photograph of several Tuskegee Airmen at Ramitelli, Italy, March 1945.

Distinguished Flying Crosses, a Silver Star, and 14 Bronze Stars. They were credited with destroying 112 German planes in combat and another 150 on the ground while eliminating hundreds of enemy trucks and rail cars, and even sinking a naval destroyer. (In 2012, George Lucas released the film *Red Tails* to retell the Tuskegee Airmen's story to a new generation of Americans unaware of their contribution.)

Active participation in the war effort led to increased pride and assertiveness by many African Americans for social change at home even before the war ended. While extolling black citizens to show loyalty to their country by supporting the fight against the nation's enemies, the African-American press continued to stress that the benefits of equal rights should come as a result. The influential Pittsburgh *Courier* led a "Double V" campaign, calling for the defeat of the Axis abroad while continuing to advocate for the end to Jim Crow at home. In 1942, the Congress of Racial Equality (CORE) organized in Chicago to push for an end to segregation through nonviolent direct action. The successful use of sit-ins by the group's black and white members, two decades before their popularity by antiwar activists and civil rights protesters during the 1960s, led to the desegregation of public facilities in Chicago, Denver, Detroit, and many other cities outside the South. Meanwhile, the legal division of the NAACP achieved a significant victory when the Supreme Court overturned the Texas white primary law in its 1944 *Smith v Allwright* decision. Blacks outside of the South also began to assert themselves politically during the war. With nearly 90 percent of southern black migrants eventually settling in the seven states with the largest electoral vote counts, African American political power rose as these states were very closely balanced between the Democrats and Republicans. As a result, northern politicians from both major parties began to woo black voters who often held the balance of power in close elections—a political development brought about by the war that would serve African Americans well in the postwar years.

Hispanics and the War

With over 350,000 serving in the military, Mexican Americans played a significant role during the war. Tens of thousands of Latinos also left agricultural work in the countryside to labor in shipyards, aircraft factories, and other war industries where they previously had been excluded. In Los Angeles, a city containing the largest Hispanic population outside of Mexico, certain Latino youths known as pachucos grew increasingly discontented with local prejudice, segregation, and poverty by expressing racial pride in numerous ways, the most noticeable being the wearing of the "zoot suit"—a men's clothing style actually originating in Harlem noted for its long jackets with padded shoulders and baggy pants accessorized with a long key chain and felt hat. Anglo civilians associated the suit wearers with increased violent gang activity and believed the amount of material used to create a zoot suit was an extravagant waste of material in wartime. White servicemen stationed in Los Angeles occasionally engaged in altercations with Latino youths who they tended to view negatively as draft dodgers and juvenile delinquents. On June 4, 1943, a group of sailors who fought with some pachucos earlier in the evening began a rampage against any Mexican-American youths they encountered, beating them while stripping off their zoot suits. With a supportive local press, local police stood idly by over the next four nights as a few thousand sailors, marines, and private citizens proceeded to enter Latino neighborhoods and randomly attack pachucos during these so-called "Zoot Suit Riots" until military authorities finally ordered the soldiers and sailors back to their bases and ships. Though local newspapers praised the servicemen for clearing the streets of "hoodlums" and the city council soon banned the wearing of zoot suits, a governor's commission later attributed racism as the main cause of the riots.

As large numbers of Latinos left farms in favor of work in war factories, an agricultural labor shortage ensued. In addition to using German POW labor, the federal government responded by arranging the Mexican Farm Labor Program Agreement (also known as the *bracero* program) to provide Mexican laborers to work legally for American farmers and ranchers for the duration of the war. The agreement guaranteed a minimum wage of 30 cents an hour and humane treatment in the form of adequate shelter, food, and sanitation. Two hundred thousand braceros eventually worked in the United States during the war, with over half laboring in California. When Texas farmers balked at the terms of the agreement, however, the Mexican government refused to allow temporary work visas for migrant farm workers to enter Texas. Nevertheless, farmers in South Texas benefited during the war from access to undocumented Mexican labor.

Native American Contributions

Twenty-five thousand Native Americans served in the armed forces (some were drafted, some volunteered), mostly in the U.S. Army serving in fully integrated units. Ira Hayes, a Pima from Arizona, earned fame as one of the Marines raising the American flag atop Mount Suribachi during the Battle for Iwo Jima depicted in Joe Rosenthal's famous Pulitzer Prize-winning photo. The most well-

Japanese-Americans transferring from train to bus at Lone Pine, California, bound for the war relocation authority center at Manzanar.
April 1942

known contribution of Native Americans came from 400 Navajo "code talkers" who served in the US Marine Corps in the Pacific and relayed coded messages in their rare language, making it impossible for the Japanese to decipher their transmissions. (The Army successfully used some Choctaw code talkers in Europe during World War I and also used a few other non-Navajo code talkers during WW II). Another 50,000 Native Americans left their reservations to perform war work, primarily on the West Coast.

The Internment of Japanese Americans

One of the most shameful episodes for the United States during the war involved the nation's treatment of ethnic Japanese residents living on the West Coast. Almost 50,000 were "Issei," or first generation aliens who often could not vote and endured other restrictions by state and federal law. Another 80,000 were "Nisei," or American-born Japanese who were legal citizens who nevertheless found themselves subject to the century-old prejudices often found in the western United States against all Asians. Despite the climate of legal discrimination and a myriad of restrictions based on local custom, many Japanese prospered in California, Oregon, and Washington as small truck farmers and fishermen.

After the attack on Pearl Harbor, fear and hysteria reigned on the West Coast as politicians, editors, and many in the general public feared that the Japanese residents would undertake espionage and sabotage missions for the enemy. Government officials did nothing to stop that perception even though the Federal Bureau of Investigation found no basis for such fears. The region's long-standing anti-Japanese racism explains much of this thinking—in Hawaii, home to a much larger Japanese population than existing on the West Coast and the location of the Pearl Harbor attack, few questioned the loyalty of the islands' Japanese Americans. Some on the West Coast also coveted Japanese-American property.

In February 1942, President Roosevelt bowed to the public clamor and signed Executive Order 9066, which authorized the U.S. military to remove any and all people from designated "military exclusion zones." Ultimately, the West Coast became the only declared zone and only people of Japanese descent were excluded. Without any legal due process, ethnic Japanese men, women, and children (including Nisei who were U.S. citizens) were ordered to report to "assembly centers," often located at fairground facilities and horse stables at racetracks, for processing and to await completion of the ten internment camps (officially known as "war relocation centers"), which would become their ultimate destination. Given less than a week to dispose of property that they could not take with them, Japanese Americans lost millions of dollars of property as they sold land, homes, and businesses at prices far below market value. Many had to simply abandon property they could not sell, returning after the war to find strangers living in their homes or farming on their lands.

Camp conditions were generally poor. Mostly located in desert or mountain areas of six western states (two were placed in Arkansas), internees were often subjected

Frank Fujita, Jr.—A Japanese Texan Prisoner of the Empire of the Rising Sun

Due to his unique situation of being the only Japanese-American combat soldier captured by Japanese forces during World War II, Frank Fujita's wartime experiences differed from those of any other Texan. Fujita's father, Frank Fujita, Sr., arrived in America from Nagasaki, Japan in 1914, ostensibly to study American methods of agriculture. Shunning such an education, however, he chose instead to work as a travelling private chef for railroad company officials. While on a layover in Illinois, he met Fujita's future mother, a white woman from Oklahoma working as a waitress in a local hotel, and they eventually married. Born in 1921, Frank Fujita, Jr. became the second-oldest of the couple's five children. Though the family often moved around Oklahoma and North Texas during his youth, the family finally settled in Abilene, Texas in 1937. Young Frank Fujita attended Abilene High School where he stood out because of his ethnicity and his incredible drawing ability, which led to his cartoons being showcased in school and local newspapers.

Following the lead of one of his friends who served in the Texas National Guard and painted a picture of excitement and adventure, Fujita received permission from his parents to join an artillery battalion of the 36th Infantry Division in 1938. In late 1941, as hostilities with Japan seemed more imminent, the U.S. Army separated Fujita's battalion from the already-activated 36th Division and shipped the unit to the Pacific Theater to form a new artillery brigade to bolster American defenses in the Philippines. Eight days after embarking from California, Fujita's convoy received word of the Japanese attack on Pearl Harbor. Diverted initially to Australia, Fujita's unit was ordered to the Dutch East Indies in January 1942 to help defend Java. Japanese forces invaded the island on March 1, 1942 and overwhelmed the Allied defenders within a week, resulting in Fujita's capture.

The first half of Fujita's 42-month long incarceration mirrored the experiences of other Allied POWs, largely because the enemy guards had not yet discovered his Japanese ancestry. On Java, Japanese guards brutally mistreated Fujita and his comrades while demanding immediate compliance to their orders and expecting the POWs to constantly bow to them. Failure to do so resulted in severe beatings. The Japanese forced the prisoners to labor on the island while being crowded in squalid camps with horrendous sanitation issues. Latrines in the camps consisted of open pits infested with disease-carrying flies. The prisoners' quarters were constantly infested with bedbugs, fleas, and lice while the food provided was meager and of poor quality, often consisting of small quantities of rice, bread, and soup infested with worms. Eventually, Fujita developed pellagra—a condition that led to cracked skin all about his body. The coating came off his tongue and the skin around his scrotum peeled off leading to unbearably painful chafing while walking.

After six months on Java, the Japanese crammed Fujita and other chosen prisoners into the holds of cargo ships and transported them to Changi prison camp in Singapore, a larger facility containing over 15,000 British and Australian prisoners. Living conditions there proved to be no better than on Java. Fujita and the other POWs ate whatever they could find—large snails, stray birds, and, in one instance, they killed and ate a small dog that turned out to be the British officers' mascot. In December 1942, Fujita and a contingent of men from his unit were again loaded into cargo ships, this time to be transported to Nagasaki, Japan—his father's former home—for hard labor at local shipyards. There the climate was much chillier than in Indonesia, with Siberian winds blowing through the cramped quarters which had no doors or windows. Thin straw mats and a few cotton blankets provided the only protection from the extreme cold. The food provided was usually a small allotment of rice and barley plus a soup consisting of discarded vegetables and fish parts. At the work site, the Japanese formed the prisoners into groups by task, with Fujita's crew used to build and maintain scaffolding for other work crews.

Fujita toiled in the shipyards for four months until a Japanese guard who could read English discovered his heritage while skimming over the prison roster. This was the moment Fujita had long feared, convinced that the Japanese would single him out and kill him for being a racial traitor even though he was a proud American. Instead, enemy officers tried in vain to teach him the Japanese language and indoctrinate him to their cause. For many months, Fujita was given lighter workloads and protected from harassment by guards. One day in August 1943, however, hateful guards took out their anger on Fujita. When their officers left the base to attend important meetings, the guards took him into a room where they took turns bending him over and smacking him full force in the back and buttocks with clubs the size of baseball bats while kicking and punching him in the face. Despite the thrashing he received, Fujita refused to fall to the ground, partly out of spite, but also because he had seen beaten prisoners who fell down receive even worse treatment, sometimes resulting in death. When the guards finally tired, they marched him back to his fellow prisoners where he promptly passed out.

> *In October 1943, the Japanese ordered Fujita to Tokyo and informed him that he would deliver propaganda messages over the radio or "his life would not be guaranteed." A dozen other coerced POWs joined Fujita in the broadcasts, mostly individuals with previous radio or entertainment experience, but there were also a couple of Americans who willingly collaborated with the enemy and were greatly despised by Fujita and the other prisoners. For the remainder of the war, Fujita passed the time delivering lackluster radio messages, observing the Allied bombings of Tokyo, and making entries into a secret diary he had kept since being captured on Java despite the Japanese military's threat to shoot any POWs caught possessing a journal.*
>
> *As the war drew to a close, Frank Fujita greatly feared that he and the other prisoners would be executed and began making preliminary plans to escape. A lack of opportunity to flee and the war's abrupt end negated such thoughts. Instead, Fujita and the other prisoners' morale soared as American planes identified their camp and dropped packages of food and medical supplies. The next day, U.S. Navy ships were spotted in Tokyo Bay with small boats heading for the prison camp located along the coast. Though physically weakened from years of mistreatment and malnourishment (his pre-war frame of 145 pounds had been reduced to 90 pounds), Fujita was so elated at the sight of American ships that he joined other POWs who foolishly jumped into the bay to swim out to the incoming boats, almost drowning in the process before being plucked out of the water by the shocked sailors.*
>
> *After the war, Fujita's secret war diary served as evidence in various war crimes trials before being returned. Though partially disabled due to his wartime treatment, Fujita eventually used his artistic talents to work as an illustrator for the Air Force. Before his death in 1996, Fujita published his memoirs based on his diary, which include many drawings and intricate maps he created to powerfully relay to his readers many important aspects of his brutal incarceration.*

to extreme hot and cold. Some died due to inability to acclimate. Individuals and families lived in barracks with little to no privacy. Though the term "concentration camp" would be associated for generations in the public mind with the Nazis, American internment camps were also concentration camps in that they forcibly kept people inside against their will with a combination of barbed wire fences and armed guards.

Some internees challenged their imprisonment in federal court, including California native Fred Korematsu, who police arrested for refusing to report to his designated assembly center. In 1944, a majority of Supreme Court justices ruled in the *Korematsu v. United States* case that the government's internment policy was constitutional, thus continuing the tradition of allowing the executive and congressional branches of the government much leeway in defining "military necessity" in times of war. During the 1980s, a government commission determined that "race prejudice, war hysteria, and a failure of political leadership" were the main factors behind the forced relocations. This admission led Congress in 1988 to issue an official apology to Japanese Americans and to grant $20,000 compensation to each of the 80,000 surviving members of the camps. Ten years later, the healing process continued when Fred Korematsu received the Presidential Medal of Freedom from President Bill Clinton.

Despite being forcibly relocated by their government, 26,000 Nisei determined to prove their loyalty left the camps and served in the U.S. Army, with over half serving in the 442nd Regimental Combat Team—an all-Japanese-American infantry regiment assigned to combat duty in Europe. The 442nd became the most decorated U.S. regiment of the entire war (21 of its members earned Congressional Medals of Honor) while sustaining the highest casualty rate (57 percent) of any similar-sized American combat unit.

VICTORY IN EUROPE, 1943-1945

Despite the common goal of defeating the Axis, a significant degree of mistrust characterized the uneasy alliance between the United States, Great Britain, and the Soviet Union during World War II. The three powers not only brought different strengths to the inevitable winning coalition—the Soviet Union had seemingly endless manpower, England had its superior navy, and the United States possessed vast natural resources and industrial capacity—they also had contrary national temperaments and interests. The Soviets sought to drive the Germans and their allies out of Russia and to establish a strong security zone in Eastern Europe while maintaining a desire to export communist ideology abroad. The English wished to defend their island and overseas empire while preventing Soviet expansion and the spread of communism in Europe. The Americans sought to defeat the Germans and Japanese, to end totalitarianism, and extend its economic reach throughout the world.

The Debate Over Strategy in Europe

One of the earliest manifestations of the potentially tense alliance involved the development of an effective strategy to defeat Germany. Bearing the brunt of Axis forces driving deep within western Russia in 1941 and 1942, the impatient Joseph Stalin demanded the western Allies open up a major **second front** against the Nazis in France as soon as possible. Such an offensive would draw away a significant number of German divisions from the Eastern Front, guarantee the survival of the USSR, and allow the Russians to counterattack. The Soviet dictator, prone to bouts of paranoia, believed western allied leaders privately hoped that the communists and fascists would kill each other off on the Russian steppes. Determined not to have the Soviets take the bulk of the punishment from German aggression, Stalin occasionally dangled the possibility of a cease fire with Hitler in order to spur American and British decision makers to action.

For their part, American military leaders generally concurred with Stalin's sentiment albeit for different reasons. Not favoring a long, drawn-out conflict, and trained since the Civil War to amass forces and hurl overwhelming firepower at the enemy's strength, American generals such as Roosevelt's Army Chief of Staff George C. Marshall wished to gather significant U.S. and British troops in England before ordering an invasion across the English Channel to hit the Nazis in northern France. Such a move would force Hitler to divert forces from Russia and keep the Soviets in the fight. After liberating Paris, the western Allied forces would drive into the heavily industrial Ruhr region of Western Germany and knock the Nazis out of the war. Marshall made plans, tentatively approved by Roosevelt, for a sizeable military buildup in England throughout 1942. Ideally these forces would not go into action until early 1943, but he also authorized a contingency for a desperate late-1942 attack if the USSR appeared to be on the verge of collapse.

British Prime Minister Winston Churchill wholeheartedly opposed the idea of a cross-Channel invasion. Stung by the heavy troop losses that Britain endured during World War I and the early stages of World War II, he favored a patient, less direct approach. Adopting the traditional viewpoint of a naval power's leader, Churchill preferred to blockade Axis ports and pick at the enemy's weak points along its overextended periphery. Not believing that sufficient American and British forces could be accumulated for a successful cross-Channel strike for many years, he tried to convince Roosevelt that an attack upon Vichy-controlled Northwest Africa showed more promise for initial success. Such a move would support English troops in their struggle against Rommel's Afrika Korps and allow the British to control the Mediterranean Sea, freeing England to resume use of the Suez Canal in Egypt to channel supplies and troops into North Africa from India. General Marshall strongly dissented against Churchill's proposal, arguing that an attack on northwestern Africa would be a mere sideshow interfering with the buildup of forces in England. If Roosevelt accepted the plan, Marshall warned that the U.S. should commit to a purely defensive posture in Europe and send all nonessential resources to the Pacific for offensive operations against the Japanese.

Roosevelt set aside Marshall's complaints and ultimately accepted Churchill's North Africa proposal, hoping that the first American ground forces would get into action against Axis troops before the midterm congressional elections set for early November 1942. Though the president also concurred with the plans for a cross-Channel invasion, the date for that attack would be pushed back until mid-1944. Stalin was furious when informed of Roosevelt's decision. Though Churchill personally traveled to Moscow to visit the dictator in August 1942, Stalin received him coldly. The seeds of mistrust had been planted anew.

Operation Torch

The attack on northwestern Africa, code-named Operation TORCH, involved 65,000 American and English troops at three landing sites in Morocco and Algeria under the overall command of U.S. General Dwight Eisenhower. Plans to land troops as far to the east as Tunisia were scrapped due to fears over German air power in the central Mediterranean and possible Spanish entry into the war disrupting Allied supply lines through the Strait of Gibraltar. French forces initially resisted all three landings and hundreds of American soldiers were killed before negotiators quickly struck an agreement with the local Vichy military commander, Admiral Jean François Darlan. In return for ordering a cease fire, the admiral was allowed to assume administrative control over French North Africa. Though many in the United States criticized the military for generously dealing with a Nazi sympathizer, the move saved additional American soldiers' lives plus Darlan was soon killed by an antifascist Free French assassin.

The successful Allied landings in Northwest Africa initiated a chain of responses by the Axis. While Italian forces moved into the French island of Corsica in the western Mediterranean, Hitler ordered Nazi forces to move into Vichy France to protect the southern coast from potential attack. German troops also began to pour into Tunisia where they linked up with scattered Vichy French forces trekking eastward from Algeria and over 200,000 German and Italian soldiers fleeing Libya after the defeat at El Alamein. The initial Allied decision not to attack Tunisia assured a hard fight

Photo shows Italian prisoners of war captured in the El Alamein area entering the "cage" preceded by their guard.

against strong defensive positions taken by Rommel in the eastern Atlas Mountains before all of North Africa could be secured. The first assaults by green American troops against Rommel's veteran Afrika Korps ended horribly, most notably at Kasserine Pass in February 1943, but time and logistics worked against Rommel who eventually had to leave North Africa due to illness. After Hitler questionably reinforced Tunisia (weakening the effort on the Russian Front in the process), Axis forces eventually found their supply lines cut off by the British Royal Navy and American air superiority. While U.S. forces under General George Patton renewed their attacks against their weakened foes from the west, British General Bernard Montgomery finally succeeded in breaking through the German and Italian lines from the east. In May 1943, over 250,000 Axis forces in North Africa, over half of them German troops, capitulated to the Allies.

The Allied Invasions of Sicily and Southern Italy

Stalin reluctantly accepted the fact that Operation TORCH meant there would be no second front established in northern France during 1942. He soon discovered that the Western Allies would not attack there in 1943 either. Before the German and Italian defeat in North Africa, the British and American high commands were already pondering their next moves. Churchill and Roosevelt agreed to a summit to take place in recently-captured Casablanca, Morocco in January 1943 to hammer out an agreement for joint action. Churchill and his military staff came to the Casablanca Conference prepared to argue for a move against Sicily as the first step to knock Italy out of the war. As a result of dogged British determination for their viewpoint and divisions among Roosevelt's commanders about how to proceed, Churchill convinced the president to authorize an attack on Sicily. In an attempt to placate Stalin's assumed anger from the further delay of establishing the Second Front in France, Roosevelt and Churchill decided to commence a strategic bombing campaign against Axis targets and publicly announce unconditional surrender as a declared Allied war aim. Stalin seethed, however, when he learned that northern France would not be the next location for a major American and British offensive, threatening to conquer Germany himself and establish a puppet state there without consulting the western Allies.

Preparations for the Sicilian invasion included an elaborate ruse designed to confuse the Germans about the location of the next Allied Mediterranean offensive (later depicted in the novel and movie *The Man Who Never Was*.) Acquiring the cadaver of a drowned Englishman, British agents handcuffed a suitcase filled with fake documents to the body, which was dumped along the Spanish coast to give the illusion that he was an important courier who had been lost in a plane crash. After the corpse's discovery, Spanish authorities gave copies of the satchel's contents to the Germans who considered them authentic. Hitler became so convinced that the next Allied move would be against Sardinia and Greece that he ordered reinforcements there but not to the real target of Sicily where over 150,000 American, British, and Canadian troops came ashore in mid-July 1943, soon followed by 300,000 more. The Italians had close to 300,000 soldiers in Sicily, but most began to reconsider their allegiance to Mussolini and showed little desire to fight. Over 60,000 German defenders provided the bulk of the resistance, benefiting from the rocky terrain to slow the Allied advance and inflict heavy casualties before evacuating the island after a five-week confrontation.

As the fighting in Sicily raged, King Victor Emmanuel ordered Mussolini's arrest (though German commandos soon rescued the deposed dictator, transporting him to northern Italy) and named Marshal Pietro Badoglio to be the new prime minister. Badgolio publicly announced Italy's continued support for the Axis but soon began secret negotiations with the Allies, finally surrendering in early September 1943 as British and American troops began to invade southern Italy. Hitler built up German strength on the Italian peninsula, ordered the occupation of Rome, and demanded the deactivation of Italian forces. German soldiers imprisoned Italians who had been fighting alongside them in Russia and massacred over 5,000 Italian soldiers in Greece when they refused the order to disarm (an episode dramatized in Louis De Bernières's novel *Captain Corelli's Mandolin*). While the Allies encountered stiff resistance securing a beachhead at Salerno, German forces under Field Marshall Albert Kesselring dug into the rough terrain of the Italian countryside and prepared for a grinding war of attrition. Though gradually driven back over the next 18 months, Kesselring succeeded in protecting Germany's southern flank for the remainder of the war. When Germany finally surrendered in May 1945, the Allies had only reached the Italian border with Austria.

Strategic Bombing

The origin of high-altitude strategic bombing can be found in the prewar writings of air power advocates who garnered the enthusiastic support of British and American air marshals wishing to distinguish their branch of the service within their countries' respective military apparatuses. In addition to advocating the combat use of aircraft for such tactical objectives as ground support attacks, the air marshals came to believe that victory in modern war could be achieved through the **"strategic" bombing** of economic targets (factories) and infrastructure facilities (such as dams, bridges, and rail stations). The marshals argued that large numbers of thickly armored bombers armed with multiple machine gun turrets and flying in tight formations without fighter escort could adequately defend themselves while dropping heavy payloads with precision from very high altitudes to deliver crippling blows to the enemy's ability to prosecute a war while receiving relatively light casualties. At the very least, they wished to try. Looking for another sign of commitment to show Stalin in lieu of opening the Second Front in 1943, Roosevelt and Churchill agreed at the Casablanca Conference to implement a combined bombing offensive against the Axis.

Prior to 1943, Germany and Great Britain had undertaken high-altitude bombing attacks against the other with minimal results. During the Battle of Britain, German bombers killed hundreds of civilians and destroyed portions of London and other English cities but did little damage to industrial targets while suffering heavy losses. Churchill ordered retaliatory strikes against German industrial cities. These counterattacks also killed many civilians and damaged many neighborhoods but failed to destroy the intended targets and resulted in significant losses to air crews. Nevertheless, in their desire for revenge and to take the horrors of war directly to the German people, Churchill and his air marshals authorized frequent "area bombings" of German cities designed primarily to kill civilians and break the morale of the survivors. To reduce the loss of planes, these raids primarily took place at night. In one notable instance, British pilots armed with incendiary devices firebombed Hamburg in late-July 1943 resulting in over 40,000 civilian deaths and the destruction of over a quarter million homes.

During the Combined Bomber Offensive of 1943, the U.S. Eighth Air Force joined the British Royal Air Force (RAF) in hitting enemy targets for the first time utilizing B-17 "Flying Fortresses." Generally opposed to nighttime area bombing (mostly on military grounds rather than moral objections), American commanders preferred to focus on daytime precision bombing of selected industrial targets even though the German and British failure to produce consistent results should have dissuaded them from the attempt. The U.S. air marshals professed more faith in the B-17s than the British Lancaster bombers and the German equivalents, plus they wanted to see how the Flying Fortresses would perform. Subsequent experience would show that American high-altitude bombing did little directly in 1943 to slow the German war effort. High-altitude "precision bombing" was, in practice, not very precise at all. A U.S. military

French General Henri Geraud, President Franklin Roosevelt, British Prime Minister Winston Churchill, and Free French military commander Charles DeGaulle discuss the course of the war against the Axis Powers at an conference of the Allies at Casablanca, January 24, 1943.
Photo credit: FDR Presidential Library.

survey estimated that only 3 percent of bombs dropped by American air crews hit their intended targets. The remaining ordinance landed on scattered fields, forests, churches, and houses across the countryside. Far from contributing to the breakdown of German public morale, resentment among civilians only stiffened as they felt unfairly targeted by enemy planes. Though the bombing campaign contributed to the Allied achievement of complete air superiority over Europe by mid-1944 (due to the great reduction of Luftwaffe numbers as German fighter pilots were shot down at unsustainable rates), that result would have occurred anyway due to the massive buildup of American air forces from 1942 to 1944. The Nazis largely maintained industrial production through 1944 while inflicting heavy losses upon Allied bomber crews. With some raids producing 20 percent losses, the B-17 proved not to be a "flying fortress." Efficient aerial attacks versus Axis strategic targets began to take place in mid-1944, resulting from the achievement of complete Allied air supremacy, the development of the P-51 Mustang to provide effective long-range fighter escort, and a shift to lower-altitude strikes by medium-sized fighter-bombers. Only then did German manufacturing and transportation facilities suffer consistent destruction. Still, the

RAF continued to undertake terror raids against enemy population centers, joined by American squadrons in a controversial February 1945 fire-bombing of Dresden in eastern Germany, which killed over 30,000 civilians for no apparent purpose other than the city had not yet been attacked.

The Combined Bombing Offensive has received intense criticism from military personnel and historians alike. While some question the morality of sinking to the level of the enemy by deliberately targeting civilians (over 300,000 German civilians were killed by Allied air raids), most have noted the tremendous cost in manpower and material needed to wage such a campaign for such relatively moderate returns. The British Bomber Command lost over 50,000 airmen in the skies over Europe. U.S. bomber crews suffered comparable combat losses in addition to losing over 35,000 in accidents. (By comparison, the entire U.S. Navy suffered only 16,000 fatalities during the war). Further, the ground personnel and resources necessary to build and maintain the heavy bomber bases in England, if diverted to support ground units, could have provided the Allies with forces comparable to an extra field army in Europe. Though easy to point out the inadequacies of the Allied air marshals' bold predictions for "victory through air power," such condemnation can only be delivered through the luxury of hindsight. Never before deployed in combat, high-altitude strategic bombers represented a genuine hope that they could be used to defeat the enemy with greatly lower casualties than witnessed in the First World War. Experience eventually showed this to be an overly optimistic illusion.

The Tehran Conference

In late-November 1943, the "Big Three" Allied leaders (Roosevelt, Churchill, and Stalin) met jointly for the first time in Tehran, Iran to discuss plans for the long-awaited cross-Channel invasion of northern France and the establishment of the Second Front. Churchill remained in favor of a postponement of the offensive (now code-named OVERLORD) in favor of continued attacks on Axis positions in the Mediterranean. Holding many strong cards at the conference as his troops continued to drive the Germans back along the Eastern Front, Stalin pressed for firm commitments on OVERLORD and would not discuss much else until they finalized its particulars. Roosevelt also strongly desired a cross-Channel attack in mid-1944, believing it important to satisfy Stalin in the short term and hopefully usher in a spirit of cooperation for the postwar years. Ultimately, the Big Three chose May 1944 as the first possible date for the invasion, which would be led by Dwight D. Eisenhower, the American general who had previously overseen the attacks on North Africa and southern Italy. Stalin received assurances that the Soviets would be able to annex the Baltic States and portions of eastern Poland (areas soon to be under Russian military control) as well as some island territories from Japan in East Asia. In exchange for these concessions, Stalin satisfied FDR by agreeing to launch a major offensive on the Eastern Front coinciding with OVERLORD, vowing to enter the war against Japan after Germany's defeat, agreeing to partition Germany upon its defeat, and promising to join a new postwar global organization.

D-Day

The buildup of men and material in England for OVERLORD continued throughout the first months of 1944. Knowing from ULTRA intercepts that the Germans expected the cross-Channel invasion to take place at Pas de Calais, located only 20 miles from southern England, Eisenhower and the British generals did everything they could to reinforce that notion. Their deception included allowing the Germans to intercept fake radio transmissions and planting fraudulent documents to be captured, which implied that Calais would be the target zone. Eisenhower also created a faux army base in southeast England to convince Hitler that armored divisions under the command of General George Patton were assembling there for a quick strike on Calais. Such ruses ultimately paid off, helping OVERLORD's success and saving many lives as Hitler kept valuable reserves in the area of Calais rather than the real attack point chosen by Eisenhower: five beaches in Normandy on the north-central French coast.

Weather considerations postponed "D-Day" until June 6, but six Allied divisions (three American, two British, and one Canadian) of 100,000 men finally came ashore in the largest amphibious invasion in world history. The attack involved 5,000 ships transporting troops and vehicles across the Channel and providing offshore bombardment. Eight hundred planes dropped American, British, and Free French paratroopers inland to support the landings while an additional 300 planes strafed German positions. Most Allied soldiers came ashore with little difficulty, the major exception being American forces on "Omaha Beach" that encountered rough seas and tenacious resistance by German defenders who pinned them down with withering artillery and machine-gun fire from cliffs overlooking the landing zone for much of the day until being finally dislodged (Steven Spielberg re-created the carnage that took place on Omaha Beach in the beginning of his 1998 film *Saving Private Ryan*.)

The Allies suffered 10,000 casualties to secure the Normandy beaches, which soon became the staging area for a massive buildup of men, vehicles, and equipment allowing for the breakout that would establish the Second Front. Within ten days, over 500,000 men came ashore. By July 1, over a million soldiers occupied the Normandy beachhead. Allied forces advanced slowly southward as they encountered strong resistance from German troops using the hedgerow-laden terrain of the "Bocage" to their advantage. In this region, high earthen banks topped by thick hedgerows lined the roads and pastures, providing the Germans with natural walls of defense that neutralized the ability of Allied armored units to maneuver. Improvising American soldiers, however, eventually developed a means to cut through the hedgerows, setting the stage for a major breakout into the French countryside.

As Allied forces drove off the Normandy beachhead, events taking place in Germany almost ended the war sooner than many had expected. On July 20, Colonel Claus von Stauffenberg, chief of staff for the Reserve Army, planted a suitcase bomb under a table at a conference attended by Hitler at his "Wolf's Lair" military headquarters in East Prussia. The explosion killed four men but only wounded Hitler and twenty others. Sensing the war was lost and that Hitler planned to destroy Germany in the process, Stauffenberg and his fellow conspirators had planned the dictator's assassination as the first step in a greater effort to seize control of the government and negotiate a peace settlement with the Allies. Hitler's survival, however, ruined the plot. In an effort to cover up his knowledge of the conspiracy, General Friedrich Fromm, commander of the Reserve Army, ordered the colonel's arrest and quick execution by firing squad. Nevertheless, Fromm and many others involved in the conspiracy, or with knowledge of it, were subsequently put on trial and executed.

A week after the attempt on Hitler, the Allies launched a major offensive, finally breaking out into the French interior. American forces under General Patton and British troops under General Montgomery now moved swiftly westward into Brittany, southward toward Paris, and eastward toward the Belgian border. On August 15, American and Free French forces landed in southern France, capturing valuable ports before driving northward. Ten days later, Allied troops entered Paris. As enemy resistance crumbled, American and British forces pressed eastward toward Germany, occupying most of Belgium and Luxembourg by mid-September. Eisenhower authorized a bold plan devised by Montgomery to swing around German defenses by striking quickly into the Netherlands, followed by a drive southward into the Ruhr region, Germany's industrial heartland. Montgomery called for 30,000 paratroopers to capture key bridges behind enemy lines, followed by the arrival of supporting armored divisions, which would secure the bridges that would serve as major pathways into the Ruhr. The operation (code-named Market-Garden) failed, however, due to a combination of bad weather, the complicated logistics of capturing bridges over 50 miles behind the front lines, and the tenacious defense of two German armored divisions in the area. The failure of Market-Garden meant the war would not end in 1944.

As winter settled on the new Western Front, Allied forces made preparations for a final Spring offensive into Germany. Hitler used the lull to organize a massive counterattack through the densely wooded Ardennes Forest area of Belgium. Pulling crucial forces from the crumbling Eastern Front, Hitler gambled that a large mobile attacking force thrown against the unsuspecting Allies could drive a wedge between the British and American armies, forcing a grand Allied retreat, and providing a tremendous morale boost for Germany. The surprise attack began on December 16, taking advantage of fog and snow that neutralized the Allied air supremacy. Over a quarter of a million men assisted by armored divisions punched a deep "bulge" 60 miles deep and 50 miles wide into the front lines. Initially caught off guard, Eisenhower quickly mobilized over 200,000 reinforcements to stabilize the Allied position. After a week of fighting, fair weather returned, allowing Allied planes to pound German forces. Soon, General George Patton led a counterstrike that shrunk the bulge and eventually compelled Hitler to order a retreat by mid-January. With almost 90,000 casualties (19,000 killed, 47,500 wounded, and 23,000 captured or missing), the United States suffered more casualties in the "Battle of the Bulge" than in any single fight during the entire war. Hitler nevertheless squandered most of his remaining reserves, losing 100,000 men. France and Belgium remained in Allied hands as Eisenhower prepared for the final thrust into Germany. Meanwhile, the Soviets continued to drive westward along the Eastern Front. By the end of January 1945, Russian forces had not only expelled the Germans from the Soviet Union, but also controlled most of Poland, Slovakia, Hungary, and Romania.

The Yalta Conference

In February 1945, Franklin Roosevelt made the long laborious trip to Yalta on the Crimean Peninsula in southern Russia to have his final Big Three summit with Winston Churchill and Joseph Stalin. Having recently defeated Thomas Dewey, the Republican governor of New York, to win an unprecedented fourth term, Roosevelt arrived with a determination to get firm commitments from Stalin on the final phase of the war and to establish the structure for postwar cooperation. At the **Yalta Conference**, the Big Three finalized many agreements that had been initially discussed at the Tehran Conference. Prescribed zones in Germany and Central Europe for American, British, French, and Russian troops to occupy for an indeterminate amount of time were established, with the German capital of Berlin (well within the Russian zone) also to be subdivided among the four Allies. Germany would be disarmed and any captured Nazi war criminals prosecuted in a postwar tribunal. Roosevelt and Churchill reluctantly allowed Stalin to annex eastern Poland. Stalin promised (though he never followed through with his pledge) to include non-communists in a new Polish coalition government and to allow free elections in Eastern European countries under Soviet occupation. Roosevelt exacted a pledge from Stalin to enter the war against Japan three months after the conquest of Germany. In return, the Soviets could take possession of the Kurile Islands and the southern half of Sakhalin Island located to the north of Japan. Finally, Stalin reaffirmed his commitment to join the new global organization that would become the United Nations.

Critics later accused FDR of "giving away" too much to Stalin at Yalta, possibly because of his obviously failing health (he died two months after the visit). In reality, the president was still in charge of his mental faculties and while Stalin got much of what he desired, Roosevelt did exact some concrete agreements from the Soviet leader. With Russian troops in control of Eastern Europe and pouring into Germany, the strategic situation greatly favored Stalin. Further, not willing to rely on the possibility of successfully developing the atomic bomb in time to make a difference in the war, Roosevelt felt it was imperative to receive Russian assistance against Japan in East Asia.

Map 25.3 Prescribed zones for a divided Berlin

End of the War in Europe

By the Spring of 1945, the end of the war in Europe was a foregone conclusion—the only questions that remained were how long would it take for the Allies to complete the task, how many more casualties would each side have to endure, how many Axis leaders would be captured alive to be brought to justice, and what would be Europe's condition when it was all over. As Allied forces pressed into Germany, the horrors of the **Holocaust** were revealed to American and British forces as they already had been exposed by the Russians in Poland. Allied troops not only liberated prisoner-of-war camps, but also the Nazi death camps where six million Jews and an equal number of other "undesirables" such as gypsies, homosexuals, mentally and physically handicapped, and various political prisoners met their fate. Only a relatively small number of emaciated victims survived to be freed. Unable to dispose of the remaining corpses in time, German guards left piles of bodies stacked like firewood several feet high. Hardened Allied veterans of modern war could barely believe that such places existed. As one soldier wrote his family: "Every day for the rest of my life, what I've witnessed here will be the first thing I remember and the last thing I forget." While the American public had heard stories of Nazi atrocities and death camps, many discounted what they heard as wartime propaganda in the same vein as they discredited stories about the Germans spread by the British during World War I. Many American military and political leaders knew better—that these camps did exist, the main purpose to efficiently kill all who entered, either immediately in gas chambers or gradually through brutal forced labor. Anti-Semitism and simple indifference explain much of the nonexistent effort to act more decisively to aid Jewish refugees or disrupt the rail lines to the death camps. While military officials contended that attacking the rail lines (or even the gas chambers themselves) would divert resources from more efficient missions designed to speed up the end of the war, targets located only a few miles away from death camps were hit multiple times in 1944 and 1945, not to mention the fact that the military occasionally took other nonmilitary considerations under advisement when determining missions.

By the end of April 1945, Allied troops in Italy finally defeated General Kesselring's forces, captured the major northern cities of Genoa, Milan, and Venice, and forced Kesselring's successor to surrender the remainder of his army group. In the end, 60,000 Allied soldiers and 50,000 German troops died fighting on the peninsula. On April 27, Italian communist partisans captured Benito Mussolini, his mistress, and staffers as they attempted to escape to Switzerland. They were all shot the next day and brought to Milan where their bodies were displayed in the city square—a place where anti-fascists had been executed during the dictator's regime. After the corpses of Mussolini and the others received significant abuse, they were hanged upside down to the delight of jubilant anti-fascists.

Meanwhile, American and British forces pressed into western Germany, capturing the Ruhr region by mid-April as German forces surrendered en masse. On April 16, Russian forces attacked Berlin. Over a two-week period they suffered 100,000 casualties driving into the central district of the German capital against diehard Nazi fighters. Wishing to avoid Mussolini's fate, Adolf Hitler committed suicide in his private bunker on April 30. Two days later, Berlin fell to the Soviets. Though sporadic fighting continued for another week away from the capital, the war in Europe was finally over.

British Prime Minister Winston Churchill, President Franklin Roosevelt, and Soviet leader Josef Stalin confer at the Livadia Palace in Yalta, in the Soviet Union, February 9, 1945.
Photo credit: FDR Presidential Library.

The victory over Germany not only revealed the atrocities of the Holocaust but also the full extent of Nazi technical prowess. Though Hitler did not allow much funding on atomic research, preferring instead to develop more "practical" weapons, by the war's end German scientists created a whole new generation of destructive technological innovations that the dictator had hoped would miraculously turn the tide of the war. Beginning in mid-June 1944, the Germans fired almost 10,000 V-1 cruise missiles on southern England (causing over 20,000 civilian casualties) and over 3,000 short-range ballistic missiles (V-2 rockets), which killed approximately 7,000 Londoners. In the final months of the war, the Germans deployed the C-2, the world's first surface-to-air guided missiles, and a small number of crude but effective jet fighters (the ME-262s). Further, German scientists had developed prototypes for air-to-air missiles as well as long-range ballistic missiles and submarine-launched missiles capable of hitting targets in the United States.

VICTORY IN THE PACIFIC, 1943-1945

Before focusing on an effective strategy to defeat the Japanese, President Roosevelt first had to overcome the intense inter-service rivalry between the Army and the Navy. General Douglas MacArthur strongly desired to become the supreme commander of American forces in the Pacific. FDR balked at the idea, not only to avoid upsetting top Navy brass but also to prevent elevating MacArthur's status to a level that might make him a formidable Republican presidential candidate. Roosevelt also dismissed the notion of naming Chester Nimitz, the head of the Pacific Fleet, supreme commander because of latter's relative lack of prestige. Ultimately, Roosevelt decided upon a compromise—command in the Pacific would be divided. MacArthur would direct operations against the Japanese in the South Pacific. From Australia, the U.S. Army would attack New Guinea and advance westward toward the Philippines. Meanwhile, Nimitz and the U.S. Navy were charged with attacking the Japanese in the Solomon Islands located to the east of New Guinea as well as advancing upon the major enemy-held island chains in the Central Pacific. Though the arrangement was politically satisfying, the arrangement proved to be an inefficient way of conducting a major war effort against a tenacious foe. While a strongly coordinated strategy would have maximized resources, the two military branches often worked independent of each other in their separate theaters of operation, possibly prolonging the war and adding to the war's cost in men and material. Nevertheless, beginning in late 1942, American forces prepared for the grim fight ahead. Though the Japanese suffered major defeats at Midway and Guadalcanal, hundreds of thousands of soldiers remained entrenched on islands across the western Pacific prepared for a grinding war of attrition. In consultation with MacArthur and Nimitz, U.S. Army and Navy war planners in Washington ultimately developed a strategy to drive westward effectively and force a Japanese surrender within three years.

President Franklin Roosevelt (center) confers with his top Pacific commanders, Army General Douglas MacArthur and Navy Admiral Chester Nimitz in Pearl Harbor, Hawaii, July 26, 1944.

The South Pacific Campaign

After forcing the Japanese withdrawal from Guadalcanal in February 1943, the U.S. Navy began a steady drive up the narrow central gap within the Solomon Islands referred to as "the Slot" by American military personnel. The heavily defended air and naval base at Rabaul on the island of New Britain located to the north of the Solomons was the ultimate goal. After a series of successful air assaults on the Japanese stronghold, however, military leaders in Washington called off plans to attack the base. Since the 100,000-man garrison had been neutralized, American lives and resources would be spared by simply sidestepping the base and moving on to the next strategic objective in the South Pacific—the Philippines.

Simultaneous to the effort in the Solomon Islands, Douglas MacArthur led an American and Australian counterattack against Japanese forces on New Guinea. With limited sealift capacity, the general ordered his troops to cross the brutal Owen Stanleys in order to capture a major Japanese position on the northeastern portion of the island. From there, MacArthur's forces spent the first half of 1944 rapidly driving westward along New Guinea's northern coast. Finally given adequate landing craft for amphibious movement, MacArthur skillfully employed a bypassing strategy to avoid strongly-held Japanese positions while infusing a strong element of surprise in his attacks deep behind enemy lines. By the summer, his forces advanced a thousand miles to western side of New Guinea, setting the stage for his promised return to the Philippine Islands.

The Central Pacific Campaign

Even more significant to the defeat of Japan than MacArthur's push to the Philippines, the U.S. Navy's successful drive through the Central Pacific island chains provided the means for the American military to hit the Japanese home islands with long-range heavy bombers. Before such bombing could commence, the Navy first had to gain control of the Gilbert, Marshall, Caroline, and Mariana Islands. Rather than attempting to dislodge the enemy from every island enclave, Admiral Nimitz used an **"island hopping"** strategy to limit the number of engagements with the Japanese. Similar to MacArthur's bypassing operations in New Guinea, Nimitz ordered specific islands to be assaulted that would yield air bases to allow American patrol planes to neutralize the remaining islands in a chain before moving on to the next objective closer to Japan. Though this approach minimized the amount of potential casualties and spent resources, brutal engagements nevertheless took place when the key islands in a chain were invaded and entrenched Japanese defenders fought tenaciously, rarely surrendering.

The Navy's first attack in the Gilberts took place in November 1943 when marines stormed the tiny Tarawa atoll. In three days of intense fighting on Tarawa's Betio Island (which covered less than three square miles), over a thousand marines lost their lives struggling to push off the landing beaches against 5,000 Japanese defenders who fought to the death. Only 17 prisoners were taken. On nearby Makin Atoll, an assault force of 6,500 U.S. Army troops attacked a much smaller force of 800 Japanese defenders. Because effective enemy sniper fire delayed completion of the task for four days, a Japanese submarine had enough time to infiltrate the supporting fleet offshore, firing torpedoes that sunk the escort carrier *Liscome Bay* at the cost of 650 sailors—one of the largest single losses for the U.S. Navy in the entire war.

Success at Tarawa and Makin allowed Nimitz to order a leapfrogging thrust at Kwajalein Atoll in the central Marshall Islands, and Eniwetok located at the western edge of the chain. In early February 1944, intense air and offshore bombardment allowed over 40,000 marines to come ashore unmolested at the northern and southern islands at Kwajalein, setting the stage for a successful four-day fight against 8,000 Japanese defenders with less than 400 marines dead—far fewer than the costly fight on Tarawa. Because Eniwetok lay within the range of Japanese ships and aircraft based at their extensive anchorage at Truk in the central Caroline Islands, Nimitz ordered massive air assaults on the bastion from carrier-based planes before advancing further. The mid-February raids destroyed over 200 aircraft and sank multiple warships, effectively neutralizing Truk as a major base of operations. The attack on Truk not only greatly aided the conquest of Eniwetok but also allowed Nimitz to safely bypass all Japanese garrisons in the Carolines to undertake operations a thousand miles to the west of the Marshalls against the Japanese in the Marianas—large islands with airstrips long enough to support long-range bombers capable of hitting the Japanese home islands.

As American forces landed troops onshore at **Saipan**, the first major island in the Marianas to be seized, Japanese naval leaders vainly tried to disrupt the invasion by sending a fleet based in the Philippines to intervene. On June 18, 1944, with most of their veterans lost by this stage of the war, the outnumbered and relatively inexperienced Japanese pilots fell in droves to their American foes who had not only grown more experienced since the beginning of the war but were now flying superior F6F Hellcats. The Japanese lost 275 of the 373 aircraft engaged compared to the United States losing 29 planes in what became officially known as the Battle of the Philippine Sea but American pilots called "the Great Marianas Turkey Shoot." On Saipan, marines with army support fought over three weeks to clear out the 30,000 Japanese defenders doggedly resisting through a series of tunnels and reinforced bunkers, at the cost of 14,000 American killed and wounded. Near the battle's conclusion, hundreds of Japanese soldiers sacrificed themselves in fruitless "banzai" charges. Meanwhile, two-thirds of the island's 12,000 Japanese civilians (mostly women and children), convinced by their military that the American soldiers would rape and kill all survivors, congregated at the northern tip of the island and killed themselves by blowing themselves up with grenades or jumping off cliffs. The Marianas campaign concluded on August 1 with the end of enemy resistance on Tinian and Guam. As the Japanese stubbornly and pointlessly fought on, many openly speculated about the potentially high level of casualties that an invasion of Japan would entail.

The Fight for the Philippines

After securing control over northern New Guinea, General MacArthur focused on the recapture of the Philippines, which would not only fulfill his promise to Filipinos to return after his flight in early 1942, but also cut off Japan from its vital oil supplies in the Dutch East Indies. MacArthur made plans for a joint operation with the Navy to attack the archipelago with the largest force yet assembled in the Pacific. Choosing to bypass the large southern island of Mindanao, the general favored first landing troops on the east-central island of Leyte in preparation for a grand thrust at the major northern island of Luzon (on which Manila was located.) On October 20, 1944, after troops secured a beachhead on Leyte, MacArthur waded ashore in front of newsreel cameras and boldly announced that his pledge to return had been fulfilled. The main fight on land and offshore, however, had yet to occur.

Japanese leaders decided to contest the Leyte landing by desperately deploying their remaining naval forces in a complex series of maneuvers designed to surprise the Americans and destroy the fleet supporting the landing. The last remaining four carriers of the Imperial Navy with its support ships bore down from southern Japan. Because the carriers only possessed a total of 100 planes with novice pilots, this fleet served as a decoy to hopefully lure the American carriers away from the Leyte area. Meanwhile, two separate Japanese naval task forces consisting of large surface ships were to converge on Leyte Gulf from the west, with one group of battleships, cruisers, and destroyers taking a route around the north of the island and another taking a southern route.

On October 23, two American submarines spotted the northern fleet and seemingly drove it off with the help of supporting aircraft. When Admiral William "Bull" Halsey received word of the decoy enemy carrier force coming from the north, the characteristically aggressive commander took the bait and ordered his carriers and major surface ships to intercept them. With the remaining battleships and cruisers sent to the south to fend off the Japanese southern attack force, the admiral left the Leyte landing zone to be defended by only five small escort carriers, three destroyers, and four destroyer escorts under the command of Rear Admiral Clifton Sprague. As Halsey chased the decoy fleet (eventually sinking all four of its carriers), the Japanese fleet which had initially been turned away swung around under cover of darkness and continued its advance to the north of Leyte. Greatly outnumbered and outgunned, Sprague's light force performed the seemingly impossible task of holding off the massive Japanese battlewagons and cruisers by executing a series of intricate diversionary maneuvers. Sprague's pilots, trained only in ground-support combat, slowed down the Japanese ships by dropping the few torpedoes they had, along with non-armor piercing bombs. When their ordinance ran out, they simply made multiple dry runs with no ammunition. Meanwhile, Sprague's destroyers and destroyer escorts laid smoke screens and made swift attacking runs with their torpedoes and deck guns. So tenacious was the defense of the Gulf that the Japanese commander, who believed he was actually facing Halsey's large carriers and capital ships, finally called off the attack. The four separate engagements from October 23-25 collectively known as the **Battle of Leyte Gulf** was the largest naval battle in world history. The victorious Americans lost a light carrier, two escort carriers, two destroyers, one destroyer escort, and 3,000 men. Meanwhile, Japanese losses were staggering: four large carriers, three battleships, ten cruisers, nine destroyers, and over 10,000 men.

U.S. forces gained control of Leyte by December, though sporadic Japanese resistance continued for several more months. MacArthur finally landed troops on Luzon in January 1945 as Japanese pilots desperately flew their bomb-laden aircraft into American ships, sinking one escort carrier, damaging another, and also hitting two battleships and five cruisers. Initially used at the end of the Battle of Leyete Gulf, these suicidal kamikaze attacks could occasionally be devastating to American ships. (Named after the Japanese phrase "divine wind," kamikaze pilots deliberately dove their planes into targets like American ships.). Though the majority of kamikazes were shot down, enough penetrated American naval defenses during the waning months of the war to do significant damage to American vessels and morale. By February, American ground forces reached Manila and proceeded to spend the entire month clearing out Japanese defenders in brutal street fighting that resulted in the deaths of almost 100,000 Filipino civilians.

The Bloody Fight for Iwo Jima and Okinawa

While the fight for Manila commenced, the U.S. Navy landed marines on the small volcanic island of Iwo Jima. Despite its size (5 miles long and 2 ½ miles across), located halfway between the Marianas and Tokyo, Iwo Jima held strategic value to the Japanese as a fighter base along the flight path for American heavy bombers, which had already begun hitting the home islands. The U.S. military wished to capture the island to eliminate its ability to serve as a Japanese fighter base, to use the airfields to house American fighter escorts, and to serve as an emergency landing strip for disabled bombers. Though small, the island's topographical features greatly aided the island's 20,000 defenders who were well supplied with artillery and machine guns. Iwo Jima possessed several rocky high points including the 550-foot Mount Suribachi, which dominated the southern tip of the island. On the beaches, volcanic ash rather than sand covered the coastline making it difficult for men and vehicles to maneuver. The island also contained countless caves, which the Japanese used to connect with underground tunnels, reinforced bunkers, and blockhouses.

Landing on Iwo Jima's southern shore on February 19, 1945, marines fought their way off the beaches for three days before capturing Mount Suribachi. The most famous American photograph of the war was soon taken when Associated Press photographer Joe Rosenthal snapped a picture of five marines and a U.S. Navy corpsman raising a large American flag over the position. The fight for Iwo Jima, however, was far from over—three of the flag-raisers would be killed before the battle ended a month later. For the next four weeks, marines fought their way northward across the grueling terrain under withering enemy fire, helped out with tanks using flamethrowers to clear out the enemy defenders. As the case at Saipan, when the last remaining Japanese soldiers realized that hope was lost, they sacrificed themselves with suicidal banzai charges. The final human cost of the battle to wipe out the entire Japanese garrison was 6,821 dead marines with over 17,000 wounded. Of all U.S. Marines killed in the Pacific, one-third died at Iwo Jima.

On April 1, 1945, the U.S. military conducted its final amphibious operation of the war, landing 180,000 marines and army personnel on the island of Okinawa. Located only 350 miles south of Kyushu, the southernmost of the main Japanese home islands, Okinawa contained airfields and anchorages that could serve as an excellent base for close-range bombings of Japan as well as a staging area for a direct attack invasion. Japanese military leaders were well aware of the island's importance and planned to hold it at all costs, reinforcing its garrison to 100,000 men – the largest force that U.S. troops would ever face during the entire Pacific war. Over fifty times larger than Iwo Jima, Japanese soldiers used defensive networks imbedded in the rough terrain similar to the earlier fight to exact high casualties and continued to fight with tenacity and desperation. Offshore, the U.S. Navy endured the largest series of kamikaze attacks of the war, losing 35 ships with 350 damaged. Ultimately, the battle for Okinawa, the bloodiest that the Americans fought in the Pacific, took six weeks to complete. The United States lost over 7,000 army soldiers and marines on the ground and another 5,000 sailors at sea due to the kamikazes. The Japanese lost 95,000 men (including 1900 kamikaze pilots) while over 7,000 defenders (mostly recent local civilian conscripts) surrendered.

The New President

While the fight for Okinawa raged, the nation learned of Franklin Roosevelt's death on April 12 from a cerebral hemorrhage and more details about the man who would succeed him. Born in the small town of Lamar, Missouri during the mid-1880s, **Harry S Truman** in many ways embodied Middle America during the first half of the twentieth century. Hard-working and determined, casually racist, and well-read but lacking a college education, the future president possessed "the manner of a country boy who had made good but never forgot his origins," according to historian David Kennedy. "He was as straightforward as a sentence without commas." Truman experienced many personal highs and lows before his perseverance began to produce dividends. After high school he undertook a series of odd jobs and enlisted in the Missouri National Guard. During World War I, Truman served as an artillery captain in France. The war impacted Truman on many levels as he observed the devastation of war firsthand, lived for the first time in a foreign land, and established personal contacts that would make possible his future political career. Upon returning home he briefly entered a business school and took night classes to seek a law degree, but quit before finishing either pursuit. He opened a haberdashery in Kansas City with a wartime buddy but the business closed after a few years.

Truman's fortunes turned when he entered Missouri politics. In 1922 he received support from the Democratic Party political machine in Kansas City run by Thomas Pendergast (the uncle of another wartime comrade) to win election as a county judge. An administrative post rather than a judicial position, Truman served as a loyal member of the political establishment throughout the 1920s. In 1934, Pendergast promoted Truman's candidacy for a U.S. Senate seat, which he won in the Democratic landslide of that year, quickly elevating the inexperienced local politician to the national stage. While earning a reputation in Washington as a solid New Dealer, Truman largely operated out of public view before Franklin Roosevelt chose him as a political compromise to be his running mate in the 1944 election. Before FDR's decision, Truman had only emerged into the national spotlight on two occasions: his dogged investigation of questionable wartime government contracts that brought the senator his largest degree of positive publicity; and, when he responded to a reporter's query about his views on the German invasion of Russia, by stating bluntly: "If we see that Germany is winning we ought to help Russia, and if Russia is winning we ought to help Germany, and that way let them kill as many as possible." While not received well by the suspicious Joseph Stalin, Truman's sentiments were commonly held in the United States and Great Britain. Truman's elevation to the presidency meant that an individual with many positive attributes but also some glaring personal limitations would direct America's participation in the closing months of World War II and oversee the use of the atomic bomb.

Naval Blockade and Fire Bombing of Japan

By the time Harry Truman assumed the presidency, Japan was a defeated nation, even if its leaders refused to accept that fact. In China, large numbers of occupation soldiers garrisoned the large cities in the eastern coastal areas, but ceded much of the countryside to the nationalist forces of Chiang Kai-Shek and communist rebels under Mao Zedong. In the western Pacific, American forces were pressing against the home islands. Japanese forces still held on to a large number of islands in the central and southern Pacific, but their troops were left to "die on the vine"—isolated and cut off from their supply lines by American patrol planes and surface ships. By mid-1945, the main Japanese islands were virtually cut off from the outside world by American minelayers and submarines. Half of Japan's merchant fleet had been destroyed with the remaining ships clinging to the shore, abandoning the high seas. Most food importation from China and Manchuria ended. As oil imports from the Dutch East Indies ceased, Japanese air and naval units suffered greatly and Japanese industry ground to a halt.

(L) Hiroshima after the bomb
(R) Second atomic bombing of Nagasaki, Japan.
August 1945

Meanwhile, Japan began to be relentlessly pummeled from the air by B-29 Super Fortresses—new heavy bombers that were larger and faster than the B-17s used in Europe with much greater range and bombload capacity. Originally launched against Japan from China in June 1944, the B-29s initially followed the same high-altitude strategic bombing tactics used in Europe—with equally ineffective results. Even after the bombers were redeployed to the Marianas for missions over Japan starting in late November and placed under the command of General Curtis LeMay, an innovative veteran commander who led strategic bombing attacks over Germany, the poor results continued. Though the American pilots had to contend with few enemy fighter planes, strong winds from the jet stream and frequent heavy cloud cover limited the success of the missions. LeMay then shifted to incendiary attacks using Napalm-B—a new flammable jelly developed by Dupont and Standard Oil designed to spread fires rapidly. For greater precision, the bombing runs would take place at a much lower altitude (5,000 feet). To avoid heavy antiaircraft fire, the general ordered the removal of most machine gun turrets and crew for increased flight speed and to attack at night. The first mission under the new guidelines took place over Tokyo on March 9, 1945. The raid destroyed 16 square miles (about a quarter of the capital city) and killed approximately 100,000 civilians by incineration or suffocation—by far the most deadly bombing of the entire war. Heartened by his success, LeMay ordered similar attacks over the next several months against 60 other Japanese cities, wiping out over half their size and killing another 400,000 Japanese civilians. While the attacks destroyed some industrial targets, they were morally indefensible—the clear purpose of the raids was to break the will of the Japanese public through terror bombing. After the war LeMay admitted the immorality of targeting civilians but consoled himself with the basic belief that all war was immoral and if one worried about such matters he wouldn't be a good soldier. He then added: "I suppose if [we] had lost the war, I would have been tried as a war criminal."

Despite the blockade and continuous aerial bombing, Japanese leaders still refused to surrender unconditionally as the Allies demanded. While some diehards in the government would never surrender under any circumstances, many held on to the vain hope that a negotiated settlement could be reached because the Americans wished to avoid the massive casualties an invasion of Japan would deliver. The Japanese sent inquiries to Joseph Stalin to ascertain if the Soviet leader was interested in brokering a peace deal, but the dictator turned away the diplomats' request for a meeting. Aware of the overture, the Truman administration nevertheless refused to deviate from the demand for unconditional surrender. Meanwhile, November 1, 1945 was set as the preliminary date for the invasion of Kyushu. With an entrenched enemy forces supported by a hostile civilian population fighting fanatically in defense of their homeland, the U.S. military estimated that American casualties would exceed a quarter of a million killed and wounded. While these figures weighed on President Truman's mind, the president hoped for positive news coming from the government's top-secret atomic research program.

The Defeat of Japan

The origins of the Allied nuclear weapons development program, code-named the **Manhattan Project**, trace back to 1939 when a small group of scientists including Albert Einstein brought the possibility of an atomic bomb being created in the near future to Franklin Roosevelt's attention. Fearing such a weapon of mass destruction in Hitler's hands, Roosevelt and Churchill decided in 1940 to secretly work together on its development (though Stalin was never told of the Manhattan Project before the bomb's use, he became aware of its development through his spy network.) Military officials informed President Truman of the first successful detonation near Alamogordo, New Mexico on July 16, 1945 while he was meeting with Winston Churchill and Stalin at the Potsdam Conference outside Berlin. Truman used the occasion to inform Stalin that the U.S. now had a bomb of immense destructive capability. Feigning ignorance of the atomic program, Stalin simply told Truman to use the weapon against Japan as soon as possible, which was indeed Truman's intention. At Potsdam, Truman, Stalin, and Clement Atlee (the new British Prime Minister who replaced Churchill after the first parliamentary elections after the collapse of Nazi Germany) issued the Potsdam Declaration, which reiterated the demand for Japan to surrender unconditionally or face "complete and utter destruction."

Though some historians have argued that Truman's primary motivation in using the atomic bomb was to keep the Soviets in line after the war's conclusion, the president and his advisors largely viewed that possibility as a side benefit. In the end, Truman believed, correctly or not, that the bomb would save American lives by ending the war sooner without the need for an invasion of Japan. In making the decision, he pushed aside strong objections raised by a cadre of scientists who had developed the weapon as well as some top military brass. Though Army Chief of Staff George Marshall concurred with Truman that the atomic weapon had to be used, Fleet Admiral William Leahy, the Chief of Staff to the Commander in Chief (equivalent of the Chairman of the Joint Chiefs of Staff today) strongly objected on moral grounds, later writing in his memoirs: "It is my opinion that the use of this barbarous weapon . . . was of no material assistance in our war against Japan. The Japanese were already defeated and ready to surrender because of the effective sea blockade and the successful bombing with conventional weapons. . . . My own feeling was that in being the first to use it, we had adopted an ethical standard common to the barbarians of the Dark Ages. I was not taught to make wars in that fashion, and that wars cannot be won by destroying women and children." General Dwight Eisenhower, the Supreme Allied Commander in Europe, also objected. In his published recollections after the war, he related details about a meeting with Secretary of War Henry Stimson in which he was informed of the bomb's existence and the government's plans to use it. "During his recitation of the relevant facts," the general wrote, "I voiced to him my grave misgivings, first on my belief that Japan was already defeated and that dropping the bomb was completely unnecessary, and secondly because I thought that our country should avoid shocking world opinion by the use of a weapon whose employment was, I thought, no longer mandatory as a measure to save American lives. It was my belief that Japan was, at that very moment, seeking some way to surrender with a minimum loss of 'face.' The Secretary was deeply perturbed by my attitude."

On the morning of August 6, 1945, a B-29 named the *Enola Gay* took off from its base on Tinian in the Marianas to drop an atomic bomb codenamed "Little Boy." Hiroshima, a port city of 340,000 located on the southern coast of Japan's largest island of Honshu, headed a list of potential targets that consisted of large urban centers with military value that had escaped firebombing. At 8:15 a.m., Little Boy detonated 2,000 feet over the city center, immediately producing an immense fireball emitting nuclear radiation and a powerful shock wave that destroyed all buildings within a mile radius of the blast point. Seventy to one hundred thousand men, women, and children (including at least 10 American prisoners-of-war) were killed directly as a result of the bombing, with the death toll reaching near 200,000 due to the effects of radiation poisoning within a few years.

After the Hiroshima bombing, Japanese diplomats renewed their efforts to involve Stalin in peace negotiations, but the Soviet leader not only demurred, he also declared war on Japan, fulfilling his promise to Roosevelt at Yalta. Sensing the war was nearing its conclusion, Stalin ordered Russian troops to attack Manchuria and to seize as much land as possible—a very demoralizing development for Japanese leaders. While they debated the merits of a possible surrender, Truman authorized the dropping of a second atomic bomb. Not only had the Japanese government failed to surrender unconditionally, but an earlier decision dictated that the second bomb should be used relatively quickly after using the first one—since the U.S. had initially only developed three bombs and it would be weeks before additional bombs would be available, Truman concurred with advisors who suggested that quick use of two bombs would have added shock value, giving the impression that the first bomb was no fluke and that the

United States had the capability of immediately destroying Japan. Hence, the crew of a B-29 named *Bockscar* left Tinian on August 9, headed for Kyushu. Their target was the city of Kokura, but with reports of bad weather, the commander decided to divert the mission to its secondary target—the port city of Nagasaki with a population of a quarter million. The hills surrounding the city limited the extent of the cataclysm, but the blast destroyed the town center and killed 40,000 immediately with an equal number succumbing by the end of the year.

The dropping of both atomic bombs and Russian entry into the war convinced many Japanese leaders that they must surrender, though most did not wish to do so unconditionally. Even after the atomic attacks, they desired guarantees for the life and position of their emperor. Emperor Hirohito's supreme war council became deadlocked between such peace advocates and the radical military elements who wished to fight on. The ruler finally interceded to break the impasse by relaying his desire to accept the Potsdam Declaration if the institution of the emperor would be retained. The council relayed this proposal to the Truman administration, which accepted the proviso with the understanding that the emperor's authority would be subject to the dictates of the Allied commander of occupation forces (General Douglas MacArthur). As Japanese leaders debated this proposal, rogue army officers desperately sought to take over the government to prevent the possibility of surrender, but their coup attempt failed. After three days of discussion, Japan accepted the modified conditional surrender terms on August 14, unofficially ending the war. Some historians later asserted, as did General MacArthur, that the war might have ended weeks earlier without the use of nuclear weapons if the U.S. had agreed, as it later did anyway, to the condition of retaining the emperor and giving him immunity from prosecution for war crimes. Regardless, Japanese officials formally signed the surrender agreement aboard the deck of the battleship *Missouri* in Tokyo Bay on September 2, thus ending the most bitter and destructive war in the history of the world.

In the final analysis, World War II should be viewed as the culmination of clashing ideologies unleashed by the disappointments created by World War I and the extreme economic hardships of the Great Depression. On the one hand, the Soviet Union, formed in the latter stages of the First World War, emerged as the world's first communist power. Ostensibly elevating the working man to cast off the chains of capitalist oppression by confiscating excess wealth and private property, diehard Bolsheviks sought to spread their ideology beyond Russia's borders. At the other extreme, the 1930s witnessed the rise of militant fascism in Italy, Germany, and Japan—an ideology that manifested itself differently in various countries but shared such common characteristics as militancy, ultra-nationalism, vehement anticommunism, and a strong aversion to the "inefficiency" of democracy. Between the extremes of communism and fascism lay the democracies of the United States, Great Britain, and France, which incorporated progressive (and occasionally socialistic) reforms to moderate its capitalist systems in order to promote efficiency and social justice while undercutting more radical proposals. While the Second World War ended the threat of militant fascism to world peace, the conflict also set the stage for a new global struggle between democratic capitalist nations led by the United States and communist countries guided initially by the Soviet Union, later to be joined by the People's Republic of China.

Chronology

1921	Washington Conference first meets.
1922	Mussolini assumes power in Italy.
1923	France and Belgium occupy the Ruhr in Western Germany after Germany fails to make its reparations payments.
1924	Dawes Plan. Coolidge withdraws U.S. troops from the Dominican Republic.
1928	Kellogg-Briand Treaty signed.
1931	Japanese occupation of Manchuria.
1933	FDR inaugurated president. Hitler becomes chancellor of Germany. Germany and Japan leave the League of Nations.
1935	First U.S. Neutrality Act passed. Italy invades Ethiopia.
1936	German troops occupy the demilitarized Rhineland.
1937	Japan attacks China. Italy leaves League of Nations.
1938	Germany annexes Austria after the Munich Conference. Germany occupies the Sudetenland.
1939	Nazi-Soviet Non-Aggression Pact signed. Germany attacks Poland. WW II in Europe begins. German takeover of Czechoslovakia.
1940	Tripartite Pact signed. Japan occupies Indochina. FDR re-elected to 3rd term.
1941	U-Boat action. Germany attacks Russia. Japan attacks Pearl Harbor. U.S. declares war on Japan. Germany and Italy declare war on the United States.
1942	Battles of Coral Sea, Midway, El Alamein, and Stalingrad. U.S. forces land in North Africa.
1943	Casablanca Conference. Allied forces invade southern Italy. Italy quits the war. Battle of Tarawa.
1944	Invasion of Normandy. Battle of Leyte Gulf. FDR elected to fourth term. Battle of the Bulge.
1945	Yalta Conference. FDR dies. Germany and Japan defeated.

Review Questions

1. Describe America's international relations during the 1920s. Was the United States aloof and isolationist, or actively engaged in foreign affairs during the decade? Explain with examples.

2. Describe the challenges that Franklin Roosevelt faced at home and abroad during the period of American neutrality before U.S. entry into World War II. How did he react to these challenges?

3. Identify and describe three turning points during World War II that culminated in the defeat of Germany, Italy, and Japan.

4. Describe the contributions of women and minority groups to the American war effort during World War II.

5. Describe the development and use of the atomic bomb during World War II.

Glossary of Important People and Concepts

Battle of the Atlantic
Battle of Britain
Battle of Midway
Battle of Stalingrad
Ethiopia
Fascism
Good Neighbor Policy
Adolf Hitler (1889-1945)
Holocaust
Isolationism
Kellogg-Briand Pact
Lend-Lease Act
Charles Lindbergh
Manchuria
Manhattan Project
Munich Conference
Benito Mussolini (1883-1945)
Nazi-Soviet Non-Aggression Pact
Neutrality Acts
Office of Price Administration (OPA)
Operation Overlord
Pearl Harbor attack
A. Phillip Randolph (1889-1979)
"Second Front"
Spanish Civil War
strategic bombing campaign
Tuskegee Airmen
Washington Naval Conference
Women Airforce Service Pilots (WASPs)
Yalta Conference

SUGGESTED READINGS

Thomas A. Bailey and Paul B. Ryan, *Hitler vs. Roosevelt: The Undeclared Naval War* (1979).

John Morton Blum, *V Was for Victory: Politics and American Culture during World War II* (1976).

Warren I. Cohen, *Empire without Tears: America's Foreign Relations, 1921-1933* (1987).

Matthew Ware Coulter, *The Senate Munitions Inquiry of the 1930s: Beyond the Merchants of Death* (1997).

Robert Dallek, *Franklin D. Roosevelt and American Foreign Policy, 1932-1945* (1979).

Roger Daniels, *Prisoners without Trial: Japanese Americans in World War II* (1993).

Robert A. Divine, *The Reluctant Belligerent: American Entry into World War II*, 2nd ed. (1979).

Justus D. Doenecke and John E. Wiltz, *From Isolation to War, 1931-1941*, 3rd ed. (2003).

Sherna Berger Gluck, *Rosie the Riveter Revisited: Women, the War, and Social Change* (1987).

Waldo Heinrichs, *Threshold of War: Franklin D. Roosevelt and American Entry into World War II* (1988).

Saburo Ienaga, *The Pacific War, 1931-1945* (1978).

Akira Iriye, *The Origins of the Second World War in Asia and the Pacific* (1987).

John Keegan, *The Second World War* (1989).

David Kennedy, *Freedom from Fear: The American People in Depression and War, 1929-1945* (2001).

Warren F. Kimball, *Forged in Battle: Roosevelt, Churchill, and the Second World War* (1997).

Michael J. Lyons, *World War II: A Short History*, 3rd ed., (1999)

National Park Service, *World War II and the American Home Front: A National Historic Landmarks Theme Study* (2007).

William L. O'Neill, *A Democracy at War: America's Fight at Home and Abroad in World War II* (1998).

Richard Polenberg, *War and Society: The United States, 1941-1945* (1972).

Richard Rhodes, *The Making of the Atomic Bomb* (1995).

Martin Sherwin, *A World Destroyed: Hiroshima and Its Legacies*, 3rd ed. (2003).

HARRY S TRUMAN

Chapter Twenty-six

THE ORIGINS OF THE COLD WAR

Woodrow Wilson told a Princeton friend in 1913 that it would be ironic if foreign rather than domestic affairs became his administration's priority. One year after making that remark World War I began. In 1910, the Mexican Revolution had erupted, which also impacted the Wilson presidency. In 1914, he sent warships and troops to that beleaguered nation to occupy the port city of Veracruz, allegedly to protect United States' interests. In 1916, Wilson sent General "Black Jack" Pershing into northern Mexico to track down Pancho Villa in retaliation for Villa's invasion of the United States and the killing of American citizens in the fall of that year. By 1914, foreign crises had enveloped the Wilson administration. As his earlier Democratic colleague, Harry Truman too found himself immersed and overwhelmed by the exigencies of foreign policy. Like Wilson, world conflict and its aftermath forced Truman to put domestic issues on the backburner and deal instead with the problems of war and peace.

In the history of the executive branch, Harry Truman was one of the most poorly prepared vice presidents to become president. His lack of readiness for the job, however, was not his fault. A large part of the blame must be placed on President Franklin Roosevelt, who met with Truman only three times between the inauguration following the 1944 election and the president's death. This lapse in communication between Truman and FDR greatly handicapped him, especially in the area of foreign affairs. As vice president, Truman had been excluded from all foreign policy discussions. He knew nothing about the Manhattan Project. The new president, Secretary of War Henry Stimson noted, was "coming into an office where the threads of information were so multitudinous that only long previous familiarity would allow him to control them." More succinct were Truman's own comments: "They didn't tell me anything about what was going on. . . . Everybody around here that should know anything about foreign affairs is out." Confronted with multiple, complex, and sensitive issues sufficient enough to intimidate any individual, Truman had to act quickly on a succession of national security issues. Although never portraying himself anything close to a foreign policy expert, ironically, some of Truman's greatest successes as president were in this realm. Indeed, Truman can be credited with establishing the foundation of America's Cold War policy upon which subsequent presidents simply added new approaches and interpretations, but the essence remained the same for over 40 years.

THE EMERGING COLD WAR

The wartime alliance between the United States and the Soviet Union had never been anything but a marriage of convenience. Defeat of the Axis powers had demanded that the two governments cooperate but collaboration scarcely lasted beyond Germany's final surrender in May 1945. From that point on, U.S.-Soviet relations steadily degenerated into a Cold War of suspicion and constant tension, if not outright hostility, that could have escalated into World War III.

Historians vary in their analyses of the origins of the Cold War. The traditional interpretation, which gained currency after the Soviet Union's collapse in 1989, asserts that Soviet expansionism, which was a continuation of the long established czarist appetite for new territory, coupled with an ideological zeal to spread international communism, was the main cause. Proponents of this view insist that the United States, to stop the spread of such totalitarianism, had to take as hard a line as possible to stop this Russian historical imperative. Other historians, called **revisionists**, view the Soviet's postwar behavior less ideologically, contending that Soviet expansionism was purely defensive, to secure "Holy Mother Russia" from future invasions. To most revisionists, Soviet aggression was rooted in a Russian history that had witnessed centuries of invasion, conquest, and subjugation of vast amounts of Russian territory and its people, producing in the process a collective paranoia and obsession with security. Revisionists maintain that since the United States had never experienced anything remotely equivalent in its history, it was impossible for American foreign policy makers in the aftermath of World War II to understand this Russian historical reality. Thus, the revisionists claim that such expansion was historically logical and necessary because the most destructive attacks on Russia had come from the West, beginning with Napoleon's invasion in 1812. Revisionists argue that the Soviet Union's obsession with securing its western borders was understandable, especially after Nazi Germany's devastating invasion in 1941.

The United States, in this view, should have tried to reassure the Soviets by seeking accommodation instead of pursuing policies that intensified Soviet fears. Also fueling Soviet fear was the memory of "the Allied-capitalist" intervention during the Red-White civil war that engulfed Russia soon after the Bolsheviks toppled the Kerensky government in October 1917. The United States, Great Britain, France, and Japan all sent troops into Russia in the summer of 1918 to help the Whites (the anti-Bolshevik forces) overthrow Lenin's regime. Allied assistance proved to no avail; the Red Army eventually crushed the White factions. The long-range affect, however, on Soviet feelings of security was important. As a result of the 1918 Allied invasion, Stalin believed he could never trust the West, that the Western capitalist powers would always welcome or take advantage of any opportunity to bring down the Soviet government and end communism. Thus, the revisionists assert, because of Western intervention during the Russian civil war, it was no wonder Stalin was leery, if not outright suspicious, of U.S. and British intentions in the aftermath of World War II.

To revisionists, the Cold War could have been avoided had the United States (the Truman administration) been willing to recognize early on the concept of "spheres of influence" that Stalin had advocated during his wartime talks with FDR and Churchill, which would have given the Soviets the security on their western borders they had wanted for decades, if not for centuries. This implied, of course, a willingness by the United States to allow for Soviet control of Eastern Europe. Therein, perhaps, can be seen the flaw in the revisionist interpretation. Given the rhetoric and propaganda of the Roosevelt administration during the war years, especially his promulgation of the "Four Freedoms," which he expected the world to embrace in the aftermath of such global destruction, there was no way either the American people or the Truman administration would tolerate Soviet oppression of millions of people. To do so would be a most egregious negation of the blood sacrifice of the tens of thousands of American dead, who believed they were fighting a war of liberation in the name of all humanity.

Still other scholars maintain that assigning blame to one side or the other obscures the deep-seated ideological dynamics that made postwar tensions between the two superpowers inevitable. These historians believe that given the great historical disparity and reality of the two nations, a clash between them was destined to occur once the common enemy had been defeated. According to this view, the Cold War was an unalterable event that no amount of American or Soviet accommodation, or understanding, could have prevented.

Compounding Truman's situation was the fact that FDR had acted as his own secretary of state, sharing with almost no one his postwar vision and plans. Roosevelt mistrusted the State Department, disagreeing with its suspicious, anti-Soviet hardliners. FDR believed that he alone had the "magic" touch when it came to dealing with the Soviets. In retrospect, if there was an area in which Roosevelt could be rightly criticized, it was his naïve insistence (and his unwillingness to listen to Winston Churchill's much more sound counsel relative to understanding Russian history) that the Western allies show Stalin that they trusted him to fulfill his postwar commitments established at Tehran (1943) and Yalta (1945). To no avail, Churchill tried to impress upon FDR that making Stalin feel secure would only serve to fuel his determination to establish Soviet hegemony over Eastern Europe, as well as control of East Germany. Although FDR was more conciliatory toward Stalin than Churchill believed was appropriate, there was little either leader could do to prevent the Red Army from advancing into Eastern Europe, especially given Stalin's determination to establish a Soviet presence there even before war's end. Moreover, perhaps FDR was using the lure of Eastern European "liberation" by the Red Army

THE ORIGINS OF THE COLD WAR | 797

The "Big Three" Allied leaders in World War II—British Prime Minister Winston Churchill, U.S. President Harry Truman, and Soviet dictator Josef Stalin—divided Europe into communist and pro-Western zones at their Potsdam Conference. Photo taken on July 23, 1945. Photo credit: Truman Library.

as a bargaining chip to get the Soviets in the war against Japan. Although the Manhattan Project was well under way, there was no guarantee the atomic bomb would have the impact all hoped it would. If the bomb failed, then FDR would welcome Soviet participation in the struggle against Japan, which he hoped would help bring that theater of the war to a quicker conclusion. Nonetheless, as Churchill warned FDR, once entrenched in Eastern Europe, Stalin would never get out, for to do so would be to negate an historical Russian imperative of relinquishing a region long viewed essential to his nation's security.

THE TRUMAN DOCTRINE AND CONTAINMENT

As the Soviets tightened their grip on Eastern Europe, all hopes for reconciliation between the two superpowers dissipated. To Truman, as Eastern European nations fell one by one under Soviet control, it was clear that Stalin had no intention of honoring his earlier commitments to promote democracy in that region, nor allow its people the right of self-determination. Despite Stalin's claims to the contrary, Truman declared such aggression blatant proof of Stalin's larger purpose of not only spreading communism but of brutally subjugating other peoples in the process. Consequently, by early 1947, the former allies were well on their way to becoming bitter adversaries, a reality that the president had accepted from the beginning, and now he was proven right. More important, if further Soviet expansion and suppression was to be stopped, Truman felt that he had to respond then before it was too late and all of Europe came under Soviet domination, making communism an even greater threat to peace and freedom than fascism ever was. If Truman continued to trust the Soviets, as FDR and others had urged, believing negotiation and diplomacy still possible, then in his mind, he would be as guilty as the French and British had been with Nazi Germany, willing to appease Hitler out of fear of provoking another war.

To Truman, it was straightforward: had the Western democracies learned nothing out of six years of horrible conflict? Allowing a new aggressor, Stalin, to have his way would be tantamount to repeating the same mistakes made with Hitler in the late 1930s. In Truman's estimation, both Stalin and Hitler were brutal dictators whose respective ideologies produced essentially the same results: totalitarianism and world domination. It was time for the United States to "buck up" and fulfill its role as the liberator of oppressed peoples and the protector of those trying to withstand the onslaught of such violent encroachment upon their freedom. Thus, from 1947 on, Harry Truman placed his personal stamp on both the presidency and American postwar foreign policy by focusing on the fight against the Soviet Union and, in the process, put into place some of the most important and enduring foreign policy initiatives in United States history. In 1947, via the initiation of the **Truman Doctrine**, the United States once and for all broke with its isolationist past and committed itself to be the protectors and champions of freedom and democracy throughout the world. From March 12, 1947, when Truman first articulated before Congress this monumental break with the isolationist past, the United States has faithfully adhered to this most seminal of departures.

A key individual in the formulation of the Truman Doctrine was **George Kennan**, a long-time State Department official. A year before the initiation of the policy, Kennan had sent to his superiors a long telegram from his diplomatic post in Moscow, outlining what became the foundation for **containment**. According to Kennan, Soviet leaders believed "there can be no permanent peaceful coexistence" between capitalism and socialism. Stalin and his regime were certain that capitalist nations, beset by internal problems, and in order to distract their

GEORGE KENNAN

respective populations from such issues, would pursue unrelenting war against socialist nations. Acting on this fear, the U.S.S.R., Kennan asserted, would try to penetrate and destabilize other nations and align them with the communist bloc. In order to survive, he concluded, the communist system needed to expand constantly. Thus, in Kennan's view, it was imperative that the United States have a foreign policy in which "the main element must be that of a long-term, patient but firm and vigilant containment of Russian expansive tendencies." The United States, Kennan further declared, must put in place a foreign policy "designed to confront the Russians with unalterable counter-force at every point where they show signs of encroaching upon the interests of a peaceful and stable world."

The potential for Soviet-inspired and aided communist takeovers in Greece and Turkey, two countries vital to U.S. and Western European security interests, prompted Truman to announce his "doctrine" and implement Kennan's strategy. In Greece, a civil war had erupted between communist–led rebels and the forces of the British-backed conservative government in Athens. The insurgents were receiving sanctuary and aid from Yugoslavia, which the Truman administration believed to be merely a Russian puppet state—a completely inaccurate assumption.

Although a communist, Marshal Josip Broz Tito, Yugoslavia's dictator, successfully maintained his nation's independence from Soviet hegemony. Thus, Yugoslavia was never a Soviet **"satellite."** The misperception, however, led Truman to believe that Stalin himself was directing the rebellion. Before the outbreak of civil war, American officials had privately criticized the sometimes brutal and ineffective British efforts to defeat the Greek leftists. Now that Great Britain could no longer economically afford to prop up the Athens government, the United States decided to intervene by drawing the enfeebled birthplace of "democracy" into the expanding American sphere of influence. "If Greece should fall under the control of an armed minority," Truman concluded in an early version of the "domino theory," the effect upon its neighbor Turkey would be immediate and serious. Confusion and disorder might spread throughout the entire Middle East."

In Truman's view, the situation in Turkey was dire; the president believed that "the primary objective of the Soviet Union is to obtain control of Turkey." He pledged that the United States would resist any Soviet "aggression" by "force of American arms" if necessary. What prompted such a response from Truman was the Soviet insistence that for security reasons, the Dardanelles come under Russian control. To the Truman White House this was a Soviet ruse for taking all of Turkey, which of course the president would not allow to happen. Truman and his fellow Cold Warriors believed Turkey to be a vital link in a global chain that must be prevented from coming under the Russian sphere. Indeed, Turkey had to be secured in the American sphere. Although the Soviets made no military move against Turkey, and although there was no direct evidence of Soviet intentions of world conquest, the United States thought the worst. With massive aid coming from the United States, Turkey naturally gravitated, as hoped, toward the American sphere of influence.

According to Truman, since the United States had emerged as the preeminent world power, with such status, came responsibility not only to ensure the nation's continued safety, but of free peoples worldwide. The United States' first gesture in helping others "who are resisting attempted subversion by armed minorities or by outside pressures" was to extend assistance to the freedom fighters in Greece and Turkey. If the United States failed to help those two beleaguered countries, Truman asserted, totalitarian communism would spread around the world and ultimately threaten the United States itself. With backing from both Democrats and Republicans, Congress passed Truman's request for $400 million in assistance to Greece and Turkey, most of it in the form of military aid. This vote signaled broad, bipartisan support for the new national security policy that came to be called containment, which Truman established as the foundation of U.S. Cold War policy. With only some minor alterations, containment remained the cornerstone of U.S. policy until the end of the Cold War.

Containment became the catchphrase for a global, anticommunist national security policy, linking all leftist insurgencies, wherever they occurred, to the notion that they were all antidemocratic movements controlled from Moscow that directly threatened the United States. To counter such alleged assaults on freedom and democracy, beginning with the Truman administration, the United States increasingly supported right-wing totalitarian regimes throughout the world but especially in the Western Hemisphere (Latin America), which saw American anticommunist policy degenerate into obsessive paranoia and blatant interventionism. Beginning in the early 1950s and over the course of the next three decades, the United States pursued the fanatically reckless policy of toppling, by using whatever means deemed effective—covert or brazen military intervention—any government suspected of being too far left ("communist" in Washington's eyes, often simply nationalistic in reality) that might threaten the hemisphere's democratic stability. After supposedly cleansing the communist threat in a particular country, the United States would then promote freedom and democracy in that nation by installing a new government, which in many instances quickly revealed itself to be an oppressive right-wing military dictatorship. As long as such a regime was pro-United States and anticommunist, the United States would help maintain such a government in power indefinitely. Regardless of the region, beginning with the Truman administration and throughout the Cold War years, the United States supported some of the most notoriously brutal dictatorships in the name of containing supposed communist expansion or takeover.

In Africa, for example, this mentality shaped U.S. policies, bringing the United States into an alliance with South Africa. In 1948, the all-white Nationalist Party instituted **apartheid**—the complete segregation and oppression of black and all "colored" (non-white) South Africans from their white counterparts and the brutal enforcement of such a policy by the minority white government. State Department officials familiar with African affairs warned that supporting apartheid in South Africa would damage U.S. prestige and credibility in the rest of the continent, but the Truman administration decided to cement such a tie with South Africa nonetheless. That country, Truman reasoned, possessed valuable raw materials (uranium for atomic weapons and manganese for steel), and a cheap labor force. Moreover, South Africa's Nationalist Party was militantly anticommunist.

The Marshall Plan

A major accomplishment of the Truman administration was the **Marshall Plan**, which also embodied the concept of containment. The Truman White House was concerned that Western Europe's postwar severe economic problems might energize leftist, pro-Soviet political movements. Indeed, the French and Italian communist parties had made significant political headway in their respective countries, and Truman feared that it was only a matter of time before both nations elected communist governments. Thus, Secretary of State George C. Marshall (a retired five-star general who oversaw all U.S. military operations during World War II) devised a plan to strengthen the economies of that region. The plan called for the Western European governments to coordinate their plans for postwar economic reconstruction with the help of funds provided by the United States. Between 1947, when the plan was implemented, until its end in 1951, the United States contributed nearly $13 billion to seventeen Western European nations to stabilize and eventually revitalize those economies. The Soviets were also invited to participate, as the plan was offered to Eastern European nations as well, but American policy makers correctly anticipated that Moscow would avoid any program that had as its intent the rebuilding or fostering of capitalism anywhere in Europe. Stalin's purpose was to keep Eastern Europe economically in submission and subservient to Soviet needs. At the end of the war, Stalin had ordered the Red Army to strip the occupied countries of valuable raw materials, which he immediately transported to the Soviet Union to help in its rebuilding process. Thus, from the beginning of the Cold War to its end in 1989, the Eastern Bloc countries not only served as a military buffer zone for the Soviets but as providers of key resources and markets for Soviet-made goods.

The Marshall Plan proved a stunning success, even though conservatives charged it was a giveaway program. To counter such accusations, Truman pointed out that the plan opened up both markets and investment opportunities in Western Europe to American business. Moreover, it helped stabilize the European economy by quadrupling industrial production within its first few years. Improved standards of living enhanced political stability, which helped undermine Western European left-wing political parties from taking over. Finally, as the program wound down, Marshall and others urged the Western European nations to create some sort of cooperative economic union, which they believed would make the Europeans' respective economies stronger and more viable and thus their citizens less susceptible to far left movements and ideologies and more willing to embrace and sustain demo-

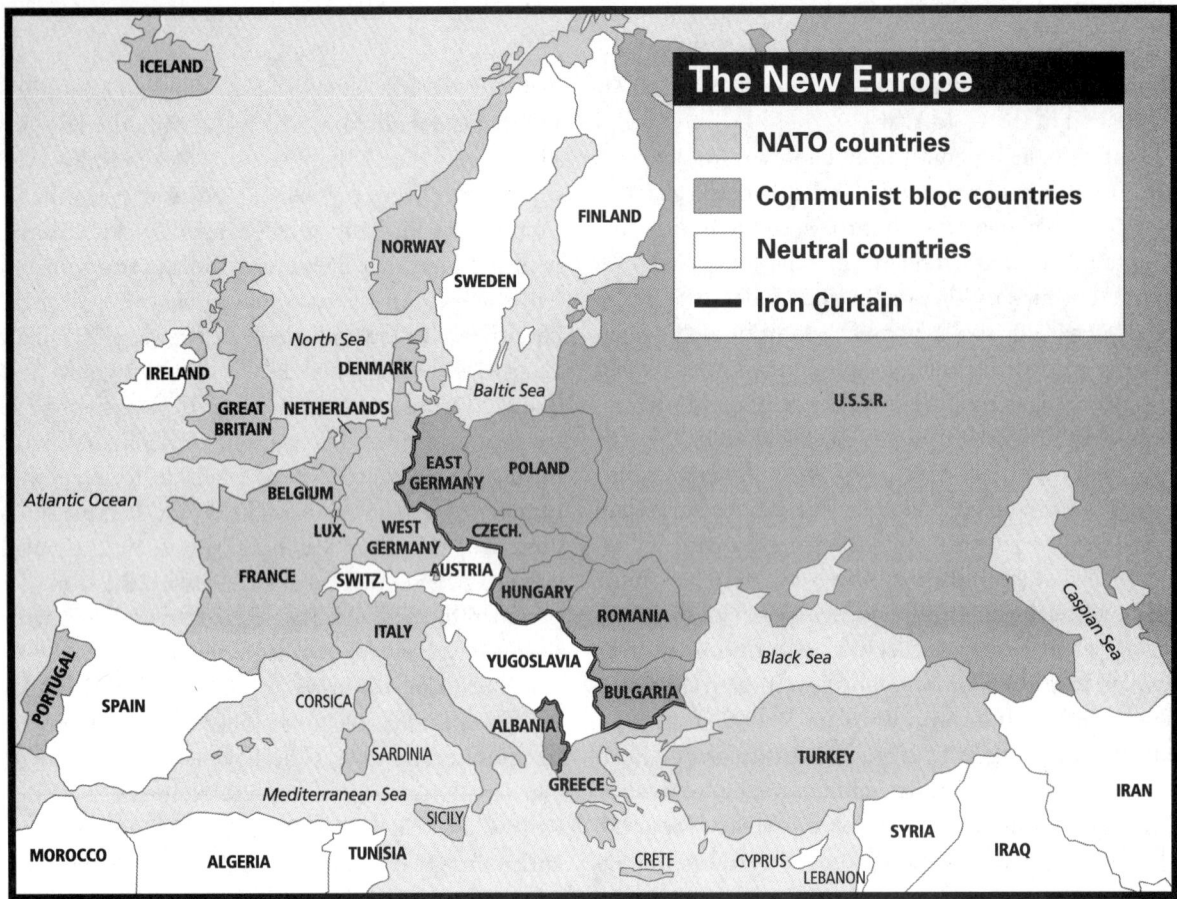

Map 26.1 Europe after 1945

cratic capitalism. In the view of many U.S. policy-makers at the time, the war had destroyed the last vestiges of European economic power and supremacy; that momentum had shifted fully to the United States upon whom they were now dependent for their economic survival, whether they liked it or not. If they hoped to regain their vitality and competitiveness, then the Europeans needed to put aside past economic grievances and divisions and engage in enterprises and trade relations that promoted their greater mutual interests and benefit. The U.S.-inspired idea of an economically united Europe gained traction, and by the late 1950s, six nations—Italy, France, West Germany and the Benelux countries (Belgium, the Netherlands, and Luxembourg) had formed the first of such associations in European history, the EEC—the European Economic Community, commonly known as the Common Market, which pledged to remove trade restrictions, to allow for the free movement of labor and capital, and to establish common trade, investment, and social welfare policies. Other Western European nations eventually joined the EEC, which became the precursor to the present-day European Union. At the time, few if any American policy makers or corporate chieftains believed the Europeans could overcome centuries-old rivalries and unite economically let alone politically; they were certain American economic dominance would continue indefinitely. By the early twenty-first century, however, "old" Europe did indeed unite economically and politically.

The Berlin Crisis

Truman and his advisers rightly concluded that the key to a revitalized Western European economy was the restoration of the German economy, a country still divided into four zones of occupation. In June 1948, Great Britain, France, and the United States agreed to initiate procedures for the partial reunification of Germany (only of their occupation zones) into a federal republic, believing the Soviets would follow suit, allowing their sector to be incorporated into the process. At this juncture, Stalin's true position on Germany became clear: from the beginning Stalin had no intention of ever allowing a reunited Germany, whom he considered (after the United States) to potentially be the greatest threat to the Soviet Union. Compelled by such fears, in June 1948, the Soviets cut off all highways, railroads, and water routes linking West Berlin, which lay entirely within the Soviet occupation zone in eastern Germany, to the French, British, and American occupation zones in western Germany.

Truman passed with flying colors this first of many Soviet challenges to the American commitment to containment with flying colors. The president knew the moment that the blockades began what Stalin intended. He also knew that, if he used military force to smash the blockades to liberate West Berlin, such action could instigate World War III. Although sympathetic to the plight of West Berliners, the American public would not sanction the use of force if it meant getting involved in another major conflagration so soon after the last one had ended. By this time too many Americans were enjoying the benefits of one of the greatest economic booms in history. They did not want to be distracted from enjoying the good life after so many years of sacrifice and deprivation. Truman was acutely aware of these factors, but he also knew that if he did not stand up to the "test" this time, Stalin would certainly try again somewhere else for he would believe Truman to be weak. The president responded with the famous Berlin Airlift, which over an 11-month period saw British and American pilots make 250,000 flights, round-the-clock, and deliver a total of 2 million tons of supplies to West Berliners. Recognizing that Truman had not only met his challenge but in effect defeated him as well, Stalin lifted the blockade in May 1949. He then created the German Democratic Republic out of his East German sector, and West Berlin survived as an enclave tied to the United States. The "two Germanys" and the divided city stood as symbols of Cold War tensions. Perhaps more important, Truman established West Berlin not only as a U.S. protectorate but as a manifestation as well of the American commitment to preserving the "status quo" in Europe. In effect, the **Berlin Crisis** made it clear that by its end (1949), Western Europe fell under the U.S. sphere of influence and Eastern Europe under Soviet domination—a situation that would remain until the end of the Cold War. Truman made it clear that the United States would never abandon West Berlin, nor have any intention of trying to occupy East Berlin, nor of **"rolling back the Iron Curtain."** The United States expected the Soviets to respect this arrangement relative to Europe, and subsequent American presidents and Soviet premiers adhered to this understanding. Thus, by 1950, the Cold War in Europe had reached an uneasy but stable point of acceptance by both belligerents.

The 1948 Election

Truman's successful Cold War policies and tough stand against the Soviets in the first Berlin Crisis no doubt helped him win the 1948 election, a victory that marked one of the most remarkable and legendary political comebacks in United States history. Only two years earlier (fall 1946) Truman's presidential ratings hit an all-time historic low when only 32 percent of the electorate approved of his performance. Insult was added to injury when, in the congressional elections of that year, the Republicans gained control of both houses of Congress for the first time since 1928. So stunned were some Democrats, believing Truman the cause of the Republican's victory, that Arkansas Senator J. William Fulbright urged Truman to name a Republican as Secretary of State and then resign so that, in order of constitutional succession in place at the time, a Republican could ascend to the Oval Office. It was obvious to Fulbright and other Democrats that their party had no chance of victory in 1948, so why not accept the inevitable now and in the process dump the man they believed responsible for their demise. Truman did not take Fulbright's advice, and, henceforth, he referred to the Arkansan as "Senator Halfbright."

Fulbright was not the only disaffected Democrat. A combination of anti-containment renegade Democrats, Republicans, isolationists, "America Firsters," and a host of other leftist organizations rallied to former FDR vice-president and Truman cabinet official Henry Wallace, who had been critical of Truman's Cold War policies from the beginning. Together with other anti-containment liberals, Wallace formed the **Progressive Party**, running as the group's standard-bearer, claiming he had "taken leave" of the Democratic Party because: "There is no real fight between a Truman and a Republican. Both stand for a policy which opens the door to war in our lifetime and makes war certain for our children." Wallace had criticized Truman's "get tough" stance with the Soviet Union, labeling such a position as bellicose, militaristic, war mongering, and purposely provocative. Truman's chances for re-election were undermined further when southern Democrats, in response to his public support for civil rights, bolted and formed the States' Rights Party, the **"Dixiecrats,"** and nominated the hardcore segregationist Strom Thurmond of South Carolina as their presidential candidate. With the Democrats in apparent complete disarray, the Republicans smelled an easy victory, if not a rout. In nominating Thomas Dewey of New York, who just four years earlier lost to FDR, Republicans were certain that they could easily beat a beleaguered and battered Harry Truman. With such forces arrayed against him, Truman entered 1948 less than hopeful about his chances for victory. The president, however, had faced tough election campaigns before, when everyone wrote him off, yet he somehow managed to snatch victory from the jaws of defeat. It would be no different this time.

In retrospect, given the strategy he adopted that garnered the support of key New Deal coalition groups, a Truman victory was almost a certainty. He also employed

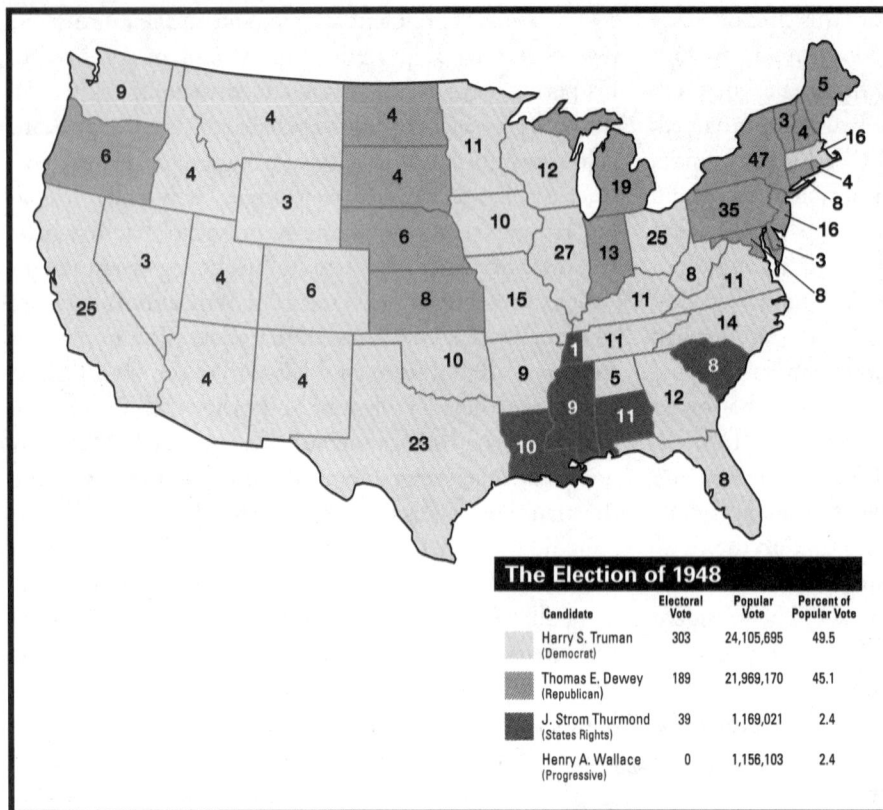

Map 26.2 The Election of 1948

the effective rhetoric of anticommunism. The architect of Truman's campaign tactics was presidential aide Clark Clifford, who told the president that he could win if he cultivated urban areas and minorities with his liberalism, while isolating Wallace in the public mind by associating him with the communists. Truman then employed the politics of anticommunism by declaring, "I do not want and will not accept the support of Henry Wallace and his communists .... These are days of high prices for anything, but any price for Wallace and his communists is too much for me."

Truman's prospects for victory grew brighter with the support of labor and the recently formed liberal organization—the Americans for Democratic Action (ADA). Two events helped persuade labor leaders to side with Truman. First, the president established his credentials as the champion of the working class by vetoing the 1947 anti-labor Taft-Hartley Act (which prohibited the "closed shop" and a series of "unfair labor practices" on the part of unions, such as secondary boycotts, strikes by federal workers, and union contributions to federal political campaigns). Although the law was passed over Truman's veto, his election seemed imperative if the harsh act had a chance of being repealed. Second, the ADA was formed by liberals such as Eleanor Roosevelt, intellectuals like Reinhold Niebuhr, and labor leaders like Walter Reuther, all of whom hoped to distance liberalism from the anti-Cold War, pro-Soviet rhetoric of the Progressive Party. "We reject any association with communists or sympathizers with communism in the United States," the ADA proclaimed. The organization staunchly supported Truman's Cold War initiatives, especially the Marshall Plan, and believed Truman to be the heir of the Rooseveltian legacy of liberalism at home.

Meanwhile, unfortunately for the Republicans, their candidate was digging his own and his party's political grave. Compared to the colorful Truman, Dewey was as exciting as a piece of chalk. Behind closed doors even Republicans complained about his bland speeches and empty platitudes. As one reporter said, "Dewey doesn't seem to walk, he coasts like a man who has been mounted on casters and given a tremendous shove from behind." Despite Dewey's lackluster personality and weak campaign, reporters, columnists, and experts thought that he would win.

Another component of the Clifford strategy was to have Truman call the Republican-dominated Eightieth Congress into a special session and ask them to pass a host of liberal measures such as social security expansion, a higher minimum wage, and national housing legislation, which he had proposed earlier. Truman employed this particular tactic to show the American people that he not only was FDR's liberal heir but that the Republicans and their candidate, despite their rhetoric to the contrary, were bent on the New Deal's destruction. All through the campaign, Dewey had said he favored such legislation, but Truman countered by arguing if that was

President Truman waving from the rear platform of a train. June 3, 1948
Photo credit: Truman Library

true, then the Republicans should vote to pass his obviously liberal agenda. The president stated that he knew the Republicans would do nothing because if Dewey won they could then dismantle what was left of the New Deal. Harry Truman hit the campaign trail with a fire in his belly rarely seen in American politics. In a whistle-stop campaign, Truman barnstormed his way across the nation, moving from town to town, stopping to denounce Dewey and Wallace from the back of a railroad car. Feisty, biting, and combative, Truman mocked the Republicans, red-baited the Progressives, and ignored the Dixiecrats as he began to win the loyalty of the 6 million people who came to hear his stump speeches. Truman accused Dewey of plotting "a real hatchet job on the New Deal," and that the governor's party was controlled by a cabal of "cunning men" who were planning "a return of the Wall Street economic dictatorship." He told farmers and workers they would be "ingrates" if they did not vote Democratic. "If you send another Republican to Washington, you're a bigger bunch of suckers than I think you are." Farmers found Truman's dire predictions of a Republican victory especially alarming because Truman told this particular bloc of voters that if Dewey won it would mean the end of farm price supports. The crowd would yell back, "Pour it on Harry. Give'm hell."

When the country awoke the day after the election, the "miracle of 1948" had happened. Truman was elected, scoring the biggest upset victory in American history, rolling up 24.1 million votes (49.5 percent) to Dewey's 22 million (45.1 percent) and a more emphatic 303 to 189 in the Electoral College. Both Wallace and Thurmond had the same popular tally, but Thurmond, thanks largely to black disfranchisement, received 39 electoral votes from the states of Louisiana, Mississippi, Alabama, and South Carolina, and one vote from Tennessee. Wanting their vote to count for something, other southern segregationists stayed inside the Democratic tent and hoped to influence the president from within. Wallace was embarrassed by his party's communist supporters and by the brutal Soviet coup in Czechoslovakia, which resulted in the murder of its anti-Soviet Foreign Minister Jan Masaryk. Riding on the president's coattails were new liberal senators Hubert Humphrey of Minnesota, Estes Kefauver of Tennessee, and Lyndon Baines Johnson of Texas.

Although it was the loyalty of voters to the memory of FDR and to his New Deal coalition that put Truman in the victory column, the president nonetheless commanded a constituency of his own by virtue of his anti-communist policies and successful Cold War initiatives. In this sense, Truman's presidency established a pattern that would persist for several decades. If Democratic candidates could avoid appearing "soft" or "weak" on national security issues, they stood a good chance of being elected president. Truman stood "tough" in 1948 and had a string of Cold War successes to bolster his credentials as someone who would not let the Soviets have their way abroad or communists at home undermine the American way of life.

Harry Truman and the Fair Deal

Although the Truman administration placed its greatest priority on constructing a global policy of containment, it also reconstructed the domestic legacy of FDR. Many New Deal liberals still believed it essential to see Roosevelt's "Second Bill of Rights" become reality and naturally looked to Truman for such action. Frustrating Truman from realizing the New Deal vision was a problem with which FDR never had to contend with during his tenure: "the politics of prosperity." As Barton J. Bernstein observed, the politics of depression allowed the Roosevelt administration to court interest groups and contributed to an economic upturn. Inflation required Truman to curb wages, prices, and profits. A growing white middle class suburban America stymied Truman's efforts at continuing with the New Deal where FDR and the war years had left off.

Truman needed to find a different approach to policy making. The 1946 debate over the Full Employment Act helped identify one. That act as initially conceived by Truman aspired to be the centerpiece of liberal hopes for a prosperous, just society. As originally drawn, it would have made the federal government responsible for providing employment for everyone who was able to work and seeking work, with the president recommending programs to sustain employment whenever his economic advisers projected a dip in the economy. Although such work programs might cause short-term budget deficits, supporters believed that in the long run full employment would generate sufficient taxes to both balance the budget and to finance social welfare programs, such as increased minimum wages and national health insurance. Full employment was the cornerstone of Roosevelt's "Economic Bill of Rights." To the conservatives (Republicans and Southern Democrats), these provisions and the phrase "full employment" smacked of European-style welfare, even socialism.

Truman could not hold the forces of reaction at bay. By the time Congress finally acted on the measure, most of its key provisions had been gutted. Instead of full employment, the new version called for maximum employment, a phrase that conceivably could justify a jobless rate of 5 or 6 percent. Other provisions stipulated that the private sector still bore the responsibility for employment, as well as general economic decision-making. The conservatives still allowed for some government management of the economy, but they made it clear that the heady days of New Deal regulation and government-sponsored job creation were over. By the time the measure finally passed, it represented a vague statement of principles rather than a plan for action, its most significant reform being the creation of a Council of Economic Advisors to provide recommendations to the president and Congress regarding long-range economic developments.

President for the first time in his own right in 1948, Truman told the American people in his State of the Union address that, "every segment of our population and every individual has a right to expect from his government a fair deal." Many have unfairly called Truman's administration "Roosevelt's Fifth Term." On the surface the Fair Deal appeared to be merely an elaboration of existing New Deal initiatives, but at a deeper level Truman's agenda was different, especially in the way such programs were to be paid for. Unlike the New Deal, the Fair Deal was based on the assumption that expansion of social welfare programs could be financed from continual economic growth. A constantly expanding economy would mean a bigger piece of the pie for white middle class Americans so they could not resent helping those left behind. "Fair Dealers," unlike their more radical counterparts of the 1930s refrained from advocating tax the rich to aid the poor programs. Few Fair Dealers, including Truman, believed in such policies.

Truman nonetheless pushed hard for repeal of the Taft-Hartley Act, a more progressive tax system, a seventy-five cent minimum wage (it was then forty cents an hour), agricultural reform, resource development, public housing, Social Security expansion, national medical insurance, federal aid to education, civil rights, and expansion of federal housing programs. Truman was confident he could get much of this agenda passed, for the 81st Congress, in which the Democrats regained majorities, initially seemed inclined to cooperate. Truman's initial optimism faded however, for the coalition of Republicans and conservative (primarily southern) Democrats proved too powerful in their obstruction to overcome. Thus, by the end of the 1949-1950 sessions, Truman had achieved only three of his goals: a minimum wage increase to fifty cents, expansion of Social Security, and public housing. Under the 1950 Social Security Act, the level of benefits was increased significantly, the retirement portions of the program were expanded, and coverage was extended to more than 10 million people, including agricultural workers.

The more expansive Fair Deal proposals either failed or were scaled back by the Republican/conservative Democratic bloc that dominated Congress. Truman's plan for a comprehensive national health-care insurance program ran into opposition, not only from congressional conservatives but from powerful medical lobbies—the American Medical Association (AMA) and the American Hospital Association (AHA). Both associations helped block any government intervention in the traditional fee-for-service medical system and steered Congress toward a less controversial alternative—federal financing of new hospitals under the Hill-Burton Act. Meanwhile, opinion polls suggested that most voters, many of whom were enrolling in private health insurance plans such as Blue Cross and Blue Shield, were simply apathetic or confused about Truman's national health proposals.

Despite these setbacks, Truman persevered, establishing unprecedented breakthroughs in the area of civil rights. Indeed, without question Truman's most lauded accomplishment as president was his civil rights initiatives, which began the long, arduous process, finally realized by the late 1960s by Lyndon Johnson. Truman supported the fight against racial discrimination more vigorously than previous presidents, including FDR. Only LBJ's commitment to this most vital of domestic issues exceeded that of Truman's.

Black Americans in 1945 looked forward to a better life, hoping that their wartime contributions both at home and abroad would at last earn them their full citizenship rights. During the war their share of defense jobs increased from 3 to 8 percent (in large part because of Truman's Senate committee). NAACP membership reached over half a million by 1945. Despite persistent racism and continued government indifference, a new sense of ferment and protest was pervasive in the land, especially in the South. Whether in northern cities or southern towns, African Americans, together with some white allies, were committed to building on the energies of the war years. Black Americans sought to secure a permanent FEPC, to abolish the poll tax, to achieve the basic right of citizenship involved in voter registration, and to outlaw forever the terrorism of lynching. Over a million black soldiers had fought in a war to preserve democracy; now many refused to accept passively a return to the status quo or to racism.

Even before becoming president, Truman had endorsed certain civil rights. As senator, he supported legislation to abolish the poll tax, appropriations for the FEPC, passage of anti-lynching legislation, and an end to the filibuster on an anti-poll tax. President Truman intervened openly with Congress to promote legislation creating a permanent FEPC, writing the chairman of the House Rules Committee that to abandon the FEPC was unthinkable. Truman met with both black and white activists to discuss anti-lynching legislation, expressing genuine sympathy for African Americans' plight. In a private meeting with southern Democrats, Truman confessed his own forebears were Confederates and that he came from a part of Missouri where Jim Crowism still prevailed. Truman, however, also told his fellow Southerners, "My stomach turned over when I learned that Negro soldiers just back from overseas, were being dumped out of army trucks in Mississippi and beaten. Whatever my inclinations as a native of Missouri might have been, as President I know this is bad. I shall fight to the end evils like this."

Truman created a Committee on Civil Rights in 1946. Comprised of such notables as Charles Wilson of General Electric, Frank Graham Porter of the University of North Carolina, and Franklin Roosevelt Jr., the committee surveyed the entire spectrum of American race relations. The commission concluded that the situation for black Americans was so desperate that, if something wasn't done soon to rectify the discrimination, repression, and murder of African Americans, the nation was on the verge of a potential race war. In its report, entitled "To Secure These Rights," the committee recommended a series of actions to correct racial inequality: the establishment of a permanent civil rights division of the Justice Department, the creation of a Commission on Civil Rights, enactment of anti-lynching legislation, abolition of the poll tax, passage of laws to protect the rights of qualified voters, desegregation of the Armed Forces, elimination of grants-in-aid from the federal government to segregated institutions, enactment of a permanent FEPC, home rule for the District of Columbia, and support for the legal attack on segregated housing. In the meantime, Truman became the first president to address a NAACP rally, declaring, "There is a serious gap between our ideals and some of our practices." Truman pledged that every man should have the right to a decent home, the right to an education, the right to a worthwhile job, the right to an equal share in making public decisions through the ballot. We must assure that these rights—on equal terms—are enjoyed by every citizen.

African Americans were elated by Truman's declaration. Truman immediately endorsed the commission's recommendations and the day after their release ordered the Justice Department to intervene in cases before the Supreme Court seeking to invalidate government-backed segregation of public schools and restrictive covenants in housing. These covenants were legal agreements that prevented racial or religious minorities (principally Catholics and Jews) from acquiring real estate in predominantly WASP neighborhoods. Thanks in large part to Truman, in 1946 the Supreme Court declared restrictive covenants illegal and began chipping away at the "separate but equal" principle that had been used since *Plessy v. Ferguson* (1896), to justify segregated schools. In 1950, again thanks to pressure from the White House, the Court ruled that under the Fourteenth Amendment racial segregation in state-financed graduate and law schools was unconstitutional. In light of these decisions, all the traditional legal arguments that had been used since *Plessy* to legitimize racial segregation in all public schools seemed open to successful challenge, which would finally come in 1954. Thanks in large part to Truman's courageous determination to obtain justice and equality for black Americans in the immediate post-war years, such an existence for African Americans might not have become a reality in later decades.

The Formation of NATO

Believing the time had arrived for the United States to establish a system of worldwide military alliances, Truman initiated an unprecedented change in American foreign policy. Since 1778, the United States had refused to join military alliances during peacetime. In April 1949, the United States, Canada, and ten European nations formed the **North Atlantic Treaty Organization (NATO)**. Three months later, the Senate overwhelmingly (82-13) ratified American membership in the alliance. The signatories pledged themselves to collective security, whereby an attack against one would automatically be considered an attack against all. The members also agreed to cooperate on economic, political, and military matters. When Cold War tensions increased in 1950, Truman sought to develop the pact's military potential. After a "great debate" in 1951, U.S. troops were assigned to NATO forces where they remained for decades. Until recently, the United States provided the bulk of NATO's soldiers.

Although the majority of Americans supported Truman's NATO initiative, some opposed the concept, believing the alliance to be a provocation to the Soviet Union. They also saw the treaty as an "entangling alliance" that defied common sense, violating foreign policy traditions that had kept the nation safe for over 150 years and threatened constitutional government by eclipsing Congress' power to declare war. Such were the sentiments of Republican Senator Robert Taft of Ohio, the treaty's most vociferous critic and "America First"advocate (isolationist). The nation's use of military force, Taft warned, could be dictated by a response to events in other countries rather than determined by the United States' own policymaking processes. Taft feared that Truman was using Cold War exigencies to augment executive power, and if the economy sagged, involve the nation in another war to end the downturn.

Although Truman believed in a powerful executive and wielded presidential power to its fullest capacity when he deemed it essential to protect the people, his presidency never even remotely approximated the power (or abuse of it), of his predecessor nor of many of his successors. Truman did believe, however, that the president was to play an active, decisive leadership role when it came to foreign policy, something conservatives such as Taft could not accept. Moreover, as Truman concluded, the United States would never have to "go it alone" against an aggressor, which in the long run would save thousands of American soldiers' lives. Thanks to Truman's and others' persuasive arguments, the NATO concept prevailed, allowing for the creation in the 1950s of other such pacts in other regions of the world that the United States deemed geopolitically important for itself and for its allies' interests.

THE FALL OF CHINA

In 1949, Truman's string of foreign policy successes, popularity, and bipartisan support for his Cold War agenda suffered a severe blow with the fall of China to the communist forces of **Mao Zedong**. Between 1945 and 1948, the United States extended a billion dollars in military aid and another billion in economic assistance to **Chiang Kai-shek's** government. But Chiang steadily lost ground to Mao's communist forces. Mao was especially popular among the Chinese peasantry, who still comprised the bulk of the country's population, because he promised them what they wanted most: land reform. In 1949, when Mao's armies forced Chiang off the mainland to the offshore island of Formosa (Taiwan), many Americans wondered how, with such massive U.S. aid, the communist forces prevailed. Republicans naturally blamed Truman for the debacle, charging his administration with selling out to the communists. The fall of China to the communists was the moment conservative isolationists and other anti-Truman groups had been waiting for. With the most populous nation on Earth succumbing to communism, the opposition was poised and ready to exploit this calamity for as much political gain as they possibly could. Financed by conservative business leaders, a powerful "**China Lobby**" emerged and denounced Truman and his new Secretary of State Dean Acheson for being soft on communism and, despite friction between Mao and Stalin, spoke of a global communist conspiracy directed from Moscow. China's fall also helped to usher in the "domino theory," which asserted that if the United States did not contain communism to China, it would spread like a deadly contagion. According to this theory, like a row of dominoes, Asia's democratic regimes would fall to communist insurgents directed and financed by Moscow and Beijing. The **domino theory** came to especially dominate Republican Cold War thinking during the 1950s.

Like so many other issues and problems, Truman inherited the China problem from FDR, who inherited it from the Hoover administration when the Chinese civil war between the forces of Chiang Kai-shek and Mao Zedong began. From the beginning of that conflict (early 1930s), the United States supported Chiang and his Nationalist movement against Mao's communists. Throughout the 1930s, FDR sent millions in aid to Chiang, who used the money on himself and in building up his army rather than improving his peoples' lives and implementing necessary reforms. Well before 1949, many Americans close to the scene had concluded that Chiang's regime had degenerated into a corrupt, vicious, and oppressive dictatorship that alienated the Chinese people, driving them by the thousands into Mao's arms. To them, Chiang seemed no different than the warlords of old who terrorized and brutally subjugated the people for their own aggrandizement. Such assessments, however, did not deter the Roosevelt administration from continuing to send aid to Chiang.

The final straw for most Chinese came with the Japanese invasion, which saw the Japanese forces ravage the Chinese countryside while slaughtering hundreds of thousands of innocent Chinese civilians in the process. In the meantime, Chiang, instead of using his army to try to stop the Japanese, continued to fight the communists. Indeed, he reached an agreement with the Japanese that he would let them have the parts of China they had conquered if they, in turn, would help him defeat Mao's communist forces. For the majority of the Chinese, Chiang's deal with the Japanese was the ultimate betrayal, and now they were ready to join with Mao, who not only was proving himself a patriot by fighting the Japanese but a liberator as well from both Japanese aggression and Chiang's corrupt tyranny.

The civil war somewhat abated from 1941-1945 as the United States insisted that Chiang use his forces to defeat Japan, and together they would worry about the communists once Japan had been defeated. No sooner did the Japanese surrender than Chiang and Mao were once again locked in a vicious civil war. Truman wanted to know why, with all this U.S. support, Chiang was not winning. In 1945-46, Truman sent George C. Marshall to China as an emissary to determine the problem. Marshall returned, disgusted with Chiang, and told the president that, in effect, the United States had been supporting the wrong side. The majority of the Chinese despised Chiang and had come to embrace Mao Zedong, and thus the communists would prevail. After hearing Marshall's assessment, Truman lost all faith in Chiang, concluding that the United States could not save the venal Nationalist regime. Indeed, they would be "throwing good money after bad." As Acheson observed, "The unfortunate but inescapable fact is that the ominous result of the civil war in China was beyond the control of the government of the United States. Nothing that this country did or could have done within reasonable limits of its capabilities could have changed the result. . . . It was the product of internal Chinese forces, forces which this government tried to influence but could not."

Truman's critics had varied motivations. Naturally, the Republicans were highly partisan. More important than the Republicans' partisan rantings were the reactions of the American people, who were unable to understand why the most powerful and wealthiest nation in the world could not prevent bad things from happening. As one observer put it, people had an "illusion of American omnipotence." When setbacks occurred—the "losing" of China, the Soviets possessing the bomb, which they announced they had in September 1949—the United States must have done something wrong. From this simplistic starting point, it was an easy next step to lash out at the scapegoats, and no one served that purpose better than the president. Although the American public and the Republicans lambasted Truman for "losing" China, the country had been "lost" long before Harry Truman became president.

THE CREATION OF THE "COLD WAR MENTALITY"

In September 1949, word reached the Truman administration that the Soviets had exploded a crude atomic device, marking the end of the U.S. nuclear monopoly. Already besieged by critics who saw a world with Soviet gains and American defeats, Truman issued reassuring public statements but privately took the advice of hard-line advisers and authorized the development of a new bomb based upon the still unproven concept of nuclear fusion. The decision to build this "hydrogen bomb" wedded the doctrine of containment to the creation of even more deadly nuclear technology, as well as intensifying the arms race with the Soviet Union.

Prompted by the events of 1949, the Truman administration reviewed its foreign policy assumptions. The task of conducting the assessment fell to Paul Nitze, a hard-liner, who produced a top-secret policy paper officially identified as **National Security Council document 68 (NSC-68)**. It provided a blueprint for both the rhetoric and the strategy of future Cold War foreign policy. The paper opened with an emotional account of a global ideological clash between freedom spread by American power, and "slavery" promoted by the Soviet Union as the center of international communism. Warning against any negotiations with the Soviets, the report urged a full-scale offensive to expand U.S. power worldwide. It endorsed covert action, economic pressure, more vigorously hyped anticommunist propaganda, and a massive military buildup. Because Americans might oppose larger military spending and budget deficits, the report warned, U.S. actions should be couched as defensive and be presented as economic stimuli rather than as a drain on national resources. In NSC-68, became redefined as simply anticommunism.

Truman initiated a problem that affected every president henceforth—how to formulate and win support for a foreign policy based on national interest rather than on moral purity. An American diplomat wrote in 1967, "There crept into the ideas of Americans about foreign policy . . . a historic note . . . a desire to appear as something greater perhaps than one actually was. It was inconceivable that any war in which we were involved could be less than momentous and decisive for the future of humanity. . . . As each war ended we took appeal to universalistic, utopian ideals, related not to the specifics of national interest but to legalistic and moralistic concepts that seemed better to accord with the pretentious significance we had attached to our war effort." As a consequence, the diplomat went on, it became difficult to pursue a policy not defined by the language of "angels or devils," "heroes" or "blackguards."

The tragedy, of course, was that such a policy offered no room for intelligence or flexibility. If the battle in the world, according to Truman, was between good and evil, believers and nonbelievers, anyone who questioned the wisdom of established policy risked dismissal as a traitor. An ideological frame of reference emerged during the Truman years through which all other information was filtered. A "Cold War mentality" consumed Americans, shaping everything, defining issues according to moralistic assumptions, regardless of objective reality. The intellectual basis for this frame of reference was provided by men such as George Kennan, to whom Truman turned for advice because of their supposed expertise in foreign affairs. It was Kennan who told Truman that the Soviet Union was a political force committed fanatically to confrontation with the United States and world domination. Twenty years later, Kennan searchingly criticized those who insisted (as he once had) on seeing foreign policy as a battle of angels and devils, heroes and blackguards. Ironically, it was Kennan again in the 1970s who declared, "the image of a Stalinist Russia, poised and yearning to attack the west... was largely a product of western imagination." However, for more than a generation, that image would shape American life and world politics.

The Politics of Anticommunism

In the years after World War II, the politics of anticommunism achieved a new pitch of hysteria and viciousness. The **House on Un-American Activities Committee (HUAC)** was first established in 1938 under the chairmanship of the hardcore conservative Democrat from East Texas, Martin Dies, to investigate anti-American propaganda, which the congressman and his henchmen believed emanated from communist cells within the nation's universities where these denizens of conspiracy found a safe haven among liberal faculty and naïve students. For all of Dies's ranting about communists, his committee's investigations found no communists hiding in the towers of academia. Nonetheless, in order to placate the redbaiters in Congress and to keep them occupied so they would not meddle in his other affairs of state, Roosevelt had allowed HUAC to be made a permanent standing committee. FDR further indulged the anticommunists when he did not veto the Smith Act, which provided a vehicle for prosecuting anyone who even advocated com-

Rep. Martin Dies, Chairman of the House Un-American Activities Committee. February 2, 1940

munism. In a postwar atmosphere suffused with fear and suspicion, opportunities were rife to use these acts for political persecution and intimidation.

The Truman administration bore at least partial responsibility for the outrages that would occur in the name of anticommunism over the next several years. To placate the rabid anticommunists in Congress who had been ranting about supposed communists in the federal government, the president, just nine days after the promulgation of the Truman Doctrine, issued Executive Order 9835, creating the Federal Employee Loyalty Program. The order gave government security officials authorization to screen two million federal employees for any hint of political deviance and also authorized the Attorney General to draw up a list of "totalitarian, fascist, or subversive organizations." Membership, affiliation, or even sympathy with such groups could then be used as a basis for determining disloyalty.

Truman's response reflected a combination of concerns. Clearly, there was a connection with the Truman Doctrine. If the country were to wage a crusade against communism abroad, a strong commitment to clean out communist subversives at home seemed a logical parallel. If, as Michigan Senator Arthur Vandenberg said, the only way to get the Truman Doctrine through Congress was to "scare the hell out of the American people" about Soviet expansionism abroad, a vigorous anticommunist program at home would serve as an appropriate complement. If

Truman hoped to get any funding for his doctrine's initiatives or for any of his domestic programs, he had to acknowledge the rabid anticommunism of the powerful chairmen of the Senate and House Appropriations Committees—Republican John Taber of New York in the House and Senator Styles Bridges of New Hampshire in the Senate. Both Taber and Bridges were convinced that communists (often defined as New Dealers during the Republican backlash of the immediate post-war years) riddled the federal bureaucracy. In acquiescing to the political conservatism of such power-brokers, Truman helped legitimize a form of political inquisition, soon to be labeled "**McCarthyism**," after the most notorious red-baiter of the Cold War era, Republican Senator Joseph McCarthy of Wisconsin. All of McCarthyism's later abuses were anticipated by Seth Richardson, the first president of the Loyalty Review Board, when he declared "the government is entitled to discharge any employee without extending to such employee any hearing whatsoever." Any "suspicion of disloyalty, however remote" could provide justification for such dismissal. Using these procedures, civil servants who at any time in their lives had criticized United States society or government policy (exercising their right of free speech) could be arbitrarily dismissed from their job without being given the right to confront their accusers. The Attorney General's list of subversive organizations allowed for HUAC and Loyalty Board henchmen to call before them and interrogate any individuals whom they "suspected" of at one time belonging to such "traitorous" groups as the Soviet-American Friendship Society—a World War II organization promoted by FDR as being essential in helping to foster good relations with the Soviet Union. Truman further alienated civil libertarians by having as his Attorney General a notorious red-baiter, J. Howard McGrath, who publicly declared that communists were "everywhere—in factories, offices, butcher shops, on street corners, and private businesses. And each carries in himself the death of our society." CIO president Phillip Murray reflected the concern of many when he asked: "What sudden threat can warrant our throwing over board the democratic principles of fair hearing and fair trial?"

Perhaps the most sensationalized of HUAC's investigations took place in 1947, when the committee launched a series of hearings about communist influence in Hollywood, long considered by right-wingers to be the bastion of political radicals. Calling some of the most popular and legendary actors, directors, and screenwriters of the era to appear before the committee ensured it a wave of national publicity. To the shock and betrayal of many of their colleagues, former New Dealers such as Walt Disney, Ronald Reagan, and Gary Cooper testified that the motion picture industry was rife with communists. To the committee's delight, this was exactly what they wanted to hear. With such confirmation, for the next several years HUAC unleashed a reign of terror in Hollywood, subpoenaing hundreds whom they hoped, out of fear of being labeled a communist, would turn on their friends and colleagues and deliver up to the committee the names of those they believed or suspected of being subversives, often on testimony lacking any real merit. Very few, if any of those subpoenaed, were communists or socialists. At the very worst they may have been momentarily captivated by such ideologies, especially during the 1930s, when democratic capitalism appeared to be on the verge of collapse. The majority of those who appeared, however, before the committee had never even flirted with such organizations as the Communist Party, and if they had attended a meeting or two, it was out of innocent curiosity, which many freely admitted to have been their single motivation.

Not all of Hollywood ran scared of HUAC. Ten "unfriendly witnesses," memorialized as the Hollywood Ten (screenwriters/directors Alvah Bessie, Herbert Biberman, Lester Cole, Edward Dmytryk, Ring Lardner, Jr., John Howard Lawson, Albert Maltz, Samuel Ornitz, Adrian Scott, and Dalton Trumbo), refused to answer the committee's questions about their political beliefs or to "name names" ("rat out" their friends and colleagues as alleged subversives) on the grounds that the hearings violated First Amendment guarantees of freedom of speech and political association. The committee charged the Hollywood Ten (around whom many stars of the day rallied such as Humphrey Bogart and Lauren Bacall, along with scores of other legendary film stars, directors, and screenwriters) with contempt of Congress, and they all served jail terms ranging from six months to a year. Hollywood studios blacklisted them (denied them employment), along with over 200 others who were accused of communist sympathies or who refused to name names. As one of those who cooperated with HUAC, a remorseful Sterling Hayden, confessed years later that he was "a rat, a stoolie, and the names I named of those close friends were blacklisted and deprived of their livelihood."

The Spy Trials

In the wake of the Hollywood purge came a series of highly publicized legal cases, which only further fueled the anti-communist hysteria slowly but insidiously enveloping more and more Americans. Whittaker Chambers, an editor at *Time* magazine, testified before HUAC that during the 1930s Alger Hiss, a high-ranking State Department official, had given him secret government documents to pass to Soviet agents. Hiss vehemently denied the charge, but a jury convicted him of perjury and he served five years in prison. As HUAC's popularity grew, ambitious young congressmen from both parties fought for membership on the committee. One such new young lion was Richard Nixon, Republican member of the House from southern California, whose dogged pursuit of Hiss won the future president his first taste of the national limelight. As Nixon's notoriety with the Hiss trial confirmed, increasing numbers of aspiring young politicos were discovering that the key to their future success in politics, regardless of party affiliation, was to jump on the politics of anticommunism bandwagon, and be there, front and center, when the crusade reached its crescendo, which had yet to happen. In the meantime, it was important to be a member of HUAC and from that position help expose to the American people the communist threat in America.

The most sensational, perverse, and prejudiced trial involved Julius and Ethel Rosenberg, a working-class Jewish communist couple from New York City (quite different from Hiss, a member of the eastern Protestant establishment). In 1951, a jury convicted the Rosenbergs of conspiracy to pass secrets concerning the atomic bomb to Soviet agents during World War II (when the Soviets were U.S. allies). Their chief accuser was David Greenglass, Ethel's brother, who had worked at the Los Alamos, New Mexico research center, where the bomb was being constructed. The case against Julius Rosenberg rested on highly secret documents that could not be revealed in court. (When they were released many years later, the scientific information they contained seemed too crude to justify the government's charge that Julius had passed along the secret of the atomic bomb, although the documents he did give the Soviets may have helped speed up their atomic program.) The government had almost no evidence against Ethel Rosenberg, and Greenglass later admitted (years after her execution) that he had lied in some of his testimony about her involvement. Prosecutors seem to have indicted her in the hope of pressuring Julius to confess and implicate others. But in the increasing atmosphere of anticommunist hysteria and fear, their conviction was certain. Even though they had been convicted of conspiracy, a far less abominable charge than spying or treason, Judge Irving Kaufman called their crime "worse than murder." They had helped, he declared to cause the Korean War and thus sentenced them to the electric chair. Despite an international outcry, the Rosenbergs were executed on June 19, 1953. The couple's two young sons, Robert and Michael, spent the bulk of their adult years trying to prove their parents' innocence. Sadly, in 2008, Julius Rosenbergs' co-defendant, 91-year-old Morton Sobell, finally admitted that Julius was indeed a

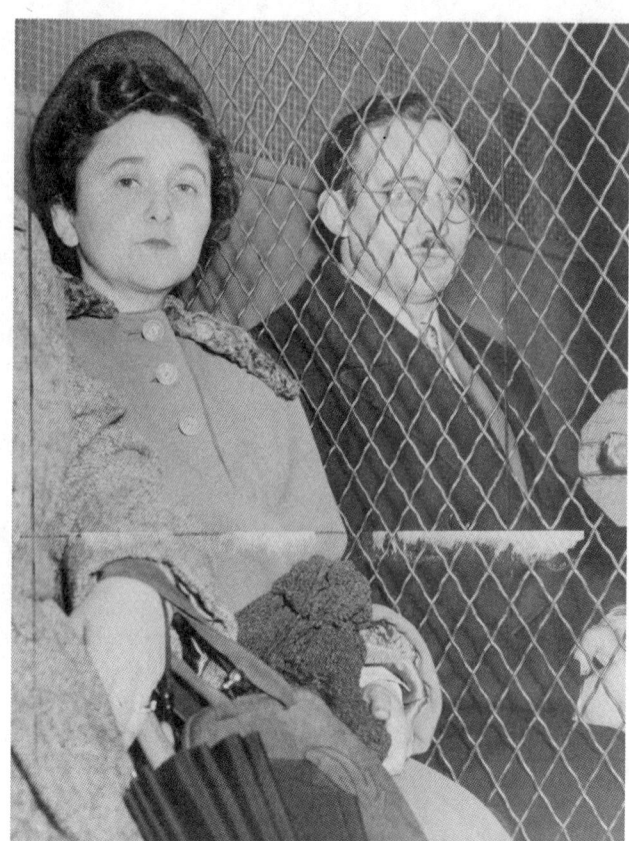

Julius and Ethel Rosenberg are separated by a heavy wire screen as they leave the U.S. Court House after being found guilty by a jury. 1951

hired Soviet spy, who received vital information from his brother-in-law David Greenglass about the Manhattan project, which he then passed on to his Soviet contacts. It is doubtful Ethel was involved in the espionage ring, and her execution was unwarranted, as well as that of her husband. Nonetheless, these trials powerfully reinforced the idea that an army of Soviet spies had infiltrated the nation and with the help of traitors such as Alger Hiss and the Rosenbergs were intent on bringing down the great democratic Republic from within.

McCarthyism

Into this atmosphere of fear, suspicion, and increasing paranoia, a little-known senator from Wisconsin emerged to exploit for personal political gain the insecurities of a generation of citizens searching to relieve them of their collective apprehension about communism. That individual was the Irish Catholic Republican Joseph McCarthy, who momentarily became one of the most popular, feared, and powerful individuals in the country between 1950 and 1954. McCarthy's witch-hunts gave a new name to the anticommunist crusade ("McCarthyism"), which, since the 1950s, Americans have come to associate with

Senator McCarthy talking to reporters after a session of his Senate Investigations Subcommittee. August 15, 1949. Credit: Dwight D. Eisenhower Library

the Red Scare of that decade. McCarthy won election to the Senate in 1946, partly on the basis of a fictional war record (he falsely claimed to have flown combat missions in the Pacific as a "tail-gunner," one of the most dangerous positions on a bomber, for which he earned the nickname "Tail-gunner Joe") but mostly because of his constituencies' growing angst about communism.

McCarthy made the first of his many outrageous accusations about communist infiltration in the government in a speech in Wheeling, West Virginia in February 1950 before a gathering of Republican women, whose mouths surely dropped to the floor when the senator pulled a piece of paper from his pocket and proclaimed that on this paper were the names of 205 "known communists" presently working for the State Department. From that moment on, "Tail-Gunner Joe" became the darling of every far-right, rabid anti-communist organization in America. Tragically, as McCarthyism gained momentum and popularity, Republicans and Democrats (sadly, both the Kennedy brothers, John and Bobby, joined McCarthy's crusade) jumped on the senator's bandwagon, hoping to advance their own careers by parlaying his popularity. From the beginning, all of McCarthy's charges were preposterous, the numbers of alleged communists constantly changed, and he never identified a single person guilty of genuine disloyalty. Nonetheless, for close to five years McCarthy and his henchmen ran amok, terrorizing with impunity thousands of Americans with their accusations and outright lies. Sadly, polls revealed that a majority of Americans supported McCarthy's reign of terror. Why? The answers were quite simple. First was that the McCarthy phenomenon reflected an age-old adage—the greater or more outlandish the lie, the more believable it becomes. In other words, no one would make such an outrageous claim as communists in the government or in other American institutions such as universities or labor unions, unless it was true.

The second answer is deeper and more reflective of American culture and society of the early 1950s. It must be remembered to whom McCarthy was speaking—a generation of Americans who had known nothing but the crises of deprivation and war; a citizenry for whom

Chills and Fever during the Cold War

In November 1953, John Moretta was summoned to appear before HUAC (The House Un-American Activities Committee) that had finally made its way to San Antonio, Texas in its mission to purge the nation of suspected communists. The committee had spent the past several months in Austin, Texas, home of the University of Texas, which since the 1930s, right-wing, anti-communists zealots were convinced had been a bastion of communist subversion in Texas. As the Martin Dies committee had found no communists among the faculty and staff in 1938, the same held true in 1953. Finding no communists at the university, the committee decided to go to San Antonio, a city considered by local anti-communist crusaders to have also had been a hotbed of communist activity and conspiracy, largely because of its support of the New Deal and because of its overwhelmingly Hispanic (primarily Mexican) population.

Moretta, the son of Italian immigrants who had brought their family to the United States in 1927 from Turin, Italy, when John was 5 years old, had just been promoted by the huge retail conglomerate, Sears Roebuck and Company, to become one of the youngest store managers in the history of the corporation. John was 31 years old at the time, was married with three young boys and another child on the way. He had been informed by the Chicago office (the company's headquarters) that he was to appear before the committee to defend himself against the accusation that he had been a member of the Communist Party, which he allegedly had join as a CCC worker in the late 1930s in southwest Texas while working on developing Big Bend National Park. If true, he would be summarily fired by Sears for being a security risk. At first John thought this was a prank by his colleagues, a tasteless joke. Communism was no laughing matter in the United States, however, especially since Senator Joseph McCarthy's reign of terror, which already had ruined thousands of innocent Americans' lives. John naturally feared that this would be his fate as well, blacklisted forever from the corporate business world that he had worked so hard to establish a career.

Moretta was also a decorated (Silver Star, Purple Heart) World War II veteran, who enlisted in the Marines soon after Pearl Harbor and who fought at Guadalcanal, Iwo Jima, and Okinawa. Thanks to the GI Bill, upon his return to the United States, Moretta finished his education at Texas A&M University, graduating in 1947 with a degree in business. In many ways, Moretta was the "poster-boy" for the immigrant American success story. Apparently little of that mattered to HUAC.

Moretta did have a left-wing "skeleton in his closet;" his father had been an active member of the Italian Socialist Party before emigrating to the United States, literally fleeing for his life. By 1927 the fascist dictator Mussolini had declared all-out war on all opposition to his regime, especially targeting Socialists and Communists for his purges, even though he once had been a devoted member of the former.

Suddenly, like others of the period, Moretta faced a nightmare. Despite his spotless record, Moretta was told by corporate headquarters that an unnamed accuser had identified him as a Communist; an individual who claimed he saw Moretta join the party and attend several meetings after "recruiters" had come to south Texas to try to attract young CCC workers—a New Deal program many McCarthyites believed to have been a Communist front organization from its inception. The burden of proof was entirely on Moretta, and he believed it would be impossible to clear his name without being able to confront his accuser, which the committee refused to reveal. Committee members told Moretta he could exonerate himself if he gave the names of others who had worked for the CCC who also had joined the party. Moretta told the committee he could not provide such information because none of the guys in his barracks joined the party and that no party recruiters had ever come to the project that he knew about. The committee refused to believe him and continued to pound away at Moretta for several days, hurling accusation after accusation at him that he would pay a high price for his lying.

Moretta refused to be intimidated; he was a man of honor—a Marine, who refused to succumb to such bullying and imputation of his character. He knew if he refused to crater to their harassment, they would eventually give up and move on to their next target. Moretta defended himself throughout the ordeal. He was confident he would ultimately prevail and clear his name and reputation. What worried him the most, however, was his employer. How would Sears Roebuck view his personal nightmare? Despite his innocence, would they nonetheless always look upon him with suspicion and thus stymie his career? Would he be eventually fired? Fortunately none of Moretta's fears ever became reality.

> One month after his subpoena, he was cleared of all charges, thanks in large measure to Moretta finding several witnesses willing to testify on his behalf: former CCC co-workers as well as his Marine commander, all of who testified that Moretta was not only a loyal American, a war hero, but also that no Communist Party recruiters had ever come to the Big Bend project while Moretta was working. Fifteen witnesses either spoke under oath on Moretta's behalf or left sworn written depositions testifying to his good character and meritorious service. One of the individuals who came forward and confirmed Moretta's stellar job performance and "upstanding citizenship" was the vice-president in charge of operations for the entire national Sears Roebuck network. Much to his relief and joy, Moretta kept his job and remained with Sears Roebuck until he retired in 1988 at age 66 as executive vice-president of the corporation's multi-billion dollar division of catalog sales.
>
> Moretta was more fortunate that some victims of the anti-Communist crusade. People rallied around him and gave him valuable support. Despite considerable mental and emotional anguish, he survived the witch-hunt of the early 1950s, but his case still reflected vividly the ugly domestic consequences of the Cold War.

the American Dream of stability, security, and prosperity had to be postponed for almost two decades. By the early 1950s, however, much to the delight of white middle-class America, the post-war economic boom, which few realized would be as impressive and bountiful, had restored to white Americans confidence that the American dream was on the horizon and, for many, had become a reality by the early 1950s. Now that stability, security, and prosperity had returned, white middle-class America was not about to let any subversive group take the good life away. To this particular generation of Americans, Joe McCarthy and his anticommunist crusade represented the safeguarding of all they had accomplished since war's end, and they rallied to the senator, believing his wild accusations and falsehoods about communist bogeymen lurking everywhere, waiting for the right moment to strike and take from Americans the good life they had worked so hard to reclaim.

With increasing numbers of Americans, corporations, and right-wing organizations behind him, and with a genius for self-promotion, McCarthy became a blustering, crass, abusive, red-baiting juggernaut, who even a popularly-elected president, Dwight David "Ike" Eisenhower, refused to criticize. Eisenhower chose to remain aloof of the anticommunist controversy, believing any counter-action would demean the office of the presidency, for it would be engaging McCarthy in the game of gutter politics, "to get into a pissing contest with a skunk," as he remarked privately in language Truman would have used publicly. As did so many other politicians, Eisenhower feared McCarthy, especially the prospect that the senator would turn on the Republican administration as he had on the Democratic. McCarthy perhaps reached the height of his shamelessness when he had the audacity to accuse Eisenhower's close friend and mentor, five-star general and former Secretary of State and Defense George C. Marshall, of being a communist. Ike said nothing publicly in Marshall's defense; he simply told the press that he refused "to get into the gutter" with McCarthy. Eisenhower's detachment from McCarthy's rantings is unforgiveable, especially when it is to be remembered that it was Marshall who had convinced FDR to appoint Eisenhower as Supreme Allied Commander. Ike owed his career to George Marshall. Although McCarthy was certainly powerful and embraced by the American people, Ike's personal popularity and presidential prestige was far greater than that of McCarthy's. Thus, Ike could have used his standing with little adverse affect on his acclaim or office to slow the senator down or hasten his demise. His refusal to challenge McCarthy represented, along with his equally detached attitude toward civil rights, a major moral blot on his presidency.

By 1952, McCarthy appeared invincible. Through his subcommittee, the Permanent Subcommittee on Investigations, McCarthy held countless hearings, hauling thousands of citizens before his inquisition, rudely and crassly leveling individuals with the most outrageous charges. His attacks went beyond individual Americans; the senator also went after the Defense Department, the Voice of America, and many other government agencies, including the CIA, as well as schools and churches. Although many Republicans initially supported his rampage as a weapon against the Truman administration, McCarthy became somewhat of an embarrassment after Eisenhower's election, but he remained popular with the American people.

McCarthy's downfall began in early 1954, when **Edward R. Murrow**, one of the nation's most respected radio and television commentators and investigative reporters, decided to take McCarthy's demagoguery head on, exposing him for the first time on television. By the time Murrow began his assault on his weekly CBS show, "See It Now," 25 million households owned at least one black and white television set. For the most part, Murrow let McCarthy's bullying words and actions speak for themselves. Only at the end of his show, would Murrow comment, often scathingly about McCarthy. The senator finally appeared on the show and tore into Murrow, calling him "the leader and the cleverest of the jackal pack which is always found at the throat of anyone who dares expose individual communists and traitors." Scholars debate the impact of these shows on the viewing public, with some insisting that their negative effect on McCarthy was minimal because most Americans preferred watching the popular police drama, "Dragnet," which aired at the same time. The effect on CBS was not negligible; almost immediately after Murrow's first broadcast sponsors pulled their spots and threatened to never return if CBS did not remove Murrow from the air. Much to the surprise of the station's corporate sponsors, the network's president, Fred Friendly, stood by Murrow, refusing to shut down the program. CBS employees rallied to Murrow and Friendly and voluntarily gave up their salaries (including Murrow and Friendly) to keep the network operating and Murrow's show on the air. Television was still coming of age at the time of the Murrow-McCarthy confrontation and had yet to become the all-powerful medium that it would by the 1960s. Nonetheless, "See It Now" did attract a great deal of attention and critical praise, and most important it inspired other media to begin to come out of hiding and criticize McCarthy as well.

McCarthy's ill-advised attempt to ferret out subversive activities in—of all places—the United States Army finally brought him down. McCarthy's stupidity was the handiwork of his chief counsel, New York attorney Roy Cohn, who was upset that his lover, G. David Schine, had been recently drafted into the Army. A year earlier Cohn and Schine had set off on a well-publicized tour of Europe in which they called for the purging of allegedly subversive literature from government libraries. The State Department panicked, and its Secretary, John Foster Dulles, issued a directive removing all the literature recommended by Cohn and Schine from United States information centers abroad. After failing to get Schine released from his two-year commitment, Cohn then tried using influence to get Private Schine as many special privileges as he could. The Army, however, refused to be brow-beaten by Cohn, and in retaliation, Cohn had his boss unwisely charge that the Army had harbored communists. The Senate established a special committee headed by South Dakota Republican Karl Mundt to hear the charges and counter charges. The nationally-televised **"Army-McCarthy" hearings** began on April 22, 1954 and lasted 36 days (for a total of 188 hours) through June 17, 1954. Unlike "See It Now," which was a prime-time evening show, the hearings were televised during the day, and since the soap operas had yet to takeover daytime television, Americans tuned into the hearings with an estimated 20 million Americans watching. For many Americans this was their first glimpse of McCarthy, and those who watched were appalled by his brutish, venal, abusive, and crass bullying of witnesses and by his sweeping accusations.

After the hearings ended, the Senate censured McCarthy for his behavior. He died three years later at the age of 48 from alcoholism. By then, the word "McCarthyism" had forever entered the political vocabulary, a short-hand for character assassination, guilt by association, and abuse of power in the name of anticommunism.

THE KOREAN WAR

One of the Truman administration's greatest controversies remains the Korean War. Although many historians blame Truman for the alleged debacle, it can be argued that event also represented, like the first Berlin Crisis, one of Truman's more outstanding moments. Once again, he confronted a blatant act of communist aggression and would have triumphed had it not been for the arrogance and defiance of one of his own generals, Douglas MacArthur, who was more culpable for the war's needless protraction. Even the American public must be reproached for their inability to understand the concept of a "limited war," which was the only type of conflict that could have been feasibly fought, given the fact that both the "greater belligerents"—the United States and the Soviet Union—possessed atomic weapons. The risk of a nuclear exchange with the Soviets was a factor throughout the war, because of the Sino-Soviet alliance signed soon after Mao Zedong's takeover in 1949. Truman understood this and wisely kept the war in perspective by not directly antagonizing the Soviets or threatening either them or the Chinese with the bomb, even though MacArthur urged such action. By pursuing such an approach, Truman prevented the war from escalating into a possible nuclear confrontation between the United States and the Soviet Union. Had the United States used nuclear weapons, especially on China after that nation entered the conflict in the fall of 1950, the Soviets, despite ideological differences with the Maoist regime, certainly would have come to their ally's aid, threatening to use their weapons of mass destruction in retaliation. Indeed, it could be argued that Truman's restraint and clarity prevented Armageddon.

On June 24, 1950, North Korean troops swept across the 38th parallel to attack South Korea. The Truman administration responded immediately to this blatant act of aggression on one of the United States' key Asian

President Truman and General MacArthur. October 15, 1950.
Photo credit: Truman Library

allies. Truman viewed the assault as another Soviet test of U.S. will and commitment to containment via its lackey state of North Korea. Although it is still not known to what degree the Soviets were behind the invasion (North Korean dictator Kim Il-sung probably had Stalin's tacit approval for the attack in an effort to unify the country, which had been divided into a communist North and noncommunist South after WW II, under Kim's control), Truman nonetheless believed Moscow was the instigator. "Korea is the Greece of the Far East," he maintained. "If we are tough enough now, if we stand up to them like we did in Greece [and Berlin] they won't take any next steps." To Truman, failing to respond to the invasion smacked of appeasement, believing that the communists were doing in South Korea exactly what Hitler, Mussolini and Japan had done in the 1930s. "Nobody had stood up to them. And that is what led to the Second World War." Truman further asserted, "if the Russian totalitarian state was intending to follow in the path of the dictatorship of Hitler and Mussolini, they [had to] be met head on in Korea."

Three days after the invasion, Truman asked the United Nations (U.N.) to authorize action to repel the North Korean attack. Fortunately for the United States, the Soviet delegate had been boycotting the Security Council to protest the U.N.'s unwillingness to seat a representative from Mao's "Red" China, and Truman gained approval for a U.N. "**police action**" to restore South Korea's border. The president appointed General Douglas MacArthur to command the U.N. effort. Although the defense of South Korea was a U.N.-sanctioned use of force to repel an aggressor (16 other member nations supplied troops for the effort, including Great Britain, Canada, Australia, France, Greece, and Turkey), the United States from the beginning provided the overwhelming majority of foreign troops immediately ordered into the fray to aid the South Korean army. The Cold War had turned hot.

North Korean forces initially routed the surprised and disorganized U.S. and South Korean troops, driving them by September 1950 all the way to Pusan on the southeastern tip of the peninsula. There they struggled to avoid being pushed literally into the sea. In a daring, and what turned out to be a tactically brilliant move, MacArthur landed 40,000 U.S. troops at Inchon, behind enemy lines in the south, in effect catching the North Korean forces in a pincer. Within two weeks, U.S. and South Korean forces had recaptured Seoul, the capital of South Korea, and had driven the North Koreans back across the 38th parallel. At this juncture the conflict should have ended, for Truman

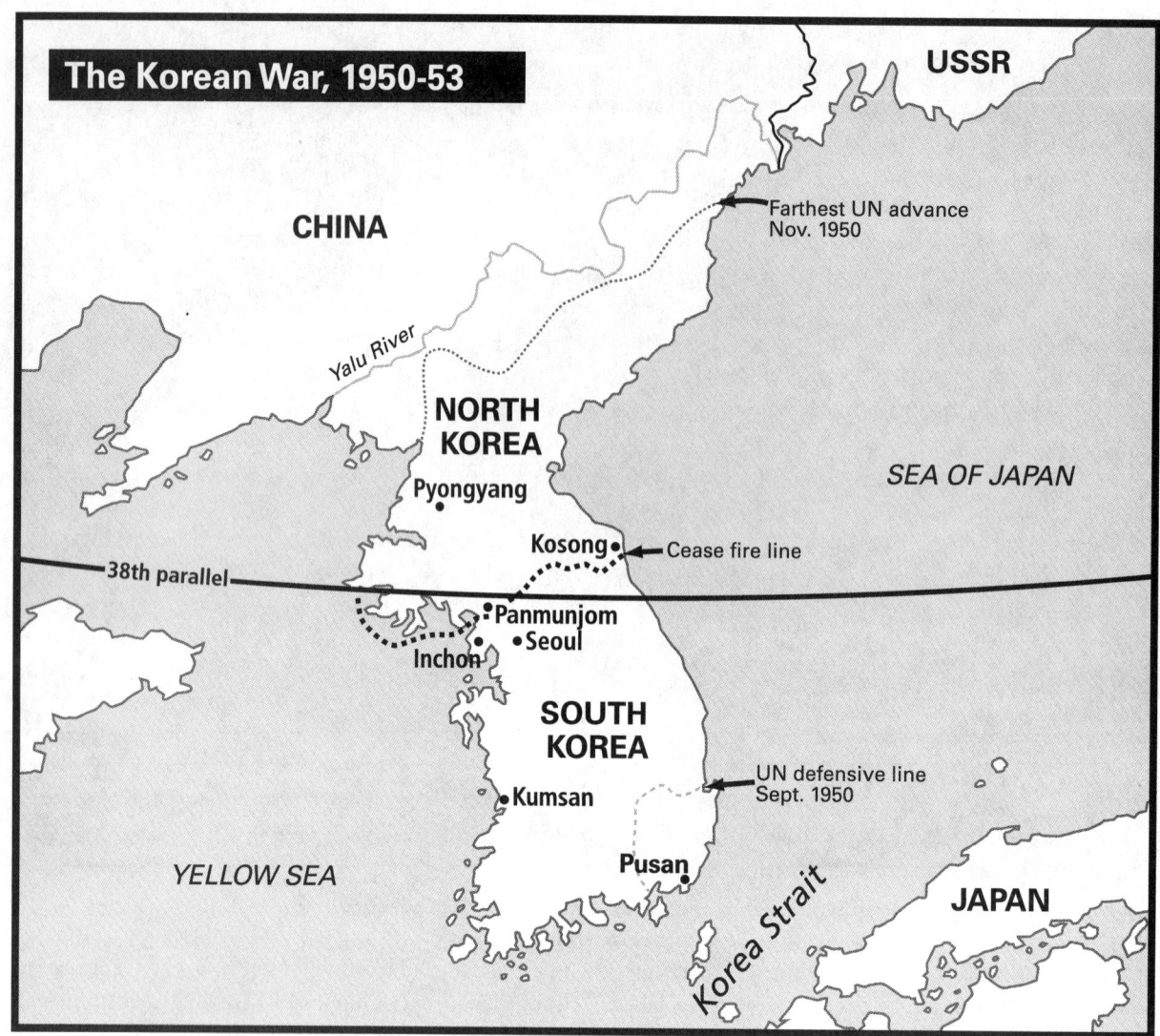

Map 26.3 The Korean War

had publicly announced even before sending U.S. troops to Korea that his objective was to restore the status quo. MacArthur's forces had accomplished that objective. The general, however, wanted an all-out victory—the end of North Korea and a united, democratic, pro-U.S. Korea. He thus persuaded Truman to let him cross the border to liberate all of Korea from communism. By the middle of October 1950, MacArthur's offensive had captured the North Korean capital of Pyongyang and by the end of the month had all but destroyed the North Korean army, whose remnants crossed into China for sanctuary. Truman did not order the general to stop, even though MacArthur's actions disavowed the president's stated goal of a police action designed to stop aggression, protect a U.S. client state, and to maintain the status quo on the Korean peninsula. Nowhere in his public pronouncements had Truman stated that he wanted to see a united, democratic Korea. Yet, even at this juncture it might have been possible to establish a mostly-united Korea under U.S.

auspices had MacArthur not proceeded with his troops to the Yalu River, the border between China and Korea. The Chinese warned that they would not "sit back with folded hands and let the Americans come to the border." Dismissing the threat, an overconfident MacArthur deployed his forces in a thin line about 12 miles south of the river. On November 25, 33 Chinese divisions (about 300,000 men) counterattacked. Within two weeks they drove U.N. forces south of the 38th parallel. By winter's end the contending armies were deadlocked at roughly the original dividing line between the two Koreas.

Largely because of MacArthur's arrogance, the war became the worst kind of conflict: a stalemate that in the end saw 33,000 American soldiers die for a return to the status quo. Although frustrated, Truman realized that to end the fighting and preserve American lives, he had to seek a negotiated peace based on the original objective of securing South Korea's sovereignty as an independent nation. MacArthur, however, felt betrayed by Truman, who he believed was selling out to the communists. The general wanted to blockade and bomb (with atomic weapons if necessary) Mao's China and to unleash Chiang Kai-shek's forces from Taiwan to invade the mainland. "In war," MacArthur insisted, "there is no substitute for victory." Truman, however, rightly feared that if MacArthur invaded China, such actions would bring the Soviet Union directly into the conflict. The president told the general, "We are trying to prevent a world war—not start one."

Despite repeated warnings from Truman to refrain from publicly challenging his policies, MacArthur continued to openly lambaste the president and his conduct of the war. Truman, exasperated, had no choice but to fire the general on April 10, 1951. The Joints Chiefs of Staff supported Truman's decision, but public opinion backed one of the most popular generals in United States history, believing Truman, not MacArthur, was responsible for the setback. Many Americans felt that the president should have allowed MacArthur to invade China, as naively confident as the general that the United States had the power to easily defeat China and the Soviet Union, disregarding the fact that the Russians possessed atomic weapons and that Stalin, if backed into a corner, would use them in Korea or elsewhere, possibly Europe. Moreover, the very idea of limited war, of containing rather than annihilating the enemy as the United States had pursued in its past wars, baffled many Americans, and the mounting casualties in pursuit of a negotiated peace angered them. It all seemed so senseless. Despite the admonishments of General Omar Bradley, Chairman of the Joint Chiefs of Staff, that MacArthur's proposals "would involved us in the wrong war at the wrong place in the wrong time with the wrong enemy," a growing number of Americans listened sympathetically to Republican charges that communist agents were in control of American foreign policy. Unfortunately for Harry Truman, the Korean War proved to be his undoing. The president lost favor with the American people who blamed him, not MacArthur, for the rising number of American casualties.

Although in the end, the Korean debacle was largely the result of MacArthur's hubris, Truman nonetheless was partially responsible. It could be said that the president's failure to demand that MacArthur pull back to the 38th parallel instead of allowing the general to establish a front so close to the Chinese border was the real issue. Like many Americans, Truman was possibly in awe of this most magnificent of generals who previously had been credited with victory in the Pacific over the Japanese—at the very least he understood MacArthur's immense popularity at home. There is possibly another reason, and if more accurate than already mentioned, then Truman was just as culpable as MacArthur for the quagmire. Perhaps Truman secretly became politically greedy and saw great opportunity if the right circumstances emerged to allow MacArthur to invade China and return that country to the democratic fold. It must be remembered that the Right and the "Asia-First" crowd had skewered the president for having "lost" China to the communists. If there was a chance to atone for that supposed fiasco, then to avoid being labeled soft on communism, Truman was willing to take the chance that perhaps MacArthur was right. If that was the real reason Truman did not demand MacArthur's retreat, then Truman was just as much to blame as the general for prolonging the war. Instead of thinking clearly rather than politically, the president may have cost the lives of thousands of more American soldiers and untold numbers of Koreans and Chinese.

The Korean conflict also accelerated the process of globalization of the Cold War. When the fighting ended, the United States found itself ever more strongly committed to greater military support for NATO. The United States also redoubled its efforts to rebuild Japan as a bastion of capitalist anti-communism in Asia. The United States also felt obligated to protect Syngman Rhee, the repressive president of South Korea. Most important for the future, the U.S. found itself more engaged in the support of another despot, Chiang Kai-shek in Taiwan, and supporting French imperialism in Indochina. By January 1953, Truman's last month in office, the U.S. was providing 40 percent of the French effort in that little-known but highly incendiary outpost of Southeast Asia. It was Truman who first involved the United States in Vietnam when he allowed the French to return to its colony after World War II. Why did Truman make such a mistake? Again, the answer lies in containment, for Truman saw a French return as a means of stopping the spread of communism in Southeast Asia, for the leader of the insurgents was Ho Chi Minh, a communist who had spent many years in Moscow. Although Ho was a Marxist, he was no Soviet puppet. He was first and foremost a nationalist who believed the United States would help liberate his country from French colonialism as a reward for his aid in defeating the Japanese during World War II. Truman, so immersed and blinded by his own anti-communist rhetoric, only saw "red" when he looked at Ho Chi Minh. Consequently, as early as 1947, Ho became an American enemy who had to be destroyed. Contrary to most Americans' knowledge, U.S. involvement in Vietnam did not begin in the 1960s but in the late 1940s when the Truman administration agreed to support the French return and pay for their presence as a deterrent to the spread of communism in that part of the world.

By 1952, the Red Scare on Capitol Hill, in conjunction with the Korean War, deeply damaged the Truman administration. Korea was the final blow. Some 5.7 million men served in the military during the conflict—about one-third of the number who served in World War II. The frustrations of stalemate and continuing casualties intensified the Red Scare and rendered Truman virtually powerless to control Congress or effectively lead the country. Well before the 1952, election it was clear that the Korean War had divided the nation and that the majority of Americans were ready for a change in leadership.

THE EISENHOWER ERA AND THE COLD WAR

The 1952 Election

So battered and bruised was the Truman administration by 1952, that although constitutionally eligible to run, Truman decided he had had enough and bowed out of the race after losing the New Hampshire primary to Tennessee Senator Estes Kefauver. Kefauver went on to win a string of northern primaries, making him the front runner for the nomination. Although a Southerner, Kefauver's support of the Truman administration's civil rights initiatives had earned him the enmity of his fellow white Southerners, who considered him a traitor. Thus it became clear that Kefauver could, ironically, win only in northern states. The search began for an alternative candidate, someone who could hold the "solid South" and hopefully win in the Midwest as well. After much hesitation and behind-closed-doors wheeling and dealing at the Democratic convention held in Chicago, Stevenson finally agreed to accept the nomination and won the right to be his party's candidate on the third ballot. In order to ensure that the South remained "solid," Democratic Stevenson chose as his running mate Alabama Senator John Sparkman, who was a strong segregationist.

Victory was for the Republican taking in 1952, so unpopular had poor Truman become and by extension his party. The Republicans had to overcome one major obstacle for victory: they had to pick the right candidate. The party's initial front-runner and favorite was Senator Robert Taft of Ohio. However, Taft was a colorless, serious, uncharismatic man, and a hard-core isolationist, whom the Eastern Establishment members of the party, led by Thomas Dewey and Henry Cabot Lodge, did not like. Internationalists dominated the eastern wing of the party, and on the home front, these individuals tended to be more moderate and progressive on some social policy issues than the Taft-led more conservative middle-western wing of the party. To the eastern Republicans, Taft simply could not win, regardless of whom the Democrats ran. Someone with great mass appeal across party lines, that was what was needed and to the more progressive-internationalists Republicans there was only one individual out there that fit the bill: General Dwight Eisenhower, currently supreme commander of NATO forces in Europe. The question was how to get "Ike" to accept and run for president as a Republican, for until now, no one knew Eisenhower's politics.

For several years, the general's glittering war record and widespread popularity had made him an attractive presidential candidate for both parties. As early as 1948, the Republicans had tried to woo him into running and even some Democrats who wanted to dump Truman approached him as well. But Ike resisted all approaches and remained as Columbia University's president. Even after he left Columbia to become supreme NATO commander, both parties continued to besiege him. By the fall of 1951, non-partisan "Ike clubs" were springing up around the country. Truman himself in November told Eisenhower that he would back him for the Democratic nomination, which seemed like a very real possibility because Democratic presidents had been responsible for all his military appointments and advancements. Moreover, Eisenhower strongly supported Truman's Cold War initiatives, including the Korean War, but there the ideological camaraderie ended. Ike was much more conservative on domestic issues, believing passionately in the necessity of balanced budgets and limited governmental intervention in the nation's socio-economic affairs. Ike was no New Dealer, and thus not for a minute did he consider running as a Democrat.

Ike found it difficult to resist Republican entreaties. Led by Dewey, Lodge, and other Eastern Establishment Republicans, who put relentless pressure on Eisenhower to run as a Republican, Ike finally succumbed and agreed from Europe to allow his name to be put on the Republican primary ballot in New Hampshire. Without leaving his NATO post or taking a stand on any of the issues, Ike won the primary 46,661 votes to 35,838 for Taft, his most formidable opponent. Several factors prompted Ike to agree to run for president as a Republican. One was his opposition to the Fair Deal, particularly its costs. Another was a disdain of Taft, who had opposed both FDR's and Truman's foreign policy agenda, and who had rallied conservative Republicans in support of both MacArthur and McCarthy, two individuals Ike held in contempt. Taft, he told a friend, "was a very stupid man . . . he has not the intellectual ability, nor any comprehension of the issues of the world." After his victory in New Hampshire, Ike convinced himself that he had a duty to the country to run, for in his mind, there was no one else out there in either party that could do the job better.

Taft's supporters were furious with Ike and the eastern wing of the party for promoting Eisenhower. To the Taft camp, Ike was an outsider who had no right to enter the GOP primaries, let alone claim the nomination. The senator's people could rant all they wanted, for whether they liked it or not, Ike possessed two qualities their candidate did not: his knowledge of world affairs was superior to Taft's and he was America's most popular hero. For these reasons Ike rolled up delegates in the primaries and, to the surprise of many pundits, squeaked out a narrow victory over Taft at the convention, which proved to be one of the party's more bitterly divisive contests. So angry was Taft that he did not come out and publicly support Eisenhower until September and only after the general promised the "Taftites" that he would implement a conservative domestic agenda. Eisenhower, however, refused unequivocally to even slightly modify his internationalism. Indeed, Ike played a major role in formulating the GOP's foreign policy platform. Naturally, the party denounced the Truman Doctrine of containment as "negative, futile, and immoral" because it "abandons countless human beings to a despotism and godless terrorism." Mindful of ethnic and anti-communist voters, the platform deplored the plight of the "captive peoples of Eastern Europe," calling for their liberation.

As his running mate, Ike chose the 38-year-old senator from California, Richard Nixon, a fiercely anti-communist partisan and a tireless campaigner. Given his age, Nixon provided a youthful balance—Ike was 62 and soon to be one of the oldest men ever elected president. Also, Eisenhower represented the Eastern Establishment wing of the party and so the Californian Nixon helped to give the ticket regional balance as well. California was the fastest growing state in the Union, second only to New York (45 electoral votes) in having the most electoral votes. (At the time Pennsylvania also had 32 electoral votes, same as California.) Nixon already had endeared himself to the rabid anti-communists within the party for his pursuit of Alger Hiss while a member of HUAC and for his staunch support of McCarthy. No sooner did Nixon become Eisenhower's running mate than he ran into trouble with the press, who reported that wealthy Californians had created a private fund for his family. Interestingly, this should not have been a big issue, for the fund was small ($16,000) and legal. Many politicians, including Stevenson, had similar "resources." However, the press, which had never liked Nixon, continued to hammer at the issue and made Ike increasingly nervous about having such a running mate, whom Ike never warmed to nor really ever liked or respected. Indeed, Eisenhower considered dropping Nixon from the ticket. Nixon, however, refused to have his political career destroyed;

During World War II, the popular image of General Eisenhower depicts him wearing a well tailored, short-waisted, smart-looking jacket, designated officially as the "Wool Field Jacket, M-1944." To the troops it was known as the ETO (European Theater of Operations) Jacket, or even more popularly as the "Ike Jacket."
Credit: of Dwight D. Eisenhower Library

he went on national television to defend himself. In a 30-minute speech, Richard Nixon received redemption and vindication. Nixon told his viewers of his ordinary Quaker upbringing, war service, and close-knit family. His wife Pat, he said, did not have a mink coat, but "she does have a perfectly respectable Republican cloth coat." Nixon then told his audience about "the little cocker spaniel dog . . . black and white spotted" that had been sent to them in Washington "all the way from Texas" at the start of the campaign. "Our little girl—Tricia, the six-year-old—named it Checkers. And you know the kids love that dog and I just want to say right now, that regardless of what they say about it, we're going to keep it."

To the surprise of many pundits, popular reaction to Nixon's **"Checkers Speech"** was overwhelmingly favorable, with many viewers breaking into tears as he spoke. Eisenhower, who nervously watched the speech, was relieved by the positive responses, concluding that his running mate had saved himself and thus his place on the ticket. Nixon was proud of what he had accomplished, believing he was a master of television and could best anyone who tried to challenge him on the screen. Perhaps most important, Nixon's performance illustrated how television was beginning to transform politics by allowing candidates (especially those with bundles of money because television "ads" or "spots" were very expensive) to bring a carefully crafted image and message directly into Americans' living rooms. The 1952 campaign became the first to make extensive use of TV ads. The GOP invested an estimated $1.5 million in television ads, bringing Eisenhower's luminous smile into millions of American homes. Parties, one observer complained, were "selling the President like toothpaste." Despite the criticism, the use of television coverage henceforth became an indispensable tool in American politics.

Stevenson ran a dignified, issues-oriented campaign in which he promised to "talk sense to the American people." As the Democratic candidate, however Stevenson all too frequently found himself having to contend with partisan assaults on the Truman administration. Republicans hammered away at the "creeping corruption" or the "mess in Washington" as they called it. The Truman years, they clamored, involved "Plunder at home, Blunder abroad." There was corruption in the administration after 1950 but it was minor, but it nonetheless existed and the president—ever loyal to friends—was slow to address it. Eventually, Truman's appointments secretary was convicted of accepting bribes, and nine federal employees of the RFC and Bureau of Internal Revenue (the IRS) went to jail.

More damaging by far to Stevenson were the incessant and shrill charges that the Democrats had been soft on communism. By 1952, the Red Scare and Korea dwarfed all other issues, including civil rights. Leading this particularly shameless and vicious assault was the Republican Right. McCarthy branded the FDR-Truman years as "twenty years of treason." Referring to "Alger—I mean Adlai," McCarthy said he would like to get onto Stevenson's campaign train with a baseball bat and "teach patriotism to little Ad-lie." Nixon labeled Stevenson "Adlai the Appeaser," declaring that Stevenson had a "Ph.D. from Dean Acheson's cowardly college of Communist Containment," and reminded voters that the country would be better off with a "khaki-clad President than one clothed in State Department pinks." Nixon and McCarthy were not alone in their red-baiting; many major newspapers were equally vitriolic and crude. The *New York Daily News*, a bitterly reactionary paper, referred to Stevenson as "Adelaide" and said that he "trilled" his speeches in a "fruity" voice, using "teacup words" that were reminiscent of a "genteel spinster who can never forget that she got an A in elocution at Miss Smith's finishing school." Such comments as those of the *Daily News*, questioning the masculinity and virility of Stevenson and other Democratic liberals were common place during the election campaign, suggesting that only rabid anti-communist and hard-boiled conservatives were real men—that Democrats, especially liberals, were too effete to stand up to the communists.

More important to the election's outcome was Eisenhower's popularity and public weariness with the Korean War. Ike's pledge to go to Korea in search of peace signaled his intention to bring the conflict to an end. As predicted, Eisenhower won a resounding victory over Stevenson. Four years later Ike would again defeat Stevenson by an even greater margin. Stevenson took nine southern and border states, thanks to Sparkman's presence on the ticket as well as his own declaration that he believed civil rights to be mainly a question for the states to handle. Another consolation for Stevenson was he got 3.14 million more votes than Truman had in 1948, thanks in part to increased voter turnout. Most important, the election was a mandate for Eisenhower, a personal triumph. Ike captured 33.9 million votes (55.4 percent of the total) to 27.3 million for Stevenson (44.4 percent of the total). Sweeping the Electoral College, 442 to 89, Ike even cracked the "Solid South," winning Florida, Tennessee, Texas, and Virginia. Ike's coattails however, were not as long as Republicans had hoped. The GOP won a razor-thin majority in Congress in 1952 but the Democrats regained control in 1954 and kept their dominance into the next decade. In 1956, Ike became the first president to be elected without his party controlling either house of Congress.

Eisenhower's victory also reflected an interesting phenomenon both at home and abroad. During the uncertain 1950s, voters seemed to find reassurance in selecting familiar, elderly, seasoned leaders to govern them. Ike seemed positively youthful compared to Winston Churchill, who returned to office as prime minister of Great Britain at age 77. Charles DeGaulle became president of France at 68, and Konrad Adenaur became chancellor of West Germany at 73 and remained in that capacity until he was well into his 80s.

Eisenhower and the End of the Korean War

Soon after entering the White House, Eisenhower, as he had promised during the campaign, went to Korea to bring about a cease-fire and, as quickly as possible, end the war. A combination of factors, including the Chinese and North Korean forces' exhaustion, led to the signing of an armistice that took effect on July 27, 1953, thirty-seven months after the war had started. A year later, a treaty was signed by the belligerents that officially ended the war and returned to the status quo antebellum—the 38th parallel once again became the boundary between North and South Korea. That dividing line is still in effect. The cease-fire accord was probably Eisenhower's single most important accomplishment in the foreign policy arena during his tenure. The agreement gave his presidential prestige a big early boost and eliminated the most bitter political issue of the era. Perhaps most important, the ending of the war allowed Americans to enjoy the good life at home, for which they credited Eisenhower's skillful diplomacy.

The Eisenhower Cold War Frame of Reference

Throughout most of his two terms as president, Eisenhower presented himself as a hard-boiled Cold Warrior, publicly talking "tough" at every occasion. Repeating his campaign's tough anti-communistic messages, he devoted much of his inaugural address to denouncing communism. "Freedom," he declared, "is pitted against slavery; lightness against dark." In his State of the Union message he added that the United States would "never acquiesce in the enslavement of any people." Despite many realities to the contrary, especially those about supposed Soviet military and missile superiority, Ike nonetheless projected to the American public a harsh rhetoric designed to reassure U.S. anti-communist allies abroad of the nation's resolve to maintain the essence of containment while strengthening American abilities to project retaliatory power. Ike believed such posturing essential to bolster NATO, which was then seeking to augment its forces and embrace West Germany. On the home front, the new president had to keep the hard-line wolves at bay such as McCarthy, who were stronger than ever before in Congress. Also motivating many of the more shrill congressional Cold Warriors (as well as Eisenhower to a certain degree) were the lucrative defense contracts that had become vital to their districts' economic development during the Korean War. The Eisenhower administration spent more than $350 billion on military-industrial contracts during the 1950s, an amount that sustained a host of corporations and defense workers throughout the country.

Perhaps motivating Eisenhower to talk tough above all other considerations was that neither he nor anyone else could be sure of Soviet or Chinese intentions. His national security advisers flooded him with reports, many of which contended that the Soviets had the capacity to deliver a knockout attack on the United States. Although knowing that the United States had far superior nuclear weaponry (both in fire-power and in numbers of atomic and hydrogen bombs) than the Soviets, Ike nonetheless could not afford to be cavalier in such circumstances. Like all U.S. presidents during the Cold War years, Ike had to take seriously a powerful adversary and thus felt obliged to frequently issue dire warnings to the American people. He was also convinced that he was dealing with an intractable foe and that any hint of softness in dealing with the Soviets were tantamount to appeasement—one of the worst epithets that a politician could be labeled with during the Cold War era. The majority of both liberals and conservatives agreed on these immutable facts of the world order. They also believed, as did Eisenhower, that the United States, the world's greatest democracy, had a moral obligation to the rest of humanity to promote democratic ideals throughout the globe.

JOHN FOSTER DULLES AND THE "NEW LOOK"

No other individual in the Eisenhower administration exerted more influence than Secretary of State John Foster Dulles, a devout and uncompromising anti-communist. Dulles believed with complete certainty that motivating all Soviet behavior was their desire to spread communist ideology and in the process takeover the world. The possibility that strategic concerns or national security

Running for re-election in 1956, President Dwight Eisenhower and First Lady Mamie Eisenhower wave to voters at a trainstop in Washington, D.C., Nov. 1, 1956.

interests might influence Soviet aggression never entered Dulles's thought process. To him, the Cold War was relatively simple: it represented if not the ultimate struggle of good and evil in world history but a conflict that was against the most dangerous, intractable, and ideologically fanatical threat to world peace in the history of mankind. Dulles, moreover, was moralistic and self-righteous; a devout Presbyterian whose Christian faith strengthened his disdain for communism, which he deplored as atheistic and unprincipled. Self-assured and pompous, he had a habit of looking up toward the ceiling (some critics thought towards God), hands calmly folded on his desk, while talking (pontificating to some of his detractors) at considerable non-stop length, not allowing others a word in edge-wise. Other critics simply described his manner as "Dull, Duller, Dulles."

Nothing did more to promote the toughness of the Eisenhower administration, especially relative to the Soviet Union, than Dulles's declaration in early 1954 of what the secretary called "massive retaliation," which became the foundation of his overall "**New Look**" containment agenda. In Dulles's view, although the United States had properly contained communism through such initiatives as the Marshall Plan, the Berlin Airlift, and the sending of troops to Korea, these were at best "emergency" reactions and in the end, inadequate. Moreover, in his mind, the Free World could not match the "mighty land power [of the combined Sino-Soviet conventional forces] of the Communist world." If that was true, then the United States must rely on its "massive retaliatory power"—the launching or delivering of atomic/nuclear weapons on American adversaries. In short, the United States, which at the time possessed more bombs and missiles than the Soviet Union, would not equivocate in attacking the U.S.S.R. directly with weapons of mass destruction if the Soviet Union threatened the security of any American ally. Dulles believed that such "bomb-rattling" during the Korean conflict had brought the Chinese to heel in Korea by 1953. He seemed to be proposing that the United States not hesitate to brandish its superior nuclear weaponry when challenged by an enemy.

Another appealing facet of the New Look was Dulles's claim that his form of containment would give the United States what he called "more bang for the buck;" that is, massive retaliation would henceforth save the American taxpayers billions of dollars by eliminating from the defense budget obsolete conventional ground and naval forces. To Dulles and his supporters, the Soviets possessed a very large advantage in ground forces, and there was no way the United States, without great costs to taxpayers, could hope to catch up. In reality, for both sides, conventional forces had become antiquated because both the U.S. and the Soviet Union had become nuclear powers and thus could destroy in seconds each other's ground forces by simply dropping a bomb or two on either one's advancing armies. To Dulles and Eisenhower, the answer was to funnel defense dollars into weaponry that counted: missiles with atomic (and soon to be nuclear warheads), jet-propelled bombers such as the new B-47s, which could fly up to 600 miles per hour and had an effective range (when refueled in the air) of 6,000 miles (by 1955 the U.S. had 400 B-47s plus another 1,350 planes capable of dropping atomic bombs on the Soviet heartland); jet fighters, armed with missiles that could shoot down incoming enemy bombers; submarines armed with missiles with atomic warheads, such as the Polaris; and aircraft carriers, upon which such bombers and planes could be easily deployed from sea. Eliminated from the budget would be obsolete warships—cruisers, frigates, and huge battleships, which meant less need for sailors and marines; tanks, field artillery, jeeps, trucks, and, of course, U.S. Army personnel and soldiers. Ike embraced Dulles's **more bang for the buck** philosophy. As a result, during his presidency, the size of the armed services fell by nearly half. Especially decimated was the U.S. Army, which lost 671,000 men and women between 1953 and 1959—a slashing that brought the total number of soldiers and personnel in the Army to 862,000. Meanwhile, the number of nuclear warheads rose from 1,000 in 1953 to 18,000 in 1960.

Many within the armed services and other critics decried these cuts, rightly protesting that the United States had lost its ability to "flexibly respond" to local crises—limited wars—throughout the world, which were becoming more and more prevalent beginning in the 1950s, especially in the newly emerging nations of Africa and Asia, which saw wars of national liberation becoming endemic in those regions as the indigenous people revolted against the last vestiges of European colonialism. Despite this shift in Cold War geopolitics, Eisenhower was determined to control defense spending. Certain that air and naval power offered sufficient security (especially when missiles became operational), Ike unequivocally supported the New Look and massive retaliation. Only a war-hero general with commanding popularity and expertise could have managed this policy without severe political damage amid 1950s Cold War fears.

Eisenhower's and Dulles's support for massive retaliation also reflected historically familiar approaches to defense: faith in high technology and aversion to large standing armies in times of peace. They also believed the policy widened American options by enabling quick retaliation—nuclear if necessary—on an aggressor's own territory. The U.S. could blast the Soviet Union instead of deploying thousands of troops and conventional weapons,

JOHN FOSTER DULLES

which were expensive to maintain and might get killed, to stop communist aggression wherever it might occur throughout the world. In this sense, the new policy was both cheaper and safer than the old containment approach of the Truman administration, which called for fighting aggression conventionally wherever it occurred. Finally, massive retaliation was not only supposed to scare the hell out of the nation's adversaries, but perhaps more frightening, it was to keep them guessing, for they would never know where the U.S. might unleash on their homeland their weapons of mass destruction. Ike and Dulles believed the Chinese and Soviets would thus think twice before challenging the United States.

To Eisenhower, the New Look promised above all to promote his vision of the good society at home. Reliance on massive retaliation would reduce the size and personnel of conventional forces, which would have been very costly to maintain at Korean War levels. The president was especially anxious to balance the budget because he feared inflation, which he was sure would badly damage the economy and intensify class divisions in American society. Perhaps most interesting, Ike's support of the New Look reflected his belief that massive defense spending would give too much power to military leaders and defense contractors. The result could be a "garrison state" that perverted priorities in order to sustain the legitimacy of its existence (the military) and the profitability of its enterprises (the private sector contractors), to the detriment of the nation's domestic well being. "Every gun that is made," Eisenhower said in 1953, "every warship launched, every rocket fired signifies, in the final sense, a theft from those who hunger and are not fed, those who are cold and not clothed." Ike's statement implied no support for expanded social welfare spending to relieve suffering—far from it, for such endeavors would unbalance the budget as well. What Ike did worry about relative to bloated military spending was that such policies would so augment the power of what he later called and feared, as "the military-industrial complex."

Critics of the New Look and Massive Retaliation

Those who opposed Dulles's policies contended that massive retaliation ran the risk that any small conflict could escalate into a "hot war" that would destroy both the United States and the Soviet Union. Critics called the doctrine "brinkmanship," warning of the danger of the Eisenhower administration's willingness to bring the world to the brink of nuclear war. Other critics complained that massive retaliation was saber-rattling of the most dangerous kind—that it frightened allies and that it would accelerate an already intense arms race. "More bang for the buck" would be matched by an equally aggressive Soviet build-up of thermonuclear weapons. Finally, critics asserted that such militarism would not deter would-be aggressors, who would act with impunity, confident that when push came to shove, the United States would not dare use nuclear weapons in the vast majority of regional conflicts. The American people simply would not allow such recklessness unless the nation's security was at risk.

There was no doubt that the New Look rhetoric was threatening to the Soviets, for Dulles also declared that if given the opportunity, the United States would "roll back the Iron Curtain." Soviet leaders surely must have thought that something was "wrong" with Dulles, for only someone who had lost all sense of reality would articulate such a challenge to Soviet security. His policies may have in fact helped the cause of Soviet hard-liners looking for reasons to accelerate their own weapons development.

The reality that an all-out war would result in "mutual assured destruction" (MAD) did succeed in making both sides cautious in their dealings with one another. But it also inspired widespread fear of impending nuclear war. Government programs encouraged Americans to build bomb shelters in their backyards, and school drills trained children to hide under their (wooden) desks in the event of an atomic attack, aiming to convince Americans that nuclear war was survivable. Following a briefing in 1955 on the outcome of a hypothetical atomic confrontation with the Soviets, Eisenhower estimated privately that the Soviet Union (which lagged in the nuclear arms race) would incur three times as many deaths as would the United States. Sixty-five percent of Americans, however, would require medical care, most of whom would be unable to get it. Ike observed, "It would literally be a business of digging ourselves out of the ashes, starting again." Such a scenario was indeed unthinkable—the most horrifying of the many calamities that could destroy the planet if the Cold War ever went hot.

Ike and the Soviets

Joseph Stalin had ruled the Soviet Union since 1927 and over the course of the next 26 years unleashed a reign of terror on his own people that probably killed more human beings than Hitler had during the Holocaust and World War II. During his dictatorship, untold numbers of Russians were either outright executed or sent to the hundreds of gulags—"work" camps in the most isolated and desolate parts of the Soviet Union—for crimes against the state. Stalin's collectivization of farms, especially in the Ukraine in the 1930s, ignited a fierce rebellion, which he suppressed with incredible brutality. At the time, few knew of Stalin's purges and other acts of totalitarian oppression. Moreover, he was psychotically paranoid, which only intensified his viciousness and cruelty. When the dictator died in 1953, millions of Russians actually felt fear because they couldn't imagine their country led by anyone else and many believed Stalin had saved their homeland from the Nazis. Others, including his hundreds of thousands of surviving victims and members of the Soviet Politburo and Central Committee, breathed a deep sigh of relief. Although relieved to be rid of such a tyrant, Stalin's death created a crisis within the Central Committee over who was to succeed him. Initially, Georgi Malenkov was elected First Party Secretary (premier), but others within the Central Committee believed him to be too much of a Stalinist and thus Malenkov was deposed. "Chaos in the Kremlin" thus ensued, a power struggle for close to two years as members of the Central Committee jockeyed with each other to become First Party Secretary. No doubt in the process, many of the rivals found themselves purged from the party; some even sent to a gulag or Siberia, or executed.

During this interregnum, the Soviets would be hard pressed to pursue their policy of "testing" the new Eisenhower administration's commitment to their New Look containment policies, whose shrill, antagonistic, and militaristic rhetoric no doubt shocked, if not scared, the Soviets for their survival. For almost two years, Dulles and his believers got away with their rabid anti-communist verbiage and threats to "nuke" the Soviets if they dared to challenge the United States or any of its allies. By 1955, however, Eisenhower, much to Dulles's and other hardliners chagrin, began having second thoughts about unequivocally supporting the New Look. Ike became convinced that rather than being blind zealots, the Soviets were reasonable and could be dealt with in conventional diplomatic terms. The president became especially interested in a rapprochement after Nikita Khrushchev came to power in 1955 and soon thereafter publicly revealed and denounced Stalin's purges and atrocities. Khrushchev also called for peaceful coexistence with the United States, signaling that he and his fellow Soviets were ready to engage in dialogue with the United States, raising, to the relief of many worldwide, that perhaps the antagonisms between the two great superpowers were lessening. Hope became reality in 1955 when Eisenhower and Khrushchev met in Geneva, Switzerland, at the first "**summit**" conference since Potsdam a decade earlier. The "spirit of Geneva" generated great hope and enthusiasm for future world peace. Russian and American delegates mingled, even in the bars, and people joked about "coexistence cocktails"—"you know, vodka and Coke." The world-renowned evangelist Billy Graham conducted a revival there, extolling the virtues of summits. Moses, he reminded this throng, (over 20,000 attended his sermon) had a summit parley and received a ten-point directive (the Ten Commandments) that heads of state would do well to examine. Perhaps most important, Khrushchev's unveiling of Stalin's murderous purges and rebuke of his policies created a crisis of belief among communists throughout the world. In the United States, the Communist Party all but withered away in light of Stalin's crimes, as three-quarters of its members abandoned the organization, believing they had been betrayed and duped by the nature of his despotic rule.

The Hungary Crisis

Unfortunately, the thaw in Cold War tensions was abruptly shaken in October 1956 with the Hungarian Revolution, an event in many ways caused by Dulles's New Look rhetoric of "rolling back the Iron Curtain." The Eastern European Soviet satellite nations had long chafed under Soviet hegemony, determined to break free of the Russian yoke. Many of these nations were encouraged that their day of liberation was imminent, especially in the aftermath of Khrushchev's denunciation of Stalinism. In mid-1956, riots in Poland forced the U.S.S.R. to make some concessions, which apparently emboldened the Hungarians to do likewise in October, with protests that soon escalated into open armed rebellion. Initially it appeared that Soviet diplomacy would end the uprising, but in early November 1956, Khrushchev became "Stalin," sending 200,000 troops and 4,000 tanks into Budapest and other areas to crush the rebellion. The Hungarians resisted for as long as they could, waiting for aid from the United States that they thought was certain to come because they had provided the entrée Dulles supposedly had been waiting for to "roll back the Iron Curtain." American assistance in any form did not come; it could not, unless one wished for World War III, and once Ike had assured the Soviets the U.S. would not intervene, the Soviets brutally put down the insurrection: some 40,000 Hungarian freedom fighters were killed and more than 150,000 fled the country. In many ways, the **Hungarian revolt** was a test of the Eisenhower-Dulles approach to containment, and the United States failed the exam. The administration's doctrine of liberation might have appealed to the Right's anti-communism and to many Eastern European Americans, but military reality and Cold War exigencies in Europe proved a sham unless the United States was willing risk an atomic war with the Soviets over Hungary, something Ike was not about to consider, regardless of Soviet brutality in crushing the rebellion. Eisenhower thus rejected CIA calls for the parachuting of arms and supplies to the Hungarian rebels and of the dispatching of American ground forces, which might have very well initiated World War III by threatening the Soviet buffer zone in Eastern Europe, thereby disrupting the status quo in Europe. In the end, Ike escaped with very little egg on his face. The real villain proved to be Khrushchev, who proved in this instance to be no less brutal than his predecessor.

The U-2 Incident

In 1958, the two superpowers agreed to a voluntary halt to the testing of nuclear weapons. The pause lasted until 1961. In 1959, Khrushchev toured the United States and had a friendly meeting with Ike at Camp David, which again momentarily generated hopes for a new era of coexistence. However, the "spirit of Camp David" ended abruptly in May 1960 when the Soviets shot down an American U-2 spy plane over their territory, near Sverdlovsk, 1,300 miles inside Russian borders. The U-2 was a supersonic jet plane that could fly at 80,000 feet (well above radar detection) and take very accurate photos of everything on the ground. The Soviets did not yet have such an aircraft, and so when the plane was recovered, with cameras intact, and the pilot (Francis Gary Powers) captured after he had bailed out (he was supposed to have committed suicide by lethal injection supplied to him by the CIA before being captured), Khrushchev felt rightly "exposed" and his nation's security at risk. Eisenhower was embarrassed and livid, as the event could not have happened at a worst moment for the United States as his administration prepared for another summit with Khrushchev to be held in Paris later in the month.

The U-2 incident was the result of an earlier attempt by Eisenhower at the 1955 Geneva Conference to promote the idea of "open skies," which at the time, Khrushchev outright rejected. At Geneva, Ike declared that the United States was prepared to swap sensitive information concerning its armed forces with the Soviet Union. He further recommended regular and frequent aerial inspection of military installations in both countries. To Eisenhower's dismay, Khrushchev found Ike's proposal contemptible, telling the president that, "In our eyes this is a very transparent espionage device. You could hardly expect us to take this seriously." To his credit, the Soviet leader saw right through Ike's proposal—an American propaganda ploy to show the world that the United States had abandoned its earlier militarism, and was now ready to do all it could to promote peace. Khrushchev also knew that after having made the proposal, Eisenhower would do little to make good his offer. Moreover, Ike knew that the Soviets already knew much more about American military installations than the United States understood about Soviet bases and sites. If Khrushchev had accepted open skies, he would have learned relatively little but would have bolstered U.S. military intelligence to the detriment of his own nation's security. Khrushchev thereby rejected the proposal.

Eisenhower initially denied the plane had been involved in espionage, stating that only a U.S. weather reconnaissance plane was missing. On May 7, 1960, however, Khrushchev produced the captured Powers, whom the Soviet premier claimed had confessed to spying and the photographic equipment that proved Powers's plane was for espionage purposes. Ike declared that the U-2 flights had been necessary because "no one wants another Pearl Harbor." To prevent another such attack the United States had to protect itself and the "Free World" by spying. Espionage activities of that sort, Ike claimed, were a "distasteful but vital necessity." Eisenhower then set out for Paris, determined to have the summit. His Soviet counterpart, however, was in no mood for dialogue on any subject, still smarting from the U-2 incident. On the conference's first day, Khrushchev arose, red-faced and angry, demanding that Ike condemn U-2 flights, renounce them in the future, and punish those responsible (the CIA). He also withdrew his invitation for Eisenhower to visit the Soviet Union. Ike was angry but kept his temper and refused to accede to Khrushchev's demands. When the Soviet leader stalked out of the room, it was clear the summit was over before it started. Unfortunately, the U-2 debacle chased away the "spirit of Camp David," ushering in a hardening of Soviet-American relations during the next two years, which became so strained that they brought the world to the brink of nuclear war in October 1962

THE EMERGENCE OF THE THIRD WORLD

Wars of national liberation erupted throughout Asia and Africa as the indigenous peoples of those regions struggled to free themselves from their European overlords, many of whom had been under European subjugation for centuries. Decolonization began when India and Pakistan (the latter carved out of India to give Indian Muslims a homeland) achieved independence in 1947. Ten years later, Britain's Gold Coast colony in West Africa emerged as the independent nation of Ghana. Other new nations—including Indonesia (once part of the Dutch empire), Malaysia (part of the British empire) Nigeria, Kenya, and Tanzania (also all formerly British colonies)—soon followed. In 1975, Portugal granted independence to its African colonies in Angola and Mozambique but not until after bloody insurrections had occurred.

The majority of new nations that emerged during the postwar years gained their independence during the 1950s and came to be called the Third World. (Countries that have emerged since the 1990s are no longer referred to as "third world" but rather by the more politically correct term, "developing" nations). The term "Third World" became the Cold War diplomatic parlance to describe the newly independent non-aligned countries (not becoming the allies or "client states" of either superpower) seeking their own model of economic development between Soviet centralized planning and free market capitalism. Those primarily African and Asian nations desirous of such status met in Indonesia in 1955 at the Bandung Conference, where the 29 attendees proclaimed their non-alignment while asserting that collectively they represented a new force in global affairs. Despite such hopes for political and economic independence to remain neutral in the Cold War, none of the countries which attended the conference could avoid being strongly affected by the exigencies of Cold War power politics.

The Cold War in the Third World

By the 1950s, the struggle for hegemony in the United States and the Soviet Union had shifted to the Third World. Both superpowers hoped to gain new allies, either for strategic geopolitical reasons or for economic interests—valuable natural resources, which many Third World nations had in abundance. Decolonization presented the United States with a complex set of choices. It created power vacuums in the former colonies into which American foreign policy makers feared communists would move. The Soviet Union strongly supported the wars for national liberation, hoping to make as many of the new nations as possible Soviet satellites. The United States naturally pursued a policy of checking Soviet influence in the Third World. Thus, several showdowns occurred during the 1950s between the U.S. and the Soviet Union in the battle for power in the Third World. Perhaps most important, containment policy unfortunately easily slid over into opposition to any government, whether communist or not, that seemed to threaten U.S. strategic or economic interests. It was during the 1950s that the Central Intelligence Agency (CIA) became one of the United States' most effective "weapons" in this particular dynamic of the Cold War.

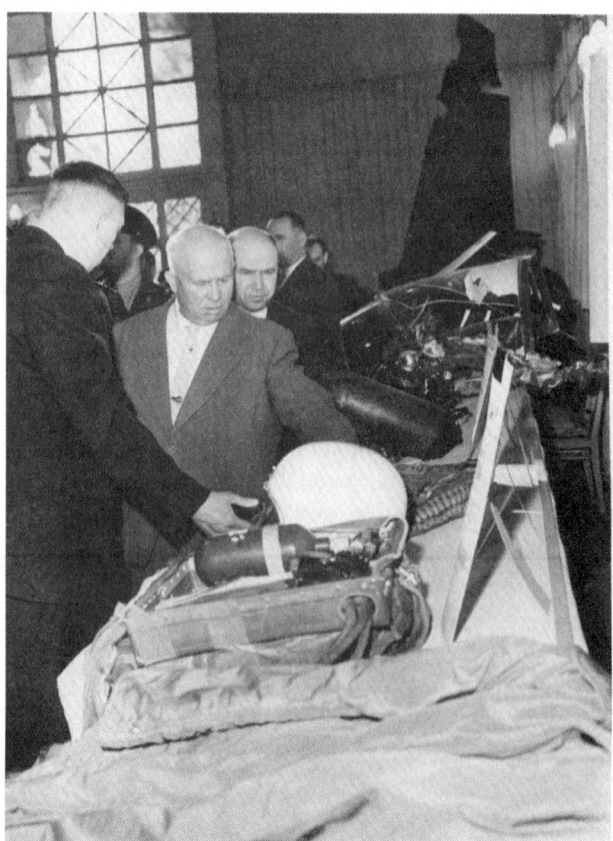

Russian leader Nikita Khrushchev inspects the remains of the American U2 spy plane that was shot down over the Soviet Union.
Credit of the Dwight D. Eisenhower Library.

The CIA, created in 1947 as an outgrowth of the wartime Office of Strategic Services (OSS), had grown slowly prior to the Korean War. Receiving presidential authorization during the Truman administration to conduct covert operations, the agency intervened in Italian politics to ensure that the Italian communist party did not come to power. The CIA expanded rapidly in the 1950s, which by the time of the Eisenhower administration had a budget of $82 million, 2,812 domestic employees and another 3,142 overseas personnel. Its number of foreign stations grew from 7 in 1948 to 47 by 1953. The head of the agency during the 1950s was Allen Dulles, John Foster's equally rabid anti-communist younger brother. The agency's first significant forays into the Third World occurred in 1953 in Iran and a year later in Guatemala. In both instances the CIA led coups that overthrew two legitimate, popularly elected governments because the United States considered their respective leaders to have been too Left (code for communists or at the very least, pro-Soviet) for American economic and security interests. In neither case were the deposed men actual communists. Indeed, in both instances the leaders were homegrown nationalists, not agents of Moscow, and both were determined to reduce foreign corporations' control over their countries' economies.

In the summer of 1953 the CIA ousted the Iranian Prime Minister Mohammad Mossadegh, whom British leaders despised because he nationalized in 1951 the Anglo-Iranian Oil Company, whose refinery in Iran was Britain's largest remaining overseas asset. The coup replaced Mossadegh with the pro-Western, fanatically anti-communist Mohammad Reza Shah Pahlavi, who agreed to a new charter that gave British and U.S. oil companies 40 percent each of Iranian oil revenues. In return, the Shah received a package of American economic aid worth $85 million for which he was to use to modernize Iran and in the process become the bastion of anti-Communism in the Middle East. In June 1954, the CIA intervened again, this time in Guatemala coming to the aid of anti-government rebels seeking to overthrow the legally elected president, Colonel Jacobo Arbenz Guzman. Upon becoming president, Arbenz made land reform a priority and such an initiative would result in confronting the powerful American-owned United Fruit Company, which owned close to half the land in Guatemala and had so for decades. Arbenz nonetheless proceeded with his agenda, expropriating (with compensation) significant UFC acreage. Naturally, the company turned to the Eisenhower administration for assistance, accusing Arbenz of being a communist who had to be gotten rid of in a hurry and Eisenhower agreed, allowing CIA pilots to join in bombing raids that helped the coup succeed. Fearing the spread of communism in Central America, Ike was highly pleased with the result. "My God," he told his cabinet, 'just think what it would mean if Mexico went communist."

Sadly, Americans seemed unconcerned that the interventions violated sovereign rights. Indeed, the ouster of both governments was a clear violation of the U.N. Charter, which forbade a member state from taking military action against another except in self-defense. John Foster Dulles was hardly challenged when he went on radio and television programs following the Guatemalan coup to call it a "new and glorious chapter for all the people of the Americas." Above all, the coups reflected the Cold War mentality of the Eisenhower-Dulles years. Dulles's coterie of true believers at the State Department argued that indigenous communist factions linked to Moscow were the key forces behind both Mossadegh and Arbenz. This was not so in either case. Although Mossadegh, out of desperation for his government's survival, belatedly turned to the Iranian Communist Party for help, he was fundamentally a nationalist. Arbenz was a reformer, not a communist. The Dulles brothers easily convinced themselves and others in the administration that communism was the cause of international unrest. The Iranian and Guatemalan coups revealed that key policy makers in the Eisenhower administration a dim awareness of the appeal of nationalism and anti-colonialism throughout the world. Over the course of the next two decades, this inability or unwillingness to understand and embrace nationalist movements would manifest itself in many regions of the world and would have grave consequences for the United States.

THE SUEZ CRISIS

The combination of anti-colonialism and nationalism also inflamed the Middle East during the Eisenhower years. Trouble began in 1954 when Gamal Abdel Nasser, a passionate and ambitious Arab nationalist, secured power in Egypt. Nasser revealed that he had plans of uniting as many Arab-Muslim speaking countries in the area as possible under Egyptian auspices, to be used primarily against both further Western exploitation of the Arab people and their resources—oil—as well as to destroy Israel, which he saw as an illegitimate, Western-backed anti-Arab state. Such a Pan-Arab union occurred in 1958 when Syria joined Egypt to create such an entity. Nasser would never have been able to assert such leadership, however, had he not two years earlier become a hero among the Arab world as a result of the Suez Crisis.

One of Nasser's rallying cries was the destruction of Israel, a nation created in the aftermath of World War II, in many ways to atone for the Holocaust by providing its survivors with a refuge. Also motivating the Truman White House to support the establishment of a Jewish state was the desire to keep the Jewish-American vote at home solidly Democratic, which it had become by 1948. Added pressure came from politically engaged American Jews who had become Zionists—supporters of a movement that called for the creation of an independent Jewish state in Palestine, which had been a British mandate since the end of World War I. Zionists in the United States embarked on a very aggressive campaign to rally American public support for such a homeland, which polls revealed some 80 percent of the people supported. Moreover, 33 state legislatures passed resolutions favoring a Jewish state in Palestine while 40 governors, 54 senators, and 250 members of the House signed petitions urging Truman to act on the issue.

As European Jews flooded into Palestine, the inevitable occurred: violence erupted between the Arabs and the Jews in the region, which the British by 1947 could no longer contain and thus sought United Nations help. The UN decided to partition the region in hopes of restoring peace, but to the Arabs such a move reflected capitulation to both U.S. and European Zionists and that Jews in Palestine would proclaim this area the nation of Israel. Virtually all of Truman's top foreign policy advisers opposed the UN resolution, fearing that such a move would provoke the Arabs into war. Marshall, Kennan, Secretary of Defense James Forrestal, and Undersecretary of State Robert Lovett all believed the creation of an independent Jewish state would jeopardize U.S.-Arab relations, thereby undermining Truman Doctrine efforts to promote stability in Turkey, Iran, and other Arab countries. They also worried that an enraged Muslim world would retaliate by cutting off oil shipments to Western Europe and the United States. These individuals also feared that if an Arab-Israeli conflict did erupt, the Jews would lose, be slaughtered, and the world would have another Holocaust. Such were the sentiments of Secretary of Defense Forrestal who told Clark Clifford that "You fellows over at the White House are just not facing up to the realities in the Middle East. There are thirty million Arabs on one side and about six hundred thousand Jews on the other. It is clear to me that in any contest the Arabs are going to overwhelm the Jews. Why don't you face up to the realities? Just look at the numbers!"

Although accurate in his number crunching, Forrestal's entreaties fell on deaf ears. Both Clifford and Truman believed it to be essential for European Jews to have a homeland, particularly in the aftermath of the Holocaust. The president appreciated the Jews' commitment to democracy and their desire to establish a new world for themselves. Moreover, Truman believed that their claim to the Holy Land was more legitimate than that of the Arabs. Finally, there were the domestic political considerations that his advisers seemed to have overlooked, such as the tens of thousands of dollars in campaign contributions Jewish Americans had made to Democratic candidates beginning with FDR. As the president said to a gathering of State Department officials, "I have to answer to hundreds of thousands who are anxious for the success of Zionism. I do not have hundreds of thousands of Arabs among my constituents." For these reasons Truman ignored Arab admonishments that Palestine was a Holy Land for Muslims (and Christians) as well as for Jews, and he held fast to the liberal hope that Jews and Arabs could learn to cooperate and that the United States could manage to get along amicably with both sides.

Truman received fierce opposition from Secretary of State Marshall who opposed the creation of a Jewish state at the Arabs' expense to such an extent that he told the president that if he proceeded along this course, "I would vote against you in this election [1948]." Nevertheless, Truman, on May 14, 1948, recognized de facto the nation of Israel. No sooner did the Israelis proclaim their state than the Arabs attacked. To the surprise of many officials who had worried about another slaughter of Jews, the Israelis ultimately won the first of many such conflicts to occur in this region of the world. American Zionists continued to pressure Truman to recognize the new Jewish state de jure by giving arms to Israel. The president drew the line, however, refusing to go any further on the "Israel question." Politically, Truman's support and de facto recognition of Israel paid the desired dividends. He received over 90 percent of the Jewish-American vote in the November election.

Truman's Arab-Israeli policies had long-range controversial results. Despite his hope for the best, Truman aligned the United States with Israel thereby alienating the Arabs and from this point on associated the United States with the continued survival of Israel. Such perceived unequivocal support for Israel engendered Muslim wrath against the United States down to the present. There were no easy solutions to the desire of European and American Jews for a safe sanctuary in the aftermath of the Holocaust. Jewish and Muslim nationalism were thus on a collision course in Palestine, and there was no policy the U.S. could pursue that would have placated both groups. Truman's decision to support the creation of a Jewish state in the Holy Land reflected humanitarian, political, and Cold War motivations and exigencies. The president believed the presence of a democratic, pro-American nation in the Middle East would help to secure the long-range interests of both the United States and its Western European allies in the region—that attempts by the Soviets to make inroads in the Middle East would be blocked by the assistance of a powerful Israel. The political considerations were hard to resist at the time. Whether Truman's hopes concerning security were correct continued to be debated decades later. Indeed, by the time of the Suez crisis, Israel's preeminence in the Middle East would be recognized.

When Nasser first came to power, Dulles hoped to use Egypt as a buffer against a Russian presence in the oil-rich Middle East. To achieve that, Dulles agreed in 1955 to lend Nasser $56 million to build a TVA-type project on the upper Nile River, the Aswan High Dam project. Nasser believed the dam's construction essential to breaking his nation's poverty and of promoting industrialization. Nasser, however, like most leaders of emerging nations at the time, wanted to be non-aligned, neutral relative to the Cold War. Although accepting Dulles's offer, Nasser could not look as if he was becoming a U.S. ally. Thus, to show his independence and to keep his Arab nationalist identity intact, he recognized "Red" China and purchased arms from the Soviet satellite of Czechoslovakia. Dulles was furious, for in the Dulles Cold War frame of reference, a nation was either with the U.S. one hundred percent or it was against the U.S., which Nasser displayed he apparently was by his engagement with communist countries. Dulles retaliated against Nasser's betrayal by rescinding the loan offer. Nasser responded by nationalizing the Suez Canal, which had been controlled until then by a joint British-French owned company. Nasser announced that the revenues from ships passing through the canal would now pay for the Aswan project. While Eisenhower and Dulles tried diplomatically to bring Nasser around, the Israelis, British, and French quietly resolved to retake the canal by force. On October 29, 1956, the Israelis attacked, smashing Nasser's ill-trained forces and began driving toward the canal. Two days later the British and French, in what was obviously a preconceived plan worked out with the Israelis, began bombing Egyptian military installations. They then landed paratroopers with the intent of retaking the canal.

Eisenhower was furious with Israel, France, and Great Britain—all American allies—who did not consult him before their attacks. He was especially irate with France and Great Britain for they had assured him that they would not use force. What worried Ike the most was the possibility of Soviet intervention on the side of Egypt, for the Soviets, ever since Dulles's shunning of Nasser, had been providing the Egyptian leader with money, arms, and anything else he might need to help him become the region's superpower. Indeed, the U.S.S.R. announced that it was prepared to use military force against the triumvirate if they did not immediately get out of Egypt. Ike warned Khrushchev that if he sent Soviet troops to Egypt, Eisenhower would do likewise to resist them. This was the tensest moment of the crisis and one of the most frightening of the entire Cold War. As Ike told one of his advisers, "If those fellows [the Soviets] start something, we may have to hit them—and if necessary, with everything in the bucket [atomic weapons]."

Fortunately, World War III was averted as cooler, saner minds prevailed. The Soviets did not intervene, and the Israelis, British and French all agreed to a cease-fire and ultimately withdrew. Nasser became a hero to other Arab nationalists, which he parlayed over the next few years into creating the United Arab Republic. The Israelis proved they had the best army in the Middle East but were restrained by the United States from annihilating the Egyptians, which no doubt would have upset greatly the already precarious balance of power in the region. Most adversely affected by the escapade were the British and French, who having embarked on a foolish military mission, had been isolated and forced to withdraw. They never regained their standing in the Middle East, which now shifted to the United States who became the major Western power in the area. Henceforth, the U.S. was the most important protector of Western oil interests in the Middle East. In 1957, the president extended the principle of containment to the region, issuing the Eisenhower Doctrine, which pledged the United States to defend Middle Eastern governments threatened by communism or Arab nationalism. In 1958 Ike dispatched 5,000 American troops to Lebanon to protect a government dominated by pro-Western Christians against Nasser's effort to bring all Arab states into a single regime under his rule.

EISENHOWER AND VIETNAM

Following a policy initiated by the Truman administration, Eisenhower funneled billions of dollars in aid to bolster French efforts to remain in Indochina as a bulwark against communist expansion. By the time of Ike's presidency, the so-called "domino theory"—the idea that if one country fell to the communist then neighboring countries would become communist pawns as well—had gained great currency with U.S. foreign policy makers relative to Southeast Asia. If a local communist like Ho Chi Minh could topple Vietnam, nearby dominoes—Thailand, Burma, Malaysia, Indonesia, maybe even Australia, New Zealand, India, and Japan, might fall next. Such a domino effect would not only deprive the Free World of resources and bases, it would also demonstrate that the United States was a paper tiger—loud but not credible when a crisis arose. Thus the Eisenhower administration was determined to see France prevail and by early 1954 was willing to cover 75 percent of France's war bill.

Despite massive American aid, the French were losing badly to rebel forces, the Vietminh, led by the resourceful Vo Nguyen Giap. Benefiting from nationalistic peasant support, the Vietminh soldiers fought bravely, shrewdly, and relentlessly while incurring huge casualties, in their effort to win their independence. By contrast, the French army was poorly led, unmotivated, its commanders arrogant and disdainful of Giap and his guerrilla forces, and refused to adapt to that style of warfare. Even Ike disapproved of the French commanders, calling them "a poor lot." General Lawton Collins, the top American adviser to the French complained that if the French didn't "get off their fannies and do something" all would be lost. The French rarely ventured into the countryside where the Vietminh concentrated, and when they did, they were ambushed and defeated. The French simply occupied the major cities of Hanoi and Saigon, waiting for the Vietminh to attack. Finally, but foolishly, the French decided in early 1954 to engage the Vietminh in what they hoped would be a decisive battle at Dienbienphu, a hard-to-defend garrison deep in rebel-held territory near the Laotian border.

At this juncture, many of Ike's advisers began clamoring for U.S. intervention, ranging from the advocacy of sending ground forces to massive airstrikes, possibly with tactical nuclear weapons. The latter idea was proposed by Air Force Chief of Staff Nathan Twining, who believed the use of atomic bombs would "clean those Commies out of there and the band could play the Marseillaise and the French would come marching out of Dienbienphu in fine shape." As the agitation for the use of atomic weapons mounted, Ike rejected the idea and finally exploded at those who continued to pressure him for their use. "You boys must be crazy. We can't use those awful things against Asians for the second time in less than ten years. My God." By early April 1954, Ike had decided that the United States would not intervene in any capacity in Vietnam to help save the French. On May 7, 1954, France's 12,000-man garrison at Dienbienphu surrendered, representing one of the most humiliating defeats in French military history, as well as a disastrous blow to French pride and resolve. Ho, Giap, and the peasant-based Vietminh had won a resounding triumph against Western colonialism.

In the aftermath of Dienbienphu, the combatants met at Geneva to work out a political settlement. Ho Chi Minh's representatives naturally demanded the formation of a united, independent Vietnam. The United States, China (an age-old enemy of Vietnam), and members of the South Vietnamese bureaucracy opposed a united Vietnam under communist control, and thus the Vietminh agreed to a temporary division of the country at the 17th parallel. The reunification of Vietnam was to take place in July 1956 following free elections that would determine a new government. Though disappointed, Ho accepted the Geneva Accords, the treaty ending this particular war of national liberation. The North, which Ho was to govern, contained the majority of the country's population. By contrast, southern Vietnam was to be ruled by a Francophile aristocratic prince named Bao Dai, who had at best only modest public support, mostly from the remaining French and Vietnamese Catholics working for the government (far outnumbered by the rest of the southern population, which was predominately peasant and Buddhist). It was obvious to everyone that come July 1956, Ho Chi Minh would win the vote in a landslide.

The Eisenhower administration was hopeful that in the two years before the election was to be held they could prop up with enough money and military aid a pro-United States, anti-communist regime in the south and, with the right candidate, defeat Ho Chi Minh in the election. It became readily clear, however, that Bao Dai would not be that individual. Increasingly, the United States turned to Ngo Dinh Diem, who became premier in 1954. Diem was a passionate Vietnamese nationalist who hated the French (although he was Catholic) and was a staunch anti-communist. Diem was also a self-centered, stubborn, and power-hungry leader. In late 1955, a referendum ousted Dai and established Diem as president of the new Republic of South Vietnam. As the July 1956 election neared, Diem announced, with American approval, the cancellation of the November voting. Ho felt betrayed, especially by the United States, whose word he believed at Geneva, and with whom he hoped to become allies with against China, who historically had been the greatest threat to Vietnamese sovereignty.

The United States' support of Diem proved the last straw for Ho, who more or less declared war on South Vietnam, determined to overthrow the U.S. puppet regime of Diem and unite his country. No sooner did Diem renege on the election than pro-Ho forces in the south, the communist-led National Liberation Front, the Vietcong, began a full-scale guerrilla revolt against the Diem government. The Eisenhower administration believed it must aid Diem with whatever he needed to crush the Viet Cong (VC) and contain communism in Southeast Asia. To Ike, here was the most important domino in the region. Soon after Diem gained complete control of South Vietnam, Eisenhower gave his version of the domino theory: "You have a row of dominos set up. You knock over the first one [South Vietnam], and what will happen to the last one is a certainty that it will go over very quickly. So you could have a beginning of disintegration that would have the most profound consequences." Ike's remarks reflected a firm American commitment to Vietnam. Over the next four years, the Eisenhower administration poured billions of dollars in economic and military aid into South Vietnam, sustaining Diem while modernizing his armed forces with all they needed to defeat the Viet Cong. By 1960, the Army of the Republic of Vietnam (ARVN) was one of the best equipped, modern armies in the world. However, ARVN for a variety of reasons and shortcomings could not defeat the VC. Most important, despite massive aid, the president refused to commit American troops. When he left the White House in 1961, there were only approximately 500 American military personnel in South Vietnam serving as advisers to the ARVN. Nonetheless, Ike's support of Diem's decision in 1956 to not hold the promised election had unforeseen but ultimately terrible results for the Vietnamese people and for American society. The refusal to agree to elections in 1956, along with Diem's rabid repression thereafter, ignited nationalist rage, civil war, increasing U.S. aid to Saigon, and full-scale American intervention by 1965. That is not to say, however, that Ike's policies made U.S. military involvement in the American-Vietnamese War inevitable. American leaders in the early 1960s could have cut their losses and gone home. Ike's decisions, which had bipartisan support, were perceived thereafter by both parties as commitments to the protection of South Vietnam from Communism. This was a highly dangerous legacy to leave.

SPUTNIK

The successful launching by the Soviet Union on October 4, 1957, of *Sputnik*, the world's first orbiting satellite, increased the American public's paranoia about communism. *Sputnik* was small, about the size of a beach ball and weighed about 184 pounds. It traveled at 18,000 miles per hour and circled the globe about every 92 minutes. A month later the Soviets sent *Sputnik II* into space. This satellite weighed 1,120 pounds and carried scientific instruments for studying the atmosphere and outer space. It even contained a dog, Laika, with medical instruments strapped to its body.

When news of these launches reached the American public, their reaction approached panic, for the *Sputniks* represented their worst fears and suspicions about the Soviet Union. Many were convinced that the satellites were simply the first step. Next, the Soviets would be landing on the moon and from there would launch atomic-warheaded missiles at the United States. Moreover, many Americans felt humiliated and ashamed, for the *Sputniks* also reflected in their minds that Soviet science, engineering, mathematics, and technology was superior to that of the United States. Such trepidation seemed to become reality as American efforts to catch up appeared to be ludicrous, failed endeavors. On December 6, 1957, a nationally televised test of the *Vanguard* missile proved deeply embarrassing. The projectile rose two feet off the ground and crashed. The press referred to the attempt as "Flopnik" and "Stay-putnik."

The American public's overreactions to the *Sputnik* launches had little to no basis, especially when it came to the United States' destructive missile capacity. No doubt for the moment, the Soviets had an edge in capacity for thrust—the ability to boost satellites into orbit but that was the extent of their supposed superiority. They lagged badly in the production of usable warheads and did not

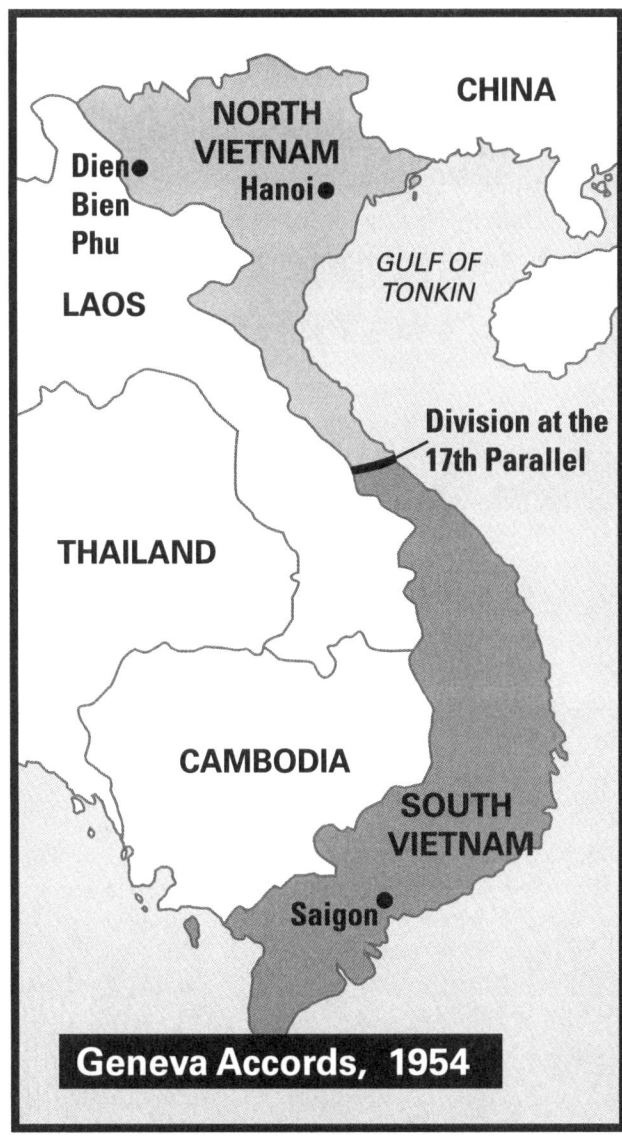

Map 26.4 The Geneva Accords

deploy an intercontinental ballistic missile during the Eisenhower years. In 1957 the U.S. had a huge advantage over the U.S.S.R. in the areas of military missile development and in nuclear weaponry, and it widened during Ike's second term. In the event of a Russian attack—which under the circumstances would have been suicidal for the Kremlin—the United States' retaliation would devastate the military and industrial power of the Soviet Union.

Although Eisenhower was hardly alarmed by the *Sputniks*, he nonetheless placated the American public's anxiety about "being behind" with some rather unprecedented, monumental legislation—The National Defense Education Act. This was historic legislation for it broke with the twentieth century practice of making states and localities solely responsible for educational funding and spending. As its title indicated, the act was sold as a defense measure, not as an endorsement for broader federal aid to schools or universities. Typical for the time, individuals who received money under the act had to sign a statement affirming their loyalty to the United States and to swear that they had never engaged in subversive activities. Ike also recommended federal aid to promote American scientific enterprises and for the learning of foreign languages. Finally, after relentless pressure from Democrats like Senator Lyndon Baines Johnson from Texas, Ike supported the establishment of the National Aeronautics and Space Administration (NASA), a civilian bureaucracy to coordinate missile development and future space exploration, headquartered in Houston, Texas.

In January 1961, shortly before leaving office, Eisenhower delivered a televised Farewell Address. Knowing that the United States was far ahead of the Soviet Union in possession of weapons of mass destruction and in other military technology, including closing the gap in the "race for space," Ike warned Americans against the clamor for a new military buildup. He urged his countrymen to think about the growing and dangerous power of what he called the "military-industrial complex," something that had worried him throughout his administration. This ever-expanding entity was the conjunction of "an immense military establishment" with a "permanent arms industry" that had an influence felt "in every office" in the land. "We must never let the weight of this combination," he exhorted, "endanger our liberties or democratic processes." Unfortunately, few Americans shared Ike's concern. Far more saw the alliance of the Defense Department and private industry as a source of jobs and national security rather than a threat to democracy or as a powerful enterprise that needed a war to sustain its preeminence and profitability. A few years later, with the United States locked in an increasingly unpopular war, Eisenhower's warning would come to seem prophetic.

Chronology

1945 Franklin Roosevelt dies.
Harry Truman becomes president.
United Nations established.
Indochina returned to French control.

1946 Iron Curtain speech—Winston Churchill.
Coal miners' strike.
1,000,000 GIs to college.
Vietnam declares its independence.
Baby Boom begins.

1947 Truman Doctrine.
Taft-Hartley Act.
Marshall Plan.
Containment policy developed by Kennan.
Central Intelligence Agency (CIA) established.

1948 Israel founded.
Berlin Blockade and Airlift.
Truman orders end to segregation in the armed forces and sends the first civil rights message to Congress.
Truman-Dewey election with Truman victor in greatest upset in American history.

1949 NATO established.
Communist victory in China.
Soviets detonate atomic bomb.

1950 Truman authorized hydrogen bomb.
Joseph McCarthy announces that there are communists in the government.
Korean War begins.
China enters Korean War and U. S. begins the longest retreat in U. S. military history.

1951 MacArthur fired for insubordination.
Rosenbergs convicted of espionage.
Armistice talks begin.
Twenty-second Amendment—limits on presidential term of office.

1952 First hydrogen bomb exploded.
Eisenhower elected president.

1953 Korean Truce signed.
CIA supported coup in Iran.
Earl Warren appointed Chief Justice.

1954 Army-McCarthy hearings.
Brown v. Board of Education of Topeka.
CIA intervention in Guatemala.
"Under God" inserted in Pledge of Allegiance.
U.S.S.R. explodes hydrogen bomb.
South East Asian Treaty Organization (SEATO) established.

1956 Interstate Highway Act.
Suez Crisis.
Eisenhower re-elected.
Hungarian Revolution.
U-2 spy plane built.
Eisenhower agrees to support Diem in Vietnam.

1957 Eisenhower Doctrine.
Civil Rights Act (first since Reconstruction).
Sputnik launched.

1958 Halt of atomic tests by U. S. and U.S.S.R.
National Aeronautical and Space Administration (NASA) founded.

1959 Castro comes to power in Cuba.
Landrum-Griffin Act passed.

1960 U-2 incident.
Second Civil Rights Act.
Election of John Fitzgerald Kennedy.

1961 Eisenhower's farewell address.

Review Questions

1. Discuss the origins of the Cold War. In your opinion, what were the most important factors leading to the breakdown of U.S.-Soviet relations.

2. How did Truman's view of the post-war world differ from that of FDR's? Most important, what did Truman conclude about the Soviet Union's foreign policy and how did he meet the foreign policy challenges presented during his presidency?

3. Describe the various dynamics involved in the formulation of containment.

4. Assess the Eisenhower presidency's "New Look" foreign policy relative to the Cold War? Why did Eisenhower institute a departure from the Truman initiatives?

5. America's Cold War policy unleashed the politics of anti-communism on the home front. What were some of the events and issues that emerged as a result? In short, define the politics of anti-communism and discuss its various manifestations beginning in the Truman years through the Eisenhower presidency.

Glossary of Important People and Concepts

Apartheid
Army-McCarthy hearings
Berlin Crisis
"Checkers Speech"
Chiang Kai-shek
China Lobby
Containment
"Dixiecrats"
"Domino Theory"
House Committee on Un-American Activities
Hungarian Crisis
Iron Curtain
George Kennan
Marshall Plan
Mao Zedong
McCarthyism
"More bang for the buck"
Edward R. Murrow
NSC-68
New Look
North Atlantic Treaty Organization (NATO)
"police action"
Progressive Party
Red-baiting
Revisionists
"rolling back the Iron Curtain"
"satellite"
Summit
Truman Doctrine

SUGGESTED READINGS

Stephen E. Ambrose, *Eisenhower: Soldier and President* (1990).

Walter La Feber, *America, Russia, and the Cold War, 1945-2006* (2008).

John Lewis Gaddis, *Strategies of Containment: A Critical Appraisal of National Security Policy During the Cold War* (2005).

____, *We Now Know: Rethinking Cold War History* (1998).

Alonzo Hamby, *Man of the People: A Life of Harry Truman* (1995).

George F. Kennan, *American Diplomacy, 1900-1950* (1951).

____, *Memoirs 1925-1950* (1967).

Michael L. Krenn, *Fall Out Shelters for the Human Spirit: American Art and the Cold War* (2005).

Ralph B. Levering, *The Cold War: A Post-Cold War History* (2005).

Ernest R. May, *American Cold War Strategy: Interpreting NSC-68* (1993).

David McCullough, *Truman* (1992).

John Ranleagh, *The Agency: The Rise and Decline of the CIA from Wild Bill Donovan to William Casey* (1986).

Richard Rhodes, *Dark Sun: The Making of the Hydrogen Bomb* (1995).

Lisle A. Rose, *The Cold War Comes to Main Street: America in 1950* (1998).

Stanley Sandler, *The Korean War: No Victors, No Vanquished* (2000).

Sam Tannehaus, *Whittaker Chambers, A Biography* (1997).

Warren A. Trest, *Air Commando One: Heinie Aderholt and America's Secret Air Wars* (2000).

Stanley Weintraub, *MacArthur's War: Korea and the Undoing of an American Hero* (2000).

David Wise and Thomas B. Ross, *The Invisible Government* (1962).

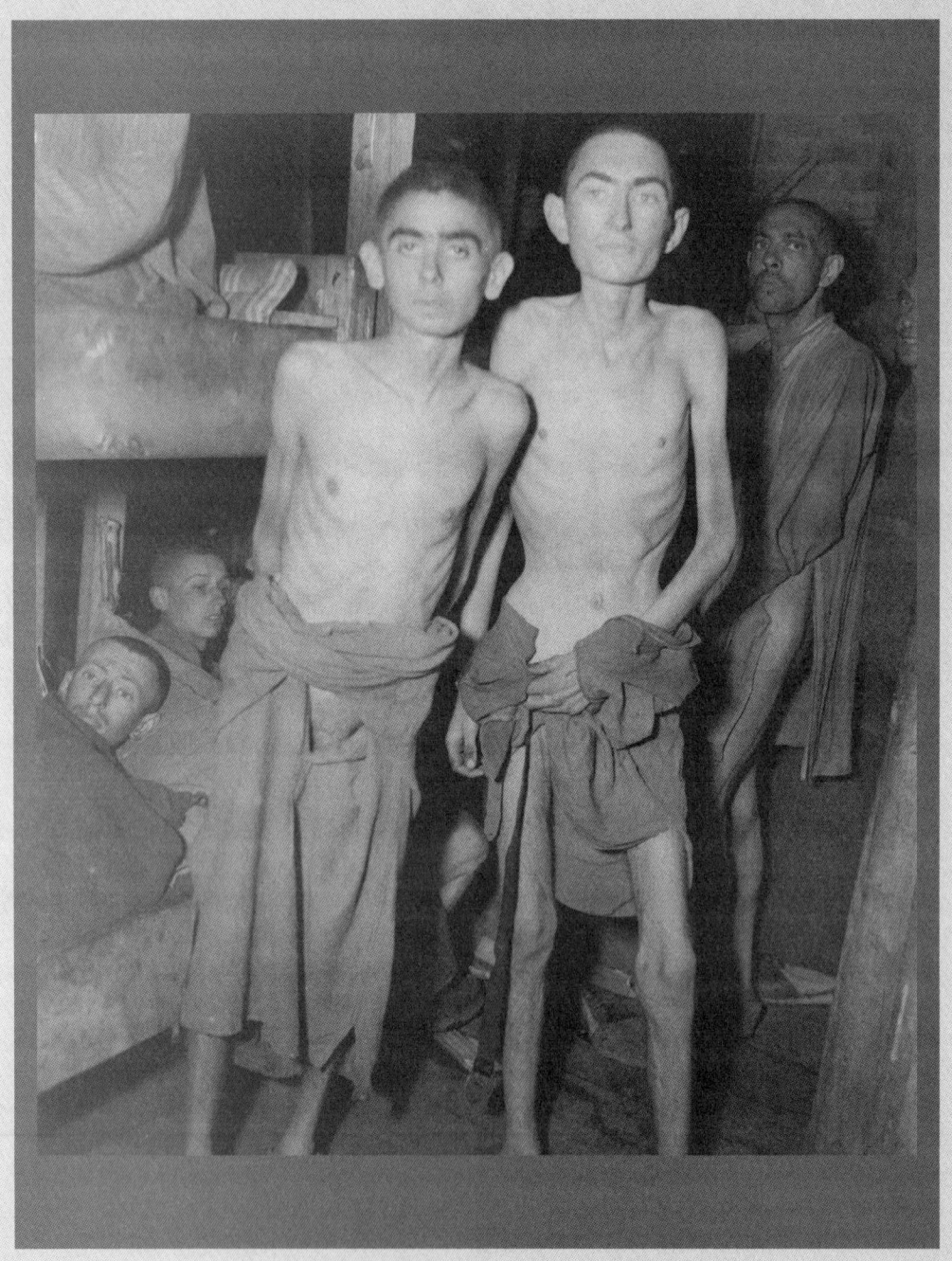

These inmates of the Amphing concentration camp in Germany were liberated by the U. S. Third Army troops. May 4, 1945

Chapter Twenty-seven

AMERICAN CULTURE FROM 1945 To 1960

During World War II, the American public knew that under Adolf Hitler, Germany exterminated Jews and other supposed racial inferiors. Not until the end of the war could Americans imagine the scope of the Nazi genocide. The George Gallup polling organization in November 1944 asked, "Do you believe that the Germans have murdered many people in concentration camps?" While 76 percent of respondents believed that mass murder had occurred in the Nazi empire, Americans badly underestimated how many victims died as a result of the German race war against Jews, Poles and other groups the Third Reich deemed inferior. According to the poll, 36 percent of those who believed people had been killed in concentration camps placed the number of victims at 100,000 or less. Slightly more than 50 percent placed the death toll at one million or less, while only 16 percent guessed the number to be two to six million.

It would be years before Americans perceived the Holocaust as an act of violence primarily against Jews. More victims in the western concentration camps were non-Jewish than in eastern camps like Auschwitz that had been liberated by Soviet troops. American soldiers, however, received a shocking lesson in the dangers of racism and intolerance. They could not anticipate the hellish landscape that greeted them as they advanced into the heart of Germany. On April 12, 1945, in Gotha, Germany, the Supreme Commander of the Allied Forces in Europe, Gen. Dwight D. Eisenhower, and two other top officers, Gen. Omar Bradley and Gen. George S. Patton, toured the Ohrdruf Concentration Camp. "The smell of death overwhelmed us even before we passed through the stockade," Bradley later recalled. "More than 3,200 naked, emaciated bodies had been flung into shallow graves. Others lay in the streets where they had fallen. Lice crawled over the yellow skin of their sharp, bony frames."

Guides took the generals past torture instruments, buildings loaded with corpses, and to a butcher's block where Nazi soldiers smashed inmates' teeth in order to steal the gold fillings. The famously tough Gen. Patton became nauseous and had to break from the tour group. Shaken, Eisenhower ordered American soldiers in the region to view the remains of Ohrdruf. "We are told that the American soldier does not know what he is fighting for. Now, at least, he will know what he is fighting against." Other soldiers liberating concentration camps across Germany had similar reactions to that of their commanding officers. "[The prisoners] were so thin they didn't have anything—didn't have buttocks to lie on; there wasn't any flesh on their arms to rest their skulls on," said William Lovelady, commander of a Third Armored Division task force liberating Nordhausen.

The starving camp survivors seemed maddened by their years of torture and abuse. GIs experienced both pity and disgust when they interacted with the inmates. Samuel Glasshow, an officer who helped liberate the Woebbelin camp, recalled his horror at inmates' reactions when offered food. "We walked inside and saw these skinny people still living," he later said, "and one of my enlisted men who walked in with me realized they were starving and we had nothing but candy bars, which we got in a ration, and one of my men gave the candy bar to one of these people who grabbed it and ran away and gulped so fast that he became unconscious and probably choked on it before someone took it away from him. These Jewish people and these Polish people were like animals, they were so degraded, and there was no goodness, no kindness, nothing of that nature, there was no sharing. If they got a piece of something to eat, they grabbed it and ran away in a corner and fought off anyone who came near them."

Some camp victims wreaked vengeance on their former tormentors while others sat in an apathetic, exhausted stupor. Still, many gathered mysterious sources of strength and overwhelmed American GIs with gratitude. Captain J.D. Pletcher later noted the range of reactions from survivors at the Gunskirchen camp. "As we entered the camp, the living skeletons still able to walk crowded around us and, though we wanted to drive deeper into the place, the milling, pressing crowd wouldn't let us," he said. "It is not an exaggeration to say that almost every inmate was insane with hunger. Just the sight of an American brought cheers, groans and shrieks. People crowded around to touch an American, to touch the jeep, to kiss our arms—perhaps to make sure that it was true. The people who couldn't walk crawled out toward our jeep. Those who couldn't even crawl propped themselves up on an elbow and, somehow, through all their pain and suffering revealed through their eyes the gratitude, the joy they felt at the arrival of Americans."

Black, brown and Anglo soldiers brought face-to-face with the horrors of Nazi genocide returned to America as changed men. The concentration camps, after all, represented the logical conclusion of racist thought popular not just in Germany, but also in America and Great Britain, before the war. Nazis gave racism a bad name. Even though American culture still included deep elements of bigotry, a perceptible change in American attitudes toward race took place after the war. More northern whites, at least, seemed ready to support the African-American campaign for desegregation in the South. **Anti-Semitism**, widely shared among even educated Americans, clearly declined partly as a reaction to the Nazi death camps. Asked in August 1945 by the U.S. Army's **Yank** magazine, "What changes would you like to see made in post-war America?" a majority agreed that they wanted, "above everything else [the] . . . wiping out [of] racial and religious prejudice." In a series of surveys conducted by the American Jewish Committee between 1946 and 1951, the number of Americans reporting that they had overheard anti-Jewish remarks during the previous year declined from 64 percent to 16 percent. The AJC also asked American Gentiles if there were "any nationality, religious or racial groups in this country that are a threat to America." In 1946, 18 percent named Jews. By 1954, the number was down to 1 percent.

In addition to shock over the crimes of the anti-Semitic Nazi regime, another factor that pushed anti-Semitism from the mainstream to the American fringe was that by 1950, 75 percent of Jews in America had been born in the United States. Jewish celebrities, such as Bess Meyerson, who won the "Miss America" beauty pageant in 1945, and Detroit Tiger Hank Greenberg, who blasted a ninth-inning grand slam homer to capture the World Series for his team the same year, won legions of Gentile admirers in the post-war years.

"A remarkable metamorphosis occurred in the United States in the two decades following the end of World War II," historian Leonard Dinnerstein concluded. "After more than half a century of increasing animosity toward the Jews, anti-Semitism in the United States suddenly began to decline . . . Laypersons and scholars both acknowledged the change by 1955. **Look** magazine believed that Hitler had made anti-Semitism disreputable, cracks about Jews that used to be taken for granted were fewer in number, and for Jews anti-Semitism in America was downgraded from a problem to an irritant." A new America was born inside the gates of Nazi death camps. The diminishing of American anti-Semitism would be only one of a legion of convulsive changes that would rock America in the 15 years from 1945 to 1960.

If anti-Semitism declined after the war, the struggle against anti-black and anti-Latino discrimination and the struggle to end sexism proved more intractable. Nevertheless, the 1950s proved to be a revolutionary decade in terms of race, gender, and sexual politics, the media, and entertainment. Millions of black and Mexican-American veterans returned home from the war doubly determined not to accept a return to a status quo of racial violence, segregation, low wages, and dilapidated schools. Millions of women who worked in factories to replace their soldier husbands and boyfriends would no longer accept domestic confinement as housewives. Stereotypically portrayed as a sleepy, conservative, introspective time, the 1950s instead saw the rise of protest movements, and redefinitions of the family, sexual morality, and popular culture. Rather than a placid time, the Beat poet Allen Ginsberg saw the era as an epoch in which the best were destroyed by madness. More accurately, it became a time in which a growing number of Americans began to confront the insanity of racism, sexism, militarism, and the ugly endurance of American poverty.

AMERICAN RACISM BEFORE WORLD WAR II

Before the war, American college professors and bestselling authors embraced the idea of white supremacy. Madison Grant, who received a law degree from Columbia University, authored *The Passing of the Great Race: or The Racial Basis of European History* (1916), and Lothrop Stoddard, who received a Ph.D. in history from Harvard, wrote

The Rising Tide of Color Against White World-supremacy (1920). Both became best sellers. These books claimed that African Americans possessed less intelligence and a greater tendency toward crime than Americans of European descent. Allowing African Americans any degree of political power, Grant and Stoddard argued, would destroy the American political system. Blacks, however, did not represent the only demographic category threatening the future of the country.

Grant, Stoddard and other scholars in the fields of anthropology, biology and history argued that Jews, Italians, Greeks, Poles and other immigrants from Southern and Eastern Europe represented racially inferior groups that, because of their supposed lower intelligence and lack of moral character, could never become productive citizens. Grant became the leading voice of the **eugenics** movement, which held that genetic heredity, rather than environment, determined not only a person's physical characteristics, but also intelligence and moral outlook. American and British eugenicists also divided Europeans into several "races," of which so-called Nordics from Northern and Western Europe were rated the best and most valuable. Only Europeans could be defined as fully human. Southern and Eastern Europeans ranked lower than Nordics, and eugenicists ranked Jews even lower. Eugenicists theorized that breeding between superior and inferior races produced offspring inferior to either parent.

Eugenicists misused Stanford-Binet IQ tests to prove America was amidst a racial crisis, a genetic meltdown that would destroy the country. To investigate the alleged impact of mass immigration to the United States from the 1880s through the first two decades of the twentieth century, eugenicists persuaded the military to submit Army recruits, many of them recent immigrants with limited command of English, to **Army IQ tests** during 1917-1918 when America became involved in the First World War. The tests required soldiers to do addition and other math problems, answer questions about American history and identify characters associated with advertising or answer other culturally based questions. Recruits filled out their answers in crowded, uncomfortable, noisy rooms under intense pressure from drill sergeants to finish. The Army submitted 1.75 million recruits to IQ testing during the war, and the results were published in 1921. The Army reported that the average American had a mental age of 13. According to the Army tests, Russian immigrants possessed an average mental age of 11.34; the Italians, 11.01; and the Poles, 10.74. Blacks supposedly held a mental age of 10.41, the lowest of all groups.

Immigration Restriction Before World War II

Groups like the American Eugenics Society (AES) sounded the alarm against American "race suicide." The AES held exhibitions across the country, telling audiences that while a new child was born in the United States every 16 seconds, the country produced a feeble-minded child every 48 seconds, and a future criminal every 50 seconds. Truly intelligent and creative children, the society warned, were born in the United States only every seven and a half minutes. Hoping to reverse what was perceived as a national decline in intelligence, state legislatures and the U.S. Congress passed a series of laws aimed at improving the country's racial stock. Between 1895 and 1913, many states had enacted laws restricting marriages involving people regarded as insane, epileptic, or mentally deficient. These laws were not strictly enforced, however, and subsequent laws became harsher.

Between 1905 and 1922, fifteen states passed bills allowing institutionalized people to be sterilized without prior consent. Doctors eventually carried out 3,233 such procedures. By 1931, twenty-eight states had such laws, and the rate of operations surged dramatically. Doctors not only performed involuntary tubal ligations and vasectomies on mental patients but on many African-American men

The humor magazine *Puck*, on the cover of its June 18, 1913 issue, satirically suggests that eugenics—the pseudo-science that aimed at breeding racially superior humans—had become so dominant in Western thought that by the second decade of the twentieth century that it, like gravity, "made the world go around."

and women simply unfortunate enough to go to eugenically minded physicians. So many blacks received these operations in one state that the procedures came to be known as "Mississippi appendectomies." By 1941, 38,087 people had been legally sterilized involuntarily across the country because of sterilization laws. Such U.S. legislation strongly influenced Nazi Germany's 1933 edict under which 3.5 million people deemed insane, epileptic, or mentally deficient were forcibly sterilized, a program publicly praised by American eugenicists throughout the decade.

Racism crossed boundaries between North and South and between the political left and right. Feminist and socialist birth control advocate **Margaret Sanger** battled enthusiastically to limit the birth rates of blacks, working class whites and the mentally disabled. "More children from the fit, less from the unfit—that is the chief issue of birth control," Sanger said. Allying with Dr. Clarence J. Gamble, a philanthropist, she later helped develop the so-called "Negro Project" encouraging birth control among southern African Americans.

Before World War II, mainstream medical publications like the *Journal of the American Medical Association* publicized and supported eugenics research. When Adolf Hitler came to power in 1933, American eugenicists along with anti-Semitic celebrities like aviation hero Charles Lindbergh and auto manufacturer Henry Ford received awards from the Nazi regime even as "race scientists" from America attended eugenicist conferences held in the Third Reich. Money from the Rockefeller and Carnegie Foundations, established by the nineteenth-century business tycoons John D. Rockefeller and Andrew Carnegie, funded eugenics research in the United States and supported the work of Nazi scientists searching for supposed racial characteristics of Jews and others. In addition, the Carnegie foundation funded the *Eugenical News* publication that in 1932 declared that "The Aryans [Hitler's term for 'pure Germans'] are the great founders of civilization . . . The mixing of blood, the pollution of race . . . has been the sole reason why old civilizations have died out." International Business Systems, now known simply as IBM, provided data processing equipment that helped Nazi Germany analyze the racial backgrounds of German citizens and to track down Jews selected for detention and murder. IBM later claimed it did not know for what purpose the equipment would be used.

Race Before and After World War II

As Nazis forcibly sterilized epileptics, alcoholics and others deemed racially unfit and as persecution of Jews intensified and became more ruthless in the late 1930s, a backlash brewed against ideas associated with the Third Reich, such as eugenics. A sterilization bill proposed in the Alabama state legislature stalled because, as one opponent to the law put it, "In my judgment, the great rank and file of the country people of Alabama do not want this law; they do not want Alabama, as they term it, Hitlerized." Politicians stopped openly advocating involuntary sterilizations, but the practice continued quietly for two decades. As part of the eugenics crusade, doctors sterilized an estimated 62,000 Americans in 30 states from the 1920s until the early 1960s, according to a study sponsored by the United States Holocaust Memorial Museum.

The war against Japan instigated intense anti-Asian bigotry. On February 19, 1942, Franklin Roosevelt signed Executive Order 9066, which authorized the incarceration of 120,000 Japanese Americans and Japanese immigrants living near the Pacific Coast in ten concentration camps in isolated sites in seven inland states. During their time in the camps, Japanese Americans lost jobs and ownership of their homes and businesses. In the post-war era it was not unusual to see businesses with "No Jap Trade Wanted" signs posted on the windows.

For the most part, however, open racism became less socially acceptable in much of the country during the 1941-1945 war years. Before World War II ended, popular singer Frank Sinatra made a short film for the United States government called *The House I Live In*, which asked Americans to not let themselves be divided by race, ethnicity and religion as they faced the common Nazi enemy. By 1945, it had been two decades since the restrictive 1924 immigration law took effect, and Anglo-Saxons no longer felt threatened by immigration from Eastern and Southern Europe. Films addressing the evils of **anti-Semitism**, such as *Gentleman's Agreement*, reached wide audiences.

By the 1940s the undeniable debt that the Nazi regime owed to American and European eugenicists became a public relations nightmare for that discipline after the liberation by American soldiers of German concentration camps. "The opposition to Nazism shaped in a dramatic fashion the refutation of racism as a legitimate intellectual stance," as historian Elazar Barkan noted. Instead of attributing unchanging intellectual and personality characteristics to individuals based on their supposed racial identity, "environmentalism, culture and human changeability gained primacy," as historian Matthew Frye Jacobson put it.

In 1945, the United Nations Educational, Scientific and Cultural Organization blamed World War II on the "doctrine of the inequality of men and races." By 1950, UNESCO issued its "**Statement on Race**," which announced that "[s]cientists have reached general agreement that mankind is one; that all men belong to the same species, *Homo sapiens.*" Humanity could not be properly divided into types, but into populations where small differences occurred based on variation of one or more genes, but these differences were small in comparison to the vast genetic similarity. UNESCO proposed replacing the term "race," which it described as hopelessly vague, with the phrase "ethnic group." The changing social climate led Anglo Christian Americans to more readily accept Jews, Italians, and Greeks as white people. Asian Americans eventually benefited from the new atmosphere. In 1952, the Walter-McCarran Act allowed Japanese immigrants to become American citizens for the first time. Generally, discrimination against the Japanese declined, though it remained the strongest in the Pacific Rim. Young internees who experienced life in the Japanese concentration camps, and the children of internees, would lead an Asian American civil rights movement in the 1960s and 1970s.

THE COLD WAR AND RACE RELATIONS

The commencement of the Cold War, a protracted global political struggle with the Soviet Union, proved as important as any event in changing how white American elites thought about race. The political leadership perceived the Soviets, armed with nuclear weapons shortly after World War II, as set on world conquest. As the colonial empires of Britain and France fell apart, several presidential administrations eagerly pursued alliances with and sought to establish bases in newly born countries across Africa and Asia. Locked in a bitter ideological war with the Soviets for hearts and minds in new independent states, the Truman and Eisenhower administrations both realized that southern lynchings of black men and women, segregation, and the disenfranchisement of African-American voters gave the United States a bad image in countries governed by people of color. With the Soviet Union presenting an image of both anti-imperialism and anti-racism, according to historian Joel Williamson, the United States found itself in a public relations bind. "The United States, offering itself as both the modern exemplar and the champion of democracy, was faced with the problem of wooing the non-white people of the Third World into the anti-Communist camp while racism ran riot at home," Williamson wrote. This pushed both Democratic and Republican administrations from 1945 to 1960 to be friendlier toward African-American civil rights than they might have otherwise.

The paradox of America presenting itself as the land of the free while African Americans faced segregation and violence, particularly in the South, did not escape the attention of even conservative publications like *Time* magazine, which observed that "in Washington, the seated figure of Abraham Lincoln broods over the capital of the U.S. where Jim Crow is the rule." Cases of racial discrimination received wide attention not only in the Soviet press, but also in newspapers and radio broadcasts in newly independent nations like India and Ceylon, and in sub-Saharan Africa. In one incident, Alabama police arrested U.S. Sen. Glen Taylor, running in 1948 for vice president on the Progressive Party ticket headed by Henry Wallace, when he entered the "colored entrance" to a Birmingham church to make a speech. The Shanghai, China newspaper *Ta Kung Pao* sharply criticized American hypocrisy. "If the United States merely wants to 'dominate' the world, the atomic bomb and the U.S. dollar will be sufficient to achieve this purpose," an editorial said. "However, the world cannot be 'dominated' for a long period of time. If the United States wants to 'lead' the world, it must have a kind of moral superiority in addition to military superiority." The fact that this criticism of American race relations appeared in a newspaper in China, a country engaged in a civil war between a conservative dictatorial regime and communists, particularly alarmed the American State Department.

PRESIDENT TRUMAN AND RACIAL POLITICS

President Harry S Truman came from a regional border state (Missouri) and occasionally used anti-black slurs in private conversation. Writing to his daughter Margaret Truman when he was a senator from Missouri, the future president once complained about black waiters at a Washington, D.C. restaurant whom he described as "an army of coons" who thought they were "evidently the top of the black social set in Washington." Once in a 1939 letter to his wife, Bess, Truman derided an African-American social occasion as "nigger picnic day." As president, however, Truman worried about the impact of racial injustice in the United States on the Cold War. Pragmatic electoral concerns also shaped his newly found interest in civil rights. From the 1920s through World War II, millions of African Americans had moved north of the Mason-Dixon line and into the West to escape the harassment of southern whites and to find better-paying jobs. Since Roosevelt's second term, African-American voters in the North and West largely supported Democrats, and in states like California and Michigan the black electorate could swing close elections. Black resentment over the influence of southern white segregationists on the Democratic Party, however, caused a drop-off in black support for the Democrats in the 1946 congressional races. Truman wanted to win these voters back.

Post-war racial violence, however, also moved the president. Black activists told Truman of an incident in Monroe, Georgia, in which whites fatally shot two African-American men. The wife of one of the victims recognized one of the white shooters, so the killers assassinated both of the men's spouses, as well. Violence against African-American servicemen in particular shocked the president. More than 1 million African Americans served in the military during the war. Black soldiers entering the war hoped to win what civil rights leaders like W.E.B. Du Bois called the "Double V"—victory against the Axis Powers and against racism at home. Just as many African-American soldiers returning from World War I suffered persecution and lynching upon returning to the United States, several shocking attacks on black veterans made headlines across the nation just after World War II. Black veterans would be outraged by the poor treatment they received upon their return to the United States, prompting many to become active in the Civil Rights Movement.

In one incident, the police chief in Aiken, S.C., severely beat Sgt. Issac Woodard, an African American, with a nightstick and gouged an eye out. Woodard had received his separation papers from the United States Army a mere three hours earlier. Hearing of this attack, Truman reportedly said, "My God. I had no idea it was as terrible as that. We've got to do something!" Truman later said incidents such as the assault on Sgt. Woodward moved him to push for civil rights. Pressed by southern members of Congress to abandon this stand, Truman said, "My forebears were Confederates.... Every factor and influence in my background—and in my wife's for that matter—would foster the personal belief that you are right. But my very stomach turned over when I learned that Negro soldiers, just back from overseas, were being dumped out of Army trucks in Mississippi and beaten. Whatever my inclinations as a native of Missouri might have been, as President I know this is bad."

On December 5, 1946, Truman established the **President's Committee on Civil Rights**, to which he predominantly appointed racial liberals. The committee issued its report, "To Secure These Rights," the following October. According to the report, the contrast between the nation's stated ideas of human equality and the widespread practice of racial discrimination served as "a kind of moral dry rot which eats away at the emotional and rational bases of democratic beliefs." With its eyes on America's global competition with the Soviet Union, the report warned that "we cannot ignore what the world thinks of us or our record."

The committee recommended a broad range of reforms including enacting a federal anti-lynching statute (designed to get around southern courts, which refused to prosecute violent crimes committed by whites against blacks); a ban on the poll tax (which reduced black voting); prohibiting by federal statute discrimination in private employment; establishing a permanent Commission on Civil Rights; increasing the size of the Justice Department's civil rights division; and strictly enforcing voting rights laws. The Commission also urged the Justice Department to file lawsuits against housing developments and neighborhood associations that used secret covenants to deny housing to racial and religious minorities; said that federal money should be denied to any public or private agency that practiced segregation; and called for the Congress to integrate all facilities in Washington, D.C., including the public school system. President Truman embraced most of these recommendations in a civil rights message to Congress on February 2, 1948.

At the Democratic National Convention that summer, southern delegates walked out when a far-reaching pro-civil rights plank was for the first time added to the Democratic Party platform. Nevertheless, Truman issued two executive orders on July 26, 1948: one that would eventually desegregate the armed forces and another that prohibited discrimination in the federal civil service. Truman first signed **Executive Order 9981** ordering the desegregation of the Armed Forces on July 26, 1948, but by January 13, 1949, only one of the Marine Corps' 8,200 officers was African Americans. Only five of the Navy's 45,000 officers were black. The Army, meanwhile, maintained a 10 percent recruiting quota for African Americans until the Korean War began in 1950. High casualties among white units in the war hastened the integration of black army troops. Not until 1953 could the Army announce that 95 percent of African-American troops served in integrated units.

During the late 1940s, Truman also used his executive powers to empanel a Commission on Higher Education that recommended an end to religious and racial quotas used at universities to limit admission of Jews and blacks. After his presidency, Truman continued to use words like "nigger" in private conversation, dismissed Martin Luther King, Jr., as a "troublemaker," and considered the Civil Rights Movement at least partly inspired by communism, but his presidency nevertheless committed the national Democratic Party to greater support for black voting rights and opposition to segregation.

BLACK POLITICAL ACTIVISM

Whether or not they had the support of the Washington political establishment, the African-American community fought most of the struggle for civil rights themselves. In October 1946, four hundred African-American children in Lumberton, N.C., staged a walkout from classes to protest the shoddy, unsafe conditions at segregated black campuses. The students held signs sadly asking, "How Can I Learn When I'm Cold?" and noting "It Rains On Me." Such grassroots protests enjoyed surprising, if still limited, success. Spending on black education increased in the South in the immediate post-war years, but that improvement was relative since allocations for African-American schools in the former Confederacy before the war had been minuscule. Nevertheless, the increased industrialization of the South as a result of the world war and the post-war economic boom gave the poorest states in Dixie more money to spend on black students. The per capita spending in Louisiana on African-American pupils rose from an almost non-existent $16 in 1940 to a still meager $116 in 1955. South Carolina passed a $75 million bond issue funded by a 3 percent sales tax increase to improve and expand black schools.

White-run southern legislatures did this because, against all odds, African Americans applied pressure to the southern power structure. The NAACP's anti-lynching campaigns had substantially reduced the number of black men, women and children murdered for racial reasons each year. White mobs murdered almost sixty African Americans annually in the five years starting with the end of World War I, from 1918 through 1922. As a result of NAACP lobbying, the Civil Rights Section of the Justice Department in the late 1930s increased federal prosecutions for police brutality and began investigating lynchings. Between 1937 and 1946, lynch mobs murdered 42 African Americans, but as a result of federal pressure, law enforcement rescued 226 potential victims. Whites lynched six African Americans in 1946, but local authorities prevented twenty-two murders.

Black political power increased as the number of African-American voters inched up across the South. American prosperity after World War II made southern blacks more impatient for improvement in their material lives, while many returning black veterans, who had fought to defeat the racist Nazi regime, insisted on change at home. Although most southern African Americans still lacked access to the ballot, the total number of registered blacks in the former Confederacy had increased from a few thousand to approximately one million by 1952. In close elections, African Americans could determine the outcome. Relative moderates like Governor Jim Folsom of Alabama and Mayor William B. Hartsfield in Atlanta actively sought the support of black voters and even promoted black voter registration. Southern legislatures also increased funding for black schools because they feared losing cases filed by the NAACP challenging segregated schools and realized they could not forever maintain the fiction that white and black campuses were "separate but equal."

Nevertheless, by the early 1950s the economic, political and academic inequalities faced by African Americans in the South remained glaring and tragic. During an NAACP inspection of white and black schools in Clarendon County, S.C., for instance, Howard University associate professor Mathew J. Whitehead found that white schools had water fountains but black students had to use a dipper to scoop water from open buckets. The school system provided white students with buses but black students living far from campuses had no access to transportation. Each white campus employed a janitorial staff, but black teachers and students had to serve as uncompensated custodians at Jim Crow schools. White schools provided seating for every student, while one black school in the county did not possess a single desk.

School Desegregation

Beginning in the 1940s, the NAACP launched a legal offensive aimed at step-by-step desegregation of American education. **Heman Marion Sweatt** forced open the doors of the University of Texas law school to African Americans in 1950. An NAACP activist in Houston since the early 1940s and a columnist for the local black-owned newspaper the *Informer*, Sweatt plunged into fundraising drives for the NAACP's lawsuit against the so-called "white primary." Democratic Party rules in Texas barred blacks from voting in primaries, which, given the party's almost complete monopoly on elective office in the first half of the twentieth century, left African Americans with no voice in partisan political races.

The NAACP successfully persuaded the United States Supreme Court to declare the white primary unconstitutional in the 1944 *Smith v. Allwright* case. A postal carrier, Sweatt fought against discriminatory policies that blocked African Americans in Texas from higher-paying positions as clerks. His work on that issue sparked his growing personal interest in a law career. Sweatt considered attending law school in Michigan but changed his mind when his father suffered a heart attack. At the urging of Dallas NAACP attorney W.J. Durham, Sweatt applied to the UT Law School, aware that the school was legally vulnerable to litigation since the state of Texas had failed to provide a law school for African-American students.

Sweatt applied, was turned down, and on May 16, 1946 filed the *Sweatt v. Painter* case.

The state of Texas scrambled to provide sham law schools for blacks to avoid a federal desegregation order. The Texas A&M regents created a "law school" for blacks by hiring two Houston lawyers to hold classes in their offices. No one enrolled. The Texas Legislature, meanwhile, moved to convert Houston College for Negroes into Texas State University for Negroes, which would provide law classes for African Americans. (TSUN would open in 1947 and eventually be rechristened Texas Southern University.) At the University of Texas, regents set aside a basement in a building south of the campus on Thirteenth Street where black students could receive law instruction from the most junior members of the faculty, although African Americans would not have direct access to the law library or other resources. Only one black student, Henry Doyle, attended the Jim Crow classes. Sweatt and the NAACP refused to accept this sham.

After years of financial hardship while waiting for the case to wind through the courts, Sweatt prevailed in his lawsuit against UT in 1950. The same day as its *Sweatt v. Painter* decision, the Supreme Court ruled in *McLaurin v. Oklahoma State Regents* that Oklahoma State University had erred when it admitted a black student to a graduate program but then required him to sit apart from white students. That momentous day in judicial history also saw the release of the Supreme Court's decision in *Henderson v. the United States*, in which the court ruled that the Southern Railway company violated the *Plessy v. Ferguson* requirement that African Americans be afforded "separate but equal" accommodations. Southern Railway, the court ruled, failed to provide a black customer, Elmer W. Henderson, the same level of service that would be provided a white customer using the same class of ticket.

Change came slowly even after the NAACP's triple victory. After the *Sweatt* decision, the University of Texas admitted 22 African Americans out of a total enrollment of 12,000, with six of the black students enrolled in law classes. The state of Texas began allowing African Americans to attend other graduate programs besides the UT law school but only if those programs were not available at Prairie View A&M, a segregated black college. According to Texas NAACP historian Michael Gillette, the reactions of whites to Sweatt and the five other African Americans in the program were mixed. Most were agreeable, Sweatt said, and he and the other integration pioneers encountered few problems as they sought access to water fountains, restrooms, school dining facilities, lounges and football games. The Friday of his first week at UT, however, Sweatt discovered, after studying late at the law library, that a large white crowd had gathered across the street and was burning a cross. Accompanied by a white friend, Sweatt made it safely to his car, only to discover that the tires had been slashed. Although a few campus liberals offered condolence, UT officials largely ignored the incident, and Austin police never made an arrest in the case.

The intense scrutiny of the press, the racism of faculty and students, and financial pressure destroyed Sweatt's marriage during his two years at UT and undermined his academic performance. Poor health added to Sweatt's difficulties as he battled a painful ulcer and missed seven weeks of classes after suffering appendicitis. He failed courses in his first year, audited the classes he failed in the fall of 1951, and re-enrolled in the spring semester of 1952, but he subsequently dropped out. Nevertheless, the *Painter* case laid the groundwork for the more famous *Brown v. the Board of Education* school desegregation decision in 1954.

The Brown Decision

During a 1950 NAACP legal strategy session, lawyers decided to challenge public school segregation head-on. Civil rights attorneys, concerned that the pronounced white southern paranoia about sexual contact between black male and white female teenagers might provoke violence, reasoned they must pursue desegregation of high schools with particular care and instead chose to work their lawsuits up grade-by-grade. The NAACP represented African-American parents who filed lawsuits against segregated school districts in Delaware, Kansas, Louisiana, South Carolina, Virginia, and Washington, D.C. These suits reached the United States Supreme Court in 1952, the court consolidating the cases under the title **Brown v. the Board of Education of Topeka, (KS)**, et. al. The court announced its decision on May 17, 1954. In overturning the 1896 *Plessy v. Ferguson* decision, Chief Justice Earl Warren spoke for a unanimous court in declaring that "In the field of public education, the doctrine of separate but equal has no place. Separate educational facilities are inherently unequal."

Unfortunately, the Supreme Court delayed its implementation of *Brown* for a year. The May 31, 1955, implementation order, known as *Brown II*, set no firm deadline for school districts to achieve integration, only urging local authorities to proceed with "all deliberate speed." The court failed to define the threshold at which a school district achieved desegregation, leaving that matter to the federal district courts. Finally, the Court provided a list of reasons school districts could use to delay implementation, such as administrative difficulties.

AMERICAN CULTURE FROM 1945-1960 / 845

As a result of all of this temporizing, the integration process dragged on for years, and more than a decade after *Brown* many southern schools remained substantially segregated. As historian Richard Kruger notes in his book *Simple Justice: The History of Brown v. Board of Education and Black America's Struggle for Equality*, "Throughout the balance of the Fifties, the South interpreted 'all deliberate speed' to mean 'any conceivable delay' and desegregation was far more a figment in the mind of the Supreme Court than a prominent new feature on the American social landscape."

The Court also unintentionally gave opponents of integration a chance to organize what came to be known as "**massive resistance**" to the *Brown* decision. Initially, white southern segregationists reacted with surprising calm to *Brown*. "No citizen, fitted by character and intelligence to sit as a justice on the Supreme Court . . . could have decided this question other than the way it was decided," an editorial in the *Knoxville Journal* proclaimed, while the *New Orleans States-Item* called for "calmness and moderation." The delays created by *Brown II*, however, allowed integration opponents to whip up fear and resentment.

"MASSIVE RESISTANCE"

In July 1954, plantation manager Robert P. Patterson organized the first "**White Citizens Council**" in Sunflower County, Mississippi. "Integration represents darkness, regimentation, totalitarianism, communism and destruction," wrote Patterson. "Segregation represents the freedom to choose one's associates." Labeled by NAACP attorney and future Supreme Court Justice Thurgood Marshall as the "uptown Klan," these organizations drew segregationist lawyers, doctors, bankers, merchants and other influential citizens and used legal and illegal methods to prevent enforcement of *Brown*. Byron De

Holding a poster against racial bias in Mississippi are four of the most active leaders in the NAACP movement, from left: Henry L. Moon, director of public relations; Roy Wilkins, executive secretary; Herbert Hill, labor secretary, and Thurgood Marshall, special counsel. 1956

La Beckwith, who assassinated civil rights campaigner Medgar Evers in 1963, belonged to a chapter of the White Citizens Council. However, these groups used their financial and political influence primarily to minimize integration. African Americans who filed integration lawsuits lost jobs and could find no further employment in the white community because of boycotts organized by the councils. Furthermore, these groups raised millions of dollars to establish private "white academies" where parents wishing their children to attend segregated campuses could send their children. At the movement's peak, about 1 million belonged to Citizens Councils across the South.

Under pressure from groups like the White Citizens Councils to take a more defiant stand against *Brown*, southern legislatures tried various ruses to avoid integration. Faced with integration orders, school officials in Little Rock, Ark., and Norfolk, Va., completely shut down their public schools. Prince Edwards County, Va., closed its public schools for eight years to avoid admitting African-American students. Some southern states provided white parents vouchers to pay for tuition at private, non-integrated schools. Other states, like Alabama, passed "pupil placement" laws that complied with the letter of *Brown* but dodged the decision's mandate for integration. These statutes ostensibly allowed students to transfer from campuses where school administrators had racially assigned them. Theoretically, black students could transfer to white schools and white students to black schools. In practice, no white students requested transfer to underfunded and overcrowded black campuses, and school administrators concocted various reasons to reject African-American students' applications to attend white majority campuses.

Attorneys general in several southern states began a coordinated legal assault on the NAACP, hoping to harass the organization into bankruptcy and to frighten its members into silence. African-American teachers made up a large percentage of the group's membership rolls, so states like South Carolina passed laws prohibiting educators from publicly advocating integration, forcing twenty-four teachers at Elloree Training School in Orangeburg County who belonged to the NAACP to step down. Needing income, however, most teachers chose to quit the civil rights organization rather than leave their jobs, a drain that decimated many local chapters. Southern legislatures also forced state and local NAACP chapters to file membership lists and the names of contributors with the government, documents that were made public. In states like Louisiana, the White Citizens Councils then used these lists to target civil rights activists for harassment, firings, and business boycotts.

In Texas, State Attorney General John Ben Shepperd pressured the state NAACP by forcing the group to cough up unpaid franchise taxes. He also insisted that the NAACP publicly file its membership list. Settling out of court, the NAACP agreed to pay the franchise taxes in return for the state agreeing not to challenge the civil rights organization's nonprofit status. Resentment over the Texas NAACP's decision to settle and the publication of membership lists prompted resignations across the state, with the number of branches plummeting from 76 to 46 and overall membership declining from almost 17,000 in 1956 to under 8,000 the following year. This followed the pattern across the South. In Louisiana during the legal war against the NAACP, branches declined from 65 to 7 and membership from just over 13,000 to under 1,700 in the year after membership lists were made public in 1955. In Alabama, the NAACP refused to hand over its membership lists and state Judge Walter B. Jones issued an injunction prohibiting the group from operating anywhere in the state, an order that stood for eight years.

The Murder of Emmett Till

The savage beating death of a 14-year-old African-American boy named **Emmett Till** in Money, Mississippi August, 28, 1955, horrified much of the world and did much to mobilize the Civil Rights Movement in the second half of the 1950s. A Chicago native, Till traveled south to visit his extended family in the Mississippi Delta when, one week into his trip, he and several friends were standing outside a white-owned grocery in the tiny town of Money. Till told his unbelieving friends that he had several white friends in the North, including friendships with white girls. The friends dared him to go inside the store and flirt with Carolyn Bryant, a white woman who worked at the cash register. Accounts conflict on what happened next, with some claiming he whistled at Bryant, others that he reached for her hand and asked her out, while according to a third version he said, "Bye, baby," as he left the store. The cashier's husband, Roy Bryant, returned from a road trip three days later and vowed that he would "teach the boy a lesson."

Just after midnight August 28, 1955, Bryant and his step-brother J.W. Milam arrived at the house of Moses Wright, where Till was staying. They threw him in the back of a pickup truck and drove him to nearby Sunflower County, where they beat him until his face was unrecognizable and shot him. Tying a seventy-pound weight to his body, Bryant and Milam threw Till's body into the Tallahatchie River. After three days, authorities discovered Till's bloated body and later arrested Bryant and Milam.

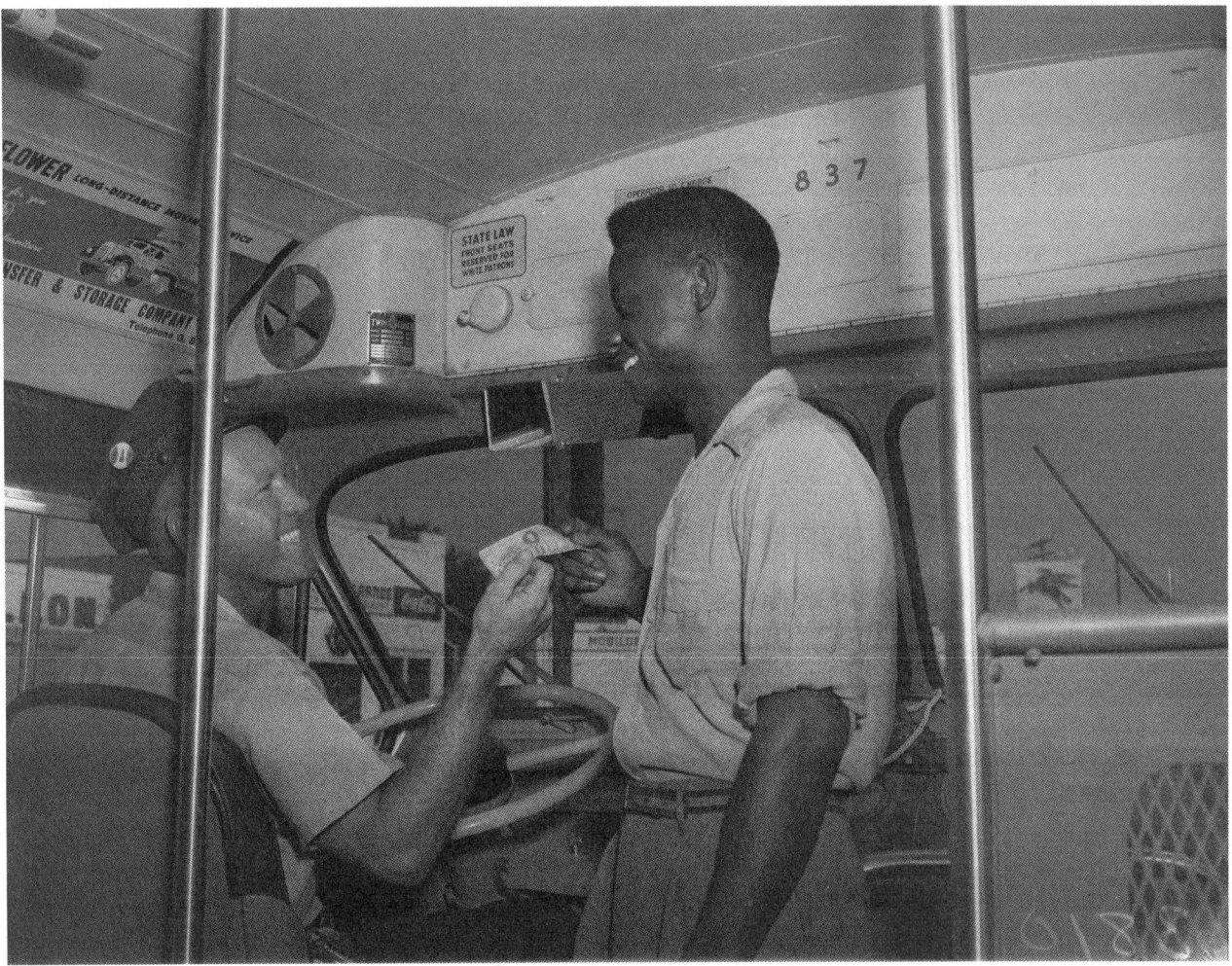

**This bus in San Antonio, Texas, 1949, has a sign above the driver's seat that states
"STATE LAW: Front Seats Reserved for White Patrons"
Credit: Institute of Texan Cultures**

Till's mother, Mamie Till Bradley, had her son's body brought to Chicago for the funeral. After seeing her son's mutilated face, she insisted on an open-casket funeral. "I wanted the world to see what they did to my baby," she said. Photographs of Till in his casket, with his face visible, appeared in *Jet*, an African-American-owned magazine, and soon shocked viewers around the world. In spite of the fact that Wright bravely identified one of the killers in the courtroom, an all-white jury took little more than an hour to acquit the defendants. Bryant and Milam, protected from further prosecution for Till's murder by the constitutional ban on double jeopardy, later admitted to the killing in a *Look* Magazine interview in return for $4000.

Rosa Parks and the Montgomery Bus Boycott

As a girl attending the Montgomery Industrial School for Girls, an institution founded in the Alabama city in 1886 by two New England missionary women, **Rosa Parks** learned a principle that would guide her entire life. "What I learned best," she recalled, "was that I was a person with dignity and self-respect, and I should not set my sights lower than anybody else just because I was black." Joining the NAACP at the age of 30, Parks became secretary of the Montgomery, Alabama branch. Parks earned a reputation as a quiet but hard worker guided by strong beliefs.

African Americans in Montgomery had planned for some time to challenge segregated seating on the city's buses. Black riders were made to sit in the back. Each bus had a "moving barrier" that divided the races. If the white section filled up, blacks were expected to move farther back and, if necessary, surrender seats to just-boarding white passengers. On December 1, 1955, Parks left her job as a seamstress at the Montgomery Fair department store and entered the bus that took her home each afternoon. Soon the 36 seats on the bus filled, with 22 black passengers in the back and 14 whites in the front. A white man stood at the front of the bus and driver J.P. Blake demanded that four black passengers sitting just behind the back of the white section move to seats farther down. The African-American passengers did not budge. After a threat from Blake, three of the riders relented. The fourth, Parks, told Blake that she was not in the white section and would remain in her seat. Blake replied that he had the authority to determine where the white section ended and the black section began and that he had the authority to arrest Parks if she refused to move. Blake told her she was under arrest. She remained seated until Blake returned with Montgomery police officers, who fingerprinted her and placed her in jail. The police charged her with violating Alabama's bus segregation laws.

The African-American community in Montgomery, who all shared humiliating experiences coping with the city's Jim Crow ordinances, quickly mobilized as word spread of Parks's arrest. The Montgomery Improvement Association (MIA) led a boycott of the city bus system with a 26-year-old Baptist minister, Martin Luther King, Jr., selected as its president. A one-day black boycott of the city's mass transit turned into a more than yearlong campaign. The MIA at first made mild demands: that black passengers be seated from back to front and whites from front to back on a first-come, first-serve basis. Originally the MIA made no demand for integration, but city officials still refused to budge.

During the **Montgomery Bus Boycott**, the MIA arranged transportation for the African-American domestic servants, sanitation workers, and janitors participating in the bus boycott to travel the often long distances to their jobs. Montgomery police began arresting drivers participating in the MIA carpools. Police arrested Dr. King for allegedly speeding, and four days later someone ignited dynamite at the homes of King and of E.D. Nixon, another boycott leader. Montgomery's white leadership hoped to break the spirit of the boycotters, but the King arrest and the terrorist attacks had the opposite effect. One maid vowed she would crawl before she got back on the city buses.

Responding to the demands of rank-and-file protestors, the MIA then vowed to continue the boycott until the city desegregated the buses. In spite of the poverty of its supporters, the MIA raised $2,000 a week to carry on its carpools, pay legal expenses, and carry on the boycott. A white grand jury indicted 115 African Americans participating in the movement, including more than 20 African-American ministers, which only strengthened the resolve of the boycotters. By February of 1956, the story made headlines around the world and donations to the cause poured in from other countries. The boycott lasted 381 days and began to adversely affect white businesses

Dwight D. Eisenhower, Arkansas Governor Orval E. Faubus and Arkansas Congressman Brooks Hays at the naval base in Newport, Rhode Island following a two hour conference on the Little Rock school integration controversy. September 14, 1957. Credit: Eisenhower Presidential Library

in downtown Montgomery. A federal court in June 1956 ruled that Alabama's and Montgomery's bus segregation laws violated the Constitution, a decision affirmed by the U.S. Supreme Court's *Browder v. Gayle* decision. Even though segregated public transportation remained the rule in the South for years to come, the Montgomery Bus Boycott made King a national civil rights leader and set the precedent for sit-ins and other mass protests that would mark the Civil Rights Movement. Other southern cities like Tallahassee and Baton Rouge would witness similar bus boycotts, and the events in Montgomery even had an international impact, with a bus boycott launched by blacks in Alexandra, South Africa, in 1957. There, protestors demanded subsidies to pay for transportation from black townships to jobs in white neighborhoods during the era of apartheid, the South African system of segregation.

The Little Rock Crisis

Such protests required much physical bravery and commitment, and very often the youngest Americans paid a

**President Dwight Eisenhower has a special broadcast on the Little Rock situation. September 24, 1957.
Credit: Eisenhower Presidential Library**

high price in the struggle for civil rights. African-American children breaking the color bar often suffered horrendous verbal and physical abuse from white students, as was the case of the nine students sent to integrate Central High School in Little Rock, Arkansas, in 1957. **Arkansas Governor Orval Faubus,** who had earned a reputation as a racial moderate, faced a tough re-election battle and decided to exploit the racial tensions sparked by a court order to desegregate the Little Rock campus. On September 2, 1957, the night before the school term began, Faubus appeared on Arkansas television and announced that it would "not be possible to restore or maintain order if forcible integration is carried out tomorrow." Faubus dispatched the Arkansas National Guard to Central High to bar the entrance of the African-American students who volunteered to integrate the high school. The black students did not attempt to enter the campus the next day, but a federal judge ordered integration to proceed. As the black students approached the next day, a large white mob gathered around Central High and yelled, "Niggers! Niggers! They're coming. Here they come!" National Guardsmen again turned back the Little Rock Nine, as the black students came to be called.

Dwight Eisenhower then occupied the White House and he had no appetite for getting involved in the **Little Rock Crisis.** The Republican president, who in 1952 had won four southern states against the liberal Democrat Adlai Stevenson, believed that the GOP had a chance of making electoral headway in the South, and he did not want to alienate segregationist voters. Eisenhower himself sympathized somewhat with white southern racial attitudes. After the *Brown* decision, he told Supreme Court Chief Justice Earl Warren, "These [white Southerners] are not bad people. All they are concerned about is to see that their sweet little girls are not required to sit in schools alongside some big black bucks." At a press conference the week the Little Rock Nine tried to enroll at the high school, Eisenhower said, "You cannot change people's hearts merely by laws."

Eisenhower's actions the year before gave civil rights supporters little hope that the president would intervene to protect the Little Rock Nine from physical danger. In 1956, a federal court mandated school desegregation in Mansfield, Texas, a small town between Dallas and Fort Worth. With the support of Texas Governor Allan Shivers, enraged white mobs surrounded Mansfield High School on August 30 and 31 in order to block the enrollment of three African-American students. Whites hanged three black-faced effigies, which dangled in front of the Mansfield High campus for days with no action from school officials. Rather than calling for Mansfield residents to respect the law, Shivers disobeyed court orders, dispatching Texas Rangers to keep the three African-American students from entering the campus.

Facing re-election in 1956, and hoping to win votes in Texas, Eisenhower took no action to enforce the desegregation order. The president allowed Governor Shivers to illegally maintain segregation, which did not end at the campus until the high school faced the loss of federal funds in 1965. Inspired by events in Mansfield, Arkansas Governor Faubus expected a similar result in Little Rock in 1957.

Ordered a second time on September 20, 1957, to implement desegregation, Governor Faubus withdrew the National Guard and predicted bloodshed as he left the state to avoid responsibility. Meanwhile, the governor's

**President Dwight Eisenhower signs the Civil Rights Act of 1957 in his office at the naval base in Newport, Rhode Island. September 9, 1957.
Credit: Eisenhower Presidential Library**

aides organized another ugly white mob that included hotheads from all across the South. A large, unruly crowd gathered at Central High School by Monday, September 23. The mob chanted, "Two, four, six, eight, we ain't gonna integrate!" and "Niggers, keep away from our school—go back to the jungle." This time the Little Rock mayor ordered the black students withdrawn.

Aware of the Cold War consequences as the news from Arkansas gained a worldwide audience, Eisenhower appeared on television to condemn the "disgraceful occurrence." A bigger mob showed up at the school on September 24. Aware of rising national and international criticism of his inaction, Eisenhower federalized the Arkansas National Guard and dispatched a thousand troops of the 101st Airborne Division to Central High to escort the Little Rock Nine safely to the campus. Armed soldiers would accompany the African-American students for several weeks, but the Little Rock Nine would face danger upon the withdrawal of the federal troops.

The coming months proved hellish for the small black contingent. One student, Melba Pattillo, suffered racial slurs and was pushed, hit, and tripped by white students. Pattillo later recalled that a small group of white students attempted to quietly help her during the ordeal, but the majority stood by in silence as an angry faction of whites subjected her to various tortures. One white student squirted acid into her eyes, almost causing permanent blindness. "If someone called me names or spat on me, or kicked me in the shin, or walked on my heel, I thought I couldn't make it one more moment," said Pattillo, who nevertheless persisted to the end of the school year.

Terrorists fired bullets into her home and the school district threatened her mother, a teacher at a black school, that her job would be eliminated. A National Guardsmen felt compassion for Pattillo and advised her not to reveal her emotional pain to her tormentors. "Warriors don't cry," he told her. Later, Pattillo recalled that the presence of reporters probably saved the lives of her family. ". . . [T]he media followed us," she said. "When houses were attacked, reporters would spend the night. The press offered us some protection. How are you going to kill someone . . . if their names are in the paper?"

One of the nine, Minnijean Brown, could take the harassment no more and poured chili on a group of white boys who were tormenting her in the school cafeteria. School officials did nothing to the boys but suspended Brown for six days. After another incident, officials suspended Brown for the remainder of the school year. Her parents transferred her to a high school in New York. Faubus, meanwhile, continued his resistance by closing down all of Little Rock's high schools in the 1958 to 1959 school year. Federal courts intervened to reopen the schools. That year, the Arkansas governor was named one of the most admired men in America in a Gallup Poll.

MEXICAN-AMERICAN ACTIVISM

From 1941-1945, close to 500,000 Mexican Americans served in the United States military out of a Hispanic population of about 2.7 million. In Los Angeles, Hispanics accounted for one-tenth of the total population but comprised one-fifth of the metropolis' wartime casualties. Hispanics made up 25 percent of the victims of the "Bataan Death March" (in which the Japanese beat, shot and marched to death captured British and American prisoners of war in the Philippines), and Mexicans and Mexican Americans earned more medals of honor than any other demographic group.

The Mexican population in the United States increased dramatically during the post-World War II period, with Mexican immigrants increasing from 5.9 percent of all newcomers to 11.9 percent at the end of the 1950s. Part of this increase resulted from the *bracero* program, in which American landowners imported Mexicans as low-paid agricultural workers. The number of *braceros* brought in from Mexico jumped from about 35,000 in 1949 to 107,000 in 1960. In 1956, the *bracero* program peaked with more than 445,000 Mexicans working on American farms that year. Many *braceros* remained in the United States after their year-long contracts expired, joining a growing number of Mexicans who fled poverty in their country by crossing the American border.

Responding to Anglo concerns about the rising number of so-called "wetbacks"—the insulting term used for Mexican immigrants who supposedly crossed the border by swimming across the Rio Grande River—the federal government launched a crackdown on undocumented workers, "**Operation Wetback**," in 1950. During the next five years, the government seized and deported nearly four million people whom authorities claimed were illegal immigrants, with Mexican-American legal residents sometimes included in the sweeps. Immigration would heavily politicize the Mexican-American community after the war, and many Hispanic political organizations battled to improve working conditions for migrant workers and to fight what they saw as harassment of the Mexican-American community, including repeated FBI investigations of Hispanic labor unions, which Anglo law enforcement insisted were communist fronts.

As with African Americans, Mexican-American veterans of World War II returned from a war against racist fascist regimes impatient with the intolerance they still encountered at home. Passage of the G.I. Bill meant

**LULAC meeting at Aztec No. 3 club on Main Street, Victoria, Texas, 1940s.
Source: Tensy Quinbar, San Antonio, Texas. Credit: Institute of Texan Cultures**

that more Mexican Americans attended college than ever before, and with increased enrollment at colleges and universities came rising expectations for a better life. The percentage of Hispanics living in towns and cities as opposed to rural areas dramatically increased after the war, reaching 65 percent in 1950, which facilitated political activism. Hispanic veterans in particular played a major role in the two primary Latino civil rights organizations of the post-war years: the **League of United Latin American Citizens (LULAC)** and the **American GI Forum (AGIF)**. Well-educated, often prosperous and urban Mexican-American elites formed LULAC in Texas in the late 1920s. LULAC's founders saw assimilation with the Anglo majority as a path toward winning acceptance in American society. They embraced a "Mexican American" identity that combined respect for Mexican traditions and pride in American citizenship. A major focus was "Americanizing" Latinos who still spoke Spanish.

"LULAC symbolized the rise of the Mexican middle class," according to historian Rodolfo Acuña. "As in the past, the organization did not really serve the interests of the poor, but, rather, reflected the philosophy of the middle class, who wanted assimilation . . . To achieve its goal, the middle-class leadership demanded constitutional and human rights for all Mexicans . . . They demanded equality as North Americans; their major goals remained equal access to education and other public and private institutions, and the enactment of state laws to end discrimination against Mexicans."

The Anglo response to Mexican Americans and immigrants in states like Texas and New Mexico varied widely, with discrimination more common and harsher in places with large Spanish-speaking populations. The law in Texas and other Southwestern states did not define Mexican Americans and Mexican immigrants as non-whites, so segregation of Latino students resulted from custom rather than statute. In such communities, authorities denied Mexican Americans access to public parks and swimming pools, and restaurants either would not serve Mexican American and Mexican patrons or would force them to take their food through a back window and eat outside. Though no formal law segregated Mexican and Mexican-American children from Anglos in Texas schools, in districts with large Latino populations, school officials routinely assigned Hispanic children to separate, crowded and poorly funded schools.

In New Mexico, teachers taught Mexican school children in Spanish, which LULAC saw as a deliberate attempt to block these pupils from economic success in an English-speaking country. Mexican children fared

Leaders of the Latino civil rights struggle gather outside the Casa Blanca restaurant in San Antonio, Texas during a celebration of victory in the landmark 1948 *Delgado v. Bastrop ISD* decision that outlawed segregation against Latino students. Pictured, from left to right: Dr. Arthur Campa, a University of Denver professor; Dr. George I. Sanchez, a professor at the University of Texas at Austin; Joe Castanuela, president of a local LULAC chapter; and Ramon Galindo, president of local Mexican-American Chamber of Commerce.
Credit: Institute of Texan Cultures

poorly in Anglo-run school districts. Hispanic students rarely finished their public school education with a high school diploma. Many non-native speakers of English ended up assigned to remedial classes. In San Antonio in 1920, 11,000 students attended the district's elementary schools, but there were only 250 high school graduates. In 1928, only 250 Mexican students attended colleges and universities in the entire state of Texas.

To address the high drop-out problem in the Mexican-American community, in 1956 LULAC President Felix Tijerina established "The Little School of the 400" program designed to teach Spanish-speaking preschool children a 400-word vocabulary of basic English words before they began first grade. Like the NAACP, from the late 1920s through the post-World War II years, LULAC helped members file lawsuits against informal school segregation in the public schools and to open access to higher education for the Mexican and Mexican-American community.

In 1946, a U.S. District court in Southern California ruled, in *Méndez v. Westminster School District*, that segregating Mexican school children violated their constitutional rights, a decision later upheld by the Ninth Circuit Court of Appeals. The dismantling of segregation in Texas began with the 1948 *Delgado v. Bastrop ISD* decision, in which a lower federal court banned school boards from placing Mexican-American students in different schools than Anglo children. The court's rationale rested on Texas's legal definition of Mexican American as white. These cases provided two of many precedents for the *Brown* decision. Later, in the 1957 *Hernandez v. Driscoll CISD* case, lower federal court justices ruled that a Texas district's practice of holding back Mexican-American children in grades one and two for four years served as a form of discrimination.

Dr. Hector Garcia formed the American GI Forum in Corpus Christi, Texas, in 1948 to serve Mexican-American veterans who frequently did not receive Veterans Administration benefits on time. Shut out by the Anglo-

AMERICAN CULTURE FROM 1945-1960 / 853

Dr. Hector P. Garcia, founder of the American G.I. Forum.   Credit: Institute of Texan Cultures

run American Legion, Garcia and others decided to form their own veterans' group. The AGIF grabbed national headlines in 1949 when it led protests against a Three Rivers, Texas, funeral home that denied the use of a chapel to the family of Army Private Felix Longoria, who died in combat in World War II. The AGIF launched an intense lobbying campaign. Lyndon Johnson, at the time a U.S. senator from Texas, successfully persuaded authorities to grant a full funeral service for Longoria at Arlington National Cemetery. Angered by the treatment of Longoria, Mexican-American veterans across the country flocked to the GI Forum, and by the end of 1949, there were 100 AGIF chapters in 23 states across the country. With its ladies' auxiliary, entire families could participate in GI Forum events, a key to its success.

The LULAC and AGIF leadership tended to be conservative, and through the 1950s often presented Mexican Americans as a white ethnic group with a distinct cultural identity but American loyalties. As such, the leaders of these groups distanced themselves from the African-American civil rights movement, were often critical of black civil rights protests, and sometimes even used racist terms to describe African-American leaders. Job competition between African Americans and Mexican Americans for the same low-paying jobs often created tensions between the groups.

REP. HENRY B. GONZALEZ, Austin, Texas 1950s

"Mexican American and African American civil rights workers during and after World War II only rarely viewed their campaigns as a common struggle for equality and full citizenship rights," observed historian Neil Foley. "Part of the reason can be traced to the immigrant status of many Mexicans, many of them unauthorized immigrants, and the deep concern of African Americans that Mexican immigrants competed with them for jobs." Groups like LULAC and AGIF focused their legal strategies not on fighting Jim Crow on principle, but on securing a consistent legal definition of Mexican Americans as whites who therefore had the right to attend better-funded white schools. Nevertheless, Mexican-American politicians like Henry B. Gonzalez of Texas threw his support behind the NAACP and black desegregation efforts. The Chicano movement of the late 1960s would bring increased efforts to unite blacks and browns in a common battle against racism.

ROSIE THE RIVETER AFTER THE WAR

During World War II, millions of women filled industrial jobs left by men serving in the military and played a critical role in producing military equipment and other products needed by the troops in Europe and Asia. Between 1940 and 1945, the number of women workers climbed by 50 percent. About 75 percent of women workers were married and most had school-age children. By 1944, the year before the war ended, 36.5 percent of women worked outside the home.

World War II profoundly affected women's perceptions of themselves and of their career expectations. Poor, working-class, and especially African-American and Mexican-American women had been forced by economic circumstances to work outside their homes. In the 1950s, more than 40 percent of African-American mothers of small children had no choice but to work outside the home. Before the war, however, many middle-class and upper-class white women at least perceived holding jobs outside of the home as an emergency option exercised when the family needed money. During the war such women experienced greater personal wealth, acquired new skills, enjoyed more freedom, and experienced a wider social experience with their workmates than ever before. "Although 95 percent of the new women employees had expected when they were first hired to quit work at the end of the war," historian Stephanie Coontz observed, "by 1945 an almost equally overwhelming majority did not want to give up their independence, responsibility and income, and expressed the desire to continue working."

After the war, however, employers laid off female workers en masse, with the percentage of women earning wages outside the home dropping to 30.8 percent in 1947. Among women who stayed in the workplace, those who had enjoyed higher wages in manufacturing jobs during the war often found themselves consigned to lower-paid, more traditional positions as secretaries. Nevertheless, by the beginning of the 1950s, the number of women earning salaries began to inch upward again. In 1952, there were two million more women in the workplace than at the peak of wartime production. A decade later, 40 percent of women aged 16 and older held jobs. Driving increased female employment, at least in part, was a rise in consumerism, created in turn by a vast expansion of mass media and advertising in the late 1940s and 1950s. While spending on food increased only by a third in the five years following World War II, and spending on clothes climbed only by a fifth, purchases of household appliances and furniture spiraled 240 percent in the same time period. The dazzling array of household products paraded in newspapers, magazines, and nightly on television shows and the radio put pressure on family incomes. Women worked so families could keep up with what came to be called the "rat race." However, even women who returned to a domestic life were influenced by their wartime experiences, and many taught their daughters that they could do whatever men could do. These women laid a foundation for the feminist movement of the 1960s.

Women in 1950s Popular Culture

Assertive women, however, were demeaned by American culture of the late 1940s, 1950s and early 1960s, and blamed for a supposed rise in juvenile delinquency, homosexuality, and other alleged social ills. Movies like **Rebel Without a Cause** (1955), *Psycho* (1960), and *The Manchurian Candidate* (1962) depicted children raised by domineering mothers with no strong male in the house as liable to become at best dysfunctional and at worst homicidal monsters.

The popular situation comedy **I Love Lucy** depicted the ditzy title heroine's dreams of a show business career as laughable. Lucy carried a mixed message. The title character, like many real 1950s women, desperately wanted a career and success outside of the boring housewife role the male-dominated culture thrust upon them. All of Lucy's attempts to become an actress, a novelist, or a singer, however, ended in comic failure. In most family-centered comedies, however, women were portrayed as happy and fulfilled homebound wives and mothers. Shows like *Father Knows Best* and *Ozzie and Harriet* featured men as the wage earners and decision makers of the family and adult women as perfectly dressed and bejeweled housewives with no life outside of keeping house and fretting about the children. In such programs, housewives did not come up with solutions to the problems facing the family but instead meekly deferred to their presumably smarter and wiser husbands. Inevitably, popular entertainment of the era suggested that single women wanted nothing more than to leave their jobs and find a husband.

In movies, unconventional women were portrayed in more sinister hues. In *Rebel Without a Cause*, the tragic hero of the film, Jim Stark, (played by teen idol James Dean) descends into juvenile delinquency in large part because of a weak father dominated by a bossy wife. At one point, Stark bitterly complains that his mother bullies his father, who in one scene wears a kitchen apron. She "eats him alive and he takes it," Stark complains, later insisting that "if he had guts to knock Mom cold once, then maybe she'd be happy and then she'd stop pickin' on him, because they make mush out of him."

Heavily influenced by the overt sexism of Freudian psychology, bestsellers like *The Modern Woman*, published in 1947, suggested that women who sought careers or higher education sought to symbolically "castrate" men. Psychiatrists regularly diagnosed women who defied the gender norms of the time by delaying childbirth, pursuing careers, or being insufficiently subservient to their husbands as neurotic or even as suffering from schizophrenia. According to Stephanie Coontz, the medical records of women hospitalized as "schizophrenic" in the San Francisco Bay area in the 1950s reveal that most of these women were subjected to forced commitment and electro-shock therapy in order to get them to accept their domestic roles and the authority of their husbands. Doctors also used electro-shock to "cure" women who sought abortions, which doctors interpreted as a sign of mental illness.

FAMILY LIFE AND THE BABY BOOM

Few women experienced the lives portrayed on popular TV shows, but that was not for lack of effort. The median age for women marrying for the first time dropped to just over 20 years in mid-decade (the median age for men was around 22.5.) It became common for couples to marry shortly after high school graduation. No generation married at higher rates than those Americans who reached maturity during World War II. About 96 percent of the women and 94 percent of the men in that group married, with the average family having between 3.2 and 3.7 children during the course of the 1950s. The so-called "**Baby Boom**" years from 1946 to 1964 saw the birth of 79 million children. Births per year soared from around 2.5 million in the 1930s and the early 1940s to a peak of 4.3 million in the late 1950s.

Psychiatrist Robert J. Lifton suggested that Americans in the 1950s had, because of anxieties produced by the war, the Holocaust, and the beginning of the nuclear age, lost their faith that scientific discoveries would inevitably make life better, freer, and safer. Lifton argued that Americans suffered from a numbing fear of nuclear annihilation in particular. Historian Elaine Tyler May believes that the Baby Boom of 1946-1964 represented a response to that anxiety. "Americans were well poised to embrace domesticity in the midst of the terrors of the atomic age," she wrote in *Homeward Bound: American Families in the Cold War Era*. "A home filled with children would create a feeling of warmth and security against the cold forces of disruption and alienation. Children would also be a connection to the future and means of replenishing a world depleted by war deaths."

Sadly, marriage and children often failed to bring the emotional and material rewards to men and women as promised on television comedies. As in other eras, family life in the 1950s featured tragically frequent incidents of child and spousal abuse, infidelity, chemical dependency, and poverty. Under state laws of the 1950s, wife-beating was not considered a crime, and psychologists and sociologists largely overlooked issues like child abuse, even in states like Colorado where in one year police recorded 302 cases of battered children, and 33 died from beatings.

Family Troubles

Even though the father of psychoanalysis, Sigmund Freud, came to conflicting conclusions about the prevalence of incest and the sexual abuse of children by family members, Freudian psychiatrists in the 1950s tended to dismiss female patients accusing their fathers of rape, claiming that such women were indulging in sexual fantasies. Not believing their abuse claims, doctors often sought to sedate their female patients. A multi-million dollar industry manufacturing tranquilizers and sleeping pills underwent explosive growth in the 1950s, and females became the major consumers. Consumption of anxiety medications climbed from 462,000 pounds nationally in 1958 to 1.15 million pounds only a year later. Men expressed shock as they became increasingly aware of discontent among women. After being swamped with responses when the magazine ran an article called "The Mother Who Ran Away," an editor of *McCall's* remarked, "We suddenly realized that all those women at home with their three and a half children were miserably unhappy."

Educated women in particular felt they were not free to express themselves intellectually. About 40 percent of Barnard College women in one survey admitted to "playing dumb" in order to attract men, but once in such relationships, they often experienced anger and frustration. In 1957, Betty Friedan began the research that led to her groundbreaking 1963 book *The Feminine Mystique*, and she found legions of thoughtful middle- and upper-class women who spent their years after college graduation with nothing more mentally taxing to do than housework. A study of young female college graduates found that those who became full-time housewives after school suffered from a more intense fear of growing old, enjoyed less confidence, were more critical of themselves, and had greater doubts about their skills as mothers than women who had paying jobs.

Many women hid inner turmoil under a passive exterior, one physician wrote in 1953, but behind the mask often lurked "an inwardly tense and emotionally unstable individual seething with hidden aggressiveness and resentment." Male doctors at the time saw women as suffering from mental illness but did not perceive as sick a society that denied smart, educated women a professional outlet.

THE DOUBLE STANDARD

Other women found themselves trapped into marriage by premarital pregnancy. According to John D'Emilio and Estelle B. Freedman, historians of American sexuality, the period after World War II saw an increase in sexual permissiveness that had actually begun in the 1920s and 1930s when young people first began in large numbers to select their own mates instead of letting their parents arrange courtships and choose their marriage partners. By mid-century, it became common for girls and boys in high school to "go steady," a commitment to a relationship that allowed these couples a greater degree of sexual exploration. Sexual contact short of intercourse became more commonplace, particularly with the great availability of automobiles and the rising prosperity of the post-war period, which provided teenagers more allowance money for entertainment. "Petting," involving prolonged kissing and physically stroking partners, became commonplace and a topic of discussion among worried parents and therapists.

Sex researcher **Alfred Kinsey** observed that in mid-century America, on "doorsteps and on street corners, and on high school and college campuses . . . [petting] may be observed in the daytime as well as in the evening hours." However as sexual activity became more common, American society gave boys greater permission to pursue sexual contact, but women who engaged in sexual acts lost social standing and became less attractive to boys as long-term partners. Boys often shunned girls with whom they had engaged in premarital sex. "How are you supposed to know what they want?" a sixteen-year-old girl complained in the 1950s. "You hold out for a long time and then when you give in to them and give your body they laugh at you afterwards and say they would never marry a slut, and that they didn't love you but were testing because they only plan to marry a virgin and wanted to see if you would go all the way."

Regardless of the stated sexual standards of the day, the work of Kinsey, a zoologist from Indiana University, made it clear that many Americans lived in secret defiance of those standards. Kinsey's dry 1948 scientific tome, *Sexual Behavior in the Human Male*, spent 27 weeks on the *New York Times* bestseller list, eventually selling 250,000 copies. The 1953 follow-up on female sexual behavior joined its predecessor at the top of the book charts. Kinsey's findings, rather than his writing style, commanded attention. Kinsey and his staff questioned 5,300 white men and 6,000 women before drawing his conclusions. Interview subjects would be questioned in great detail on up to 521 items on his survey.

Among his controversial findings: 90 percent of men had engaged in premarital intercourse; 50 percent had engaged in extra-marital affairs; about 33 percent had at least one homosexual "experience"; that nearly all men had found a "sexual outlet" by the age of 15; and 95 percent reported they violated a law at least once while achieving orgasm (by, for instance, violating state laws against oral sex or homosexual acts, or by sexual acts with an underage partner.) Fewer women violated supposed American sexual standards, but the Kinsey results still startled the media and the average reader. According to Kinsey, more than 75 percent of women masturbated, 90 percent engaged in petting, 50 percent had sex before marriage, and a 25 percent had participated in extramarital affairs. According to Kinsey, Americans were more sexual than was publicly acknowledged and also more hypocritical about sex than was commonly admitted.

PORN IN THE U.S.A.

Confusing, contradictory messages about sex dominated American popular culture following World War II. "Soldiers who had graced their barracks and even their planes with photos and drawings of 'pinup' girls returned from Europe and Asia laden with pornography obtained abroad," according to D'Emilio and Freedman.

"They soon found a new genre of magazines available to fill their acquired tastes." In 1953, Hugh Hefner began publication of **Playboy**, a men's magazine that featured photos of nude women and frank discussions of sexuality. As the readership grew and became more prosperous, the magazine eventually also included celebrity interviews, music and movie reviews, and commentary on politics. Hefner described his attitudes toward sex as the "Playboy philosophy," and he encouraged his male readership, which reached one million by the end of the 1950s, to "enjoy the pleasures that the female has to offer without becoming emotionally involved." *Playboy* presented an upside-down image of American gender politics in which Hefner sympathized with the socially climbing male audience, 25 percent of whom were college-aged, whom he depicted as put upon by money-grabbing women. Hefner depicted marriage as a financial trap, urging men not to become one of the "sorry, regimented husbands trudging down every woman-dominated street in this woman-dominated land."

Sex scandal-driven periodicals like *Confidential* became the forerunners of today's supermarket tabloids. Magazines posing as male fitness periodicals and featuring muscle-bound male models in swimsuits served as softcore gay pornography. Even paperback novels sold at dime stores featured suggestive titles or titillating covers (such as in the case of the Bantam edition of *The African Queen*, which featured a drawing of a naked man arising from the water.) These publications joined *Playboy* in the increased eroticization of American culture. Perhaps sensing the shift in public attitudes toward sex and aware of the actual widespread sexual behavior uncovered by Kinsey, the United States Supreme Court began in the 1950s to take a more liberal stand on pornography cases brought by prosecutors against writers, photographers, publishers, booksellers and performers of adult material, setting an ever-higher bar for what could be considered "obscene." In a case that overturned a Michigan obscenity statute, the court ruled that the law in question would "reduce the adult population of Michigan to reading only what is fit for a child."

The Cost of Sexual Hypocrisy

Even though American teenagers had greater knowledge of and made more use of contraceptives in the 1950s, unwanted pregnancies still haunted many adolescent girls. In 1957, 97 out of every 1,000 girls from age 15 through 19 gave birth for the first time, in contrast to 52 of every 1,000 girls 26 years later. As Stephanie Coontz writes, "A surprising number of these births were illegitimate. " Coontz notes that the illegitimacy rates can't be accurately estimated because women giving birth out of wedlock weren't counted in statistics if they lived with their parents. To avoid scandal, parents often sent their daughters to homes for unwed mothers and urged them to put their children up for adoption. Overall, the period from 1944 to 1955 saw an 80 percent climb in the adoption of children born outside of marriage.

Many women forced into early marriage or to raise children as single parents experienced poverty, but they were hardly alone. After World War II, women who continued to work outside of the home found it hard to get the type of high-wage, challenging jobs they held in the early 1940s. Men returning from the war took back manufacturing jobs in the defense, steel, and automobile industries. Women once again could only find low-wage jobs as secretaries and domestics. In any case, a high number of men and women did not enjoy the economic boom time of the period from 1945 to 1960. One out of four Americans met the official definition of poverty in the 1950s, including one-third of children. African-American women and their children faced a double bind, and by 1959, 55 percent of the black population lived in poverty, one more instance of how real American family life in the 1950s differed from the fantasy projected in popular culture.

OPPRESSION AND THE BIRTH OF THE GAY RIGHTS MOVEMENT

During the war, millions of gay men and women left their small towns and farming communities where they had lived lonely lives of isolation and entered the military where for the first time they met large numbers of other gays. As a 20-year-old gay draftee wrote a friend, life in the military provided freedom from parental and neighborly scrutiny. "You see, the Army is an utterly simplified existence for me," he said in a letter. "I have no one to answer to as long as I behave during the week and stay out of the way of the MPs [military police] on weekends. If I go home, how can I stay out all night or promote any serious affair? My parents would simply consider me something perverted and keep me in the house."

After the war, many homosexuals from middle America settled in cities that already had substantial, established gay communities like New York, San Francisco and Los Angeles. Gay servicemen often evaded detection because military psychiatrists, given the job of screening out homosexuals, relied on stereotypes of effeminate gay men and masculine lesbians. Gay men turned to YMCA dormitories and public parks, along with the more traditional gathering places like bathhouses and gay bars, to find sexual and romantic partners and to connect with a larger community. Kinsey's report on the prevalence of homosexual behavior among men, and his estimate that gays constituted between 4 to 10 percent of the population, bolstered the confidence of the community even as positive images of lesbian relationships appeared in the paperback novels of Ann Bannon and Paula Christian.

The Cold War, however, sparked a new wave of anti-gay oppression. Some allies of the red-baiting Wisconsin Senator Joseph McCarthy claimed that homosexuality represented part of a communist conspiracy to undermine American masculinity, the family, and the country's military resolve. Government officials claimed that gay government workers posed a security risk because they were weak and vulnerable to blackmail by Soviet agents. In 1950, a State Department official revealed that his office had fired dozens of employees for suspected homosexuality. Republican members of Congress charged that gays had infiltrated President Truman's administration while the party's national chair, Guy Gabrielson, sent a letter to thousands of party activists, warning that "sexual perverts" were "perhaps as dangerous as actual communists." In June 1950, the Senate authorized an investigation into "homosexuals and other moral perverts" serving in the government.

In December 1950, the government issued a report, "Employment of Homosexuals and Other Sex Perverts in Government" that charged, "The lack of emotional stability which is found in most sex perverts and the weakness of their moral fibre makes them susceptible to the blandishments of foreign espionage agents . . . [and] easy prey to blackmailers." A purge of gay government workers ensued in which employees faced the loss of a job. Investigators warned the targets of the gay witch hunt that their lifestyles would be publicly revealed and they could face criminal prosecution if they did not provide names of other homosexuals working in federal agencies.

The number of government employees sacked during the "gay scare" increased by twelve times in the period between 1950 and 1953. Shortly after being sworn in as president, Dwight Eisenhower issued an executive order barring any gay man or woman from working for the federal government. A gay purge happened in the military, with annual discharges doubling through the 1950s. Even companies doing business with the federal government began screening employees for "homosexual tendencies."

Media outlets like the magazine *Newsweek* piled on. Responding to Kinsey's findings, the magazine argued against the tolerance for gays that Kinsey implicitly advocated, declaring that "the sex pervert, whether a homosexual, an exhibitionist, or even a dangerous sadist, is too often regarded as merely a 'queer' person who never hurts anyone but himself. Then the mangled form of some victim focuses public attention on the degenerate's work." *Newsweek* held out the hope that modern psychiatry might help gays discover the "error" of their ways but called for tough legal measures against homosexuals, warning that, "The sex pervert [should not] be treated as a coddled patient, but as a particularly virulent type of criminal."

The federal gay purge probably inspired increased harassment of homosexuals by local police departments, which increased raids on gay bars and bathhouses. Police frequently beat gay suspects. Washington, D.C. police arrested more than 1,000 suspected gays a year in the early 1950s, with other police sweeps of gay hangouts taking place in cities like Baltimore, Miami, New Orleans, and Dallas. So pervasive became homophobia, author Barbara Ehrenreich suggested, that men remained with wives they wanted to leave because of the fear they might be accused of being gay if they left to live on their own. The psychiatric profession, meanwhile, defined homosexuality as a mental illness and many gays found themselves involuntarily committed to mental hospitals where, like unconventional women, they found themselves subjected to electro-shock therapy or to insulin injections aimed at causing "curative" seizures.

Ironically, two of the top figures promoting the Red Scare and its related Gay Scare were Roy Cohn, the closeted gay attorney for Sen. Joseph McCarthy's Committee on Government Operations, and FBI director J. Edgar Hoover. It was rumored of Hoover that he was gay and a cross dresser. Most gay men like Cohn, and possibly Hoover, stayed in the closet and a few tried to prove their heterosexuality by being publicly anti-gay. Watching a climate of fear settle over the gay community, however, Henry Hay created what could be described as the first gay civil rights organization in the United States, the **Mattachine Society**. "The country, it seemed to me, was beginning to move towards fascism and McCarthyism; the Jews wouldn't be used as a scapegoat this time—the painful example of Germany was still too clear to us," Hay said later. ". . . It was obvious that McCarthy was setting up a pattern for a new scapegoat and it was going to be us—Gays. We had to organize, we had to move, we had to get started."

The Mattachine Society derived its name from the Italian word mattachino, which referred to medieval court jesters who risked telling the king painful truths. The first chapter of the society formed in Los Angeles in 1951, with affiliates soon popping up in Boston, Philadelphia, Chicago, Denver and Washington, D.C, the latter city the epicenter of the Gay Scare. In its founding statement of principles, the group sought to consciously imitate other "minority" groups like "the Negro, the Mexican, and the

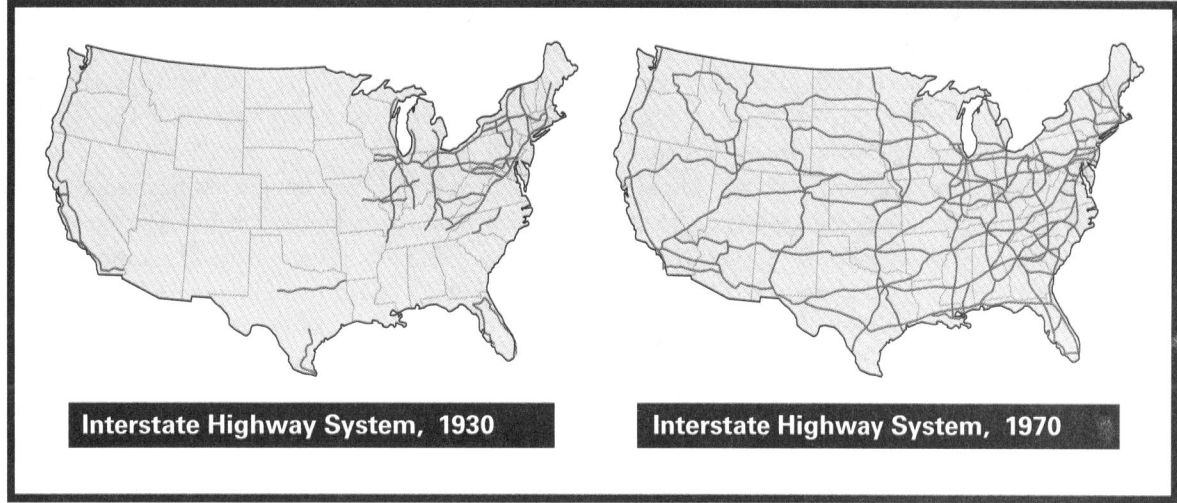

Map 27.1 The Interstate Highway and Defense System Act of 1956 authorized federal funds to build the highways that crisscrossed the nation.

Jewish people," in developing an "ethical homosexual society" and to campaign against "discriminatory and oppressive legislation" and assist "our people who are victimized daily as part of our oppression."

The year 1951 also saw publication of *The Homosexual in America*, written by Edward Sagarin (who published under the pseudonym Donald Webster Cory). He contended that gays represented a discriminated-against minority group due civil rights and wrote, "there is no homosexual problem except that created by heterosexual society." Sagarin told his audience that, "What the homosexual wants is freedom—not only freedom of expression, but also sexual freedom." A gay American had the right to use his body, he said, "so long as he does not use the force of violence, threat, or superior age, so long as he does not inflict bodily harm or disease upon another person; so long as the other person is of sound mind and agrees to the activity." Unless the gay man would "rise up and demand his rights" then "he will never get them, but until he gets those rights he cannot be expected to expose himself to the martyrdom that would come should he rise up and demand them." Gays remained trapped in this political paradox, unable to expect others to respect their human dignity but facing horrible consequences for coming out of the closet through political activism, through the 1960s. It would not be until the Stonewall Riot in New York City in 1969 that the gay civil rights movement would make significant headway.

ON THE ROAD

One of the most long-lasting, and often overlooked, transformations in American life from 1945 to 1960 came in the form of the interstate highway system. In 1956, the U.S Congress passed the **Interstate Highway Act**. President Dwight Eisenhower supported the bill as an aid to national defense. During World War II, the American military worried about attacks on the American Pacific coast by the Japanese and on the Atlantic coast by the Germans. A highway bill had passed in 1944, but Eisenhower, who had been impressed by the German autobahn highway system that had been constructed by the Nazis, wanted superhighways for America. Automobile manufacturers lobbied for highway construction as well.

This sign for the Interstate Highway System salutes President Dwight Eisenhower, who initiated the system in the 1950s.

Crews built 46,000 miles of road with $130 billion in federal funds. As journalist Eric Schlosser notes, "The new highways spurred car sales, truck sales, and the construction of suburban homes."

At the same time highways spread across the country, auto companies like General Motors began to buy mass transit systems like urban trolley cars and train systems in order to shut down the competition. GM bought 100 different trolley systems in major cities like New York, Baltimore, Chicago, Los Angeles and smaller cities like Tulsa, Oklahoma and El Paso, Texas, and promptly tore them down. City buses manufactured by GM replaced the trolley systems the company had destroyed.

Americans quickly came to prefer driving their own cars to being passengers on public transportation. Schlosser notes that unlike railroad, subway and trolley companies, carmakers did not have to pay for the construction of their roadways and therefore did not have to pass the cost on to their customers. This created an illusion of the car as a cheap way to travel. Cars offered other immediate advantages. "The automobile offered a sense of independence and control," as Schlosser writes. "Daily travel was freed from the hassles of rail schedules, the needs of other passengers, and the location of the trolley stops." Tragically, the spread of highways and America's infatuation with cars also increased pollution and the country's dependence on oil, problems that would not begin to be acknowledged until the 1960s and 1970s.

A new industry, fast food, grew symbiotically with the spread of the highway system. The new highway system of the 1950s provided a marketing strategy for the fast food emporiums rising in the next decade. Located strategically on off-ramps, these restaurants offered quick, cheap, predictable meals to harried and wearied travelers who increasingly drove long distances from their downtown jobs to the suburban homes or who trekked across the ever more accessible breadth of the country in search of sales opportunities and business contacts. McDonald's, Kentucky Fried Chicken, and other national fast food chains began to conquer the American landscape by the 1960s. Meanwhile the explosion of fast-food restaurants, destined to contribute to an epidemic of American obesity by the late twentieth century, followed the winding network of interstates.

Fast-food restaurants also established a pattern of American business relying on low-wage, low-skilled non-union workers, often teenagers, providing nationally standardized products. "America's main streets and malls now boast the same Pizza Huts and Taco Bells, Gaps and Banana Republics, Starbucks and Jiffy Lubes . . . Almost every facet of American life has now been franchised or chained," Schlosser wrote. "From the maternity ward at a Columbia/HCA hospital to an embalming room owned by Service Corporation International . . . a person can now go from cradle to grave without spending a nickel at an independently owned business." That trend began in the 1950s.

The year 1956 saw not just the beginning of highway construction across the nation but also the opening of America's first indoor shopping mall in Edina, a suburb of Minneapolis, Minnesota. With more and wider roadways available and car ownership on the increase, retail outlets increasingly moved from urban downtowns to outlying suburbs. The prototypical post-war suburb, with blocks of affordable, modest-sized, look-alike homes, arose in Levittown, New York, a 17,500-home community designed by William Levitt specifically for veterans returning from World War II and their wives and children. Increasingly, Americans moved from large cities to nearby suburbs, with the suburban population doubling from 36 million to 72 million from 1950 to 1970. Part of this population shift resulted from "white flight" as Anglo families sought neighborhoods farther from the growing African-American and Mexican-American communities within the major cities. The move of so many Americans farther from the urban core led to the economic deterioration of inner cities. Corporations, manufacturers and retail outlets soon also fled to suburbs offering lower taxes. The combined effect would be increased traffic, higher highway fatalities and urban sprawl.

TV NATION

Americans grew addicted to television in the 1950s. The number of households with television sets grew from a few thousand in 1946 to 15 million six years later. By 1955, two-thirds of American households owned a TV. Television served as the most effective medium for advertising to date. Soon, "Marlboro Men"—handsome cowboys riding horses on the American plains—made cigarette smoking appear masculine and glamorous, while other products ranging from cars to aftershave and mouthwash appeared. Hygiene products suddenly acquired sex appeal through the use of attractive male and female actors. Advertisers spent only $170 million on television advertising in 1950, but just five years later TV's advertising revenues surpassed $1 billion. The success of television dramatically affected radio programming, as the soap operas, police dramas and comedies that had appeared on the older medium became staple TV fare. Radio increasingly became a medium for music, news and talk shows.

A few serious programs, such as Edward R. Murrow's CBS news program *See It Now*, graced the airwaves. A series of 1954 *See It Now* broadcasts investigating the unethical behavior and unsubstantiated charges of Sen. Joseph McCarthy contributed to the Wisconsin politician's fall. Another CBS series, *Playhouse 90,* featured serious drama starring respected actors, with some episodes such as "The Miracle Worker," about teacher Anne Sullivan's education of the deaf, mute and blind Helen Keller, and "Judgment at Nuremburg" about Nazi war crimes. Both episodes later became acclaimed movies. However, broadcasters preferred what they considered the "least objectionable" content, airing dramas and comedies that steered clear of controversial subjects.

Rod Serling, writer of a *Playhouse 90* episode, "Requiem for a Heavyweight," recalled scripting a drama for the *United States Steel Hour* about an elderly Jew murdered by a bigot who is acquitted of the crime by a small-town jury. Asked by a reporter if the script was a comment on the Emmett Till murder, Serling said, "If the shoe fits . . ." Hearing this and afraid of offending southern audiences, sponsor U.S. Steel demanded several script changes, including making the murder victim an unspecified foreigner, removing the word "lynch" from the script and requiring characters to repeatedly say, "This is a strange little town," so it would not seem the program was criticizing any specific American community.

Serling had similar problems with sponsors regarding a drama he wrote that he set in the United States Senate. He was forbidden to deal with any contemporary political issues. The final approved script had the characters loudly arguing about made-up issues in such vague language that it bordered on incomprehensible. "In retrospect, I probably would have had a much more adult play had I made it science fiction, put it in the year 2057, and peopled the Senate with robots," Serling later said. "This probably would have been more reasonable and no less dramatically incisive." Serling, in fact, would soon turn to science fiction, creating the series **The Twilight Zone,** a show first airing in 1959. *The Twilight Zone* dealt with many controversial themes such as McCarthyism, nuclear weapons, the Holocaust, racism and other issues but often in a disguised manner that avoided the detection of wary censors or advertisers.

Most airtime became relentlessly bland. Critics soon called television the "idiot box." As Newton Minow, the controversial chair of the Federal Communications Commission in the early 1960s, put it, "When television is good, nothing is better. But when television is bad, nothing is worse. I invite you to sit down in front of your TV set and keep your eyes glued to that set until the station signs off. I can assure you that you will observe a vast wasteland."

Almost all programs lacked African American, Mexican American and Asian actors. The only program on the TV schedule with an all-black cast in 1951-1952 was the CBS comedy **Amos 'n' Andy,** a spin-off of a long-popular radio series that had starred two white actors in black face. In spite of the lack of other black performers on network television, the NAACP led a campaign for the cancellation of the show, which catered to white-held stereotypes of African Americans. In spite of good ratings, the show eventually could find no sponsors. CBS cancelled the program after its second season, and black people almost completely disappeared on the networks until the 1960s.

Television and Professional Sports

Before television became a feature of most Americans' homes, professional baseball reigned as the country's favorite sport. With its intricate strategy, slow pace and long pauses between action, baseball represented a perfect sport for radio. The integration of professional baseball after World War II, however, made its debut on television a culturally significant event. The National League and American League had segregated in the late nineteenth century through an informal "gentleman's agreement." As a result, up until the end of World War II, talented African American professional players spent their careers in several black baseball associations that came to be known as the "**Negro Leagues.**" **Jackie Robinson** broke the National League's color barrier on April 15, 1947.

A child of sharecroppers, Robinson attended UCLA and lettered in four sports, but lacking financial resources, he left college just short of graduation. After the Japanese attacked Pearl Harbor, Robinson enlisted in the Army, earning the rank of second lieutenant. Robinson, however, was arrested by military police and court martialed after he refused to move to the back of a bus while in Texas. Robinson eventually faced charges of insubordination but was acquitted and received an honorable discharge. After the war, he played for the Kansas City Monarchs in the Negro Leagues, but his talent caught the attention of the Brooklyn Dodgers organization. Robinson first played for the Dodgers on April 15, 1947 and stayed with the team until his retirement in 1956. During his career, he endured verbal abuse from fans and fellow players who called him "nigger." Some racist players deliberately injured him, and the St. Louis Cardinals at one point said they would refuse to play against him.

Nevertheless, Robinson's talent and courage allowed him to outlast his detractors, and he opened the door for other future Hall of Fame black players in the National League, such as Ernie Banks, Hank Aaron, and Willie Mays. Playing for the New York Giants baseball team,

Mays dominated sports headlines during the 1955 season when he recorded 51 home runs and stole 24 bases. The American League took longer to desegregate, but the sight of black professional players on television in broadcast markets often far removed from professional franchises and playing such a commanding role in what had long been considered the "national pastime" helped erase white myths about black physical inferiority and may have helped ease racism.

Wilt Chamberlain, drafted first by the Philadelphia Warriors, and Bill Russell, star of the National Basketball Association's Boston Celtics, became the first African-American athletes to completely dominate what had previously been an all-white professional sports league. Drafted by the Celtics in 1956, Russell would guide the team to nine NBA championships in 10 years, his speedy, agile play often inspired by the anger he felt at the racism he encountered across the country. Chamberlain played first for the barnstorming, all-black Harlem Globetrotters from 1958 to 1959 before signing with the Warriors, who played in his hometown of Philadelphia. He redefined the center position, and in 1962, he led the league, scoring an average of 50.4 points a game, including an all-time record of 100 points against the New York Knicks.

No sport benefited more from the popularity of television in the 1950s than professional football. The National Football League began play in the 1920s, but had taken a distant back seat not only to professional baseball, but to college football as well. Pro games rarely sold out and were usually played at college stadiums or professional baseball fields converted for football use. If pro games received any newspaper coverage, it usually appeared on the inside of the sports section. The biggest baseball stars like Joe DiMaggio pulled salaries of $100,000 a year or more. In contrast, most pro football players earned less than $6,000 a year, barely above the average American worker's $5,000 annual income, and had to supplement their income with jobs at car dealerships, grocery and liquor stores, or with furniture movers to pay their bills. Even the big stars, like Baltimore Colts quarterback Johnny Unitas, earned only $17,550 the year his team won the championship.

Football, however, with a larger ball and faster pace than baseball, proved an ideal match for television. "Professional football... now flowered under the sympathetic eye of the camera, its importance growing even as the nation was being wired city by city and house by house for television," wrote journalist and author David Halberstam. "Suddenly, professional football had become a new super sport, the first true rival to Major League baseball for the nation's affection."

When NFL games began to be broadcast on television on Sunday afternoons, the audience for the game grew, and by the late 1950s, 37 percent of the American public watching TV in that time slot tuned in to pro football games. The NFL championship game received national television broadcast coverage for the first time in 1956, and the size of the audience increased each year. A turning point in American sports history happened on December 28, 1958, when the New York Giants played the Baltimore Colts in the NFL title game. The contest, played in New York's Yankee Stadium, failed to sell out due to cold weather and because a two-week newspaper strike had sharply limited press coverage of the upcoming game. The broadcast was blacked out in the nation's largest city, though some wily New Yorkers placed taller antennas on their apartment buildings and caught broadcasts from Philadelphia.

Seen in black-and-white across the nation, the championship became the first game in NFL history to go into overtime and it thus extended into prime time—the peak hours of television viewing. With the game tied 17-17, the Colts reached the goal line in the first overtime period when a fan accidentally tripped over a cable and blackened TV screens across the country. The NBC broadcasting crew sent someone onto the field to delay the game while an engineer discovered the source of the broadcast interruption and reconnected the cable. The nation was wired in just in time to see the Colts score a game-winning touchdown.

The dramatic game vastly expanded pro football's television audience, which had grown to the point that by 1960 football fans could support an NFL rival, the American Football League. Competition between the leagues created a salary arms race that brought NFL wages closer to baseball standards. Both leagues took a gamble by creating franchises in the South, where college football remained the region's favorite sport. Competitive pressures led the Dallas Cowboys of the NFL, the Dallas Texans of the AFL (a team that would become the Kansas City Chiefs in 1963), and the AFL's Houston Oilers to sign black players even though those Texas cities still enforced segregation laws. The American Football League, uncertain of its financial future, desperately searched for stars and drafted players from previously ignored historically black colleges like Grambling University. The AFL soon had a higher percentage of black players than the NFL.

The arrival of star black players like Abner Haynes of the Texans helped hasten the demise of Jim Crow in the state. This process accelerated as the NFL in the mid-1960s opened franchises in New Orleans and Atlanta and the AFL in Miami. Soon, integrated pro basketball and baseball franchises started play in Dixie. From the Civil War to the early 1960s, the South had been culturally isolated from the rest of the nation, but the arrival of professional sports helped bridge the regional distance. Southern sports fans, it turned out, could cheer for black players as long as they helped their favorite teams win games. Meanwhile, football became the new national pastime. By the end of the 1960s, pro football eclipsed baseball as the nation's most popular sport, and NFL teams, by the end of the century, could demand millions from cities for the right to host to a franchise.

SUBTERRANEAN REBELS

Beatniks later became an icon of the 1950s, but they inspired fear and derision in their own era. Decades later, the leaders of the Beats could not agree where the label applied to their generation came from. Jack Kerouac said it came from the phrase, "beat it!" meaning "leave me alone." Others suggested "beat" referred to the rhythms of the jazz music Beatniks admired. One Beat author, John Clelon Holmes, claimed it referred to being exposed, suffering raw nerves or being "beat," or exhausted, in a world of nuclear threat, political crisis and painful social conformity. Whatever the origin of the term, the Beats embraced sexual rebellion, a sometimes condescending admiration of black culture, experimentation with marijuana and other drugs, and a rejection of the materialism and blandness of 1950s culture.

Four major authors defined the Beat movement: Kerouac, who authored the seminal novel **On the Road**; William S. Burroughs, writer of the disjointed and nightmarish novel *Naked Lunch*; and the openly sexual poets Gregory Corso and Allen Ginsberg, the latter whose collection of poems **Howl** celebrated homosexuality and sparked an obscenity case. The quartet's careers blossomed in the late 1940s and early 1950s.

The four became close companions, with Kerouac, Ginsberg and Burroughs first meeting in the early 1940s and Corso joining the gang by 1950. These authors became characters in each other's novels and poetry and critiqued each other's writings. To this quartet and the Beat writers who followed, American culture in the 1950s smothered individualism and creativity. Dim-witted TV comedies, frozen foods, maddeningly repetitive and depersonalized neighborhoods such as Levittown, and the constant hypocritical praise for the "nuclear family" represented a phony, living death for Beat novelists and poets.

The Beats wrote in a self-consciously slapdash, helter-skelter style that reflected their hatred of dehumanizing, super-efficient corporations and bureaucracy. Giant companies like the computer firm IBM or the Ford Motor Company reminded the Beats of Nazi-like totalitarianism. "A bureau takes root anywhere in the state," William Burroughs wrote in *Naked Lunch*. "Turns malignant like the Narcotics Bureau, and grows and grows, always reproducing more of its own kind, until it chokes the host if not controlled or excised. Bureaus cannot live without a host, being true parasitic organisms . . . Bureaucracy is as wrong as a cancer . . ." Burroughs undermined linear thinking and the normal organization of a novel with a mad glee in *Naked Lunch*, a book in which vignettes were randomly sorted to defy any conventional sense of narrative.

The Beat writers celebrated brutal self-honesty, merging the personal and the political even as they painfully confessed sexual anxiety and self-doubt, politically incorrect thoughts, homosexual crushes, and moments of petty violence and criminality. Their lives often proved as chaotic as their writing. Such was the case with Allen Ginsberg, a gay Jew whose mother was an institutionalized schizophrenic and who was sent to a mental institution himself, and William Burroughs, a heroin addict who accidentally killed his wife trying to shoot an apple off her head in imitation of William Tell during a drug binge in Mexico. Ginsberg only had to look to his friends for inspiration when he wrote the opening lines of "Howl," his groundbreaking 1956 poem:

> I saw the best minds of my generation destroyed by madness, starving hysterical naked, dragging themselves through the negro streets at dawn looking for an angry fix

The erection of the interstate highway system had smoothed over regional accents and local distinctiveness even as the rise of chain stores and restaurants had homogenized the American landscape. In response, Beats wanted to rediscover the unique and the authentic. Wishing to escape the plastic bubble of urban America, Jack Kerouac exclaimed in one letter, "I want to be left alone. I want to sit in the grass. I want to ride my horse. I want to lay a woman naked in the grass on the mountainside. I want to think. I want to pray. I want to sleep. I want to look at the stars . . . I want to get and prepare my own food, with my own hands, and live that way . . ."

Beats idealized African Americans as living genuine lives as an oppressed people alienated from mainstream culture. The mostly white beatniks could be maddeningly unaware of black suffering and exoticized African Americans as noble savages close to nature. Kerouac, author of works like *The Subterraneans* and *The Dharma Bums*, achieved fame with his epic novel *On the Road*, which followed the aimless wanderings of Salvatore Paradise and

Dean Moriarty as they drive across America, get drunk, read poems, and make love. Marked by unrealistic and condescending depictions of African Americans, *On The Road* in one scene features the narrator thinking as he strolls through the streets of Denver that he wishes he "could exchange worlds with the happy, true-hearted, ecstatic Negroes of America." Kerouac reduces African Americans to childlike noble savages and never acknowledges the violence, poverty and political marginalization experiences by such "happy Negroes."

The pace of the book, alternating between languid and frantic, derived from the art of African-American bebop musicians. Bebop artists broke the mold of the big band jazz music dominant in the early 1940s. As rebels, they earned the adoration of Beats like Kerouac. Exemplified by artists such as Charlie Parker and Dizzy Gillespie, Bebop focused on individual performers who rejected the limits of conventional tonality. Bebop influenced other art forms. Jackson Pollack brought a Bebop sensibility to his paintings, a series of wild color splashes that led some critics to dismiss him as "Jack the Dripper." Comedian Lenny Bruce, whose standup routines touched on political issues such as segregation and popular culture, and who explicitly attacked the hypocrisy of American attitudes toward sex (often using four-letter words that would get him arrested for obscenity) also derived his style from Bebop musicians and became a Beat icon.

The most visible Beat leaders such as Kerouac and Burroughs came of age in the 1930s and 1940s. Primarily older men and women, some of them Korean War veterans, occupied the original Beat enclave in Venice West near Los Angeles. In later Beat communities, such as North Beach near San Francisco, and Greenwich Village in the late 1950s, the population was mostly between the ages of 18 and 28 and more closely resembled the stereotypical youthful image of finger-snapping artists hanging out at coffee houses and reading poetry presented in the mass media.

Older audiences saw the Beats as threatening, and the television comedy *The Many Lives of Dobie Gillis* marginalized the movement with the portrayal of the satirical Beatnik character Maynard G. Krebbs, who devoted his life mostly to avoiding work. Nevertheless, many new Hollywood actors in the 1950s took their cues from the Beat movement and became major youth culture idols along the way. The acting technique of stars such as James Dean, Marlon Brando, Paul Newman, and Montgomery Clift derived much from the attitude of characters in novels like *On the Road*. Movies such as *The Man with the Golden Arm* (1956), that starred popular singer Frank Sinatra as a jazz-playing junkie, and *All the Fine Young Cannibals* (1959), featuring Robert Wagner, aimed to capture the romance of the Beat hipster scene. Films like *Rebel Without a Cause* and *The Wild One* (1953) tried to capture Beat nihilism and rebelliousness. Not surprisingly, many of these films won a large audience of alienated teenagers eager to escape neighborhoods of look-alike homes and conformist values. Dean, who died in a car crash in 1955 at age 24 after starring in just three major films, and Brando both became major icons for a generation of frustrated and bored suburban kids.

"SEDUCTION OF THE INNOCENT": The Comic Book Wars

Many World War II soldiers had not left their teens, and they brought youthful reading habits with them to the front. Comic book publishers provided free copies of *Superman*, *Batman*, the detective series *Dick Tracy*, and science fiction fare to appreciative servicemen during World War II. Many of these young men continued to feed their new comic book habit when they returned to the United States. The expanding youth market of the **Baby Boom** era supplemented veterans as the readership for comic books grew exponentially in the late 1940s and early 1950s. After the war, many comic books took a more sexual and violent turn. Perhaps frightened and deeply marked by the horrors of the Second World War, the Holocaust, the atomic bombings of Hiroshima and Nagasaki, and the war that had just broken out in Korea, young readers enjoyed escaping into the fantasy bloodshed regularly featured in the popular new "horror comics" like *Tales from the Crypt*, *The Crypt of Terror*, *The Vault of Horror* and *Weird*, many published by EC, a company run by William M. Gaines.

The content of the horror comics reflected the youthful distrust of the phony pieties surrounding institutions such as marriage, the family, and even the "American Pastime." In these stories, weaklings turn the tables on the strong, thus appealing to youths coping with schoolyard bullies or the random dictates of their parents. In one story, a housewife can no longer stand the tyranny of her obsessively neat, orderly husband. She murders him and when police arrive they see jars containing body parts labeled kneecaps (2), toes (10), heart (1), etc. The wife, Eleanor, tells a detective, "I remember wanting to show him I could be neat! I wanted it to be a neat job! I cleaned up everything when I finished!" In another horror tale, "Foul Play," a ruthless baseball player murders an opponent by sliding into him with poisoned spikes. The victim's teammates take revenge by dismembering the murderer and, during a ghoulish midnight game, using his limbs as bats and his organs as bases.

Gaines's horror comics also published illustrated versions of budding science fiction writers like Ray Bradbury. His artists intentionally defied convention, drawing villains to resemble the pope and heroes to bear a striking resemblance to Soviet dictator Joseph Stalin. Gaines also published *Mad Magazine*, founded in 1952, which in its early years parodied other comic books like *Superman*, the teenage comedy *Archie*, and even Walt Disney's *Mickey Mouse*.

With the horror comics adding to the violent content common on television police dramas and Westerns, many figures like **Dr. Frederic Wertham**, a famous Freudian psychiatrist, began to warn of the alleged effects of popular culture on young people. Wertham's 1954 book *The Seduction of the Innocent: The Influence of Comic Books on Today's Youth* attacked comic books like *Batman* for the supposed subliminal homosexual relationship between the title hero and his youthful sidekick Robin. Wertham claimed that comic books glorified violence as a solution to all problems, and that the industry generally promoted juvenile delinquency and anti-social behavior with its illustrations of gore and scantily clad women. "All comic books with their words and expletives in balloons are bad for reading, but not every comic book is bad for children's minds and emotions," Werthem wrote. "The trouble is that the 'good' comic books are snowed under by those which glorify violence and crime."

Pressure built up for policing the industry and a bill passed the state legislature in New York, where most of the comic books were published. Had it become law, the bill would have regulated what themes and images could appear in such publications. New York Governor Thomas Dewey vetoed the bill, but the controversy only increased after an issue of *Panic*, another humor magazine like *Mad* published by William Gaines, released an issue with a cover illustration called "The Night Before Christmas." The drawing featured Santa Claus in a sled decorated with a "Just Divorced" sign and a meat cleaver, two daggers and an ash can tied to the rear. New York City police arrested an EC comics staffer on charges of selling "disgusting" literature when they objected to the content of another Gaines publication.

A Senate investigating committee held a special hearing in New York City, and Gaines agreed to testify. On a diet that involved taking dexedrine, a stimulant that kept the publisher from sleeping, Gaines arrived at the hearings feeling groggy. Sen. Estes Kefauver of Tennessee held up a cover of one EC comic and, pointing to its typically gory cover said, "This seems to be a man with a bloody axe holding a woman's head up, which has been severed from her body. Do you think that's in good taste?" Gaines replied, "Yes, sir, I do—for the cover of a horror comic. A cover in bad taste, for example, might be defined as holding the head a little higher so the blood could be seen dripping from it . . ." Gaines went on in more graphic detail oblivious to the shocked murmur building up in the hearing room. The next day journalists mocked Gaines's claim that the cover was in good taste, with one, Max Lerner, concluding that, "This means that society is a jungle—a proposition we cannot accept."

Fearing public backlash and the possibility of boycotts, comic book publishers responded to the New York hearings by forming the Comics Magazine Association of America, which in turn created the Comics Code Authority. The CCA would give or withhold from each issue of each comic book a seal of approval. To earn the seal, comic book stories could not in any way create sympathy for criminals; cause disrespect for police, judges, or other government officials; had to always present good as triumphing over evil; and could never use lurid or gory images to accompany the content. The code forbade the words "terror" or "horror" in comic book titles, as well as scenes of bloodshed, cannibalism, or sadism. Urging his wholesalers not to submit to censorship, Gaines protested, "This is what our forefathers came to America to escape." Gaines decided to stop publishing the horror comics, he claimed, because that's what parents wanted, but he also knew that distributors and stores that sold comic books would no longer carry publications like *Tales from the Crypt*.

With bland content now mandated voluntarily by the industry, comic book sales plummeted. For instance, in 1955, DC Comics (which published *Superman* and *Batman*) sold 10.5 million copies of all its publications. Two years later, sales had dropped by more than 50 percent. Meanwhile, Gaines switched his focus to *Mad Magazine*, which expanded its focus to satirize politics, television programs, popular music, social movements, and advertising. Publishing *Mad* as a "magazine," Gaines would not have to worry about compliance with the comic books code. *Mad* became far more rebellious and anti-establishment than any of the horror comics had ever been. Using famous comedy writers like Stan Freberg, Tom Lehrer, Ernie Kovacs, and Bob and Ray in addition to its usual staff writers, *Mad* became a major inspiration for later comedy television programs like *Saturday Night Live* and *The Simpsons* and the online newspaper parody *The Onion*.

ROCK 'N' ROLL

Horror comics may not have survived the early 1950s, but the Baby Boom audience that read these publications

THE COMICS CODE
Code For Editorial Matter

General Standards Part A:

1) Crimes shall never be presented in such a way as to create sympathy for the criminal, to promote distrust of the forces of law and justice, or to inspire others with a desire to imitate criminals.
2) No comics shall explicitly present the unique details and methods of a crime.
3) Policemen, judges, government officials, and respected institutions shall never be presented in such a way as to create disrespect for established authority.
4) If crime is depicted it shall be as a sordid and unpleasant activity.
5) Criminals shall not be presented so as to be rendered glamorous or to occupy a position which creates the desire for emulation.
6) In every instance good shall triumph over evil and the criminal punished for his misdeeds.
7) Scenes of excessive violence shall be prohibited. Scenes of brutal torture, excessive and unnecessary knife and gun play, physical agony, gory and gruesome crime shall be eliminated.
8) No unique or unusual methods of concealing weapons shall be shown.
9) Instances of law enforcement officers dying as a result of a criminal's activities should be discouraged.
10) The crime of kidnapping shall never be portrayed in any detail, nor shall any profit accrue to the abductor or kidnapper. The criminal or the kidnapper must be punished in every case.
11) The letters of the word "crime" on a comics magazine shall never be appreciably greater than the other words contained in the title. The word "crime" shall never appear alone on a cover.
12) Restraint in the use of the word "crime" in titles or subtitles shall be exercised.

General Standards Part B:

1) No comic magazine shall use the word "horror" or "terror" in its title.
2) All scenes of horror, excessive bloodshed, gory or gruesome crimes, depravity, lust, sadism, masochism shall not be permitted.
3) All lurid, unsavory, gruesome illustrations shall be eliminated.
4) Inclusion of stories dealing with evil shall be used or shall be published only where the intent is to illustrate a moral issue and in no case shall evil be presented alluringly nor so as to injure the sensibilities of the reader.
5) Scenes dealing with, or instruments associated with walking dead, torture, vampires and vampirism, ghouls, cannibalism, and werewolfism are prohibited.

General Standards Part C:

All elements or techniques not specifically mentioned herein, but which are contrary to the spirit and intent of the Code, and are considered violations of good taste or decency, shall be prohibited.

Dialogue:
1) Profanity, obscenity, smut, vulgarity, or words or symbols which have acquired undesirable meanings are forbidden.
2) Special precautions to avoid references to physical afflictions or deformities shall be taken.
3) Although slang and colloquialisms are acceptable, excessive use should be discouraged and wherever possible good grammar shall be employed.

Religion:
Ridicule or attack on any religious or racial group is never permissible.

Costume:
   1) Nudity in any form is prohibited, as is indecent or undue exposure.
   2) Suggestive and salacious illustration or suggestive posture is unacceptable.
   3) All characters shall be depicted in dress reasonably acceptable to society.
   4) Females shall be drawn realistically without exaggeration of any physical qualities.

NOTE: *It should be recognized that all prohibitions dealing with costume, dialogue, or artwork applies as specifically to the cover of a comic magazine as they do to the contents.*

Marriage and Sex:
   1) Divorce shall not be treated humorously nor shall be represented as desirable.
   2) Illicit sex relations are neither to be hinted at nor portrayed. Violent love scenes as well as sexual abnormalities are unacceptable.
   3) Respect for parents, the moral code, and for honorable behavior shall be fostered. A sympathetic understanding of the problems of love is not a license for moral distortion.
   4) The treatment of love-romance stories shall emphasize the value of the home and the sanctity of marriage.
   5) Passion or romantic interest shall never be treated in such a way as to stimulate the lower and baser emotions.
   6) Seduction and rape shall never be shown or suggested.
   7) Sex perversion or any inference to same is strictly forbidden.

Code For Advertising Matter:

These regulations are applicable to all magazines published by members of the Comics Magazine Association of America, Inc. Good taste shall be the guiding principle in the acceptance of advertising.

   1) Liquor and tobacco advertising is not acceptable.
   2) Advertisement of sex or sex instructions books are unacceptable.
   3) The sale of picture postcards, "pin-ups," "art studies," or any other reproduction of nude or semi-nude figures is prohibited.
   4) Advertising for the sale of knives, concealable weapons, or realistic gun facsimiles is prohibited.
   5) Advertising for the sale of fireworks is prohibited.
   6) Advertising dealing with the sale of gambling equipment or printed matter dealing with gambling shall not be accepted.
   7) Nudity with meretricious purpose and salacious postures shall not be permitted in the advertising of any product; clothed figures shall never be presented in such a way as to be offensive or contrary to good taste or morals.
   8) To the best of his ability, each publisher shall ascertain that all statements made in advertisements conform to the fact and avoid misinterpretation.
   9) Advertisement of medical, health, or toiletry products of questionable nature are to be rejected. Advertisements for medical, health or toiletry products endorsed by the American Medical Association, or the American Dental Association, shall be deemed acceptable if they conform with all other conditions of the Advertising Code.

would serve as the fans for one of the most durable creations of the decade: rock 'n' roll. The ultimate origins of rock music can be found in the ring shouts of West Africa. A form of praying, singing, and dancing performed as participants stood in a circle, ring shouts broke out during weddings, funerals and other religious rituals throughout West and Central Africa, the ancestral homeland of most African Americans. According to historian of African-American culture Sterling Stuckey, these ceremonies served as "a means of achieving union with God."

Music critic Robert Palmer describes the music brought from Africa to North America as sharing many traits with later rock music. "It was participatory; often a song leader would be pitted against an answering chorus, or a solo instrument against an ensemble, in call-and-response fashion," Palmer said. "It sometimes attained remarkable polyrhythmic complexity and always had a kind of percussive directionality or rhythmic drive."

Over the 200-plus years of American slavery, African music forms blended with European folk melodies and structure as the inspiration for work songs used by blacks to keep time, raise spirits and make moral comment on their slave masters as they worked in the fields. Slave songs also led to black gospel music while the West African call-and-response style formed the structure of both jazz and blues songs composed by black artists in the early twentieth century along the Mississippi River from Chicago to Memphis to New Orleans. Another source for rock music came from the boogie style of piano-playing inspired by the hectic pace of life in African-American urban neighborhoods. With the structure of a blues band centered on a lead singer backed by the guitar, drums, bass and piano in various combinations, the way was paved for the rise of rock music.

The basic form of the rock song was in place when the folklorists John and Alan Lomax recorded a black gospel group performing music in Mississippi in 1934 that, with its steady drumbeat, blues-style melodies and singing rhythms, evoked the slave past while anticipating the future of American popular music. Singing in a style called "rocking and reeling" that incorporated drums, guitars and horns then prevalent in many Southern African American Pentecostal churches, the band performed the song "Run Old Jeremiah," which the Lomaxes recorded for the Library of Congress. The lead vocalist blurted in a gravelly voice:

> O my Lord
> O my Lordy
> Well, well, well
> I gotta rock
> you gotta rock

> Wah wah ho
> Wah wah wah ho

The hand-clapping beat and nonsense syllables would become hallmarks of 1950s rock music. As the music evolved, a new invention—the electric guitar—entered the sound mix. By 1940, pioneer blues artists like T-Bone Walker regularly played electric guitar riffs as part of stage performances. If rock primarily derived from African heritage, however, rural southern white and black musicians fed off of and challenged each other, with Bob Wills and the Texas Playboys playing white backwoods country and western music blended with urban African-American blues and the sophisticated big band sounds from the East Coast to create a new genre called western swing music.

Such musical blending became easier with the development of sound recording in the late nineteenth and early twentieth century and the wider distribution of music records, in the bulky form of 78 rpm "records" by mid-century. The creators of rock 'n' roll could carry on a musical dialogue over a much vaster geographic space than previously imaginable, adding greatly to the emerging rock genre's range of expression. As radio formats changed from comedy and drama programming to music, white children in the late 1940s and early 1950s saw a chance to rebel and experience greater sexual expression as they danced to "race records"—blues songs recorded by black performers like Big Mamma Thornton and Fats Domino.

Memphis became an incubator for rock music by the early 1950s. Guitar masters like B.B. King stretched the boundaries of urban blues even as record producer Sam Phillips assembled a stable of artists that would dominate American youth music for the next decade beginning with the self-named Phillips Records, which opened for business in 1950, and then at Sun Records starting in 1952. Over the years, Phillips would polish raw talents like Jerry Lee Lewis, Carl Perkins, Roy Orbison, and Johnny Cash at tiny studios, launching them into national stardom.

Phillips acted as B.B. King's producer and in 1951 worked with musician Ike Turner on a recording of "Rocket 88," a number in praise of the American automobile and highlighted by a fuzzy, highly amplified electric guitar playing to a boogie rhythm. The lyrics and the arrangement have led many music historians to label "Rocket 88" as the first rock 'n' roll single. "Rocket 88" would soon also be recorded by Bill Haley and the Comets. Haley later released the hit "Rock Around the Clock," a top-seller featured on the sound track of the juvenile delinquency-themed movie *The Blackboard Jungle*.

Haley would be one of many white artists who made hit versions of songs originally written and performed by

AMERICAN CULTURE FROM 1945-1960 / 869

black musicians and composers. Most African-American performers remained uncompensated when white singers recorded hits based on their songs. Nevertheless, the rapid rise of rock music opened the door for black performers like Fats Domino, Little Richard, and Chuck Berry to win an army of young white fans and to reach an even larger audience through variety programs like *The Ed Sullivan Show*. No black or white artist, however, matched the popularity or fame of **Elvis Aaron Presley,** born to a dirt-poor Tupelo, Mississippi, family in 1935.

Presley spent his childhood listening to gospel music at his parents' First Assembly of God Church. "Since I was two years old, all I knew was gospel music; that was music to me," Presley later recalled. "We borrowed the style of our psalm singing from the early Negroes. We used to go to these religious singings all the time. The preachers cut up all over the place, jumping on the piano, moving every which way . . . I loved the music. It became such a part of my life it was as natural as dancing . . . a way to escape from the problems and my way of release."

Sam Phillips would produce and engineer a custom-made record for anyone who came into his studio for $2 a side. In 1954, Elvis Presley appeared at the studio to record a pair of songs for his mother. Presley lobbied Phillips to record him for a professional release and the collaboration produced a single of the old blues number, "That's All Right." Phillips delivered a tape of the session to a Memphis radio station where a friendly disc jockey played the song six times in a row to an enthusiastic listening audience. By the time the record was finally released, there was a back order of 5,000 copies in the Memphis area, before the recording reached number one on the city's country and western sales charts. By mid-1955, Presley enjoyed his first national country and western hit.

Signed by the flamboyant agent "Colonel" Tom Parker, who would over the years cheat his protégé out of millions of dollars, Presley would become the first rock 'n' roll superstar. He recorded a remarkable string of number one hits such as "Heartbreak Hotel," "Hound Dog," and "Jailhouse Rock." Presley's curling upper lip, untamed bangs and erotically charged dance moves led teenage girls in his audience to scream and weep. His openly sexual approach to music stirred controversy and attracted gigantic audiences when he appeared on the *Milton Berle* and *Ed Sullivan* television shows. Parents worried that Presley's music would inspire sexual promiscuity among excited teenage girls. Alarmed by the clear influence of black music on white performers like Presley and other rock stars, the secretary of the North Alabama White Citizens Council warned in a 1956 television message that "Rock and roll is a means of pulling the white man down to the level of the Negro. It is part of a plot to undermine the morals of the youth of our nation."

In 1950s, adults also perceived rock 'n' roll as "children's music," as comedian Tom Lehrer put it. Newspapers and magazines disparaged youth culture and paid it scant attention. When an airplane crash in 1959 killed rock stars Buddy Holly, Ritchie Valens, and J.P. Richardson, famous as the "Big Bopper," many newspapers ran the story on inside pages. But rock 'n' roll would be

**President Dwight Eisenhower receives a group of prominent civil rights leaders.
(L to R) Lester Granger, Dr. Martin Luther King, Jr., E. Frederic Morrow, President Eisenhower, A. Philip Randolph, William Rogers, Rocco Siciliano, and Roy Wilkins.
June 23, 1958
Credit: Eisenhower Presidential Library**

influenced by politically oriented folk-music recorded by singer-songwriter Bob Dylan and others in the early 1960s, and would exercise a profound effect on the adult politics of war and civil rights in the coming decade. Young whites who eagerly bought rock records featuring songs written by or first performed by black musicians or released by black artists themselves developed an appreciation for African-American culture that deeply influenced the attitudes of the Sixties generation.

THE LASTING INFLUENCE OF THE 1950s

In 1971, singer-songwriter Don McLean released an epic hit song, "American Pie," which traced in symbolic language the journey of American politics and culture from the time of the plane crash that killed Buddy Holly and his fellow rock stars in 1959 to the assassinations and climate of fear that menaced society by the end of the 1960s. In McLean's lyrics, Buddy Holly's death is characterized as the "day the music died," but more broadly the songwriter suggests that America passed from a more innocent time just after World War II to an epoch of disillusionment and division during the Vietnam War.

That image of the 1950s as placid and monotone resulted from a conscious propaganda effort by American elites, according to English scholar Alan Nadel. He argues in *Containment Culture: American Narrative, Postmodernism and the Atomic Age* that the politically powerful in the immediate post-World War II era sought not only to contain communism—to prevent the Soviet empire from expanding beyond Eastern Europe—but to contain the revolutionary changes in family life that had taken place during the Great Depression and World War II. In the tumultuous 16-year period from 1929 to 1945, women had often served as the primary breadwinners for the family and managed the home alone while their husbands wandered off in search of work or to fight in Europe and Asia. These women had experienced, often for the first time, relatively decent wages and the wider social circle at factory shop floors, and came away from these experiences yearning for a life beyond the home.

The expectations, frustrations, and dreams that fueled the Women's Movement of the 1960s and 1970s—what Betty Friedan would call "the problem with no name"—were in place by the early 1950s. The African American Civil Rights Movement, meanwhile, had already reached full tilt and blacks had already scored some of their most important legal victories in their campaign for equality before 1960, starting with the 1954 *Brown v. Board of Education* decision. Mexican-American politics remained largely shaped by conservatism, but young Mexicans had before them the model of black protestors. The triumphs and tragedy of the African American civil rights campaign in the Fifties inspired a more radical *Chicano* generation a decade later. Turmoil marked the Fifties, with only some of the ferment under the surface.

American sexual attitudes had always been more varied than the myth promoted by the decade's situation comedies. Most did not live the tame, bland, conformist existence portrayed on programs like *The Donna Reed Show*. Behind the walls of those suburban homes, Americans experimented with premarital sex, adultery, homosexuality and alternative family structures. If the 1960s would be characterized as the "Sexual Revolution," the first shots of that rebellion had been fired in the late 1940s and the 1950s. The popular culture reflected this more open sexuality in advertising. Movies, suffering a loss of audience because of the growing ownership of television sets, also became more frankly erotic in content.

Behind a sexual opening up of the culture loomed a growing awareness of the mass market provided by those millions of children born during the Baby Boom. In the earliest days of television, children's programs rapidly expanded and advertisers realized they could go over the heads of parents and aim their commercials for toy guns, Barbie Dolls and G.I. Joe soldiers directly at children. As these children reached a rebellious adolescence, they wanted music, magazines, and movies that pushed the cultural envelope, that pierced the veil of the hypocritically Victorian middle class. Their parents' generation, with its supposedly more traditional values, had forced their children to live in the shadow of nuclear mushroom clouds.

By the late twentieth century, conservatives would hail the 1950s as the "anti-1960s," in other words a golden age of sexual discretion, intact nuclear families, patriotism, traditional values, and a respect for authority. Hollywood movies of the era, however, reveal a wide array of anxieties haunting what one 1970s television sitcom called *Happy Days*. The plot of movies from 1945 to 1960 reflect fears not just about the role of men in the post-war world, the impact of more assertive women on society, and the menace of juvenile delinquency. Movie audiences in the 1950s also shared with Hollywood screenwriters worries about the dangers of conformity and McCarthyism (the subtext of the 1956 science fiction classic *Invasion of the Body Snatchers*), and the threat to human survival posed by nuclear weapons (an anxiety evident in a flood of movies about monsters created by radiation such as 1954s *Godzilla and Them!*, and 1955's *It Came From Beneath the Sea*.) Monsters ranging from giant ants to masculinized, ambitious women terrified Americans, many of whom had only to glance at their backyard bomb shelters to be reminded of how fragile their suburban world had become.

The 1950s, however, served as the necessary prelude to the decade of hippies, war protestors, and youth rebellion that would shortly follow. Teenagers who engaged in "heavy petting," who read horror comics, who idolized movie stars like James Dean and rock stars like Elvis, had already walked away from the worldview of their parents. Many youths in the 1960s would conclude that Auschwitz and Hiroshima consumed one world and that a new one must rise from its ashes, but doubts about America's religious values and cultural priorities, its Cold War politics, about the media and the country's leaders, sank deep roots in the fifteen years from 1945 and 1960.

Chronology

1944 *Smith v. Allwright* decision.

1946 President's Committee on Civil Rights issues its report, "To Secure These Rights."
Post war "Baby Boom" begins.

1947 Jackie Robinson breaks Major League Baseball's color barrier.

1948 Executive Order 9981 ordering desegregation of the military.
Delgado v. Bastrop ISD ruling.
Alfred Kinsey's *Sexual Behavior in the Human Male* becomes a bestseller.

1950 United Nations Educational, Scientific and Cultural Organization issues its "Statement on Race."
Sweatt v. Painter decision.

1951 The Mattachine Society forms.

1952 Walter-McCarran Act.

1953 *Playboy Magazine* begins publication.

1954 *Brown v. Board of Education* decision.
The first "White Citizens Council."
Fred Werthem's book *The Seduction of the Innocent: The Influence of Comic Books on Today's Youth* is published.

1955 Emmett Till beaten to death.
Montgomery Bus Boycott begins.

1956 Interstate Commerce Act.
Allen Ginsberg's *Howl* and *Other Poems* is published.
Elvis Presley makes television performances.

1957 The Little Rock school desegregation crisis.
Jack Kerouac's novel *On The Road* is published.

1959 Buddy Holly, Ritchie Valens and J.P. "The Big Bopper" Richardson, die in a plane crash.

Review Questions

1. What factors led to the decline of scientific racism and to President Harry Truman's support for Civil Rights for African Americans after World War II?

2. What legal cases led to the overturn of segregation at public schools and colleges and in what ways did white Southerners resist implementation of these decisions?

3. What changes happened in the lives of American women after World War II and how were women portrayed in the culture?

4. What themes did the Beatniks explore in their novels and their poetry and what impact did they have on the broader American culture.

5. How did American adults view youth culture—comic books, science fiction, and rock 'n' roll—in the 1950s?

Glossary of Important People and Concepts

American GI Forum
Anti-Semitism
Army IQ tests
Baby Boom
Brown v. Board of Education of Topeka (1954)
Eugenics
Executive Order 9981
Orval Faubus
Howl
I Love Lucy
Interstate Highway Act of 1956
Alfred Kinsey
Little Rock Crisis
League of United Latin American Citizens (LULAC)
Mad Magazine
"Massive Resistance"
Mattachine Society
Montgomery Bus Boycott
On The Road
"Operation Wetback"
Rosa Parks
Playboy
President's Committee on Civil Rights
Elvis Presley
Rebel Without A Cause
Jackie Robinson
Margaret Sanger
"Statement on Race"
Sweatt v. Painter (1950)
Emmett Till

SUGGESTED READINGS

Robert H. Abzug. *Inside the Vicious Heart: Americans and the Liberation of Nazi Concentration Camps* (1985).

Rodolfo Acuña. *Occupied America: A History of Chicanos* (1988).

Elazar Barkan. *The Retreat of Scientific Racism: Changing Concepts of Race in Britain and the United States between the World Wars* (1993).

Edwin Black. *War Against the Weak: Eugenics and America's Campaign to Create a Master Race* (2003).

Mark Bowden. *The Greatest Game Ever: Giants vs. Colts, 1958, and the Birth of the Modern NFL* (2008).

Taylor Branch. *Parting The Waters: America in the King Years, 1954-63* (1988).

Stephanie Coontz. *The Way We Never Were: American Families and the Nostalgia Trap* (2000).

Arnoldo de León. *Mexican Americans in Texas: A Brief History* (1999).

John D'Emilio and Estelle B. Freedman. *Intimate Matters: A History of Sexuality in America* (1997).

Leonard Dinnerstein. *Anti-Semitism in America* (1994).

Mary L. Dudziak. *Cold War Civil Rights: Race and the Image of American Democracy* (2000).

Melvin Patrick Ely. *The Adventures of Amos 'n' Andy: A Social History of an American Phenomenon* (1991).

Adam Fairclough. *Better Day Coming: Blacks and Equality, 1890-2000* (2001).

Neil Foley. *Quest for Equality: The Failed Promise of Black-Brown Solidarity* (2010).

Byrne Fone. *Homophobia: A History* (2000).

Edward Halsey Foster. *Understanding the Beats* (1992).

Raymond H. Gesselbracht. *The Civil Rights Legacy of Harry S Truman* (2007).

Michael Lowery Gillette, "Heman Sweatt: Civil Rights Plaintiff," in Alwyn Barr and Robert A. Calvert, eds., *Black Leaders: Texans for their Times* (1981).

Allen Ginsberg. *Howl and Other Poems* (1956).

Sherna Berger Gluck. *Rosie the Riveter Revisited: Women, the War and Social Change* (1988).

Albert Goldman. *Ladies and Gentlemen, Lenny Bruce!!* (1971).

Stephen Jay Gould. *The Mismeasure of Man* (1981).

Peter Guralnick. "Elvis Presley" in Anthony DeCurtis, and James Henke with Holly George-Warren, *The Rolling Stone Illustrated History of Rock & Roll* (1992).

David Halberstam. *The Fifties* (1993).

Frank Jacobs. *The Mad World of William M. Gaines* (1972).

Jack Kerouac. *On the Road* (1957).

Richard Kluger. *Simple Justice: The History of Brown v. Board of Education and Black America's Struggle for Equality* (1975).

Arthur and Kit Knight. *The Beat Vision: A Primary Sourcebook* (1987).

Stephen Krensky. *Comic Book Century: The History of American Comic Books* (2008).

Edward J. Larson. *Sex, Race and Science: Eugenics in the Deep South* (1995).

William J. Leuchtenburg. "The Conversion of Harry Truman." AmericanHeritage.com. http://www.americanheritage.com/articles/magazine/ah/1991/7/1991_7_55.shtml (1991).

Elaine Tyler May. *Homeward Bound: American Families in the Cold War Era* (1988).

David Morgan. "Yale Study: U.S. Eugenics Paralleled Nazi Germany," February 15, 2000 *Chicago Tribune*.

Alan Nadel. *Containment Culture: American Narratives, Postmodernism, and the Atomic Age* (1995).

Peter Novick. *The Holocaust in American Life* (1999).

Robert Palmer. "Rock Begins" in Anthony DeCurtis, and James Henke with Holly George-Warren, *The Rolling Stone Illustrated History of Rock & Roll* (1992).

Michael Phillips. *White Metropolis: Race, Ethnicity and Religion in Dallas, 1841-2001* (2006).

Eric Schlosser. *Fast Food Nation: The Dark Side of the All-American Meal* (2002).

Amilcar Shabazz. *Advancing Democracy: African Americans and the Struggle for Access and Equity in Higher Education in Texas* (2006).

Harvard Sitkoff. *The Struggle for Black Equality, 1954-1980* (1981).

Gregory Stephenson. *The Daybreak Boys: Essays on the Literature of the Beat Generation* (1990).

Sterling Stuckey. *Slave Culture: Nationalist Theory and the Foundations of Black America* (1987).

David Quentin Voigt. *American Baseball Volume III: From Postwar Expansion to the Electronic Age* (1979).

Frederic Wertham. *The Seduction of the Innocent: The Influence of Comic Books on Today's Youth* (1954).

Joel Williamson. *A Rage for Order: Black-White Relations in the American South since Emancipation* (1986).

Marc Scott Zicree. *The Twilight Zone Companion* (1982).

The entrance to the "Negro Waiting Room" at the Katy Depot in San Antonio, Texas in 1956.

Chapter Twenty-eight

REFORM AND BACKLASH UNDER KENNEDY AND JOHNSON

In Mississippi, during the civil rights campaign of the 1950s and early 1960s, white people had a license to kill African Americans. In Liberty on September 25, 1961, a member of the all-white state legislature, E.H. Hurst, murdered an African-American man and former childhood friend, Herbert Lee, when the latter tried to register as a voter. In front of a cotton gin, Hurst shot Lee in the head as he sat in the cab of his truck. Lee fell out of the vehicle, and his body was left lying in an expanding pool of blood for two hours before a black undertaker picked up the body.

A farmer and father of nine, Lee had been active in the voter registration drive conducted in the black community by the Student Nonviolent Coordinating Committee (SNCC). He acted as a chauffeur for the group's leader, **Robert Paris Moses**, *a Harlem native who moved to the rural community to head the campaign. Even though Hurst murdered Lee outdoors in broad daylight in front of several witnesses, a coroner's jury ruled the death a justifiable homicide. Hurst claimed that Lee owed him money and became threatening when the politician demanded payment. Hurst also told the jury he had accidentally pulled the trigger on his .38 pistol. One African-American witness, Louis Allen, had been threatened and out of fear testified before the jury that the five-foot-four Lee had tried to strike Hurst, who stood more than six feet, in the head with a tire iron.*

By October, a federal grand jury had convened to consider indicting Hurst for violating Lee's civil rights. Allen told Moses that he was willing to recant his earlier statements and would testify that Hurst killed Lee without provocation. Moses called the U.S. Department of Justice and tried to get *protection for Allen, but the DOJ turned him down. Later, an FBI agent tipped off the local sheriff's department that Allen was planning to testify against Hurst. Allen was attacked, the assailant breaking the witness's jaw with a flashlight. Shortly thereafter, on January 31, 1964, an assassin killed Allen with three shotgun blasts. That killer also was never punished.*

THE SIT-IN MOVEMENT

Even though the United States Supreme Court had ruled school segregation unconstitutional in the *Brown v. Board of Education* decision in 1954, by 1959 more than 99 percent of black and white students in the South still attended Jim Crow campuses. Across the former Confederacy, states denied African Americans the right to vote in spite of a **1957 civil rights law** passed by Congress that reaffirmed the Fourteenth and Fifteenth Amendments to the U.S. Constitution. These amendments guaranteed voting rights regardless of race or color. Throughout the South, blacks who asserted their constitutional rights to vote, or to sit near white people in movie theaters or on buses, faced getting fired or physical violence.

Tired of continued discrimination, four African-American students at North Carolina A&T College in Greensboro, N.C., Ezell Blair, Franklin McCain, Joseph McNeil, J.R. David Richmond, and white NAACP member Ralph Johns planned a direct blow against local segregation laws. After buying school supplies to establish that they were paying customers, the five staged a "**sit-in**" at the segregated lunch counter at the town's F.W. Woolworth Company department store February 1, 1960. "We believe, since we buy books and papers in the other part of the store, we should get served in this part," one of the students told a wire service reporter from United Press International. The demonstrators asked for coffee. A black dishwasher, fearful of losing her job, castigated them. "You're acting stupid, ignorant," she said. A white policeman closely watched the students and struck his billy club against the palm of his hand. C.L. Harris, the store manager, chose to ignore the five protestors. "They can just sit there. It's nothing to me." The five protestors sat at the lunch counter for hours as some white customers, assuming the men didn't know any better, told them that they were at a "whites only" counter. Others cursed them while a small number patted them on the back and expressed support.

Protestors proved much harder to ignore the next day. Twenty-five participated in a second sit-in. On the third day, 85 showed up. The fourth straight day of sit-ins included white students from the University of North Carolina's Women's College in Greensboro. Soon, North Carolina students staged sit-ins at theaters, drugstores, and other businesses in a dozen towns across the state. Sit-ins bedeviled Jim Crow businesses outside of the state, in Hampton, Virginia; and in Chattanooga and Nashville, Tennessee. In Little Rock, Arkansas, sit-in participants sported buttons that said, "I am wearing 1959 clothes with 1960 dignity." On the seventh day of the campaign, civil rights demonstrators held 54 sit-ins in fifteen cities and nine states across the former Confederacy. Eventually 70,000 Americans would participate in the sit-in movement of 1960, and 3,000 would be arrested, with the demonstrations breaking out even as far away as Nevada.

If the first sit-ins were spontaneous, as the movement spread, such demonstrations became more organized, with students receiving training in the non-violent techniques established by civil rights leaders like **Martin Luther King, Jr.**, and his allies in the 1950s. Over Easter weekend, 1960, Ella Baker of the Southern Christian Leadership Conference (SCLC) (a group led by King) presided over a meeting of sit-in protestors from across the country dubbed the "Sacrifice for Dignity" at Shaw University in Raleigh, North Carolina. Baker urged the students to form their own civil rights organization, independent from older groups like the NAACP and the Congress of Racial Equality. They formed the Student Nonviolent Coordinating Committee (better known as the SNCC or "Snick") to direct the national sit-in campaign. In Nashville, protestors received a list of "Do's" and "Don'ts": "Do show yourself friendly on the counter at all times.

Do sit straight and always face the counter. Don't strike back or curse back if attacked. Don't laugh out. Don't hold conversations. Don't block entrances."

Stores resisting desegregation soon displayed signs that proclaimed "No Trespassing" and "We Reserve the Right to Service the Public as We See Fit." The protests were now receiving national media attention. As the non-violent sit-ins spread, whites often responded with brutality. At Nashville lunch counters, angry local whites burned the backs of black women with lit cigarettes, while in Biloxi, Mississippi, whites shot and wounded ten African Americans gathered at a public beach. As newspaper photographers snapped pictures and television cameras rolled, whites hit well-dressed, well-behaved black students, poured ketchup and mustard on their heads and pulled them off of stools.

Such scenes had a profound impact on newspaper and magazine readers and television viewers across the country, with African-American activists winning sympathy from white audiences in the North, Midwest, and the West Coast. Even white southern elites cringed at the spectacle of crude hoodlums bullying the brave and dignified sit-in participants. Long portrayed as inferior and uncivilized, African Americans projected an intelligent and even saintly image as they endured the blows of uneducated thugs. "Here were the colored students, in coats, white shirts, ties, and one of them was reading Goethe and one was taking notes from a biology text," wrote conservative and segregationist newspaper columnist James J. Kilpatrick of the *Richmond News Leader*. "And here, on the sidewalk outside, was a gang of white boys come to heckle, a ragtail rabble, slack-jawed, black-jacketed, grinning fit to kill, and some of them, God save the mark, were waving the proud and honored flag of the Southern States in the last war fought by gentlemen. Eheu. It gives one pause."

In the North, blacks and whites organized boycotts of chain stores that practiced segregation in the South such as Walgreen's, Woolworth's and S.H. Kress stores. Yolanda Betzbeze Fox, a white former Miss America, protested at Woolworth's stores in New York City, telling reporters, "I'm a Southern girl, but a thinking girl." These sympathy boycotts put serious economic pressure on chain stores whose Dixie affiliates practiced segregation in the South, prompting a variety of reactions ranging from the closing of lunch counters to ending Jim Crow practices.

Change happened more rapidly in the border South. Four theaters and six lunch counters announced an end to segregation in Nashville, Tennessee, on May 10, 1960. Eager to avoid business disruptions and bad publicity, white business leaders and black political leaders worked out plans to quietly desegregate downtown department stores in Galveston and Houston. In Dallas, city leaders formed a Committee of 14 with seven whites and seven blacks. The committee convinced several stores such as Woolworth's and Walgreen's in the spring of 1960 to desegregate lunch counters. Nevertheless, sit-ins broke out all over Dallas, starting in October 1960. In the spring of 1961 a group of fifty-eight white and two black theology students from Southern Methodist University sat in at the lunch counter at the University Drug Store across the street from the college campus. Students began a sit-in at the Titche-Goettinger department store in downtown Dallas.

According to 1960s chronicler Todd Gitlin, the sit-in movement in the first months of the new decade formed a sharp demarcation between the 1950s and the 1960s. "History rarely follows the decimal system as neatly as it did in 1960," the sociology professor wrote in *The Sixties: Years of Hope, Days of Rage*. "Suddenly the campus mood seemed to shift . . . What had been underground flowed to the surface. After all the prologues and precursors, an insurgency materialized, and the climate of opinion began to shift, the way spring announces itself with scents and a scatter of birdsong before the temperature climbs to stay."

THE 1960 PRESIDENTIAL ELECTION

Surprisingly, presidential candidates largely overlooked the civil rights struggle in the 1960 election. Several signs pointed to a favorable year for the Democrats, out of power in the White House for the eight years of Dwight Eisenhower, but the party still relied heavily on its Southern segregationist wing. Senator **John F. Kennedy** of Massachusetts, who waged an unsuccessful campaign to win the party's vice presidential nomination in 1956, opened the race as a top contender because of family money, a highly publicized war record, his personal attractiveness, and the glamour of his wife, the former Jacquelyn Bouvier. Kennedy feared alienating key white southern politicians as he fought an uphill primary battle with two-time presidential nominee Adlai Stevenson, the favorite of the liberal wing, and Senate Majority Leader **Lyndon Johnson** of Texas, who had the support of many key Democratic leaders in the South such as U.S. House Speaker Sam Rayburn, who also hailed from the Lone Star State.

Kennedy avoided discussing civil rights issues as much as he could during his primary battle, and he actively courted and won an early endorsement from arch-segregationist Alabama Gov. John Patterson. Noting that Eisenhower had pulled southern whites into the Republican camp in his 1952 and 1956 campaigns against Stevenson, the eventual GOP nominee, Vice President Richard Nixon, also sought the backing of whites in Dixie who supported Jim Crow laws.

Eisenhower, a World War II hero, would not be on the ballot in 1960, the first of many political problems facing the Republican Party. The Soviet Union's launch of the **Sputnik** space satellite in 1957 panicked many American voters, who feared that the Russians had rapidly caught up or even surpassed the United States in technology and that this might make the country militarily vulnerable. Voters also remembered the 1957-1958 "Eisenhower" recession, in which five million Americans lost their jobs. Reductions in federal spending and tight Federal Reserve Board policies that made borrowing more expensive resulted in reduced consumer spending, which caused the sharpest economic downtown since the end of World War II. In the 1958 off-year elections, Democrats picked up 16 seats in the United States Senate and 49 seats in the House of Representatives to claim a commanding majority. The Republicans controlled only 14 of the lower 48 state legislatures.

Democratic candidates spent the next two years playing on voter fears that the Soviet Union had achieved nuclear supremacy and warned of a non-existent "missile gap" between the two countries. Eisenhower's winter of

Senator Lyndon B. Johnson, Senate Majority Leader, looking out a window, September 1955.
Photo credit: Library of Congress.

discontent grew colder still in May 1960 with the shooting down of American pilot **Francis Gary Powers'** U2 spy plane over the Soviet Union. Eisenhower then suffered the indignity of a Paris summit in which Soviet leader Nikita Khrushchev revealed the American president had lied about aerial espionage over the Soviet Union, got denounced by the Russian premier, and then had to cancel a flight to Japan because of anti-American riots in Tokyo. These events, plus the 1959 Cuban Revolution followed by overtures toward an alliance with the Soviet Union by the island nation's leader Fidel Castro, led many American voters to wonder whether Republicans had lost control of both domestic and international events. "The nation was threatened by a missile gap," writes historian Allen J. Matusow of the American mood at the beginning of 1960. " . . . but Eisenhower was more worried about the budget. The nation needed spiritual inspiration, but Eisenhower was playing golf. The nation needed strong leadership and an activist government, but Eisenhower was old, tired, and increasingly dominated by reactionary advisers."

Democratic Primaries

In spite of their many advantages going into the 1960 presidential race, the Democrats almost lost. Kennedy had essentially run for the presidency since 1957. That year saw publication of his second book, *Profiles in Courage*, a series of biographical sketches of eight senators who defied the wishes of their party or risked political popularity because of principle. There have been persistent rumors that Kennedy family friend and speechwriter Ted Sorenson had ghostwritten the book. In any event, the work became a bestseller and established Kennedy's intellectual credentials. He then won a massive majority in his Senate re-election bid in 1958. Kennedy toured the nation, developed relationships with politicians across the country to build a network of support, and sent aides to acquire political intelligence on opponents and learn about local issues.

Nevertheless, Kennedy had to fight to win over liberals in his own party. His wealthy father, Joseph P. Kennedy, a former ambassador to England, had been seen as an appeaser of Hitler's Germany in the days leading to World War II. The elder Kennedy was a close friend of Red-baiting Sen. Joseph McCarthy. Bobby Kennedy, the Senator's younger brother, had been the minority Democrats' lead staff attorney advising McCarthy's Permanent Subcommittee on Investigations, which had the job of finding alleged communist subversion in the federal government. Finally, during debates on a 1957 Civil Rights Act, John Kennedy had sided with southern segregationists on some issues. Liberals did not trust him because they felt that during his Senate career, as Eleanor Roosevelt said, he had shown "more profile than courage."

Kennedy's obvious intelligence, charm, humor and good looks, however, proved to be potent political weapons. Aware that party leaders wanted a more experienced candidate, like Adlai Stevenson, as the nominee, Kennedy decided to demonstrate his popularity through a series of primary victories. The big challenge came in the West Virginia primary contest against Minnesota Senator **Hubert Humphrey**. Many expected Kennedy's Catholicism to be a problem with West Virginia's overwhelmingly Protestant voters. The only other serious Catholic candidate for president in American history had been Democratic nominee Al Smith in the 1928 presidential race and Smith lost badly, to a large degree because Protestant voters believed that a Catholic president would be subservient to the pope and would weaken American independence.

In speeches Kennedy told voters, "I refuse to believe that I was denied the right to be president on the day I was baptized." During a television broadcast in West Virginia, he said, ". . . [W]hen any man stands on the steps of the capitol and takes the oath of office of president, he is swearing to support the separation of church and state . . . And if he breaks that oath, he is not only committing a crime against the Constitution, for which the Congress can impeach him—and should impeach him—he is committing a sin against God." Kennedy beat Humphrey in the West Virginia primary by a comfortable margin and convinced Democratic Party elders that a Catholic could win the general election. Humphrey dropped out of the

HUBERT HUMPHREY

race and at the Democratic National Convention that summer, Kennedy outmaneuvered his chief rivals, Lyndon Johnson and Adlai Stevenson, to capture the Democratic nomination on the first ballot. In a controversial move protested even by his brother and campaign manager Bobby, Kennedy selected Johnson as his running mate. The move was aimed to comfort southern Democrats but antagonized party liberals who questioned Johnson's commitment to civil rights.

Civil Rights and the 1960 Campaign

On the Republican side, New York Governor **Nelson Rockefeller** attempted to frustrate Vice President Richard Nixon's campaign for the GOP nomination by appealing to liberals within the party on civil rights. Many African Americans grew disgusted with the continued dominance of southern segregationists in the Democratic Party and had voted for Eisenhower in 1956. Some African Americans felt reassured by Eisenhower's use of the National Guard to integrate Central High School in Little Rock, Arkansas, in 1957. Nelson Rockefeller believed that the Republicans had a chance to win the black vote in 1960 and that this could give the party an edge in close races in major northern and midwestern states. Rockefeller demanded a stronger than planned civil rights plank in the 1960 Republican platform and Nixon, also hopeful of winning black support, acquiesced. The platform pledged "vigorous enforcement of civil rights laws," support for "court orders for school desegregation" and creation of "a Commission on Equal Job Opportunity" and "Action to ensure that public transportation and other government authorized services shall be free from segregation."

Nixon tripped over himself trying not to alienate black voters while at the same time hoping to carry white southern voters as successfully as Eisenhower had in 1952 and 1956. Kennedy, meanwhile, described segregation as "irrational" but was largely unaware of the conditions faced by African Americans in the South and seemed to have little emotional investment in the issue. Yet, he realized that the black vote could swing six of the eight most populous states his way in the November elections. Liberal advisors persuaded him to reach out to African Americans. Once, while driving his red convertible through Georgetown on his way to the Senate, Kennedy spotted Harris Wofford trying to get a cab. Wofford was an attorney advising the Democratic campaign on civil rights. Kennedy pulled over, picked Wofford up, and, as his left hand tapped on the car door, the senator said to him, "Now in five minutes, tick off the ten things that a president ought to do to clear up this goddamned civil rights mess." Kennedy soon promised that with a "stroke of the pen" he would end discrimination in federally funded housing. An incident in Georgia, however, provided an important, lucky opportunity for the Democrat to win over African-American voters.

On October 19, less than a month before the election, police arrested civil rights leader Martin Luther King, Jr., along with 53 other African-American protestors at Rich's Department Store in Atlanta, for refusing to leave tables at the segregated Magnolia Room Restaurant. Five days later, authorities released the other protestors from jail, but King was sentenced to four months' hard labor for supposedly driving with a suspended license and was transferred to Reidsville State Prison. Members of the King family feared that the minister would be murdered while in custody.

Nixon instructed aides to tell the press that the Vice President would offer no comment on the issue. The Kennedy campaign, however, saw an immediate opportunity to gain ground with African-American voters. Wofford feared for King's safety and sent an urgent message to Kennedy, who was campaigning in Chicago and in Michigan. Kennedy placed an immediate call to Mrs. King and told her he would see if he could assist the family.

Campaign manager Bobby Kennedy phoned the judge who had sentenced King. "It just burned me up . . . to think of that bastard sentencing a citizen to four months of hard labor for a minor traffic offense and screwing up my brother's campaign and making our country look ridiculous in front of the world," Bobby Kennedy later said. ". . . I made it clear that if he was a decent American he would let King out of jail by sundown." It took a little longer, but within days authorities released the minister from jail. The incident got relatively little coverage in the white press, but word spread quickly in the African-American community. The civil rights leader's father, the influential minister Martin Luther King, Sr., had said that, "I had expected to vote against Senator Kennedy because of his religion. But now he can be my president, Catholic or whatever he is. It took courage to call my daughter-in-law at a time like this. He has the moral courage to stand up for what he knows is right. I've got all my votes and I've got a suitcase and I'm going to take them up there and dump them in his lap."

A blue-bound election pamphlet distributed to African-American church congregations quoted the elder King's endorsement and spread among black congregations in the days leading to the presidential election. Kennedy himself later laughed at the mixed message contained in the African-American minister's words. "He was going to vote against me because I was a Catholic, but since I called his daughter-in-law, he voted for me. That's a helluva bigoted statement, wasn't it? Imagine Martin

Luther King, Jr., having a bigot for a father." Then, acknowledging the controversies surrounding Joseph P. Kennedy, Kennedy grinned as he observed, "Well, we all have fathers, don't we?" Kennedy had won over black voters worried about his Catholic background, but his religion continued to be an issue with white Protestants.

The Catholic Issue Returns

As Kennedy became a more serious contender for the White House, several prominent Protestant ministers, such as evangelist **Billy Graham**, bestselling author Norman Vincent Peale, and W.A. Criswell (head of the largest Southern Baptist congregation in the world, First Baptist Church of Dallas), warned that a Catholic president represented a threat to religious freedom in America. Graham told one audience, "A man's religion cannot be separated from his person; therefore where religion involves political decision, it becomes a legitimate issue. For instance, the people have the right to know a Quaker's view on pacifism or a Christian Scientist's view on medical aid, or a Catholic's view on the secular influences of the Vatican."

Kennedy had in fact repeatedly split with the Catholic Church on numerous issues, for instance backing bills that provided federal funds for public schools but not funding for parochial schools, and opposing the appointment of an American diplomat to Vatican City. Nevertheless, Reverend Peale presided over a national meeting that Billy Graham had helped organize, the National Conference of Citizens for Religious Freedom, intended to fuel public worries about Kennedy's religion. Graham's father-in-law, Dr. Norman Bell, made a speech in which he claimed that the Roman Catholic Church is a "political system that like an octopus covers the entire world and threatens those basic freedoms and those constitutional rights for which our forefathers died in generations past." John Kennedy concluded he had no choice but to directly address the issue as he had in the West Virginia primary, and the forum he chose was the Greater Houston Ministerial Association on September 12. This was a city suspicious about Kennedy's stands on civil rights and with a strong anti-Catholic bias in the white Protestant community. Many historians, journalists and political scientists rate it as the future president's finest performance in the campaign.

"I believe in an America where the separation of church and state is absolute—where no Catholic prelate would tell the President (should he be a Catholic) how to act, and where no Protestant minister would tell his parishioners for whom to vote," Kennedy said. "[An America] where no church or church school is granted public funds or political preference—and where no man is denied public office merely because his religion differs from the president who might appoint him or the people who might elect him." The press covering the event interpreted this as the moment when Americans grew comfortable with the idea of a Catholic president. For the rest of the campaign Kennedy largely focused on Eisenhower's handling of the Cold War and the sluggish economy, and tried to shift blame for these failings to Richard Nixon.

Television and the Kennedy-Nixon Debates

Television news came of age during the 1960 presidential campaign, and the signal moment arrived when Nixon and Kennedy debated four times on national network television. A champion college debater, Nixon had judged Kennedy's acceptance speech at the Democratic National Convention during the summer as a failure and, in a moment of overconfidence, agreed to appear on a television stage with the junior senator from Massachusetts. Kennedy advisers, aware that many voters feared that the relatively young and inexperienced Democratic nominee lacked the qualifications to serve as president in the nuclear age, hoped that a respectable showing in TV debates would erase any advantage Nixon enjoyed from his eight years in the Eisenhower administration, including two stints in which Nixon acted as president when Eisenhower suffered heart attacks.

Nixon kept a promise to campaign in all 50 states and maintained an exhausting schedule right up to the day of the first of four television showdowns. Kennedy, by contrast, allowed himself time to rest. Ill and suffering from a painful knee injury, Nixon arrived at the CBS television studios in poor shape for the critical first debate. Pale, tired and underweight, he suffered from an unfortunate tendency to sweat heavily on his upper lip, which bore a heavy "five o'clock shadow" even after the candidate shaved. Nixon tried to cover the stubble with ineffective, light, "lazy shave" makeup that only highlighted the uneven facial hair. Reportedly, a Nixon campaign aide asked Robert Kennedy his assessment of the Republican's makeup. As Kennedy biographer Ralph G. Martin tells the story, "Bobby noted Nixon's paleness, his sunken cheeks and shadowed eyes, and replied, 'Terrific! Terrific! I wouldn't change a thing!'"

Eighty million Americans watched the first debate, which marked a shift in American culture in which Americans increasingly got their information from television rather than newspapers. In the years to come, expensive television advertising and staged events for network cameras would become at least as important in the thinking of campaign strategists as stump speeches, rallies, and campaign buttons. Always the lifeblood of politics, money became even more central to any potential political candidate's prospects.

Following their first TV face-off, the consensus of the media and the political world was that a cool-headed Kennedy had triumphed and achieved his primary goal of attaining presidential stature standing next to nervous Richard Nixon. Nixon, stumbling over his words, directed his comments toward his debate opponent and often did not look at the camera, and he often appeared to be talking down to the Democrats. Kennedy, with a better understanding of television, directed his comments to the TV audience. "Nixon was best on radio simply because his deep resonant voice carried more conviction, command, and determination than Kennedy's higher-pitched voice and his Boston-Harvard accent," wrote *New York Herald Tribune* reporter Earl Mazo. "But on television, Kennedy looked sharper, more in command, more firm—his was the image of a man who could stand up to Khrushchev."

There was scarcely any distance between the two candidates on the issues. The sharpest difference came over Fidel Castro's regime in Cuba. Kennedy had been briefed by the State Department about CIA plans to overthrow Castro, who was moving toward an alliance with the Soviet Union. During the debates, Kennedy pushed for a more aggressive stance toward Castro. Not wanting to tip off the secret CIA planning to the Russians, Nixon attacked Kennedy's posture as reckless, but ended up making himself, in the intense Cold War climate of the day, look weak and vacillating.

THE REASONS FOR KENNEDY'S VICTORY

The election was a squeaker. Kennedy carried only 49.7 percent of the popular vote as opposed to Nixon's 49.5 percent, a raw vote difference of 118,550 ballots out of nearly 69 million votes. Nixon would suggest that Kennedy won the Electoral College 303 to 219 because corrupt Democratic political boss Richard Daley, mayor of Chicago, stuffed ballot boxes. In Illinois, Kennedy's margin was 8,856 out of a total of 4.75 million. Voting results in Chicago were suspicious. At Precinct 50, Ward 222 registered voters somehow cast 74 votes for Kennedy and three for Nixon. Regardless, even if one accepts Nixon's later claims that Kennedy stole the state's Electoral College votes, as Matusow points out, "Illinois' 27 electoral votes would have been insufficient to produce a Nixon majority in the Electoral College."

What made the election so close in spite of all the advantages enjoyed by the Democrats? It appears that despite Kennedy's performance before the Houston ministers in the fall, many southern and western Democrats abandoned their nominee because of religion. The Democratic Party as a whole won 5 percent more votes in total than Kennedy did. In the South, Kennedy lost 17 percent of voters who normally cast Democratic ballots, a total of a million votes. He also lost votes from Democrats in the Midwest and the Plains States. Kennedy seems, however, to have clearly lost only two states because of anti-Catholic sentiment: Tennessee and Oklahoma.

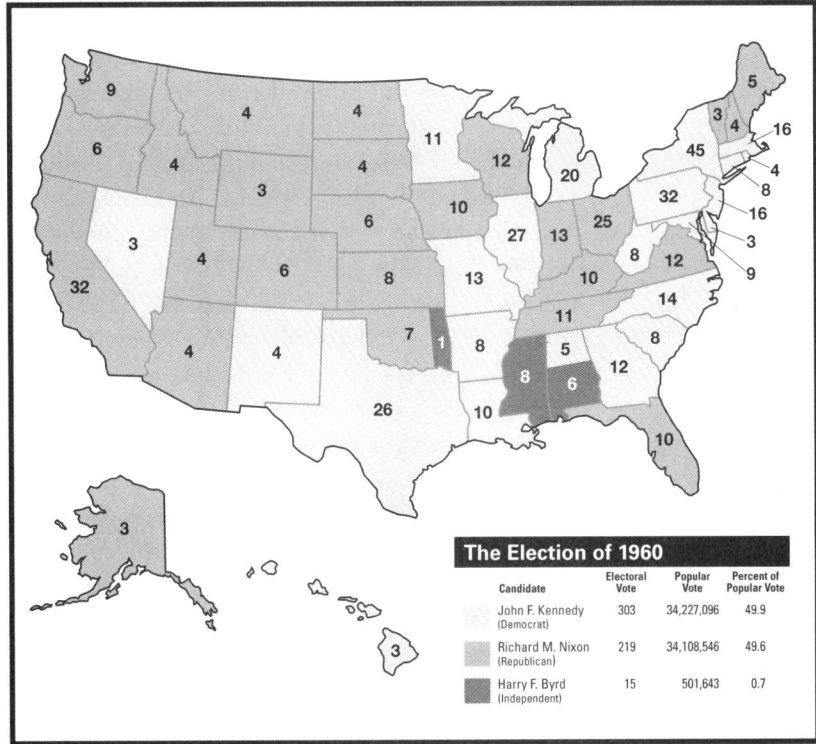

Map 28.1   The Election of 1960

President and Mrs. Kennedy arrive at the National Guard Armory in Washington for the Inaugural Ball. Jan. 20, 1961 Photo credit: Abbie Rowe, National Park Service/JFK Library

Kennedy, however, did extremely well among Catholic voters, carrying 80 percent as opposed to the usual 67 percent carried by Democratic presidential candidates. In the industrial Midwest states, his gains among Catholics offset losses from anti-Catholic voters. He also lost few southern whites on the civil rights issue even though he was more vocal than Nixon in his support of integration. Meanwhile, even though at the start of the Democratic Convention Kennedy was the least popular among the party's major candidates among African Americans, on election day he carried 70 percent of black votes. This constituency provided his margin of victory in South Carolina and Texas, and also may have pushed him over the top in nine other states, including electoral-vote rich Michigan, New Jersey, and Pennsylvania. Whatever his emotional distance regarding the civil rights struggle, Kennedy probably owed his presidency to African Americans.

THE "NEW FRONTIER"

At the time, the words struck the audience in Washington, and the larger television audience around the world, as an eloquent promise of American resolve to make the world a better place. On a day when eight inches of snow fell and the temperature was 22 degrees (which felt like 7 degrees when the wind chill was considered) Kennedy still stirred his heavily bundled inaugural audience on January 20, 1961 with this bold notice: "Let every nation know, whether it wishes us well or ill, that we shall pay any price, bear any burden, meet any hardship, support any friend, oppose any foe, in order to assure the survival and the success of liberty."

The words proved tragically prophetic. The audience could not know it, but in their drive to pay any price and bear any burden, Kennedy and his two successors would commit American prestige, money, and troops in increasing numbers to oppose what was seen as a global communist menace in Cuba, Vietnam, Cambodia and Laos. A decade after Kennedy's inaugural speech, with its promise of an aggressive foreign and military policy, Americans would tire of both the price and the burden of extending what Kennedy called "the **New Frontier**" around the globe. The first act in a tragic drama would unfold within weeks in Cuba.

The Bay of Pigs Fiasco

During the Eisenhower administration, the CIA formulated a plan for the invasion of Cuba and the overthrow of Fidel Castro. The agency informed Kennedy that the plan was ready for implementation soon after he took office. Kennedy, a fan of the *James Bond* spy novels written by British author Ian Fleming, liked the boldness of the scheme and signed off on the operation. On April 17, 1961, a force of 1,400 CIA-trained and armed Cuban exiles landed at the **Bay of Pigs** in Cuba. The CIA had failed to notice the presence of coral reefs in the bay. The reefs tore the undersides of several landing craft. Swamps surrounded the landing site, trapping the invaders. Castro responded quickly, and Cuban ground forces and attack planes quickly routed the invaders. As the invasion quickly went awry, Kennedy cancelled a planned air strike for fear it would reveal the degree of American complicity in the invasion. The incident would foster in Kennedy a strong distrust of the military and intelligence leadership that had assured him that Cubans would support the invasion and that the invasion would succeed. Publicly, a shaken president took responsibility for the failure. "Victory has a hundred fathers and defeat is an orphan," he told a press conference.

The failure of the invasion inspired a Cuba obsession within the Kennedy administration. In the coming months, the CIA concocted a variety of schemes to overthrow Castro. The agency's "Operation Mongoose," involved plans to sabotage the Cuban economy and concocted outlandish plots for killing Castro. Knowing that the Cuban leader liked to scuba dive, the CIA drew up an assassination scheme that involved planting explosives in a colorfully painted shell in hopes it would draw Castro's attention. Another plan would have infected the dictator's diving suit with a fungus that would cause a painful skin infection. Because Castro liked to smoke cigars, CIA planners discussed planting in Castro's possession an exploding cigar with enough firepower to kill him. The CIA knew that Mafia kingpins wanted to get even with Castro because he had closed down lucrative casinos in Havana and eliminated mob-run drug and prostitution rings in the island capital. The intelligence agency offered $150,000 to mob leaders Sam Giancana, Santos Trafficante and Johnny Roselli in return for a successful assassination of Castro, but all attempts failed. The Cuban leader remained in power until his resignation for health reasons in February 2008. Meanwhile, the failed Bay of Pigs invasion and the plots against Castro worsened U.S.-Soviet relations and set the stage for the **Cuban Missile Crisis**.

The Kennedy-Khrushchev Clash

Kennedy and Soviet leader Nikita Khrushchev finally faced off against each other directly in a summit in Vienna in June 1961, just two months after the Bay of Pigs disaster. Many Kennedy advisors wanted the president to cancel the meeting, expecting it would result only in escalating tensions, but Kennedy wanted to present himself as a strong, resolute leader willing to stand up to his adversaries face-to-face. The meeting proved to be another disaster. Khrushchev berated Kennedy, whom he saw (in the wake of the Cuban incident) as weak and indecisive. Kennedy wanted Khrushchev to back down in his support of communist insurgencies in Southeast Asia, but the Soviet leader insisted that the USSR had a moral obligation to support what he called "**wars of liberation.**" The two leaders also butted heads on the issue of **Berlin**. The city had been divided in two since the end of World War II, with the Western allies controlling the western part of the city and the Soviet Union and its allies controlling the east. At various times, the Soviets had cut off access to West Berlin, which was surrounded by East Germany. Khrushchev told Kennedy that the Soviet Union was ready to diplomatically recognize East Germany as a separate country. The East German government would determine whether western people and goods could enter West Berlin. Kennedy replied that the United States would defend West Berlin at all costs. A report said the meeting ended with "table banging and talk about missiles flying."

Kennedy returned home worried that the Soviets were contemplating starting a nuclear World War III. He went on national television calling up the reserves and asking for the public to support doubling the size of the military draft, the mass construction of bomb shelters, increased funds for civil defense, and a boost in the military budget by $3 billion. Kennedy also concluded that the United States would have to increase its involvement in Vietnam in order to demonstrate that his administration would not tolerate further communist expansion.

Meanwhile, through the summer 6,000 East Germans fled to West Berlin every day. In response the East German government constructed a 12-foot wall, complete with sniper nests, which would divide the city until the fall of the communist regime in 1989. After a year had passed, the Berlin Wall was more than seven miles long and fences were placed around the remaining almost 92 miles of East Berlin. Over the years at least 163 men and women died attempting to cross from East to West Berlin. Meanwhile the Soviet Union resumed testing nuclear weapons, and Kennedy responded in kind.

CHAPTER TWENTY-EIGHT

The Cuban Missile Crisis

The Bay of Pigs misadventure had a terrifying sequel. Alarmed by America's attempts to unseat him, Castro pleaded for more visible support from the Soviet Union. Khrushchev ordered the installation of Soviet nuclear missiles in Cuba capable of striking any major city on the American East Coast. By the fall of 1962 American spy planes had photographs of the missile sites under construction. That October, the world came as close as it ever did to a nuclear holocaust.

Why did Khrushchev make such a provocative move? "Khrushchev would have understood if Kennedy had left Castro alone or destroyed him in the Bay of Pigs invasion nineteen months before," Kennedy biographer Martin wrote. "But when he saw a young president rash enough to strike at Cuba but not bold enough to finish the job, Khrushchev decided he was dealing with an inexperienced leader who could be intimidated and blackmailed. That's when he gambled with the missiles."

Kennedy's military advisers proposed a wide range of options, including bombing the missile sites or an invasion of Cuba. Dean Acheson, Harry Truman's Secretary of State, pushed for a bombing raid. Kennedy knew such actions would put Khrushchev's credibility on the line and that the Soviet premier might respond with a nuclear strike against the United States. United Nations Ambassador Adlai Stevenson urged the president to tell Khrushchev that the United States would dismantle its nuclear missile bases in Turkey and evacuate the U.S. military base at Guantanamo Bay in Cuba in return for Khrushchev removing the missiles sites under construction on the island. Kennedy responded that the Russians would interpret this as a sign of weakness and become more aggressive.

Kennedy opted for a naval blockade of Cuba, what he called a "quarantine," which would intercept Soviet ships carrying missile parts. Kennedy addressed the American people in a national TV and radio broadcast October 22, 1962. Referring to Allied appeasement of Adolf Hitler's aggression in Europe, Kennedy told a riveted audience, "The 1930s taught us a clear lesson: aggressive conduct, if allowed to go unchecked and unchallenged, ultimately leads to war."

Four missile sites in Cuba were fully operational, and nuclear warheads were already on the island. Nineteen American ships stood between Cuba and a fleet of 25 Soviet vessels. Ship captains were ordered to stop any vessel with a cargo hold large enough to contain a nuclear warhead. Soviet vessels approached the American ships, but half turned back while the other half stopped their advance. "Doomsday didn't happen that day because we were lucky," a Kennedy advisor later recalled.

On October 26-27, the White House received two very different teletype messages from Khrushchev. In one, the Soviet leader insisted that the missiles in Cuba were for defensive purposes only and that the Russian ships that approached Cuba did not carry weapons. Khrushchev urged Kennedy to ratchet down the tension so as to not "... doom the world to the catastrophe of thermonuclear war." Khrushchev suggested that Kennedy promise that he would not invade Cuba. In return, the Soviet Union would withdraw military advisors from the island. The next day, the White House received an angrier message from Moscow. This time, the Soviet leader insisted that the United States withdraw nuclear warheads from Turkey before the Kremlin would consider removing missiles from Cuba. The Kennedy team worried that such a move, made publicly, would undermine the confidence of NATO allies in American assurances of protection. Presidential advisers argued over how to respond to the mixed messages coming out of Moscow. Which one reflected the Soviet government's current thinking? Still smarting from the Bay of Pigs, Kennedy dismissed the more aggressive suggestions of military leaders like General Curtis LeMay. Meanwhile, a plume of smoke wafted from chimneys at the Soviet Embassy as staff, worried about the likelihood of war, began burning secret documents.

The president's brother, Attorney General Robert Kennedy, proposed a simple solution to the dilemma. The younger Kennedy suggested that the president ignore the angry second message and respond positively to the more friendly and conciliatory first teletype. A positive response was sent, but the Soviets were warned not to reveal the American agreement to pull missiles out of Turkey. (Kennedy had already planned this course of action anyway.) Meanwhile, Bobby Kennedy warned Soviet ambassador Anatoly Dobrynin that the military was pressuring President Kennedy, and might even overthrow him unless he took a tough stand. The attorney general then cautioned that unless the missiles were removed, a bombing raid would be authorized.

For several hours, the Cabinet awaited what they feared would be Armageddon. Then, on Sunday morning, October 28, a radio bulletin announced that Khrushchev had accepted Kennedy's terms for ending the standoff. Many in the Cabinet felt they had won a major showdown with the Soviets after embarrassing diplomatic defeats at the Bay of Pigs and the Vienna Summit. Upon hearing the news, Secretary of State Dean Rusk exclaimed, "We were eyeball to eyeball and I think the other fellow just blinked."

In the coming year, the United States dismantled the missiles in Turkey, a telephone "hotline" to the Kremlin was installed in the Oval Office to facilitate instant communication between the American and the Soviet leaders, and the two countries began hammering out an agreement on ending testing of nuclear weapons in the atmosphere. A new tone had been set in American-Soviet relations.

"Both the United Sates and its allies have a mutually deep interest in a just and genuine peace and in halting the arms race," Kennedy said in a speech to graduating students at American University on June 10, 1963. "Agreements to this end are in the interests of the Soviet Union as well as ours . . . For, in the final analysis, our most basic common link is that we all inhabit this small planet. We all breathe the same air. We all cherish our children's future. And we are all mortal."

THE SPACE RACE

The rivalry between the United States and the Soviet Union extended even into outer space, begun almost four years before Kennedy became president. Fear spread across the country when, on October 4, 1957, the Soviets successfully launched *Sputnik I*, the first artificial satellite into orbit around the earth. Americans immediately worried about the military implications of the Soviet scientific achievement and that a fleet of spacecraft far beyond any American defense system could bombard the United States with nuclear warheads. The Soviets launched *Sputnik II*, with a dog named Laika on board, in November. Worried about not just the military aspects of Soviet space flight but also the blow to the prestige of the United States, which had been seen as the world's scientific leader, the Eisenhower administration inaugurated a crash space program to catch up with the Soviets. The United States put an unmanned craft of its own, *Explorer I*, into orbit on February 1, 1958.

This first American spacecraft sent data back to Earth, producing an important scientific discovery, the Van Allen Radiation Belts. By July 29, 1958, President Eisenhower had signed legislation creating the National Aeronautics and Space Administration, which would plan future space missions, design new spacecraft, and determine priorities in what was already being called a "space race" with the Soviet Union.

Many blamed the American education system for allowing the U.S. to fall behind the USSR in space technology. Congress passed, and Eisenhower signed the National Defense Education Act, which aimed to improve math and science programs at public schools and universities

A gathering at the White House to watch the liftoff of the *Mercury* spacecraft that will make John Glenn the first American in outer space. (From left to right): Vice President Lyndon Johnson, presidential advisor Arthur Schlesinger, Admiral Arleigh Burke, President John Kennedy and the First Lady, Jacquelyn Kennedy. Photo credit: Cecil Stoughton, White House/JFK Library.

The crew of *Apollo 1* (at left) burned to death because of high oxygen content and an electrical malfunction in the command module of *Apollo 1* in May 1965. (At right) The powerful Saturn V complex at Rocket Park at the National Space and Aeronautics Agency, Johnson Space Center, in Houston, Texas.

across the country. NASA soon announced the beginning of the Mercury space program, which would culminate in manned flights in space. Soviet scientists continued to give the United States headaches, sending out unmanned space ships on three separate missions. One vessel flew past the moon, another struck the lunar surface, and a third took the first-ever photographs of the dark side of the moon.

Always romantically attracted to adventure, Kennedy approved the **Apollo program,** which aimed to land humans safely on the moon. American scientists felt even more pressure when the Soviets sent the *Vostok I* into Earth orbit carrying cosmonaut Yuri Gagarin, who on April 12, 1961 became the first human in outer space. By this time scientists working for the American government had developed powerful *Saturn V* rockets that could carry heavy payloads deep into space. Many of the scientists involved in the space program, like Dr. Werner Von Braun, formerly developed deadly war rockets for Nazi Germany but had been brought to the United States as part of what the military called "Operation Paperclip." The United States government decided that it was in the national interest to ignore the war crimes committed by some of the German scientists if they could help the country keep up with the Soviets in the arms and space races.

American astronaut Alan Shepard became the second man in space on May 5, flying onboard the first of the **Mercury program** rockets. Kennedy now felt confident enough to announce even bolder plans for NASA. During a May 25, 1961 speech before Congress, he announced, "I believe that this nation should commit itself to achieving the goal, before this decade is out, of landing a man on the moon and returning him safely to the earth. No single space project in this period will be more impressive to mankind, or more important for the long-range exploration of space; and none will be so difficult or expensive to accomplish."

Kennedy accelerated the *Mercury* program. By February 20, 1962, astronaut John Glenn became the first American to orbit Earth, making the round trip three times and spending what was then a record 34 hours in space. Soon the United States launched the Telstar TV satellite, which made worldwide television broadcasts possible for the first time. In May 1965, a year and a half after Kennedy's death, Ed White became the first American to conduct a space walk. Even when three astronauts, White, Virgil "Gus" Grissom, and Roger "Bruce" Chafee burned to death inside the command module of *Apollo I* on January 27, 1967, Americans felt confident that the United States would meet its goal of landing on the moon by the end of the 1960s.

THE WARREN COURT

During the 1960s, civil rights marchers sought to revolutionize American race relations as they assaulted the citadels of segregation. Kennedy dramatically energized the office of the presidency, transforming it into the dynamic center of the federal government after what he saw as the long eight-year slumber of the Eisenhower years. Scientists, meanwhile, shattered humanity's bondage to planet Earth through the space program. Yet, ironically, one of the most revolutionary forces in the decade was a collection of nine mostly elderly, wealthy white men: the United States Supreme Court as led by Chief Justice Earl Warren.

President Eisenhower appointed Warren, the Republican governor of California and the GOP's nominee for vice president in 1948, as chief justice in 1953. Eisenhower saw Warren as a middle-of-the-road personality like himself who would preside over a cautious court. While some justices initially dismissed Warren as a politician rather than a genuine legal mind, the new chief justice's mellow, humble personality allowed him to earn respect and warm regard from his colleagues. Warren proved talented in winning over justices to his legal viewpoints and in presenting to the world an image of a united Supreme Court in even the most controversial cases. The year after his appointment, Warren provided the leadership that led to the historic *Brown v. Board of Education* school desegregation decision.

Warren had missed the initial arguments in the case but was on hand for the second round of arguments. After that session, the justices discovered that a 5-4 majority favored overturning the *Plessy v. Ferguson* "separate but equal" decision. Warren, however, said that the authority of such an important decision would be undermined if the Court remained almost evenly split. He insisted on a unanimous decision and gradually persuaded the remaining four justices that segregation could be justified only on the assumption that African Americans were intellectually inferior. Through a slow process, Warren won over the entire court. Warren himself delivered the Court's unanimous decision.

Brown was just the beginning of a long, remarkable and controversial string of decisions. Under Warren, a previously conservative Court shifted sharply in a liberal direction. Eisenhower later said that appointing Warren as chief justice seat was "the biggest damned-fool mistake I ever made."

The **Warren Court** outraged social conservatives with a pair of 1963 rulings regarding school prayer. In 1960, after discovering that her son William was compelled to participate in daily group prayers at his junior high school, outspoken atheist Madalyn Murray brought a lawsuit against the Baltimore school district. A Maryland district court and the state appellate court rejected her arguments that the school prayers violated the United States Constitution's ban on government "establishment" of religion. Murray's appeals eventually reached the Supreme Court, which combined *Murray v. Curlett* with the similar *Abington School District v. Schempp* case. Murray argued that the Constitution provided an "unalienable right to freedom from religion as well as freedom of religion." In an 8-1 opinion, the Court ruled that mandated school prayers indeed violated the Constitution's establishment clause. Murray later filed an unsuccessful suit to get the phrase "In God We Trust" removed from American currency.

In a series of rulings from 1957 to 1987, a divided Court chipped away at state anti-pornography laws and greatly expanded the permissible sexual content of books, magazine, and movies. In the 1957 *Roth v. United States* case, a 6-3 majority overturned the obscenity conviction of Samuel Roth, who sold a publication called "American Aphrodite," which included nude photos of women. In the majority opinion, the Court ruled that "sex and obscenity are not synonymous" and that only material that appeals to "prurient interests" could be considered a violation of federal anti-pornography laws. In its 1966 *Memoirs v. Massachusetts* case, the justices overturned lower court rulings, which banned the eighteenth-century book *Memoirs of a Woman of Pleasure* (also known as *Fanny Hill*) based on its alleged obscenity. The majority deemed that a "book cannot be proscribed unless it is found to be utterly without redeeming social value." In the following years, the Court routinely dismissed attempts to ban books, magazines, photos and films as obscene.

Sexual freedoms also expanded under the Warren Court. In the 1965 *Estelle v. Griswold* case, the Court ruled a Connecticut law to be unconstitutional that outlawed the use of contraceptives. By a 7-2 vote, the justices ruled that the statute violated the right of privacy indirectly provided by the Constitution through the Ninth and the Fourteenth Amendments and the penumbras of other rights provided under the national charter. The Court's reasoning would later provide the basis for the *Roe v. Wade* decision that legalized abortion in the first two trimesters of pregnancy. Meanwhile, several states had repealed laws deeming publications providing information on contraception as obscene. In 1960 the Federal Food and Drug Administration approved the marketing of the birth control pill, an event many feminists hailed as a moment of liberation. With the pill, many argued, adults could decide when to have children and how many, and women could be freed to have an active sex life and pursue a career.

The Warren Court also greatly upset conservatives by greatly expanding the rights of criminal defendants with its 1963 *Gideon v. Wainwright* and 1966 *Miranda v. Arizona* decisions. In *Gideon*, the Court held that under the Sixth Amendment to the Constitution, which guarantees the right of those accused of a crime to have "the assistance of counsel," impoverished criminal defendants have to be provided lawyers if they cannot hire one on their own. In the *Miranda* decision, the Supreme Court ruled that any person interrogated while in police custody had to be informed of his/her rights, including the right to not speak without a lawyer present. "In case after case," legal scholar Lawrence M. Friedman wrote, "the Supreme Court [under Warren] took the side of the prisoner, requiring strict adherence to the principles of fair search, arrest and trial—principles which, it sometimes seemed, the judges created themselves. These were dramatic cases. On the one side, the state; on the other, some broken figure of a man, shuffling into court, a drunk, a gambler, a dope addict, a four-time loser, a petty thief, a creature at the bottom of the ladder. The Warren Court sided with this underdog (and his lawyers) often enough, and forcefully enough, to draw cries of pain from the temples of law and order."

FREEDOM RIDERS

Events in Cuba, the confrontation with the Soviets, and the mounting communist guerilla war in Vietnam consumed the Kennedy administration. Even the space race was part of a "twilight struggle" with the Soviets. The president quickly lost his enthusiasm for domestic matters and believed that foreign policy afforded him more freedom of action. In spite of Kennedy's victory in the 1960 presidential election, the Democrats had lost 22 seats in the House and two seats in the Senate. Kennedy could reliably count on only 180 votes in the 435-member House to support liberal legislative proposals. In 1961, the Kennedy administration witnessed 16 of its 23 proposed bills on domestic issues go down to defeat.

Segregationist Democrats from the South served as chairs of the important House and Senate committees, and they allied with conservative Republicans to block much of the president's agenda. Civil rights issues, therefore, proved particularly vexing since the Kennedy administration didn't want to alienate powerful Southerners in the Congress. Civil rights leaders, however, refused to make their cause subservient to Kennedy's long-term strategic interests. Recent federal court orders had mandated desegregation of interstate transportation terminals. In the spring of 1961, James Farmer, executive director of the Congress of Racial Equality, announced that black and white "**freedom riders**" would test the willingness of the federal government to enforce these Court decisions by boarding buses and traveling across the South. Farmer, described by historian Mark Hamilton Lytle as "a large, charismatic figure with the voice of Darth Vader, wanted to provoke a confrontation that would force the slow-moving Kennedy administration to take action." As Farmer put it, "We felt we could count on the racists of the South to create a crisis so that the federal government would be forced to enforce the law."

Seven African Americans and six whites boarded two buses in Washington, D.C., in May 1961, headed for the dangers of violently segregationist Alabama and Mississippi. The Freedom Riders knew the peril they faced. One, future Georgia Congressman John Lewis, declared that he was ready to "give up all if necessary for the Freedom Ride." Lewis paid a heavy cost early in the odyssey. As he attempted to enter a whites-only restroom in Rock Hill, South Carolina, a gang of whites blocked Lewis's entry and clubbed and beat him. Physical injury became a regular feature of the journey, and white police and sheriff's deputies refused to provide the Freedom Riders any physical protection or to prosecute those guilty of assault. The federal government had still not intervened as the buses headed toward Alabama.

Sheriff "Bull" Connor and Police Violence

Angry whites carrying sticks and metal bars lined the streets of Anniston, Alabama as the Freedom Rider buses entered town. With local police nowhere to be seen, the mob slashed two tires on the lead bus. When the tires flattened, the bus stopped and the crowd shattered the bus windows. A southern white man who boarded the bus in Atlanta, Eli Cowling, went to the door, pulled a gun, and held the mob back for 15 minutes. Later it turned out that Cowling was an undercover police officer sent by Alabama Governor John Patterson, who worried about the damage to the state's image if one of the protestors were murdered.

Cowling, however, was unable to prevent one man from thrusting a bomb into a broken window. The passengers ran out of the bus and crawled out of the shattered windows, only to be beaten by the frenzied throng. The beatings stopped when Cowling fired his handgun in the air and threatened to kill the next person who hit anyone. A group from a nearby house went outside to check on the passengers and to offer refuge while shaking their heads and saying, "It's a shame." Meanwhile, a group of state troopers arrived and exchanged warm greetings with the mob leaders. The mob also attacked the second

President Kennedy, Director F.B.I. Hoover, and Attorney General Kennedy, White House, Oval Office. Feb 23, 1961 Photo credit: Abbie Rowe, National Park Service/JFK Library

bus, which nevertheless reached the Birmingham terminal where another gang beat the riders with lead pipes, baseball bats, and bicycle chains. After the pummeling, one rider needed 53 stitches on the head. Birmingham **Police Commissioner Eugene "Bull" Connor** claimed that none of his officers arrived to rescue the Freedom Riders because they had taken the day off for Mother's Day. In fact, an FBI informant had passed word to the agency's director, J. Edgar Hoover, that Connor had promised the local Ku Klux Klan a free 15 minutes to beat the protestors. Hoover, the head of a deliberately segregated agency who was convinced that Martin Luther King, Jr. and other civil rights leaders were communist agents, sat on the information.

As news coverage of the civil rights campaign increased, the president sent John Seigenthaler, a top aide to the attorney general, to Alabama to persuade officials there to protect the Freedom Riders. Seigenthaler escorted the battered demonstrators from Birmingham and onto a plane that flew them to New Orleans. James Farmer then announced that more Freedom Rides would follow. This angered President Kennedy, who yelled at his civil rights adviser Harris Wofford, "Tell [the protestors] to call it off! Stop them!" Kennedy was preparing for his Vienna summit with Khrushchev and didn't want the image of bloodied civil rights activists broadcast around the world during his face-off with the Soviet leader.

Farmer then decided only reluctantly to give a green light to student activists Diane Nash and John Lewis to pull together another group of eight Freedom Riders who traveled back to the scene of the previous violence in Birmingham. On May 17, they arrived in the city, only to have Connor place them in "protective custody." Alabama state troopers drove them to the Tennessee border and dumped them at a highway, leaving them vulnerable to attack. They hid in an African-American family's home, ate for the first time in three days, and called activists in Nashville who provided transportation back to Birmingham.

On To Montgomery

Frightened of violence, Greyhound bus drivers refused to transport the Freedom Riders. Bobby Kennedy, resigned to the fact that the rides would continue, called the Greyhound Company superintendent and insisted that the company comply with recent Court decisions. "Somebody better get in the damn bus and get it going and get these people on their way." The following morning a Greyhound bus carried the riders to Montgomery,

Alabama. Streets appeared abandoned when the bus arrived at the city's depot. Residents had been notified in advance of the travel itinerary. When riders stepped out of the bus, whites poured out of surrounding buildings, shouting, "Niggers, kill the niggers." A member of the mob beat one rider until he suffered a spinal cord injury. The mob also attacked an NBC television network cameraman, smashing him in the head with his equipment until he passed out. John Doar, an attorney with the Justice Department's Civil Rights Division, desperately phoned Bobby Kennedy from the scene while Seigenthaler was struck in the head, a protective helmet dented, as he tried to escort two women bus riders from the scene. Through all the violence, the police took no action.

Americans across the country felt shock when they saw film and photos of the attack. Even *The Atlanta Constitution*, a newspaper that had adamantly opposed integration, expressed shock at the mob action and the lack of police protection for the protestors. "If the police, representing the people, refuse to intervene when a man—any man—is being beaten to the pavement of any American city, then this is not a noble land at all. This is a jungle."

Incidents like this began to turn northern whites from neutrality or indifference to the hardship faced by southern blacks to sympathy. As Farmer had guessed at the start of the Freedom Rides, the movement would gain greater support if whites were imperiled in the desegregation struggle. A wide television audience watched an interview with one badly injured white protestor from Wisconsin who declared, "We will take hitting. We'll take beatings. We will accept death. But we are going to keep coming until we can ride anywhere in the South . . . as Americans . . ."

Negotiations Behind the Scene

The Riders pressed on to Jackson, Mississippi. The Kennedy brothers secured a promise from Mississippi Senator James Eastland that the Riders would be safe on their journey across the state as long as the administration did not object if the protestors were arrested and jailed for traveling "with the avowed purpose of inflaming public opinion." Hellish conditions awaited the Freedom Riders in the Jackson jails. Police packed as many as 14 prisoners in cells meant to accommodate only two. Some prisoners were forced to do outside labor in sweltering heat. The blankets smelled of urine. During chilly nights, guards intentionally opened windows in order to expose the protestors to cold, only to close them during the day when temperatures soared to triple digits. Guards and inmates beat the Riders whenever they started singing "freedom songs."

With a certainty that the Freedom Rides would continue until segregation ended on public transportation, and the equal certainty that the Freedom Rides would embarrass the president before the world, Robert Kennedy prodded the Interstate Commerce Commission and pressured the operators of bus terminals to quietly take down the "whites only" signs across the South. Worried about the economic repercussions of continued violence, several southern communities removed the Jim Crow signs without news coverage or protestors. "We created a crisis situation," Farmer later recalled. "It was worldwide news and headlines and everybody was watching it—people all over the world. The attorney general had to act and he did."

INTEGRATING "OLE MISS"

John Kennedy's inaugural speech deeply moved an African-American veteran of the Air Force, James Meredith, who attempted to register at the all-white University of Mississippi at Oxford. In spite of his excellent grades and his service in the military, the university's admissions office turned down his application. Meredith filed a lawsuit and a federal court ruled that the university had to admit him as a student. On September 20, 1962, Mississippi Gov. Ross Barnett personally blocked Meredith's way as he attempted to register at the admissions office. Angry over Barnett's obstruction of a federal order, Robert Kennedy sent 500 federal marshals to "**Ole Miss**," as the campus was known. Meredith registered and checked into his dorm room without violence.

However, on September 30, an agitated mob of students and non-students from across the South gathered to chant, "Two, four, one, three, we all hate Kennedy." The mob began throwing rocks at the federal marshals, and the marshals responded by firing tear gas canisters into the crowd. The crowd grew into the thousands.

Soon a riot broke out with the white mob throwing not just rocks, but acid, bricks, Molotov cocktails, and buckshot fired from rifles. As a result of the mêlée, 160 marshals were wounded, with 28 hit by bullets. Two men were killed, a jukebox repairman who happened to be at the wrong place at the wrong time, and a French news cameraman. Monitoring events through the night, Kennedy ordered 5,000 army troops to the campus before dawn. In the end, Meredith attended Ole Miss for two semesters, enduring anger, threats and harassment from fellow students. Events at Mississippi deeply shaped John and Robert Kennedy. "The President . . . found that bolder action on race issues would not necessarily

Integration at Ole Mississippi University
James Meredith walking on the campus of the University of Mississippi accompanied by U. S. marshals.
October 1, 1962

destroy his political base in the South," wrote historian Robert Weisbrot. "Although leaders in Mississippi and neighboring Alabama harked back to dark images of Reconstruction, in other Southern states the reaction to the president's use of troops was milder. Many officials recognized that Kennedy had responded patiently to [Gov.] Barnett's provocations and ordered Army units only as a last resort in the face of unrelieved mob violence."

"BOMBINGHAM" AND THE UNIVERSITY OF ALABAMA

Martin Luther King, Jr., and other civil rights leaders knew it would take more dramatic direct actions to keep the administration focused on the issue. They planned a series of boycotts aimed at department stores in downtown Birmingham, the Alabama capital where the Freedom Riders had received their worst beatings and where city officials shut down all parks rather than comply with a Department of the Interior order to desegregate them. King deliberately started the campaign during Easter time, knowing that the city's African-American community spent a substantial sum every year buying holiday clothes at the city's segregated department stores. These stores would not allow black customers to try on clothes and made them buy any product they touched. When activists began their sit-ins and picketing on April 3, 1963, Sheriff Connor showed surprising restraint, ordering his officers not to use billy clubs or any other violent techniques to break up the protests.

After eight days of protests, a state court ordered King to stop the campaign. King was arrested and held for three days—symbolically, as it turned out—from Good Friday to Easter Sunday. Eight southern ministers and rabbis issued a statement praising Birmingham officials for enforcing the law, criticizing King and other civil rights leaders for increasing racial tensions and calling their boycott "unwise and untimely," and urging black leaders to wait until southern society was ready to accept the type of changes the freedom movement demanded. The statement provoked King to write his "**Letter From a Birmingham Jail**," a masterpiece of American literature that would later be included in his book, *Why We Can't Wait*. A black trusty lent him a pen and scraps of paper, and King composed his letter in a dimly lit cell. In the April 16, 1963 letter, King explained to southern moderates why the movement could afford no more patience:

> Perhaps it is easy for those who have never felt the stinging darts of segregation to say, "Wait." But when you have seen vicious mobs lynch your mothers and fathers at will and drown your sisters and brothers at whim; when you have seen hate filled policemen curse, kick and even kill your black brothers and sisters; when you see the vast majority of your twenty million Negro brothers smothering in an airtight cage of poverty in the midst of an af-

fluent society; when you suddenly find your tongue twisted and your speech stammering as you seek to explain to your six year old daughter why she can't go to the public amusement park that has just been advertised on television, and see tears welling up in her eyes when she is told that Funtown is closed to colored children, and see ominous clouds of inferiority beginning to form in her little mental sky . . . when you take a cross county drive and find it necessary to sleep night after night in the uncomfortable corners of your automobile because no motel will accept you; when you are humiliated day in and day out by nagging signs reading "white" and "colored" . . . when . . . you are forever fighting a degenerating sense of "nobodiness"—then you will understand why we find it difficult to wait. There comes a time when the cup of endurance runs over, and men are no longer willing to be plunged into the abyss of despair.

King's letter was published and quoted in newspapers and church bulletins across the country. He was finally released on April 20. By the time King stepped outside the jail, the boycott had lost steam. "We have scraped the bottom of the barrel of adults who would [risk going to jail]," one protestor explained to King. King and his top lieutenants then agreed to recruit high school students to participate in the protests. By May 2, more than 900 children had gone to jail for participating in the protest. Connor reverted to form. On May 3, officers stormed the **Sixteenth Street Baptist Church**, where more than 1,000 boycotters had gathered. As the protestors left the church, police aimed fire hoses at the congregants with sufficient force to knock both children and adults to the ground and tear skin from their bodies. Police began to wildly swing their billy clubs even as they released police dogs that began biting old and young alike. White attacks continued for four days, and some of the younger African Americans lost patience with non-violence and began throwing rocks and soda bottles at the police.

Sales at downtown Birmingham stores dropped to almost nothing during what traditionally had been a profitable season. Local merchants were also facing pressure from northern suppliers who were appalled by the televised violence and the possibility that the boycott movement might spread to affect their businesses. The downtown merchants hammered out a compromise with King on May 10: In return for desegregation of the stores, the protestors would end the boycott. Alabama Gov. George Wallace and Sheriff Connor attacked the agreement, with Connor urging whites to boycott stores that had integrated.

In the aftermath of the Birmingham campaign, two dynamite explosions blasted the home of King's brother, a Birmingham minister, while another dynamite blast destroyed part of the Gaston Motel where the movement leadership had set up headquarters. African Americans again took to the streets and hurled rocks and other weapons at police who responded by again clubbing the protestors. Birmingham became known as "Bombingham."

RACIAL TENSIONS AND THE FINAL MONTHS OF THE KENNEDY ADMINISTRATION

Even as the administration wished the civil rights issue would fade from public attention, protests against segregation broke out across the country. In 1963, civil rights activists marched not just for desegregation but also for better jobs and better schools, not just in southern cities like Jackson, Mississippi and Raleigh, North Carolina, but also in cities like Los Angeles and Philadelphia. Approximately 75,000 Americans participated in civil rights marches in May 1963 alone.

Alabama **Governor George Wallace** stood blocking the entrance to Foster Auditorium at the University of Alabama as two African-American students, Vivian Malone and James A. Hood, armed with a court order mandating their admission, attempted to enter the building. Wallace won election the previous year promising to resist integration. During his inaugural speech on January 14, 1963, he declared, "Segregation now! Segregation tomorrow! Segregation forever!" The Kennedys negotiated with Wallace, who agreed he would step aside to let the students inside the building once he had finished making a speech. President Kennedy nationalized the Alabama National Guard to guarantee Wallace's compliance.

That night in a national broadcast, the president made his strongest statement ever in support of civil rights. The speech, written by aide Ted Sorenson, was not finished until minutes before airtime. "We are confronted primarily with a moral issue," Kennedy told his audience. "It's as old as the Scriptures and is as clear as the American Constitution . . . If an American, because his skin is dark, cannot eat lunch in a restaurant open to the public, if he cannot send his children to the best public school available, if he cannot vote for the public officials who represent him, if, in short, he cannot enjoy the full and free life which all of us want, then who among us would be content to have the color of his skin changed and stand in his place? Who among us would then be content with the counsels of patience and delay? . . . Are

Vivian Malone, one of the first African Americans to attend the University of Alabama, walks through a crowd that includes photographers, National Guard members, and Deputy U.S. Attorney General Nicholas Katzenbach to enter Foster Auditorium to register for classes. June 11, 1963

we to say to the world, and much more importantly to each other that this is a land of the free except for Negroes; that we have no second class citizens except Negroes; that we have no class or caste system, no ghettoes, no master race except with respect to Negroes?" The same evening as this dramatic speech, the field secretary of the Mississippi NAACP, Medgar Evers, was shot to death in the driveway of his Jackson, Mississippi home.

On June 19, 1963, the president submitted to Congress a sweeping civil rights bill that strengthened voting rights laws, empowered the attorney general to file school desegregation lawsuits, gave the president the power to end federal funding of state programs that racially discriminated, and outlawed segregation in public accommodations such as restaurants, movie theaters, hotels and motels, stores, and stadiums. Civil rights leaders wanted more, such as a ban on job discrimination, but Kennedy told movement leaders that the bill went as far as it could if it were to have any chances to pass the Congress. Because of the opposition of most southern Democrats, Kennedy would have to rely on support from liberal Republicans.

The March on Washington

To put pressure on Congress to pass the bill and perhaps strengthen it, civil rights leaders like King organized a "**March on Washington**" to be held in late August. The Kennedys strongly opposed the rally, fearing wavering members of Congress might resent the show of force, that violence might break out, or that a small turnout might undermine momentum for the legislation. When it became clear that the march would take place, the Kennedy team essentially stage-managed the event, insisting that speeches be cleared with them beforehand.

Governor Wallace, attempting to block integration at the University of Alabama, stands defiantly at the door while being confronted by Deputy U.S. Attorney General Nicholas Katzenbach. June 11, 1963

About 250,000 people showed up for the August 28. The din made it hard for the massive throng to hear folksingers like Joan Baez; Bob Dylan; and Peter, Paul, and Mary; and the gospel singer Mahalia Jackson. The world, however, listened as national TV broadcast King's famous "I Have a Dream" speech. In ministerial cadences, King mesmerized the marchers in Washington and the vast television audience with these words:

> As we walk, we must make the pledge that we shall always march ahead. We cannot turn back. There are those who are asking the devotees of civil rights, "When will you be satisfied?" We can never be satisfied as long as the Negro is the victim of the unspeakable horrors of police brutality. We can never be satisfied, as long as our bodies, heavy with the fatigue of travel, cannot gain lodging in the motels of the highways and the hotels of the cities. We cannot be satisfied as long as the Negro's basic mobility is from a smaller ghetto to a larger one. We can never be satisfied as long as our children are stripped of their selfhood and robbed of their dignity by signs stating "For Whites Only". We cannot be satisfied as long as a Negro in Mississippi cannot vote and a Negro in New York believes he has nothing for which to vote. No, no, we are not satisfied, and we will not be satisfied until justice rolls down like waters and righteousness like a mighty stream.

Kennedy declined to speak at the event but agreed to meet the organizers after the successful march. He greeted King with words echoing the civil rights leader's earlier speech: "I have a dream." Rather than provoke a backlash, the march gave momentum to the civil rights bill, which was approved by the House Judiciary Committee and referred to the full House on October 23, 1963. Kennedy had feared that support of civil rights would lose him the critical support of southern Democrats, but polling by Louis Harris in November 1963 indicated he had gained more support than he lost by lending his support to the civil rights bill. Kennedy still sought to repair the gulf between the northern and southern wings of the Democratic Party when he decided to make an appearance in Dallas, Texas, later that month.

Four Little Girls

Whatever euphoria civil rights activists might have felt in the wake of the March on Washington gave way to bitter tears on September 15, 1963. That Sunday an explosion rocked the 16th Street Baptist Church in Birmingham during services. A bomber had tunneled under the church basement and set off a bundle of dynamite underneath the girls' restroom, killing four young girls dressed in white, three 14-year-olds named Cynthia Wesler, Carole Robertson and Addie Mae Collins, and one 11-year-old named Denise McNair. The explosion during the church's annual "Youth Day" injured 20 other worshippers. When the bomb exploded, Sunday school students had been debating the day's topic, "The Love That Forgives." McNair's father, upon discovering her body, stood holding one of her white dress shoes and screamed, "I'd like to blow the whole town up."

The United Klans of America targeted the church because it had served as a meeting place for civil rights leaders. The explosion also came in the wake of voting rights campaigns conducted by King's Southern Christian Leadership Council (SCLC) and the Congress of Racial Equality (CORE), and the dispatch of National Guard units to enforce a desegregation order for Birmingham schools. King often discussed future demonstrations at the 16th Street church. Alabama Gov. Wallace had been exploiting racial tensions to enhance his popularity with white voters, and one week before the explosion *The New York Times* published an interview in which Wallace said that the state needed a "few first-class funerals" to stop the civil rights protests.

Carole Robertson's family wanted a private service, but the other three girls had a joint public funeral on September presided over by King. "At times life is hard, hard as crucible steel," King said. In an atmosphere of high tension and continued bombing threats, 8,000 mourners attended the service, including 800 black and white Birmingham pastors. As the historian Taylor Branch notes, the service was the largest interracial meeting of ministers in the city's history. It took until November 1977 for the bomber, Robert Chambliss, to be found guilty and sent to prison. Juries eventually convicted three accomplices and sentence them to prison terms as well. King, however, blamed Wallace, writing to him, "the blood of four little children ... is on your hands. Your irresponsible and misguided actions have created in Birmingham and Alabama the atmosphere that has induced continued violence and now murder." Sorrow and anger over the bombing did, however, intensify the effort to pass major civil rights legislation in 1964.

THE KENNEDY ASSASSINATION AND ITS IMPACT

President Kennedy decided to visit Dallas in order to mend a deep rift between Texas Democratic Governor

**Swearing in of Lyndon B. Johnson as president, Air Force One, Love Field, Dallas, Texas.
November 22, 1963 Photo credit: LBJ Library Photo**

John Connally, an ally and friend of Vice President Lyndon Johnson, and the Lone Star State's liberal Senator Ralph Yarborough. Many Kennedy aides worried about the trip. Dallas had acquired a reputation as a city of right-wing crackpots.

Uncertain of carrying Texas in the 1960 presidential campaign, Kennedy sent his running mate Lyndon Johnson to make an appearance in Dallas in the closing days of the race. On November 4, Johnson and his wife Lady Bird appeared at the Adolphus Hotel in downtown Dallas for a speech. After the speech the pair were assaulted by a well-dressed mob led by Dallas' rightwing Republican Congressman Bruce Alger. Calling LBJ "Late Blooming Judas" because of his role in passing the 1957 civil rights bill, the hostile throng spat upon the Johnsons, and pulled on Lady Bird's hair and clothes.

Less than a month before JFK's visit, another reactionary mob spat upon United Nations Ambassador Adlai Stevenson after he made an October 26, 1963 speech to the Dallas Council on World Affairs marking United Nations Day. The protestors rocked Stevenson's limousine back and forth before a driver finally managed to race the ambassador to safety. Dallas's business leaders feared that another embarrassing incident like the assault on Stevenson would be a fatal blow to the city's international image, prompting Mayor Earle Cabell to beg Dallas's citizens to give the president a friendly reception. The police received orders to "spot any agitator quickly and . . . remove him before trouble could start."

Kennedy arrived in Dallas on November 22, 1963. Riding in a limousine with the top removed so Dallas could get a better look at the president and the first lady, Kennedy smiled broadly at the crowd and waved right up until the moment the car passed the School Book Depository near the triple underpass in downtown Dallas. Three shots rang out, with bullets hitting Kennedy in the neck and, fatally, in the head. Rushed to Dallas's Parkland Hospital, Kennedy was soon declared dead. Instead of a right-winger, police arrested Lee Harvey Oswald, an employee of the Book Depository and a self-styled leftist who supported Fidel Castro's regime in Cuba and defected briefly to the Soviet Union before returning to a life of loneliness and frustration in Texas. Oswald himself would be assassinated by a Dallas nightclub owner with orga-

> ### Where were you when President Kennedy was shot?
>
> Inauguration day in 1961 was crisp and cold with snow piled everywhere in Washington. Matching the untypical weather was the address that John F. Kennedy gave that day. It was a call to patriotism and selfless dedication to the good of the nation. As Kennedy called the nation to ask "what you can do for your country," he set the youth of all races afire with the notion that they could change the nation and even the world. The drama of this beginning was matched three years later with the drama of its end. The shock of the assassination was such that over thirty years later, 300,000 Americans wrote to advice columnist, "Dear Abby," to answer the question, "Where were you when President Kennedy was shot?"
>
> "I was in the Peace Corps and had been teaching English in a small town in Thailand for just two months. The shy young Thai student who lived with me came and told me in Thai that President Kennedy had died. I couldn't imagine why he would die suddenly, and said, 'Oh, you must mean that his father has died.' No, no, she said, and kept explaining in Thai what had happened. I didn't know the Thai word for 'assassinate' so I couldn't understand her. Finally she got her English lesson book and pointed to a drawing of a fellow shooting a gun, next to the sentence, 'He fired a shot.' Then I knew."   M.J.B. Van Nuys, CA.
>
> "I still feel the loss as if a member of my family had been killed. I was twenty years old that year and just about idolized John Kennedy. I don't think I will ever forget."   M.B. Gadsden, AL.
>
> "My husband and I were working in the yard as it was a beautiful November day. I could hear the telephone ringing and ringing. I finally went in to answer it, and it was Mrs. L., a woman who liked to be first with any news. She told me that John Kennedy had been killed. I yelled for my husband to come in as I turned on the TV. We spent the next four days in front of the TV crying and wondering what would happen next."
> MGK, Ruffs Dale, PA.

nized crime ties, Jack Ruby, who claimed he murdered the suspect out of respect and sorrow for the president's widow, Jackie Kennedy.

The president's murder, and the rapid killing of his suspected assassin, spawned a host of conspiracy theories that blamed the Russians, the Cubans, the Mafia (angered by Bobby Kennedy's work as a lawyer for a Senate committee investigating organized crime in the 1950s), Teamsters Union boss Jimmy Hoffa (jailed for corruption after prosecution by the Kennedy administration), and even Vice President Johnson. The new president, seeking to quell suspicions, appointed a blue-ribbon panel chaired by Supreme Court Chief Justice Earl Warren and including future President Gerald Ford, then a congressman from Michigan, to investigate the assassination. The Warren Commission concluded that Oswald acted alone, but a large percentage of the population continued to doubt the official government version of events.

In the decade that followed Kennedy's death, a period that would see government lies about the Vietnam War exposed and the revelations about the Watergate scandal during the Nixon administration, the assassination in Dallas ushered in an era of cynicism. "Fatalism flourished," wrote one-time student activist Todd Gitlin. "[T]he power of the will to prod history in the right direction was blunted. One common conclusion was that even the steadiest of institutions, the august presidency, was fragile indeed ... The Warren Commission Report, released on September 27, 1964, was shoddy enough, but something else was operating to discredit it; a huge cultural disbelief that an event so traumatic and vast in its consequence could be accounted for by a petty assassin."

LBJ: UNLIKELY CIVIL RIGHTS ALLY

Lyndon Johnson might be the most complicated figure in American political life in the mid- and late-twentieth century. Often crude, he nevertheless proved to be perhaps the greatest political tactician of his era. The graduate of Southwest Texas State Teachers College, a small Central Texas campus, he often suffered from an inferiority complex in the company of the Ivy Leaguers peopling the Kennedy administration, yet his ambitions bordered on the grandiose. A small-town Southerner, Johnson would use the word "nigger" in private conversation but still devoted much of his public life to promoting civil rights and fighting poverty. An inveterate compromiser, Johnson would also propose some of the boldest reform legislation in American history.

Mrs. Kennedy and her children leave the Capitol building. (L-R) Peter Lawford, Attorney General Kennedy, Patrica Kennedy Lawford, Caroline Kennedy, Mrs. Kennedy, John F. Kennedy Jr. November 24, 1963
Photo credit: Abbie Rowe, National Park Service/JFK Library

Johnson's early career as a grade-school teacher would shape his political worldview. During the 1928-29 school year, he taught fifth-, sixth- and seventh-graders at a tiny, segregated Mexican-American school in Cotulla, Texas, just south of San Antonio. Three-quarters of the Mexican population in the town, according to Johnson biographer Robert Dallek, lived in "hovels or dilapidated shanties without indoor plumbing or electricity." The parents worked at area ranches and farms for "slave wages." Johnson would later recall that his heart broke looking at students "mired in the slums . . . lashed by prejudice . . . buried half-alive in illiteracy." He remembered looking at their eyes and seeing "a quizzical expression on their faces" as they wondered, "Why don't people like me? Why do they hate me because I am brown?"

Johnson was often harsh and sometimes intolerant as a teacher, using corporal punishment if he caught students speaking Spanish, but he also felt empathy for his young charges' poverty. Johnson would say, "I was determined [to help] those poor little kids. I saw hunger in their eyes and pain in their bodies. Those little brown bodies had so little and needed so much I was determined to spark something inside of them, to fill their souls with ambition and interest and belief in the world, to help them finish their education. Then the rest would take care of itself." Johnson may have underestimated the power of racism to deter educated, ambitious people of color, but he devoted himself to his students, distributing toothpaste sent to him by his mother and starting extracurricular activities like debate, track, baseball, spelling bees, and band.

Johnson carried his conflicted personality, which was both bigoted and empathetic, to his job as director of the New Deal-created National Youth Administration in Texas from 1935 to 1937. Though he sometimes accommodated local anti-Mexican prejudice in his hiring of unemployed youths on projects such as constructing roadside parks, he was more assertive in recruiting and promoting African Americans. Under Johnson, the NYA created Freshman College Centers for students who had received a high school education but could not, with their small NYA salaries, afford tuition at local colleges. Under this program, students could take a pair of college courses tuition-free, improving their education and their resumes at the same time.

898 / CHAPTER TWENTY-EIGHT

A Political Force of Nature

In 1937, the congressman in Johnson's U.S. House district died. Johnson ran for the open seat as a supporter of the New Deal and Franklin D. Roosevelt. A close friend of House Speaker Sam Rayburn, Johnson remained in the House for 11 years and was named head of the Democratic Congressional Campaign Committee in 1940. He ran unsuccessfully for the Senate in a special election in 1941. Johnson served in the Navy in 1942 but returned to his House seat at the insistence of President Roosevelt. Johnson ran for the Senate again in 1948 in a heated and controversial race against the archconservative and segregationist former Texas Governor Coke Stevenson, winning the Democratic primary by only 87 votes. Johnson earned the ironic nickname "Landslide Lyndon" as a result of this election and charges of voter fraud dogged him the rest of his political life, although Stevenson himself certainly engaged in ballot box stuffing in the same election.

Early in his Senate career, Johnson intervened in the controversy surrounding Private Felix Longoria. Longoria was killed in the Philippines during a volunteer mission in the closing days of World War II, and his body was shipped to a cemetery in Three Rivers, Texas. But the funeral director refused to allow a wake to be held in the chapel, supposedly because there had been disorder at previous Mexican-American funerals and because "the whites would not like" sharing the funeral grounds with Mexicans. Dr. Hector Garcia, a Corpus Christi Mexican American civil rights activist, contacted Johnson, who arranged a funeral with full honors at Arlington National Cemetery on February 16, 1949. Johnson and a personal representative of President Harry Truman attended the service with the Longoria family.

In 1955, Johnson's peers selected him as Senate Majority Leader. Franklin Roosevelt had predicted that Johnson might become the first southern president since antebellum times. With a White House bid in mind, in the late 1950s Johnson positioned himself as a racial moderate. He was pointedly not asked to sign the so-called "**Southern Manifesto**" circulated among and supported by 101 members of the House of Representatives and the United States Senate. The 1956 document condemned the Supreme Court's 1954 *Brown* school desegregation order. Johnson, the Senate majority leader who was distrusted by his Dixie colleagues as a racial liberal, joined Tennessee senators Estes Kefauver and Albert Gore, Sr., as the lone southern standouts in the Senate who did not lend their names to the Manifesto.

The "Johnson Treatment" is displayed here with Louis Martin (top-L) at a reception for the Democratic National Committee delegates on April 20, 1966, in the Red Room of the White House, Abe Fortas (R), associate justice of the Supreme Court in July 1965, at the White House, and with Senator Richard Russell (bottom) on December 17, 1963, in the Cabinet Room of the White House.
Photo credit: LBJ Presidential Library

Lyndon Johnson also gave his critical support to the 1957 Civil Rights Act, the first voting rights law passed by the Congress since Reconstruction. Under this law, Congress established the Justice Department's Civil Rights Division. The law empowered this division to investigate claims of voter harassment and racial discrimination by election officials. The Justice Department now could prosecute individuals conspiring to deny voting rights. The law also established a six-member United States Civil Rights Commission, which examined cases where voters were denied the ballot because of race. Johnson also proposed in 1959 a federal civil rights mediation board where disputes over elections could be resolved.

Johnson entered the 1960 Democratic presidential primary race, losing to Kennedy. He was selected as running mate because the party faithful worried about their prospects in Texas, a state that had gone for Eisenhower twice in the previous two presidential elections. Kennedy and Johnson proved a mismatch. The president and his brother Bobby saw Johnson as unsophisticated, and they underestimated his political skills. Johnson also bridled at serving as junior partner to the younger Kennedy; he had served longer in the Senate than Kennedy and in that chamber had ranked higher as Majority Leader.

Nevertheless, when Johnson spoke up, it could be with force. Johnson later recounted an anecdote: He was vice president and he asked his African-American cook and her husband to drive him from Washington, D.C., to Texas. Their route took them through Alabama, Mississippi and Louisiana, and the entourage could find no restaurants or restrooms open to two of the three passengers. "Two people who worked for the Vice President of the United States peeing in a ditch . . . That's not right," Johnson would later drawl. As historian Matusow notes, Johnson was passionate, if ineffective, as head of the president's Committee on Equal Employment Opportunity and he "urged Kennedy to tour every Southern state to tell white people in person that segregation was morally wrong, utterly unjustifiable, and in violation of the tenets of Christianity."

JOHNSON AS PRESIDENT

Because of his origins in a highly conservative and segregationist state like Texas, many liberals worried about Johnson's political intentions when the Kennedy assassination thrust him into the presidency. Johnson, however, pushed through at breakneck speed a torrent of legislation unmatched since Franklin Roosevelt's famed first 100 days in office. Johnson skillfully used the memory of the widely mourned Kennedy to win support for civil rights

Harry Truman and LBJ (day of Medicare Bill Signing). July 30, 1965

and anti-poverty legislation, a program he dubbed "**The Great Society**." Aimed at the 20 percent of the American population living below the poverty line, this war was fought through programs like the Job Corps designed to provide training to historically underemployed populations. Head Start provided preschool educations for children living in poverty in order to allow them to catch up with students from more advantaged backgrounds.

Under Johnson, $1.5 billion in aid was sent to public and private schools. Medicare and Medicaid became the most important domestic programs created since the establishment of the Social Security Administration three decades earlier. Medicare provided health insurance coverage for Americans aged 65 and older, while Medicaid, which shared administration by the federal government and the states, provided access to health care for the poor. Johnson believed that Kennedy's death lent momentum for these programs, but most of all for civil rights.

"Everything I had ever learned from the history books taught me that martyrs have to die for causes," said Johnson, who called Kennedy "too conservative for my taste" in a later interview. "John Kennedy had died but his 'cause' was not really clear. That was my job. I had to take the dead man's program and turn it into a martyr's cause."

The 1964 Civil Rights Act

Johnson frequently invoked his martyred predecessor as he pushed, needled and cajoled the Congress toward passage of his top legislative priority, the **1964 Civil Rights Act**. The law banned segregation at public facilities and racial discrimination in the work place, empowered the attorney general to initiate lawsuits against segregated school systems, and allowed the federal government to withhold funds from schools refusing to comply with desegregation orders. In the Senate, Richard Russell of Georgia launched a filibuster, relying on a team of 18 colleagues who attempted to talk the bill to death, claiming the proposed law would lead to "amalgamation and mongrelization of the races."

Meanwhile, in the House of Representatives, Democratic leaders joined by liberal Republicans defeated more than 100 "poison pill" amendments that would have gutted the legislation or made it unacceptable to a congressional majority. Attempting to kill the bill, Congressman Howard Smith of Virginia introduced an amendment banning employment discrimination against women as well as African Americans. Representative Emanuel Celler of Brooklyn, one of the House liberals, objected, saying the amendment would overturn traditional gender roles and that it ignored the "biological differences" between men and women. Smith responded by mocking Celler's hypocrisy. Mistakenly thinking that adding women's rights to the civil rights bill would kill the legislation, southern segregationists joined with feminists to approve Smith's amendment. One critic said that Smith "outsmarted himself," and the bill passed by an overwhelming 290-130 vote.

Senator Hubert Humphrey of Minnesota, soon to become Johnson's vice president, urged Senate Minority Leader Everett Dirksen, not previously a supporter of civil rights legislation, to join the cause. On June 10, 1964, Dirksen announced his support for a cloture vote, which would end the filibuster and allow a vote on the bill. The cloture motion passed 71-29, with four votes more than needed to close debate. The front lines of the battle for social justice, however, would not be found in Washington, D.C., but in the backwoods of Mississippi.

FREEDOM SUMMER

A younger generation of black protestors was not content to wait upon the slow workings of the United States Senate. The NAACP, representing an older generation, fought segregation through a series of lawsuits. Martin Luther King Jr.'s Southern Christian Leadership Conference (SCLC) sought to defeat Jim Crow through political lobbying, negative publicity about southern discrimination, and acts of non-violent resistance, such as sit-ins at segregated lunch counters. With a younger membership, the Student Nonviolent Coordinating Committee (SNCC) favored direct action against injustice, led by local civil rights campaigners. SNCC's membership resented King and other civil rights "celebrities" they accused of swooping in at the end of a campaign and claiming credit for the hard grassroots work of locals.

To the Civil Rights Movement's surprise, the president's brother, Attorney General Robert Kennedy, signaled in late 1961 that he would help groups like SNCC receive financial support from liberal charities, such as the Taconic Foundation, if the civil rights organizations focused on voter registration in the South. Worried that its mild civil rights record guaranteed that Kennedy would lose southern states to the Republicans in the 1964 re-election effort, the administration no doubt hoped that an increase in the number of friendly black voters in states like Mississippi would provide a counter to white segregationists. Many in SNCC feared the White House was using them, but the cash-strapped group found Bobby Kennedy's offer one they couldn't refuse. SNCC, the NAACP and the Congress of Racial Equality (CORE) launched the Voter Education Project in April 1962.

More than $870,000 (about $5.5 million in today's dollars) poured into the Voter Education Project from the Taconic Foundation, the Stern Family Fund, and the Field Foundations. Over the next two years, the project registered for the vote more than a half-million African Americans in the South, but the overwhelming majority of these voters lived in big cities. The large numbers of rural southern blacks remained largely unregistered, and in Mississippi, the project had added only 4,000 new voters. Just under 400,000 African Americans remained unregistered there. By 1964, even though African Americans made up 42 percent of the total population they comprised only 6.7 percent of registered voters.

Mississippi became a focus of the registration drive. Having seen so many African Americans injured or killed over civil rights, and a victim of an attempted murder himself, Bob Moses in the fall of 1963 invited the participation of white students from colleges like Harvard, Yale and Stanford. His vision of a nation transformed into a "Beloved Community" included blacks and whites. Moses moved ahead with plans for a "**Freedom Summer**" in 1964, in which hundreds of white volunteers would join black activists to increase the number of African American voters across Mississippi. Most of the 900 student volunteers who arrived from out of state for the campaign were well-off white students from elite universities.

Martin Luther King, Jr. talks with President Lyndon B. Johnson in the Oval Office, White House. December 3, 1963 by Yoichi R. Okamoto. Photo credits: LBJ Library Photo

The Schwerner, Chaney, and Goodman Murders

Civil rights dominated the headlines in 1964. The Twenty-fourth Amendment to the U.S. Constitution, banning poll taxes, had been submitted to the states in 1962 and was ratified January 23, 1964. Meanwhile, during Mississippi's "Freedom Summer" volunteers not only registered black voters but set up 30 "Freedom Schools" to offer children an alternative to the state's dilapidated, underfunded Jim Crow schools. On top of reading, writing and arithmetic, college students taught their young black students African-American history, and lessons on the importance of voting and the philosophy of the Civil Rights Movement. CORE and other groups also helped organize the **Mississippi Freedom Democratic Party** (MFDP) as an alternative to the white supremacist state Democratic Party. The MFDP held separate primaries and elected an alternative slate of delegates to the Democratic National Convention to be held in the summer of 1964. The MFDP would challenge the credentials of the all-white, segregationist delegation during the convention and demand that the national Democratic Party recognize its integrated slate as the legitimate representatives of Mississippi.

Michael Schwerner, 24, was among the white men and women who responded to Bob Moses's call to bring democracy to Mississippi. A native of Manhattan's Lower East Side and a CORE volunteer, Schwerner had already registered African Americans in Meridian, Mississippi, when he returned to that state for Freedom Summer. Schwerner was joined by a local African American man, James Chaney, a 19-year-old high school dropout drawn to the civil rights movement in spite of his family's fears, and Andrew Goodman, a Queens College anthropology major from New York who had never before been in Mississippi.

On June 21, the three traveled to investigate a report that Mount Zion United Methodist Church in Philadelphia, Mississippi, the spiritual home of a black congregation, had been torched by white supremacists. The local Ku Klux Klan and White Citizens Council closely monitored the trio's movements, and Neshoba County Deputy Sheriff Cecil Price, a Klansman, arrested them for alleged speeding. While held in the county jail in Philadelphia, the three were not allowed to make phone calls. Meanwhile, Price arranged for Klansmen to ambush them after they were released from jail. Around 10:30 p.m. Price let the activists out of their cells and told them to leave town. Price followed them in his squad car and, after crossing the town limits, he pulled them over. A Klan ambush party then yanked Schwerner, Chaney and Goodman out of the car. When Schwerner was pulled from the car, a man with a pistol said, "You still think a nigger's as good as I am?" before shooting the civil rights worker in the chest. The Klansmen savagely beat

Chaney. A doctor who later examined the body of the young African American said that in his 25-year career he had "never witnessed bones so severely shattered." The Klansmen fatally shot all three and buried their bodies in an earthen dam.

Nationwide shock over the disappearance of two white men active in civil rights moved President Lyndon Johnson to insist that FBI Director J. Edgar Hoover dispatch agents to find the missing activists. Hoover, who had not hired an African American for any job other than custodian or driver in his four-decade tour as FBI director, had contempt for the civil rights movement and particularly despised Martin Luther King, whom he suspected as a communist agent. FBI agents had infiltrated the Klan and other racist groups in the South and frequently failed to warn the targets of planned violence of pending danger. Hoover initially resisted involvement, but when President Johnson insisted, the agency director dispatched scores of agents to Mississippi.

After being paid $25,000, an FBI informant told agents to look for the bodies in the dam at the Bogue Chitto Swamp. Navy divers and FBI agents found not only the bodies of Schwerner, Chaney and Goodman, but also the corpses of seven other black men murdered by whites and dumped there over the years.

State and local authorities refused to charge the perpetrators with murder, so the U.S. government secured federal indictments against Price, Neshoba County Sheriff Lawrence Rainey and 16 other defendants. They were charged with depriving Schwerner, Chaney and Goodman of their civil rights. A jury found seven of the defendants, including Price and Klan Imperial Wizard Samuel Bowers, guilty on October 20, 1967. Authorities released all those convicted within six years. After an investigation by a Mississippi journalist and by high school students competing in a National History Day contest, enough evidence was uncovered to lead to the arrest and conviction for murder of another killer, preacher Edgar Ray Killen, in 2005. Killen, then 80, received a sentence of three consecutive 20-year sentences.

The murders of the three young men in Mississippi turned public sentiment strongly in favor of the 1965 Voting Rights Act. For many African Americans, however, the case also served as a reminder that the establishment valued white life much more than black life. Soon, black activists in large numbers would part from their white allies and seek a separate black identity that rejected what they saw as the sick values of American society. "I am sick and tired of going to the funerals of black men who have been murdered by white men," said CORE activist David Dennis, angry tears streaming down his cheeks, during the funeral for James Chaney. "I've got vengeance in my heart tonight . . . If you go back home and sit down and take what these white men in Mississippi are doing to us . . . if you take it and don't do something about it . . . then God damn your souls."

THE MISSISSIPPI FREEDOM DEMOCRATIC PARTY

Lyndon Johnson had long felt like an unwanted interloper, and was rankled that some Democrats saw him as an illegitimate heir to the Kennedy throne. Thus, Johnson hoped that the 1964 Democratic National Convention that summer in Atlantic City would be his coronation, an untarnished celebration of that year's many legislative accomplishments. Unfortunately, in spite of movement in the direction of expanded black civil rights, the signs loomed of a national white backlash against reform legislation, and the atmosphere threatened to spoil the Democratic celebrations. George Wallace, the segregationist governor of Alabama, entered the Democratic presidential primaries and carried 34 percent of the vote in Wisconsin, 30 percent in Indiana, and a shocking 43 percent in Maryland. When Wallace's insurgent campaign failed to unseat Johnson, many of these voters began drifting to Republican nominee Barry Goldwater, who portrayed civil rights laws as the intrusion of a growing and increasingly tyrannical federal government into states' rights. Rioting in Harlem and other American cities in the summer of 1964 provoked white anger and increased Johnson's fear of a challenge on the right.

The president, however, perceived a more direct challenge from southern African Americans seeking to put a stop to the all-white segregationist delegations from the South that had been a feature of Democratic Conventions since the 1830s. The Mississippi Freedom Democratic Party (MFDP) had been organized during Freedom Summer. Using a black panther as its symbol, the MFDP planned to challenge the credentials of Mississippi's all-white delegation on the floor of the 1964 convention. The MFDP held its own primaries, with black representatives from cities and rural communities across the state, as well as four white delegates. The delegates would charge that the Mississippi regulars conducted primaries that ignored black voting rights and were thus in violation of federal law and could not be legally seated.

President Johnson didn't want a credentials fight at his convention. Seeking to not embarrass the president, liberals proposed seating both the all-white Mississippi regulars and the Freedom delegation. Governor Paul Johnson of Mississippi told the president his delegation would walk out if forced to share a place with the dissenters. Johnson promised Hubert Humphrey a position as his running mate if he could persuade the Freedom delegation to drop its credentials challenge.

A compromise was offered that would allow two Freedom delegates to sit with the regulars while sixty-six other Freedom Party members could sit as non-voting observers with other delegations. Unwilling to accept even this watered-down proposal, and a demand that they pledge loyalty to the Democratic presidential ticket, the all-white regular delegation walked out of the convention along with the Alabama delegates. The walkout didn't spread, however, which Lyndon Johnson declared as victory. The convention voted to insist that the 1968 Mississippi delegation had to be integrated. Hubert Humphrey was rewarded with this outcome by being named Johnson's running mate.

The Democratic ticket overwhelmingly defeated GOP nominee Goldwater that November. The Arizona senator frightened off mainstream voters with a convention nomination speech in which he declared, "I would remind you that extremism in the defense of liberty is no vice! And let me remind you also that moderation in the pursuit of justice is no virtue!" Later, Goldwater dismissed the hydrogen bomb as "merely another weapon." The night before the general election, the Johnson campaign ran an ad in which a young girl pulled petals from a daisy and counted them, then a voiceover counted down to a missile launch and the screen filled with footage of a mushroom cloud. The ad was designed to remind voters of the dangers of nuclear weapons, and to imply that Goldwater's attitude toward them was irresponsible.

The next day, Johnson carried 61 percent of the popular vote and beat Goldwater 486-52 in the Electoral College. Goldwater's sweep of the Deep South states of Louisiana, Mississippi, Alabama, Georgia and South Carolina, where he carried the votes of whites angered by Johnson's support of civil rights legislation, represented the only cloud on the political horizon for the Democrats.

BLOODY SUNDAY

Lyndon Johnson might have gotten his way regarding the Mississippi Freedom Democratic Party at the 1964 Democratic convention, but Martin Luther King would force the president's hand regarding passage of a voting rights act in 1965. For his next voting rights campaign, King targeted Selma, Alabama, where only 383 of about 15,000 African Americans were registered. King chose Selma not only for the obvious suppression of black voting but because he could count on an overreaction by Dallas County Sheriff Jim Clark. This man had acquired a reputation for out-of-control anger and violence.

The campaign started in January 1965. King announced that the campaign would climax with a 54-mile march on March 7 from Selma to the statehouse in Montgomery, the one-time capital of the Confederacy. That day, 600 marchers crossed the Edmund Pettus Bridge onto state Highway 80 before state troopers, who arrived in squad cars adorned with Confederate flags, halted the march. The state police charged into the crowd wielding billy clubs and firing tear gas canisters. State police chased the marchers back across the bridge with Sheriff Clark shouting, "Get those goddamned niggers!"

Deputies carried on what was essentially a police riot in Selma's black neighborhoods that day, seizing a young black man from inside a church and throwing him through a stained-glass window decorated with an image of Jesus. Footage of the police violence interrupted ABC's broadcast of the film *Judgment at Nuremberg*, and the ugly scenes played on televisions around the world. The event came to be known as "**Bloody Sunday**."

King had been warned of an assassination plot by the Johnson administration and so was not present at the march but, after hearing of the injuries suffered by his friends and allies, he announced a second march. Johnson worked out a deal with Wallace, however. King could bring the marchers to the bridge, but they would halt when ordered to by the state troopers. The protestors would then bow in prayer and leave. Sadly, violence still broke out the night of the second march on March 9, when thugs beat to death James Reeb, a white minister from Massachusetts who had participated in earlier protests.

Johnson had wanted a "cooling off" period for civil rights legislation and hoped to focus on Medicare and other parts of his "Great Society" agenda, but the scenes on Bloody Sunday outraged him, and he made a voting rights bill a priority. Johnson would also step in to allow King and his fellow marchers to complete their symbolic trek from Selma to Montgomery. Johnson federalized the Alabama National Guard for the third march, which began on March 21. With 1,900 guardsmen shielding them from violence, by the fourth day the marchers numbered 25,000 protestors and included entertainers like the musical group Peter, Paul and Mary, United Nations Ambassador Ralph Bunche, and longtime activists like Roy Wilkins, A. Philip Randolph, and Whitney Young. On March 25, King spoke from the steps of the Alabama State Capitol, where Jefferson Davis had been sworn in as president of the Confederacy in 1861.

The protestors happily sang freedom songs at the end of the long journey to Montgomery. This moment represented in many ways a final hurrah for King's movement. A deep generational split over the tactics of non-violence and incremental reforms would cause the young members of SNCC to move in a more radical direction, to be followed by more confrontational groups such as the Black Panthers. Too many African Americans got tired of African American non-violence provoking white brutality. The night of March 25, Viola Liuzzo, a white woman from Detroit, had volunteered to help transport marchers. The mother of five was driving with a black passenger on Highway 80, the main route to Montgomery, when a car occupied by four Klansman pulled alongside her and fatally shot her in the head. Gary Thomas Rowe, an informant on the FBI payroll, testified against the other three Klansmen, who were never convicted of the murder but sent to prison for 10 years for violation of the 1871 Ku Klux Klan Act.

VOTING RIGHTS ACT

"Bloody Sunday," followed by the Liuzzo murder, gave momentum to passage of the 1965 Voting Rights Act. The act prohibited devices employed by southern legislatures to keep African Americans from voting, such as literacy tests, which were supposedly equally enforced for black and white voters but were manipulated to systematically deny African Americans the ballot. The law also empowered the U.S. Justice Department to monitor elections in order to prevent intimidation and harassment of black voters in districts with a history of such behavior.

On August 3, the House passed the measure by a 4-1 margin, and the next day the Senate passed the legislation 79-18. Johnson signed the bill into law August 6 in the President's Room, where, in 1861, Abraham Lincoln signed a law declaring free any slaves forced into service with the Confederate Army. Johnson passed out 89 pens he used to sign the law, with Rosa Parks (who started the Montgomery bus boycott) and Vivian Malone (who had to be escorted into the University of Alabama by federal marshals when the university was integrated in 1963) two of the recipients.

A jubilant atmosphere attended the signing ceremony, but Johnson knew the political dangers of pushing for such revolutionary change. "I have signed away the South for a generation," he is said to have commented after he signed the bill into law. Johnson had no way of knowing if African Americans would vote in significant numbers after the bill's enactment. He could count on, however, an angry southern white backlash. He would live long enough to see his sad prophecy come true, as former segregationist Democrats essentially became segregationist Republicans across Dixie.

As a result of this law and the 1964 Civil Rights Act, segregation slowly faded across the South. Decades later many students across the country would still attend overwhelmingly white or predominantly black and brown schools. But in terms of black voter registration, the impact of the 1965 Voting Right Act was dramatic. In the states of Virginia, South Carolina, Georgia, Alabama, Mississippi and Alabama, black registration overall went from 31 percent to 57 percent by the late 1960s. In the Deep South, the results were more dramatic, with black registration climbing from 32 to 60 percent in Louisiana, 19 to 53 percent in Alabama, and from 6 percent to 44

Signing of the Voting Rights Act President Lyndon B. Johnson moves to shake hands with Dr. Martin Luther King while others look on. LBJ Library photo by Yoichi Okamoto, 08/06/1965

Martin Luther King and Malcolm X waiting for a press conference. March 26, 1964

percent in Mississippi. In Dallas County, Alabama, where the Selma campaign had just taken place, the number of registered voters rocketed from 320 to 6,789. The number of black elected officials in the South also sharply climbed. In the six states mentioned above, the number of black elected officials grew from 70 to about 400.

"BY ANY MEANS NECESSARY"

Even with these gains, the frustrations of watching Martin Luther King Jr.'s non-violent campaign against segregation and racism so frequently encounter murderous violence from powerful southern whites led many African Americans to question King's tactics and to embrace the concept of self-defense. The leader of this alternative approach to black resistance was a man born Malcolm Little, who would later achieve international fame as Nation of Islam Minister **Malcolm X.**

In his bestselling book *The Autobiography of Malcolm X* (1965), Malcolm described his father, Baptist preacher Earl Little, and his mother M. Louise Norton, as dedicated followers of Marcus Garvey, the controversial founder of the United Negro Improvement Association. In the early 1920s, Garvey contended that black people in the Western Hemisphere could achieve political freedom only by returning to the African homeland. Until an independent "Empire of Africa" was created, Garvey said, blacks should struggle to attain complete separation from whites, creating their own "homeland" within the United States. African Americans should only do business with members of their own race, he said, and if attacked they should fight back, returning blow for blow. Earl Little became a preacher, carrying Garvey's message to blacks in Nebraska when Ku Klux Klan nightriders appeared at the Little home and warned the family to leave Omaha.

Less than two years after Malcolm was born, the family resettled in Lansing, Michigan. According to the autobiography, a white hate group called The Black Legion, angered by Earl Little's activism, set fire to the family home in late 1929. Earl Little built a new home outside East Lansing but died on September 28, 1931, after being hit by a streetcar. Malcolm X later described his father's death as an assassination. Louise Little suffered a breakdown eight years later, and Michigan courts divided the eight Little children among several foster families.

In spite of making high grades through his eighth year of public school, Malcolm said he became bitter and rebellious when a previously supportive white English teacher asked him what he wanted to do for a living. When Malcolm said he wanted to become a lawyer, the teacher told him "that's no realistic goal for a nigger" and advised him to become a carpenter. Disillusioned, he became a petty criminal before spending time in a detention home. Malcolm's problems prompted his move in 1941 to Boston, where he lived with his half-sister Ella. He soon drifted to the fringes of Boston's underworld, where he remade himself as "Detroit Red," a zoot-suited con artist, dope dealer, burglar and pimp. He was arrested in February 1946 and given a seven-year sentence on several felony charges including illegal breaking and entering.

Surprisingly, his arrest gave Malcolm an opportunity for self-education, with the future minister copying by hand a dictionary word for word and voraciously reading at the prison library. At this time, his brothers Philbert and Reginald exposed him to the teachings of the Nation of Islam (NOI), a religious sect founded around 1930 in Detroit and led by Elijah Muhammad. According to the NOI, whites were an inherently evil race created in ancient times by a sinister black scientist named Yacub. On judgment day the NOI deity, Allah, would destroy whites and save the black race. Until then, blacks should win the favor of Allah by surrendering vices such as alcohol, avoiding impure foods such as pork, and educating themselves about the past achievements of the black race. NOI members were taught to not vote or participate in politics in any way. Rather than integrate into a racist white society, blacks should embrace complete segregation from white society and dedicate themselves to establishing a financially and politically independent black homeland.

Upon his release from prison in 1952, Malcolm replaced his last name with an "X" to represent the African family name lost under slavery. He soon rose as a full-time NOI minister and distinguished himself as Elijah Muhammad's most effective recruiter and spokesman. An imposing figure, standing about six feet, five inches, with a lanky physique, light skin, closely cropped reddish hair and grayish eyes which peered intensely through horn-rimmed glasses, Malcolm mixed fiery words with politeness and charm.

Malcolm X denounced middle-class black leaders as "Uncle Toms" and labeled Martin Luther King, Jr. a "chump" for advocating integration, declaring that "an integrated cup of coffee was insufficient pay for 400 years of slave labor." Malcolm also ridiculed King's "I Have a Dream" speech, insisting that independence, not integration, represented the only true path to African-American freedom.

By 1964, Malcolm X was outranked only by Republican presidential candidate Barry Goldwater as the most sought-after speaker on college campuses. With Malcolm's evangelism, the NOI grew from a few hundred adherents to 100,000 or more members by the early 1960s. Malcolm grew frustrated by the NOI's refusal to participate in politics and the civil rights struggle while men like King directly challenged white authority.

Malcolm later wrote that he became disillusioned with the Rev. Elijah Muhammad after learning that the chief NOI minister had affairs with several secretaries and fathered six illegitimate children. Malcolm also became outraged at what he saw as financial improprieties by church officials. In December 1963, when Malcolm described the recent assassination of President John F. Kennedy as a case of "chickens coming home to roost," Muhammad, for all his rhetoric about black assertiveness and self-defense, feared a white backlash and suspended Malcolm from his ministry for ninety days.

On March 8, 1964, Malcolm publicly severed his ties with the Nation of Islam. By this point, he had become knowledgeable about orthodox Islam and came to see the variant led by Elijah Muhammad as heretical. Malcolm sought closer ties with King, stating that both men sought black freedom. Plunging into mainstream politics, he now urged his followers to register to vote and to fight to make voting rights a reality in the South. He founded both Muslim Mosque, Inc., and the Organization of Afro-American Unity, which sought to make the rights of black Americans an international issue.

Taking the required Muslim hajj to Mecca in Saudi Arabia, Malcolm for the first time encountered Muslims of all races experiencing spiritual brotherhood. He wrote that he no longer saw all whites as devils but would only hold individual whites accountable for their actions. Malcolm embraced the Sunni branch of Islam and adopted a new name, El-Hajj Malik El-Shabazz.

Malcolm began receiving death threats from his former colleagues in the NOI. Unknown assailants firebombed his New York home, which had been awarded to him by the NOI for his ministerial work, on February 14, 1965. Just four days later, the NOI evicted him from the residence. On February 21, Talmadge Hayer repeatedly shot Malcolm at the start of a speech at the Audubon Ballroom in New York. A grand jury indicted Hayer, Norman 3X Butler, and Thomas 15X Johnson, all members of the NOI, for Malcolm's murder. On the day after the assassination, Elijah Muhammad denied involvement with the killing.

Malcolm's influence increased after his death with the publication of *The Autobiography of Malcolm X*, co-written by Alex Haley, who would gain fame himself in the 1970s as the author of *Roots*. Members of the Student Nonviolent Coordinating Committee (SNCC) increasingly came under the posthumous influence of Malcolm and radicalized, even throwing white members out of the group in the name of black independence.

Director Spike Lee's 1992 film biography *Malcolm X* sparked a renaissance of interest in Malcolm's career and the growth of a merchandising empire that included caps inscribed with the letter "X." Rap recordings in the late twentieth century sampled his speeches, and his face haunted many videos. In popular culture, Malcolm X remains a divisive figure, an anti-hero in his guise as the street-smart hustler who rejected inter-racial cooperation as unrealistic and a hero as the self-educated minister who redeemed himself from an intellectual ghetto.

Long Hot Summers

For Lyndon Johnson and the Democratic Party, the era of peaceful reform ended with shocking abruptness in the mid-1960s. Rather than a racial millennium, the immediate aftermath of the landmark civil rights legislation from 1964 to 1965 brought explosive urban uprisings across the country and angry backlash from the white working and middle classes. A mere five days after Johnson signed the Voting Rights Act, a riot exploded in the Watts neighborhood of Los Angeles. "Watts was a neighborhood of single-family detached homes that did not look like a 'slum' at all," historians Maurice Isserman and Michael Kazin observed. "But it had all the problems of more congested urban neighborhoods, including poor schools, high unemployment, and a high crime rate that included a growing drug abuse problem." The riot started when Lee Minikus, a white police officer, arrested Marquette Frye, an African American who had just consumed two beers with his brother Ronald, for speeding.

As a possibly intoxicated Frye began to resist arrest, a rumor spread rapidly through the crowd that police had beaten Frye's mother and pregnant girlfriend. One woman spat at a police officer and was pushed into a police car. Tempers rose on the hot summer day and the crowd, which included many who had been roughly treated by Los Angeles police, began throwing rocks and bottles. About 5,000 Watts residents, chanting "Burn, baby, burn," began torching buildings, looting stores, and firing handguns.

The **Watts Riot** lasted for six days and took the lives of 34 people (32 of them black), injuring another 900, leaving hundreds homeless, and destroying neighborhood businesses. Black businessmen tried to save their businesses by posting signs in windows that said, 'Soul Brother," meaning that the establishment was African American owned. King would tour the riot zone days later and was shocked when young people yelled to him, "We won." King shot back with a question. "How can you say we won when [32] Negroes are dead, your community is destroyed and whites are using the riots as an excuse for inaction?" Watts' angry young men gave an answer filled with bitterness over the persistence of racism and the failure of liberal reform to bring improvement to the lives of black Americans more quickly: "We won because we made them pay attention to us."

An Undeclared Civil War

In this new period, more defiant and, to some whites, more threatening black voices like those of Stokely Carmichael and H. Rap Brown, both members of SNCC who later affiliated with the **Black Panther Party**, received bigger audiences. Carmichael in particular liked to talk of what he called "Black Power," which he described as "bringing the country to its knees . . . you are talking of a movement that will smash everything Western Civilization has created."

The months of June through August 1967 became known as the "long, hot summer," as riots in 127 cities claimed at least 77 lives and a total of a half-billion dollars in property destroyed. One riot broke out in Plainfield, New Jersey, on July 14, 1967, but the worst urban upheaval exploded in Detroit July 23, 1967. There, police conducted a series of raids on buildings where after-hours drinking and illegal gambling regularly took place. By the time the police conducted their fifth raid, they encountered a party celebrating the return home of two servicemen. Police conducted mass arrests, hauling 82 to jail. During the lengthy raid, a mob gathered and, as in Watts, rumors of police brutality echoed across the black community. By 5 a.m., someone had thrown a bottle at a police car window, even as someone else threw a garbage can through a store window. Looters, including not just the unemployed but people with jobs and whites as well as blacks, began shattering storefronts.

Reportedly, some rioters began to dance as a Molotov cocktail-sparked fire destroyed one building. Twenty-five mph winds spread the sparks, lighting flames throughout the city. Fire soon raged across a 100-block area. Detroit police and the Michigan National Guardsmen began widespread shooting, killing thirty. United States Army units calmed the situation down, and after five days the riot burned itself out. A total of 33 African Americans and 10 whites died in the melee, which caused $250 million in damages to homes and businesses. Much of Detroit turned into a burned-out shell. Michigan Gov. George Romney described Detroit as looking like it "had been bombed on the west side."

TWO NATIONS

In 1968, President Johnson appointed a commission made up of representatives of the establishment civil rights organizations, politically centrist businessmen and politicians to explain the causes of race riots that had torn American cities apart during the previous three summers. Chaired by Illinois Governor Otto Kerner, the commission attributed the violence to a spirit of "hopelessness" felt by many blacks, Hispanics, and even poor whites in the inner city. Urban slums served as homes, the commission reported, to "men and women without jobs, families without men, and schools where children are processed instead of educated, until they returned to the streets—to crime, to narcotics, to dependency on welfare, and to bitterness and resentment against society."

The culprit, the commission declared, was white racism that created racial segregation and discrimination, race-based income disparity, lax law enforcement in ghettoes, white flight from urban areas to the suburbs, and a lack of financial development and business investment in inner cities. In cities hit by riots, according to the commission, blacks were twice as like to be unemployed, and those who had jobs earned only 70 percent of what whites earned. Black residents of riot-torn communities were three times more likely to live in substandard and overcrowded housing. In cities like Detroit and Los Angeles, the **Kerner Commission's** final report said, "Actions to ameliorate Negro grievances have been limited and sporadic; with but with few exceptions, they have not significantly reduced tensions . . . In several cities, increasing polarization is evident, with continuing breakdown of inter-racial communication, and growth of white segregationist or black separatist groups."

The commission recommended further reforms including expansion of public housing and urban renewal programs, provision of subsidies for low-income families so they could purchase homes, improved procedures for filing grievances against abusive police officers and a larger, non-confrontational police presence in urban neighborhoods, and increased attention by the national media to the challenges faced by minority communities in the inner city. Unless such steps were taken, the commission report warned, the United States would become "two societies, one black, one white—separate and unequal."

BLACK IS BEAUTIFUL

As the racial divide deepened, no group struck greater fear in white America than the Black Panther Party, established by Bobby Seale and Huey P. Newton in October 1966 in Oakland, California. Party members wore black military-style berets and openly displayed firearms as they advocated the establishment of a socialist nation that would provide for black and other "oppressed Americans'" free health care, self-determination, improved and non-racist education, quality housing and a cessation of police brutality. The Panthers established health clinics, classes on self-defense, free clothes and meals for schoolchildren and so on. In 1967, the California state legislature and Gov. Ronald Reagan were disturbed enough by the group that these normally pro-gun politicians pushed through a bill outlawing the carrying of loaded weapons in public. The Panthers appeared at the state legislature in Sacramento bearing arms during debates on the measure. Panthers also regularly pursued white policemen in black neighborhoods as a means of preventing police brutality.

Black nationalists and separatists deeply influenced black culture in the 1960s, even if few African Americans supported the ideology of radicals. Polls conducted in the mid-and late 1960s revealed that most African Americans still saw King as the leader of the civil rights cause and only approximately 15 percent of the black population identified with Black Nationalism. In the wake of Malcolm X and the Panthers, however, black studies curricula spread to colleges and universities across the country and eventually were offered at public schools. Black Nationalists rejected the notion that white people represented the universal standard of beauty. The slogan "Black is Beautiful" inspired African Americans and, at an admittedly glacial pace, black models and actresses began to appear in advertising, magazines and movies. Hairstyles like the "Afro," in which African Americans refused to straighten their hair in order to meet white expectations, and African-inspired clothing such as dashikis became popular among young American blacks. Many African Americans rejected their "slave names" and adopted new Muslim or African names as a means of restoring a heritage and identity partly lost during slavery.

White Backlash

The race riots from 1965 to 1967, and the emergence of groups like the Black Panthers, became a final, decisive factor in shattering the liberal consensus forged by the national Democratic Party from the time of Franklin Roosevelt until the middle of Lyndon Johnson's one full term as president. News stories of rising crime rates prompted fears about personal safety among middle-class and working-class whites. Increased drug use among young people and a more frankly secular and sexualized mass media made socially conservative whites worry that their control of the culture was slipping away and that the country was sliding into anti-patriotic decadence.

The urban riots, for some middle-class and working-class whites, served as a final straw. To many resentful whites, some openly embracing racism, politicians like Johnson had created welfare programs and handed greater political power to an ungrateful black population that wanted government handouts rather than jobs. The first signs of this white backlash came as early as 1964 when an avowed segregationist governor like Wallace could do so well in Democratic Party primaries held in states north of the Mason-Dixon line. Also, that year 65 percent of Californian voters approved Proposition 14, a measure that reversed a law earlier passed by the state legislature that banned home sellers from discriminating against racial minorities. (Both the California and then the United States Supreme Court later overturned Proposition 14.) White anger found its voice in the successful 1966 California gubernatorial campaign of former actor Ronald Reagan, who overwhelmingly defeated liberal incumbent Democratic Gov. Pat Brown, carrying almost 58 percent of the vote.

The off-year congressional elections that year were a disaster for Johnson and the Democrats. That November, 27 of the 48 Democratic House freshmen elected as part of Johnson's 1964 landslide lost office. Of the 10 new governors elected that fall, nine were Republicans, and the GOP now controlled 12 of 13 Western state legislatures. The number of Americans identifying themselves as Republicans increased. Author Rick Perlstein argues that the conservative coalition in Congress—made up of segregationist southern Democrats and northern Republicans—doubled after the 1966 elections. The now former governor of California Pat Brown was certain why he and other Democrats had been drubbed. "Whether we like it or not, people want a separation of the races," he said. "Maybe they feel Lyndon Johnson has given them [blacks] too much. People can only accept so much and then they regurgitate."

1960-1967: THE BEST OF TIMES

The curses of poverty, unemployment, crime, poorly funded and understaffed schools, and malnutrition still haunted African-American communities. Nevertheless, it would be wrong to assume that the voting rights laws, legislation requiring access to public accommodations regardless of race, anti-poverty programs and anti-discrimination mandates passed by Kennedy and Johnson had no impact.

For instance, during the 1960s, black unemployment dropped 34 percent. From 1959 to 1967, the poverty rate among African Americans dropped from a staggering 55.1 percent to a still much too high but significantly better 39.3 percent. (By 1970, the poverty rate among African Americans dropped further to 33.5 percent.) The poverty rate for all Americans in that time period dropped from 22.4 to 14.2 percent. Before the 1960s, a large percentage of African Americans held low-paying custodial or domestic jobs, or worked as under-compensated farm labor. During the 1960s, the number of blacks holding jobs in higher-paid technical, professional and clerical fields doubled, and the length of time African Americans stayed in school increased by an average of four years.

Largely because of civil rights laws and the Voting Rights Act of 1965, African Americans gained unprecedented clout in local, state and national politics during the Kennedy-Johnson era. Just one year after Johnson signed the voting rights law, an additional 450,000 southern blacks registered to vote. More black voters meant more black office holders. Between 1960 and 2000, the number of African-American officeholders sharply climbed from just 300 to nearly 9,040. African Americans have been elected mayor of many of the nation's largest cities, including New York, Los Angeles, Chicago, Washington, D.C., Dallas, Atlanta, Philadelphia, and Detroit. Without the 1965 Voting Rights Act, it is highly unlikely that Barack Obama, whose mother was white and whose father was a black native of Kenya, could have been elected president in 2008.

Before the civil rights laws of 1964 and 1965, African-American employees often had to walk blocks to find a designated "colored" restroom. The NAACP published travel guides indicating which lunch counters, restrooms, pools, parks, and hotels were open to African Americans. In a matter of weeks after passage of the landmark 1964 Civil Rights Act, "whites only" restrooms, water fountains, and seating in theaters, sports stadiums and restaurants disappeared across the South. Between 1964 and 1974, the United States Justice Department filed suits against 500 school districts and more than 400 gas stations, hotels and motels, restaurants and lunch counters, bars and truck stops that still segregated black patrons.

It wasn't just African Americans who benefited from Kennedy's New Frontier and Johnson's Great Society. Increased government spending on both defense and domestic projects helped create 8.4 million new jobs from 1960 to 1966. Spending on health and education increased 59 percent and on urban development by 76 percent. The average family saw a 30 percent gain in real income from 1960 to 1968. Counting all racial categories, at the beginning of the 1960s, 40 million Americans lived in poverty. A decade later, the poverty rate dropped to 24 million, a decline from 20 percent of the population to 12 percent.

The Kennedy-Johnson years saw the development of a more equitable criminal justice system. Johnson established public television and public radio, which gave Americans access to information, music and news not subject to the pressure of commercial popularity or pressure from sponsors. Laws passed in this era provided greater protection for privacy, increased rights for women, a sharper division between church and state, and an explosion of scientific and technological innovations. Literacy rates rose dramatically. In addition to space travel, the era saw the rapid improvement in the power and efficiency of computers, and better prospects for patients with cancer and other lethal diseases. Life spans lengthened and the population generally enjoyed better health from the 1940s until the late 1960s, an age of political liberalism.

1960-1967: THE WORST OF TIMES

In spite of all these achievements, the problems faced in the 1960s proved maddeningly hard to solve. Johnson's programs to fight poverty and racial discrimination proved the least popular initiatives of his presidency among white voters who began to feel they were too highly taxed for the benefit of racial minorities. Before the disastrous 1966 midterm elections, a poll in July of that year revealed that a majority of Americans favored cuts in anti-poverty and urban renewal programs, rent subsidies and welfare expenditures, and showed that they wanted the savings to be used to increase spending on the Vietnam War. Most Americans, according to polls, approved spending on the space program and programs to curb pollution, but an astonishing 90 percent were against further civil rights legislation. A Gallup survey indicated that 88 percent of Americans thought that more hard work and effort would solve black poverty, rather than more government assistance. By 1967, after another round of urban riots, 52 percent of Americans believed that Johnson had moved "too fast" on the issue of integration. By 1966, President Johnson despaired that Americans were more excited about the prospects of humans landing on the moon than they were about any successes of the war on poverty.

According to George Lipsitz, a professor of ethnic studies at the University of California at San Diego, much of the celebrated civil rights and anti-poverty legislation of the Kennedy and Johnson years was either designed to fail or foundered because of white bureaucrats' unwillingness to enforce anti-discrimination laws. The newly established Equal Employment Opportunity Commission lacked enforcement powers such as the ability to issue "cease and desist orders against discriminating employers. The EEOC could do no more than offer its services as a non-binding arbitrator between discriminated against individuals and discriminating employers. Underfunding, understaffing and a lack of administrative will to tackle entrenched job discrimination made the EEOC a paper tiger. By 1967, the agency received an average of 23 discrimination complaints a day. By 1972, only about half of the 80,000 cases referred to the EEOC had ever been investigated.

Given the loopholes, and bad faith on the part of many government administrators charged with enforcement of civil rights legislation, it is no wonder that many of the most promising of the Kennedy-Johnson civil rights and anti-poverty measures fell short of their promise. Even after the Kennedy-Johnson reforms, African Americans still suffered significantly higher poverty rates than whites. This is attributable in part to a sharp increase in the number of single-parent homes in black America. This, as political scientist Andrew Hacker points out, is a recent phenomenon. In 1950, he notes, single women headed only 17 percent of black homes, a lower rate than exists in 2010 for whites. By 1970, the percentage of black homes headed by single women stood at 34.5 percent. Hacker proposes several reasons for this. According to Hacker, looser attitudes toward sex outside of marriage have contributed to the increase, as well as the rise of a more negative attitude by men toward marriage. According to the federal government, most absent fathers in recent decades have ended up paying no child support or less than the splitting couple had agreed upon.

Black women were particularly hard hit by the absence of the father's income, since both black men and women earned significantly less than their white peers. Even with an increase in black wages from 1960 to 1970, African-American men climbed from $669 earned for every $1,000 earned by whites in 1960 to only $704 per each $1,0000 earned by whites in 1970. Black women experienced a much more dramatic growth in wages but still lagged considerably behind whites. In 1960, black women earned $696 per $1,000 paid to whites and only $851 per $1,000 for whites in 1970.

After the Kennedy-Johnson initiatives, white flight aggravated the poverty of black neighborhoods. The United States Census Bureau reported that about 900,000 whites moved from cities to the suburbs each year between 1965 and 1970. This mass movement started in part in reaction to the riots in the larger cities. Whites concluded it was no longer safe to live inside the nation's metropolises. White parents also feared sending their children to the same schools as black and Latino children. The sad irony was that once schools were legally mandated to desegregate, the schools re-segregated because of the white migration. With the fleeing whites went white-owned businesses and white money, and urban school districts, now with a minority majority population, would struggle to make up the decrease in tax revenues.

In the end, Lyndon Johnson's dream of winning the war on poverty and ending racial strife was sacrificed on the altar of the Vietnam War. The war consumed an ever larger percentage of the budget. Total American military expenditures grew from more than $295 billion in 1964 to over $354 billion in 1967. With major increases in both domestic and military spending, inflation began to rise each year, from 1.28 percent in 1964 to 4.27 percent in 1968, Johnson's last full year in office. Johnson steadily lost interest in battling poverty and discrimination as he became obsessed with avoiding the onerous fate of being the "first" American president to supposedly lose a war. By 1967-1968, Johnson began cutting domestic programs in order to support a deepening war effort in Southeast Asia. Dr. King would come out against the war, seeing in it the defeat of his campaign for social justice.

"A few years ago there was a shining moment in [the civil rights] struggle," King said in a New York speech April 4, 1967, exactly one year before his assassination. "It seemed as if there was a real promise of hope for the poor, both black and white, through the poverty program. There were experiments, hopes, new beginnings. Then came the buildup in Vietnam, and I watched this program broken and eviscerated as if it were some idle political plaything of a society gone mad on war. And I knew that America would never invest the necessary funds or energies in rehabilitation of its poor so long as adventures like Vietnam continued to draw men and skills and money like some demonic, destructive suction tube."

The African-American poet Langston Hughes once famously asked, "What happens to a dream deferred? Does it dry up like a raisin in the sun? Or fester like a sore—and then run? . . . Maybe it just sags like a heavy load. Or does it explode?" Unbelievably, after the heartaches of the Kennedy, Medgar Evers and Malcolm X assassinations, the Schwerner, Chaney and Goodman murders, the 16th Street Baptist Church bombing, and the holocausts that consumed Watts, Detroit and scores of other cities, national turmoil did not subside as 1967 wound to a close. In the coming months, the frustrated dreams of Americans would explode, creating terrifying chaos and violence that would dwarf the murderous previous three years. The year 1968 would be marked by the fall of a president, two more political assassinations, the widest and most bitter riots, a massacre in a remote village in Vietnam, and the rise of a new president whose administration would transform into a criminal enterprise. By the end of 1968, the dreams of too many Americans had transformed into a nightmare.

Chronology

1960 Sit-ins at lunch counters.
John Kennedy elected president.

1961 Peace Corps.
Alliance for Progress.
Bay of Pigs.
Berlin Wall erected.

1962 Cuban Missile Crisis.
James Meredith enrolls at Old Miss.

1963 Civil Rights demonstrations in Birmingham.
March on Washington.
Test Ban Treaty.
Diem assassination.
Kennedy assassination.
Betty Friedan, *The Feminine Mystique*.

1964 Job Corps.
Head Start.
Mississippi Freedom Summer.
Civil Rights Act.
Economic Opportunity Act.
Gulf of Tonkin Incident.
War on Poverty.
Johnson-Goldwater election.

1965 Americanization of Vietnam War.
Assassination of Malcolm X.
Medical Care Act.
Civil Rights March: Selma to Montgomery.
Voting Rights Act.
Watts riot.
Grape strike in California.
Opposition to draft.

1966 Black Power.
National Organization of Women (NOW).

1967 Anti-War Demonstrations.
Race riots in Newark, Detroit.
March on Pentagon.
Thurgood Marshall, first African-American appointed to the U. S. Supreme Court.

1968 Tet Offensive.
Indian Civil Rights Act.
Johnson not to seek re-election.
Martin Luther King, Jr. assassinated.
Robert F. Kennedy assassinated.
Violence at Democratic Convention.
Vietnam Peace talks.
Nixon elected president.

Review Questions

1. How did the sit-in movement mark a change in strategy for the Civil Rights Movement and where else did leaders use the tactic of "direct action"?

2. What political factors, including the Cold War, religion, race, and media technology, shaped the 1960 presidential election?

3. What major events marked the American relationship to the communist world during the Kennedy and Johnson administrations?

4. What were the most important domestic initiatives that comprised the "Great Society," including civil rights reforms?

5. What underlying factors caused the urban unrest of the mid- and late-1960s?

Glossary of Important People and Concepts

Apollo Program
Bay of Pigs Invasion
Berlin Crisis of 1961
Black Panther Party
"Bloody Sunday"
Civil Rights Act of 1957
Civil Rights Act of 1964
Sheriff Theophilus Eugene "Bull" Connor
Cuban Missile Crisis
Freedom Riders
Freedom Summer
Great Society
Hubert Horatio Humphrey
Lyndon Baines Johnson
John F. Kennedy
Kerner Commission
Martin Luther, Jr. King
"Letter From a Birmingham Jail"
March on Washington
Mississippi Freedom Democratic Party
Robert Parris Moses
"New Frontier"
"Ole Miss"
Francis Gary Powers
Profiles in Courage
Nelson A. Rockefeller
Sixteenth Street Baptist Church Bombing
Southern Christian Leadership Council (SCLC)
Southern Manifesto
Sputnik
Warren Court
Watts Riot
Malcolm X

SUGGESTED READINGS

Taylor Branch. *Parting the Waters: America in the King Years, 1954-1963*. 1988.
Roger Bruns. *Martin Luther King, Jr.: A Biography*. 2006.
Clayborne Carson. *In Struggle: SNCC and the Black Awakening of the 1960s*. 1981.
Dan T. Carter. *The Politics of Rage: George Wallace, The Origins of the New Conservatism, and the Transformation of American Politics*. 1995.
Paul A. Carter. *Another Part of the Fifties*. 1983.
Peter Collier and David Horowitz. *The Kennedys: An American Drama*. 1984.
Patrick L. Cox and Michael Phillips. *The House Will Come to Order: How the Texas Speaker Became a Power in State and National Politics* (2010).
Robert Dallek. *An Unfinished Life: John F. Kennedy, 1917-1963* (200.
____, *Lone Star Rising: Lyndon Johnson and His Times, 1908-1960* (1991).
____, *Flawed Giant: Lyndon Johnson and His Times, 1961-1973* (1998).
John D'Emilio and Estelle B. Freedman. *Intimate Matters: A History of Sexuality in America* (1997).
Marshall Frady. *Martin Luther King, Jr.: A Life* (2005).
Lawrence M. Friedman. *A History of American Law* (1985).
Todd Gitlin. *The Sixties: Years of Hope, Days of Rage* (1987).
John Gunther. *Inside USA* (1947).
Andrew Hacker. *Two Nations: Black and White, Separate, Hostile, Unequal* (1992).
Maurice Isserman and Michael Kazin. *America Divided: The Civil War of the 1960s* (2000).
Susan Jacoby. *Freethinkers: A History of American Secularism* (2004).
Martin Luther King, Jr. *Why We Can't Wait* (1964).
Richard Kluger. *Simple Justice: The History of Brown v. Board of Education and Black America's Struggle for Equality* (1975).
George Lipsitz. *The Possessive Investment in Whiteness: How White People Profit from Identity Politics* (1998).
Mark Hamilton Lytle. *America's Uncivil Wars: The Sixties Era From Elvis to the Fall of Richard Nixon* (2006).
Ralph G. Martin. *A Hero for Our Time: The Intimate Story of the Kennedy Years* (1983).
William Martin. *With God On Our Side: The Rise of the Religious Right in America* (1996).
Allen J. Matusow. *The Unraveling of America: A History of Liberalism in the 1960s* (1984).
Stephen P. Miller. *Billy Graham and the Rise of the Republican South* (2009).
Anne Moody. *Coming of Age in Mississippi* (1968).
Rick Perlstein. *Nixonland: The Rise of a President and the Fracturing of America* (2008).
Kevin Phillips. *Wealth and Democracy: A Political History of the American Rich* (2002).
Michael Phillips. *White Metropolis: Race, Ethnicity and Religion in Dallas, 1841-2001* (2006).
Harvard Sitkoff. *The Struggle for Black Equality, 1954-1980* (1981).
Robert Weisbrot. *Freedom Bound: A History of America's Civil Rights Movement* (1990).
Theodore H. White. *The Making of the President: 1960* (1961).
Tom Wolfe. *The Right Stuff* (1979).
Malcolm X (as told to Alex Haley). *The Autobiography of Malcolm X* (1964).

President John F. Kennedy and Vice President Lyndon B. Johnson

Chapter Twenty-nine

ROLLING THUNDER: The Vietnam War Under Kennedy and Johnson

World War II had presented the United States Army with a unique problem in the history of armed conflict. After the war, the Army Air Force (the Air Force didn't become a separate military branch until 1947) discovered that less than one percent of its pilots ranked as "aces," meaning they had shot down at least five enemy planes. Aces accounted for up to 40 percent of all enemy aircraft downed. Most pilots, the command discovered, never shot anyone down. Another study found that only one in seven infantry soldiers used their weapons even in combat.

As military historian Gwynne Dyer notes, by the Second World War, "with the increased dispersion of infantrymen and their escape from direct observation by their comrades, their fundamental disinclination to kill had become the dominating factor, even when a unit was directly engaged in combat . . . Men will kill under compulsion—men will do almost anything if they know it is expected of them and they are under strong social pressure to comply—but the vast majority of men are not born killers."

Dyer notes that basic training changed after World War II, becoming more violent and more centered on killing and dehumanizing the potential enemy. Early in training, American recruits were given "pugil-sticks." Equipped with helmets and gloves, two recruits faced off against each other with sticks heavily padded on each end and then struck each other with those weapons until one of the men fell to the ground. Dyer, in his study of the language used by drill instructors at the Marine training facility at Parris Island, heard the DI shouting the following at recruits:

You want to rip his [the enemy's] eyeballs out, you want to tear apart his love machines, you want to destroy his privates, you don't want to have nothing left of him. You want to send him home in a Glad Bag to his mammy! Hey, show no mercy to the enemy, they are not going to show it on you. Marines are born and trained killers. You've got to prove that every day.

Post-World War II basic training camps built on earlier traditions of converting independently minded people into component parts of a fighting unit. Hair was shaved off, look-alike uniforms were issued, and the recruit was not referred to by name, but by insulting labels given by the drill instructors, names that drew on racial slurs and mockery of the recruit's physical and personality traits. Before the recruit could assimilate into a new identity as a member of the Corps or the Army, DIs shattered many of the larger society's norms. In this era when women were a tiny percentage of the armed services, drill sergeants encouraged misogyny, with women referred to generically by names like "sluts" or "Suzy Rottencrotch." The sergeants defined war as the ultimate expression of masculinity and told recruits that real men killed the enemy.

"We are reluctant to admit that essentially war is the business of killing," General George Marshall wrote in 1947. This was no longer the case on military training bases by the 1950s. During the Korean War, the Army estimated that 50 percent of soldiers fired their weapons in combat. By the Vietnam War, the military placed killing the enemy front and center in training future soldiers. As one Marine Corps drill sergeant and Vietnam veteran told Dyer in an interview in the 1980s:

> The Vietnam era was, of course, then at its peak, you know, and everybody was motivated more or less towards, you know, the kill thing. We'd run PT in the morning, and every time your left foot hit the deck you'd have to chant, "kill, kill, kill, kill." It was drilled into you mind so much that it seemed like when it actually came down to it, it didn't bother you, you know? Of course, the first one always does, but it seems to get easier—not easier because it still bothers you with every one that, you know, that you actually kill and know you killed.

BEARING ANY BURDEN

Like many of his generation, John F. Kennedy's worldview had been largely shaped by events in Europe in the late 1930s. Kennedy remembered how British Prime Minister Neville Chamberlain repeatedly appeased German dictator Adolf Hitler, stepping aside as the Nazi government violated the Versailles Peace Treaty, built up the armed forces, and annexed Austria before forcibly taking over Czechoslovakia.

Committed to Truman's policy of containing communism, Kennedy had favored funding the French War in Indochina, first as a congressman and then as a senator. Kennedy saw the communist regime in Moscow, like the Nazi regime in Germany, as engaged in an aggressive campaign to dominate the world. Appeasement of the communists, he argued, would only encourage more aggression from the Soviets. The United States must back anti-communist regimes wherever they stood, even in small corners of the world like Southeast Asia, to prevent "the onrushing tide of Communism from engulfing all Asia." This aggressive stance formed the context for his pledge in his inaugural address in which he promised to "pay any price, bear any burden, meet any hardship, support any friend, and oppose any foe to assure the survival and success of liberty." When Kennedy took office as president on January 20, 1961, Vietnam did not top his foreign policy concerns. Kennedy had no great enthusiasm for committing American troops to support South Vietnam, but he was also unwilling to remove the American military "advisors" already placed there.

The year 1954 saw the French surrender in Vietnam and the **Geneva Peace Accords**, which established separate North and South Vietnamese governments, called for national elections and unification of the two sections in 1956, and allowed Vietnamese to settle where they wished for 300 days after the accord took effect. The South Vietnamese government was headed by a pro-American Catholic dictator, **Ngo Dinh Diem**. By 1955, 900,000 North Vietnamese Roman Catholics requested transportation south. In the end only 90,000 successfully resettled in South Vietnam, where they became a resented religious minority.

In 1957, Diem decided not to hold an election unifying North and South Vietnam as called for in the Geneva Accords. In response, the communists launched a guerilla campaign, assassinating more than 400 South Vietnamese officials. The guerillas organized 37 military companies by the end of the year. The North Vietnamese started transporting weapons and other supplies on the Ho Chi Minh Trail, which crossed into Laos and Cambodia before winding into South Vietnam. In 1960, the war escalated with the formation of the National Liberation Front, or the "Vietcong," as they were labeled by the Diem regime. The North Vietnamese regular army amply supported the NLF. The size of the North Vietnamese Army, at the same time, grew with Hanoi's implementation of a universal conscription law.

THE DIEM REGIME

Diem knew that he could not win a fair election against **Ho Chi Minh**, the North Vietnamese leader who was widely admired as an ardent fighter for Vietnamese independence from France, then against Japanese occupation during World War II. Arguing that if elections were held in 1956 the communists in the North would be able to coerce 100 percent support from their citizens, Diem cancelled the elections and received full American support for his decision.

Born to a well-off family in the city of Hue, Diem lacked a rapport with the poor farmers who made up most of the South Vietnamese population. He had been active in anti-communist politics under the colonial regime, and the French appointed him governor of Phan Thiet Province. When the French placed the Emperor Bao Dai on the Vietnamese throne, they insisted Diem serve as interior minister. Diem resigned, however, when the French refused his request to form a Vietnamese legislature. During World War II, he formed a political party seeking Vietnamese independence. Angered, his former French patrons sought his arrest.

After the war, the French changed course and appointed Diem prime minister. With Ho Chi Minh's Democratic Republic of Vietnam firmly entrenched in the North by 1954, the government in Paris formally dissolved the colony of French Indochina and proclaimed the birth of the Republic of Vietnam. The Diem government staged a corrupt referendum and voters were asked to choose between living under a monarchy ruled by the Emperor Bao Dai or a republic under a Diem presidency.

South Vietnamese policemen combed neighborhoods, knocked on doors, and told the occupants their lives would be in danger if they chose not to vote. Diem would improbably claim 98.2 percent of the vote. In Saigon, with its population of 450,000 registered voters, Diem managed to win 605,025 votes. Intended to establish Diem's legitimacy, the election instead reinforced the president's image as a corrupt dictator.

Diem was a wealthy man in a country of poverty. He was a Catholic in a land with a Buddhist majority. He was a man of poor political skills in a badly divided nation. This is the man the United States chose to back against Ho, widely regarded as a patriot and a hero in the wars against the Japanese and the French. Ho's popularity in the North only grew in the 1950s when he implemented badly needed land reform. Before the communist regime implemented land redistribution, 60 percent of the population owned only 11 percent of the land. Even though the communists used ruthless methods to achieve their ends, including the executions of between 3,000 and 15,000 landowners, according to one historian of the land reform campaign, most peasants approved of the government action.

Not popular, except with Catholics, Diem made only haphazard attempts to build public support and never embraced the idea of democracy. Americans refused to push him in that direction as long as he remained reliably anti-communist. Diem described his political philosophy as "personalism" in which the population owed the ruler absolute obedience. As Vietnam War historian Bernard Fall noted, Diem believed that "compromise has no place, and opposition of any kind must of necessity be subversive and must be suppressed with all the vigor the system is capable of." In South Vietnam, land remained in the hands of the few. Bureaucrats in the Diem government became infamous for greed. Reluctant to share power, Diem abolished local elections and asserted his authority to appoint village and provincial officials.

Incompetent South Vietnamese government officials routinely demanded bribes and Diem personally controlled drug trafficking in the country. The dictator shut down newspapers that criticized him. Dissidents who spoke out against the Diem dictatorship faced arrest and torture, and some simply disappeared. By the time Diem and his brother **Ngo Dinh Nhu**, the head of the South Vietnamese secret police, were killed during a 1963 military coup, 50,000 languished in prisons on political charges. The government detained many dissidents, communist and non-communist alike, in so-called reeducation centers where interrogators abused them and attempted to brainwash them into supporting the regime. Yet U.S. President Dwight Eisenhower hailed Diem as a "tough little miracle man," and later, Kennedy's Vice President Lyndon Johnson crowned him as the savior of Southeast Asia.

CAUTIOUS ENGAGEMENT

Kennedy harbored doubts about Diem but for two years felt he had no choice but to support the shaky regime. As Stanley Karnow, journalist and chronicler of the Vietnam War, put it, Kennedy "rejected a withdrawal from Vietnam, but he balked at plunging into total war, a prospect he could not even envision." When one Kennedy advisor, George Ball, predicted that the United States might eventually have to send 300,000 troops to fight North Vietnam, Kennedy shot back, "Well, George, you're supposed to be one of the smartest guys in town, but you're crazier than hell. That will never happen." Ball actually underestimated the eventual American commitment in Southeast Asia. Later, during the Johnson administration, the United States had a half-million troops in South Vietnam.

By April 1961, Kennedy had assembled a Vietnam task force charged with forming a strategy to prevent communist domination of South Vietnam. These advisors debated the wisdom of placing American combat troops in South Vietnam, an idea that Diem opposed at the time, arguing that it would make him appear to be a puppet of the United States. The administration's hand was tipped by an escalation of guerilla warfare waged by the communist NLF. In October, the communist Vietcong forces staged attacks causing heavy South Vietnamese Army of Vietnam (ARVN) casualties at South Vietnamese bases in the Phuoc Thanh and Darlac provinces. His confidence shaken, Diem now asked for American combat soldiers and a bilateral defense pact between the United States and South Vietnam. Meanwhile, **Maxwell Taylor,** a favored general in the Kennedy camp, toured the region and returned to Washington urging the commitment of American ground forces.

Taylor's recommendations included dispatching to South Vietnam an increased number of military advisors as well as three squadrons of combat helicopters flown by American pilots. Taylor also urged the secret deployment of 8,000 combat troops, supposedly to help the Diem regime deal with a flood in the Mekong River

Vice President Lyndon B. Johnson standing among a group of Vietnamese and American soldiers during a visit to Saigon, South Vietnam. May 12, 1962

Delta. To discourage the North Vietnamese regular Army (the NVA) from increasing its aid to South Vietnamese guerillas, Taylor suggested a bombing campaign against North Vietnam. Taylor embraced the so-called "**domino theory**"—the argument that if South Vietnam fell to the communists, neighboring countries would be swallowed by the "red tide" until, as Vice President Johnson said, American troops would have to fight "on the beaches of Waikiki" in Hawaii.

Kennedy remained skeptical about escalation. He predicted to his friend and advisor, the historian Arthur Schlesinger, "The troops will march in, the bands will play, the crowds will cheer, and in four days everybody will have forgotten. Then we will be told we have to send in more troops. It's like taking a drink. The effect wears off, and you have to take another." Tragically, Kennedy overcame his reluctance. By the time Taylor had toured South Vietnam in late 1961, the number of American military advisors had grown to 3,000 and would reach 16,000 by the time of the America president's murder in 1963. By the end of 1961 American pilots flew combat missions for the first time, bombing NLF (Vietcong) and North Vietnamese targets under the cover story that they were training South Vietnamese crews.

Meanwhile, the increased number of American military advisors supervised a South Vietnamese offensive against the Vietcong. Using combat helicopters, ARVN forces enjoyed an unprecedented mobility. The larger American presence and the increased military hardware briefly turned momentum. But, as historian George Herring points out, even with the choppers and new electronic communications and surveillance equipment, and with the use of defoliation chemicals that stripped trees in South Vietnam of leaves, the rice paddies and dense jungles of the South provided heavy cover for Vietcong bases.

The loud arrival of helicopters signaled an assault by American and ARVN soldiers on the ground, giving guerillas the chance to melt into the environment. VC soldiers quickly figured out how to down the low-flying choppers with small arms, and sometimes stayed concealed until the helicopters departed, when they would launch a surprise attack on the landing party. At the same time, the communist insurgents increased in strength. By the spring of 1962, the Vietcong numbered, according to one estimate, 300,000 male and female soldiers and 1 million supporters among South Vietnamese civilians.

Quarantine

The domino theory presumed that political ideas like communism spread like viruses. The American military sought to quarantine Vietnamese peasants from radical political thought. Using a plan drawn up by British military advisor Robert Thompson, President Diem and his brother Nhu for years had advocated the construction of so-called "strategic hamlets." Under this plan, the Americans and South Vietnamese, beginning in 1962, sought to prevent Vietcong contact with peasants, a major source of support for the guerillas. Once placed inside these hamlets, the peasants living there could hold village elections giving at least the semblance of political empowerment to the countryside farmers. Inside the hamlets, the peasants would also enjoy access to schools and medicine.

Dependent on peasants for food and shelter, the VC would be cut off from life support by the stockade fences surrounding the strategic hamlets. Roger Hilsman, a Kennedy advisor, urged the implementation of the program, which he hoped would reduce the Vietcong to "hungry, marauding bands of outlaws devoting all of their energies to remaining alive."

The South Vietnamese military tried to persuade poor farmers to voluntarily move into the villages and, if that failed, to force them at gunpoint. Soldiers posted at the hamlets monitored and inspected all who entered the village compound. The South Vietnamese government later fraudulently proclaimed that more than 4 million people, about a third of the population, had been successfully relocated. In reality, only 10 percent of the hamlets provided any security from VC penetration. The hamlets failed in their most important objective: isolating peasants from contact with the Vietcong. Old men armed with swords and flintlock rifles often provided the so-called security. In most cases, the VC entered and exited hamlets at will and collected money, intelligence and food from the residents.

The South Vietnamese government forced the hamlet farmers to pay for construction of their new homes and for the fences surrounding the artificial villages even though the U.S. government already had paid for these materials. South Vietnamese officials also stole supplies such as American-provided food and seeds. Strict curfews hampered peasants' attempts to farm. Meanwhile, those living in the hamlets faced arbitrary searches, detention and demands for bribes. The chief impact of the program was to inspire anger against the Diem government.

"A BUDDHIST BARBECUE SHOW"

No group felt more alienated under President Diem than South Vietnam's Buddhist majority. In government appointments, Diem heavily favored fellow Catholics, and the president frequently directed his police to throw their weight around during the springtime buildup to the Buddha's birthday, May 8. The waves of arrests would show "the VC that the Government was strong and make opponents of the Government afraid," said a South

Buddhist monk Thich Quang Duc, burning himself to death to protest persecution of Buddhists in Vietnam, as other monks look on, Saigon, 1963.

Vietnamese Catholic priest. Leading up to May 8, 1963, secret police launched a crackdown in the old capital city of Hué against Buddhists who had begun speaking out against Diem's policies.

Diem decided to mark the Buddha's 2,527th birthday by harshly enforcing a law banning the display of any flags other than that of the Republic of South Vietnam. Recently, the central government had ordered the widespread display in Hué of Vatican flags in honor of Diem's brother, Archbishop Ngo Dinh Tuc. The hypocrisy outraged the local population, and many flew Buddhist banners from their homes. Nine Buddhists celebrating the birthday died when fired upon by South Vietnamese troops. Ten thousand Buddhists marched two days later to protest the killings, and Diem responded in a typically hamfisted way, ordering the mass arrests of outspoken Buddhist monks and their backers. Labeling such monks as communists, Diem placed guards around the most important pagodas in the country.

The Buddhist clergy captured world attention on June 11, 1963. On that day, a monk named **Thich Quang Duc** exited a car and sat in the lotus pose at a busy Saigon intersection in front of the Cambodian embassy. Other monks chanted while two doused the 66-year-old with gasoline. Quang Duc lit a match and burned to death while a man with a microphone declared, "A Buddhist priest burns himself to death. A Buddhist priest becomes a martyr." Only his heart remained unburned, and this became a sacred relic and symbol of the rightness of the Buddhist protests against Diem.

As the shocking images of this public suicide reached the United States, for the first time Americans realized how deep the opposition to Diem ran and how badly they had been misled by the Kennedy administration about Vietnamese support for American policies. No moment better captured the growing distance between Diem's inner circle and the South Vietnamese population than the reaction of the president's sister-in-law, Madame Ngo Dinh Nhu, to the death of Quang Duc, widely considered a saintly hero. Nhu contemptuously said she would "clap hands at seeing another Buddhist barbecue show." The monk's death sparked a summer of demonstrations at public schools and colleges, and five more Buddhists set themselves ablaze by the end of October 1963.

Kennedy realized the United States had become too close to Diem. He replaced the American ambassador to South Vietnam, Frederick Nolting, who had a close friendship with Diem, with **Henry Cabot Lodge**, a Republican whose appointment would make American policy in Southeast Asia a bipartisan affair. Kennedy also sent Diem a clear message that he wanted Nhu removed from the government and his despised wife out of the

Map 29.1 Vietnam

public picture. The administration believed that it "was Ngo Dinh Nhu who had alienated the country and oppressed the Buddhists," according to historian Marilyn B. Young. "If only Diem would only rid his top governing councils of Nhu and his wife, the country would rally to his support. Blaming Nhu exempted the rest of American policy from close examination, and Nhu was such a convincing villain."

Nhu remained in the government, and in August, instead of building bridges to the Buddhists, Nhu dispatched a private military force disguised as regular ARVN units to arrest popular Buddhist clergy and attack pagodas. (Nhu hoped the public would blame the attacks on ARVN commanders, who he increasingly thought were disloyal to the regime.) Even Madame Nhu's mother and father, the South Vietnamese United Nations observer and the ambassador to Washington respectively, resigned in protest against the Buddhist crackdown.

In August Kennedy ordered a reduction of American aid to Diem. By September, Nhu and his brother had completely outlived their usefulness to the administration. Nhu sent word to Ho Chi Minh that the Diem government was interested in negotiating a possible ceasefire with North Vietnam, directly contradicting the U.S. position. Lodge and other Kennedy officials signaled to top South Vietnamese generals that they would not object to a military overthrow of President Diem.

"A PROMISING *COUP D'ETAT*"

In September, Kennedy gave a television interview to CBS News in which he signaled his growing dissatisfaction with Diem. "In the final analysis, it's their war," he said. "They're the ones who have to win it or lose it. We can help them as advisors but they have to win it." By the fall of 1963, the most respected military officer in South Vietnam, General Duong Van Minh, had requested a meeting with Lou Conein, a CIA operative. Minh, whose troops were mostly Buddhist and hated Diem and the Nhus, told Conein that the war was being lost and would be hopeless unless there was a change in the South Vietnamese leadership.

Minh didn't want or expect American help with a *coup d'état*. He just wanted to make sure the United States wouldn't interfere and attempt to prevent it. Kennedy fretted that American involvement in the coup might wind up in another Bay of Pigs-style disaster. Ambassador Lodge advocated giving passive American approval to a coup. "Lodge felt that all the charges against the Ngo family were true, that Nhu could not be separated from Diem, that the war was being lost, that since there was going to be a coup anyway, the U.S. position should be to neither encourage it (except perhaps slightly, by not discouraging it) nor thwart it," journalist **David Halberstam** later reported. Lodge reassured the administration, characterizing the plot as a "promising *coup d'état*."

Word reached Lodge and Kennedy officials in Washington that the coup would start on November 1. Shortly after 1 p.m. troops involved in the overthrow took over key control points in Saigon, such as the central police station and Saigon's radio station where a rebel soldier proclaimed a revolution over the airwaves. Diem frantically called Lodge, who disingenuously told the American ally that he was unsure of the American government's feelings about the military overthrow. Seconds later, Lodge made the American viewpoint clear. "Now I am worried about your physical safety," Lodge told Diem, never admitting he had been in contact with the plotters. "I have a report that those in charge of the current activity offer you and your brother safe conduct out of the country if you will resign . . . If I can do anything for your physical safety, please call me."

Now aware that his American friends were complicit in the overthrow, Diem and Nhu fled to a Catholic Church where they were arrested and murdered on November 2 in the back of armored personnel carrier. After shooting both, soldiers vented their rage at Nhu, stabbing his body multiple times after his death. The new military junta wiped out most traces of the Diem government. "One day photographs and statues had been everywhere, but not just of Diem, but of his sister-in-law as well, a personality cult," Halberstam said.

> The next day it was all gone, the statues smashed, the posters ripped through, his likeness left only on the one-piastre coin. In the streets, the population mobbed the generals and garlanded the troops with flowers . . . When Lodge himself walked through the streets, he was cheered like a presidential candidate. For the Americans it was a high moment, yet it would soon be followed by darkness; the reality of how bad the war was going would now come home as the death of Diem opened the floodgates of reporting and allowed officers to tell the truth.

"The Prospects Now Are For a Shorter War"

President Kennedy died as well 20 days later, leaving the war in the hands of Vice President Lyndon Johnson. A clear transition took place in President Kennedy's thinking about Vietnam in the final days of his administration. Kennedy asked his commanding officers to draw up contingency plans for a withdrawal. Maxwell Taylor, the chairman of the Joint Chiefs of Staff, issued a memo on

General Maxwell Taylor at National Security Council meeting in the Cabinet Room of the White House, Washington D.C. April 2, 1965. Credit: LBJ Library

October 4, 1963, which called for the removal of 1,000 military personnel by the end of the year and in which Taylor said that "all planning will be directed towards preparing Republic of Vietnam forces for the withdrawal of all United States special assistance units and personnel by the end of the calendar year 1965." Additionally, Kennedy's budget for the fiscal year ending June 30, 1964 envisioned no major expansion of troop levels, thereby suggesting no plans existed for an escalation of troops in Southeast Asia.

Just after Diem's overthrow, Ambassador Lodge declared, "The prospects now are for a shorter war." More sober assessments followed as 1963 shaded into 1964. Diem's regime had reduced South Vietnamese agriculture to a shambles. The forced relocations disrupted planting and harvesting, crop yields were down, the poor faced hunger and, at the instigation of the ever more numerous VC, peasants had happily dismantled the strategic hamlets they had learned to hate.

Saigon's political chaos since the coup added to American troubles. General Minh proved to be an incompetent political leader, a "model of lethargy, lacking both the skill and the inclination to govern" as Stanley Karnow described him. General Nguyen Khanh overthrew Minh, after three months, in January 1964. South Vietnam went through seven changes of government after the Diem coup until the military appointed a civilian, Phan Khac Suu, as president on October 26, 1964. Suu held the presidency until June 14, 1965, when Nguyen Van Thieu began his decade-long autocratic leadership, which would last until the waning days of the South Vietnamese Republic. **Secretary of Defense Robert McNamara** derided the South's military leaders as "so preoccupied with essentially political affairs" that ARVN soldiers in the field lacked clear direction.

Subsequently released taped White House conversations from the first half of 1964 show that McNamara repeatedly urged Johnson to consider withdrawal of American forces from Vietnam within two years. Johnson shot back that Kennedy and McNamara had hurt the war effort and soldiers' morale in late 1963 by openly discussing such a possibility. McNamara never aired his doubts publicly and even urged the president to begin an "education" campaign on the need for combat troops even though the defense secretary believed the war was possibly unwinnable.

Johnson, meanwhile, felt torn between two contradictory impulses, which he believed to be inextricably entwined. The future of the Democratic Party, he believed, depended on the success of his "Great Society" programs such as the "war on poverty" and Medicare. But the United States would lose face and its influence in the world if he were perceived to be the first president to "lose a war," a feckless accommodator who retreated in the face of communist "aggression."

As Johnson told his biographer, the historian Doris Kearns Goodwin, "I knew from the start that I was bound to be crucified either way I moved. If I left the woman I loved—the Great Society—in order to get involved in that bitch of a war on the other side of the world, then I would lose everything at home. All my programs. All my hopes to feed the hungry and shelter the homeless . . . But if I left the war and let the Communists take over South Vietnam, then I would be seen

Secretary of Defense Robert McNamara pointing to a map of Vietnam at a press conference. April 26, 1965.

as a coward and my nation would be seen as an appeaser, and we would . . . find it impossible to accomplish anything for anybody on the entire globe."

Unable to choose between contradictory demands, Johnson made what proved to be a very expensive choice: he opted for both guns and butter. Even as the ARVN displayed its continued weakness in combat against the VC, General Taylor became a major voice for escalating the American role in South Vietnam. The increasing use of North Vietnamese regular troops in South Vietnam made the ARVN's task more difficult. Taylor argued that until the South Vietnamese forces could stand on their own, the American military would have to bear the burden of halting communism in Southeast Asia.

That summer, Lodge resigned as ambassador in order to run for the Republican nomination for president. Johnson replaced him with General Taylor and made General William Westmoreland the new commander of the U.S. military advisory group. The president now relied on an inner circle more hawkish (pro-war) than Kennedy's. Johnson, meanwhile, worried about the challenge on his right from Republican presidential nominee Barry Goldwater.

"EXTREMISM IN THE DEFENSE OF LIBERTY"

Johnson wanted to win big in the 1964 presidential . He sensed that voters saw his ascendancy to the White House as illegitimate, an accident created by a tragedy. He worried about living up to the already mythic memory of his martyred predecessor. He obsessed over the possible political challenge within his own party by the late president's brother Robert Kennedy, who made no secret of despising Johnson. He felt acutely the prospects of a major political realignment represented by the surprising success of George Wallace, Alabama's segregationist governor, in northern states' primary elections. Archconservative Wallace voters, resenting Johnson's civil rights efforts, could not be counted on to vote for LBJ in November. Johnson also refused to appear less anti-communist or less manly than the far right-wing presidential nominee of the Republican Party that year, Senator Barry Goldwater of Arizona.

Goldwater famously said in his acceptance speech in San Francisco in July that "Extremism in the defense of liberty is no vice." Until November, he would hammer the Democrats for being soft on communism, arguing that past Democratic presidents like Franklin Roosevelt had handed over domination of Eastern Europe to the Soviet Union, that Harry Truman had "lost" China to the communists and failed to "win" the Korean War, and that the Kennedy-Johnson team had bungled the liberation of Cuba at the Bay of Pigs and were losing the Vietnam War. Johnson sought to politically neutralize Vietnam as an issue.

Aides spent the first half of 1964 drafting a congressional resolution they hoped to have introduced and approved during the summer that would give the president an unlimited free hand to conduct the war in Southeast Asia. Johnson believed that the resolution would enhance his credibility on the world stage, particularly in dealing not just with the North Vietnamese but the Soviets and the Chinese as well. The resolution would also get congressional Republicans, including Goldwater, on board as publicly supporting the president's actions in Vietnam. It would be a bipartisan war, and Goldwater would be tied in knots, unable to oppose the resolution because it would make him look soft on communism, but unable to criticize the actions of an administration he had just handed a blank check. Even before the resolution had been debated, the Pentagon drew up plans for an extensive bombing campaign against North Vietnam, identifying ninety-four key targets.

The Johnson administration began intense lobbying of congressional leaders seeking support for the war powers resolution. **Senator J. William Fulbright** of Arkansas, later to become a chief critic of the war, even suggested that in a nuclear age the president's war powers granted by the U.S. Constitution might have to be expanded—even to the point of removing from Congress the exclusive power to declare war. "I wonder whether the time has not arrived, or indeed has already passed, when we must give the executive a measure of power in the conduct of our foreign affairs that we hitherto jealously withheld," he said.

The effort stalled because Johnson decided that he could not risk the resolution's defeat. **Senator Mike Mansfield**, the majority leader from Montana, had favored a negotiated settlement in Vietnam while **Senator Wayne Morse** of Oregon had spent his career resisting efforts to expand presidential power at the expense of Congress. The two could endlessly delay consideration of the resolution, which National Security Advisor McGeorge Bundy warned Johnson would persuade Europeans that Americans were divided over the war and that the United States should begin negotiations with Ho Chi Minh. Events in the far-off Gulf of Tonkin, however, would bring the resolution roaring back to life.

"Not a Ship, Nor the Outline of a Ship . . ."

Since the division of the country into North and South Vietnam in 1954, Americans had trained and dispatched

Vietnamese agents across the border to assassinate communist officials, train anti-government guerillas, sabotage bridges and other infrastructure, recruit spies, and so on. These efforts had proved spectacularly unsuccessful.

Underpaid and demoralized South Vietnamese officials, operating in an atmosphere of rampant corruption, proved easy targets for North Vietnamese spies. In contrast, it proved hard to infiltrate the highly disciplined, dedicated government agencies in the North. Of the 80 espionage and sabotage teams sent to North Vietnam in 1963, nearly 100 percent of the agents had been killed or captured.

These efforts, however, heightened the suspicions of the North Vietnamese government, which nervously awaited an expected escalation of American forces in the South. Ho Chi Minh anticipated that the Americans would try to inflict damage on the North and had convinced the Soviet Union and the Chinese government to provide sophisticated anti-aircraft batteries, radar, missiles and other defensive weapons. The American military conceived a plan in which South Vietnamese commandos would attack and activate North Vietnamese radar transmitters, allowing the signals to be intercepted by American intelligence ships, which could then pin down the location of these defense installations. American aircraft could then destroy communist radar sites and anti-aircraft guns, enabling American bombers to destroy larger targets within North Vietnam.

This would require the Americans and the South Vietnamese to patrol the waters near North Vietnam's coastline, considered vulnerable to attack by the communist military command. The naval destroyer *U.S.S. Maddox* became one of the first ships dispatched to conduct naval intelligence probes in late July 1964. Superiors instructed Captain John J. Herrick, the ship's commander, to maneuver no closer than eight miles from the coast or four miles from its islands. North Vietnam had never declared the limits of its territorial waters. When they ruled the region, the French had set the limit at three miles from its coast, but Hanoi was likely to follow China's lead and regard 12 miles as the line of demarcation.

The afternoon of July 30, four swift boats manned by South Vietnamese commandoes attacked the North Vietnamese island of Hon Me, seven miles off the coast, then Hon Ngu, an island just three miles from the busy port of Vinh. The *Maddox* intercepted radar signals and transmitted the information to the CIA. The vessel stayed in the area and, in the early morning of August 2, 1964, the crew faced off against hundreds of North Vietnamese junks. On high alert and anticipating an attack, Captain Herrick radioed to the Seventh Fleet Command that he expected an imminent attack.

A technician on board the *Maddox* informed Herrick that he had intercepted a North Vietnamese message suggesting the enemy vessels were preparing for "military operations." Herrick requested permission to withdraw, but instead his superiors ordered him to remain, and the *Maddox* moved within 10 miles of the Red River Delta. Technicians intercepted new orders from the North Vietnamese ships to attack the destroyer after refueling. Herrick told his crew to fire if enemy craft came within 10,000 yards. Soon the *Maddox* unleashed repeated salvos on the North Vietnamese junks.

After a twenty-minute battle, the *Maddox* barely suffered a scratch but seriously damaged two North Vietnamese vessels and sank a third. Johnson gave the Navy orders to send the ship back to the Gulf of Tonkin, this time accompanied by a second vessel, the *Turner Joy*. Naval commanders ordered the ships to buzz the North Vietnamese coast even more closely. Rear Admiral Robert B. Moore contacted Herrick, telling him to treat North Vietnamese vessels as "belligerents from first detection." As the *Maddox* approached its objective on August 4, thunderstorms played havoc with the ship's equipment. Sonar and radar operators signaled to the captain that North Vietnamese vessels had fired 22 torpedoes at them, even though no enemy ships had been seen and none of the charges hit their supposed targets. The *Maddox* opened fire. Technicians then warned of more torpedoes on the way.

Captain Herrick dispatched pilots to find the attacking ships. Commander James Stockdale, who would later be shot down over North Vietnam and spend 1965-1973 as a prisoner of war before being promoted to admiral, flew one of the planes. (Independent presidential candidate Ross Perot would tap Stockdale as his running mate in 1992.) Flying over the Gulf, Stockdale radioed back, "Not a ship, not the outline of a ship, not a wake, not a reflection, not the light of a single tracer bullet. Nothing." The captain sent a report to naval command, cautioning that an error may have been made in reading the sonar.

McNamara later said that Johnson reacted to the Gulf of Tonkin "on the belief that it was a conscious decision on the part of the North Vietnamese political and military leaders to escalate the conflict and an indication that they would not stop short of winning." McNamara later claimed that both he and the president were trapped in the assumptions of the Cold War, the idea that Vietnam was a chess piece used by the Soviets as part of a larger game ending in communist world domination. In spite of the ambiguities of the incident, Johnson also knew the political advantages that could be realized from exaggerating events. As the Pentagon spoke of "a second deliberate attack," the president addressed the nation on television, declaring that "Repeated acts of violence against the armed forces of the United States must be met not only with defense, but with positive reply."

That positive reply came in the form of the first major American bombing raid against North Vietnam. American aircraft bombed four North Vietnamese patrol bases and an important oil storage depot, destroying or damaging twenty-five North Vietnamese vessels. The North Vietnamese downed two American planes in the engagement, including one carrying Everett Alvarez, Jr., of San Jose, California, who would become the first American prisoner of war in the Vietnam conflict and would remain in Communist custody for another nine years.

The guns aboard the *Maddox* had barely cooled when the war powers resolution was reintroduced to the Congress. Known popularly as the "**Gulf of Tonkin Resolution**," the document declared that, "the Congress approves and supports the determination of the President as Commander in Chief, to take all necessary measures to repel any armed attack against the forces of the United States, and to prevent further aggression." President Johnson would behave as if the resolution, passed on August 7 by a 414-0 vote in the House of Representatives and opposed only by Senators Wayne Morse and Ernest Gruening of Arkansas in the upper chamber, represented a virtual declaration of war. Congress surrendered its constitutional prerogative to decide on matters of war and peace, and for nine years the House refused to shape war policy through its power of the purse for fear of being accused of not supporting the troops. Johnson won a monopoly on decision making while parceling out responsibility to congressional Democrats and Republicans alike. Meanwhile, Johnson's approval rating jumped from 42 to 72 percent, according to a Lou Harris poll.

INTO THE STONE AGE

Armed with a mandate from the voting public in the 1964 presidential race and the Gulf of Tonkin Resolution, Johnson felt politically strong enough to push a more aggressive approach in Indochina.

Johnson spent early 1965 relying on a heavy bombing campaign in North Vietnam aimed at breaking the communists' will to fight and the Hanoi regime's ability to supply men and arms to the South. The ostensible rationale for the bombing campaign came with the Battle of Pleiku, in which eight Americans died on February 7, 1965. Called "Operation Rolling Thunder," the bombing of North Vietnam lasted from March 1965 until November 1968, involving two million sorties in which more than one million tons of bombs were dropped.

In all, 7,078,032 tons of bombs would be dropped by Americans on North and South Vietnam from 1964 until 1973, as compared with the total of 2,057,244 tons dropped by American pilots in all theaters of World War II. This came to about 1,000 pounds for every Vietnamese man, woman and child. Johnson put great stock in the American monopoly on air power and wanted strict

---

GULF OF TONKIN RESOLUTION
Joint Resolution of Congress
H.J. RES 1145 August 7, 1964

Resolved by the Senate and House of Representatives of the United States of America in Congress assembled. That the Congress approves and supports the determination of the President, as Commander in Chief, to take all necessary measures to repel any armed attack against the forces of the United States and to prevent further aggression.

Section 2. The United States regards as vital to its national interest and to world peace the maintenance of international peace and security in Southeast Asia. Consonant with the Constitution of the United States and the Charter of the United Nations and in accordance with its obligations under the Southeast Asia Collective Defense Treaty, the United States is, therefore, prepared as the President determines, to take all necessary steps, including the use of armed forces, to assist any member or protocol state of the Southeast Asia Collective Defense Treaty requesting assistance in defense of its freedom.

Section 3. This resolution shall expire when the President shall determine that the peace and security of the area is reasonably assured by international conditions created by action of the United Nations or otherwise, except that it may be terminated earlier by concurrent resolution of the congress.

control of targets so the conflict would not spin out of control. The president reportedly boasted, "they can't even bomb an outhouse without my approval." Bombing raids on an almost entirely rural country like North Vietnam, however, produced meager military results, and the South Vietnamese military continued to perform poorly. The communists, meanwhile, seemed poised for an offensive in the South's Central Highlands. Johnson reluctantly gave approval to an expanded air campaign with fewer restrictions.

"My solution to the problem [of communist advances] would be to tell the North Vietnamese communists frankly that they've got to draw in their horns and stop their aggression or we're going to bomb them into the Stone Age," declared Air Force **General Curtis LeMay.** Operation Rolling Thunder didn't stem North Vietnam's momentum, but it did become the rationale for a larger commitment of ground troops.

Two battalions of Marines waded ashore at Danang on March 8, 1965, along with tanks and howitzers, to protect the airbase there—the first American combat units dispatched to Vietnam. "[T]hey were welcomed by South Vietnamese officials and by pretty Vietnamese girls passing out leis of flowers," Herring wrote. "It was an ironically happy opening for what would be a wrenching experience for both countries."

The administration decided to lengthen the bombing campaign to a year (it would be extended to more than three years) and to put 40,000 combat troops "in country." Eventually more than 500,000 Americans would be fighting and dying in Southeast Asia. To avoid the possibility of a devastating engagement such as the French experienced in 1954 at Dien Bien Phu, troops would be assigned to protect limited, 50-mile enclaves around American bases. These enclaves, the Americans hoped, would prevent the communists from scoring a knockout blow while giving the air war a chance to cripple the enemy.

SOLDIERS' STORIES

At the beginning of America's involvement in the Vietnam War, draftees made up only 21 percent of the armed forces fighting there. Many volunteer Marines and soldiers like Philip Caputo felt inspired by President Kennedy's call to national service and sought excitement not available in their sleepy hometowns. "I joined the Marines in 1960 partly because I got swept up in the patriotic tide of the Kennedy era but mostly because I was sick of the safe, suburban existence I had known most of my life," Caputo recalled in his Vietnam memoir, *A Rumor of War*. Caputo remembered his youthful desire for adventure while growing up in Westchester, Illinois, near Chicago.

There was small game in the woods, sometimes a deer or two, but most of all a hint of the wild past, when moccasined feet trod the forest paths and fur trappers cruised the rivers in bark canoes. Once in a while, I found flint arrowheads in the muddy creek bank. Looking at them I would dream of that savage, heroic time and wish I had lived then, before America became a land of salesmen and shopping centers. This is what I wanted, to find in a commonplace world a chance to live heroically. Having known nothing but security, comfort, and peace, I hungered for danger, challenges and violence.

Vietnam brought out the best and the worst in American fighting men. Sandra Collingwood, a community development worker in Vietnam during the war, recalled seeing soldiers sharing food rations with Vietnamese villagers. Journalist Anne Allen remembered meeting a six-year-old Vietnamese boy in Saigon who had been informally adopted by American GIs, who gave him child-sized fatigues that he always wore, and taught him English, including the four-letter words that peppered the troops' daily speech. The boy, called Dewey, served as a translator for the soldiers and was brought along when the Americans negotiated with prostitutes. Once he finished negotiating terms, the soldiers rewarded Dewey with a soft drink for his translation work, and the boy was sent on his way. Allen reported that Dewey loved "his" GIs.

Sexual relations between soldiers and local women became commonplace, even though these women were looked down upon by other Vietnamese as no better than prostitutes. Many times, soldiers made promises to their "in-country" girlfriends that they didn't keep, and the relationships ended when the men returned stateside.

Vietnamese women who had American boyfriends or had borne a child of an American might be beaten or rejected by their parents, and most Vietnamese men would not even consider marrying them. "When you gave birth to a mixed kid, in the countryside, they hold many prejudices against you," said Mai Thi Kim, whose mother had a relationship with an American naval officer who became her father. "... I was very bitter and shameful when they looked down on me that way." Biracial children faced ridicule by peers who called them "con lai" (half-breed) or "bui doi" (the dust of life).

The Vietnam War included scenes of deep compassion and horrifying cruelty. Doctors serving in Vietnam persuaded friends in the United States to send griseofulvin, a treatment for the terrible cases of ringworm. One doctor, Lawrence H. Climo, described GIs making poverty wages offering to pay for medical care for the daughter of a **Montagnard** tribesman who had been released from a local charity ward. As the girl's condition worsened from lack of food and water, local soldiers pooled resources to save her life. With money collected from servicemen, Climo was able to place the girl in a "pay" ward at the hospital, where she recovered.

"I save food from the officers' mess (hot dogs, vegetables, etc.) and bring it to a hospitalized Montagnard with nutritional deficiencies and to a young girl low on . . . red blood cells," Climo later recalled. "The hungry family, visitors and other patients gather about me." Meanwhile, the United States Agency for International Development made available powdered milk, protein supplements and wheat for the underfed patients recovering in the Montagnard charity hospital.

Military medical crews provided the first effective care for many Vietnamese suffering from treatable diseases, like tuberculosis and leprosy, that in some cases had almost disappeared in the West. Many of his patients suffered from parasites like pinworm and hookworm. Typhoid fever, malaria, and anemia claimed many Montagnard victims. About 50 percent of the children born near Climo's station died before they reached age five. Many diseases stemmed from haphazard or nonexistent sanitation. "There were no latrines for the families living with the patients," Climo remembered. "They defecated outside the windows. Behind the surgery ward was a black, foul-smelling, fly-infested streamlet with pooled feces, urine and infected waste." Climo, and the rest of his Army 33rd Advisory Team, spent their time outside of the hospital wards constructing shelters for families, sanitary facilities and hospital furniture.

"I never saw so many guys cry as I did while I was in Vietnam," one nurse said after she returned from the war. "I went over to Vietnam thinking that Army doctors were hard asses. It's just not so," she said. One night a 21-year-old Vietnamese girl cleaned the floors of the medical barracks. A flammable liquid had been used to remove wax, but a soldier struck a match on the floor while the woman was scrubbing the surface, and she burst into flames.

A surgeon named Paul treated her. "When he got to her, she was 100 percent second- and third-degree burns," the nurse said. "Plus, she had inhaled a lot of smoke. Usually these people are going to die, so you let them. The thing was, she was still conscious and talking, and her kidneys were still working. So he had to try and save her . . . Burn victims shed the inside of their lungs. It's like getting sunburned on the inside and peeling. She would cough up her lungs and she'd be bleeding and slowly choking to death. She could speak English. She would hold on to Paul and beg him to not let her die."

The doctor disappeared for an hour, saying he had to think about what treatment he should try next. The nurse found him in a room the size of a closet. "He was in there crying his eyes out," she said. 'What am I going to do? I never should have started that IV on her. I never should have put that catheter in her. But she was alive when she came in and I had to do something. I can't trach her. She'll live six weeks and then she'll die horribly. What am I going to do with her?'" The doctor and the nurse did the only thing they could—as the woman slowly died they changed her dressings and tried to reassure her that they wouldn't let her die, even as they decided to discontinue heroic measures.

Bad Chemistry

If medics experienced death firsthand, for some soldiers American military technology made killing an abstract, distant experience. This, in turn, encouraged an indifference to Vietnamese lives. More than 58,000 Americans lost their lives in the war, and 300,000 suffered injuries, making it the fourth costliest in American history and creating psychological scars still shaping American politics five decades later. These numbers, however, pale alongside Vietnamese casualties. The South Vietnamese military suffered 224,000 deaths and 1 million injured. The government of Vietnam announced in 1995 that 1.1 million communist troops, including the North Vietnamese Army and the Vietcong, died; and 600,000 were wounded during the American war from 1964 to 1973. The number of civilian casualties, North and South, remains controversial, but most estimates place the number between 1 and 2 million.

The American air war played a prominent role in Vietnamese military and civilian deaths. In 1961 and 1962, the U.S. military began experimentation with a variety of counter-insurgency tactics aimed at crippling the Vietcong guerillas. Military scientists developed defoliants aimed at poisoning food supplies for the communist forces and stripping bare the trees in forests and jungles where the VC camped and launched surprise attacks. The plan was to deny the VC food and places to hide. In the six years between 1962 and 1968, the United States military sprayed almost 700,000 acres of farmland with "Agent Blue," a chemical compound damaging rice crops, which caused hunger among peasants in the Vietnamese countryside.

Pilots participating in Operation Ranch Hand dropped highly carcinogenic chemical compounds like **Agent Orange** on Vietnam beginning in January 1962, with 100 million pounds dumped over four million acres in South Vietnam over the next eight years. The bombings and the defoliants destroyed about half of the country's timberlands. Decades after this campaign, Vietnamese as well as American veterans of the Vietnam War suffered from side effects of Agent Orange and other defoliants, including chronic lymphocytic leukemia, Hodgkin's disease, lung cancer, non-Hodgkin lymphoma, multiple myeloma and prostate cancer. After the war, American veterans reported abnormally high rates of children born with spina bifida, or lacking arms and/or legs, or with Down syndrome. Agencies like the Red Cross estimate that by 2003, a half-million Vietnamese had died from health complications caused by Agent Orange and other chemicals used during the war and that 650,000 still suffered health problems. The Vietnam food chain is still poisoned by dioxins introduced into the soil and water by defoliants.

Americans also dropped 400,000 tons of bombs containing a petroleum-based jelly made of polystyrene, gasoline and benzene known as **Napalm-B**. This fire-starting agent burns at 1,000 degrees Fahrenheit, and the military used it to destroy villages suspected of being enemy bases, to clear areas with heavy foliage to allow airborne surveillance, and to terrify the Vietcong and their supporters. Victims of napalm suffered as the chemical created a burning sensation and ate away skin to the muscle layer. One American soldier later recalled witnessing an accidental napalm attack against a friendly village:

> A hooch [hut] went up in a ball of flame, and a woman and a couple of kids came running out of its suffocating core, the burning jelly charring the soles of their feet black. One of the men hurdled the concertina wire [surrounding the village] . . . and pulled them screaming out of the fire, but there was no way to put out napalm; it was made to cling to human flesh and keep eating inward until it burned itself out.

Nurse Holland spent part of her tour of duty working in the "Vietnamese ward" at a hospital in Chu Lai. She frequently dealt with the casualties of America's chemical warfare. "Mostly we had women and children and elderly men," she said.

> Some of the children came in with napalm burns. Most of them were burned pretty badly and when you touched them a white, powdery dust would come off of their skin. It was like their skin was evaporating. It had a really pungent odor of burned flesh and chemicals. Their beautiful country and their homes and family were torn apart and yet they managed to survive. They took care of one another and would absorb people from other families who weren't even blood relatives. They were warm and caring. Family members were always in the hospital.

"Killing is the Easiest Part"

American ground troops felt unprepared for the physical demands of fighting in Vietnam, where temperatures often soared as high as 120 degrees Fahrenheit, the heat enhanced by high humidity. Salt tablets became part of a soldier's necessary survival tools. Meanwhile, fire ants and leeches tormented soldiers, leaving the surface of the skin painfully itchy and fiery red. Abrasive elephant grass growing as tall as eight feet also tore at the troops' skin. Rubber and bamboo trees so densely crowded the jungle landscape that the sun at times could not be seen in broad daylight. Soldiers often could move no more than 100 feet in one hour, even as they were overwhelmed by the smells of gunpowder, sulfur, diesel fuel and rotting corpses.

"War is not killing," one soldier said. "Killing is the easiest part of the whole thing. Sweating twenty-four hours a day, seeing guys drop all around you of heatstroke, not having food, not having water, sleeping only three hours a night for weeks at a time, that's what war is. Survival."

Soldiers feared so-called "Bouncing Bettys," land mines with a spring that activated an explosive when stepped on. The explosive propelled four or five feet into the air and sprayed metal shards and other cutting projectiles downward and outward. Such explosives could kill several infantrymen at the same time. Even in the cities, soldiers had to watch out for hidden explosives in abandoned toys and even in the bodies of dead Vietnamese. On top of these dangers, soldiers and Marines witnessed women and small children tossing hand grenades at Americans and sometimes discovered that Vietnamese to whom they had grown close were secretly fighting for the Vietcong. It became increasingly difficult to distinguish friends from foes.

Search and Destroy

Before long, American soldiers felt contempt for their purported ARVN allies, who were seen by many as cowardly and corrupt. "Only thing they beat us to was

This group of South Vietnamese soldiers with American soldiers are in a jungle sweep of another hamlet. February 12, 1962.

the chow line," one soldier in Charlie Company, Omega Harris, remembers thinking. Otherwise, the ARVN troops timidly stayed behind the lines and let Americans do the fighting, he and his fellow "grunts" thought. After patrols, the ARVN men returned clean. Harris believed they spent their time in the brush napping.

If GIs hated the VC and North Vietnamese enemy, these warriors earned the Americans' grudging respect. "[S]ome came to envy the enemy his skills at war and his sense of calling to it—a commitment, wanting in themselves, to a cause worth dying for," wrote Peter Goldman and Tony Fuller. ". . . To the men, the enemy seemed unafraid of anything, perhaps excepting B-52s and Cobra attack helicopters—anything, that is, that [the U.S. military] could bring to bear against him in the normal course of business."

General Bruce Palmer, Jr., Westmoreland's chief deputy, admitted years later, "Our greatest battle successes occurred when the enemy chose to attack a U.S. unit well dug in and prepared to defend its position." Offensive operations, however, proved much more difficult. "It was a tough, risky business, for our troops, moving into and searching a hostile area, were exposed to enemy ambush, mines, and booby traps. Frequently they suffered casualties without ever seeing or contacting the enemy. After they stopped moving, they often hoped for an enemy attack and an opportunity to inflict heavy casualties."

Palmer called this an "offensive-defensive" tactic, though it became better known by the term coined by another Westmoreland aide: "search and destroy." As it evolved, search and destroy usually meant transporting, usually by helicopter, ground troops to enemy positions, obliterating the enemy forces, and then returning to the American lines. The American commanders needed to instill confidence in their South Vietnamese allies and were concerned that they couldn't patiently wait for the enemy to make a frontal attack, especially after they figured out the high casualty rates such tactics guaranteed.

In spite of the risks, commanders decided they had to take the fight to the enemy. Underestimating the North Vietnamese and Vietcong level of commitment, American commanders assumed that the American technological advantage would mean they would prevail in a war of attrition. U.S. commanders assumed that high enough casualties would force the outgunned communists to sue for peace. To accomplish this, Westmoreland asked for more troops, a total of 450,000 by the end of 1966.

The Vietcong and NVA proved willing to suffer large numbers of combat deaths and injuries and quickly adapted to American combat tactics and strategies. The Americans expended huge amounts of ammo and often had little to show for it. For instance, at the Battle of the Battangan Peninsula in August 1965, the Americans used 6,000 Marines, two naval destroyers, a squadron of Phantom and Skyhawk jets, napalm, and 3,000 rounds of ammo. While they killed 573 communist fighters and took 122 prisoners, and lost only 46 dead and 204 wounded, three-fourths of the communist troops slipped away, melting into the general population and able to fight another day.

The Americans suffered 300 casualties in an encounter with North Vietnamese regulars at the **Battle of the Ia Drang Valley**, in the vicinity of several villages, in August. Naval batteries pounded the villages, which were also destroyed by napalm. Fighting in close quarters for a month, the NVA lost 1,500 dead as American B-52 bombers dropped 500-pound bombs and fired more than 33,000 rounds of 105-millimeter howitzer ammo. As in the Battle of the Battangan Peninsula, the U.S. military declared victory after Ia Drang, but the NVA learned an important tactical lesson that would affect the future war: The tremendous advantages Americans enjoyed in the air and the greater firepower of American ground weapons became significantly less important if the Vietnamese battled at close quarters, which made it much harder for American firepower to claim only enemy lives.

Such fighting proved unnerving to 18- and 19-year old soldiers, more and more of whom were draftees in dark, unfamiliar and heavily wooded terrain. Search and destroy missions based on rooting out Vietcong bases of operations often put Americans in the position of destroying entire villages. The Americans would use Zippo cigarette lighters to burn down huts, destroy chickens and water buffalo that could be used to feed communist soldiers, and then moved on, leaving behind an angry, hungry and homeless population. The Vietcong use of traps, as well as women and young children as soldiers, increased the paranoia of American troops. Seeing potential assassins everywhere, American soldiers frequently shot neutral and friendly Vietnamese, which greatly increased the support for the communists.

"The only thing they told us about the Viet Cong was that they were gooks," one Marine later said. "They were to be killed." Barely out of high school, many fighting men were set on a hair trigger. Broadly worded orders given by superiors made tragedies more likely. On August 5, 1965, Marines approached the village of Cam Ne. Helicopters had buzzed the village and warned the people living there to evacuate. Marines approaching the village were told that they could assume anyone left behind was a "VC."

"They told us if you receive one round from the village, you level it," said Private First Class Reginald Edwards. "So we was coming into the village, crossing over the hedges . . . Not only did we receive one round, three Marines got wounded right off . . . So you know how we felt." Edwards received an order to shoot a fleeing elderly man. "Caught my man as he was comin' through the door. But what happened was it was a room full of children. Like a schoolroom. And he was runnin' back to warn the kids that the Marines were coming. That's who got hurt. All those little kids and people."

The Marines burned Cam Ne to the ground. CBS newsman Morley Safer was there to capture the scene and, in a devastating report later aired to a national television audience, reported that two of three Marines injured had been hit by friendly fire. The village had been destroyed for the actions of what was apparently just one sniper. Safer tried to help villagers escape and discovered that they had not understood the orders to evacuate, which had been given in English.

"The day's operation burned down 150 houses, wounded three women, killed one baby . . . and netted these four prisoners," Safer told his audience. "Four old men who could not answer questions put to them in English. Four old men who had no idea what an ID card was. Today's operation is the frustration of Vietnam in miniature. There is little doubt that American firepower can win a military victory here. But to a Vietnamese peasant whose home . . . means a life of backbreaking labor . . . it will take more than presidential promises to convince him that we are on his side."

This report marked one of the first critical accounts of the war to appear in the American media, which had dutifully supported the military effort, bought into the domino theory, and had accepted that the Vietnam conflict was not a civil war in which the United States supported an unpopular side against forces seen by many in Vietnam as patriotic. Instead, like the government, most of the press saw Vietnam as part of a global chess game played between the Americans and the Soviets.

"Feasting on the Body"

Over the years the Cam Ne tragedy was repeated countless times. Officers told infantrymen that every Vietnamese represented a potential assassin. Communist troops reinforced this lesson by fighting ruthlessly, executing 39,000 South Vietnamese officials and members of the armed forces. (The United States also had an assassination program, Project Phoenix, that targeted Vietcong agents operating in South Vietnam and may have recorded 21,000 successful killings.) The communists saw themselves as defending their country from invaders. American soldiers joked that they were fighting the wrong Vietnamese and compared ARVN troops unfavorably to determined NVA and VC fighters. Nevertheless, U.S. infantrymen often saw their enemies as heartless killers.

The Vietcong use of child soldiers in particular sharpened GI distrust of the native population. As another soldier told author Mark Baker, "You can't tell who's your enemy. You got to shoot kids, you got to shoot women. You may be sorry that you did. But you might be sorrier if you didn't. That's the damned truth." Not just fear, but the desire for revenge over lost buddies, and resentment over dangerous assignments played a role in both large- and small-scale atrocities.

Vietnamese woman and children and American military advisor sit amid ruins of village in South Vietnam which was burned by government troops because it was thought to have been a Viet Cong stronghold. 1963

One GI told Baker of an incident when he was part of a team that had been in the field three weeks and were running security in a "free-fire zone." A Vietnamese man and his daughter approached riding a Lambretta, a motorbike. The soldiers decided to stop them and were angered when they saw the man had a can of American pears. "Here we are in the field, we don't know what pears is," the soldier later remembered. "They got pears! And we don't have pears." One soldier grabs the can and opens it with his bayonet. The other GIs wanted their share. "We were fighting, literally fighting to eat pears. Food! It wasn't fresh, but it was something other than the shit they put together chemically and pressed into a can. It was like the man brought me steak and potatoes and I was back in my mother's house eating Sunday dinner."

The soldiers became angrier over the pears and began to interrogate the Vietnamese man how he had gotten his hands on the cargo. The older man explained that he worked at an American mess hall and that the can had been given to him by GIs. "The GIs gave you pears?" the furious soldiers yelled. "For that, we're going to screw your daughter." As the young woman wept, the GIs pulled her pants down as one of the men put a gun to her head.

"Why are you doing this to me?" the girl cried in English. Turning their fury back on the father, they tore his identification card that the Vietnamese were required to carry. "Hey, we got a VC here, fellas. A VC stealing government stuff, huh?" The soldiers began shooting the man, who was in his forties. "As I said, we was in a *free-fire zone*. We just started pumping rounds into him until the guy just busts open. He didn't have a face anymore.

> Baby-san, she was crying. So a guy just put a rifle to her head and pulled the trigger just to put her out of the picture. Then we started pumping her with rounds . . . And everybody was laughing about it. It's like seeing the lions around the just killed zebra . . . The whole pride comes around and they start feasting on the body.

The longer the war dragged on, the bigger the gulf between the supposed liberators and the intended recipients of liberation. "Too many of us forgot that Vietnamese were people," one soldier said. "We didn't treat them as people after a while."

RACIAL MATTERS

Racism shaped the Vietnam War in two ways: how American soldiers treated each other, and how they saw and treated the Vietnamese. Growing up in a culture saturated with white supremacist ideas, American soldiers often brought their racist baggage with them to Vietnam. Many black veterans reported being called "nigger" and being singled out for punishment as early as boot camp. In Vietnam, closer relationships developed between whites and blacks on the front—where soldiers depended on each other for survival—than in the rear, where whites and blacks segregated in housing and in friendships.

Richard J. Ford III, an infantryman who served in Vietnam in 1967-1968, remembered a fight that broke out between black soldiers returning from a dangerous combat mission and whites at a military police barracks. "One time we saw these [Confederate] flags in Nha Trang . . . They was playing hillbilly music. Had their shoes off dancing. Had nice, pretty bunks. Mosquito nets over top the bunks. . . Air conditioning. Cement floors. We just came out the jungles. We dirty, we smelly, hadn't shaved. We just went off. We turned the bunks over, started tearing up the stereo. They just ran out. Next morning, they shipped us back up."

African-American soldiers, who suffered death rates out of proportion to their share of the U.S. forces, suspected that white officers singled them out for dangerous combat duty. For this and other reasons, early on the Vietnam War became controversial in the African-American community. In the early 1960s, Malcolm X saw the war as white America's imperialism against people of color. For years, the mainstream civil rights organizations held back, not wanting to antagonize allies in the Kennedy and Johnson administrations. Dr. Martin Luther King, Jr., however, had attacked the war in accordance with his pacifist beliefs. By 1967, his words became sharper as he expressed fears that programs he favored, such as the War on Poverty, would be sacrificed to feed the ever-costlier war in Southeast Asia. Johnson's anti-poverty initiatives had raised people's hopes, King said, but the war was "an enemy of the poor." As had others, King pointed to the irony of black men fighting for the freedom of others while being denied basic dignity at home. "We were taking the young black men who had been crippled by our society and sending them 8,000 miles away to guarantee liberties in Southeast Asia which they had not found in Southeast Georgia and East Harlem," King said. "So we have been repeatedly faced with the cruel irony of watching Negro and white boys on TV screens as they kill and die together for a nation that has been unable to seat them together in the same schools."

Racial violence at home, such as in the Watts riot of 1965, the Detroit riot in 1967, and the King assassination in 1968, deepened the divide between black and white soldiers in the field. At the same time, American soldiers often perceived a deep racial divide between themselves and their Vietnamese hosts. One soldier in Vietnam, Norman Nakamura, believed anti-Vietnamese racism fed both casual abuse of the local population, such as throwing empty cans at children walking on a roadside, and major atrocities such as the massacre of the village of My Lai in 1968. "For some G.I.'s in Vietnam, there are no Vietnamese people," Nakamura wrote in a guest column in the June/July 1970 edition of the publication *Gidra*. "To them the land is not populated by people but by 'Gooks,' considered inferior, unhuman animals by the racist-educated G.I. Relieved in his mind of human responsibility by this grotesque stereotype, numerous barbarities have been committed against these Asian peoples, since 'they're only 'Gooks.'"

Drawing on America's mythology of the Old West, their minds filled with scenes from movies in which the cavalry mowed down droves of murderous "redskins," troops in Vietnam often called themselves "cowboys" and the natives "Indians." As in the Asian theater of World War II, American soldiers were more likely to shoot soldiers who had surrendered than had their peers fighting in Europe during the First and Second World Wars. Like Anglo soldiers fighting the Japanese, American soldiers also sometimes collected and even mailed home "trophies" of their Vietnamese killed, such as severed ears.

THE HANOI HILTON

A common GI experience in the war was bewilderment when locals seemed indifferent to the fate of Americans. Other soldiers felt they were the targets of icy hatred. Undoubtedly war atrocities like those mentioned above, even in the context of extreme communist bloodshed, belied the supposed purpose of the American war effort. The killing of civilians, the burning of villages, and the dropping of napalm alienated the South Vietnamese population, even those who previously had been anti-communist but who now saw a North Vietnamese victory as preferable to American occupation.

A perception of American cruelty may have contributed to, or at least provided a rationale for, the inhumane treatment suffered by American GIs languishing in North Vietnamese prisons. Downed bomber pilots and flight crews made up most of the 591 prisoners of war released as part of "Operation Homecoming" at the end of the war. In April 1993, Harvard economist Stephen Morris discov-

Lieutenant Commander John McCain, a POW in the Vietnam War, April 24, 1973.
Photo by Thomas J. O'Halloran, *U.S. News & World Report* Magazine Photograph Collection

ered North Vietnamese documents indicating that Hanoi held 1,205 American prisoners as late as September 1972, a short time before prisoner releases began. Whether the discrepancy between the number of American prisoners released through Operation Homecoming and the number mentioned in the report represents a clerical error, a translation mistake, or evidence of the mass killing of American POWs remains a mystery. When the United States pulled combat forces out of Vietnam in 1973, about 2,000 servicemen remained unaccounted for. A larger number of Vietnamese soldiers remain missing.

Released prisoners, including future Arizona senator and 2008 Republican presidential nominee John McCain, reported being tortured. North Vietnamese guards beat prisoners with rifle butts, clubs and fists, deprived them of sleep and adequate nutrition and mocked them when news arrived of tragedies in the prisoners' families. Many were forced to sit through interminable "re-education" sessions and were told 5,000 years of Vietnamese history through the Hanoi regime's perspective. Withholding medicine became a common method of weakening prisoner resistance. Interrogators sometimes sought intelligence, but just as often they simply wanted to shatter the spirit of their hostages. The POW camp at Hao Lo gained particular infamy and was given the sarcastic name "**Hanoi Hilton**."

Porter Halyburton served as pilot in a two-man Navy F-4 Phantom that was shot down while bombing a bridge on a road connecting the North Vietnamese capital, Hanoi, to China. Parachuting over hostile territory, he quickly fell into the hands of North Vietnamese soldiers who put him in an animal shed, giving him rice, water, and cigarettes until a jeep arrived to carry him to Hanoi.

"They told me, 'If you cooperate with us, and repent for your crimes, we will move you to a nice camp, a really nice place. You'll be with all your friends. You'll have nice food and you can play games and write to your family. But if you refuse, we'll move you to a worse place.'"

Halyburton refused to provide the information sought by interrogators and wound up in a facility his captors called "the Zoo." He spent days in the dark before guards transferred him to a coal storage area. "Ants, rats, mosquitoes by the ton," he said to author Christian J. Appy. "They would put my shitty little bowl of rice outside the door and leave it there for hours. By the time they finally gave it to me, it was completely covered with ants. It was inedible. I had dysentery by then and was getting disheartened. I hadn't talked to an American in months. The constant interrogation and indoctrination were wearing me down."

The North Vietnamese forced POWs to march through Hanoi, handcuffed two-by-two. Made to bow their heads, the prisoners suffered a blow to the back of their heads every time they looked up. At the urging of the guards, the crowds screamed, "Yankee imperialists! Air pirates! Murderers!" The North Vietnamese then confined Halyburton in a remote prison nicknamed "The Briarpatch." The guards wanted him to write a confession. "First, they just beat the crap out of you to soften you up," he said.

> Or they made you sit on a little wooden stool for days . . . After that, the torture began. The method they used on me we called "max cuffs." Your arms were pulled up behind your back and then they put these handcuffs on the upper part

of your arm. Then they tied a rope on your wrists and pulled it up. I could actually see the fingertips over the top of my head when they did that. It pressed the nerves against the bone. It was like molten metal flowing through your veins—just indescribable pain.

This last round of abuse broke Hayburton's resistance. He signed confessions, gave biographical information and listed all his flights over North Vietnam. They asked him to write the same information over and over. "Psychologically, I think this was more damaging than the physical torture because you felt like you completely failed," he said. "You had given up. You had capitulated. You had violated the code of conduct. You let everybody down." It was only after the war that he found out that his breakdown had been universal.

THE "TELEVISION WAR"

The destruction of villages like Cam Ne, the murder of South Vietnamese civilians by American and ARVN troops, drug use by the military, and the surprising resilience of the Vietcong and the NVA provided memorable media coverage. For the first time, America fought a war in which the overwhelming majority of the country's households included at least one television set. Two years after the end of the Korean War, in 1955, 64.5 percent of homes had access to television. A decade later, 92.6 percent did.

Networks provided some combat coverage during the Korean War, though film was often broadcast days later. Bigger budgets for network news provided speedier transportation of Vietnam combat coverage, still shot on motion picture film that had to be developed before it could be screened and edited. If editors believed that the story was important enough, the film would be transported to Japan, developed and transmitted via satellite to network headquarters in the United States. Starting in the mid-1960s an ever-growing number of homes could watch war coverage in color. The mid-1960s also marked the first time that more Americans told pollsters that they received news primarily from television than from radio or newspapers. Also by the mid-1960s, evening network news broadcasts had expanded from the 15-minute format used by CBS and NBC in the 1950s to a full half-hour. The expanded time provided more opportunities to cover the war. These factors converged to make Vietnam the first "television war" or the "living room war."

President Johnson obsessed over network coverage of the war and had three televisions in the Oval Office set to ABC, CBS, and NBC when the news came on every evening. Johnson called network anchors to praise them when their coverage pleased him but would give them obscenity-strewn tongue lashings when the coverage was critical. "This is your president, and yesterday your boys shat on the American flag," Johnson once screamed at CBS News President Frank Stanton after a negative report.

In the beginning, most coverage of the war supported the American military's point of view uncritically. A *Boston Globe* survey of the 39 largest daily newspapers' editorials revealed that as late as 1968, not one advocated withdrawal from Vietnam. Initially, even the most skeptical reporters, such as Morley Safer of CBS News, David Halberstam and Harrison Salisbury of *The New York Times*, and Peter Arnett of the Associated Press, initially accepted the Cold War argument that South Vietnam represented an important battlefront against world communism and that American defeat there would allow the Russians to dominate all of Southeast Asia. Criticism focused mostly on tactics.

Pleased with the early coverage, the military brass relied on voluntary press guidelines, counting on reporters to not release information that would be useful to the enemy. Overwhelmingly, reporters adhered to those guidelines. The Department of Defense did prohibit photographs or film in which wounded or dead American soldiers could be identified, unless families had been notified or had given the news agency permission. Network news editors followed the informal rules even though the undeveloped film they received from the front often had not passed through a military censor.

To war critics, far too many reporters relied exclusively on military spokesmen and official press releases for their stories. Some covered the war from the relative safety and comfort of Saigon hotels, rarely following troops into the field. The American media, with notable exceptions, gave little coverage to how the war affected the Vietnamese.

The cozy relationship between the press and the Defense Department began to unravel, however, as the war dragged on and reporters tired of hearing about a "light at the end of the tunnel" that receded ever farther in the distance. Told repeatedly that the Vietcong and the North Vietnamese would soon collapse, reporters instead saw an enemy that seemed highly motivated and determined even as the South Vietnamese military seemed increasingly dispirited, corrupt and incompetent. Many reporters, however, risked their lives to experience the war as lived by the American soldiers, with sixty-three journalists killed during combat action in Vietnam.

"Our Worst Enemy"

A commonly believed post-Vietnam legend suggests that a politically liberal press opposed the Vietnam War from the start and unfairly portrayed the military as filled with drug-crazed baby killers, and that this undermined public support of the war. In reality, not only did newspapers support the war on the editorial pages, both the print and the electronic media sat on stories that would have increased opposition to the war. Yet, when he ordered American troops into Laos in 1971, President Richard Nixon declared, "Our worst enemy seems to be the press!" Regardless of Nixon's resentments, from the time of the Gulf of Tonkin incident on, a broad consensus developed among elites in support of the Vietnam War, encompassing leading Democrats and Republicans, much of academia, newspaper publishers, television executives, and business leaders.

The American public at large did not share this sentiment. As of March 1966, most Americans still supported Johnson's actions in Vietnam, but this support was soft. A majority told pollsters they would approve of a withdrawal of troops and free and fair elections in South Vietnam even if that meant a political victory by the Vietcong. Johnson's advisors opposed both of these options, as did most newspaper editorial boards. By August 1968, the broader American public had turned against the war. That month, a Gallup poll showed that 53 percent of the American public thought American involvement in Vietnam had been a mistake. The gap between elites and the rest of the country grew deeper through the end America's involvement in war in the early 1970s.

Opposition to the war ran inversely to educational attainment. According to a Gallup Poll taken in January 1971, 73 percent of the American public favored withdrawal from Vietnam. The percentage favoring withdrawal was highest, 80 percent to 20 percent, for those with only a grade-school education. Among high school graduates, 75 percent favored withdrawal. The most educated remained the most supportive of the war. Among college graduates, only 60 percent favored withdrawal while 40 percent backed continued military involvement. As will be discussed later, however, a desire for the war to end did not mean that the American working class supported the college student-based peace movement.

Since press coverage generally favored the war, one can only conclude that—contrary to the myth—the majority of Americans rejected what they were told by the media about Vietnam and put more stock in the experiences of their family and that of their neighbors. "[E]xercising their own independence of mind, and displaying a substantial measure of contempt for all those in the press and government who had sought to manipulate them over the years, Americans had used their common sense," author William M. Hammond wrote. "If more bombing and more killing had earlier proved to be of no avail, and if the South Vietnamese had shown few of the traits necessary for survival, why prolong the struggle? Enough was enough."

CLASS WARFARE

The Vietnam War deepened the class divide in American society. About 80 percent of the 2.5 million American men who served in the Vietnam War came from the poor or working class. Meanwhile, "[t]he institutions most responsible for channeling men into the military—the draft, the schools, and the job market—directed working class children to the armed forces and their wealthier peers towards college," according to author Christian G. Appy. "Most young men from prosperous families were able to avoid the draft, and very few volunteered. Thus America's most unpopular war was fought primarily by the nineteen-year-old children of waitresses, factory workers, truck drivers, secretaries, firefighters, carpenters, custodians, police officers, sales people, clerks, mechanics, miners and farmworkers . . ."

Enlistees from blue collar families ranged from a low of 52 percent in the Vietnam-era Air Force to a high of 57 percent for the Marine Corps. From 1966 to 1971, 79.7 percent of servicemen had 12 years or less of education. High school dropouts outnumbered college graduates in the military by 3-1. For most of the war, soldiers fighting and dying in Vietnam were also disproportionately African American.

In the early years of the war, African Americans, often coming from poor backgrounds, were more likely to volunteer for the military or to lack the college deferment or other means of avoiding Vietnam service. They made up 20 percent of combat deaths. (African Americans in the mid-1960s comprised 11 percent of the American population.) For most of the war, African Americans re-enlisted at a higher rate than whites. Even though African-American enlistments trailed off at the end of the war, they still represented a larger percentage of wartime deaths (12.5 percent) than they represented in the general population.

If it was a rich man's fight and a poor man's war, part of the reason rests with local draft boards, charged with ruling on requests for deferments. The membership of these boards drew overwhelmingly from the affluent. A 1966 national study found that only 9 percent of members of draft boards came from blue collar backgrounds, while 70 percent were professionals, public officials, managers, and mid-level bureaucrats. These boards tended to favor the deferment requests of the upper class and were more skeptical of applications from lower income brackets.

Part of the working class opposition to the war perhaps stemmed from the fact that their children disproportionately had to serve in Vietnam and casualties from Vietnam more often came from poor and working class neighborhoods. A firefighter who lost a son in Vietnam told interviewer Robert Coles:

> I'm bitter. You bet your goddamn dollar I'm bitter. It's people like us who give up our sons for the country. The business people, they run the country and make money from it. The college types, the professors, they go to Washington and tell the government what to do . . . But their sons, they don't end up in the swamps over there, in Vietnam. No, they get deferred, because they're in school. Or they get sent to safe places. Or they get out with all those letters they have from their doctors . . . Let's face it; if you have a lot of money, or if you have the right connections, you don't end up on the firing line in the jungle over there, not unless you *want* to.

Dodging the Draft, Elite Style

Until 1971, the American draft laws granted deferments for those attending college. College students disproportionately came from the middle and upper classes. Future political leaders like President Bill Clinton, Vice President Dick Cheney, Deputy Defense Secretary Paul Wolfowitz—an architect of the American invasion of Iraq in 2003—and House Speaker Newt Gingrich all received college deferments during the Vietnam War. Another recipient of a college deferment, future House Majority Whip Tom DeLay, claimed that, "So many minority youths had volunteered . . . that there was literally no room for patriotic folks like myself."

Placement in the reserves and the state National Guard units became another way elites with political connections avoided combat duty in Vietnam. Only 15,000 National Guard and reserve soldiers actually served in Vietnam, out of a total of more than a million men. The National Guard became such a popular means of avoiding Vietnam that by 1968, the waiting list for enlistment reached 100,000 names.

"Throughout the country, the reserves and the guard were notorious for restrictive, 'old boy' admissions policies," wrote Appy. "In many places a man simply had to have connections to get in. For the poor and the working class it was particularly difficult to gain admission." Appy notes that the number of college graduates in the Army reserve equaled three times the number in the regular Army. Blacks, who disproportionately came from the poor and the working class, comprised only 1.45 percent of the National Guard in 1964. As the Guard became a refuge for well-connected white men, the black percentage of the Guard dropped to 1.26 percent by 1968. Future political leaders who avoided Vietnam service through this means include Vice President Dan Quayle and President George W. Bush.

Considering such evidence, sociologist James Loewen observes that even though elites proved less likely to serve in combat, they more strongly supported the war. He suggests that more than mere hypocrisy was involved. He argues that elites internalized the values of the ruling class and felt allegiance to policies formed in Washington. Loewen also believes that a major function of the American educational system is indoctrination. "The more schooling, the more socialization, and the more likely the individual will conclude that America is good." Thus, Loewen suggests elites on major newspaper editorial boards, in network newsrooms, in policy institutes, in the Pentagon and in the executive branch of the federal government continued to have a faith in the Vietnam War effort when objective evidence suggested the war was a failure. Less invested in a system that provided them fewer rewards and in which their influence was denied, working class and poor people were more likely to favor an end to the war.

The Whole Thing is a Mess

This didn't mean that the poor and the working class identified with the peace movement. Appy explains the paradox this way. "Working class people opposed college protestors largely because they saw the anti-war movement as an elitist attack on American troops by people who could avoid the war," he said. ". . . How, they wondered, could college students possibly claim to be victims (of police brutality, of bureaucratic college administrators, of an inhuman corporate rat race that provided meaningless work) when they were so obviously better off than workers who endured far more daily indignity and mind-numbing labor?"

A fireman interviewed by Coles captured the conflicted feelings of the working class. "I hate those peace demonstrators," he said. "Why don't they go to Vietnam and demonstrate in front of the North Vietnamese?. . .

Protest vigil for peace taken outside the Alamo, San Antonio, Texas, on Feb. 4, 1967.

The whole thing is a mess. The sooner we get the hell out of there the better. But what bothers me about the peace crowd is that you can tell from their attitude, the way they look and what they say, that they don't really love this country. Some of them almost seem glad to have a chance to criticize us . . . To hell with them! Let them get out, leave, if they don't like it here! My son didn't die so they can look filthy and talk filthy and insult everything we believe in and everyone in the country—me and my wife and people here on the street, and the next street, and all over.

Problems Troubling and Unresolved

The leaders of the anti-war movement did come from college campuses rather than assembly lines. Risking accusations of undermining America's struggle against the Soviet Union in the Cold War, the "New Left," as it came to be known, certainly rejected what it saw as American militarism. American military might, symbolized by the hydrogen bomb, provoked more fear than security in the minds of the men and women who would lead the opposition to the Vietnam War in the 1960s. **Todd Gitlin**, a sociologist who served as president of the Students for a Democratic Society in 1963-1964 and became a leader in many of the radical movements of the decade, remembered that

> Rather than feel grateful for the Bomb, we felt menaced. The Bomb was the shadow hanging over all human endeavor. It threatened all the prizes . . . The Bomb that exploded in Hiroshima gave lie to official proclamations that the ultimate weapon was too terrible to be used. It had been used.

A peace moratorium at Trinity University, San Antonio, Texas, on Oct. 14, 1969.

The existence of the hydrogen bomb, with its capacity to destroy all life on Earth, led college students like Gitlin to conclude that institutions like the universities, the military, and the federal government had failed in their basic mission of nurturing and protecting life, liberty and the pursuit of happiness. America rotted from racism, greed and militarism. Some form of radical change would be necessary to keep the madmen in Washington from vaporizing the world in a mushroom cloud.

The New Left sprang from the socialist and communist Old Left of the 1930s and from the armies of idealistic young people, black, white, and brown, who participated in the Civil Rights campaigns of the 1950s and early 1960s. Many leaders of the New Left were "red diaper" babies, the children of communist and socialist activists. These young men and women grew up perceiving a link between capitalism and working class poverty. Religious intolerance, anti-Semitism, racism, and sexism served as weapons used by capitalists to turn workers against each other, a game of divide-and-conquer that left America's labor force poor and politically disenfranchised.

The **Students for a Democratic Society (SDS)** originated as a youth chapter of the League for Industrial Democracy, a socialist group that once claimed the authors Upton Sinclair and Jack London as members. The SDS would soon split from the Old Left, which focused almost entirely on workplace fairness and economic inequality, to tackle issues of personal freedom.

Al Haber, a jazz and folk music fan who admired the revolutionary ballads composed by the singer/songwriter Woody Guthrie, led the SDS chapter at the University of Michigan, a hotbed of civil rights and anti-nuclear weapons activism. Haber asked his friend, **Tom Hayden**, to compose the so-called *Port Huron Statement*, a manifesto of youthful radicalism, to be presented and debated at an SDS national convention June 11-15, 1915. The Port Huron Statement distilled much of the New Left's political dreams in the 1960s.

For the most part, the 64-page statement consists of a rather pedestrian laundry list of left-wing demands for cuts in military spending, increased investment in social welfare programs, and support for civil rights reforms. But the statement's emphasis on values marked the document as truly revolutionary. For the first time, the New Left spelled out the radical 1960s worldview. The decade's revolution should be about more than higher wages for workers and gaining voting rights for African Americans. The family, the attitudes toward materialism, education, and conformity would all need to change. According to the statement:

We regard men as infinitely precious and possessed of unfulfilled capacities for reason, freedom, and love. In affirming these principles we are aware of countering perhaps the dominant conceptions of man in the twentieth century: that he is a thing to be manipulated, and that he is inherently incapable of directing his own affairs. We oppose the depersonalization that reduces human beings to the status of things . . .

The goal of man and society should be human independence: a concern not with image or popularity but with finding a meaning in life that is personally authentic; a quality of mind not compulsively driven by a sense of powerlessness, nor one which unthinkingly adopts status values, nor one which represses all threats to its habits, but one which . . . openly faces problems which are troubling and unresolved; one with an intuitive awareness of possibilities, an active sense of curiosity, an ability and willingness to learn.

Whites overwhelmingly made up the New Left, which drew its inspiration from African-American groups like the Student Nonviolent Coordinating Committee (SNCC.) In conscious imitation of SNCC's community organizing campaigns, which trained the poor in how to obtain assistance for food, help for utility payments and dealing with landlords, and to inform parents about preschool and other programs available for needy children, Hayden moved into a poor neighborhood to "create an interracial movement of the poor."

The New Left rejected the leadership model of the Old Left communist and socialist parties, which to a much greater degree rested on rigid hierarchy and strict adherence to party doctrine. This allowed both creativity and an openness to leadership from unexpected sources.

The minds of young activists opened to a broader world through college, by television and movies, by popular music, and the opportunities provided by programs like the Peace Corps in which idealists could both explore the world and help the poor and struggling in Africa, Asia, and South America. Young, curious minds explored Eastern religions, saw traditional Native American societies as an alternative to Western cultures built on possessiveness, and rediscovered the literature and art created by earlier dissidents such as the Transcendentalist writers Ralph Waldo Emerson and Henry David Thoreau. These cultural trends led the New Left to push against the provincialism, bigotry and violence they saw in America and in Vietnam.

SDS members began their campaign to save the world by going to the American South to risk their lives in civil rights sit-ins, freedom rides, marches, and protests. White members wanted to employ the direct-action tactics of groups like SNCC to address a wider range of issues, including the Vietnam War. In any case, by the mid-1960s many whites felt that the major battles connected with the civil rights struggle had been won. At the same time, black nationalists in groups like SNCC began to insist on their independence from white allies and began nudging them out of the movement. White activists moved on to peace activism.

A small core of peace activists, made up mostly of Unitarians and pacifist Quakers, had protested American foreign policy since the beginning of the Cold War. Protests against the Vietnam War at first drew little media attention. In New York in May 2, 1964 a dozen men burned their draft cards during a rally held by the Student Peace Union. Lyndon Johnson's decision to launch Operation Rolling Thunder in February 1965 intensified opposition. A new tactic, the teach-in, made its debut at this time. Teach-ins involved professors, students and off-campus activists gathering at a college to raise awareness of and interest in the anti-war movement through discussions, debates, study sessions, and film screenings. Activists held a teach-in that October at the University of California at Berkeley.

Also in March, SDS members picketed at the Oakland Army Terminal, the point of departure for troops headed to Vietnam, and organized the first mass protest against the war on April 17, 1965. About 20,000 protestors assembled for an SDS-sponsored anti-war rally in Washington, D.C. Folk singers like Joan Baez and Judy Collins performed as civil rights veterans such as Robert Moses denounced the American war effort. Moses pointed to the hypocrisy of Americans supposedly battling for democracy in Vietnam when the white South routinely denied African Americans the right to vote and economic opportunity. "What kind of America is it whose response to poverty and oppression in Vietnam is napalm and defoliation," the printed announcement for the rally asked, while its "response to poverty and oppression in Mississippi is . . . silence?"

As a result of the April protest, SDS chapters formed at 300 campuses across the nation, more than 100,000 students joining the cause. The SDS and similar groups targeted Reserve Officer Training Corps (ROTC) programs at university campuses, picketed Central Intelligence Agency recruiters visiting colleges, protested against companies like Dow Chemical that manufactured war materials such as napalm and Agent Orange, and rallied against university science, chemistry and engineering departments conducting weapons research and development for the Pentagon. Other forms of anti-war activism included letter-writing campaigns aimed at newspapers and the Congress, withholding of taxes owed, and acts of civil disobedience such as blocking the movement of trains carrying troops.

The Burning of Norman Morrison

Norman Morrison committed the most riveting, and the most shocking, act in the history of the young anti-war movement on November 2, 1965 when the 31-year-old Quaker, inspired by the protest of Buddhist monks in South Vietnam two years earlier, doused himself with gasoline, struck a match, and burned himself to death in front of the Pentagon. That afternoon his wife, Anne Morrison, remembered picking up the couple's older children, five-year-old Christina and six-year-old Ben. Norman Morrison had already left the family's Baltimore home with their one-year-old daughter, Emily, and had driven to the Pentagon complex in Washington, D.C., the headquarters of the most powerful military in the world. Accounts vary, but many witnesses said Morrison, a pacifist, handed Emily to someone just before setting himself ablaze at 5:20 in the evening, just under the window of Defense Secretary Robert McNamara's office. Morrison would be one of eight Americans who burned themselves to death in protest of the Vietnam War.

Morrison had been moved by an account about the napalm attack by American forces on the South Vietnamese village of Duc Tho published the previous day in the leftist newspaper *I.F. Stone's Weekly*. The paper quoted a French priest crying, "I have seen my faithful burned up in napalm. I have seen the bodies of women and children blown to bits." Anne Morrison remained uncertain of the details of that traumatic day, but she believes she discussed the article with her husband just before lunch. Norman Morrison cut the article out, and before his suicide he stopped by a U.S. Post Office and mailed a letter telling his young wife, "Know that I love thee, but I must act for the children of the priest's village." Morrison's wife received the letter after his death became international news.

"So he did care immensely about the Vietnamese, but he also wanted to stop the war for America's sake, so that no more of our soldiers would get killed either," recalled his widow, who remarried in 1967 and became known as Ann Morrison Welsh. "And so we wouldn't lose our sense of moral dignity and integrity. He was afraid that if we kept fighting in Vietnam we would lose some of our conscience. And I think that we did." Like so many family members who lost loved ones in Vietnam, Anne Welsh would feel the absence of this domestic war casualty. Years later, she told Vietnam historian Christian G. Appy, "It took me a long time to face Norman's death because I was so shocked and horrified. The next morning I didn't want to get out of bed. But, here are three children. They need breakfast. They had to be taken care of. So you just move on."

"No Vietcong Ever Called Me Nigger"

That long-time leftist figures like Beat poet Allen Ginsberg opposed the war surprised no one. Ginsberg participated in the mass protest at the Army Terminal in Oakland, California, October 15, 1965 in which members of the Hell's Angels motorcycle gang tore down signs, and beat protestors they called "communists." Ginsberg, Ken Kesey (the author of the novel *One Flew Over the Cuckoo's Nest*) and others pleaded with Angels leader Sonny Barger to not disrupt the next day's protests, and they spent the night taking LSD. There was no trouble with the Angels at the next day's protest.

The public reacted with greater surprise when Dr. Benjamin Spock, the author of the 1946 bestseller *Baby and Child Care*, became a peace activist in the early 1960s, joining the Committee for a Sane Nuclear Policy, which opposed the use and spread of nuclear weapons. In 1967 he signed "A Call to Resist Illegitimate Authority," a document that argued that, "the war is unconstitutional and illegal. Congress has not declared a war as required by the Constitution." The manifesto contended that because the war violated American constitutional law and human decency, "every free man has a legal right and a moral duty to exert every effort to end this war, to avoid collusion with it, and to encourage others to do the same." Spock and other signatories such as the Rev. William Sloane Coffin encouraged young men to not cooperate with military conscription by refusing to turn in their draft registration cards, to claim conscientious objector status in order to

Dr. Benjamin Spock (center, foreground) leading a march to the United Nations to demand a cease-fire in Vietnam. 1965

avoid combat duty, and urged soldiers in Vietnam to refuse to follow "illegal and immoral orders."

At an October 1967 protest in Boston, more than 1,000 war resisters handed over their draft notices to Coffin, who later presented the documents to the Department of Justice. (Some of the cards turned out later to be blank sheets of paper.) In 1968, the Justice Department secured the indictment of Coffin, Spock, the philosopher Marcus Raskin, author Mitchell Goodman, and graduate student/activist Michael Ferber for aiding and abetting others to violate the Selective Service Act. An appeals court overturned Spock and Ferber's convictions and ordered new trials for Coffin and Goodman in 1969. The Justice Department then opted to drop the charges against the two remaining defendants.

The boxer **Muhammad Ali** became the most famous war dissenter not just in the United States but the world. Ali had first gained fame as Cassius Clay, the brash young boxer who claimed a gold medal at the Summer Olympics in Rome in 1960. In a culture that expected deference even from African-American celebrities, Clay taunted his future opponents in rhyme, proclaiming, "I am the greatest!" and changing his name upon his conversion to Islam by the radical black minister Malcolm X.

In 1967, he refused induction after being drafted, declaring, "I ain't got no quarrel with the Vietcong. No Vietcong ever called me Nigger." Ali went further, questioning the justice of the war. "Why should they ask me to put on a uniform and go ten thousand miles from home and drop bombs and bullets on brown people in Vietnam while so-called Negro people in Louisville are treated like dogs and denied simple human rights?" The federal government prosecuted him for draft dodging, and a jury convicted him. He stayed out of prison while lawyers appealed, but all of the major boxing commissions stripped him of his titles and banned him from fighting. He was not allowed to travel, and, instead, he earned a living from speaking fees. Ali lectured at Harvard and other universities where anti-war sentiment grew the strongest. The U.S. Supreme Court overturned his conviction on June 28, 1971. In the 1970s, Ali earned his titles back in the ring.

Armies in the Night

The anti-war movement in the Johnson era reached a crescendo in 1967. A new draft policy launched that year ended the deferments granted for postgraduate education. Aimed at making the controversial conscription program fairer to working class constituents, this policy frightened and radicalized the previously apathetic middle class and affluent white students who enrolled in graduate school programs. A new contingent of young people suddenly felt they had a personal stake in ending the war.

That spring, the National Mobilization Committee Against the War, known by members as "The Mobe" and made up of pacifists, leftist radicals, and more conventional liberals, staged anti-war events in New York and San Francisco. Convergence developed between the protest movement and the more apolitical hippie counterculture, which had drawn thousands of young people that summer to the Golden Gate city to celebrate what was optimistically dubbed "The Summer of Love." Momentum steadily built toward the year's climax, the **March on the Pentagon** on October 21.

The rally, attended by 70,000 protestors called "armies of the night" by the novelist Norman Mailer, opened at a cultural touchstone, the Lincoln Memorial, where Martin Luther King, Jr., had delivered his "I Have a Dream Speech" four years earlier. About 100,000 showed up for the anti-war march. Spock, Mailer and the poet Robert Lowell spoke against American militarism to a colorful audience that included anti-war activist Abbie Hoffman sporting peace beads and an

Protesting the Vietnam War: The March on the Pentagon. Washington D.C. on October, 21, 1967
Credit: LBJ Library

Uncle Sam hat. The contrast with the short hair and the suits and ties that characterized the attire favored at the 1963 March on Washington could not have been more striking. Looking at his audience, Mailer thought of the flamboyant costumes donned by the rock band the Beatles for the cover photo on their landmark 1967 album *Sgt. Pepper's Lonely Hearts Club Band*, the biggest hit on the radio that summer. These "legions of Sgt. Pepper's Band," Mailer wrote in his account of the event, *The Armies of the Night: History as a Novel/The Novel as History*, "assembled from all the intersections between history and the comic books, between legend and television, the Biblical archetypes and the movies."

The largely white anti-war protestors differed from King's protestors beyond their clothing. If King preferred a dignified movement that aimed at persuasion and moral force, the March on the Pentagon made clear the late-'60s trend toward outrageous street theater, sarcasm and confrontation. Popular chants—such as "Ho, Ho, Ho Chi Minh/The NLF is gonna win"—supported the North Vietnamese and Vietcong forces still seen as the enemy by many in middle America. One protest sign cruelly mocked a president many liberals still supported: "LBJ, Pull Out Now, Like Your Father Should Have Done" while other protestors rhythmically asked the Commander in Chief, "Hey, hey, LBJ/How many kids did you kill today?"

The protestors moved from the Lincoln Memorial to the Pentagon. Some protestors later claimed to urinate on the side of the Pentagon complex while some threw rocks at the phalanx of federal marshals, soldiers and National Guardsmen who ringed the complex. Other protestors hurled rocks at the office windows. As he nervously watched from his office window, McNamara insisted that none of the 3,000 troops and 1,800 Guardsmen load their rifles without his authorization.

Some protestors placed flowers in the barrels of soldiers' M-14 rifles. Picketers pushed back against the defensive perimeter, with about 3,000 attempting to break through police lines. A small group eventually succeeding in entering the Pentagon, provoking nervous and angry building security to rough up the intruders. Eventually, authorities arrested 681, mostly for charges ranging from disorderly conduct to breaking police lines.

At one point, police fired tear gas canisters. The protestors had a surprisingly sympathetic audience in one of the Pentagon offices. Though he continued to publicly support the war and predict its victorious outcome, Robert McNamara had concluded that Vietnam was hopeless from a military standpoint. McNamara's son Craig had turned against the war and had become a peace activist who pinned a Vietcong flag on his bedroom wall. Robert McNamara was in the process of suggesting to the president gradual withdrawal from the war. Watching the March on the Pentagon, McNamara felt nostalgia for the civil rights activists of earlier days. "I could not but help but think that had the protestors been more disciplined—Gandhi-like—they could have achieved their objective of shutting us down," McNamara said later.

APOLOGIES AND FORGIVENESS

Aware that he might not win in Vietnam, Lyndon Johnson worried about the erosion of political support at home. He faced a re-election campaign in 1968. In 1967, he had been forced to raise taxes to pay for his "Great Society" programs and the Vietnam War. The public would accept higher taxes only if an end to the Vietnam War was in sight. At the same time, his commander in Vietnam, General Westmoreland, sent Johnson a memo suggesting that in order to meet military objectives he would need another 200,000 troops in addition to the nearly 500,000 troops already there. Yet, Johnson knew that an expansion of American involvement on that scale would be a political disaster.

Fearing the anti-war movement's apparent momentum, Johnson tried to disrupt it by dispatching CIA agents, in violation of U.S. law, to spy on peace advocates. The agency compiled dossiers on more than 7,000 citizens. Grand juries indicted draft resisters while the FBI infiltrated the peace movement and attempted to discredit its leaders by spreading false information about alleged sexual affairs, crimes, and other fabricated misdeeds that reached family members, friends and sometimes the media. Undercover FBI *agents provocateurs* incited activists to commit illegal acts just so they could be arrested. These illegal activities of the FBI, part of its COINTELPRO (Counter Intelligence Program), were not uncovered until Senate investigations in the mid-1970s.

Unable to suppress public dissent against his Vietnam policy, the president sought to eliminate disagreement within his cabinet. McNamara had expressed too much skepticism to Johnson about the war, and LBJ quietly fired him, replacing him with Clark Clifford, a lawyer and a Washington insider widely thought to be more of a hawk than McNamara. (In fact, after the communist Tet Offensive in early 1968, Clifford would form a group within Johnson's inner circle to persuade the president to draw down forces in Vietnam.)

No figure in American politics had played a more complicated, contradictory role in the Vietnam disaster than McNamara. One of the chief architects of the war, and an enthusiastic supporter of Operation Rolling Thunder, the former Ford Motor Company executive has since tried to reshape his image, to place blame for the war squarely on Johnson, and to suggest that he had much in common with war protestors like Norman Morrison.

"I remember reading that General [William Tecumseh] Sherman in the Civil War, the mayor of Atlanta pleaded with him to save the city and Sherman essentially said to the mayor, just before he torched it and burned it down, 'War is cruel. War is cruelty,'" McNamara told filmmaker Errol Morris in the 2003 documentary *The Fog of War*, "... He [Sherman] was trying to save the country. He was trying to save our nation and in the process he was prepared to do whatever killing was necessary. It's a very, very difficult position for sensitive human beings to be in. [Norman] Morrison was one of those. I think I was."

Since 1965, Morrison's widow had struggled to understand her husband's act and the Vietnam War itself. Anne Welsh, in an interview for the book *Patriots: The Vietnam War Remembered From All Sides*, said that for years she suppressed the urge to mourn, to feel resentment over her husband's suicide, or to do anything that might harm the anti-war movement. Anger came years later. Her son with Norman, named Ben, was diagnosed with cancer. But until then, "... The war was still going on and I wanted to honor Norman's memory and his sacrifice," she said. "I wanted to work to end the war in every way I could. So I didn't give myself liberty to grieve." She continued:

> Then in 1970, Ben got sick. He was eleven. At first we thought it was just growing pains. But it got worse, so we went to the doctor and found out it was cancer. We went to Sloan Kettering and for almost five years we tried to save his life. We saved his leg but we didn't save his life. He died in 1975.
>
> When Ben was really sick, I felt anger toward Norman for the first time. I had remarried and I had support from my husband but it was not the same as having Ben's dad present. I thought, "God, Norman, why aren't you here?" ... Around 1990 or '91 I really let my emotions out. Finally my daughters were at an age where we could sit down together and really look back at what their dad had done. Christina was so hurt by her father's leaving because she loved and remembered him well and he didn't even tell her good-bye. I had shielded them, and the act kept them from wanting to look at it. We just talked about it and expressed our anguish and our grief and our sadness. We were finally able to face what it did to our family.

McNamara did not witness Morrison's death but said the event haunted him. Years later, when he had admitted publicly that Vietnam had been a mistake (though he put ultimate responsibility on President Johnson and not himself), Anne Welsh said she was moved. "In 1995 I read Robert McNamara's *In Retrospect* and felt moved to express my appreciation to him for his acknowledgment that the war was a mistake," she said. "I just felt it was unusual for a public official to admit error, even decades later in hindsight. So I wrote him a letter. It obviously moved him, perhaps in part because most of the reactions to his book were negative, even venomous." Welsh said McNamara phoned her in response.

> He said he was gratified and surprised by the forgiveness I had expressed. We had an amazingly relaxed conversation, almost as if we knew each other. He talked about how he hadn't been able to talk to his family about Norman's death even though they were all deeply affected by it and wanted to talk. I said that I hadn't talked enough about it with my children either in those years. So I just felt this little bit of kinship with him as a parent and a human being. It was almost as if we hadn't been on opposite sides of the chasm that had split our country apart.

The reconciliation between McNamara and Anne Morrison Welsh would not be the norm in post-Vietnam America. In the years that followed the Kennedy-Johnson debacle in Vietnam, the war more often divided than united public opinion. Just as the shadow of the Civil War shaped American politics for a half-century after the last shot was fired, political debates since the 1960s have largely centered on the meaning of the war and its ultimately unsuccessful conclusion.

Some liberals would argue that the Vietnam War symbolized the perils of American hubris, the notion that this nation is the world's policeman and has the right to impose its political and economic priorities on the world. The United States cannot force an unpopular regime on another people without paying a high price, such liberals would argue. The United States cannot successfully present itself as a defender of democracy when it backs oppressive regimes like the government of South Vietnam on the pretense that such dictatorships are anti-communist. The American effort failed in large degree because the government did not live up to the values embodied in the United States Constitution.

Some conservatives would argue that Johnson failed to "win" the war because he was unwilling to pay the political price and held back from using the full might of the American military. Johnson's half-measures, these conservatives would suggest, represented appeasement of communists in the Soviet Union and China who were determined to dominate the world. Vietnam, conservatives like Ronald Reagan would insist, had been a worthy cause and had failed because of a lack of will on the part of weak politicians.

"[W]ho can doubt that the cause for which our men fought was just?" President Reagan asked in a speech at the Washington, C.D., Vietnam Memorial in 1988. "It was, after all, however imperfectly pursued, the cause of freedom; and they showed uncommon courage in its service. Perhaps at this late date we can all agree that we've learned one lesson: that young Americans must never again be sent to fight and die unless we are prepared to let them win."

The Vietnam War has been an issue in almost every presidential election in the ensuing four decades. Dissatisfaction with Johnson's war helped Richard Nixon win the presidency in 1968, and Nixon would cruise to reelection in 1972 partly by accusing Democratic nominee George McGovern of being soft on the North Vietnamese and partly by announcing a peace agreement with the communists just before Election Day. Democrat Jimmy Carter promoted his presidential bid by emphasizing his honesty to a public well aware of the dishonesty of Johnson and Nixon on the Vietnam issue.

Republican presidents Ronald Reagan and George H.W. Bush won the White House vowing to restore American military might supposedly lost in the wake of the Vietnam fiasco. After directing a brief and successful war in response to the invasion of Kuwait by Iraqi dictator Saddam Hussein, in 1991, Bush spoke of the U.S. overcoming a "Vietnam Syndrome" of defeatism. Controversies erupted over prominent politicians' use of college deferments or National Guard service to avoid Vietnam combat: Bush's vice president, Dan Quayle; Democratic President Bill Clinton; and Republican President George W. Bush, to name a few. America was involved in two wars in 2004, in Afghanistan and Iraq, but much of the presidential campaign that year centered on George Bush's National Guard service and on Republican efforts to discredit the two Purple Hearts earned during the Vietnam War by Democratic nominee John Kerry.

The deep political divisions opened by the Vietnam War were already shaping American life by December 1967. In the next year these divisions would produce the collapse of a presidency, two political assassinations, another series of race riots, a major political convention marked by police beating and tear-gassing demonstrators, and the election of a new president promising "law and order" who would be forced out of office after he was accused of lawbreaking. Meanwhile, no one doubted America's importance to the world, but its power seemed diminished and useless to tame international chaos. "[T]he destiny of the human race depends on America," the Black Panther Eldridge Cleaver said. ". . . like passengers in a jet forced to watch helplessly while a passel of drunks, hypes, freaks and madmen fight for the controls."

Chronology

1954 The Viet Minh defeat the French at Dien Binh Phu.
The French Indo-China War ends.
Geneva Peace accords are signed.
Ngo Dinh Diem dictatorship of South Vietnam begins.

1957 Diem announces there will be no reunification election.

1960 National Liberation Front, or "Vietcong," is formed.
John F. Kennedy defeats Richard Nixon.
Eisenhower Administration has assigned 900 military advisors to South Vietnam by the end of the year.

1961 President Kennedy forms a Vietnam policy task force to explore America's options.
Kennedy dispatches 100 Special Forces troops to South Vietnam.
American pilots fly the first combat missions of the against North Vietnamese and NVA targets.

1962 The "Strategic Hamlet" program.

1963 The Army of Viet Nam (ARVN) is defeated by communist forces on January 2.
Buddhist anti-Diem protests begin May 8 with the self-immolation of Thich Qunag Duc.
American government gives tacit support to an anti-Diem military coup.
Military draws up plans to withdraw 1,000 military advisors from South Vietnam and to remove all American forces by the end of 1965.

Nov. 1-2: Diem and his brother are murdered, and a military dictatorship establishes control over South Vietnam.

Nov. 22 President John F. Kennedy is assassinated.
By the end of the year, 16,000 American troops are stationed in South Vietnam.

1964 Robert McNamara reports to President Johnson that the Vietcong control 40 percent of the countryside and 90 percent of the provinces near the Saigon.

May 2 Protestors in New York burn their draft cards.

Aug. 2 The *USS Maddox* in the Tonkin Gulf .

Aug. 4 *Maddox* and the *Turner Joy* falsely report an attack from North Vietnamese vessels.

Aug. 7 Gulf of Tonkin Resolution.
Johnson defeats Barry Goldwater.

1965: Operation Rolling Thunder.

March 8 Two battalions of Marines sent to Vietnam to protect the American air base at Da Nang.

March 9 President Johnson authorizes the use of napalm.

April 17 President Johnson offers to economically develop North Vietnam in return for a peace agreement in his "peace without conquest" speech.
20,000 gather in Washington, D.C., to protest the war.

June 28 President Johnson announces he will double the monthly draft call and will increase troop levels to 125,000.
Battle of Ia Drang in August.
Poet Allen Ginsberg, author Ken Kesey and others picket at the Army Terminal in Oakland, California on October 15.
Norman Morrison burns himself to death in front of the Pentagon .
American troop levels reach 184,000 by the end of the year. By the end of December, 2,255 Americans have died in Vietnam.

1966 American troop levels reach 385,300, and 8,398 have died there by the end of the year.

1967 Martin Luther King begins to speak out against the Vietnam War.
March on the Pentagon.
American troop levels reach 485,500 and casualties reach 19,951.

Review Questions

1. By what steps did the United States get involved in the Vietnam War, and what assumptions, such as the "Domino Theory," drove this process?

2. What advantages did the North Vietnamese and the National Liberation Front enjoy in their war?

3. How did the American government mislead the public about the war in Vietnam, including its depiction of South Vietnamese support for the Saigon government, the facts surrounding the Gulf of Tonkin incident, enemy casualty rates, and the communist forces' will to fight?

4. What factors contributed to human rights abuses by the American, South Vietnamese and North Vietnamese forces in the Vietnam War?

5. How did the Vietnam War aggravate class tensions within the United States, and how did these tensions shape public perception of the peace movement?

Glossary of Important People and Concepts

Agent Orange
Muhammad, Ali
Battle of Ap Bac
Battle of Ia Drang Valley
Domino Theory
William J. Fullbright
Geneva Peace Accords of 1954
Todd Gitlin
Gulf of Tonkin Resolution
David Halberstam
Hanoi Hilton
Tom Hayden
Ho Chi Minh
Edward Lansdale
Curtis LeMay
Walter Lippman
Henry Cabot Lodge, Jr.
Mike Mansfield
March on the Pentagon
Robert McNamara
Montagnards
Norman Morrison
Wayne Morse
Napalm-B
Ngo Dinh Diem
Ngo Dinh Nhu
Nguyen Van Thieu
Operation Rolling Thunder
Port Huron Statement
Project 100,000
"Search and Destroy"
Students for a Democratic Society (SDS)

SUGGESTED READINGS

Christian G. Appy, *Working-Class War: American Combat Soldiers and Vietnam* (1993).

____, *Patriots: The Vietnam War Remembered From All Sides* (2003).

Mark Baker, *Nam: The Vietnam War in the Words of the Men and Women Who Fought There* (1981).

Lawrence H. Climo, "Dr. Lawrence H. Climo Recalls His Vietnam War Service," *Vietnam* (April 2003).

Philip Caputo, *A Rumor of War* (1977).

Gail Dolgin and Vicente Franco, directors, *Daughter from Danang* (2002) American Experience website, http://www.pbs.org/wgbh/amex/daughter/peopleevents/p_gis.html.

Gwynne Dyer, *War* (1985).

James Ebert, *A Life in a Year: The American Infantryman in Vietnam* (2004).

Bernard Fall, *The Two Vietnams: A Political and Military Analysis* (1967).

Francis Fitzgerald, *Fire in the Lake: The Vietnamese and the Americans in Vietnam* (1972).

George Q. Flynn, *The Draft: 1940-1973* (1993).

Marvin E. Gettleman, et al., eds., *Vietnam and America: A Documented History* (1985).

Todd Gitlin, *The Sixties: Years of Hope, Days of Rage* (1987).

Peter Goldman and Tony Fuller, *Charlie Company: What Vietnam Did to Us* (1983).

David Halberstam, *The Best and the Brightest* (1969).

William M. Hammond, *Reporting Vietnam: Media and Military at War* (1998).

Paul Hendrickson, *The Living and the Dead: Robert McNamara and Five Lives of a Lost War* (1996).

George C. Herring, *America's Longest War: The United States and Vietnam, 1950-1975* (1986).

Stanley Karnow, *Vietnam: A History* (1983).

Paul Kusch, *All American Boys: Draft Dodgers in Canada From the Vietnam War* (2001).

James Loewen, *Lies My Teacher Told Me: Everything Your American History Textbook Got Wrong* (1995).

Norman Mailer, *Armies of the Night: History as a Novel, the Novel as History* (1968).

Allen J. Matusow, *The Unraveling of America: A History of Liberalism in the 1960s* (1984).

Robert McNamara, *In Retrospect: The Tragedy and Lessons of Vietnam* (1996).

Errol Morris, director, *The Fog of War* (2003).

Bruce Palling, director, *Vietnam: A Television History* (1983). http://www.pbs.org/wgbh/amex/vietnam/trenches/mia.html

Bruce Palmer, Jr., *The 25-Year War: America's Military Role in Vietnam* (1984).

Neil Sheehan, *A Bright Shining Lie: John Paul Vann and America in Vietnam* (1988).

Winnie Smith, *American Daughter Gone to War: On the Front Lines With an Army Nurse in Vietnam* (1992).

Steve Stibbens, et. al, *Ambassadors in Green: A Pictorial Account of U.S. Marines in Vietnam, the Battles They Fought, the Hardships They Endured* (1971).

Wallace Terry, *Bloods: An Oral History of the Vietnam War by Black Veterans* (1984).

Tom Wells, *The War Within: America's Battle Over Vietnam* (2005).

Marilyn B. Young, *The Vietnam Wars: 1945-1990* (1991).

Dror Yuravlivker, "'Peace without Conquest': Lyndon Johnson's Speech of April 7, 1965," *Presidential Studies Quarterly* (August 24, 2006).

ROBERT KENNEDY

Chapter Thirty

THE NIGHTMARE YEAR, 1968

As the first major Democratic showdown loomed in the Indiana primary on May 7, Robert Kennedy drew large crowds that responded to his appearances with frightening intensity. The multiple tragedies of 1968 and the dreams that his supporters projected upon Kennedy delicately balanced the candidate at a thin intersection of hope and doom. Friends warned Kennedy that someone would kill him. The question for some was whether he would be slain by someone who despised him or someone motivated by a twisted sense of love.

Kennedy's fans screamed and wept at his appearances, their faces marked by and their voices touched with pain over past losses and a despairing, wounded hope for a better tomorrow. Bobby's older brother, President John Kennedy, had been assassinated five years earlier; and the recent murder of civil rights leader Martin Luther King, Jr., as well as the bloodshed in Vietnam and a series of race riots that had ripped apart American cities had taken their toll on the emotions of the younger Kennedy's followers. His audiences reached out to the New York Senator as a refuge from the madness.

"The crowds were savage," recalled RFK adviser John Bartlow Martin. "They pulled his cuff links off, tore his clothes, tore ours. In bigger towns, with bigger crowds, it was frightening." Kennedy biographer Evan Thomas related how a Kalamazoo, Michigan, housewife reached into Kennedy's open campaign car, grabbed for the candidate, and came away with a trophy—one of Robert's shoes.

Kennedy would stand in his open top car as it slowly inched through admiring, emotional throngs, briefly touching the hands, arms and faces of grasping admirers while his aide Bill Barry desperately held him from behind, trying to keep him from being pulled away. "Not so tight, you're going to break my back," Kennedy was once heard pleading. Nevertheless, on another occasion a woman yanked his head down by pulling on his tie while another woman pulled him off the car completely.

These were violent scenes in a violent year. Two political murders darkened the year, as did the slaughter by American soldiers of the civilian residents of a Vietnamese village named My Lai. In 1968, nearly 16,000 American soldiers died in Vietnam and another 99,000 suffered injuries, the bloodiest year yet of the war in terms of American casualties.

The war also came home. The United States turned on itself, with the conflict between whites and blacks, pro-war "hawks" and anti-war "doves," between college students and the working class, and between rich and poor often punctuated with bloodshed. "Nineteen sixty-eight was the pivotal year of the sixties; the year when all of a nation's impulses towards violence, idealism, diversity and disorder peaked to produce the greatest possible hope—and the worst imaginable despair," observed Charles Kaiser, author of **1968 in America: Music, Politics, Chaos, Counterculture, and the Shaping of a Generation***.*

In 1920, the Irish poet William Butler Yeats looked back at another time of multiple horrors, the First World War, and composed one of the landmarks of modern literature, a poem called "The Second Coming." Looking at Europe's post-war landscape, Yeats wrote:

Things fall apart; the centre cannot hold;
Mere anarchy is loosed upon the world,
The blood-dimmed tide is loosed, and everywhere
The ceremony of innocence is drowned;
The best lack all conviction, while the worst
Are full of passionate intensity.

Yeats's words perfectly describe 1968. It was a year in which the bullet carried more power than ideas. Along with the 1930s, Kaiser argued, 1968 was a time when "large numbers of Americans wondered out loud if their country might disintegrate." This epic year was a time when political heroes became martyrs, idealism turned to rage, and cities in Vietnam and the United States became funeral pyres.

REVOLUTIONS & STUDENT UNREST ON COLLEGE CAMPUSES

Up Against the Wall

Like the unstable subatomic particles studied by physicists, in 1968 political disputes over topics ranging from the seemingly trivial (the construction of a gymnasium), to the essential (the Vietnam War), to the existential (how one could find meaning in a life under depersonalized industrial capitalism), set off chain reactions that at times appeared to shake the very foundations of Western society. Nowhere was this more the case than on college campuses around the world. There, revolution seemingly joined reading and "'ritin" and "'rithmetic" as one of the four "R's." The year 1968 saw student rebellions at Columbia University in New York; in Paris, France; and in Mexico City. These youthful uprisings aimed at greater academic freedom, genuine democracy, socialism, and an end to imperialist wars.

A student revolt at Columbia University in New York City captured 1968 in a microcosm. There the students protested against capitalism, the Vietnam War, the university's involvement in developing war technology, and institutional racism. Mostly affluent and overwhelmingly white, most of the students at the school didn't care that the university had broken ground for a new gymnasium that would intrude on the mostly African American and poor Harlem neighborhood next to the campus. Morningside Park, an undeveloped 30-acre plot on the eastern side of the campus, had always served as the border between Columbia and Harlem.

Planned since 1959, the gym would cost $8.4 million ($52.6 million in 2010 dollars), and Columbia promised to construct public facilities, including a swimming pool, open to Harlem residents. Proposed spending on the gym, however, outstripped planned university spending on the local community by five to one. By the time of its ground-breaking in February 1968, the project had become a target of discontent for Black Power advocates in Harlem, who derided it as "Gym Crow." White anti-war activists attending Columbia took a longer time to notice the dispute.

Student activism focused on the on-campus recruitment conducted by Dow Chemical, the manufacturer of Napalm-B (the cancer-causing, flammable chemical agent used to burn communist troops and destroy villages in South Vietnam) and the Central Intelligence Agency. The campus chapter of the leftist Students for a Democratic Society also objected to Columbia University's participation in the Institute for Defense Analyses (IDA), which developed weapons and "counter-insurgency" strategies against guerrilla forces such as the Vietcong. Military research and weapons development constituted about 46 percent of Columbia's total budget by 1968. Finally, campus SDS leader **Mark Rudd** and other members of the anti-war group objected to a campus-wide prohibition on indoor demonstrations as a violation of free speech.

In 1968, Columbia had a tiny number of African-American students. An on-campus group, the Students' Afro-American Society, according to historian Kaiser, acted more like a book club and a debating society than a locus of political activism. That changed with the election of Black Nationalist Cicero Wilson as SAS president in the spring semester of 1968. Wilson grew up in the African-American ghetto of **Bedford Stuyvesant** in Brooklyn. Wilson was the first member of the SAS who had lived "on the streets." As one SDS member put it, he was "a tough, city black kid. He really was crucial, for while he was not flamboyant, he exerted a kind of moral force on the other guys. He wasn't a 'Negro'; he was the equivalent of Malcolm X."

Unlike Malcolm, Wilson quickly showed a willingness to work with white activists on campus. He found a kindred spirit in SDS leader Rudd. A Jewish kid with relatives who survived the Holocaust, Rudd knew the dangers of failing to oppose evil. Already a self-described radical, Rudd believed that the Vietnam War was evil, as were the "liberals" who supported it. "They [liberals] can rationalize anything," Rudd later said. "There will always be slums, they say, there will always be wars . . . a radical doesn't accept that."

On March 27, students protested against Columbia's contribution to war technology by occupying part of Low Library, the location of university administration offices, in open defiance of the ban against indoor demonstrations. Students occupied the building and demanded to meet Columbia President **Grayson L. Kirk,** who sat on the board of the IDA. Kirk's reign as campus president bordered on autocratic.

The Occupation

On April 23, about 400 students gathered at a sundial on the southern side of the campus. Speakers representing the SDS and the SAS denounced the construction of the gym, the IDA, the Vietnam War and the college discipline policies. The crowd reached an emotional crescendo when SAS leader Wilson spoke. Wilson suggested that oppressed residents of Harlem might join student radicals in reclaiming the land Columbia University sat on. "You people had better realize that you condone Grayson Kirk with his rough riding over the black community. But do you realize that when you come back, there may not be a Columbia University? Do you think that this white citadel will be bypassed if an insurrection occurs this summer?"

Students tried to break the locks on the doors of the Low Library and, thwarted, charged toward the gym construction site. Tearing down the fence surrounding the dig, the protestors tangled with police. A student occupation of Hamilton Hall, and of Columbia University, began. Henry Coleman, the Columbia College acting dean, went to his office in Hamilton and promptly became a hostage of the protestors. By the fourth day, demonstrators controlled five buildings. Students decorated the occupied buildings with pictures of Cuban revolutionary Che Guevara, Soviet revolutionary leader Vladimir Lenin and Malcolm X.

The university suspended construction of the new gymnasium, which was never completed at the Morningside Park site. A different one would eventually be built inside the campus. The students made five other demands before they would leave the buildings they controlled: the end of Columbia's affiliation with the IDA; the reversal of the ban on indoor demonstrations; the dropping of criminal charges against the student demonstrators; the release of six prisoners already arrested for protests against the IDA; and amnesty from suspensions and other discipline for the protest participants. The university rejected amnesty for the protestors and on April 30, the New York City police gathered in military formation and stormed the occupied buildings, ejecting the protestors.

"Policemen who might have dreamed of sending their sons to such a prestigious place waded into the crowds of privileged Ivy League students to create the closest thing to class warfare ever witnessed on the Columbia campus," Kaiser noted. Pacifists wearing green armbands tried to stand between the police and the protestors but were beaten with nightsticks and blackjacks. Police forced one group of protestors to run a gauntlet, with officers raining down blows with clubs and other weapons. "Some of the students inside Avery and Mathematics Halls were dragged facedown over marble steps leading to police vans waiting on Amsterdam Avenue," Kaiser said. Faculty members, innocent bystanders, a *New York Times* reporter, and even members of a pro-administration conservative students group suffered beatings by the police. Several hundred were injured, and police reported that 720 had been arrested.

In response, a general strike paralyzed the campus. The administration summoned Rudd and four other student protest leaders to the dean's office on May 21 to face disciplinary actions. The four refused to attend the hearing. About 350 students once again occupied Hamilton Hall. Events unfolded as they had on April 30, with 68 students injured and 177 arrested. Nevertheless, the protesting students got most of what they wanted. Columbia University ended its affiliation with IDA, and the prohibition against indoor demonstrations was reversed. The university dropped trespassing charges against most of the students and loosened campus rules restricting the access of women to male students on campus. Rudd would be charged with riot, incitement to riot and trespass. Columbia suspended him, making him eligible for the military draft, but he sought an occupational deferment on the grounds that he was a "professional revolutionist." Rudd ended up flunking his Army physical.

Admitting that he authorized a fire to be set at Hamilton Hall, Rudd later said the campus occupation for him served as a crossing of a philosophical Rubicon. "Caught up in 'total war' mode, beyond rage and without limits anymore . . . I had crossed over the line of nonviolent protest." The next year Rudd would form the Weather Underground, an offshoot of the SDS that dedicated itself to "bringing the war home" and using terrorism, including the bombing of buildings and bank robberies, to overthrow the American government.

THE TAKING OF THE *PUEBLO*

At the same time campus demonstrations rocked the country, the United States suffered serious setbacks in foreign policy that seemed to threaten its position in the world. Entering what would be the most difficult year yet for the Vietnam War, the United States almost stumbled into a second war against North Korea.

On January 11, 1968, the **U.S.S. *Pueblo*** departed from a Japanese port on an espionage mission off the North Korean coast. The North Koreans captured the ship and held the crew prisoner for almost a year while the Pyongyang regime presented evidence that the *Pueblo* had entered the communist nation's territorial waters. Conservatives in the Congress called for a military strike against North Korea, and President Johnson received angry letters complaining about his perceived failure to strongly respond.

The American command should have seen this incident developing. The Navy had previously come close to mothballing the *Pueblo*, which had a history of problems with navigation, and speed, and with its communication equipment. Yet the Navy sent this vessel to monitor Soviet and North Korean sonar, radar and radio transmissions and to observe the movement of Soviet and North Korean vessels. The *Pueblo*, slow and hard to maneuver, also suffered from inadequate defenses, according to historian Mitchell B. Lerner, including guns that overheated and were accurate only from a short range.

The ship's translators, Robert Hammond and Robert Chicca, were not up to the jobs assigned them. "Their task of monitoring and translating Korean communications was crucial for the ship's safety, since they were relied on to warn the officers of any impending danger," Lerner wrote. ". . . Yet neither Hammond nor Chicca was qualified for this critical position. Their training consisted of a nine-month course in Korean at the Defense Language Institute . . . Neither had used the language for years, and their skills had deteriorated to such an extent that neither could read Korean without a dictionary. In fact, Hammond's fluency was so poor that while in captivity the North Koreans beat him repeatedly because his personnel file stated that he could speak Korean, but he was so inept at it that they believed he was trying to conceal this ability." In spite of all of these problems, the Navy sent the ship near the coast of an enemy with no clear set of commands for the crew on what to do if they were detected and stopped by North Korean ships.

The *Pueblo's* mission took place amid signs that the North Korean government had embarked on a more aggressive course towards the United States and its South Korean ally. The North Korean navy had seized twenty South Korean vessels in the last three months of 1967. On January 17, thirty-one North Korean Army officers had crossed the South Korea border as part of a plot to assassinate President Park Chung Hee. The hit squad reached the South Korean presidential palace on January 22 when stopped by a South Korean policeman. In the ensuing gun battle, eight South Koreans and five members of the assassination squad died.

As Lerner notes, North Korean dictator **Kim Il-Sung** had domestic political reasons for his more aggressive stance towards South Korea and his belligerent approach to the *Pueblo* crisis. The North Korean economy slowed significantly in the 1960s. As industrial and agricultural production fell, the low wages paid North Koreans led most families to suffer as prices rose. Underwear cost North Korean workers almost two weeks' wages. Severe shortages of beef and pork made these items unavailable for most North Koreans.

Kim also faced serious challenges within the North Korean communist leadership from moderates who wanted a less provocative foreign policy towards South Korea. Acting aggressively towards a United States vessel, therefore, served Kim's domestic political needs by creating a crisis in which opposition to the dictator would seem like treason. If the United States had viewed North Korea as an independent state rather than as a pawn, the military establishment might have been more cautious in how it deployed spy ships near the North Korean coast.

The North Koreans seized the *Pueblo* on January 23, 1968. One crewman died during a faceoff with the North Korean Navy, and the other 82 were arrested. The North Koreans claimed their territorial waters extended 12 miles from their shore and that the *Pueblo* had crossed this line. Lerner believes that American administration officials told the truth when they said the *Pueblo* was captured in international waters. The seizure of the *Pueblo* proved devastating to American security. The capture of communications equipment and classified documents, combined with information provided by a Soviet-paid spy operating in the United States, Navy Officer John Walker, Jr., allowed the Soviets to decode approximately 1 million American messages. The Soviets were able to tip off the North Vietnamese about American bombing raids in advance, allowing the Hanoi military to prepare defenses, which resulted in downed American bomber planes.

Under torture, the *Pueblo* crew signed several statements indicating they had committed crimes against the North Korean people. To win the release of the prisoners, an American negotiator on December 23 signed a statement written by the North Koreans in which the American government apologized for the incident. The North Koreans released the 82 surviving crew members. The statement the Americans signed was humiliating, but in one important way, the resolution of the *Pueblo* crisis marked a rare and important achievement for the Johnson administration that year. In this case, the United States was able to avoid armed conflict, a rare foreign policy triumph that year.

A DRASTICALLY DIFFERENT KIND OF WAR

During the summer of 1967, congressional leaders confronted Lyndon Johnson about the immense costs of both the Vietnam War and Johnson's beloved "Great Society" social programs. By this point the war cost $20 billion a year (more than $127 billion a year in 2009 dollars.) To pay the bills for these expensive projects, the president would have to propose tax increases and/or budget cuts. Johnson opted for a 10 percent tax surcharge to be assessed on all corporate and individual taxpayers. "Until that moment, most Americans had not been asked to do anything or pay anything to support the war," journalist Dan Oberdorfer wrote.

> For most of them, the conflict was remote from their personal lives and experience . . . For all the talk of coffins coming back, it is likely that the vast majority of 200,000,000 Americans did not know personally any of the 13,000 men who had been killed in action in Vietnam from 1961 to the summer of 1967. More Americans than that died *per year* from accidental falls, twice as many died *per year* from cirrhosis of the liver and four times that many died *per year* in motor vehicle accidents.

Nevertheless, disturbing signs abounded that the war would take a more violent turn. By the summer of 1967, American military commanders received intelligence indicating a buildup of North Vietnamese forces in Khe Sanh in the far northwestern corner of South Vietnam, not far from the Demilitarized Zone (DMZ) dividing the two countries. Commanders dispatched Marines to reinforce the base against an anticipated North Vietnamese Army (NVA) assault. The North Vietnamese and National Liberation Front (Vietcong) troops began bombarding Khe Sanh and laid siege to the base. American air superiority allowed the military to keep Khe Sanh supplied. As fighter planes attacked communist anti-aircraft batteries, helicopters dropped ammunition, food and other essentials to the Marines below. The siege lasted 77 days and resulted in 703 American and South Vietnamese deaths and 2,642 wounded.

Many journalists, politicians and historians later agreed that the **Battle of Khe Sanh**, which began on January was an intentional distraction, aimed at forcing American commander Gen. William Westmoreland to divert resources to an unimportant corner of South Vietnam as part of a grand strategy. Such analysts believe that the communists intended to draw American troops away from multiple cities across South Vietnam in preparation for a campaign launched on January 30 that came to be known as the **Tet Offensive**.

Americans had negotiated a ceasefire with the North Vietnamese during Tet season, a Vietnamese Lunar New Year celebration. The Americans anticipated a quiet holiday. Instead, close to 70,000 communist soldiers launched a surprise attack at the beginning of Tet, on January 30. The North Vietnamese and their NVA allies attacked more than 100 cities and towns, including 39 of South Vietnam's 44 provincial capitals.

Caught by surprise, the military leadership had no idea how many communist troops had been thrown into the campaign and how many had been held in reserve. The North Vietnamese and their NLF allies also startled the Americans with their abrupt change of tactics. The communists had always tried to avoid direct confrontation with the better-armed U.S. military, preferring ambushes and hit-and-run attacks. For the Tet Offensive, suddenly the communists fought as an effective conventional army.

When the Vietcong seized control of the South Vietnamese city of Hue, they carried with them a detailed enemies list that included top South Vietnamese soldiers and residents who had collaborated with the American-supported regime in Saigon, Americans, Germans and Filipinos. During the weeks communists held the city, they massacred between 3,000 and 6,000 supporters of the "puppet regime" in Saigon.

Four thousand communist troops struck the South Vietnamese capital of Saigon. Ho Chi Minh, the North Vietnamese leader, and his officers displayed a keen awareness of the importance of press coverage to their military campaign. They launched the offensive in the dead of the night, including the all-but-doomed assault on and occupation of the American embassy by 19 guerillas, in sufficient time for film to be shot, processed and transmitted from Japan just in time for the evening news broadcasts in America. The battle at the embassy captured the attention of the world press. Film of a battle unfolding at the embassy, the center of American power in Southeast Asia, made a mockery of Johnson administration claims that victory over the communists was at hand.

One of the Great Pictures of the Vietnam War

One searing image from the Tet Offensive fixed in the American mind the brutality of the Vietnam War and the distance between the spin offered by Johnson and his cabinet and the ugly realities on the ground. On February 1, **General Nguyen Ngoc Loan**, the chief of South Vietnam's national police, conducted a spontaneous street execution of a communist guerilla. Images of the killing reached newspaper readers and television viewers around the world. Loan had ruthlessly crushed a dissident Buddhist movement in Hue two years before. During the Tet Offensive, Communist soldiers had killed several of his men, including a major who was a close friend, along with the major's wife and children. That day, Associated Press photographer **Eddie Adams** and Vo Suu of the National Broadcasting Company cruised around the gun-blasted South Vietnamese capital, eventually approaching the An Quang temple. They spotted South Vietnamese marines who held in custody a man in black shorts and a checkered shirt, with his hands tied behind him. They led the prisoner to General Loan, who carried a pistol.

Loan used the gun to wave away a gathering crowd, stretched his right arm towards the prisoner's temple, and pulled the trigger. "The man grimaced—then, almost in slow motion, his legs crumpled beneath him and he seemed to sit down backwards, blood gushing from his head as it hit the pavement," Stanley Karnow, author of *Vietnam: A History*, writes. "Not a word was spoken. It all happened instantly, with hardly a sound except for the crack of Loan's gun, the click of Adams's shutter, and the whir of Vo Suu's camera." Loan calmly holstered the pistol, walking away and telling the NBC photographer, "'These guys kill a lot of our people, and I think Buddha will forgive me.'"

Adams's camera had captured the moment when the bullet from Loan's gun first struck the prisoner's temple. Transmitting that picture with radio transmitters to the AP's New York office, Adams had photographed one of the iconic and most devastating images from the Vietnam War. "Everyone knew it was a prizewinner," author Don Oberdorfer wrote, "one of the great pictures of the Vietnam War." The next day, Adams's photograph appeared on the front pages of newspapers around the world. NBC broadcast film of the incident shot by Vo Suu in color as part of *The Huntley-Brinkley Report*. As Kaiser observed, "This image did more damage to the idea that America was bringing civilization to South Vietnam than any other event . . . It was an honest portrait of the brutality of war and the ruthlessness of our Vietnamese ally" even if viewers did not understand the brutality of the North Vietnamese and Vietcong during the Tet Offensive.

The Johnson administration's efforts to manage the news from South Vietnam suffered another body blow on February 7. The American military organized a field trip

Vietcong prisoner, Nguyen Van Lém, being executed by police chief General Nguyen Ngoc Loan in Saigon.
February 1, 1968   Credit: Library of Congress

Secretary of Defense Robert McNamara on the telephone January 10, 1964   Credit: LBJ Library

for reporters to Ben Tre, the capital of Kien Hoa province, that had been home to 35,000. The town lay in ruins and the battle there produced a high number of civilian casualties. One major told AP reporter **Peter Arnett,** "It became necessary to destroy the town to save it." If Adams's and Suu's photography captured the savagery of the Vietnam War, the quote reported by Arnett captured the war's insanity. The tremendous technological advantage the United States brought to the war obviously had failed to crush the North Vietnamese and the Vietcong's will to fight, but the advanced weaponry clearly had destroyed much of America's South Vietnam ally and its people.

Years of empty assurances from President Johnson and Secretary of Defense Robert McNamara about success in Vietnam lay in ruins. The Tet Offensive can be considered the death knell of Johnson's credibility with the American voting public. A substantially larger percentage of Americans believed that the United States was losing the war in Vietnam in late February 1968 than had the previous November. The number saying America was losing went up from 8 to 23 percent in that four-month period, according to a Gallup organization poll, while the number believing that America was making military "progress" dropped from 50 percent to 33 percent.

Losing the Most Trusted Man in America

From a pure tactical standpoint, the Tet Offensive represented a disaster for the North Vietnamese military and its NLF allies. Ho Chi Minh and other North Vietnamese leaders had hoped that the offensive would spark a popular uprising against the Saigon regime, but they were sorely disappointed. The communists were unable to hold positions they had taken and were forced, bloodied and disappointed, to melt back into the jungles. While the Americans had lost about 2,000 men between January 30 and early March, the highest death toll in a single campaign yet for the United States in the war, and the South Vietnamese lost 4,000, the North Vietnamese and Vietcong suffered almost a mortal wound. Credible estimates put communist deaths at 50,000 deaths in one month.

Westmoreland described the offensive to reporters as a failed "go for broke" move similar to the German Ardennes Offensive in 1944-1945 that led to the Battle of the Bulge. The American general celebrated a victory on the ground, but the communist leadership had additional objectives that Tet season. North Vietnamese military strategist **Vo Nguyen Giap** hoped the offensive would demoralize the American public and increase impatience in the United States for an end to the conflict. "Giap's long-range strategy was to continue to bleed the Americans until they agreed to a settlement that satisfied the Hanoi regime," said Karnow. "For that reason, the Communists were willing to endure terrible casualties during the Tet campaign, as they did throughout the war. The Tet Offensive was not intended to be a decisive operation, but one episode in a protracted war that might last 'five, ten, or twenty years.'" Karnow noted what Ho had warned the French twenty years earlier. "You can kill ten of my men for every one I kill of yours. But even at those odds, you will lose and I will win."

Considered the most trusted man in America, CBS News anchor Walter Cronkite traveled to South Vietnam in February 1968 with the objective of measuring how close the United States was truly to winning in Vietnam or whether victory was any longer possible. In the days before the internet, in which only three television networks competed for national news audiences, an anchor like Cronkite enjoyed out-of-size influence. One politician described Cronkite as a man who "by mere inflection of his deep baritone voice or by a lifting of his well-known bushy eyebrows . . . might well change the vote of thousands of people." On February 27, CBS broadcast *Report from Vietnam by Walter Cronkite*. The Nielsen ratings service later estimated that nine million Americans watched the report. Among them was a nervous Lyndon Johnson who dreaded a critical broadcast. Johnson's worst fears were realized as Cronkite editorialized at the program's conclusion:

It now seems more certain than ever that the bloody experience of Vietnam is to end in a stalemate . . . To say that we are closer to victory today is to believe, in the face of the evidence, the optimists who have been wrong in the past. To suggest that we are on the edge of defeat is to yield to unreasonable pessimism. To say we are mired in stalemate seems the only realistic, yet unsatisfactory, conclusion . . . [I]t is increasingly clear to this reporter that the only rational way out then will be to negotiate, not as victors but as an honorable people who lived up to their pledge to defend democracy and did the best they could.

The anchor's words thunderstruck President Johnson, who said, "If I've lost Cronkite, I've lost Middle America." In fact, a substantial percentage of Americans had grown skeptical of the war before Cronkite's broadcast. Support for the president dropped, but there was no significant increase in opposition to the war, nor a decline in support for the war. The tone of news coverage, however, permanently changed. Before Tet, war supporters appearing on network news broadcasts outnumbered critics by more than 6-1. It was only after Tet that critics and war supporters achieved parity on the evening news.

Personnel shifts at newspapers by 1968 also changed press coverage as the pro-administration and pro-war "old guard" moved out of the newsrooms to management positions or retired, their places taken by younger, more skeptical reporters. War correspondents who came of age during the height of the Cold War in the 1950s moved on and made room for a new generation of college-educated reporters more likely to have absorbed the anti-war sentiments prevailing at many college campuses.

*The Banality of Evil:
A Massacre at My Lai*

The Tet Offensive provided the most memorable photographic image of the Vietnam War and the Battle at Ban Tre, its most ironic, unforgettable quote. The mass murder by American soldiers of four hundred unarmed women, children and elderly in My Lai provided the war's great moment of infamy. In spite of American slavery, genocide aimed at Native Americans, human rights abuses committed again Filipino guerillas in the late nineteenth and early twentieth century, and imperialism aimed at Mexico and much of Latin America in the previous two centuries, an enduring American self-image was that of the United States as uniquely moral, a people who fought selflessly against evil forces such as the Nazis and godless communists. The cruel, ruthless killing of a small Vietnamese village gave lie to that self-satisfying myth.

In many ways, My Lai simply represented the cold, horrible logical conclusion of General Westmoreland's decision to fight a war of attrition, in which the communists supposedly would flinch as casualties mounted. As **Philip Caputo,** a Marine who later wrote extensively and critically about the American experience in Vietnam, observed:

Our mission was not to win terrain or seize positions, but simply to kill: to kill Communists and kill as many of them as possible. Stack 'em up like cordwood. Victory was a high body count, defeat a low kill ratio, war a matter of arithmetic. The pressure on unit commanders to produce enemy corpses was intense, and they in turn communicated it to their troops . . . It is not surprising, therefore, that some men acquired a contempt for human life and a predilection for taking it."

Nevertheless, the men of **Charlie Company,** who carried out the four-hour massacre at the village the Americans called My Lai 4, went above and beyond that homicidal imperative. Writing about Nazi mass murderer Adolf Eichmann, the scholar Hannah Arendt marveled at what she called the "banality of evil." Charlie Company was extraordinary only in its ordinariness. Of the most infamous murderers in the company, **Lt. William Laws Calley,** historians of the My Lai massacre Michael Bilton and Kevin Sim said, "His averageness had made him so invisible at one college he had attended that all anyone could remember about him was that he paid his rent regularly. In a similar vein, it was reported that he never drove too fast and would often mow the lawn and do jobs about the house." A post-massacre study by the Army documented that Charlie Company had a 20 percent higher ratio of high school graduates than the Army as a whole, and that in other aspects—such as IQ test scores and amount of training—these men matched Army norms.

Most of the company's soldiers were between 18 and 22 and almost half were African American. The **Peers Report,** commissioned by the Army, analyzed the causes of the My Lai Massacre and concluded that the perpetrators of the atrocity were "generally representative of the typical cross section of American youth assigned to combat units throughout the Army." As Lt. Calley later testified, the only lesson that came through during their stateside training loud and clear was that every Vietnamese represented a potential enemy. "It was drummed into us, 'Be sharp!' On guard! As soon as you think these people won't kill you, ZAP! In combat you haven't friends! You have enemies!'" Calley later recalled.

Soon after it arrived "in country" Charlie Company found itself in Quang Ngai Province, which, the men had been briefed, represented a hotbed of NLF resistance. Commanders sent the newest, greenest wave of American soldiers on "Search and Destroy" missions in the Quang Ngai countryside. Lt. Calley filled with stories about the North Vietnamese and Vietcong using children as soldiers, saw local youths as killers in waiting. "All the men loved them," Calley later told investigators. "Gave the kids candy, cookies, chewing gum, everything. Not me. I hated them. I was afraid of Vietnamese kids." One soldier later described Calley as a "glory hungry person . . . the kind of person who would have sacrificed all of us for his own personal advancement." Calley grew so despised by the men of Charlie Company that a price was put on his head.

As Bilton and Sim point out, early in January 1968, a pattern was set in the company where soldiers committed human rights abuses that were ignored or even praised by superior officers. Paranoia overcame the soldiers, particularly after the launch of the Tet Offensive. On February 11, one of Charlie Company's radio operators, Ron Weber, died after a shot ripped a kidney from his body, the first death experienced by the unit. On February 13, nearby Bravo Company came under fire in a battle resulting in one soldier's death and wounds for five others. Charlie Company had yet to find one Vietcong soldier, much less inflict one confirmed casualty. Any remaining restraints unraveled in one incident when Calley and a G.I. named Herbert Carter interrogated an old man, beat him, and threw him down a well before Calley shot him with an M-16. One soldier, Dennis Conti, became infamous for raping Vietnamese girls. After one assault, Conti cut braided hair off one of his victims and used this "trophy" to decorate his helmet.

Bitterness among the Americans deepened with the explosion of a mine that killed three members of Charlie Company on February 25. The American soldiers blamed the locals for not warning them about the mines. On March 14, one of the most popular men in the unit, Sgt. George Cox, stepped on a booby trap, which exploded, ripping him to pieces, causing another soldier to lose two legs, and a third to lose an arm and a leg as well as his eyesight. By the end of March, Charlie Company had seen five soldiers die and 23 suffer injuries, some severe.

On March 15, Task Force Barker, which included Charlie Company, received the assignment to clear out local villages of suspected Vietcong fighters. The task force was named after **Lt. Col. Frank A. Barker,** the commander of the operation. The men of Charlie Company were primed for vengeance. Task force officers later claimed that Barker ordered the destruction of the "houses, dwellings, and livestock" in the My Lai area, though some say this was implied rather than clearly demanded. Many officers, including Capt. Ernest Medina, told their men that anyone they found in the village the morning of the operation was probably a Vietcong fighter. "He [Medina] stated that My Lai . . . was a suspected VC stronghold and that he had orders to kill everybody that was in the village," Max D. Hudson, a weapons squad leader, told the Army Criminal Investigation Unit later.

The operation started at sunup on March 16. The four-hour reign of terror began with indiscriminate artillery barrages. There was no return enemy fire. One soldier, Michael Bernhardt, reported later that when soldiers stepped off helicopters they began firing the minute any Vietnamese was spotted, and the victims were left on the ground wounded or dying.

An old Vietnamese man stood in a field next to a water buffalo and put his hands in the air to indicate he was a non-combatant. Lt. Calley passively watched as several men in the unit shot the elderly man to death. A platoon medic began wildly shooting cows, buffalo and other animals. Conti forced a woman about 20 years old to have oral sex with him, coercing her by putting a gun to the head of her four-year-old child. Two hours into the operation, not a weapon had been found, not a shot fired at the Americans, nor a single NVA soldier located, much less killed.

A group of soldiers assigned to the First Platoon gathered about 60 Vietnamese villagers. The group included children ranging in age from infancy to around 12 and 13, as many as 15 old men, and 10 younger women, along with a group of very elderly women. Calley yelled at a group of soldiers, "I want them killed." Calley and another soldier fired into the civilians from ten feet away. "The Vietnamese screamed, yelled and tried to get up," Bilton and Sim wrote.

> It was pure carnage as heads were shot off along with limbs; the fleshier body parts were ripped to shreds . . . Mothers had thrown themselves on top of the young ones in a last desperate bid to protect them from the bullets raining down on them. The children were trying to stand up. Calley opened fire again, killing them one by one.

Calley moved on. The lieutenant stood near a ditch filled with children. A two-year-old climbed away from his mother and got to the top of the ditch. Calley spotted the toddler, yanked up the child, flung him back into the ditch and shot him. Elsewhere, soldiers sodomized women with their rifles, sometimes before shooting them in the genitals, while others joined Conti in rape.

Uncommon Valor

Individual soldiers tried to save villagers by getting them to hide in their huts, but such men sadly formed a minority at My Lai. Heroism proved to be in short supply, but helicopter pilot Hugh Clowers Thompson of Georgia, attached to the 123rd Aviation Battalion, emerged as one of the few brave men in a scene of mass murder. "Thompson was a character," Bilton and Sim later wrote. "He was also an exceptional pilot who took danger in his stride. If there was an enemy to find he would seek them out and kill them . . . Ruthless in winking out the VC, Thompson was also a very moral man. He was absolutely strict about opening fire only on clearly defined targets . . . He wanted to kill them cleanly and made it absolutely clear to his gunners that he wanted to see a weapon first before they opened fire."

Thompson and his crew flew near My Lai 4 to provide assistance if the infantry came under attack, and would also drop smoke sticks marking where he had spotted wounded soldiers and civilians. Thompson dropped a stick near a wounded Vietnamese civilian woman lying in a rice paddy. Thompson watched as a group of soldiers approached the woman. He lowered the chopper near the wounded woman and announced her presence to the soldier. A man wearing captain's bars approached the unarmed woman, prodded her with his foot and then shot her.

Shaken, Thompson and his men flew to another site where they saw dozens of civilians lying dead and dying in a ditch while a cluster of GIs sat nearby taking a cigarette break. Aware that he was witnessing a war crime, Thompson ordered his men to take off and he spotted a group of 10 civilians, including children, fleeing towards a crudely made bomb shelter. Soldiers from the 2nd Platoon chased them. Thompson ordered his men to land the helicopter between the civilians and the chasing soldiers. He ordered his gunner, Larry Colburn, to shoot the American soldiers if they began to fire upon the villagers. "Open up on 'em—blow 'em away," he screamed to his gunner.

Thompson began to personally evacuate terrified civilians from the bunker. Meanwhile, he had been screaming over the radio to gunship commanders about the unfolding massacre and pleaded for help with the evacuations. Thompson and his men continued to look for survivors and he spotted a ditch that contained at least 100 victims. Thompson could see something moving. While the rest of Thompson's men trained their machine guns on the soldiers of Task Force Barker, Colburn spotted what the helicopter crew was looking for: "[a] child, about age 3, covered in blood and slime, but not seriously injured." A soldier handed the child, "limp and . . . like a rag doll" to Colburn. "Thompson, who had a son about the same age, was crestfallen and decided to fly immediately to the ARVN hospital in Quang Ngai. The child, in a clear state of shock, lay across [another soldier's] . . . lap. Colburn noticed the blank look on its face and saw, too, for the second time that day, that tears were streaming down Thompson's cheeks," wrote Bilton and Sim.

When Thompson got the helicopter back to base, he emerged from the craft, throwing his helmet on the ground. He informed his section leader about the massacre, and the information crawled its way up the serpentine military command structure. By this time, Task Force Barker was ordered to cease fire. As many as 500 villagers in My Lai 4 and the immediate surrounding area had been butchered. The Army's newspaper, *Stars and Stripes*, initially reported that Charlie Company and other units involved in the massacre had encountered enemy resistance. Written by Sgt. Jay Roberts, who had been present at My Lai and had witnessed the murder of civilians, the story made no mention of the atrocities and made the patently false claim that 128 enemy fighters had been killed by Task Force Barker. This fabrication was undercut only paragraphs later when Roberts admitted that only three weapons had been found in the villages. Roberts quoted Lt. Barker as saying, "The combat assault went like clockwork." The story of My Lai would remain hidden from the American public for more than a year.

A DARK NIGHT OF THE SOUL

The tragedies and failures of Vietnam created opportunities for Lyndon Johnson's political enemies. A president once seen as a sure bet for a second full term now seemed vulnerable. No Johnson enemy stood taller in the public mind than Robert F. Kennedy, the younger brother of slain President John Kennedy. Johnson and the younger Kennedy had never liked each other, and this mutual antagonism became harsher when Johnson took control of the White House. Robert Kennedy resented Johnson as a crude, uncultured interloper, and Johnson raged at the condescension shown to him by the attorney general and others belonging to the late president's circle of friends.

Bobby, as he was known to intimate associates, was haunted by JFK's assassination. "Robert Kennedy seemed devoured by grief," biographer Evan Thomas wrote. "He literally shrank, until he appeared wasted and gaunt. His clothes no longer fit, especially his brother's old clothes— an old blue topcoat, a tuxedo, a leather bomber jacket with the presidential seal—which he insisted on wearing and which hung on his narrowing frame . . . he appeared to be in physical pain, like a man with a toothache or on the rack. Even walking seemed difficult to him, though he walked for hours, brooding and alone."

Bobby had always occupied third place among the four Kennedy brothers, taking a backseat to his older brothers Joe and John, who were considered more handsome and were thought to be promising future political stars by the family patriarch Joseph Kennedy, Sr. After the death of Joe, Jr., in World War II, John took up the family mantle. Bobby, smaller than his older brother, less articulate, less spontaneous, and less confident than Jack, served a subordinate role in his father's mind. Bobby was raised to sacrifice his own ambitions and dreams in service of John's rise to greatness.

Now, once the most powerful member of his brother's cabinet, Kennedy continued as attorney general under a new president who didn't trust him. Top Democrats tried to convince Lyndon Johnson to name Kennedy his running mate for the 1964 presidential race, but by that time the two hated each other too much for such an alliance to gel. Johnson called Kennedy "a grandstanding runt" while Kennedy described Johnson as "mean, bitter, vicious—an animal in many ways." Johnson, instead, named Minnesota Sen. Hubert Humphrey to the number two spot.

Unable to stand working for Johnson any longer, Kennedy resigned as attorney general. He moved to New York to run for the United States Senate in 1964. A lifelong resident of Massachusetts, Kennedy had to deal with accusations that he was an opportunistic "carpetbagger." Much to Kennedy's chagrin, he depended on Johnson's considerable coattails to win the race. He won the Senate seat by 700,000 votes, 2 million fewer votes than Johnson carried in New York.

Kennedy did not enjoy his time in the Senate. During his three-plus years in that body he was unable to pass a single major piece of legislation he had authored. As early as April 1965, Kennedy doubted that the Vietnam War could be won in conventional military terms. That month, he urged Johnson to halt the bombing of North Vietnam. The president complied with this wish for a brief time, but soon resumed "Operation Rolling Thunder." At a press conference in November 1965, Kennedy started to tell reporters that he did not "agree personally" with young people who burned their draft cards, "but if a person feels that strongly . . ." A reporter interrupted. 'What about giving blood to the North Vietnamese?" the journalist asked. "I think it's a good idea . . . in the oldest traditions of this country," Kennedy replied. The press, still strongly pro-war, reacted hysterically. *The New York Times* suggested that if Kennedy wanted to "help" the North Vietnamese then, "why not go whole hog? Why not light out for the enemy country and join its armed forces?"

In February 1966 Kennedy made his boldest break with Johnson yet, declaring during another press conference that the United States should seek a negotiated settlement with North Vietnam and perhaps even include the National Liberation Front, the political arm of the Vietcong, in a coalition government. However, Lyndon Johnson's aides began quoting the late President Kennedy on the necessity of resisting communist victory in Southeast Asia. Ever loyal to the memory of his brother, and not wanting to tarnish John Kennedy's legacy by criticizing the Vietnam War, Bobby again fell silent on the issue. "I'm afraid that by speaking out I just make Lyndon do the opposite out of spite," the New York Senator told friends. "He hates me so much that

Although Bobby Kennedy deeply resented the man who replaced his brother as president, Lyndon Johnson, he depended on LBJ's help to win his New York Senate race in 1964. Here, LBJ, right, appears with Kennedy on of that year's campaign stops. Credit: LBJ Library.

if I asked for snow, he would make it rain, just because it was me."

Last Crusades

Having grown up in a family in which he felt like an underdog, Kennedy believed he understood the desperation of impoverished African Americans and Latinos. During the period from 1966 to 1968, Robert Kennedy seemed to instinctively seek out the dispossessed. Invited to speak in South Africa, where the ruling white supremacist regime had imposed apartheid, a rigidly enforced system of racial separation and oppression of the black majority, Kennedy took up the challenge. Kennedy visited the poverty-stricken black townships lying on the outskirts of South Africa's major cities. A crowd of approximately 15,000 attended Kennedy's speech at the University of Cape Town. Realizing his audience was filled with activists committed to justice but afraid of their authoritarian government, Kennedy urged his listeners not to feel powerless. As he told his audience:

Few will have the greatness to bend history itself; but each of us can work to change a small portion of events and in the total of all those acts will be written the history of this generation... It is from numberless diverse acts of courage and belief that human history is shaped. Each time a man stands up for an ideal, or acts to improve the lot of others, or strikes out against injustice, he sends forth tiny ripples of hope, and crossing each other from a million different centers of energy and daring these ripples build a current which can sweep down the mightiest walls of oppression and resistance...

Hunger and deprivation became personal issues for the wealthy and privileged politician. In 1967, serving on the Senate Labor Committee's Subcommittee on Poverty, Kennedy attended hearings in rural Mississippi. "Appalled by the testimony, he went out into the fields," biographer Evan Thomas wrote. "Kennedy was hardly new to scenes of want and deprivation, but he was still shocked by the living conditions of poor blacks in the Delta. The stench and vermin in the windowless shacks overwhelmed his senses. He sat down on a dirty floor and held a child who was covered with open sores. He rubbed the child's stomach, which was distended by starvation. He caressed and murmured and tickled. No response. The child was in a daze."

(Left) Senator Robert Kennedy and Donald Benjamin (Central Brooklyn Coordinating Council for Bedford Stuyvesant) join kids at a playground. (Right) Senator Kennedy discusses school with a young boy. February 4-5, 1966.

Kennedy, who mocked himself as someone who had made a D in his college economics class, struggled for an answer to poverty. He launched an experiment in the neighborhood of Bedford Stuyvesant in Brooklyn. Poor and with a population that was 82 percent African American and 12 percent Puerto Rican, "Bed-Stuy," as it was known, became the scene of a riot in 1964 after a police shooting of a black teenager. After a February 1966 tour of the neighborhood, Kennedy met with business leaders and the wealthy heads of charitable foundations to see if a program combining government incentives such as tax breaks and grants with private investment capital could be marshaled to create quality jobs in the neighborhood.

Along with his fellow New York Senator Jacob Javits, Kennedy secured passage of an amendment in November 1966 to the Economic Opportunity Act originally passed in 1964. The new provision created the Special Impact Program. This law allowed the creation of the Bedford Stuyvesant Development and Service Corporation. The agency included one board made up of members of the local community that would determine which projects were most needed while another board sought corporate investment dollars and provided management expertise. In the last four decades, the program has provided job placement services, opened an arts academy and the Billie Holliday Theatre (named after the legendary jazz singer), constructed 2,200 housing units, and provided $60 million in mortgage financing to about 1,500 Bed-Stuy residents.

CLEAN FOR GENE:
AN UPSET IN NEW HAMPSHIRE

The Kennedy family had always placed a high premium on action and courage, but as the 1968 presidential campaign opened, and anti-war activists tired of waiting for Robert to announce his candidacy, war critics began to accuse him of political cowardice. Anti-war activists looked for someone else to pick up the mantle. Minnesota **Sen. Eugene McCarthy** had become one of the early skeptics of the Vietnam War. McCarthy became one of only five senators to vote for a motion to repeal the Gulf of Tonkin Resolution, which had given Johnson the authority to pursue the Vietnam War. A quiet, deeply religious Catholic and a published poet, he could not have had a more different personality than Lyndon Johnson, the backslapping, larger-than-life president. He often spoke with the cool, detached air of an intellectual and often irritated his campaign staff with what seemed his lack of passion. However, his opposition to the Vietnam War, and his resentment over the increase of executive

Senator Eugene McCarthy at a meeting in the Cabinet Room. October 3, 1966   Credit: LBJ Library

power that came in the Johnson years, pushed him into the unlikely arena of presidential politics.

With no other Democrat willing to mount a credible challenge to Johnson's misadventure in Vietnam, McCarthy announced his entry into the primaries on November 30, 1967. McCarthy benefited from lucky political timing. During the month leading up to the campaign season's opening New Hampshire primary, the news was filled with reports on the Tet Offensive. As the only man standing up to Johnson within the Democratic Party, McCarthy received the enthusiastic support of anti-war college and high school students from all across the country.

These volunteers mounted a "children's crusade" to topple President Johnson and end the war. "McCarthy's cause attracted some of the youngest, smartest, most independent, best-educated and worst-paid staff members in the history of American politics," Kaiser notes. McCarthy's effort relied on a determined and effective ground game. The campaign lacked money, which meant it could not buy much radio or television advertising. Volunteers worked day and night to invite virtually every New Hampshire voter to receptions where the candidate would appear. Voters who showed up, according to Kaiser, received "a personalized thank-you, with McCarthy's signature forged by a student from Rutgers."

Unpaid campaigners knocked on nearly every door in the state and spoke to virtually every person who intended to vote in the Democratic presidential primary. The Johnson campaign, in contrast, suffered from arrogance and obliviousness to the changed political environment created by Tet. Johnson also suffered from high expectations. An incumbent president would be expected to win by a landslide in his party's primaries, so all McCarthy needed was a respectable showing in order to be seen as the victor. McCarthy's election night tally on March 12 exceeded any television and newspaper pundit's highest expectations. The Minnesota senator won 42.4 percent of the New Hampshire primary vote, with President Johnson receiving only 49.5 percent.

The New Hampshire results gave Bobby Kennedy the opening he had been looking for. Kennedy announced he was entering the presidential sweepstakes four days later, on March 16. Kennedy received flack from Democratic voters who accused him of splitting the peace vote, but Kennedy was certain that McCarthy had no realistic chance of capturing the Democratic nomination, much less of defeating the likely Republican nominee, former Vice President Richard Nixon.

THE WISE OLD MEN

Even before New Hampshire in November 1967, a distraught Lyndon Johnson began to despair about the war. He had convened a meeting of longtime friends, advisers, and political insiders—a group dubbed the **"Wise Old Men"**—to Washington, D.C., to discuss the future plan of attack. Included in the discussion was **Clark Clifford**, an attorney soon to be appointed McNamara's replacement as defense secretary, former national security advisor McGeorge Bundy, and Supreme Court Justice (and, like Clark, a longtime Johnson confidant) Abe Fortas. The men received typically glowing reports from military officers on the progress being made in the war. "I don't believe one single Wise Man raised any serious questions," Clifford later recalled of that first convocation. Only Bundy raised an objection and that only as the meeting was breaking up. "I've been watching you across the table," Bundy said. "You're like a flock of buzzards sitting on a fence, sending the young men off to be killed. You ought to be ashamed of yourselves." No one responded to Bundy.

That was before the Tet Offensive. As the embarrassing scenes unfolded at the American Embassy in Saigon and Khe Sanh, only Secretary of State Dean Rusk and National Security Adviser Walt Rostow remained solidly committed to the status quo in Vietnam within the president's inner circle. The new Secretary of Defense, Clarke Clifford, already parted with Johnson over the war.

Experienced Washington hands had expected Clifford, selected to replace the wavering McNamara precisely because of his steadfast faith in the Vietnam effort, to be a hawk (a supporter of the war). The Tet Offensive shook up Clifford, who changed his mind about the war early in his tenure as defense secretary. "I had personal daily and hourly access to civilians and all the top military," he recalled later. ". . . I was finding out, in constant contact with the joint chiefs, that we had no real plan to win the war. All we were going to do was just keep pouring men in there . . ." Clifford interrogated officers on whether there was any sign that the North Vietnamese government and military had lost any of its will to fight and the cabinet official was told no. Meanwhile, the budget office placed the cost of 206,000 more troops that General Westmoreland had recently requested at $2 billion for the last four months of the fiscal year and up to $12 billion for the following fiscal year.

"Will three hundred thousand more men do the job?" Clifford asked the Pentagon, which remained unable to give a definite answer. He then asked how long it would take for the United States to win the war. Again, military leaders could not give him an answer with any confidence. "It all began to add up to the realization that we'd been through a period of never-never land in thinking that we were going to win this," Clifford said. The defense secretary decided he must prevent the administration from deepening even further America's commitment to the Vietnam War and, if possible, to find an honorable way out of the conflict.

In the wake of the Tet Offensive, Johnson asked the Wise Old Men to gather again at the State Department on March 25. Once again, they received glowing reports from the military. The Tet Offensive had been a defeat for the North Vietnamese and their allies. The communists supposedly had suffered heavy casualties and would be unable to recover. Though they couldn't specify when this would happen, Pentagon officials told the Wise Men that the war would soon end in an American victory. The Wise Men, however, had become skeptics.

As historian Taylor Branch observed, Bundy "chilled the Cabinet Room" with his first words. "Mr. President, there is a very significant shift in most of our positions since we last met." Bundy bluntly told the president, "We must begin steps to disengage." At a second day of discussions on March 26, former Secretary of State (under President Truman) Dean Acheson said that the American public did not support the war and the United States had no right to militarily impose a corrupt, dictatorial government on South Vietnam. Someone in the room objected that the United States was not imposing its will. Acheson lost his temper and blurted out:

> What in the name of God have we got five hundred thousand troops out there for? Chasing girls?

You know damned well this is what we're trying to do—to force the enemy to sue for peace. It won't happen—at least not in any time the American people will permit.

Johnson realized he no longer had the confidence of his own cabinet. The negative feedback from the Wise Men and McCarthy's showing in New Hampshire moved President Johnson towards making a decision he had contemplated at least since the fall of 1967. The president had been scheduled to make a televised speech in prime time about the Vietnam War on March 31. Clifford got the president to change the first line of his speech from "I want to talk to you about the War in Vietnam" to "I want to talk to you about peace in Vietnam." The final draft of the speech included a bombing halt in North Vietnam. Johnson told his speech writers that he would provide the concluding remarks himself.

By the morning of March 31, Johnson's daughter Lynda's husband, Chuck Robb, was serving with the Marines in Vietnam. His other son-in-law Patrick Nugent was due to ship out to Vietnam shortly. The war had been hard on Lynda and Johnson's other daughter Lucy, who had to deal with protestors from their generation chant-

President Lyndon Johnson reads a story about the bombing halt in *The Evening Star*. November 1, 1968

ing, "Hey, Hey, LBJ/How many kids did you kill today?" outside the White House. That morning, according to Kaiser, Johnson had an intense conversation with Lynda, who wanted to know why her husband, Robb, had to "fight for people who did not even want to be protected?" The president told his wife Lady Bird that he "wanted to comfort her [Lynda], and I could not."

During the speech, Johnson told his audience that the United States would end bombing of North Vietnam as part of an effort to kick-start peace talks. At the end, he looked up from the paper copy of his speech and said directly into the camera that he "did not want the presidency to become involved in the partisan divisions that are developing this political year.

> With our hopes and the world's hopes for peace in the balance every day, I do not believe that I should devote an hour or a day of my time to any personal partisan causes or to any duties other than that of the awesome duties of this office—the presidency of your country. Accordingly, I will not seek, and I will not accept, the nomination of my party for another term as your President.

President Lyndon Johnson listens to a tape sent by Captain Charles Robb, his son-in-law, from Vietnam. July 31, 1968

President Lyndon B. Johnson addresses the nation announcing a bombing halt in Vietnam and his intention not to run for re-election. March 31, 1968. Credit: LBJ Library

Some of Johnson's most sharp-tongued critics now praised the president's statesmanship. Even the president's chief nemesis, Bobby Kennedy, had words of praise for Johnson, describing the president's decision as "truly magnanimous" and offering to meet with the president to discuss "how we might work together in the interest of national unity during the coming months." That Wednesday, North Vietnam finally agreed to start peace talks with the United States.

MARTIN LUTHER KING, JR., AND BLACK POWER

The brief moment of good feeling created by the president's withdrawal from the race and the announcement of peace talks with North Vietnam would shatter at the hands of an assassin on April 4. By 1968, Martin Luther King, Jr., had spent decades staring into the chasm of death. As enumerated by sociologist Michael Eric Dyson, King's brushes with mortality included two impulsive, youthful attempts at suicide. On January 30, 1956, unknown assailants firebombed King's home during the ultimately successful Montgomery, Alabama, bus boycott. Eleven months later someone fired a shotgun at his door. Five weeks after that came another bombing attempt, the would-be murderer planting a dozen sticks of dynamite on his front porch. On September 20, 1958, a mentally unbalanced woman who believed that King's civil rights activism was placing African Americans such as herself in danger named Izola Ware Curry stabbed King deeply with a letter opener during a book signing at Blumstein's Department Store in Harlem. The blade came perilously close to severing King's aorta.

During a speech before the Southern Christian Leadership Council in 1962, a large Neo-Nazi marched to the stage and began beating King. He spoke quietly and calmly to the attacker even as the blows continued. When shocked SCLC members finally subdued the white supremacist, King pleaded with them, "Don't touch him! Don't touch him! We need to pray for him." Throughout his life as a civil rights leader, he received death threats. Planes he boarded had to be checked for bombs.

By early 1968, King battled not just mortality but deepening depression. He knew the FBI was harassing and spying on him, and he felt increasingly isolated from some former white supporters and from many younger people in the black community. Men like **Stokely Carmichael** began to mock King's non-violent approach to protest. Carmichael led the Student Nonviolent Coordinating Committee (SNCC), a black civil rights group that had expelled white members in order to chart a course free of white domination. Carmichael, who coined the phrase "Black Power!" as a rallying cry, belittled King's Southern

Christian Leadership Council, which financially relied on donations from sympathetic white liberals. In August 1967 H. Rap Brown, a chairman of SNCC, traveled to Cambridge, Maryland where local Ku Klux Klansman and other white racists had recently demonstrated against black civil rights and urged a black audience to "Burn this town down . . . where you tear down the white man, brother, you are hitting him in the money . . . Don't love him to death. Shoot him to death." That night African Americans in Cambridge rose up for a night of arson and looting.

By 1968, King also faced verbal assaults and harassment from law enforcement because of his decision to expand his crusades from assaults on discrimination to the problem of poverty and the tragedy of the Vietnam War. He not only charged that the war drained badly needed money from the president's avowed war on poverty but said that the violence used by the American government in Vietnam spawned a general social sickness that manifested in urban riots. "As I have walked among the desperate, rejected, and angry young men, I have told them that Molotov cocktails and rifles would not solve their problems," King said. "They asked me if our own nation wasn't using massive doses of violence to solve its problems, to bring about the changes it wanted . . . I knew that I could never again raise my voice against the violence of the oppressed in the ghettos without having first spoken clearly to the greatest purveyor of violence in the world today—my own government . . . Somehow, this madness must cease." King urged his listeners who objected to the war who got snared in the military draft to claim conscientious objector status. For the first time, northern liberal editorialists blasted King with the venom he usually received from southern segregationists.

The FBI War on MLK

By 1968, FBI Director **J. Edgar Hoover** had spent almost 14 years trying to destroy Martin Luther King. Hoover had led the agency, originally known as the Bureau of Investigation, since 1924. Hoover had grown up in segregated Washington, D.C., and his attitude towards blacks reflected a white southern cultural background. Hoover "believed blacks were basically lazy and unreliable," according to biographer Richard Hack. "He was, if nothing else, a gentleman of the Old South who believed that blacks were fine 'in their place,' which to Hoover meant as servants, handymen, laborers, and field workers." The FBI's hiring practices reflected Hoover's personal racist values. Until his death in the 1970s, the FBI was "basically an all-white organization," as Hack observes.

The few blacks who had been hired by the Bureau worked exclusively for Hoover. James Crawford, his chauffeur, was expected to be on call around the clock, and even worked weekends at the director's home on general maintenance and gardening—on FBI wages . . . Hoover had a black driver at his exclusive disposal in Los Angeles and another in Miami. [These were] the black men of the FBI.

At the start of the civil rights movement he advised the Eisenhower administration that white southern parents had a reasonable fear of black students attending the same schools as their children, where they would share bathrooms and gymnasiums with white students, because "colored parents are not as careful in looking after the health and cleanliness of their children." Unwilling to believe that blacks could analyze the problems they faced in American society and create a movement of their own to address those issues, the FBI director decided that men like King had to be puppets of the Soviet government.

King obsessed Hoover. The director focused on King's relationship with Stanley Levinson, who in the early 1950s had given the Communist Party USA financial advice. Levinson later severed his relationship with the group. Hack, however, writes that Hoover held fast to the idea of "once a communist, always a communist." Both with and without the legal authorization of the Kennedy and Johnson administrations, the FBI director authorized the wiretapping of Levinson's phones and those of the SCLC. Agents also tapped the phones in the hotel rooms occupied by King and other civil rights leaders.

Hoover had remained director of the FBI in spite of abundant evidence of his incompetence. The director was slow to respond to the rise of gangsters like Bonnie and Clyde and John Dillinger in the 1930s, had insisted that the Mafia did not exist even as organized crime took over several cities in the 1940s and 1950s, and had spent the McCarthy era wasting agency resources chasing a mass communist conspiracy that proved to be a phantom. Part of the secret of his survival, in spite of his widely rumored homosexuality, was his exploitation of the FBI to spy on the sexual habits of the most powerful figures in Washington, D.C. Agents placed microphones in hotel walls and mattresses and snapped secret pictures documenting affairs and sexual preferences, information that ended up in Hoover's "Obscene File," a compilation of erotic dirt on those who could cause the director trouble. Presidents, senators and congressmen feared crossing Hoover for decades. This was one way that Hoover convinced Bobby Kennedy to agree to wiretapping King. The attorney general's brother had numerous affairs. Some presented danger to more than just President Kennedy's political future and the health of his marriage. One girlfriend, Judith Exner, was also the mistress of Mafia boss Sam Giancana. More seriously, another mistress, Ellen Rometsch, was also an East German spy. Though he disliked and distrusted the FBI director, Robert Kennedy thought it best to keep Hoover happy.

This made the Kennedy administration the unwilling partner in Hoover's private war against King, a war that continued after Johnson took office. On January 5, 1964, King and his lieutenants checked into the Willard Hotel in Washington, D.C., and FBI agents planted a microphone in his suite. At the same time, King's face appeared on *Time*'s cover as the publication's "Man of the Year," the FBI recorded King, other officials from the SCLC and two women drinking and having sex. According to Hack, Hoover listened to parts of the tape in his office and, in a celebratory mood, declared, "This will destroy the burr head."

After Hoover briefed President Johnson on the matter, LBJ suggested that the information should be made available to the press "for the good of the country." To Hoover's frustration, however, the press did not take the bait. Hoover raged when King's stature increased upon winning the 1964 Nobel Peace Prize. Unable to smear him publicly, Hoover sought to frighten King out of politics. With the director's approval, the FBI anonymously sent a package to King that contained an edited audiotape of King's extramarital sexual encounters with a threatening letter:

> King, look into your heart. You know you are a complete fraud, and a great liability to all of us Negroes . . . King, like all frauds, your end is approaching. You could have been our greatest leader. You, even at an early age, have turned out not to be a leader, but a moral imbecile . . . The American public, the church organizations that have been helping—Protestant, Catholic, and Jews will know you for what you are—an evil, abnormal beast . . . You are done.
>
> King, there is only one thing for you to do. You know what it is.

This extraordinary note, written by the leaders of a government law enforcement agency, sexually blackmailed a private citizen and, by implication, urged him to commit suicide. By this time, Hoover had launched the **COINTELPRO** program. This program sought to disrupt and sew internal conflict within civil rights, Black Nationalist and anti-war groups that had violated no U.S. laws but simply drew the ire of Director Hoover.

FBI agents infiltrated protest groups, spread false stories that movement leaders had committed crimes such as embezzlement, started sexual rumors aimed at creating conflict between activists, forwarded fake evidence that key leaders were actually police, FBI or CIA spies, and so on.

Meanwhile, feeling pressure from all sides, deeply sad and tired, King had every incentive to withdraw from public life in the spring of 1968. Instead, he pressed on.

"The Day of Violence is Here"

King spent the early months of 1968 planning a Poor People's March, based on his triumphant 1963 March on Washington. King conceived of the march as a means of responding to a noticeable white backlash to the African American freedom struggle. Many whites, in contradiction of objective evidence, now believed that black people had gained unfair advantages over white people. Across the country, white voters reacted angrily to the urban uprisings in places like the Watts neighborhood of Los Angeles, in Detroit, and in Newark. White voters who had backed liberal, or at least moderate, Democrats began in 1966 to support conservative "law and order" Democrats and Republicans who promised to crack down on lawless inner city youths and drug-taking anti-war protestors.

King hoped that by focusing on poverty he would be attacking an issue that transcended race. Whites, in fact, constituted the largest number of poor people in America, poor whites heavily concentrated in deep southern states like Mississippi and the hills of Kentucky and Tennessee. Poverty, King suspected, lay behind the white resentments that fed anti-black racism. Details of the planned march remained vague even as a humble strike by sanitation workers created what became an enormous distraction.

Mostly African American, Memphis sanitation workers lived below the national poverty line even though they worked full-time. About 40 percent received such low wages that they qualified for welfare. The workers lacked health insurance coverage, paid vacation time, a pension plan, and any place at the work site to shower or eat. These collectors carried heavy, leaky garbage containers, which often showered them with rotting food, dirty diapers and maggots. Tragedy struck on February 1. As Taylor Branch describes the incident:

> Foreman Willie Crane's five-man crew had headed for the dump in one of the compressor trucks . . . Only two of the four collectors could squeeze into the driver's cab after hauling their tubs on foot, and the two junior men normally jockeyed from handholds and footrests on the outside . . . [T]orrential

cloudbursts late Thursday drove them through side-loading splits into the huge storage cylinder itself . . . Crain heard screams . . . Investigators would conclude that a freak shift by an onboard shovel may have shorted wet wires to the separate motor. A witness looking through her kitchen window said she saw one man struggle almost out before his raincoat or something grabbed and pulled him back down head first, leaving parts of both legs exposed.

The compressor fatally crushed both sanitation workers, Echol Cole and Robert Walker. Unable to take any more exploitation, 930 of the city's 1,100 sanitation workers launched the **Memphis Sanitation Workers' Strike** on February 12, 1968 and demanded safety equipment, paid days off during rain, better pay, benefits and recognition of their American Federation of State, County, and Municipal Employees Union.

King saw that the fight of the Memphis sanitation workers fit perfectly into his **Poor Peoples' Campaign**, and though advisors—worried about the ugly atmosphere in Memphis—urged him to not get involved, he supported their cause and agreed to appear there. King arrived in town on March 28 and because of flight delays at the Atlanta airport, he was late for a scheduled protest rally. Events spun out of control.

A group of thirty black students with rocks and clubs marched down Beale Street, heart of the city's blues district. Suddenly the protestors heard loud pops that sounded like gunshots. The sound, instead, marked the cascade of shattered storefront windows being broken by angry marchers along Beale and Main Streets. The day saw nine police officers injured, including one beaten by five enraged teenagers with sticks used to support protest placards. In addition, two hundred protestors would be arrested and sixty injured. One police officer backed a 16-year-old suspected rioter into a stairway and blasted him point blank with a sawed-off shotgun.

Feeling completely defeated, that night King watched Memphis news coverage of the riot. King considered canceling the Poor People's March. The rioting was a gift to the movement's enemies in the FBI, he said. "Maybe we just have to admit that the day of violence is here," he said in a tone of resignation. "And maybe we just have to give up and let violence take its course." Eventually, he overcame his defeatism and said he had to try to organize a peaceful rally in Memphis before he could successfully lead one in Washington, D.C. Meanwhile, the garbage piled up in Memphis, a reality the city would face for 64 days.

"I've Been to the Mountaintop"

A bomb scare delayed King's return to Memphis on April 3. The longtime activist had been through many such warnings before. When King arrived, an army of uniformed and undercover Memphis police and FBI agents followed him. He should have been the safest man in America. Hoover, however, violated normal FBI policy, refusing to inform the civil rights leader of death threats. King checked into Room 306 at the Lorraine Motel, a location advertised in the local press.

King was scheduled to speak to sanitation workers that night at the city's Mason Temple but, as tornados and harsh thunderstorms struck the region, received a report that only 2,000 were at that night's massive speaking venue that could hold up to 14,000. King asked his aid, the **Reverend Ralph Abernathy,** to speak in his place. Abernathy sensed upon arrival the crowd's disappointment when they didn't see King enter the hall as well. Abernathy called King and told him the Mason Temple was "a core crowd of sanitation workers who had braved a night of hellfire to hear him and they would feel cut off from a lifeline if he let them down."

Cheers rattled the building when the audience spotted King, who would treat them to the most prophetic speech of his career. King recalled significant highlights of the civil rights struggle. He then compared himself to Moses, who according to the Bible led the Israelites out of slavery in Egypt but was allowed by God to see the Promised Land only from the summit of a mountain.

> Well, I don't know what will happen now. We've got some difficult days ahead. But it doesn't matter with me now. Because I've been to the mountaintop. And I don't mind. Like anybody I would like to live—a long life—longevity has its place. But I'm not concerned about that now. I just want to do God's will. And I've looked over. And I have seen the promised land. And I may not get there with you, but I want you to know tonight that we as a people will get to the promised land! So I'm happy tonight! I'm not worried about anything! I'm not fearing any man! My eyes have seen the glory of the coming of the Lord!

The night of King's epic speech at the Mason Temple, an escaped convict named **James Earl Ray** also arrived in Memphis after driving from Atlanta. Ray, a small-time crook previously convicted of armed robbery targeting gas stations and liquor stores, broke out of a Missouri prison April 23, 1967. Living in hiding, he heard rumors of southern businessmen who would pay a bounty to anyone who killed King. Reading in the newspapers that King was staying at Room 306 at the Lorraine Motel, Ray rented a cheap room at Bessie Brewer's flophouse, conveniently across a parking lot from where King was staying. Among Ray's few belongings was a .30-06 Remington Gamemaster rifle.

The afternoon of April 4, King was in a jolly mood, and several fellow ministers and the activists gathered in Room 306, swapping good-natured jokes about each other, about women they knew and about their past together. The group planned an early supper before a mass meeting to discuss the upcoming Memphis March. The Rev. Jesse Jackson's civil rights group Operation Breadbasket had a band scheduled to perform that night. From the balcony of the Lorraine Motel, King shouted to the band's saxophonist Ben Branch that he wanted the group to play the black spiritual "Precious Lord, Take My Hand." The song's lyrics powerfully evoked King's recent life.

> Precious Lord, take my hand,
> Lead me on, let me stand
> I'm tired, I'm weak, I'm alone
> Through the storm, through the night
> Lead me to the light.

"Play it real pretty," King told Branch. "O.K., Doc, I will," Branch promised. King turned back toward his room to get a topcoat. It was 6:01 p.m. In seconds, the sharp report of a rifle cracked through the sky. From across the street, Ray had put in his sights a man called a spiritual leader, a modern Moses, a revolutionary, Nobel laureate, an agitator, and a subversive—and pulled the trigger. The bullet sailed through the air and passed through King's jaw and neck, leaving an enormous wound. The bullet severed the knot from King's necktie, which flew off and landed far from his body. King collapsed. His closest friends ran to be with him, stood next to his lifeless body sprawled on the balcony, and pointed in the direction of the dingy flophouse across the parking lot where the rifle blast had erupted. King was 39 years old.

AFTERMATH OF A KILLING

That night, as news spread that the leader of the most successful non-violent reform movement in American history had died, riots exploded in 110 American cities. In Minneapolis, a man seized with disbelief declared he would kill the first white man he saw. He then shot his neighbor six times. Fires erupted in Boston, the birthplace of the American Revolution, and Winston-Salem, the scene of peaceful sit-ins in an earlier, now-distant era.

One city remained quiet that night. Sen. Robert Kennedy spent the late afternoon of April 4 flying from Washington, D.C., to Indiana, where an important presidential primary loomed. Kennedy had enjoyed wide and enthusiastic support among black and poor voters, and he could expect a friendly audience that night in the Indianapolis ghetto. On the campaign plane, reporter Johnny Apple of *The New York Times* leaned toward the candidate with the shocking news that King had been shot. Apple later said that Kennedy, probably struck with memories of his brother's murder, "sagged. His eyes went blank."

Bobby Kennedy and Martin Luther King had shared a cold, tense relationship. In love with the idea of coolness under pressure, Kennedy disliked what he saw as the excessive emotion of King's rhetorical and political style. He found the preacher pompous and believed the black minister lacked the Kennedy's family's style of self-deprecating gallows humor. As his brother's attorney general and chief political captain, Kennedy had resented the spotlight King had often placed on America's ugly race relations, which Robert believed placed President Kennedy in an embarrassing political light. Sadly, Kennedy and King more often saw each other as antagonists.

When the plane landed in Indianapolis, aides told Kennedy that King had died. Reports of riots developing across the country began to filter in. The city's police chief feared unrest, thought the white politician would be unsafe facing a black audience, and advised him to cancel his appearance. Around one thousand people had shown up to hear the Kennedy brother speak. The crowd, about 70 percent African American, had not yet heard the news about King. It would be Kennedy's job to tell them. He would speak off the cuff and from the heart. As complicated as his feelings were about King, the still-mourning brother understood the deep feeling of loss his audience would soon feel. "Ladies and gentlemen, I'm only going to talk to you just for a minute or so this evening because I have some very sad news for you all, and I think sad news for all our citizens and people who love peace all over the world," Kennedy said, gingerly feeling his way toward the awful truth. "And that is that Martin Luther King was shot and was killed in Memphis, Tennessee." The audience screamed and many murmured in disbelief, "No, no." Kennedy then improvised the best speech in his tragically brief political career.

In spite of the terrible emotions that now enveloped Kennedy's audience, the crowd cheered an honest expression of loss and a hope for reconciliation. There were no riots that night in Indianapolis, which became a rare exception. Kennedy called Coretta Scott King and

> ### ROBERT KENNEDY ON THE DEATH OF MARTIN LUTHER KING
>
> *Ladies and Gentlemen—I'm only going to talk to you just for a minute or so this evening. Because I have some very sad news for all of you, and I think sad news for all of our fellow citizens, and people who love peace all over the world, and that is that Martin Luther King was shot and was killed tonight in Memphis Tennessee.*
>
> *Martin Luther King dedicated his life to love and to justice between fellow human beings. He died in the cause of that effort. In this difficult day, in this difficult time for the United States, it's perhaps well to ask what kind of a nation we are and what direction we want to move in.*
>
> *For those of you who are black—considering the evidence evidently is that there were white people who were responsible—you can be filled with bitterness, and with hatred, and a desire for revenge.*
>
> *We can move in that direction as a country, in greater polarization—black people amongst blacks, and white among whites, filled with hatred toward one another. Or we can make an effort, as Martin Luther King did, to understand and to comprehend, and replace that violence, that stain of bloodshed that has spread across our land, with an effort to understand, compassion and love.*
>
> *For those of you who are black and are tempted to be filled with hatred and mistrust of the injustice of such an act, against all white people, I would only say I can also feel in my own heart the same kind of feeling. I had a member of my family killed, but he was killed by a white man.*
>
> *But we have to make an effort in the United States, we have to make an effort to understand, to get beyond these rather difficult times.*
>
> *My favorite poet was Aeschylus. He once wrote: "Even in our sleep, pain which cannot forget falls drop by drop upon the heart, until in our own despair, against our will, comes wisdom through the awful grace of God."*
>
> *What we need in the United States is not division; what we need in the United States is not hatred; what we need in the United States is not violence and lawlessness, but is love and wisdom, and compassion toward one another, and a feeling of justice toward those who still suffer within our country, whether they be white or whether they be black.*
>
> *So I ask you tonight to return home, to say a prayer for the family of Martin Luther King, yeah that's true, but more importantly to say a prayer for our own country, which all of us love—a prayer for understanding and that compassion of which I spoke. We can do well in this country. We will have difficult times. We've had difficult times in the past. And we will have difficult times in the future. It is not the end of violence; it is not the end of lawlessness; and it's not the end of disorder.*
>
> *But the vast majority of white people and the vast majority of black people in this country want to live together, want to improve the quality of our life, and want justice for all human beings that abide in our land.*
>
> *Let us dedicate ourselves to what the Greeks wrote many years ago: to tame the savageness of man and make gentle the life of this world.*
>
> *Let us dedicate ourselves to that, and say a prayer for our country and for our people. Thank you very much.*

provided a plane to fly King's body back to Atlanta. The United States, he probably realized, turned a corner to a meaner reality that night.

At the corner of 14th and U Streets in Washington, D.C., Stokely Carmichael spoke to a mob of 400. "Go home and get your guns," he said. "When the white man comes he is coming to kill you. I don't want any black blood on the street. Go home and get you a gun and then come back because I got me a gun." The next day, Friday, fires roared just two blocks from the White House. Riot troops gathered on the White House lawn. Violence had not reached so close to the president's mansion since British troops ransacked the city and burned the White House down in 1814. Across the country, 39 died and 2,500 suffered injuries.

After Robert Kennedy's performance in Indianapolis, black leaders began asking him to make speeches to African-American audiences to calm the waters. Kennedy became white America's emissary to its anguished and angry black population. Temporarily suspending his campaign schedule, Kennedy spoke on the King assassination in Cleveland on April 5. He wove together political assassination, the violence of poverty, and American violence in places like Vietnam.

Referring to King's death, and by implication his brother's death in Dallas, Kennedy noted that, "[T]here is another kind of violence, slower but just as deadly, as the shot, or the bomb in the night. This is the violence of institutions: indifference and inaction and slow decay. This is the violence that afflicts the poor, that poisons relations between men because their skin has different colors. It is the slow destruction of a child by hunger, and schools without books and homes without heat in the winter."

Kennedy delivered to the Cleveland audience his own prophetic oration on the heartbreaking American addiction to gunplay. "This is a time of shame and sorrow," Kennedy said. "It is not a day for politics. I have saved this one opportunity, my only event today, to speak briefly to you about this mindless menace of violence in America which again stains our land and every one of our lives... It is not the concern of one race. The victims of violence are black and white, rich and poor, young and old, famous and unknown. They are most important of all, human beings whom other human beings loved and needed. No one—no matter where he lives, or what he does—can be certain who will suffer from some senseless act of bloodshed. And yet it goes on, and on. Why?"

"IF YOU DO NOT DO THIS, WHO WILL DO THIS?"

Jules Witcover covered Bobby Kennedy's 1968 presidential campaign for the Newhouse News Service. After the King assassination, Witcover argued in his book *85 Days: The Last Campaign of Robert Kennedy*, the halting, unsure New York Senator found his voice.

Kennedy, perceived to be an East Coast liberal, faced a tough challenge in one of his first presidential primaries in Indiana, a conservative state that in the early 1920s had been an epicenter of the revived Ku Klux Klan. Kennedy calibrated his message to his Indiana audience, reminding crowds that he had once been the nation's "chief law enforcement officer," and promising to be tough on crime. However, unlike later so-called "New Democrats" like Bill Clinton who embraced the death penalty and bashed programs like welfare to contrast themselves with traditional liberals, Kennedy did not abandon his emphasis on poverty even to his Indiana audiences.

He did not pander, but often defied his audience, at the risk of angering them, to sacrifice the privileges of a middle-class existence for the sake of their country. During one April 26 campaign stop he addressed doctors and medical students at the University of Indiana. In spite of his well-off, all-white, conservative audience, Kennedy chose that evening to call for government-provided health care for the poor. "Where are you going to get all the money for these federally subsidized programs you are talking about?" one irritated student asked. "From you," Kennedy answered bluntly, provoking boos and hisses from the crowd. Unfazed, Kennedy reminded the audience that those who have received much from their country should give much in return. "If you do not do this, who will do this?" Kennedy pushed even harder. "You sit here as white medical students, while black people carry the burden of the fighting in Vietnam."

In the Indiana primary, Kennedy intensity won out over McCarthy cool. Kennedy won 42 percent of the vote. Governor Roger Branigan, running as a stand-in for Vice President Hubert Humphrey (who had entered the presidential race but chose to avoid primaries, relying instead on winning Democratic Convention delegates through the party caucuses run by political professionals) won 31 percent, while McCarthy finished a disappointing third at 27 percent. Nevertheless, Robert Kennedy had been expected to carry more than 50 percent of the vote. In spite of his clear win, Thomas points out, the victory was not perceived as a "knockout" and so the primary battle with McCarthy continued.

"On to Chicago"

When Kennedy lost the Oregon primary on May 28, it marked the first time a son of Joseph Kennedy had lost a political race since the first time John Kennedy ran for a position in student government at Harvard. With a middle-class electorate and a state population with few African Americans or Latinos, Kennedy's themes of economic justice and racial reconciliation did not resonate with Oregon voters. With Vice President Humphrey enjoying the support of Johnson and lining up a multitude of party regulars who would serve as delegates at that summer's Democratic Party Convention, the next primary, in California, was do-or-die for Kennedy's campaign.

Throughout his campaign, Kennedy had had trouble winning over Jewish voters. Bobby's father ,Joseph Kennedy, was widely known as an anti-Semite who, as American ambassador to Great Britain, had urged President Franklin Roosevelt to avoid war with Adolf Hitler's Germany. To reassure these voters, Kennedy endorsed the sale of more weapons to Israel during the campaign.

Just the year before, the State of Israel had defeated Egypt, Jordan and Syria in a lightning-quick attack that came to be known as the Six-Day War. As a result of the war, Israel now occupied a large swath of what used to be Jordanian territory on the West Bank of the Jordan River, including the eastern half of Jerusalem. A Jordanian living in California named **Sirhan Sirhan** had already been angered by a news photo of Bobby Kennedy wearing a Jewish head covering called a yarmulke. Now, he heard that Kennedy called for further American military support for Israel. Sirhan owned a gun and bought a box of ammo for his small .22 caliber handgun. Sirhan determined to take action.

The night of the California primary, Kennedy won 46 percent of the vote to McCarthy's 42. Late that night, Kennedy reached the Ambassador Hotel in Los Angeles to be interviewed by reporters and to thank supporters. Shortly before midnight, Kennedy went down to the ballroom, the crowd erupting in joy when he emerged. Kennedy spoke under the stifling hot lights of the TV cameras. "What is quite clear [is] that we can work together in the last analysis, and that what has been going on within the United States over a period of the last three years—the divisions, the violence, the disenchantment with our society; the divisions, whether it's between blacks and whites, between the poor and the more affluent, or between age groups or on the war in Vietnam—that is we can start to work together. We are a great country, an unselfish country and a compassionate country . . . My thanks to all of you, and on to Chicago."

As he departed, as he had so often during the 85-day quest for the president, he "reached down and shook hands with some [of the crowd] . . . and touched some outstretched fingers." Kennedy's handlers guided the candidate out of the ballroom and through the kitchen corridor. At about 12:13 a.m. June 5, Sirhan was standing on a low tray-stacker when Kennedy passed. The young man stepped off the tray stacker, raised his pistol-bearing right hand over a cluster of Kennedy staffers, and aimed at the senator's head. He fired one shot, then after a brief pause, several more quick shots. Kennedy "threw his hands up to his face, then staggered back, falling to the grey concrete floor on his back—his eyes open, his arms over his head, his feet apart," Witcover said. ". . . He was alive, but grievously wounded; blood flowed from behind his right ear. In back of him, others were hit and fell."

Kennedy still lived as his wife Ethyl stroked her dying husband's face and chest. Still conscious, he asked, "Is everybody else all right?" An ambulance crew lifted him onto a stretcher as Ethyl cried out, 'Gently, gently." Kennedy closed his eyes, never to awake, as Ethyl wept, "Oh, no, no, don't . . ." Meanwhile, the audience in the ballroom heard the news and let out a terrible scream. Doctors pronounced Kennedy dead at 1:44 a.m. June 6, 1968. His body lay in state at St. Patrick's Cathedral in New York and would be buried at Arlington National Cemetery in Washington, D.C., next to President Kennedy.

News coverage of the service switched to breaking news that King's assassin, Ray, had been arrested in London. Somehow, the almost penniless unemployed drifter, after killing King, successfully crossed the border and reached Toronto, Canada and with a forged passport flew to London and then reached Lisbon, Portugal, where he purchased a second fake Canadian passport. Flying back to London's Heathrow Airport, Ray carried a loaded pistol as he tried to board a plane to Brussels, Belgium. The Canadian Mounted Police matched his photo to those provided by the FBI of King's wanted assassin, and arrested him. Knowing that FBI Director J. Edgar Hoover despised Kennedy as much as he hated Martin Luther King, "Kennedy's friends wondered whether J. Edgar Hoover had timed the announcement to upstage his enemy one last time in the middle of his funeral," Kaiser wrote.

The rituals that Americans observed to say goodbye to prominent political figures—those enacted for John Kennedy, Medgar Evers, Malcolm X and Martin Luther King, Jr., now marked the passing of Robert Kennedy. As with services for Abraham Lincoln 103 years earlier, a train bore Kennedy from New York to the nation's capital. "As they had for Lincoln, many thousands—perhaps, for RFK, a million people, lined the tracks," Thomas wrote. ". . . [A]long the route of the train, Boy Scouts and firemen braced at attention; nuns, some wearing dark glasses, stood witness; housewives wept. Thousands and thousands of black people waited quietly in the heat . . ."

"POOR RICHARD"

On the right, politicians like California Gov. Ronald Reagan and former Vice President Richard Nixon insisted that the violence consuming America in 1968 stemmed from permissive parents who had mollycoddled the young. Lacking discipline, those brats now protested at college campuses and refused to fight for their country in Vietnam, the conservatives claimed. The Supreme Court, dominated by liberals, had gone soft on crime. Progressives in Congress, with their welfare programs, had created a spoiled underclass that expected something for nothing and who, when they didn't get their way, rioted.

Former Vice President Richard Nixon had been nursing personal grudges and mining white resentment since he lost his presidential contest against John Kennedy in 1960. Born in 1913 in Yorba Linda, California, the child of two intensely religious Quakers, Nixon was described by authors Maurice Isserman and Michael Kazin as a "solitary and unsmiling child." The family suffered numerous tragedies, including the deaths of two of Nixon's brothers before he finished college. "Early on he concluded that life was a grim and no-holds-barred struggle, in which success came only to those who persevered at any cost," the authors said.

Nixon always felt insecure about his poor parents and his education, attending small Whittier College in California rather than the prestigious, expensive Ivy League schools favored by the affluent. Nevertheless, through hard work he won a scholarship to Duke University in North Carolina, where he earned a law degree. After serving in the Navy in the South Pacific during World War II, he returned to Whittier and practiced law with a small firm. Always ambitious, Nixon challenged incumbent liberal Congressman Jerry Voorhis, whom Nixon characterized with great inaccuracy as a supporter of "Communist principles." Already, Nixon had acquired a reputation as a dirty campaigner, but to the young congressman this was the only way to challenge the unfair advantages of wealth and prestige enjoyed by his political opponents.

Nixon was named to the House Un-American Activities Committee, where his flair for red-baiting would get a choice platform. Nixon seized an opportunity to get attention when *Time* magazine editor and former communist Whittaker Chambers testified before the committee that while he was a member of the party he had helped Alger Hiss, an adviser in Franklin Roosevelt's State Department, make copies of secret State Department documents. Chambers said the copies were made so he could transmit them to the Soviet government. Hiss, Chambers claimed, was a fellow communist.

In testimony, Hiss denied the charges, and he then sued Chambers for slander. With great theatricality, Nixon revealed microfilmed copies of State Department documents that had been discovered, under Chambers' direction, in a hollowed-out pumpkin at the editor's Maryland farm. The "Pumpkin Papers," as they became known, attracted page-one headlines and Nixon promoted the evidence as proving "the most serious series of treasonable activities . . . in the history of America." Because of the statute of limitations, Hiss was immune from espionage charges, but he was convicted for perjury and received a five-year sentence in federal prison. Hiss continued to deny the charges for the rest of his life.

Nixon won fame from his involvement in the Hiss case, which he used to his advantage in 1950 when he ran for the United States Senate against liberal Democrat Helen Gahagan Douglas. Again, he smeared his opponent as a communist sympathizer, calling her a "pink lady." Nixon won again. When he ran for president in 1952, the moderate Eisenhower picked as running mate the conservative Nixon to broaden his appeal and to help him earn California's electoral votes.

Nixon had his first of many political near-death experiences during the 1952 campaign. News stories revealed that Nixon had received possibly illegal contributions from wealthy supporters to reimburse the California senator for his campaign expenses. Nixon defended himself on national television, misleadingly characterizing his income as meager. Referring to his wife, Nixon said his family didn't have much money. "It isn't very much, but Pat and I have the satisfaction that every dime that we've got is honestly ours," Nixon said. "I should say this—that Pat doesn't have a mink coat. But she does have a respectable Republican cloth coat. And I always tell her that she'd look good in anything." At the end of the speech, Nixon did admit to receiving from one contributor the gift of a dog for his daughters, which the children named Checkers. "And you know, the kids, like all kids, love the dog and I just want to say this right now, that regardless of what they say about it, we're gonna keep it," Nixon said.

Many establishment Republicans cringed at the scandal and what some called Nixon's "Poor Richard" speech. Critics began calling Nixon "Tricky Dick." Nevertheless, the Californian's performance won support from the public and ensured he would remain on the Eisenhower ticket.

In Exile

Nixon once predicted he would literally die if he had to leave politics. Nixon took his loss to Kennedy in the 1960 presidential election as a personal repudiation and he desperately wanted to win back public approval. In 1962, he ran for California governor against the Democratic incumbent, Edmund "Pat" Brown. A moderate on civil rights during his Senate career and a supporter of some social programs, Nixon had fallen out of touch with the right-wing drift of the California Republican Party during his sojourn in Washington.

Right-wingers were less than enthusiastic about Nixon, and many did not turn out on Election Day. Pat Brown, meanwhile, charged that Nixon had no interest in serving as governor and that he would exploit the office in order to run for president again. Nixon lost to Brown by approximately 52 percent of the vote to 47 percent.

Nixon held a bitter press conference upon losing the California governor's race. "And as I leave the press, all I can say is this: for sixteen years, ever since the Hiss case, you've had a lot of fun—a lot of fun—that you've had an opportunity to attack me, and I think I have given as good as I have taken," he told a crowd of reporters. ". . . [A]s I leave you I want you to know—just think of how much you are going to be missing. You won't have Nixon to kick around anymore, because, gentlemen, this is my last press conference."

Across the country, journalists panned Nixon's performance at the press conference, which they said showed the man to be resentful and un-presidential. ABC broadcast a 30-minute news special, *The Political Obituary of*

Richard Nixon. "Barring a miracle, his political career ended last week," *Time* proclaimed. Nixon stayed in the background during the 1964 presidential campaign, although he dropped big hints that he would again accept the Republican nomination if asked. Nixon also said that if the GOP nominated Sen. Barry Goldwater of Arizona, the extremely conservative frontrunner, this development would be a "tragedy" for the party. Yet, when Goldwater received the nomination, Nixon alone among prominent Republicans campaigned across the country for Goldwater, making 156 speeches on his behalf. Nixon realized that the conservative delegates who supported Goldwater at the 1964 Republican National Convention would be in charge for the 1968 convention. Having campaigned for both conservative and liberal Republican candidates across the country in 1964, and again in 1966, Nixon would soon collect his chits. "Every side owed him something," historian Rick Perlstein said.

"Pointy-headed Bureaucrats"

Nixon found political gold in tapping white anger against African Americans. As part of his comeback plans the former vice president already implemented what would come to be known as the "Southern Strategy" during his presidential administration. Nixon watched with intense interest and fear the career of segregationist Alabama Governor George Wallace, who had performed surprisingly well in northern Democratic primaries in 1964. Politicians like Wallace, Nixon and former Hollywood actor Ronald Reagan perceived the growing white backlash in the United States, even in places as far from the South as California, where 65 percent of voters in 1964 approved Proposition 14, a measure that overturned a previously passed fair-housing law prohibiting home sellers from discriminating against racial minorities.

As the 1968 presidential season dawned, Wallace sought out disaffected whites across the country as he launched the American Independent Party, a third-party vehicle for his presidential ambitions. A Detroit newspaper columnist derided Wallace's constituency, which included Klansman and Neo-Nazis, as "kooks." Wallace scoffed. "The other side's got more kooks than we do," he insisted, adding, "kooks got a right to vote too." Wallace successfully tapped into a culture, shaped by Joe McCarthy-era claims of secret communist plots to take over America (ideas still promoted by J. Edgar Hoover) and doubts over the official conclusions regarding the JFK assassination, increasingly attuned to conspiracy theories. The race riots that had wracked the country, Wallace claimed, were the product of a sinister plan to destroy America launched by "pointy-headed" bureaucrats in Washington who were taking their orders directly from communist leader Fidel Castro in Cuba.

He spoke in racial code, of lazy people on welfare, and the collapse of law and order. "You people work hard," he told a white, blue-collar California audience, "you save your money, you teach your children to respect the law." Yet, Wallace said, when someone burns down a city and murders someone, "'pseudo-intellectuals' explain it away by saying the killer didn't get any watermelon to eat when he was 10 years old." Furthermore, Wallace claimed, "the Supreme Court is fixing it so you can't do anything about people who set cities on fire."

Wallace also included leftist professors, immoral Hollywood movies and "long-haired hippies" in his list of "sinister forces destroying America." While the Northeast press derided Wallace for his simple-minded and often crude rhetoric, voters found the renegade candidate refreshingly blunt. "You don't have to worry about figuring out where he stands," a steelworker in Youngstown, Ohio, told one reporter. "He tells it like it really is." Few expected that Wallace could get on the ballot in California, but on January 2, 1968, Wallace announced that he had collected the required 100,000 signatures. A Gallup Poll at the time showed 11 percent of California voters supporting Wallace for president.

Last Man Standing

Nixon benefited when his chief opponents within the GOP dithered or imploded. New York **Governor Nelson Rockefeller**, the liberal who mounted the main challenge to Barry Goldwater in 1964, couldn't make up his mind about entering the race, and his indecision undercut whatever support he might have received. For a time, Michigan Governor George Romney ran as a substitute for Rockefeller. Considered handsome by many and a moderate elected in a Democratic state, Romney fatally wounded his campaign during a September 4, 1967 interview. Romney seemed to favor a negotiated settlement in Vietnam, but he hesitated to say so clearly for fear of being seen as soft on the Vietnamese communists. Asked about his inconsistency, Romney commented on a tour he once had taken in Vietnam. "When I came back from Vietnam in 1965, I just had the greatest brainwashing that anyone can get when you get over to Vietnam," he said. "Not only the generals, but also the diplomatic corps over there, and they do a very thorough job." Romney had tried to describe the intense and dishonest salesmanship the military engaged in regarding the war, but as the historian Rick Perlstein observed, "What people heard was the word *brainwashing*," which implied to many voters that Romney was weak-minded. He also seemed to imply that the military, an institution still highly regarded by most Americans, was dishonest. Once very competitive with Nixon, Romney was trailing Nixon by a 6-1 margin just before the New Hampshire primary in March 1968, the first contest in the Republican nomination process, and he dropped out of the race shortly before the casting of ballots.

Nixon saw Ronald Reagan as his chief obstacle. In California, Reagan had handily defeated Pat Brown, the man Nixon lost to in 1962, in the 1966 gubernatorial contest. As the top elected official in the state with the most electoral votes, he immediately became a presidential contender. During his gubernatorial campaign, he sounded many of the same themes as Nixon and Wallace, though in a more appealing, Hollywood star fashion. Always an advocate of tax cuts for the rich, Reagan still resonated with working-class audiences by appealing to their resentments against what blue-collar voters saw as spoiled and unappreciative college students who burned the flag and rioted rather than taking advantage of going to college and learning.

Within 10 days of his election as governor, Reagan gathered his advisors at his Pacific Palisades home and discussed a presidential campaign for the first time. Reagan's first two years as governor, however, let the air out of his ambitions. When tax cuts he pushed for created a deficit, he then presided over the largest tax increase in state history. A so-called homosexual scandal broke out. The newspaper columnist **Drew Pearson** revealed the presence of gays on Reagan's staff, and in this intensely homophobic era the story tarred Reagan's reputation. Reagan purged gays from the state government, but as journalist and author Theodore White wrote, "From this blow, the Reagan campaign never recovered."

Nixon won the nomination at the Republican National Convention in Miami on the first ballot, August 7, 1968. Nixon's nomination largely resulted from the failures of the other candidates. He nevertheless gave one of the best speeches of his career when he accepted the nomination the next night. "As we look in America, we see cities enveloped in smoke and flame. We hear sirens in the night... We see Americans hating each other, fighting each other; killing each other at home." Little did Nixon know that night that his words could be describing the Democratic National Convention in Chicago, August 26-29. The nation would watch in horror as police rioted, demonstrators bled and a major political party committed suicide in front of television cameras.

"The Whole World is Watching"

Like Nixon, Vice President Hubert Humphrey had sought the presidency for eight years. Unlike Nixon, however, Humphrey had to answer for the unpopularity of Johnson's war in Vietnam. Humphrey avoided the party's primaries, preferring to campaign behind the scenes, lining up the support of Democratic Party bosses who controlled a majority of the delegates who would attend the Democratic Party Convention in August. Approximately 80 percent of Democratic primary voters had supported the chief anti-war candidates, Bobby Kennedy and Eugene McCarthy. However, the math that mattered was that in thirty-three states, pro-administration party officials chose who would attend the convention. Throughout the 1968 campaign, Humphrey would not clearly break with the president on Vietnam.

To the young, rebellious voters who backed Eugene McCarthy and Bobby Kennedy in particular, Humphrey seemed the embodiment of a hack machine politician. "A balding man who dyed his remaining hair an implausible shade, often sounded fatuous, and seemed unable to free himself from the yoke of a dubious president, Humphrey came across to many as a parody of all the establishment's failures," Charles Kaiser wrote. "He hardly needed any additional disadvantages in his quest for younger supporters. However, by ignoring the primaries, and getting nearly all his delegates through the party's power brokers, the vice president was making a difficult situation impossible."

A bad atmosphere pervaded Chicago even before the Democratic National Convention started. Several strikes—by telephone installers, electrical workers, and bus and taxi drivers—made communication and transportation difficult. Daley turned the International Amphitheatre, where the Democrats convened, into a war zone. Barbed wire that could be electrified surrounded the building, as did a literal army of 12,000 police officers working 12-hour shifts, 6,000 National Guardsmen as well as another 6,000 soldiers who, as Kaiser noted, "were armed with rifles, flamethrowers, and bazookas."

Anti-war activists planned a confrontation in Chicago during the convention. The **Youth International Party**, or Yippies, and other activists anticipated that the Chicago Police, under corrupt and almost dictatorial Democratic **Mayor Richard Daley**, would respond with violence to anti-war protestors outside the Democratic Convention. A bloody clash, Yippies like Jerry Rubin and Abbie Hoffman hoped, would prove that the United States had become a police state.

Daley had given his police department "shoot to kill orders." The city banned any permits for groups wanting to camp at city parks. Protestors ignored the order and occupied Lincoln Park. Late on the Sunday night before the convention opened, the police charged into the protestor encampment determined to clear the anti-war protestors from the area. Yippies and others yelled, "Pigs!" and cried "Oink, oink," prompting many officers to shout, "Kill the Commies!" as they cracked the heads of young people with nightsticks. A Chicago police officer shouted an obscenity at a *Newsweek* magazine reporter when he displayed his press credentials and clubbed him on the head and body. Police injured ten journalists that evening.

While pro-Johnson delegates at the convention shot down a Vietnam peace plank, around 10,000 protestors gathered in nearby Grant Park. On Wednesday, disappointed and angry Eugene McCarthy supporters (who realized that the fix was in and that the convention would anoint Humphrey as the nominee) joined Yippies and the more conventional anti-war types who had participated in earlier events like the March on the Pentagon. One demonstrator donning an army helmet attempted to remove the American flag from a flagpole at Grant Park and was mauled by police. Another group took the flag down and replaced it with a red T-shirt, provoking what a later investigative commission would call a "police riot." Swinging nightsticks and pelting the protestors with tear gas and Mace, Chicago police launched a full-scale crackdown. As TV cameras rolled, network coverage shifted from the chaos inside the convention to the street violence outside. Broadcasts gave viewers a close-up look as police bloodied protestors and innocent bystanders as well. Police pushed onlookers, reporters and demonstrators on the sidewalks of Michigan Avenue through plate-glass windows fronting the Hilton Hotel. Meanwhile, protestors chanted, "The Whole World Is Watching."

The disorder inside the convention hall often matched the battle raging outside. On the second night of the convention, television viewers saw Daley's security people punch CBS News reporter Dan Rather in the stomach, prompting the anchor of the network's convention coverage, Walter Cronkite, to remark, "I think we've got a bunch of thugs here, if I may be permitted to say so."

Humphrey's inevitable nomination served as a harder truth for protestors and many delegates. Just before midnight the night of the Grant Park riot, the vice president had secured enough votes for the nomination. His nomination defined the term "Pyrrhic victory." More relevant than the nomination was the image fixed in the minds of the voters, of the Democrats as a party of violence and anarchy. In contrast, the relatively calm Republican convention projected an image for Nixon and the GOP as the forces of law and order.

During the convention, more than 12,009 had been arrested. A total of 65 journalists covering the convention had been assaulted and/or arrested. Area hospitals reported treating 111 demonstrators, while volunteers with the Medical Committee for Human Rights reported treating more than 1,000 at the scenes of protests. Polls afterwards showed that a clear majority of Americans supported the actions against the protestors taken by the mayor and his police department. At a press conference on September 9, Daley, famous for being tongue-tied, announced, "The policeman isn't there to create disorder, the police is there to preserve disorder."

"IF YOU MEAN IT, WE'RE WITH YOU"

A year that often seemed to presage a revolution ended instead in a counter-revolution. The luck Nixon enjoyed in the race for the Republican nomination held up during the fall. Remembering painfully his fall in the 1960 debates with John Kennedy, the Republican avoided sharing a stage with Humphrey and relied instead on a sophisticated media strategy that foreshadowed the style of presidential candidates ever since. Meanwhile, Humphrey struggled to dig himself out of the hole created by the Chicago convention, and the long-shot Wallace third-party campaign fatally stumbled.

By September 27, a Gallup poll placed Humphrey fifteen points behind Nixon and a mere seven points ahead of Wallace. Desperate, the Humphrey campaign spent $100,000 to buy 30 minutes on national television TV time. Humphrey made a conditional promise that, if elected president, he would halt bombing in North Vietnam if the communists would "restore" the Demilitarized Zone separating North and South Vietnam that had been repeatedly violated in recent months. "As president, I

Ex-Governor George Wallace of Alabama during the news conference in which he announced his candidacy for the presidency on a third-party ticket.
February 8, 1968   Credit: Library of Congress.

would be willing to stop the bombing of the North as an acceptable risk for peace," he told the audience. Johnson had warned Humphrey to not make that promise and was furious when Hubert delivered the talk anyway. When the vice president spoke soon thereafter at the University of Tennessee for the first time in weeks, he did not have to deal with protestors and some students held a sign that said, "IF YOU MEAN IT, WE'RE WITH YOU."

More important, labor unions finally leapt into the campaign, providing volunteers and money when Humphrey most needed it. Humphrey received a big boost from mistakes by the Wallace campaign. The former Alabama governor had trouble getting someone to agree to run with him. Wallace approached Ezra Taft Benson, the former Secretary of Agriculture under Dwight Eisenhower to be his running mate and was turned down and also considered asking Harlan Sanders, better know as "Col. Sanders" of Kentucky Fried Chicken Fame. The nod for the vice presidential candidacy instead went to Air Force Gen. Curtis LeMay, who had directed the air war against the Japanese in World War II, and became commander of operations during the Berlin Airlift in 1948 when the Soviet Union cut West Berlin from NATO.

In his public statements, LeMay had expressed his frustration with America's "phobia" about using nuclear weapons. Wallace held an October 3 press conference alongside LeMay broadcast by the three television networks. Beforehand, Wallace had urged the general to not talk about nuclear weapons. *Los Angeles Times* reporter Jack Smith asked LeMay if the United States could win the Vietnam War "without nuclear weapons." "We can win this war without nuclear weapons," LeMay said.

I think there may be times when it would be most efficient to use nuclear weapons. However, the public opinion in this country and through the world throw up their hands in horror when you mention nuclear weapons just because of the propaganda that's been fed to them. I've seen a film of Bikini Atoll [in the Pacific] after 20 nuclear tests, and the fish are all back in the lagoons, the coconut trees are growing coconuts, the guava bushes have fruit on them, the birds are back.

Humphrey benefited from the LeMay gaffe, with some Wallace supporters concluding that the American Independent Party and its top two candidates were irresponsible and dangerous. Many of these voters drifted back to the Democratic Party, and Humphrey had erased most of Nixon's lead going into the last days of the campaign.

BRANDING NIXON

Nixon's strategy, meanwhile, focused on avoiding mistakes. He sought to carefully control his public appearance as his media team devised a strategy to make the candidate's television appearances an advantage instead of a fatal weakness. In addition to not debating Humphrey, where he might slip, he avoided press conferences where he might be tripped up by a question from a skeptical reporter.

Nixon instead taped a series of ten television programs in which he answered questions from pre-screened voters before an audience of around 200 committed supporters. The audience and the pre-selected questioners sat in a semi-circle around Nixon. Audience members were told beforehand to applaud when Nixon answered and to get up and surround him at the end of these taped encounters so the last thing the television audience would see was Nixon shaking hands with a friendly crowd. Journalists had to watch these performances on monitors in a nearby room. Worried about the tendency of his upper lip to sweat when he was hot, Nixon ordered the air conditioner in the studio to run at full blast. The tapes played regionally so the topics could center on issues of concern to particular subsets of voters.

These extended political commercials were the brainchild of Roger Ailes, later a media consultant for President Ronald Reagan and president of Fox News. A minor crisis developed before one taping in Philadelphia when a staffer had placed a Jewish psychiatrist on the panel. Nixon didn't like Jews and held a deep suspicion of the psychiatric profession. The man was dropped from the panel before taping and Ailes made a suggestion for a substitute. "A good, mean Wallacite cabdriver," he said. "Wouldn't that be great? Some guy to sit there and say, 'Awright, Mac, what about those niggers?'" Nixon could then act shocked, Ailes reasoned, deplore the man's language, but then talk about law and order and "states' rights"—in short offer a reasonable version of the cabbie's anti-black resentments. Ailes went outside the studio and found a cabdriver who matched the desired description.

In front of a friendly audience, Nixon did not sweat, he smiled often enough, did not lose his temper, and he handled the rare tough question with relative calm and grace. During the campaign, Nixon also promised he had a secret plan to end the war. Ailes and other figures on the campaign successfully re-branded Nixon as a steady, tough and experienced potential president who would pursue a tough course with Vietnamese communists but would soon end the war, and who would not tolerate the lawlessness that had marked recent years.

Nixon's approach proved to be a winning one, though

THE NIGHTMARE YEAR, 1968 / 977

it barely succeeded. The networks did not call the November election until 9 a.m. the next morning. Nixon won 43.4 percent of the vote, and 301 Electoral College votes, and Humphrey carried 42.7 percent of the popular vote, with 191 Electoral College votes.

Wallace had one of the most successful third-party campaigns in U.S. history. He carried 13.5 percent of the popular vote and received 46 votes in the Electoral College, but he won states only in his Deep South home base—Alabama, Arkansas, Louisiana, Mississippi and Georgia. Adding the Wallace and the Nixon votes, together, which represented 57 percent of the vote, the election represented a firm rejection of Johnson's policies and their perceived effect on creating an atmosphere of dangerous permissiveness. Many white voters in particular had grown tired of the revolution in civil rights and the indecisive results in Vietnam and wanted a return to what they saw as normality.

1968: THE "WHAT-IFs"

Few years in American history inspire as many of what historians call "counter-factual propositions" as the year 1968. For instance, what would have happened if Lyndon Johnson had not dropped out of the Democratic presidential race and decided to run for a second full term? Bobby Kennedy would never have directly challenged a sitting Democratic president and most likely would have lived to run for president in 1972, leaving McCarthy alone in a quixotic quest to challenge the Johnson juggernaut. Clearly, because of the president's continued control over about 66 percent of the delegates who would have attended the Democratic convention, Johnson would have easily won re-nomination. After that, the speculation gets murkier, but given the mood of the time, it is hard to imagine Johnson triumphing in November.

What if Johnson had dropped out, and Kennedy had entered the primaries, but had not been murdered in California? Back in 1988, on the twentieth anniversary of Bobby Kennedy's assassination, historian Arthur Schlesinger, a close friend of the New York senator, speculated that Bobby would have catapulted from his victory in the California primary to the Democratic nomination. He then would have beaten Richard Nixon in the November presidential election. Winning the White House, Kennedy would have ended the Vietnam War much sooner, cutting in half the number of names now on that tragic Vietnam Memorial in Washington.

President Robert Kennedy, Schlesinger speculated, would have continued the reform tradition of the New Deal and New Frontier, might have achieved racial reconciliation between whites and blacks and, by defeating Nixon, would have prevented the national malaise ushered in by Watergate and the later failed presidencies of Gerald Ford and Jimmy Carter. That's a huge, messianic burden

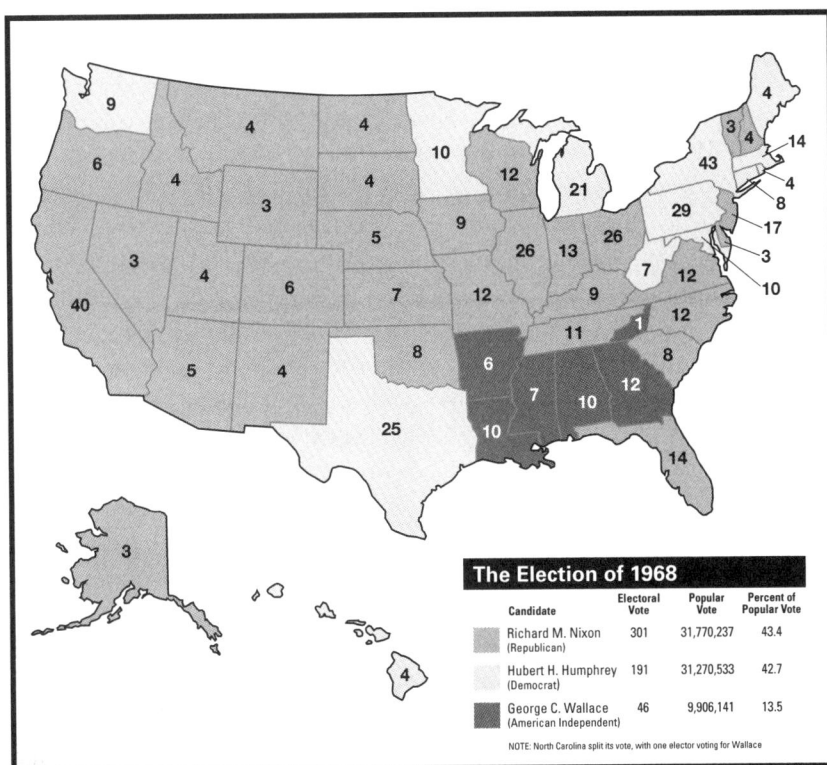

Map 30.1   The Election of 1968

for a one-term U.S. attorney general and four-year senator from New York to bear, a similar one that has been thrust upon the shoulders of Bobby's similarly-martyred brother John F. Kennedy. The idolization of both Kennedys represent prime exhibits of what historians refer to, usually with derision, as the "Great Man" theory of history—the notion that the times are shaped not by larger forces like industrialization or racism but by bold individuals of unique vision who rise above the moment and bend the world to their will.

There's reason to think that the world would have changed less dramatically had Bobby Kennedy lived. If he had reached the White House and fulfilled his campaign promise to withdraw from Vietnam, South Vietnam likely still would have fallen to the communists. Republicans and conservative Democrats would have pilloried him as the man who "lost Southeast Asia," much as Harry Truman had been condemned as the man who supposedly lost China in 1949. There likely would have been a post-war recession, as happened under Nixon, when defense spending inevitably declined. White Americans still would have been frightened by the rise of assertive black nationalist groups like the Black Panthers, and liberal judges probably still would have ordered school busing in places like Boston, sparking a white backlash that has defined American politics for nearly four decades.

In any case, the deindustrialization of the Northeast and the growing support for free trade in both parties that started in the 1960s would have eroded the strength of the union vote so essential to the Kennedy family's national political ambitions. Bobby Kennedy would have been a more progressive president than Nixon, and may have been less divisive, but he likely would have had as mixed a record as president as his older brother.

What if Martin Luther King had survived 1968? Although he was overwhelmingly admired by African Americans, by 1968 signs abounded that his influence within the left wing of the black community had ebbed. He could not have prevented continued violence by various white-controlled police departments and white supremacists acting alone or as part of an underground. Likely, he could not by himself turn back the embrace by some African Americans of more violent action in response. More radical alternatives to King, like the Black Panther Party, had risen by the time of his death.

King had taken on a far more difficult crusade than southern desegregation at the end of his career. During his campaign against poverty, he called for a massive redistribution of wealth, a solution controversial even among the liberals who normally would have been his allies. In any case, solving poverty would have been a much more difficult feat than getting "whites only" signs taken down from water fountains. Alienated from at least some more radical African Americans, he likely would have lost white support as well.

In the end, this is all speculation. We can be certain only about what actually happened. The year 1968 marked a triumph not of reform or liberalism but of retrenchment and conservatism. As president, Nixon proved as reluctant as Johnson to be the "first president to lose a war." As a result, the war dragged on for four more years, and about 30,000 more Americans died in the conflict. Johnson's last year in office marked the last time that the federal government recorded a balanced budget until Bill Clinton's second term in the late 1990s. The start of the Nixon years would launch three decades of debt that would leave the funding for federal budget dependent on China's purchase of U.S. bonds.

Nixon's insecurities and fears would infect his presidency, leading to the Watergate scandal. Even before burglars working for the Nixon re-election campaign broke into Democratic Party headquarters on June 17, 1972, the deception of the Gulf of Tonkin Resolution, and the constant lies surrounding American progress in Vietnam had pushed Americans into greater skepticism of and alienation from the federal government.

The twin assassinations of Martin Luther King and Bobby Kennedy in 1968, joined with the earlier murder of John Kennedy, led many Americans to doubt the official finding of guilt and to suppose that the federal government, up to the highest offices, played a hand in the murders. The public increasingly concluded that corruption in government was business as usual, leading them to doubt the likely benefits of heroic reform programs that had been promised as part of The New Frontier and The Great Society. Fueled in part by white anger against what was seen as the excesses of the 1960s, and particularly the near-anarchy of 1968, America entered a long political period of conservative dominance starting with Nixon's election to the White House. Conservative Republicans would control the White House for 28 of the next 40 years and both houses of Congress for 12 of those years.

Humphrey's defeat and Democratic nominee George McGovern's crushing defeat by Nixon in 1972 convinced Democrats as well that the days of big government liberalism had ended. The next three Democratic presidents – Jimmy Carter, Bill Clinton, and Barack Obama—would try to rule from the center-right of American politics, and spend much of their political lives criticizing the party's left wing. Meanwhile, King's life and words would be whitewashed. His birthday would become a holiday and his most provocative and radical statements would be forgotten. Conservatives would distort the meaning of his words during the March on Washington, in which he wished for men to be "judged not by the color of their skin, but by the content of their character," to mean that King would have been opposed to affirmative action opening job opportunities to people of color, even though King had supported such programs, and even suggested he backed reparations to African Americans for the centuries of unpaid slave labor. Safely dead, King was remade by white America as a non-threatening figure whose innocuous dream of equality, white America falsely claimed, had been already achieved.

Author Charles Kaiser once interviewed folk/rock star Bob Dylan and asked him about the events in 1968. "All those things like that deaden you," Dylan said. "They kill part of your hope. And enough of those blows to your hope will make you deader and deader and deader, until a person is existing without caring any more . . ." America left 1968 sad, exhausted and a little bitter, feeling not hope but a nostalgia for a largely fictitious and presumed Golden Age of Innocence. In the 1970s, Americans came to believe they lived in a declining empire.

Chronology

Jan. 5, 1968	Alexander Dubcek becomes head of the Communist Party in Czechoslovakia.
January 23	North Koreans seize the *U.S.S. Pueblo*.
January 30	Tet Offensive.
February 27	*Report from Vietnam by Walter Cronkite*.
March 12	Eugene McCarthy wins 42.4 percent of the vote in the New Hampshire Democratic Primary.
March 16	My Lai Massacre. Bobby Kennedy announces he is entering the Democratic race for president.
March 22	A wave of protests start in France.
March 27	Student occupation of Columbia University.
March 31	Lyndon Johnson announces that he will not seek another term as president.
April 4	Martin Luther King, Jr., is assassinated.
June 4	Bobby Kennedy is assassinated in the Ambassador Hotel in Los Angeles.
June 8	Arrest of James Earl Ray, the assassin of Martin Luther King. Bobby Kennedy is buried.
August 20-21	The Soviet Union, and most of its Warsaw Pact allies, invade Czechoslovakia.
August 26-29	The Democratic National Convention becomes a scene of chaos. Hubert Humphrey wins the nomination of the Democratic Party for president.
October 2	Mexican government troops massacre up to 400 protestors in the Plaza de Tres Culturas in the District of Tlateloco.
October 17	U.S. Olympic sprinters Tommie Smith and John Carlos make a "black power" salute after winning first and third place medals in the Olympics in Mexico City.
November 6	Richard Nixon is elected president.
December 23	North Korea releases the crew of the *U.S.S. Pueblo*.

Review Questions

1. How did American assumptions about the Cold War lead to the capture of the *U.S.S. Pueblo*?

2. What factors possibly led to the My Lai Massacre?

3. What challenges did the Democratic Party face in the 1968 presidential race?

4. Why did J. Edgar Hoover seek to undermine Martin Luther King, Jr. and his movement?

5. What strategy did Richard Nixon follow in winning the presidency in 1968?

Glossary of Important People and Concepts

Ralph Abernathy
Eddie Adams
Peter Arnett
Lt. Col. Frank Barker
Battle of Khe-Sanh
Bedford-Stuyvesant
William Laws Calley
Philip Caputo
Stokely Carmichael
Charlie Company
Cesar Chavez
Clarke Clifford
COINTELPRO
Richard J. Daley
Alexander Dubcek
J. Edgar Hoover
Kim il-Sung
Grayson Kirk
Eugene McCarthy
Memphis Sanitation Strike
Nguyen Ngoc Loan
Andrew Russell "Drew" Pearson
The Peers Report
Poor Peoples' Campaign
Pueblo Crisis
James Earl Ray
Nelson Rockefeller
Mark Rudd
Bashir Sirhan Sirhan
Tommie Smith
Tet Offensive
Võ Nguyên Giáp
"Wise Old Men"
Jules Witcover
Youth International Party

SUGGESTED READINGS

David L. Anderson, ed., *Facing My Lai: Moving Beyond the Massacre* (1998).

Michael Bilton and Kevin Sim, *Four Hours in My Lai* (1992).

Taylor Branch. *At Canaan's Edge: America in the King Years, 1965-1968* (2006).

Archie Brown, *The Rise and Fall of Communism* (2009).

Dan T. Carter. *The Politics of Rage: George Wallace, The Origins of the New Conservatism, and the Transformation of American Politics* (1995).

Robert Dallek. *Flawed Giant: Lyndon Johnson and His Times, 1961-1973* (1998).

Brian Dooley, *Robert Kennedy: The Final Years* (1996).

Michael Eric Dyson. *April 4, 1968: Martin Luther King Jr.'s Death and How It Changed America* (2008).

Ingrid Gilcher-Holtey, in Martin Klimke and Joachim Scharloth, eds., "France" in *1968 in Europe: A History of Protest and Activismm 1956-1977* (2008).

Doris Kearns Goodwin. *Lyndon Johnson and the American Dream* (1976).

Richard Hack. *Puppetmaster: The Secret Life of J. Edgar Hoover* (2007).

J. Edgar Hoover. *Masters of Deceit: The Story of Communism in America* (1958).

Maurice Isserman and Michael Kazin. *America Divided: The Civil War of the 1960s* (2000).

Charles Kaiser, *1968 in America: Music, Politics, Chaos, Counterculture, and the Shaping of a Generation* (1988).

Stanley Karnow, *Vietnam: A History* (1983).

Mitchell B. Lerner, *The Pueblo Incident: A Spy Ship and the Failure of American Foreign Policy* (2002).

Joe McGinniss. *The Selling of the President, 1968* (1969).

Michael C. Meyer and William L. Sherman, *The Course of Mexican History* (1991).

Don Oberdorfer, *Tet: The Turning Point in the Vietnam War* (1984).

Rick Perlstein. *Nixonland: The Rise of a President and the Fracturing of America* (2008).

Mark Rudd, *Underground: My Life With SDS and the Weathermen* (2009).

Arthur M. Schlesinger, Jr., *Robert Kennedy and His Times* (1978).

Evan Thomas, *Robert Kennedy: His Life* (2000).

Robert Weisbrot. *Freedom Bound: A History of America's Civil Rights Movement* (1990).

Theodore H. White. *The Making of the President: 1968* (1969).

Jules Witcover, *85 Days: The Last Campaign of Robert Kennedy* (1969).

Chapter Thirty-one

AMERICAN FRUSTRATION AND DECLINE IN THE 1970s

When investigative reporter Seymour Hersh discovered that American soldiers had butchered about 400 unarmed civilians in the village the military called My Lai on March 16, 1968, he could not sell the story to major publications like **The Washington Post** *or* **The New York Times** *but instead had to sell the scoop to the small, left-leaning and newly formed Dispatch News Service. A story, headlined "Lieutenant Accused of Murdering 109 Civilians," appeared on November 15, 1969 in thirty mid-sized newspapers across the country, which paid $100 each, before it was picked up by major news outlets.*

Hersh informed readers that platoon leader William L. "Rusty" Calley had received orders to strike at communist guerillas supposedly hiding in My Lai and to "shoot anything that moved." Soldiers killed unarmed elderly people, women and children, Hersh reported, and 90 percent of the company had participated in the slaughter.

The Cleveland Plain Dealer *received official Army photos of the mass murder and ran them with a second Hersh dispatch published November 20. On November 25, one of the whistleblowers, Paul David Meadlo, told his story on* **CBS News**. *Meadlo had not discussed My Lai with his family before giving the interview. His mother found out the details about My Lai watching him on television. "He wasn't raised up like that," Myrtle Meadlo said. "I raised him to be a good boy and I did everything I could. They came along and took him into the service. He fought for his country and look what they done to him. They made a murderer out of him..." In early December, graphic My Lai photos were published in color by* **Life** *magazine, featuring (as author Rick Perlstein describes them), a "boy with a stump where his leg should be; a pile of adult and infant corpses lying on a dusty road like broken toys; and woman splayed in rape position..."*

News of My Lai surfaced during an angry era of American politics, an age of white backlash against black protestors, of adult exasperation with the young, and of American resentment of the world. Instead of outrage, many Americans rallied to the defense of William Calley (who faced a military trial for murder) and the other men of Charlie Company who took part in the massacre.

Perlstein, in his book **Nixonland: The Rise of a President and the Fracturing of America**, *notes the wide support for the massacre in the American public. 'What do they give soldiers bullets for—to put in their pockets?" one elevator operator in Boston said. "It sounds terrible to say we ought to kill kids, but many of our boys beings killed over there are just kids, too." A reader of the Plain Dealer wrote to the editor that, "Your paper is rotten and un-American." Others insisted that the story was fake, the result of a liberal conspiracy. "The story was planted by Vietcong sympathizers and people inside the country who are trying to get us out of Vietnam sooner."*

Calley defended himself by saying he was only following orders. A military court in Fort Benning, Georgia convicted Calley and sentenced him to life imprisonment. Calley was sent to serve his sentence at Fort Leavenworth in Kansas. The American Legion post in Columbus, Georgia, promised to raise $100,000 for Calley's appeal. The group issued a statement that said, "The real murderers are the demonstrators in Washington who disrupt traffic, tear up public property, who deface the American flag. Lieutenant Calley is a hero . . . we should elevate him to saint."

Across the country cars sported bumper stickers that demanded "Free Calley" while a Nashville radio station released a record with a reading done in William Calley's voice as "The Battle Hymn of the Republic" played in the background. The record sold 200,000 copies, and some radio stations played the disc around the clock, breaking in only to ask for donations to Calley's defense fund. The White House conducted a poll and found that 78 percent of the American public disagreed with the Calley verdict while about 51 percent wanted him completely exonerated. In spite of being advised by White House counsel John Dean that Calley's trial was airtight legally, President Richard Nixon, a Republican, saw an opportunity to ride a growing backlash against antiwar protestors and he ordered the lieutenant released from the stockade until his appeal was decided.

"And a man convicted by fellow army officers of slaughtering twenty-two civilians was released on his own recognizance to the splendiferous bachelor pad he had rented with the proceeds of his defense fund . . . " Perlstein wrote, "complete with padded bar, groovy paintings, and a comely girlfriend, who along with a personal secretary and a mechanical letter-opener helped him answer some two-thousand fan letters a day." Meanwhile, Calley's sentence was repeatedly reduced by Nixon and then commuted to time served. He was released in November 1974. Calley resumed a quiet life after his brief reign as an American anti-hero.

THE SOUTHERN STRATEGY

Richard Nixon preferred to work in solitude. He hated the handshaking, the backslapping, and the give-and-take essential to any political career. Nixon once described himself as an introvert in an extrovert's business. "Most politicians, good and bad, are men who can't stand to be alone," presidential biographer Richard Reeves said. "Nixon did not like to be with people."

Much of his discomfort came from his embarrassment over economic hardships during his childhood, the trauma he shared with his parents when two of his brothers died of tuberculosis, and his resentment at what he saw as easier life enjoyed by others, such as the family he came to obsessively hate—the wealthy and glamorous Kennedys. Nixon's father had been withdrawn emotionally, and so was the president. He left nothing to chance and memorized what he was going to say when he was going to meet people. Even as president, Nixon wrote daily messages to himself to overcome his feelings of inferiority.

Henry Kissinger, who served as Nixon's national security advisor and then as his secretary of state, did not have the kindest of words for his former boss after both men had left public office. "He was a very odd man," Kissinger said. ". . . He is a very unpleasant man. He was so nervous. It was such an effort for him to be on television. He was an artificial man in the sense that when he met someone he thought it out carefully so that nothing was spontaneous, and that meant he didn't like people. People sensed that. What I never understood is why he became a politician. He hated to meet new people. Most politicians like crowds. He didn't."

Elliott Richardson, a longtime Nixon associate, said of the 37th president, "He wanted to be the Architect of his Times." In fact, he was to a large degree a product of his times.

One of the most perceptive politicians of his era, he quickly recognized shared grievances. The Nixon coalition brought together those, as Perlstein notes, who resented "condescending and self-serving liberals 'who make their money out of plans, ideas, communication, social upheaval, happenings, excitement,' at the psychic expense of the great, ordinary . . . mass of Americans from Maine to Hawaii." Nixon began to call such culturally conservative Americans the "Silent Majority," a group involving "millions of people in the middle of the American political spectrum who do not demonstrate, who do not picket or protest loudly."

Nixon and his aides sought to walk a tightrope, wanting to appear moderate compared to explicit racists like Alabama segregationist governor and presidential candidate George Wallace, while still appealing to Wallace's resentful southern white constituency. This approach came to be known as the "**Southern Strategy**." During his career in the United States House and the Senate, Nixon acquired the reputation of a racial moderate, so much so that for a time he was seriously competitive for the African-American vote in his presidential race against John Kennedy. While vice president, Nixon supported the United States Supreme Court decision *Brown v. the Board of Education*, a step further than President Eisenhower was willing to take. He backed civil rights bills introduced in the Congress in the 1950s and the 1965 Voting Rights Act, and met publicly with Civil Rights leader Martin Luther King, Jr. in 1957. Nixon, nevertheless, "thought, basically, they [African Americans] were genetically inferior . . . He thought they couldn't achieve on a level with whites," said **John Ehrlichman**, White House counsel and assistant to the president for domestic affairs.

Audio tapes Nixon made in the Oval Office when he was president revealed he frequently used the word "nigger" and other slurs to refer to blacks. Nixon told his personal secretary, Rosemary Woods, that it would take 500 years for African Americans to catch up with whites. Nixon claimed, according to biographer Reeves, "that there had never in history been a successful or adequate black nation. Nixon also said that the Irish were mean drunks as a "natural trait," and that Italians "just don't have their heads screwed on right." Nixon, in particular, harbored a deep distrust of Jews, whom he described as "disloyal" and out to get him. "The Jews voted 95 percent against me," Nixon complained. Even the Jews he was close to, such as Kissinger and speech writer William Safire, had to deal with the president's anti-Semitism. Nixon would contemptuously refer to Kissinger as "my Jew-boy" while the senior diplomat was in the same room.

Nixon, however, to a large degree kept these prejudices close to his vest. "When Nixon embraced a 'southern strategy' that involved turning his back on the civil rights movement, his actions were dictated more by a cool calculation of political advantage than by any personal racial animosities," historians Maurice Isserman and Michael Kazin write. Seeking to build Republican support in the South, Nixon and **Attorney General John Mitchell** in 1969 asked the courts to delay enforcement of the desegregation of Mississippi schools. "Do only what the law requires," Nixon wrote in a memo. "Not one thing more." When expiration of the 1965 Voting Rights Act approached in 1970, Nixon unsuccessfully urged Congress to allow the law to lapse.

Affirmative Action

Nixon did pursue one policy that seemed, on the surface, to be friendly to the civil rights movement, supporting federally enforced guidelines regarding the hiring of African Americans and other "minorities" in private employment. This policy came to be known as "**affirmative action**." Under affirmative action, starting in 1970, all federal agencies and contractors had to meet "numerical goals and timetables" in hiring a proportionally representative number of African Americans, Mexican Americans, women and other groups that had been historically discriminated against. Many on the right criticized this program as creating a quota system that would reward less qualified applicants with jobs based on their race or gender.

Nixon, according to Isserman and Kazin, liked affirmative action for several complex reasons. "Compared to job training programs, or public works, it was a low-cost strategy for the government to boost black employment," they said. "It also fit in with his belief that 'black capitalism' would prove the solution to America's racial problems; government regulations also required the 'set-aside' of a percentage of government contracts for minority businesses. The new black middle class, who were the beneficiaries of federal largesse, might decide that economic self interest dictated a vote for Republican candidates in the future." Nixon also liked the prospect of forcing Democrats to choose between their white working class voters who would see affirmative action as an assault on the privileges of union seniority, and their African-American supporters who might benefit from affirmative action.

Compared to later Republican presidents like Ronald Reagan and George W. Bush, much of Nixon's domestic agenda was relatively liberal. In his first term, Nixon placed his name on legislation doubling the budget for the National Endowment for the Arts and the National Endowment for the Humanities. He proposed that the federal government guarantee a yearly income for all Americans. He signed laws increasing welfare spending in programs like Social Security, Aid to Families with Dependent Children (AFDC) and food stamps, and signed into law the creation of the Occupational Safety and Health Administration (OSHA) and the Environmental Protection Agency (EPA).

However, he implemented cost-benefit reviews of all environmental regulations, watering down their effectiveness, and tried to eliminate the Office of Economic Opportunity, which had been the agency charged with implementing President Johnson's War on Poverty. Nixon also launched what he called "devolution"—passing authority over programs from the federal government to the states. In conservative states where the leadership did not desire to interfere with big business and did not believe in wealth redistribution, this meant that environmental and anti-poverty programs were half-hearted at best.

NIXONOMICS

Nixon faced a major political challenge because of the economy. Lyndon Johnson's high spending on domestic programs and the Vietnam War had sparked inflation in the Democrat's later years in office. During the first half of the 1960s, through both the Kennedy and the Johnson administrations, inflation stood at a negligible 1 percent. By 1968, Johnson's last year in office, inflation quadrupled to 4 percent. In Nixon's first year in office, 1969, inflation rose to 7 percent.

While incomes for Americans improved steadily for 25 years from 1945 to 1970, the long boom began to ebb. To curb inflation, Nixon cut spending on both domestic programs and the military, increasing unemployment, which reached 6 percent by 1971. For the first time, the

**Richard M. Nixon flashes the "V" for "victory" sign.
Photo credit: Nixon Presidential Library.**

economy experienced both rising joblessness and inflation. Baffled economists combined "stagnation" and "inflation" to term the phenomenon "stagflation."

Even worse for American workers, the European and the Japanese economies began to expand faster than the United States' in the 1970s, and the United States started running trade deficits, meaning it bought more products overseas than it sold to the rest of the world. As Americans made fewer products for the international market, and Japanese cars and electronics took a larger share of the American market, the number of manufacturing jobs began a sharp decline that would continue in the early twenty-first century. One million American manufacturing jobs in the auto, steel, electronics and garment making industries disappeared between 1966 and 1971. A recession began in 1970. The American stock market became erratic, with the Dow Jones Industrial Average dropping from slightly under 1,000 to just over 800. More than 100 businesses with shares traded on the stock exchange went out of business.

Nixon believed in free-market principles, including the positive effects of reduced government regulation, but felt forced to change course because of the grim economic and political realities he faced. In August 1971, Nixon began to issue by executive orders a "New Economic Policy" that imposed a three-month freeze on wages and prices, a 10 percent tax on imports (a policy designed to boost sales of American-made goods), and took American currency off the gold standard. At the same time, the Democratic-controlled Congress boosted spending on Social Security and military veterans while Nixon accelerated government purchases of goods such as trucks, office supplies, and even toilet paper. A mild recovery began. Unemployment dropped to below 5 percent by 1972 while earnings again rose by about 4 percent in both 1971 and 1972.

Acid, Amnesty, and Abortion

The year 1972 did not bring a return to boom times, but for a while the economy improved enough to no longer be a major political handicap for Nixon.

Nevertheless, Nixon approached his re-election campaign with dread. An unknown factor was the Twenty-Sixth Amendment to the Constitution, which gave the vote to 18-year-olds and had been ratified in 1971. Revulsion that young Americans had been considered old enough to kill and die in the Vietnam War but not old enough to select their leaders propelled passage of the amendment. The youth vote was assumed to be anti-war, a distinct disadvantage for the president. Nixon had other worries. "He began seeing 1972 in apocalyptic terms," Perlstein said. "Any imaginable Democratic candidate was 'irresponsible domestically' and 'extremely dangerous internationally.' He had come to understand something profound in his two years as president, in all those afternoons brooding alone in his hideaway office in the Executive Office Building—the kind of profundity too deep to share with the mere public: 'America has only two more years as the number one power.' America had either to 'make the best deals we can between now and 1975 or increase our conventional [military] strength. No Democrat can sell this to the country.'" This sense of doom led Nixon to believe he was justified in doing anything to guarantee that he won re-election.

Chaos within the Democratic Party made Nixon's task easier. After the disastrous 1968 presidential nominating convention in Chicago, liberals (led by presidential contender and South Dakota **Senator George McGovern**) rewrote party rules to ensure that women, young people, African Americans and other traditionally disenfranchised constituencies would get fair representation in the 1972 convention to nominate the party's presidential ticket. These changes would prove to be a big advantage for McGovern in that year's Democratic nomination contest. The leading Democratic contender, the environmentalist but moderate **Senator Ed Muskie** of Maine (who had served as Hubert Humphrey's running mate in 1968), collapsed due to his poor performance in the New Hampshire primary. When polls in New Hampshire predicted Muskie would win two-thirds of the state's votes, the Nixon campaign focused early on destroying Muskie's presidential bid.

Aiming to sow bitter division within the Democratic Party, the Nixon campaign sent a fake "Citizens for Muskie" letter to Florida Democrats that accused candidate Sen. Henry "Scoop" Jackson of being arrested for "homosexual activity" and of having a secret love child. The letter also falsely stated that former Vice President Humphrey had been arrested for drunk driving while visiting a prostitute.

The highly conservative *Manchester (New Hampshire) Union Leader* newspaper printed two harsh articles that accused Muskie of using an anti-French-American slur, "Canuck," on one occasion. The Nixon re-election campaign faked the evidence for that charge, an explosive accusation in a state with a large French-American community. The newspaper also smeared Muskie's wife Jane as an alcoholic. Just before the New Hampshire primary, Muskie held a press conference in front of the *Union-Leader* offices and then appeared to break down in tears. (Muskie later said that the moisture on his cheek was melting snow.) New Hampshire voters questioned whether Muskie was tough enough to be president. Muskie won the primary, beating McGovern by 46 to 37 percent of the vote, but he was expected to do much better in a state next to his native Maine. The press interpreted Muskie's numerical win as a strategic loss. Later, when Muskie finished a disappointing fourth in Florida, the man many believed to be the strongest Democratic candidate against Nixon in November, dropped out of the race.

Nixon, meanwhile, worried that George Wallace, an outspoken segregationist, would take enough votes away from him as a third-party candidate in 1972 to deny him re-election. A would-be assassin's bullet cut short Wallace's Democratic Party insurgency. Arthur Bremer shot him during a campaign stop at a shopping mall in Wheaton, Maryland, on May 15. Bullets also hit three other people. The attack left Wallace paralyzed. He would be a paraplegic the rest of his life. Upon hearing about the shooting, Nixon and his staffers discussed whether they could plant left-wing political literature, or even pro-McGovern and Edward Kennedy campaign materials, in Bremer's hotel room in order to make it look like the president's political opponents had inspired the shooter. Law enforcement agencies, however, had already secured the hotel room.

The false stories about Muskie's wife and the proposed planting of literature in Bremer's room constituted part of what Nixon's re-election campaign called "**dirty tricks**." According to an October 10, 1972 article by *Washington Post* reporters **Bob Woodward** and Carl Bernstein, the Committee to Re-elect the President's (or, as it was called, "CREEP") dirty tricks included spying on other candidates, forging inflammatory letters to supporters and newspapers using the letterheads of other candidates and stealing confidential campaign files. These dirty tricks would culminate in the wiretapping of the Democratic National Headquarters at the Watergate Hotel in Washington, D.C., causing a scandal that would come to be known as simply as "**Watergate**."

The result of the Democratic primary campaign pleased Nixon operatives as the candidate the Republicans regarded the weakest potential Democratic nominees, McGovern, won the nomination. Seen as sincere and idealistic, McGovern certainly was the favorite of those new Democratic voters between the ages of 18 and 21 who were drawn to his strong opposition to the Vietnam War. Unfortunately for the Democrats, the McGovern campaign fell apart almost as soon as it was clear that McGovern would be the nominee. Sensing that McGovern's presidential quest was doomed, the best-known and most popular Democrats, such as Massachusetts Sen. Edward Kennedy, Humphrey, and Muskie turned McGovern down when he asked them to serve as his running mate. McGovern eventually went through 24 names of possible running mates before finally selecting the little-known freshman **Senator Thomas Eagleton** of Missouri.

The Democrats' platform, adopted by the convention, called for an immediate withdrawal from Vietnam, abolition of the draft and a minimum guaranteed income even as McGovern himself proposed legalization of marijuana and abortion rights. To many working class white voters, this agenda leaned too far to the left. Almost immediately, McGovern's nomination was overshadowed by the news that, unknown to McGovern, Eagleton had received repeated electroshock therapy as a treatment for chronic depression. Even though Eagleton had concealed his health issues, McGovern declared that he was behind his running mate "1,000 percent." Behind the scenes, McGovern pressured Eagleton to step down. It turned out later that Eagleton had been the source of an anonymous quote reported by conservative columnist Robert Novak that the Democratic nominee was "for amnesty [for Vietnam draft dodgers], abortion, and legalization of pot."

The Nixon campaign picked up on this phrase, and McGovern was labeled the candidate of "acid [LSD], amnesty, and abortion." Eagleton would be replaced on the Democratic ticket by Kennedy in-law Sargent Shriver, the first director of the Peace Corps. After this incident, voters doubted McGovern's competence. Following the Democratic National Convention, Democratic mayors, governors and members of Congress often refused to campaign at McGovern's side. Nixon also would not agree to debates with the Democrat. McGovern probably made his already hapless campaign hopeless when he made a speech in October promising the immediate withdrawal of U.S. forces from Vietnam without even setting as a precondition the return of hundreds of American prisoners of war from North Vietnam.

Shortly before Election Day, Secretary of State Henry Kissinger announced that "We have now heard from both Vietnams and it is obvious that a war that has been raging for ten years is drawing to a conclusion . . . We believe that peace is at hand." Nixon later admitted that he delayed peace talks with North Vietnam because he knew that Americans would be reluctant to hand presidential power to what was perceived as a weak Democratic candidate while the war was still going on.

Election Day 1972 resulted in one of the biggest landslides in American history, with Nixon winning 61 percent of the vote and losing only Massachusetts and the District of Columbia in the Electoral College. Nixon even won 35 percent of Democratic voters. Young people did not turn out in the numbers expected and were not as solidly Democratic as many had predicted. In spite of Nixon's overwhelming success, the president had no coattails. Republicans lost a pair of seats in the Senate, giving the Democrats a 57-43 majority, and picked up only 12 new seats in the House of Representatives, where the Democrats still claimed a commanding 243-192 edge.

Stagflation

Nixon never cared for the wage and price controls he implemented in his first term and, with his re-election secured, he lifted these caps in January 1973. Unfortunately, he unleashed devastating inflation with high employment causing **stagflation**. Worldwide economic growth in 1972 spurred big demand for almost every item while the devaluation of the dollar Nixon imposed reduced the cost of American goods for overseas markets by 10 percent.

The overheated consumer demand boosted wholesale prices by an incredible 20 percent in the first half of the year, resulting in an 8 percent spike in consumer prices. In June, Nixon relented and placed a 60-day freeze on all prices. Not wanting to sell at artificially low prices, some producers responded by holding back goods from the market. This created shortages. Nixon again changed course and began easing price controls. To prevent events from spinning out of control, the Federal Reserve Board increased the prime interest rate from 10 to 12 percent, which cooled down the economy.

The good news did not last. Americans didn't know it, but they were at the dawn of a new and harder economic reality dominated by de-industrialization, the rise of America as a lower-wage service-sector economy, increasing workplace automation that reduced the number of jobs available, and a decline in union membership along with a deterioration of the average family's standard of living. Adjusted for inflation, real wages would decline by 2 percent a year from 1973 to the 1990s. Poverty rates had fallen through the 1960s to a low of 11 percent in 1973 but would climb through the 1970s to 15 percent by 1982.

THE FIRST ENERGY CRISIS

On shaky ground, the American economy took another major hit in late 1973 when the Arab members of the Organization of Petroleum Exporting Countries (OPEC) staged an oil boycott of the United States following that year's Arab-Israeli War. The second Middle Eastern war in six years, the so-called Yom Kippur War, began on October 6 during the Jewish holiday when Egypt, Jordan and Syria (along with military units provided by Iraq and Libya) attempted to retake land (the Sinai Peninsula, the West Bank and the Golan Heights) occupied by Israel since the overwhelming defeat of the Arabs in 1967's Six-Day War.

With Israel initially caught ill-prepared, Egyptian forces successfully crossed the Suez Canal and began to retake chunks of the Sinai. Saudi Arabia and other energy-rich Arab states increased the price of oil to frighten Western countries from rushing to Israel's defense. Frightened about her nation's survival, Israeli Prime Minister Golda Meir's cabinet discussed using the nuclear weapons the Israelis had already developed.

Worried that the Israeli use of nuclear weapons would provoke the Soviet Union to use its arsenal to defend its Arab allies, Nixon and Secretary of State Henry Kissinger began airlifting military supplies to help the Israelis. American jets delivered more military equipment and ammunition to the Israelis in 1973 than they had brought to the besieged city of West Berlin during the 1948-1949 airlifts. The tide of the war turned. Israeli troops recovered, surrounded Egyptian forces in the Sinai and reached within 20 miles of the Syrian capital of Damascus. The United States and the Soviet Union brokered a truce. A cease-fire was signed November 11. In retaliation for American aid to the Israelis, Saudi Arabia, Kuwait, Iraq and Libya cut off all oil shipments to the United States and reduced their shipments to the rest of the world by 5 percent. About 35 percent of American oil supplies in 1973 came from foreign sources. The embargo hit the

Map 31.1 Israel, Six Day War 1967

United States in a vulnerable spot, as workers since World War II had moved to suburbs farther and farther away from their jobs. About 85 percent of American workers drove to work every day.

In Northern Virginia near the national capital, shortages became acute, and motorists waited as long as three hours to fill their tanks. Gas prices at the pump quadrupled from 30 cents a gallon to $1.20 (or from $1.46 to $5.82 in 2011 dollars) at the height of what was widely called "**The Energy Crisis**." Shortages forced a rationing system on service station owners. Owners of vehicles with license plates ending in even numbers could buy gasoline only on even-numbered days while those with plates ending in odd numbers could refuel only on odd days. Many gas stations limited purchases to ten gallons per customer. Violence broke out at some gas stations.

Nixon tried a patchwork of temporary fixes. At Nixon's prompting, the Congress banned gasoline purchases on Sunday and extended daylight saving time from January 6, 1974 to February 23, 1975, controversial because this forced many school children to wait at bus stops in the dark or for their parents to drive them to campuses before sunrise. Furthermore, in 1974 the Congress set a national maximum highway speed limit of 55 miles per hour.

OPEC lifted the embargo on March 18, 1974, but the damage to the economy had been done. OPEC set oil prices at $11.65 a barrel, up from $1.80 in 1970. (In 2011 dollars, the increase was from $7.87 to $50.92 a barrel.) High gasoline prices rippled through the economy. Wholesale prices jumped by 18 percent in 1973, and then consumer prices increased an average of 12 percent the following year. The overall inflation rate wobbled between 8 and 10 percent. Meanwhile, from January 1973 to December 1974, the Dow Jones Industrial average dropped 45 percent.

THE "NIXON DOCTRINE"

The **1973 Energy Crisis** revealed the limits of American global power, as did the continued U.S. frustrations in Southeast Asia. As mentioned before, Nixon wanted to be an architect of the world order, and he and his chief foreign policy advisor, Henry Kissinger, would later take credit for strategic planning they claimed not only ended American military involvement in Vietnam, but also opened diplomatic relations with China and achieved a more peaceful relationship with America's chief Cold War rival, the Soviet Union. In fact, Nixon's foreign policy represented less a well-planned global strategy than a series of at-times skillful improvisations in response to rapidly shifting global events.

From the beginning, the key player in Nixon's foreign policy was national security advisor Kissinger. Later elevated to secretary of state by Nixon and kept on by Nixon's successor, **Gerald Ford**, Kissinger saw himself as a hard-bitten pragmatist. His Jewish family had fled Nazi Germany in 1938. Highly intelligent, Kissinger received a Ph.D. from Harvard University in 1954, and became a professor of government and international affairs there the same year. He impressed Nixon with his sharp mind, his pragmatism and the sweep of his vision for American foreign policy.

Nixon saw a clear American victory in Vietnam as already impossible by the time he took office in 1969. Early on, the White House unveiled the so-called "**Nixon Doctrine**" in which the United States would rely on allies such as Japan, and unsavory regimes such the white supremacist apartheid government in South Africa, the dictatorship ruling Pakistan, and the Shah's ruthless monarchy in Iran to bear more of the responsibility for checking the spread of communism. Key allies would be protected by America's nuclear shield, but other nations would be expected to "assume the primary responsibility

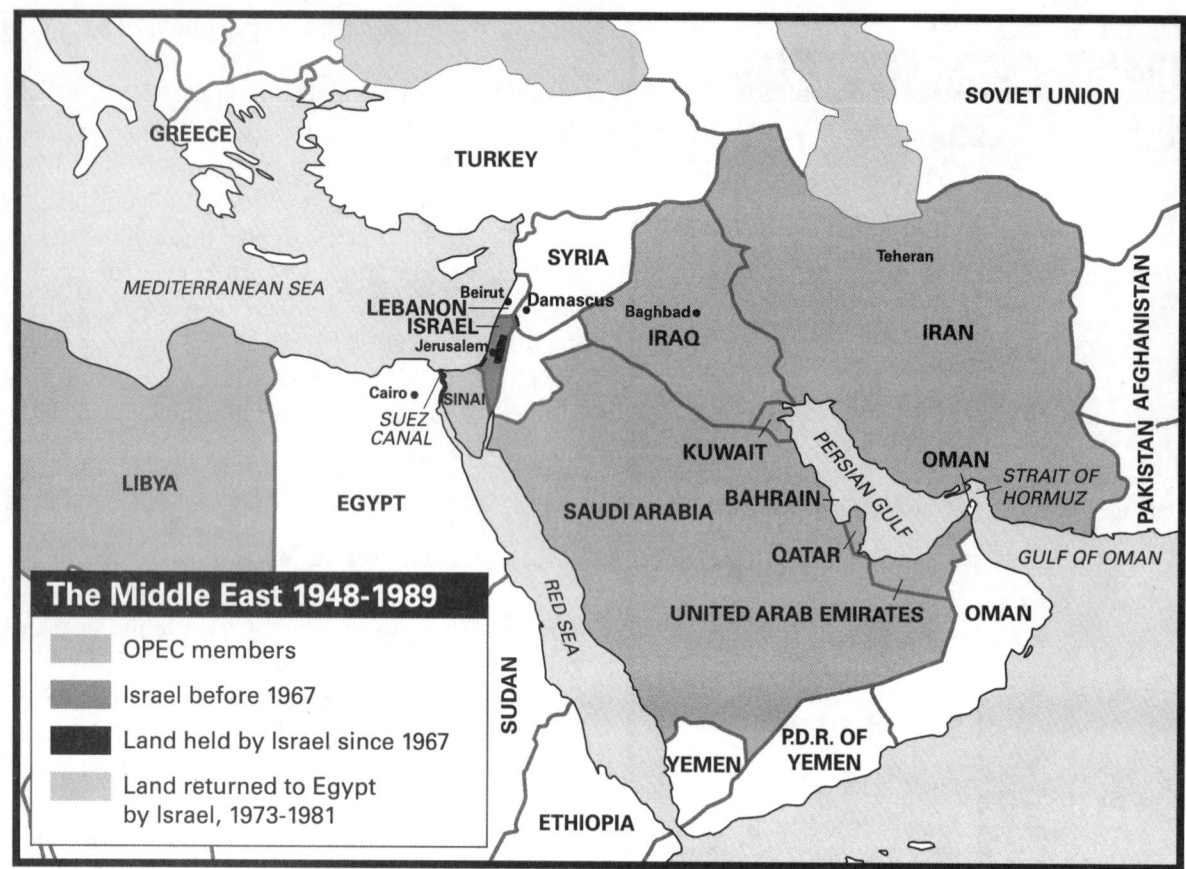

Map 31.2 The Middle East 1948-1989

of providing the manpower for [their] own defense," as diplomatic historian William Bundy puts it.

A balance of power between the Americans and the Soviets became Nixon and Kissinger's obsessive priority. Human rights and self-determination in the developing world did not enter into their calculations. As part of the Nixon Doctrine, American sales of fighter planes, tanks, radar, anti-aircraft weapons, and other military hardware to American allies escalated dramatically in the Nixon years from under $2 billion to more than $15 billion. Pro-American nations like Iran and South Vietnam would control some of the largest militaries in the world, forces armed with some of the most sophisticated weapons. In the early 1970s, with Washington's encouragement the Shah of Iran spent $35 billion of that nation's oil revenues upgrading and expanding the military, mostly on American-manufactured weapons, even though life expectancy in Iran was only 50, childhood mortality remained high, and six out of every ten Iranians remained illiterate. In many American client states, health and education took a back seat to the larger needs of the Cold War.

A Coup in Chile

The Nixon Doctrine would claim human rights victims around the globe. Chile represents one heart-breaking case in point. On September 4, 1970, a Marxist, Salvador Allende Gossens, won a democratic election for the presidency of Chile, a mineral-rich nation whose border snakes along more than half of South America's Pacific coast. Chile had been one of the most stable nations in Latin America since the writing of its 1839 constitution, a country generally ruled through an ostensible democracy controlled by a small elite. Chile was of interest to the United States primarily because of its rise as the world's leading producer of copper, used in building motors, generators, cables, and wires. By the late twentieth century, two American mining companies dominated Chile's copper industry and International Telephone and Telegraph controlled Chile's phone services.

Allende, the leader of Chile's Socialist Party, rose to political prominence in the 1960s. "Despite Chile's relatively prosperous position among South American nations, millions of its people lived in desperate poverty, and this genuinely moved Allende," wrote journalist Stephen Kinzer. He advocated peaceful revolution, through democratic elections. IT&T and other companies that gave money to Nixon's 1968 campaign asked for the president's help in preventing Allende from taking power, and Nixon obliged, asking the CIA to instigate a coup. In addition, many in Chile's business community and military were fiercely anti-communist and had convinced themselves

**The Shah of Iran, President Nixon, and Mrs. Nixon in formal attire for a state dinner in the White House.
October 2, 1969   Photo credit: Nixon Presidential Library**

that Pinochet would destroy their country and they happily accepted the outside assistance Nixon provided.

The CIA encouraged military leaders to overthrow their democratic government. After Allende was sworn in as president in 1970, American companies conspired to not fill orders for spare parts, which forced the closing of factories operating in Chile. Nevertheless, Allende stood up to American pressure and persuaded the Chilean Congress to nationalize the copper industry and then the national phone company controlled by IT&T. The CIA's destabilization campaign, however, began to wreck Chile's economy and weakened Allende's government by 1972. The CIA successfully recruited Chilean General Augusto Pinochet to lead a military coup, which toppled the Allende regime on September 11, 1973. Using American weapons and money, soldiers seized control of police stations, government buildings, and radio stations. Rebel airplanes, believed flown by American pilots, fired rockets into the presidential palace. Pinochet's military dictatorship later claimed that Allende committed suicide rather than surrender, while others say he was murdered.

In the first days of the Pinochet dictatorship, approximately 13,500 civilians were arrested. "Thousands ended up in the two main football stadiums in Santiago," wrote journalist Naomi Klein. "... Inside the National Stadium, death replaced football as a public spectacle. Soldiers prowled the bleachers with hooded collaborators who pointed out 'subversives'; the ones who were selected were hauled off to locker rooms and skyboxes transformed into makeshift torture chambers. Hundreds were executed. Lifeless bodies started showing up on the side of major highways or floating in murky modern canals."

One of the victims was the left-wing Chilean folksinger Victor Jara. Soldiers broke the performer's hands to deny him his ability to play the guitar and later shot him 44 times. In the days immediately after the coup, the Pinochet regime executed 3,200, imprisoned 80,000 and forced 200,000 more to flee. Many Chileans who survived torture reported that unidentified persons who spoke English with American accents oversaw their brutal interrogations. By the year after the coup, 1974, Chile's economy shrank by 15 percent and unemployment, which had been 3 percent under Allende, skyrocketed to 20 percent. By 1988, Chile's economy stabilized but 45 percent of the population had fallen below the poverty line. This was the Nixon Doctrine in action. Allies were rewarded for being anti-communist, even if they were brutally anti-democratic and poorly served their people.

Cracks in the Communist World

Kissinger and Nixon sought to reduce the overwhelming pressure on the American military by easing tensions with the Soviet Union, a chief supplier of weapons to North Vietnam. Nixon's pursuit of warmer relations with Mos-

**President Nixon meets with China's Communist Party Leader, Mao Zedong.
February 29, 1972, Photo credit: Nixon Presidential Library**

cow came to be known by the French term détente. Nixon and Kissinger quickly exploited a dangerous conflict that developed in the communist world in 1969. The Soviets and the Chinese almost came to war, exchanging gunfire along the Ussari River that separated the two nations near Vladivostok in far East Asia. The Soviets responded to the incident by increasing their military presence there from 70,000 to 240,000 soldiers. Soviet leaders became convinced that China represented a serious threat to its security. At one point the Soviet Defense Ministry compared Chinese leader Mao Zedong to Adolf Hitler. The Nixon White House sought to play both nations off of each other.

The White House realized that if the U.S. cultivated a friendlier relationship with China, the Soviet Union—suffering from consumer shortages and feeling the economic strain of the long Cold War—would feel threatened on two fronts. The Kremlin might become more attentive to American foreign policy concerns, such as pressuring the North Vietnamese to make peace. The American president also saw China as an ascending power.

Since the triumph of the communists in the 1949 Chinese Revolution, the United States had never recognized the Beijing regime as the legitimate Chinese government and had successfully prevented the People's Republic's admission to the United Nations. The breakaway Nationalist regime in Taiwan still held China's seat in the UN. This put the United States at odds with the rest of the Western alliance, and the People's Republic took China's seat at the UN on October 25, 1971, over U.S. objections.

Even with this dispute, on December 8, 1970, Chinese Premier Zhou Enlai (the second most powerful man in the country) sent Nixon a letter through Pakistani diplomats to discuss the future American relationship to Taiwan. Beginning in 1971, Kissinger opened up a secret diplomatic dialogue with Zhou. Kissinger faked an illness so he could without detection spend a week in China in July of that year to negotiate a new phase in American-Chinese relations.

The first sign of a thaw in Sino-American relations came on April 6 of that year when, at the end of the World Table Tennis Championships in Japan, the American team captain received an invitation by the Chinese captain to play a week of exhibition matches in Beijing. The invitation came from Chinese Communist Party leader Mao.

**President and Mrs. Nixon at the Great Wall of China.
February 24, 1972. Photo credit: Nixon Presidential Library**

The American team was the first official U.S. delegation in the country since the 1950s.

Kissinger arranged for a week long visit in China by President Nixon, from February 21 to 28, 1972, the first appearance by an American leader in that nation since the 1949 revolution. The visit greatly enhanced Nixon's standing with the American public. Never one for understatement, Nixon described the visit as "the week that changed the world." In fact, it was just a start for fuller relations between the United States and China. The United States established full diplomatic relations with China under President Jimmy Carter on January 1, 1979 and recognized Taiwan as just part of a single Chinese nation, even though Americans continued to give aid to the anti-communist regime on the island.

The opening to China, as Nixon and Kissinger expected, inspired the Soviets to move toward détente—the French term Kissinger used to describe warmer relations between Washington and Moscow. Nixon visited Soviet leader Leonid Brezhnev in Moscow in May 1972, striking a deal that allowed the Soviets, suffering from inefficient farming, to buy American wheat and leading to the **Strategic Arms Limitation Treaty (SALT I)**. The United States and the USSR agreed to cap the number of intercontinental ballistic missiles either side could install. Under SALT, both the Americans and the Russians pledged to not develop new anti-ballistic missiles, which could have provoked an expensive arms race.

"Peace With Honor"

Nixon's evolving relationship with the Soviets and the Chinese had less impact on the Vietnam War than he hoped. The Russians wanted the war to end. "[T]he Soviet Union was fed up with the war," journalist Stanley Karnow wrote in *Vietnam: A History*. "Its massive aid program to North Vietnam, a region outside its true realm of interest, was draining its domestic economy." The Chinese, at the same time, were worried about the massive buildup of Soviet troops along its border and sought a closer relationship with the Americans as a protection against Russian aggression. The Beijing government knew support of North Vietnam would complicate that objective.

Yet, the worries of the Russians and the Chinese were of no concern to North Vietnam. The North Vietnamese saw themselves as fighting a war of national independence, not as serving as pawns for communist super-states. The relationship between North Vietnam and Russia strained badly as the Kremlin increasingly urged a settlement. The Vietnamese, furthermore, had a difficult and often hostile relationship with China stretching back centuries.

Nixon had no grand scheme to cut this Gordian knot. As with détente and the opening to China, Nixon and Kissinger improvised. Nixon said repeatedly that he was seeking "peace with honor." To the outside world this meant that the United States would not withdraw until it had guaranteed the survival of a non-communist South Vietnam. To Nixon's inner circle, this meant getting out of Vietnam without making Nixon appear like he was "the first president of the United States to lose a war." By the time he was sworn in as president, Nixon believed that a clear military victory in Vietnam was impossible but hoped he could leave behind a stable, adequately strong South Vietnam as American forces withdrew.

He hoped to achieve this through what the White House called "**Vietnamization**," simply another application of the "Nixon Doctrine." Nixon hoped to replace American soldiers in Vietnam with South Vietnamese troops heavily armed with U.S.-provided weaponry.

At the same time, Nixon tried to frighten the North Vietnamese into accepting American terms utilizing what he called "the madman theory." As Nixon told **White House Chief of Staff H.R. "Bob" Haldeman**, "I want the North Vietnamese to believe that I've reached the point where I might do anything to stop the war. We'll just slip the word to them that, 'for God's sake, you know Nixon is obsessed about Communists. We can't restrain him when he's angry—he has his hand on the nuclear button' and [North Vietnamese leader] Ho Chi Minh himself will be in Paris in two days begging for peace."

By April 30, 1969, the number of American military personnel in Southeast Asia reached a record 543,000. Troop levels would drop from this peak for the rest of the war. American hopes for an end to the war briefly perked up when Ho died on September 2, 1969, but the communist leader's successors instead vowed to continue the struggle until "there is not a single aggressor in the country."

Operation Menu

Within weeks of the president's 1969 inauguration, generals convinced Nixon to launch an intensive bombing campaign aimed at destroying North Vietnamese "sanctuaries," supply routes and weapons depots the communists had created in neighboring, neutral Cambodia. Nixon kept the bombing campaign, dubbed "Operation Menu" secret from the public and even the Congress. From its launch in February 1969 until 1973, Operation Menu resulted in 3,600 missions dropping 500,000 tons of bombs on eastern Cambodia. Bombers also attacked communist positions in Laos as well. The Cambodian government led by Prince Norodom Sihanouk had been fighting a low-intensity war with communist forces that called themselves the "Khmer Rouge." (The Khmers are Cambodia's largest ethnic group while "Rouge" is French for "red," the symbolic color of the international communist movement.) The Khmer Rouge represented one of the most fanatical communist forces in the world. Their leader, Soloth Sar, went by the *nom de guerre* "Pol Pot." Winning a scholarship, he briefly studied at a university in Paris, where he became a Marxist before dropping out and returning to his homeland. By 1962 Pol Pot rose to the leadership of the Cambodian Communist Party.

Meanwhile, Prince Sihanouk could see the strength of the North Vietnamese Army and sought to avoid confrontation with these forces by avoiding an alliance with the United States. He allowed the North Vietnamese to use his territory to supply troops and provide hiding places outside the grasp of the United States military.

American planes began to follow and strafe Vietcong and North Vietnamese soldiers as they crossed into Cambodia, but sometimes they hit civilians. By 1966, Sihanouk claimed that "hundreds of our people" had been killed in American attacks. As American bombers caused approximately 150,000 deaths of mostly unarmed peasants during Operation Menu, from March 1969 to May 1970, the Khmer Rouge enjoyed more support and began to control more territory. "[T]he carpet bombing of Cambodia's countryside by American B-52s," wrote historian Ben Kiernan. ". . . was probably the most important single factor in Pol Pot's rise."

Nixon aides like Bob Haldeman always said that if there had been no Vietnam War, there would have been no Watergate scandal. In May 1969, the *New York Times* revealed the bombing campaign in Laos and Cambodia. Angered and wanting to know who revealed the secret military operation to the press, Nixon ordered FBI wiretaps of four reporters and 13 government officials. Without court authorization, these illegal wiretaps started the Nixon White House pattern of lawbreaking and violations of civil liberties, which would continue and expand until Watergate forced Nixon's resignation in August 1974.

The Moratorium

Nixon's war plans depended on his ability to convince the Vietnamese that the American public was as resolute about the war as the communists. As historian Ronald H. Spector said, Nixon had most of the public with him regarding Vietnam early in his presidency. A May 1969 Harris poll revealed that only 9 percent of the American public would approve a peace settlement that left the door open to an eventual communist victory. "Like Johnson and Nixon," Spector wrote, "the majority of Americans in 1968 and 1969 wanted to 'get out' but 'didn't want to lose.'"

This didn't prevent between 1 million and 2 million Americans from participating in the so-called "**Moratorium**," simultaneous protests against the Vietnam War, on October 15, 1969. About 100,000 protestors participated in Boston Commons alone. Another 250,000 participated in events staged in Washington, D.C. Supporters of the protests wore black armbands and paid respect to servicemen who had died in the war. Future president Bill Clinton, on a Rhodes scholarship, helped organize a demonstration of 1,000 people who picketed in front of the American embassy in London. Protestors in Newton, Kansas, rang a bell every four seconds with each toll representing a fallen soldier while a funeral procession unfolded in Milwaukee. In Houston, the names of the war dead were read out, one reader pausing and choking up when he came upon the name of a friend.

Furious that the Moratorium protests might make him look weak to the North Vietnamese, Nixon dispatched his tart-tongued **Vice President Spiro Agnew** to smear the mass movement as the work of traitors. Nevertheless, as *Time* magazine put it, the middle class presence at the day's events gave "new respectability and popularity" to the anti-war movement. Nixon dismissed the protests, insisting that, "Under no circumstances will I be affected."

"An Age of Anarchy"

Irritated by Cambodian Prince Sihanouk's neutrality, the Americans supported Cambodian General Lon Nol when he overthrew the government in 1970 and launched a more aggressive war against the Khmer Rouge forces. The Americans provided Nol with more weapons but did not respect him enough to consult him before the United States launched an invasion of Cambodia in March. The American public was informed of the invasion on April 30, 1970. Nixon claimed that a super "headquarters for the entire Communist military operation in South Vietnam" lay in the Cambodian jungles and that destroying that base was a key to American victory. Anticipating a new round of protests, Nixon in a televised address delivered a call to arms aimed at his supporters in the continuing strife within America:

> We live in an age of anarchy. We see mindless attacks on all the great institutions which have been created by free civilizations in the last five hundred years . . . I would rather be a one-term President and do what I believe is right than to be a two-term President at the cost of seeing America become a second-rate power and to see this nation accept the first defeat in its proud 190-year history . . . It is not our power but our will and character that is being tested tonight.

After the speech, telegrams sent to the White House praising the president outnumbered those criticizing him by a 6-1 margin. While visiting the Pentagon, Nixon said of anti-war protestors, "You see these bums, you know, blowing up the campuses. Listen, the boys that are on college campuses today are the luckiest people in the world, going to the greatest universities, and here they are, burning up the books, storming around about this issue . . . you name it. Get rid of the war and there will be another [issue.]" On May 2, *The New York Times* informed the public of a secret bombing campaign that had begun in North Vietnam, the first such bombings in the North since Johnson had suspended the attacks in 1968. The bombing, and the invasion of Cambodia, angered senators and members of the House who believed that the president, by not consulting with the legislative branch before taking military actions, was essentially suspending the part of the Constitution that gave the power to declare war exclusively to the Congress.

Four Dead in Ohio

Shortly after Nixon announced that U.S. forces had invaded Cambodia, anti-war protests opened at **Kent State University** in Ohio. The protestors set fire to the ROTC (Reserve Officer Training CORP) building and burned an American flag. Students then tried to set fire to the campus library. On May 2, Ohio Governor James Rhodes ordered state National Guard units to the campus and pledged to use "every force possible" to quell the disorder. On May 3, the Guardsmen used tear gas to disperse a crowd in front of the university president's residence. Guardsmen gored two students with the sharp edges of their bayonets while the protestors hurled rocks at the troops.

Close to noon on May 4, Guardsmen faced a hail of rocks thrown by the protestors. They fired canisters of tear gas and advanced on a crowd of angry students. "The Guardsmen feared they were out of tear gas and panicked as the protestors threw rocks and chanted, 'Pigs off campus! Pigs off campus!'" Perlstein wrote. At around 12:24 p.m. several of the troops dropped to one knee and fired in the direction of a group of students "in a parking lot beyond the fence," firing 67 rounds in 13 seconds. Thirteen students, "mostly bystanders," fell, with one paralyzed and four (Allison Krause, William Schroeder, Jeff Miller and Sandra Lee Scheuer) killed.

Two of the deceased were 19 years old; the other two were 20. Many of the victims were not in any way involved with the protests and were simply walking to class when struck by bullets.

Later that week to prevent protests, 448 campuses closed. Demonstrations took place at more than 1,100 schools with an estimated 2 million students going on strike. On May 14 at Jackson State College in Mississippi, an historically black college, two African-American students died during an uprising when police fired into a dormitory. Many in Nixon's "Silent Majority" loudly cheered the action of the National Guard at Kent State and the crackdowns elsewhere and insisted the students, even if they were bystanders, deserved what happened to them. A Gallup poll indicated that 58 percent of Americans blamed the students for their deaths.

Angry that Mayor John Lindsay of New York lowered flags at half-staff in honor of the Kent State dead, 200 construction workers, so-called hardhats, charged into an anti-war rally, beating the protestors with fists, pipes and hammers. Many of the blue-collar workers shouted, "Kill the Commie bastards" and "Love it [America] or leave it." It was later revealed that the New York City police knew the assault would happen and chose to stand by and let it unfold. A few weeks later, thousands of hardhats staged a patriotic rally in support of the war that reached New York's financial district. Stockbrokers saluted the construction workers, showering them in ticker tape.

A picture of a 14-year-old girl, Mary Ann Vecchio, kneeling beside the body of a dead student at Kent State and lifting her arms as if in prayer, won a Pulitzer Prize for the photographer John Filo. Printed in newspapers around the world, the picture became an iconic image of America at war with itself and inspired the rock star Neil Young to pen the song "Ohio."

> Tin soldiers and Nixon's coming/
> We're finally on our own/
> This summer I hear the drumming/
> Four dead in Ohio/
>
> Gotta get down to it/
> Soldiers are gunning us down/
> Should have been done long ago/
> What if you knew her/
> And found her dead on the ground?/
> How can you run when you know?

"The song was banned from Ohio playlists at the urging of Governor Rhodes," Perlstein wrote, "That helped send it shooting up the hit parade: one more scene in the new American civil war." In October, a grand jury cleared the Guardsmen involved in the shooting, though it indicted students for arson and other offenses prior to the massacre. If Nixon's political objective had been to divide and conquer the country, by this point it appeared he had won.

"Collapsing in the Field"

Nixon announced an American withdrawal from Cambodia on June 30, 1970, and by then dropped reference to the communist headquarters, which had proven to be largely a myth. Vietnamization was already clearly failing. In 1971, the United States played a support role as it directed a South Vietnamese invasion of neighboring Laos. Again, the justification was the presence of a North Vietnamese supply line—the so-called Ho Chi Minh Trail—in a nearby neutral nation. This operation ended in disaster as the South Vietnamese army performed poorly. South Vietnamese officers in charge of the operation proved to be incapable.

Regardless of the readiness of their South Vietnamese allies, the number of American personnel in South Vietnam, Cambodia and Laos dropped from approximately 536,100 in 1968 to 156,800. American combat deaths dropped from 20,600 in 1968 (Johnson's last year directing the war effort) to 1,380 in 1971. "The simple truth is that Nixon's strategy in this period amounted to a managed retreat," historian William Bundy argues. Vietnamization had an unintended consequence, however. It badly demoralized the soldiers remaining in combat who had no desire to be the last to die in a cause the Nixon administration had essentially given up on. Morale also declined as draftees made up an ever-larger percentage of troops in the field. In 1965, only 21 percent of the combat troops in Vietnam were drafted. After 1970, draftees made up about 70 percent of the combat force. (Nixon and the Congress acted to end the draft in 1973.)

In the early 1970s, many military officers worried that the armed services in Southeast Asia were in a state of mutiny. A new word, "fragging," had entered the military vocabulary. **Fragging** referred specifically to the murder of commanding officers in combat, usually when the officer made an unpopular decision, was inept, demeaning to soldiers, or put his men unnecessarily in harm's way. The term comes from the small percussion fragmentation hand grenades often used in such homicides. In one such incident, Private Gary Hendricks had been ordered to stand guard at night near the Da Nang Airbase. Sergeant Richard Tate discovered Hendricks asleep while on duty and "gave the private a tongue lashing, but took no further action," according to historian Peter Brush. Around midnight the following day, Hendricks threw a fragmentation grenade into a bunker occupied by Sergeant

Tate. "The grenade landed on Tate's stomach and the subsequent blast blew his legs off, killing the father of three from Asheville, North Carolina, who had only three weeks left on his tour of duty," said Brush. Hendricks confessed to the murder and was convicted by general court-martial. His death sentence was reduced to life in prison. Hendrick's case was but one of 209 fragging incidents resulting in 34 deaths in 1970. By July 1972, Army officials believed 551 fraggings had killed 86 and injured more than 700.

By the last years of the Vietnam War, the military command uncovered numerous cases of "bounty hunting" in which soldiers raised money to pay someone to murder an unpopular and/or dangerous officer. Soldiers also began to openly defy orders. In 1971 in Laos, a captain ordered two platoons to charge into withering enemy fire. The soldiers said no. "A lieutenant colonel pleaded, then ordered," Perlstein wrote. "Fifty-three still refused. They also refused to give their names. No disciplinary action was taken. The brass also feared that the mutiny would spread brigade-wide.

The American army was collapsing in the field. "I just work hard at surviving so I can go home and protest the killing," explained one GI. At Fort Bliss, soldiers were calling commanding officers by their first names, who in turn passed anyone through basic training who promised he wouldn't go absent without leave (AWOLs went up fivefold between 1966 and 1971) . . . In Vietnam, soldiers wrote semi-seditious slogans on their helmet headliners ("The unwilling, led by the unqualified, doing the unnecessary, for the ungrateful . . .) and, caught in infractions, responded, 'What are you going to do about it, send me to 'Nam?'"

Drug use spiraled among soldiers, according to one official report. The American command in Saigon estimated that 65,000 soldiers operating in the theater were "on drugs" in 1970. An American helicopter pilot, Fred Hickey, reported that entire units —from privates to the commanding officers—were "doing heroin."

Unit cohesion collapsed as American units turned not only on their officers but also on each other. Hickey told Stanley Karnow that in his unit, GIs split into factions, "the red necks from Texas and the Deep South who hated the California and New York liberals, and vice versa . . . The blacks were moving into their black power thing, and they got militant . . . Everybody seemed to be at everybody else's throat. You had to speak softly, mind your own business, sleep with a weapon at all times, and only trust your closest buddies, nobody else. I had a knife attached to my boot."

Meanwhile, an ever-larger number of soldiers returning home became harsh critics of the war, with **Vietnam Veterans Against the War** (VVAW), formed in 1967, eventually claiming 25,000 members. The group staged the 'Winter Soldier Investigation" in January 1971. The WSI served as a mock war crimes trial, in which members of the group described human rights violations they had witnessed while in Vietnam. On April 23, the VVAW staged another protest, including almost 1,000 veterans, in which they tossed their medals and combat ribbons on the U.S. Capitol steps. The most prominent members of the VVAW, future Massachusetts senator and presidential candidate John Kerry, spoke for many who had battled in Vietnam during two hours of testimony before the Senate Foreign Relations Committee on April 22. The war violated American principles, Kerry argued, and it was immoral to ask for further sacrifice for a cause entirely in vain. "We are asking Americans to think about . . . how do you ask a man to be the last man to die in Vietnam?" Kerry asked. "How do you ask a man to be the last man to die for a mistake?"

THE PENTAGON PAPERS

Richard Nixon deeply believed in secrecy and felt threatened whenever White House discussions became public knowledge. This extended even to public knowledge about debates within previous administrations. His volcanic temper exploded, therefore, with *The New York Times*' 1971 publication of what came to be known as "**The Pentagon Papers**," a huge collection of government memos on Vietnam from the period just after World War II to the Kennedy and Johnson administrations that had been archived and analyzed by the Defense Department under the order of former Defense Secretary Robert McNamara in 1967. The documents spanned 47 volumes, complete with 3,000 pages of commentary by unnamed government historians. The papers revealed that several Democratic and Republican administrations had intentionally misled the American public about the military's success in Vietnam and the stability and strength of the United States' ally South Vietnam.

The Nixon administration rushed to the federal courts to halt publication of the documents after the *Times* published three installments. The Justice Department won a temporary retraining order to stop further publication by the *Times* and the *Washington Post*, which had begun to publish its own series. On June 30, 1971, the United States Supreme Court lifted the order, holding that freedom of the press stood paramount over administration concerns about secrecy.

Nixon was not done with the matter. "I want to know who is behind this, and I want the most complete investigation that can be conducted," Nixon shouted. "... I don't want excuses. I want results. I want it done, whatever the costs." Nixon's secret investigation revealed the source of the leak, **Daniel Ellsberg**, a Pentagon official during the McNamara era. Egil "Bud" Krogh, a White House assistant, sought to damage the reputation of Ellsberg and prevent further press leaks. "Anyone who opposes us, we'll destroy," Krogh said. "As a matter of fact, anyone who doesn't support us, we'll destroy." The team Krogh assembled to "plug" leaks became known as the "**White House Plumbers**." The Plumbers, which included White House Special Counsel Charles Colson, former CIA Agent E. Howard Hunt, and retired FBI agent G. Gordon Liddy, would play a key role in Watergate.

They compiled a White House "enemies list" of 200 names, including celebrities such as liberal actor Gregory Peck, star of the movie version of *To Kill a Mockingbird*, Super Bowl-winning New York Jets quarterback Joe Namath, reporter Daniel Schorr of CBS News and print journalist Stanley Karnow. The Plumbers put Ellsberg under surveillance and in one of their many illegal acts, burglarized the office of his psychiatrist hoping to find damaging evidence about his mental health. A grand jury had indicted Ellsberg for theft of the *Pentagon Papers,* and he went on trial in January 1973, but all charges were dropped on May 11 after news broke about the Plumbers' burglary. During the summer of 1974, a jury convicted White House aides Ehrlichman and G. Gordon Liddy of violating the psychiatrist's civil rights and sent the pair to federal prison.

THE CHRISTMAS BOMBING

By the start of 1972, the president could correctly point out that he had withdrawn more than 400,000 troops from Southeast Asia. Now, combat deaths were down to about 10 a week. Kissinger was secretly negotiating with the government committee that had run North Vietnam since Ho's death. Yet, the war was going to take one more bloody turn that year.

The North Vietnamese launched their "Easter Offensive" on March 30, with more than 120,000 North Vietnamese Army and Vietcong soldiers initially overwhelming South Vietnamese forces in the northern provinces, the Central Highlands and the area just north of the capital, Saigon. "Equipped with Soviet artillery, rockets and tanks," the North Vietnamese made big gains. The Americans, on the other hand, had only 6,000 combat soldiers left of the 70,000 remaining in Vietnam. South Vietnam had a million armed soldiers, but they were stretched to the breaking point.

North Vietnam was beating the South Vietnamese forces badly because, as Nixon observed in his diary, "the enemy is willing to sacrifice in order to win, while the South Vietnamese simply aren't willing to pay that much of a price in order to avoid losing." Politically unable to re-introduce combat troops, Nixon pounded North Vietnam and communist positions in South Vietnam with bombs, American B-52s flying about 50,000 sorties south of the demilitarized zone that separated the two countries. The bombing in the North was sustained and brutal, with 125,000 tons of bombs dropped there, and hospitals, schools, and other civilian targets destroyed along with military objectives like roads, bridges, and oil facilities. Hanoi, the North Vietnamese capital, suffered much of the damage. Americans also bombed Haiphong Harbor, a key supply depot for the communists, and placed a naval blockade on the North, creating food shortages and other hardships. By the time "Operation Linebacker" ended in October, North Vietnam had suffered 100,000 casualties. By the end of 1972, the Americans couldn't "win" with air power alone, and the North Vietnamese couldn't protect themselves from bombers. Hanoi signaled it was ready to talk again.

The combat in 1972, however, produced one more searing image from the war. On June 8, South Vietnamese pilots accidentally dropped napalm on a South Vietnam village and Nick Ut photographed a young girl, Kim Phúc, who had torn off her burning clothes and was running down a road near Trang Bang screaming as the chemicals burned her flesh. The napalm burned her skin at almost 1,500 degrees Fahrenheit. Phúc, who eventually defected to Canada, underwent 17 surgeries to overcome her injuries. Ut won a Pulitzer Prize for his photo, another scarring image from a long, divisive war. As it was published around the world, even more Americans questioned the sanity of continuing the conflict.

One last act remained in the almost 30-year drama. Talks between Kissinger and the North Vietnamese representative to the peace talks, Le Duc Tho, resumed on August 1. Kissinger told the American public that peace "was at hand" just before the November election showdown with McGovern, but the talks stalled again. Nixon responded with the so-called "Christmas Bombing" in December, in which U.S. planes dropped more ordnance than in the first two years of the Nixon administration. A Vietnamese physician, Nguyen Luan, later recalled how, after a bomb hit one hospital, he had to amputate the limbs of patients so he could remove them from the rubble. The North Vietnamese shot down 26 American aircraft. By now, both sides were exhausted. The North Vietnamese no longer demanded the removal of South Vietnamese President Thieu. All remaining differences

Photograph showing Vietnamese children, including Kim Phúc, running and crying after napalm was dropped from South Vietnamese Skyraider airplanes on their village of Trang Bang. June 8, 1972

between Le Duc Tho and Kissinger were resolved, and a truce was signed January 27, 1973 that allowed Nixon to declare, "We have finally achieved peace with honor."

"NOTHING MORE TO SAY AFTER THAT": Aftermath of the Vietnam War

Under the peace terms, the Americans agreed to remove all troops, including military advisers, from South Vietnam. The U.S., South Vietnam, and the North also agreed to exchange prisoners of war. North Vietnamese troops could maintain their positions in South Vietnam, as could Vietcong guerillas. In essence, the truce was a surrender document, not much different from what the president could have gotten from Hanoi when he first took office in 1969. In all, 58,193 Americans died in Vietnam, almost 21,000 under Nixon's watch, as well as close to 2 million Vietnamese. At least 150,000 soldiers and medical personnel suffered injuries. The United States spent $138 billion in military aid plus $8.5 billion in economic aid, a total of about $743 billion in 2011 dollars.

Henry Kissinger and Le Duc Tho received Nobel Peace Prizes for the truce in 1973, in spite of Kissinger's involvement in invasions of Cambodia and Laos and his likely involvement in the Chile coup the same year. The comedian and musical satirist Tom Lehrer supposedly retired from performing upon hearing the news. "It was at that moment that satire died," Lehrer reportedly said. "There was nothing more to say after that." Kissinger and Le Duc Tho's Peace Prize became even more ironic since the Vietnam War didn't actually end until two years later.

The Democratic Party-dominated Congress in November 1973 passed the **War Powers Act**, overriding Nixon's veto. Congressional leaders knew that the free hand given several consecutive administrations, culminating in the Gulf of Tonkin Resolution in 1964, had resulted in the Vietnam quagmire. Alarmed particularly by Nixon's unauthorized invasion of Cambodia and bombing campaigns there, members of the House and Senate sought to reassert their voice in military policy. Under the War Powers Act, the president has to notify the Congress within 48 hours of any military deployment where battle conditions prevail or are likely to prevail. If the Congress does not sign off on the military action, the president has to withdraw troops within 60 days.

The Hanoi government clearly saw the peace agreement as merely a pause in the action. Fighting between the North Vietnamese and Vietcong and South Vietnam began almost immediately after the American departure. North Vietnam launched a new full-scale offensive in 1975. By then, North Vietnam boasted the fifth largest military in the world. It anticipated that the final phase of the war would take two years, but final victory came in only 55 days.

Coordinated attacks across the country began on March 10. Just three days later, hoping to consolidate his forces in the southern third of the country, Thieu ordered a withdrawal from the northernmost provinces and the Central Highlands. This triggered a panic as South Vietnamese soldiers, police and other government officials fled in droves, struggling to flee on clogged roads and arriving as refugees in Saigon, which became virtually the last government stronghold by April 1975. Gerald Ford, who assumed the American presidency when Nixon was forced to resign August 9, 1974, had already declared that no American combat soldiers would rescue the South one more time. He authorized "Operation Frequent Wind," which eventually evacuated more than 7,000 American personnel and 150,000 South Vietnamese officials and family members who feared retribution from the North Vietnamese government. As thousands of locals fought their way into the American embassy compound, American television crews filmed some South Vietnamese being pushed away from overcrowded helicopters or grabbing the skids and holding on as the crafts took off from the embassy roof. The morning of April 30 the last American personnel, 10 Marines, departed and North Vietnamese forces poured into Saigon, which they quickly renamed "Ho Chi Minh City" after the late Communist leader.

The collapse of Saigon marked the start of a mass Vietnamese diaspora. For months before the fall of the Thieu government, South Vietnamese had heard rumors of a planned bloodbath in which the victorious communists would commit mass murder against their political opponents. Some fled by foot to nearby countries. Thousands who came to be known as "**boat people**," those who had worked for or supported the South Vietnamese government or served in its military or its intelligence services, put together rickety sea craft. They sailed until they met friendly vessels and were placed in refugee camps and tent cities across East Asia. Some eventually reached the United States.

About a quarter million Vietnamese-born refugees made it to the United States between 1975 and 1980, settling in large numbers in states like California and Texas. Reminders of a lost war, the refugees often received a harsh reception in the United States. In 1981, armed Klansman led by Vietnam War veteran Louis Beam harassed the new Vietnamese community, burned crosses, hanged effigies and torched boats owned by Vietnamese fishermen near Galveston, Texas. A Gallup Poll taken in 1975 showed that Americans opposed admitting the refugees by a margin of 54 percent to 36 percent. The House of Representatives rejected a bill that would have provided $327 million in aid to the refugees. "Those sons of bitches," President Gerald Ford said when he heard about the vote.

In the nearly four decades since the war ended, 40,000 Vietnamese have died or have been injured by land mines and unexploded bombs left behind in Southeast Asia. About 12 to 18 percent of the bombs dropped during the war didn't explode, only to blow up when discovered by farmers, children, and others who, if they survived, were left with missing limbs.

Meanwhile, digging up the explosives cost Vietnam about $1,000 each and disturbing the soil exposed the local population to the cancer-causing defoliant Agent Orange. During the 1960s, until a 1970 lab study demonstrated that **Agent Orange** caused birth defects in animals, American planes dropped 12 million gallons of the chemical compound, a cancer-causing defoliant created by Dow Chemical, on the Vietnamese countryside to strip trees as a means of exposing communist fighters. The heaviest spraying took place during "Operation Ranch Hand" between 1967 and 1969. Up to one million Vietnamese children have suffered birth defects as a side effect of the chemical, with another half-million injured during the initial chemical drops. Since then, cancer rates in Vietnam exploded and soldiers and servicemen from the United States, Australia and other countries that fought there have reported skin rashes; cancers of the skin, lung, brain and prostate; non-Hodgkin lymphoma, Hodgkin's lymphoma and unusual rates of handicaps in their children.

THE KILLING FIELDS

There was no more tragic aftermath to the Vietnam War than the rise of the Khmer Rouge in Cambodia. During the Operation Menu bombing campaign that began in 1969, Cambodian President Lon Nol noted a sharp increase in the number of communist guerillas operating in his country. At the same time, Lon Nol's government proved ineffective, corrupt and cruel. Cambodia's economy began to collapse, which added to the Khmer Rouge's momentum. Food prices escalated wildly.

Nixon's invasion of Cambodia created 700,000 refugees by the end of 1970. Eventually 540,000 tons of bombs fell on the tiny country, and the number of refugees by the end of 1971 reached a staggering two million people out of a total population of about seven million. "Pol Pot's Communist Party of Kampuchea (CPK) . . . used the bombing's devastation and massacre of civilians as recruitment propaganda and as an excuse for its brutal, radical policies and its purge of moderate communists," noted historian Ben Kiernan.

By March 1973, American bombing raids encompassed the entire country, with 3,000 civilians dying in just three weeks. One evening a mass funeral procession unknowingly walked into a bombing target area, and hundreds were killed. One villager told an interviewer in April, "The bombers may kill some communists, but they kill everyone else too." Armed by the North Vietnamese, the Khmer Rouge became a tightly-disciplined, dedicated and ruthless fighting force. On April 17, 1975, the remnant of Lon Nol's forces collapsed. The Khmer Rogue marched into Phnom Penh and took effective control of the nation they renamed Democratic Kampuchea. Pol Pot declared the start of "Year Zero." Cambodia would be rebuilt from the ground up and become an almost entirely agricultural society in which all private ownership was banned and the family abolished. The Khmer Rouge closed down newspapers and television stations, prohibited the use of money, and shuttered schools. Small children as well as adults became part of a mass agricultural work force. The regime also expelled foreigners. Pol Pot ordered all of the 2 million persons living in Phnom Penh to evacuate. Soldiers went through hospitals, shot patients too weak or ill to move, and forced the rest to join a mass march to the countryside.

About 20,000 died in the forced march, those falling shot by soldiers. In mass agricultural camps, men and women lived separately and ate meals communally. Children were separated from parents and casual conversation was suppressed, and some were executed for laughing. Workdays, beginning at 4 a.m., lasted 18 hours, followed by mandatory lectures on communism. Overwork, combined with paltry food rations (amounting to 90 grams of rice a day) caused starvation and death from exhaustion. The Khmer Rouge murdered any civilians they caught eating the food they were harvesting.

About 2 million Cambodians died during less than four years of rule by the Khmer Rouge. Democratic Kampuchea became, as the North Vietnamese regime described it, "a land of blood and tears, hell on earth." The Khmer Rouge remained in power until a series of Cambodian border raids provoked Vietnam to invade on December 25, 1978. The Vietnamese took control of Phnom Penh in January 1979, set up a puppet government, and the Khmer Rouge lost control of the majority of the country, continuing a guerilla war against the new government from remote outposts mostly in the western part of the country for 17 years. The Vietnamese withdrew in 1990. The Khmer Rouge collapsed in 1997-1998, with Pol Pot placed under arrest by his own forces. He died in April 1998, 23 years after launching his brief, nightmarish reign.

A CANCER CLOSE TO THE PRESIDENCY: The Watergate Scandal

The cluster of scandals that became known by the shorthand phrase "Watergate" started well before the morning of June 17, 1960, when Washington, D.C. police arrested five men employed by Nixon's Committee to Re-Elect the President after they broke into the Democratic National Committee headquarters located in the Watergate Hotel (just one mile from the White House.) As already noted, by the time of the break-in, Nixon's campaign had engaged in extensive "dirty tricks" targeting the Muskie campaign. Nixon had already violated the law by authorizing illegal wiretaps to determine who had leaked the information on American bombing in Cambodia and Laos and had formed the "Plumbers Unit." It was the White House Plumbers Unit that broke into the Watergate Hotel in order to repair bugging devices planted there during an earlier break-in.

Nixon wanted the Plumbers to reveal what he thought was a criminal relationship between Democratic National Chair Lawrence O'Brien and the reclusive billionaire Howard Hughes, who also had contributed money to Nixon. Discovering those theoretical links was the original purpose of bugging O'Brien's Washington headquarters. When police nabbed the five Watergate burglars, the Plumbers—including former CIA agent Bernard Barker and James W. McCord (a security coordinator for the Republican National Committee and CREEP)—wore business suits and carried the bugging equipment and $2,300 in cash in a series of $100 bills with sequential serial numbers. Sensing something unusual about this break-in, newly hired *Washington Post* police reporter Bob Woodward attended the burglars' arraignment and was startled to hear McCord tell the judge about his former job at the CIA. Woodward also discovered that the burglars carried address books that listed the name and phone number of Howard Hunt, another former CIA agent and a Nixon White House consultant. Woodward called Hunt's number and asked what he had to do with the burglars. "Good God," Hunt exclaimed before he hung up.

Third-rate Burglary

Early in the morning of June 17, 1972, five men broke into the Democratic Party headquarters at the Watergate apartment and office complex only a mile from the White House. They wore surgical gloves and carried lock-picking tools, camera, mace, and wire-tapping devices to replace faulty bugs installed in an earlier break-in. The techniques used by the burglars were so primitive and the equipment so shoddy that they would have "appalled the CIA, the Mafia, the New York Police Department or the KGB," in the words of one observer. The incompetent criminals carefully placed tape across the latches of the spring locks on the door to the Democratic headquarters. A guard on a routine inspection noticed the tape and removed it. The burglars, noting that the tape was no longer in place, re-installed it in the same conspicuous way. The guard, returning an hour later, alertly observed the reappearing tape and summoned the police.

The Nixon administration had targeted Washington to demonstrate its commitment to law and order. The newly effective Washington patrol system rushed a car to the scene at 2:00 A. M. On the sixth floor of the Watergate building, the police burst in to discover the culprits who pleaded, "Don't shoot, we give up." The inept criminal band included four Cuban-Americans who thought they were striking a blow against Castro, and James McCord, the "wire man." McCord was a former CIA agent and current security chief for the Committee to Re-elect the President (CREEP). The cash they carried in $100 bills could be easily traced through serial numbers to CREEP. Papers found on the perpetrators linked them to two CREEP officials: E. Howard Hunt, a former CIA agent, and G. Gordon Liddy, a former FBI employee.

The logic behind the break-in was difficult to discern. Apart from the size of its considerable debts, it is hard to figure out what possible secrets of any significance could have been discovered by tapping the phone of the Democratic National Committee. The burglars, undoubtedly, were comfortable in the belief that their superiors in CREEP (who now included John Mitchell, the former attorney general) could easily cover up the episode and arrange for their release.

*Despite these expectations, a grand jury indicted the five burglars, as well as Hunt and Liddy. The administration quickly developed a cover story to ensure that any links to criminal activities stopped at Hunt and Liddy. The break-in, according to this tale, had been "deplorable, an excess of zeal, unauthorized, illegal, regrettable." Neither the media nor the public picked up Democratic cries of a cover-up in the 1972 election campaign. There was nothing to link the White House to this "third-rate burglary." President Nixon won a landslide re-election victory. After thanking White House Counsel John Dean, for his role in containing the damage, the president darkly threatened all of those he believed "have tried to do us in." All his enemies were "asking for it and they are going to get it." A lawyer for the **Washington Post** was "a guy we've got to ruin . . . We are going to fix that son-of-a-bitch." How had such an intoxicating victory turned into such a dark moment? Would the beleaguered White House staff be able to contain what Dean described as a "cancer on the Presidency"?*

White House Press Secretary Ron Zeigler dismissed the incident as a "third rate" burglary. Woodward and another *Washington Post* reporter, Carl Bernstein, turned Watergate into a full-time beat. The pair of investigative journalists demonstrated that the Nixon campaign had created an illegal $350,000 election "slush fund" in which money from donors was "laundered" through Mexican bank accounts to conceal the source of the money. The money was then used to pay for dirty tricks. Woodward and Bernstein proved a connection between the break-in and the president's re-election campaign, but still Watergate had no effect on the 1972 election.

The scandal grabbed the public's attention in January 1973 when a Washington jury convicted the Watergate burglars, Howard Hunt and Liddy, of conspiracy and burglary charges. Threatened with a long prison term, McCord began to provide the court details about the Plumbers and other illegal White House operations. The Senate empaneled a Select Committee on Presidential Campaign Activities chaired by the colorful, story-telling, longtime segregationist North Carolina **Sen. Sam Ervin**. The Watergate suspects began to talk to investigators. **White House Counsel John Dean** warned Nixon on March 21, 1973 that, "We have a cancer within, close to the presidency, that's growing. It's growing daily. It's compounding. It grows geometrically now, because it compounds itself."

"Stonewall It"

Speaking with the president, Dean laid out the financial demands in return for silence from the Watergate burglars. "Hunt is now demanding another $72,000 for his own personal expenses; $50,000 to pay his attorney's fees . . . wanted it by the close of business yesterday," Dean said. The White House lawyer hoped to alert Nixon to the dangers of the White House submitting to blackmail. Instead, Nixon asked, 'How much money do you need?" Hoping to scare the president off from committing bribery, Dean said, "I would say that these people are going to cost a million dollars over the next two years." Nixon didn't blanch. "We could get that . . . If you need the money, you could get the money. I know where it could be gotten."

The president eventually authorized his legal advisor to raise $75,000 in "hush money" to ensure Hunt would remain silent about criminal acts and White House involvement. Nixon told other aides on March 22, "I want you all to stonewall it, let them plead the Fifth Amendment, cover up, anything else." Unknown to Dean and others, Nixon had been secretly audiotaping his Oval Office conversations. Convinced that he was making history, Nixon had requested systematic taping of his conversations so he could retrieve every word he uttered in the Oval Office. The secret taping indeed preserved his place in history but not in the way Nixon imagined. The recordings had just caught the president ordering an aide to bribe witnesses in a criminal case.

Federal Judge John Sirica pressured McCord to cooperate with investigators, and McCord accused Dean and others of ordering a cover-up to conceal the White House connection to Watergate. Dean, in turn, implicated more White House officials including top Nixon lieutenants Haldeman and Ehrlichman. On April 30, 1973, Nixon went on television to address the widening Watergate scandal and to announce the resignation of Haldeman, Ehrlichman, and Dean.

Sadly for the country, the drama dragged on for more than another year. Hoping he could convince the public that he wanted to get to the bottom of the matter, Nixon appointed **Archibald Cox** as special prosecutor to investigate the Watergate matter. That summer, Ervin's committee held televised hearings. Commercial networks broadcast five hours of the hearings each day. About 85 percent of the American public told pollsters that they watched some part of the hearings. Even Republican senators began to criticize the president, with moderate Sen. Howard Baker of Tennessee famously asking, "What did the president know and when did he know it?" A turning point came in July 1973 when former White House staffer Alexander Butterfield revealed the existence of the White House tapes.

An unrelated scandal involving Vice President Spiro Agnew further tarred the administration. Agnew had been the administration's conservative lightning rod, making fiery speeches attacking the supposedly liberal media, war protestors, and black radicals. But now he faced charges that while Baltimore County executive and governor of Maryland he had accepted $147,500 in bribes, sometimes delivered to the governor's mansion in brown paper bags, from businesses seeking state contracts. He continued to accept the bribes when he assumed the vice presidency. He had also failed to report the illegal income on his tax forms. Shortly after pledging in a speech that he would not "resign if indicted," Agnew stepped down on October 10, 1973, after pleading no contest to one count of tax evasion.

For the first time ever, the Twenty-Fifth Amendment to the United States Constitution, ratified in 1967 and adopted in the wake of President Kennedy's assassination, required a president to appoint and the Senate and House to confirm a replacement vice president. (Previously, if a vice president vacated the office through death, succession to the presidency or some other reason, the office remained open until the next presidential election.) Nixon sought a non-controversial replacement and selected House Minority Leader Gerald Ford of Grand Rapids, Michigan, to serve as the next vice president. Bland but pleasant and not heavily ideological, Ford struck many as a feasible president, and he was approved by the Senate 92-3 and the House by a 387-35 margin. Democrats would not have wanted to place Agnew in the White House through impeaching Nixon, but Ford's appointment emboldened the Democrats' investigation of presidential wrongdoing.

"The Saturday Night Massacre"

The Senate and Special Prosecutor Cox demanded that the White House turn over the tapes, but Nixon refused, citing "executive privilege," the legal argument that presidents need candid advice from their advisors in order for the Executive Branch to function and that the Constitution's "Separation of Powers" doctrine allows presidents to keep certain conversations from public scrutiny. Angered by Cox's persistence regarding the tapes, Nixon on the evening of October 20, 1973 ordered his Attorney General Elliott Richardson to fire the special prosecutor. Richardson resigned rather than comply. William D. Ruckelshaus stood next in line in the Justice Department, and Nixon fired him minutes later when he also refused to follow orders. Finally, the Solicitor General, Robert Bork (later unsuccessfully nominated by Ronald Reagan to the United States Supreme Court) carried out Nixon's command. The incident became known as the "**Saturday Night Massacre**" and deepened the growing public perception that Nixon had something to hide.

On Nov. 1, Nixon was forced to name a new special prosecutor, Leon Jaworski, who continued to press the White House to release the tapes. On March 1, 1974 a federal grand jury returned indictments against seven former top White House officials, including one-time Attorney General Mitchell, Haldeman, Ehrlichman, and special counsel (and later Christian evangelist) Charles Colson, on charges of conspiracy to obstruct justice. The grand jury named Nixon as an "unindicted co-conspirator." With increasing evidence gathering against Nixon, who was also charged with ordering IRS audits of political opponents, the House Judiciary Committee began impeachment hearings in March, the first such event since Andrew Johnson's impeachment proceedings just after the Civil War.

Aware that the tapes themselves contained evidence of criminal wrongdoing, Nixon instead released 1,200 pages of heavily edited transcripts of Watergate-related conversations. Nixon's reputation took a further hit as the publicly prudish president was revealed as an angry, foul-mouthed man whose many obscenities were replaced in the transcripts by the soon-to-be infamous phrase "expletive deleted." Senate Minority Leader Hugh Scott, a member of the president's own party, called the president's words in the transcript "deplorable, shabby, disgusting, and immoral."

The transcripts did not satisfy Jaworski, who petitioned the Supreme Court to order the White House to release 42 tapes. The Supreme Court ruled unanimously in 1974 in *United States v. Nixon* that the president must comply with the request. Included among the recordings was a June 23, 1972 conversation that revealed that, in contradiction to his public statements, Nixon knew that the Watergate burglars were tied to the re-election campaign and that former Attorney General Mitchell had helped plan the break-in. Stories circulated during Nixon's last week in office, from August 2-9, 1974, that the president was drinking to the point of intoxication. Son-in-law Edward Cox told frightened listeners that Nixon was "up walking the halls last night, talking to pictures of former presidents—giving speeches and talking to the pictures on the wall."

Between July 27 and 30, the Judiciary Committee approved three articles of impeachment—abuse of powers, obstruction of justice and defiance of House Judiciary Committee subpoenas—but turned down two proposed articles related to his use of public money to improve his personal property and his bombing of Cambodia without

Members of the White House staff watch as Richard Nixon, who announced his resignation as president the night before, leaves the White House August 9, 1974 with his wife Pat and accompanied by his successor, Vice President Gerald Ford and his wife Betty.

congressional approval. Nixon's voter approval rating had dropped to 24 percent. With Democrats controlling more than two-thirds of the votes in the chamber, it was clear that the House of Representatives would vote to impeach the president, leaving the matter in the hands of the Senate where a two-thirds vote was necessary for conviction. Nixon would be the first president to stand trial in the Senate in 106 years.

Complying with the Supreme Court, on August 5 Nixon released three tapes containing damaging conversations demonstrating his hands-on management of a criminal cover-up. This was the so-called "smoking gun," and the president's remaining support in the Senate vanished. The deciding moment came on August 7 when a delegation of Republican senators, including former GOP presidential nominee Barry Goldwater and Hugh Scott of Pennsylvania told the president that he could count on maybe only 16 to 18 members of the upper chamber to vote for acquittal. That night, Nixon met with Kissinger and, with tears in his eyes, asked the former professor, "Will history treat me more kindly than my contemporaries?" The president sobbed and then asked Kissinger to pray with him. The president kneeled and "Kissinger felt he had no alternative but to kneel down,

President Ford announcing his pardon of Richard Nixon from the Oval Office. September 8, 1974.
Photo credit: Gerald R. Ford Library

too," Woodward and Bernstein wrote in their book, *The Final Days*. "The President prayed out loud, asking for help, rest, peace, and love. How could a President and a country be torn apart by such small things?"

Nixon announced his resignation—the first by an American president—during a televised speech the next night, August 8, from the Oval Office. Before retreating to his home in California the next day, he said goodbye to his cabinet as the live television cameras looked on. The August 9 farewell speech was classic Nixon, at different times eloquent, self-pitying and defiant. "Always remember," he told his staff, "others may hate you—but those who hate you don't win unless you hate them, and then you destroy yourself." Sadly, it was advice Nixon never took to heart.

A FORD, NOT A LINCOLN

A generally quiet man who spoke in a slow monotone, Ford was born Leslie Lynch King in 1913, but renamed himself later in life in honor of his stepfather. An all-star football center at the University of Michigan, Ford received contract offers from two National Football League teams, the Detroit Lions and the Green Bay Packers but decided instead to attend Yale Law School. There, he worked as an assistant football and boxing coach and graduated in the top third of his class before seeing combat duty in the United States Navy during World War II. He won his first race for the United States House in 1948 and never carried less than 60 percent of the vote in his home district.

By 1950, he won a spot on the House Appropriations Committee. Ford voted against Lyndon Johnson's Medicare and public housing programs. Genial, well-liked, and seen as honest, he nevertheless acquired a reputation among liberals as someone out of touch with the poor and as being sub-par intellectually. Lyndon Johnson famously put him down as someone who played "too much football without a helmet." Nevertheless, Johnson appointed him to serve on the Warren Commission that investigated President Kennedy's assassination, and Ford became a vigorous defender of its controversial conclusions. In 1965, he rose to the position of House Minority leader and from that point on his ambition was to become House Speaker, which he described as the "greatest job in the world." By 1973 he gave up hope that Republicans would ever gain a majority in the House and decided that he would run for only one more term and return to Michigan. Then Nixon selected him to be vice president.

Ford won easy confirmation as vice president from the Senate in December 1973. When Nixon resigned and he was sworn in as president, he jokingly contrasting himself with a luxury car, saying he was, "a Ford, not a Lincoln." Exhausted by Vietnam and Watergate and the lies that surrounded both issues, Americans responded with relief when Nixon stepped down and Ford assumed the presidency. "The outpouring of goodwill towards Ford in the first week of his presidency was immense," wrote Bob Woodward. "There was a sense of cleansing and simplification. Nixon's crisis had created the feeling of national siege. Ford had punctured the tension." On the morning Ford assumed the office, the press extensively wrote about how the new president toasted his own English muffins. He asked the Marine Corps Band to not play "Hail to the Chief" at his swearing-in, saying that he would prefer the University of Michigan fight song. His words were also winningly humble. "My fellow Americans, our long national nightmare is over," he said. "Our Constitution works; our great Republic is a government of laws and not of men. Here, the people rule." With a few short words and simple gestures, Ford generated a lot of support. His first major act as president, however, would inspire cynicism and anger.

"A Full, Free, and Absolute Pardon"

Ford worried that the continuing controversy surrounding Nixon, and the prospect of a criminal trial for the former president, would consume the country and make governing a nation already buffeted by scandal, high inflation, and the continued conflict with the Soviet Union even more difficult. He later said that he spent about 25 percent of his time "listening to lawyers argue what I should do with Mr. Nixon's papers, his tapes, et. cetera." Ford's honeymoon with the press and the American public came to a crashing halt on September 8, 1974, on a Sunday morning when he announced on television that he had granted Nixon a "full, free, and absolute pardon" for "all offenses against the United States" Nixon "has committed or may have committed."

The reaction was immediately angry and harsh. Ford faced accusations that he had agreed to pardon Nixon in return for gaining the White House. In October, Ford appeared before a House Subcommittee on Criminal Justice to deny any corrupt deal had been made related to the Nixon pardon, but the damage was done. As *Time Magazine* put it, "the exhilarating atmosphere of honesty and belief that surrounded Gerald Ford in his first month in office . . . that unreal glow is gone, and it will probably never return." After the pardon, Ford's approval rating seldom climbed over 50 percent.

His political problems deepened with the fall elections in 1974. The Democrats picked up 43 seats in the House where they would hold a better than 2-1 margin, 291-144, and picked up three more seats in the Senate, which they now commanded by a 61-39 edge. Democrats now served as governors in 36 states. It was the Republican Party's worst performance since the 1932 landslide when Franklin Roosevelt crushed Herbert Hoover. Even Ford's old congressional district went to the Democrats. Although the results could be traced to Nixon's misdeeds, Washington insiders saw Ford as politically weakened.

An athletic man, Ford's image took another hit in June of 1975 when during a trip to Europe and following a mostly sleepless night, Ford slipped down the metal steps leading from Air Force One, falling to the tarmac. Photographs and film footage of the event filled newspapers and television coverage, and soon every Ford stumble caught media attention. By the time Ford fell while skiing in Vail, Colorado, the president's alleged clumsiness added to his reputation as an intellectual lightweight, became a running joke and a staple of a popular new TV variety series that debuted in the fall of 1975, *Saturday Night Live*. The support from his first month in the White House long gone, Ford could not shake the image of a dimwitted stumbler.

THE REFORM CONGRESS

The new heavily Democratic Congress believed it had won a mandate to reform government, and it focused on limiting what it saw as presidential powers run amuck. The Congress had already passed the War Powers Act while Nixon was still in office. More directly addressing the abuses of Watergate, the 93rd Congress passed the Federal Election Campaign Act of 1974 that, in an attempt to limit the influence of special interests, allowed for the first time public financing of presidential campaigns. The Congress also amended the Federal Election Campaign Act of 1971 that placed limits on the size of political contributions in federal elections, put in place stricter requirements on candidates to report the source of their campaign funds and the details of their expenditures, and created the Federal Election Commission, which was given the job of enforcing campaign finance laws.

These reforms suffered fatal flaws. Over the years, the FEC has been reluctant to enforce rules, and the limits on corporate, union and personal donations simply inspired the creation of so-called "third party" groups that operated under no limitations in fundraising and spending as long as they supported "positions"—like support of free trade—and not particular candidates. The Republican Party became particularly adept at creating so-called "PACs" or political action committees in the 1970s and 1980s, such as the National Conservative Political Action Committee (NCPAC) that raised record amounts of money from big business to support Ronald Reagan and other right-of-center candidates in presidential elections.

Even as they tried to prevent future corruptions of the political process, Democrats uncovered past misdeeds. Already accustomed, after the Johnson and Nixon administrations, to distrusting the government, the public received another round of shocks with the **Church Committee Hearings** in 1975. In late 1974, investigative reporter **Seymour Hersh**, the man who had revealed the My Lai Massacre, reported that the CIA had illegally spied on American citizens. This prompted the U.S. Senate in 1975 to empanel an 11-member committee chaired by Idaho Democrat Frank Church that would investigate past abuses by the CIA, the FBI, the National Security Agency and the Internal Revenue Service. The committee interviewed 800 witnesses, conducted 250 closed door "executive sessions" and held 21 public hearings over the next nine months.

The committee exposed the existence of the FBI's COINTELPRO (Counter-Intelligence Program) in which undercover agents infiltrated protest groups such as the Black Panthers and attempted to disrupt them through spreading false rumors about leaders and encouraging members to violate the law so the agency could justify a crackdown. Investigators further discovered that in the 1950s, the CIA had experimented with the use of the hallucinogenic drug lysergic acid diethylamide (LSD), first developed in 1938 as a truth serum that could be used to get information from Soviet and other communist prisoners. The agency gave LSD to 1,000 soldiers without their knowledge in the 1950s.

In one case, Dr. Frank Olson, a civilian employee of the U.S. Army, unknowingly drank a potion that contained LSD. Olson panicked when he started exhibiting symptoms of paranoia and schizophrenia, and in 1953 jumped from a ten-story window while awaiting treatment. Responding to reports that American soldiers captured by the North Koreans during the Korean War from 1950-1953 had been "brainwashed" into defecting, the CIA launched Project BLUEBIRD, experimenting on mental patients, who had not given informed consent, subjecting them to isolation, sleep deprivation, and repeated electroshock sessions to see how prisoners of war might respond to such treatment.

The panel released a two-foot-thick report, without the endorsement of Republican committee members, in May 1976. The hearings resulted in the creation of the Senate's permanent Select Committee on Intelligence, charged with monitoring the actions of intelligence agencies, and also added to the sense of many Americans that the government was out of control and often acted as an enemy rather than a protector of ordinary citizens.

"Whole Dollars and Seemingly All at Once"

Seen as an accidental occupant of the White House, President Ford could not even count on the loyalty of his cabinet, which included many leftovers from the Nixon administration. On May 12, 1975, Khmer Rouge forces seized control of the American merchant ship, the **S.S. Mayaguez**. The Cambodian government held the 39-person crew hostage for 65 hours before Ford ordered a military rescue mission. The crew was safely removed, but at the cost of 41 American military deaths. Ford's approval ratings shot up 11 percent after the costly rescue, but this political gain quickly faded.

Fatal to Ford's long-term prospects was a sinking economy. By 1974, American automakers were losing sales because of the availability of cheaper Japanese cars that recorded better gas mileage. The auto industry laid off about half its workforce that year, and the unemployed found few replacement jobs to match their experience and skills. America's industrial dominance in the world was crumbling. Factories with a high-paid union work force in so-called "Rust Belt" states in the Northeast and Midwest shut down so owners could take advantage of the low wages in the so-called "Sun Belt"—the stretch of states from Georgia to California—where so-called "right-to-work" laws and police harassment had kept union membership at a minimum. Rust Belt cities like Pittsburgh; Cleveland; Youngstown, Ohio; and Detroit, already crippled by corrupt local governments, urban uprisings and bad race relations, experienced high unemployment even as prices for consumer goods skyrocketed through the 1970s.

As Yanek Mieczkowski notes, the 1970s were the first decade since the Great Depression in which Americans lost wealth. A low point in the Ford years came in 1974 when inflation cracked double digits, hitting a painful 12.2 percent, the highest level that Americans had experienced since 1946. Americans who had rarely experienced significant price increases in the 1950s and 1960s underwent sticker shock. "Things went up not just a few cents, or gradually," one Seattle woman complained, "but whole dollars and seemingly all at once."

After Nixon ended the gold standard, the value of the dollar dropped versus other currencies. European and Japanese customers could buy American food for less, which drove up the price tag for groceries in the United States. The Russians had a series of bad harvests, driving them to buy more American commodities. A shortage of fuel supplies in America meant that farmers here could not harvest a large portion of their crops. Together, these factors resulted in the price of farm and food products increasing almost 8 percent during just the first month of the Ford presidency.

As under Nixon, inflation combined with high unemployment to further stagger Americans. Unemployment soared from 5.3 percent when Ford first took office in August 1974 to 8.3 percent a year later. Industrial workers with or without high school diplomas suffered more in an economy in which American manufacturing increasingly became a thing of the past. Ford tried to curb inflation by encouraging Americans to voluntarily cut back on consumption. In imitation of the "Blue Eagle" National Recovery Administration logo during the New Deal, the administration released "WIN!" (**Whip Inflation Now!**") buttons. His formerly warm relationship with the Congress grew bitter as he set a modern mark for presidents in exercising the veto to stop Democratic job bills and other economic stimulus programs he saw as too expensive and inflationary. Ford vetoed 66 bills during his two-and-a-half years as president, the fourth highest per-year average in American history. Congress was able to override only 18 of the vetoes, meaning that the government was often in gridlock during the economic crisis.

Welfare Queen

Ford presided over a divided, deeply troubled government during deeply troubled times. The president had never won an election in an area larger than a congressional district, and the economy and his media image seemed to be working against him. The right wing of the Republican Party, which temporarily retreated after the debacle of the Barry Goldwater campaign in 1964, had been slowly and surely taking over the GOP in the Nixon years, and the movement's leader, Ronald Reagan, smelled blood. In spite of Ford's clear record of fiscal conservatism, Reagan objected to the president's continuation of détente towards the Soviet Union. Following the expiration of his term as California governor in 1975, he confidently launched a full-time rebel campaign against his party's incumbent president.

Many did not take the former Hollywood actor, who had once co-starred with a chimpanzee in the movie *Bedtime for Bonzo*, seriously. The economy began to improve as 1976 approached, and Ford sought to enhance his prospects with conservatives by convincing his liberal vice president, Nelson Rockefeller, to step down as running mate. However, Ford underestimated the ideological commitment of the Republican right. After losing in early primaries like New Hampshire, Reagan scored an upset in North Carolina and began attacking Ford as part of the liberal establishment, weak on defense, and an appeaser towards the Soviet Union who let the United States slip to a "second-rate power." Reagan also accused Ford of failing to rein in the excesses of the liberal welfare state and made numerous, repeated false claims on the campaign. A favorite, racially-charged tall tale of his concerned a "welfare queen" who supposedly used 80 false identities, had a dozen Social Security cards and allegedly cashed in on veteran's benefits from four husbands.

When pressed for details such as the name of this welfare cheat, Reagan and his campaign couldn't produce any supporting evidence. Such stories were fictions. The tale was aimed straight at angry southern white men who believed that black malcontents in the 1960s had manipulated liberal guilt to gain undeserved benefits. The stories got Reagan's audience riled, so he kept telling them regardless of their authenticity.

Reagan went off to win primaries in Texas, Alabama, Georgia, and Indiana before Ford regained his stride. Ford did not seal his win until the Republican National Convention in Kansas City, and he eked by 1,187 delegates to 1,070. Reagan supporters almost knocked Ford's acceptance speech out of prime time with a noisy demonstration that kept the president from addressing the nation until 10:40 p.m. Eastern. The primary campaign had been brutal and expensive, and the president started deep in the hole.

"ESTABLISHING JUSTICE IN A SINFUL WORLD"

"Washington" was a dirty word by the time of the 1976 presidential election and the Democratic nominee, James Earl Carter, started a tradition whereby White House hopefuls ran not on their diplomatic or executive experience but on their status as "outsiders" and their zeal to clean out the corruption and dysfunctions of the capital city. Born in rural Plains, Georgia, a small community of only 500 people, on October 1, 1924, Carter was the son of a successful businessman who operated a peanut warehouse and owned considerable real estate. Carter entered the United States Naval Academy where he excelled, finishing 16th out of a class of 822 Midshipmen. He graduated in 1951 and spent seven years in the Navy, serving on the *Seawolf*, the prototype of the Navy's nuclear-powered submarine. He left the Navy as his father began to suffer ill health. After his father's death, Carter spent years rebuilding the family's peanut business, which suffered during a prolonged drought in the early 1950s.

Carter proved to be a good businessman and the peanut warehouse flourished, but politics fascinated him. He served two terms in the Georgia state senate from 1963-1966 and established a reputation as a moderate who emphasized the need to help the poor. He attacked the corrupt relationship between the state's politicians and special interests. When he lost in the 1966 Georgia Democratic gubernatorial race, the intensely driven farmer suffered a bout of depression. Always a religious man, the Southern Baptist re-committed his life to Christianity. As biographer Burton I. Kaufman notes, he was deeply influenced by the theologian Reinhold Neibuhr, who once declared that, "the sad duty of politics is to establish justice in a sinful world."

Jimmy Carter became famous for his toothy smile and for his commitment to human rights, but when competing, he occasionally could be hardnosed. He again ran for governor in 1970 and, as Kaufman notes, he appealed directly to segregationists, attacking mandatory school busing to achieve racial balance, making a campaign stop at an all-white private academy. He attacked liberals like Hubert Humphrey and told reporters, "I am and always have been conservative . . . I'm basically a redneck." Carter won and served as Georgia governor from 1971-1975.

In spite of his toying with racists, Carter behaved differently as governor. Carter famously ordered a portrait of the late civil rights leader Martin Luther King, Jr., to be displayed in the Georgia statehouse and said that segregation had no future in Georgia politics. During his one term as governor, the number of African Americans holding state jobs grew from 4,850 to 6,684. In addition, he modernized Georgia's services for the mentally ill and passed some of the state's most progressive laws on the environment. He remained fiscally conservative. By 1972, he was already thinking of running for president.

Carter campaigned for the 1976 nomination promising to bring "a government as good as its people." New Democratic Party rules required that delegates at the national convention accurately reflect the share of black, brown and women voters in the party. Reflecting this post-McGovern effort to make the Democratic Party more democratic, a record number of states, 30, decided to hold presidential primaries in 1976. (Only 21 states held primaries in 1972.) While his opponents still thought they could rely on party professionals to win the nomination, Carter campaigned hard to appeal to women and African-American voters, and conducted a door-to-door campaign in early caucus and primary states like Iowa and New Hampshire.

The Georgia politician also got his biggest break when the most formidable of his rivals, **Sen. Edward Kennedy,** decided not to enter the presidential contest. Kennedy concluded that it was too soon after the 1969 Chappaquiddick incident. Seven years earlier, Kennedy left a party honoring those who had served on his late brother Robert's presidential campaign and drove off a Massachusetts bridge near the Chappaquiddick ferry, killing his passenger, 28-year-old Mary Jo Kopechne. Kennedy had been drinking at the party and left the scene before police arrived. For many voters inside and outside the Democratic Party, Chappaquiddick forever disqualified the youngest of the Kennedy brothers from ever serving as president. The African-American vote was key for Carter. He won 90 percent of the African-American vote in North Carolina. Black voters would be a significant part of Carter's coalition in November. Carter had the Democratic nomination locked up before the summer.

"No Soviet Domination of Eastern Europe"

By August, Carter enjoyed a 15-point advantage over Ford in opinion polls. The Republican incumbent hit Carter hard on the vagueness of his campaign promises. Carter also worried some Jewish and Catholic voters because of his campaign references to being a "born-again" Christian. Some were concerned Carter's personal faith would play too big a role in his policy decisions.

During the Republican National Convention, Ford dramatically challenged Carter to a series of debates. None had been held since the famous Kennedy-Nixon debates in 1960. Carter agreed, and the two nominees debated three times, with a fourth debate held by Carter's running mate, Senator Walter Mondale of Minnesota, and Ford's vice presidential nominee Senator Robert Dole of Kansas. As the debates approached, Ford had pulled even or passed Carter in some public opinion polls.

In the second debate, Ford made a mistake that may have cost him the election. The Ford administration had recently signed the **Helsinki Accords**, a 1975 agreement in which the United States, Canada, the Soviet Union and 32 other nations committed to recognize European boundaries established just after World War II, to cooperate in scientific research and economic development, and to respect human rights such as free speech and freedom of religion. Not a formal treaty, the agreement was non-binding on the signatory nations, but many conservatives in the United States saw this accord as surrendering Eastern Europe to permanent Soviet occupation. During the second debate, on October 6, 1976, a reporter asked Ford what the United States had gained in return for "an agreement that the Russians have dominance in Eastern Europe?" Ford said, "There is no Soviet domination of Eastern Europe, and there never will be under a Ford administration . . . I don't believe that the Yugoslavians consider themselves dominated by the Soviet Union. I don't believe the Romanians consider themselves dominated by the Soviet Union. I don't believe the Poles consider themselves dominated by the Soviet Union."

Ford had recently visited Eastern Europe and had been impressed by what he saw as the determination of Poles, Czechs, and others living under military domination by the Soviet Union to achieve political independence. It was the will of the people there to not live under Russian control that Ford referred to, not the present-day control the Soviets exercised in the region. Nevertheless, the remarks reinforced the perception that Ford was not very smart or competent. Ford's remarks also angered voters of Eastern European descent who longed for their homelands to overthrow Soviet occupation. Ford made the mistake worse when he failed to clearly explain what he meant.

Ford's performance in the debates stalled the major comeback the Republican ticket had made. In spite of their mistakes, however, Ford almost pulled off an upset. Carter won only 50.1 percent of the popular votes to Ford's 48 percent and the Electoral College was also close, with Carter carrying 297 votes to Ford's 240. Carter owed his victory to African Americans (he carried 5/6ths of the black vote). Blue Collar voters had turned on McGovern, but Carter carried 60 percent of this important Democratic constituency. Carter also won 54 percent of the white southern vote, the highest percentage for a Democrat since 1948. (McGovern had won just 27 percent of white Southerners.)

Power Failure

Crippled with a weakened economy, high energy costs, and the unexpected rise of a militant anti-American regime in Iran, Carter faced immense challenges to his leadership throughout his term. The Congress was filled with reformers eager to roll back presidential power after the abuses of the Nixon administration. Carter was also philosophically at odds with many members of his own party. "He didn't fit neatly into the existing wings of the party," said Carter's chief domestic policy advisor, Stuart Eizenstat. "He was neither a typical southern conservative nor a Kennedy liberal." This odd position between the wings of the party often left him with few allies, a situation made worse with his personality.

He often seemed stubborn to congressional leaders, made little attempt to form personal relationships with important senators and congressmen and often seemed self-righteous, openly threatening recalcitrant legislators that if they stood in his way he could, as president, appeal over their heads to their constituents. He despised as corrupt the ordinary horse-trading involved in getting legislation passed. "Every time I see Carter, he makes me feel like a political whore," said Jim Wright, a congressman from Fort Worth, Texas, who would later become Speaker of the House. Carter also hated delegating authority and stretched himself thin as he micromanaged his administration. Furthermore, he had trouble setting priorities, which limited his ability to lobby effectively for his most important initiatives.

Meanwhile, the economy was particularly vulnerable due to America's continuing dependence on expensive foreign oil. Carter directed his Secretary of Energy, Ford's former Defense Secretary James Schlesinger, to draft a comprehensive energy plan that aimed at reducing American dependence on Middle Eastern petroleum, expanded natural gas production, increased use of alternative energy sources such as nuclear energy and coal, and encouraged conservation. Carter and Schlesinger had not consulted Congress when the administration revealed its complicated 100-point plan, which raised the ire of both environmentalists (because of its support for increased coal and nuclear energy use) and the oil industry (because of its advocacy of federal gasoline taxes as a means of reducing consumption.) Congress rejected the plan, and the United States again would suffer serious energy shortages in 1979 after a revolution in Iran.

The near meltdown of a nuclear reactor at **Three Mile Island** near Harrisburg, Pennsylvania on March 28, 1979 also thwarted Carter's push for increased use of nuclear energy. A failure of a pump and valve caused one of the reactors to overheat, and clouds of radiation appeared in the skies. The area around Harrisburg was evacuated. Just before the accident, American audiences had seen the movie *The China Syndrome* in which a nuclear power plant experienced a similar malfunction.

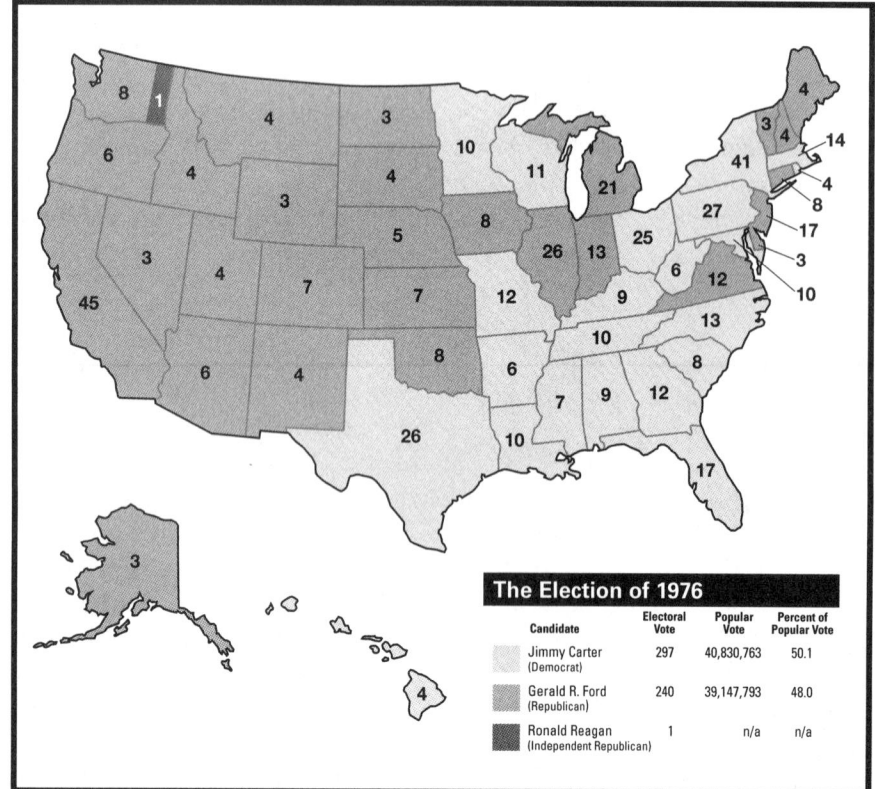

Map 31.3 The Election of 1976

President Jimmy Carter and Rosalynn Carter at the Inaugural Ball.
January 20, 1977   Photo credit: Jimmy Carter Library

(The title refers to the theory that a nuclear meltdown in America would cause a chain reaction that would blow a radioactive hole in the Earth's crust from the United States to China.) The movie, the incident at Three Mile Island, and another incident July 16, 1979 when a dam burst near Church Rock, Mexico, and flooded uranium mines and filled the Rio Puerco River Valley with ninety million gallons of radioactive waste water, proved politically fatal to advocates of nuclear energy like Carter. As more nuclear power plants already approved for construction went on line, the amount of electricity provided by nuclear power doubled from 11 to 22 percent from 1979 to 1982. Yet, construction of new power plants, already controversial, faced far more fierce opposition and no new plants approved after 1974 ever became operational.

"The Great Inflation"

Like Nixon and Ford, Carter faced unusually high inflation yet had to combat unemployment at the same time. Inflation climbed from 5.2 percent when Carter first took office to 7 percent in 1978. Because of escalating energy costs, certain commodities rose in price more sharply. In 1978, for instance, meat prices shot up a stunning 18 percent. Economists have called the period "the Great Inflation." When he first took office, Carter had proposed public works projects to reduce unemployment, but conservative opposition in the Congress stymied that. He then focused on trying to balance the budget. At the same time, he persuaded the Congress to increase spending on Social Security, Medicare, and Medicaid. His policies were a muddle, and many of the weaknesses in the American economy were beyond his ability to control.

In spite of the rising price of gasoline, American auto manufacturers in Detroit continued to build big gas guzzlers, driving consumers to buy imports. The American steel industry also began to collapse. Many steel plants, such as in Youngstown, Ohio, had not updated technology in decades while by the 1970s European and Japanese industry had completely recovered from World War II and were using cutting-edge machinery. Because of technological improvements, Japanese steel cost 15 to 20 percent less than American steel, allowing them to sell under the price of American steel. Tens of thousands of jobs in the American steel industry would disappear during the 1970s.

Human Rights

Carter's foreign policy produced perhaps his greatest political triumph, a peace treaty between Egypt and Israel. It also produced his greatest defeat, the holding of

American hostages by the radical Islamist regime in Iran for more than a year. Carter wanted his foreign policy to represent a clean break with what he saw as the callousness and amorality of the Nixon/Ford years. He wanted to move away from an era in which the United States would support brutal dictatorships in nations like Chile as long as those governments opposed communism. He declared that "human rights" would be the cornerstone of his foreign policy.

Carter criticized the Soviet Union's treatment of political dissidents, which caused strain between the two countries. He spoke out against the mistreatment of political prisoners, the shutdown of opposition newspapers, and the lack of elections in countries ruled by tyrants in Latin America, Africa and Asia. As part of this effort, the Congress, with Carter's support, cut off military and financial aid to the brutal and corrupt Nicaraguan dictatorship of Anastasio Somoza Debayle. A revolutionary group, who called themselves the Sandinistas, overthrew the 46-year-old Somoza regime in the summer of 1979.

Carter outraged conservatives when he signed a treaty giving control of the Panama Canal Zone to Panama in the year 2000. The negotiations were a continuation of talks dating back to when Panamanians had staged anti-American protests outside the 10-mile-wide Canal Zone in 1964. Panamanians and others in Latin America saw the canal as a symbol of American bullying and imperialism. Carter and Canal Zone President Omar Torrijos signed two treaties in 1978, one guaranteeing the neutrality of the Canal Zone (meaning that use of the canal could not be blocked to international vessels for political reasons) and another that provided for joint U.S.-Panamanian control of the canal until December 31, 1999, when full control would pass to the government of Panama. Already running for president, former California Gov. Ronald Reagan belittled Torrijos as a "tin-horn" dictator and proclaimed to cheering audiences, "We built it! We paid for it! It's ours and we're going to keep it!" The U.S. Senate ratified the treaties in March and April of 1978. The agreement greatly improved the United States' relationship to Latin America. Reagan, however, would cite the treaty as a sign of American retreat and weakness under Carter, and the issue would help fire up the conservative base in the two years leading up to the 1980 presidential elections.

"Just Waiting for the Proper Invitation"

Carter earned broader plaudits for his role in securing what came to be known as "the Camp David Accords." Egypt had borne the brunt of Arab-Israeli wars in 1948, 1956, 1967, the unofficial so-called "War of Attrition" from 1967-1970, and in 1973, suffering far more casualties (more than 15,000) than any other Arab state. Military expenses put a strain on the weak Egyptian economy and that of their more prosperous enemies next door, the Israelis. Egyptian President Anwar Sadat believed that the greatly improved performance of his military in the 1973 Yom Kippur War (as opposed to the humiliation of the Six-Day War in 1967), gave him enough prestige and credibility to resolve the Arab-Israeli conflict. In a November 9, 1977 speech to the Egyptian Parliament, he declared he would do anything to achieve peace. "I am ready to go to the Israeli parliament itself and discuss it with them," Sadat proclaimed.

Five days later, Walter Cronkite interviewed Sadat on his prime time CBS News broadcast and Sadat repeated his offer, saying that he could make the trip to Jerusalem within days. "I'm just waiting for the proper invitation," Sadat said. Cronkite then interviewed Menachem Begin, Israel's newly elected prime minister and head of the right-wing Likud Party, who extended the invitation. On November 20, Sadat became the first Arab leader to visit Israel and, as promised, he made a speech to the Knesset, the Israeli Parliament, and spoke with other Israeli leaders. During his speech, Sadat proclaimed he was there to break down "the barriers of suspicion, fear, illusion, and misrepresentation" that had divided Arabs and Israelis. Sadat was immediately denounced by hardline Arab leaders like Libyan dictator Muammar Gaddafi and the head of the Palestine Liberation Organization, Yasser Arafat, who believed that Israel occupied land stolen from the Palestinians and that the Jewish state had no right to exist.

Carter invited Begin and Sadat to Camp David, a presidential retreat in Maryland built during the Eisenhower administration, for peace negotiations. Under pressure at home, Sadat pressured Begin for some concessions to the Palestinians who had been forced from their homes during the Israeli War of Independence in 1948 and were living in squalid refugee camps in the Israeli-occupied West Bank of the Jordan River, and in Arab nations like Jordan and Lebanon. The three world leaders conferred at Camp David for 13 days, and at different points Begin and Sadat threatened to leave with no agreement signed. In each case, Carter was able to persuade the two sides to continue negotiations. Unable to resolve the conflict over the Israeli-occupied West Bank, the Golan Heights (in Syria) and the Gaza Strip (adjoining the Sinai Peninsula), the Camp David agreement became simply an accord between Egypt and Israel that Carter would declare a "framework of peace" in the entire Middle East. The Israelis agreed to return the Sinai Peninsula to Egypt, and in return Egypt agreed to diplomatically recognize Israel. Begin and Sadat agreed to continue negotiating the Palestinian issue. The two Middle Eastern leaders

Menachem Begin, Jimmy Carter, and Anwar Sadat during one of the Camp David Summit meetings.
September 7, 1978 Photo credit: Jimmy Carter Library

signed a formal peace treaty on these terms in 1979. The state of war that had existed between Egypt and Israel officially ended after 30 years. Carter played a major role in achieving this breakthrough, but it would be Begin and Sadat who would be awarded the Nobel Peace Prize.

The agreement made Sadat a marked man in the Arab world. The Palestinians felt abandoned by the largest Arab nation. Several Arab countries withdrew their diplomats in Cairo and hit the poverty-stricken nation of Egypt with economic sanctions. To make up for these losses, Egypt and Israel became the two largest recipients of American foreign aid. Egyptians enraged by Camp David assassinated Sadat while he viewed a parade honoring troops on the anniversary of the Yom Kippur War in October 1981. In spite of the promise for peace Camp David represented, the final status of the Golan Heights, the West Bank and the Gaza Strip remained unresolved as of 2011, and most Palestinians live in poverty with few opportunities.

"The Peacock Throne"

The United States had been deeply involved in Iranian politics since 1953 when the CIA, at the direction of the Eisenhower Administration and at the urging of the British government, overthrew the democratically elected government of Prime Minister Mohammad Mossadegh. The Iranian leader had angered the West when he seized control of the Anglo-Iranian Oil Company. The British firm, through bribes to the Iranian monarchy, made huge profits off of Iran's most valuable economic resource while contributing little to the Iranians themselves. In spite of its vast oil reserves, by the 1950s Iran remained a poor country. Mossadegh wanted Iranians to profit from their own oil and for the money to be invested in Iranian schools, colleges, agricultural projects and hospitals. He also wanted to limit the power of the Shah, the nation's strongly pro-Western emperor Mohammad Reza Pahlavi.

Pahlavi had ascended the so-called "peacock throne" in Iran in 1941 and, when the CIA engineered a coup against Mosaddegh, he rolled back democratic reforms. The Shah "became increasingly isolated and dictatorial," as author Stephen Kinzer reported. He crushed dissent and spent huge amounts of money on weaponry—$10 billion in the United States alone—between 1972 and 1976. His secret police force, SAVAK, tortured and killed dissidents or had them deported. The Shah seemed oblivious to the suffering of his people, living in vast luxury while many families worried whether they would have enough to eat. In 1971, the Shah threw a massively expensive celebration of the 2,500th anniversary of the establishment of the Persian Empire. The party, held in the ruins of the ancient Persian royal desert city of Persepolis, cost up to $300 million ($1.5 billion today). This lavish soiree unfolded in a country where the average person earned only $500 a year (about $2,700 annually in 2011 dollars).

There was no more ferocious critic of the Shah, of his closeness to the United States, and his support for the state of Israel than Iran's extremely conservative religious leader, the Ayatollah Ruhollah Khomeini. The Ayatollah also objected to the Shah's so-called 1961 "White Revolution," which not only involved the distribution of limited government-owned land to the poor, and profit-sharing for workers, but also voting and education rights for women and the creation of a Literacy Corps to extend education to the countryside. The Shah arrested Khomeini, and he was expelled from the country, and by 1978 living in Paris. Opposition to the Shah came not just from mullahs—individuals trained in Muslim religious law—but also from secular intellectuals who wanted a more democratic government.

In spite of his support for human rights, Carter visited Iran in late December 1977 and praised the dictator for creating "an island of stability in one of the most troubled areas of the world." Carter proclaimed that the Shah had won "the respect and the admiration and love" of his people, had been a good ally, and ranked among the world's great leaders. In spite of American support, the Shah's regime began to unravel in the late 1970s when an economic slowdown produced rising unemployment and inflation, which reached a catastrophic 50 percent. Riots broke out, starting in January 1978, with protestors in the large cities like the capital, Tehran, numbering in the millions. In August 1978, a fire at a movie theater in Abadan killed 377 people. Most Iranians believed the Shah had set the fire. The Shah ordered a crackdown, and police killed some 8,000 demonstrators, including 700 at one protest in Jaleh Square in Tehran. The Shah then imposed martial law, and Khomeini responded by calling a general strike. Strikes by oil workers brought the Iranian economy to a standstill. When soldiers refused to follow orders to shoot at protestors, the Shah realized his life and his family's lives were in danger, and he fled into exile.

The Ayatollah arrived at the airport in Tehran on February 1, 1979, as a returning hero. Khomeini soon ruled by religious decree, making his interpretation of Islam the law of the land. Music was banished, women were forced to wear traditional head coverings, supporters of the Shah were executed, and religious minorities like Zoroastrians and Christians were persecuted.

"Malaise"

The chaos surrounding the Iranian Revolution caused a drop in the world's supply of oil by 2 million to 2.5 million barrels of oil a day between November 1978 and June 1979, causing crude prices to more than double from $14 to $35 a barrel. Gasoline prices at the pump climbed to an unprecedented 90 cents a gallon (about $2.67 in 2011 dollars), and drivers sometimes spent hours in line at the gas stations during the **Energy Crisis of 1979**. Violence broke out. In Los Angeles, one person attacked a pregnant woman accused of cutting in line. Some carried guns when they went to fill up. Cases of gas poisoning increased as some tried to steal gasoline from their neighbors' cars by sucking on hoses. Angry drivers sported bumper stickers saying "Carter—kiss my gas."

By January of 1980, inflation roared at a devastating 18.2 percent, the highest in six years. The prime interest rate stood at 18.5 percent in April of that year, causing home sales to drop by 6 percent and higher unemployment in the construction trades. Unemployment reached 7.8 percent in 1979, and most economists expected it to go higher in 1980.

Religious in his orientation, Carter believed he detected a crisis in the American spirit, caused by the economic troubles of the decade, the lost war in Vietnam, political assassinations and Watergate. Carter decided to make a speech that addressed the despair many Americans felt. It would be the most prophetic speech of his career. "All the legislation in the world can't fix what's wrong with America," he said. Americans, he said, had found themselves in a new age of limits. The country would have to learn how to find happiness in harder times. "In a nation that was proud of hard work, strong families, close-knit communities and our faith in God, too many of us now tend to worship self-indulgence and consumption," Carter said. "Human identity is no longer defined by what one does but by what one owns."

Carter urged Americans to think of future generations and conserve energy. He pledged to limit oil imports, and to increase funding for research into alternative energy sources such as solar power. He called on Americans to approach the energy crisis with the same spirit that suffused the *Apollo* mission that placed the first humans on the lunar surface just a decade earlier. "[T]he solution of the energy crisis can also help us to conquer the crisis of spirit in our country," he said. "It can rekindle our spirit of unity, our confidence in the future, and give our nation and all of us individually a new sense of purpose."

Initial reaction to the speech was strongly positive. According to author Kevin Mattson, in his book, *What The Heck Are You Up To, Mr. President? Jimmy Carter, America's Malaise and the Speech That Should Have Changed The Country*, "[t]housands of Americans telephoned [the White House], 84 percent of them supporting the speech." Unfortunately, Carter quickly squandered what he gained from the speech. Just two days later, he impulsively fired and asked for the resignation of five cabinet officers. It made Americans again think the administration was clueless, lurching from one action to another with no grand plan. The Carter years seemed like a parade of crises. The economy continued to be shaky

AMERICA HELD HOSTAGE

Foreign affairs took an ugly turn on December 24, 1979, when the Soviet Union invaded Afghanistan to prop up a friendly communist regime, starting a decade-long war that would hasten the fall of the Soviet government. It would also mark the first appearance on the world stage of Osama bin Laden, who later became the mastermind of the September 11, 2001 terrorist attacks on New York City and Washington, D.C. He was an anti-Soviet fighter in the mountainous nation of Afghanistan. American-Soviet tensions rose sharply, and in retaliation for the invasion, Carter decided to cancel America's participation in the summer Olympics scheduled to take place in Moscow the next summer.

Clouds appeared elsewhere in the Middle East. Distracted by his Egyptian-Israeli diplomacy, Carter was slow to react to the Iranian Revolution. The new "Islamic Republic of Iran" demanded that the Shah be returned to government custody to stand trial for his human rights abuses and put pressure on other governments to not give him sanctuary. Students began holding angry demonstrations in Iranian cities, shouting, "Death to America!" and burning the American flag.

The Shah shuttled with his family from Egypt to Morocco to the Bahamas and then to Mexico. In Mexico, doctors diagnosed him as suffering from cancer. Carter allowed the Shah to enter the United States to receive medical treatment. In response, on November 4, 1979, more than 3,000 student radicals, at the behest of the Iranian government, took over the American embassy in Tehran and began holding those inside hostage. The Iranians also seized control of most of the embassy files.

Khomeini said there would be no release of the 66 hostages until the Shah was sent back to Iran to stand trial. Two weeks after the initial embassy takeover, the Iranians did release five women and eight African-American men. Another hostage was let go in July 1980 when he began to suffer symptoms of multiple sclerosis. Carter for a long time retreated to the White House, eager to let Americans know that he was focused on winning the release of the hostages and had no time for ordinary politics. In fact, he created the impression of being besieged, an image reinforced by a new TV news show on ABC that debuted in 1979, *America Held Hostage*. Hosted by Ted Koppel, the show focused on each day's developments concerning the hostage drama. Each episode was labeled by the number of days since the crisis began—for instance, "Day 100." The show eventually became a permanent network feature and became the TV program *Nightline*. As the number of days grew higher, already low approval ratings for Carter dropped even further. The United States froze Iranian assets held in America.

The Iranian government demanded access to that money, and other reparations for the nation's suffering during the Shah's rule and the hand over of the Shah himself. The Shah left the United States on December 15, 1979 and stayed in Panama, where Omar Torrijos was repaying a debt to Carter for the Canal treaties. The Shah died in Egypt on July 27, 1980. With negotiations hopelessly deadlocked, patience running thin, and Carter aware of the political damage being done to him, the president authorized a military mission to rescue the hostages on April 24-25. Malfunctioning helicopters forced Carter to abort the mission. Eight Marines died in the rescue attempt and five suffered injuries. "The photographs of the wreckage—an Air Force plane crashed into some of the helicopters in the Iranian desert—became the symbol of America's and Carter's impotence," Bob Woodward wrote.

THE MORAL MAJORITY

Some Americans drew a religious message from America's troubles. Religious conservatives believed that the various recent social revolutions, such as feminism, gay rights, the experimentation with drug use and open sexuality, and the legalization of abortion had brought the wrath of God upon the nation. A majority of people who called themselves born-again Christians had voted for Carter in 1976, but they were disillusioned with him by 1979. On April 26, the Rev. Jerry Falwell of Virginia held his first "I Love America!" rally that featured the flag, gospel songs and political preaching. Falwell had opposed ministers getting involved in politics when Martin Luther King, Jr. and other ministers had led the African-American civil rights movement. At that time, the pro-segregationist Falwell claimed that the word of God would be corrupted if it were mixed with a political agenda. But since then, Falwell had been angered by the Supreme Court's 1973 *Roe v. Wade* decision that legalized abortion in the first two trimesters. He fiercely opposed the ongoing campaign for the Equal Rights Amendment (ERA) to the United States Constitution, which would have federally outlawed gender discrimination.

Falwell formed a group called the Moral Majority, dedicated to electing candidates who supported what Falwell and other Christian Right activists called "family values." The Moral Majority registered conservative

After 444 days the Iranian hostage crisis ended, but it destroyed Carter's chances for re-election.

Christian voters, bought ads attacking the positions taken by liberal candidates on issues like school prayer and abortion, and issued "report cards" for members of Congress and presidential candidates on "moral" issues, including their support for weapons systems like the B-1 bomber. It delivered votes almost exclusively for the Republican Party. The hostage crisis, inflation, and other American problems, Falwell and his allies like the Rev. Pat Robertson argued, stemmed from a lack of moral leadership by Carter and what they saw as a liberal-dominated Congress.

During the 1970s, Christians built an alternative media, with the Rev. Pat Robertson, son of a former segregationist senator, building the Christian Broadcasting Network, carried across the nation that mixed the gospel with a segment in which the TV minister offered news commentary. Falwell talked about Jesus, current events, and his own take on issues during his sermons on his TV show, *The Old-Time Gospel Hour*, which was also syndicated nationwide.

Ronald Reagan, opposed to abortion and gay rights and sharing the TV preacher's enthusiasm for a big defense budget, openly sought the support of Christian conservatives after he won the Republican nomination in the summer of 1980. Reagan appeared at the Religious Roundtable National Affairs Briefing in Dallas, Texas, in August 1980, and at a press conference expressed doubt concerning the theory of evolution. In a speech to the large assembly, which included Falwell, Robertson, and anti-ERA activist Phyllis Schlafly, Reagan said, "I know you can't endorse me, but I endorse you."

The 1980 election would mark the marriage of the Religious Right with the Republican Party. It helped the Republican Party and candidates like Reagan that most of the Christian Right was not just culturally conservative but economically conservative as well. White voters had increasingly opposed welfare programs and, slammed by high oil prices and growing tabs at the grocery store, they also became increasingly impatient with high taxes. In November 1978, voters placed anti-tax referenda on the ballot in sixteen states, and 12 of these measures passed. The most notable such measure was Proposition 13 in California, tirelessly supported by businessman Howard Jarvis. Proposition 13 limited property taxes in California to 1 percent of the property's value. Property taxes in California had escalated dramatically during the 1970s. Anti-tax sentiment was a powerful force going into the 1980 elections. The Republican nominee, Reagan, was able to unite both fiscal and religious conservatives that year, and reshaped his party for decades to come. The GOP remained in favor of low taxes and against government regulations, but opposition to abortion, and gay rights, and support for legalizing directed school prayer and tax support for church schools increasingly became litmus tests for hopeful Republican candidates.

"THERE YOU GO AGAIN": THE ELECTION OF RONALD REAGAN

Inflation, high unemployment, and the Iranian hostage crisis turned out to be too much for Jimmy Carter to overcome as he ran for re-election in 1980. The Democratic president first had to battle a challenge from Democratic Sen. Edward Kennedy that lasted until the party's national convention. Kennedy was unable to overcome the suspicions regarding the Chappaquiddick incident, and he never could articulate a clear argument for his candidacy, but he left Carter badly damaged politically. During the August 11-14 Democratic National Convention at Madison Square Garden in New York City, Kennedy's rousing concession speech got more applause than Carter's acceptance speech. At the end of the convention, red, white and blue balloons failed to release at the right moment, an unfortunate omen for Carter's fall campaign.

Carter faced not just Reagan, but moderate Republican Congressman John Anderson of Illinois who dropped out of the GOP primaries when it was apparent he couldn't win the party's conservative base; Anderson instead ran as an independent. The Carter campaign ignored Anderson, and the race tightened as the Carter campaign called attention to the many fact errors Reagan made on the campaign trail, such as when he claimed that "80 percent" of pollution comes from "plants and trees." Once again, as happened in 1960 and 1976, a televised presidential debate played a decisive role. Carter and Reagan faced off in Cleveland on October 28 and Carter showed a command of facts, but many voters saw the president as grim and aggressive. "In terms of style and images . . . Reagan was the clear winner," Jimmy Carter biography Burton Kaufman wrote. "Appearing relaxed, reasonable, and informed and avoiding any obvious mistakes, he effectively undermined the single concern that had propelled Carter into a virtual tie with him in the polls—that he was not up to the job of chief executive. He also came off as warmer than the president and more intimate with the voters, often fending off Carter's jabs with a sorrowful shake of the head followed by 'aw, shucks,' or 'there you go again.'" Reagan asked viewers, "Are you better off than you were four years ago?" Whether or not it was his fault, it was impossible for Carter to deny that most Americans were worse off economically in 1980 than they had been in 1976.

Reagan won in a landslide, receiving 51 percent of the popular vote to Carter's 41 percent and Anderson's 7 percent. Carter won only the states of Georgia, Maryland, Minnesota, Rhode Island, and West Virginia and the District of Columbia as Reagan beat him in the Electoral College 489 to 49. Carter made his concession speech early in the night, which caused Democratic voters in the West to not show up at the ballot box, a mistake that helped lose the Democratic Party's control of the Senate. The election was held on Day 365 of the hostage crisis. After the election, Carter worked with determination to finally secure the release of the hostages, but even with the issues resolved, the Iranians waited until minutes after Reagan was sworn in on January 20, 1981 to free them after 444 days of captivity. It was salt in Carter's psychic wounds, and he would retreat into depression for months, until he re-emerged as a leader of numerous humanitarian causes.

AMERICANS GET ANGRY

One of the hit movies of 1976 was the cynical comedy *Network*. The plot centered on a burned-out, lonely TV news anchor, Howard Beale, who is going to be fired because of poor ratings. Beale announces to the audience he will kill himself on the air during the next broadcast. The ratings soar, he keeps his job, and instead of a newscaster Beale becomes the "mad prophet of the airwaves." One night he delivers this sermon:

> I don't have to tell you things are bad. Everybody knows things are bad. It's a depression. Everybody's out of work or scared of losing their job. The dollar buys a nickel's worth; banks are going bust; shopkeepers keep a gun under the counter; punks are running wild in the street, and there's nobody anywhere who seems to know what to do, and there's no end to it.
> We know the air is unfit to breathe and our food is unfit to eat. And we sit watching our TVs while some local newscaster tells us that today we had fifteen homicides and sixty-three violent crimes, as if that's the way it's supposed to be! We all know things are bad—worse than bad—they're crazy.

Beale admits he doesn't have a solution to the myriad problems of 1970s America, but he has a first step on the road from powerlessness and despair gripping his audience. "I don't want you to protest," Beale says.

> I don't want you to riot. I don't want you to write to your Congressman, because I wouldn't know what to tell you to write . . . All I know is that first, you've got to get mad. You've gotta say, 'I'm a human being, goddammit! My life has value! . . . I want you to get up right now and go to the window, open it, and stick your head out and yell, 'I'm as mad as hell, and I'm not going to take this anymore!!'

Americans got angry during the 1970s. In fact, tax protestor Howard Jarvis in California titled his memoir, *I'm as Mad as Hell!* They expressed this rage in ways great and small. In 1980, they voted out an incumbent president, and the Democrats lost 12 seats in the United States Senate. A more meaningful statistic might be the number of voters who expressed disgust at both Republicans and Democrats and indifference to the political process by declining to vote. About 63.1 percent of registered voters participated in the presidential election between John F. Kennedy and Richard Nixon in 1960. The percentage

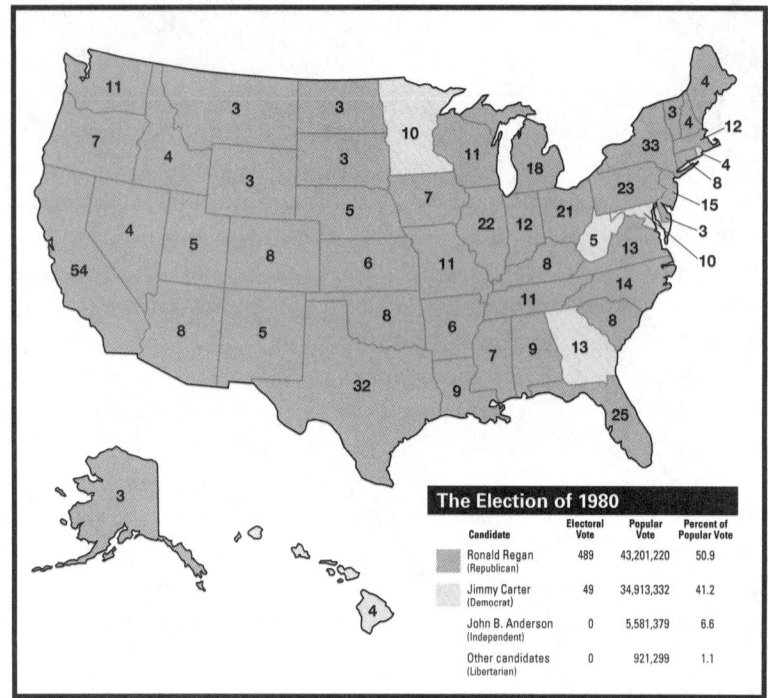

Map 31.4 The Election of 1980

declined slightly to 60.6 in 1968. By 1980, barely over half—52.6 percent—cast a ballot in the election between Carter and Reagan.

Americans beat up each other in gas lines and even rioted over disco music. In 1979, a Chicago disc jockey named Steve Dahl quit working for one radio station when it dropped its rock format and switched to all-disco. At his new radio home at WLUP-FM, he created the Disco Destruction Army. He convinced Bill Veeck, the owner of the Chicago White Sox, to stage a "Disco Demolition Night" during a game against the Detroit Tigers on July 12. Fans who brought a disco record to Comiskey Park got a big discount on their tickets. The records were collected and, as fans chanted, "Disco sucks!" Dahl blew up a mountain of vinyl. In a frenzy, fans poured out of their seats, some jumping from dangerous heights, and tore up chunks of the field and began tearing up seats. Police plunged into the crowd and made arrests, and there was so much damage and unrest that the second game of the double-header was cancelled.

"Some people pondered what the rampage meant," author Kevin Mattson notes. "It was certainly the country's first full-fledged riot against disco . . . Gay and civil rights groups worried . . . that this was a revolt against anything upsetting heterosexual whiteness, the stoner equivalent of the Moral Majority. There was some truth to the charge. But in a place like Chicago, economic resentment mattered as much." Mattson points out that the late 1970s saw a proliferation of pricey discos on North Street that drew affluent young urban professionals—those who would be called "yuppies" by 1984. "The kids who cheered Dahl were the long-haired working-class guys who had problems affording the paraphernalia—gold chains and polyester suits – necessary for discotheques."

If the specific target of their rage, disco music, was irrational, Dahl's fans felt the fear that their lives might not be as prosperous as their parents'. The 1970s marked the start of a long decline in the American middle class that continues into the twenty-first century. Starting in the Nixon years and continuing through the Obama administration, wealth redistributed from the poor and middle class to the already wealthy. Increasingly, families depended on two wage earners to make ends meet. In 1960, only 19 percent of married women with children of pre-school age worked outside of the home; by 1995, 64 percent did. The average work year expanded by 184 hours during the last four decades of the twentieth century. In 1977, the poorest two-fifths of Americans held 17.2 percent of the national wealth, but only 14.9 percent by 1999. The middle fifth saw their share of the national wealth decline from 16.4 percent to 14.7 percent. The richest one-fifth, however, saw their share of the national wealth climb from 44.2 percent to 50.4 percent.

The Vietnam War and the Iranian hostage crisis proved to frustrated Americans in the 1970s that the United States could no longer impose its will on the world. Watergate and the Church hearings proved that Americans could no longer trust their government. According to surveys, the percentage of Americans who trusted their government to "do the right thing" fell sharply from 75 percent in 1964 to only 36 percent by the time Nixon resigned in 1974. This had a profound effect on American politics as voters no longer trusted the government to accomplish big things like the moon landing or the kind of massive public works projects that characterized the New Deal. In later decades proposals for big government projects like President Bill Clinton's and Barack Obama's health-care reforms in 1993-94 and in 2009-2010 ran into a buzz saw of skepticism. Skepticism of government served a conservative agenda as both Republicans and Democrats moved further right after the 1970s.

Americans' distrust deepened as they were battered by successive waves of inflation, unemployment, and the disappearance of decent wages and benefits. It was no accident that as the glittery escapism of disco faded from the music scene in the late 1970s, one of the rising music stars, Bruce Springsteen, became a troubadour for the troubled and alienated working class. His song, "The Promised Land" voiced the frustrations of many Americans:

> There's a dark cloud rising from the desert floor/
> I packed my bags and I'm heading straight into the storm/
> Gonna be a twister to blow everything down/
> That ain't got the faith to stand its ground/
> Blow away the dreams that tear you apart/
> Blow away the dreams that break your heart/
> Blow away the lies that leave you nothing/ but lost and brokenhearted.

Writers like the journalist Tom Wolfe ridiculed the 1970s as "The Me Decade," but narcissism was a luxury of the well-to-do, those pampered enough to be frivolous. For working Americans, the decade marked the start of the Great Squeeze, an age in which they could not find enough hours in the week or earn enough money to guarantee their children a college education, or themselves a secure job and a comfortable retirement. Working class Americans began to sense that the social contract had been broken. As another Bruce Springsteen song recorded in the twenty-first century put it,

> We sent our sons to Korea and Vietnam/
> Now we're wondering what they were dyin' for.

Chronology

1969 Richard Nixon sworn in as 37th president.
My Lai Massacre.
Nixon begins bombing campaign in Cambodia.
The Moratorium takes place across the nation.

1970 American troops invade Cambodia.
Protests are held at Kent State University.

1971 Twenty-Sixth Amendment is ratified.
The *New York Times* publishes *The Pentagon Papers*.

1972 Nixon visits China and the Soviet Union.
SALT I treaty is signed.
Break-in at Watergate.
Nixon wins re-election.
Christmas Bombing of North Vietnam.

1973 Peace accords in Vietnam take effect.
Senate Watergate hearings begin.
The CIA instigates a coup in Chile.
Vice President Spiro Agnew is forced to resign.
The Yom Kippur War.
"Saturday Night Massacre."

1974 Richard Nixon resigns as president.
Gerald Ford becomes the 38th president.
Ford pardons Nixon.

1975 The South Vietnamese government surrenders.
The Khmer Rouge takes over of Cambodia.
The *Mayaguez* incident.

1976 Jimmy Carter is elected president.

1977 Panama Canal Treaty is ratified.

1978 Camp David Peace Accords.
The Iranian Revolution starts

1979 The Shah of Iran is overthrown and Ayatollah Ruhollah Khomeini becomes "Supreme Leader."
The United States formally recognizes China.
Egypt and Israel sign a formal peace treaty.
Three Mile Island accident.
American hostages are seized by militants in Iran.
The Soviet Union invades Afghanistan.
Carter cancels American participation in the 1980 Summer Olympics in Moscow.

1980 Ronald Reagan is elected the 40th president.

Review Questions

1. In what ways did the Vietnam War prompt the Watergate Scandal?

2. What was the "Nixon Doctrine" and how was it applied in Vietnam, Iran, and Chile?

3. What were President Richard Nixon's objectives in improving relations with China?

4. What factors caused "stagflation" in 1973 and the economic slowdown in 1979-1980?

5. Describe how President Jimmy Carter applied and failed to apply his policy of "Human Rights" in his relationship with other world leaders.

Glossary of Important People and Concepts

Affirmative Action
Spiro Agnew
Boat People
Church Committee Hearings
Archibald Cox
John Dean
Dirty Tricks
Thomas Eagleton
Daniel Ellsberg
John Ehrlichman
Energy Crisis (1973)
Sam Ervin
Jerry Falwell
Gerald R. Ford
Fragging
H.R. "Bob" Haldeman
Helsinki Accords
Kent State Massacre
George McGovern
Mayaguez
John N. Mitchell
Moratorium
Edmund Muskie
Nixon Doctrine
Pentagon Papers
Elliott Richardson
Southern Strategy
Stagflation
Three Mile Island
Watergate

SUGGESTED READINGS

W. Carl Biven, *Jimmy Carter's Economy: Policy in an Age of Limits* (2002).

Peter Brush, "The Hard Truth About Fragging: Unprecedented Decline of Morale and Discipline Spawned a Phenomenon Forever Tied to the Vietnam War," *Vietnam* (July 28, 2010), http://www.historynet.com/the-hard-truth-about-fragging.htm. Accessed July 11, 2011.

___, "Higher and Higher: Drug Use Among U.S. Forces in Vietnam," *Vietnam Magazine*, Vol, 115, No. 4 (December 2002), pp. 46-53, 70., http://www.library.vanderbilt.edu/central/Brush/American-drug-use-vietnam.htm. Accessed July 11, 2011.

William Bundy, *A Tangled Web: The Making of Foreign Policy in the Nixon Presidency* (1998).

David Frum, *How We Got Here: The 70s, The Decade That Brought You Modern Life – For Better or Worse* (2000)

Seymour M. Hersh, *The Price of Power: Kissinger in the Nixon White House* (1983).

Maurice Isserman and Michael Kazin. *America Divided: The Civil War of the 1960s* (2000).

Burton I. Kaufman, *The Presidency of James Earl Carter* (1993).

Stanley Karnow. *Vietnam: A History* 1983.

Ben Kiernan, *The Pol Pot Regime: Race, Power, and Genocide in Cambodia Under the Khmer Rouge, 1975-79* (1996).

Stephen Kinzer, *Overthrow: America's Century of Regime Change From Hawaii to Iraq* (2006.)

____, *All The Shah's Men: An American Coup and the Roots of Middle Eastern Terror* (2003).

Naomi Klein, *The Shock Doctrine: The Rise of Disaster Capitalism* (2007).

Mark Hamilton Lytle, *America's Uncivil Wars: The Sixties From Elvis to the Fall of Richard Nixon* (2006).

Kevin Mattson, *What The Heck Are You Up To, Mr. President? Jimmy Carter, America's Malaise and the Speech That Should Have Changed the Country* (2010).

Allen J. Matusow, *The Unravelling of America: A History of Liberalism in the 1960s* (1984).

Yanek Mieczkowski, *Gerald Ford and the Challenges of the 1970s* (2005).

Rick Perlstein, *Nixonland: The Rise of a President and the Fracturing of America* (2008).

Kevin Phillips, *Wealth and Democracy: A Political History of the American Rich* (2002).

Richard Reeves, *President Nixon: Alone in the White House* (2001).

Bruce J. Schulman, *The Seventies: The Great Shift in American Culture, Society and Politics* (2001).

William Shawcross, *Sideshow: Kissinger, Nixon and the Destruction of Cambodia* (1979).

___, *The Shah's Last Ride: The Fate of an Ally* (1988).

Ronald H. Spector, *After Tet: The Bloodiest Year in Vietnam* (1993).

Wyatt Wells, *American Capitalism, 1945-2000: Continuity and Change from Mass Production to the Information Society* (2003).

Bob Woodward, *Shadow: Five Presidents and the Legacy of Watergate* (1999).

Bob Woodward and Carl Bernstein, *All The President's Men* (1974).

____, *The Final Days* (1976).

Wasteland, a shop on San Francisco, California's Haight Street, was once the center of the "hippie movement."

Chapter Thirty-two

AMERICAN CULTURE AND THE COUNTERCULTURE OF THE 1960s and 1970s

A musical celebrating hippies, drugs, the anti-war movement, and free love, **Hair** *became one of the surprise Broadway hits in the late 1960s. Opening at the Biltmore Theater in April 1968, the play shocked audiences with its occasional nudity, frequent profanity, embrace of interracial sex, and tolerance of homosexuality. The production mixed an almost naïve hope for peace and love with acidly cynical putdowns of establishment political figures like Lyndon Johnson and Richard Nixon.*

Hair *opened with "The Age of Aquarius," a song destined to become a Top 40 hit. The song brimmed with optimism. The lyrics proclaimed the dawn of a new era of human consciousness.*

> *When the Moon is in the seventh house*
> *And Jupiter aligns with Mars*
> *Then peace will guide the planets*
> *And love will steer the stars*

Like so much of the 1960s and 1970s, paradox almost overwhelmed **Hair***. In spite of the sunny mood of the opening number, by the climax one of the major characters has decided to not dodge the draft, reports for duty, is sent to Vietnam and, by the closing number, lies dead on the stage as the rest of the cast sings with sadness, "Let the Sunshine In." The emotional kaleidoscope of 1960s always mixed hues of activism and alienation, new frontiers and apocalyptic doom.*

The historian Rick Perlstein noted that if one scanned the American bestsellers lists as the Sixties shaded into the Seventies, it would seem that America had fallen into terminal decline. Books predicting stock market crashes, death-dealing ecological disasters, and even the imminent Second Coming of Jesus sold in the millions. Observing the cultural landscape in California, **New York Times** *reporter Steve Roberts noted in 1971, "Prophets of doom are as common as girls in bikinis (there are even a few prophets of doom in bikinis). Some predict the whole state will break off and sink into the Pacific—probably this month."*

Twentieth century Protestants increasingly embraced "pre-millennial dispensationalism"—the belief that soon Christians will be taken up to heaven in an event called "the Rapture" so they would not suffer a seven-year series of natural disasters and wars causing millions of deaths (a period believers call "the Tribulation.") The Tribulation would end, such evangelicals believed, with the emergence of a Satanic figure called the Antichrist who would become a dictator of the world before being defeated by Jesus and his angels. Hal Lindsey, a former tugboat captain and graduate of the Armageddon-oriented Dallas Theological Seminary, brought these ideas to a broad audience and became one of the 1970s' most successful prophets of doom, writing that decade's bestselling non-fiction book **The Late, Great Planet Earth***. Formerly an evangelist for the Campus Crusade for Christ, Lindsey grew sideburns, a moustache and longer hair and filled his book with the language of the 1960s youth counterculture, using a popular term for LSD hallucinations when* he described the Rapture as "the ultimate trip" and calling the Antichrist "the weirdo beast." Lindsey frightened his audience, insisting that images of fire and blood in the Biblical Book of Revelation were predictions of nuclear war. The Bible, Lindsey insisted, was as current as today's headlines. "The rebirth of Israel, an increase in natural catastrophes, the threat of war with Egypt and the revival of interest in Satanism and witchcraft . . . were foreseen by prophets from Moses to Jesus as being the key signals for the coming of an Antichrist. And a war which will bring man to the brink of destruction."

California cult leader Charles Manson led his followers on a killing spree that claimed seven victims in the summer of 1969. Their intention was to produce a race war between blacks and whites he believed that the Bible predicted. Religion did not inspire all late-1960s and early 1970s doomsday prognosticators. A novel, **The Andromeda Strain** by Michael Crichton, depicted the human race as threatened with extinction by a killer virus delivered to the planet by a fallen space satellite. According to Perlstein, a non-fiction book called **The Population Bomb** by Paul Ehrlich "went into a new paperback printing every couple of weeks." The book predicted a human population explosion leading to mass famine and warfare over diminishing resources. "While you are reading these words, four people will have died from starvation," the back cover grimly proclaimed, "most of them children."

Dread of religious or secular Armageddon haunted movies and music as well. One hit film, **The Planet of the Apes**, takes place after a nuclear war has allowed mutant apes to take over Earth and enslave a human race that has lost the power of speech. Meanwhile, a 1969 number one song by the folk duo Zager and Evans, "In The Year 2525," warned listeners that,

> In the year 6565/
> you won't need no husband/
> won't need no wife/
> You'll pick your son, pick your daughter too/
> from the bottom of a long glass tube.

As the author Perlstein notes, "The public appetite for doom was bottomless."

ORGANIZATION MEN:
The Suburbs and the Birth of the 1960s Counterculture

America slouched towards Armageddon in the blandest of settings, the American suburbs. Parents in the 1960s, after living through the Great Depression, World War II, the creation of dangerous nuclear weapons, and the start of a possibly world-destroying "Cold War" with the Soviet Union craved a predictable, safe life. Instead, they found anxiety as the TV news bombarded them with fears of nuclear destruction and of communist spies hidden deep within every important American institution, from the highest level of government, to college campuses, to the church around the corner.

Disposable incomes rose by 49 percent between 1940 and 1964, but as author and 1960s protestor Todd Gitlin noted, greater personal wealth did not seem to buy everyone peace of mind. In post-war America, patients with more money in their pocket increasingly spent it on psychoanalysis. The number of psychiatrists practicing in the United States rose by a factor of six between 1940 and 1964. A central icon of the era was the character Linus from the popular comic strip "Peanuts." Highly intelligent, Linus nevertheless clung desperately to a security blanket. Linus' older sister Lucy opened up a booth where she offered psychological services to the strip's other children for 5 cents a pop. Anxiety, it seemed, even shadowed the newspaper "funny pages."

It became a sign of status for Anglos to move from crowded and dirty cities filled with unhappy racial and ethnic minorities to all—or mostly—white suburbs. In post-war America, bedroom communities spread like mushrooms after a rain with about 1 million Americans moving from cities or rural areas to suburbs every year during the 1950s, until about 25 percent of the country lived in such communities by 1960. The number of Americans living in suburbs sharply angled upwards from around 36 million to approximately 74 million. Residents often left communities where they had longstanding family ties and friendships to arrive in a constantly changing suburban landscape where trees and other signs of nature were leveled to make way for endlessly expanding rows of houses. Discontent, however, brewed under the placid exterior of these neatly groomed look-alike homes.

In popular books such as Herman Wouk's *Marjorie Morningstar* and Sloan Wilson and Jonathan Franzen's *The Man in the Gray Flannel Suit* (both published in 1950), the male business heroes are not completely beaten down by demanding bosses, long hours, and ever-longer commutes, but they mourn the time away from wives and children and regret when they succumb to carnal temptations offered by a life spent away from the home.

In Arthur Miller's 1949 play *Death of a Salesman*, Willy Loman discovers too late in life that, in his relentless drive for corporate success and middle-class respectability, he has lost emotional fulfillment and his integrity. He can only measure his worth through the eyes of his more successful peers, and their disdain as he ages and his failures pile up proves lethal. His wife begs their sons to respect their father and his sacrifices:

> I don't say he's a great man. Willie Loman never made a lot of money. His name was never in the paper. He's not the finest character that ever lived. But he's a human being, and a terrible thing is happening to him. So attention must be paid. He's not to be allowed to fall in his grave like an old dog. Attention, attention must finally be paid to such a person.

Loman commits suicide, with only his wife and his ungrateful sons to note his passing. By Loman's own measure his lack of material success meant he had become a nonentity. In addition to novels and plays, several non-fiction works in the post-war era critiqued American materialism, such as David Reisman, Nathan Glazer and Reuel Denney's *The Lonely Crowd* (1950), C. Wright Mills' *White Collar: The American Middle Classes* (1951) and William Whyte's *The Organization Man* (1956).

This simmering discontent with the values of post-World War II America bubbled to the surface during several episodes of the hit television show **The Twilight Zone**, which ran on CBS in the early 1960s. In *The Twilight Zone*, technology, Cold War paranoia, and corporate culture turned the small towns and suburbs of America into alienated islands of poisonous suspicion. In a 1960 episode, "The Monsters are Due on Maple Street," a peaceful, all-American suburb turns into a hothouse of paranoia after the electricity in a neighborhood goes out. A child who has been reading perhaps too much science fiction excitedly speculates that the power outage is the first step in an invasion by space aliens. Ethnic, class and social tensions arise as the once friendly neighbors remember innocent past incidents that in the heat and the darkness now seem sinister. A neighbor who tinkers with mysterious machinery in his basement is accused of being a secret space invader because he was seen one night glancing at the stars. Another whose lights come on while all the other houses remain dark becomes a new target of doubt.

One man is fatally shot, and a riot breaks out. At the episode's conclusion, we discover that real space aliens have been turning the lights on and off, knowing that the stress of the unfamiliar would terrify these alienated suburbanites and lead them to destroy each other. The aliens can take over once the humans have done the killing for them. The episode obviously comments on the McCarthy-era Red Scare, when Americans destroyed each others' lives on flimsy or non-existence evidence of communist subversion, but it also speaks loudly of the loneliness and social isolation prevailing in the suburbs.

"WHAT ARE YOU REBELLING AGAINST?": The Childhood of 1960s Radicals

Many white children growing up from the late 1940s through the 1950s saw the frustrations of their mothers, felt the unhappiness of their parents, were horrified by the monotony and emotional coldness that accompanied the pursuit of material wealth, and witnessed the thrilling black struggle for freedom in the South unfolding on their television screens. As they entered their teens, they demanded a life less conformist and with more immediate emotional rewards. They eagerly read books like the 1951 novel *The Catcher in the Rye* by J.D. Salinger, in which an angry teenager named Holden Caulfield furiously condemned adults he considered "phonies." Holden hates materialism. "Goddamn money," he grumbles at one point. "It always ends up making you blue as hell."

Caulfield lives in a society dominated by cars, in which kids escaped the supervision of their parents by "cruising," making out in "lovers' lanes" and at drive-in movie theaters. If other teens found sexual freedom behind the wheel, Caulfield saw the car as one more expensive toy that brought only temporary happiness and failed to fill the spiritual emptiness of modern life, one more oppressive machine that commands time and money. "Take most people, they're crazy about cars," Caulfield says. "They worry if they get a little scratch on them, and they're always talking about how many miles they get to a gallon, and if they get a brand-new car already they start thinking about trading it in for one that's even newer. I don't even like *old* cars. I mean they don't even interest me. I'd rather have a goddamn horse. A horse is at least *human*, for God's sake."

The entire American value system would be up for reappraisal in the 1960s and the young would be inspired by 1950s pop culture. In the 1953 movie *The Wild One*, Marlon Brando played a character named Johnny, the leader of a motorcycle gang. Brando and his crew upset a quiet, sleepy town. At one point, he's in a bar standing next to a jukebox. A young woman asks, "Hey, Johnny, what are you rebelling against?" Brando looks at her with amusement and says, "What've you got?"

Children and teenagers who admired these actors like Brando and James Dean and films like *Rebel Without a Cause* would later lead the so-called "New Left" of the 1960s. These young people would aim their revolutionary zeal at a much broader range of targets than the "Old Left," which focused on union organizing and opposition to segregation and other pragmatic issues. The New Left had a wider agenda, tackling conventional thought not just on race and economic class, but also questioning traditional definitions of masculinity and femininity, the structure of the family, and the morality of private property. New Leftists would incorporate Eastern religions like Hinduism and Buddhism as alternatives to middle class Christianity and Judaism. More explicitly political and goal-oriented than the Beatniks of the 1950s, early 1960s political dissenters, according to historians Maurice Isserman and Michael Kazin, advocated:

- Rejection of militarism, the Cold War, and the deepening American misadventure in Vietnam.
- Racial and class equality, overturning the traditional America hierarchy based on wealth and status.
- Direct democracy bypassing the well-financed interest groups that dominated the adult political world.
- Sexual frankness instead of phony modesty and moral hypocrisy.

If American society was oppressive, and the older generation brought the world pollution and war, young dissenters argued what was needed was a new culture, what came to be known as the "counterculture." The rebels of the 1960s raged against Willie Loman-style anonymity, and proclaimed that "less is more" as they questioned the value of big institutions ranging from public schools to supermarkets to the federal government. Older Americans, the New Left believed, falsely equated consumerism with happiness, ever-harder labor with moral rectitude, and loyalty with knee-jerk flag-waving.

The New Left would eventually question existing power structures: the political dominance of the West over the developing world in Africa, Asia and Latin America; the vestiges of white power that trampled the rights of blacks, browns and Native Americans; the political and economic dominance of men over women; the oppression of gays and bisexuals at the hands of heterosexuals. At its best, the 1960s counterculture would become an expansive, inclusive movement, as the era's premiere troubadour, **Bob Dylan** sang, ringing chimes of freedom for "each an' ev'ry underdog soldier in the night," tolling

> for the rebel, tolling for the rake
> Tolling for the luckless, the abandoned an' forsaken
> Tolling for the outcast, burnin' constantly at stake
> An' we gazed upon the chimes of freedom flashing.

"THE ORDER IS RAPIDLY CHANGIN'": Bob Dylan and 1960s Protest Music

The multiple crusades of the 1960s and 1970s marched forward to a kaleidoscopic soundtrack blending several musical genres from the blues to Indian sitar instrumentals. Racism, sexism and the environment would become the subject matter for much of the music.

By 1961, a 20-year-old Minnesota native, Robert Allen Zimmerman, had already started performing under the stage name Bob Dylan. The young man was soon a mainstay in New York City's Greenwich Village folk music scene. A rock fan as a child, who loved the records of Little Richard and Buddy Holly, Dylan also drew inspiration from African-American folk performer Lead Belly, early blues singers like Blind Lemon Jefferson, folk artist Woody Guthrie, and Beat poets and authors like Allen Ginsberg and Jack Kerouac.

Not everyone loved his nasal, sometimes raspy voice. But Dylan brought passion to his performances and touched the hearts of educated young people drawn by his outcast image. Early in his career, Dylan performed with just an acoustic guitar and a harmonica held by a neck brace, which gave a greater intimacy to his concerts. He shared the impatience of many young people in the early 1960s. In one of his most famous songs, 1964's "The Times They Are A-Changin,'" he commanded the older generation to step aside if they weren't willing to make the world a more decent, fair place:

> Come mothers and fathers
> Throughout the land/
> And don't criticize
> What you can't understand/
> Your sons and your daughters
> Are beyond your command/
> Your old road is
> Rapidly agin'/
> Please get out of the new one
> If you can't lend your hand/
> For the times they are a-changin'.

Dylan gave sophisticated political analysis in his protest songs, seeing even violent racists, such as the assassin of the Mississippi civil rights leader Medgar Evers, as being manipulated by southern politicians in a deadly game of divide-and-conquer. Politicians served only the rich and divided the black and white poor in order to prevent meaningful change, as he suggested in the song "Only a Pawn in Their Game" (also released in 1964):

A South politician preaches to the poor white man/
"You got more than blacks, don't complain/
You're better than them, you been born with white skin"/
They explain/
And the Negro's name/
Is used it is plain/
For the politician's gain/
As he rises to fame/
And the poor white remains/
On the caboose of the train/
But it ain't him to blame/
He's only a pawn in their game/

Most of his songs, such as the classic protest ballad, "Blowin' In The Wind" (1963) and the surrealistic "Mr. Tambourine Man" (1965) became hits only when recorded by pop music groups like Peter, Paul, and Mary and rock bands like The Byrds. Dylan was perhaps more important in how he influenced other artists than in anything he wrote or sang himself. His most important fans were the British rock band the **Beatles**, whose records began dominating the American music charts in January 1964. Many historians believe that the hysterical fan enthusiasm the band generated—dubbed "Beatlemania" by the press—came not only from their great songwriting talent and charming intelligence, but the proximity of their first American concert and TV performances to the assassination of President John Kennedy. "On an emotional level, what Beatlemania achieved for many young people was a restoration of the feelings of hope and sheer intensity that many feared had died forever with John Kennedy," wrote author Charles Kaiser.

Before the band landed at John F. Kennedy Airport in the United States on February 7, 1964, their single "I Want to Hold Your Hand" had already sold almost 3 million copies. About 40 percent of the population watched their first performance on American television, on the variety program *The Ed Sullivan Show*. The Beatles openly admired African-American blues and early rock stars like Chuck Berry, leading a much larger white audience to appreciate those artists. "It was the black music we dug," singer, guitarist and composer John Lennon said. "We felt that we had the message, which was, 'Listen to this music. When we came here . . . nobody was listening to rock 'n' roll or to black music in America. We felt as though we were coming to the land of its origin, but nobody wanted to know about it."

The Beatles also set a trend for men wearing long hair. Guitarist George Harrison's interest in the music of India and in Hinduism intensified young people's interest in all things Eastern. Most important, the Beatles expanded the range of issues and styles that could be explored in popular songs. Making unprecedented use of unusual electronic musical instruments like the mellotron, Indian sitars, and studio techniques like playing tapes of music performances backward, the Beatles created a richly varied sound. Beginning in 1965, Bob Dylan became a major influence in their song writing as they explored issues as varied as loneliness ("Eleanor

This "Head Shop" on Haight Street in the Haight-Ashbury section of San Francisco, California, where the hippie movement was headquartered in the 1960s. Taken between 1980 and 2006

Rigby" in 1966), teen runaways ("She's Leaving Home" in 1967), and the dangers of political violence ("Revolution" in 1968).

The Beatles' success inspired Dylan to transition from acoustic folk singer to rock star, which brought him a much wider audience with hits such as "Like a Rolling Stone" (1965). The Beatles' lyrics, meanwhile, became more complex (and incomprehensible to some) after Dylan introduced them to marijuana during their first meeting in August 1964 and the Beatles began openly experimenting with LSD, a psychedelic drug. Lennon caused Beatles fans to frantically search for hidden meanings in his lyrics with the release of songs like "Lucy in the Sky With Diamonds" in 1967:

> Follow her down to a bridge by a fountain,
> Where rocking horse people eat marshmallow pies.
> Everyone smiles as you drift past the flowers,
> That grow so incredibly high.

Critics pointed out the initials of the song spelled out "LSD" and accused the Beatles of promoting drug use. Nevertheless, "Lucy" was just one hit off the most influential rock album of all time, *Sgt. Pepper's Lonely Hearts Club Band* (1967). The mid- and late-1960s music of Bob Dylan and the Beatles made the adult world for the first time take youth culture and rock music seriously. Previously ridiculed as children's music, rock started getting reviewed in serious magazines like *Newsweek* and the era's songs began to be studied as literature on college campuses.

"TUNING IN AND DROPPING OUT": The Hippie Culture

After recording two albums of topical and protest songs, Dylan released an introspective album in 1964, *Another Side of Bob Dylan*. The record included love songs and musings of how hard it is to maintain personal integrity in a corrupt world. Bob Dylan's politically motivated folk fans felt betrayed when he began singing more symbolic, personal lyrics and especially when he—as they saw it—"sold out" by performing with a rock band. Dylan would reply that he was simply returning to the music he loved and that he didn't want to be beholden to any particular ideology. In fact, the quest for personal authenticity Dylan pursued at this time was a journey shared by many in the 1960s generation. Many Sixties rebels rejected politics in favor of personal freedom and spiritual enlightenment.

So-called hippies dropped out of mainstream society because they saw nuclear weapons, the Vietnam War, and industrial pollution as symptoms of a sick society poisoned by greed. San Francisco's Haight-Ashbury district became America's most famous hippie enclave, drawing thousands of teenagers and young adults, especially during the so-called "Summer of Love" in 1967. Hippies soon competed with the Golden Gate Bridge as one of the city's tourist attractions. Thousands of other colonies, however, such as the "The Farm" in south central Tennessee and the New Buffalo Community in Arroyo Hondo, New Mexico, sprang up across America. Residents in these communes often cooperatively farmed, renounced private property and even shared sexual partners. Hippies embraced instinct over rationality and spontaneity over routine.

Hippies tended to be less educated, less traveled and less focused than the New Left revolutionaries. The hippies focused on genuine emotions and living for today rather than seeking some distant and possibly unattainable political objective. Members of political groups like the Students for a Democratic Society saw the hippies as foolish and self-indulgent, and their dependence on drugs and sexual hedonism as a dangerous distraction from youth resistance to the Vietnam War and against racism.

"LISTEN TO THE COLORS OF YOUR DREAMS": Hippies and Psychedelic Drugs

Marijuana, a natural product, remained the drug of choice in the 1960s, almost as common among young people as beer was among their parents. Yet, if hippies called for a return to nature, much of the ecstasy they experienced came from a laboratory-produced chemical. As noted by historians Maurice Isserman and Michael Kazin in *America Divided: The Civil Wars of the 1960s*, D-Lysergic acid diethylamide, or LSD as it became more famously known, was invented by the Swiss chemist Albert Hoffman at pharmaceutical firm Sandoz Laboratories in 1943. Hoffman hoped to find a cure for migraines by synthesizing a compound made from rye fungi that he had mixed five years earlier and set aside. While combining chemicals, Hoffman spilled a small amount of concentrated LSD on his fingertips and the substance was absorbed through his skin.

Hoffman hallucinated wildly, experiencing the world's first "acid" trip. In his diary, he wrote that he experienced a "remarkable but not unpleasant state of intoxication, characterized by an intense stimulation of the imagination and an altered state of the awareness of the world." Hoffman later recalled "fantastic, rapidly changing images of a striking reality and depth, alternating with a vivid kaleidoscopic play of colors," a sense-juggling dream state that continued for three hours.

Hoping he would find a practical application for the drug, Hoffman mailed out LSD to the ever-expanding roster of psychiatrists practicing in 1940s America. Psychiatrists in private practice, universities and the CIA experimented with the drug. The CIA, hoping the drug could be used to achieve mind control or as a more effective truth serum, administered LSD to several test subjects without their knowledge. One test subject "ran across a bridge over the Potomac River and went temporarily mad before his colleagues rescued him," wrote Isserman and Kazin. "Every automobile, he swore, looked like a bloodthirsty monster."

LSD got its greatest publicity boost when Beatle Paul McCartney admitted in an interview taking it and when references to trips began to appear in John Lennon's lyrics, such as when he urged his listeners to "listen to the color of your dreams" in the 1966 song "Tomorrow Never Knows." A Harvard psychiatrist, **Dr. Timothy Leary,** became the chief evangelist for LSD as a means of discovering inner peace and expanded consciousness. Leary received a small sample of Sandoz acid in early 1961 and tested the substance on himself and his Harvard colleagues. In their 1963 *Harvard Review* article, "The Politics of Consciousness Expansion," Leary and his research partner Richard Alpert wrote, "The social situation in regard to consciousness-expanding drugs is very similar to that faced sixty years ago by those crackpot visionaries who were playing around with horseless carriages. Of course, the automobile is external child's play as compared to the unleashing of cortical energy, so the social dilemma is similar."

Leary believed that the magic of acid was that it could cause users to question social norms and conventional beliefs, a desirable goal in a society warped by racism and violence. In 1961, Leary conducted experiments at the Concord State Prison in Massachusetts. He gave LSD to prisoners and "guided" them through their hallucinations. Leary later claimed it helped the convicts "rethink" the mental "games" that turned them into lawbreakers. Leary famously advised students to "Turn on, tune in, drop out." Leary's outspoken advocacy of drug use and his uncontrolled distribution of LSD led to his firing by Harvard and the closing of his Psychedelic Research Project on the campus. Leary moved to Millbrook, an upstate New York estate, where he sought to "create a new organism and a new dedication to life as art."

One of the first LSD test subjects was future author **Ken Kesey,** who would later write *One Flew Over the Cuckoo's Nest* (1962), a novel about inmates in an insane asylum that became a cult hit in the 1960s counterculture. Like many who took LSD, Kesey believed that he had found a key to understanding the universe. In the mid-1960s, Kesey led a group that dubbed itself the Merry Pranksters, in winding, acid-drenched bus rides across America. Wanting to celebrate the publication of his second novel, *Sometimes a Great Notion*, Kesey and the Pranksters painted a school bus in Day-Glo colors, installed a first-rate sound system, named it "Further" and zigzagged across the country Taking not just LSD, also smoking marijuana and popping amphetamines, the Pranksters introduced friendly people they encountered to acid and staged "happenings"—spontaneous events featuring drugs, rock music and light shows. In 1966, the Pranksters started staging "Acid Tests"—LSD raves—in the Bay area. (LSD did not become illegal until that year.) The rock band the Grateful Dead, then called the "Warlocks," provided the soundtrack as psychedelics were passed out like candy. Journalist Tom Wolfe later immortalized the Merry Pranksters' adventures in the book *The Electric Kool-Aid Acid Test*.

After the anecdotes from doctors concerning patients who suffered psychotic episodes after taking acid, Congress convened three hearings investigating LSD use in 1966. The Food and Drug Administration then released a report to the press that cited a few isolated incidents of bizarre behavior from LSD users. In one case, Los Angeles police reported arresting two young men after the pair was seen chewing tree bark while tripping on acid. The report created a national panic. Research did indicate that approximately two percent of LSD users suffered from serious psychological or emotional side effects from the drug, but a majority of these cases had already exhibited mental illness before LSD use. In any case, possession and sale of the drug became a felony on October 6 of that year.

"BLACK POWER"

If many on the left saw hippies as shallow and self-indulgent, the African American Civil Rights Movement won broad acceptance from youth protestors, as an authentic revolution striving for justice. Until the mid-1960s, the "Movement," as it was known, had been biracial. White students participated in sit-ins, the Freedom Rides and the voter registration drive during Mississippi's "Freedom Summer."

But the presence of whites in the movement had always caused tension. In his *Autobiography*, former Nation of Islam Minister Malcolm X tells how, after speaking at a New England college, "one little blonde co-ed" whose "clothes . . . carriage and . . . accent" suggested "Deep

South breeding and money" searched for him and later located Malcolm at one of his favorite restaurants on Lennox Avenue in Harlem. With pain in her voice, she asked, "Don't you believe there are any *good* white people?" Malcolm replied, "People's *deeds* I believe in, Miss, not their words." She then asked the Black Nationalist what she, as a white person, could do to advance African-American freedom. "Nothing," Malcolm replied coldly. The young woman fled the restaurant in tears.

Malcolm later regretted his words and, according to friends like author Alex Haley (who helped the minister write his *Autobiography*), he often spoke of the incident. "I regret that I told her she could do 'nothing,'" he wrote. "I wish now that I knew her name, or where I could telephone her, and tell her what I tell white people now when they present themselves as being sincere, and ask me, one way or another, the same thing that she asked." However, in 1966 some African American civil rights leaders like **Stokely Carmichael**, who had coined the phrase "Black Power!" believed that white people within the movement held black people back. Too many whites assumed leadership positions in the Civil Rights Movement, which held back black independence, Carmichael argued. To black radicals, the white philanthropists who supported the NAACP and other groups were just trying to stave off a real revolution against a capitalist system that was inherently racist. In any case, by 1965 many white activists believed that the Civil Rights Act of 1964 and the Voting Rights Act of 1965 meant the black freedom struggle had already met its goals.

As civil rights historian Robert Weisbrot noted, "Like most slogans, 'Black Power' could mean all things to all people . . . [to some] it referred to racial pride and racial solidarity, and black leadership of institutions for Afro-American progress . . ." On the other hand, NAACP Executive Director Roy Wilkins blasted the slogan in 1966, claiming that, "No matter how endlessly they try to explain it, the term 'black power' means anti-white power," Wilkins claimed. The controversy over the phrase "black power" was as much part of what was called in the 1960s the "Generation Gap," the gulf of perception between Baby Boomers and their parents, as it was a black-white conflict.

"TOMISM"

In the mainstream media, African Americans had been mostly invisible until the post-World War II era. In the movies, in the 1950s and 1960s, African-American actor **Sidney Poitier** became the first black movie superstar, but his career revealed the limits of what whites would accept from black performers. The handsome, deep-voiced, Bahamian-born actor worked a series of low-paying jobs and slept in the restroom of a bus terminal when he moved to New York as a teenager. A stage actor, his first big movie break came in the 1950 film *No Way Out* in which he portrayed a doctor with a white racist as a patient. Poitier played a series of characters who were not angry, imminently reasonable and idealistic and often middle class. By the end of 1950s, he played the leading man in civil rights-friendly films like *The Defiant Ones* (1958) in which he portrayed a convict chained to a white prisoner (Tony Curtis). The two escape, become unchained, and at one point Poitier rescues Curtis, which results in Poitier's recapture. This movie became one of Poitier's biggest hits, and earned him his first Oscar nomination for best actor, but white and black audiences perceived the message differently.

"Good" negro characters in American films had long sacrificed themselves in the interest of white characters, their hopes, fears and aspirations surrendered in service to the usual white hero. "When he saved his honky brother, he was jeered at in ghetto theaters," film historian Don Bogle wrote in his book *Toms, Coons, Mulattoes, Mammies & Bucks: An Interpretive History of Blacks in American Films*. To younger African Americans particularly, the Poitier character struck them as an "Uncle Tom," a black person who deliberately subordinates himself to whites. Poitier finally won a best actor Academy Award for his role in the 1963 film *Lilies of the Field*. Poitier played a likable former soldier traveling across the Arizona desert who discovers a group of white nuns hoping to build a chapel. In *Guess Who's Coming to Dinner* (1967) he depicted a prosperous, well-respected doctor nominated for the Nobel Prize who travels to the suburbs to meet his white fiancée's parents, played by Katharine Hepburn and Spencer Tracy. Poitier doesn't wear the African-inspired dashikis popular among many young Black Nationalists of the time, but instead is dressed in a perfect, bourgeois suit and tie. Poitier's character doesn't shout "Black Power!" His future in-laws express the mild discomfort with their daughter's romantic choice necessary for melodrama, but they mouth no ugly racism and everyone is at peace in the end. The film was so tame it didn't inspire much controversy, even in the South.

On television, the treatment of African Americans was often similarly condescending. A rare exception challenging such limits placed on black performers was the science fiction series **Star Trek**, cancelled by NBC after just three seasons in 1969. Although its depiction of women was sexist, *Star Trek* featured a rare multi-racial, multi-ethnic cast. The Starship *Enterprise* featured an East Asian officer, Mr. Sulu, a nationalistic Russian, Mr.

Twelve protestors stage a sit-in demonstration at the White House in relation to civil rights. March 11, 1965

Chekov, and a proudly Scottish engineer stereotypically named "Scotty." The two lead actors, William Shatner and Leonard Nimoy (playing Captain James Kirk and Mr. Spock), were both Jewish, a rarity in American television at the time. The Mr. Spock character, born of a human mother and a father from the planet "Vulcan," could be seen as a metaphor for the increasingly diverse, hybrid nature of American culture in 1960s.

Meanwhile, the ship's communications officer, Lieutenant Uhura, played by African-American actress Nichele Nichols, proudly bore an African name. Comedian and actress Whoopi Goldberg later recalled what a powerful impact seeing a beautiful black actress not playing a cleaning lady had on her as a child. "Well, when I was nine years old *Star Trek* came on. I looked at it and I went screaming through the house, 'Come here, mum, everybody, come quick, come quick, there's a black lady on television and she ain't no maid!' I knew right then and there I could be anything I wanted to be . . ." Black actors on *Star Trek* often broke out of the subservient roles typical in movies of the era, portraying doctors and other professionals. In one episode, Shakespearean actor William Marshall (who would play an African vampire called "Blackula" in a 1970s film) portrayed a character hailed as the galaxy's greatest computer genius.

Racial conflict was a frequent theme on the show. Repeatedly, the character Spock had to deal with the southern bigotry of "Bones" McCoy, the ship's physician who hailed from Georgia. Frustrated with Spock's reliance on cold logic rather than emotion, McCoy frequently lashed out, calling the spaceship's science officer a half-breed and a "freak." In another 1969 episode, "Plato's Stepchildren," Kirk and Uhura engaged in the first interracial kiss on an American dramatic series (the African-American entertainer Sammy Davis, Jr., briefly kissed singer Nancy Sinatra on a variety program two years earlier.) Gene Roddenberry, the series producer, struggled with NBC censors who were afraid of negative reaction from TV stations in the South. Even though the amorous Kirk was portrayed in the series as relentlessly pursuing women across the galaxy, even aliens, he and Uhura are depicted as being forced into their kiss by cruel aliens with telekinetic powers. Nichols later noted, "We received one of the largest batches of fan mail ever, all of it very positive . . . almost no one found the kiss offensive." The audience, even in the South, was apparently ahead of the Hollywood television studio, Desilu, which produced the show. Though it drew small audiences while broadcast by NBC, *Star Trek* became vastly more popular as reruns in syndication, sparking a revived interest in science fiction and creating an audience for the enormously successful **Star Wars** series of movies, which began in 1977, and several space-themed films by director Steven Spielberg, including *Close Encounters of the Third Kin*d (also released in 1977.)

"BLACK IS BEAUTIFUL"

In spite of increased visibility in the media, African Americans struggled against a larger American culture that associated beauty with white skin and demeaned African-

American intelligence and talent. Such negative messages about blackness even poisoned black-owned media. In the 1960s, the African American-owned newspaper *The Dallas Express* carried advertising for hair straighteners and skin bleach, which suggested to readers that kinky hair and black skin were unattractive and a social impediment. "Enjoy the Light Side of Life with new, improved 'Skin Success' Bleach Cream," one ad promised. "Now you can enjoy the popularity and admiration that goes with a lighter, fairer complexion."

African-American politicians, authors and poets argued that before blacks could free themselves from white oppression, they would have to free themselves from feelings of self-hatred and inferiority. They embraced the term "Black" as a sign of pride in their skin color and called themselves "Afro-Americans" in solidarity with their lost family on the Mother Continent. This quest for internal liberation inspired a "Black is Beautiful" movement. African-American activists urged both men and women to don natural "Afro" hairstyles. As the poet **Nikki Giovanni** proclaimed, referring to the oppressive white minority apartheid regime in South Africa in "Of Liberation":

If 10% honkies[whites] can run south Africa
then
10% Black people (which has nothing to do with Negroes)
can run America
These are facts
Deal with them . . .

Everything comes in steps
Negative step one: get the white out of your hair
Negative step two: get the white out of your mind
Negative step three: get the white out of your parties
Negative step four: get the white out of your meetings

In the 1960s, black Americans sought to reconnect with their African heritage. Poets like Giovanni, Leroi Jones, (who divorced his white wife, began wearing African-style dress, and adopted the African name **Imamu Amiri Baraka**), Gwendolyn Brooks, and Gil-Scott Heron wrote of the beauty of black skin, the nobility of black culture, and the need for African Americans to liberate themselves from Euro-American expectations.

Inspired by such artists and Malcolm X, so-called Black Nationalists rejected what they saw as the hopelessly idealistic dream of a just, multi-cultural America. They concluded that African-American freedom would come when black people lived under black leaders, were served by black institutions, and supported black businesses. Some Black Nationalists went as far as the Nation of Islam, advocating the creation of a separate black homeland within the United States. Turning away from Martin Luther King's non-violent approach to civil disobedience, many Black Nationalists embraced self-defense as a necessity in a violent white supremacist society. In 1966, Bobby Seale and Huey Newton, two southern-born African-American students who had attended Merritt College in the Oakland area in Alameda County in Northern California, formed the **Black Panther Party** for Self Defense on October 15, 1966 to counter police abuse and killings of black youths in ghetto neighborhoods.

Seale and Newton were moved to arm themselves after an April 1, 1967 incident in which a black child named Denzill Dowell was shot to death by police in the nearby town of Richmond. Police claimed Dowell, who suffered from a painful hip injury, had fled from arrest. Seale, Newton and the other Panthers armed themselves and began to shadow police officers operating in their neighborhood. "Armed patrols of young male Black Panthers accosted police in the act of mistreating local Negroes and recorded evidence of abuses, often narrowly avoiding shootouts with incensed officers," Weisbrot observed.

"What set the Black Panthers apart from black nationalist groups was their conviction that the problem was one of class as well as race, their belief that the enemy was the white ruling class, not 'whitey,'" wrote historian of feminism Alice Echols. ". . . In fact, the Panthers encouraged white radicals to assume the role of support troops for the black movement." California law banned carrying loaded weapons only inside a car, and the Panthers made a point of parading in wealthy white neighborhoods to "let them find out what it was like to have hostile forces stalking your streets with guns." The Panthers also provided books and free breakfast programs for children, programs that received a lot less attention from the media.

As Echols notes, the Panthers were "more incendiary in their rhetoric than in their actions." Yet the Panthers, bearing firearms, and exhorting their followers to "Off a Pig!" (kill a cop) provoked a white overreaction. Don Mulford, a conservative California Republican in the state assembly, introduced a gun control measure prohibiting citizens from carrying loaded weapons in public places. The Panthers arrived at the California state capitol on May 2, 1967 carrying loaded shotguns and rifles in protest before police forced them out of the building. The California Legislature passed the law, and Gov. Ronald Reagan, later hailed by conservatives as a defender of gun owner rights, signed the measure into law.

Law enforcement declared war on the Panthers. Chicago police in coordination with the FBI, on December 4, 1969, assaulted the home of Panther leader **Fred**

Hampton. Officers fatally shot Hampton, 21, and his body guard Mark Clark, 22, multiple times even though both apparently were unarmed at the time of the raid. A filmmaker who rushed to the scene later said that the police leaving the building were smiling, celebrating and hugging each other. Ballistics tests showed that no guns were fired from within Hampton's house, but 76 bullets were fired from outside. It was later revealed that an FBI spy within the Panthers had slipped Hampton a drink laced with sedatives that would make it harder for him to defend himself. The violence of the raid was so excessive that the Cook County district attorney, his assistant and eight Chicago police were indicted by a federal grand jury, but all were gradually acquitted. Overall, 26 Black Panthers died violently, mostly at the hands of police, between April 1968 and December 1969.

ROOTS

Black nationalism transformed depictions of African Americans in movies and television in the 1970s. ABC broadcast the "mini-series" ***Roots***, based on African American author Alex Haley's book of the same name. Like the book, the series told the story of Haley's family, from the capture of an African ancestor named Kunte Kinte as a slave in the 1700s, to the life of "Chicken" George, who lives to see emancipation in the Reconstruction era. ABC executives worried about the show, scheduling the program in January when TV audiences were smaller than other parts of the year, as author Dominic Sandbrook pointed out, because the mini-series "had almost no sympathetic white characters and depicted a brutal world of rape and racism." Yet, the series served as a cathartic moment for a massive black and white audience. The eight-part program, which debuted January 23, 1977, became the most watched television program of the season, with 100 million viewing the final installment. *Roots* struck a deep emotional chord. "My children and I just sat there crying," recalled an African-American public relations director in Nashville. "We couldn't talk. We just cried."

For many African Americans, *Roots* instilled pride in the strength and endurance of their ancestors and prompted black families to explore their genealogy. African Americans booked tours to Africa in large numbers. Among white viewers, the show provoked an awareness of American injustice and empathy for the African-American freedom struggle. "I never knew such horrible things happened," a high school senior in Missouri said. "I wasn't very proud of my ancestors. Since the movie I have felt sorry for our black population and whenever I see a black person I wonder if any of my ancestors tortured them."

LATINO PROTESTS

The African American civil rights movement profoundly inspired Latinos after World War II. Latinos represented one of the fastest-growing populations in the United States after the war, with approximately 6 million people of Mexican descent living in the Southwestern United States from California to Texas. A large cluster of Cuban immigrants had settled in Florida, and the major urban centers in the Northeast now included a large number of residents of Puerto Rican descent. Many Mexicans had settled in the United States as a result of the bracero, or agricultural guest worker program, between Mexico and the United States, from 1942 to 1964. After World War II, Latinos of all ethnicities became increasingly aware that their larger numbers could translate into greater political power.

Mexican Americans had primarily voted for the Democratic Party, but by the late 1950s many had concluded that Democrats took them for granted. To address these frustrations, activists like Bert Corona and Edward Quevedo formed the Mexican American Political Association (MAPA) in California in 1959, and the group recruited Mexican-American candidates for public office. During the 1960s, *Viva Kennedy!* clubs formed all over the Southwest as the largely Catholic Mexican American population rallied behind their co-religionist. After Kennedy's election, older Latino civil rights organizations such as the League of United Latin American Citizens (LULAC) and *Viva Kennedy!* joined together, following a 1961 meeting in Victoria, Texas to form the Political **Association of Spanish-Speaking Organizations (PASO)**, which would shake the political world with local elections in the small town of Crystal City, Texas.

Crystal City was an agricultural community where Mexican Americans made up 80 percent of the population. Many lived in poverty and attended poorly funded schools. The city council was all-Anglo in 1963. Juan Cornejo, a member of the local Teamsters Union at the Del Monte cannery in Crystal City (a politically powerful local business), and a PASO organizer, launched a successful campaign to get Mexican Americans to pay the poll tax and register to vote. As a result of the drive, Mexican Americans constituted almost 70 percent of voters. Cornejo then helped boost the city council candidacies of five Mexican-American candidates, who came to be known as *los cinco*. The candidates included a grocery store clerk, a truck driver, and the owner of a camera store. The Anglo power structure cracked down on this attempt by Mexican Americans to take over the city council and the Del Monte plant fired numerous workers for wearing campaign buttons supporting *los cinco*. After intervention from the Teamsters Union, the workers were rehired.

The city government reduced the number of polling places within Mexican-American neighborhoods from three to one. Some workers continued to be physically threatened and then the Del Monte plant ordered overtime production during the election to keep their Mexican American workers from voting. "The Mexicans are trying to take over our town," complained an Anglo worker at a local gas station. Nevertheless, the Mexican American slate won the election and held all seats on the new Crystal City Council. The PASO faction would lose control of the city government by 1965. Nevertheless Anglos would never again hold a monopoly on power in Crystal City. Events in Crystal City politically energized Latinos across the United States, and especially in Texas.

CÉSAR CHÁVEZ AND THE UNITED FARM WORKERS

Among Latino leaders, **César Chávez** enjoyed a unique ability to appeal to "center Mexican American organizations, along with the left," as the historian Rodolfo Acuña wrote. In so doing, he became the "only Mexican American leader to be so recognized [as a national Latino spokesman] by the mainstream civil rights and antiwar movements." Chávez first achieved notice when Filipino workers in the Agricultural Workers Organizing Committee (AWOC) on September 8, 1965 organized a strike against grape growers in the Delano region of California's San Joaquin Valley. Earlier that year, the U.S. Labor Department had ordered that *braceros* (guest workers from Mexico) working in the Coachella Valley receive pay of $1.40 an hour ($10.40 an hour in today's dollars.) The grape pickers were receiving 30 cents, or $2.15 an hour less in today's dollars. Filipino and Mexican workers walked off the job, demanding the same pay as the braceros.

Chávez became a champion of the grape pickers' cause. Born in Yuma, Arizona, in 1927, Chávez was the child of a union activist and a member of the United Farm Labor Union. He recalled being abused by teachers who punished students who spoke Spanish. One teacher made him wear a sign that said, "I am a clown. I speak Spanish." He was deeply influenced by Pope Leo XIII's papal 1891 encyclical *Rerum Novarum* in which the Catholic leader urged church members to support workers' rights and fight for social justice. Chávez also studied the career of India's non-violent independence leader Mahatma Gandhi. In 1962, Chávez moved to Delano to work as a union organizer, focusing on recruiting Mexican field hands. By 1964, the National Farm Workers Association, the grape pickers' union, had a membership of 1,700.

The charismatic Chávez won support across the country from Anglo Protestant civil rights activists. As a result of pressure from the growing number of Latino members in groups like the United Auto Workers, and the significant support of liberal Catholic priests, the grape strike became a national cause. The NFWA started a grape boycott that hurt growers, grocers and wine manufacturers. The boycott eventually persuaded some of the biggest grape growers and wine manufacturers like Gallo, Christian Brothers, and Paul Masson to sign multi-year contracts with higher pay with the grape pickers.

Other growers continued to resist. The United States government undermined the union and, by 1969, bought more than 4 million pounds of boycotted grapes, some sent to troops in Vietnam. Nevertheless, the boycott spread to Canada and Europe, and by 1970, the strike in its fifth year, major growers in the San Joaquin and the Coachella Valley signed contracts with the NFWA. By the spring of 1971, the major lettuce growers recognized the United Farm Workers Union and offered contracts with higher wages.

CHICANISMO

By the late 1960s, Black Nationalism became a model for younger Latinos who had tired of the more modest goals of assimilation and desegregation sought by groups like LULAC. Younger activists began to adopt the term **Chicano** to refer to their community. *Chicano* "had historically been a pejorative term applied to lower-class Mexicans," Acuña wrote. "Working class people themselves, however, had always used it playfully to refer to each other." Linking themselves to the poor, *Chicanos* rejected the materialism of their elders and declared their solidarity with African Americans, Cubans, the Viet Cong and others they saw as victims of *Gringo* (Anglo) imperialism and capitalism.

Chicanos rejected the approach taken by older Mexican-American political groups like LULAC and the GI Forum. In spite of all LULAC and AGIF's efforts to win Anglo tolerance, Mexican-American children still attended poorly funded and segregated schools where most teachers were Anglo and could speak only English. The emphasis of LULAC on Mexican Americans and Mexican immigrants learning English and becoming flag-waving patriots had not won Anglo respect for Mexican-American culture. *Chicanos* now insisted on "the retention of Mexican cultural traditions—language, ceremonies, songs, family" and proudly declared their "racial and cultural distinctiveness."

One *Chicano* activist, Rodolfo "Corky" Gonzalez (a former boxer and Democratic Party activist) established in 1966 the Crusade for Justice in Denver, which battled for reform of the local courts and police department, economic justice, and the inclusion of *Chicanos* in school lessons. "The Crusade became highly nationalistic; at one point Gonzalez considered appealing to the United Nations for a plebiscite in the Southwest to determine whether the people—*la raza*—might desire independence from the United States," historian Bruce J. Schulman said. Gonzalez took advantage of a Denver teachers' strike and got volunteers from the Crusade to teach not only core courses like math and biology, but also classes on Spanish and Mexican culture and *Chicano* history.

This embrace of cultural difference, which came to be known as *Chicanismo*, found a following among young Houston, Texas, Latinos in the mid-1960s. When the Anglo-run Houston school board attempted to dodge sending white children to desegregated schools by designating Mexican-American children as white and grouping them with African Americans, *Chicano* youths resisted. *Chicanos* launched a two-and-a-half-week strike involving 3,500 students who refused to attend Houston schools in August and September 1970. *Chicanos* set up *huelga* or strike schools, so Mexican-American children could continue their lessons and learn more about their culture and history. As a result of the strikes, more bilingual Mexican-American teachers were hired by the Houston district, the curriculum was rewritten so students would be exposed to positive portrayals of Mexican Americans and physical improvements were made at some minority-majority schools. The Houston school board, however, never recognized *Chicanos* or Mexican Americans as a separate racial category, and brown and black children continued to bear the burden of desegregation. Houston *Chicanos*, however, deeply influenced the future shape of Mexican-American politics across Texas and the country for the next four decades. Similar student walkouts occurred in the late 1960s and early 1970s in California, Colorado, New Mexico and in major cities across the country.

BACK TO WOUNDED KNEE:
The American Indian Movement

Beginning in the late 1960s, and through the 1970s, Native Americans emerged from the political shadows and launched a "Red Power" movement to protest poverty, lack of jobs and poor health care on reservations, the disrespect shown Indian history and culture in American movies and television, and the lengthy list of treaties with Indian nations signed and broken by the federal government. In the early 1960s, as the historian James Wilson wrote, conditions in "most Indian communities were appalling . . . more than 90 percent of their housing was substandard; their infant mortality rate was more than twice the national average; their incidence of preventable diseases such as tuberculosis, meningitis, and dysentery exceeded the general population's by anything up to a hundred times; their average age of death was 43 years [as opposed to almost 70 for the general population]; and, with unemployment running between 40 percent and 80 percent, their average family income was only around 20 percent of their Anglo-American neighbors."

The political ferment of the 1960s moved young Native Americans to take direct action against oppressive white laws. The National Indian Youth Council (NIYC), for instance, conducted "fish-ins" in 1964 to assert tribal fishing rights in Oregon, Washington, and Idaho where pollution and the construction of dams, along with the intrusion of commercial fishing companies, had sharply reduced fish stocks in local streams, lakes and rivers. The three state governments had implemented conservation laws that applied equally to non-Natives and Natives, even though for the latter group the fish were "not only the staple food . . . but also one of the central *motifs* of their cultures." Indians had also been promised by nineteenth century treaties with the federal government that they would be allowed to fish in "their usual and accustomed" places. Young Native Americans blamed the depletion of local trout and salmon not on Indian fishers but on commercial fisheries. The NIYC began to deliberately disobey local fishing laws, and game wardens arrested the protestors. As the arrests multiplied, the protests began to draw national attention.

In 1966, under escalating pressure the Justice Department announced that it would defend in court, upon request, any Native person protected by federal treaties charged with violating state fishing regulations. The **American Indian Movement**, founded in 1968 by two members of the Chippewa Nation, George Mitchell and Dennis Banks, became perhaps the most influential and powerful "Red Power" group among Native Americans. Formed in Minnesota, AIM organized "patrols to protect Indians from police brutality" and used federal funds to "establish 'urban alternative' schools, where Native American children who had dropped out of the school system could develop greater cultural awareness and self-respect and learn how to survive in both the Indian and non-Indian worlds."

Native American groups in the late 1960s and early 1970s sought to speak not just for individual tribes, but for all indigenous people victimized by white oppression.

Such was the approach when an invading force that called itself "Indians of All Tribes" on November 20, 1969 seized control of Alcatraz Island, a closed federal prison in San Francisco Bay. The force included 300 Native Americans from 50 different Indian nations. The occupiers laid siege for 19 months, demanding that the government turn the property back over to its proper Indian owners and calling for the construction of an Indian cultural center on the site that would include an "Indian college, museum and ecology center." Federal marshals ousted the last 15 Native American protestors on June 11, 1971.

The cultural center was not built, but one leader of the **Alcatraz occupation** believes the action had a positive impact on the indigenous community. "Alcatraz was a major turning point in my life," said one Native American, Francis Wise. "For the first time in my life, I was proud to be an Indian and an Indian woman. I grew up in an all-white area. It was very difficult. You were constantly struggling to maintain any kind of positive feeling, any kind of dignity. Alcatraz changed all that."

A dynamic new leader of AIM, **Russell Means,** continued to raise the visibility of the Indian cause by staging protests at two sites cherished by white America: Mount Rushmore, the sculpted tribute to four American presidents (George Washington, Thomas Jefferson, Abraham Lincoln and Teddy Roosevelt) created on a mountain on Indian land in South Dakota, and at the *Mayflower II*, the replica of the Pilgrim ship in the harbor at Plymouth, Massachusetts.

The Indian movement, and the Indian-admiring white counterculture, dramatically changed the way whites saw Native Americans. Prior to the late 1960s, Westerns had consistently been the most popular American movie genre and in these films, Native Americans were almost always portrayed as inarticulate buffoons, or menacing killers with no regard for the life of the defenseless. Westerns began to disappear from theaters by 1970. One of the few to be released that year, *Little Big Man*, had as its hero a man interviewed in modern times at the epic age of 121, Jack Crabb (played by Dustin Hoffman.) Crabb, audiences learn, spent his life being captured back and forth by whites and by an Indian tribe that called themselves "The Human Beings." It is the Native Americans who are funny, wise, and compassionate in the film, and the whites who are drunks, fools, and murderers. George Armstrong Custer, the Army Indian fighter long portrayed in American folklore as a hero, is conceived in this film as a ruthless killer willing to step over the bodies of murdered Indian children and unarmed women as he pursues military and political fame.

In the Oscar-winning film *One Flew Over the Cuckoo's Nest* (1973), an insane asylum run by a heartless, autocratic nurse serves as a metaphor for the United States during the Cold War and the Vietnam War. The hero (Randall Patrick McMurphy, played by Jack Nicholson) finds his strongest, most steady ally in a Native America, nicknamed with ironic humor "Chief," who shows compassion and intellectual clarity as the inmates rise up in rebellion. In contrast to real life, it is the Native American who is the only inmate able to escape the clutches of a mad American society by the film's end.

Indian pride fueled another protest action at Wounded Knee, South Dakota, scene of a late-nineteenth-century massacre of Native Americans by the U.S. Army. On February 27, 1973, about 200 Native Americans armed themselves and took over the Pine Ridge Indian Reservation in Wounded Knee to overthrow a corrupt Indian leader enjoying white support who tried to crush AIM. "The young kids tied eagle feathers to their braids, no longer unemployed kids, juvenile delinquents or winos," recalled one participant, Mary Crow Dog. More than 300 National Guardsmen and U.S. marshals surrounded Wounded Knee village, filled with "hundreds of Sioux and—at various times—members of 64 other tribes and a handful of black, chicano, and Euro-American supporters who had managed to slip past the government roadblocks," as author James Wilson said.

This siege lasted 71 days. Across America, Native American and *Chicano* protestors rallied in support of the Indians and some were killed by police violence. Shootouts at Wounded Knee killed two Indians, with one federal marshal injured. In May, the Indians agreed to lay down their weapons. "Appropriately, perhaps, the Wounded Knee siege was the high-water mark of Native American activism," Wilson observed. "Although the radical movement continued in 1974, for instance AIM established the International Treaty Council to try to win recognition of Native American sovereignty from the UN and other nations—it was never again able to attain the same level of public awareness and support. With U.S. withdrawal from two conflicts—the Vietnam War and the War on Poverty . . . the country gradually drifted towards a much more consensual, cautious mood . . ."

DAYS OF RAGE

As African American civil rights groups such as the Student Nonviolent Coordinating Committee (SNCC) and the Black Panthers embraced self-defense and more confrontational tactics, a new anti-war group, **The Weather Underground**, arose. Named after a line in the Bob Dylan song *Subterranean Homesick Blues*, that included the lyrics, "You don't need a weatherman to know which way the winds blows," so-called Weathermen engaged in domestic terrorism. They called for "anti-imperialist action in which a mass of white youths tear up and smash wide-ranging imperialist targets such as . . . high schools, draft boards and [military] induction centers, pig [police] institutes, and pigs themselves."

The revolutionary group held "jail breaks" in which they "liberated" classrooms—taking over school facilities to lecture students about revolution. The Weathermen vowed to "bring the war home." Announcing the start of "Days of Rage" on October 8-11, 1969, the Weather Underground attacked Chicago's wealthy Gold Coast neighborhood, vandalizing cars and police vehicles, shattering store windows, and attacking random individuals. Both police and members of the Underground suffered injuries. Six Weathermen suffered gunshot wounds and police arrested 250 rioters.

The Weathermen conducted a series of successful and attempted bombings, including the detonation of a pipe bomb at the San Francisco police department headquarters in February 1970. On March 6, 1970, Weathermen gathered in a Greenwich Village townhouse prepared a bomb they intended to set off at a military officers' dance at Fort Dix in New Jersey. An incorrectly connected wire caused the bomb to explode, killing three members of the terrorist cell. In 1971-1973, members of the Underground set off several explosions at the U.S. Capitol, the Pentagon, the ITT headquarters in New York City and the United States State Department. Classified as a domestic terrorist organization by the FBI and under intense pressure from other law enforcement agencies, the top Weathermen like Mark Rudd and Bernadine Dohrn went into hiding during the bombing campaigns, using a series of fake identities. Gradually members of the Underground resurfaced and charges against most members were dropped because of illegal investigative tactics used by the police.

The chief impact of the Weather Underground was to damage the image of the anti-war movement, which overwhelmingly opposed violence. The "Days of Rage," the bombings, and images of Black Panthers carrying weapons frightened many middle class and working class white Americans. As one worker said, "What I don't like about the students, the loudmouthed ones, is that they think they know so much they can speak for everyone, because they think they're right and the rest of us aren't clever enough and can't talk like they can."

SILENT SPRING

One way in which young protestors sought a more authentic life was through a closer relationship to nature. Even as many Americans marveled at the technology that made space travel possible, and marveled at big cars, highways, new television sets and oversized factories, young people came to disdain the belching smokestacks of foul, smelly industrial waste. A 55-year-old woman became the unlikely inspiration to an emerging, youth-oriented environmental movement. The year 1962 saw the publication of *Silent Spring* by **Rachel Carson**, a zoologist who charged that the chemical pesticides used in American agriculture killed birds and left their eggshells dangerously thin. The problem worsened markedly in 1942 when farmers started spraying fields with DDT, a chemical that killed insects on contact. The United States Department of Agriculture's 1957 fire ant eradication program, involving intense use of DDT, provoked Carson's scientific investigation of pesticides. "Chemicals are the sinister and little-recognized partners of radiation in changing the very nature of the world—the very nature of life," Carson said.

> Since the mid-nineteen forties, over 200 basic chemicals have been created for use in killing insects, weeds, rodents and other organisms described in the modern vernacular as pests, and they are sold under several thousand different brand names. The sprays, dusts and aerosols are now applied almost universally to farms, gardens, forests and homes—non-selective chemicals that have the power to kill every insect, the good and the bad, to still the song of birds and the leaping of fish in the streams—to coat the leaves with a deadly film and to linger on in soil—all this, though the intended target may be only a few weeds or insects. Can anyone believe it is possible to lay down such a barrage of poisons on the surface of the earth without making it unfit for all life? They should not be called "insecticides" but "biocides."

In May 1963, President Kennedy's Scientific Advisory Committee issued a report on pesticides that vindicated Carson's warnings. Dr. Jerome B. Wiesner declared that the unregulated use of pesticides represented "potentially a much greater hazard" to survival of life on the planet than radioactive fallout from atomic weapons. Carson's efforts led to a nationwide ban on DDT and other chemical pesticides and helped inspire the environmental movement of the late 1960s. Scientific investigation after Carson's death from breast cancer in 1964 demonstrated that chemicals such as DDT found their way inside humans and caused soft-tissue cancers.

MERCY, MERCY ME: The American Environmental Movement

Pollution became a topic addressed both in newsmagazines like *Time* and humor magazines largely read by kids, such as *Mad*. A major oil spill off the Santa Barbara, California coastline in 1969 outraged not just committed environmentalists, but also middle-class voters who saw a beautiful beach spoiled and worried about the chemicals entering their bodies. Radio stations in the early 1970s gave heavy rotation to songs like John Denver's "Colorado Rocky Mountain High" that celebrated the glories of unspoiled nature and Joni Mitchell's "Big Yellow Taxi" that mourned the loss of wilderness. "You paved paradise and put up a parking lot," Mitchell caustically sang.

The Beat poet Gary Snyder saw a connection between the industrial assault on the environment and the Vietnam War. Snyder compared trees to African Americans and the Vietnamese. All were victims of modern American capitalism. Entertainer Marvin Gaye, known primarily for love songs and sexy rhythm and blues tracks, devoted a large part of his 1971 *What's Going On?* album to environmental issues. In his hit song "Mercy, Mercy Me," Gaye offers the following plaint:

> Ah, mercy, mercy me/
> Things ain't what they used to be/
> Where did all the blue skies go?
> Poison is the wind that blows from the north, south and east/
> ... Oil wasted on the ocean and upon our seas/
> Fish full of mercury/
> ... Radiation underground and in the sky/
> Animals and birds who live nearby/
> Are dying.

The public in large numbers celebrated the first "**Earth Day**" April 22, 1970. The initial push for Earth Day came from Democratic Senator Gaylord Nelson of Wisconsin who believed the health of the planet to be "the most critical issue facing mankind" and who, borrowing an idea from the anti-Vietnam War movement, encouraged a nationwide "teach-in" about the environment in which Americans would be educated about the harm of industrial pollutants, the devastation of wildlife, and related issues.

When April 22 arrived, about 10 million Americans, plus millions more across the globe, celebrated Earth Day by hiking, planting trees, picking up litter and so on. Earth Day became an annual event and promoted the growth of grassroots environmental activism. Sensing the popularity of the issue, President Richard Nixon signed into law the Clean Air Act of 1970, which for the first time established national air quality standards and set caps on harmful emissions by automobiles. Privately, Nixon had little interest in the environment. "I think interest in this will recede," he wrote in an internal memo. He later dismissed the environmental movement as "crap" for "clowns."

Nixon badly underestimated the concern over pollution. One in four Americans named the environment as the "nation's most pressing problem," according to historian Dominic Sandbrook. Responding to public pressure, the Congress passed a spate of environmental laws in the early 1970s, including the statute that created the Environmental Protection Agency (EPA) in 1970. The Endangered Species Act in 1973 protected not only endangered animals but also the habitats they depended on that were threatened by economic development. The Safe Drinking Water Act of 1974 gave the EPA the power to set standards in terms of chemical content for water across the United States.

The movement remained mostly white and middle and upper class, but environmentalists learned much from the sit-ins and non-violent protest tactics of the African American Civil Rights Movement. Organizations like the Abalone Alliance in California used civil disobedience, using up to 2,000 activists to occupy and block entrances of work crews at the Diablo Canyon nuclear power plant located near a fault line by San Luis Obispo, California. The protestors, however, failed to stop the opening of the plant. Such defeats did not dim the idealism of committed environmentalists. According to the *New York Times*, the spontaneous "back-to-nature movement" had created 2,000 communes and 5,000 collective farms by the beginning of the 1970s.

At Red Rocks in Colorado, 25 people shared a geodesic dome where they "cooked, worked, slept, healed the sick, gave birth; all children born in the dome received the surname 'Red Rocks.'" Such grassroots activists at times irritated mainstream environmentalist groups like the Sierra Club, particularly those more radical elements who embraced "**Deep Ecology**," the belief that animals and even trees and plant life have rights that need to be balanced with human needs. Groups like Earth First! inspired by the radical 1975 novel *The Monkey Wrench Gang* by Edward Abbey, alarmed more conventional activists as they used sabotage to stop forest logging and vandalized laboratories engaged in animal research.

Two incidents in the 1970s dramatized the need for environmental regulation. In Niagara Falls, New York, the Hooker Chemical & Plastics Corporation had poured 22 tons of toxic chemicals into a dry canal called **Love Canal** between 1947 and 1952 and concealed the dump with layers of clay soil. The local school district, short of cash and experiencing a local population boom requiring construction of new campuses, bought the land from Hooker for $1 and built an elementary school on top of the poisonous underground stew. Other schools were rapidly constructed nearby. As the community later grew to a population of 75,000, residents complained of bad smells in their basements and of chemicals leaking to the surface that sometimes caught fire. Heavy rains and melted snow following a blizzard exposed more of the waste. The affected area covered 36 square blocks. EPA investigators would later find higher-than-normal rates of miscarriages and birth defects, elevated levels of toxic chemicals in the milk of breast-feeding mothers and increased cancer rates in the neighborhood.

New York Department of Health Commissioner Robert Whalen proclaimed the Love Canal site a threat to human health in 1978. Four months later, authorities placed a barricade around the old landfill and ordered the closing of the 99th Street School that had been built on top of the dump. The New York state government purchased the entire neighborhood and evacuated around 800 families. In response to the crisis, the Congress in 1980 passed the Comprehensive Environmental Response Compensation and Liability Act, better known as the "Superfund" law. The law set aside federal money to aid states in cleaning up toxic waste sites near residential areas. Love Canal became the first Superfund-designated site. Love Canal area was not declared clean by the federal government until 2004. The publicity surrounding Love Canal and the near meltdown of the **Three Mile Island** nuclear power plant near Harrisburg, Pennsylvania on March 28, 1979, deepened the public distrust of American corporations and increased awareness of the immense dangers posed by industrial capitalism to the natural world.

"THE PROBLEM WITH NO NAME"

The collapse of the civil rights coalition by the mid-60s led to the birth of several other freedom struggles, including those of women and gays. Women who fought against segregation and for black voting rights became the leaders of the 1960s feminist movement. CBS television produced a documentary on the "trapped housewife" in 1960 that featured the journalist Marya Mannes, who argued that the Cold War made employment of women in professions a political necessity. The United States couldn't compete with the Soviet Union is it continued to ignore the talent and brainpower of suppressed women. "We have for years been wasting one of the resources on which our strength depends and which other civilizations are using to their advantage," she said.

In her 1963 bestselling book *The Feminine Mystique*, author **Betty Friedan** described the frustration and boredom felt by many educated suburban housewives as the "problem with no name." Friedan's book described the agonies of middle-class white American women who found themselves locked into lives as domestic servants to their husbands, burdened with washing diapers, raising children in isolation from adult company, waxing floors and preparing the big meals expected by their husbands.

Friedan, who worked during the 1950s at so-called "women's magazines," all edited by men, blamed the media for promoting the myth that healthy women could find true purpose and glory only in playing the role of wife and mother. Conducting an extensive survey of middle class and affluent women similar to herself, Friedan blamed the "feminine mystique"—which glorified only women who played a traditionally subservient role to men—as the cause of an outbreak of depression, anxiety, emotional withdrawal, anger and infantilization of adult women and their daughters. The book found an understanding audience, and *The Feminine Mystique* became a best-seller, with more than a million copies purchased.

The publication of her book occurred almost simultaneously with the release of a report by the President's Commission on the Status of Women, a blue-ribbon panel chaired by former First Lady Eleanor Roosevelt. The report documented widespread discrimination against women regarding employment, pay and promotion at the workplace, and in colleges and universities. President John F. Kennedy responded to the report by signing an executive order directing federal agencies to hire employees "without regard to sex." Kennedy also threw his support behind the Equal Pay Act of 1963, which prohibited employers from paying employees differently based on gender. The persistence of sexism in American life, plus the release of the commission's report and Betty Friedan's book, inspired the rise of what would be called the second wave of feminism (the first wave was the women's suffrage campaign from 1848 to 1920).

"The Bunny Law"

The Equal Pay Act and the anti-sex discrimination provisions of the 1964 Civil Rights Act had a dramatic impact on women's experiences in the workplace. The law empowered the newly created Equal Employment Opportunity Commission (EEOC) to enforce provisions against racial and sexual discrimination. At first EEOC administrators laughed at the concept of gender discrimination, an insensitivity reinforced by the male-dominated press that frequently scoffed at the idea of male and female equality. Editorialists railed that men

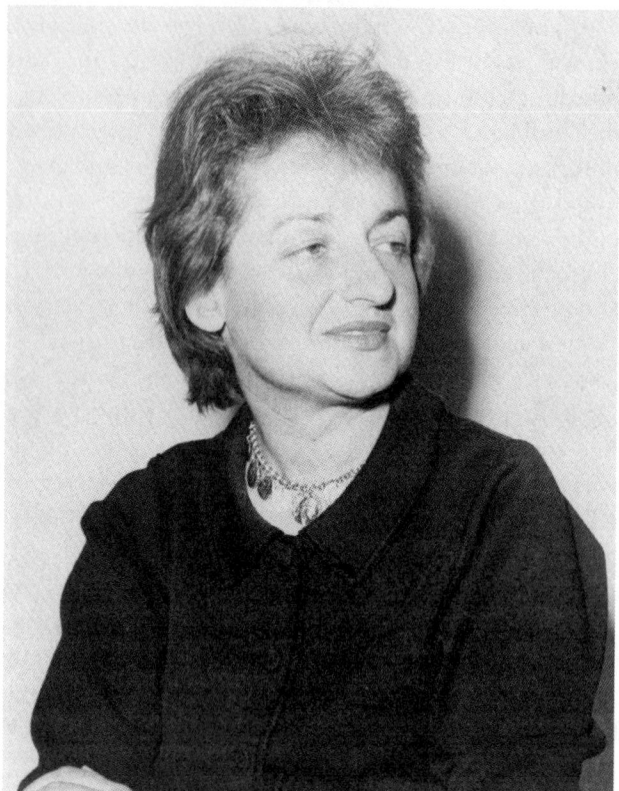

BETTY FRIEDAN, 1960
Credit: Library of Congress

and women were biologically suited for different kinds of work. Would feminists protest, they joked, if a man were refused a job as a Playboy bunny, a waitress dressed in what was basically a one-piece bathing suit adorned with a fluffy bunny tail and bunny ears who served drinks at the nightclubs owned by Hugh Hefner, the publisher of *Playboy*, a popular men's magazine? Newspapers caustically dubbed the anti-sexual-discrimination provisions of Title VII of the Civil Rights Act as the "bunny law."

Feminists did not find such condescending attitudes from men amusing. Women still faced substantial legal obstacles. State laws in the 1950s and 1960s did not take spousal abuse seriously. Several states placed barriers to women serving on juries. Connecticut prevented women from obtaining birth control. Through the early 1960s, it was typical for classified ads to specify, "Help Wanted: Male." In Texas, until 1967 a woman technically could not sign a contract to work without her husband's permission.

By the late 1960s, many women had been active in the Civil Rights and Anti-War movements, yet suffered marginalization by male protestors. Men rarely listened to the ideas of their female comrades and sometimes made them the objects of crude jokes or as weapons to entice their political opponents. "Girls Say Yes to Boys Who Say No," was a frequent slogan used by men in the anti-draft movement. Women acted as voter registrars and recruiters, often facing physical danger. Yet, at the civil rights offices, men expected these women to perform menial tasks like typing and making coffee, even demanding sexual favors. Reportedly, when asked "What is the position of women in SNCC [the Student Non-Violent Coordinating Committee]?", African American civil rights activist Stokely Carmichael crudely replied, "The position of women in SNCC is prone."

Women activists realized that they would have to form their own civil rights group to be heard. In 1966, feminists formed an organization named, at Betty Friedan's suggestion, the **National Organization for Women (NOW)**. Overwhelmingly white, NOW at first catered primarily to older, more affluent, professionals—lawyers, government workers, and women working in the media. Like the NAACP, NOW primarily battled gender discrimination through lobbying Congress and state legislatures and litigation rather than through "direct action" protests.

The original NOW leadership came from a comfortable, upper middle-class culture, and often showed a lack of imagination and had a limited vision of how feminism should change society. Women were entitled to more than access to professional jobs, as younger activist and historian Sara Evans suggested in her memoir *Personal Politics: The Roots of the Women's Liberation in the Civil Rights Movement and the New Left*. Women still received substantially lower salaries than men. To truly end discrimination, women had to directly challenge American society's belief in male supremacy, the assumption that men were smarter, stronger and were natural leaders whose work deserved greater financial compensation, and that women were irrational, less reliable and should be submissive.

Glass Ceilings

In spite of male hostility, feminists successfully won a place for women in American politics. In 1968, women constituted only 13 percent of the delegates to the Democratic National Convention and 17 percent of the Republican National Convention delegates the same year. Feminists realized that women's issues would not be taken seriously unless more women were elected to public office. There were no women in the United States Senate in 1968 and only nine women in the United States House out of 435 members the same year. In 1971, veteran feminists like Friedan, civil rights campaigner Fannie Lou Hamer, and those belonging to the tiny circle of women in the United States Congress like Bella Abzug and Shirley Chisholm who in 1968 became the first black woman elected to the House, organized the National Women's Political Caucus to increase the number of women members of Congress, governors, legislators, mayors and city council members.

The 1970s would see the election of Ella Grasso as governor of Connecticut and Dixie Lee Ray as the chief executive in Washington State. Mary Anne Krupsak won election as the lieutenant governor of New York under the slogan, "She's Not One of the Boys" while Abzug won a seat in the New York congressional delegation, declaring that, "This woman belongs in the house—The House of Representatives." All these women were Democrats.

Feminists in the 1960s and 1970s wrote, voted for, and successfully lobbied for several landmark laws benefiting women. For instance, Title IX of a 1972 federal law, the Education Amendments Act, banned sex discrimination in university admissions, faculty hiring and college athletics, which slowly and steadily increased the number of women earning advanced degrees. In 1960, only 1.7 percent of women 25 years old and beyond had an education beyond a bachelor's degree, compared to 4.4 percent of men. By 2009, the numbers had reached near parity, with 10.1 percent of women and 11.1 percent of men taking course work beyond a four-year diploma. By 2000, women between the ages of 25 and 29 for the first time constituted a majority of those holding at least a master's degree, with women representing 58 percent of MAs in that age group.

Nevertheless, in the 1970s a considerable gulf existed between law and enforcement. Women found they still hit unofficial barriers to their career advancement, a glass ceiling above which they could never rise. Women's pay remained unequal in the workplace even though the Equal Pay of 1963 had been strengthened by two Supreme Court decisions. In *Schultz v. Wheaton Glass Co.* (1970), the court majority held that jobs don't have to be identical in order for the Equal Pay Act to apply, but only have to be "substantially equal." This ruling meant that an employer could not alter job titles or make minor alterations in job descriptions for women employees to justify paying them less. In the 1974 *Corning Glass v. Brennan* case, the Supreme Court ruled that employers could not legally pay women less because that was the "going market rate" paid in a locality or pay men more for doing the same work "simply because men would not work at the low rates paid women." In spite of the law and such court rulings, however, by 2010 women still earned only 78 cents for every dollar earned by their male peers.

The Failure of the Equal Rights Amendment

The continued barriers to women in the workplace sparked a movement to add an **Equal Rights Amend-**

**Fannie Lou Hamer at the Democratic National Convention, Atlantic City, New Jersey, August 1964.
Credit: Library of Congress**

ment to the United States Constitution. "Equality of rights under the law shall not be denied or abridged by the United States or by any state on account of sex," said the first section of the brisk, 56-word proposed amendment. A version of the ERA, as it was called, had been written by Alice Paul in 1923 and had been introduced in every session of Congress since, until the modern version passed both houses of Congress in 1972. A seven-year deadline was placed on ratification, and the amendment went to the states. "In the beginning, the ERA seemed certain to pass," historian Bruce J. Schulman wrote. Hawaii became the first state to ratify it, on the very day it passed the Congress. Three days after congressional passage, the amendment had also been approved by Delaware, Idaho, Iowa, Nebraska, and New Hampshire. Within five years, the ERA had been ratified by 35 states, just three short of the 38 needed for it to become part of the Constitution. Majority opinion supported the ERA, with the amendment winning the backing of as much as 74 percent of voters polled in 1974. Opponents never represented even a third of voters.

Bella Abzug at a press conference for National Youth Conference for 1972. November 30, 1971
Credit: Library of Congress

Momentum had undeniably slowed by 1977. The ERA was partly a victim of feminism's successes. With laws already on the books banning discrimination in hiring and pay, some Americans found the need for the amendment less urgent. As Schulman pointed out, the states that had not passed the ERA were heavily concentrated in the highly conservative and religiously fundamentalist South and Western Mormon areas, which saw the proposed amendment as a threat to the traditional, "God-mandated" role of women as mothers and homemakers. The amendment was a "definite violation of holy scripture," declared TV evangelist **Jerry Falwell,** who insisted that the Bible defined "the husband as the head of the wife." Conservative Southern Protestants saw the amendment as one more assault on traditional values by the same liberals who had ended racial segregation. Many of the ERA's opponents like Falwell had also supported Jim Crow.

A conservative woman who had campaigned for Barry Goldwater for president in 1964, **Phyllis Schlafly**, led the group STOP ERA and would battle the entire feminist agenda. "Superficially, Schlafly seemed an odd candidate to lead women against feminism," Schulman said. "A master organizer and brilliant speaker, she had run for public office, published several books, and lectured around the nation. In 1970s terms, she appeared the model of a liberated woman." Schlafly was conservative across the board, supporting the war in Vietnam, and opposing gay rights, social welfare programs and federal involvement in education. A strongly independent woman, she acted submissive when it suited her political purposes, often telling her audiences that she was speaking to them only because she had her husband's permission.

Schlafly warned that the ERA would end special protections for women, who might become eligible for the draft and placed in combat. Men would be "free to abandon their wives without the obligations of alimony or child support," as Schulman summarizes her arguments. Schlafly also warned that the ERA would result in unisex restrooms in public buildings and the legalization of gay marriage. Congress extended the deadline for ratification until 1982, but no more states passed the amendment. Support for the ERA had been on the platform of both major parties, but the Republican Party—at the behest of conservative presidential candidate Ronald Reagan's supporters—removed its pro-ERA plank in time for the 1980 national convention. The ERA has been re-introduced in Congress every session since 1982 but has failed to pass.

Congresswoman Shirley Chisholm announcing her candidacy for the presidential nomination. Jan. 25, 1972.
Credit: Library of Congress

Activist Phyllis Schafly wearing a "Stop ERA" badge, demonstrating with other women against the Equal Rights Amendment in front of the White House, Washington, D.C., February 4, 1977. Credit: Library of Congress

"Back Alley Abortions"

Feminists in the 1960s argued that because women lacked political power, they had lost control of their own bodies. Abortion was a felony in 49 states and the District of Columbia as of 1967. Abortion was allowed in some states in a narrow range of exceptional cases, with 42 states allowing the procedure to save the life of the mother. In other states, doctors could perform abortions to prevent "serious permanent bodily injury" or harm to the woman's health. Mississippi was the only state to allow abortion for rape victims or in cases of incest.

The procedure had continued with surprising frequency in spite of the ban. At a 1955 Planned Parenthood Conference, zoologist, researcher and author Alfred Kinsey, based on his extensive interviews with Americans about their sexual habits, estimated that between 200,000 and 1.2 million abortions took place a year in the United States. In spite of its frequency and widespread acceptance in the medical community, their underground nature often made abortions dangerous. Dr. Mildred Hanson recalled one incident during her childhood involving an illegal abortion. "In 1935, when I was 11 years old, my mother left our Wisconsin house on a bitter February night and dashed to the farm next door to help an ailing woman who'd had an illegal abortion," Hanson told an interviewer. "Our neighbor was writhing in pain so severe that she was having convulsions and was chewing her lip raw. It took her two days to die of blood poisoning. She left six children behind—and left me with firsthand knowledge of the injustice of illegal abortion."

In some cases, desperate women performed abortions on themselves, inserting sharp objects in their cervix to induce a miscarriage or douching themselves with bleach. By the 1960s, momentum was on the side of abortion law reformers, with the American Law Institute promoting a "model law" for states that would allow abortion to protect the life or health of the woman, in cases of rape or incest or if the fetus showed severe abnormalities.

As journalists James Risen and Judy L. Thomas noted in their book *Wrath of Angels: The American Abortion War*, the abortion controversy gained a human face because of an Arizona woman named Sherri Chessen Finkbine. The mother of four and the host of the Phoenix version of the children's television program *Romper Room*, the pregnant Finkbine suffered high blood pressure and took high doses of thalidomide, which had been widely prescribed around the world as a cure for morning sickness. Her husband had obtained the drug in Europe, where reports surfaced of thousands of badly deformed babies with facial malformations, missing arms and legs, heart defects and mental impairment born to women who had taken the drug. Finkbine's doctor warned her that she faced a great risk of having a highly deformed child.

Her doctor said she would have to get approval from a three-doctor medical board at Phoenix's Good Samaritan Hospital before she could have an abortion. Arizona state law allowed abortion only to save the mother's life, but doctors sometimes interpreted the statute broadly. Worried that other women might take the drug, Finkbine called the *Arizona Republic* newspaper and agreed to be interviewed only if her identity was protected. After the story was published, hospital administrators worried about being prosecuted, and cancelled the hearing on whether the abortion could take place.

Finkbine sued and her name was now on the public record and her picture was soon in newspapers and on TVs across the country. Finkbine started getting death threats in the mail. "We received pictures of me from the paper, and there'd be an ice pick or a dagger with blood spewing," she said later. "We'd receive manure in the mail. I was called a baby killer . . . and a murderess . . . We had to change our phone number dozens of times."

Finkbine realized that her case had become too controversial for her to receive permission for an abortion in Arizona or elsewhere in the United States. She flew to Sweden where she had to be certified as mentally ill before she could have the abortion. "The doctor told her that the thirteen-week-old fetus had been so severely deformed that it would have never survived," Risen and Thomas wrote. When the Finkbines returned to Arizona, the FBI had to escort their children to school. "I never got to do *Romper Room* again," Finkbine later said. "I was told by the vice president of the NBC affiliate that I was unfit to handle children." Most Americans did not agree with the TV executive. A Gallup Poll revealed that half of all respondents thought that Finkbine had done the right thing and only 32 percent opposed her actions. The Finkbine case galvanized forces lobbying for more liberal abortion laws.

Roe v. Wade

By 1967, several states passed the American Law Institute's "model law" for abortion. In 1967, Colorado passed a law based on the model legislation, quickly followed by North Carolina. Such reforms received the endorsement of the American Baptist Convention and the American Medical Association's House of Delegates shortly thereafter. A poll taken by *Modern Medicine* revealed that almost 87 percent of American doctors supported liberalizing abortion laws. This information helped persuade the California legislature, which passed a more permissible abortion law signed by Gov. Ronald Reagan, later touted as a hero by the anti-abortion movement. By 1969, Arkansas, Delaware, Georgia, Kansas, Maryland, New Mexico, and Oregon had all passed reform laws.

In the early 1970s, Norma McCorvey, described by Risen and Thomas as a "street smart high school dropout, a drug user, a lesbian and a victim of abusive men and neglectful parents" was in Dallas, pregnant a third time after giving up one child for adoption and having another taken away by her mother. McCorvey did not want to deliver another child but was turned down by a doctor who told her abortion was illegal in Texas. She tried to end the pregnancy herself using a home remedy of peanuts and castor oil, a concoction that only succeeded in making her ill. McCorvey went to an illegal clinic in Dallas. "Nobody was there," she said later. "It was an old dentist office. Then I saw dried blood everywhere and smelled this awful smell." Dallas police had shut down the clinic just before McCorvey's visit. She fled the scene and agreed to talk to two lawyers she had been told were seeking to challenge the Texas anti-abortion law. Those lawyers, Linda Coffee and Sarah Weddington, filed a class action suit against Dallas District Attorney Henry Wade claiming that the Texas anti-abortion law, which allowed the procedure only to save the patient's life, violated the constitutional right of privacy.

The case worked its way up to the United States Supreme Court, which on January 22, 1973, ruled in ***Roe v. Wade*** by a 7-2 margin, that the Constitutional right to privacy was "broad enough to encompass a woman's decision whether or not to terminate her pregnancy" during the first two trimesters (or first six months.) Judge Harry Blackmun, who wrote the majority opinion, held that a woman had an unqualified right to an abortion in the first trimester, and the states could only require the abortion be carried out by a qualified person. The states could only regulate the practice to protect the life and health of the mother in the second trimester. In the final trimester, Blackmun wrote for the court, the fetus is viable (able to survive outside its mother's body). At that point, states could regulate or even ban the practice. Strict abortion laws in Texas and most other states were overturned.

Abortions became much more common after the *Roe* decision. The Alan Guttmacher Institute estimated that by the end of 1973, the first year of legal abortions nationwide, almost 745,000 such procedures were performed in the United States for women between the ages of 15 and 44, the number going up to 1 million the following year. For the rest of the decade, the Catholic Church represented the only major institution opposing *Roe*. The Bishops' Conference and Catholic-supported anti-abortion groups chose an incremental path of lobbying Congress for tighter restrictions and campaigning for anti-abortion candidates for president who might appoint judges who would reverse *Roe*. For some Catholics who

> ## ROE v. WADE, 410 U.S. 113 (1973)
>
> *Below is the majority decision, which was written by Justice Harry Blackmun.*
>
> We forthwith acknowledge our awareness of the sensitive and emotional nature of the abortion controversy, of the vigorous opposing views, even among physicians, and of the deep and seemingly absolute convictions that the subject inspires. One's philosophy, one's religious training, one's attitudes toward life and family and their values, and the moral standards one establishes and seeks to observe, are all likely to influence and to color one's thinking and conclusions about abortion.
>
> In addition, population growth, pollution, poverty, and racial overtones tend to complicate and not to simplify the problem.
>
> Our task, of course, is to resolve the issue by constitutional measurement, free of emotion and of predilection. We seek earnestly to do this....
>
> The Constitution does not explicitly mention any right of privacy. In a line of decisions, however, ... the Court has recognized that a right of personal privacy, or a guarantee of certain areas or zones of privacy, does exist under the Constitution. In varying contexts, the Court or individual Justices have, indeed, found at least the roots of that right in the First Amendment ... in the Fourth and Fifth Amendments ... in the Ninth Amendment ... or in the concept of liberty guaranteed by the first section of the Fourteenth Amendment ....
>
> This right of privacy ... is broad enough to encompass a woman's decision whether or not to terminate her pregnancy. The detriment that the State would impose upon the pregnant woman by denying this choice altogether is apparent. Specific and direct harm medically diagnosable even in early pregnancy may be involved. Maternity, or additional offspring, may force upon the woman a distressful life and future. Psychological harm may be imminent. Mental and physical health may be taxed by child care. There is also the distress, for all concerned, associated with the unwanted child, and there is the problem of bringing a child into a family already unable, psychologically and otherwise, to care for it. In other cases, as in this one, the additional difficulties and continuing stigma of unwed motherhood may be involved. All these are factors the woman and her responsible physician necessarily will consider in consultation.
>
> On the basis of elements such as these, appellant and some amici argue that the woman's right is absolute and that she is entitled to terminate her pregnancy at whatever time, in whatever way, and for whatever reason she alone chooses. With this we do not agree..... The Court's decisions recognizing a right of privacy also acknowledge that some state regulation in areas protected by that right—is appropriate. As noted above, a State may properly assert important interests in safeguarding health, in maintaining medical standards, and protecting potential life. At some point in pregnancy, these respective interests become sufficiently compelling to sustain regulation of the factors that govern the abortion decision. The privacy right involved, therefore, cannot be said to be absolute....
>
> We, therefore, conclude that the right of personal privacy includes the abortion decision, but that this right is not unqualified and must be considered against important state interests in regulation ....
>
> Our conclusion that Art. 1196 is unconstitutional means, of course, that the Texas abortion statutes, as a unit, must fall.

saw abortion as the murder of the unborn, this approach was tantamount to standing by and doing nothing while innocents were murdered.

The Birth of the Anti-Abortion Movement

John O'Keefe, a Maryland Catholic who had opposed the Vietnam War and lost a brother in that conflict, began a "direct action" campaign against abortion clinics, consciously imitating the civil rights protestors who "sat in" at segregated lunch counters to end Jim Crow laws. O'Keefe believed that God had led him to oppose the Vietnam War, support Civil Rights and now to oppose abortion. He believed that abortion was another symptom of a sick American society addicted to violence, whether on battlefields or inside a woman's womb.

The Catholic Bishops' Conference and mainstream anti-abortion groups like the National Right to Life Committee secured passage in 1976 of the "Hyde Amendment" authored by Rep. Henry Hyde, an Illinois Republican. This law prohibited the use of Medicaid funding for abortions and effectively denied poor women the same access to the procedure allowed better-off women. Nevertheless, men like O'Keefe concluded that such legal limitations on what they saw as murder were not enough. A non-violent protest at the Sigma Reproductive Health Services Clinic in Rockville, Maryland, on August 2, 1975, launched a new, more confrontational era in anti-abortion activism. Six women staged a sit-in between the waiting room and the procedure rooms while protestors sang, prayed, passed out anti-abortion literature, and tried to persuade women to not go inside. The protest got little press attention. O'Keefe and other charismatic Catholics continued to dominate the movement, staging sit-ins with small numbers of protestors.

This would change by the late 1970s when leadership of the anti-abortion movement was taken over by conservative evangelical Protestants. O'Keefe had been heavily influenced by the non-violent philosophy of Martin Luther King, Jr. New anti-abortion activists came from the political right and felt no tie to the traditions of the anti-war and civil rights movements, and would use greater attention-grabbing protest tactics. Soon, prominent preachers on television like Pat Robertson and Jerry Falwell, and anti-ERA campaigner Phyllis Schlafly joined the anti-abortion movement and gave it financial muscle and, particularly within the Republican Party, political power.

As they turned more radical, anti-abortion protestors began to call their blockades "rescues." They sought to "rescue the unborn" by closing down clinics, if possible permanently. The first known act of anti-clinic violence happened at a Planned Parenthood clinic in Eugene, Oregon, in March 1976 when a man named Joseph Stockett set the building on fire and received a five-year sentence for arson. The next February, an arsonist also targeted a Planned Parenthood clinic in St. Paul, Minnesota. In the 1980s, anti-abortion violence escalated, with protestors chaining themselves to clinics, threatening the lives of doctors, pouring noxious chemicals in clinic vents, bombing facilities and eventually assassinating abortion services staff. The struggle over abortion became—to use Risen and Thomas's term—a "war," a struggle of absolutes in which one side saw themselves engaged in a moral crusade equivalent to the struggle against slavery. Extremists believed that killing some was necessary to prevent murder of others.

STONEWALL

It was not the feminist movement alone that challenged the definition of masculinity and femininity in American society. "Most postwar Americans understood sexuality as a spectrum running from most manly to most womanly," historian Bruce J. Schulman wrote. "They assumed that homosexual men were effeminate, lesbians masculine. For a man to prove his heterosexuality, he had to eschew any effeminate behavior or trait." As Schulman argued, during the 1950s and 1960s a focus of the gay rights movement was to point out that these stereotypes were invalid, that "homosexual men were regular guys, professionals, working men." Promoting tolerance of sexual orientation, he said, became almost secondary to changing the image of the gay community. By the late 1960s, however, a new generation of gay activists wanted to move on from confronting stereotypes. The rise of the "Gay Liberation Movement," which sought acceptance of homosexuality as an example of human diversity, was greatly aided by the development of large gay communities with thriving subcultures in places like San Francisco's Castro District. Perhaps the most critical moment in the history of gay activism happened on June 27, 1969 when New York City police conducted a raid on a nightspot, the Stonewall Inn, on Christopher Street in the heart of the metropolis' gay community. "The 'Stonewall' catered to a young and largely nonwhite clientele, including many drag queens," Schulman said. Police routinely harassed patrons at gay night spots, with customers rounded up and arrested, but on this night something different happened. The usual arrests were unfolding as police seized control of the Stonewall and loaded up the patrons into a police van when a lesbian began to struggle against arresting officers.

As news of the uprising spread through the city, upwards of 1,000 protestors arrived on the scene. Gay men, who had been routinely beaten and humiliated by police, fought uniformed officers and covered buildings on Christopher Street with graffiti that read, "Gay Power!" The police department dispatched a riot squad to quell the disturbance, but demonstrations continued in New York for days. Within a short time, gay men in New York had formed the Gay Liberation Front, a group that consciously modeled itself on groups like the Black Panthers. Similar organizations calling for not just acceptance of homosexuals, but political power for gays, spread throughout the country.

Gay bars had long been gathering spots for the community, but after Stonewall, restaurants, legal clinics, newspapers, churches and synagogues aimed at the gay public opened in cities across America. Gay rights advocates won one of their most significant political victories in 1974. Until that year, the American Psychiatric Association defined homosexuality as a mental illness in its *Diagnostic and Statistical Manual of Mental Disorders* (DSM). In pursuit of curing this so-called disease, doctors subjected gay patients to castration, overdoses of insulin, electro-shock and "aversion" therapy. Activists demanded the profession provide objective evidence that gays were less well adjusted than heterosexuals or drop

A coalition of gay and lesbian activists gather for a parade in downtown Des Moines, Iowa on June 28, 1983 to kick-off the start of National Gay and Lesbian pride week.

the designation. A committee could find no scientific evidence that gays were not mentally healthy. In 1974, the psychiatric group voted to drop homosexuality from the DSM. The following year, the United States Civil Service Commission dropped its prohibition on the hiring of gays in the federal government. City governments in Boston, Detroit, Houston, Los Angeles, San Francisco and Washington, D.C. included a ban on anti-gay discrimination in their civil rights ordinances.

The gay subculture, which had for decades strongly influenced American music and Broadway theater, reached a mass audience through the disco music craze in the late 1970s. One group, the Village People, featured singers and dancers dressed as masculine archetypes (an Indian in feathered headdress, a policeman, a cowboy, etc.) and had a string of novelty hits beginning in 1977, including "Macho Man" and "Y.M.C.A." (the latter an inside joke for the gay community because YMCAs had, for much of the twentieth century, served as a place for men to make sexual hookups.)

Inevitably, gays faced a fierce counteroffensive from those describing themselves as defenders of "traditional values." A gay-rights ordinance in Dade County, Florida, inspired a repeal campaign led by singer and former Miss Oklahoma **Anita Bryant**, who had a Top 40 hit song, "Paper Roses" in 1960. Bryant, who at one point called gays "human garbage," had become a fixture in TV commercials for Tupperware, Coca-Cola, Holiday Inn, and the Florida Citrus Commission, for whom she promoted drinking orange juice. When Dade County passed a law banning discrimination in employment, housing and public accommodations for gays, she organized protestors, and claimed that if socially accepted, gays would sexually assault children. "As a mother, I know that homosexuals cannot biologically reproduce children, therefore, they must recruit our children," she said. "If gays are granted rights, next we'll have to give rights to prostitutes and to people who sleep with Saint Bernards and to nail biters." Bryant formed a group called "Save Our Children" and nearly 70 percent of Dade County voters elected to overturn the anti-discrimination ordinance June 7, 1977.

Within the next year, voters reversed anti-discrimination ordinances in Eugene, Oregon, St. Paul, Minnesota, and Wichita, Kansas. The biggest battle came in California where conservative state Senator John Briggs placed a referendum on the state ballot that would have allowed school districts to fire gay employees or anyone discovered to be publicly or privately "advocating, imposing, encouraging or promoting homosexual activity." After a string of political defeats, the gay community effectively organized and put together an impressive coalition to oppose the "Briggs Initiative" as it was known. Labor rallied to the defense of gay members belonging to teacher unions, the largest-circulation newspapers in the state editorialized against it and even conservative Governor Ronald Reagan opposed the law, calling it an attack on free speech. In an editorial, Reagan (who as a Hollywood actor had worked with many gays) asked what would happen if a student upset about a bad grade made a false accusation of homosexuality against a teacher. More than 58 percent of voters cast "no" ballots on November 7, 1978, and the measure was even rejected in Briggs' base in Orange County.

Such elections drew gays into politics and brought to the limelight the first openly gay politicians. In 1980, the Democrats included a gay rights plank in their national platform. However, anti-gay attitudes remained at high levels in the American public. Only 27 percent of the American public believed that gays should be allowed to teach in elementary schools, according to a 1977 Gallup poll. Only 26 percent in 1978 said they would vote for a "well-qualified" gay candidate for president. For three years in a row after her anti-gay campaigns, readers of *Good Housekeeping* named Anita Bryant "Most Admired Woman."

Harvey Milk's political career captured the triumph and tragedy of gay politics in the 1970s. A Navy veteran and former Wall Street investment banker, Milk moved to San Francisco and opened a camera shop on Castro Street in 1972. Milk organized the Castro Village Association, a merchants' organization in the neighborhood famous for its large gay community. A mayor and a County Board of Supervisors governed both the city and the county of San Francisco. After losing three times as an openly gay candidate in races for the Board of Supervisors when elections were held on a city-wide basis, the "Mayor of Castro Street" finally won an election on January 8, 1977 when the county races were broken into individual districts.

Milk received letters of admiration and praise, as well as ugly threats from across the country. "I thank God," read one letter from a 68-year-old lesbian, "I have lived long enough to see my kind emerge from the shadows and join the human race." More sinister was another note that said, "Maybe, just maybe, some of the more hostile in the district may take some potshots at you—we hope!!!" Milk took such threats in stride. One of his biggest accomplishments was passage by the board of an anti-discrimination ordinance that prohibited businesses from firing individuals based on sexual orientation. He also supported free public transportation and called for a citizens' commission to oversee the San Francisco Police Department.

Yet, Milk seemed to sense his life was in danger, and he made a tape recording on November 18, 1977, leaving a note that the message was to be played only after his death. "If a bullet should enter my brain, let that bullet destroy every closet door," he said. Milk was assassinated just nine days later by Dan White, a mentally imbalanced man who had recently resigned from the Board of Supervisors over the issue of pay and then became enraged when San Francisco Mayor George Moscone would not reinstate him. On November 27, White, a conservative Catholic and former police officer, fire fighter and military veteran, arrived at city hall, sneaked into the building with a handgun, fatally shot the mayor and then killed Milk, shooting him five times. Insult was added to injury at Dan White's trial when defense attorneys successfully kept gays and people of color off the jury and argued that at the time of the murders White suffered from "diminished capacity" mentally from eating too much junk food, the so-called "Twinkie defense." The jury convicted White of voluntary manslaughter, rather than first-degree murder, and he was sentenced to only seven years and eight months in prison. A mob of 3,000 gay men and women rioted the night of the verdict May 21, 1979, leaving more than 160 hospitalized, including 61 police officers, and more than $1 million in damages across the city.

"A CIVILIZATION WITHOUT INSANITY": Religious Experimentation in the 1960s

The injustice of this planet led activists to want to change this world. For others, oppression and economic injustice led them to turn away from their here-and-now and focus on what they hoped would be a happier afterlife. Drug use, particularly consuming LSD, had been widely seen as a spiritual exercise that allowed one to escaped doomed Western civilization. Now young people in the Sixties and Seventies sought more natural means to expand their minds and looked to ancient wisdom available in India, China, and Japan. In America, young people turned to Tibetan and Zen Buddhism. Others experimented with the mysticism of Sufi Islam. The Hare Krishna sect, in which devotees surrendered personal property, shaved their heads, wore orange or yellow robes, took a Sanskrit name, and danced and chanted the name of the Hindu deity Krishna, as they begged for donations became a common sight at American airports by the 1970s. Other young people, including feminists offended by the exclusion of women from the clergy in many mainstream churches, embraced nature-worshiping "Wiccan" beliefs.

New religions also arose, such as the Church of Scientology founded by one-time science fiction writer **L. Ron Hubbard**. "A civilization without insanity, without criminals and without war, where the able can prosper and honest beings can have rights, and where man is free to rise to greater heights, are the aims of Scientology," Hubbard once wrote to his followers.

Hubbard served in the United States Navy during World War II, and later claimed that he received serious injuries that left him "[b]linded with injured optic nerves and lame with physical injuries to hip and back . . . a supposedly hopeless cripple." Hubbard would tell his followers that he miraculously healed himself while lying in a military hospital bed, using the methods that later became Church of Scientology practice. Hubbard said he discovered that the mental exercises he used to repair his body could cure depression, alcoholism and other mental maladies.

He codified these techniques in a 1950 book *Dianetics: The Modern Science of Mental Health*, which charted 28 weeks on the *New York Times* bestseller list. "Written in a bluff, quirky style and overrun with footnotes that do little to substantiate its findings," journalist Lawrence Wright noted, "'Dianetics' purports to identify the source of self-destructive behavior—the 'reactive mind,' a kind of data bank that is filled with traumatic memories called 'engrams,' and that is the source of nightmares, insecurities, irrational fears, and psychosomatic illnesses. The object of Dianetics is to drain the engrams of their painful, damaging qualities and eliminate the reactive mind, leaving a person 'Clear.'"

Scientologists had their personalities tested, received treatments that were supposed to address past pains and current anxieties, and paid for ever more expensive courses that progressively revealed the cosmic truth as understood by Hubbard, that humans are occupied by the souls of aliens tormented in a disastrous war that unfolded millions of years ago and that these alien presences cause the mental illnesses Scientology claims to cure.

Many young people in the Sixties and the Seventies moved quickly from one belief system to the next, sometimes blending wildly divergent beliefs like a theological smoothie. Wade Clark Roof, a sociologist, came across one upper-class Jewish woman, "Mollie" from New York who told him she tried out "holistic health, macrobiotics, Zen Buddhism, [and] . . . Native American rituals." She told Roof she joined a "commune," read about reincarnation and started attending Quaker meetings. Mollie was not typical. "Of course, such spiritual alternatives never attracted more than a small fraction of Americans who adhered to one variety or another of Judaism and Christianity," wrote Isserman and Kazin. "Even in the San Francisco Bay Area, mecca for unorthodox faiths, fewer than 10 percent of the population seems to have taken part in any manifestation of the new religions."

"Revolutionary Suicide"

Nevertheless, the search for truth and happiness for some young people turned desperate, leaving them vulnerable to ruthless con artists. **Jim Jones**, a preacher and faith healer, founded the Peoples Temple Christian Church Full Gospel in Indianapolis. A crusader against racism who embraced Marxism, Jones launched programs to aid the poor and the hungry. He presided over an integrated congregation that often met hostility from white residents in a city that had been dominated by the Ku Klux Klan in the 1920s. Appointed to the Indianapolis Human Rights Commission, Jones used his position and the support of local civil rights groups like the NAACP to advance desegregation of the city police department, local businesses and other institutions. Jones received numerous threats as he began adopting Korean, Native American and African-American children.

Jones's inner demons soon overwhelmed his idealism. He staged fake miracle cures to bring in more congregants and to fill church coffers. Dependent on drugs and alcohol, and sexually exploiting members of his church, Jones became obsessed with what he saw as the pending end of the world and paranoid about an establishment he believed was plotting his demise. Jones relocated his church and his congregation to Northern California, which he believed would be spared a coming nuclear war. He eventually established a headquarters in San Francisco where his charitable work and anti-racism activism earned him enough credibility that Mayor George Moscone appointed him to lead the city's Housing Authority Commission. By this point, still telling his followers that a nuclear war would soon happen and now insisting that the United States government wanted to kill him and destroy the People's Temple, Jones in 1973 rented a remote plot of land surrounded by jungle in Northern Guyana for a communal farm that he dubbed "Jonestown."

More than 900 members emigrated there, where they found a life of relentless labor, clearing the jungle, building housing, cultivating crops and listening to Jones's increasingly doomsday-oriented sermons. Preaching that U.S. government forces would soon come to destroy the Temple, Jones led his followers in suicide drills in which members drank what they were told was Flavor-Aid filled with the poison cyanide. Reports from relatives of Temple members that their loved ones had become disaffected with Jones but were being held against their will in South America led the San Francisco-area Congressman Leo Ryan to travel to Jonestown on November 14, 1978. With him were 17 concerned relatives of People's Temple members and an NBC News crew.

After difficult wrangling, the group was allowed to inspect Jonestown on November 17. When Ryan left the next day, 14 Temple defectors joined him. Jones ordered the assassination of Ryan and his group. Temple hitmen murdered the Congressmen and four others at a nearby airstrip. Jones's long awaited apocalypse had arrived, and the heavily sweating and stern minister called on members to engage in an act of "revolutionary suicide." Eventually 909 people in Jonestown, including more than 300 children, were found dead. Most drank cups of poisoned Flavor-Aid under the watchful gaze of Jones's private army. Jones shot himself in the head.

"A God in Your Universe"

California served as home base not just for the People's Temple, Scientology, and the Charles Manson family, but also a number of so-called consciousness-raising groups like **Erhard Sensitivity Training** or est. Born Jack Rosenberg, Werner Hans Erhard had already experimented with Scientology and Zen Buddhism and had failed at selling cars and encyclopedias before launching est, according to Schulman. Erhard vaguely claimed to have had some profound spiritual insight while driving on a California freeway. He told perspective students that est would make them "throw away" their belief systems, break down their old personalities and let them recreate a healthier version of themselves. Students who attended the group training seminars, which cost $250 a pop, were given infrequent food, little sleep and and few bathroom breaks and were sometimes stuck in a conference room for eight hours with trainers who shouted verbal abuse in order to break down their defense mechanisms.

Trainers taught students that failure, illness, romantic frustration, etc., were always a product of the individual's unhealthy thinking and not of random chance or normal human frailty. Once beaten down, the students took "responsibility" for their failures and were told they could now achieve virtually anything they wanted as long as they didn't defeat themselves. "You are omnipotent," Erhard would tell his devotees. "You are a god in your universe." As historian Dominic Sandbrook wrote, ". . . Not all customers emerged satisfied, and psychiatric journals reported that several people, some already vulnerable, had been driven to near madness."

In the 1960s and 1970s, transactional analysis, primal scream therapy, Esalen, Rolfing and other pop psychology therapies, as well as the endless list of bestselling self-help books like *I'm O.k., You're O.k.* and *Looking Out For Number One* shared what journalist Peter Marin labeled "the new narcissism." Perhaps Sixties youth grew tired of battling intractable problems like poverty and racism, but these fads all reflected a withdrawal from the wider world and what Marin called "selfishness and moral blindness." Marin described how he heard two speakers at the Esalen Institute claim that "the Jews must have wanted to be burned by the Germans." Marin asked the women what they would say to a child trapped in a famine and one said, "What can I do if a child is determined to starve?" Tom Wolfe called the Seventies the "Me Decade," a time Marin said, of "a retreat from the worlds of morality and history, an unembarrassed denial of human reciprocity and community."

THE PROMISE AND THE DISAPPOINTMENT OF AMERICAN CULTURE, 1960-1980

Both the liberal political establishment, represented by the Kennedy administration, and the youth counterculture that arose in its wake started the period from 1960 to 1980 with a broader sense of purpose than the narcissistic pursuit of self-fulfillment. The administrators of Kennedy's New Frontier, filled with hubris, saw their mission as saving the world from communism. The more idealistic members of the Kennedy administration hoped to usher in an America freed from segregation and poverty. Meanwhile, counterculture youths saw a world poisoned with militarism and corrupted by the undemocratic dominance of wealthy, straight, Protestant, English-speaking Anglo men. They fought to create a world in which African Americans, Mexican Americans, Native Americans, women, gays and the poor would have a voice. Both sets of idealists looked outward to make the world a better place rather then inward for self-justification.

Two overlapping journeys in the summer of 1969 illustrate these separate, Homeric quests for a better world: the *Apollo 11* moon landing on July 20, 1969 and the staging of the **Woodstock Music and Art Fair** in upstate New York, August 15-18. For millions of Americans the manned moon landing marked the emotional highlight of a difficult, often depressing decade, a rare moment of unity in a divisive time. A party atmosphere surrounded Cape Kennedy in Brevard County on Florida's east coast on the morning of July 16. About 1 million visitors flocked to the launch site. Counterculture youths had dubbed as "happenings" their large gatherings to share emotional experiences stimulated by mood-altering chemicals. The *Apollo* launch was a "happening" for the older generation.

"From Titusville to Melbourne, thousands of cars converged on huge regions stretching as far west as Orlando," author Dan Parry wrote. "With the freeways blocked by the worst jams in Florida's history, some drivers used the wrong side of the road since no-one was headed in the opposite direction. Only the wealthy, or well-connected, managed to avoid the crowds by arriving in private aircraft, and then boarding one of the hundreds of boats choking the Banana River. Meanwhile thousands of people, who were settled among their barbecues, beer coolers and bottles of pop, were either lounging around or else trying out their cameras, telescopes and binoculars." Elsewhere, space tourists set up tents and camper vans or cooled off at the local bars where a "'lift-off martini' would set you back $1.25, while for those who really wanted to live it up there was the 'moonlander' consisting of crème de menthe, crème de cacao, vodka, soda, and a squeeze of lime, topped with an American flag."

Inside the space center, officials set up bleachers for establishment celebrities and important officials including former President Johnson, the first man to fly solo across the Atlantic, Charles Lindbergh, and *Tonight Show* host Johnny Carson. NASA set up a "press enclosure" for 3,500 reporters from around the world. African Americans were offended that all the *Mercury*, *Gemini* and *Apollo* astronauts had been white, but even more by the fact that black school children lived in crumbling urban neighborhoods with deteriorating schools while the federal government wasted money on what they saw as space tourism and the terrible misadventure in Vietnam. The Rev. Ralph Abernathy, who became president of the Southern Christian Leadership Conference following the assassination of Martin Luther King, Jr., led 100 protestors to the gates of the Kennedy Space Center, to protest what he saw as badly misplaced priorities. The money spent on moon landings, he said, should instead be used to feed the poor. NASA officials invited Abernathy into the VIP section to watch the liftoff. Even Abernathy, there to protest, found himself overwhelmed by the drama.

He considered himself "one of the proudest Americans as I stood on this soil." Later, after a moment of reflection, his ambivalence returned. "There's a great deal of joy and pride," he said, "For that particular moment and second I really forgot the fact that we have so many hungry people in the United States of America . . . This is really holy ground. And it will be more holy once we feed the hungry, care for the sick, and provide for those who do not have houses."

About 600 million people around the world, 20 percent of the Earth's population, watched on television or listened on the radio when Neil Armstrong announced at 4:18 p.m. EST on July 20 that "The Eagle has landed." ("The Eagle" was Apollo 11's landing craft, the so-called lunar module.) When an announcer at Yankee Stadium in New York informed the fans of the Eagle's touchdown, the crowd of 16,0000 let out a whoop of celebration, belting out "The Star-Spangled Banner." In Britain, television networks provided their first all-night broadcast, allowing audiences there to see the landing live.

Apollo lunar modules would land on the Moon five more times between November 14, 1969 and December 19, 1972 (because of dangerous mechanical problems, the *Apollo 13* mission had to be cut short before it reached the moon). By this point television audiences had grown bored with the moonwalks and few paid attention to the last lunar voyage, *Apollo 17*. The last mission in the series, *Apollo 18*, was scrubbed due to objections to the moon program's continuing high costs.

Always controversial, when the *Apollo* program ended in 1972, it had cost the taxpayers $25.4 billion, or about $129 billion in 2011 dollars. That amounted to, when adjusted for inflation, $11.7 billion a mission at a cost of about $630 per person in the U.S. Many scientists believe that more information could have been obtained at less expense with unmanned craft. Nevertheless, lunar rocks and soil brought back to Earth by the astronauts have provided solid evidence supporting the "giant impact theory" concerning the Moon's origins. According to this theory, a Mars-sized object collided with the Earth early in its history. Scattered debris from this impact, through gravity, coalesced to create the Moon.

Apollo 11 was the first manned mission to land on the Moon. The first steps by humans on another planetary body were taken by Neil Armstrong and Buzz Aldrin on July 20, 1969. The astronauts also returned to Earth the first samples from another planetary body.

Technology developed for *Apollo* greatly accelerated the development of, as Sharon Guadin for *Computerworld* magazine wrote, robotics, the integrated circuit, laptop computers, nanotechnology, and technological advances in aeronautics, transportation and the health-care industries. Micro-electromechanical systems, supercomputers and microcomputers, software and microprocessors are also technological spin-offs resulting from NASA's lunar quests. "Without the research and development that went into those space missions, top companies like Intel Corps may not have been founded," reported Guadin, "and the population likely wouldn't be spending a big chunk of work and free time using laptops and Blackberries to post information on Facebook or Twitter." Freeze-dried food, the credit card swiping devices used by retailers, and liquid-cooled clothing used by firefighters also trace their origins to the *Apollo* program.

To older Americans, the moon mission provided supposedly objective evidence that American capitalism was superior to Russian communism because the United States got to the moon first. It confirmed the power of rational thought, and that with determination and unity Americans could do anything. For some, like the poet Archibald MacLeish, the photos of the Earth taken by *Apollo* astronauts served as an eloquent warning to humanity of the loneliness and fragility of the planet and the consequent need for peace and understanding. "To see the earth as it truly is," MacLeish wrote, "small and blue and beautiful in that eternal silence where it floats, is to see ourselves as riders on the earth together, brothers on that bright loveliness in the eternal cold—brothers who know now they are truly brothers."

Many counterculture figures, by contrast, saw the space mission with its segregated all-male crew leaving garbage and planting an American flag on the surface as evidence that humans were just transporting racism, sexism, pollution, and imperialism elsewhere in the cosmos. *Apollo* was an expensive diversion, a typical example of establishment excess. The truth lay in inner, not outer space. About 400,000 gathered in upstate New York for a journey of a different sort. Promoters organizing the Woodstock Music and Art Fair had rented 600 acres of farm land from Max Yasgur to see one of the most storied music lineups in history, including longtime folk music legend Joan Baez, the English rock band The Who, blues-inspired, scorching Texas vocalist Janis Joplin, the band most associated with extended musical LSD raves (The Grateful Dead), and emerging guitar legends Carlos Santana and Jimi Hendrix.

On the surface, Woodstock was about the counterculture—the alternative values embraced by young people by the late 1960s that questioned aspects of mainstream society like capitalism, but at this festival, appearances were often deceiving and not just because of the mind-altering drugs gobbled there. As historian David P. Szatmary documents, "Woodstock represented a well-calculated business venture. The planning and promotion of the festival has been masterminded by two astute businessmen—John Roberts, a young millionaire who graduated from the University of Pennsylvania, and Joel Rosenman, a Yale Law School graduate . . ." The festival organizers were out to make a buck and hoped to charge those in attendance $18 a head, but "the state police closed the New York Thruway [and] . . . long hairs from throughout the country parked their cars and walked miles to the site," as historian John C. McWilliams observed. "As the crowd grew . . . promoters realized the futility of trying to collect a fee . . ." Many newspapers and television stations predicted a disaster and, as McWilliams argued, "it should have been.

> With very little security and almost no police protection, severe food shortages, a limited medical staff, inadequate toilet facilities, drugs everywhere, and a fierce thunderstorm that turned the field into a swamp, a disaster did seem inevitable. Some people suffered from dehydration, and several experienced bad drug trips, but remarkably there was no rioting. At Woodstock, the hippies gave peace a chance . . . After three days of continuous music, three deaths were reported – two drug related and a third when a tractor accidentally ran over a person in a sleeping bag. A sense of community among the crowd fostered cooperation and civility . . . The police chief in nearby Monticello called the festival throng "the most courteous, considerate, and well-behaved group of kids that I have ever been in contact with in my twenty-four years of police work." Despite the drugs, unsanitary conditions, a three-hour wait to use a pay telephone, and shortages of almost everything, no violence—not even a fistfight—occurred.

During the *Apollo* mission on the moon, astronauts were sealed in airtight suits to protect them from the cold, the lack of oxygen and the absence of air pressure in space. Their helmets and suits came between them and a new world. The Woodstock festival immersed its audience in tastes and smells, with flesh pressed against flesh and oozing mud squishing between everyone's toes and fingers. The audience felt inducted into a new, psychically bound "Woodstock Nation," as one participant Glenn Weiser remembered.

"That was the first revelation of Woodstock.—the sheer size the counterculture had grown to. Every town had its hippies, but now enormous numbers of us had massed in one area. Friday afternoon brought home to everyone how broad-based the movement had become . . . [T]he second revelation of Woodstock [was] the brotherhood that developed as an entire crowd of young people high on psychedelics got acquainted with those sitting next to them . . . There was a feeling of immediate friendship, and the sense of a group mind at work." Some hoped magic would result, a world transformed not through space age technology but through good will.

And I dreamed I saw the bombers/riding shotgun in the sky," Joni Mitchell later sang of the concert, "And they were turning into butterflies/ above our nation.

The vision of a better world that fueled both quests proved to be an illusion. Moon landings ended much sooner than anyone expected, and by 2011 the future of the American space program was in question. The space shuttle program ended that year, and NASA had no new manned journeys to space planned by the end of the year. If Archibald MacLeish hoped that the image of the world from space would inspire brotherhood, that dream had completely crumbled by the time of a civil war in Bosnia in the 1990s that produced the worst genocide in Europe since the Holocaust and other heartless slaughters in Rwanda in the 1990s and in the Sudan in the opening years of the twenty-first century.

The dreams Woodstock inspired also quickly shattered. Just four months after the concert, the English rock band, the Rolling Stones, staged a show at the Altamont Raceway in northern California. A cancellation of an earlier show meant that the concert's producers had a single day to prepare for the arrival of an audience of about 300,000. "Sanitary facilities were inadequate, the sound system, terrible; the setting cheerless," author Allen J. Matusow wrote. "Lots of bad dope, including inferior acid spiked with speed, circulated through the crowd. Harried medics had to fly in an emergency supply of Thorazine to treat the epidemic of bad trips and were busy administering first aid to the victims of the random violence."

Much of the trouble came because the Rolling Stones had decided, upon the recommendation of the Grateful Dead, to hire the Hell's Angels motorcycle gang to guard the stage in return for $500 worth of beer. Drunk and strung out on drugs, the Angels "indiscriminately clubbed people for offenses real and imagined." The clubbing continued when the Stones got on stage. Lead singer Mick Jagger stopped singing at one point to beg the Hell's Angels to stop the violence, but to no avail. Jagger resumed the concert, and darkly sang the band's recent hit "Sympathy for the Devil":

> I watched with glee
> While your kings and queens
> Fought for ten decades
> For the gods they made
> I shouted out
> "Who killed the Kennedys?"
> When after all
> It was you and me.

"Midway though [the song]," Matusow said, "only a few feet from the stage, an Angel knifed a black man named Meredith Hunter to death." In retrospect, the event seemed like the death of the 1960s and the start of a more desperate decade of diminished expectations in which bombers didn't turn into butterflies.

The counterculture to a large degree was a byproduct of the prosperity produced in the post–World War II American economy. The middle-class and affluent whites who dominated the counterculture enjoyed the luxury to dream of alternatives to the status quo. "By solving the problem of want, industrial capitalism undermined the very virtues that made this triumph possible, virtues like hard work, self-denial, postponement of gratification, submission to social discipline, strong ego-mechanisms to control the instincts," Matusow argued. ". . . Unprecedented affluence after World War II created a generation of teenagers who could forgo work to stay in school. Inhabiting a gilded limbo between childhood and adult responsibility, these kids had money, leisure, and unprecedented opportunity to test taboos." A revolution was needed in a culture in which rape was treated as a male privilege in marriage and in which millions of African Americans, *Chicanos*, and Native Americans were disenfranchised and treated as subhumans. Among affluent whites, however, both the Baby Boomers and their parents were deceived by the unusual economic comfort of the 1950s and the 1960s and suffered from unrealistic expectations of what was possible, financially, morally and spiritually.

The protest movements and the counterculture that sustained them did expand the realm of the possible in American life. Though not yet reflective of American diversity, corporate board rooms, universities, the Congress, state legislatures, police departments, the medical field, movies and television programs have never again been as stiflingly white, Anglo, Protestant and male as these institutions were before the 1960s and 1970s.

Without the Civil Rights Movement, it's hard to imagine a President Barack Obama. Black men and women serve as mayors and sheriffs in cities once ruled by the Ku Klux Klan. Without a women's rights movement, it's hard to imagine the political career of Hillary Rodham Clinton. Without the environmentalist movement, the construction of nuclear power plants may not have halted in the 1980s, and it's difficult to see how recycling could have become part of the average American's life. The Women's Movement shattered rigid conceptions of masculinity and femininity, opening doors for fathers to have more affectionate, open relationships with their children, the creation of the Women's National Basketball Association, and the musical careers of such gender benders as David Bowie in the 1970s, Prince in the 1980s, and Lady Gaga in the twenty-first century. The gay rights movement has forced the heterosexual community to reconsider discrimination at the workplace, in the military, in politics and in marriage.

Just as 1950s and 1960s protestors drew on and modified the tradition of dissent that flowered in the Great Depression, the organizers of marches for immigrant rights in recent years and the Occupy Wall Street demonstrations calling for economic fairness that riveted America in 2012 borrow much of their style and their substance from the 1950s and 1960s. Black music reached white audiences in the 1950s mostly when performed by white artists. Beginning in the 1980s, rap became the dominant genre and it addressed black themes performed by black artists to a large, integrated audience. Youth culture once dismissed as disposable trash became the topic of graduate school seminars.

Radicals in the 1960s, however, didn't want mere reform or changes in public taste. They dreamed of revolution. And the youth movements from the 1950s to the 1970s fell far short of that. Like Tantalus in the Greek myth, these generations thought themselves surrounded by limitless opportunity and endless pleasure—whether in the form of material comfort, a freer society, a more just world, or a life unshackled by punishing Puritanism—that lay within easy reach. The crushing economic contraction of the 1970s, however, cruelly pulled away these treasures, feeding a resentment that would give rise to a different, conservative age of indulgence.

One of the central political figures of the 1980s would not be a hippie but a straight-laced Baptist minister in Virginia, Jerry Falwell, who made a career of bashing unions. Falwell had supported segregation and had not baptized African-American members in his church until 1971. He would blame the 2001 terrorist attacks at the World Trade Center and the Pentagon on feminists and the legalization of abortion, and would describe AIDS as "the wrath of God against homosexuals." Men like Falwell hated everything about the 1960s and 1970s counterculture and the Virginia minister would become the most visible leader of evangelical Christians who would sweep Ronald Reagan into power in the 1980 presidential race. The view of the Woodstock audience had been inclusive. The creators of *Apollo* imagined an expansive future. Falwell wanted a narrower, more restrictive America. He wanted gays back in the closet, and women back at home. While he condemned the sexual excess and drug abuse of the 1960s counterculture, however, Falwell would in the years after the 1980s show blindness towards another type of excess.

When Ronald Reagan was sworn into office January 20, 1981, "The inaugural festivities had been in full swing since the weekend . . . In 1976 [at Jimmy Carter's inaugural], all the events had been open to the public, and most had been free. Now a simple ball ticket cost $100 ($274 in 2011 dollars) . . . the tarmac at Washington National Airport so crowded with private jets that some had to be turned away," as Dominic Sandbrook said. At a time of high inflation and skyrocketing unemployment, Nancy Reagan wore a dress "that cost enough to keep fifty people in food stamps for a year." The inaugural festivities cost taxpayers $16 million [almost $44 million in today's dollars.]

At one banquet at Union Station, Sandbrook wrote, "tables were piled high with gourmet food prepared by the finest French chefs; stuffed clams and raw oysters, lobsters and scallops, éclairs and brioches, carpaccio and chardonnay." In spite of expensive decorations, however, Union Station was decaying after years of neglect and one failed attempt at renovation during the 1976 bicentennial celebrations. "Even as Reagan's guests circulated around the gourmet tables, some noticed mold in the ceiling and cigarette burns in the carpet."

As the wealthy inaugural attendees "swallowed their expensive cakes and pastries, they tried to ignore the shabby drunks and derelicts, a small army of the capital's homeless, gathering outside the doors, drawn by the aroma of the food," according to Sandbrook. "First one, then another slipped past security and made for the tables, and for a few glorious moments the forgotten Americans found themselves shoulder to shoulder with the rich and the famous. But it was only for a minute or two, then the guards were on them, and the illusion was broken, and they were outside, shivering with cold as Washington toasted a new era."

The inaugural foreshadowed the next thirty years of American history. Reagan would slash spending on public housing, and federal aid to cities would be cut by 60 percent during his eight-year presidency. A consequence was a massive increase in the number of homeless, which in America by the late 1980s had swollen to "600,000 on any given night—and 1.2 million over the course of a year. Many were Vietnam veterans, children, and laid-off workers." Meanwhile, Reagan tripled the federal debt from $900 billion to $2.7 trillion ($5.1 trillion as of 2011), spent to a large degree on military hardware. From Reagan's first year in office to 2011, the United States federal government would run deficits 27 out of 31 years and would decline to raise taxes for expensive wars and other military adventures in Lebanon, Grenada, Panama, the Persian Gulf, Somalia, Bosnia, Serbia, Haiti, Afghanistan, Iraq, Pakistan, Libya and elsewhere. As of 2011, the total federal debt reached $14 trillion. Many questioned whether America adequately funded schools, much less moon missions. By 1981, America did not find a Woodstock Nation of peace and love, or a New Frontier in outer space, but a Darwinian world of rich and poor drowning in red ink.

Chronology

1962 Rachel Carson's book *Silent Spring* is published.

1963 *The Feminine Mystique* by Betty Friedan.
Sidney Portier becomes the first African American to win an Oscar for best actor for his performance in the movie *Lilies of the Field*.
Mexican Americans sweep elections, taking control of the city council in Crystal City, Texas.

1964 Bob Dylan releases "The Times They Are-A Changin."
The Beatles reach wide American audience on "The Ed Sullivan Show" on CBS.
Title IX of the 1964 Civil Rights Act bans sex discrimination in education and the workplace.

1965 The Agricultural Workers Organizing Committee launches a strike against grape growers in California's San Joaquin Valley.

1966 The National Organization of Women (NOW).
The phrase "Black Power" and "black is beautiful" come to be widely used by African-American protestors.
Television series *Star Trek* debuts on NBC.

1967 Beatles record and release their land-mark album, *Sgt. Pepper's Lonely Hearts Club Band*.

1968 American Indian Movement (AIM) is formed.
Hair opens on Broadway.
Feminists protest outside the Miss America pageant.

1969 The "Stonewall Riot," breaks out.
The Woodstock Music and Art Fair unfolds.
Native American protestors seize control of the former federal prison on Alcatraz Island.
The Chicago Police and FBI agents fatally shoot Black Panther leader Fred Hampton.

1970 "Earth Day" is held April 22.
Clean Air Act.
Environmental Protection Agency (EPA).

1972 Congress submits the Equal Rights Amendment but ratification narrowly fails.

1973 *Roe v. Wade*.
Wounded Knee occupation.

1974 American Psychiatric Association drops its definition of homosexuality as a mental illness in its Diagnostic and Statistical Manual of Mental Disorders.
Safe Drinking Water Act is enacted.

1976 Congress passes the Hyde Amendment.

1977 *Roots* debuts on television.
Singer Anita Bryant leads a successful campaign to overturn a Dade County, Florida gay rights ordinance.
Harvey Milk becomes the first openly gay candidate to win a seat on the San Francisco Board of County Supervisors.

1978 Love Canal declared a threat to human health.
California voters reject the anti-gay "Briggs Initiative" in a referendum November 7.

1979 Three Mile Island nuclear power plant accident.

1980 The EPA "super fund" to clean toxic wastes sites is created by Congress.

Review Questions

1. What social and economic factors led to the rise of the 1950s and 1960s counterculture and what values did 1960s and 1970s protestors generally embrace?

2. How did Black Nationalists differ from early civil rights protestors in terms of their focus and their tactics and how did *Chicano* protestors differ from participants in older Mexican American groups like LULAC?

3. What factors led to the failure of the Equal Rights Amendment?

4. How did the anti-abortion movement change over the years, particularly as control of the movement passed from liberal Catholics to conservative evangelical Protestants?

5. What contributions did Bob Dylan and The Beatles make to popular music in the 1960s?

Glossary of Important People and Concepts

Alcatraz Occupation
All In the Family
American Indian Movement
The Beatles
Black Panther Party
Susan Brownmiller
Anita Bryant
Stokely Carmichael
Rachel Carson
César Chávez
Chicano Movement
Consciousness-Raising
Deep Ecology
Bob Dylan
Earth Day
Equal Rights Amendment (ERA)
Erhard Sensitivity Training (est)
Jerry Falwell
Betty Friedan
Jim Jones
Love Canal
Charles Manson
Harvey Milk
The National Organization of Woman (NOW)
Roe v. Wade
Roots
Phyllis Schlafly
Three Mile Island
The Weather Underground
Wounded Knee Occupation

SUGGESTED READINGS

Rodolfo Acuña, *Occupied America: A History of Chicanos* (1988).

Donald Bogle, *Toms, Coons, Mulattoes, Mammies & Bucks: An Interpretive History of Blacks in American Films* (1996).

Paul Boyer, *When Time Shall Be No More: Prophecy Belief in Modern American Culture* (1992).

Clayborne Carson, *In Struggle: SNCC and the Black Awakening of the 1960s* (1981).

John D'Emilio and Estelle B. Freedman, *Intimate Matters: A History of Sexuality in America* (1997).

Peter Drier, "Reagan's Legacy: Homelessness in America," *Shelterforce Online*, May/June 2004, http://www.nhi.org/online/issues/135/reagan.html.

Alice Echols, *Daring to be Bad: Radical Feminism in America, 1967-1975* (1989).

Sara Evans, *Personal Politics: The Roots of Women's Liberation in the Civil Rights Movement and the New Left* (1979).

David Farber, *The Age of Great Dreams: America in the 1960s* (1994)

___, *The Sixties: From Memory to History* (1994)

Todd Gitlin, *The Sixties: Years of Hope, Days of Rage* (1987)

Sharon Guadin, "NASA's Apollo Technology Has Changed History: Apollo Lunar Program Made A Staggering Contribution to High Tech Development" *Computerworld*, July 20, 2009, http://www.computerworld.com/s/article/9135690/NASA_s_Apollo_technology_has_changed_history?taxonomyId=11&pageNumber=1

Charles Kaiser, *1968 in America: Music, Politics, Chaos, Counterculture, and the Shaping of a Generation* (1988).

Norman Mailer, *Of A Fire on the Moon* (1969).

Allen J. Matusow, *The Unraveling of America: A History of Liberalism in the 1960s* (2009).

Matt S. Meier and Feliciano Rivera, *The Chicanos: A History of Mexican Americans* (1972).

John C. McWilliams, *The 1960s Cultural Revolution* (2000).

Dan Parry, *Moon Shot: The Inside Story of Mankind's Greatest Adventure* (2009).

Rick Perlstein, *Nixonland: The Rise of a President and the Fracturing of America* (2008).

Michael Phillips, *White Metropolis: Race, Ethnicity and Religion in Dallas, 1841-2001* (2006).

James Risen and Judy L. Thomas, *Wrath of Angels: The American Abortion War* (1998).

Dominic Sandbrook, *Mad As Hell: The Crisis of the 1970s and the Rise of the Populist Right* (2011).

Guadalupe San Miguel, *Brown, Not White: School Integration and the Chicano Movement in Houston* (2001).

David P. Szatmary, *Rockin' In Time: A Social History of Rock and Roll* (1987).

Bruce J. Schulman, *The Seventies: The Great Shift in American Culture, Society and Politics* (2001).

Robert Weisbrot. *Freedom Bound: A History of America's Civil Rights Movement.* 1990.

Sean Wilentz, *Bob Dylan in America* (2010.)

James Wilson, *And the Earth Shall Weep: A History of Native America* (2000).

Tom Wolfe, *The Right Stuff* (1979).

Lawrence Wright, "The Apostate: Paul Haggis vs. The Church of Scientology," *The New Yorker*, February 14, 2011.

Malcolm X (as told to Alex Haley), *The Autobiography of Malcolm X* (1964).

Marc Scott Zicree, *The Twilight Zone Companion* (1982).

Chapter Thirty-three

THE RISE OF CONSERVATISM:
Ronald Reagan to George H. W. Bush

Although credited with ideas and policies that ended several years of stagflation, in reality the Reagan presidency marked the beginning of one of the most protracted periods of income inequality in American history. The theme of money, status, and power came to dominate popular culture in the 1980s. Reagan himself set the tone when he responded to a reporter's question asking him what was best about America. "What I want to see above all," Reagan replied, "is that this remains a country where someone can always get rich." Many thousands of Americans realized the Reagan credo, making fortunes in the expansive and lucrative sectors of the economy: stock trading, real estate, business services, defense contracting, and high-tech industries. A step below those who made millions in these various enterprises were the aspiring, college-educated, middle-management professionals among the Baby Boomers, the "yuppies" (young urban professionals) of the upper middle class, with their conspicuous consumption of gourmet foods, designer clothes, expensive automobiles, and the purchasing of homes in gentrified neighborhoods. (A gentrified neighborhood is a poor one that has been refurbished and where the poor residents have been replaced by more affluent ones.)

The nation's economy expanded significantly during the 1980s; wealth was created and money was made but this wealth, as believed by Reagan and his supporters, did not "trickle down" into the pockets of ordinary working Americans. Real income for the majority of the American working class declined during the Reagan years. By the close of the Reagan-Bush era (1992), the number of poor people in America had reached 36.9 million, or 14.5 percent of the population. At the time of Reagan's inauguration in 1981, the government had classified about 26.1 million people as poor, 11.7 percent of the population. While the United States during the 1980s and early 1990s became home to more billionaires than ever before, ordinary working Americans were coupon clipping and heading to WalMart looking for the cheapest possible necessities with which to feed, clothe, and clean their families. All across the nation's landscape, dollar stores proliferated on land that once sustained factories. While millions of Americans struggled to barely make ends meet on minimum wage incomes, executive, managerial, and CEO salaries accelerated at rates that would have shocked even the original Robber Barons of the late nineteenth century.

The Reagan-Bush era ushered in a feminization of poverty. Despite a growing rate of labor force participation in the 1980s, the majority of women gainfully employed earned less than a living wage. Even if employed, women usually lost ground following a divorce, especially with the end of alimony payments in most instances. Moreover, the decade witnessed a dramatic increase in "dead-beat fathers"—men who defaulted on child-support payments within one year after separation and then disappeared for years and paying nothing until they were found and ordered by the courts to make restitution or spend time in jail. The financial damage caused by their abandonment to wives or girlfriends and their children had long taken its toll. Whereas divorced men enjoyed a sizable increase in their standard of living, divorced women suffered a significant decline in their quality of life. During the 1980s, the number of poor families headed by women increased nearly 70 percent.

A sharp rise in teenage pregnancy reinforced this pattern. An increasingly high percentage of these mothers were too young to have gained sufficient education or skills to secure jobs that would pay them enough to support themselves and their children. Even with income supplements from AFDC (Aid to Families With Dependent Children) and food stamps, it was impossible for these single mothers to keep their families above the poverty line. By 1992, female-headed households, comprising 13.7 million people, accounted for 37 percent of the poor. African American and Latino women and their children made up the overwhelming majority of those living in poverty and despair.

In the following excerpt taken from David Shipler's in-depth study of income inequality, **The Working Poor: Invisible in America**, the problem of crushing income inequality that exploded during the Reagan-Bush years and its debilitating physical and psychological impact on the lives of millions of ordinary American citizens is revealed. "Christie did a job that this labor-hungry economy could not do without. Every morning she drove her battered 1986 Volkswagen from her apartment in public housing to the YWCA child-care center in Akron, Ohio, where she spent the day watching over little children so their parents could go to work. For her services, she received a check for about $330 every two weeks. She could not afford to put her own children in the day-care center where she worked. Christie is a single mom with two young children."

"Like a great many Americans, Christie suffered from stress and high blood pressure. She had no bank account because she could not keep enough money long enough. Try as she might to shop carefully, she always fell behind on her bills and was peppered with late fees. Her low income entitled her to food stamps and rental subsidy, but whenever she got a pay raise, the government reduced the benefits and she felt punished for working. She was trapped on the treadmill of welfare reform, running her life according to the ever-changing rules of welfare retrenchment. Initially the new laws combined with the good economy to send welfare caseloads plummeting. As states were granted flexibility in administering time limits and work requirements, some created innovative consortiums of government, industry and charity to guide people into effective job training and employment. In the 1990s this approach was dubbed 'workfare' and represented a total rejection of the paternalistic liberal 'welfare state' idea of the 1960s. The problem with workfare was that most available jobs had three unhappy traits: they paid low wages, offered no benefits (especially health insurance) and led nowhere."

"Many who do find jobs," concluded the Urban Institute "lose other supports designed to help them such as food stamps and health insurance, leaving them no better off—and sometimes worse off—than when they were not working."

"Christie considered herself such a case. In her wallet was a computerized credit card look-alike issued by the state of Ohio. On the second working day of every month she slipped the card into a special machine at Walgreens and entered her ID number. A credit of $135 was loaded onto her chip. This was the form in which her food stamps was now issued. This was her first portion of income each month. The money was to be used for food only and not for cooked food or pet food. Christie spent this $135 immediately at the grocery but only a few days later she had to find more money for food. In order to justify receipt of this assistance to the state, every three months Christie had to take a half-day off from work (losing money) and take all her pay stubs, utility bills, and rent receipts to a caseworker who applied a state-mandated formula to figure the food stamp allotment and her children's eligibility for health insurance. When Christie completed a training course and earned a raise of 10 cent per hour, her food stamps dropped by $10 per month."

"The arithmetic of Christie's life added up to tension and you had to look hard through her list of expenditures to find fun or luxury. On the fifth she received her weekly support check from Kevin (her boyfriend and father of her son). Christie received nothing from her daughter's father who was serving a long prison sentence for assault. The same day she put $5 worth of gas in her car and the next day spent $6 of her own money to take the daycare kids to the zoo. The eighth was payday and her entire $330 paycheck disappeared in a flash. First was a $3 charge to have the check cashed (a poor person's tax like many of the associated fees with money orders, very low bank accounts, etc.). Immediately, $172 went for rent, including a $10 late fee because she never had enough to pay by the first of the month. Then, because it was October and she had started a plan for Christmas, she paid $31.47 at a store for presents that she had put on layaway, another $10 for gas, $40 to buy shoes for her two kids, $5 for a pair of corduroy pants at a second hand shop, another $5 for a shirt, $10 for bell bottom pants, and $47 bi-weekly for car insurance. The $330 was gone. She had no insurance on her TV, clothes, furniture, or other household goods. Utilities and other bills got paid out of her second check toward the end of the month. Her phone usually cost about $43 per month, gas for the apartment $3, electricity $46 and prescriptions between $8 and $15. Her monthly car payment ran $150, medical insurance $72 and cable TV $43." As Shipler wryly observed, "Recreation for Christie and Kevin centered on food and drink. Occasionally she budgeted $15 for a bottle of Paul Masson brandy."

A PERSPECTIVE ON RONALD REAGAN'S 1980 ELECTION VICTORY

To fully comprehend the Reagan presidency's impact on the nation, it is essential to first examine the political, sociocultural, and economic forces that had been gaining momentum since 1968 that helped Reagan and other

THE RISE OF CONSERVATISM: Ronald Reagan to George H W. Bush

conservatives to defeat liberal Democrats, and in the process establish the Republican Party as the majority party by the early twenty-first century. These various impulses coalesced in the formation of a "**New Right**" movement, propelling Reagan and other conservatives to power in the 1980s. The individual most responsible for creating the blueprint strategy for the conservative (and Republican) resurgence was Kevin Phillips. In his manifesto, *The Emergence of a Republican Majority,* Phillips outlined what would become for the next 30 years the fundamental Republican strategy for winning elections at both the national and state levels. Phillips correctly contended that the majority of white middle-class Americans had grown weary of New Deal liberalism. These "silent" or "forgotten" Americans, as Richard Nixon called them, shared a common revulsion against militant minority groups, student activists, and arrogant intellectuals, all of whom along with a Northeastern liberal media elite had come to dominate the Democratic Party.

Phillips believed that if the Republican Party focused its message of patriotism, law and order, and rugged individualism on these particular groups living in the Sun Belt—the states of the old South or former Confederacy, including Texas, and western states like California, New Mexico, Oklahoma, Arizona, and Colorado—they would not only win in 1968 but for years to come, for they would have successfully and dramatically changed the nation's political demographics, shattering in the process the Democratic Party's close to 100 years of southern hegemony. The "Solid South" would become Republican and with such a base help carry the party to successive electoral victories, especially at the national level. Phillips' assertion proved prescient as most southern states became so-called "red states," reliably Republican.

Why such concerted effort on the Sun Belt states? The answer was relatively simple: the region since 1945 had become a magnet for both the American people and modern industry. It had become the natural home for political and cultural conservatism as well as the center of a revitalized, aggressive, and doctrinaire evangelical Protestantism. By the time of Reagan's election, it was clear that the majority of "**Sun Belters**" had remained traditional in racial attitudes and still suspicious of northeast elitism. In the thirty years after the war, these

Nancy Reagan looks at her husband, Ronald Reagan, as he takes the oath of office as 40th President of the United States. January 20, 1981.
Photo credit: Reagan Presidential Library

states' populations more than doubled. Cities like Phoenix, Arizona, sky-rocketed in population from 65,000 to 755,000, and Houston from 385,000 to 1.4 million. The Sun Belt also became a haven for the new high-tech industries of aerospace, plastics, chemicals, electronics, and ultimately computers. Scientists, engineers, and other tech specialists flocked to the new industrial research parks in North Carolina, Florida, Texas, and especially to California, which by the end of the 1970s became synonymous with the computer industry. Indeed, the Santa Clara valley of the central coast region of northern California, an area once encompassed by fruit orchards and farms, was renamed "Silicon Valley," for as *Fortune Magazine* noted the 25-mile stretch from Santa Clara to south San Jose boasted "the densest concentration of innovative industry that exists anywhere in the world."

Moreover, these states provided Nixon and future Republicans with the ideal constituency for their calls for "law and order." Their attacks on the Supreme Court for its excessive liberalism resonated well with Sun Belters, as did their extolling and applauding Westerners and Southerners for their devotion to the traditional values of hard work, patriotism, and family. The New Right mobilized voters around volatile social issues and middle American outrage at the excesses of the 1960s, which such individuals perceived as a concentrated assault on the most basic values and institutions of society—the family, the church, patriotism, and sexual morality.

Although the New Right had its origin in traditional conservatism, notably anticommunism, the movement accelerated in popularity by exploiting the anger among increasing numbers of white middle-class Americans against policies recently introduced to the national agenda: busing, affirmative action, feminism, abortion (the 1973 *Roe v. Wade* decision), school prayer, and new attitudes of permissiveness toward pornography and sexual freedom. By the late 1970s, the Republicans grasped the anger and hostility among traditional Democrats toward these issues and seized the opportunity to exploit such outrage for political gain. In effect, by 1980, the Republican Party, through its New Right supporters, claimed to be speaking for the average American while accusing and labeling the Democrats as the voice of liberal Democrats and their allies.

For New Righters the 1970s represented the beginning of the culture wars, with conservatives rushing to defend against the liberal assault on the family and other cherished values and traditional morality. The New Righters devoted countless hours and money opposing the Equal Rights Amendment, defending the "right to life" of fetuses, and seeking to ban homosexuals from teaching in the public schools. Many New Right conservatives were convinced that a conspiracy existed, spearheaded by liberal Democrats and their special interest allies, such as gays and lesbians, to destroy, as one New Righter declared, "everything that is good and moral here in America."

Ronald Reagan and the "Moral Majority"

Bolstering the New Right was evangelical Christianity, which by the end of the 1970s declared the support of more than 50 million Americans that cut across all Protestant denominations. Exploiting this resurgence of "born again" Christians were fundamentalist "televangelists" such as Jerry Falwell and Pat Robertson, and a host of others, who through weekly talk shows, either on television or the radio, like the *700 Club* or *Praise the Lord (PTL)*, reached millions of Americans. Falwell's *Old Time Gospel Hour* was broadcast on 225 television stations and 300 radio stations. From his base of operations in Lynchburg, Virginia, Falwell galvanized his followers into the **Moral Majority** movement to "fight the pornography, obscenity, vulgarity and profanity that under the guise of sex education and 'values clarification' literally pervades the literature of the public schools." Robertson urged his listeners to condemn the "humanistic/atheistic/hedonistic influence on American government. We have enough votes to run the country," Robertson, declared, "and when the people say 'we've had enough,' we're going to take over."

Leaders like Falwell and Robertson made it clear that politics had become religion and religion had become politics. In their view, America had become a Sodom, rife with all manner of vice, corruption, and licentiousness. It was the Evangelical Right's duty to God and country to cleanse the nation of such sin, and thus in sermons and literature, they condemned abortion, the ERA, homosexuality, and for the restoration of school prayer. Falwell, who became the most dominant, visible, outspoken, and richest spokesmen for the Evangelical Right, declared that "We're going to single out those people in government who are against what we consider to be the Bible, moralist position." Leaders like Falwell expected the faithful come election time to vote according to prescribed fundamentalist criteria, which meant for candidates who were "pro-family" (code for pro-life), for the restoration of school prayer, and opposition to gay rights.

The New Right also perfected the concept of direct mail, which became their most important vehicle for direct political action. This approach was the brainchild of the Texas conservative Richard Viguerie, who idolized such reactionary figures as Joseph McCarthy and Douglas

MacArthur. Prompting Viguerie to develop this medium was the 1974 finance reform law that limited the amount of money any individual could contribute to a political campaign. Instead of seeing this restriction as a handicap to the conservative impulse, Viguerie and his supporters saw the situation as a massive opportunity to mobilize grass-roots support for right-wing causes. Viguerie also saw direct mail as a means to personal wealth, which occurred by 1980, when his firm RAVCO reported an annual income in the millions of dollars. Serving virtually all the single issue causes of the New Right, direct mail threatened to revolutionize 1970s politics.

Perhaps what made this approach so effective was the personal nature of each letter sent. Not only were recipients' individual names on the letterhead but the requests for money or support were also intimate as well. One letter from right-wing congressman Philip Crane, for example, asked more than 80,000 citizens to join his *personal advisory* committee, as well as to make a financial donation. Direct mail, Viguerie announced boldly, "Allows a lot of conservatives to by-pass the liberal media and go directly into the homes of the conservatives in this country... There really is a silent majority in this country, and the New Right now has learned how to identify them and communicate with them."

Most direct mail letters were purposely strident, seeking to anger voters by exploiting their fears on certain issues. "The shriller you are," another fundraiser declared, the easier it was to recruit supporters. Thus, one anti-abortion mailing called on voters to "stop the baby killers. These anti-life baby killers are already organizing, working and raising money to re-elect pro-abortionists like George McGovern. Abortion means killing a living baby, a tiny human being with a beating heart and little fingers . . . killing a baby boy or girl with burning deadly chemicals or a powerful machine that sucks and tears the little infant from its mother's womb." Frequently accompanied by graphic pictures, such literature almost inevitably evoked a response, and usually it came in the form of a donation for the cause.

The final component of the conservative revival was the establishing of right-wing "**think tanks**" on an academic par with their liberal counterparts. Since World War II, liberals had dominated public policy and thus the national agenda and debate on critical issues through studies from the Brookings Institution, the Ford Foundation, and the Rockefeller Foundation. Although the founders of the latter two institutes were hardly liberals, over time, especially during the 1930s, both think tanks became liberal bastions. However, by the late 1970s, conservative think tanks had emerged, such as The Heritage Foundation, funded by millions of dollars from archconservative Joseph Coors (of Coors Brewery). For the first time in American history conservatism generated an intellectual class and a place for them to gather. Indeed, the Heritage Foundation promulgated most of the task force ideas of the Reagan administration. Another of such brain trusts was the American Enterprise Institute, committed to conservative positions on both domestic and foreign policy. They were aided by yet another "neo-conservatism" (the belief that the United States should engage in a more aggressive unilateral foreign policy based on solely U.S. national interests) expressed in such publications as *Commentary* magazine and *The Public Interest*.

By the late 1970s, the New Right had become one of the most visible and powerful political forces in American history. Through the Conservative Caucus, a sort of national directory headed by Richard Viguerie and Howard Phillips, the New Right sought to coordinate the activities, agenda, and direction of the conservative movement. The Conservative Caucus wove together in one monolithic reactionary enterprise virtually every conservative organization from the National Right to Work Committee to the National Right to Life Committee, to the Committee for the Survival of a Free Congress, and the Swift Boat Veterans for the Truth, which helped defeat John Kerry in his presidential election bid.

By 1980 the New Right had embraced the candidacy of Ronald Reagan for president. They also claimed direct responsibility since 1976 for the defeat in the United States Senate of Gaylord Nelson in Wisconsin, Birch Bayh in Indiana, John Culver in Iowa, Frank Church in Idaho, and George McGovern in South Dakota. "We aim to take control of the culture," one New Right leader declared, and the election results—Reagan's victory and the defeat of such liberal lions as those noted above—seemed to suggest that the aim had been accomplished. Indeed, many pundits as well as Democrats, such as Massachusetts moderate Senator Paul Tsongas, interpreted Reagan's victory and the defeat of men like Bayh, Church, and McGovern as a right-wing sweep.

THE REAGAN YEARS

By the 1950s and the advent of television, Reagan's engaging and homey personality made him into one of television's most popular prime-time hosts. Thanks to his television career, Reagan also became one of the most sought after public speakers, telling huge audiences why they should buy a particular product or support a certain cause. One of Reagan's favorite yarns and one that reveals the essence of Reagan's personality was the story about

That Old Time Religion: American Evangelism in Historical Perspective

The election of a confessed born-again Christian to the White House in 1976, Jimmy Carter witnessed the beginning of yet another evangelical Protestant revivalism in American history. By the late 1970s up to the present, not only had this brand of "good old time religion" reappeared yet again, but to the surprise and disquiet of many Americans, especially progressives, who emerged out of the 1960s certain that such "fanaticism" had long since died, the evangelism preached by the new faithful had become (and continues to be) more politicized, shrill, self-righteous, intolerant, and polarizing than any such past evangelical manifestations had ever been. The doctrine of salvation delivered by evangelists is not one of hope and redemption for all, but rather the fire and brimstone of condemnation. Much of the nation's current "culture wars" can be attributed to the divisive effects of the current brand of evangelism being propagated.

Throughout the nation's history, evangelism had been a powerful socio-cultural force. From the revivals on the Kentucky frontier in 1801 to a long series of urban revivals led by Charles Finney, Dwight L. Moody, and others, evangelical piety pervaded American life. While missions, Sunday schools, and tract societies spread the faith in the cities, preachers and missionaries carried the Word to isolated rural areas. For all their passion and devotion to delivering God's message, rarely if ever did these individuals attempt to "confuse" politics with religion; they saw their primary responsibility to uplift individuals to God's forgiving grace and help them to live better lives. If at any time they crossed that line of mixing politics and religion it was in the name of reform, of which many nineteenth century evangelicals were in the forefront, such as the antislavery movement and other impulses for the betterment of society—to help individuals to save themselves, not to condemn individuals for their differences.

By the close of the nineteenth century evangelism seemed to wane. From the 1890s to the 1920s, the liberal Social Gospel dominated the mainstream Protestant ethos. In the more rural and isolated areas of the South, Great Plains, and West, however, fundamentalist evangelicals fought back, resisting the "sins" of modernism and codifying the fundamentals of their faith. As many politicians from those regions supported the anti-progress crusade, once elected, they passed laws in their respective states that ran the gamut from prohibition to anti-immigration restrictions, to the forbidding of the teaching of evolution in public schools. Never before had the separation of church and state been so blatantly defiled. To such individuals, the Bible was to be taken literally and the resurrection and Second Coming of Jesus Christ, Judgment Day, was at hand, or so declared one of the most popular evangelists of the 1920s, Aimee Semple McPherson, whose Los Angeles radio show attracted huge followings.

Evangelism witnessed somewhat of a decline during The Great Depression and World War II years, but no sooner was the war over and the faith reappeared, perhaps more vibrant and appealing than ever thanks to individuals such as Billy Graham, who became the most legendary of all such preachers. Graham was the rarity however among the majority of his post-WWII peers. He respected the sanctity of the separation of church and state, and his message was always one of acceptance, tolerance, compassion, forgiveness, and humanity, and love. In many ways Graham almost single-handedly resurrected the evangelical movement in America, and thanks to him, organization such as Youth for Christ emerged as well as new churches such as the Assemblies of God and other charismatic or "pentecostal" groups that featured divine healing and highly emotional worship, which attracted throngs of individuals for a variety of reasons. In the 1970s and 1980s, with mainstream Protestantism in decline, evangelicalism attracted waves of new adherents. Evangelical/fundamentalist paperbacks sold by the millions. Bible-centered or defined fundamentalist independent churches proliferated across the land. TV preachers, ranging from Oral Roberts to Jimmy Swaggert to Jerry Falwell, became celebrities as millions tuned into their respective "Gospel Hour." Evangelical missionaries even made inroads into Catholic Latin America, winning thousands of converts there, much to the chagrin of the Catholic Church.

*By the end of the 1980s scholars could no longer ignore the evangelical phenomenon, especially as it became more powerful politically and more reactionary on socio-cultural issues. In **American Evangelism: Conservative Religion and the Quandary of Modernity**, (1983), sociologist James Davison Hunter examined how evangelicals both resist and accommodate contemporary trends in a process he called "cognitive bargaining." For example, evangelical authors published many self-help books offering techniques for achieving personal happiness and emotional well-being—popular general themes among most Americans—but written from a specifically evangelical theological*

> *perspective, which is to say, from a very fundamentalist, conservative, viewpoint. In* **Culture Wars: The Struggle to Define America** *(1991), Hunter presented religious conservatives as the key players for the nation's soul. "America," he wrote, "is in the midst of a culture war that reverberates not only within public policy but within the lives of ordinary Americans everywhere."*
>
> *What were or are the political implications of this war? Some of the true believers repudiated the wicked world and withdrew into their own spiritual realm. At its most extreme, the separatist impulse that produced the likes of David Koresh and his Branch Davidians, whose members barricaded themselves in a heavily armed compound near Waco, Texas to await "the End." In April 1993, after a long standoff with federal agents, Koresh and most of his followers perished in a fiery "holocaust" that tragically fulfilled their prophecies of a final Armageddon-like confrontation.*
>
> *Koresh was an extreme and fleeting rarity. Most alarmingly turned to politics to realize their moral vision. The most notorious of such potentially dangerous individuals was the televangelist Jerry Falwell, whose organization, the Moral Majority, passionately and righteously supported the conservative resurgence supposedly led by Ronald Reagan, who, ironically, in reality was pretty much an a-religious individual and certainly not a fundamentalist fanatic or bigot. Nonetheless, Falwell and other reactionary evangelicals such as Pat Robertson wrapped themselves in Reagan's mantle throughout the decade. In the 1990s Robertson became especially politically active via his Christian Coalition, through which mobilized conservative activists ran for school board, city council, and other local offices, hoping to build a righteous nation starting at the grassroots level. It was through such organizations as the Christian Coalition that Robertson and other evangelicals hoped to gain control of the Republican Party and dictate its social issues agenda, which they succeeded in accomplishing by 2010 in conjunction with their Tea Party allies.*
>
> *Scholars observing this trend believed that driving the evangelical momentum was the decline in traditional denominational loyalties and the gravitation of such "seekers" to the more charismatic yet simple, black and white, good and evil evangelical doctrine, especially that expressed by Falwell and his like. Falwell and others also developed special-agenda groups such as the Christian Action Council, the Christian Heritage Center, the National Pro-Family Coalition, and scores of others that pursued specific causes while sharing a common goal. Nineteenth-century evangelicals had also formed single-issue campaigns such as the 1895 Anti-Saloon League but had lacked the computer-based direct-mail techniques available to their modern successors. Rallying around what they saw as defining moral issues, politically active religious conservatives embraced symbolic crusades such as creationism, school prayer, and family values, while battling abortion, pornography, sex education, homosexuality, radical feminism, sexual permissiveness in the media, sex education in the schools, government support for "obscene" art, and the worldview that they denounced as "secular humanism." As one liberal pundit declared, the latter term to the conservative evangelicals has become "a label used by the Far Right to attack virtually everything they disagree with about the schools and society at large."*
>
> *Mark Twain once dismissed reports of his death as "greatly exaggerated," and the same might be said of evangelical religion in America. Amid turbulent world events and unsettling social changes at home millions of Americans still find meaning and reassurance in religious beliefs and folkways. As they enter the public arena to apply their religious vision to public policy, and regardless of how one may personally feel about such participation, there is no denying that even since its inception in the early nineteenth century evangelicalism has played a central role in U.S. history and life.*

two young brothers, one of whom was an inveterate pessimist, the other an incurable optimist. Their parents tried to remedy their respective outlooks by giving them very different presents on gift-giving holidays such as Christmas and their birthdays. Despite such largesse, the pessimist cried in the corner, certain all the toys he had been given would break. The optimist, carefully examining a pile of horse manure, plunged happily into the dung, digging furiously and exclaiming confidently that, "I just know there's a pony in here somewhere."

The optimist's comment reflected the confidence, and frequent naiveté and simplicity, that came to define the Reagan presidency. Throughout his tenure Reagan was like the optimist. As he had during his campaign, he repeatedly rejected the notion that the country was at the abyss, about to enter an era of limits and declension. Reagan refused to accept such notions, endlessly telling Americans that they possessed all the right stuff to not only resurrect the nation from its alleged malaise but to take the United States to unimaginable new heights of domestic prosperity and international respect and presence. Reagan believed unequivocally that Americans were God's chosen people, and thus if they did not rise to their calling, if they did not fulfill their righteous, God-ordained endowment to spread democracy and American ideals about the world, they would not only disappoint God but humankind as well. In his inaugural address, he exhorted Americans to "believe in ourselves and to believe in our capacity to perform great deeds, to believe we can still resolve the problems which now confront us. Why shouldn't we believe that? We are Americans."

That Reagan sincerely embraced such tenets was obvious to everyone who knew him or heard him speak. Reagan possessed a simple, pure vision that dissenting voices could not penetrate, let alone alter. The country was in trouble, but contrary to the naysayers and other pessimists, the problems were not insurmountable. As Reagan told Americans, all that was required was for "a new sheriff to ride into town" to clean up the mess—to rescue America, restore confidence, and sweep away all the doubters and skeptics who insisted on talking about problems rather than solutions.

Reagan's faith in the capacity of Americans to transcend all problems and emerge triumphant in every encounter, whether at home or abroad, knew no bounds. Reagan's media-savvy aides and advisors ensured such a message came across loud and clear to the American people. As one of Reagan's top "spin-doctors," Michael Deaver, later proclaimed, "We kept apple-pie and the flag going the whole time." In 1984, Deaver and others made "Its Morning Again in America" the central theme of Reagan's feel-good campaign for reelection. Then, as always, they carefully managed his public appearances, providing television reporters with a "line-of-the-day" sound bite, always optimistic phrase for use in the evening news. Presented this way, Reagan was a national master of ceremonies for the New Right.

Some of the goals Reagan advanced, such as winning the Cold War, bolstering traditional values, and propagating the American dream of upward social mobility, resonated well with millions of voters. Reagan represented the triumph of New Right conservatism, and thus when he blamed liberals for being soft on communism or "permissive" about developments at home, he found a receptive audience among millions of citizens. Reagan's domestic agenda focused on using the commanding power of the presidency to dismantle the New Deal/Great Society legacy, obliterating what was left of the welfare state. Reagan's obsession with destroying the liberal ethos contradicted his supposed worship and desire to emulate FDR, his only real political hero. While paying lip service to his mentor, Reagan denounced environmentalists, condemned welfare recipients as too "lazy" to get a job, and labeled the Soviet Union an "evil empire."

Reagan left one of the most enduring personal legacies of any twentieth-century president. The Reagan credo characterized the 1980s. Two qualities imbued the essence of the Reagan canon: the tendency with which he believed in a few fundamental ideas and the extraordinary skill to communicate those beliefs to the American people. To Reagan, liberalism—big government and the welfare state—were responsible for most of the nation's problems. Such an onus needed to be lifted from the American people's backs. The military, however, was good, the sole exception to the evil of government, and warranted unlimited support. Relative to foreign policy and reflecting a 1950s Cold War mentality reminiscent of John Foster Dulles, the Reagan creed advocated a dangerous heating up of tensions with the Soviet Union because the purpose of American foreign policy was to fight communism wherever and whenever it appeared (hence the need for a strong military). To Reagan, the Soviet Union personified evil, the United States naturally good. It was incumbent upon the United States in the service of all humanity to extirpate from the world such a menace. On the domestic scene, slashing taxes would accomplish the dual goals of making America rich and abolishing deficits. These ideas became a religious principle, articles of faith upon which Reagan grounded his presidency.

Reagan, we know now, was one of the nation's most detached executives, relying on a handful of loyal supporters to implement his vision. From the very beginning of the Reagan presidency, his closest advisors knew he would be disengaged from the daily development of policies. They knew their man was a "delegator." Reagan simply had no interest for or intellectual information about the details of the decision-making process. Thus, few insiders were surprised when he made such statements that ICBM's could be called back after launching or that U.S. submarines did not carry nuclear missiles. Although columnists such as David Broder commented sarcastically that "when someone approaches Reagan bearing information, he flees as if from a leper's touch," Reagan apologists dismissed such criticism, declaring that unlike past presidents such as Jimmy Carter who became mired in the supposed minutiae of his office, Reagan did not, allowing him more time to develop his vision.

Regimenting Reagan's daily routine was his wife, Nancy, and his closest aides. Their objective was not only to ensure Reagan's freshness but to conserve his energies for the limited tasks he *had* to carry out. His wife and aides so circumscribed his day that what few responsibilities he had to perform could be completed as efficiently as possible. Their goal was to keep Reagan sharp enough to present the big decisions and policies of his administration to Congress and the public in a sufficiently clear manner.

The key to such an approach was the quality of people the president called on to implement his vision. In addition to his wife, three other individuals were responsible for running the Reagan White House and implementing the Reagan agenda: Edwin Meese (who served as attorney general), Michael Deaver (his deputy chief of staff), and James Baker (who became chief of staff and then Secretary of the Treasury). These men were powerful insiders; in effect, they ran the government. They sat at the Cabinet table with the president, a fact that bothered many Cabinet members; Meese, not the president, defined the Cabinet's agenda and moderated its discussions; and no one, not even the National Security Advisor, had direct access to the president without their approval. It was only a matter of time before the flaws of such an insulated and detached approach to governing would adversely affect the Reagan presidency. As Martin Anderson, the Reagan White House economic advisor, noted, "if any of his personal staff chooses to abuse his or her position, and deliberately withholds key information or misleads him, Reagan is helpless and disaster can strike." Anderson described perfectly the fundamental cause of the Iran-Contra debacle, which resulted largely from Reagan's detached and dependent approach to governing the country.

For the moment, however, such dangers seemed only real to embittered Democrats still reeling from Reagan's landslide victory. What mattered was not the new president's executive style or his personal policies, rather it was Reagan's passionate call for Americans to support the simple beliefs of his credo. If they did, he promised he would resurrect the nation from whatever doldrums it may have fallen so that America would once more stand tall, and no one, anywhere, would ever again think about challenging the strongest power on earth.

Domestic Policy Agendas

No sooner did Reagan enter the Oval Office than he began to make good his campaign promise to dismantle the remnants of the Great Society, cut taxes, and expand the military-industrial complex. Reagan proceeded to perform radical surgery on the nation's economy and welfare system. In 1981, Congress agreed to cut more than $25 billion from welfare programs (with hundreds of billions more planned for future years), while slashing taxes over five years by $750 billion. Perhaps more important and ominous for the future was Reagan's securing of congressional approval to increase over a five-year period defense spending to the staggering amount of $1.2 trillion. With such a mandate, Reagan appeared to be fulfilling his pledge that during his watch the United States would not only reestablish itself as the greatest superpower but that never again would the United States be subject to humiliation at the hands of the Soviet Union.

To Reagan, all of the country's socioeconomic ills since the late 1960s resulted from the continued expansion of the federal government and the welfare state. If the federal government's presence in the daily life of the nation was minimized and if all but the most essential social welfare programs or entitlements (i.e., social security) could be eliminated, then all would be right again in America, for the private sector would once again be responsible for the nation's well-being.

Reagan made the end of affirmative action one of his priorities. He ordered his Attorney General William French Smith to fight such programs in the federal courts and packed the Civil Rights Commission and (Equal Employment Opportunity Commission (EEOC) with individuals dedicated to reversing the racial and gender policies of previous administrations. Reagan slashed food stamp benefits, eliminated 300,000 Comprehensive Employment and Training Act (CETA) jobs, cut AFDC funds—leading to a reduction of more than 10 percent in the welfare rolls—and lowered the benefits of an additional 300,000 families receiving welfare assistance.

Deregulation

Reagan proved equally passionate about deregulation, especially when it came to the environment, which he believed must be delivered to the private sector to promote economic growth. Reagan saw all the environmental protection laws passed since the presidency of Theodore Roosevelt as one of the greatest handicaps to domestic economic expansion, for such laws prevented businesses access to vital resources and land essential for development. Reagan thus ordered EPA (Environmental Protection Agency) administrator Anne Burford to delay imposing penalties on chemical companies responsible for toxic waste dumps. No one perhaps better reflected the Reagan credo relative to the environment than Secretary of the Interior James Watt. Watt, from Wyoming, worked tirelessly to open federal wilderness areas, forestlands, and coastal waters to oil and gas companies and developers. He also undermined endangered species programs and cut initiatives to protect environmentally threatened regions. Before coming to Washington, Watt had headed the Mountain States Legal Foundation, an organization which spearheaded the so-called Sagebrush Rebellion of western conservatives seeking to open public lands to private development.

Watt's disdain for conservationists did more to galvanize the environmental movement than any previous individual. In response to Watt's extreme positions, membership in the Sierra Club, the Wilderness Society, and other environmental organizations skyrocketed. More than a million conservationists signed petitions demanding Watt's removal. After a series of public relations gaffes, Watt resigned in 1983.

Only on implementing New Right social issues did the Reagan administration fall short, but even in this capacity—on questions such as abortion, school prayer, and busing—the president enthusiastically endorsed New Right positions, frequently using executive power to back up his words. New federal rules banned the circulation of birth control information or abortion advice without parental consent, and wherever possible, Justice Department lawyers argued the New Right position on social issues that came before federal courts. As a result of such actions, by the end of Reagan's second term, the Supreme Court had substantially removed previous rulings on "set aside" programs for minority and women contractors, while threatening to overturn *Roe v. Wade*. In all such activity, the administration's agenda reflected two fundamental convictions of Reagan: that the least government was the best government, and that allowing the private sector to once again reign supreme offered the surest guarantee of sustained prosperity and growth.

Reaganomics

To the New Right, Reagan, and the Republicans the key to their success was to redeem the economy from the Keynesian ideas liberals had implemented since the late 1930s. Inspired by British economist John Maynard Keynes, American liberals since the 1930s had used government spending to stimulate the economy during economic slowdowns. Spending had often been financed by relatively high taxes on upper income brackets. Such adherence, the Right believed, had caused the economic downturns of the 1970s and early 1980s. Reagan and his supporters believed the first step in their crusade was to sharply reduce personal and corporate income taxes, especially the former, which he proposed to reduce by 30 percent over the next three years. Reagan's zeal for lower taxes was both ideological and personal. He embraced the fundamentals of supply-side economics, an anti-Keynesian approach first introduced by a University of Southern California economics professor, Arthur Laffer, the "**Laffer Curve**."

Reagan charged a conservative, David Stockman, to head the Office of Management and Budget (OMB). Stockman, was a devoted disciple of the supply-side theory. According to Stockman, sharp reductions in personal income taxes would encourage savings and investments, especially among employers and investors, who Stockman believed would want to make even more money by using their tax savings to expand their businesses by increasing production, which in turn would create more jobs. Such greater entrepreneurial activity would spur rapid economic growth, which would hike personal income, bringing in greater tax revenues, even at the lower rates. Deregulation of industry, in turn, would free businesses to compete more efficiently in the marketplace. Repealing environmental protection measures would release energy and resources for private development. Cutting back social welfare payments to the elderly and poor would bolster self-reliance and initiative. The overall goal, Stockman later said, was "a minimalist government, a spare and stingy creature which offered evenhanded public justice, but no more." Millions of citizens might suffer in the short run, but, in the long run, the country would be strengthened "by abruptly severing the umbilical cords of dependency that ran from Washington to every nook and cranny of the nation."

Despite the defection of some Democratic stalwarts such as Senator Lloyd Bentsen of Texas, who supported **Reaganomics**, the majority of Democrats opposed the concept, rightly claiming that the tax cuts would benefit the rich more than the poor, exacerbating economic inequality. The opposition also correctly asserted that the program would expand budget deficits because the president was calling for huge increases in defense spending. One could not massively expand military spending, cut taxes sharply, and still have a balanced budget. The insanity of such policies became apparent by 1982 when in that year budget deficits soared to over $100 billion, which was more than three times the largest deficit incurred during the Carter years. By 1983 the deficit reached $300 billion. "No one imagined how bad the outcome would be," Stockman later observed. "It got away from us."

Reagan must be held responsible for what George H.W. Bush called "**voodoo economics**." When Stockman realized that politicians, especially the Democrats who made the sustaining of the welfare state their political lifeblood, weren't going to turn against their handiwork, cutting social security and Medicare benefits to the elderly, he tried to curtail defense spending and persuade Reagan to raise revenues. The president, however, turned a deaf ear to such a plea, despite bipartisan support for such measures. "Everyone was ready," said Stockman, "But Reagan said no. He wouldn't allow it. He didn't believe there was a problem. That was his selectivity on the facts of life. The whole thing got turned into a cynical, politicized, surreal substitute for sane fiscal government." As Reagan and his aides lobbied hard for the bill in March 1981, it became clear that the measure would not pass as easily as Reagan blithely had hoped.

As the impasse intensified, fate dealt Reagan a cruel but politically auspicious hand. On March 30, 1981, deeply troubled twenty-five-year-old **John Hinckley** tried to assassinate Reagan as he left a speaking engagement at a Washington hotel. Firing six times with a .22 caliber pistol, Hinckley hit James Brady, Reagan's press secretary, in the head. The shot permanently disabled Brady. Other gunfire bloodied a Washington policeman and a Secret Service agent. One of Hinckley's bullets ricocheted off the presidential limousine, hitting Reagan under his left arm. The bullet eventually lodged in his lung close to his heart. An ambulance rushed him to the nearest hospital where doctors found him bleeding profusely. Surgeons operated on him for two hours to remove the bullet and save his life. Reagan's brush with death kept him in the hospital until April 11.

While Reagan recuperated, news releases informed a frightened public not only how close they came to losing their president but, perhaps more important politically, how calm and good-humored he had been. As he was being taken into the operating room, Reagan quipped to his wife, Nancy, "Honey, I forgot to duck." As doctors were about to put him under, he remarked, "Please tell me you are all Republicans." Polls recorded that his courage and joviality had caused his popularity to soar, with more than 70 percent of the people giving him favorable ratings.

Upon his return to the White House, Reagan kept a low profile until April 28, 1981, when he emerged to give an eagerly awaited television speech to a joint session of Congress. Still recovering, he seized this emotionally charged occasion to call upon the legislators to enact his economic program. How could Congress defy such a popular and courageous man? Indeed, he appeared to be reprising one of his more immortal Hollywood roles, that of the great Notre Dame football legend, George Gipp, only this time "the Gipper" lives, returning to the playing field with even greater vigor and intensity than before. (Reagan played Notre Dame football legend Gipp in the 1940 movie *Knute Rockne All-American*. Gipp died, prompting Notre Dame coach Rockne to fire up the Fighting Irish by asking them to "Win one for the Gipper." Reagan's friends often called him "The Gipper.") For the next four months Reagan and his aides unleashed upon Congress one of the most ferocious lobbying campaigns witnessed in years, with Reagan personally meeting 69 times with 467 members of Congress. The president's persistence paid off. In July, Congress passed slightly modified tax and budget bills, thanks largely to the defection of "boll weevil" (conservative) Southern Democrats, whom Reagan had won over during the preceding months. In securing the measures, Reagan greatly advanced conservative economic ideas, thereby driving liberals—then and

Secret service agents rush an assailant who fired six shots at President Reagan as he was leaving the Washington Hilton on March 30. This photo released by the White House shows the door on the presidential limousine being closed (right) after Reagan was pushed in, and Press Secretary James Brady and patrolman Thomas Delahanty on the ground after being hit by gunfire.

thereafter—onto the defensive. His triumph impressed many seasoned observers. Reporters declared a "Reagan Revolution" in fiscal policy. Hedley Donovan of *Fortune* wrote that the tax and budget acts represented the "most formidable domestic initiative since the Hundred Days of Franklin Roosevelt." At last, it seemed, the United States had a president who could oil the gears of government and make them turn.

Soon after the passage of the tax and budget bills, Reagan endeared himself further among the New Righters by refusing the right of the federal employees who were members of the **Professional Air Traffic Controller's Organization (PATCO)** to strike for better pay and benefits. When union members voted to strike, Reagan rejected their demands and threatened to fire them if they did not return to work in 48 hours. Reagan believed such a strike to be illegal, even though he was the first American president to have served as the head of a union—the Screen Actor's Guild of Hollywood—and who had received PATCO's endorsement in 1980. Nonetheless, Reagan held firm in his belief that if the workers went out on strike they would be endangering the nation's well being. Many Americans agreed and supported Reagan's tough stance. When his 48-hour decree passed, Reagan announced that 38 percent of the strikers had returned to work and that military controllers would replace those who were still on strike. After firing more than 11,000 air traffic controllers, Reagan reassured the nation that air travel was safe and that flight schedules had returned to 80 percent normal. Reagan's action destroyed the union and sent a unmistakable anti-union message to the rest of the nation's labor organizations, making it clear that the heyday of union power and the striking worker was coming to an end.

Reagan's actions signaled to the American public that he could be, and often was, a stubborn man of conviction. Conservatives were euphoric, more confident than ever that they, at last, had in Reagan truly one of their own. His image as a consistent defender of a core of ideas helped him repeatedly to deflect all criticism, causing opponents to lament that he was a **"Teflon president"**—nothing stuck to him.

Equally appalling to liberals was Reagan's open hostility to large-scale spending for social welfare, especially when this frugality was contrasted to the lavishness of Nancy Reagan's lifestyle and the glitter of the celebrations that surrounded the inaugural ceremonies. Nancy Reagan's wardrobe for these events was said to have cost $25,000. It seems the Reagans simply brought Hollywood excess and self-indulgence to the nation's capital and expected the American people to hold them in awe as many once did when both husband and wife were on the silver screen. As Speaker of the House Tip O'Neill exclaimed, "When it comes to giving tax breaks to the wealthy of this country, the president has a heart of gold." A joke circulated in Washington that Reagan's right hand didn't know what his far right hand was up to. Liberals, however, did not laugh. Many believed Reagan was deliberately running up deficits via tax cuts and military spending in order to starve social programs. This, they charged, was **"Reagan's Revenge,"** a plot to destroy the welfare state, or what was left of the programs after years of chipping away at the overall system.

While implementing Reaganomics, Stockman and his cohorts at the OMB also faced the immediate problem of inflation, which had reached 13 percent by the last year of the Carter presidency. The Federal Reserve Board, under the leadership of Paul Volcker as chairman, led the charge, pushing interest rates ever higher in hopes of forcing Americans to save and invest rather than spend, which if they continued to do, would only push prices higher. This harsh medicine, coupled with a drop in oil prices, did its job. Inflation fell to around 4 percent in 1983 and held steady thereafter. The high interest rates, however, necessary to curb inflation soon brought on the worst recession to hit the country since the 1930s. Unemployment shot up to 10 percent by 1982, and because of earlier cuts in funding for social welfare programs, the plight of the poor worsened. Moreover, as interest rates remained high, America's European allies screamed in pain as money flowed out of their countries and into the coffers of U.S. banks where their money earned unprecedented interest. As the dollar rose in value relative to foreign currency, the situation made U.S. goods more expensive abroad but allowed Americans to consume in great quantities the much cheaper foreign products. Such a scenario led to a dramatic decline in American exports and the simultaneous staggering increase in Americans buying TV's, stereos, automobiles, and a host of other products made in Japan and other countries. The result was a mind-numbing trade imbalance or U.S. deficit (the gap between exports and imports) that reached a whopping $111 billion by 1984. By that year, the United States was well on its way to becoming for the first time in decades a "debtor nation."

The industrial heartland was especially hit hard, reeling under the triple blows of slumping exports, particularly of capital goods, foreign competition, and technological obsolescence. The hard-hit auto plants, aging steel mills, and other heavy industries of the Midwest, Mid-Atlantic, and Northeast laid off workers with many plants closing their doors forever. In the years 1979-1983, 11.5 million U.S. workers lost their jobs as a result of plant closings and general decline in heavy manufacturing. As a result, thousands left the "Rust Belt" and headed to the booming high-tech, oil, and petrochemical dominated economies of the Sun Belt states, particularly California and Texas, where cities like San Jose and Houston respectively became the permanent home of these new "**Okie**" migrants. This influx caused the populations of Sun Belt cities like Houston to explode. By 1983, Houston had become the fourth largest city in the country, with over 4 million residents, only New York, Los Angeles, and Chicago were larger. Not since the Dust Bowl days of the Great Depression had the country witnessed such a massive exodus of people from one part of the nation to another. To be sure, farmers suffered as well. Wheat exports fell 38 percent from 1980 to 1985, and corn exports by 49 percent. In foreclosure sales, the family farm was about to disappear from the American landscape.

Soaring federal deficits added to the economic muddle. Reagan's tax cuts reduced federal revenues without immediately producing the predicted business boom, while soaring military expenditures far exceeded domestic spending cuts. With the economy sputtering and budget deficits escalating, Reagan in 1982-1983 grudgingly accepted a reduction in military appropriations, a slowing of cuts in social programs, new emergency job programs, and various tax increases his administration disguised as "revenue-enhancement measures." Such a reversal, however, came too late to save the Republicans from defeat in the 1982 congressional elections. In that year, the Democrats gained 26 House seats, signifying what appeared to be a clear rejection of supply-side economics.

By 1983, the "Gipper" was back on top as the economy rebounded. Encouraged by tax cuts, falling interest rates, and evidence that inflation had been tamed at last, consumers went on a buying binge, unemployment dropped, and Reagan's popularity revived. The recovery was by no means universal. African Americans especially continued to suffer, with their income declining relative to whites, and the percentage of those living in poverty increased. But the welfare of black Americans had never been a priority for Reagan, and for much of the rest of the nation (white America) the economic indicators were positive. By 1984 unemployment declined to 7.5 percent, and the automobile industry recovered its vitality, as did the housing market, which witnessed a boom in starts. It was the most vibrant economy since the early 1960s, and despite continued high interest rates and deficits, people felt good. Continued growth seemed likely, and the nation acquired once more a sense of confidence. Less sanguine individuals such as David Stockman and others, however, knew it would only be a matter of time before the massive deficit spending would bring economic catastrophe. The "Teflon President" would escape the fallout of his own making, but his successor, George H.W. Bush, would not.

The overall economic picture of the mid-1980s, though improved, was uneven. While many of the wealthy prospered as never before, the real wages of full-time male production workers continued to stagnate. As in the 1970s, job-seekers frequently complained that the fastest growing occupations were in the low-paying jobs of the service sector—waiters and waitresses, nurses, janitors, cashiers, and truck drivers. As American manufacturing declined because of less expensive imported goods, or as increasing numbers of businesses sent their production overseas in search of cheap labor markets, blue-collar American workers lost what for many were good-paying jobs. At the very least, they had earned enough money to support an acceptable middle-class existence. As a result of supply-side policies, such individuals not only lost decent paying jobs, but if they wanted to continue to work, they had to either completely retrain for another industry or take low-paying service sectors jobs in the meantime in order to put food on the table.

With better times came a wave of stock-market speculation reminiscent of the 1920s. The bull market began in August 1982 and lasted for five years. Entrepreneurs like Donald Trump, a Manhattan real estate mogul, and Ivan Boesky, a supposed genius at stock transactions, became millionaire celebrities by playing the market and engaging in a variety of other speculative ventures. The same mania to get rich quick that affected Americans in the 1920s engulfed many of their 1980s counterparts, and in many instances producing a "new breed" of the affluent, derisively referred to as "**yuppies**"—young urban professionals, many of whom had entered the ranks of the upper middle class by either investing in the stock market or by working in one of the many "boiler room" brokerage firms that proliferated across the nation during the 1980s.

Yuppiedom also connoted a certain lifestyle of consumerism on an unprecedented scale, not only in quantity but in finery as well. As former hippies and radicals entered the ranks of middle class respectability and responsibility, they purchased the very best their money could buy—VCR's, personal computers, telephone answering machines, cable TV, and remote controls—the latest, most expensive electronic gadgets that did not exist in 1970. The German-made BMW became a yuppie's personal car of choice, as did expensive, exotic vacations, and a new home, outfitted with the latest in house-ware accessories, in the best suburban neighborhoods.

Critics asserted that while 1970s culture, the Me Decade, had been greedy and self-absorbed, their cupidity paled in comparison to their 1980s counterparts' grasping. Thanks to Reagan's message, yuppies were becoming icons, inspiring others to want to plunge their hands into the cornucopia of goods that had seduced the United States into becoming a nation of uninhibited consumers.

Not only did stock market speculation flourish in the 1980s, but so did corporate mergers and the further consolidation of various businesses into the hands of fewer and fewer owners. Chevron bought Gulf Oil in 1984 for $13 billion; General Electric acquired RCA (and its subsidiary NBC) for $6.3 billion in 1986. Conservatives naturally embraced and touted conglomeration, asserting that mergers helped the United States weed out its inefficient companies, invest in recent technology, and outperform foreign competition. Critics charged that such compression caused the "downsizing" and "outsourcing" of employment, wiped out well-managed small businesses, enriched already fat CEOs, smashed labor unions, and inflated prices. In the meantime, the stock market roared on. Banks and savings and loan companies, newly deregulated and flush with deposits of eager investors, ladled out billions to developers planning shopping malls, luxury apartments, condominiums, retirement communities, and office buildings.

Nowhere was this frenzied, self-indulgent, and ostentatious speculation more manifest and abundant than in Houston, Texas, the city that came to symbolize the limitless opportunities of unfettered corporate capitalism. Houston's downtown skyline, proliferation of malls, high-rise office buildings and apartment complexes reflected the freebooting capitalism unloosed by the Reagan administration's laissez-faire policies. By the mid 1980s, however, as oil prices plummeted and savings and loan scandals rocked the nation, Houston, "Boom Town USA," experienced one of the worst recessions in its history. It appeared by the late 1980s that no region or city, regardless of how prosperous or allegedly recession-proof, could escape the long-range repercussions and inherent flaws of Reaganomics.

REAGAN CONFRONTS THE WORLD

The Soviet Union, and Crises in the Middle East and Central America

Many Americans felt a new sense of pride and confidence that Reagan not only would restore U.S. honor, respect, and might around the globe, but, in the process, win the Cold War and usher in an "American Century," a "Pax Americana," in which all the nations of the world would benefit. The New Right and the movement's Evangelicals saw in Reagan the triumph of fundamentalist, millennial American Christianity over the forces of communism. It was before a convention of evangelicals that Reagan demonized the Soviet Union as "the focus of evil in the modern world." To the Soviet Union he declared a new policy of moral superiority. The arms race, he declared, was a struggle of "good versus evil, right against wrong." To back up his antagonistic rhetoric, Reagan lobbied and eventually won congressional approval for a 41 percent increase in defense spending. With such funding he pledged to build 17,000 new nuclear weapons.

During his first term, Reagan made no move to engage in arms control negotiations with a series of elderly and dying Soviet leaders even as his harsh rhetoric moved Leonid Brezhnev to put his military on alert status."

Possible Armageddon almost occurred when Soviet MiG fighter jets shot down a civilian Korean airliner in the fall of 1983. The act was one of incompetence and confusion on behalf of the Soviets, not one of wanton aggression. Soviet military officials genuinely believed the plane to be a spy intruder. Reagan, however, ignored all evidence that confirmed the attack as one of miscalculation and, instead, seized on the event to lead a worldwide condemnation of the Soviet Union. Reagan, of course, led the name-calling, labeling the Soviets as "inhumane," "barbarous," and "uncivilized," and accusing them of a "massacre," implying that the Soviet strike reflected the premeditated murder of innocent civilians.

Perhaps nowhere in the world was Reagan's obsession with communism more intense than in the Western Hemisphere, especially in desperately poor Central America, where two nations, caught up in revolutionary turmoil, El Salvador and Nicaragua, became fixations for the Reagan administration. As he told a joint session of Congress in May 1983, "The national security of all the Americas is at stake. If we cannot defend ourselves there, we cannot expect to prevail elsewhere... and the safety of our homeland would be put at jeopardy." In El Salvador, the Reagan White House backed the right-wing military junta in its brutal suppression of all opposition. Certain the regime was fighting to preserve "democracy" in El Salvador, Reagan allowed the CIA and other U.S. covert agencies to send advisors to help the Salvadoran army put down the supposed communist insurgents. With such approval from Washington, the Salvadoran government unleashed a vicious reign of terror on its own citizens, with U.S.-trained paramilitary death squads roaming the Salvadoran countryside slaughtering thousands of innocent people over the course of several months. By 1984, El Salvador had been saved from communism. A U.S.-favored moderate, Jose Napoleon Duarte, won the

1984 presidential election, ending the rule of the military junta. However, under Duarte the killing of opponents continued. The Reagan administration naturally saw nothing wrong with the removal of communists from El Salvador and thus supported the Duarte dictatorship.

In Nicaragua, the Carter administration, in an attempt to atone for decades of United States-backing of the brutal Anastasio Somoza regime, had initially granted aid to the Sandinista revolutionaries, who overthrew Somoza in 1979. No sooner did Reagan enter the White House than he reversed this policy, claiming the leftist **Sandinistas** were turning Nicaragua into another Marxist state like Castro's Cuba. Although certainly no great fans of U.S. policy toward Central America and without question socialists in their economic vision for their country, the Sandinistas had no intention of becoming a Soviet lackey state. However, Reagan's attitude and policies, which cut off all aid to Nicaragua because they had gone red, left the Sandinistas no choice if their country and regime was to survive but to turn to Cuba and the Soviet Union for assistance. As the Sandinistas drifted deeper into the Cuban-Soviet camp, the more determined Reagan became to overthrow the regime. In 1982, with Reagan's blessing, the CIA organized and financed a 10,000 man anti-Sandinista guerrilla army called the *contras*, based in neighboring Costa Rica and Honduras, with the avowed purpose of bringing down the Marxist dictatorship of Nicaragua.

Reagan and other conservatives referred to the *contras* as freedom fighters but as recently de-classified documents have shown, the majority of the individuals comprising the force were ex-Somoza thugs, mercenaries, and many were heavily involved and profiting from drug smuggling (cocaine) for **Manuel Noriega** of Panama and for the Colombian cartels. With full-fledged U.S. support, the *contras* conducted raids, planted mines, and carried out sabotage in Nicaragua. Their terrorist activities naturally caused the death of several thousand innocent civilians over the course of several years of covert operation.

Many Americans grew alarmed as details of this secret war against the Sandinistas leaked out. Thus, in 1982, led by Democratic congressman Edward Boland from Massachusetts, the House passed an amendment—the **Boland Amendment**—prohibiting the CIA and Defense Department from using funds to overthrow the Sandinistas. The administration, however, ignored the resolution and continued to funnel money contributed by foreign governments and right-wing groups in the United States to the *contras*. Such clandestine operations increasingly came under the auspices of the National Security Council, which became the conduit for delivering the covert aid. The two men most responsible for the venture, as well as for what would become known as the Iran-Contra scandal, were National Security Council (NSC) director, Robert MacFarlane, and his gung-ho staff assistant, Marine Lieutenant Colonel Oliver North.

The continuing turmoil and conflict in the Middle East that had so frustrated the Carter presidency also affected the Reagan administration. Determined to stop the spread of militant Islamic fundamentalism, with its call for jihad against Western corruption and imperialism, the United States sided with Saddam Hussein's Iraq in its eight-year war (1980-88) with Iran. The conflict resulted in an estimated 1.5 million Iraqi and Iranian deaths, devastated both nations' economies, and created millions of refugees. U.S. support of Iraq only served to embolden Saddam Hussein, who believed he could dominate the Middle East for he was certain the United States would sanction his pretensions because he would be a countervailing force against the more radical Iranians and equally ambitious Hafez Assad of Syria.

Meanwhile, the conflict between Israel and the Palestinians and their Arab allies dragged on. Because of America's growing dependence on foreign oil, particularly from the Middle East (most notably Saudi Arabia), as well as its deep emotional bond with Israel, which resulted in billions of dollars of military aid and other assistance, the

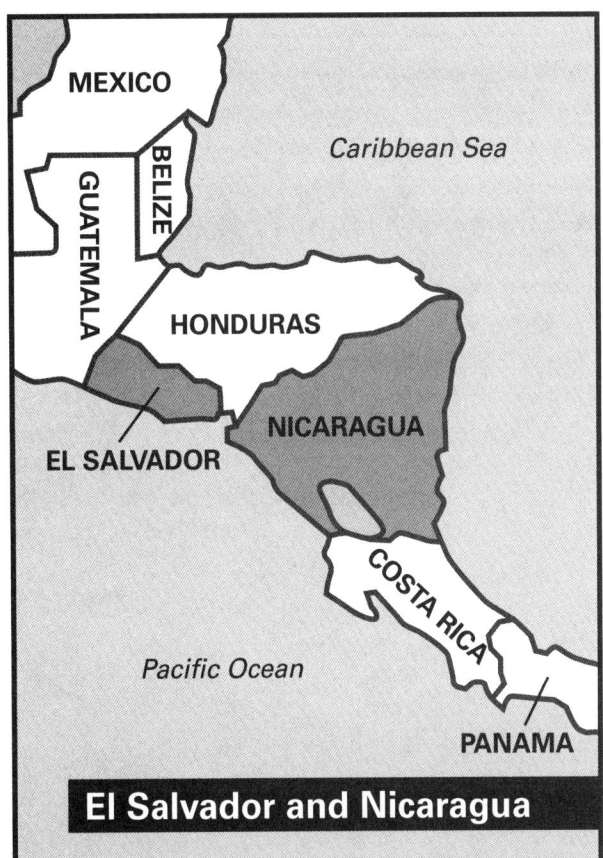

Map 33.1 El Salvador and Nicaragua

Reagan administration was no different than any of its predecessors in failing to achieve peace in the region. No matter how much impartiality the United States tried to demonstrate to the region's Arab/Muslim countries, such as giving substantial aid to Egypt, they knew that in the end America would always side with Israel.

Since Israel was established in 1948, millions of Arabs called Palestinians (who had once lived in Jewish-held lands) had settled in refugee camps in nearby Arab countries such as southern Lebanon. Groups aiming at the establishment of a Palestinian state, such as the Palestinian Liberation Organization (PLO), had used the camps as a launching ground for guerilla strikes against Israel. An unofficial war had long waged between the Israelis and the PLO along the Lebanese border. In 1981, Israel and the PLO concluded a cease-fire. The PLO, however, continued building up forces at its base in southern Lebanon. In June 1982, when an extremist faction within the PLO shot and critically wounded Israel's ambassador to Great Britain, Israel retaliated. Israeli troops under General Ariel Sharon, Israel's defense minister, invaded Lebanon, defeated the PLO, forcing its leaders, including Yasser Arafat, to flee Lebanon. The Israeli invasion only served to intensify the already bloody civil war in Lebanon between Christian and Muslim factions for control of the nation's government. Both the United States and Israel favored the Christian forces, for a Christian-dominated Lebanon not only would secure Israel's southern border with a friendly power but also hopefully give the United States, as well, a non-Muslim ally in the region. With Sharon's approval, a Lebanese Christian militia force entered two Palestinian refugee camps near Beirut to search out armed gunmen. The raid's purpose changed dramatically into one of bloody revenge for the assassination a few days earlier of Lebanon's Christian president. The Christian partisans massacred as many as 700-800 camp residents, including women and children. An Israeli commission of inquiry found Sharon negligent for allowing the militiamen to enter the camp and recommended his dismissal but found no evidence that Sharon knew of the planned slaughter in advance. Sharon resigned as defense minister but remained in the government.

After the Beirut massacre, Reagan ordered two thousand marines to Lebanon as part of a multinational peacekeeping force. Reagan, oblivious to how Lebanon's Muslim militias would see his initiative, was courting disaster, for the Muslims naturally saw the Americans as favoring Israel and the Christian side. Thus, in October

The Reagans honor the victims of the bombing of the American Marines barracks, in Beirut, Lebanon, at Andrews Air Force Base, Maryland. April 23, 1983. Photo credit: Reagan Presidential Library

U. S. Marines walk down a street of Greenville, Grenada after landing near the town.

1983, a Shiite Muslim on a suicide mission crashed an explosive-laden truck into the poorly guarded U.S. barracks, killing 239 marines. In early 1984 Reagan withdrew the surviving marines.

The Reagan administration quickly rebounded from the Beirut disaster by invading the tiny West Indies island of **Grenada**, allegedly to protect the lives of American medical students threatened by a supposed Castro-manipulated Marxist dictatorship. In reality, there was very little evidence that the American medical students studying on the island were in any danger from the Grenada regime, but Reagan administration felt the need for decisive action after the Beirut fiasco and invaded the island with 10,000 troops. After a day of skirmishing with 750 Cuban laborers constructing a new airport (only 110 of them were soldiers), Reagan declared a great American victory and the public's display of enthusiasm for Reagan and for such a trivial affair was absurd. Of course, the Reagan public relations experts exploited such a *cause celebre* to its fullest political potential for the president and the Republican Party, which now assumed the mantle of having restored America's military might by vanquishing a threat to American security, a petty, left-leaning dictatorship on a microscopic Caribbean island. As the political commentator Elizabeth Drew noted soon after the Grenada hoopla died down, "Reagan is a political phenomenon—a man who by force of personality and marvelous stage management superimposes himself over his own mistakes."

THE ELECTION OF 1984

As the 1984 election neared, liberal Democrats and many independents criticized Reagan for excessive military spending, Cold War belligerence, massive budget deficits, cuts in social programs, and assaults on the government's regulatory powers. The majority of Americans, however, dismissed such accusations, believing Reagan had redeemed America from its supposed malaise both at home and abroad. They touted his delivering of a booming economy with an end to the inflation that had wracked the country for several years prior. They applauded his tough stance with the Soviets and the rebuilding of America's military might. Even feminists welcomed his 1981 nomination of Sandra Day O'Connor as the first woman justice on the Supreme Court. The 1984 Republican convention, brilliantly staged for TV by the powerbrokers of the Republican National Committee (RNC), became a Ronald Reagan love-fest, hammering home the themes of patriotism, prosperity, and, above all, the personality of Ronald Reagan, the individual most responsible for the nation's resurrection.

After Senator Edward Kennedy declined to enter the presidential campaign, former Vice President Walter Mondale emerged as the early favorite in the party's primary race. Colorado Senator Gary Hart and the Reverend Jesse Jackson of Chicago, however, ran surprisingly strong campaigns. Receiving support from so-called "yuppies," Hart—like Bill Clinton in 1992—often criticized unions and presented himself as a different type of Democrat who advocated new ideas that would free from the party old-fashioned, New Deal-style, big government liberalism and win back some Reagan supporters and younger, college educated. Jackson, hoping to be the first-ever black major party nominee, promised to unite through his campaign a "rainbow coalition" of African Americans, Hispanics, displaced white-ethnic blue-collar workers, and all other citizens negatively affected by the Reagan Revolution.

Mondale, descending from Norwegian stock, the son of a minister and piano teacher, epitomized the nation's heartland virtues of hard work, compassion, and public service. He was also the anointed heir of Hubert Humphrey, one of the Democratic Party's and liberal America's most beloved and genuine progressives. A student leader at Macalester College, Mondale became Humphrey's protégé as Minnesota's attorney general then moved on to the U.S. senate. Mondale was bright, worked hard, and his colleagues respected him. After Jimmy Carter chose him as his running mate in 1976, Mondale became a full partner in the Carter administration, participating on a daily basis in governing the country and in making major decisions. He knew the tensions, ambiguities, and challenges of the Oval Office better than any person except the president himself. Mondale was ready.

Mondale believed he could win—not easily—to be sure, but he was confident that if he could pull together the old New Deal coalitions, add a few allies, and appeal to Americans' sense of "fairness," maybe he could pull off a victory. Mondale believed that when shown the truth and the reality of Reaganomics, that it had promoted a class struggle on behalf of the rich, they would reject both Reagan and the New Right agenda, returning to the liberal ethos.

With equal conviction, Mondale believed voters had become alarmed by Reagan's militarism and Cold War belligerence. Polls revealed that more than 70 percent of Americans supported a nuclear freeze with the Soviet Union. Three-quarters of a million people had demonstrated in New York City on behalf of such disarmament. Reagan's increased production of weapons not only fueled out-of-control deficits but also created the possibility of confrontation with the Soviets. There was, ample evidence from polls that most citizens were deeply troubled by the possibility of Central America turning into a new Vietnam and wished as well for a shift in Soviet-American relations from confrontation to cooperation.

Mondale was confident that he could put together a coalition of Democratic loyalists and challenge the president. He put his efforts toward reclaiming these lost Democrats, going to the AFL-CIO, the National Education Association, the NAACP and other civil rights groups, and women's organizations for support. According to public opinion polls, the most significant new political phenomenon was the "gender gap." Women differed from men by 10 to 15 points on issues such as war and peace or social justice at home. Thus, Mondale cultivated the support of groups like NOW. He also solicited the trade unions, all the while selling his case on fairness at home and relaxation of tensions abroad, especially with the Soviet Union.

With the party establishment, unions and other traditional liberal groups behind him, Mondale should have easily sewn up the nomination. Instead, Hart upset him in the New Hampshire primary and would win other big contests like Massachusetts, Florida, Ohio, and California. Hart won almost all of the states west of the Mississippi. Jesse Jackson won states with large black constituencies such as South Carolina. Louisiana, and Washington, D.C., and split the delegates in Mississippi, thus becoming the first African American to ever win a major party state presidential primary or caucus. Mondale didn't sew up the nomination until after the final round of primaries.

Mondale plodded on. Hoping to secure the liberal base, he gave Jesse Jackson center-stage at the Democratic convention and then boldly chose Congresswoman Geraldine Ferraro of New York as the first female vice-presidential candidate in history. In the process he further alienated the disaffected white, working-class Democrats.

That anyone could have defeated Reagan in 1984 seems absurd. The economy was booming, inflation was done, and America was strong again. Before Reagan's 1980 election, Americans had been held hostage in Iran for over a year, United States athletes had boycotted the Moscow summer Olympics, the economy was stagnant, and American morale had sunk to its lowest level since the Great Depression. By the time of the 1984 election, all that had changed. American athletes, led by Carl Lewis in track and field, swept the gold at the Los Angeles Olympics (helped in no small amount by the nonparticipation of Soviet and Eastern European athletes), a new patriotism permeated the country, and the United States had demonstrated its reinvigorated military prowess in

Grenada as well as in the construction and significant increase in nuclear weapons, cutting-edge aircraft (the stealth bomber), and nuclear-powered, multi-war-headed, missile-laden submarines. Nothing seemed impossible any longer. "Just about every place you look," one Reagan ad declared, showing a man painting a white picket fence, "things are looking up. Life is better—America is back—and people have a sense of pride they never thought they'd feel again." As one Reagan advisor observed, "I almost feel sorry for Mondale having to go up against this . . . it's almost like running against *America*."

That had been the Republican campaign strategy from the moment the 1984 election began. As a Republican staff memo instructed: "Paint Reagan as the personification of all that is right with, or heroized by America. Leave Mondale in a position where an attack on Reagan is tantamount to an attack on America's idealized image of itself—where a vote against Reagan is, in some subliminal sense, a vote against a mythic AMERICA."

In the face of such odds, all Mondale could do was to hammer way at the fact that for many Americans the Reagan years had not brought "Morning again in America" but rather endless dark nights and days of poverty, despair, and discrimination. As Mondale told a Cleveland audience, in Reagan's America "it's all picket fences and puppy dogs. No one's hurting, no one's alone. No one's hungry. No one's unemployed. No one gets old. Everybody is happy." However, there was another America, Mondale declared—the poor, the disabled, the unemployed, and the victims of bigotry.

On election day, Reagan won in a devastating landslide, rolling to victory with 59 percent of the popular vote and taking 49 out of 50 states in the Electoral College for a total of 525 electoral votes to Mondale's 13. Although the Democrats retained control of Congress and remained strong at the state and local levels, the Republicans' post-1968 dominance of the White House—interrupted only by what now seemed a momentary aberration, Jimmy Carter's single term—continued.

Falling Apart

It was only a matter of time before Reagan's detached, dependent, and uninformed style of governance would catch up with him. During his first term Reagan escaped accountability for the flaws of his disengagement largely because of extraordinary good luck and because his immediate staff brilliantly buffeted him from too much public exposure. One of the biggest mistakes Reagan made during his second administration was to reshuffle his White House staff, sending to new positions the very men who had so remarkably insulated him during his first

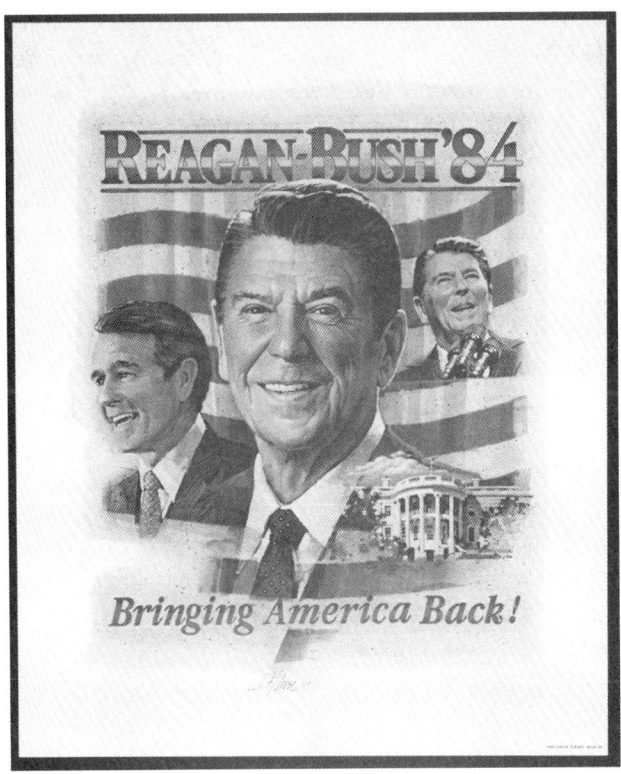

four years. James Baker became Secretary of the Treasury while the former head of that department, Donald Regan, became Reagan's new chief of staff. Unlike James Baker, Regan could not relate to Nancy Reagan, and thus during the second term, Nancy, not the chief of staff, exerted overwhelming influence on the president. She always had her husband's ear, but during the second term her presence and control of the president knew no bounds.

More devastating to Reagan was his increasing detachment from foreign policy decisions and the delegating of such crucial matters to a group of individuals who came to believe they had the authority and the right to take the law into their own hands. Reagan's uninvolvement in the details of governing resulted in him becoming an accomplice in his administration. By the fall of 1987, the Reagan presidency seemed poised to self-destruct.

Even before the **Iran-Contra Affair** emerged, the flaws of Reaganomics began to adversely affect the economy. Sky-high federal deficits grew worse, surging to over $200 billion in 1985 and 1986, and hovered at about $150 billion for the next two years. This, coupled with the trade gap, which soared to $170 billion by 1987, made the United States the world's largest debtor nation. The interest on the national debt alone took as much money as it cost to run nine government departments, including Labor, Commerce, Education, and Agriculture. It required the output of 1.5 million American workers simply to pay the interest on the debt it owed to the rest of the world. In the face of such realities, one economist concluded, "the potential for disaster is great."

Despite such pitfalls, Reagan's second term was not a complete domestic lost cause; there were some important legislative achievements. Most notable among them was the **1986 Immigration Reform and Control Act**, which for the moment outlawed the hiring of illegal aliens, strengthened border controls, and offered legal status to aliens who had lived in the United States for five years. The other important domestic initiative of Reagan's second term was the 1986 tax reform. This particular bill made the system fairer by eliminating many deductions—"loopholes"—which had favored the rich and establishing uniform rates for taxpayers at comparable levels. The law removed some 6 million low-income Americans from the income-tax rolls as well. With his appointment of Sandra Day O'Connor, an Arizona conservative and protégé of Barry Goldwater, Reagan also began the reshaping of the Supreme Court and the federal judiciary into increasingly more conservative institutions.

The Iran-Contra Affair and Other Scandals

The most devastating blow to Reagan's credibility and popularity arose from his administration's effort to control events in Latin America. Late in 1986, a Beirut newspaper reported the disturbing news that a year earlier the United States had shipped, via Israel, 508 antitank missiles to the anti-American Iranian government. Admitting the sale, Reagan claimed his goal with the armaments sale had been to encourage moderate elements in Tehran to rise up against the militant fundamentalist regime and to gain the release of U.S. hostages held in Lebanon by the Iranian-supported terrorist organization Hezbollah. The Beirut release was just the tip of the iceberg of a contempt for the law that would reach deep into the bowels of the Reagan White House. Prompting such intrigue was the intractability of the hostage problem, especially the desire to secure the release of an American CIA officer. Although Reagan himself had always insisted that the United States would never negotiate with terrorists, or ransom the hostages, he evidently failed to understand that this was exactly the nature of the bargain proposed by his aides, especially by members of what was becoming a renegade National Security Council led by Robert McFarlane and then by Admiral John Poindexter who, along with his sidekick, Marine Lieutenant Colonel Oliver North, took the initiative to a whole new level of deceit and abuse of power. Much to their credit, neither Secretary of Defense Caspar Weinberger nor Secretary of State George Schultz supported any aspect of the scheme. Sadly, their wisdom fell on deaf ears. As the transactions became murkier and more complicated, even McFarlane advised calling a halt to the entire affair.

Most explosive was the revelation that North, with Poindexter's and others' approval on the NSC, had secretly diverted profits from the Iran arms sales to the Nicaraguan *contras* at the very time the Boland Amendment had been passed, forbidding precisely such clandestine support in the overthrow of governments. To Oliver North and other true believers, the law was not only irrelevant but a severe retardant in America's fight against communism in the Western Hemisphere. Desperate to circumvent the congressional restraint, North and other NSC staffers solicited third-country and private contributions for the freedom-fighting *contras*. Over an 18-month period, North and his minions received $32 million for their cause from Saudi Arabia. As the intrigue deepened and more and more players became involved, it became inevitable that word would leak, and it did, spilling across the front pages of not just every American newspaper but all the major publications throughout the world. The Reagan administration naturally tried to skirt the issues but as it became apparent that a cover-up was impossible, Reagan declared that the venture had the best of intentions—to begin to cultivate the anti-Khomeini forces in Iran, which hopefully would result in the mullah's overthrow. Eventually all the "cover" stories were discounted, the plan to divert money to the contras revealed, and an administration that had railed against its allies for talking to terrorists was exposed as having both betrayed its own exhortations and violated its own laws.

In November 1986, Reagan appointed the so-called "Tower Commission," headed by former Texas Senator John Tower, former Secretary of State Edmund Muskie, and former National Security Adviser Brent Scrowcroft to investigate the scandal and issue its findings. Reagan testified before the commission and, at different times, claimed to have approved the arms sales to Iran, and at other times to have not remembered whether he did. The report, issued in February 1987, criticized Reagan's failure to monitor the actions of his national security team and his detachment from day-to-day operations at the White House.

In May 1987, a joint House-Senate investigative committee opened televised hearings on the scandal. Perhaps most startling were the revelations made by Poindexter, North, and others that they believed they had the power to create a secret government beyond the control of laws and institutions, free to pursue a hidden agenda that they alone would have the right to define. During the hearings Poindexter declared that he had the right to lie to Congress and the press, on his own authority, without going to Reagan, since he knew what the president wanted, and after all, the people had chosen the president. Poindexter believed it was more important to refuse to inform the president of details in order to guarantee Reagan "plausible deniability" than to bring important issues for decision to him. Members of Congress were shocked by Poindexter's presumption.

Even more terrifying was North's testimony. Not only did North confess that he, Poindexter, and CIA Director William Casey (who died of a cerebral hemorrhage the day before he was to testify) had planned from the beginning of the arms sales for the funds to go to the contras but to finance as well "an overseas entity capable of conducting activities similar to the ones we conducted here." Even more unsettling was North's arrogance and obvious disdain for the commission for having the audacity to impugn his patriotism, which he believed his every action in the operation reflected. After watching the North spectacle one columnist wrote that, "What we see here is a combination of right wing fervor, militaristic nationalism, and religiosity reminiscent of the stirrings of authoritarianism in Europe." Most distressing, the American public initially embraced North as a national hero, more impressed by his protestations of patriotism than by his reckless disregard for the law.

Even though the scandal seemed a sickening replay of the 1974 Watergate crisis, it was the very prospect of having yet another president, in little over a decade, having to resign in disgrace for the abuse of power that in the end saved Reagan from humiliation and kept his popularity in tact. The American people simply did not want to have to endure the embarrassing spectacle of having the world watch yet another one of their leaders either resign or be removed from office for their wrongdoing. To avoid such a disgrace, the American people decided that for the good of the country, it would be better to exonerate even the worst of the culprits like North, and certainly the president, than to have to endure another Watergate debacle. Thus, the Tower Commission found no positive proof of Reagan's knowledge of illegalities but roundly criticized the lax management style and contempt for the law that had pervaded the Reagan White House. In 1989, after his indictment by a special prosecutor, North was convicted of obstructing a congressional inquiry and destroying and falsifying official documents. The conviction was later reversed on the technicality that some testimony used against North had been given under a promise of immunity. Although less damaging than Watergate, the Iran-Contra scandal dogged the Reagan administration's final years as a gross abuse of executive power in a zealous campaign to overthrow a Latin American government the White House found objectionable. Indeed, for a moment is seemed the "Teflon" had finally worn off. Even Republican Dick Cheney of Wyoming, Gerald Ford's former chief of staff noted "You have to say it's a pretty fundamental flaw that would allow a lieutenant colonel on the White House staff to operate in defiance of the law."

Despite the magnitude of the Iran-Contra crisis and the revelations about the Reagan White House the scandal brought to the fore, Reagan's personal popularity seemed unaffected. Drawing on his training as an actor, he possessed the uncanny ability to communicate warmth and sincerity and to shrug off damaging implications with a disarming joke. Within months of the hearings' ending, Reagan acted as if nothing seriously had happened. He was still the "Gipper" whom the American people believed in and loved, and despite that little mishap called Iran-Contra, it was still "Morning in America." Benefiting Reagan most was the turn of events abroad, which would allow his presidency to end on a triumphant note.

Reaching New Heights

Rescuing the Reagan administration from despair was the leader of the president's arch-nemesis, the Soviet Union, Mikhail Gorbachev, who accepted Reagan's rather harsh and unilateral ground rules for ending the Cold War. What made such an historic event possible was the complete about-face both men took—Reagan, one of this nation's most fervid anticommunists since the late 1940s, became the defender of détente, while the leader of totalitarian communism transformed into a champion of democracy.

Many Americans (especially Republicans) still boast that it was Reagan's shrewd diplomacy and handling of Gorbachev that made the Soviets accept a "zero option"

Lt. Col. Oliver North takes the oath before the House Foreign Affairs Committee. His vigorous defense of his actions in the Iran-Contra affair made him a cult hero to many on the political right, eventually leading to his unsuccessful campaign for the U.S. Senate in 1994.

agreement relative to their nuclear missiles in Europe (in effect Reagan demanded that the Soviets dismantle the Warsaw Pact and remove all their missiles from their Eastern European bases). In reality, the Soviet system was collapsing by the mid-1980s, leaving Gorbachev and his followers no choice but to seek a rapprochement with the United States so Russia could survive without enduring another upheaval like that of 1917, which brought the Bolsheviks to power. By the time Gorbachev became Soviet Premier, the years of Cold War competition with the United States had finally taken its toll. The Soviets simply could not keep pace with the more dynamic and abundant United States economy, an economy that could provide its citizens with the most enviable standard of living in the world while simultaneously producing the most advanced weapons of mass destruction and conventional armaments, from planes, to ships, to infantry rifles. By the beginning of Reagan's second term, the old hardliners had all either died (Yuri Andropov and Konstantin Chernenko, Gorbachev's two older predecessors) or had been cast aside by a younger generation of leaders like Gorbachev, anxious to reform Russia before it was too late.

Affecting the Soviet Union by the time of Gorbachev's ascendancy were the repercussions of the 1979 Soviet invasion of Afghanistan, which had become for the Soviet Union a "Vietnam quagmire." Just as American military might could not, in the end, subdue the Vietcong, neither could Soviet superiority defeat the Afghani insurgents fighting a similar guerrilla war with arms supplied by the United States and other countries. The Soviets not only were losing a very costly war but was causing the Russian people a multitude of deprivations at home. Soviet consumers waited in lines for hours for basic necessities such as meat, bread, and toilet paper, while the government spent billions on new rockets, tanks, and trying to hold on to a country, Afghanistan, which the majority of Soviet citizens believed was a horrible waste of Russian lives and resources. Gorbachev agreed so within a year of becoming premier he pulled all Soviet troops out of Afghanistan and gave the country back to its people, which sadly fell under the control of the Taliban, an Islamic fundamentalist faction that took over Afghanistan in the early 1990s. The Taliban created one of the most oppressive regimes in the world—a far more repressive government than the one the Soviets had installed when they invaded the country in 1979.

The final motivating factor for Gorbachev to seek détente with the United States was the Reagan administration's attempt to develop a space satellite defense system, which, if successful, would render any future retaliatory missile attacks or first-strikes by the Soviets futile—the

President Reagan and Vice President Bush meet with Soviet General Secretary Gorbachev on Governor's Island, New York. December 7, 1988
Photo credit: Reagan Presidential Library

Strategic Defense Initiative (SDI) or the "Star Wars" defense system after the popular movie. The proposed technology would use laser-beams to build an umbrella of protection that would destroy any incoming missile. Millions were spent on "Star Wars" over the years, but such a system proved too costly and impractical and tests on early prototypes were less than impressive. Nevertheless, Gorbachev feared the United States might develop such a weapon, forcing his cash-strapped country into a new, expensive arms race in which the Soviets were already behind. Gorbachev agreed that it was time to end this ridiculous no-win war of nerves and saber rattling with the United States and build a new Russia. He announced his commitment to *glasnost* and *perestroika* (openness, freedom, and decentralization) at home while simultaneously announcing massive cuts in Soviet arms production and a new policy of close cooperation with the United States and its western allies.

The question now became was the Reagan administration up to the task. Fortunately for world peace, Ronald Reagan rose to the occasion, having four summits with

Gorbachev in two and a half years. In 1987, the two leaders signed the Intermediate Nuclear Forces Treaty (INF), providing for the removal of 2500 U.S. and Soviet missiles from Europe. This treaty, for the first time, eliminated an entire class of existing nuclear weapons rather than merely limiting the number of future weapons as SALT I had done. It, in turn, led to Reagan's historic visit to Moscow in May 1988, where the two leaders strolled and chatted in Red Square in front of the Kremlin. Historic in themselves, the INF treaty and Reagan's trip to Moscow proved a mere prelude to more dramatic events. They marked, in fact, nothing less than the beginning of the end of the Cold War. That one of America's most dedicated Cold Warriors should be the president to preside over its final phase remains one of the great ironies of recent United States history. Nonetheless, Ronald Reagan could leave the White House as the man who took one of the greatest steps toward world peace since World War II. But whatever Reagan's part (and it should not be ignored or downplayed), the triumph was above all a gift of Mikhail Gorbachev, who for his own reasons had entered onto the world stage with his own commitment to radical change for his country, which would most assuredly impact the United States. Indeed, as one Soviet leader humorously but poignantly announced, "We are going to do something terrible to you Americans; we are going to deprive you of an enemy."

When Ronald Reagan likened his presidency to a sheriff who had come to town to clean out all the "bad guys," he projected an image of himself that baffled many foreign observers. The answer was simple. It was Reagan the actor who held the key to the political history of the 1980s. He himself wondered out loud how any president who had *not* been an actor could survive the Oval Office. In his daily routine he carried out the role assigned to him. At moments of the highest drama, he aspired to Academy Award levels of performance. It was in Moscow, before a group of intellectuals and artists that Reagan articulated his view of the presidency, declaring that acting had helped him greatly "in the work I do now." Cleverly acknowledging the work of the famous Russian director Serge Eisenstein, he went on to tell his audience that, "The most important thing is to have the vision. The next is to grasp and hold it. To grasp and hold a vision, to fix it in your senses, that is the very essence, I believe of successful leadership." In many ways, Reagan had grasped and held onto his vision. He had gotten "inside a character, a place, and a moment." Because he was so successful at playing the part, regardless of what his critics said or continue to say, Reagan left an indelible mark on history.

THE REAGAN LEGACY: GEORGE H. W. BUSH

The person who would politically bridge the decades of the 1980s and 1990s was George H.W. Bush, Ronald Reagan's loyal vice-president. Although somewhat tarnished by Iran-Contra and other scandals, Reagan left the White House with his reputation and popularity in tact. Leaving on such a positive note boded well for George Bush, who could claim that his unflinching support for the president made him Reagan's logical successor. The Republican Party agreed, and with virtually no opposition from within the party's ranks, George H.W. Bush easily captured the Republican nomination. Accepting his party's endorsement to carry forward the "Reagan revolution," Bush called for a "kinder, gentler America" and pledged "Read my lips: no new taxes." As his running mate, he selected the affable but rather bland Indiana Senator Dan Quayle. It was to be Bush's good fortune to preside over the final dissolution of the Cold War and the unchallenged rise of the United States to military supremacy in the world. It was to be Bush's misfortune to inherit an economy wasting away under bloated deficits (the national debt had tripled from $1 trillion in 1981 to $3 trillion by 1988) and industrial inertia. It would be Bush's inability to effectively address such pressing economic issues that destined him to be a one-term president. Although not to blame for these problems, Bush, nonetheless, like his predecessor in many ways, blithely believed they would all go away in due time without much effort from him. Perhaps, had Bush possessed Reagan's theatrical wit and charm, the same "Teflon" so-to-speak, he might too have escaped unscathed and been reelected. Such was not to be George Bush's good fortune.

Although possessing no core political identity other than being attached to Reagan and elected to office in his own right only twice (two terms in the United States House representing Houston), Bush's identification with Reagan proved to be enough to get him elected. The Democrats, on the other hand, had far more serious problems to overcome if they hoped to recapture the White House. First, and probably most devastating, was the loss of their party's core, blue collar, industrial, ethnic, Catholic workers, who had gravitated to the Republican Party in 1984, "the Reagan Democrats." Also, by 1988, the transformation of the white South into a Republican stronghold was almost complete. Hurting the party was the loss to a sex scandal of its leading contender Senator Gary Hart of Colorado. The Reverend Jesse Jackson once again sought the nomination, winning states like Michigan in the primaries and for a while boasting the most delegates. To many pundits' surprise, however, a relative dark horse, the dry, serious, high-tech governor of Massachusetts, Michael Dukakis, ended up the winner. To "balance" his ticket and in hopes of winning back at least some of the southern states such as Texas, Dukakis chose as his running mate the moderate from the Lone Star State, Senator Lloyd Bentsen. Dukakis owed his victory to a superior campaign organization, certainly not to his charisma or to his vision for the country, which many people in his own party had difficulty discerning.

In the electoral race that followed both candidates paid, at best, lip service to the profound issues facing the country. They favored TV-oriented "photo opportunities" and "sound bites." Bush visited flag factories and military plants. In one of the more ridiculous-looking so-called photo ops (events staged so the press can take photographs), Dukakis proved his toughness on defense by posing in a tank, with only his head popping out of one of the vehicle's portals like a jack-in-the-box. Editorial writers grumbled about the "junk-food" campaign, but fleeting visual images, catch phrases, and twenty-second spots on the evening news had seemingly become the essence of presidential politics.

Bush stressed and identified himself with Reagan's achievements, while keeping his distance from the Iran-Contra scandal, which he repeatedly told the public, he was completely "out of the loop." Later evidence revealed that Bush knew more of the intrigue than he told the public in 1988. Emphasizing peace and prosperity, Bush pointed to better Soviet relations, low inflation, and the 14 million new jobs created during the 1980s—an achievement unmatched by any other industrial nation. What Bush failed to note was the sector that experienced the most prodigious job growth was the military-industrial complex. Since the arms race component of the Cold War was now over, there soon would begin the layoffs in those defense industries stimulated by Reagan's expenditures. It would only be a matter of time before unemployment would rise, ultimately affecting the Bush administration.

In response, Dukakis emphasized his accomplishments as governor. "This election is not about ideology, it's about competence," he insisted. Dukakis hammered at the failures of the "Swiss-cheese" Reagan economy and urged "Reagan Democrats" to return to the fold. But throughout the campaign Dukakis appeared edgy, dispassionate, defensive, and simply lackluster. His dismissal of ideology made it difficult for him to define his vision for the country. Liberals chafed at Dukakis' centrist position on many issues and were especially upset by his less than enthusiastic support for social welfare legislation. They wearied of his stock phrases and his repeated boasts of his managerial skills.

The campaign reflected the extraordinary hold that appeals to law and order, "negative images," fear, and patriotism still exerted on the American public. The Dukakis team allowed the Republicans to paint Dukakis as weak on every issue that appeared to be important to voters. The Bush team ran some of the most blatantly racist and scurrilous campaign ads ever seen on television, portraying Dukakis as a cold, effete, unpatriotic, anti-religious, soft on crime, opposed to the death penalty, liberal/intellectual. The most infamous ad depicting Dukakis in such light was the one focusing on Willie Horton, a black inmate who had been convicted of rape and assault and who, on a weekend furlough, had terrorized a Maryland (white) couple, raping the woman. The Willie Horton piece showed a revolving door letting people out of prison (black folk) and accused Dukakis of pampering criminals and endangering law-abiding citizens. "Never had the appeal to racism been so blatant and raw," the *New Yorker's* Elizabeth Drew wrote. However, as Bush campaign strategist Lee Atwater boasted, "If I can make Willie Horton a household name, we'll win the election." He was right. On November 8, 1988, Bush carried forty states, giving him 426 electoral votes, while garnering 54 percent of the popular vote. Dukakis prevailed in only ten states plus the District of Columbia for 112 electoral votes. Although losing the White House yet again, the Democrats retained control of both houses of Congress and most state legislatures.

THE GEORGE H.W. BUSH PRESIDENCY

In asking Americans to become a "kinder, gentler" people, and evoking the image of citizens helping one another through volunteer work, Bush seemed to be attempting to break from the harsh social policies of the Reagan years. Bush was no right-wing ideologue—a conservative on some issues, but Bush's politics, attitudes, and beliefs reflected more the moderate internationalism of the traditional Eastern Establishment wing of the Republican Party. Much to the dismay of his party's more doctrinaire conservatives, Bush did not pander to their interests or succumb to their evangelical rantings for enactment of their New Right agenda. Still the question remained: could he, or would he, deliver on both a foreign and domestic initiative for change. Not surprisingly, Bush deftly and purposefully handled most of the foreign policy crises that came his way. Although criticized by the more hawkish hard-right members of his party's supporters for not being more aggressive or assertive on specific issues, the majority of the American people, including Democrats, agreed that Bush was sure-handed and effective in pursuing his goals.

The Cold War Ends

The collapse of Soviet power, symbolized by the toppling of the Berlin Wall in November 1989, proceeded with breathtaking rapidity during Bush's presidency. Communist regimes fell across Eastern Europe, and the East German communist state ceased to exist. Germany reunited for the first time since 1945. Estonia, Latvia, and Lithuania, the Baltic republics forcibly annexed by the Soviet Union prior to World War II, declared independence; Solidarity won free elections in Poland; even in Romania, where the harshest hard-line Stalinist dictator, Nicolae Ceausescu, had brutally oppressed his people for years, was overthrown and publicly executed in a display of democratic fervor that swept through the "satellite states" of the Soviet bloc. Although some criticized Bush for not responding more boldly to these democratic uprisings, his cautious approach made eminent sense. To have reacted with the Cold War mentality might well have caused a violent counter-revolutionary reaction, especially from the Soviet armed forces already smarting from Gorbachev's demilitarization policies. Indeed, by the time of Bush's inauguration, Gorbachev was already feeling pressure from both the right and left within his country to either move Russia toward greater democracy and privatization or to suppress dissent and maintain the status quo. Were he to lose power to the hardliners, such a coup would reverse many of the positive changes that had already occurred, particularly in Eastern Europe. Thus, Bush wisely but judiciously bolstered Gorbachev, publicly applauding his every effort to change Russia and doing what he could to tangibly support his initiatives. Bush correctly believed that the best way to sustain Gorbachev in power was to continue détente by disarmament initiatives. Bush responded to Gorbachev's overtures on arms control by cancelling the nuclear-alert status of U.S. bombers and agreed to terminate plans to build mobile long-range missiles. Through a series of summits, the two super-power leaders arrived at stunning breakthroughs on new arms control treaties that promised to reduce dramatically the nuclear weapons arsenals of the world.

Bush's diplomatic aplomb was further tested in August 1990 when the hardliners in the Soviet military, in a last-ditch effort to reassert control, attempted a coup, which to the surprise of the world was thwarted by an outpouring of citizens rallying behind their nationalist leader Boris Yeltsin, who had become Gorbachev's most serious rival. Yeltsin had recently won an election as president of Russia, part of the Soviet Union. The coup greatly damaged Gorbachev's credibility while bolstering popular support for Yeltsin and the further democratization of Russian society. Within weeks of the coup's defeat, the USSR disappeared, dissolving into 15 different nation states. By now more a bystander than a player, Bush had committed his only major error—recognizing too late Yeltsin's ascendancy and Gorbachev's decline. Bush recovered quickly, however, and made Yeltsin into an ally, beginning a new coalition wherein both world powers would act in concert to enforce peace around the globe.

One issue of vital concern was the future of the Soviet arsenal of 27,000 nuclear weapons, based not only in Russia but in newly independent Ukraine, Belarus, and Kazakhstan as well. Secretary of State James Baker worked to ensure the security of these weapons and, more importantly, to win the cooperation and promise from these republics' regimes in preventing further nuclear proliferation, especially the selling of these weapons and nuclear technology to other nations or terrorist groups. As strategic talks with Yeltsin and other leaders went forward on these issues, Bush promoted further good will by announcing major reductions in the U.S. nuclear arsenal.

For decades the superpowers had backed their client states and rebel insurgencies throughout the Third World. As the Cold War faded, the prospect for solving some local disputes brightened. In Nicaragua, Bush proved himself to be much less of an evangelical anticommunist than his predecessor, abandoning Reagan's failed policy of financing the *contras* war against the Sandinistas. Moreover, by the time Bush entered the White House, the Sandinista government was self-destructing, having recently lost its most important patron, the Soviet Union, leaving only Castro's Cuba to sustain the Marxist regime, which Fidel could not do alone. Bush also distanced himself from the *contras* upon learning of their ties to the Colombian drug cartels and other questionable support groups. Bush and Congress worked out a program aimed at reintegrating the more reputable *contra* factions into Nicaraguan life and politics. Bush's willingness to reach an accord with the Sandinistas paid off in that country's 1990 elections, which saw a multiparty coalition of anti-Sandinistas emerge victorious.

Poverty, ignorance, and economic exploitation still plagued Latin America. Open guerrilla warfare continued in Peru, Bolivia, and Colombia, largely the result of conflict between government forces trying to smash the powerful drug lords and their well-armed militias. The flow of cocaine and heroin from those countries to U.S. cities reached epidemic proportions, and the Bush administration determined to stop the trade by getting rid of the individuals who served as the conduits. In December

1989, concern over the drug traffic led to a U.S. invasion of Panama to capture its dictator, General Manuel Noriega, who for years had been on the CIA's payroll. Noriega was found to have been accepting bribes and kickbacks from the cartels to permit drugs to pass through Panama and then on to the United States. Convicted of drug trafficking, he was given a 40-year sentence in 1992. He was extradited from a United States prison in 2007 to France where he faced charges of money laundering and homicide. Found guilty, he received a seven-year sentence, but was extradited in 2011 to his native Panama to face more charges. He was still being held in a Panamanian prison in 2012.

There might have been a more compelling reason for Bush to want to remove Noriega. According to documents, as well as to individuals within the Reagan administration, most notably Caspar Weinberger and George Shultz, and despite his repeated protestations to the contrary, Bush's involvement in the Iran-Contra scandal was extensive. According to Weinberger and Shultz, not only was Bush "*in* the loop," he had also strongly advocated for the arms sales and the using of the proceeds to fund the *contras*. Most startling were the revelations relative to Noriega, who claimed that Bush knew of his drug trafficking but looked the other way as long as Noriega funneled some of his take to the *contras*, which he agreed to do through the CIA. Thus, there was possibly a great deal more involved in Bush's Panama invasion that just the supposed war on drugs. For the moment these revelations did no dramatic harm to Bush—he continued to stick by his "out of the loop story." What they did do was raise questions about his candor and integrity. Further investigation into Bush's involvement in Iran-Contra was about to proceed when on August 2, 1990, Iraq shocked the world by invading the neighboring nation of Kuwait. Americans now had a more important crisis to worry about than whether George H.W. Bush had lied about his role in the Iran-Contra affair. To most Americans that was an episode that was over and done with, and the majority of citizens were glad it was.

Operation Desert Storm

Iraq's dictator, Saddam Hussein, had long dismissed Kuwait's ruling sheiks as puppets of Western imperialists and asserted Iraq's claims to Kuwait's vast oil fields. To a degree, Hussein's proclamations of sovereignty were historically legitimate, but none of the great powers in the past were about to acknowledge their validity, especially since Kuwait had become one of the Western industrial powers most important suppliers of oil. Moreover, under Saddam, Iraq had become a general menace throughout the Middle East, causing fear to the other Arab nations, as well as Israel. Iraq's military program, including both chemical and nuclear weapons projects, worried many governments. During the Iran-Iraq war, however, the United States had favored Iraq over Iran and even assisted Iraq's military buildup. We now know that such aid to Iraq, which included not just arms but providing Hussein with satellite photos of Iranian positions, continued through the Reagan and Bush administrations. Bush, even more than Carter or Reagan, had the closest ties with the dictator. He opposed as president a congressional attempt to impose sanctions on Iraq for its use of chemical weapons against the Kurds, an ethnic minority in Northern Iraq, and arranged for $2 billion in agricultural credits. Only 10 months before the attack on Kuwait, Bush issued a National Security directive ordering all government agencies to strengthen their ties with Iraq. Just a few days before the invasion, the U.S. ambassador to Iraq reassured Saddam that the U.S. wanted to maintain good relations with him and that the Bush administration had no opinion regarding Iraq's territorial dispute with Kuwait. Thus Saddam was justifiably shocked when Bush turned on him after he invaded Kuwait, for all along he had believed the United States would not only look the other way but even support his annexation of Kuwait as legitimate. As one reporter noted, "During a decade of extensive contacts with Washington, nothing whatever had occurred that could have led him [Saddam Hussein] to expect it"—Bush's complete about-face and determination to drive the Iraqis out of Kuwait.

Why such an abrupt change in policy? The answers were relatively simple: oil and Israel. Kuwait was and still is one of Europe's main oil suppliers and for the sake of solidarity with the Europeans, Bush had to respond with force. During his campaign, *Newsweek* ran a critical cover story on Bush headlined "The Wimp Factor." The magazine questioned Bush's political principles because of his apparent unwillingness to take a strong stand on any important issue or clearly articulating any solutions to vexing problems. He appeared nothing more than a loyal yes-man to Reagan. This dogged him through the early months of the campaign, but he addressed this supposed liability by delivering mean-spirited ads on television. The ads were supposed to have shown the public that George Bush could be tough on the issues that mattered. Saddam's invasion of Kuwait simply provided Bush with the perfect opportunity to reaffirm in the eyes of his own citizens, as well as in those of the world, that George H.W. Bush would stand up to bullying and aggression. Lastly, Saddam Hussein's rantings about destroying Israel could never be tolerated by any U.S. president, and in defense of the U.S.'s long-time ally and friend, Bush had to help protect Israel from such possible attacks.

Bush wisely built a consensus for a clear military objective—Iraq's withdrawal from Kuwait—and once that had been accomplished, the use of force ended then and there. There would be no invasion of Iraq proper to oust Saddam Hussein.

In his call to arms Bush eventually got the full support of Congress, the United Nations, and, most important, the American people. If United Nations' imposed economic sanctions failed to remove the Iraqis from Kuwait, Bush was ready to deploy more than four hundred thousand U.S. troops to Saudi Arabia from where the offensive to drive the Iraqis out of Kuwait would be launched. The United Nations mandated that Saddam withdraw from Iraq by January 15, 1991. On January 12, 1991, on divided votes, the Senate and the House endorsed military action against Iraq to commence on January 16, 1991. Most Democrats voted against war, favoring continued economic sanctions instead. The air war began on January 16, 1991. For six weeks B-52 and F-16 bombers pounded Iraqi troops, supply depots, and command targets in Baghdad, Iraq's capital. The air forces of other nations participated as well because this was not just a U.S. war but a United Nation's collective security response to an act of aggression. To the surprise of the coalition forces, even Syria, which was no friend of the United States, joined the cause, largely because its equally ambitious dictator Hafez Assad saw his country's involvement in the conflict as his chance to weaken a rival. Asad had long wanted Syria to become the dominant Arab power in the Middle East but such pretense could not be accomplished as long as the United States bolstered Saddam Hussein.

In retaliation, Saddam fired Soviet-made Scud missiles against Tel Aviv and other Israeli cities, as well as against the Saudi capital, Riyadh. Americans watched transfixed as CNN showed U.S. Patriot missiles streaking off to intercept incoming Scuds. As portrayed on television, the war seemed a glorified video game. The reality of many thousands of Iraqi deaths, military and civilian, hardly affected the national consciousness. Bush learned from a past president's mistake: Lyndon Johnson did not censor the Vietnam conflict; instead he allowed Americans to watch in "living color" on the nightly news American soldiers in actual combat, and frequently they watched the young men die before their very eyes. Bush was not about to let such a reality undermine his war effort, and thanks to CNN reporters broadcasting live from a Baghdad hotel room, the only fighting the American public saw on their television sets were the bombs exploding in Baghdad after being dropped by U.S. bombers on their targets. Bush handled the conflict with the greatest of diplomatic and political dexterity.

On February 23, 1991, two hundred thousand U.S. troops under General H. Norman Schwarzkopf moved across the desert toward Kuwait. Although rain turned the roadless sands to soup, the army pushed on from their base in Saudi Arabia.. Knowing they could not defeat the overwhelming military might of the United States, especially on land, and no doubt at this juncture despising Saddam Hussein for having placed them before such a juggernaut, Iraqi soldiers either fled or surrendered en masse. U.S. forces destroyed 3,700 Iraqi tanks while losing only three. More than 300 Iraqi soldiers died for every allied casualty. With Iraqi resistance crushed, Bush declared a cease-fire, and Kuwait's ruling family returned from various save havens where they had sat out the war. U.S. casualties numbered 148 dead—including 35 killed by "friendly fire" and 467 wounded. Perhaps the most important lesson Bush learned from the past was that once the announced objective had been attained—in this instance, Iraq driven out of Kuwait—the military operation was over. Despite pressure from Schwarzkopf and other generals to push on into Iraq and remove Saddam Hussein, Bush refrained from such action. Although Bush was tempted to "unleash Stormin' Norman" on Iraq, he wisely listened to the more judicious advice of his Chairman of the Joint Chiefs, Colin Powell.

Despite some sporadic, half-hearted campus protests, the war enjoyed broad public support. After the victory celebrations, however, the outcome seemed less than decisive. Saddam still held power. His army brutally suppressed uprisings by Shiite Muslims in the south and ethnic Kurds in the north. Saddam agreed to grant U.N. inspection teams access to his weapons-production facilities but reneged on his agreement within a few years. Despite the stunning military victory of 1991, Iraq remained a thorn in the flesh for the United States and its U.N. allies.

The Politics of Frustration

In the afterglow of **Operation Desert Storm**, George Bush's popularity reached an all-time high of 91 percent. The lightning victory seemed to vindicate Bush, with many suggesting that anyone who had opposed the war faced political extinction. Bush's monumental (but momentary) public acclaim in the early summer of 1991 made many prospective Democratic candidates reluctant to seek their party's nomination, for they did not want to become another Alfred Landon or Walter Mondale, suffering a humiliating electoral defeat and then historical oblivion. Many decided to give 1992 a pass, assuming no one could even remotely challenge Bush. Such Democratic trepidation was based on a short-term perspective. The popularity of a triumphant commander-in-chief could fade in the face of other discontents, whether in foreign policy matters or at home. In Bush's case it was the latter, a recession caused by the final fallout of Reaganomics, which inevitably was going to negatively affect Reagan's successor, which just happened to be George Bush. By the late fall of 1991, Bush's lassitude and ineffectuality in domestic matters had caused his ratings to drop below 50 percent. The *New York Times* described Bush as "shrewd and energetic in foreign policy, but clumsy and irresolute at home. The domestic Bush flops like a fish, leaving the impression that he doesn't know what he thinks or doesn't much care, apart from the political gains to be extracted from an issue." As the *Times* accurately observed, Bush cared little if anything about domestic policies, had no ideas on how to proceed, and appeared content to mouth platitudes about things not being *that* bad.

By January 1992, unemployment was over 7 percent; new jobs were concentrated in service industries; and even huge firms like IBM and Xerox were beginning to flounder. Yet, instead of alarm, Bush responded with indifference, even complacency. "I don't think it's the end of the world even if we have a recession," Treasury Secretary Nicholas Brady said. "We'll pull out of it again. No big deal." Rather than devise a new approach, Bush advisors recommended standing pat. "Frankly," Bush's chief of staff John Sunnunu said in November 1991, "this president doesn't need another single piece of legislation."

The Bush administration thus ignored the realities of a major sea of change in people's attitudes toward politics, even as all around it the tide was rushing out. Eight months after the Gulf War, fewer than 40 percent of the American people felt comfortable with the way the country was moving. A deep-seated malaise seemed to be sweeping the land. There were problems no one was addressing, issues that for too long had been swept under the rug, first with Reagan and now with Bush. Perhaps no other event better encapsulated this frustration, anger, despair, and disillusionment than the **south-central Los Angeles race riots** that exploded in April 1992 after the verdict acquitting the police who had been shown beating black motorist Rodney King on videotape. For several days the release of anger and pent-up frustration raged, leaving some forty persons dead and millions in property damage, reminding the nation of the desperate conditions in its inner cities. The Bush administration did little to remedy these issues. In 1990, when Congress passed a bill broadening federal protection against job discrimination, Bush vetoed the measure, claiming that such legislation encouraged racial quotas in hiring. When Bush came to Atlanta in 1992 to observe Martin Luther King Day, King's daughter, a minister, ask bitterly, "How dare we celebrate in the midst of a recession, when nobody is sure whether their jobs are secure?"

Government officials and corporate executives were going to jail for betraying their obligation to the people. Suddenly an election that had looked like a coronation of the incumbent became a wide-open contest, evoking passions not seen in the political arena for three decades.

DOMESTIC UPHEAVAL

United States culture in the late 1970s and 1980s revealed contradictory tendencies. On the one hand, movies, TV, and popular music provided escapism, and many middle-class citizens immersed themselves in a frivolous materialism and a careerist pursuit of wealth and status not seen since the 1920s. Perhaps most important and alarming was the emergence of a conservative backlash coupled with a resurgence of evangelical religion around which conservatives organized politically to achieve their vision of a better America. At the same time, activists found expression in a revived women's movement, a gay-rights campaign, and support for environmental causes. On the economic front, the 1980s and early 1990s saw equally divergent tendencies. The 1980s, although bracketed by recessions, brought a boom that suffused part of Reagan's America with a glow of prosperity. Millions of Americans, however, mostly in the inner cities seemed permanently frozen out of a high-tech economy that increasingly demanded education and specialized skills. Many African Americans entered the ranks of the middle class, but the majority remained mired in inner city poverty and hopelessness. Throughout the era growing immigration from Latin America and Asia reshaped the nation's ethnic and demographic profile.

Internationally, U.S.-Soviet relations worsened in the late 1970s and early 1980s but improved dramatically in Reagan's second term. Brightening prospects on one front were matched by heightened menace elsewhere. The Middle East, in particular, wracked by ancient conflicts, brought moments of illusory hope interspersed with frustration and tragedy. As the 1980s ended, a rising tempo of terrorist attacks suggested that the nation was entering a period no less dangerous than that which Americans had faced during the darkest days of the Cold War.

Chronology

1981 Ronald Reagan takes office as president.
Hostages released from Iran.
Severe recession begins (to 1983).
Researchers identify cause of AIDS.
Sandra Day O'Connor appointed first female Supreme Court justice.
Reagan survives wounds from assassination attempt.

1982 U. S. supports contra war against Sandinista government in Nicaragua.
Equal Rights Amendment dies.

1983 U. S. invades Grenada.
Terrorist attack in Beirut kills American Marines.
U. S. pulls out of Lebanon.
Reagan proposes Strategic Defense Initiative.

1984 Democrats choose Geraldine Ferraro, first woman vice presidential candidate.
Reagan re-elected as president.

1985 Mikhail Gorbachev becomes leader of Soviet Union.

1986 Iran-contra scandal begins to leak out.
U. S. bombs Libyan targets.
Insider trading scandals rock Wall Street.
Challenger space shuttle blows up after takeoff.

1987 Congressional hearings held on Iran-contra.
Stock market suffers record decline.
Gorbachev comes to Washington.

1988 George H.W. Bush elected president.

1989 Berlin Wall is torn down.
Communism collapses in Eastern Europe.
U. S. invades Panama.
Chinese government crushes prodemocracy students in Tiananmen Square.
Alaska hit by massive oil spill from *Exxon Valdez*.

1990 Bush and Congress agree on tax increases to reduce budget deficit.
Federal Clean Air Act is passed.
Iraq invades Kuwait.
Gorbachev wins Nobel Peace Prize as Soviet troops withdraw from Eastern Europe.

1991 Soviet Union disintegrates as Soviet republics declare independence.
U. S. ousts Iraqi army from Kuwait in Gulf war (Operation Desert Storm).

Review Questions

1. Discuss the social factors that produced the New Right and the Moral Majority.

2. Why have many historians referred to the Reagan presidency as the "Reagan Revolution"?

3. Describe "Reaganomics" and what kind of economic thinking or theories did such policies reflect?

4. Many Americans believe that Reagan's hard line with the Soviets was responsible for ending the Cold War. Do you agree or disagree? Would the Cold War have ended regardless of Reagan's "tough talk"?

5. By the close of the Gulf War in the fall of 1991, George H.W. Bush had attained the highest popular approval rating of any president in modern history; a year later he was soundly defeated by Bill Clinton. What happened in that short time to cause the Bush presidency to unravel? What were some of the issues in the Bush presidency (many of which he inherited from his predecessor) that came to the forefront?

Glossary of Important People and Concepts

Boland Amendment
Contras
Geraldine Ferraro
Grenada
John Hinckley
Immigration Reform and Control Act of 1986
Iran-Contra Affair
"The Laffer curve" or supply-side economics
Moral Majority
"neo-cons"
new "Okie" migrants
New Right
Manuel Noriega
Operation Desert Storm (the First Gulf War)
Professional Air Traffic Controller's Organization (PATCO)
"Reagan's Revenge"
"Reaganomics"
Sandinistas
south-central Los Angeles race riots, 1992
Strategic Defense Initiative (SDI) or "Star Wars"
"Sun Belters"
"Teflon president"
"think tanks"
"voodoo economics"
Yuppies

SUGGESTED READINGS

Mary Francis Berry, *Why ERA Failed* (1986).

Michael Beschloss and Strobe Talbott, *At the Highest Levels: The Inside Story of the End of the Cold War* (1993).

Bryan Burroughs and John Helyar, *Barbarians at the Gate: The Fall of RJR Nabisco* (1990).

Lou Cannon, *President Reagan: The Role of a Lifetime* (1990).

Theodore Draper, *A Very Thin Line: the Iran-Contra Affair* (1991).

Lawrence Freedman and Efraim Karsh, *The Gulf Conflict, 1990-1991* (1993).

Andrew Hacker, *Two Nations: Black and White, Separate, Hostile, Unequal* (1992).

Haynes Johnson, *Divided We Fall: Gambling with History in the Nineties* (1994).

——, *Sleepwalking Through History: America in the Reagan Years* (1991).

Michael Katz, *The Undeserving Poor: From the War on Poverty to the War on Welfare* (1989).

Jonathan Kozol, *Rachel and Her Children: Homeless Families in America* (1988).

Alex Kotlowitz, *There Are No Children Here: The Story of Two Boys Growing Up in the Other America* (1991).

Nicholas Lemann, *The Promised Land: The Great Black Migration and How it Changed America* (1989).

Martin Lowy, *High Rollers: Inside the Savings and Loan Debacle* (1994).

Kevin Phillips, *The Politics of Rich and Poor: Wealth and the American Electorate in the Aftermath of the Reagan Presidency* (1990).

Arthur M. Schlesinger Jr., *The Disuniting of America* (1991).

Randy Shilts, *And the Band Played On: Politics, People and the AIDS Epidemic* (1987).

James B. Stewart, *Den of Thieves* (1991).

Gary Wills, *Reagan's America: Innocents At Home* (1987).

——, *Under God: Religion and American Politics* (1990).

William Julius Wilson, *The Truly Disadvantaged* (1987).

President Bill Clinton giving the 1999 State of the Union Address

Chapter Thirty-four

A DIVIDED AMERICA: Bill Clinton to George W. Bush

It was clear and pleasant on that September 11 morning. United Airlines Flight 93, scheduled to depart Newark at 8:01 for San Francisco, took off 40 minutes late. There were only 40 aboard the plane; 15 of them had decided to take that flight at the last minute. There was the usual combination of business and pleasure travelers. One passenger, with a heavy heart, was recovering the remains of a stepson killed in an auto accident on his honeymoon.

At 9:28, four Middle Eastern men wearing bandanas hijacked the plane. One claimed to have a bomb strapped to his body. An air-traffic control tape revealed that the pilot yelled, "Get out of here!" This was followed by a breathless terrorist announcing, with bizarre decorum, "Ladies and gentlemen, here, it's the captain. Please sit down. Keep remaining sitting. We have a bomb on board." But the passengers did not passively remain seated. Through more than two dozen in-flight phone calls, they learned that three planes had crashed into the World Trade towers and the Pentagon with horrendous consequences. Jeremy Gluck, a former college judo champion, told his wife that there were three other passengers as big as he. Mark Bingham had played on a championship college rugby team. Tom Burnett, a former high school quarterback, informed his wife that "a group of us" were planning to get control of the plane. Todd Beamer, a baseball and basketball player in college, prayed with a telephone operator he had reached. She heard him say, "Let's roll," at the end of their conversation. A flight attendant told her husband, "They're forcing their way into the cockpit." The passengers seemed to have broken into the cockpit using a food cart as a battering ram. In those final desperate minutes, a ferocious struggle took place. At 10:03 the Boeing 757 crashed into an old strip mine outside of Shanksville, Pennsylvania. All aboard died, but they had prevented the plane from reaching its destination, the Capitol or the White House.

The passengers on Flight 93 were not the only heroes of the 9/11 atrocity. Thousands of fire fighters, police officers, emergency medical technicians, and ordinary people rushed to the Twin Towers to help. Partially as a result of failures of communication in their rescue efforts, 343 fire fighters died. One woman, after descending 80 floors, along with dozens of others, found the stairway blocked. A fire fighter broke through an office wall with his ax, locating a way out. "Come this way – move quickly," he shouted, illuminating the path with his flashlight. She and the others made it to the street at 10:24, four minutes before the north tower collapsed. The survivors did not include the firefighter. "He stayed there because there were more people behind us," she recalled.

Mohammed Salman Hamdani, a Muslim Pakistani, was a research technician at Rockefeller University who had experience as an emergency worker, so he dashed into the towers to assist in the rescue efforts. He was never heard from again. There were insulting rumors about his disappearance and loyalty to America that were dispelled by the recovery of his remains.

The events of 9/11 penetrated the consciousness of Americans who previously had a sense of invulnerability. Although, "we all know that we are going to die," one observer noted, "Americans see suffering and death as aberrations." The

9/11 catastrophe "presented us with this massive reminder of death, and how unpredictable, uncontrollable and arbitrary death can be," a social psychologist commented. The public saw the ghastly details on television: the towers collapsing, the people jumping, the billows of smoke, and felt it personally. "Everybody felt that it had happened to them." The stories of heroism were a balm to wounded souls. The people on Flight 93 acted quickly when they learned about the unthinkable. The son of one of the passengers said, "I think it is a message to the world that the American spirit is alive and kicking."

THE 1992 ELECTION: Bill Clinton and the Triumph of Neo-Liberalism

The recession following the Gulf War opened the door for a Democratic victory in 1992. As is always true, the party out of power not only has to have a distinct, clear message of change to present to the people, but the right person to articulate that vision and energize the party faithful. That person, William Jefferson Clinton, the 45-year-old, six-term governor of Arkansas, surfaced in the summer of 1991.

Clinton claimed to represent a "New Democrat" in ideology and vision, believing the party had to "center" itself and cultivate a new relationship with the middle-class, especially with its more upwardly mobile, affluent members who since the 1980s had moved to the right along with many traditional working-class Democrats. If the Democrats hoped to win the presidency as well as maintain the Democratic Party as the majority party, Clinton believed that it was time for the Democrats to shed its New Deal/Great Society heritage and embrace instead a new look that reflected the interests and concerns of middle-class voters. Beginning in 1968, large numbers of white middle-class Americans had come to resent traditional liberalism, believing it had overwhelmingly catered to the underprivileged and disenfranchised at their expense. Such "favoritism" (whether real or perceived) caused widespread white middle-class alienation and defection, resulting in the emergence of the "Reagan Democrats" and Republican presidential landslide victories beginning in 1980.

To promote his party's new agenda, Clinton, along with other neo-liberals (a moderate who wanted to reduce federal spending and favored other conservative ideas like tougher penalties for criminals, created the Democratic Leadership Council (DLC) in the late 1980s. In 1990, Clinton became the DLC's chairman. From that position, he began putting together a new coalition of middle-class Democrats. In the summer of 1991, Clinton believed the time was right for him to test whether the middle-class was ready to rejoin a redefined and refocused Democratic Party by announcing that he was running for the party's nomination. To the surprise of many, including the stalwarts of his own party, there emerged a groundswell of support throughout the country for Clinton's new message.

Although confident he could bring back the wayward middle-class Reagan Democrats to the party, Clinton had to contend with the unsuspected and potentially damaging third-party candidacy of Texas billionaire **H. Ross Perot**, who many Clinton Democrats feared could hurt their candidate's presidential prospects. Like Clinton, Perot had great populist appeal with his straight-talking, outspoken views on everything and a remarkable capacity to be in the right place at the right time. Perot claimed to speak for the forgotten Americans, who were sick of big government and were tired of both major parties' political broken promises. Perot appealed to those who were ready for a take-charge kind of guy, who could look under the hood, tell them what was wrong, and proceed to fix the damage without fanfare.

Perot's party, "United We Stand, America," called for cutting the deficit and balancing the budget. Although allegedly "a-ideological," Perot articulated a political philosophy that was essentially conservative/libertarian, which called for less government involvement in people's

Ross Perot, January 24, 1990.
Photo credit: UTSA's Institute of Texas Cultures

lives. His inherent conservatism was tempered by a populist reality that many Americans still wanted a government responsive to the common people's needs. Perot's folksy straight-talk more than anything else, however, appealed to many disaffected voters, cutting across partisan lines and causing Democrats and Republicans to reevaluate their traditional third-party perceptions and calculations.

Helping Perot and others disseminate their respective messages to larger audiences was the emergence of talk-show "journalism," hosted by such celebrities as Oprah Winfrey, Geraldo Rivera, and Phil Donahue. All provided politicians with an outlet to reach the American heartland via television. By the early 1990s, Larry King's one-hour show on CNN had become the prize media site for any aspiring candidate. Perot used his friendship with King persuading the interviewer to let him on his program. King allowed Perot the airtime, and their one hour discussion helped to catapult Perot overnight into one of the most popular third-party alternatives in several decades.

Unfortunately for Clinton, it would only be a matter of time before his notorious philandering past would come to the fore. Clinton and his politically savvy staff and wife, Hillary, knew the question would arise and had prepared to address the inevitable. Clinton did a masterful job of convincing the press that such indiscretions were behind him when his 12-year affair with Gennifer Flowers hit the tabloids and then the legitimate press. Clinton's campaign entered a free fall in the polls. Indeed, it looked as if his gambit for the Democratic nomination was over. Clinton, however, was not about to bow out of the race, choosing instead to address the issue directly, with his wife by his side. Thus on Super Bowl Sunday (January 1992), the Clintons appeared on one of television's most respected, legitimate news programs, CBS' *60 Minutes*. They did what no political couple had ever done before—confess to past marital problems. They told the TV audience, however, that those problems had been worked out.

To the Clintons' and their campaign's great relief, their ploy worked: sufficient numbers of Americans forgave Clinton for his wandering. Indeed, after losing the New Hampshire primary to Massachusetts Senator Paul Tsongas, the Clinton campaign became a juggernaut of one primary victory after another. By the end of Super Tuesday in March 1992, Clinton had wrapped up the Democratic nomination. The attacks on his personal behavior (such as his alleged Vietnam War draft-dodging, involvement in antiwar protests while at Oxford University, and his pot-smoking) still dogged him. Clinton was even behind in the June polls to Ross Perot. If Clinton hoped to even have a chance to compete, he had to find a way to define himself and his program in such a way that the American people would have a positive reason to support him.

Clinton concluded that he had to focus on the issue or issues that affected the majority of Americans. It quickly became apparent to the Arkansan what that issue was. As the sign in Clinton's Little Rock campaign headquarters blared, "IT'S THE ECONOMY, STUPID."

Black voters rallied to the Clinton campaign. Even as governor of Arkansas, Clinton had connected with African Americans. His ability to relate to the African-American community, especially in the South, earned him the honor and recognition among many black Africans of being the nation's first "black president." Clinton also publicly celebrated multiculturalism, asserting it to be a positive development, enriching the American character by endowing our national personality with a more global perspective.

The rapid unraveling of the Bush presidency helped Clinton. Not only were real incomes declining for the lower middle-class and working class, but Republicans around the country began expressing dissatisfaction with the administration's inertia. Compounding Bush's economic woes was the reemergence of a revitalized Republican Far Right led by individuals such as Patrick Buchanan. Such conservatives never saw Bush as one of them. Bush tried to make peace with the right wing of his party by unwisely turning over the opening night of the Republican national convention in Houston, Texas to Buchanan and the equally shrill fundamentalist minister Pat Robertson. Both men called for a cultural and religious war to cleanse the nation of feminists, homosexuals, pro-choice advocates, and other alleged deviants, all of whom they claimed were undermining the country's traditional moral underpinnings. To both men, diversity and multiculturalism, if not checked soon, would cause the end of an America they believed was meant to be a Judeo-Christian nation.

Despite the debacle at the Republican convention, Bush continued to believe he could win. By invoking the pride of Desert Storm, he would be returned to office. Reality set in, however, by mid-summer as Bush trailed Clinton in some polls by 15 points. At that juncture, Bush asked long-time friend and adviser, Secretary of State James Baker, to leave his cabinet position and take over his campaign.

While Bush's campaign stalled, Clinton further amplified his image as a New Democrat by choosing as his running mate a generational peer, Tennessee senator Al Gore, Jr. Clinton's selection of Gore surprised many primarily because he was a fellow Southerner, which flew in the face of conventional wisdom that a candidate should never choose a running mate from his own region of the country. Clinton believed that by selecting Gore he could win more southern states, essential to a Democratic victory. Since the Nixon years, the South had been increasingly gravitating toward the Republican Party; by the end of the Reagan era, the "Solid South" now meant overwhelmingly Republican. Thus, with a fellow Southerner on the ticket, Clinton was confident he would at least win a few key southern states. It paid off because in the election, Clinton took Arkansas, Louisiana, Georgia, Tennessee, and Kentucky—all states that four years earlier went to George H.W. Bush.

Bill Clinton won because he possessed a strategy, a vision, and a campaign apparatus prepared to implement a winning plan. By contrast, *Time* observed that Bush was "feckless, confused, whining, and rudderless." Clinton successfully brought back to the Democrats a good number of Reagan defectors. Bush seemed oblivious to the common folk Reagan had so skillfully cultivated. Bush seemed unable to shed his blue-blood persona and image and connect with the average person. As a result, Bush won a lower percentage of popular votes (37 percent) than Barry Goldwater in 1964, Herbert Hoover in 1932, or George McGovern in 1972, three presidential candidates beaten handily by their opponents. Indeed, no incumbent since William Howard Taft (in 1912 against Woodrow Wilson and TR) had fared so poorly. Bush won a majority only among white Protestant Southerners. In the Electoral College Clinton won handily, 370-168, carrying 32 states and the District of Columbia. In contrast to Bush winning only a majority among Southerner white Protestants, Clinton carried the Jewish, African American, and Latino vote by large margins. Perot's candidacy hurt Bush more than Clinton. The Texas billionaire gained no electoral votes but did attract 19 million popular votes. Perhaps most surprising, about 55 percent of eligible voters went to the polls, a turnout that reversed 32 years of increasing voter apathy.

Most interesting were the poll revelations that women (both black and white), especially those in the workplace, had favored the Clinton-Gore ticket because they believed they would benefit from the kind of social programs that Clinton and most Democrats promoted. Compared to their male counterparts, fewer working women had employer-funded health insurance; conversely, children and their single-parent working mothers were the overwhelming recipients of Food Stamps and Medicare/Medicaid. Given such status of many working women, it was no surprise that they would vote for a ticket that promised programs that would ameliorate their plight.

The election saw female representation in the House of Representatives nearly double, from 28 to 47, while the number of women in the Senate tripled, from 2 to 6. The Democratic victory bode well also for African Americans, who saw their presence in the House climb to 41 members, an all-time high.

Perhaps such an improved turnout can be attributed to Clinton's appeal among Baby Boomers, for they were electing one of their own and took great pride in the

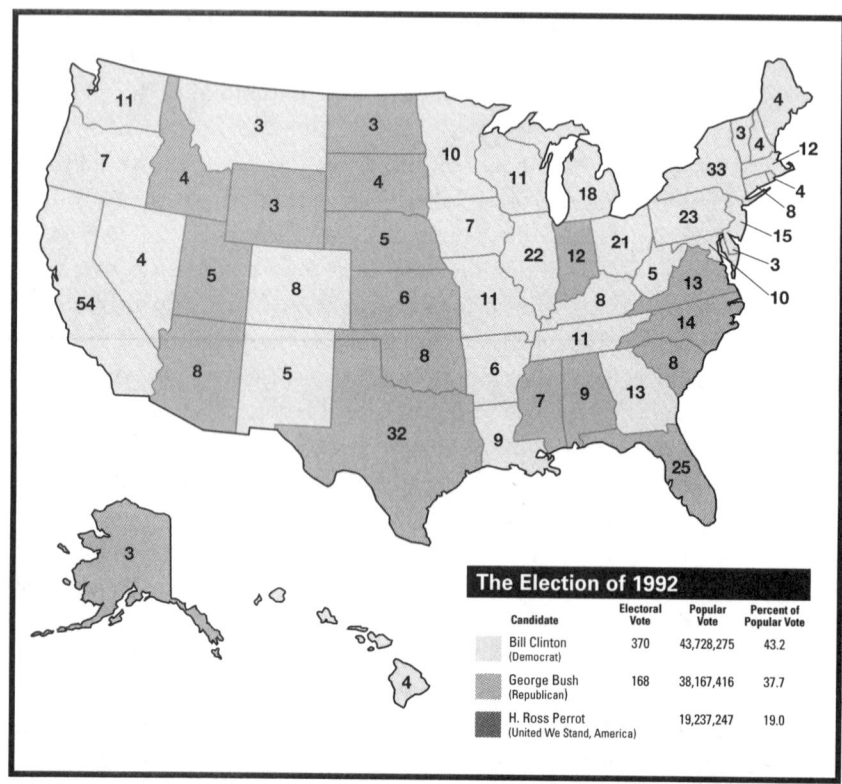

Map 34.1 The Election of 1992

Bill Clinton shaking hands with John F. Kennedy.
Photo credit: Consolidated News, Arnie Sachs

fact that their day in the political sun had finally arrived. Clinton projected the image of a youthful, exuberant, and thoughtful leader with an equally accomplished wife who promised to be a full partner in the White House, perhaps potentially more powerful in the public arena than any First Lady since Eleanor Roosevelt. As one writer noted, to many Baby Boomers, Clinton was "our generation's second chance."

THE CLINTON YEARS

The Clinton presidency can be divided into two phases. From early 1993 to the fall of 1994, the Clinton administration pursued an ambitious agenda of socio-economic reform. Whatever progress Clinton had made toward change, however, he undermined by political miscalculation and shortsightedness. As a result, the Republicans swept to victory in the 1994 congressional elections, after which his administration reflected little more than an effort to survive in office by accommodating congressional conservatives. Yet, despite an innate penchant for self-destructive behavior, which did not reach full potential until his second term, Clinton implemented many successful initiatives both at home and abroad.

Clinton embraced diversity by appointing to his cabinet three African Americans—Mike Espy as Secretary of Agriculture; Ron Brown as Secretary of Commerce, and Jesse Brown as Secretary of Veteran Affairs—and two Latinos—Henry Cisneros as Secretary of Housing and Urban Development, and Federico Pena as Secretary of Transportation. Clinton's initial cabinet also included three women—Janet Reno as Attorney General, Donna Shalala as Secretary of Health and Human Services, and Hazel O'Leary as Secretary of Energy. As his first nomination to the Supreme Court, Clinton chose Ruth Bader Ginsburg, only the second woman to sit on this nation's highest tribunal. And as representative to the United Nations, Clinton named Madeline Albright, who would also become the country's first female Secretary of State during his second term.

On social issues Clinton claimed several victories during his first term. He ended the Reagan era's ban on abortion counseling in family planning clinics; pushed through Congress a family leave program for working parents; established **AmeriCorps** (reminiscent of LBJ's VISTA), which allowed students to repay college loans through community service; and secured passage of the **Brady Bill**, which instituted a five-day waiting period for the purchase of hand guns. In conjunction with the Brady Bill, Clinton also pushed through a crime bill that banned the manufacture, sale, or possession of nineteen different assault weapons. He also won new funding for police and prison modernization as well as for a youth-oriented job corps.

Without question, one of Clinton's boldest yet questionable accomplishments was his deficit reduction initiative, which he made a priority over the middle-class tax cuts and social investment programs in infrastructure, education, environmental technology, and health care he had promised voters in the campaign. In retrospect, it appears Clinton was paying only lip-service to such endeavors during his run for the White House. Once in office, he dropped the fight for large-scale infrastructure spending and the jobs such a program would have created in favor of a more conservative and moderate-pleasing plan of deficit reduction. Before Clinton introduced his plan, and even before his inauguration, he brought together in Little Rock industrial leaders, financiers, and academics to educate the American people and his own team of advisors about the appropriate combination of deficit reduction and stimulus in the economic agenda he would introduce once he became president. The result was a carefully crafted package that would cut in half the annual deficit as part of the total expenditures, raise taxes on the wealthy, and put in place a mechanism for sustained economic growth. To sweeten the proposal and help create new jobs, Clinton offered an economic stimulus program that would inject $30 billion into the economy through various federal programs and incentives.

Despite their own avowed commitment to deficit reduction, the Republicans refused any cooperation with Clinton. Senate minority leader Robert Dole told the president that he would not get a single Republican vote. The Republicans then successfully filibustered against the stimulus package. To secure a one-vote victory in the Senate for the overall deficit-reduction bill, Clinton sacrificed an energy tax. In the end, the legislation turned out to be a great success. The bill proved critical to ending the seemingly interminable round of huge federal deficits, while encouraging record-setting economic growth and prosperity. Perhaps no other Clinton initiative better reflected the neo-liberal ethos than his deficit reduction measure, which revealed that the ideology's adherents were fiscal conservatives. As a result, Clintonian economic policies mollified Wall Street bond traders and generated the lower interest rates that Clinton's more orthodox advisers thought necessary for business investment and economic recovery.

"Don't Ask, Don't Tell"

In 1993, Congressional Republicans immediately got the Clinton agenda off track. They made an issue of Clinton's campaign promise to end discrimination against gay men and women by the U.S. military. Homosexual behavior had been banned by the United States military since the founding of the republic. In 1950, during a time of fears that gays posed a security risk because they were supposedly more vulnerable to blackmail, Harry S. Truman signed the Uniform Code of Military Justice. This standardized procedures for kicking gay soldiers out of the military. In 1982, President Ronald Reagan's Defense Secretary Casper Weinberger pushed for a more aggressive effort to purge gays from the armed services and the White House issued a directive declaring that "homosexuality is incompatible with military service," encouraging investigators to find and force from the service anyone caught in homosexual acts or who admitted to being gay or bisexual.

While running for president in 1982, Bill Clinton promised gay rights groups that he would issue an executive order lifting the ban, a move still unpopular with the general public. In the first days of his presidency, Republicans, with the aid of conservative Democrats like Senator Sam Nunn of Georgia, brought the issue front and center and began drafting legislation continuing the gay ban. To prevent the passage of a law that might prove difficult to reverse, Clinton compromised and in December 1993 issued a new directive banning the military from interrogating service members and recruits about their sexual orientation, but allowing the military to expel soldiers and sailors if their homosexuality or bisexuality were uncovered, a policy that came to be known as **"Don't Ask, Don't Tell"** (DADT). A witch hunt still continued, with soldiers and sailors blackmailed, and officers improperly spying on members of the service to uncover their sexual behaviors, with the military expelling 14,346 people from the service because of their sexual orientation between 1993 and the repeal of DADT in 2011 Clinton's attempt to appease both the gay community and those opposed to ending the military ban against gays ending up pleasing no one. Gays felt Clinton had broken a promise, cultural conservatives saw Clinton's efforts as radical, and other voters found the issue insignificant at a time of economic suffering. Clinton came to be seen as a "waffler"—someone afraid to fight for principle. "It was the grimmest start of any presidency in generations," the *New Republic* declared.

Health-care Reform

From the beginning everyone knew that Clinton's presidency would rise or fall on his success in passing health-care reform, guaranteeing some form of basic, adequate coverage to every American citizen. By 1992, the United States was the only developed industrial nation in the world without such a system. All European countries had long since instituted national health-care programs, some even before World War II. For the first time in almost 50 years, it seemed possible to resurrect the idea, for nearly 40 million Americans were totally without health-care coverage. To many liberals, the right to health care was as fundamental in a democracy as the right to vote. For Clinton, economic reform and health-care reform were symbiotic: a permanent cure for huge deficits required harnessing the explosive rate of inflation in health-care costs. In Clinton and other liberals' view, health-care reform represented the most massive, important social legislation in all of twentieth-century American history, making even Social Security pale in comparison. Clinton was also keenly aware of the future political benefits such reform could bring both him and his party. If he could tie the middle-class to the Democratic Party through providing universal national health insurance, Clinton could solidify at least for another generation his party's dominance. The Republicans were determined to defeat it.

A multitude of reasons explain why Clinton's health-care reform initiative ultimately went down to crushing defeat. One of Clinton's most fatal errors was to give responsibility for drafting the proposal to a task force headed by his wife and his old friend and fellow Rhodes Scholar, Ira Magaziner. Although by everyone's account Hillary Clinton was brilliant, hard driving, a master of detail, and a charismatic leader, she did not accept criticism easily nor tolerate dissenting views. Magaziner possessed an equally overbearing and overwhelming personality—the quintessential "policy wonk" who believed that non-politically motivated experts could devise such legislation if left alone to do their work. The project became policy-making by secret, led by individuals who were often seen as arrogant and dismissive as they rode roughshod over those they believed were less bright and competent.

Compounding the personality problems of the task force was the exclusion of Congress, especially the wheelers and dealers who are key to getting such controversial legislation passed. Not only were important legislators left out of the process but so were equally vital members of the administration, such as Secretary of Health and Human Resources, Donna Shalala, and Secretary of the Treasury, Lloyd Bentsen. Both cabinet members had handled more health-care legislation than anyone on the task force and no doubt resented being snubbed.

Not surprisingly, the measure produced by this process was extraordinarily complicated and sophisticated—with a provision for any and every eventuality—and completely incomprehensible to the average citizen. Nearly 1350 pages in length, the Clinton health-care package arrived on the Hill almost a full year after the president had taken office. The initiative immediately incurred the venom of both Republicans and Democrats, with the former especially harsh in their criticisms. Utah Republican Senator Bob Bennett denounced the bill as "incredibly bloated, complex, unresponsive, and incomprehensible; symbolic of everything people hate about government." Even supporters expressed anxiety, and the lobbyist for America's senior citizens openly worried "about the complexity of this [plan] and the ability of people to feel comfortable with something that is so complicated. If you're explaining it, people's eyes glaze over."

There was little doubt Clinton could have avoided such attacks and concerns had he gone to the American people with broad outlines of a program and worked with congressional committees to draft the appropriate legislation. For a brief time, however, Clinton overcame the plan's cumbersomeness and inaccessibility. In a speech before Congress and the nation in September 1993, he explained the measure's most salient points—quality care, savings, simplicity, and security. At that moment the president was clearly in his element, rising to the occasion with a memorable address that stirred even his opponents in the audience. One Republican senator called Clinton's speech "the most comprehensive, brilliantly presented analytical dissection of everything that is wrong with the present health-care system" that he had ever heard. Yet, almost immediately, Clinton allowed the momentum he had created to dissipate.

Other issues distracted him such as the **North American Free Trade Agreement (NAFTA)**. Labor unions fiercely opposed NAFTA, which they correctly anticipated would result in high-paying manufacturing jobs being shipped to low wage job markets overseas. Clinton had to rely on Republicans in the Congress to pass NAFTA, and he paid a heavy political price. Clinton's support of the bill made many working class voters furious, particularly in declining industrial states like Ohio and Michigan. The labor vote would not turn out for Democrats at the usual level in the 1994, one factor leading to the Republican takeover of Congress for the first time since the 1950s that year. This also dampened labor efforts to support Clinton's health-care reform efforts. Meanwhile, the Magaziner task force labored away trying to produce a legislative draft—a process that would take two more months. Suddenly the wind in Clinton's health-care sails disappeared, to be replaced by inaction, confusion, and demoralization, especially among reform advocates who saw passing from their control the best chance they would ever have to secure success.

Into the vacuum strode the Republican opposition, which had been waiting to savage the president's plan precisely because of its gargantuan size, its incomprehensibility, and its apparent threat to small business and individual choice. The Republicans, however, didn't get very far in their effort to destroy the proposal. Clinton rebounded once again toward the end of his first year with some notable legislative successes such as the ratification of NAFTA, the Brady Bill, passage of his deficit reduction package, creation of Americorps, and a new, more liberal voter registration bill, all of which helped Clinton regain momentum on his health-care initiative. Then bad press coverage of the Whitewater land deal overwhelmed Clinton. The Republican Congress launched an investigation into a murky Arkansas land deal involving the president and the First Lady while Bill Clinton was still governor. The Clintons lost money on the investment, but Republicans made confusing charges of criminal misconduct and got a special prosecutor, Kenneth Starr, appointed to investigate the matter. A White House lawyer and close friend of the Clintons, Vince Foster, committed suicide. Right-wing talk show hosts like Rush Limbaugh spread the false claim that Foster had been murdered because he knew something about Whitewater, even though repeated police investigations confirmed that the man's gunshot wounds were self-inflicted. Stories also still percolated about the president's marital infidelities, prompted in part by a sexual harassment lawsuit filed by an Arkansas woman, Paula Jones.

Notwithstanding a determined last-minute effort by Senate moderates to devise a compromise plan, the Clinton health-care initiative was doomed. As late as December 1993, Clinton enjoyed a 17-point margin of approval for his proposal; by March 1994, all support had evaporated with a new majority now saying they opposed health-care legislation.

To a large extent Clinton was responsible for the defeat of health care, and he openly admitted his culpability to reporters. "We made the error of trying to do too much, took too long, and ended up achieving nothing," he declared in an interview with Haynes Johnson and David Broder. Compounding his legislative digressions was the fact that Clinton went outside the system with his task force approach, slighting and thus alienating key congressional leaders as well as vital members within his own administration, whose knowledge and experience in health-care matters would have been most valuable to his cause. Finally, he failed on the critical terrain of timing and momentum, which any politician will admit is perhaps the most important factor in determining a bill's success or failure.

THE 1994 REPUBLICAN COUNTER REVOLUTION

The Right's Momentary Triumph

Largely as a result of Clinton's failed health-care proposal, the Republican opposition seized the opportunity to initiate its counterrevolution against Clintonian liberalism. The Republican right, led by such stalwarts as Newt Gingrich in the House and Texan Phil Gramm in the Senate, had been waiting since the first day of the Clinton's presidency to, as Gramm put it, "blow this train [Clinton's administration] up." After the health-care debacle, Gin-

Senator Dick Durbin (D-IL) talks at the podium on the issue of handgun control. In the wheelchair to his left is James Brady, who was hit by gunfire when John Hinkley shot at President Reagan. The Brady Act is a congressional law mandating that state law enforcement agencies conduct criminal background checks prior to allowing an individual to purchase a handgun.

grich insisted that Republicans unite in total opposition. Even Senator Bob Dole of Kansas, certainly no Far Right ideologue, joined with the hardliners, not wanting to jeopardize his hopes for the 1996 Republican presidential nomination. Clinton faced an implacable opposition that brooked no dissent and set out from the beginning to demonize the president. Referring to several famous, decisive battles, Gingrich believed health-care reform would be the Democrats' "Stalingrad, their Gettysburg, their Waterloo." In short, Gingrich would defeat Clinton and proceed to lead a Republican counterrevolution that would attempt to destroy the liberal ramparts that the Democrats had built over the preceding six decades.

Two years after *Time* magazine called him the "second chance" for the sixties generation, Clinton received a resounding vote of no confidence from the American people. In the 1994 mid-term congressional elections, the Republican Party gained 9 Senate seats, 52 House seats, and 11 governorships, winning control of both houses of Congress in the process. As one member of the Democratic Leadership Conference observed, "The New Deal is over; the nails are in the coffin; New Deal liberalism is dead and buried." As Democratic consultant Ted Van Dyke believed, "It's over. The president is done. He's finished. He's like the old cartoon where the guy has just had his head sliced off in a fencing match. He just hasn't noticed it yet, but as soon as he tried to turn or stand up, his head is going to topple right off his back."

Gingrich emerged as the main architect of his party's counterrevolutionary agenda, the "**Contract With America**." The contract consisted of ten objectives, but the most immediate and urgent were cutting taxes, passing a balanced budget amendment, and reducing the bloated government bureaucracy and radical welfare reform. From his position as the newly-elected Speaker of the House, Gingrich sought to whip his minions into united, disciplined soldiers committed to enacting their own anti-Rooseveltian "hundred days," certain the American people wanted such reform. One after another, bills were brought to the floor for votes. There were no hearings; legislators did not even know what they were voting on. Clinton, of course, became an object of ridicule: an emasculated, irrelevant bystander, watching an unstoppable machine tear to pieces not only his agenda, but the last vestiges of New Deal liberalism as well. The counterrevolution appeared triumphant. "We are finally seeing where [the Republican contract has] been carrying us," Russell Baker acidly noted in the *New York Times*. "Dr. Kevorkian is now waiting in the parlor. He's about to be shown upstairs to finish off the government we have known for sixty years." (Kevorkian was a Michigan pathologist who advocated the legalization of euthanasia for suffering, terminally ill patients. In the early 1990s he began assisting such people to commit suicide and was acquitted of murder three times before being convicted of second degree murder in 1999.)

Contributing significantly to the resurgence of the Republican Party was the appearance of re-energized conservative, evangelical religious sentiment across the nation. The movement had somewhat abated during the Reagan-Bush years, largely because evangelical leaders believed both presidents supported their agenda, at least tacitly. However, with the allegedly non-believing Clintons and their liberal cohorts in charge of the government, the evangelicals believed it was time to resurrect their crusade against the godless and liberals. Clinton's notorious philandering and his wife's feminism only added fuel to the evangelical fire. The Religious Right perceived the Clintons and their supporters as the most un-Christian administration to ever inhabit the White House.

The Religious Right gained control of important local institutions such as school boards, city councils, and other public forums. There also emerged within this movement, more extremist sects who sought to remove themselves entirely from the temptations of contemporary American society. One such group of dissidents was the **Branch Davidian** cult led by David Koresh, who established their church (a barracks-style compound) near Waco, Texas in the early 1990s. Federal officials had long suspected that Koresh and his followers were a potentially dangerous para-military organization who had been stockpiling illegal firearms. Equally attracted to the fundamentalist fringe were white-supremacist militia organizations, which also rejected contemporary America. This radical fringe of conservatism believed that the federal government represented the greatest threat to American freedom and in order to protect their rights, they believed it essential to arm themselves to fend off oppressive authority. Such was the platform of groups like Aryan Nation, *Posse Comitatus*, and other self-proclaimed "Christian patriots." Such fanatics found safe havens for their withdrawal and fortresses in the more remote rural regions of the Far West and Rocky Mountain states.

In early 1993, U.S. Bureau of Alcohol, Tobacco, and Firearms (ATF) agents went to Waco to arrest Koresh and his followers for the illegal possession of firearms. When the ATF approached the buildings, Koresh and his followers opened fire, killing four agents. After the initial skirmish, a 51-day stand-off ensued. Finally, Attorney General Janet Reno approved a new assault on the compound. A fire broke out during this raid and eventually 86 members of the sect, including 25 children, died.

For Far Right extremists, the Waco debacle transformed Koresh into a martyr who had defended both gun

The Multiculturalism Debate

E Pluribus Unum, the nation's motto declares: "Out of many, one." As a result of the rights revolutions of the 1960s and early 1970s, the ideal of a common national culture has proven illusionary, which has witnessed the proliferation of greater assertiveness among increasing numbers of ethnic Americans to preserve their respective cultural identities and heritage against the indignation and tirades of "old stock" (WASP) Americans who demand such uniformity. The debate spilled over into the classroom, especially in the disciplines of history and literature and how they should be more "inclusive" to diversity and multiculturalism—two dynamics many WASP Americans struggle to embrace.

The multiculturalism debate has taken many forms, as advocates for women, African Americans, Native Americans, Hispanics, Asian Americans, and gays and lesbians protested the way traditional education had ignored or marginalized them. Even evangelical Christians, once the dominant culture group, complained that the academic world slighted them and devalued their beliefs. In English departments throughout institutions of higher education, academics debated whether to continue to teach the literature of "dead white European males" or to offer students new courses to increase their awareness of works by women, persons of color, and Third World writers. Historians producing textbooks and their respective publishers scrambled to give more space not only to "minorities."

Not all academicians rushed headlong to "revise" either American history or literature. Their arose the inevitable "backlash" to this supposed obsession among "the liberal elite" and other left-leaning revisionists to be more "politically correct," "sensitive," and "inclusionary," even though, according to traditionalists, the various peoples demanding inclusion had produced very little intellectually or aesthetically to warrant such recognition. In short, the **pluribus** had prevailed over the **unum**. Such were the assertions of such scholars as E.D. Hirsch, Jr. (***Cultural Literacy: What Every American Needs to Know*** (1987) and of the University of Chicago classicist Alan Bloom, an unabashed elitist who lamented the erosion of standards, which he believed the "political correctness" movement had caused, while calling for the resurrection of an intellectual elite who would regenerate the great themes of Western (white) Civilization and bring them back into the American college classroom. Bloom disdained the politics, social conflict, and mass culture, which he contended reflected the potential divisive nature of multiculturalism. Even the venerable, liberal historian Arthur Schlesinger Jr., in The Disuniting of America (1991), urged a renewed effort to define a common core of American citizenship and culture. Finally, historians warned that the impulse to enhance the self-esteem of minority groups might encourage "shoddy history."

The dispute naturally spilled over into politics as individuals from Lyn Cheney, (spouse of former vice-president Dick Cheney, who was also Defense Secretary under George H.W. Bush) whom Reagan appointed as head of the National Endowment for the Humanities, used her agency to battle multiculturalism, to the reactionary columnist Pat Buchanan, who briefly ran for president in 1992 and who at the Republican Convention in Houston in that year, rallied the Right-wing of the party by stridently summoning cheering supporters to take back "our cities, our culture, and our country," all of which in Buchanan's view had fallen into the hands of "minorities," the majority of whom had no cultural or historical legacy of "greatness." Buchanan's remarks reflected the obvious inherent racism and ethnocentrism to be found in the multicultural debate, especially in those opposed to inclusion. Such individuals have idealized, erroneous notions about an America that never really existed in which there was a supposed sense of cultural unity and intellectual harmony. Such has never been the case in the nation's history, and a close look at history from ancient Greece onward shows not harmony but conflict remarkably similar to our current own fragmentation and raucous conflicts.

In reality, it has only been in the last 25 years that U.S. historians have become more inclusive and thus more accurate in their interpretations of the nation's historical past and development. Until the late 1980s, most courses in both history and literature did focus on the exploits and writings of white males elites of European origin. In U.S. history courses, Indians appeared solely as a quickly vanishing foe, blacks mainly as victims of slavery, and Hispanics and Asian Americans hardly at all. Absent as well was working class culture, of whatever ethnic character. Few women merited notice, but the historical experience of women as a whole—one-half of the population—was pretty much ignored. As these groups asserted themselves politically, they demanded recognition in the pages of both history and literary texts. The multiculturalism debate has in fact pumped new energy into education. Textbooks and course syllabi now more closely reflect the ethnic and gender realities of the larger society. Students vigorously debate issues of gender, race, and social class that they once accepted without question.

ownership and Christian separatism (the belief of some extremists that Christians should withdraw from a supposedly anti-religious American society and create their own homeland governed by Old Testament laws). Tragically, it was only a matter of time before one of their militia groups would seek revenge for Koresh's murder. The nation became acutely aware of the violent nature of such groups when, on April 19, 1995, precisely two years after the Waco incident, Timothy McVeigh and Terry Nichols, two ex-U.S. Army soldiers associated with right-wing militias, exploded a fertilizer truck bomb in front of the **Alfred P. Murrah Federal Building in Oklahoma City,** killing 168 people. At the time, it was the most deadly terrorist attack on U.S. soil. Though initial news reports of the tragedy openly speculated that the attack might have been the handiwork of a militant Islamic terrorist organization, authorities arrested McVeigh within hours of the bombing on a misdemeanor traffic violation and charged him in connection with the bombing just three days later. After a trial in federal court, a jury convicted McVeigh of capital murder and conspiracy to overthrow the government. He was given the death penalty (carried out in June 2001), while Nichols received a life sentence without the possibility of parole.

Domestic terrorism also assumed political and ideological manifestations. Medical clinics that provided abortion services to women became prime targets. Although the ratio of abortions to live pregnancies had been declining since the late 1970s, rabid right-to-lifers became even more bellicose in the 1990s. **Operation Rescue** emerged as the vanguard of such fanaticism, which launched its crusade against abortion in a much-publicized blockade of three abortion clinics in Wichita, Kansas in September 1991. Although the blockade ended peacefully after 46 days, anti-abortion protests became increasingly violent in its aftermath. Several doctors and other medical providers were murdered outside their clinics in the early 1990s. In 1994, with Bill Clinton's support, Congress passed the Freedom of Access to Clinic Entrance Act, which provided protection to any abortion clinic requesting such service. Despite the passage of the act, the attacks on clinics continued throughout the rest of the decade, resulting in 19 bombings of abortion clinics and the murder of 42 doctors, nurses, and other medical providers.

Perhaps nowhere at the time did Gingrich Republicanism resonate better than in California, where voters in 1994 enacted a state ballot initiative—**Proposition 187**—to halt illegal immigrant access to vital social services such as prenatal and childbirth care, child welfare, public education, and non-emergency health care. The measure's passage reflected the belated effect of the 1978 property tax revolt in California, which had frozen most property taxes, costing local government more than $200 billion in badly needed revenue. One of the most disastrous repercussions of this earlier conservative backlash was the end of California's reign for having the best public education system in the nation from the elementary school to the university. By the 1990s, the state's schools, particularly at the elementary and secondary levels, had deteriorated sharply, to levels that had historically been associated with the far poorer South.

The passing of Proposition 187 also reflected white Californians' historical tendency toward nativism and racism. Similar to the bigotry toward Asians in the late twentieth and early twenty-first centuries, conservative white Californians were greatly dismayed by the large numbers of Mexican immigrants flooding into their state, blaming them for California's economic declension. An infamous TV spot broadcast during the 1994 campaign showed illegal Mexican immigrants pouring through a San Diego border checkpoint, with the ominous background voice declaring "They keep coming." The statute galvanized California's Latino population, who would soon take out their anger in the polls against Republican politicians. As a result, the Republican Party lost a majority of Mexican-American voters in the state for at least a generation. Although federal courts later overturned Proposition 187, the immigration controversy only intensified in the coming years, becoming one of the most divisive issues affecting the nation.

The country's political polarization was matched by growing racial tensions, first displayed in the riots in south-central Los Angeles in the aftermath of the Rodney King trial and then again in 1995, as tens of millions of Americans watched with rapt attention the murder trial of football legend O.J. Simpson for allegedly having killed his former white wife, Nicole, and her white male friend, Ronald Goldman. For nine months Simpson's televised trial saturated the airwaves and print media from the most respected publications to the tabloids. The spectacle even captivated the international community. Sixty percent of all African Americans believed Simpson innocent while 75 percent of white Americans believed him guilty. Simpson's high-powered defense team led by legendary African-American trial lawyer, Johnny Cochran, exploited the nation's racial divide, charging detectives who investigated the murder with racism and portraying their client as the victim of a racially tainted system of justice—the same prejudiced system that had acquitted four years earlier the police who had beaten Rodney King. Simpson's acquittal in October 1995 by a jury of nine blacks, two whites, and one Hispanic once again revealed the racial biases that still constituted the diverging social and legal realities of white and black Americans. News of the verdict precipitated outpourings of jubilation in many African-American communities throughout the nation. To others, the justice system favored the wealthy who could afford the services of slick lawyers who could expertly plant the seeds of reasonable doubt in the minds of jurors in ways better than less-skilled attorneys for poor defendants.

The decade of the 1990s also witnessed the resurgence of Black Nationalism and separatism as the Black Muslim movement led by the frequently impolitic and inflammatory Louis Farrakhan attempted to attract alienated black males to his crusade for greater black solidarity. Answering Farrakhan's call for such a cause, hundreds of thousands of African-American men participated in a "**Million Man March**" in 1996 to the nation's capital where they peacefully assembled on the mall in Washington, D.C. to affirm their unity and dignity. Leaders of the march, the largest African-American political rally in the capital, made no demands on the government but implored black men to refrain from behaviors injurious not only to themselves but the black community as well and devote themselves to redeeming the black family and the African-American community, both of which had witnessed moral and economic decline since the 1980s. Although often shrill, white-baiting, and anti-Semitic in his speeches, Farrakhan nonetheless believed that the black community traveled on a path of self-destruction if black men, in particular, did not assume greater responsibility by embracing their role as fathers and caretakers and as the progenitors of black pride and solidarity.

Another important episode involving the national racial divide took place in 1996 when California enacted an initiative that banned affirmative action in the University of California system relative to student admissions criteria and hiring by state agencies, further polarizing white and black Americans Since the late 1960s, most university administrators and corporate executives had supported affirmative action, for they saw diversity as a key to business success in a multiracial society. Reputable studies demonstrated that African Americans admitted to mostly white universities as a result of affirmative action graduated as readily as any other group of students, thereby implying that they simply needed equal access to opportunity. Research further showed that African-American graduates started careers in the professions, government, and in the private sector in numbers even greater than their white peers. Nonetheless, conservatives argued that affirmative action had become code for "reverse discrimination," and that African Americans, women, and other minorities received preferential treatment when it came to job opportunities and admission to universities. As a result, white males had become the victims of prejudice. Conservatives further argued that affirmative action made a mockery of the sanctity of advancement by merit. The debate over affirmative action turned into an argument over the degree to which racism (and sexism) remained a reality in American society.

On affirmative action and other issues, Congressional Republicans could claim no national consensus. As Gingrich and his cohorts actively challenged the liberal landscape, they never stopped to think that perhaps they might be pushing the people too fast and too hard to accept their counterrevolution. Indeed, only 38 percent of eligible voters had turned out at the polls in the Republican landslide of 1994, perhaps reflecting that the American people did not embrace the Gingrich Revolution and the Republican "Contract" with America as enthusiastically as the party believed. The Gingrich Republicans ignored the reluctance of the American people to take radical leaps, either backward or forward, without adequate discussion and negotiation. Within a few months of what appeared to be the end of liberalism, the American people began questioning the wisdom of policies enacted so quickly. Were there not some government programs worth preserving, even expanding, such as those protecting the environment? Equally alarming to many Americans was the fact that a high percentage of the newly-elected Republicans had no prior political experience and had won simply because of their ideological connection to powerful Far Right groups such as Ralph Reed's Christian Coalition. As a result, increasing numbers of Americans wondered whether the individuals just elected were acting in their interests or were they nothing more than the pawns of conservative special interest groups. To many Americans, vilifying Clinton seemed to be what motivated these Republicans rather than serving the nation. By September 1995, less than a year after their supposed mandate, conservatives found themselves "on the run," as 58 percent of the American people disapproved of the job Congress was doing.

Although bruised and battered, Clinton, to the surprise of many, came out fighting, determined to triumph over those trying to destroy his presidency. In the months between the Republicans' victory and his reemergence, Clinton developed a new strategy for reclaiming and redefining the vital center of American politics. The Democrats had lost the 1994 congressional elections because Clinton's health-care proposal, NAFTA, and other measures had alienated the white middle class, who felt betrayed because he had assured them in 1992 that he was a new Democrat with fresh ideas. Clinton had promised voters that he was not a traditional liberal. Yet, the Republicans succeeded in 1994 to paint him with that "old" Democratic brush. If Clinton hoped to once again "come back" (Bill Clinton earned the nickname the "Comeback Kid" for his second-place finish in the New Hampshire primary in 1992.), he had to recast his image back into the New Democrat mold that brought him to the Oval Office.

In 1995 the president and Congress battled over the budget. Republicans forced a 28-day government shutdown starting in late 1995 when they refuse to authorize an interim appropriations resolution for temporary funding to keep agencies operational. The impasse resulted in nonessential federal government employees and many government services being suspended.

After the confrontation ended, Clinton flooded Congress with an array of measures, including a bill that put 100,000 new police on the streets, giving life sentences to criminals convicted three times of felonies, limiting to two years people on welfare, cutting the deficit, and even addressing the controversial issue of affirmative action, which he agreed the initiative's excesses had to be kept in check. As Clinton said, "mend it, don't end it." Clinton's agenda reflected a retrenchment of liberal policies. Naturally, Clinton's legislative barrage went far toward bolstering and reinforcing his image as a reasonable centrist as opposed to the radical Republicans in Congress. The strategy worked; by the end of 1995, Clinton's poll ratings were soaring while those of Newt Gingrich and the Republican Congress plummeted.

Clinton's counterattack became complete when he declared in his State of the Union Address in January 1996 that, "The era of big government is over." With that one line, Clinton took all the wind out of the Republican sails. No longer could the Republicans criticize either Clinton or his party for being traditional liberals, advocates of big government, and still tied to the old New Deal coalitions. Indeed, no matter how hard Republicans tried to paint Clinton as a classic liberal, the president could dismiss such charges by pointing to deficit reduction, a tough crime bill, and a commitment to welfare reform.

THE 1996 ELECTION: Clintonian Liberalism Vindicated and Triumphant

For many observers, the 1996 presidential election was over the day Bill Clinton gave his January 1996 State of the Union address. Yet, the Republicans continued to believe that Clinton's resurgence was momentary and fleeting. With such confidence, the party chose the moderate senator from Kansas, Robert Dole, as their standard bearer. They wisely stayed away from Gingrich and other hard-right candidates. Although frequently vituperative in his attacks on Clinton, Dole was comparatively benign compared to his more rabid Republican colleagues. His criticism of Clinton was rarely personal or mean-spirited. He focused his assaults on Clintonian liberalism and the policies it had produced, as well as on the Democratic Party's alleged excesses. People trusted Dole (he had a 62 percent approval rating in 1995, compared to 35 percent for Gingrich and 45 percent for Clinton), and he appeared to put country over partisanship. On the downside, Dole was the oldest person ever to run for president—he was 73 at the time, a World War II veteran—and despite his good health, he was of another generation. To many Americans, especially among the majority Baby-Boomers, he represented a step backward. Also undermining Dole's chances was the fact that extreme right groups, such as the Christian Coalition, still had tremendous influence within the party. Clinton could thus portray Dole and the Republicans as extremists. Never a person given to soaring rhetoric, Dole's unimpassioned speeches and phlegmatic personality created the image that the senator, although an individual of unimpeachable integrity and pragmatism, lacked vision and energy. As his own chief campaign strategist observed, "Dole's strength is [that] what you see is what you get. Dole's weakness is [that] what you see is what you get."

Within weeks it became clear that the younger more charismatic Clinton possessed the advantage. The Clinton staff brilliantly portrayed Dole as Gingrich clone, always picturing the two together, intimating that by association Gingrich was Dole's running mate, not New York congressman and ex-Buffalo Bills quarterback, Jack Kemp. By Election Day, it was a foregone conclusion that Clinton would triumph in one of the most amazing political comebacks in modern American history. Winning almost 50 percent of the popular vote and 70.4 percent of the Electoral College, Clinton succeeded in his strategy of presenting himself as a centrist running against an older generation captive of narrow interests and shrill partisanship. In contrast to 1992, independent candidate Ross Perot's impact was minimal in 1996 (he garnered only 8 percent of the popular vote compared to 19 percent four years earlier), and his presence hurt the Republicans more than the Democrats. Clinton without question benefited from a burgeoning economy. He ran particularly well among African Americans, women, and Hispanics. The Latino electorate, which had increased substantially over recent decades, swung sharply to the Democrats, largely because of the Republicans' anti-immigration positions. As a result, Mexican American voters began migrating to the Democratic Party. In both 1996 and 1998, their wholesale shift into the Democratic column locked up

Bill, Hillary, and Chelsea Clinton walking down Pennsylvania Avenue. January 20, 1997.
Photo credits: Clinton Presidential Materials Project

California for Clinton and his party, and in subsequent elections, the Latino vote helped to turn the Golden State solidly "blue."

Although soundly defeating Dole, Clinton's victory was not a mandate. Despite some loss of seats in the House, the Republicans retained control of Congress, even gaining additional seats in the Senate and several new governorships. Democrats still held a majority of seats in state legislatures, a sign that many voters found ticket splitting (voting for both Democrats and Republicans at varying levels of office) to be a sensible course. Many experts concluded that voters had made a decision for "divided government," not for one party over another. In the minds of many Americans, a balanced government was what was now needed. Reforms, yes, if targeted to specific problems and limited in expense and a leaner government, yes, but not if it meant jeopardizing the environment, entitlements such as Medicare, or government guarantees of fundamental rights. In essence, the American people seemed to be directing their political leaders to stay the middle course.

BILL CLINTON AND THE WORLD:
Clintonian Foreign Policy

In foreign affairs, the Clinton administration made important inroads. For nearly half a century, anticommunism and the global rivalry with the Soviet Union determined much of the nation's policymaking agenda. With the breakup of the Soviet Union and the dissolution of the Eastern Bloc, the United States no longer had to worry about monolithic communism and thus needed to redefine national security to fit a multipolar world. To the surprise of many who believed his understanding of foreign policy issues and *realpolitick* was marginal at best, Clinton understood this and promoted an expansive, internationalist vision of improved relations with the United Nations (UN), reinforcing the North Atlantic Treaty Organization (NATO), advancing human rights and democracy abroad, reducing nuclear threats, working on global environmental concerns, and advocating free-market policies. Clinton believed the United States could replace the Cold War strategy of containment with a foreign policy that reflected larger humanitarian goals in conjunction with an equally important objective of enlarging "the world's free community of market democracies" under U.S. leadership.

With the United States now indisputably the world's dominant power, Clinton believed he could settle long-standing international conflicts by moral suasion and bring about the end of totalitarians' repression and brutality by making the support for human rights the most important foundation in international relations. It was on this basis that the "Clinton Doctrine" evolved.

Clinton Doctrine and The People's Republic of China

The first application of the Clinton Doctrine occurred during the president's first year in office in response to tensions that had emerged between the United States and the People's Republic of China (PRC). Clinton inherited a less than cordial relationship with the PRC from his predecessor, who had been pressured by Congress to impose economic sanctions on China in the aftermath of the Tiananmen Square massacre. That particularly violent oppression by China's totalitarian government resulted in the killing by government troops of some 3,000 pro-democracy demonstrators and the wounding of 10,000 more in the summer of 1989. International television news agencies broadcast the massacre and subsequent attacks live, provoking condemnation of the Chinese government around the world. The Bush administration was especially embarrassed by this crisis, for the president had recently negotiated a series of trade agreements with China, extending to "Most Favored Nation" status, which, would allow Chinese goods to enter U.S. markets after paying minimal tariffs, if any.

During the 1992 election campaign, Clinton accused Bush of "coddling" China despite that nation's reputation for being one of the world's worst violators of human rights. No sooner was Clinton in the White House, than all such rhetoric ceased. Indeed, Clinton completely reversed his position, declaring that he believed China had seen the error of its ways and that the U.S. should now be looking for "hopeful seeds of change." The new president thus recommended restoring China's **Most Favored Nation status**, despite the PRC's continued religious and cultural persecution in Tibet. The PRC remained a formidable world power, with the planet's greatest number of human beings, the fastest growing economy, a nuclear arsenal, and a veto in the UN Security Council. In short, Clinton believed his predecessor's economic sanctions to be too harsh, leading to reprisals that could backfire on the United States by adversely affecting the nation's economy. Clinton believed that the most effective way for the United States to advance democracy in totalitarian countries such as China was to promote free enterprise, which Clinton believed would ultimately force from within the collapse of politically oppressive regimes. Clinton used the same approach in other countries noted for their human rights repressions such as Turkey, Saudi Arabia, and Indonesia.

Middle East

Clinton strongly supported the Oslo (Norway) Accords, negotiated between Israel and the Palestine Liberation Organization (PLO) in which Israel for the first time in its history recognized the PLO's legitimacy to speak and govern on behalf of the Palestinian people living in Israeli territory. The accords appeared to be a monumental step

Prime Minister of Israel, Yitzhak Rabin, President Clinton, and Yasser Arafat, chairman of the Palestine Liberation Organization, shaking hands in an electrifying ceremony. September 1993 Photo credits: Clinton Presidential Materials Project

toward peace in the Middle East. Unfortunately, when it came time for implementation, both sides retracted, with local Israeli officials expanding Jewish settlements on Palestinian land in the West Bank—a part of Jordan seized by Israel during the 1967 Six-Day War. Such action by the Israelis upset the Palestinians because the West Bank was the region they had hoped would become the new Palestinian state. Compounding the territorial issues was the corruption, powerlessness, and inability of the new Palestinian Authority, which became the PLO's governing body in the West Bank, to stop the rise of extremist groups from other Arab countries infiltrating into the area determined to bring about the violent destruction of Israel. Clinton worked assiduously to try to make the accords work, for he knew that one of the main keys to peace and stability in all the Middle East was the ending of the long-standing enmity between Israel and the PLO. By the end of his presidency, Clinton had succeeded in bringing the two belligerents to Camp David to try to work out a final peace treaty, hoping to leave a legacy similar to that of Jimmy Carter's, who delivered the milestone Camp David Accords at the end of his tenure, establishing an enduring peace between Egypt and Israel. Such good fortune was not in the cards for Clinton, whose attempt at rapprochement failed. Tragically, violence once again became the order of the day between Israel and the PLO. An Israeli opposed to the peace process assassinated Prime Minister Yitzhak Rabin in 1995 and his government was soon replaced with hardliners favoring a more combative stance towards the Palestinians. When Yassir Arafat died in 2004, Palestinian extremists took control of the Gaza Strip bordering Egypt and they frequently fired rockets into Israel, provoking a violent response from their antagonists.

Africa

Clinton found it difficult to balance concern for human rights with the nation's strategic and economic interests and to formulate clear guidelines for humanitarian intervention abroad. Perhaps nowhere during the Clinton years did this contradiction more tragically and graphically appear than in the central African nation of Rwanda, which in 1994 witnessed one of the worst interethnic civil wars. Members of the Hutu ethnic group controlling the Rwandan government began openly encouraging violence against the ethnic Tutsis by private citizens, and Hutu militias launched a campaign of genocide. Over 800,000 people were slaughtered and 2 million more fled the country while the Clinton administration did nothing but utter rhetorical condemnations. The UN and the French (Rwanda had once been a French colonial possession) ultimately intervened with troops, but only after the killing had decimated the country. In retrospect Clinton knew he tragically mishandled the Rwandan crisis and that his failure to intervene to stop the butchery will forever taint his legacy. In the end, Clinton sacrificed his own inherent sense of humanity to appease the more callous, non-interventionist mentality of those advisers and citizens who believed that only those regions of the world of the most vital interest to the United States warranted American intervention to stop acts of brutal violence upon innocent people. Tragically, Rwanda did not fall into that category.

One of the most perplexing issues confronting Clinton involved revamping the U.S. military for the post-Cold War world and under what exigencies should U.S. troops be sent abroad either as peacekeepers or to help restore order or to protect a legitimate government from revolutionary forces from either the right or the left wanting to overthrow it. Americans were torn on these issues, some believing it was time for retrenchment, or a new isolationism and "America first," while others maintained that the worst thing the United States could do was to turn its back on the world. Clinton sought a middle ground between the isolationists and those wanting new, more expansive international commitments.

Clinton's policies were tested early in his first administration with several trouble spots sparking debate. In the African country of Somalia, ravaged by famine and civil war, powerful, brutal warlords took over the country. In the final days of his administration, President George H.W. Bush ordered American troops, under the umbrella of a UN humanitarian mission, into Somalia to help deliver food and provide relief support. As local warlords increased attacks on the multi-national peacekeeping force, and killed rising numbers of soldiers from Pakistan and other countries involved in the relief effort, American soldiers intensified their effort to capture the chief instigator of the assaults, warlord Mohamed Farrah Aidid. Unfortunately, the mission ended disastrously as U.S. troops suffered well-publicized and graphically depicted casualties in the media. The public, more in an isolationist mood than a humanitarian disposition, pressured Clinton to pull American forces out, which he did in the spring of 1994. In retrospect it appeared Clinton had miscalculated the American public's readiness to deploy troops to liberate oppressed people, particularly those living in underdeveloped nations. For many Americans, seeing a dead U.S. soldier being dragged through the streets of a Somali city by a jubilant mob who were ostensibly recipients of the West's good will was more than they could bear. Many Americans were no longer willing to sacrifice their young men to what some saw as the vicious brutality of an ungrateful people.

Other Crises

Closer to home, in Haiti, U.S. interests seemed clearer, and Clinton vowed to help reestablish Haiti's ousted president, Jean Bertrand Aristide (who was deposed again in 2004). In September 1994, the first 3,000 of a projected 15,000 American troops landed in Haiti in cooperation with the UN, and last minute negotiations by former president Jimmy Carter persuaded the Haitian military to peacefully step aside. After six months with Aristide in power and political institutions functioning again, U.S. soldiers handed over the peacekeeping to UN forces. In the former Yugoslavia, the United States also committed troops, under NATO auspices, to halt the massacre of Bosnian Muslims by Christian Serbs and to oversee a cease-fire and peace building process that all parties to the conflict accepted in the 1995 U.S.-brokered **Dayton (Ohio) Accords**.

Beginning in 1998, the United States found itself once again in conflict with Iraqi president Saddam Hussein, who was now reneging on the agreements he had signed at the end of the Gulf War and refused to permit international inspectors to examine military sites in his country. Clinton responded by ordering a series of American bombing strikes at military targets inside Iraq.

In 1999 the president faced the most serious foreign policy crisis of his presidency, once again in the Balkans. This time the conflict involved a province of Serbian-dominated Yugoslavia—Kosovo—most of whose inhabitants were Albanian Muslims. Reminiscent of the Bosnian crisis, a savage civil war erupted in the region with Serbian forces accused once again of committing unspeakable atrocities on their enemies. Clinton and the world knew that Yugoslav president, the Christian Serb Slobodan Milosevic, was nothing more than a brutal dictator, pursuing another ethnic cleansing of his country. Clinton tried negotiating a settlement, but all such efforts failed. Thus, the president decided he had no choice but to use force to stop the genocide. Clinton unleashed a bombing campaign against the Serbs, which was successful in stopping Milosevic from engaging in further acts of genocide. The intense bombing of Serb forces resulted in a cease-fire and eventual withdrawal of Serb troops from Kosovo. No doubt Clinton's resolve and his willingness to use force to stop the genocide were responsible for the withdrawal and the possibility of future peace in the Balkans.

During the Clinton years, human rights played an increasingly important role in international affairs. By the 1990s hundreds of nongovernmental agencies had emerged throughout the world defining themselves as protectors of human rights. These various organizations ranged in focus from health care and women's issues to the rights of indigenous peoples like the Aborigines of Australia and the descendants of the original inhabitants of the Americas. Two of the most important were Amnesty International and Human Rights Watch, for their specialty was monitoring how governments treated their citizens. The proliferation of these coalitions not only strongly influenced world public opinion but, perhaps more importantly, provided justification for interventions in matters once considered to be the internal affairs of

Map 34.2 Breakup of Yugoslavia

sovereign nations. As a result of the human rights crusade, new institutions emerged for the purpose of finding and punishing those who had violated the rights of their citizens or those of another nation. The Rwandan genocide produced a UN-sponsored war crimes court that sentenced the country's former prime minister to life in prison. An international tribunal put Yugoslav president Slobodan Milosevic on trial for authorizing the massacre of thousands of Albanian civilians in Kosovo. Spanish and British Human Rights courts wanted to arrest and charge former Chilean dictator Augusto Pinochet with the murder of thousands of Chileans in the 1970s but Pinochet was too old and too ill to stand trial, eventually dying while the tribunals debated. It remained to be seen whether these initiatives would evolve into an effective international system of protecting human rights across national boundaries.

During the 1990s and first years of the new century, anxiety about international terrorism escalated. Americans within their own borders felt safer from terrorist attacks than the citizens of many other countries. Americans' sense of security, however, from such reprisals was shaken on February 6, 1993, when a small group associated with **Osama bin Laden,** a radical anti-American Saudi, bombed the World Trade Center in New York City. The terrorists used a rented van loaded with explosives that they parked and then exploded in an underground parking area under the Trade Center. The blast killed six people and injured a thousand more. The bin Laden-associated terrorists declared that their action was one of retaliation for U.S. policies in the Middle East. The attack represented the most destructive act of foreign terrorism committed on U.S. soil up to that time. In response, Congress, with Clinton's wholehearted approval, passed the Antiterrorism and Effective Death Penalty Act of 1996, which greatly expanded the budget and powers of federal authorities to monitor likely terrorists. Despite increased surveillance of terrorist organizations, bin Laden's Al Qaeda cadre struck another lethal blow. On August 7, 1998, car bombings of U.S. embassies in Kenya and Tanzania injured more than 5,500 people and killed 225. Although in the aftermath of these attacks the Clinton administration put forth concerted efforts to track down the culprits and break up terrorist bands such as Al Qaeda, bin Laden and his followers as well as other terrorist organizations seemed to disappear or go so far underground that U.S. intelligence could not find them. Unfortunately, Al Qaeda and its leader, Osama bin Laden, were regrouping and rearming, preparing to unleash upon the United States the most devastating attack on American soil in America's history.

Trade Agreements

One of Bill Clinton's principal foreign policy goals was to lower trade barriers, thus expanding U.S. global markets, which he believed essential to sustain the nation's economic boom and prosperity. Building on the Reagan-Bush legacy, Clinton argued that such policies would not only boost prosperity but also help promote democracy around the world. Consequently, his administration consummated several historic trade agreements. Despite opposition from labor unions who feared a loss of jobs, Clinton strongly backed the North American Free Trade Agreement (NAFTA), which called for cutting tariffs and eliminating other trade barriers between the United States, Canada, and Mexico over a 15-year period. After adding new provisions on labor and environmental issues in December 1993, Clinton muscled the bill through Congress in a close vote that depended on Republican support. NAFTA took effect on January 1, 1994. Then in early 1995, Mexico's severe debt crisis and a dramatic devaluation of its peso prompted Clinton to extend a $20 billion loan from America's Exchange Stabilization Fund, an unprecedented act that stabilized the Mexican economy. Clinton realized that economic chaos in Mexico could easily lead to political upheaval there, which in turn could impact the United States adversely, especially if violence erupted.

In the same context as NAFTA, Clinton completed the Uruguay Round of the General Agreement on Tariffs and Trade (GATT) in late 1993, and in early 1994, GATT was replaced by a new World Trade Organization (WTO), a more powerful multilateral group created to enlarge world trade by implementing new agreements and mediating disputes. Similarly, in February 1994, the U.S. ended its 19-year-old trade embargo against Vietnam, and American businesses began establishing relations with a regime that had once been cast as a major threat to U.S. global interests. Surprisingly, Clinton did not make such an overture to Cuba, which, excluding the missile crisis of the early 1960s, had never been a threat in any capacity to the United States. Apparently Clinton worried about the intense backlash reaching any understanding with the Castro regime would inspire in the often fiercely anti-Castro Cuban American community in Florida, a critical state on the Electoral College map. Moreover, many Americans still feared communism, and since Fidel was a professed Marxist, the U.S. simply could not have relations with such a regime.

THE CLINTON ECONOMY

Bill Clinton owed a great deal of his popularity to the booming economy that he presided over during his second term. The recession of 1990-91, which Clinton exploited to defeat George H.W. Bush, ended by Clinton's second year in office. From that point on, economic expansion continued for the rest of the decade. By his last year in office, national unemployment was below 4 percent, a figure not seen since the mid-1960s. Many economists had insisted that if unemployment remained that low, inflation would inevitably occur, the result of excessive consumer spending because everyone earned income from a job. Much to these economists' surprise, prices barely rose during the boom because rising world-wide oil production kept energy costs low, and weak unions and increased global competition made it difficult for workers to demand significant pay raises or for corporations to raise prices. The Clinton boom became the longest uninterrupted period of economic growth and general prosperity in the nation's history. Clinton not only garnered great political capital from the boom, but economic expansion also gave him the opportunity to address the massive budget deficits that he inherited from Bush and Reagan. Clinton worked assiduously to balance the federal budget—a primary focus of the fiscal conservatives traditionally associated with the Republican Party. Since protracted economic growth produced increased tax revenues, Clinton during his second term witnessed a balanced budget and budget surpluses—not only an accomplishment for a Democratic president but a rare occurrence for the majority of post-World War II presidents.

THE LEWINSKY DEBACLE AND THE CLINTON PRESIDENCY

No sooner was Bill Clinton reelected to his second term than his penchant for self-destruction began, minimizing the significance of even his positive accomplishments in domestic and foreign affairs. Clinton's undoing began at the height of his confrontation with Gingrich over the national budget in 1995. The government, in effect, was shut down because Congress failed to pass a year-long appropriations measure. The White House was operating around the clock, staffers and politicians running in and out with the latest news and strategies. One night, a 23-year-old intern named Monica Lewinsky brought dinner (pizza) to the president. Long attracted to Clinton, Lewinsky by her own admission initiated what became a torrid mutual seduction that supposedly never escalated to intercourse but did involve repeated oral sex, which on one occasion resulted in a semen stain on the blue dress Lewinsky was wearing. After about a year Clinton abruptly ended the affair. Phone calls, notes, and presents, however, between the two continued for several more months. Most damaging to the president was Lewinsky's sharing of her affair with a friend, Linda Tripp, who, unbeknownst to Lewinsky, was tape-recording their conversations. Almost a year after Clinton's second inauguration, the country began to learn piece by piece all the lurid details of Bill Clinton's tryst with a White House intern.

The Lewinsky story exploded into national (as well as world) headlines. Clinton's situation worsened with a sexual harassment lawsuit filed by a former Arkansas state employee named Paula Jones along with his alleged involvement in a shady land speculation enterprise called Whitewater. Compounding Clinton's problems was the appointment of arch-conservative Kenneth Starr as special prosecutor for the Whitewater investigation. In the meantime, Paula Jones had filed a federal lawsuit against Clinton, and over the president's objections, the Supreme Court unanimously ruled in May 1997 that the Jones lawsuit should not be deferred until Clinton left office, arguing that it would not sufficiently preoccupy the president to prevent him from conducting his presidential duties. On January 17, 1998, in testimony under oath in the Paula Jones case, lawyers surprised the president by asking if he ever had sex with Monica Lewinsky. Clinton declared, without hesitation, he had not. At the same time, a federal appeals court granted Kenneth Starr's request that his investigative purview in Whitewater be expanded to include the Lewinsky case. On January 21, Clinton unfortunately dug his grave deeper when he flatly denied ever having an affair with Lewinsky. "There is no sexual relationship," he said before TV cameras and later said, "I never had sex with that woman." Hillary Clinton, as she had done in the past, "stood by her man," telling the press that the story had no validity and that it was simply another manifestation of a right-wing conspiracy to destroy her husband.

While Clinton swore that no affair had taken place, evidence continued to mount that confirmed he was lying. Clinton lied to everyone, for the now famous (or infamous) blue dress stain revealed via a DNA test that the semen did come from Bill Clinton. Such undeniable evidence put the last nail in Clinton's coffin, making even his most ardent defenders suspicious that once again the Republican caricature of "Slick Willie" had more truth than falseness to it.

Called to testify before a grand jury Starr had convened to consider the Whitewater-related allegations,

Clinton finally admitted to what had now become a given, "I did have a relationship with Ms. Lewinsky that was not appropriate." By September 1998, Starr told Congress that he had "substantial and credible information" that Clinton had committed offenses that constituted grounds for impeachment because he lied when questioned about the Lewinsky affair in his deposition in the Paul Jones lawsuit. For the next three months, the nation watched as Congress heard and debated four different counts under which Starr wished Clinton indicted. On two of those four counts, most importantly that of perjury, the House of Representatives voted for impeachment. In the end, the U.S. Senate, acting as the jury of Clinton's guilt or innocence, acquitted him of the charges, allowing him to remain in office.

For many Americans, presidential lying about an affair did not constitute a national crisis, particularly when there were more serious issues to deal with. Although Clinton lied about his affair with Monica Lewinsky and did commit adultery, his actions did not violate the constitutional provisions of his office, nor did they at any time place the nation's welfare in jeopardy. Nonetheless, the impeachment process rendered immaterial whatever else Bill Clinton hoped to accomplish. He not only was a lame duck in the sense that he could not run again but also in his ability to push through any more meaningful legislation. Despite Clinton leaving office with his popularity higher than it had been when he began his presidency, his questionable moral behavior came back to haunt the Democratic Party and its candidate for the Oval Office in the 2000 election.

THE 2000 ELECTION

Although the 2000 presidential campaign started out with some interesting individuals seeking their respective party's nomination, in the end, the two nominees, Vice President Al Gore for the Democrats and Texas governor George W. Bush for the Republicans, delivered to the American people one of the most lackluster, boring hustings not seen since perhaps the 1988 contest between Michael Dukakis and George H.W. Bush. The end result proved far more important and engendered greater popular interest and concern than either candidate mustered during the entire campaign. At the outset, both eventual nominees had potentially formidable opponents. Gore had to contend with New Jersey Senator Bill Bradley, a former New York Knicks basketball star and Rhodes Scholar from Princeton. Bradley had always been more a progressive than a neo-liberal, possessing an almost Lincolnesque modesty and simplicity but deeply and sincerely committed to restoring to the Democratic Party the traditional liberal ethos. Expert on many issues and passionately devoted to racial justice, Bradley presented himself as a serious thinker. Though highly intelligent, Bradley proved to be a dull speaker and, as a centrist like the vice president, he was never able to articulate a clear difference between his positions and that of the Clinton/Gore administration. The campaign between Gore and Bradley bored the public and the former senator dropped out of the race before the end of the primary season. For his running mate, Gore chose centrist Senator Joseph Lieberman of Connecticut, the first Jewish vice-presidential nominee.

Arizona Senator John McCain, Bush's leading opponent, also represented a challenge to politics as usual. A Vietnam War hero and former prisoner of war, McCain had gained notoriety and acclaim within both parties by his advocacy of campaign finance reform, including legislation that would cap soft money contributions and the influence of big donors on the political process. McCain also articulated progressive ideas and policies on gay rights, the environment, immigration, and the forgotten plight of Native Americans. McCain was refreshingly candid and unafraid to speak his mind on a variety of other issues. Like Bradley, McCain seemed a breath of fresh air to programmed politicians whose every word was scripted by political consultants. Perhaps most important, McCain gave Bush a real scare, his integrity and honesty shining through for many Democrats and independents as well as Republicans. Bush's advisors ran a dirty campaign against McCain, and before the critical South Carolina primary an unknown group allied with Bush distributed a campaign flier that featured a picture of McCain's adopted daughter from Bangladesh. The flier aimed its pitch at racists and implied that McCain had fathered an illegitimate daughter with a black woman. McCain lost South Carolina and his campaign never recovered. However, the Arizona senator did not get the nomination. In the end, Bush rallied the support of party professionals and the Far Right on issues like abortion and in the process successfully painted McCain with the brush of a "renegade" who could not be trusted to adhere to party orthodoxy. Bush also won his party's nomination on the first ballot at the Republican convention held in Philadelphia. Bush chose as his running mate, Dick Cheney, former Secretary of Defense under Bush's father.

As the campaign entered its final months, the public came to associate Gore with the Clinton administration, which many believed had become rife with deceit and moral lassitude, especially in its last years. Many Democrats, including Gore, felt they had to distance themselves from Clinton as if he were a moral leper. Gore felt especially duped by Clinton, for he had stood by the president

Vice President Al Gore speaks at the 1997 dedication of the FDR Memorial, Washington D.C.

100 percent, defending his denials of an affair and praising his leadership. When the truth of Clinton's relationship with Monica Lewinsky came to light, Gore appeared a naïf. As the campaign progressed into the fall months, Bush appeared overall to be more genuine, less contrived in his responses, warmer, and more approachable. By contrast, Gore seemed detached, often condescending, and lacking in spontaneity and personality. Bush seemed more gracious and occasionally able to depart from his script as when he told one harsh questioner who asked what should be done about all those "bastards" born to women on welfare: "First, sir, we must remember that it is our duty to love all the children." Only occasionally did Gore respond spontaneously, and when he did, he seemed awkward and rambling in his articulation. He slavishly stuck to his script, as though anything he said that his consultants had not approved might be damaging to his campaign.

The 2000 Post-Election Debacle

By Election Day the race appeared a toss-up, so few Americans were surprised that the election proved to be one of the closest in history. No one, however, could have predicted just how close. Gore won the popular vote by 540,000 of 100 million votes cast, or one-half of one percent. Victory in the Electoral College hinged on which candidate had carried Florida. There amid widespread confusion at the polls and claims of voter suppression, fraud, and manipulation, Bush claimed a margin of a few hundred votes. In the days after the election, Democrats demanded a hand recount of the Florida ballots for which machines could not determine a voter's choice. The Florida Supreme Court agreed that such a request be granted. At this juncture, it began to dawn on Americans that this election might not be over for weeks.

Over a month after the election, on December 12, 2000, the Supreme Court ordered by a 5-4 vote, a halt to the recounting of the disputed ballots in the south Florida counties of Palm Beach, Broward, Miami-Dade, and Duval. The Court also allowed the state's secretary of state, Katherine Harris, to certify that Bush had carried the state and, therefore, won the presidency.

The *Bush v. Gore* decision represented one of the most peculiar verdicts in Supreme Court history. By the late 1990s, the Court had become much more federalist in outlook and rulings, returning increasing powers back to the states, especially affecting individuals claiming to be victims of discrimination and negating the power of Congress to force states to carry out federal government policies. Thus, in a move totally opposite of its new stance, the Court intervened at the state level to overturn the Florida Supreme Court decision regarding the state's election laws. Both Gore and Bush supporters and other observers did not expect the Court's intervention because the matter did not seem to raise a federal constitutional question. The justices defended their decision by invoking the "equal protection" clause of the Fourteenth Amendment, which they claimed required that all ballots within a state to be counted in accordance with a single standard—something impossible to accomplish given the wide variety of machines and paper ballots used in Florida. In effect, the Court's majority ordered the vote-counting process stopped because Florida voters were being treated unequally; only certain counties (Palm Beach, Miami-Dade, and Broward) had been singled out, which the Gore camp should not have allowed. Rather, they should have insisted upon a total manual recount of the entire state, which they had initially and then unwisely rejected. Perhaps most disturbing about the Court's intervention was the declaration that its ruling only pertained to this single case—that this new constitutional principle would not be applied to other states that had voting systems as complex as Florida's.

Rarely had a decision so intensely divided the Court or the nation. The dissenting judges wrote with disdain and contempt of the Court's majority decision. Justice John Stevens declared that the ruling "can only lend credence to the most cynical appraisal of the work of judges throughout the land." Justice David Souter seconded Stevens' assessment, stating "there is no justification for denying the State the opportunity to try to count all dis-

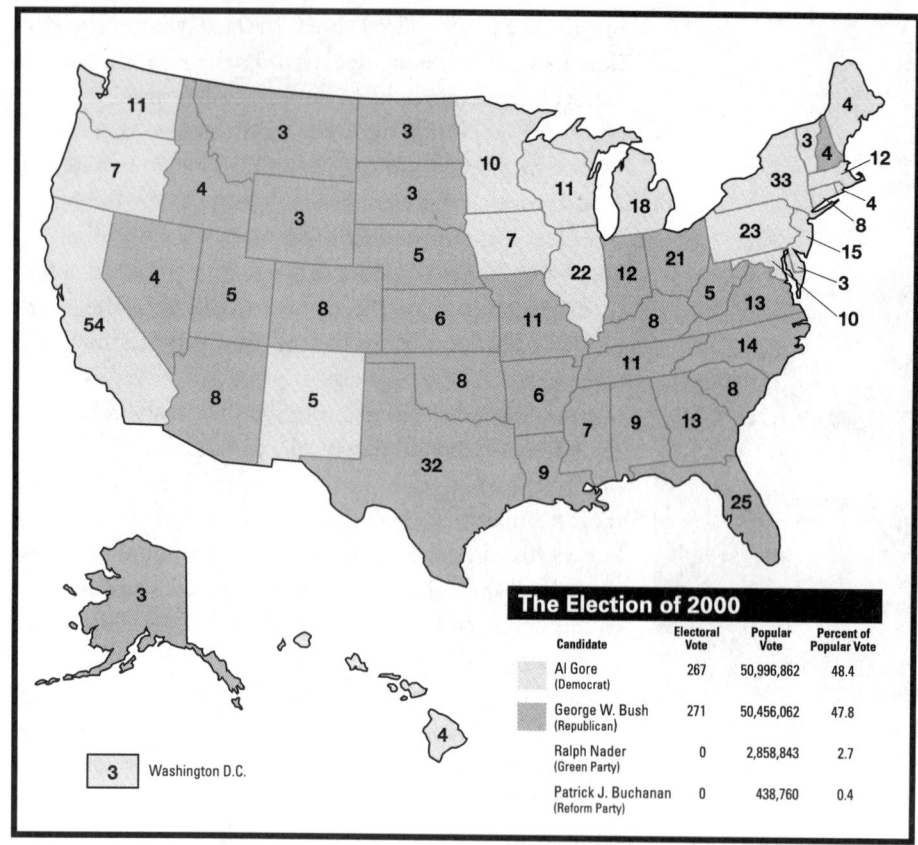

Map 34.3 The Election of 2000

puted ballots now;" and Justice Stephen Breyer, recalling the bitterness engendered in the nation by the 1857 *Dred Scott* decision upholding the notion that escaped slaves should be considered property and thus could not sue in court because they were not citizens, labeled *Bush v. Gore* another "self-inflicted wound—a wound that may harm not just the court but the Nation." According to the dissenters, the Court had violated "the basic principle, inherent in our Constitution and democracy, that every legal vote should be counted." The depth of feeling dividing the justices was one not seen in decades. The Court had become as bitterly divided as the country, and the discord would continue over many issues for several years. An election that had been one of the most lackluster in recent history unleashed a torrent of passions, but once it was over, a majority of Americans were relieved that the country would not have to endure months of agonizing and uncertainty.

Subsequent reviews by eight news organizations (most notably the *New York Times*), revealed contradictory results. If the Supreme Court had allowed a recount of votes only in the four counties where such an effort was requested by the Gore campaign, the vice president would have lost the election, the reviews concluded. If all disputed ballots from Florida had been reviewed, then Gore could have possibly managed an extremely narrow victory for Florida's electoral votes. One of the main reasons Gore lost in Florida was that 600,000 to 800,000 residents, mostly Latino and African-American males, were ex-felons who had been disenfranchised for life. Though felons from this racial demographic were more likely to vote for Democrats, the Democratic Party in Florida supported the policy of lifetime felony disenfranchisement out of the fear of being labeled soft on crime. Placed in this context, the Democrats helped place Bush in the White House. (In 2007, Florida's clemency board voted to allow the state's non-violent ex-felons to regain the right to vote but in March 2011 Florida's Republican governor, Rick Scott, approved a new rule requiring non-violent convicted felons to wait five years before applying to have their voting rights restored. By 2012, only four states permanently disenfranchised all persons convicted of felonies unless the governor intervened to restore the right to vote.)

In addition to the disfranchisement of ex-felons, the candidacy of Green Party presidential nominee Ralph Nader also hurt Gore's ability to win Florida. A life-long liberal social activist, Nader stated that he entered the presidential race to provide citizens with an alternative to the two major political parties he believed were irreparably dominated by corporate special interests. Though he knew he had no chance to win, Nader campaigned in an effort to publicize his views and to reach 5 percent of the national vote so his party would qualify for federal funding

President Bush with son, George W. Bush, and baseball broadcaster, Joe Morgan, in the locker room in Arlington, Texas, April 8, 1991. Photo credit: George Bush Presidential Library

in the next election. Nationally, he garnered 2,882,995 votes, or 2.74 percent. In Florida, Nader received 97,421 votes. Because many more of Nader's supporters would have voted for Gore rather than Bush if he was not on the ballot (though many would have stayed at home), the conclusion is clear that Gore could have gained several thousand additional votes given that scenario.

A Challenged Democracy

The 2000 election revealed a troubled American political system. The Electoral College, contrived by the founders to ensure that the nation's elite ruled rather than the common folk, gave the White House to a candidate not supported by the majority of voters. In a country that prided itself on being the most advanced technologically, a voting system was put in place using the latest innovations that bewildered voters and produced an outcome that could not be reliably determined, plunging the nation into political and legal crises for over a month. The 2000 campaign also reflected the belief among many citizens that money dominated politics. Counting both the congressional and presidential race, the contests cost over $1.5 billion, mostly raised by wealthy individuals and corporate donors. Such exorbitant spending reflected the interconnectedness that existed between power in the economic marketplace and power in the marketplace of politics and ideas.

Perhaps more alarming was Americans' widespread retreat from public life, which saw the increasing privatization of government services while millions of Americans (mostly white middle class) insulated themselves from their fellow citizens by taking up residence in homogenous suburban-gated communities. The very idea of a shared public sphere seemed to be dissolving. With politicians and political parties still viewed with suspicion and contempt and neither candidate able to generate much enthusiasm, voter turnout remained far below that of other democracies. Nearly half of eligible voters did not bother to go to the polls, and in state and local elections, turnout usually ranged between 20 and 30 percent. More people watched the 1960 Kennedy-Nixon debates than the Bush-Gore debates in 2000, even though the population of the country had increased by 100 million. Completely ignored by both Bush and Gore for most of the campaign were substantive issues like health care, race relations, and economic inequality.

AMERICAN EXCEPTIONALISM

Despite Americans' increasingly sedentary lifestyles, leading to an increase in obesity and related health problems, people lived longer and healthier lives in 2000 compared to previous generations, while enjoying a level of material comfort unimagined a century before. In 1900, the average annual income was $3,000 in today's dollars. The typical white American still had no indoor plumbing, no telephone or car, and had not graduated from high school. Forty years into the century, one-third of American households still did not have running water. In 2000, health conditions had improved so much that the average life expectancy for men had risen to 74 and for women to 79 (from 46 and 48 in 1900). Over 14 million Americans of all colors attended college in 2000, more than three times the figure for 1960. In 2000, one American in seven was older than 65, as Baby Boomers in particular were living longer than any previous generation. Such a fact sparked worries about the future cost of health care and the survival of the Social Security system. The figure also suggested that people would enjoy far longer and more productive retirement years than in the past. On the other hand, poverty, income inequality, and infant mortality rates (particularly acute in the nation's African-American and Latino communities) in the United States considerably exceeded that of other economically advanced countries.

Many of the changes affecting American life, such as the transformed role of women, better health and longer life expectancy, the spread of suburbanization, and the decline of industrial employment, have taken place in all economically advanced countries. Although still enjoying an overall better quality and abundance of life than most of the world, in key areas the United States lagged far behind its comparably wealthy, primarily European counterparts. Prevailing ideas of freedom in the United States are still more individually and materially oriented than in other developed countries. The idea of broad social welfare provided by the government is denounced by most white middle-class Americans. In 2003, when asked whether it was more important for the government to guarantee freedom from want for all Americans or greater guarantees to pursue individual advancement, only 35 percent of Americans selected freedom from want, as opposed to 58 percent in Germany, 62 percent in France and Great Britain, and 65 percent in Italy. The beginning of the new century also witnessed an increasingly more religious American society, with 60 percent of Americans agreeing with the statement that "religion plays a very important part in my life," while the comparable figure was 32 percent in Britain, 26 percent in Italy and only 11 percent in France. Perhaps more interesting was the revelation that one in three Americans said he or she interpreted the Bible literally and that over 50 percent of Americans believed the nation was providentially protected and "blessed by God" as His "chosen people." It appeared that religion and nationalism had become symbiotic by the beginning of the twenty-first century, reinforcing one another far more powerfully in the United States than in the more secular nations of Western Europe.

Other manifestations of American exceptionalism were more disturbing. Among developed countries, the United States was by far the most violent society with the highest rate of murder using guns. In 2004, the last year that comparative statistics were available, there were 14,121 murders with guns in the United States, as opposed to 473 in Germany, 201 in Canada, 84 in Great Britain, and 26 in Japan. As the new administration was about to take office, it remained to be seen whether a conception of freedom, based on materialism, acquisitiveness, and the continued glorification of individual self-fulfillment unrestrained by government, or a common public culture would emerge to define Americans in the twenty-first century.

THE BUSH AGENDA

A startling contrast to Bill Clinton, George W. Bush was low-key, relaxed, and projected an understated style, conveying to the American people a sense that simple priorities and values would define his administration. While Clinton administration staff prided themselves on who could work the most 20 hour days, Bush wanted his people to be able to eat dinner with their families at a normal hour. According to the *New York Times*, Bush wanted to run the White House "with the crisp efficiency of a blue-chip corporation." To that end, Bush projected an approach to power similar to that of his father's administration. Bush turned to one of his father's closest advisers, James Baker, for advice on how to launch his presidency. Baker urged Bush to identify two or three major objectives for his first year and to pursue their goals quickly with dogged determination. Bush defined a tax cut, education initiatives, and a defense build-up as his priorities. Baker also assisted Bush in his Cabinet appointments, asserting that he should appoint retired four-star general and former head of the Joint Chiefs of Staff, Colin Powell, as Secretary of State. For the other key cabinet position, Secretary of Defense, Baker believed long-time Republican official Donald Rumsfeld to be the best choice. With the appointments of Powell and Rumsfeld, the Bush inner team seemed, in many respects, like the first Bush presidency. Perhaps more important and impressive, Bush appointed more women, African Americans, and Latinos to key senior appointments than any of his Democratic predecessors.

In a gracious and elegantly written Inaugural Address, Bush conveyed the message that he intended to be the president of all the American people. Not known for his ability to speak spontaneously, let alone with compelling power, Bush nonetheless chose superb speechwriters, who sculpted his official statements, including the Inaugural Address, which impressed one critic as "by far the best in forty years. . .tightly constructed," with its rhythms flowing "pleasingly." Perhaps most impressive was Bush's message that he was most concerned about those at the bottom of society who he wanted to elevate. "We know that deep, persistent poverty is unworthy of our nation's promise," he declared. "And whatever our views of its cause, we can agree that children at risk are not at fault. Abandonment and abuse are not acts of God, they are failures of love."

No sooner did Bush take office than his commitment to inclusion fell by the wayside, revealing a conservatism that appealed to the Republican Party's far right base. In a rapid series of initiatives, Bush terminated U.S. aid to international family planning agencies, placating the anti-abortion groups in the United States who saw such organizations as part of a pro-choice cabal. He rescinded the prohibitions of logging in Western forests, which greatly offended conservationists. He proposed an energy package that greatly favored the big oil interests, which endorsed drilling for new oil in the Arctic National Wildlife Refuge, a sanctuary that most environmentalists and citizens in general believed inviolable. Most revealing was Bush's advocacy of the "privatization," via the nation's churches (mostly Protestant), of the social welfare system. His "faith-based" program provided federal funds to church-related organizations which offered relief and care for communities' indigent and dispossessed. Such an initiative overjoyed the Religious Right. Liberals opposed this program not only for the obvious assault on the welfare state but also because it violated the sanctity of the separation of church and state.

As disturbing as the above measures were to progressives, nothing revealed Bush's inherent conservatism more than his tax plan, which reversed completely Bill Clinton's program by once again shifting the burden of taxation onto the middle class and even the poor. Under Clinton, the tax rate on the rich went as high as 39 percent, while taxes for the majority of Americans—80 percent of the nation's population—went down. Bush's initiative reversed Clinton's structure, in effect putting in place a regressive system that benefited the rich and placed more of the burden on the rest of the taxpaying public. The Bush plan called for the biggest tax cut in history, giving back to taxpayers $1.3 trillion through 2010. When broken down relative to recipients, it became abundantly clear that the rich were the primary beneficiaries. The top 1 percent of taxpayers received 43 percent of the tax break. Most disturbing, the bottom 20 percent of taxpayers received on average an additional $15 the first year, and $37 by the third year. By contrast, the top 1 percent received, on average, $13,469 in the first year, rising to $31,201 by the third year. One tax research group estimated that by 2010, the Bush plan gave back a "bonus" of $774 billion to the richest 1 percent of the nation.

With the economy slowing by 2001, Bush was able to convince Congress that his plan would stimulate new growth. The initiative was not new—fundamentally it was the same assertion that taxes needed to be cut for the wealthy so that they could invest the money they saved in taxes in economically productive activities. Such a scenario did not occur in the 1980s and, likewise, did not occur during the Bush years because relatively few wealthy individuals put their money from their tax cuts back into the economy to expand growth.

Bush and Foreign Policy Pre-September 11

Unlike his father and Bill Clinton, both of whom pursued American interests abroad and relations with both adversaries and allies within a multilateral context, George W. Bush and his foreign policy team implemented a much more unilateral approach in the international arena. Not since the 1950s had United States foreign policy emphasized such freedom of action, unrestrained by international treaties and institutions. During the 2000 campaign, Bush criticized the Clinton administration's penchant for nation-building—U.S. aid to help stabilize countries in chaotic regions of the world. Bush believed such assistance to be a waste of money, thus it was time for a retrenchment in this particular arena of U.S. foreign policy. Since one of his priorities was to expand the nation's military capability, soon after taking office Bush announced plans to continue with the Reagan era's efforts to create a missile defense system—in effect SDI or "Star Wars." Such an initiative, however, called for the U.S. to withdraw from the 1972 Anti-Ballistic Missile Treaty, negotiated with the former Soviet Union, which forbade the deployment of such systems. Bush also withdrew U.S. support of the Comprehensive Nuclear Test Ban Treaty. Bush's disavowal of both those treaties made it clear to our allies, as well as to potential adversaries, that like Ronald Reagan, George Bush believed in American military might as the best deterrent and thus the military-industrial complex had to be revitalized and promoted in the name of national security and projection of American power abroad.

Finally, Bush vetoed U.S. membership in an International Criminal Court for trying violators of human rights, fearing that the Court would assert jurisdiction over Americans. On the surface it appeared Bush believed it was time for the U.S. to return to a semi-isolationist status, when in reality nothing could have been further from the truth. If anything, Bush was preparing the American people to embrace a new approach toward foreign policy—"unilateralism"—the belief that it was essential for the United States to determine what role it should play in world affairs based on its own best interest and security; and the right to take whatever action necessary to maintain its safety and presence abroad. Put simply, Bush believed it was time for the United States to abandon the axioms that had guided multilateral and collective security pacts since the end of World War II, the cornerstones of American foreign policy for the past several decades.

Perhaps no other Bush action reflected better this new policy than the president's announcement that the United States would not adhere to the 1997 Kyoto Protocol, which sought to combat global warming—a slow rise in the earth's temperature, caused by gases released by the burning of fossil fuels such as coal and oil, that remain in the upper atmosphere, trapping heat reflected from the earth. Since the 1990s, when significant ice melting and glacier recession in Greenland and the Antarctic, was discovered, scientists had been warning that such activity could have disastrous climatic, ecological, and environmental effects worldwide. Some 180 nations, including the United States, had agreed to accept the goals set in the Kyoto Protocol for addressing the emission of "greenhouse" gases. Since the United States at the time burned far more fossil fuels than any other nation, Bush's repudiation of the treaty on the grounds that it would hurt the American economy, infuriated much of the world, as well as environmentalists at home.

After seven and a half months in office, Bush had accomplished much—Congress had passed the largest tax cut in history. He initiated an educational reform program, "No Child Left Behind." Most importantly, Bush began a reorientation of American foreign and military policy. His rejection of the Kyoto Protocol made it clear that, like most Republicans, to Bush the environment and economic growth were directly in opposition, and corporate interests superseded those of conservation and ecology. Bush also displayed a willingness to pander to the agenda of the evangelicals, for instance supporting state initiatives banning marriage for gay couples. In short, the George Bush that emerged after seven plus months in office, notwithstanding his rhetoric about concern for the downtrodden and dispossessed, proved fundamentally to be a traditional Republican conservative. Then came September 11, 2001, a day that would transform forever America, alter the international situation, the domestic political environment, and the Bush presidency itself.

September 11, 2001

With the weather brilliantly clear up and down the East Coast, four planes prepared to take off for California—American Airlines Flight 11 and United Airlines Flight 175 from Boston, American Airlines 77 from Washington, and United Airlines 93 from Newark. All were jumbo jets, with full tanks of fuel for the 3,000 mile journey across the United States. Being a Tuesday morning, each plane carried a passenger load far below normal. Unknown to the passengers and flight crew, on board each aircraft were groups of Muslim extremists, mostly from Saudi Arabia, Egypt, and Syria and who were members of Al Qaeda, a jihadist organization formed in the early 1990s by the son of a Yemeni construction billionaire, Osama bin Laden. (Jihadists in the Middle East believe they are in a holy war against an overbearing, militarily dominant, and morally corrupt Western World and the state of Israel.)

Seizing control of each plane shortly after it reached cruising altitude, the terrorists broke into the respective cockpits, killed or disabled the pilots, took control of the aircraft and steered the planes—now deadly missiles—toward their targets. The first plane, American 11, struck the North Tower of New York City's World Trade Center at 8:46 a.m. Seventeen minutes later, United Airlines 175 slammed into the South Tower, which collapsed in a heap within an hour. Thirty minutes later the North Tower fell. Meanwhile, American Airlines 77 dive-bombed into the Pentagon just outside the nation's capital. Only United Airlines 93 was still aloft. On board, a heroic group of passengers—knowing from cell phone conversations what had happened in New York—refused to let their jet plane become another missile. Instead they assaulted the terrorists, resulting in the plane crashing into a field near Shanksville, Pennsylvania located 60 miles southeast of Pittsburgh. None of the terrorists or passengers survived.

Americans sensed the bottomless horror of what had just happened. A journalist, heading for a meeting inside the Trade Center, suddenly found himself on an observation deck halfway up the tower. "I didn't know it wasn't an exit," he said. "And it was just covered with dozens of shoes. High-heels, Strapons. . . . There were bodies, luggage, torsos. People were jumping [leaping from flames]. At first I didn't know they were people, but I realized they were flailing on the way down . . . people lining up and dropping, too many people falling." A short distance away on a Brooklyn Heights roof with his wife, novelist John Updike watched as "the South Tower fell straight down like an elevator, with a tinkling shiver and a groan of concussion distinct across miles of air. We knew we had just witnessed thousands of deaths; we clung to each other as if we ourselves were falling." Mil-

Reactionary Muslim terrorists of the Al Qaeda organization, led by Osama bin Laden crashed an American Airline flight into the Pentagon with the resulting destruction shown here.

lions watched on television as repeatedly, hour after hour, newscasts showed footage of the second plane penetrating the South Tower and exploding in flames, each time experiencing anew a profound awareness that someone, some extraordinary force, had grabbed hold of Americans' sense of security with such awful violence. As a result of 9/11, all Americans' lives would be changed in countless ways that would never permit the old ways of doing and thinking to return.

Most disturbing to Americans was the fact that the horrible outrage committed on the nation's soil, resulting in the death of over 3,000 citizens, was not the wanton act of a group of renegade individuals, acting out of desperation or futile rage, but rather the planned, calculated handiwork of a tightly-knit organization that had been operating within the United States for several years, diligently preparing their perfectly coordinated attacks. Many of the terrorists were "sleepers" inserted into a culture, carrying on normal lives, buying cars, getting jobs, mixing with neighbors, awaiting word from their leaders, who had mastermind the plans for destruction in their training camps years earlier. The attackers functioned in small "cells" of four or five, with one member serving as the link to a larger structure. To those who later analyzed what had happened, the genius of the planning was almost eerie. As one retired CIA officer declared, "I've never seen an operation go that smoothly."

The complex attacks had been carried out by Al Qaeda, an army of Islamic fundamentalists formed by Osama in Ladin, who began his career battling the West as a guerilla warrior fighting the Soviets in Afghanistan in the 1980s. For a time, East Africa became Al Qaeda's base of operations. By the time of the assault on the World Trade Center, bin Laden had moved his Al Qaeda operation to Afghanistan. There he found both a safe refuge and wholesale support for his operations against the United States and its allies from the **Taliban**, another Muslim fundamentalist extremist group, who had taken over that poor beleaguered country in the aftermath of the Soviet withdrawal in the late 1980s. From his base in Afghanistan, bin Laden built a worldwide network of terrorist cells, sustaining their operations from his own sizeable personal family fortune and from secret donations. With abundant financial support, bin Laden recruited, indoctrinated, and trained thousands of eager, mostly young Muslim males for his holy war against the West, especially the United States. By September 11, Al Qaeda had operatives in more than 40 countries and had already been using them. In 1993, Al Qaeda had launched the truck bombing attack on the World Trade Center. Five years later, Al Qaeda struck again, perpetrating the explosions that ruined the American embassies in Nairobi, Kenya and Dar es Salaam, Tanzania. In October 2000, Al Qaeda organized a deadly sea assault on the *USS Cole*, killing 17 sailors and injuring another 39 as the destroyer lay docked in the Yemeni port of Aden. All such attacks reflected what became known as the "Ladenese Epistle" (first announced in 1996 and then more ominously reiterated in 1998), in which bin Laden declared that Al Qaeda's objective was to push the United States out of the holy land (the Middle East) and that "to kill Americans and their allies, both civil and military, is an individual duty of every Muslim who is able, in any country where this is possible." Such rhetoric made it abundantly clear to the world that bin Laden believed himself to be the new *mahdi*, and, thus, if ordained by God to redeem the

Historians will certainly view the destruction of the World Trade Center in New York City, on September 11, 2001, as a turning point in American foreign, as well as domestic policy.©Danny C. Sze Photography

Muslim world and faith from Western greed, secularism, and corrupting culture, then the United States, the most "satanic" of all Western nations, would become his most important target. (The "*mahdi*" or "guided one" is a figure many Muslims believe will appear at the end of time to usher in an era of peace and justice. This figure is generally more important in the theology of Shiite Muslims than Sunnis like bin Laden.) When bin Laden set his sights on New York's landmark World Trade Center, one reporter noted "the attack was not only against a nation or government, but against a symbol, the twin towers of Sodom and mammon."

At the time of the attack, few Americans were aware of the extent of bin Laden's network and its purpose. Such was not the case for intelligence experts in Washington and elsewhere. The Clinton administration was fully aware of Al Qaeda's activities. Soon after the first truck bombing attack on the World Trade Center, law enforcement agencies rounded up bin Laden's lieutenants responsible for the deed, convicted them, and sent them to prison. After the bombing of the U.S. embassies in Nairobi and Dar es Salaam, President Clinton ordered missile attacks on a site believed to be bin Laden's headquarters in the mountains of southern Afghanistan, but the terrorist fled the area an hour before the missiles struck. Overall, the anti-terrorist campaign was low-key and unsuccessful, as if neither the Clinton administration nor the new Bush administration wanted to alarm the American people that attacks were more imminent than they appeared. Compounding this cavalier attitude was the inability of U.S. intelligence agencies to cooperate with each other, especially in the realm of information-sharing about what they knew about Al Qaeda's activities. There were individuals, however, within both administrations who warned about the likelihood of an attack on U.S. soil. Such was the belief of William Cohen, Clinton's Secretary of Defense, who predicted a direct terrorist attack on the U.S. in an op-ed article in the *Washington Post* in the summer of 1999. A commission chaired by former Senators Gary Hart and Warren Rudman concluded that terrorism represented the most dire threat to the nation, but their report fell on largely deaf ears. Richard Clarke, one of Bush's national security advisors, also believed that an attack was coming sooner rather than later. While he was on one of his frequent vacations in Crawford, Texas, on August 6, 2001, Bush received a briefing paper entitled " Bin Laden Determined To Strike in U.S." The briefing mentioned the possibility of terrorists hijacking airplanes and using them as weapons. Bush reportedly dismissively said to the intelligence official after the paper was read to him, "All right. You've covered your ass now." As former State Department official Leslie Gelb noted, despite repeated warnings "that the terrorist threat to America was far greater and more imminent than a missile attack to be defended by the President's [George W. Bush] proposed missile defense system [Star War's redux], very little has been done."

September 11 made soothsayers of the above individuals, providing a dramatic wake-up call to a nation engaged in what one security expert called "a lengthy sleepwalk." At the time of the attacks, President Bush was in a Florida elementary school, reading to children as part of a promotional junket for his education reform initiative. Fearful that the White House might be targeted as well, the Secret Service insisted that the president not return to Washington until it was safe. Bush agreed but remained in constant communication with Vice President Cheney and other White House officials. As it turned out, the Secret Service was correct. The White House was probably the original terrorist objective of the plane that crashed into the Pentagon. Clearly shaken, Bush nevertheless understood the need for the American people to hear from him as soon as possible. That afternoon the president appeared on national television to tell the American people they would endure and prevail. Although his initial comments were reassuring, it was his address nine days later to a joint session of Congress that the president demonstrated a gravitas that gave most Americans a sense that there was a sure hand at the helm in a moment of unprecedented crisis. The president conveyed a clear sense of being up to the challenges before him. The country's enemies, Bush declared, "hate our freedoms, our freedom of religion, our freedom of speech, our freedom to assemble and disagree with other." In later speeches, Bush repeated this theme. Why did terrorists attack the United States? His answer: "Because we love freedom, that's why. And they hate freedom."

The heart of Bush's message was that the **war on terrorism** would be unlike any other war the nation had fought. There would be no decisive battles or victories, no unconditional surrender, nor even clear evidence of battles fought or enemies engaged and possibly not even any visible achievements such as the capture or death of bin Laden. Rather, this would be an unrelenting war of stealth, covert missions, secret forays and the employment of whatever tactic or strategy essential, for as long as it would take, to extirpate this "evil" from the world. Bush also made it clear that prosecution of the war might well entail invading countries that supported terrorism. Yet, Bush remained clear on the objective: "Our enemy is a radical network of terrorists and every government that supports them." In that context, "every nation in every region now has a decision to make. Either you are with us, or you are with the terrorists." Perhaps most important, September 11 forced Bush to embrace a new commitment to coalition politics. The war on terrorism would be a multilateral effort, requiring cooperation of governments throughout the world in intelligence gathering, military and economic sanctions, use of airspace and bases, and actual warfare. Gone for the moment was the unilateralism that had defined the first eight months of Bush's foreign policy frame of reference. In the global village the world had become, it was hard to imagine a solution to either terrorism or hunger and poverty without nations working together in support of their mutual interests.

Even before the president's September 20 speech, people throughout the country demonstrated their sense of resolve and sympathy for the victims by outbursts of intense patriotism not seen in several decades. Almost overnight, American flags were displayed outside homes, businesses, and public buildings. Public servants like firemen and policemen became national heroes. After two decades in which the dominant language of American politics centered on deregulation and individualism, the country, for the moment, experienced a renewed feeling of common social purpose. Citizens of all backgrounds shared a sense of having lived through a traumatic ordeal. The Bush administration benefited hugely from this patriotism and identification with the government. The president's popularity soared. As in other crises, Americans looked to the federal government, and especially the president, for reassurance, leadership, and decisive action. Bush seized this opportunity to give his administration a new direction and purpose, and greater power.

September 11 also exposed the nation's economic vulnerabilities. Even before the attacks, the country was in the throes of a recession. But the attacks revealed the degree to which an entire network of economic connections could be imperiled. With the airline industry as the only most obvious example, it became clear that economic prosperity depended on the psychological buoyancy and health of the society as a whole. With people scared to travel, and anxious about their future well-being, no economy, no matter how robust in its structure, could prosper. As the months after September 11 rolled by, the nation fell further into recession. A $5 trillion projected surplus disappeared overnight due to both the Bush tax cuts and new spending for homeland security and defense. Jobs fled the country as more multi-national corporations as well as U.S.-owned manufacturers outsourced their enterprises to countries with lower wage expectations—code for developing nations with a cheap, exploitable labor market, such as China, India, and Mexico. Such was the fate suffered by the folk of Galesburg, Illinois, where Maytag, one of the largest manufacturers of washing machines, refrigerators, and other home appliances, decided to move its operation to Mexico and close its factory in Galesburg where workers earned an average wage of $15 an hour. At its Mexican plant, Maytag would only be paying an average wage of $2 an hour. Such a trend had begun during the late-Clinton years, but during the Bush era, outsourcing became even more endemic among the nation's manufacturing sector, leading to a slow but steady rise in unemployment. Indeed, Bush became the first president since Herbert Hoover to see the economy lose jobs over the course of a four-year term.

During the first Bush administration, the sectors that had expanded the most in the previous decade contracted rapidly. The computer industry slashed over 40 percent of its jobs during the first two years of the Bush White House. Thanks to the Internet, jobs such as computer programmers and other highly skilled technology positions could be shifted to India, which had a large number of well-educated persons willing to work for far less than their American counterparts. Employment in the media, advertising, and telecommunications industries also fell. The president responded to the economic downturn by supporting the Federal Reserve's policy of reducing interest rates and proposing another round of tax cuts. In 2003, Bush signed into law a $320 billion tax reduction, one of the largest in American history. As he initiated two years earlier in accordance with his belief in the supply-side theory, the cuts again benefited the wealthy and corporations, reducing their tax burden significantly so they could supposedly reinvest their savings in the economy, expand production, and hire more people. The tax cuts coupled with the continued deregulation of the economy only fueled the speculation, greed, over-expansion, leveraging, higher executive and CEO salaries and bonuses, and a whole host of other economic malpractices already rampant within the economy, caused the greatest financial crisis since the Great Depression in the summer and fall of 2008.

By the beginning of 2004, however, the Bush administration could boast that the economy was healthy. In that year, the economic growth rate was 4.2 percent, though job creation was proceeding more slowly than during previous recoveries. Because of the continuing decline of union membership (which reached a record post-World War II low of 8 percent of private sector employees in 2006), the failure of Congress to raise the minimum wage, which remained stagnant at $5.15 per hour for ten years, (thereby steadily falling in real value), the continuing shift of higher-paying manufacturing jobs overseas, and the regressive tax cuts, economic inequality continued to increase. The real income of average American families fell slightly despite the economic recovery. The number of citizens without health insurance continued its upward climb, reaching 16 percent of the population by 2005. In short, Bush's economic agenda proved only to benefit the top 5 percent of the population.

The Price Paid for "Freedom"

The war on terror became one of the greatest challenges to American civil liberties since the McCarthy era of the early 1950s. However, 9/11 greatly affected the sanctity of this most cherished quality of American life. In the immediate aftermath of the attacks, Congress rushed to pass the Patriot Act, which conferred unprecedented powers on law enforcement agencies charged with preventing the new, vaguely defined crime of "domestic terrorism." Such agencies could now wiretap, perform surveillance, open letters, read e-mail, and obtain personal records from third parties like universities and libraries, all without a suspect's knowledge. Although the Bush administration made a point of discouraging anti-Arab and anti-Muslim sentiment, there was little doubt that citizens with such a background would be the most likely to be investigated or profiled under the act. Under the direction of Attorney General John Ashcroft, the Justice Department unleashed measures to deal with suspected terrorists, all with the president's approval. Ashcroft ordered that federal authorities be permitted to eavesdrop on conversations between lawyers and their prisoner clients, called in 5,000 Islamic students for questioning, detained more than 600 aliens without identifying them, and proposed the creation of military tribunals to hold trials, in secret, of suspected terrorists who were not United States citizens.

As the Bush administration rounded up suspected terrorists abroad, a detention facility was opened for them at the American military base at Guantanamo Bay, Cuba. There, the captives of the war on terror were incarcerated with many forced to endure grueling, if not brutal, interrogations, including "water-boarding" (in which someone being interrogated has water poured over their covered face to create the sensation of drowning) and other forms of physical and mental abuse to extract information. Bush stated that these so-called "enhanced interrogation techniques" were not instances of torture, implying that inflicting pain to gather intelligence was completely different than inflicting pain for punishment or revenge, even though the United States executed Japanese military officers for waterboarding American POWs during World War II. Nevertheless, on this issue the Bush administration made it clear that the United States would not be bound by international law in prosecuting its war on terror. Bush officials were especially eager to disavow the Geneva Convention and the International Convention against Torture, both of which regulate the treatment of prisoners of war and prohibit torture and other forms of physical and mental coercion. In January 2002, the Justice Department issued a memorandum stating that the convention's mandates do not apply to captured members of Al Qaeda because they were "unlawful combatants," not members of regularly constituted armies. White House counsel Alberto Gonzales, who later became attorney general, advised the president that the Geneva Accords were

Map 34.4 Afghanistan

quaint and obsolete in this new kind of war. A year later, February 2003, Bush issued a directive denying Al Qaeda and Taliban prisoners the Geneva protections. As a result of the administration's rejection of the Geneva Accords, prisoner abuse became widespread through U.S. detention camps, the most appalling at Abu Ghraib prison in Iraq, where it became known that prisoners were beaten, subjected to electric shocks, attacked by dogs, and forced to strip naked and lie atop other prisoners. Such forms of abuse also occurred at Guantanamo. In addition, the CIA set up a series of jails in foreign countries as part of a extraordinary "rendition" of suspects, some of whom were naturalized U.S. citizens but were of Arab/Muslim background, who were kidnapped and hauled to prisons in Egypt, Yemen, Syria, and to the former communist states of eastern Europe where they were tortured in order to obtain information for the war on terrorism. Once such activities became public, especially the photos of the Abu Ghraib prisoners, the image of the United States as a country that adheres to allegedly the highest standards of civilized behavior and the rule of law became serious, if not irreparably, damaged.

Wire-tapping, arrests without warrants, imprisonment without writs of *habeas corpus*, and torture of prisoners of war became common practices as a result of 9/11, and the majority of the American people accepted such practices out of fear and in the name of national security.

Barry Goldwater's reactionary declaration in 1964, "that extremism in defense of liberty is no vice and that moderation in pursuit of justice is no virtue," seemed to become the new reality in the United States. The president's press secretary, Ari Fleischer, warned Americans to "watch what they say," and Attorney General John Ashcroft declared that criticism of administration policies aided the country's terrorist enemies.   Although rightfully consumed by their own tragedy, many Americans nonetheless wanted to know why 9/11 occurred and what motivated the individuals involved. Only since the event have Americans become aware of the profound social and economic fissures threatening to envelop the Muslim world and bring Islamic fundamentalists to power, whose mission is the destruction of the West, especially the United States. Many Arabs have been deeply angered by America's at-times unquestioning support for Israel and its continued occupation of the West Bank, which supporters of the Palestinian cause believe should belong to a new Palestinian nation. The often rough Israeli treatment of Palestinian prisoners is blamed on the United States, and many Arabs resent America administrations trumpeting the need for democracy and human rights while the U.S. has supported oppressive, dictatorial regimes in Egypt and Saudi Arabia. In nations like Egypt, the unemployment rate was often between 25-30 percent. Princes in Saudi Arabia enjoying support from Western corporations built

$300 million dollar palaces while the poor become poorer. Islamic fundamentalism provides a simple answer to these egregious inequalities: the United States, with its consumer culture, modernity, and capitalist greed, arrogantly seeks to take over the world and destroy all in its way, so say the clerics and other Muslim fundamentalists. Such sentiments clearly illustrate not only the seething rage and hatred a minority of Muslims outside the United States have for the nation, but the depth and complexity of the challenges facing the United States if it were to defeat bin Laden and his terrorism as well as the need to address the springs of discord and oppression that for so long have fed his and other's apocalyptic vision.

The United States Counterattacks

When intelligence reports indicated that Osama bin Laden was still in Afghanistan, Bush demanded that the Taliban surrender the Al Qaeda leader. When the Taliban refused, Bush initiated hostilities on October 7, 2001 by launching an invasion of Afghanistan, code-named "Operation Enduring Freedom," hoping to bring down the Taliban government and kill bin Laden in the process. By December 2001, the combination of American bombing and ground combat by the Northern Alliance (anti-Taliban Afghanis) in conjunction with special forces from the U.S. Army and Marines had overthrown the Taliban government. A new pro-United States coalition government was installed in the capital of Kabul. The new regime repealed Taliban laws denying women the right to attend school and prohibiting movies, music, and other expressions of Western culture but found it difficult to extend its control over the rest of the country, especially the more remote mountain regions where the Taliban fled and regrouped.

Bush repeatedly insisted that the Taliban's overthrow marked only the beginning of the war on terrorism. In his State of the Union address in January 2002, the president no doubt shocked many listeners by declaring that three countries in particular—Iraq, Iran, and North Korea—formed an "**Axis of Evil**," the nations most responsible in his view for terrorism by providing safe sanctuaries for such individuals as well as the development of "weapons of mass destruction"—nuclear, chemical, and biological—that posed the greatest threat to the United States. No matter how convincing Bush's rhetoric, evidence abounded that none of those countries were involved in any capacity with the 9/11 attacks, nor had they ever cooperated with one another. Indeed, Iraq and Iran had fought a long and bloody war in the 1980s, and the present dictator of Iraq, Saddam Hussein, was an ambitious megalomaniac determined for his country to dominate the Middle East. In Hussein's view, Iran blocked such objectives. Bush officials followed up the president's "axis of evil" declaration with the promulgation in September of 2002 of the National Security Strategy. Invoking the altruism of freedom as the basis of its purpose, NSS declared that henceforth the objective of U.S. foreign policy would be to not only extend the benefits of freedom by fighting terrorists but also tyrants around the world as well. In order to accomplish such a noble crusade, the United States must maintain an overwhelming preponderance of military power, greater than any other country in the world, which would prevent any other nation from challenging the United States' overall strength or its dominance in any region that the United States believed vital to its interests and security. Most important, the Bush administration abandoned the Cold War doctrine of deterrence, which George H.W. Bush and Bill Clinton both maintained, and replaced that tradition with the concept of "preemptive war." If the United States believed a country was a possible future threat to its security, the U.S. would attack that nation first.

Not since the days of John Foster Dulles had the United States issued such an aggressive, militaristic, and alarming manifesto. Bush's "Axis of Evil" speech, coupled with the announcement of the NSS, sent shock waves around the world, with many persons overseas fearing that the United States was claiming the right to act as a world policeman in violation of international law. Similar to the earlier battle against communism, the war on terrorism, under the new policy, saw the United States forge closer ties with repressive governments in strategic areas of the world such as Pakistan and the republics of Central Asia that consistently violated human rights. As a result, charges quickly arose within the international community, even from close allies, that an imperialist mentality had taken hold of the Bush administration as a result of 9/11 and that the United States intended to use its overwhelming military, economic, and even cultural power to establish a new American empire. Despite the existing economic downturn, the United States still accounted for just under one-third of global economic output and more than one-third of global military spending. Its defense budget exceeded that of the next twenty powers combined. The United States maintained military bases on virtually every continent, and its navy had a presence on every ocean. Thus, the new imperialists believed the United States had a responsibility to use its overwhelming power not only to better secure the nation but also to impose order in a dangerous world, even if this meant establishing its own rules of international conduct. The talk of a new American empire alarmed many who did not desire to

A DIVIDED AMERICA: Bill Clinton to George W. Bush / 1123

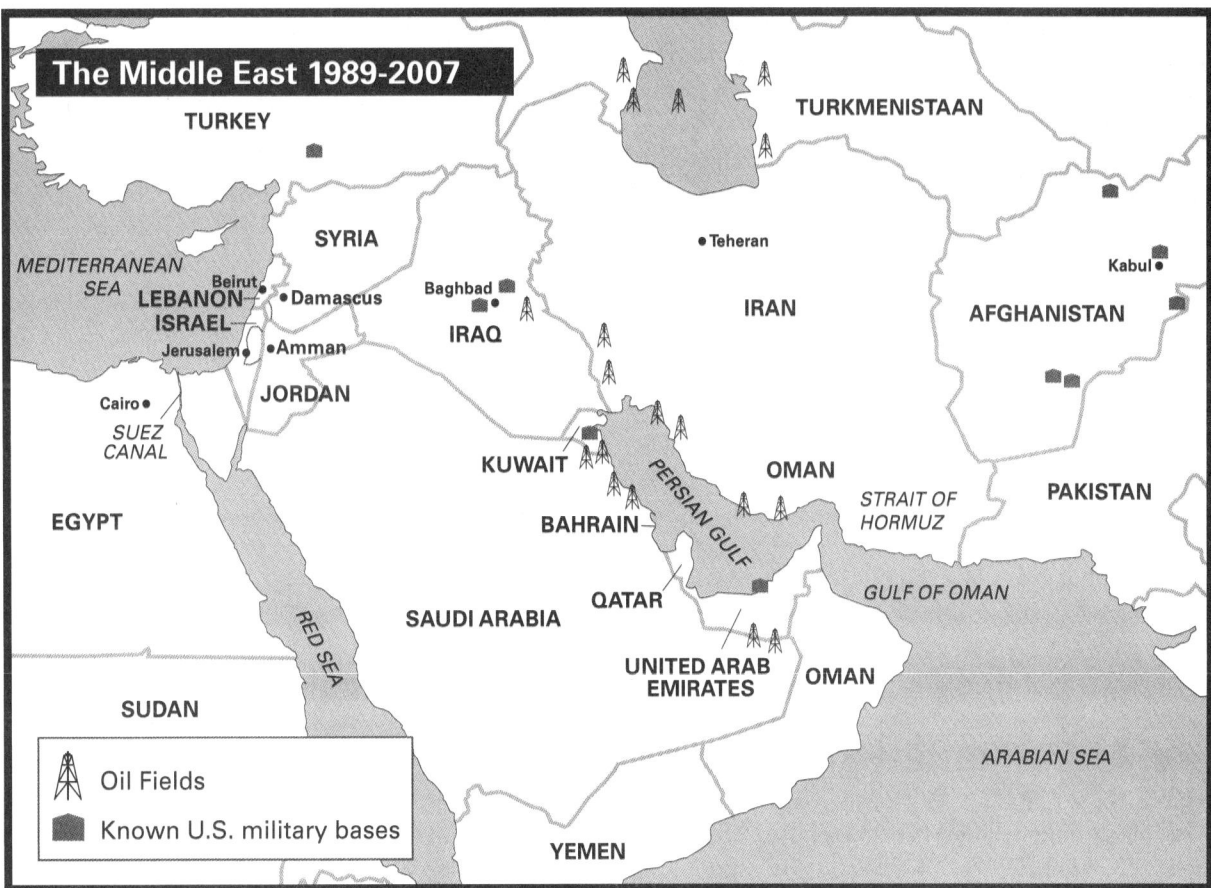

Map 34.5 The Middle East 1989-2007

have the United States reconstruct the world in its own image.

No sooner was the NSS promulgated than its real intention became apparent: the overthrow of Saddam Hussein. Almost from the moment Bush entered the White House, Hussein's overthrow was a priority, especially among the inner circle who surrounded and advised the president, individuals such as Vice President Dick Cheney, Secretary of Defense Donald Rumsfeld, and Deputy Defense Secretary Paul Wolfowitz. All three played key roles in developing a strategy and justification for a war against Iraq. First, they asserted that such a conflict would illustrate the United States' commitment to freedom, certain that the majority of Iraqi people would welcome with open arms the overthrow of Saddam Hussein, embrace the American forces as liberators, and, of course, would soon establish a democratic government, which would allow for an early departure of American soldiers. Initially, Secretary of State Colin Powell opposed such a scenario, asserting that the conquest and democratization of Iraq would require hundreds of thousands of American troops, that rebuilding the nation would take much longer than other cabinet officials believed, and that such an undertaking should not be put into effect without the support of America's allies. Powell's sound reckoning fell on deaf ears, especially those of the president who wholeheartedly embraced such a crusade against such a dangerous tyrant. As a result of his protestations, Powell found himself increasingly marginalized within the administration.

Rumsfeld and other administration officials had to find a legitimate pretext, something that would convince the world as well as citizens at home, that the overthrow of Saddam Hussein was necessary for both global and American security. Although definitely a brutal dictator, Hussein was not an Islamic fundamentalist, nor had any evidence linked him to 9/11. To further vilify the Iraqi leader, the administration stated that Hussein had developed an arsenal of chemical and bacterial "weapons of mass destruction" and that he was seeking to acquire nuclear arms. Hussein had started research programs into developing nuclear weapons and had used chemical weapons in the 1980s Iran-Iraq War and against the minority Kurds in northern Iraq, but his efforts to develop weapons of mass destruction apparently ended with his defeat in the 1991 Gulf War. These charges prompted the United Nations to authorize the sending of a team of weapons inspectors to Iraq to see if the president's accusations were true. Soon after, the UN team reported that

Hussein had no such weapons of mass destruction, the White House accused the inspectors of being inconclusive in their findings, and that they would never uncover Hussein's military capabilities. Early in 2003, despite his original misgivings, Secretary of State Powell delivered the administration's case before the United Nations Security Council. He claimed that Hussein possessed a mobile chemical weapons laboratory, had hidden weapons of mass destruction in his many palaces, and was seeking to acquire uranium in Africa to build nuclear weapons. Every one of his assertions later proved to be false. No doubt Powell felt duped and betrayed by the Bush White House, resigning soon after the president's reelection in 2004. Nevertheless, shortly after Powell's address, the president announced his intention to go to war with or without UN approval. In a vote reminiscent of the 1964 Tonkin Gulf Resolution before the Vietnam War, Congress voted overwhelmingly to authorize the president to use force if he deemed it necessary in the name of national security.

THE IRAQ WAR

As the Bush administration's patience with the UN inspections grew thin and it became a certainty that the United States would invade Iraq with or without UN approval, antiwar protests emerged throughout the world. Although large-scale protests took place in the United States, bringing together veterans of the Vietnam antiwar movement and a diverse group of young activists, their protests had little impact on the majority of Americans who supported the president and his policies.

Of greater importance in challenging the administration's push for war was the opposition presented by veteran foreign policy experts, many of them members of previous Republican administrations such as Brent Scowcroft, the first president Bush's national security adviser. Scowcroft warned that the current Bush administration's preoccupation with Iraq deflected attention from its real enemy, Al Qaeda, which remained capable of launching terrorist attacks. Scowcroft and others insisted that the United States could not unilaterally transform the Middle East into a bastion of democracy as the president and his advisers claim was the nation's long-term objective. Moreover, Afghanistan was still not stabilized. The invasion of Iraq forced the United States to put the war against the Taliban and Al Qaeda in Afghanistan on the back burner, which over time allowed them to recruit more individuals and reclaim sizeable portions of the country.

Both traditional foes of the United States like Russia and China, and strong allies like Germany and France, refused to support a preemptive strike against Iraq. Unable to obtain approval from the United Nations, the U.S. attacked Iraq anyway in March 2003, with Great Britain as its only substantial ally. President Bush called the war "Operation Iraqi Freedom." Its purpose, he declared, was to defend our freedom and bring freedom to others. For all of Hussein's posturing and boasting of his nation's military might, his forces proved no match for the overwhelming fire power of the United States. Within a month, American troops occupied Baghdad. American forces captured Hussein, who was subsequently put on trial before an Iraqi court for violation of human rights and other crimes against humanity. Late in 2006, the court found Hussein guilty of ordering the murder of many Iraqis during his reign and was executed by hanging.

No sooner did President Bush jubilantly claim victory in Iraq by piloting a fighter jet onto the deck of an aircraft carrier followed by a speech delivered with a large "Mission Accomplished" banner serving as a backdrop, than the situation in Iraq unraveled. It soon became apparent that Bush's cadre of advisors had no sound reconstruction plans or nation-building agenda, and perhaps most revealing and devastating, no exit strategy. Rather than parades welcoming the American troops as liberators, looting and chaos followed the fall of the Hussein's regime. With too few U.S. troops to establish order, mobs routinely sacked libraries, museums, government offices, and businesses with impunity, while also seizing large caches of weapons. An insurgency quickly developed that targeted American soldiers and Iraqis cooperating with the occupation forces. Sectarian violence soon swept throughout the country as a civil war emerged between Sunni and Shiite Muslims, the former a minority of the Muslim population in Iraq but under Saddam Hussein they had dominated the government and army. To the Shiite majority, it was time for revenge. Despite holding a number of elections, which the Bush administration created much fanfare about, the United States found it impossible to create an Iraqi government strong enough to bring order and stability to the country. Most disturbing, American intelligence agencies revealed that Iraq had become (to the Bush administration's contrary assertions) what it had not been before—a haven for terrorists bent on attacking Americans. The invasion of Iraq, contrary to the Bush administration's righteous claims, seemed to have accomplished very little other than the death of hundreds of thousands of Iraqis, the creation of tens of thousands of Iraqi refugees, and by the end of December 2012, 4,488 Americans killed and another 33,184 wounded. Most important, the U.S. invasion completely destabilized the region, not only increasing Muslim antipathy for the United States, but disrupting the region's balance of power, leading to Iran becoming the most powerful and menacing country in the

Middle East. As long as Saddam Hussein was in power in Iraq, the likelihood of Iran becoming such a power and threat to both the region and the United States would have been much less a reality. With a completely devastated Iraq, no counterbalance existed to contain the growing power of Iran.

Initially the Bush administration had estimated that the war would cost $60 billion, to be paid for largely by Iraq's own oil revenues. By early 2006, expenditures had reached $200 billion and climbing fast while the insurgency prevented Iraq from resuming significant oil production. Some economists and policy makers have estimated that the war will end up costing the United States nearly $2 trillion.

The 2004 Election

As a result of the Iraq war's protraction and with the economy still ailing, Bush's popularity by 2004 declined. Democrats believed that with the right candidate they could retake the White House. A host of Democrats vied for the presidential nomination, including former Vermont governor Howard Dean, Senator Bob Graham of Florida, Senator John Edwards of North Carolina, Representative Richard Gephardt of Missouri, Representative Dennis Kucinich of Ohio, Senator John Kerry of Massachusetts, and Reverend Al Sharpton of New York. Though Dean initially rallied the strongest antiwar advocates, it became clear after the first few primaries that Kerry would be the nominee. The first Catholic to run for president since John Kennedy, Kerry was also married to Teresa Heinz, the widow of an heir to the Heinz Foods dynasty, which proved to be a great boon to his campaign's financial well-being. A decorated Vietnam War combat veteran who served as commander of a small coastal patrol craft known as a "swift boat," Kerry came home in 1969 after receiving his third Purple Heart and soon joined the antiwar movement. By nominating Kerry, Democrats hoped to put forth a candidate whose military experience would insulate him from Republican charges that Democrats were anti-military and too soft on terrorism to be trusted to protect the nation from further terrorist attacks. Simultaneously, the party believed his antiwar credentials would appeal to voters opposed to the invasion of Iraq. For his running mate, Kerry chose the dynamic and charismatic Senator John Edwards.

No sooner did the campaign begin than a well-funded anti-Kerry organization emerged—the "Swift Boat Veterans for the Truth." Led by a fellow Navy and Vietnam War veteran, John O'Neill, the group publicly questioned Kerry's heroism as a fabrication. Kerry unwisely ignored their attacks, leading many voters to believe that there was some truth to the accusations. Also hurting Kerry was his appearance before a congressional committee in 1971 in which he denounced the war in Vietnam, followed by his participation in an antiwar demonstration where he joined other disgruntled veterans in throwing their medals and ribbons over a fence erected at the steps of the Capitol. To many Vietnam War veterans, including those who opposed the war (as well as soldiers who served in other conflicts), the disparaging of such honors defiled the memory of those who served and died without ever being recognized for their service. Indeed, these actions proved to be the major motivating factor behind the Swift Boaters' desires to thwart Kerry's candidacy.

Most important, Kerry proved an ineffective candidate. Aloof and lacking the common touch, he failed to generate the same degree of enthusiasm among his supporters as Bush did among his core followers. Kerry's inability to explain why he voted in favor of the Iraq War Resolution in the Senate only to denounce it later as a major mistake enabled Republicans to portray him as lacking the kind of resolve necessary in dangerous times. Meanwhile, Karl Rove, Bush's cunningly brilliant political adviser, worked assiduously to mobilize the Republican Party's conservative base, which he believed would turn out in droves to vote for Bush because the president was in tune with them on social issues such as opposition to gay rights, same sex marriage, and abortion.

Despite Kerry's lackluster persona, polls predicted a very close election. Bush won a narrow victory, with a margin of 3 percent of the popular vote and 34 electoral votes. Both sides spent tens of millions of dollars in advertising and mobilized new voters—nearly 20 million since 2000. In the end, only three states voted differently than four years before. Kerry carried New Hampshire while New Mexico and Iowa swung to the Republicans. Some pundits believed Kerry lost such a close race not because of his personality or less than enthusiastic campaigning but because the Republicans dominated the evangelical Christian vote. Fundamentalists voted overwhelmingly for Bush. Most important to the outcome were the attacks of September 11 and the sense of being engaged in a worldwide war on terror. No American president who sought reelection during wartime has ever been defeated. The key to victory for Bush was the public's lingering fear that another terrorist attack was imminent, and that it would be better to have an experienced leader in charge.

THE BUSH SECOND TERM

President Bush believed his reelection was a "mandate" for the direction he wanted to move the country, both at home and abroad. He wanted to make permanent the tax reductions Congress had passed during his first term. He believed he could gradually transform Social Security from a public pension system into a privatized "401-K" form of retirement. Meanwhile he continued the Iraq War. Bush believed the United States had to persevere in Iraq until a regime amenable to U.S. influence was securely in place.

The president succeeded in moving the Supreme Court decisively to the right on social and civil liberty issues. In 2005, Sandra Day O'Connor, the first woman to be appointed to the Supreme Court, announced her retirement. O'Connor's decision to step down was followed shortly thereafter by the death of Chief Justice William Rehnquist. Bush now had the rare opportunity to appoint not just one, but two justices. Bush wasted no time in filling the vacancies. He nominated, and the Senate confirmed two jurists he was confident would align themselves with conservative justices Antonin Scalia and Clarence Thomas. A 50-year old appellate jurist who had once worked in the Reagan Justice Department, John Roberts, succeeded Rehnquist as Chief Justice. Roberts proved to be a qualified choice but such was not the case for Bush's other nominee, Harriet Miers, his long-time family friend and White House counsel. Even right-wing pundits were outraged by Bush's selection of Miers, for she possessed at best the most meager qualifications. Bush eventually retracted, removing Miers for consideration and quickly nominated in her place Samuel Alito, a staunchly conservative federal district court judge, who was confirmed in early 2006 after a hard-fought Senate battle.

Although successfully moving the Supreme Court to the right, the rest of Bush's political agenda fell far short of realization. Bush's attempt to partially privatize social security by creating private investment accounts paid with money diverted from the system's trust fund failed. Americans were skeptical of the initiative and turned decisively against this proposed reform. Elderly Americans were especially wary since their modest but guaranteed monthly Social Security check provided stability, often determining whether they would eat, pay their utility bills, and keep a roof over their heads.

The Unraveling of the Bush Presidency

By the close of 2005 the American people had grown tired of polarizing politicking. Equally important to the demise of the Bush presidency was the disastrous Iraq war, which appeared to have no end in sight. The American people grew increasingly weary of the administration's talk about how the U.S. was winning over the Iraqi people to freedom and democracy and how increased U.S. troop levels (known as "the **surge**") had the insurgents on the run if not on the verge of defeat. The surge failed to crush the insurgents, and there was no real decrease in the sectarian violence that continued to wrack the country.

For most Americans, the war was peripheral in their daily lives. They were more concerned by the economy that had become inextricably tied to a global market, the dynamics of which they could not understand nor effectively change. **Outsourcing** of jobs and services became the order of the day, as increasing number of U.S. corporations, looking for greater profits and cheaper labor costs, moved many, if not all, of their company's components overseas. Even when Americans called on the telephone about the balances on their credit cards, they spoke with someone living and working abroad for the credit card company. Such outsourcing greatly disturbed and angered Americans, most important of which was the reality that tomorrow they could lose their job to a foreigner all because of the profiteering that had become the *modus operandi* for many American corporations.

Hurricane Katrina

Perhaps no natural disaster in the history of the United States revealed more inherent flaws of an administration than **Hurricane Katrina**, which slammed into the Gulf Coast on the morning of August 29, 2005. The storm destroyed tens of billions of dollars in property from the Florida Panhandle to Louisiana. However, it was the havoc that the storm surge wreaked on the levees of New Orleans that caused the massive flooding in one of the nation's major metropolitan areas. To many Americans, Katrina opened their eyes to the incompetence and detachment of the Bush presidency as over 100,000 citizens, mostly black, poor, and working class, were stranded with no means to leave the city as water rushed in from the broken levees. The majority of New Orleans' more affluent white residents who owned cars had left the city days a few days earlier before the storm hit. Also revealed to Americans was how poor and desperate the city's African-American population had been for generations. New Orleans had long been one of the nation's favorite cities to visit, annually attracting hundreds of thousands of tourists. For decades tourism had been one of Louisiana's most important industries. Drawing people to the "Big Easy" was the city's fame and mystique of being the nation's most exotic, eclectic, and carefree urban environments, whose cuisine was unlike any other in the country and could only be found in New Orleans. The majority of visitors, however, rarely ventured beyond the main tourist enclaves, and they never saw the squalor, crime, and

A DIVIDED AMERICA: Bill Clinton to George W. Bush / 1127

general destitution that was endemic among the city's majority black population. They were thus shocked at seeing such plight graphically covered by the television news cameras that arrived in New Orleans days before the Bush administration responded to the calamity, especially images of the thousands who rode the storm out packed inside the Superdome football stadium where some elderly and infirmed people died. Hundreds of the city's inhabitants died during and after Hurricane Katrina made landfall, most of them residents of low-income neighborhoods. They not only drowned but also fell victim to the heat, sickness, and dehydration because of an inept evacuation plan and to an excruciatingly slow response from National Guard units and the Federal Emergency Management Administration (FEMA). As a result of Katrina, more than 1.5 million Gulf Coast residents became homeless, eventually finding shelter in schools, sports arenas, hotels, and trailers in Houston, Baton Rouge, Memphis, and other southern and even northern cities. Images of the destitution and destruction of a major American city caused many Americans to wonder why the U.S. government was promising so much abroad but could deliver so little at home.

Katrina made apparent the racial and class divisions that still existed in American cities. Some asked what would the government's response have been had New Orleans been a majority white city? Bush's failure to respond swiftly and decisively resulted in the resignation of Michael Brown, FEMA's director, who in many ways became the scapegoat for the Bush administration's overall mishandling of the Katrina disaster. Politically, the hurricane response caused a sharp decline in Bush's overall approval rating. A year after Katrina, corruption and continued mismanagement of the reconstruction process pervaded practically every facet of the recovery program. Less than half the money ($70 billion) that had been appropriated to assist victims had been spent; $2 billion had been lost to fraud and waste; $900 million worth of mobile homes never got to individuals or went unused because they were inappropriate housing for a flood plain. Because of the overall political and financial mistakes and waste that ensued during reconstruction, only 35 percent of the city's population returned to the Crescent City; the other 65 percent decided that the New Orleans they had loved and that had been one of the nation's most famous and unique cities would never be the same again and thus chose to live permanently elsewhere.

(clockwise from the top) Damaged by the 2005 Hurricane Katrina is a barber shop loated in the Ninth ward, New Orleans, Louisiana, (April 13, 2006) the Waffle House torn apart on the Biloxi, Mississippi coast, (April 12, 2006) and only steps left of a home. March 3, 2006. Credit: Library of Congress

REPUBLICANS DIVIDED AND DEFEATED

By the summer of 2006 there appeared to be no end in sight for the Iraq War. So disillusioned did the American people become with the Bush White House that in the November elections of 2006 they handed the president and his party a devastating blow, electing Democratic majorities to both houses of Congress for the first time since 1994.

Although the war's growing unpopularity was the central issue of the 2006 campaign, scandals and legal issues proved to be equally devastating to both the president and his party. In April 2006, Texan Tom DeLay, the powerful House Majority Leader, resigned amid indictment on campaign finance corruption charges. Other Republicans followed suit for similar malfeasance allegations, most notably those congressmen associated with Jack Abramoff, a notorious influence peddler and rabid Republican partisan. Most appalling was the abrupt resignation of Florida House member Mark Foley who had solicited former congressional pages for homosexual encounters. Finally, the vice president's office, through Dick Cheney's chief of staff, I. Lewis "Scooter" Libby, was responsible for the vindictive "outing" of a covert CIA operative, Valerie Plame, because she and her husband (also a former CIA agent) publicly disclosed many of the administration's lies about the presence of mass destruction in Iraq. Libby was found guilty of perjury and obstruction of justice and sentenced to 30 months in prison in June 2007 but never served a single day's confinement because President Bush commuted his sentence two weeks later.

The Iraq War perpetually plagued the Bush White House. Public opinion polls in 2006 revealed that more than two-thirds of the American people considered Bush's conduct of the war misguided. Among some of the conflict's chief critics were a sizable number from the military establishment—recently retired upper echelon officers who fixed much of the blame for the war's debacle on Secretary of Defense Donald Rumsfeld, who they charged with failing to provide an effective exit strategy for U.S. troops in that war-torn country. Secretary of State Colin Powell later found out that he had been deceived by other members of the administration concerning Hussein's weapons of mass destruction, thus it should have surprised few Americans when Powell declared his support for Democratic nominee Barack Obama in October 2008.

The 2006 midterm elections became a referendum on Iraq. By November 2006, the majority of Americans no longer equated the conflict in Iraq with the war on terror. Increasing numbers of initial supporters of the war within the Democratic Party moved decisively toward a rapid withdrawal policy of American troops from Iraq. As Americans went to the polls that November they vented their frustrations toward the Bush administration by delivering to the president and his party one of the most searing repudiations in American electoral history. The Democrats captured both houses of Congress. Republicans, in even some of the most secure "red states," lost their congressional seats largely the result of an unpopular president and his policies.

A WIRED NATION AND MASS CULTURE TRENDS

Health Care and AIDS

Although the end of the Cold War by the early 1990s relieved Americans of external anxieties caused by that conflict, on the home front citizens confronted a variety of unsettling changes despite the booming economy. Complex biomedical issues, soaring medical costs, the AIDS crisis, mass culture changes, and the ongoing computer and information-technology revolution all made the late 1990s and early twenty-first century an uneasy time.

One of the more perplexing issues confronting Americans was the fact that we were living longer than any previous generation. Thanks to improved medications, breakthroughs in medical research, increased awareness of health issues, and the importance of diet and physical fitness, longevity for many Americans is a reality. Consequently, the nation's population is aging, and this has created an array of ethical issues as not all Americans enjoy quality of life as they get older. Now, as never before, families discuss assisted suicide for the terminally ill, the soaring cost of nursing-home care, of medications to sustain life or to fight off debilitating afflictions, and general financial support for the elderly whose fixed incomes from social security and retirement pensions are no longer ample for self-sufficiency. Feminist pioneer Betty Friedan, now in her early eighties, addressed this issue in *The Fountain of Age* (1993). "Grey Power" made the headlines in 1998 when NASA sent seventy-seven-year-old former "Right Stuff" astronaut-now-Senator John Glenn of Ohio on a ten-day space mission on the latest shuttle. "Children will look at their grandparents differently," declared a NASA official.

Life's beginnings also engendered controversy, and many of these issues were not related to abortion, which continues to be in the forefront of the national dialogue. As childless couples sought help from science, problems of medical ethics arose. Fertility drugs sometimes produced multiple births ranging from twins to sextuplets, and the science-fiction prospect of human cloning moved a step closer to reality in 1997 when Scottish scientists cloned a sheep called Dolly. Cries of eugenics, natural selection, and Social Darwinism were heard throughout the globe.

A stark reminder of corporate power-related health crises came in 1998 with the release of tobacco industry documents revealing the deliberate targeting by the companies of children and young people for their products. President Clinton again urged tougher controls on cigarette advertising and sales to minors. In 2002, after decades of health warnings, statistics indicated that 26 percent of Americans still smoked, including 17 percent of high school seniors.

The nation also continued to face the scourge of AIDS, the fatal disease first identified in 1981. AIDS spreads by the direct transmission of body fluids. The most susceptible populations are sexually active homosexuals or bisexuals, persons having unprotected sex with infected individuals, drug users sharing needles, and babies born to infected mothers. Early in the epidemic blood transfusions also spread the virus. With no cure in sight, public-health agencies urgently advised protective measures, including the use of condoms. By 2002, 486,000 Americans had died of AIDS. By the late 1990s, however, fewer Americans were dying from the afflictions, primarily the result of improved therapies, prevention education, and more cautious sexual practices. Nevertheless, 45,000 new cases were reported in North America in 2006, swelling the total to nearly 1 million Americans infected with AIDS or HIV, a virus that is a precursor of AIDS.

Some fundamentalists believed that AIDS was a punishment for what they saw as the sin of homosexuality and opposed any major public investment in finding a cure. The Clinton and George W. Bush administration, however, pushed ahead with research and improving the availability or treatments for the disease. The Clinton and George W. Bush administrations ignored their rantings, as both presidents urged Congress to fund research for a cure while AIDS activists continued to pressure for expanded research budgets and quicker testing of experimental drugs. Hospice organizations and support networks continued to help sufferers, and a giant AIDS quilt made of panels crafted by victims' friends and relatives toured the nation in October 1992.

The AIDS epidemic had a particularly devastating impact in the arts and entertainment worlds. Nineteen-fifties and early 1960s screen star Rock Hudson, a closet homosexual, died of AIDS in 1985. The popular pianist Liberace, long suspected of being gay, succumbed in 1987. One of the most shocking revelations came in the early 1990s when NBA superstar Earvin "Magic" Johnson announced he was HIV positive (the result of heterosexual philandering) and then later in the same time period tennis pro Arthur Ashe also revealed that he too was HIV positive, infected from a blood transfusion. Ashe died in 1993, along with legendary Russian ballet dancer Rudolph Nureyev, who also had AIDS. Plays such as Larry Kramer's *The Normal Heart* (1985) and Tony Kushner's *Angles in America* (1993), Jonathan Larson's musical *Rent* (1996), and movies such as *Philadelphia* (1993), starring Tom Hanks and Denzel Washington, examined the socio-cultural affects the affliction had on individuals, even those not homosexual, and how society viewed those with AIDS as social pariahs, much in the same way people had regarded lepers for centuries.

As the AIDS epidemic peaked in America in the 1990s, its global toll worsened. Total HIV/AIDS cases worldwide reached 42 million in 2002, with the virus reaching pandemic proportions in Sub-Saharan Africa. Region in Asia and Eastern Europe also revealed high numbers of reported cases. From 1986 through 2001, the United States contributed $1.6 billion to multinational and UN initiatives to combat HIV/AIDS, malaria, and tuberculosis in the developing world.

No doubt U.S. generosity abroad relative to ameliorating deplorable health and medical conditions in developing countries has made a difference. Ironically, at home, health care in the richest country in the world is abysmal on many levels. In 2000, U.S. health-care spending totaled $1.3 trillion, representing 13 percent of GDP (gross domestic product). In 2009 spending almost doubled, reaching $2.5 trillion and reflecting 17.3 percent of GDP. As the nation's 75 million baby boomers reach retirement age beginning in 2010, annual Medicare costs will soar still higher, threatening massive budget deficits. Charges of waste, inefficiency, and government overpayments to hospitals, physicians, and other health-care providers have added concerns about runway costs.

With Medicare threatening to spiral out of control, Congress intervened. In 1997 the Senate voted to raise the age for Medicare eligibility from 65 to 67 while increasing the premiums for more affluent retirees. The House demurred but the trend was clear as Congress set up an advisory panel to address a problem that if not dealt with could have devastating national and individual ramifications. In 2007, 62.1 percent of all individuals who filed for bankruptcy claimed that high medical expenses to be their primary reason. Health maintenance organizations (HMO's) often pass on the costs to their customers by increasing monthly premiums, reducing benefits, increasing deductibles, and raising co-payment fees for prescriptions and other services. Stories mount of patients denied needed treatment by their HMO or literally being pushed out of the bed too soon after surgery, all for cost-cutting reasons (to increase profit). Americans became outraged at such shoddy treatment for which they were paying exorbitant costs. Both the federal and state governments responded, as regulatory measures were put in place with the Clinton administration pushing through Congress a "bill of rights for health-care consumers," which set mandatory HMO guidelines and required HMOs to inform consumers about their policies and coverage. Despite their price-gouging and benefit-reduction schemes, the HMO's did moderate the inflationary increases in health-care costs. By 2000, 26 percent of Americans had some sort of HMO plan, in contrast to 4 percent in 1980, and an ever-growing number of the nation's doctors worked full-time or part-time for an HMO. The corporate and mass media consolidation trend of the 1990s and early 2000s proved to be transforming U.S. health care.

Entertainment

Health-care worries and other concerns did not prevent Americans from seeking entertainment as an escape for their anxieties. Movies, television, theme parks, professional sports, gambling casinos, video games, and the pop music industry all provided leisure-time diversion. In 2001, some 600,000 human beings—second only to the number of people who toured the White House—visited Graceland, Elvis Presley's garish Memphis mansion. In the motion picture industry fantasy extravaganzas dominated production as the two top-grossing movies of 1996, *Independence Day* and *Twister*, both loaded with special effects, dealt respectively, with invading aliens and killer tornadoes. In 1997, Hollywood released yet another James Cameron blockbuster, *Titanic*, a romantic story of a young couple's ordeal aboard that ill-fated vessel's 1912 sinking in the freezing waters of the North Atlantic. As computer animation technology became more sophisticated, real and simulated action in movies became barely distinguishable as witnessed in 2002's number one grossing movie, *Spider Man*, which was full of computerized special effects and based on a popular comic-strip character, one of the first of such genre Hollywood would profitably produce in the coming years.

During the 1990s, *Seinfeld* dominated the sit-com field as it portrayed a group of self-absorbed New Yorkers confronting in wildly bizarre ways the petty irritations of everyday life and tried, with little success, to hold jobs and sustain long-term relationships. Television also continued to influence politics profoundly. Campaigns increasingly became barely distinguishable from toothpaste promotion, as political aspirants turned to advertising conglomerates to advise them on how to best "package" themselves for the voting or constituent consumer. The candidates' commercials featured manipulative visual images, superficial sound bites, and attack ads discrediting their respective opponents. Thanks to his Hollywood years, Ronald Reagan personified and defined this particular form of political manipulation, and although Bill Clinton's easy emotion ("I feel your pain") provoked ridicule, it was effective. The line between politics and entertainment blurred in 1998 when Minnesotans elected a professional wrestler, Jesse Ventura, as their governor, and again in 2003 when Californians threw out in a recall vote Democratic Governor Gray Davis and elected legendary Hollywood action star Arnold Schwarzenegger to the governor's mansion.

The year 2000 marked the beginning of the proliferation of low-budget TV "reality" shows. Despite their lack of intellectual and aesthetic sophistication and integrity, millions of Americans would not dare to miss their favorite "reality" show, whether it was watching individuals on an island engaging in a quasi-*Lord of the Rings* existence for money—one million dollars—for the winner in *Survivor*, to *Joe Millionaire*, which featured mostly objectified young women competing for the favor of a wealthy bachelor. One of the most popular of such venues to emerge, was *American Idol*, in which amateur pop singers hoped to secure a recording contract and possible stardom by having their talent scrutinized by three already-established entertainment figures. *The Simple Life* (which aired on Fox Television from 2003-2007), sent two rich young socialites (Paris Hilton and Nicole Richie) to live on a farm—or "from penthouse to the outhouse," as the show's billing announced. Another show featured aging British rock star Ozzy Osbourne, founder of the heavy metal band Black Sabbath, who had lived a very dissipated life, rife with hard-core drug addiction while a rocker, but had "sobered up" and now he and his family were on television going about their normal daily lives.

Americans' passion for entertainment required spending mind-boggling sums of money. The 2002 sales of CDs, which by the late 1990s had replaced cassette tapes in popularity, reached 624 million. Although a staggering number, it was lower than the previous two years as more young people "shared" (actually stole) music on the Internet, a practice the music industry combated in the courts. Corporate conglomerates increasingly dominated mass culture. The Disney Corporation, one of the largest in the world, generated $25 billion in revenue in 2002 from its various income sources, which included ABC, ESPN, Pixar, and the theme parks Disney World in Orlando, Florida and Disneyland and California Adventure in Anaheim, California. In 2001-2002 Disney's toy sales alone reached $2 billion. The media giant Viacom (also

$25 billion in 2002 revenues) controlled Paramount Pictures, Blockbuster video rental, 15 book publishing companies, 28 television stations, 140 radio stations, and the Showtime, Nickelodeon, and MTV television channels, with MTV having affiliates in fourteen foreign markets. If one individual came to define writ large the consolidation process of mass culture, it was the billionaire conservative Australian mass media mogul Rupert Murdoch, who became a U.S. citizen in 1985. By 1997, after decades of acquisitions, Murdoch's parent corporation, the holding company News Corporation, owned 789 businesses in 52 countries, including Twentieth-Century Fox Movie Studio, *The Wall Street Journal*, *The New York Post*, *TV Guide*, and publishing company *Harper Collins*, which he eventually sold to yet another publishing conglomerate, the British-based Pearson/Longman. In addition to these major enterprises, Murdoch owned 22 television stations, including his pride and joy, the unabashedly right-wing mouthpiece *Fox News* and the Los Angeles Dodgers baseball team. According to the *Washington Post*, Murdoch's "planet-girdling ring of satellite TV system" could theoretically broadcast simultaneously to 75 percent of the Earth's population.

Not all Americans embraced the growing commercialization and consolidation of mass entertainment. One such individual was *Time* magazine columnist Michael Elliot, who in an October 2003 essay deplored how even a "minor" children's night of festivities such as Halloween had been appropriated for profit by capitalist conglomerates such Halloween Express, a franchise operation selling such products as schlocky plastic pumpkins that moaned ominously when someone walked by. The company had 70 stores in 21 states and according to Elliott, the chain had "turned an innocent night of excitement for children into something run by and for adults. Halloween for me is the gaudiest example of the infantilization of American culture. It's up there with McDonald's Happy Meals or Hollywood's decision to concentrate on making kid's films for grownups. In time, infantile societies become degraded, unable to meet the realities that face them."

Personal computer

While entertainment became more commercialized, the personal computer revolution accelerated. By 2001, 56.5 percent of American households had personal computers, compared to only 41 percent just four years earlier. By the beginning of the new millennium, the laptop and even smaller versions could be seen everywhere in use. By the beginning of the new century, a handful of conglomerates dominated the computer-software industry, with the most legendary king of them all, Seattle's Microsoft, founded by Harvard drop-out Bill Gates III. By the late 1990s Gates was the richest person in America with $9 billion in cash and a stock-market valuation of $160 billion—three times that of General Motors. Like the infamous Standard Oil of the Gilded Age, Microsoft crushed or bought out weaker competitors. The competition, however, initially led by Jobs, tried to fight off Microsoft, bringing suit under federal anti-trust laws, charging that Microsoft engaged in "unfair competitive practices" such as installing its own Internet browser, Explorer, in its Windows 95 operating system. In a 2001 settlement the Justice Department placed a number of restrictions on the company claiming that its mandates would "stop Microsoft's unlawful conduct and restore competition to the software industry." As was the case during the Gilded Age, the government's response to Microsoft's monopoly proved to be more bravado than of any real substance— a slap on the wrist as Microsoft remains to this day the most dominant force in the software industry.

The PC made possible the multi-billion dollar video-game industry, revolutionized personal communications through an electronic message system called e-mail, and opened a vast world of information exchange and discussion through the Internet. Developed in rudimentary form by the Defense Department in 1969, the Internet took on a life of its own in subsequent decades. By 2001 more than half of U.S. households had Internet access. The World Wide Web, created in Geneva in the early 1990s and featuring images, movement, and sound, offered an even richer Internet environment. Unlike the corporate consolidation of the software industry under the auspices of Microsoft, the Internet initially experience no such attempted "hostile takeover," and thus ran amok with its service, which allowed for abuse and perversions by various individuals and enterprises. Such free-wheeling led to calls for censorship in the United States and Congress responded by passing the 1996 Communications Decency Act. A year later the Supreme Court ruled this law unconstitutional, shifting the burden of monitoring what minors viewed on the computer screen from the government to parents. Alarming parents most was the proliferation of pornographic websites on the Internet. Civil libertarians applauded the Court's decision to strike down the 1996 law while anti-pornography groups declared that the Court's ruling represented another blow to morality and decency in the United States. Moralists were somewhat mollified when the Court amended its earlier decision by supporting the 2000 Children's Internet Protection Act, which required libraries to install anti-pornography filters on their public computers.

It was only a matter of time before the Internet became commercialized, as practically every major U.S.

retailer, from L.L. Bean to Victoria's Secret to Nike to Omaha Steaks, sold their products via websites. Amazon.com marketed books, CD's, and a variety of other products, while eBay allowed individuals to buy and sell through "bidding" or "bartering," everything from baseball cards to fur coats. The computer revolution inspired both utopian visions and great alarm among a broad cross-section of the American population; not just among moralists. In education, for example, some critics believed that computer-based teaching programs—Distance Education courses—encouraged rote memorization and stifled creativity, let alone denying the student the enriching and stimulating interaction of the classroom experience. Others, led by Seymour Papert of MIT, argued that imaginative, interactive programs could stretch pupils' imaginations—*The Children's Machine: Rethinking School in the Age of the Computer* (1993). Perhaps the greatest complaint was that constant computer use and engagement in the various "games" and activities available, especially by impressionable young people, (even adults some have contended), numbed moral sensibilities, especially by computer games that feature extreme violence without consequences. Such critics assert that the virtual reality of the computer can become more real for users than the actual world around them—that computer reality becomes their reality to the point that many individuals, both adults and adolescents, can no longer distinguish life in the real world from the world they experience on the computer screen. Underscoring such fears, teachers reported that school kids were bonding emotionally with their digital pets (a fad of the late 1990s) and grieving when they died from lack of feeding. Perhaps most disturbing was the danger of one losing their identity as people assumed different personalities and roles in the Internet chat room. To such observers of the computer revolution, the Internet was the ultimate postmodern phenomenon, a portent of the dissolution of any stable reality.

Computer access was unevenly distributed—the majority of computer owners and those connected to the larger world it presented were white middle-class Americans. 61 percent of white households owned at least one computer in 2001. By contrast, only 37 percent of black households and only 40 percent of Hispanic families had access to a computer in 2001. Even more telling, the average annual family income of computer owners was $75,000 or higher in 2001 while computer access fell off sharply further down the income scale. Trumpeted by many as the great socio-economic and cultural leveler, the computer revolution in many ways simply reinforced the divisions of American society along lines of class, race, and ethnicity. Nonetheless, the new electronic world spawned a vast progeny of personal computers that, together with cell phones, DVD players, digital cameras, pagers, and other innovations, were creating a wired society of instant communication and nonstop entertainment.

Chronology

1992 Bill Clinton elected president.
Major race riot in Los Angeles follows "not guilty" verdict in Rodney King case.

1993 Janet Reno becomes first female attorney general.
Israel and the PLO sign Oslo peace accord.
U. S. soldiers killed in humanitarian mission in Somalia.
Congress approves NAFTA.
Terrorist bomb explodes in World Trade Center in New York City.
Clinton announces policy for gays in military.
Family and Medical Leave Act.

1994 U. S. troops intervene in Haiti.
Nelson Mandela elected president of South Africa.
Republicans win control of Congress after declaring "Contract with America."
General Agreement on Tariffs and Trade (GATT) establishes World Trade Organization (WTO).

1995 Oklahoma City bombing, killing 169.
Israeli Prime Minister Yitzhak Rabin assassinated.
Dayton Accords.

1996 Personal Responsibility and Work Opportunity Reconciliation Act.
Clinton re-elected president.
Comprehensive nuclear test ban treaty signed by leaders of nuclear powers.

1997 Madeleine Albright becomes first female Secretary of State.
Supreme Court clears way for Paula Jones civil suit against President Clinton.

1998 Monica Lewinsky case embroils Clinton presidency.
Democrats gain seats in Congress.
Clinton impeached.
United States bombs terrorist sites in Afghanistan and Sudan
United States bombs Iraq.

1999 Nuclear Test Ban treaty rejected in Senate.
Senate trial fails to approve articles of impeachment.
United States, with NATO, bombs Serbia.

2000 George W. Bush elected president.

2001 September 11. Terrorists attack World Trade Center and Pentagon.
United States attacks Afghanistan, driving out Taliban government.
USA Patriot Act.

2002 Republicans gain 6 House and 2 Senate seats in election.
No Child Left Behind Act.
Department of Homeland Security established.

2003 War with Iraq.
Prescription drug coverage added to Medicare.

2004 Bush re-elected for a second term.

2005 Hurricane Katrina.

Review Questions

1. Define neo-liberalism and how this ideology differed from that of the traditional liberalism that had informed the Democratic Party since FDR.

2. What were some of Clinton's major policy and program accomplishments? What were some of his failures and why in both cases are they considered to be successes or failures?

3. One of the most searing and traumatic even in U.S. history remains the terrorist attacks on New York City on September 11, 2001. How did it change Americans' view of the world and of themselves in relation to the rest of the world?

4. Discuss the United States "war on terror." Has the U.S. won that war or is it a conflict that is unwinnable? Have the American people grown weary of the war?

5. What technological innovations have transformed the American entertainment industry?

Glossary of Important People and Concepts

AmeriCorps
Axis of Evil
Osama bin Laden
Brady Bill
Branch Davidian cult
Most Favored Nation Status - China
Contract With America
Dayton Accords of 1995
"Don't Ask, Don't Tell"
Hurricane Katrina
Million Man March
Most Favored Nation Status
North American Free Trade Agreement (NAFTA)
Oklahoma City bombing
Operation Rescue
"outsourcing"
Ross Perot
Proposition 187
Taliban
Troop "Surge"
War on Terror

SUGGESTED READINGS

Richard Bernstein, *Out of the Blue: the Story of September 11* (2002).

Bryan Burroughs and John Helyar, *Barbarians at the Gate: The Fall of RJR Nabisco* (1990).

Greg Critser, *Fat Land: How Americans Became the Fattest People in the World* (2002).

Martin Duberman, *Stonewall* (1993).

Lawrence Freedman and Efraim Karsh, *The Gulf Conflict, 1990-1991* (1993).

Andrew Hacker, *Two Nations: Black and White, Separate, Hostile, Unequal* (1992).

Christopher Jencks, *The Homeless* (1994).

Haynes Johnson, *Divided We Fall: Gambling with History in the Nineties* (1994).

Michael Katz, *The Undeserving Poor: From the War on Poverty to the War on Welfare* (1989).

Joe Klein, *The Natural: The Misunderstood Presidency of Bill Clinton* (2002).

Alex Kotlowitz, *There Are No Children Here: The Story of Two Boys Growing Up in the Other America* (1991).

Nicholas Lemann, *The Promised Land: The Great Black Migration and How it Changed America* (1989).

Jere Longman, *Among the Heroes: United Flight 93* (2002).

Martin Lowy, *High Rollers: Inside the Savings and Loan Debacle* (1994).

David Mervin, *George Bush and the Guardianship Presidency* (1996).

Timothy Phelps and Helen Winternitz, *Capitol Games: Clarence Thomas, Anita Hill and the Story of a Supreme Court Nomination* (1992).

Kevin Phillips, *Wealth and Democracy* (2001).

Arthur M. Schlesinger Jr., *The Disuniting of America* (1991).

Randy Shilts, *And the Band Played On: Politics, People and the AIDS Epidemic* (1987).

James B. Stewart, *Den of Thieves* (1991).

Sanford J. Unger, *Fresh Blood: The New American Immigrants* (1995)

Gary Wills, *Under God: Religion and American Politics* (1990).

President Barack Obama and First Lady Michelle Obama, along with former
President George W. Bush and former First Lady Laura Bush, paused at the
North Memorial Pool of the National September 11 Memorial in New York City. The North
Memorial pool sits in the footprint of the north tower, former World Trade Center.
Credit: Official White House Photo by Chuck Kennedy

Chapter Thirty-five

BARACK OBAMA: A Milestone in United States History

By the mid-1970s more and more people found employment in the booming technology industry. One such individual was **Steven Jobs,** *who along with friend and partner, Stephen Wozniak, founded Apple Computer in 1977, one of the nation's first personal computer companies and ultimately one of the world's largest and most profitable computer conglomerates—not bad for two college drop-outs. Jobs and Wozniak built a prototype PC in the Jobs' family garage. Jobs and Wozniak's initial customers were local hobbyists, but as the PC craze caught fire in 1977, they decided to officially formalize their enterprise into Apple Computer. By 1980, sales had soared to $139 million. Apple made Fortune list of the nation's top 500 corporations faster than any other company in history. IBM introduced its first PC in 1981, and other companies rushed into the market. Thanks to Jobs and Wozniak, the computer revolution was under way.*

Although Jobs became the more legendary of Apple's two founders, it was actually Wozniak who conceived of a series of user-friendly personal computers with Jobs in charge of marketing. The duo sold their Apple I computers for $666.66. The Apple I earned the corporation $774,000. Apple then produced its second model, the Apple II, which put the company in the vanguard of the PC revolution, with sales increasing 700 percent three years after its release. So profitable had their enterprise become that by 1980, Jobs and Wozniak decided to take their company public. On the first day of trading, Apple had an assessed market value of $1.2 billion. Not bad remuneration in four years time for two individuals who started their venture with "capital" received from the sale of a Volkswagen bus (Jobs) and a scientific calculator (Wozniak).

Jobs's life story reads like that of the legendary entrepreneurs and inventors of the late nineteenth century. As an infant, Jobs was adopted by Paul and Clara Jobs and named Steven Paul Jobs. Clara worked as an accountant while Paul received a pension from service in the Coast Guard and an income as a machinist. The family lived in a modest suburban community in the non-descript town of Mountain View, California, which happened to be in the heart of California's burgeoning "Silicon Valley." By the mid-1980s, what was once a small town of mostly fruit orchards had become the center of one of the nation's most important and glamorous new industries: the epicenter of the computer revolution. As a boy, Jobs and his father would work on electronics in the family garage, taking apart and reconstructing electronic apparatus. After graduating from high school in 1973, Jobs enrolled at Reed College, one of the nation's premier small liberal arts colleges in Portland, Oregon. After only six months in school, however, Jobs dropped out, spending the next 18 months auditing a variety of the college's creative classes, such as calligraphy, which Jobs later claimed was instrumental in developing his love of typography.

In 1974 Jobs took a position with Atari, at the time one of the country's leading designers of video games, which were becoming a craze that has lasted down to the present. Jobs tenure with Atari was brief—four months—and Jobs left for India to find "spiritual enlightenment," traversing the country and experimenting with psychedelic drugs, most frequently with LSD. He returned to the United States in early 1976. Within months of his return, he and Wozniak partnered and started Apple Computers. In a 2007 interview with ABC News, Wozniak spoke about why he and Jobs "clicked" so well: "We both loved electronics and the way we used to hook up digital chips. Very few people, especially back then, had any idea what chips were, how they worked, and what they could do. I had designed many computers so I was way ahead of him in electronics and computer design but we still had common interests. We both had an independent attitude about things in the world." Indeed, Jobs and Wozniak are credited with revolutionizing the computer industry by democratizing the technology and making the machines smaller, cheaper, intuitive, and accessible to everyday consumers. Apple's ground-breaking products, which include the iPod, the iPad and the iPhone, are now considered to be dictating the evolution of modern technology.

Hillary Clinton

THE 2008 ELECTION

Few elections in the history of the United States have been as momentous as that of 2008, which produced a resounding victory for not only the Democratic Party but also the election of the nation's first African-American as president. Illinois Senator Barack Obama's overwhelming victory over his Republican rival, Arizona Senator John McCain, proved to be historic in many ways. Even the Democratic primary was unprecedented, as Obama not only defeated a host of male party stalwarts, but also the woman who proved to be his main challenger, former First Lady (then a U.S. Senator representing New York) **Hillary Clinton**. She was the first female in American history to have a good chance at winning a major party's presidential nomination. (Maine Senator Margaret Chase Smith had previously sought the Republican nomination in 1964 and Congresswoman Shirley Chisholm ran for the 1972 Democratic Party nomination.) After a hard-fought battle, Clinton finally acknowledged that Obama had won more delegates to win the Democratic Party's nomination on the first ballot. Her concession fortunately occurred before the party convention in Denver, Colorado. Such a gesture by Clinton avoided what could have easily become a party-dividing donnybrook at the convention, which no doubt would have hurt the Democrats' chances of victory in November. Obama's primary triumph and eventual presidential victory reflected one of the most organized, disciplined, grass-roots organizations ever put together by a presidential contender in either party. From the moment he announced his candidacy in January 2007, and over the course of the next year, Obama, his staff, and his legions of supporters throughout the country created a campaign strategy that not only raised enormous money for presidential campaign but successfully garnered the support of Americans from all classes, regions, color, and even political affiliations. Even some moderate Republicans alienated by the Bush regime supported Obama.

Ensuring victory for Obama was his message of "change," which after eight years of Republican rule and a president who had failed on many fronts to deliver what he had promised both at home and abroad, a majority of American people heartily welcomed. Obama wrapped himself in a liberal mantle, but not one that harkened back to the liberalism of the Great Society years. Instead, he fused New Deal ideology with an overlay of the centrist, neo-liberalism of the Bill Clinton years. Indeed, this has become the "new" liberalism of the twenty-first century and one that Obama brilliantly articulated to the American people. To the surprise of many Democrats, especially Clinton supporters, Obama did not choose his former contender as his running mate, which would have created the most unprecedented ticket ever in United States history—an African-American male and a white female, together seeking the highest offices bestowed by the American people. No doubt such a combination would have engendered a very serious crisis of conscience for many Americans, particularly among the more conservative members of the white middle and working class, regardless of gender, religion, or party affiliation. During the primary campaign, Hillary Clinton had great appeal among blue collar Americans. In fact, many Democratic strategists worried that without her presence on the ticket, Obama could easily lose this key Democratic voting bloc

> ### *Race in America in the 21st Century*
>
> *Many observers wondered whether the 2008 election of America's first black president, Barack Obama, would improve race relations in America. A New York Times poll in July 2000 had revealed an enduring racial divide. Perceptions of racial realities made it seem like whites and blacks were "living on different planets." While 51 percent of blacks believed that too little had been made of problems facing black people, 75 percent of whites thought there was too much or just the right amount of attention given to those issues. Although 58 percent of whites felt that blacks and whites had "about an equal chance of getting ahead," 57 percent of blacks maintained that whites had a better chance of succeeding. Blacks were four times more likely than whites to say that blacks were treated less fairly in the workplace, shops, restaurants, and places of entertainment. The poll also made it clear that, even in the modern world, most Americans did not live, work or worship with those of other races. A December 2010 poll, perhaps surprisingly, showed little change. In fact, the percentage of blacks who believed that whites had a better chance of getting ahead than blacks rose to 64 percent. There were still few areas of regular contact reported with other races. Blacks who experienced or witnessed examples of discrimination based on race had risen from 62 to 70 percent. One positive note came out of the 2010 census. It reported that racial segregation was the lowest in a century as a rising black middle class moved into fast-growing white areas in the South and West. Segregation declined in three-quarters of America's largest cities. Southern cities as Atlanta and Miami were among the least segregated, while there was still substantial racial segregation in the so-called "ghetto belt" of the Northeast and Midwest.*

to his Republican opponent. Such a possibility never materialized; Obama took the blue collar vote in key industrial working class states such as Pennsylvania and Ohio, which helped to ensure his victory. For his running mate, Obama turned to Joseph Biden, a veteran senator from Delaware who had been one of Obama's primary opponents. Obama's choice reflected the need to enhance his foreign policy portfolio as well as hopefully bring back the wayward blue collar vote, which Hillary had so overwhelmingly won. In both instances Biden proved to have been a wise choice.

On the Republican side, to the surprise of many, especially the conservative wing of his party, the moderate "maverick" Senator John McCain of Arizona captured the nomination from two more right-leaning candidates, former Massachusetts Governor Willard "Mitt" Romney and former Arkansas Governor Mike Huckabee. As Clinton and Obama slugged it out from January to June, McCain moved ahead in the polls. However, the "Bush factor" had yet to come into play and the economy, showing signs of impending calamity, had yet to reach the crisis point. Indeed, McCain, much to his subsequent chagrin, continued to declare that the "economy was fundamentally sound." His chances for victory diminished rapidly after his selection of first-term Alaska Governor Sarah Palin as his vice-presidential choice. Selecting her only a few days before the national convention, a good number of Republicans, especially the moderates, were shocked by such a choice. Yet, for a few weeks after the Republican ballyhoo in Minneapolis, the "Palin Factor" appeared to have a positive affect for the McCain campaign. Conservative Republicans celebrated her selection, proclaiming her to be the fresh, new, young, attractive look they needed to win. Moreover, Palin expressed support for the Far Right agenda, endearing her to that wing of the party.

As the presidential campaign rolled into the fall months, the economy continued its precipitous decline, forcing both candidates in October to return to Washington to vote on a $600 billion stimulus (bail out) package for all the banks and major Wall Street brokerage firms that had gone under. Such a financial calamity could not have been worse for McCain. Obama brilliantly tied him to George Bush in every speech he delivered, declaring that McCain was no different than George Bush in mentality and policy, and thus responsible for the present crises both at home and abroad. Perhaps the biggest mistake McCain made was to allow the Republican Right to highjack his campaign. McCain earned a reputation for being a "maverick" within his party, often expressing moderate views on many social issues such as immigration and election reform. Had he remained true to his own brand of Republicanism, he might have given Obama a much closer election fight. McCain, however, allowed the right wing of his party to take control of his campaign, dictate the strategy, and even choose his running mate. Such a decision more than likely cost him the election. The American people had become so alienated and disillusioned with George Bush, with whom they had come to associate with the Republican Right, that if McCain expressed the same ideology he would only be uttering what the American public no longer wanted to hear.

Compounding McCain's woes was Sarah Palin. Whenever she spoke in an unmanaged way, especially in press interviews, she uttered the most inarticulate and uninformed thoughts for vice-presidential candidate. Palin's repeated gaffes and general inability to express coherent explanations of policy matters caused increasing numbers of Americans to genuinely fear the consequences if the governor became president of the United States should McCain die in office. No matter how hard Republican spokespersons tried to bolster Palin as a viable running mate, their arguments fell on deaf ears. As the economy worsened, it became increasingly clear as Election Day approached that Obama would win. In the end, Obama won 53 percent of the popular vote and the Electoral College by a 365-173 margin.

BARACK OBAMA: New Deal Liberal or Neo-Liberal Centrist?

The American people held high expectations for Barack Obama as his presidency began. Like FDR, Obama inherited from his Republican predecessor an economic calamity and pundits from across the ideological spectrum constantly drew parallels between Obama's triumph and that of FDR's victory 76 years earlier. Even both candidates' message was eerily similar: hope and change—words that resonated well with an American public battered by unprecedented economic problems. Unlike FDR, Obama also had to contend with two costly and protracted wars, as well as an international scene in which the United States was isolated, generally mistrusted, and in some areas of the world, outright disdained. Much of the world's suspicion and hostility toward the United States was the result of the Bush Doctrine and its preemptive foreign policy agenda. Unlike FDR, Obama entered the Oval Office confronted by serious crises both at home and abroad, which if not aggressively addressed would have serious and detrimental long-range consequences for the nation.

The Financial Crisis

During the presidential campaign, then-Senator Barack Obama returned to Washington in the middle of the election campaign to help pass emergency legislation designed to shore up the nation's crumbling financial system, which began its declension in the summer of 2008. The failure of several major Wall Street brokerage firms such as Lehman Brothers, Behr-Stearns, and Merrill-Lynch, as well as the risk of collapse to insurance giant AIG, Citibank, and the Bank of America, precipitated the crisis, which was averted by massive federal government **bail outs** of hundreds of billions of dollars. Contributing to the financial meltdown of the businesses was the practice of millions of dollars in bonuses and other perks to corporate executives regardless of company performance, and the investment for quick profits in a variety of speculative enterprises, most notably in the housing market through

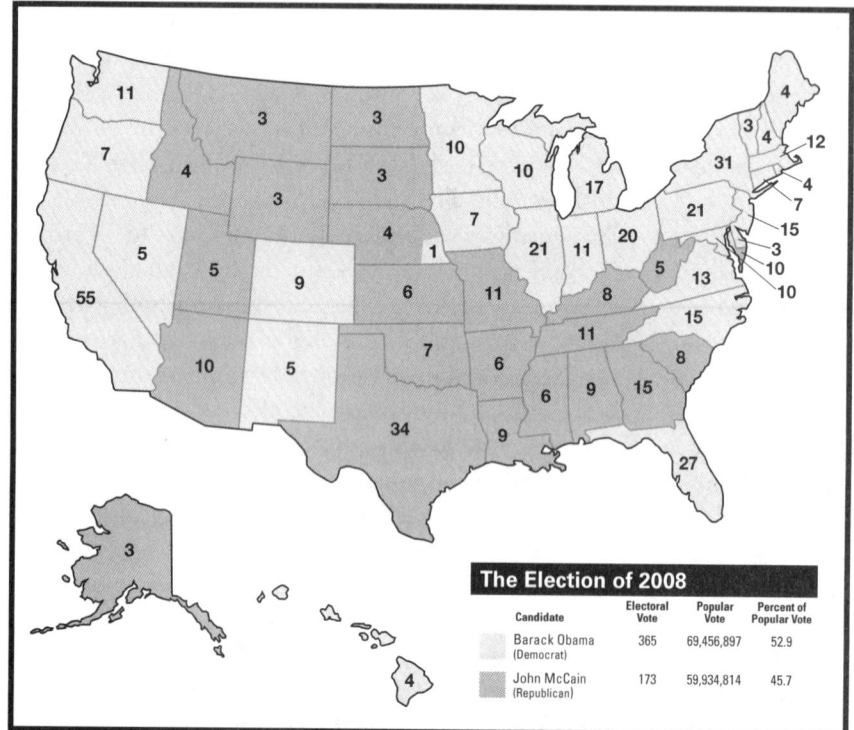

Map 35.1 The Election of 2008

mortgage-backed securities, or those based on the cash flows of mortgage loans. Created by Wall Street, this device became an unregulated investment that was highly lucrative as long as most borrowers continued to make their mortgage payments. The system collapsed, however, with devastating effects on investors and several key financial institutions as an increased number of homeowners defaulted. Some could not keep up with their payments due to simple over-borrowing. Many others, however, defaulted because of the resetting of their adjustable-rate loans, which had very low introductory interest rates for the first few years then rose based on formulas tied to various lending indexes, leading outrageously-high fixed rates (some as high as 16 percent) for the duration of the loans. Still others became victims of the deceptive practices of some lenders who lured unwary customers into mortgages with hidden terms they did not understand (so-called "predatory lending"). The previously booming housing market simultaneously contracted, with housing prices plummeting so fast that overnight it seemed homeowners found themselves "underwater" on their mortgages—they owed more on their home than it was worth. Such individuals tried to sell their homes, but as financially-strapped banks and mortgage lenders (who before the recession had been extraordinarily lenient) began to tighten their credit requirements, fewer potential buyers could qualify for new loans. Thus, millions of Americans found themselves having to pay exorbitant interest rates on a home of steadily decreasing value, so unprecedented numbers of foreclosures not seen since the Great Depression. By the time of Obama's inauguration, thousands of once middle-class suburban neighborhoods, especially the huge new housing developments ("tract" home communities) became half-finished, abandoned, deteriorating, over-grown "ghost towns," inhabited by homeless vagabonds and other dispossessed individuals. Particularly devastated by the recession were the states of California, Florida, Nevada (especially the Las Vegas area), and Arizona, states which had witnessed the most dramatic increases in new home construction and inflated home values over the previous decade.

The collapse of the housing market soon reverberated throughout the rest of the economy, causing hundreds of home-construction related businesses to close their doors, driving up unemployment. By Inauguration Day (January 20, 2009), in the prior six months over 2 million Americans had lost their jobs while millions more joined the ranks of the underemployed, which reached 17 percent by March 2010. Since the recession began in December 2007, the United States had lost 8.4 million jobs. Equally serious, job opportunities for recent college graduates greatly decreased with only a few occupations such as health care, engineering, and education providing employment possibilities on a full-time basis. The national unemployment rate had reached 10 percent and in some states such as California and Michigan, the rate had reached 12 percent and 15 percent respectively.

Because of the flailing auto industry's concentration in the greater Detroit metropolitan area, the Motor City saw its unemployment skyrocket to 25 percent by spring 2009. By that time, both General Motors and Chrysler had gone bankrupt, with plant closings and related industries, including dealerships, shutting down across the nation, leading to thousands of more Americans becoming unemployed. To prevent unemployment from going even higher as a result of the collapse of the Big Two, the Obama administration decided to bail out, in the form of a quasi-"receivership," both General Motors and Chrysler. Both corporations were placed under government auspices in return for billions in bail out dollars. The respective CEO's of each company were to restructure their corporations according to government guidelines to ensure future solvency and maintain employment. Free market believers and other conservatives criticized the president for his alleged government "takeover" of GM and Chrysler, accusing Obama of being a big-government liberal if not a closet "socialist." Conservatives also asserted that because of their poor management and business practices in general, GM and Chrysler should have been allowed to go under instead of the American people bailing out yet another set of failed enterprises. Although such assertions have a degree of validity, the Obama administration nonetheless sought for political and economic reasons to take actions that would preserve the jobs of thousands of workers.

For the new Obama administration, creating jobs became a priority. Soon after entering the Oval Office, President Obama urged Congress to pass a job-stimulus initiative, the $787 billion **American Recovery and Reinvestment Act**, which the administration declared would create or save 3.5 million jobs by the end of 2011. This package, the largest stimulus program in the nation's history, created or saved 640,000 jobs, though the final amount Congress authorized fell far short of the much-higher level of spending that many liberal economists believed would be necessary to generate a robust economic recovery.

Republicans condemned the administration's jobs initiative. "The trillion dollar 'stimulus' isn't working, and no amount of phony statistics can change that," railed House Minority Leader **John Boehner** of Ohio. "The president and his economic team promised the stimulus would create jobs immediately and unemployment would stay below 8 percent. But America has lost more than three million jobs since then, and the unemployment rate is nearing double digits." Although Boehner's partisan views and statistics were skewed, he nonetheless presented a valid criticism overall—the stimulus program had a minimal effect on unemployment.

Many progressives believed Obama had a misplaced sense of priorities and missed a prime opportunity to reform the American capitalist system. Upon his inauguration, Obama had such a moment, for he had large popular support and momentum to bring about significant structural change to the U.S. economy. After over a year in office, however, Obama lost much of that initiative, squandering his mandate by not using his office as the "bully pulpit" to lead the reform impulse. While few presidents have had the opportunity to reshape this nation, even fewer chief executives have entered the White House with a 76 percent approval rating. No sooner was Obama inaugurated than many pundits believed they were about to witness another historic Hundred Days, in which broad sweeping reforms and regulations of the private sector (particularly the nation's financial institutions) would occur in conjunction with an equally aggressive jobs initiatives. No such bold enterprises came from the Obama administration, even though much talk came from the White House about refurbishing the nation's infrastructure, as well as promoting jobs by making the United States a "greener," more energy self-sufficient country.

Equally disappointing for liberals was Obama's timidity relative to private sector reforms, especially the nation's banking, investment, and insurance corporations, all of which continued to pay huge bonuses to their executives regardless of company performance. Most egregious to large numbers of Americans was the doling out of another $700 billion in bail out money to such businesses without meaningful reform and regulation of the nation's entire financial edifice in order to avoid a repeat of another Wall Street collapse. Although President Obama was lauded for his attempts to work with the Republicans in a non-partisan fashion, it became clear that the GOP had no such desire and committed to pursue a policy of obstructionism. Although labeled a liberal by the Republican opposition, in action, rhetoric, and policy, Barack Obama's presidency and his agenda soon reflected the centrist, neo-liberalism—a brand of liberalism first articulated and put into action by Bill Clinton. Although embraced by the American public during the prosperous 1990s, and politically successful in bringing back to the Democratic Party the white middle class, many Americans questioned if continued adherence could rectify the economic crisis. Progressives demanded a return to a more traditional liberalism, with greater government activism to ameliorate the calamity and restore hope and confidence in the nation's future, as well as to rejuvenate a sense of common purpose and faith in government.

The Health-Care Debate

No issue of the early Obama administration defined the president's purpose, direction, and agenda than the narrow passage in late-March 2010 of a Democratic Party-sponsored health-care reform bill. In both houses of Congress, voting fell along strict party lines, with no Republicans in either chamber supporting the bill. Without question, the bill represented the most sweeping social legislation since the mid-1960s, when a Democratic president, Lyndon Johnson, along with fellow Democrats and some Republicans created Medicare and Medicaid. Prior to the health-care reform bill passage, the United States was the only advanced nation without universal health care, and it also had by far the world's highest health-care costs.

On November 19, 1945, Harry Truman stated facts that are true to this day: "People with low or moderate incomes do not get the same medical attention as those with high incomes. The poor have more sickness, but they get less medical care. We should resolve now that the health of this nation is a national concern; that financial barriers in the way of attaining health shall be removed; that the health of all its citizens deserves the help of all the nation." Nearly 65 years later, President Barack Obama made Truman's wish come to pass. The bill intended to eliminate medical discrimination, mandating coverage for an additional 30 million Americans (leaving only 6 percent of the total population uninsured), and provide premium subsidies for low-income Americans. Perhaps most important, the reform bill attempted to control health-care costs. The Congressional Budget Office gave the measure its financial approval by announcing that the initiative would reduce the deficit by $138 billion in its first decade, amounting to approximately $1.2 trillion in its second decade. The reform bill promised to be fiscally responsible while taking major steps toward dealing with rising health-care costs.

For President Obama, the health-care reform bill was transformative. When he began his administration, he was hopeful that he could achieve his reform agenda with Republican support. His campaign pledge to work across party lines was not a realistic possibility. No sooner did he begin his presidency and start to implement his progressive policies than the Republicans became obstructionists, determined to defeat the president's every initiative for change, labeling him a "tax and spend liberal." After months of enduring escalating vitriol about his policies, Obama gave up the pursuit of bipartisanship. The president preferred to be more of a consensus leader than a warrior. However, as demonstrated by his determination to see health-care reform pass, he quickly transformed into a focused and passionate fighter. Ultimately, Obama simply ignored critics and secured passage of the legislation.

No sooner did the health-care reform bill pass than GOP leaders vowed to pursue its repeal, declaring that such action would be the major theme of their fall congressional campaign. The partisan struggle against the measure quickly shifted from Congress to the states and their federal courthouses. Led by several states' respective attorney generals, Republicans challenged the reform by declaring that its stipulation mandating that all adults have health insurance coverage or be subject to tax penalties (which had been demanded by insurance companies as the price for agreeing to cover individuals with pre-existing conditions) violated both state sovereignty and individual rights.

The Tea Party Movement

The day before the health-care vote in the House, President Obama assembled House Democrats and in an unscripted exhortation told them why they needed to pass reform: "Every once in a while a moment comes when you have a chance to vindicate all those best hopes that you had about yourself, about this country, where you have a chance to make good on those promises that you made and this is the time to make true on that promise. We are not bound to win, but we are bound to be true. We are not bound to succeed, but we are bound to let whatever light we have shine."

When the president first introduced his health-care initiative in early summer 2009, he immediately became confronted with a surprisingly shrill opposition that appeared in town hall meetings throughout the country held by both Democrats and Republicans to gauge the peoples' temperament about the proposed reform bill. Even before the health-care bill had been introduced, groups of individuals had gathered across the country to protest the Wall Street and automobile company bail outs and to ventilate an outrage at perceived government handouts and entitlements, certain such programs would inevitably lead to increased taxation. In its early phases, the "**Tea Party**" **movement** was a tax revolt, with its members identifying their cause against current government "tyranny" with that of colonial Americans against the alleged oppressive policies of the British government during the 1760s and 1770s. Colonial protest against

Tea Party gathering in Freedom Plaza (just off the Mall) Washington D.C. March 15, 2010.   Credit: RTNews

Parliament's decrees climaxed with the 1773 Boston Tea Party, an event in American folklore and historical mythology that is considered the "defining" act of American resistance to British oppression. Hence, the assumption by the current tax "rebels" of the name "Tea Party."

Many Republicans, particularly at the state level, joined in with the protesters, exhorting them in their tirades against the excesses of big government, which they naturally ascribed to the Obama administration. The health-care bill simply galvanized this initially populist groundswell (though backed by wealthy reactionary donors) into a full-fledged nationwide protest movement, holding its first national convention in early February 2010. Over 600 people attended the conference, which also saw Sarah Palin and other right-wing notables show up to give rousing speeches endorsing the movement's crusade against big government, which meant the Obama administration and the Democratic Party.

Comprised mostly of ultraconservative Americans and libertarians, the "Tea Partiers" claimed to speak for those Americans supposedly fed up with excessive big government. They overwhelmingly favored Republicans over Democrats, but many despised both parties and their respective leadership while supporting libertarian policies and candidates. They tended to be more secular-oriented individuals, although they held anti-abortion views and opposed gay rights. Most proclaimed themselves to be independents, a "People's Party" reminiscent of the Populist movement of the 1890s. However, to compare the Tea Partiers with the Populist movement of the late nineteenth century would be a gross historical inaccuracy. The 1890s Populists were in favor of *more, not* less government regulation of private enterprise, and supported direct participation in the economy to address inequities. The Tea Party movement was critical of the government in general. The country witnessed blatant disrespect, if not outright hate for a president and his policies, at demonstrations, rallies, and conventions. Many Tea Partiers, were unabashedly malicious in their denunciations of the Obama administration exhibiting shameless placards and slogans, reflecting cynicism and hate. The Republican establishment often quietly acquiesced to the Tea Partiers. Many congressional Republicans and those aspiring to office openly pandered to the movement, believing that their party could use their support to sweep back into power. Leaders within the Republican establishment cautioned against giving the Tea Partiers too much influence within the party, fearing their policies could affect the viability of Republican candidates in general elections against the Democrats

THE 2010 CONGRESSIONAL ELECTIONS

Despite passage of the health-care bill, the Obama administration continued to lose the confidence of the American people, largely because the president's various economic stimuli and reforms had failed to fix the economy, especially to reduce the high rate of unemployment, which by the 2010 November elections hovered around 10 percent. That number only reflected the Labor Department's official statistics, those people reporting to be out of work and who were still looking for jobs. It did not include the number of underemployed Americans, which was much higher, or those citizens who had simply given up looking for any kind of work. If those numbers had been included in the overall unemployment rate, the nation would have been looking at a much more alarming figure of around 17 percent. Republicans and their Tea Party allies seized on these statistics, exploiting the growing despair among Americans out of work or in danger of losing their jobs and naturally blamed the president's economic policies, which they claimed were wrong and that the president *did not do enough* when he had the chance to end the economic downturn.

The Obama stimulus, which in retrospect amounted to a few token work programs, was almost 40 percent tax cuts, which was far too cautious and meager to turn the economy around. Despite warnings from economists that such an anemic approach would do little to ameliorate unemployment, the administration forged ahead, more concerned about achieving bipartisanship. During his first two years, the president consistently tried to reach across the aisle. He praised Ronald Reagan for restoring American dynamism, adopted GOP rhetoric about the need for government belt-tightening even in the face of a recession, and offered symbolic freezes on spending and federal wages. Conservatives continued to denounce Obama as a socialist. Perhaps most important historically for the president, Americans forgot (or never knew) that Reagan often gave ground on policy substance—most notably, when he enacted multiple tax increases during his second term as the potential for stagflation reared its ugly head. On this issue, as well as on many other matters, both Reagan and the Republican leadership of his era were willing to work with their Democratic counterparts to try to find ideological and policy common ground to ensure economic stability and security.

By 2010, Congressional Republicans had made it clear that they had no desire to engage in bipartisanship with the president or with his party. House Minority Leader John Boehner and Senate Minority leader Mitch McConnell were determined to discredit the president so much that come the 2010 congressional elections

Representative John Boehner is the third representative from the state of Ohio to serve as Speaker of the House of Representatives. He served as the Republican House Minority Leader from 2007 until the election of 2010 gave the Republicans control of the House. Boehner was then elected Speaker. Credit: RTTNews

the Republicans would sweep back into power in both houses of Congress. Once in control, they planned to continue to stymie the president's agenda until he could be defeated in the 2012 presidential election. Thus, as the November elections neared, the Republicans pursued a policy of complete obstruction of any presidential or Democratic-sponsored legislation designed to try to address the economic crisis.

From the liberals, one heard the criticism that Obama had yet to become the true progressive that they believed they elected in 2008. Rather, they got instead an overly cautious centrist cut from the same ideological cloth as Bill Clinton, but lacking the former president's willingness and fire to engage head-on the right-wing ideologues who constantly attempted to destroy his administration. Being the nation's first black president may also explain Obama's refusal to be overly confrontational. He repeatedly presented himself as a conciliator. Rather than a lack of focus, Obama suffered primarily from a lack of audacity—to take head-on aggressively his right-wing adversaries. Perhaps, if he had unleashed a counter-assault on the Republicans and if he had acted more boldly, the president and his party might not have gotten the "shellacking" (to use the president's words) that they received in the mid-term congressional elections.

Many in the nation believed that Obama truly represented the hope and change that had been a long time in coming. Instead, to the subsequent dismay of his supporters, Obama chose a safer course—a medium-sized stimulus package that was clearly not up to the task. In early 2009, many economists were frantically warning the president that his administration's proposals were not bold enough. By late 2009, the economic worriers had been right. The economic stimulus programs were much too limited in scope and depth.

Obama's lack of leadership, and, at times, general fortitude, cost his party dearly as Republicans swept back into control of the House of Representatives in 2010. (The Democrats maintained control of the Senate by a margin of 51 to 47.) Obama was not solely to blame for the House elections, so were key party leaders such as Senate Majority Leader Harry Reid and House Speaker Nancy Pelosi, both of whom failed to deliver an aggressive, positive, action-oriented message. The Democratic leadership proved at times as inept as the president and thus lost the public confidence. Moreover, the party suffered from defections, as many **"Blue Dog" Democrats** sided on key issues on the economy with their Republican cohorts. Many of these Democrats, nevertheless, lost their re-election bids. Without the president running to attract the party faithful, Democrats suffered mightily in legislative, gubernatorial, and congressional races across the country.

The 2010 election results revealed that in the House, Republicans picked up a net total of 63 seats, erasing gains achieved by Democrats in 2006 and 2008. Although the sitting president's party usually loses some congressional seats in a mid-term election, the 2010 results witnessed the highest loss of a party in a House midterm election since 1938. Commanding 242 seats to the Democrats' 193, the Republicans gained control of the most House seats since 1946, when the American people repudiated Harry Truman. The Republicans commanded 242 House seats to the Democrats 193. Pundits claimed that four interrelated issues led to such a popular rejection of both the president and his party: frustration and anger with Obama's inability to fix the economy, opposition to the Affordable Care Act ("**Obamacare**"), the overall weak economy for which Americans blamed Obama, and the Tea Party's favorite issue—deficit reduction.

No sooner did the Republicans take over the House than they began their assault on the president's agenda. In early 2012, Obama started to find his angry voice and began taking the Republicans to task for their policies of unfairness. He compromised on the Bush tax cuts, extending them temporarily, but in return the Republicans agreed to maintain middle-class payroll tax cuts as well as extend the jobless benefits for several more months. Obama also succeeded in getting relief for homeowners by mandating that the nation's largest banks, i.e., Wells Fargo, Bank of America, Citicorp, etc., stop sitting on their billions of bail out money and begin extending new loans to prospective home owners as well as help Americans to keep their homes, in other words, to help them to avoid foreclosure by refinancing their current loans at affordable rates. The Obama administration did not aggressively address the unemployment issue, although he asked for billions more from Congress for a new attempt at that most pressing issue, and he did receive sufficient moneys with which to initiate more government-sponsored job programs. Perhaps most important for the Obama administration was the fact that the unemployment rate had been steadily dropping in the opening months of 2012. As of early spring of that year, unemployment had dropped to 8.3 percent, which was encouraging, though the nation was still far from being out of trouble.

After several months of heated debate in both houses of Congress, in the summer of 2010, the legislature finally passed the **Dodd-Frank Wall Street Reform and Consumer Protection Act,** which the Obama administration had been advocating for over a year. The bill's passage represented a significant legislative victory for the president, who had promised since his early White House days to rein in Wall Street's reckless behavior, which had caused the financial system's near collapse in 2008. It was repeal of earlier regulatory measures such as the long-standing New Deal Glass-Steagall Act by the Clinton administration in 1999 that had opened the flood gates for Wall Street's abuse of the nation's financial edifice. The Dodd-Frank bill established an independent consumer bureau within the Federal Reserve to protect borrowers against "**predatory lenders**" whether it be home mortgages, credit cards, or other lender-borrower situations. The legislation also gave the government new power to seize and shut down large, troubled financial companies, such as the failed investment bank Lehman Brothers, before their collapse could cause a ripple effect and bring other banking houses down, which the 2008 collapse revealed were more intimately connected than anyone realized. Dodd-Frank set up a council of federal regulators to watch for threats to the financial system, such as those that appeared in 2008.

Also under the new rules, the vast market for derivatives, complex financial instruments that helped fuel the crisis, are now subjected to government oversight. The bill also addressed the out of control, obscene paying of huge monetary bonuses and other benefits to corporate executives, many of who were directly responsible for the abuses and high-handed manipulations and deceptions that had caused the crisis. All such activities and transactions will come under government scrutiny while shareholders gain more say on how corporate chieftains are compensated. When the president heard that the bill had passed, he declared that the measure would "protect consumers and lay the foundation for a stronger and safer financial system, one that is innovative, creative, competitive, and far less prone to panic and collapse." The bill's co-sponsor, Senator Christopher Dodd of Connecticut, was confident that the legislation would help restore Americans' faith in the badly battered financial system.

In the Senate, the bill passed by a vote of 60-39, with three Republican senators, Scott Brown of Massachusetts along with Olympia Snowe and Susan Collins of Maine, voting for the measure. Senator Russell Feingold of Wisconsin was the lone Democrat who opposed the bill, asserting that it did not go far enough in regulating Wall Street. Feingold was not alone in his criticisms that Dodd-Frank was too weak in bringing Wall Street bankers and financiers to task for what they had done. Many liberals criticized Dodd-Frank for failing to more aggressively alter the structure of Wall Street and for leaving so many critical decisions to federal regulators, who missed many of the warning signs before the 2008 crisis. Meanwhile, Republicans typically argued that the bill created bigger, more intrusive government. These critics joined with leaders in banking and business communities in insisting that the new regulations would undermine the U.S. economy's competitiveness, stifle job growth, and kill jobs at a time when unemployment was still high. By 2012, none of the Republicans' dire forecast had come true. Nonetheless, at the time of the bill's passing, Senate Minority Leader Mitch McConnell (R-Ky.) declared that "The White House will call this a victory but as credit tightens, regulations multiply, and job creation slows even further as a result of the bill, they'll have a hard time convincing the American people that this is a victory for them." Despite Republican attempts to vilify the measure in the eyes of the American people, their castigations did not have the desired political result, which was to use the measure against President Obama in his re-election bid. By election time, unemployment had dropped to 7.8 percent, with over three million jobs created or restored since Obama had been in office. Even the deficit shrank faster than anticipated since Obama came to the White House: "From fiscal 2009 to fiscal 2012, the deficit shrank 3.1 percentage points, from 10.1 percent to 7 percent of GDP," according to *Investor's Business Daily*.

THE OBAMA ADMINISTRATION AND THE WORLD

No president in American history had inherited a tenser, more uncertain, and potentially volatile international scenario than Barack Obama. No president ever assumed the fighting of two costly wars simultaneously, and only a handful of presidents had ever had to do as much to repair the image of the United States abroad. As a result of the Bush administration's "first-strike" policy and disregard for the international community's concerns, global opinion of the United States had reached an all-time low. Probably at no other time since the end of World War II had America's credibility been so universally questioned and respect for its preeminence challenged in many regions of the world. By the close of the Bush administration, surveys of world opinion revealed that even in Western Europe large numbers of people viewed the United States as a threat to world peace. Obama thus made foreign policy a priority. He renounced the Bush Doctrine's unilateralism and preemptive approach in dealing with the nation's potential adversaries. The president sought to return American foreign policy to the traditional post-World War II principle based on multilateral action and collective security pacts. The president believed that the best way to show the world that his administration had no intention of pursuing or continuing with any of the Bush administration's policies was to bring his new message of peace and multilateral cooperation through such organizations as the United Nations, as well as directly to those countries that had become the most suspicious and fearful of U.S. intentions. One of Obama's first sojourns out of the United States was to the Middle East, where in Egypt he assured the Arab-Muslim world that his administration wanted to cultivate better relations with them and did not see them as enemies of the United States, but rather as allies in the fight against the terrorist extremists that had perverted an inherently peaceful faith.

Obama's overtures to the Muslim world naturally raised concerns that such a gesture would alienate Israel who might feel he was abandoning them in favor of developing stronger ties with Arab countries. Obama visited Israel as a candidate in 2008, and since taking office, he has repeatedly confirmed America's commitment to them while exalting the U.S.-Israeli friendship. As every president before him since Truman, Obama assured the Israelis that he too considered them to be one of United States' closest allies.

Obama also worked assiduously to repair America's relations with Europe, assuring European leaders that the days of the United States acting unilaterally were over and that the United States was ready to cooperate with the European nations on a variety of concerns, ranging from continued nuclear disarmament and talks with the Russians to acting in unison on the issue of global warming. On the latter topic, the Obama administration had high hopes that the United States could reclaim its leadership when it came to preserving the world's environment and addressing the effects of global warming. In December 2009, representatives from 193 nations met in Copenhagen, Denmark to establish legally-binding pacts toward limiting greenhouse gas emissions, which most scientists believe to be causing the earth's warming temperatures and climate change. Such was the commitment made by the United States in accepting the mandates of the 1997 Kyoto Protocol, though the Bush administration had declared that America would no longer abide by its provisions. Obama personally addressed the conference, telling its attendees that the United States was ready to do its part and support any initiatives established by the conference to reduce greenhouse gas emissions. The president's words, however, fell on largely deaf ears as the gathering failed to reach any sort of consensus or pact that would become a legally-binding mandate among all the signatories.

Despite the **Copenhagen Conference** setback, President Obama's other international initiatives, especially his overtures toward peace and reconciliation with adversaries (such as Iran), and his reassertion that the U.S. is always willing to negotiate and compromise rather than act wantonly and belligerently, earned the president the 2009 Nobel Peace Prize. Obama became only the third sitting president (Theodore Roosevelt and Woodrow Wilson were the first two) to win the award. Although recognized by the world for his leadership, many Americans, especially Republican critics, believed the president to be undeserving of such distinction,

The Club of Rome, The Environmental Movement and the Issue of Global Warming

Forty years ago humanity was warned that by chasing ever greater economic growth, civilization was sentencing itself to ultimate extinction. Such foreboding came from The Club of Rome, a blue-ribbon multi-national association of business leaders, scholars, and government officials gathered together by the Italian tycoon, Aurelio Peccei, to research where decades of accelerated technological and industrial development was taking mankind. The Club's collective efforts and dire forecast appeared in a slim 1972 volume called **The Limits of Growth.** *Club members discerned their predictions from an intricate series of computer models developed by MIT professors. The book caused a sensation, believing that humanities' wants were on a collision course with the world's finite resources and that a "crisis point," if not the apocalypse, would soon visit mankind in the form of famine, overpopulation, the depletion of essential natural resources, the end of industrial production, and a completely polluted environment.* **The Limits of Growth** *was neither the first nor the last publication to assert that the end was near due to the disease of modern development. Although mostly forgotten these days, in its own time, the publication was a mass phenomenon, selling 12 million copies in more than 30 languages and being acclaimed by the* **New York Times** *as "one of the most important documents of our age."* **The Limits of Growth** *helped set the terms of debate on crucial issues of economic, social, and particularly environmental policy that remains embedded in the public consciousness four decades later.*

If the 1950s and early 1960s had been a period of technological optimism, by the early 1970s, the mood in advanced industrial nations had begun to turn grim. Rachel Carson's 1962 book, **Silent Spring,** *had raised concerns about pollution, helping to ignite the environmental movement. Paul Ehrlich's 1968 book,* **The Population Bomb**, *argued that humanity was breeding itself into oblivion. The first Earth Day (April 1970) was marked by pessimism about the future, and later that year, U.S. President Richard Nixon created the Environmental Protection Agency to address the multitude of abuses that Americans had heaped on their environment since the Industrial Revolution. This was the context in which* **The Limits of Growth** *resonated. Its genius was to bring together in one argument the concerns over pollution, population, and resources. Founded in 1968 and declaring to be "a project on the predicament of mankind," the Club of Rome had set as its mission the gathering of the world's best analytical minds to find a way "to stop the suicidal roller coaster man now rides."*

The Club's analysis was fairly straightforward. As death rates dropped significantly (due to advances in medical research that cured or prevented a host of maladies) and birthrates increased, especially in developing nations, population increased. As each person consumed more food and products, meeting the total demand required "an enormous input of resources." This depleted the resource reserves available, making it ever harder to fulfill next year's resource demands. As the population keeps growing, a staggering increase in the death rate driven by a lack of food and health services will kill a large part of civilization. The culprit is clear: "The collapse occurs because of non-renewable resource depletion." **The Limits of Growth** *contended that even if pollution and population growth were controlled, the world's resources would eventually be exhausted and food production would decline back to the subsistence level. The authors argued that the only way to avoid such a catastrophe was through policies that forced people to have fewer children while simultaneously cutting back on their consumption of material goods and prioritizing recycling, durability, and sustainability. If such programs were put into effect, world society would be stabilized at a level significantly poorer than the present one. Since most people saw such a solution as wildly unrealistic, the real truh was simple—the world was screwed. Such was* **Time** *magazine's 1972 conclusion on its assessment of* **The Limit's of Growth**'s *message, headlined "The Worst Is Yet to Be?": "The furnaces of Pittsburg are cold; the assembly lines of Detroit are still. In Los Angeles, a few gaunt survivors of a plague desperately till freeway center strips, backyards, and outlying fields, hoping to raise a subsistence crop. London's offices are dark, its docks deserted. In the farm lands of the Ukraine abandoned tractors litter the fields: there is no fuel for them. The waters of the Rhine, Nile, and Yellow rivers reek with pollutants. Fantastic? No, only the grim inevitability if society continues its present dedication to growth and 'progress.'"*

Although much of what **The Limits of Growth** *asserted has yet to manifest itself to the degrees contended by the book's authors, and since its publication, it has been roundly criticized for its anti-economic growth position, there is undeniably one topic on which the book was prescient: the issue of environmental pollution, which has caused global warming. The year 1998 was the hottest ever recorded, and nine of the ten hottest years occurred in the 1990s. In 1998 the National Oceanographic and Atmospheric Administration reported that average temperatures worldwide had increased by a degree since 1900, with the warming trend increasing, and pinpointed pollutant*

> emissions as the likely cause and the U.S. as the most egregious "emitter." The United States' per capita pollutant emissions of some twenty metric tons per year sharply contrasts with Europe's average of around eight metric tons per capita. The long range consequences of global warming, scientists warned, could include agricultural disruptions, the inundation of coastal cities from melting polar icecaps, and malaria epidemics as malaria-carrying mosquitoes expanded their range.
>
> The early twenty-first century saw a decline of environmental awareness, and the current recession has only diminished further Americans' concerns for the well-being of their physical environment. Recent polls found a sharp decline in those who considered environmentalism a "very serious" issue, from 52 percent in 2008 to less than 25 percent in 2012. Hopefully, as the U.S. economy continues to improve and Americans are less distracted by financial worries, there will be a renewed concern for environmental issues, for accumulating scientific evidence clearly shows the potential for the grim realities forecasted forty years ago by the Club of Rome and **The Limits of Growth**.

claiming he had done nothing substantive or extraordinary to earn the prize.

After several months of careful deliberation and consultation with his top military advisers, Obama decided in early December 2009 to send an additional 30,000 troops to Afghanistan (commonly referred to as "**the surge**"). The president based his decision on his belief that in order to impress the Taliban (which had increased in size and strength since the American invasion of Iraq in 2003) that the United States was not going to simply abandon the country to their tyranny, more U.S. "**boots on the ground**" would be required. Because of the Bush administration's preoccupation with Iraq, the Taliban had not only revitalized but became a threat as well to Pakistan, which the United States could ill afford to see fall to such a regime. Obama also believed that Osama bin Laden was still alive and operating out of the mountain border between Afghanistan and Pakistan. In his announcement during an impromptu visit to Afghanistan in late March 2010, Obama stated that the United States' objective was not only to ensure the survival of the Karzai government by forcing the Taliban to the peace table, but in the process, hopefully finish off Al Qaeda and its leaders, especially bin Laden.

Early in his administration, Obama announced his intention to have all U.S. combat operations in Iraq come to an end by August 31, 2010. Beginning at that time, the United States would begin to withdraw all but 35,000-50,000 American troops, with the remaining soldiers staying to help further stabilize the country and protect its democratically elected government until Iraqi security forces became strong enough to handle the insurgency. As of 2012, the war in Iraq cost $900 billion, the lives of 4,386 Americans soldiers, and the wounding of another 31,716 (the number of insurgents killed by U.S. or coalition troops is approximately 55,000). Since the war began in March 2003, over 600,000 Iraqi civilians have lost their lives with another 2.25 million becoming displaced persons in Iraq and with another 2 million Iraqis becoming refugees now living in either Syria or Jordan. Most disturbing was the latest poll taken of Iraqis in which 82 percent opposed continued U.S. and coalition presence in their country. President Obama obviously took to heart such revealing numbers and decided it was time for the United States to withdraw from what had become the most protracted war in American history.

Narrowing the Struggle

Despite Bush's blanket approach to the war on terrorism, there was reason for concern about the Tehran government. Iran's most recent elections in the summer of 2009, completely rigged in favor of the hardcore mullahs and, Mahmoud Ahmadinejad, witnessed widespread street demonstrations against the regime, which were viciously repressed. Moreover, there was little doubt that Iran had nuclear capabilities, but whether the government intended to continue development for domestic energy purposes or to build weapons of mass destruction had yet to be determined by the Obama administration. Despite tension between Iran and the United States over its nuclear program, the Obama White House believed a continued cold war with Iran made little sense. Iran's Shi'ite theocrats had a mostly hostile relationship with Al Qaeda's anti-Shi'ite leaders. In both Iraq and Afghanistan, Iran has caused trouble for the United States largely out of fear that if the U.S. prevailed in both countries, Iran would be the next target for invasion and occupation. President Obama, however, believed that if the U.S. government could convince Iran's government that America had no intention of invading Iran, then Washington and Tehran could cooperate to achieve their common objective in both Afghanistan and Iraq, which was smashing Al Qaeda.

Another problem facing the Obama White House was the fact that the United States was not as strong militarily in the early 2000s making the Iranian government and the Taliban less inclined to negotiate. With the U.S. mired in two wars, the Iranians were less afraid of American military power and continued their nuclear programs, while the Taliban had little incentive to break their ties with Al Qaeda. It became hard for Obama to win at the negotiating table without conclusive victory on the battlefield. Therein lay the irony of Obama's "New Look": his perceived need to escalate conflicts and tensions by sending more troops to Afghanistan and possibly pushing new sanctions against Iran, in order to gain the diplomatic muscle essential to negotiate, but in such a way that concessions or compromises did not look like American defeats.

THE END OF OSAMA BIN LADEN AND THE ARAB SPRING

After ten years on the run, the Obama administration finally found Osama bin Laden's hiding place in Pakistan and launched a **Navy raid** in which bin Laden was killed. Americans breathed a deep sigh of relief, as did the people of many other countries. In the wake of bin Laden's death, Obama faced other challenges globally, especially in the Middle East where the so-called "**Arab Spring**" uprisings saw several countries of that region undergo profound revolutions, some of which toppled long-standing U.S. allies such as Hosni Mubarak in Egypt, while another (with the aid of NATO air strikes) overthrew the long-standing American nemesis Gaddafi of Libya. Tunisia and Yemen also underwent revolutions to oust long-standing dictators while tiny Bahrain witnessed sporadic unrest, sometimes ending in violent confrontation between protesters and government forces, largely the result of sectarian issues between the nation's minority Sunni rulers and the majority Shi'a population, demanding greater civil and religious freedoms. Syria also descended into a vicious civil war. **President Bashar al-Assad** (son of longtime dictator Hafez al-Assad) brutally suppressed an uprising that continued into 2012 without any outside military help. The Obama administration publicly condemned Assad's violent repression, which saw thousands of Syrians, both civilian and rebels, killed. Although the president publicly denounced Assad's use of force and called for him to step down, the United States did not militarily intervene. The U.N. Security Council failed to unanimously approve sanctions against Assad, as both China and Russia, two of the council's permanent members, voted against any interference.

In the fall of 2011, in the wake of Arab spring and in response to the Tea Party Movement, tens of thousands of American citizens, initiated a nation-wide massive protest movement not seen since the days of 1960s student activism—**Occupy Wall Street**. At first, the demonstrators, from across a wide demographic, gender, age-group, and occupation spectrum of America—rallied

Members of Barack Obama's cabinet follow developments on May 1, 2011 as NAVY storms terrorist Osama bin Laden's compound in Pakistan and kill him. Vice President Joe Biden and President Obama sit on the left near Brigadier Gen. Marshall B. "Brad" Webb while Secretary of State Hillary Clinton and Defense Secretary Robert Gates sit on the right. Credit: Official White House Photo by Pete Souza.

President Barack Obama delivers the State of the Union address in the House Chamber at the U.S. Capitol in Washington, D.C., Jan. 24, 2012. (Official White House Photo by Pete Souza)

along Wall Street in New York City to let the bankers and financiers know that the people held them responsible for the nation's current condition. Indeed, activist film maker Michael Moore wanted them arrested for their crimes. From the moment that the first groups gathered in front of the Wall Street banks and brokerage firms, the police made their lives uncomfortable with constant harassment. Not to be intimidated or deterred, the Occupiers persevered for several months before finally being forced out. All the while, a good number of similar protests emerged in a multitude of other American cities where participants rallied under the same cause and banner, as well ultimately being harassed by police until being forced to disband. The movement's purpose was simple: to make it clear to both parties and the president that the people had had enough of the plutocrats' abuse and that they should be punished for having plunged the nation into its worst economic crisis since the Great Depression. Only a handful of politicians came out to support the movement. President Obama who not only counted many Wall Street firms among his supporters, but also included many pro-Wall Street economists among his closest economic advisers, refrained from making any substantive comments about the protests.

THE 2012 PRESIDENTIAL ELECTION

At the onset of the 2012 presidential election, unemployment hovered over 8 percent and consumer confidence remained low. Combined with an international scene fraught with a multitude of uncertainties from a nuclear Iran to continued unrest in the Middle East, and a European economy that seemed to be contracting daily as the count of countries on the verge of economic collapse grew, Republicans seemed confident of recapturing the White House. They could blame President Obama and his lack of leadership for much of what had occurred, especially on the home front. Although much of the Republican criticism of the president's performance was ill-founded and blown greatly out of proportion, it did appear that after almost three full years in office, Obama had very little other than health-care reform to show of great domestic accomplishment—no significant jobs programs, no energy policy, and no meaningful financial institutional reform. Other than "**Obamacare**," the president had no signal achievement of consequence to present to the American electorate come November 2012. Not considered to be major achievements by many were the president's courageous repeal of "don't ask, don't tell," and his open support for same sex marriage. In any previous presidential election year, Obama's open endorsement of such measures would not only have aroused much public debate but unrelenting criticism by his political opponents. Such was not the case in 2012 as the economy and its recovery became the overarching issue for both candidates and their respective campaigns. Nonetheless, the president's overall approval rating had plummeted to below 45 percent—the lowest in his brief tenure. What was once a "given"—the president's re-election—became a very close race for Barack Obama.

Almost from the moment the president took office, polls (a Harris as well as a *New York Times/CBS News*) consistently showed that a majority of Republicans and Tea Partiers believed President Obama to be a Muslim and a socialist—assertions repeatedly propagated by the right-wing media. As Humphrey Taylor, chairman of the Harris poll, pointed out, the hatred of presidents is nothing new but "What I think is different this time is the large numbers of people whose beliefs about this president are pretty weird or false."

Another ongoing manifestation brought out during the campaign was the assertion by those Americans, the "Birthers," that Obama was not and never had been a citizen of the United States. The "Obama haters" had propagated this accusation in 2008 and did so again in 2012. Fortunately such fear-mongering and even race-baiting was dismissed as craziness by most Americans, even Republican voters, and they focused on the real issues affecting their lives such as jobs, health care, and the deficit.

Despite the attempts by such groups as the "**Birthers**" to vilify the president, in the end the president triumphed once again." On Election Day, to the shock of overly-confident Republicans who believed their candidate would win, the opposite occurred. The president won 51.1 percent of the popular vote while former Massachusetts governor **Mitt Romney** garnered only 47.2 percent. In the Electoral College, the margin of the president's victory was even greater: 332-206, with Obama winning all the battleground states but one, North Carolina. As reflected in the Electoral College vote, the GOP had the steadfast support of the Civil War Confederate States of America as well as the "border states" of Missouri and Kentucky (but not Maryland) and the agricultural/cattle states of the Great Plains. The president's "coattails" also proved longer than expected as the Democrats picked up seats in both the Senate and the House; in the former, the Democrats enjoyed a 53-45 majority increased by two independent New England senators who caucused with the Democrats, while in the latter they narrowed the gap to 233-200 (with two seats vacant).

As Republicans dig out from a defeat, they need to acknowledge significant failures. Party and right-wing media attempts to demonize the president and the ongoing obstructionist approach to his agenda did not work. Tea Party support was there but not to the degree anticipated. Perhaps more important, the Republican Party is less the wave of the future than a remnant of the past. Opposing immigration reform was probably a bad idea. Latino voters heard the Republican immigration harsh tone and drew the sensible electoral conclusions. Voters also heard its anti-feminism, anti-gay rights (marriage in particular), and general anti-multiculturalism on most current social issues, which led to the party's repudiation and Romney's fairly resounding defeat. A longing for balanced budgets is not what drove most voters to the polls. They found the president's focus on greater job creation via a more meaningful stimulus package to be much more appealing and thus voted accordingly. Adding to the Republicans' woes was the sizeable middle and upper middle-class suburban component to the president's victory who embraced essential government functions such as aid to education.

Republicans, especially the conservatives who are currently driving the party, will have to take these issues to heart, and if they are reflective, be a party willing to engage both the president and his party to move the country forward economically as well as socio-culturally. Republicans criticized Romney for his comment that his defeat was the result of the president having handed out "extraordinary financial gifts" to his base (meaning entitlements or welfare) during his first term. Many Republicans felt compelled to denounce Romney for such a statement. Such Republicans appeared to be accepting the fact that government measures aimed at uplifting a variety of Americans were not "bribes" for particular groups of "takers," but programs and policies that designed to serve the common good.

In many ways the 2012 Republican defeat mirrored that of 2008 in the sense that Mitt Romney and John McCain both failed to realize that the majority of Americans are moderates, especially on social issues and frequently on fiscal matters as well. In the first debate Romney pivoted almost effortlessly to the center, which is where elections are won. During the Republican primaries, Romney abandoned his inherent moderate Republicanism, embracing instead the Far Right agenda of his party in order to win the primaries. Every one of the Republican contenders did the same. Romney's selection of Paul Ryan as his running mate confirmed this propensity. Romney projected the image (exploited by the Obama campaign) of being a "flip-flopper" on the major issues, whether it was tax cuts, balancing the budget, or foreign policy matters. The electorate never knew which Romney would show up on a given day—the moderate, former governor of liberal Massachusetts, or the right-wing zealot convert. Romney's equivocating aside, the election results revealed that the American people certainly knew which Republican Party would be in charge in Washington and that alarmed sufficient numbers of voters to re-elect the president.

Also contributing to Obama's re-election was the strong endorsements from such stalwart Republican statesmen as retired four-star general and former Chairman of the Joint Chiefs, and ex-Secretary of State Colin Powell and the popular mayor of New York, Michael Bloomberg. Hurricane Sandy also helped the president by giving him the opportunity (which he surely did not want, given the storm's catastrophic effects) to act presidential—to demonstrate leadership in a time of domestic crisis. One of the president's biggest Republican carpers, New Jersey Governor Chris Christie, much to the horrible chagrin of fellow party members, praised the president for his unhesitating attention and non-partisan approach in helping his state. Finally, the October jobs report bolstered the president's re-election bid as unemployment dropped to 7.8 percent—sanguine news for the president who had inherited an economy with an overall unemployment rate of over 10 percent.

For much of the last decade, Americans across the political and socio-economic spectrum have been haunted by the fear that the United States is a nation in decline. Citizens have asked why it is that the United States did a better job 40 years ago in promoting opportunity than it does now. If the president is looking for a single, unifying theme to his second term it should be to make sure that the vast majority of Americans feel good about themselves and their country; that the United States and its citizens are once again "on the move." Obama has addressed the problem of income inequality, a drop in the standard of living of many working Americans, the loss of well-paying jobs, especially in manufacturing, and curtailed access to education. Speeding the economic recovery will solve some of these problems. Only time will tell if Barack Obama over the course of his second term can deliver the American people out of their feeling of apprehension about their nation's future.

Chronology

2008 Barack Obama elected president

2009 The Obama administration initiates several bailouts of banks as well as GMC and Chrysler

2010 Obama Health-Care Plan passes
Obama announces troop withdrawal from Iraq by 2011
Obama escalates U.S. forces in Afghanistan
Emergence of the Tea Party Movement
November elections brought Republican control of the House as well as victory in many state legislatures and governorships.
Passage of the Dodd-Frank Wall Street Reform and Consumer Protection Act (July).
Shooting in Fort Hood, Texas.

2011 Arab spring and the end of totalitarian regimes in Egypt, Libya, and Tunisia.
Osama bin Laden finally found and killed.
Shooting in Tucson, Arizona.

2012 Occupy Wall Street Movement.
Barack Obama re-elected for a second term.
Shooting in Aurora, Colorado.
Shooting in Newtown, Connecticut.
Hurricane Sandy.

2013 President Obama announces new measures to prevent gun violence.

Review Questions

1. What factors, issues, personalities, and ideologies contributed to Barack Obama's election victories in both 2008 and 2012?

2. Define "Obama liberalism" and how it differs from that of his more "traditional" liberal predecessors.

3. What various economic dynamics coalesced by 2008 to cause the financial crisis and subsequent economic downturn?

4. Why did President Obama's Affordable Health Care Act generate so much controversy?

5. What foreign policy issues did President Obama inherit from his predecessor, especially in the area of U.S. relations with the Arab/Muslim world?

Glossary of Important People and Concepts

Mahmoud Ahmadinejad
Arab Spring
American Recovery and Reinvestment Act
bail outs
President Bashar al-Assad
Blue-Dog Democrats
John Boehner
"Boots on the ground"
Hillary Clinton
Copenhagen Conference
Death of Osama bin Laden
Dodd-Frank Wall Street Reform and Consumer Protection Act
Steven Jobs
"the surge"
Obamacare
global warming
Occupy Wall Street
"predatory lending"
Mitt Romney
Tea Party Movement

SUGGESTED READINGS

Richard Bernstein, *Out of the Blue: the Story of September 11* (2002).

Michel Chossoduvosky and Andrew Marshall, *The Global Economic Crisis: The Great Depression of the 21st Century.* (2010).

David Corn, *Showdown: The Inside Story of How Obama Fought Back Against Boehner, Cantor, and the Tea Party.* (2012).

Greg Critser, *Fat Land: How Americans Became the Fattest People in the World* (2002).

Martin Duberman, *Stonewall* (1993).

Mickey Edwards, *The Parties Versus the People: How to Turn Republicans and Democrats into Americans.* (2012).

Pamela Geller, Robert Spencer, and John Bolton, *The Post-American Presidency: The Obama Administration's War on America.* (2010).

Michael Haas, *Mr. Calm and Effective: Evaluating the Presidency of Barack Obama.* (2012).

Andrew Hacker, *Two Nations: Black and White, Separate, Hostile, Unequal* (1992).

Arthur Goldwag, *A History of Fear and Loathing on the Populist Right.* (2012).

Amy Goodman, Denis Moynihan, and Michael Moore, *The Silenced Majority: Stories of Uprisings, Occupation, Resistance, and Hope.* (2012)

Christopher Jencks, *The Homeless* (1994).

Haynes Johnson, *Divided We Fall: Gambling with History in the Nineties* (1994).

Jodi Kantor, *The Obamas* (2012).

Michael Katz, *The Undeserving Poor: From the War on Poverty to the War on Welfare* (1989).

Daniel Klaidman, *The War on Terror and the Soul of the Obama Presidency.* (2012).

Alex Kotlowitz, *There Are No Children Here: The Story of Two Boys Growing Up in the Other America* (1991).

Nicholas Lemann, *The Promised Land: The Great Black Migration and How it Changed America* (1989).

Martin A. Levin, Daniel DiSalvo, and Martin Shapiro, *Building Coalitions, Making Policy: The Politics of the Clinton, Bush, and Obama Presidencies.* (2012).

Jere Longman, *Among the Heroes: United Flight 93* (2002).

Kevin Phillips, *Wealth and Democracy* (2001).

Joseph A. Pika and John Maltese, *The Politics of the Presidency.* (2012).

Arthur M. Schlesinger Jr., *The Disuniting of America* (1991).

Randy Shilts, *And the Band Played On: Politics, People and the AIDS Epidemic* (1987).

James B. Stewart, *Den of Thieves* (1991).

Raymond Sturgis, *His Love and Dream for America: A Presidency Rising Above Conflicts and Challenges.* (2011)

Ron Suskind, *Confidence Men: Washington, Wall Street, and the Education of a President.* (2011).

Sanford J. Unger, *Fresh Blood: The New American Immigrants* (1995)

Gary Wills, *Under God: Religion and American Politics* (1990).

Bob Woodward, *Obama's Wars* (2012).

APPENDIX A

Declaration of Independence

Congress, July 4, 1776

When, in the course of human events, it becomes necessary for one people to dissolve the political bonds which have connected them with another, and to assume, among the powers of the earth, the separate and equal station to which the laws of nature and of nature's God entitle them, a decent respect to the opinions of mankind requires that they should declare the causes which impel them to the separation.

We hold these truths to be self-evident: That all men are created equal; that they are endowed by their Creator with certain unalienable rights; that among these are life, liberty and the pursuit of happiness; that, to secure these rights, governments are instituted among men, deriving their just powers from the consent of the governed; that whenever any form of government becomes destructive of these ends, it is the right of the people to alter or to abolish it, and to institute new government, laying its foundation on such principles, and organizing its powers in such form, as to them shall seem most likely to effect their safety and happiness. Prudence, indeed, will dictate that governments long established should not be changed for light and transient causes; and accordingly all experience hath shown that mankind are more disposed to suffer, while evils are sufferable, than to right themselves by abolishing the forms to which they are accustomed. But when a long train of abuses and usurpations, pursuing invariably the same object, evinces a design to reduce them under absolute despotism, it is their right, it is their duty, to throw off such government, and to provide new guards for their future security. Such has been the patient sufferance of these colonies; and such is now the necessity which constrains them to alter their former systems of government. The history of the present King of Great Britain is a history of repeated injuries and usurpations, all having in direct object the establishment of an absolute tyranny over these states. To prove this, let facts be submitted to a candid world.

He has refused his assent to laws, the most wholesome and necessary for the public good.

He has forbidden his governors to pass laws of immediate and pressing importance, unless suspended in their operation till his assent should be obtained; and, when so suspended, he has utterly neglected to attend to them.

He has refused to pass other laws for the accommodation of large districts of people, unless those people would relinquish the right of representation in the legislature, a right inestimable to them, and formidable to tyrants only.

He has called together legislative bodies at places unusual, uncomfortable, and distant from the depository of their public records, for the sole purpose of fatiguing them into compliance with his measures.

He has dissolved representative houses repeatedly, for opposing, with many firmness, his invasions on the rights of the people.

He has refused for a long time, after such dissolutions, to cause others to be elected; whereby the legislative powers, incapable of annihilation, have returned to the people at large for their exercise; the state remaining, in the mean time, exposed to all the dangers of invasions from without and convulsions within.

He has endeavored to prevent the population of these states; for that purpose obstructing the laws for naturalization of foreigners; refusing to pass others to encourage their migrations hither, and raising the conditions of new appropriations of lands.

He has obstructed the administration of justice, by refusing his assent to laws establishing judiciary powers.

He has made judges dependent on his will alone, for the tenure of their offices, and the amount and payment of their salaries.

He has erected a multitude of new offices, and sent hither swarms of officers to harass our people and eat out their substance.

He has kept among us, in times of peace, standing armies, without the consent of our legislatures.

He has affected to render the military independent of, and superior to, the civil power.

He has combined with others to subject us to jurisdiction foreign to our constitution, and unacknowledged by our laws, giving his assent to their acts of pretended legislation:

For quartering large bodies of armed troops among us;

For protecting them, by a mock trial, from punishment for any murder which they should commit on the inhabitants of these states;

For cutting off our trade with all parts of the world;

For imposing taxes on us without our consent;

For depriving us, in many cases, of the benefits of trial by jury;

For transporting us beyond seas, to be tried for pretended offenses;

For abolishing the free system of English laws in a neighboring province, establishing therein an arbitrary government, and enlarging its boundaries, so as to render it at once an example and fit instrument for introducing the same absolute rule into these colonies;

For taking away our charters, abolishing our most valuable laws, and altering fundamentally the forms of our governments;

For suspending our own legislatures, and declaring themselves invested with power to legislate for us in all cases whatsoever.

He has abdicated government here, by declaring us out of his protection and waging war against us.

He has plundered our seas, ravaged our coasts, burned our towns, and destroyed the lives of our people.

He is at this time transporting large armies of foreign mercenaries to complete the works of death, desolation and tyranny already begun with circumstances of cruelty and perfidy scarcely paralleled in the most barbarous ages, and totally unworthy the head of a civilized nation.

He has constrained our fellow-citizens, taken captive on the high seas, to bear arms against their country, to become the executioners of their friends and brethren, or to fall themselves by their hands.

He has excited domestic insurrections among us, and has endeavored to bring on the inhabitants of our frontiers the merciless Indian savages, whose known rule of warfare is an undistinguished destruction of all ages, sexes, and conditions.

In every stage of these oppressions we have petitioned for redress in the most humble terms; our repeated petitions have been answered only by repeated injury. A prince, whose character is thus marked by every act which may define a tyrant, is unfit to be the ruler of a free people.

Nor have we been wanting in our attentions to our British brethren. We have warned them, from time to time, of attempts by their legislature to extend an unwarrantable jurisdiction over us. We have reminded them of the circumstances of our emigration and settlement here. We have appealed to their native justice and magnanimity, and we have conjured them, by the ties of our common kindred, to disavow these usurpations, which would inevitably interrupt our connections and correspondence. They, too, have been deaf to the voice of justice and of consanguinity. We must, therefore, acquiesce in the necessity which denounces our separation, and hold them, as we hold the rest of mankind, enemies in war, in peace friends.

We, therefore, the representatives of the United States of America, in General Congress assembled, appealing to the Supreme Judge of the world for the rectitude of our intentions, do, in the name and by authority of the good people of these colonies, solemnly publish and declare, that these United Colonies are, and of right ought to be, FREE AND INDEPENDENT STATES; that they are absolved from all allegiance to the British crown, and that all political connection between them and the state of Great Britain is, and ought to be, totally dissolved; and that, as free and independent states, they have full power to levy war, conclude peace, contract alliances, establish commerce, and do all other acts and things which independent states may of right do. And for the support of this declaration, with a firm reliance on the protection of Divine Providence, we mutually pledge to each other our lives, our fortunes, and our sacred honor.

JOHN HANCOCK

BUTTON GWINNETT	THOS. NELSON, JR.	RICHD. STOCKTON
LYMAN HALL	FRANCIS LIGHTFOOT LEE	JNO. WITHERSPOON
GEO. WALTON	CARTER BRAXTON	FRAS. HOPKINSON
WM. HOOPER	ROBT. MORRIS	JOHN HART
JOSEPH HEWES	BENJAMIN RUSH	ABRA. CLARK
JOHN PENN	BENJA. FRANKLIN	JOSIAH BARTLETT
EDWARD RUTLEDGE	JOHN MORTON	WM. WHIPPLE
THOS. HEYWARD, JUNR.	GEO. CLYMER	SAML. ADAMS
THOMAS LYNCH, JUNR.	JAS. SMITH	JOHN ADAMS
ARTHUR MIDDLETON	GEO. TAYLOR	ROBT. TREAT PAINE
SAMUEL CHASE	JAMES WILSON	ELBRIDGE GERRY
WM. PACA	GEO. ROSS	STEP. HOPKINS
THOS. STONE	CAESAR RODNEY	WILLIAM ELLERY
CHARLES CARROLL OF CARROLLTON	GEO READ	ROGER SHERMAN
GEORGE WYTHE	THO. M'KEAN	SAM'EL HUNTINGTON
RICHARD HENRY LEE	WM. FLOYD	WM. WILLIAMS
TH. JEFFERSON	PHIL. LIVINGSTON	OLIVER WOLCOTT
BENJ. HARRISON	FRANS. LEWIS	MATTHEW THORNTON
	LEWIS MORRIS	

APPENDIX B

The Constitution of the United States of America

PREAMBLE

We the people of the United States, in order to form a more perfect union, establish justice, insure domestic tranquility, provide for the common defense, promote the general welfare, and secure the blessings of liberty to ourselves and our posterity, do ordain and establish this Constitution for the United States of America.

ARTICLE I.—THE LEGISLATIVE ARTICLE

Section 1. All legislative powers herein granted shall be vested in a Congress of the United States, which shall consist of a Senate and a House of Representatives.

House of Representatives: Composition, Qualification, Apportionment, Impeachment Power

Section 2. The House of Representatives shall be composed of members chosen every second year by the people of the several States, and the electors in each State shall have the qualifications requisite for electors of the most numerous branch of the State Legislature.

No person shall be a Representative who shall not have attained to the age of twenty-five years, and been seven years a citizen of the United States, and who shall not, when elected, be an inhabitant of that State in which he shall be chosen.

Representatives and direct taxes shall be apportioned among the several States which may be included within this Union, according to their respective numbers, *which shall be determined by adding to the whole number of free persons, including those bound to service for a term of years and excluding Indians not taxed, three-fifths of all other persons.* The actual enumeration shall be made within three years after the first meeting of the Congress of the United States, and within every subsequent term of ten years, in such manner as they shall by law direct. The number of Representatives shall not exceed one for every thirty thousand, but each State shall have at least one Representative; *and until each enumeration shall be made, the State of New Hampshire shall be entitled to choose three, Massachusetts eight, Rhode Island and Providence Plantations one, Connecticut five, New York six, New Jersey four, Pennsylvania eight, Delaware one, Maryland six, Virginia ten, North Carolina five, South Carolina five, and Georgia three.*

When vacancies happen in the representation from any State, the Executive authority thereof shall issue writs of election to fill such vacancies.

The House of Representatives shall choose their Speaker and other officers; and shall have the sole power of impeachment.

Senate Composition: Qualifications, Impeachment Trials

Section 3. The Senate of the United States shall be composed of two Senators from each State, *chosen by the legislature thereof,* for six years; and each Senator shall have one vote.

Immediately after they shall be assembled in consequence of the first election, they shall be divided as equally as may be into three classes. The seats of the Senators of the first class shall be vacated at the expiration of the second year, of the second class at the expiration of the fourth year, and of the third class at the expiration of the sixth year, so that one-third may be chosen every second year; and if vacancies happen by resignation or otherwise, during the recess of the legislature of any State, the Executive thereof may make temporary appointments until the next meeting of the legislature, which shall then fill such vacancies.

---

*Passages no longer in effect are printed in italic type.

No person shall be a Senator who shall not have attained to the age of thirty years, and been nine years a citizen of the United States, and who shall not, when elected, be an inhabitant of that State for which he shall be chosen.

The Vice President of the United States shall be President of the Senate, but shall have no vote, unless they be equally divided.

The Senate shall choose their other officers, and also a President *pro tempore*, in the absence of the Vice President, or when he shall exercise the office of President of the United States.

The Senate shall have the sole power to try all impeachments. When sitting for that purpose, they shall be on oath or affirmation. When the President of the United States is tried, the Chief Justice shall preside: and no person shall be convicted without the concurrence of two-thirds of the members present.

Judgment in cases of impeachment shall not extend further than to removal from the office, and disqualification to hold and enjoy any office of honor, trust or profit under the United States; but the party convicted shall nevertheless be liable and subject to indictment, trial, judgment and punishment, according to law.

Congressional Elections: Time, Place, Manner

Section 4. The times, places and manner of holding elections for Senators and Representatives shall be prescribed in each State by the legislature thereof; but the Congress may at any time by law make or alter such regulations, except as to the places of choosing Senators.

The Congress shall assemble at least once in every year, and such meeting *shall be on the first Monday in December, unless they shall by law appoint a different day.*

Powers and Duties of the Houses

Section 5. Each house shall be the judge of the elections, returns and qualifications of its own members, and a majority of each shall constitute a quorum to do business; but a smaller number may adjourn from day to day, and may be authorized to compel the attendance of absent members, in such manner, and under such penalties, as each house may provide.

Each house may determine the rules of its proceedings, punish its members for disorderly behavior, and with the concurrence of two-thirds, expel a member.

Each house shall keep a journal of its proceedings, and from time to time publish the same, excepting such parts as may in their judgment require secrecy; and the yeas and nays of the members of either house on any question shall, at the desire of one-fifth of those present, be entered on the journal.

Neither house, during the session of Congress, shall, without the consent of the other, adjourn for more than three days, nor to any other place than that in which the two houses shall be sitting.

Rights of Members

Section 6. The Senators and Representatives shall receive a compensation for their services, to be ascertained by law and paid out of the treasury of the United States. They shall in all cases except treason, felony and breach of the peace, be privileged from arrest during their attendance at the session of their respective houses, and in going to and returning from the same; and for any speech or debate in either house, they shall not be questioned in any other place.

No Senator or Representative shall, during the time for which he was elected, be appointed to any civil office under the authority of the United States, which shall have been created, or the emoluments whereof shall have been increased, during such time; and no person holding any office under the United States shall be a member of either house during his continuance in office.

Legislative Powers: Bills and Resolutions

Section 7. All bills for raising revenue shall originate in the House of Representatives; but the Senate may propose or concur with amendments as on other bills.

Every bill which shall have passed the House of Representatives and the Senate, shall, before it become a law, be presented to the President of the United States; if he approve he shall sign it, but if not he shall return it with objections to that house in which it originated, who shall enter the objections at large on their journal, and proceed to reconsider it. If after such reconsideration two-thirds of that house shall agree to pass the bill, it shall be sent, together with the objections, to the other house, by which it shall likewise be reconsidered, and if approved by two-thirds of that house, it shall become a law. But in all such cases the votes of both houses shall be determined by yeas and nays, and the names of the persons voting for and against the bill shall be entered on the journal of each house respectively. If any bill shall not be returned by the President within ten days (Sundays excepted) after it shall have been presented to him, the same shall be a law, in like manner as if he had signed it, unless the Congress by their adjournment prevent its return, in which case it shall not be a law.

Every order, resolution, or vote to which the concurrence of the Senate and House of Representatives may be necessary (except on a question of adjournment) shall be presented to the President of the United States; and before the same shall take effect, shall be approved by him, or being disapproved by him, shall be repassed by two-thirds of the Senate and House of Representatives, according to the rules and limitations prescribed in the case of a bill.

Powers of Congress

Section 8. The Congress shall have power

To lay and collect taxes, duties, imposts and excises, to pay the debts and provide for the common defense and general welfare of the United States; but all duties, imposts and excises shall be uniform throughout the United States;

To borrow money on the credit of the United States;

To regulate commerce with foreign nations, and among the several States, and with the Indian tribes;

To establish an uniform rule of naturalization, and uniform laws on the subject of bankruptcies throughout the United States;

To coin money, regulate the value thereof, and of foreign coin, and fix the standard of weights and measures;

To provide for the punishment of counterfeiting the securities and current coin of the United States;

To establish post offices and post roads;

To promote the progress of science and useful arts by securing for limited times to authors and inventors the exclusive right to their respective writings and discoveries;

To constitute tribunals inferior to the Supreme Court;

To define and punish piracies and felonies committed on the high seas and offenses against the law of nations;

To declare war, grant letters of marque and reprisal, and make rules concerning captures on land and water;

To raise and support armies, but no appropriation of money to that use shall be for a longer term than two years;

To provide and maintain a navy;

To make rules for the government and regulation of the land and naval forces;

To provide for calling forth the militia to execute the laws of the Union, suppress insurrections, and repel invasions;

To provide for organizing, arming, and disciplining the militia, and for governing such part of them as may be employed in the service of the United States, reserving to the States respectively the appointment of the officers, and the authority of training the militia according to the discipline prescribed by Congress;

To exercise exclusive legislation in all cases whatsoever, over such district (not exceeding ten miles square) as may, by cession of particular States, and the acceptance of Congress, become the seat of the government of the United States, and to exercise like authority over all places purchased by the consent of the legislature of the State, in which the same shall be, for erection of forts, magazines, arsenals, dock-yards, and other needful buildings;—and

To make all laws which shall be necessary and proper for carrying into execution the foregoing powers, and all other powers vested by this Constitution in the government of the United States, or in any department or officer thereof.

Powers Denied to Congress

Section 9. *The migration or importation of such persons as any of the States now existing shall think proper to admit shall not be prohibited by the Congress prior to the year 1808; but a tax or duty may be imposed on such importation, not exceeding $10 for each person.*

The privilege of the writ of habeas corpus shall not be suspended, unless when in cases of rebellion or invasion the public safety may require it.

No bill of attainder or ex post facto law shall be passed.

No capitation, or other direct, tax shall be laid, unless in proportion to the census or enumeration herein before directed to be taken.

No tax or duty shall be laid on articles exported from any State.

No preference shall be given by any regulation of commerce or revenue to the ports of one State over those of another; nor shall vessels bound to, or from, one State, be obliged to enter, clear, or pay duties in another.

No money shall be drawn from the treasury, but in consequence of appropriations made by law; and a regular statement and account of the receipts and expenditures of all public money shall be published from time to time.

No title of nobility shall be granted by the United States; and no person holding any office of profit or trust under them, shall, without the consent of the Congress, accept of any present, emolument, office, or title, of any kind whatever, from any king, prince, or foreign state.

Powers Denied to the States

Section 10. No State shall enter into any treaty, alliance, or confederation; grant letters of marque and reprisal; coin money; emit bills of credit; make anything but gold and silver coin a tender in payment of debts; pass any bill of attainder, ex post facto law, or law impairing the obligation of contracts, or grant any title of nobility.

No State shall, without the consent of the Congress, lay any imposts or duties on imports or exports, except what may be absolutely necessary for executing its inspection laws: and the net produce of all duties and imposts, laid by any State on imports or exports, shall be for the use of the treasury of the United States; and all such laws shall be subject to the revision and control of the Congress.

No State shall, without the consent of Congress, lay any duty of tonnage, keep troops or ships of war in time of peace, enter into any agreement or compact with another State, or with a foreign power, or engage in war, unless actually invaded, or in such imminent danger as will not admit of delay.

ARTICLE II.—THE EXECUTIVE ARTICLE

Nature and Scope of Presidential Power

Section 1. The executive power shall be vested in a President of the United States of America. He shall hold his office during the term of four years, and, together with the Vice President, chosen for the same term, be elected, as follows:

Each State shall appoint, in such manner as the legislature thereof may direct, a number of electors, equal to the whole number of Senators and Representatives to which the State may be entitled in the Congress; but no Senator or Representative, or person holding an office of trust or profit under the United States, shall be appointed an elector.

The electors shall meet in their respective States, and vote by ballot for two persons, of whom one at least shall not be an inhabitant of the same State with themselves. And they shall make a list of all the persons voted for, and of the number of votes for each; which list they shall sign and certify, and transmit sealed to the seat of government of the United States, directed to the President of the Senate. The President of the Senate shall, in the presence of the Senate and House of Representatives, open all the certificates, and the votes shall then be counted. The person having the greatest number of votes shall be the President, if such number be a majority of the whole number of electors appointed; and if there be more than one who have such majority, and have an equal number of votes, then the House of Representatives shall immediately choose by ballot one of them for President; and if no person have a majority, then from the five highest on the list said house shall in like manner choose the President. But in choosing the President the votes shall be taken by States, the representation from each State having one vote; a quorum for this purpose shall consist of a member or members from two-thirds of the States, and a majority of all the States shall be necessary to a choice. In every case, after the choice of the President, the person having the greatest number of votes of the electors shall be the Vice President. But if there should remain two or more who have equal votes, the Senate shall choose from them by ballot the Vice President.

The Congress may determine the time of choosing the electors, and the day on which they shall give their votes; which day shall be the same throughout the United States.

No person except a natural-born citizen, *or a citizen of the United States at the time of the adoption of this Constitution*, shall be eligible to the office of President; neither shall any person be eligible to that office who shall not have attained to the age of thirty-five years, and been fourteen years a resident within the United States.

In case of the removal of the President from office or of his death, resignation, or inability to discharge the powers and duties of the said office, the same shall devolve on the Vice President, and the Congress may by law provide for the case of removal, death, resignation, or inability, both of the President and Vice President, declaring what officer shall then act as President, and such officer shall act accordingly, until the disability be removed, or a President shall be elected.

The President shall, at stated times, receive for his services a compensation, which shall neither be increased nor diminished during the period for which he shall have been elected, and he shall not receive within that period any other emolument from the United States, or any of them.

Before he enter on the execution of his office, he shall take the following oath or affirmation: —"I do solemnly swear (or affirm) that I will faithfully execute the office of President of the United States, and will to the best of my ability preserve, protect, and defend the Constitution of the United States."

Powers and Duties of the President

Section 2. The President shall be the commander in chief of the army and navy of the United States, and of the militia of the several States, when called into the actual service of the United States; he may require the opinion, in writing, of the principal officer in each of the executive departments, upon any subject relating to the duties of their respective offices, and he shall have power to grant reprieves and pardons for offenses against the United States, except in cases of impeachment.

He shall have power, by and with the advice and consent of the Senate, to make treaties, provided two-thirds of the Senators present concur; and he shall nominate, and by and with the advice and consent of the Senate, shall appoint ambassadors, other public ministers and consuls, judges of the Supreme Court, and all other officers of the United States, whose appointments are not herein otherwise provided for, and which shall be established by law: but the Congress may by law vest the appointment of such inferior officers, as they think proper, in the President alone, in the courts of law, or in the heads of departments.

The President shall have power to fill up all vacancies that may happen during the recess of the Senate, by granting commissions which shall expire at the end of their next session.

Section 3. He shall from time to time give to the Congress information of the state of the Union, and recommend to their consideration such measures as he shall judge necessary and expedient; he may, on extraordinary occasions, convene both houses, or either of them, and in case of disagreement between them, with respect to the time of adjournment, he may adjourn them to such time as he shall think proper; he shall receive ambassadors and other public ministers; he shall take care that the laws be faithfully executed, and shall commission all the officers of the United States.

Section 4. The President, Vice President and all civil officers of the United States shall be removed from office on impeachment for, and on conviction of, treason, bribery, or other high crimes and misdemeanor.

ARTICLE III.—THE JUDICIAL ARTICLE

Section 1. The judicial power of the United States shall be vested in one Supreme Court, and in such inferior courts as the Congress may from time to time ordain and establish. The judges, both of the Supreme and inferior courts, shall hold their offices during good behavior, and shall, at stated times, receive for their services a compensation which shall not be diminished during their continuance in office.

Jurisdiction

Section 2. The judicial power shall extend to all cases, in law and equity, arising under this Constitution, the laws of the United States, and treaties made, or which shall be made, under their authority;—to all cases affecting ambassadors, other public ministers and consuls;—to all cases of admiralty and maritime jurisdiction;—to controversies to which the United States shall be a party;—to controversies between two or more States;—*between a state and citizens of another state*;—between citizens of different States;—between citizens of the same State claiming lands under grants of different States, and between a State, or the citizens thereof, and foreign states, citizens or subjects.

In all cases affecting ambassadors, other public ministers and consuls, and those in which a State shall be party, the Supreme Court shall have original jurisdiction. In all the other cases before mentioned, the Supreme Court shall have appellate jurisdiction, both as to law and fact, with such exceptions, and under such regulations, as the Congress shall make.

The trial of all crimes, except in cases of impeachment, shall be by jury; and such trial shall be held in the State where said crimes shall have been committed; but when not committed within any State, the trial shall be at such place or places as the Congress may by law have directed.

Treason

Section 3. Treason against the United States shall consist only in levying war against them, or in adhering to their enemies, giving them aid and comfort. No person shall be convicted of treason unless on the testimony of two witnesses to the same overt act, or on confession in open court.

The Congress shall have power to declare the punishment of treason, but no attainder of treason shall work corruption of blood, or forfeiture except during the life of the person attained.

ARTICLE IV.—INTERSTATE RELATIONS

Full Faith and Credit Clause

Section 1. Full Faith and credit shall be given in each State to the public acts, records, and judicial proceedings of every other State. And the Congress may by general laws prescribe the manner in which such acts, records and proceedings shall be proved, and the effect thereof.

Privileges and Immunities; Interstate Extradition

Section 2. The citizens of each State shall be entitled to all privileges and immunities of citizens in the several States.

A person charged in any State with treason, felony or other crime, who shall flee from justice, and be found in another State, shall on demand of the executive authority of the State from which he fled, be delivered up, to be removed to the State having jurisdiction of the crime.

No person held to service or labor in one State, under the laws thereof, escaping into another, shall, in consequence of any law or regulation therein, be discharged from such service or labor, but shall be delivered up on claim of the party to whom such service or labor may be due.

Admission of States

Section 3. New States may be admitted by the Congress into this Union; but no new State shall be formed or erected within the jurisdiction of any other State; nor any State be formed by the junction of two or more States, or parts of States, without the consent of the legislatures of the States concerned as well as of the Congress.

The Congress shall have power to dispose of and make all needful rules and regulations respecting the territory or other property belonging to the United States; and nothing in this Constitution shall be so construed as to prejudice any claims of the United States, or of any particular State.

Republican Form of Government

Section 4. The United States shall guarantee to every State in this Union a republican form of government, and shall protect each of them against invasion; and on application of the legislature, or of the executive (when the legislature cannot be convened) against domestic violence.

ARTICLE V.—THE AMENDING POWER

The Congress, whenever two-thirds of both houses shall deem it necessary, shall propose amendments to this Constitution, or, on the application of the legislatures of two-thirds of the several States, shall call a convention for proposing amendments, which, in either case, shall be valid to all intents and purposes, as part of this Constitution, when ratified by the legislatures of three-fourths of the several States, or by conventions in three-fourths thereof, as the one or the other mode of ratification may be proposed by the Congress; *provided that no amendment which may be made prior to the year one thousand eight hundred and eight shall in any manner affect the first and fourth clauses in the ninth section of the first article*; and that no State, without its consent, shall be deprived of its equal suffrage in the Senate.

ARTICLE VI.—THE SUPREMACY ACT

All debts contracted and engagements entered into, before the adoption of this Constitution, shall be as valid against the United States under this Constitution, as under the Confederation.

This Constitution, and the laws of the United States which shall be made in pursuance thereof; and all treaties made, or which shall be made, under the authority of the United States, shall be the supreme law of the land; and the judges in every State shall be bound thereby, anything in the Constitution or laws of any State to the contrary notwithstanding.

The Senators and Representatives before mentioned, and the members of the several State legislatures, and all executive and judicial officers, both of the United States and of the several States, shall be bound by oath or affirmation to support this Constitution; but no religious test shall ever be required as a qualification to any office or public trust under the United States.

ARTICLE VII.—RATIFICATION

The ratification of the conventions of nine States shall be sufficient for the establishment of this Constitution between States so ratifying the same.

Done in Convention by the unanimous consent of the States present, the seventeenth day of September in the year of our Lord one thousand seven hundred and eighty-seven and of the Independence of the United States of America the twelfth. In witness whereof we have hereunto subscribed our names.

GEORGE WASHINGTON
President and Deputy from Virginia

New Hampshire
JOHN LANGDON
NICHOLAS GILMAN

Massachusetts
NATHANIEL GORHAM
RUFUS KING

Connecticut
WILLIAM S. JOHNSON
ROGER SHERMAN

Virginia
JOHN BLAIR
JAMES MADISON, JR

South Carolina
J. RUTLEDGE
CHARLES G. PINCKNEY
PIERCE BUTLER

New York
ALEXANDER HAMILTON

New Jersey
WILLIAM LIVINGSTON
DAVID BREARLEY
WILLIAM PATERSON
JONATHAN DAYTON

Pennsylvania
BENJAMIN FRANKLIN
THOMAS MIFFLIN
ROBERT MORRIS
GEORGE CLYMER
THOMAS FITZSIMONS
JARED INGERSOLL
JAMES WILSON
GOUVERNEUR MORRIS

Delaware
GEORGE READ
GUNNING BEDFORD, JR.
JOHN DICKINSON
RICHARD BASSETT
JACOB BROOM

Maryland
JAMES MCHENRY
DANIEL OF ST. THOMAS JENIFER
DANIEL CARROLL

North Carolina
WILLIAM BLOUNT
RICHARD DOBBS SPRAIGHT
HU WILLIAMSON

Georgia
WILLIAM FEW
ABRAHAM BALDWIN

THE BILL OF RIGHTS
The first ten Amendments (the Bill of Rights) were adopted in 1791.

AMENDMENT I.—RELIGION, SPEECH ASSEMBLY, AND PETITION

Congress shall make no law respecting an establishment of religion, or prohibiting the free exercise thereof; or abridging the freedom of speech, or of the press; or the right of the people peaceably to assemble, and to petition the government for a redress of grievances.

AMENDMENT II.—MILITIA AND THE RIGHT TO BEAR ARMS

A well-regulated militia being necessary to the security of a free State, the right of the people to keep and bear arms shall not be infringed.

AMENDMENT III.—QUARTERING OF SOLDIERS

No soldier shall, in time of peace, be quartered in any house without the consent of the owner, nor in time of war, but in a manner to be prescribed by law.

AMENDMENT IV.—SEARCHES AND SEIZURES

The right of the people to be secure in their persons, houses, papers, and effects, against unreasonable searches and seizures, shall not be violated, and no warrants shall issue but upon probable cause, supported by oath or affirmation, and particularly describing the place to be searched, and the persons or things to be seized.

AMENDMENT V.—GRAND JURIES, SELF-INCRIMINATION, DOUBLE JEOPARDY, DUE PROCESS, AND EMINENT DOMAIN

No person shall be held to answer for a capital, or otherwise infamous crime, unless on a presentment or indictment of a grand jury, except in cases arising in the land or naval forces, or in the militia, when in actual service in time of war or public danger; nor shall any person be subject for the same offense to be twice put in jeopardy of life or limb; nor shall be compelled in any criminal case to be a witness against himself, nor be deprived of life, liberty, or property, without due process of law; nor shall private property be taken for public use without just compensation.

AMENDMENT VI.—CRIMINAL COURT PROCEDURES

In all criminal prosecutions, the accused shall enjoy the right to a speedy and public trial, by an impartial jury of the State and district wherein the crime shall have been committed, which district shall have been previously ascertained by law, and to be informed of the nature and cause of the accusation; to be confronted with the witnesses against him; to have compulsory process for obtaining witnesses in his favor, and to have the assistance of counsel for his defense.

AMENDMENT VII.—TRIAL BY JURY IN COMMON LAW CASES

In suits at common law, where the value in controversy shall exceed twenty dollars, the right of trial by jury shall be preserved, and no fact tried by a jury shall be otherwise reexamined in any court of the United States, than according to the rules of the common law.

AMENDMENT VIII.—BAIL, CRUEL AND UNUSUAL PUNISHMENT

Excessive bail shall not be required, nor excessive fines imposed, nor cruel and unusual punishments inflicted.

AMENDMENT IX.—RIGHTS RETAINED BY THE PEOPLE

The enumeration in the Constitution, of certain rights, shall not be construed to deny or disparage others retained by the people.

AMENDMENT X.—RESERVED POWERS OF THE STATES

The powers not delegated to the United States by the Constitution, nor prohibited by it to the States, are reserved to the States respectively, or to the people.

PRE-CIVIL WAR AMENDMENTS

AMENDMENT XI.—SUITS AGAINST THE STATES
[Adopted 1798]

The judicial power of the United States shall not be construed to extend to any suit in law or equity, commenced or prosecuted against one of the United States by citizens of another State, or by citizens or subjects of any foreign state.

AMENDMENT XII.—ELECTION OF THE PRESIDENT
[Adopted 1804]

The electors shall meet in their respective *States*, and vote by ballot for President and Vice President, one of whom, at least, shall not be an inhabitant of the same State with themselves; they shall name in their ballots the person voted for as President, and in distinct ballots the person voted for as Vice President, and they shall make distinct lists of all persons voted for as President, and of all persons voted for as Vice President, and of the number of votes for each, which lists they shall sign and certify, and transmit sealed to the seat of the government of the United States, directed to the President of the Senate;—the President of the Senate shall, in the presence of the Senate and House of Representatives, open all the certificates and the votes shall then be counted;—the person having the greatest number of votes for President shall be the President, if such number be a majority of the whole number of electors appointed; and if no person have such majority, then from the persons having the highest numbers not exceeding three on the list of those voted for as President, the House of Representatives shall choose immediately, by ballot, the President. But in choosing the President, the votes shall be taken by States, the representation from each State having one vote; a quorum for this purpose shall consist of a member or members from two-thirds of the States, and a majority of all the States shall be necessary to a choice. And if the House of Representatives shall not choose a President whenever the right of choice shall devolve upon them, before *the fourth day of March* next following, then the Vice President shall act as President, as in the case of the death or other constitutional disability of the President.

The person having the greatest number of votes as Vice President shall be the Vice President, if such a number be a majority of the whole number of electors appointed; and if no person have a majority, then from the two highest numbers on the list the Senate shall choose the Vice President; a quorum for the purpose shall consist of two-thirds of the whole number of Senators, and a majority of the whole number shall be necessary to a choice. But no person constitutionally ineligible to the office of President shall be eligible to that of Vice President of the United States.

CIVIL WAR AMENDMENTS

AMENDMENT XIII.—PROHIBITION OF SLAVERY
[Adopted 1865]

Section 1. Neither slavery nor involuntary servitude, except as a punishment for crime whereof the party shall have been duly convicted, shall exist within the United States, or any place subject to their jurisdiction.

Section 2. Congress shall have power to enforce this article by appropriate legislation.

AMENDMENT XIV.—CITIZENSHIP, DUE PROCESS, AND EQUAL PROTECTION OF THE LAWS
[Adopted 1868]

Section 1. All persons born or naturalized in the United States, and subject to the jurisdiction thereof, are citizens of the United States and of the State wherein they reside. No State shall make or enforce any law which shall abridge **the privileges or immunities** of citizens of the United States; nor shall any State deprive any person of life, liberty, or property, without **due process of law**; nor deny to any person within its jurisdiction the **equal protection of the laws**.

Section 2. Representatives shall be apportioned among the several States according to their respective numbers, counting the whole number of persons in each State, excluding Indians not taxed. But when the right to vote at any election for the choice of Electors for President and Vice President of the United States, Representatives in Congress, the executive and judicial officers of a State, or the members of the legislature thereof, is denied to any of the male inhabitants of such State, being twenty-one years of age and citizens of the United States, or in any way abridged, except for participation in rebellion, or other crime, the basis of representation therein shall be reduced in the proportion which the number of such male citizens shall bear to the whole number of male citizens twenty-one years of age in such State.

Section 3. No person shall be a Senator or Representative in Congress, or Elector of President and Vice President, or hold any office, civil or military, under the United States, or under any State, who, having previously taken an oath, as a member of Congress, or as an officer of the United States, or as a member of any State legislature, or as an executive or judicial officer of any State, to support the Constitution of the United States, shall have engaged in insurrection or rebellion against the same, or given aid or comfort to the enemies thereof. Congress may, by a vote of two-thirds of each house, remove such disability.

Section 4. The validity of the public debt of the United States, authorized by law, including debts incurred for payment of pensions and bounties for services in suppressing insurrection or rebellion, shall not be questioned. But neither the United States nor any State shall assume or pay any debt or obligation incurred in aid of insurrection or rebellion against the United States, or any claim for the loss or emancipation of any slave; but all such debts, obligations and claims shall be held illegal and void.

Section 5. The Congress shall have power to enforce, by appropriate legislation, the provisions of this article.

AMENDMENT XV.—THE RIGHT TO VOTE
[Adopted 1870]

Section 1. The right of citizens of the United State to vote shall not be denied or abridged by the United States or by any State on account of race, color, or previous condition of servitude.

Section 2. The Congress shall have power to enforce this article by appropriate legislation.

AMENDMENT XVI.—INCOME TAXES
[Adopted 1913]

The Congress shall have power to lay and collect taxes on incomes, from whatever source derived, without apportionment among the several States, and without regard to any census or enumeration.

AMENDMENT XVII.—DIRECT ELECTION OF SENATORS
[Adopted 1913]

Section 1. The Senate of the United States shall be composed of two Senators from each State, elected by the people thereof, for six years; and each Senator shall have one vote. The electors in each State shall have the qualifications requisite for electors of (voters for) the most numerous branch of the State legislatures.

Section 2. When vacancies happen in the representation of any State in the Senate, the executive authority of such State shall issue writs of election to fill such vacancies: Provided, that the Legislature of any State may empower the executive thereof to make temporary appointments until the people fill the vacancies by election as the Legislature may direct.

Section 3. This amendment shall not be so construed as to affect the election or term of any Senator chosen before it becomes valid as part of the Constitution.

AMENDMENT XVIII.—PROHIBITION
[Adopted 1919; Repealed 1933]

Section 1. *After one year from the ratification of this article the manufacture, sale, or transportation of intoxicating liquors within, the importation thereof into, or the exportation thereof from the United State and all territory subject to the jurisdiction thereof, for beverage purposes, is hereby prohibited.*

Section 2. *The Congress and the several States shall have concurrent power to enforce this article by appropriate legislation.*

Section 3. *This article shall be inoperative unless it shall have been ratified as an amendment to the Constitution by the legislatures of the several States, as provided by the Constitution, within seven years from the date of the submission thereof to the States by the Congress.*

AMENDMENT XIX.—FOR WOMEN'S SUFFRAGE
[Adopted 1920]

Section 1. The right of citizens of the United States to vote shall not be denied or abridged by the United States or by any State on account of sex.

Section 2. The Congress shall have power to enforce this article by appropriate legislation.

AMENDMENT XX.—THE LAME DUCK AMENDMENT
[Adopted 1933]

Section 1. The terms of the President and Vice President shall end at noon on the 20th day of January, and the terms of the Senators and Representatives at noon on the 3rd day of January, of the years in which such terms would have ended if this article had not been ratified; and the terms of their successors shall then begin.

Section 2. The Congress shall assemble at least once in every year, and such meeting shall begin at noon on the 3rd day of January, unless they shall by law appoint a different day.

Section 3. If, at the time fixed for the beginning of the term of the President, the President-elect shall have died, the Vice President-elect shall become President. If a President shall not have been chosen before the time fixed for the beginning of his term, or if the President-elect shall have failed to qualify, then the Vice President-elect shall act as President until a President shall have qualified; and the Congress may by law provide for the case wherein neither a President-elect nor a Vice President-elect shall have qualified, declaring who shall then act as President, or the manner in which one who is to act shall be selected, and such persons shall act accordingly until a President or Vice President shall have qualified.

Section 4. The Congress may by law provide for the case of the death of any of the persons from whom the House of Representatives may choose a President whenever the right of choice shall have devolved upon them, and for the case of the death of any of the persons from whom the Senate may choose a Vice President whenever the right of choice shall have devolved upon them.

Section 5. Section 1 and 2 shall take effect on the 15th day of October following the ratification of this article.

Section 6. This article shall be inoperative unless it shall have been ratified as an amendment to the Constitution by the Legislatures of three-fourths of the several States within seven years from the date of its submission.

AMENDMENT XXI.—REPEAL OF PROHIBITION
[Adopted 1933]

Section 1. The eighteenth article of amendment to the Constitution of the United States is hereby repealed.

Section 2. The transportation or importation into any State, Territory, or Possession of the United States for delivery of use therein of intoxicating liquors, in violation of the laws thereof, is hereby prohibited.

Section 3. This article shall be inoperative unless it shall have been ratified as an amendment to the Constitution by conventions in the several States, as provided in the Constitution, within seven years from the date of submission thereof to the States by the Congress.

AMENDMENT XXII.—NUMBER OF PRESIDENTIAL TERMS
[Adopted 1951]

Section 1. No person shall be elected to the office of President more than twice, and no person who has held the office of President, or acted as President, for more than two years of a term to which some other person was elected President shall be elected to the office of President more than once. But this article shall not apply to any person holding the office of President when this article was proposed by the Congress, and shall not prevent any person who may be holding the office of President, or acting as President, during the term within which this article becomes operative from holding the office of President or acting as President during the remainder of such term.

Section 2. This article shall be inoperative unless it shall have been ratified as an amendment to the Constitution by the legislatures of three-fourths of the several States within seven years from the date of its submission to the States by the Congress.

AMENDMENT XXIII.—PRESIDENTIAL ELECTORS FOR THE DISTRICT OF COLUMBIA [Adopted 1961]

Section 1. The District constituting the seat of Government of the United States shall appoint in such manner as the Congress may direct:

A number of electors of President and Vice President equal to the whole number of Senators and Representatives in Congress to which the District would be entitled if it were a State, but in no event more than the least populous State; they shall be in addition to those appointed by the States, but they shall be considered for the purposes of the election of President and Vice President, to be electors appointed by a State; and they shall meet in the District and perform such duties as provided by the twelfth article of amendment.

Section 2. The Congress shall have power to enforce this article by appropriate legislation.

AMENDMENT XXIV.—THE ANTI-POLL TAX AMENDMENT
[Adopted 1964]

Section 1. The right of citizens of the United States to vote in any primary or other election for President or Vice President, for electors for President or Vice President, or for Senator or Representative in Congress, shall not be denied or abridged by the United States or any State by reason of failure to pay any poll tax or other tax.

Section 2. The Congress shall have power to enforce this article by appropriate legislation.

AMENDMENT XXV.—PRESIDENTIAL DISABILITY, VICE-PRESIDENTIAL VACANCIES
[Adopted 1967]

Section 1.   In case of the removal of the President from office or his death or resignation, the Vice President shall become President.

Section 2.   Whenever there is a vacancy in the office of the Vice President, the President shall nominate a Vice President who shall take office upon confirmation by a majority vote of both Houses of Congress.

Section 3.   Whenever the President transmits to the President pro tempore of the Senate and the Speaker of the House of Representatives his written declaration that he is unable to discharge the powers and duties of his office, and until he transmits to them a written declaration to the contrary, such powers and duties shall be discharged by the Vice President as Acting President.

Section 4.   Whenever the Vice President and a majority of either the principal officers of the executive departments or of such other body as Congress may by law provide, transmit to the President pro tempore of the Senate and the Speaker of the House of Representatives their written declaration that the President is unable to discharge the powers and duties of his office, the Vice President shall immediately assume the powers and duties of the office as Acting President.

   Thereafter, when the President transmits to the President pro tempore of the Senate and the Speaker of the House of Representatives his written declaration that no inability exists, he shall resume the powers and duties of his office unless the Vice President and a majority of either the principal officers of the executive department{s} or of such other body as Congress may by law provide, transmit within four days to the President pro tempore of the Senate and the Speaker of the House of Representatives their written declaration that the President is unable to discharge the powers and duties of his office.   Thereupon Congress shall decide the issue, assembling within forty-eight hours for that purpose if not in session.   If the Congress, within twenty-one days after receipt of the latter written declaration, or, if Congress is not in session, within twenty-one days after Congress is required to assemble, determines by two-thirds vote of both Houses that the President is unable to discharge the powers and duties of his office, the Vice President shall continue to discharge the same as Acting President; otherwise, the President shall resume the powers and duties of his office.

AMENDMENT XXVI.—EIGHTEEN-YEAR-OLD VOTE
[Adopted 1971]

Section 1.   The right of citizens of the United States, who are eighteen years of age or older, to vote shall not be denied or abridged by the United States or by any State on account of age.

Section 2.   The Congress shall have power to enforce this article by appropriate legislation.

AMENDMENT XXVII.—VARYING CONGRESSIONAL COMPENSATION
[Adopted 1992]

No law varying the compensation for the service of the Senators and Representatives shall take effect until an election of Representatives shall have intervened.

APPENDIX C

PRESIDENTIAL ELECTIONS

Year	Name	Party Vote	Popular Vote	Electoral College Vote
1789	George Washington	Federalist		69
1792	George Washington	Federalist		132
1796	John Adams	Federalist		71
	Thomas Jefferson	Democratic-Republican		68
1800	Thomas Jefferson	Democratic-Republican		73
	John Adams	Federalist		65
1804	Thomas Jefferson	Democratic-Republican		162
	Charles C. Pinckney	Federalist		14
1808	James Madison	Democratic-Republican		122
	Charles C. Pinckney	Federalist		47
1812	James Madison	Democratic-Republican		128
	George Clinton	Federalist		89
1816	James Monroe	Dmocratic-Republican		183
	Rufus King	Federalist		34
1820	James Monroe	Democratic-Republican		231
	John Quincy Adams	Democratic-Republican		1
1824	John Quincy Adams	Democratic-Republican	108,740	84
	Andrew Jackson	Democratic-Republican	153,544	99
	William Crawford	Democratic-Republican	46,618	41
	Henry Clay	Democratic-Republican	47,136	37
1828	Andrew Jackson	Democrat	647,286	178
	John Quincy Adams	National Republican	508,064	83
1832	Andrew Jackson	Democrat	687,502	219
	Henry Clay	National Republican	530,189	49
	Electoral votes not cast			2
1836	Martin Van Buren	Democrat	765,483	170
	William Henry Harrison	Whig	550,816	73
	Hugh White	Whig	146,107	26
	Daniel Webster	Whig	41,201	14
	Total for the 3 Whigs		739,795	113
1840	William Henry Harrison	Whig	1,274,624	234
	Martin Van Buren	Democrat	1,127,781	60
1844	James K. Polk	Democrat	1,338,464	170
	Henry Clay	Whig	1,300,097	105
1848	Zachary Taylor	Whig	1,360,967	163
	Lewis Cass	Democrat	1,222,342	127
	Martin Van Buren	Free-Soil	291,263	
1852	Franklin Pierce	Democrat	1,601,117	254
	Winfield Scott	Whig	1,385,453	42
	John P. Hale	Free-Soil	155,825	
1856	James Buchanan	Democrat	1,832,955	174
	John Fremont	Republican	1,339,932	114
	Millard Fillmore	Whig-American	871,731	8

Year	Candidate	Party	Popular Vote	Electoral Vote
1860	Abraham Lincoln	Republican	1,865,593	180
	John C. Breckinridge	Democratic	848,356	72
	Stephen Douglas	Democrat	1,382,713	12
	John Bell	Constitutional Union	592,906	39
1864	Abraham Lincon	Unionist (Republican)	2,206,938	212
	George McClellan	Democrat	1,803,787	21
	Electoral votes not cast			81
1868	Ulysses S. Grant	Republican	3,013,421	214
	Horatio Seymour	Democrat	2,706,829	80
	Electoral votes not cast			23
1872	Ulysses S. Grant	Republican	3,596,745	286
	Horace Greeley	Democrat	2,843,446	
	Thomas Hendricks	Democrat		42
	Benjamin Browns	Democrat		18
	Charles Jenkins	Democrat		2
	David Davis	Democrat		1
1876	Rutherford B. Hays	Republican	4,036,572	185
	Samuel Tilden	Democrat	4,284,020	184
	Peter Cooper	Greenback	81,737	
1880	James A. Garfield	Republican	4,453,295	214
	Winfield S. Hancock	Democrat	4,414,082	155
	James B. Weaver	Greenback-Labor	308,578	
1884	Grover Cleveland	Democrat	4,879,507	219
	James G. Blaine	Republican	4,850,293	182
	Benjamin Butler	Greenback-Labor	175,370	
	John St. John	Prohibition	150,369	
1888	Benjamin Harrison	Republican	5,447,129	233
	Grover Cleveland	Democrat	5,537,857	168
	Clinton Fisk	Prohibition	249,506	
	Anson Streeter	Union Labor	146,935	
1892	Grover Cleveland	Democrat	5,555,426	277
	Benjamin Harrison	Republican	5,182,690	145
	James B. Weaver	People's	1.029,846	22
	John Bidwell	Prohibition	264,133	
1896	William McKinley	Republican	7,102,246	271
	William J. Bryan	Democrat	6,492,559	176
	John Palmer	National Democratic	133,148	
	Joshua Levering	Prohibition	132,007	
1900	William McKinley	Republican	7,218,491	292
	William J. Bryan	Democrat	6,356,734	155
	John C. Wooley	Prohibition	208,914	
	Eugene V. Debs	Socialist	87,814	
1904	Theodore Roosevelt	Republican	7,628,461	336
	Alton B. Parker	Democrat	5,084,223	140
	Eugene V. Debs	Socialist	402,283	
	Silas Swallow	Prohibition	258,536	
	Thomas Watson	People's	117,183	
1908	William Howard Taft	Republican	7,675,320	321
	William J. Bryan	Democrat	6,412,294	162
	Eugene V. Debs	Socialist	420,793	
	Eugene Chafin	Prohibition	253,840	

Year	Candidate	Party	Popular Vote	Electoral
1912	Woodrow Wilson	Democrat	6,296,547	435
	William Howard Taft	Republican	3,486,720	8
	Theodore Roosevelt	Progressive	4,118,571	86
	Eugene V. Debs	Socialist	900,672	
	Eugene Chafin	Prohibition	206,275	
1916	Woodrow Wilson	Democrat	9,127,695	277
	Charles E. Hughes	Republicn	8,533,507	254
	A.L. Benson	Socialist	585,113	
	J. Frank Hanly	Prohibition	220,506	
1920	Warren Harding	Republican	16,143,407	404
	James M. Cox	Democrat	9,130,328	127
	Eugene V. Debs	Socialist	919,799	
	P.P. Christensen	Farmer-Labor	265,411	
	Aaron Watkins	Prohibiton	189,408	
1924	Calvin Coolidge	Republican	15,718,211	382
	John W. Davis	Democrat	8,385,283	136
	Robert La Follette	Progressive	4,831,289	13
1928	Herbert Hoover	Republican	21,391,993	444
	Alfred E. Smith	Democrat	15,016,169	87
	Norman Thomas	Socialist	267,835	
1932	Franklin D. Roosevelt	Democrat	22,809,638	472
	Herbert C. Hoover	Republican	15,758,901	59
	Norman Thomas	Socialist	881,951	
	William Foster	Communist	102,785	
1936	Franklin D. Roosevelt	Democrat	27,752,869	523
	Alfred M. Landon	Republican	16,674,665	8
	William Lemke	Union	882,479	
	Norman Thomas	Socialist	187,720	
1940	Franklin D. Roosevelt	Democrat	27,307,819	449
	Wendell Willkie	Republican	22,321,018	82
1944	Franklin D. Roosevelt	Democrat	25,606,585	432
	Thomas E. Dewey	Republican	22,014,745	99
1948	Harry S. Truman	Democrat	24,179,345	303
	Thomas E. Dewey	Republican	21,991,291	189
	Strom Thurmond	Dixiecrat	1,176,125	39
	Henry Wallace	Progressive	1,157,326	
	Norman Thomas	Socialist	139,572	
	Claude A. Watson	Prohibition	103,900	
1952	Dwight D. Eisenhower	Republican	33,936,234	442
	Adlai Stevenson II	Democrat	27,314,992	89
	Vincent Hallinan	Progressive	140,023	
1956	Dwight D. Eisenhower	Republican	35,590,472	457
	Adlai Stevenson II	Democrat	26,022,752	73
	T. Coleman Andrews	States' Rights	111,178	
	Walter B. Jones	Democrat		1
1960	John F. Kennedy	Democrat	34,226,731	303
	Richard M. Nixon	Republican	34,108,157	219
	Harry Byrd	Democrat		15
1964	Lyndon B. Johnson	Democrat	43,129,566	486
	Barry Goldwater	Republican	27,178,188	52

Year	Candidate	Party	Popular Vote	Electoral
1968	Richard M. Nixon	Republican	31,785,480	301
	Hubert H. Humphrey	Democrat	31,275,166	191
	George Wallace	American Independent	9,906,473	46
1972	Richard M. Nixon	Republican	47,170,179	520
	George McGovern	Democrat	29,171,791	17
	John Hospers	Libertarian		1
1976	Jimmy Carter	Democrat	40,830,763	297
	Gerald R. Ford	Republican	39,147,793	240
	Ronald Reagan	Republican		1
1980	Ronald Reagan	Republican	43,904,153	489
	Jimmy Carter	Democrat	35,483,883	49
	John Anderson	Independent candidacy	5,719,437	
1984	Ronald Reagan	Republican	54,455,074	525
	Walter F. Mondale	Democrat	37,577,137	13
1988	George Bush	Republican	48,881,278	426
	Michael Dukakis	Democrat	41,805,374	111
	Lloyd Bentsen	Democrat		1
1992	Bill Clinton	Democrat	43,727,625	370
	George Bush	Republican	38,165,180	168
	Ross Perot	Independent catdidacy	19,236,411	0
1996	Bill Clinton	Democrat	45,628,667	379
	Bob Dole	Republican	37,869,435	159
	Ross Perot	Independent catdidacy	7,874,283	0
2000	George W. Bush	Republican	49,820,518	271
	Albert Gore Jr.	Democrat	50,158,094	267
	Ralph Nader	Green Party	7,866,284	
2004	George W. Bush	Republican	62,040,610	286
	John Kerry	Democrat	59,028,439	251
	Ralph Nader	Green Party	463,653	
2008	Barack Obama	Democrat	66,882,230	365
	John McCain	Republican	58,343,671	173
2012	Barack Obama	Democrat	60,459,974	332
	Mitt Romney	Republican	57,653,982	206

APPENDIX D

Members of the Supreme Court of the United States

Chief Justices	State App't From	Appointed by President	Service
Jay, John	New York	Washington	1789-1795
Rutledge, John*	South Carolina	Washington	1795-1795
Ellsworth, Oliver	Connecticut	Washington	1796-1799
Marshall, John	Virginia	Adams, John	1801-1835
Taney, Roger Brooke	Maryland	Jackson	1836-1864
Chase, Salmon Portland	Ohio	Lincoln	1864-1873
Waite, Morrison Remick	Ohio	Grant	1874-1888
Fuller, Melville Weston	Illinois	Cleveland	1888-1910
White, Edward Douglass	Louisiana	Taft	1910-1921
Taft, William Howard	Connecticut	Harding	1921-1930
Hughes, Charles Evans	New York	Hoover	1930-1941
Stone, Harlan Fiske	New York	Roosevelt F.	1941-1946
Vinson, Fred Moore	Kentucky	Truman	1946-1953
Warren, Earl	California	Eisenhower	1953-1969
Burger, Warren Earl	Virginia	Nixon	1969-1986
Rehnquist, William H.	Virginia	Reagan	1986-2005
Roberts, John G., Jr.	Maryland	Bush, G. W.	2005-

Associate Justices			
Rutledge, John	South Carolina	Washington	1790-1791
Cushing, William	Massachusetts	Washington	1790-1810
Wilson, James	Pennsylvania	Washington	1789-1798
Blair, John	Virginia	Washington	1789-1796
Iredell, James	North Carolina	Washington	1790-1799
Johnson, Thomas	Maryland	Washington	1791-1793
Paterson, William	New Jersey	Washington	1793-1806
Chase, Samuel	Maryland	Washington	1796-1811
Washington, Bushrod	Virginia	Adams, John	1798-1829
Moore, Alfred	North Carolina	Adams, John	1799-1804
Johnson, William	South Carolina	Jefferson	1804-1834
Livingston, Henry Brockholst	New York	Jefferson	1806-1823
Todd, Thomas	Kentucky	Jefferson	1807-1826
Duvall, Gabriel	Maryland	Madison	1811-1836
Story, Joseph	Massachusetts	Madison	1811-1845
Thompson, Smith	New York	Monroe	1823-1843
Trimble, Robert	Kentucky	Adams, J. Q.	1826-1828
McLean, John	Ohio	Jackson	1829-1861
Baldwin, Henry	Pennsylvania	Jackson	1830-1844
Wayne, James Moore	Georgia	Jackson	1835-1867
Barbour, Philip Pendleton	Virginia	Jackson	1836-1841
Catron, John	Tennessee	Jackson	1837-1865

*ActingChief Justice; Senate refused to confirm appointment.

McKinley, John	Alabama	Van Buren	1837-1852
Daniel, Peter Vivian	Virginia	Van Buren	1841-1860
Nelson, Samuel	New York	Tyler	1845-1872
Woodbury, Levi	New Hampshire	Polk	1845-1851
Grier, Robert Cooper	Pennsylvania	Polk	1846-1870
Curtis, Benjamin Robbins	Massachusetts	Fillmore	1851-1857
Campbell, John Archibald	Alabama	Pierce	1853-1861
Clifford, Nathan	Maine	Buchanan	1858-1881
Swayne, Noah Haynes	Ohio	Lincoln	1862-1881
Miller, Samuel Freeman	Iowa	Lincoln	1862-1890
Davis, David	Illinois	Lincoln	1862-1877
Field, Stephen Johnson	California	Lincoln	1863-1897
Strong, William	Pennsylvania	Grant	1870-1880
Bradley, Joseph P.	New Jersey	Grant	1870-1892
Hunt, Ward	New York	Grant	1873-1882
Harlan, John Marshall	Kentucky	Hayes	1877-1911
Woods, William Burnham	Georgia	Hayes	1880-1887
Matthews, Stanley	Ohio	Garfield	1881-1889
Gray, Horace	Massachusetts	Arthur	1882-1902
Blatchford, Samuel	New York	Arthur	1882-1893
Lamar, Lucius Quintus C.	Mississippi	Cleveland	1888-1893
Brewer, David Josiah	Kansas	Harrison	1889-1910
Brown, Henry Billings	Michigan	Harrison	1890-1906
Shiras, George, Jr.	Pennsylvania	Harrison	1892-1903
Jackson, Howell Edmunds	Tennessee	Harrison	1893-1895
White, Edward Douglass	Louisiana	Cleveland	1894-1910
Peckham, Rufus Wheeler	New York	Cleveland	1896-1909
McKenna, Joseph	California	McKinley	1898-1925
Holmes, Oliver Wendell	Massachusetts	Roosevelt T.	1902-1932
Day, William Rufus	Ohio	Roosevelt T.	1903-1922
Moody, William Henry	Massachusetts	Roosevelt T.	1906-1910
Lurton, Horace Harmon	Tennessee	Taft	1910-1914
Hughes, Charles Evans	New York	Taft	1910-1916
Van Devanter, Willis	Wyoming	Taft	1910-1937
Lamar, Joseph Rucker	Georgia	Taft	1911-1916
Pitney, Mahlon	New Jersey	Taft	1912-1922
McReynolds, James Clark	Tennessee	Wilson	1914-1941
Brandeis, Louis Dembitz	Massachusetts	Wilson	1916-1939
Clarke, John Hessin	Ohio	Wilson	1916-1922
Sutherland, George	Utah	Harding	1922-1938
Butler, Pierce	Minnesota	Harding	1923-1939
Sanford, Edward Terry	Tennessee	Harding	1923-1930
Stone, Harlan Fiske	New York	Coolidge	1925-1941
Roberts, Owen Josephus	Pennsylvania	Hoover	1930-1945
Cardozo, Benjamin Nathan	New York	Hoover	1932-1938
Black, Hugo Lafayette	Alabama	Roosevelt F.	1937-1971
Reed, Stanley Forman	Kentucky	Roosevelt F.	1938-1957
Frankfurter, Felix	Massachusetts	Roosevelt F.	1939-1962
Douglas, William Orville	Connecticut	Roosevelt F.	1939-1975
Murphy, Frank	Michigan	Roosevelt F.	1940-1949

Byrnes, James Francis	South Carolina	Roosevelt F.	1941-1942
Jackson, Robert Houghwout	New York	Roosevelt F.	1941-1954
Rutledge, Wiley Blount	Iowa	Roosevelt F.	1943-1949
Burton, Harold Hitz	Ohio	Truman	1945-1958
Clark, Tom Campbell	Texas	Truman	1949-1967
Minton, Sherman	Indiana	Truman	1949-1956
Harlan, John Marshall	New York	Eisenhower	1955-1971
Brennan, William J., Jr.	New Jersey	Eisenhower	1956-1990
Whittaker, Charles Evans	Missouri	Eisenhower	1957-1962
Stewart, Potter	Ohio	Eisenhower	1958-1981
White, Byron Raymond	Colorado	Kennedy	1962-1993
Goldberg, Arthur Joseph	Illinois	Kennedy	1962-1965
Fortas, Abe	Tennessee	Johnson L.	1965-1969
Marshall, Thurgood	New York	Johnson L.	1967-1991
Blackmun, Harry A.	Minnesota	Nixon	1970-1994
Powell, Lewis F., Jr.	Virginia	Nixon	1972-1988
Rehnquist, William H.	Arizona	Nixon	1972-1986**
Stevens, John Paul	Illinois	Ford	1975-2010
O'Connor, Sandra Day	Arizona	Reagan	1981-2006
Scalia, Antonin	Virginia	Reagan	1986-
Kennedy, Anthony M.	California	Reagan	1988-
Souter, David H.	New Hampshire	Bush, G. H. W.	1990-2009
Thomas, Clarence	Georgia	Bush, G. H. W.	1991-
Ginsburg, Ruth Bader	New York	Clinton	1993-
Breyer, Stephen G.	Massachusetts	Clinton	1994-
John Roberts	Maryland	Bush, G. W.	2005-
Alito, Samuel A., Jr.	New Jersey	Bush, G. W.	2006-
Sonia Sotomayor	New York	Obama	2009-
Elena Kagan	New York	Obama	2010-

Notes: The acceptance of the appointment and commission by the appointee, as evidenced by the taking of the prescribed oaths, is here implied; otherwise the individual is not carried on this list of the Members of the Court. Examples: Robert Hanson Harrison is not carried, as a letter from President Washington of February 9, 1790 states Harrison declined to serve. Neither is Edwin M. Stanton who died before he could take the necessary steps toward becoming a Member of the Court. *Chief Justice Rutledge is included because he took his oaths, presided over the August Term of 1795, and his name appears on two opinions of the Court for that Term.

[The foregoing was taken from a booklet prepared by the Supreme Court of the United States.]

**Elevated.

APPENDIX E
ADMISSION OF STATES INTO THE UNION

State	Date of Admission	State	Date of Admission
1. Delaware	December 7, 1787	26. Michigan	January 26, 1837
2. Pennsylvania	December 12, 1787	27. Florida	March 3, 1845
3. New Jersey	December 18, 1787	28. Texas	December 29, 1845
4. Georgia	January 2, 1788	29. Iowa	December 28, 1846
5. Connecticut	January 9, 1788	30. Wisconsin	May 29, 1848
6. Massachusetts	February 6, 1788	31. California	September 9, 1850
7. Maryland	April 28, 1788	32. Minnesota	May 11, 1858
8. South Carolina	May 23, 1788	33. Oregon	February 14, 1859
9. New Hampshire	June 21, 1788	34. Kansas	January 29, 1861
10. Virginia	June 25, 1788	35. West Virginia	June 20, 1863
11. New York	July 26, 1788	36. Nevada	October 31, 1864
12. North Carolina	November 21, 1789	37. Nebraska	March 1, 1867
13. Rhode Island	May 29, 1790	38. Colorado	August 1, 1876
14. Vermont	March 4, 1791	39. North Dakota	November 2, 1889
15. Kentucky	June 1, 1792	40. South Dakota	November 2, 1889
16. Tennessee	June 1, 1796	41. Montana	November 8, 1889
17. Ohio	March 1, 1803	42. Washington	November 11, 1889
18. Louisiana	April 30, 1812	43. Idaho	July 3, 1890
19. Indiana	December 11, 1816	44. Wyoming	July 10, 1890
20. Mississippi	December 10, 1817	45. Utah	January 4, 1896
21. Illinois	December 3, 1818	46. Oklahoma	November 16, 1907
22. Alabama	December 14, 1819	47. New Mexico	January 6, 1912
23. Maine	March 15, 1820	48. Arizona	February 14, 1912
24. Missouri	August 10, 1821	49. Alaska	January 3, 1959
25. Arkansas	June 15, 1836	50. Hawaii	August 21, 1959

APPENDIX F

POPULATION GROWTH

Year	Population	Percent Increase
1630	4,600	
1640	26,600	478.3
1650	50,400	90.8
1660	75,100	49.0
1670	111,900	49.0
1680	151,500	35.4
1690	210,400	38.9
1700	250,900	19.2
1710	331,700	32.2
1720	466,200	40.5
1730	629,400	35.0
1740	905,600	43.9
1750	1,170,800	29.3
1760	1,593,600	36.1
1770	2,148,100	34.8
1780	2,780,400	29.4
1790	3,929,214	41.3
1800	5,308,483	35.1
1810	7,239,881	36.4
1820	9,638,453	33.1
1830	12,866,020	33.5
1840	17,069,453	32.7
1850	23,191,876	35.9
1860	31,443,321	35.6
1870	39,818,449	26.6
1880	50,155,783	26.0
1890	62,947,714	25.5
1900	75,994,575	20.7
1910	91,972,266	21.0
1920	105,710,620	14.9
1930	122,775,046	16.1
1940	131,669,275	7.2
1950	151,325,798	14.5
1960	179,323,175	18.5
1970	203,302,031	13.4
1980	226,542,199	11.4
1990	248,718,301	9.8
2000	281,421,906	13.1
2010	308,745,538	9.7

GLOSSARY OF IMPORTANT PEOPLE AND CONCEPTS

Abernathy, Ralph (1926-1990): After the King assassination directed the Southern Christian Leadership Conference (founded by King) and organized the SCLC Poor People's March on Washington during the summer of 1968.

Abortion laws: Abortion was generally legal in the United States until the second half of the 19th century when the American Medical Association lobbied for outlawing forms of abortion that endangered women. More restrictive laws became the norm by the early 20th century and remained in place until the *Roe v. Wade* decision.

Adams, Eddie (1933-2004): An Associated Press photographer who took a Pulitzer Prize winning photograph of Police Chief Nguyen Ngoc Loan executing a suspected communist during the 1968 Tet Offensive.

Adamson Act: Federal law passed in 1916 establishing an eight-hour workday for railroad workers.

Affirmative Action: A federal policy launched in 1970 in which all federal agencies and contractors had to meet "numerical goals and timetables" in hiring a proportionally representative number of African Americans, Mexican Americans, women and other groups that had historically experienced discrimination.

Affordable Health Care Act: The attempted reform of the nation's health-care system. Providing all Americans with some sort of health-care coverage will become law for millions of Americans by 2014.

Agent Orange: A cancer-causing chemical defoliant dropped on South Vietnam during the Vietnam War to deny the communist National Liberation Front and the North Vietnamese Army jungle cover.

Agnew, Spiro (1918-1996): Vice President under President Nixon who was forced to resign October 10, 1973 because of charges that he accepted bribes while a Baltimore County Executive and Governor of Maryland.

Agricultural Adjustment Act (AAA): Federal law of the New Deal era that restricted agricultural production by paying farmers subsidies and government purchases of farm commodities.

Ahmadinejad, Mahmoud: President of Iran, whose constant saber-rattling with a supposed nuclear arsenal has caused significant tension between Iran and the United States and general alarm throughout the Middle East and Arabia.

Al-Asad, Bashar: President of Syria attempting to put down protracted uprisings against the totalitarian regime.

Alcatraz Occupation: An occupation of a former federal prison by Native American protestors calling for construction of a Native American Cultural Center on Alcatraz Island in San Francisco Bay that lasted from November 20, 1969 to June 11, 1971

Ali, Muhammad (1942-): Then known as Cassius Clay, Ali won a gold medal in boxing in the heavyweight class during the 1960 Rome Olympics, capturing his first professional boxing title against Sonny Liston in February 1964. Announcing his adherence to the Nation of Islam, Ali changed his name. Convicted for draft evasion, Ali won on appeal but had to win back in the boxing ring the championships that had been stripped from him.

All In the Family: A satirical television series that ran on CBS from 1971-1979 and dealt with issues like racism, the war in Vietnam, feminism, and religion.

American Civil Liberties Union (ACLU): Formed by Helen Gurley Flynn to combat the illegality of the Red Scare and the blatant violation of numerous individuals' constitutional rights in the name of national security.

American Expeditionary Force (AEF): Term given to the eventual 2 million U.S. troops who served in France during WWI. The AEF was commanded by General John J. "Blackjack" Pershing.

American Federation of Labor: Founded by Samuel Gompers in aftermath of Haymarket Square. A new union out of the ashes of the Knights of Labor. Gompers organized the AFL by craft rather than industry, and thus the AFL became a union of mostly skilled workers.

American GI Forum: A Latino civil rights organization formed in Corpus Christi, Texas, in 1948 by Dr. Hector Garcia to help Mexican-American veterans experiencing trouble receiving Veterans Administration benefits.

American Indian Movement: "Red Power" group formed by George Mitchell and Dennis Banks that aimed at ending police brutality victimizing Native Americans, promoting pride in American Indian history and advancing education for young Native Americans.

American Protective League (APL): A government-endorsed agency headed by businessman A.M. Briggs, organized to help curb dissent at home, especially among the German-American community and end union activities, especially strikes that could hamper the war effort.

American Recovery and Reinvestment Act 2009: Passed by the Obama administration in an effort to address the nation's high unemployment caused by the 2008 Great Recession.

AmeriCorps: A Clinton initiative in which students could repay college loans through volunteering in community service projects and programs.

Amos 'n' Andy: A spin off of a popular radio show that had featured two white actors portraying stereotypical African-American characters, this 1951-1952 CBS comedy series featured the only all-black cast on television but was the subject of an NAACP boycott because of the demeaning way the program depicted black people.

Antebellum: Term used by historians to describe the pre-Civil War period (1820-1860) in United States history. It is especially applicable to the pre-war South.

Anthracite Coal Strike: A 1902 walkout of Pennsylvania coal miners that resulted in Theodore Roosevelt establishing the first federal arbitration commission to settle a major labor disagreement.

Anti-Saloon League (ASL): Leading national organization that campaigned for the prohibition of alcoholic beverages.

Anti-Semitism: a hatred of Jews, often tied to a belief that Jews secretly control the world politically and financially.

Antrim, Henry, also known as "William Bonney" or "Billy the Kid" (c. 1859-1881): A drifter and outlaw accused of the murders of more than 20 people. Antrim's misdeeds were mostly the product of legend.

Apartheid: The white South African government's policy beginning after WWII of establishing an officially segregated society based on color.

Apollo Program: The space program inaugurated by the Kennedy administration that resulted in manned flights to the moon with landings by the crews of *Apollo* 11 and 12, and *Apollo* 14 through 17 from 1969 until 1972.

Arab Spring: The populist uprisings that began in Egypt and Tunisia in early 2011 and spread throughout the Middle East and even into the Gulf states (Yemen and Bahrain) that overthrew long-standing dictatorships.

Army IQ tests: Tests administered to 1.75 million recruits during World War I, from 1917-1918. The Army reported in 1921 that the average American had a mental age of 13. The Army reported that the scores of immigrants of Eastern and Southern European descent were even lower, sparking a panic that increased support for an immigration restriction law passed by the United States in 1924.

Army-McCarthy hearings: Televised congressional hearings authorized by Eisenhower after McCarthy had accused the Army of being infiltrated by communists. Hearings proved to be McCarthy's downfall as public turned against him after seeing his crass, brutal behavior on television.

Arnett, Peter (1934-): One of the Associated Press' top reporters covering the Vietnam War. Arnett quoted an officer making one of that conflict's most famous statements. After an American military attack devastated the town of Ben Tre during the Tet Offensive, the officer told Arnett, "It became necessary to destroy the town to save it."

Axis of Evil: Term used by the George W. Bush administration to initiate the Bush Doctrine of preemptive strikes on the nation's perceived enemies or threats to national security. The three nations the Bush administration considered the greatest dangers to the U.S. were Iran, Iraq, and North Korea.

Baby Boom: The sharp increase in live births in the United States between the years 1946 to 1964 when approximately 77 million children were added to the population. Baby Boomers had a great impact on the American economy and their taste deeply shaped American culture from the 1950s until the present.

Bail outs: The use of billions of dollars in government, taxpayer-generate revenue to bolster or save the nation's major car companies, banks, and other significant capitalist enterprises from going under.

Ballinger-Pinchot Affair: Chief Forester Gifford Pinchot's much-publicized disagreement with Interior Secretary Richard Ballinger over conservation matters that resulted in President Taft's firing of Pinchot.

"Ballyhoo": label given to the raucous behavior often associated with the Roaring 20's.

Baraka, Imamu Amiri, also known as Leroi Jones (1934--): Poet and dramatist who increasingly called for African Americans to move away from the goal of integration in a racist society and towards black economic, cultural and political independence.

Barker, Lieutenant Colonel Frank (1928-1968): The commander of American Forces in My Lai who died in a military plane crash June 12, 1968.

Battle of Ap Bac: A major battle between National Liberation Front (Vietcong) forces and the South Vietnamese Army on January 2, 1963, that revealed the weakness of the South Vietnamese military.

Battle of (the) Atlantic: Naval fight between German submarines and Allied supply convoys to Europe during WW II.

Battle of Britain: Air battle over England in 1940 that led to Hitler calling off his planned invasion of the British Isles.

Battles of Chateau-Thierry and Belleau Woods: Two of the most important engagements U.S. soldiers fought during World War I that proved to be turning points, stopping massive German offensives that had the Americans not been there, probably would have ended the war with a German victory.

Battle of Ia Drang Valley: One of the first combat engagements between North Vietnamese regulars and the United States military, in which 300 Americans died and 1,500 NVA soldiers were killed.

Battle of Khe Sanh: A battle between American forces and a combination of North Vietnam regulars and guerillas from the National Liberation Front that lasted from January 21 until April 8, 1968.

Battle of Leyte Gulf: Largest naval battle in world history fought in October 1944. The Japanese failed to prevent the American invasion of the Philippines.

Battle of Little Bighorn (also known as "Custer's Last Stand"): The battle in the Seventh Cavalry led by General George A. Custer were defeated by the Cheyennes and Sioux led by Sitting Bull and Crazy Horse in '876.

Battle of Midway: Pivotal naval battle fought in 1942 which ended Japanese offensive naval operations in the Pacific.

Battle of Saipan: Key battle in the Marianas in 1944 noted for the tenacious Japanese military defense and a mass suicide by several thousand Japanese civilians.

Battle of Stalingrad: Turning point battle fought in southern Russia from late-1942 to early 1943 resulting in a massive German defeat and the loss of Nazi momentum on the Eastern Front.

Bay of Pigs Invasion: A failed attempt to overthrow dictator Fidel Castro in April by anti-Castro Cubans.

Beatles: The most successful rock band in the 1960s, formed by singer/songwriter John Lennon in England in 1960 and recording several top-selling and highly influential albums including 1967's *Sgt. Pepper's Lonely Hearts Club Band* until their breakup in 1970.

Bedford Stuyvesant: A poor Brooklyn neighborhood populated mostly by African Americans and Puerto Ricans in the 1960s.

Berlin Crisis of 1961: The Soviets blockade of land to U.S. access to West Berlin.

Bessemer process: The ability to fabricate steel cheaply by using pig iron rather than more expensive grade iron. This process, adopted by Andrew Carnegie, catapulted him to the forefront of steel production in the U.S.

bin Laden, Osama (1957-2011): Leader of the Islamist extremist organization Al Qaeda who declared war on the West in the 1990s and was responsible for not only the 9/11 attacks on the Pentagon and the World Trade Center but the earlier bombing of the WTC in New York during the Clinton administration.

Black Codes: Laws passed denying many rights of citizenship to free blacks by the newly-elected southern white governments during presidential reconstruction.

Black Panther Party: Established in Oakland, California, emphasizing black economic and political power.

Bland-Allison Act 1878: The federal government's return to issuing silver coins and silver certificates; that is paper money backed by silver.

"Bloody Sunday": The violent attack by Alabama state troopers on civil rights protestors as they crossed the Edmund Pettus Bridge on March 7, 1965.

Blue Dog Democrats: Conservative Democrats who vote with their Republican counterparts in both the House and Senate.

Boat People: South Vietnamese refugees who fled by sea from their homeland after the collapse of the Saigon regime in 1975.

Boehner, John: As a result of the 2010 congressional elections, the Republicans took control of the House of Representative and elected conservative Minority Leader John Boehner of Ohio as Speaker.

Boland Amendment: A provision added to spending bills passed between 1982 and 1984 by the U.S. House to stop the CIA and Defense Department from funding the rightwing *Contra* rebels.

Bolsheviks: The communist revolutionary faction led by V.I. Lenin that overthrew the Provisional Government, established after the toppling of Czar Nicholas II.

Bonus Army: World War I Army veterans who demonstrated in Washington D.C. for the advance payment of their service bonuses. Hoover ordered the U.S. Army to drive the veterans and family members out of Washington.

"Boomers" and "Sooners": The terms refer to whites who seized land in what was then called the Indian Territory (modern-day Oklahoma) before the area was legally opened to white settlement on March 2, 1889.

"Boots on the ground": Term used to describe the Obama administration's troop escalation in Afghanistan, which the president believed would be required to defeat the Taliban insurgents.

Boxer Rebellion: A Chinese nationalist rebellion against the European imperialist powers that occurred in May 1900 and lasted for over two months.

Brady Bill: A law passed by Congress in response to the attempted assassination of President Ronald Reagan in which press secretary James Brady was severely wounded.

Brain Trust: The members of FDR's official cabinet as well as advisors, the majority of whom came from the nation's top universities and were experts in economic planning and other facets of macroeconomic theory.

Branch Davidian cult: An extremist religious cult led by David Koresh, who established his church on the outskirts of Waco, Texas.

Brown v. Board of Education of Topeka (1954): A Supreme Court decision that ruled "separate but equal" public schools violated the Constitution.

Brownmiller, Susan (1935--): A self-described radical woman who authored the pioneering 1975 classic detailing the history of sexual abuse against women, *Against Our Will: Men, Women and Rape*.

Bryan, William Jennings (1860-1925): The three-time Democratic presidential nominee from Nebraska who served as the party's standard bearer in 1896, 1900 and 1908.

Bryant, Anita (1940--): A singer and former Miss America Pageant contestant from Oklahoma who successfully led the campaign against gay rights legislation in Dade County Florida and campaigned against homosexuality across the country in the 1970s.

Buchwald, Art (1925-2007): A popular and Pulitzer Prize-winning American newspaper columnist and political satirist for *The Washington Post*.

Buffalo Soldiers: African-American soldiers attached to the United States Army's Ninth and Tenth Cavalry Regiments. These units performed bravely in Indian wars in the West, explored unmapped regions, built forts and guarded railroad and telegraph lines from the New Mexico Territory to the Wyoming Territory.

"Bull Moose" (Progressive) Party: Theodore Roosevelt's third party organized for the 1912 election (disbanded in 1916).

Bureau of Indian Affairs: Established in 1824 as part of the War Department, the BIA was given responsibility for physically protecting Native Americans, controlling trade with indigenous peoples, and supervising their relocation to reservations.

Burke, Martha Jane, also known as "Calamity Jane" (c. 1852-1903): A former prostitute who became a trick equestrian and sharpshooter performing for William "Buffalo Bill" Cody's "Wild West" show.

Calley, William Laws (1943--): The only soldier found guilty of murder related to the My Lai Massacre. Calley was convicted in a military trial and sentenced to life in prison, but his sentence was commuted by President Richard Nixon and he was released in 1974.

1184 / GLOSSARY

Camp Logan Riots, August 1917: One of many violent confrontations between white and black Americans that occurred during and after World War I. This particular incident involved black soldiers stationed in Houston, Texas who staged an uprising against local racism and white police brutality.

Capital goods: Finished products such as steel, iron, locomotives, rolling stock for railroads, lumber, machine parts, such as ball-bearings, tool dyes' etc. Such bi-products of industrialization were considered to be durable goods that lasted a long time.

Caputo, Philip (1941--): A U.S. Marine lieutenant during the Vietnam War, Caputo became a journalist and author after his military career, writing a gripping memoir of his Vietnam experiences, *A Rumor of War*, released in 1977

Carmichael, Stokely, also known as Kwame Ture (1941--): A civil rights activist who participated in the sit-in campaigns of the early 1960s, Carmichael joined the Student Non-Violent Coordinating Committee (SNCC) in 1964 and headed the organization the next year.

"carpetbaggers": Name given to all northern whites who migrated south allegedly to take advantage of a prostrated southern people and economy.

Carson, Rachel (1907-1964): The author of the 1962 environmental classic *Silent Spring*, which demonstrated the dangers to the ecology of pesticides.

Caudillo: Spanish word for a regional warlord or chieftain who has complete political control of that area and its inhabitants many of whom become fiercely loyal to that individual.

Charlie Company: An army military unit that carried out much of the My Lai Massacre.

Chávez, César (1927-1993): Co-founder of the United Farm Workers who used non-violent tactics to improve working conditions for largely Mexican-American agricultural labor.

"Checkers Speech": A televised speech given by Richard Nixon during the 1952 presidential campaign to challenge corruption charges. Positive response to the speech convinced GOP presidential nominee Dwight Eisenhower to keep Nixon as his running mate.

Chiang Kai-shek (1887-1975): The corrupt dictator of China from 1925 until 1949 who abused his own people while accepting billions in aid from the United States; an ardent anti-communist, he failed to stop Mao Zedong's communist revolution.

Chicano Movement: Inspired by Black Nationalists, the Chicano Movement promoted pride in Mexican culture, the Spanish language, and political autonomy for their community.

China Lobby: Term used to describe those individuals determined to see overthrown rightwing leader Chiang Kai-shek back in power in China and the overthrow of Mao Zedong's communist government.

Church Committee Hearings: A Senate investigation in 1975 into misdeeds by the CIA, the FBI and other intelligence agencies

Civil Rights Act of 1957: The first voting rights law passed by the Congress since Reconstruction, establishing the Justice Department's Civil Rights Division.

Civil Rights Act of 1964: A law banning segregation at public facilities and racial discrimination in the work place.

Civil Works Administration (CWA): A work-relief program initiated by FDR focusing on unemployed blue-collar American males, providing jobs in a variety of small-scale infrastructure projects.

Civilian Conservation Corps (CCC): One of many federally-sponsored job initiatives enacted by President Franklin Roosevelt to address unemployment.

Clayton Act: Antitrust legislation passed in 1914 that banned specific business practices including price discrimination and interlocking directorates.

Cleburne Demands: Members of the Southern Alliance gathered in Cleburne, Texas, in 1886 to draft a list of demands calling for state legislatures and the Congress to regulate railroads, outlaw land speculation, increase access to credit for farmers, and issue paper and silver currency to expand the money supply.

Clifford, Clark (1906-1998): A Washington attorney and adviser to several Democratic presidents, including Harry Truman, John Kennedy, Lyndon Johnson and Jimmy Carter. Clifford served as Robert S. McNamara's replacement as secretary of defense in the last year of the Johnson administration.

Clinton, Hillary (1947--): Secretary of State in Obama administration and previous Democratic presidential candidate (2008), who challenged Obama for the Democratic nomination.

Cody, William F. "Buffalo Bill" (1846-1917): The producer of a series of "Wild West" stage shows that starred famous Native Americans like Sitting Bull, rope twirlers and trick shooters such as Annie Oakley (Phoebe Butler). Cody's show crisscrossed America and Europe for three decades.

COINTELPRO: An FBI program that sought to disrupt and sew internal discord within civil rights, black nationalist, and anti-war groups during the 1960s.

Committee on Public Information (CPI): A government wartime propaganda agency headed by George Creel to promote the American war effort at home especially among the various immigrant communities, whose loyalty the Wilson administration wanted to ensure.

Commission-style government: A form of local government whereby individual commissioners are responsible for managing specific aspects of city government.

Comstock Lode: One of the biggest silver and gold deposits ever discovered in North America, which yielded up to $500,000,000 worth of precious metals from the Virginia Range in Western Nevada between its discovery in 1859 and 1879 when the deposits were exhausted.

Congress of Industrial Organizations (CIO): Union founded in 1935 by UMW leader John L. Lewis and Sidney Hillman of the Amalgamated Clothing Workers, for the purpose of organizing all non-union workers regardless of skill, occupation, gender, race, or religion.

Connor, Sheriff Theophilus Eugene "Bull" (1897-1973): The public safety commissioner in Birmingham, Alabama, at the height of the Civil Rights Movement in the early 1960s.

Consciousness-Raising: A technique used by feminists to make individuals aware how sexism had shaped their lives and how common the experiences of rape, spousal abuse, and job discrimination were in American life.

Consumer goods: A commodity or product produced for immediate, short-term, purchase and use by the general populace, designed with planned obsolescence and limited durability in mind.

Containment: The fundamental premise that the U.S. would "contain" communism (preventing its expansion), wherever and whenever it threatened democratic governments and free people in the world.

Contract With America: The 1994 "counter-revolution" led by Republican House Minority Leader Newt Gingrich against the Clinton administration.

Contras: Right wing rebels determined to overthrow the leftist *Sandinista* regime in Nicaragua. President Ronald Reagan referred to the guerrillas as "freedom fighters" and through the CIA and other agencies supported them with money and arms.

Coolidge, Calvin (1872-1933): staunchly conservative Republican President of the United States from 1923-1929.

Copenhagen Conference: An attempt by 193 nations to re-affirm and expand the 1997 Kyoto Protocol on the issue of greenhouse gas emissions. President Obama appeared at the conference, assuring its attendees that the U.S. was committed to accepting the Kyoto Protocol and that the nation would also reclaim its leadership in future initiatives.

Coughlin, Father Charles (1891–1979): A populist demagogue who also started out as a supporter of Franklin Roosevelt but moved first to the left then to the extreme right, supporting the fascist dictators in Europe, Benito Mussolini and Adolf Hitler.

Court Packing Plan (1937): The attempt by President Franklin Roosevelt to stack the United States Supreme Court with pro-New Deal justices by increasing the number of justices from 9 to 15, as well as establish a mandatory retirement age of 70 for all justices.

Cox, Archibald (1912-2004): The former Solicitor General under President John Kennedy appointed Watergate Special Prosecutor in 1973 who was fired by President Richard Nixon during the so-called "Saturday Night Massacre."

Coxey, Jacob and Coxey's Army: A protest movement in response to the Depression of 1893-97 organized by Jacob Coxey who urged the government to create public works projects to ameliorate the 25 percent unemployment that engulfed the nation. Coxey also led the first "march on Washington" to try to convince the government to intervene in the crisis and offer help to the people.

Crédit Mobilier: A Grant administration scandal involving the siphoning off of millions of dollars in government funds to a "dummy company" to build the Union Pacific Railroad. The railroad company owners sold bogus stock to greedy Congressmen, who believed they could make a quick buck.

"Crime of '73": When the federal government ceased minting both gold and silver coins and a return to minting only gold coins and the backing of greenbacks with gold only.

Cuban Missile Crisis: The face-off between the United States and the Soviet Union when the American military discovered on October 12, 1962, that the USSR was constructing nuclear missile launch sites on Cuba in response to the American-organized Bay of Pigs invasion the year before.

Daley, Richard J. (1902-1976): The famously corrupt and autocratic head of the Democratic Party political machine running Chicago who served as mayor from 1955 to 1976 and presided over the violent police response to protestors during the 1968 Democratic National Convention.

Darrow, Clarence (1857-1938): defense attorney for John Scopes at the "Monkey Trial."

Dawes Severalty Act: An 1887 law passed by the United States Congress that authorized the president to distribute land to individual Indians provided they broke all ties to their tribes.

Dayton Accords (1995): The U.S.-brokered peace initiative by the Clinton White House to end the genocidal civil war in the former Yugoslavian province of Bosnia between Bosnian Christian Serbs and their Muslim counterparts.

Dean, John (1938--): Served as White House Counsel to President Richard Nixon during the Watergate Scandal and plead guilty to obstruction of justice in 1973 and who received a reduced sentence in return for testifying for the prosecution.

Debs, Eugene (1855-1926): A labor leader and former Indiana congressman who ran as the Socialist candidate for presidency four times, including the 1912 election against Theodore Roosevelt, Woodrow Wilson, and William Howard Taft.

Deep Ecology: The belief that animals and even plants have inherent rights.

de Lôme Letter: The stolen communiqué of the Spanish ambassador to the United States in which de Lôme insulted President William McKinley. The letter found its way to American newspapers, further inflaming the increasing anti-Spanish temperament of the American people, leading to the Spanish-American War of 1898.

Diem, Ngo Dinh (1901-1963): The dictator of South Vietnam from 1954 until his overthrow and assassination in a November 1963 military coup.

Direct Primary: the popular election of nominees from a political party for a public office.

Dirty Tricks: Unethical and illegal campaign tactics, including writing fake, inflammatory letters using the letterhead of opponents, planting false, damaging stories in the press, espionage and theft of confidential files used by the Nixon reelection campaign in 1972.

"Dixiecrats": A third-party movement that emerged during the 1948 election that was anti-civil rights and pro-"states' rights" (pro-segregation).

Dodd-Frank Wall Street Reform and Consumer Protection Act: A measure the Obama administration lobbyied for since the Wall Street collapse, passed by Congress in July 2010. The bill massively overhauled the nation's financial system. The bill re-established the government's regulatory powers over the financial system, safeguarding the system from future abuses, which had caused the 2008 collapse.

"Dollar diplomacy": Foreign policy initiatives of Teddy Roosevelt's successor in the White House, William Howard Taft, supporting U.S. corporations that invested in Latin American countries.

Domino Theory: The belief that if South Vietnam fell to the communists, then communist regimes would be established across Asia.

"Don't ask, Don't Tell": The government's policy toward gays in the military during the Clinton and Bush administrations. Known gay and bisexual men and women were expelled from the service but could remain in the military provided they kept their sexuality secret.

Doughboys: Name given to U.S. soldiers who fought in World War I, dating back to the Mexican-American war of 1846-1848 when U.S. soldiers marching through Mexico had their uniforms covered in chalky white dust that turned to a doughy type of substance when their uniforms got wet.

Dubcek, Alexander (1921-1992): The Communist Party leader from January until August 1968 in Czechoslovakia, who ushered in a period of greater press and artistic freedoms and looser control of the economy. This time came to be known as the "Prague Spring."

Dust Bowl: The Great Plains area of the U.S. that suffered choking dust storms in the 1930s because farmers had overworked the land, stripping it of topsoil and nutrients, causing the dirt to become very thin.

Dylan, Bob (1941--): A widely influential singer/songwriter who began recording in the 1960s who frequently dealt with political themes.

Eagleton, Thomas (1929-2007): A Democratic Senator from Missouri selected by Democratic presidential nominee George McGovern as his running mate in 1972 who was forced to step down from the ticket when it was revealed he had received electro-shock therapy for depression.

Earth Day: An annual event started April 22, 1969, that aims to increase awareness of pollution and the importance of the natural environment.

Ehrlichman, John (1925-1999): White House Counsel and Assistant to the President for Domestic Affairs under President Nixon, later convicted of conspiracy, perjury, and obstruction of justice related to the Watergate Scandal.

Eighteenth Amendment: A provision prohibiting the sale and manufacture of alcoholic beverages in the United States until repealed in 1933.

Ellsberg, Daniel (1931--): A Pentagon military analyst who leaked the "Pentagon Papers," a secret history commissioned by the Pentagon of the American military involvement in Vietnam, to *The New York Times* and the *Washington Post*.

Energy Crisis (1973): A fuel shortage kicked off when the Organization of Petroleum Exporting Countries boycotted oil shipments to the United States in response to American support for Israel in the 1973 Yom Kippur War.

Energy Crisis (1979-1980): A fuel shortage caused by the Iranian Revolution and the 1980 invasion of Iran by Iraq.

Equal Rights Amendment (ERA): A proposed amendment to the United States Constitution approved by Congress in 1972 that fell three states short of the required three-fourths of the states needed for ratification.

Erhard Sensitivity Training (EST): One of several "encounter groups" offered as an alternative to traditional psychology and psychiatry that became popular in the 1960s and 1970s.

Ervin, Sam (1896-1985): A Democratic Senator from North Carolina who chaired the Senate Select Committee to Investigate Campaign Practices that investigated Watergate in the summer of 1973 and revealed the existence of the secret White House taping system.

Espionage Act: Of 1917 made it a crime to interfere with U.S. military operations, including the promotion of insubordination in the military or interference with military recruitment.

Ethiopia: An East African kingdom attack by Italy in 1935.

Eugenics: The racist pseudo-science of producing superior humans through selective breeding.

Executive Order 9981: An order issued by President Harry Truman on July 26, 1948, that mandated the desegregation of the United States Armed Forces by January 13, 1949.

Falwell, Jerry (1933-2007): The conservative, anti-feminist, anti-gay activist Baptist pastor of the Thomas Road Baptist Church in Lynchburg, Virginia, and co-founder in 1979 of The Moral Majority.

Faubus, Orval (1910-1994): The segregationist Democratic Governor of Arkansas from 1955 to 1967. Faubus ordered the Arkansas National Guard to prevent the school's integration but President Dwight Eisenhower nationalized the Guard and implemented the order.

Federal Emergency Relief Administration (FERA): First direct welfare assistance/relief program ever enacted in U.S. history in which the federal government authorized money for the poor as well as other assistance such as food, clothing, and medicine, for free to recipients.

Federal Reserve Act: Federal law passed in 1913 establishing the Federal Reserve System as the nation's central banking system under direction of the Federal Reserve Board.

Federal Trade Commission: Independent agency of the federal government created in 1914 to eliminate anti-competitive business practices by enforcing the nation's antitrust statutes.

Ferraro, Geraldine: (1935-2011): First woman ever chosen in U.S. history to be a vice-presidential running mate. Ferraro had been a several term Democratic member of the House from New York when Walter Mondale, Democratic nominee, chose her as his running mate in 1984.

Fifteenth Amendment: A Reconstruction-era amendment that bars states from interfering with the right to vote based on "race, color, or previous condition of servitude."

Fireside Chats: Radio speeches made by Franklin Roosevelt that aimed to reassure voters and to inform citizens of his New Deal programs and their purpose.

Foraker Act 1900: The law that established Puerto Rico as a U.S. "territory" and gave the U.S. the right to annex Puerto Rico without any provision for making the island an American state and its people citizens.

Ford, Gerald R. (1913-2006): The 38th President of the United States who assumed office upon the resignation of Richard Nixon on August 9, 1974. He was the first person to serve in the White House without being elected either as president or vice president.

Ford, Henry (1863-1947): Founder of the Ford Motor Company who revolutionized the manufacturing of automobiles by improving assembly line techniques.

"Forty Acres and a Mule": A Radical Republican proposal during Reconstruction to destroy the pre-Civil war plantation/slave-owning elite by confiscating their property and redistributing it to freedmen in allotments of 40 acres.

Fourteen Points: Woodrow Wilson's peace plan for the World War I period that called for global disarmament, free trade, open diplomacy and the creation of the League of Nations. The League would mediate disputes between nations and guarantee the safety and territorial integrity of member states.

Fourteenth Amendment: A Reconstruction-era amendment passed in 1866 that officially made the freedmen U.S. citizens while prohibiting the states from denying such individuals all the rights and privileges guaranteed any citizen of the United States.

Fragging: The assassination of a superior officer, which happened with increasing frequency towards the end of the Vietnam War.

Friedan, Betty (1921-1996): A leading feminist and author of the influential and bestselling 1963 book, *The Feminine Mystique*, that described the frustrations of educated women with few career opportunities in 1950s and 1960s America.

Freedmen's Bureau: First federally-sponsored and funded welfare agency created during Reconstruction to help the freedmen adjust to their new status while providing education, protection, and other services.

Freedom Riders: Seven African Americans and six whites who boarded interstate buses and rode through the South in the spring of 1961 to test federal enforcement of a court order desegregating interstate transportation terminals.

Freedom Summer: A civil rights campaign conducted by the Student Non-Violent Coordinating Committee (SNCC) and allied groups in the summer of 1964 to increase African-American voter registration in the state of Mississippi, to encourage black political activism there and to provide alternative schools for African-American children in place of the badly under-funded segregated schools provided by the state.

Freud, Sigmund (1856-1939): Austrian psychologist who pioneered the clinical approach of treatment through dialogue with patients.

Fulbright, J. William (1905-1995): A Democratic Senator from Arkansas who, after initially supporting Johnson's policies in Vietnam, became one of the war's toughest critics.

Fundamentalism: The Protestant movement within many denominations characterized by strict adherence to theological doctrines, especially a literal interpretation of the Bible.

Fusion: The partial merger of the Democratic Party with the People's, or Populist, Party for the 1896 presidential election.

Garvey, Marcus (1887-1940): Black nationalist leader who founded the United Negro Improvement Association (UNIA).

Geneva Peace Accords of 1954: The agreement signed between Ho Chi Minh and the French that established separate North and South Vietnamese governments.

Gentlemen's Agreement: An accord reached between the U.S. and Japan over the Japanese immigration issue. Japan agreed to halt further immigration of its citizens to the U.S., while President Teddy Roosevelt agreed to stop white Californian's persecution of Japanese immigrants as well as their segregation in the school system.

Geronimo (1829-1909): A Chiricahua Apache chief who led Indian resistance in northern Mexico and the American Southwest from the 1870s until his capture in modern-day Arizona in 1886.

Giáp, Võ Nguyên (1911--): The principal communist military commander in the First Indochina War against the French (1946-1954) and in the Vietnam War (1960-1975.)

Giovanni, Nikki (1943--): A poet, educator, and civil rights activist who advocated black cultural pride in collections like *Black Feeling/Black Talk* (1972).

Gitlin, Todd (1943--): President of the leftist Students for a Democratic Society from 1963-1964, Gitlin became a leader of the anti-war movement during the Vietnam era.

"Gold Bug": Politicians in the late 19th century who favored keeping all U.S. currency backed by gold.

Good Neighbor Policy: Franklin Roosevelt's foreign policy toward Latin America based upon noninterference in the domestic affairs of Latin American nations.

"Goo-goos": Pejorative used by the Americans for the Filipino insurgents who resisted for several years U.S. occupation and control of their islands in the late 1890s and early 1900s.

Gospel of Wealth: The belief of some of the richest Americans in the late 19th and early 20th centuries that God had blessed them with such wealth because of their virtue. This idea that God had rewarded the rich was used as an argument against the wealthy being required to pay workers higher wages or financially support government services for the poor.

Graham, William Franklin "Billy" (1918--): A leading Southern Baptist preacher estimated to have converted 2.5 million people in evangelical crusades around the globe since 1949, Graham formed friendships with several American presidents, including Harry Truman, Lyndon Johnson, Richard Nixon, and Bill Clinton. During the 1960 presidential race he drew criticism for suggesting that John Kennedy, a Roman Catholic, would have divided loyalties, split between the Vatican and the United States, should he win the presidency.

Grand Army of the Republic: Name given to Union Civil War veterans who became a powerful lobby during the Gilded Age over the issue of pensions and other benefits for Union Army combatants.

Grange (Patrons of Husbandry): The first farmers' union formed in the late 1860s to help small farmers in particular deal with railroad abuse and exploitation of their condition.

"Grantism": Refers to government officials acting in a corrupt, unethical way. Derives from the many scandals that erupted during the Grant administration from 1869 to 1877. The term became subsequently synonymous with any administration tainted by such abuses of power.

Great Railroad Strike of 1877: The first major strike in the nation's most important industry, caused by wage cuts, some as high as 35 percent. Railroad workers walked off the job at all major rail lines from St. Louis east. Violence ensued in many states, with the death toll over 100 and resulting in millions of dollars in property damage and lost railroad revenue.

Great Society: President Lyndon Johnson's social welfare programs, including Medicare, Medicaid, Head Start, the Job Corp, and VISTA. Also included in this legislative agenda were cultural initiatives such as creation of the Public Broadcasting System, the National Endowment for the Arts and the National Endowment for the Humanities.

Great White Fleet: President Teddy Roosevelt's dispatch of the nation's largest 16 battleships on a world tour for the purpose of displaying to the world the U.S.'s military and industrial might.

Greenback Labor Party: A third-party movement that emerged during the 1870s that championed a monetary system based on paper currency, the greenbacks, a move that would help out southern and western farmers.

"Greenbacks": Paper currency printed by the federal government during the Civil War to finance the northern war effort. Their issue caused widespread, exorbitant inflation in the North while taking the dollar off the gold standard.

Grenada: A small Caribbean island on which Cuban dictator Fidel Castro helped install a supposedly communist government. President Ronald Reagan sent American troops to invade the island in 1984 on the pretext of rescuing U.S. citizens attending medical school there.

Gringo: Mexican/Spanish language pejorative for all foreigners who had taken over their nation's economy during the dictatorship of Porfirio Diaz during the late 19th and early 20th centuries. However, the term subsequently became mostly associated with Americans.

Gulf of Tonkin Resolution: A congressional resolution that gave the American president authority to "take all necessary measures to repel any armed attack against the forces of the United States, and to prevent further aggression."

Halberstam, David (1934-2007): A Pulitzer-Prize winning journalist and longtime reporter for *The New York Times*, Halberstam provided what was then rare critical coverage of Vietnam and also wrote about the Civil Rights Movement of the early and mid-1960s.

Haldeman, H.R. "Bob" (1926-1993): White House Chief of Staff under President Nixon convicted of obstruction of justice and conspiracy in 1975 in relation to the Watergate conspiracy.

Half-Breeds: A moderate Republican faction in the late 19th century led by James G. Blaine of Maine that favored civil service reform.

Hampton, Fred (1948-1969): A leader of the Black Panther Party in Illinois fatally shot as he lay in his bed in his apartment in Chicago by city police and the FBI on December 4, 1969.

Hanoi Hilton: An infamous North Vietnamese prisoner of war camp in Hao Lo where captured American soldiers were tortured and subjected to "brain washing."

Harding, Warren G. (1865-1923): A conservative Republican President of the United States from 1921 to 1923 whose administration became embroiled in the "Tea Pot Dome Scandal."

"Harlem Renaissance": An African-American cultural movement expressing racial pride through the arts during the 1920s and 1930s.

Hay-Bunau-Varilla Treaty (1903): A questionable deal made between the United States and the newly formed country of Panama and its supposed ambassador, Philipe Bunau-Varilla, who actually had been director of the French company who originally contracted to build a canal. The treaty granted the U.S. the right to build the canal across the country of Panama.

Hay-Herrán Treaty (1901): Arrangement made between Secretary of State John Hay and Colombian ambassador Tomas Herran, who agreed to allow the U.S. to build a canal across the Colombian province of Panama for a one-time payment of $10 million and an annual rental fee of $250,000.

Hay-Pauncefote Treaty (1901): Agreement between the U.S. and Great Britain releasing the U.S. from its earlier 1850 obligation of having to build a canal in modern-day Panama in conjunction with Great Britain.

Hayden, Tom (1939--): A leader of the Students for a Democratic Society who drafted The Port Huron Statement, a document highly influential on the student left of the 1960s. Married for a time to actress Jane Fonda, Hayden became highly involved in protesting the Vietnam War, served in the California State Assembly from 1982-1992, and later became an animal rights activist.

Haymarket Square: Site of a bombing during a strike for the eight-hour workday in Chicago. Workers at the McCormick farm machinery plant went on strike and while demonstrating a bomb was thrown into the police crowd, killing six cops and causing a riot in which 50 people were wounded and 10 dead, 4 others besides the police.

Hays, William H. (1879-1954): The first president of the Motion Pictures Association of America who developed the voluntary code for filmmaking designed to produce films without objectionable material that dominated the industry until replaced by the Movie Ratings System in the late 1960s.

Helsinki Accords: An international agreement signed by the United States, Canada, the Soviet Union and 32 other nations that recognized the boundaries set in Europe at the end of World War II.

Hepburn Act: Federal law passed in 1906 that empowered the Interstate Commerce Commission to fix reasonable maximum railroad rates (subject to court review) based on inspection of railroad company records. The legislation marked the first time that the federal government regulated rates or prices of an American business.

Hersh, Seymour (1937--): An American investigative reporter who in 1969 broke the news of the My Lai Massacre in South Vietnam the previous year and the existence of an secret American program that spied on U.S. citizens.

Hinckley, John (1955--): Attempted to assassinate President Ronald Reagan in March 1981. Reagan was seriously wounded but recovered.

Hitler, Adolf (1889-1945): Nazi dictator of Germany.

Ho Chi Minh (1890-1969): The communist leader of the Vietnamese independence movement who directed the resistance to the Japanese occupation of Vietnam during World War II, then the Viet Minh forces that defeated France in the 1946-1954 Indochina War. After the Geneva accords, Ho became the leader of North Vietnam and directed communist efforts to push American military forces out of South Vietnam from the mid-1950s until his death in 1969.

Holocaust: The murder of six million Jews and "undesirables" by the Nazi regime during WW II.

Homestead Act: A law passed by the United States Congress in 1862 that allowed farmers to obtain 160 acres of public land for free, as long as they cultivated it for five years. Farmers also had the option of buying the land for $1.25 an acre if they cultivated it for six months.

Hoover, Herbert (1874-1964): The Commerce Secretary under President Warren Harding and Calvin Coolidge who won election as President of the United States in 1928. .

Hoover, J. Edgar (1895-1972): The first director of the Federal Bureau of Investigation, from 1924 until his death in 1972, Hoover played a key role in fanning fears of communist conspiracies during the McCarthy period of the 1950s and used illegal tactics to disrupt civil rights and anti-war groups in the 1960s.

Horizontal integration: Perfected by J.D. Rockefeller in the oil industry whereby one corporation or company gains complete control of a particular phase of production. In Rockefeller's case, Standard Oil controlled the refining process, perhaps the most important phase of transforming crude oil to a usable commodity such as heating oil.

House Un-American Activities Committee (HUAC): Right-wing Texas Congressman Martin Dies first chaired HUAC. Established in 1937, it investigated the influence of American communists and those sympathetic to fascism in the United States. HUAC would hold hearings on supposed communist subversion in Hollywood and American universities and strongly influenced the later Senate investigations of Soviet infiltration by Joseph McCarthy.

Howl and Other Poems: A controversial 1956 collection of poems celebrating homosexuality and exploring madness by one of the leaders of the Beat Movement, Allen Ginsberg.

Hubbard, L. Ron (1911-1986): Science fiction author, founder of the Church of Scientology, and creator of the so-called "science of the mind" Dianetics.

Humphrey, Hubert Horatio (1911-1978): A Senator from Minnesota, the vice president of the United States from 1965 to 1969 under Lyndon Johnson, and the 1968 Democratic nominee for the presidency, Humphrey stood as an advocate of Franklin Roosevelt-style liberalism, supporting social welfare programs and civil rights measures throughout his political career.

Hundred Days: The first three months of FDR's presidency (March to May, 1933), in which some of the more crucial programs and policies of the New Deal were enacted. Key legislation such as the Glass-Steagall Act, the FDIC, and the Securities and Exchange Act were passed and put into immediate effect.

Hungarian revolt: An uprising against Soviet domination that broke out in the Eastern European country in the fall of 1956.

Hurricane Katrina: One of the nation's worst natural disasters that caused the destruction of much of New Orleans in the summer of 2005.

I Love Lucy: A popular situation comedy starring Lucille Ball that aired on the CBS television network from 1951 to 1957.

Immigration Reform and Control Act of 1986: A law passed by Congress during the Reagan administration addressing the ongoing problem of illegal immigration. The law outlawed the hiring of illegal aliens, strengthened border controls, and offered legal status to aliens who had lived in the U.S. for five years.

Indian Reorganization Act of 1934: This legislation gave tribal lands back to Native Americans lost under the 1887 Dawes Act, grating them all manner of autonomy and ending the "assimilationist" crusade of the 1920 in which white authorities wanted to forcibly integrate Indians into white society.

Industrial Workers of the World (IWW): A radical leftist union, whose members were nicknamed the "Wobblies." The IWW welcomed all workers, regardless of skill, industry, gender, race, or ethnicity while advocating strikes to obtain worker rights.

Interlocking directorates: A business structure pioneered in the late 19th and early 20th centuries by businessmen like J.P. Morgan in which members of one corporation sit on the boards of supposed competitors.

Internment camps: Prison camps established for Japanese American civilians during WW II.

Interstate Commerce Act 1887: First federal regulatory agency in the history of the U.S. government, empowering the Interstate Commerce Commission to investigate and oversee railroad activities but the ICC could not mete out fines and other punishments for violators.

Interstate Highway Act of 1956: A bill passed by the United States Congress that authorized $130 billion to construct 46,000 miles of roads connecting the eastern coast of the United States to the western coast.

Iran-Contra Affair: A scandal during the Reagan presidency that involved the illegal sale of arms to Iran, a U.S. enemy, to pay for the release of hostages held in Lebanon by terrorist groups allied with the Iranian regime. The money from the arm sales went towards arming the *Contras*, a right-wing guerilla army seeking to overthrow the leftist *Sandinista* regime in Nicaragua, in direct violation of a congressional ban on such assistance to the Central American rebels.

"Iron-clad oath": An oath of allegiance all southern white males had to swear in which they promised that they in no way aided or abetted the Confederate cause. If able to take such an oath, they could vote and run for office in state elections.

Iron Curtain: A term used by Winston Churchill in a 1947 speech given in the United States to describe the boundary between Soviet-dominated Eastern European countries and Western Europe. Afterwards, "Iron Curtain" countries were those controlled by the Soviets.

Irreconcilables: Fierce congressional opponents of both the League of Nations and Treaty of Versailles, who were determined to defeat both. Members were hardcore isolationists.

"island hopping": The American military strategy during World War II in the Pacific of bypassing many Japanese-held islands after capturing key points in an island chain and isolating the remaining Japanese forces in the area.

Isolationism: The movement to isolate the United States from involvement in foreign conflicts in Europe and Asia during the 1930s.

James-Younger Gang: A criminal band of bank and train robbers active in Missouri and neighboring states in 1870s and 1880s led by two brothers, Jesse and Frank James.

Jazz: Musical style originating in the southern United States at the turn of the twentieth century blending African and European musical traditions.

"jingoism": A term originally coined in Great Britain in the 1870s that described an aggressive, militarist foreign policy using war and conquest to build an empire.

Jobs, Steven: Jobs, along with partner Steve Wozniak, founded one of the world's first PC's, naming their company Apple Computers. Since the company's founding in 1976, Apple has led the way in computer-related technological devices, ranging from the iPad to the iPhone series.

Johnson, Lyndon Baines (1908-1973): A Democratic member of the Texas delegation in the House of Representatives from 1937 to 1949, a senator from 1949 to 1961 (including a stint as Senate Majority Leader from 1955-1961), the vice president from 1961 to 1963, and president from 1963-1969, Johnson ascended to the White House after John Kennedy's assassination. Johnson created social welfare programs such as Medicare and Medicaid, Project Head Start and what he called "The War on Poverty."

Jones, Jim (1931-1978): A minister, faith healer and founder of the People's Temple who led more than 900 followers in a mass suicide in Guyana following his complicity in the murder of Congressman Leo Ryan and four others.

The Jungle: Upton Sinclair's 1906 novel that attempted to draw attention to the plight of the working class and to promote socialism, but ended up generating public outrage over unsanitary meatpacking conditions and passage of the Meat Inspection Act.

Kellogg-Briand Pact: Treaty signed in 1928 by the U.S., France, and thirteen other nations (later joined by forty additional nations), which officially renounced war as an instrument of foreign policy.

Kennan, George (1904-2005): Considered by most Cold War historians to be the individual who had the most influence on the development of the containment policy adopted by President Harry Truman.

Kennedy, John F. (1917-1963): The 35th President of United States. Kennedy's administration has been associated with the start of the *Apollo* moon mission, troubled relations with the Soviet Union characterized by the Bay of Pigs invasion and the Cuban Missile Crisis, the start of the Vietnam War, and his administration's occasional support of the Civil Rights Movement. An assassin, Lee Harvey Oswald, murdered Kennedy in Dallas, Texas, November 22, 1963.

Kerner Commission: A panel appointed by President Lyndon Johnson to investigate the causes of urban riots in the United States between 1965 and 1968.

Kesey, Ken (1935-2001): Author of the important 1962 novel *One Flew Over the Cuckoo's Nest*. Kesey formed a group called The Merry Pranksters, a band of hippies who traveled the country and held LSD "raves" that usually featured music and free samples of the drug.

Keating-Owen Act: Federal legislation outlawing the shipment across state lines of items manufactured in whole, or in part, by labor under the age of 14. The U.S. Supreme Court ruled the law unconstitutional in 1919.

Kelley, Florence (1859-1932): Progressive reformer who campaigned for regulating the working conditions and the wages and hours of women and children.

Kennedy, Edward (1932-2009): A Massachusetts Senator, younger brother of President John F. Kennedy and Senator Robert Kennedy, and unsuccessful challenger to President Jimmy Carter in the 1980 Democratic presidential race.

Kent State Massacre: The fatal shooting of four students and injuring of nine others at the Kent State University campus on May 4, 1970, by National Guardsmen during protests over the American invasion of Cambodia.

Kissinger, Henry (1923--): President Nixon's National Security Advisor and Secretary of State under Nixon and President Gerald Ford.

Kerensky, Alexander (1881-1970): Leader of Russia's first attempt at parliamentary, democratic government following the overthrow of Czar Nicholas II in the Russian Revolution in February 1917.

Keynesian economic theory: Economic theory put forth by the British economist John Maynard Keynes that depressions and general economic downturns can be rectified by governments increasing spending, inflating the money supply, reducing taxes, and lowering interest rates to improve demand or consumer purchasing power.

Kim Il-Sung (1912-1994): Dictator of North Korea during the time of the *Pueblo* crisis in 1969.

King, Martin Luther, Jr. (1929-1968): The primary leader of the African-American civil rights movement from the Montgomery Bus Boycott until his assassination in Memphis, Tennessee, April 4, 1968. For many, King's 1963 "I Have a Dream Speech" during the March on Washington on August 28, 1963 summarized the highest ideals of the 1960s protest movement.

Kinsey, Alfred (1894-1956): An American sex researcher whose books *Sexual Behavior in the Human Male* (1948) and *Sexual Behavior in the Human Female* (1953) documented much higher rates of premarital sex, marital infidelity, sexual experimentation among teens, and homosexuality in the American population than previously assumed.

Kirk, Grayson (1903-1997): President of Columbia University from 1953 to 1968 who resigned following the student protests and the occupation of the campus from March until May 1968.

Knights of Labor: One of the nation's first prominent labor organizations, formed in 1869 and reaching the peak of its strength in the 1880s. The union allowed both unskilled and skilled workers to join, as well as women and African Americans.

Ku Klux Klan: A white supremacist group that aimed to destroy the Reconstruction-era Republican Party in the South, to force the withdrawal of Union troops from the region, and to terrify African Americans into not voting or demanding better working conditions.

"Laffer Curve" or supply-side economics: Anti-Keynesian economic theory proposed by University of Southern California economist Arthur Laffer, which advocated cutting both corporate and personal taxes in order to stimulate economic growth. Such savings would theoretically encourage producers to make more products and thus create more jobs, which would put more money in people's pockets, leading to prosperity.

La Follette, Robert (1855-1925): Progressive Republican governor of Wisconsin later elected to the U.S. Senate. In the 1924 presidential election, he ran as a third-party candidate for the presidency.

Laissez-faire: A notion by 18th century English economist Adam Smith that capitalism operates for the greater benefit of all individuals if free from government interference and other artificially imposed restraints.

Lansdale, Edward (1908-1987): A United States Air Force Major General who served in both the Office of Strategic Services and its successor, the Central Intelligence Agency. Beginning in 1953, Lansdale was an aggressive advocate of a deeper American military commitment in South Vietnam and stronger support for South Vietnamese dictator Ngo Dinh Diem.

League of Nations: The "fourteenth point" of Wilson's grand post-World War I peace plan that called for the creation of a world organization to address global disputes before they escalated into war.

League of United Latin American Citizens (LULAC): A Latino civil rights group formed in 1929 in Corpus Christi, Texas, that sought to end discrimination against Hispanics and also sought to promote "Americanism" in the community through English language classes.

Leary, Timothy (1920-1996): A former professor of psychology and researcher at Harvard University who in the 1960s, became an advocate of the psychedelic drug LSD, claiming it would create a more peaceful world, and the man who coined the famous phrase, "Turn on, tune in, and drop out."

LeMay, Curtis (1906-1990): An American Air Force general who directed the controversial firebombing of Tokyo and other cities during World War II, and headed the Berlin airlift when the Soviets cut off supplies to West Berlin. He called for bombing Cuba during the 1962 Cuban Missile Crisis and wanted to expand air attacks on civilian targets in North Vietnam during the Johnson administration. LeMay ran for vice president on the American Independent Party ticket with segregationist former Alabama Governor George Wallace in 1968.

Lend-Lease Act: Legislation pushed by Roosevelt in 1941 that empowered the president "to sell, transfer title to, exchange, lease, lend, or otherwise dispose of" any American defense articles to the government of any country whose defense the president deemed vital to the protection of the United States.

"Letter From a Birmingham Jail": The letter was written by Martin Luther King, Jr., in 1963 while he was held in jail after violating an Alabama state court order to stop a boycott of Birmingham's segregated department stores. Soon published, the letter condemned the inaction of so-called "moderates" who stood by while southern states denied African Americans their constitutional rights.

Lindbergh, Charles A. (1902-1974): First pilot to fly solo across the Atlantic Ocean in 1927. He was a famous isolationist aviator who clashed with the Roosevelt Administration over foreign policy during the 1930s.

Lindsey, Hal (1929--): A Christian evangelical author who wrote the bestselling book of the 1970s, *The Late, Great Planet Earth*.

Little Rock Crisis: The battle over desegregation at Little Rock, Arkansas' Central High School in 1957. Arkansas Governor Orval Faubus dispatched the state National Guard to prevent black students from entering the school, forcing Dwight Eisenhower to nationalize the Guard and enforce a federal court's desegregation order. In response, Faubus shut down all of Little Rock's high schools in the 1958-1959 school year.

Loan, Nguyen Ngoc (1930-1998): The chief of South Vietnam's national police who was captured in an infamous news photo taken during the Tet Offensive executing a suspected communist fighter.

Lodge, Henry Cabot, Jr. (1902-1985): A Senator from Massachusetts and the Republican vice presidential nominee in 1960, Lodge served from 1963-1964 as ambassador to South Vietnam, where he was a supporter of the military coup against President Ngo Dinh Diem.

Long, Huey (1893-1935): Popular Louisiana governor and senator who in 1934 began sharply criticizing the New Deal from the political left.

Love Canal: A site in Niagara Falls, New York, where a neighborhood in 1978 had to be evacuated because of the long-term dumping of toxic chemicals.

Lusitania: A British luxury liner sunk in 1915 during World War I by a German submarine on the suspicion that U.S. arms manufacturers were smuggling weapons onboard such ships. De-classified U.S. government documents confirmed the German suspicion.

McCarthy, Eugene (1916-2005): A liberal and anti-Vietnam War Senator from Minnesota who challenged

President Johnson in the 1968 New Hampshire primary whose surprisingly strong showing forced LBJ to drop out of the race. He ran for president again in 1972 (as a Democrat) and in 1976 (as an independent.)

McCarthyism: Term used to describe the "witch hunts" for alleged communists in the United States in the early 1950s, led by Senator Joseph McCarthy of Wisconsin.

McGovern, George (1922--): A South Dakota Senator who led liberal opposition to the Vietnam War and captured the Democratic nomination for president before losing in a landslide to President Nixon in 1972.

McNamara, Robert Strange (1916-2009): The Ford Motor Company executive who served for seven years as President John Kennedy's and President Lyndon Johnson's Secretary of Defense and the chief architect of American military strategy in South Vietnam from 1965 to 1968.

McNary-Haugen bills: Legislation twice vetoed by Calvin Coolidge that would have created an agricultural export-dumping program in an effort to boost domestic farm prices.

McPherson, Aimee Simple (1890-1944): Theatrical fundamentalist preacher who opened the first megachurch in Los Angeles in 1923.

Mad Magazine: A satirical publication launched in 1952 that originally parodied comic books but expanded to humorously comment on politics and American culture.

Mahan, Alfred Thayer (1840-1914): American naval officer who wrote one of the most influential military history books in United States history, advocating for the United States to not only become a world power but the process by which such status was to be attained through sea power.

Malcolm X or Malcolm Little (1925-1965): A former street hustler converted by the eccentric Nation of Islam sect who as an NOI minister became a leading advocate of black self-assertion and black self-awareness before his assassination in New York on February 21, 1965.

Manchuria: A loosely-governed Chinese province taken over by Japan in 1931.

Manhattan Project: A secret joint American and British research program that developed the atomic bomb.

Mansfield, Mike (1903-2001): A Democratic Senator from Montana and an early critic of the Vietnam War.

Manson, Charles (1934--): The leader of a California cult who directed followers to murder Hollywood actress Sharon Tate and six others during a spree on August 8-9, 1969.

Mao Zedong (1893-1976): Leader of the Chinese Communist Party who fiercely battled the Japanese invaders of his country in the 1930s and 1940s before winning in 1949 the long civil war he waged against the U.S.-supported Chiang Kai-Shek dictatorship.

March on the Pentagon: An anti-war protest staged by 70,000 demonstrators opposed to the Vietnam War who marched from the Lincoln Memorial in Washington, D.C., to the Pentagon where they clashed with soldiers and police.

March on Washington: A civil rights rally held on the Mall in Washington, D.C., August 28, 1963 that galvanized congressional support for a proposed civil rights law passed the following year.

Marshall Plan: An initiative put forward by Secretary of State George C. Marshall to provide American loans and investment to the devastated economies of Europe in order not only to revitalize those economies but to prevent possible communist takeovers, especially of western Europe.

"Massive Resistance": The attempt by southern states to undermine implementation of the Supreme Court's *Brown* decision requiring desegregation of public schools through closing public schools, passing laws allowing white parents to receive vouchers for attending all-white private schools, harassment lawsuits against the NAACP, and so on.

Mattachine Society: The first American gay civil rights organization, formed in Los Angeles in 1951.

Mayaguez: A merchant ship seized by the Khmer Rogue government in Cambodia on May 12, 1975 and held for less than three days until a military rescue. Thirty-nine were rescued by Marines, but 41 died in the operation.

Means, Russell (1939--): A leader of the American Indian Movement who led protests for Native American rights at Mount Rushmore and the *Mayflower II* during the early 1970s.

Meat Inspection Act: A federal law passed in 1906 empowering the U.S. Department of Agriculture to establish regulations for the sanitary processing of meat products and to provide for regular inspections of meat processing facilities.

Medicine Lodge Treaty of 1867: A coerced agreement that relocated Arapaho, Cheyennes, Comanches, Apaches, and Kiowas onto reservations to be shared with already resident Bannocks, Navajos, Shoshones, and Sioux. Eventually more than 100,000 people scrabbled for existence on these lands, which became infamous for malnutrition, disease, alcoholism and depression.

Mellon, Andrew W. (1855-1937): Secretary of the Treasury under Harding, Coolidge, and Hoover who favored tax reduction for corporations and the wealthy to spur investment during the 1920s.

Memphis Sanitation Strike: A job walkout beginning February 11, 1968 by the Tennessee city's sanitation workers, who demanded higher wages, better benefits and recognition of their union. Dr. King was murdered in Memphis while attempting to help the strikers.

***Mercury* Program**: The American space program improvised by the Eisenhower administration after the Soviets successfully launched *Sputnik* satellites in orbit around the Earth. *Mercury* culminated in America's first manned outer-space orbits of Earth.

Milk, Harvey (1930-1978): The political leader of the San Francisco gay community who was assassinated shortly after becoming the first openly gay candidate to win a seat as supervisor on the San Francisco County Board of Supervisors.

Million Man March: Reflected the resurgence in the 1990s of black nationalism and separatism among many alienated black males. Events such as the Million Man March on Washington, led by the leader of the Black Muslims, Louis Farrakhan, made no demands on the government but rather represented a gathering to exhort black males to refrain from behaviors and lifestyles injurious to not only themselves but the black community in general.

Mississippi Freedom Democratic Party: Organized during Freedom Summer in 1964, the MFDP challenged the credentials of Mississippi's all-white delegation on the floor of the 1964 Democratic National Convention.

Mitchell, John N. (1913-1988): Attorney General under Richard Nixon who, as head of the Committee to Re-Elect the President in 1972, directed the illegal activities such as wiretapping that came to be known as the "Watergate Scandal" and was convicted of perjury, conspiracy and obstruction of justice in 1975.

Montagnards: A tribal people of South Vietnam who allied themselves with the United States during the Vietnam War.

Montgomery Bus Boycott: A 381-day civil rights campaign begun December 1, 1955 against Montgomery, Alabama's segregated public transportation that begun by Rosa Parks, an African American woman who refused to surrender her seat to a white man.

Moral Majority: A rightwing Christian organization formed in 1979 by television evangelist Jerry Falwell to encourage political activism among evangelicals. The group urged the banning of abortion, the reinstitution of prayer in public schools, opposed the teaching of evolution and fought against gay rights. .

Moratorium: A nationwide protest on October 15, 1969 against the Vietnam War involving up to 2 million people who read the names of war dead, tolled bells, and held funeral processions to symbolize their opposition to administration policy

"More bang for the buck": A euphemism for saving the tax payers money relative to the 1950s defense budget. The policy, advocated by Secretary of State John Foster Dulles during the Eisenhower administration, was meant to save Americans billion in tax dollars by curtailing the production of "obsolete" weapons, and in favor of a larger nuclear arsenal, and a technologically advanced Air Force and submarine fleet.

Morrison, Norman (1933-1965): A committed Quaker who burned himself to death in front of the Pentagon in protest against the Vietnam War on November 2, 1965.

Morse, Wayne (1900-1974): First elected Senator from Oregon as a Republican in 1944, he became a Democrat in the mid-1950s and would be one of the most vocal opponents of the Vietnam War.

Moses, Robert Parris (1935--): A leader of the 1960s Civil Rights Movement who became field secretary for the Student Non-Violent Coordinating Committee (SNCC).

Most Favored Nation Status—China: An attempt by the Clinton administration to improve relations with China by allowing Chinese products to enter the U.S. marketplace with minimal to no tariffs.

"Muckrakers": Theodore Roosevelt's label for the Progressive Era's investigative reporters.

Mugwumps: The faction within the Republican Party that advocated civil service reform and other measures to try to put party leadership in the hands of competent, dedicated, loyal Republicans, not party hacks and placemen.

Muller vs. Oregon (1908): A United States Supreme Court decision upholding the constitutionality of an Oregon state law limiting the working hours of women.

Munich Conference: A meeting between the leaders of Germany, Italy, Great Britain, and France which led to an agreement allowing Germany's annexation of Czechoslovakia's Sudetenland.

Munn v. Illinois (1877): A U.S. Supreme Court decision that allowed the states to regulate railroads operating lines and networks within their state boundaries.

Murrow, Edward R. (1908-1965): CBS news commentator and television pundit who was one of the first to challenge McCarthy publicly in the national media.

Muskie, Edmund (1914-1996): A Democratic Senator from Maine and Hubert Humphrey's running mate in 1968, whose campaign for president was heavily targeted for sabotage by the Committee to Re-Elect the President in 1972.

Mussolini, Benito (1883-1945): The fascist dictator of Italy from 1922 to 1943 who allied his nation with Adolf Hitler's Germany during World War II.

Napalm-B: A fire-starting chemical used by the United States military during the Vietnam War; it caused a high number of civilian deaths and injuries.

National American Woman Suffrage Association (NAWSA): Leading national organization that campaigned beginning in the 1890s for women's right to vote.

National Industrial Recovery Act (NIRA): Legislation passed in 1933 during the early New Deal designed to rejuvenate American industry through reforms, such as establishing a minimum wage, shorter work hours, and abolishing child labor.

National Organization of Woman (NOW): A feminist organization founded in 1966 by Berry Friedan and dedicated to ending job, wage, and educational discrimination against women.

National Origins Act: A law passed by Congress in 1924 that reduced the maximum level of legal foreign immigration to 150,000 while altering the nationality quotas to 2 percent of the number of each nationality residing in the United States in 1890

National Security Council document 68 (NSC-68): A position paper issued in 1950 by Paul Nitze, a member of President Harry Truman's National Security Council, which defined America's Cold War conflict with the Soviet Union as a life and death struggle between good and evil, freedom and slavery.

National Union Party: A third-party coalition formed by conservative Republicans, northern Democrats, and other Unionists to represent a compromise between the Radical Republicans and the Democrats while supporting Andrew Johnson's policies.

Navy Seals and the death of Osama bin Laden: Perhaps the Obama administration's most significant foreign policy accomplishment. In the late spring of 2011 Navy Seals found and killed bin Laden in his secret compound in Pakistan.

Nazi-Soviet Non-Aggression Pact: An agreement between Germany and the Soviet Union in 1939 in which the two powers pledged mutual neutrality and secretly authorized the partition of Poland.

Negro Leagues: African American professional players spent their careers in several black baseball associations known as Negro Leagues.

"neo-cons": Former liberal Democrats who moved to the right after 1968 over foreign policy issues. Although not nearly as stridently conservative on social issues as the New Right, the neo-cons remained hardcore anti-communists.

Neutrality Acts: Legislation passed by Congress between 1935 and 1937 that outlawed the selling of arms or the issuance of loans to nations at war and only allowed the trading of non-military items to nations at war on a "cash and carry" basis.

New Deal: The name given by President Franklin Roosevelt to his programs aimed to ameliorate the effects of the Great Depression.

New Departure: A movement by moderate and liberal southern whites in the late 1860s to find a middle ground between white backlash extremism and the Radical Republicans agenda of black equality. Advocates believed in treating freedmen fairly, decently, and enfranchising them. They nonetheless remained white supremacists.

"New Frontier": John F. Kennedy's term for his legislative program during his 1960-1963 presidency. Included were moderate support of African American civil rights, vigorous backing of the American space program, and continuation of Harry Truman and Dwight Eisenhower's policy of containing communism.

New Look: Name given to John Foster Dulles' approach toward containment; it called for the buildup of U.S.'s atomic weapons capability, first-strike delivery and the threat of massive retaliation against the Soviets if they made any aggressive moves in the world.

"New Okies": Term used to describe the tens of thousands of migrants who left the Northeast and Mid-East and Mid-West during the early 1980s because of the massive loss of jobs in heavy manufacturing, which defined the economies of many of those states in those regions.

New Right: Conservative movement that emerged during the 1970s that exploited for political gain voters' social issue concerns such as abortion, gay rights, and even continued civil rights.

Nhu, Ngo Dinh (1910-1963): The influential brother of Ngo Dinh Diem who headed South Vietnam's secret police and initiated the strategic hamlet program, Ngo Dinh Nhu died alongside his brother in the November 1963 military coup.

Nineteenth Amendment: Ratified in 1920, the amendment that forbade states from denying an individual from voting because of their gender.

Nixon Doctrine: The policy of relying on allies receiving military equipment and financial aid from the United States to bear the burden of resisting communist expansion in their region of the world.

Noriega, Manuel (1934--): Panamanian dictator who George H.W. Bush overthrew in 1989 for his involvement with the South American (primarily Colombian) drug cartels. He served time in prison in the United States and France following his capture by U.S. forces.

North American Free Trade Agreement (NAFTA): A pact ratified during the Clinton administration that went into effect in 1994 that established complete free trade between Mexico, the U.S., and Canada. NAFTA served part of President Bill Clinton's goal of expanding U.S. global markets, which he believed could only occur via free trade.

North Atlantic Treaty Organization (NATO): A collective security alliance created in 1949 between the United States, Canada and several mostly Western European nations that aimed to counter the military threat posed by the Soviet Union and its satellite states in Eastern Europe.

Northern Securities Company: A consolidated railroad system put together by investment banker J.P. Morgan during the 1890s in response to the economic panic of that decade. It reflected the increasing consolidation of the American economy by the wealthy in the late 19th century and was dissolved by order of the U.S. Supreme Court in 1904.

Northwestern, Southern and Colored Alliances: Farmers' groups formed in the 1880s that addressed the issue of price gouging by railroads and grain elevator operators. The alliances lobbied for laws regulating how much these businesses could charge. These groups also formed cooperatives, attempting to sell commodities at an agreed-upon price in hopes of earning a higher profit.

Obamacare: Derisive name given to the Affordable Health Care Act by conservatives and Republicans, who believe that the measure was designed to "socialize" medicine/health care in the United States. Opposition groups also condemn the act for allegedly costing too much and of forcing all Americans to have or buy health care coverage.

Occupy Wall Street: A massive protest movement against the nation's present plutocracy and their hegemony over the nation's economic system. The protesters believed these individuals were responsible for the nation's financial collapse and continued economic woes, such as unemployment.

Office of Price Administration (OPA): A government agency that oversaw price restrictions and rationing programs during World War II.

"Okies": Nickname given to those mid-Westerners fleeing the Dust Bowl in the 1930s. One of the hardest hit states was Oklahoma and thus a high percentage of those emigrants came from that state. Most "Okies" headed west, for California where many found a new lease on life in that state's vast undeveloped farmland in its inland valleys.

Oklahoma City bombing, 1995: Domestic terrorist attack killing 168 people at the Murrah Federal Building in Oklahoma City in 1995. The bombers, Timothy McVeigh and Terry Nichols, carried out the attack in response to the fiery standoff between federal law enforcement and members of the Branch Davidian sect in Waco, Texas, in 1993.

"Ole Miss": Nickname for the University of Mississippi at Oxford. A riot broke out on the campus on September 30, 1962 after the Kennedy administration enforced a court order that the school enroll James Meredith, an African-American student.

On The Road: A seminal 1957 novel of the Beat generation of the 1950s written by Jack Kerouac.

Open Door Policy: Term used by Secretary of State John Hay to describe U.S. relations with China, which, by 1900, had been cut up by the European imperial powers into spheres of influence. After occupying a specific region of China, the Europeans then closed off their sphere from all outside trade. The United States was the only major world power without a sphere in China and thus locked out of the lucrative China trade.

Operation Desert Storm (the First Gulf War): The 1991 U.S.-led military invasion of Kuwait, in response to Iraq's conquest of that nation the previous year.

Operation Overlord: Code name for the 1944 Allied invasion of Normandy during World War II.

Operation Rescue: A radical anti-abortion organization that initiated the "war in Wichita, Kansas" in 1991 in their attempts to shut down several abortion clinics or planned parenthood centers in that city.

Operation Rolling Thunder: An intensive bombing campaign against North Vietnam from March 1965 to November 1968 in which more than 7 million tons of explosives were dropped.

"Operation Wetback": A federal government crackdown on undocumented Mexican workers carried out in 1950.

"outsourcing": The sending of American jobs overseas to under-developed or developing countries with a much cheaper labor market. Hundreds of U.S. corporations are engaged in such activities, which began during the latter Clinton years and became especially popular during the George W. Bush administration, and devastated the U.S. job market, especially in the manufacturing sector.

Over There: One of the most popular, patriotic wartime songs ever written in U.S. history by Irish-American vaudevillian George M. Cohan, for which Cohan received a Congressional Medal of Honor from Woodrow Wilson for helping the war effort. The song became the war's unofficial anthem.

Parks, Rosa (1913-2005): An African-American activist in the NAACP who launched the Montgomery Bus Boycott.

Political Association of Spanish-Speaking Organizations (PASO): Created in 1961 in Victoria, Texas, formed to mobilize Latino voters and to support Latino candidates.

Paul, Alice (1885-1977): "Militant" woman suffragist leader and advocate for the Equal Rights Amendment (ERA), first proposed in 1923.

"Peace Without Conquest": A speech made by President Lyndon Johnson April 7, 1965 in which he pledged $1 billion in economic aid to North Vietnam if the Hanoi government would accept the independence of South Vietnam.

Pearl Harbor attack: Japanese sneak attack upon the U.S. Navy's Pacific base in Hawaii on December 7, 1941 that led to America's entry into World War II.

Pearson, Andrew Russell "Drew" (1897-1969): A syndicated American newspaper columnist and opponent of McCarthyism whose "Washington Merry-Go-Round" nevertheless often included questionable allegations against public figures. Many attribute the suicide of President Truman's Defense Secretary James Forrestal to Pearson's newspaper attacks. In 1968, Pearson wrote columns accusing Bobby Kennedy of concocting plots to kill Cuban dictator Fidel Castro.

Peers Report: The findings of an Army Committee formed to investigate the My Lai Massacre.

Pendleton Act: One of the most broad-sweeping reform measures of the federal government's civil service system, passed in 1883, which established the modern procedure for positions within the federal bureaucracy.

Pendleton Plan: A proposal by Ohio Democratic Senator George H. Pendleton to make greenbacks permanent as the nation's legal tender, thus ending decades of only specie—hard money, gold and silver coins—as the nation's legitimate currency in circulation.

Pentagon Papers: An official, secret Pentagon history of the Vietnam war, complete with vast collections of memos produced by government officials on the conflict put together by orders of Lyndon Johnson's Defense Secretary Robert McNamara and published by *The New York Times* and the *Washington Post* in 1971. Publication of these papers would lead President Nixon to order the formation of the White House Plumbers unit.

People's or Populist Party: A third political party formed in the 1890s that sprang from various farmers movements in the last three decades of the 19th century and elected members of Congress and state legislatures in the elections of 1892, 1894, and 1896.

Perot, Ross (1930--): The founder of EDS, a Texas high-tech firm, who led one of the more popular third party movements in American history. Perot ran as an independent in the 1992 presidential race.

Pinchot, Gifford (1865-1946): Head of the U.S. Forest Service from 1905 to 1910 and main conservation advisor to President Theodore Roosevelt.

Playboy: A "men's" magazine featuring nude photos of women, along with interviews with famous people, movie reviews and other cultural commentary that began publication in 1953.

Platt Amendment: Approved by the Congress in 1903, this measure recognized the right of the United States to annex Cuba as a "protectorate."

Plutocrat: A term used to describe the newly rich and powerful industrial magnates who emerged during the Gilded Age in the late 19th century.

Poitier, Sidney (1927--): The Bahamian-born performer and first black movie star to win an Academy Award for best actor, who performed in a number of civil rights-friendly films in the 1950s and 1960s such as *Lilies in the Field* and *Guess Who's Coming to Dinner?*

"Police Action": Term used to describe U.S. response to aggression that did not involve a full declaration of war; a "limited war" for a specific reason and for a specific period of time. The Truman administration first used the term to describe the Korean War, fought from 1950-1953.

Poor Peoples' Campaign: Martin Luther King, Jr.'s last protest effort, in 1968, aimed at forcing the federal government to focus on black, white and brown poverty. After King's death, organization of the drive fell to Dr. Ralph Abernathy, a close King associate.

Port Huron Statement: Presented and debated at the Students for a Democratic Society national convention in Port Huron, Michigan, from June 11-15, 1962, the Statement (drafted by Tom Hayden) called for cuts in military spending, increased investment in social welfare programs, and support of civil rights reforms and condemned American materialism and excessive competitiveness.

Powers, Francis Gary (1929-1977): The pilot of an American U2 spy plane shot down over the Soviet Union in May 1959. His capture led to one of the dangerous superpower confrontations of the Cold War.

"Predatory lending": Mortgage companies that sold adjustable-rate high interest loans to unsuspecting homebuyers, many of whom did not qualify with sufficient income to own a home or once in possession could not keep up with the escalating mortgage interest and payments. Such a practice led to unprecedented foreclosures beginning a year before the Wall Street collapse.

Presidential Reconstruction: The period from 1863 to 1866 which saw the Executive Branch rather than Congress responsible for Reconstruction of the South at the end of the Civil War. President Abraham Lincoln believed that Reconstruction was a presidential responsibility because the secession of southern states was illegal and that it was the president's job to put down rebellions.

President's Committee on Civil Rights: A committee formed by President Harry Truman in 1946 that issued a report the following year, "To Secure These Rights." The report concluded that segregation laws and racial discrimination in the United States hurt its standing with newly independent nations in Africa and Asia and recommended enactment of a federal anti-lynching statute; a ban on the poll tax; prohibiting by federal statute discrimination in private employment; establishing a permanent Commission on Civil Rights; increasing the size of the Justice Department's civil rights division; and strictly enforcing voting rights laws.

Presley, Elvis (1935-1977): One of the bestselling recording artist of all times, Presley introduced to white audiences in the 1950s numerous songs originally performed by black artists and ushered in the era in which the youth market came to dominate the music industry.

Professional Air Traffic Controller's Organization (PATCO): A powerful union that went on strike in 1981 demanding more pay and less hours for its members. President Ronald Reagan eventually ordered the firing of over 11,000 workers. His action signaled the start of a long decline in American union influence and activism.

Profiles in Courage: A 1957 bestseller by Senator John F. Kennedy, thought to have been ghostwritten by Ted Sorenson, that told the stories of eight United States senators who defied the wishes of their political party to make a principled political stand.

Progressive Party: A third-party movement led by former Vice President and Secretary of the Interior Henry Wallace in the 1948 presidential campaign. The party opposed the Truman Doctrine—using American military and economic might to halt Soviet expansionism—as militaristic and needlessly provocative toward the Soviet Union.

Progressivism: Term given to the diverse reform efforts of the late 19th century and early 20th century responding to the social, political, and cultural changes caused by the Industrial Revolution.

Project 100,000: A defense department program that allowed 300,000 enlistees to join the military during the Vietnam War although they could not meet entry test requirements.

Proposition 187: An anti-illegal immigrant referendum approved in 1994 by California voters that denied undocumented workers and their children access to vital social services such as prenatal and childbirth care, child welfare, public education, and non-emergency health care. Courts ruled the law unconstitutional, preventing Proposition 187 from ever being implemented.

Protectorate: Term used in the late 19th and early 20th century by American imperialists as code word for conquered lands not intended to become states.

Public Credit Act: Law passed in 1869 that allowed for the redemption of all government bonds in gold, while pledging to bring greenbacks (paper currency) on par with gold as well.

Public Works Administration (PWA): Established under the auspices of the National Industrial Recovery Act, passed in 1933 during the Roosevelt administration. The program hired tens of thousands of unemployed and underemployed Americans to build the Hoover and Grand Coulee dams, thousands of new schools and public libraries, and the 100 mile causeway linking Florida to Key West.

***Pueblo* Crisis**: An incident that began when North Korean ships attacked and boarded the *U.S.S. Pueblo* on January 23, 1968, killing one sailor and taking 82 prisoners. The North Koreans claimed the ship had entered their territorial waters. After negotiations, the United States government apologized, and the crew was released on December 23, 1968.

Pure Food and Drug Act: Federal law passed in 1906 creating the Food and Drug Administration to test and approve drugs before being allowed for sale on the market.

Race-baiting: Politicians use of race as a campaign issue, exploiting white racism and fear of black equality.

"Race Suicide": A fear promoted by white supremacist racial theorists in the late 19th and early 20th centuries that supposedly inferior African Americans, and immigrants from Eastern and Southern Europe and Mexico, were reproducing faster than supposedly superior Anglo-Saxons.

Radical Republicans: Republicans opposed to President Abraham Lincoln and Andrew Johnson's Reconstruction policies from 1863-1868. The Radicals believed the South should be punished for their "treason" and that the freedmen should become full-fledged United States citizens and their new status protected by the federal government.

Randolph, A. Phillip (1889-1979): Leader of the Brotherhood of Sleeping Car Porters, the largest African American labor union in the country, whose mobilization of blacks for a potential mass march on Washington led President Franklin Roosevelt in 1941 to issue Executive Order 8802, which forbade discrimination by defense industry employers or government agencies based on race, color, creed, or national origin.

Ray, James Earl (1928-1998): An armed robber who assassinated civil rights leader Martin Luther King, Jr., on April 4, 1968.

"Reaganomics": President Ronald Reagan's policies based on the theory of supply-side economics.

"Reagan's Revenge": Term used by liberal Democrats for Reagan's attempts to destroy the last remnants of the liberal welfare state by massive military spending and tax cuts which drove up the deficit. The deficit then would be used as an excuse to eliminate or slash programs like food stamps.

Rebel Without A Cause: A 1955 movie starring James Dean as a troubled juvenile trying to find his identity in spite of his domineering mother and his emasculated father.

Reconstruction Acts of 1867: Represented the end of Presidential Reconstruction and the beginning of Congressional or Radical Reconstruction. These laws restarted the political process in the South, with the 10 unreconstructed southern states divided into five military districts administered by Army generals.

Red-baiting: The labeling of individuals or ideas as being "communist," a political tactic common during the Red Scare in 1919 and in the McCarthy era in the 1950s.

Red Scare: The first outbreak of hysteria over communist subversion in 1919 in the aftermath of World War I.

Reservationists: Those congressional Republicans and Democrats who, in 1919, opposed the Treaty of Versailles ending World War I, especially Article 10 of the League of Nations charter, which called for collective security among League members to deal with aggressor nations.

Revisionists: Those historians of the post-World War II era who believe the United States was more responsible or culpable for initiating the Cold War rather than the Soviet Union. They see the Truman administration from 1945-1953 as short-sighted, historically oblivious to Russian history, and, in short, the aggressor in the sense of trying to create a post-war world order in which the United States dominated.

Richardson, Elliott (1920-1999): The Attorney General under President Nixon who resigned in 1973 rather than fire Watergate Special Prosecutor Archibald Cox in part of what came to be known as the "Saturday Night Massacre."

"Roaring Twenties": Stereotypical depiction of the 1920s as a carefree period characterized by people dressing and behaving in nontraditional ways.

Robinson, Jackie (1919-1972): a baseball player who in 1947 became the first African American to play in the major leagues since the late 1880s. Robinson played first and second baseman for the Brooklyn Dodgers until 1956.

Rockefeller, Nelson (1908-1979): A liberal Republican who served as governor of New York from 1959 to 1973, was the chief opponent to archconservative Barry Goldwater in the 1964 Republican presidential contest and ran against Richard Nixon in 1968.

Roe v. Wade **(1973)**: The controversial United States Supreme Court decision that legalized abortion in the first two trimesters of pregnancy.

"Roll back the Iron Curtain": A pledge made by John Foster Dulles, U.S. Secretary of State from 1953-59, to liberate communist nations in Eastern Europe from Soviet domination. Dulles announced that if the U.S. were ever given the opportunity, they would "roll back the Iron Curtain."

Romney, Mitt: Republican presidential nominee in 2012, who after a grueling Republican primary, lost in the general election to incumbent President Barack Obama by a substantial margin in the Electoral College.

Roosevelt Corollary: President Theodore Roosevelt's addendum to the Monroe Doctrine, in which he announced that the U.S. had the right to intervene in the internal affairs of any nation in the Western Hemisphere if the U.S. deemed it essential for "hemispheric security and stability."

Roosevelt, Theodore (1858-1919): Progressive Republican who served as governor of New York before becoming the 26th President of the United States (1901-1909). He later became the candidate of the Progressive ("Bull Moose") Party in the 1912 presidential election.

Roots: An award-winning eight-part mini-series broadcast by the ABC television network between January 23-30, 1977, that chronicled the history of author Alex Haley's family from the enslavement in Africa of Kunte Kinte to his ancestor's freedom in the Reconstruction-era South.

Root-Takahira Agreement (1908): Accord between the United States and Japan that recognized Japanese control of southern Manchuria, a Chinese province.

"Rough Riders": Nickname given to Theodore Roosevelt's all-volunteer military outfit of individuals ranging from cowboys, Ivy League graduates, Hispanics, and an assortment of European immigrants, who went to Cuba during the 1898 Spanish-American War.

Rudd, Mark (1947--): A leader of the Students for a Democratic Society who helped organize the student occupation of Columbia University in the spring semester of 1968. Later, he participated in the violent Weather Underground movement.

Rural Electrification Administration (REA): A New Deal program during Franklin Roosevelt's administration that, in the 1930s, brought federally funded electrical power and other utilities to rural areas where such services had been unavailable.

Russo-Japanese War: An important conflict in East Asia between two rival Asian powers, Japan and Russia between 1904-05. The war shocked Europeans and white Americans as supposedly inferior Asians handily defeated an important European empire.

Sacco, Ferdinando Nicola (1891-1927) and Bartolomeo Vanzetti (1888-1927): Italian immigrant anarchists convicted of murder in 1921 following an armed robbery in South Braintree, Massachusetts and executed after a controversial trial and six-year round of highly-publicized appeals.

Safer, Morley (1931--): A Canadian-born American television journalist who brought the brutality of the Vietnam War to viewers with his coverage for CBS of the destruction of the Village of Cam Ne in 1965.

Sand Creek Massacre: A November 29, 1864 attack on Cheyenne women, children and elderly men carried out by a white militia, the "Colorado Volunteers," that left 200 dead.

***Sandinistas*:** Marxist/leftist insurgents who had overthrown the vicious and corrupt Anastasio Somoza dictatorship in Nicaragua in 1979 and implemented land reform and forged a close relationship with the communist governments in the Soviet Union and Cuba.

Sanger, Margaret (1879-1966): Birth control advocate who organized the American Birth Control League in 1921 and which, by 1942, became Planned Parenthood. She also supported eugenics and, with Dr. Clarence J. Gamble, promoted the "Negro Project" aimed at reducing African-American reproduction in the South.

Santo Domingo Affair: The attempt by the Grant administration in 1869 to annex the present-day country of the Dominican Republic. This ended in political disaster for President Ulysses Grant who failed to consult with key Republican senators before drawing up a treaty with the Dominican leadership, and who didn't lobby for ratification of the agreement.

"satellite": A term used to describe the Eastern bloc nations controlled by communist, pro-Soviet governments.

Saturday Night Massacre: An incident on October 20, 1973 when Richard Nixon ordered his Attorney General Elliott Richardson to fire Watergate Special Prosecutor Archibald Cox, only to see Richardson resign and then his successor William D. Ruckelhaus also resign rather than comply. Nixon's orders were finally carried out by Solicitor General Robert Bork, a future unsuccessful Supreme Court nominee

"scalawags": A pejorative term given during the Reconstruction Era in the 1860s and 1870s to southern whites who had supported the Union during the Civil War and the Republican Party during Reconstruction.

***Schenck v. United States* (1919):** A United States Supreme Court decision upholding the constitutionality of both Espionage Act and Sedition Act on the grounds that during times of war the need for state security supersedes the free speech rights of individual citizens.

Schlieffen Plan: A German military plan first formulated after the Franco-Prussian War in 1870-1871 that called, in the event of another war with the French, for the army to invade Belgium as a means of more quickly reaching Paris. This plan leaked out during World War I (1914-1918) and played a role in Great Britain entering the war on the side of the French.

Schlafly, Phyllis (1924--): A political conservative, opponent of abortion and gay rights, and leader, during the 1970s, of the successful opposition to the Equal Rights Amendment.

Scopes "Monkey Trial": A trial in Dayton, Tennessee in 1925 of teacher John Scopes for teaching evolution in violation of state law.

"Search and Destroy": A tactic used by the Americans in the Vietnam War of transporting, usually by helicopter, ground troops to enemy positions, obliterating the enemy forces, and then returning to the American lines.

"Second Front": The long-awaited western front against Nazi Germany established in France after the invasion of Normandy in 1944. Since 1942, Soviet leader Joseph Stalin had pressured England and the United States to open a second front to relieve the pressure created by German army units that had invaded Russia in 1941.

Sedition Act of 1917: Measure passed by Congress that made illegal criticism of American wartime policy as well as public dissent from war-related domestic policies.

Selective Service Act: The draft instituted by the Wilson administration in 1917 to ensure the nation's armed services had adequate manpower for World War I. All men between the ages of 18 and 30 had to register with the federal government for possible conscription.

Settlement houses: Houses established in urban slums where college-educated social workers lived and provided the poor with vital social services.

Sherman Antitrust Act 1890: A federal law that forbid businesses to conspire to restrain trade or to create monopolies and empowered the federal government to investigate such trusts. The law was mostly used to stop unions from staging strikes. The statute was not extensively used to break up business monopolies until the presidency of Theodore Roosevelt from 1901-1909.

1204 / GLOSSARY

"Sick industries": industries such as coal mining, textile manufacturing, and railroads plagued by excessive productive capacity with declining demand and labor conflict during the 1920s.

Sirhan, Bashir Sirhan (1944--): A Palestinian immigrant who fatally shot Robert Kennedy on June 4, 1968 after being angered by Kennedy's support for Israel.

"Sit-Ins": A type of direct-action protest launched by students at North Carolina A&T College in Greensboro, N.C., on February 1, 1960 against a segregated Woolworth's lunch counter. Black students refused to move from whites-only seats at lunch counters, buses, theaters and other businesses.

Sitting Bull (1834-1890): A Hunkpapa Sioux chief credited with prophetic visions in which he saw white soldiers falling into Native American hands. Sitting Bull was one of three Native American leaders who defeated General George Armstrong Custer's forces at the Little Big Horn River in present-day Montana on June 25, 1876.

Sixteenth Street Baptist Church Bombing: A September 15, 1963 terrorist bombing set off by a member of the Ku Klux Klan, Robert Chambliss, during Sunday school classes. The explosion killed four African-American children: Cynthia Wesler, Carole Robertson, Addie Mae Collins, and Denise McNair.

Smith, Tommie (1944--): An American sprinter who won a gold medal in the 200-meter dash during the 1968 Olympics in Mexico City. Along with bronze metalist John Carlos, he made a "black power" salute during the medal ceremony in protest of discrimination against African Americans.

Social Darwinism: The application in the late 19th and early 20th century by social scientists such as Herbert Spencer in England and William Graham Sumner in the U.S. of Charles Darwin's theory of natural selection in nature to human society. As there were higher and lower orders of species in the animal kingdom, so there were superior and inferior individuals and races among people.

Social Security Act (1935): A social insurance program funded by payroll taxes and employer matching funds to provide retirement funds for Americans age 65 and older and financial assistance to those with disabilities, as well as survivor's benefits for dependent spouses and children.

South Central Los Angeles Race Riots, 1992: Caused by the acquittal of the LA police officers who brutally beat, while being video-taped, African American motorist Rodney King for allegedly resisting arrest. When the news of their acquittal by an all-white jury in a suburb of LA reached the public, the ghetto of south-central LA exploded into one of the worst race riots in U.S. history, in which 40 people died.

Southern Christian Leadership Conference (SCLC): The civil rights organization that formed during the Montgomery Bus Boycott in 1955. Martin Luther King, Jr. led the group from its formal creation in 1957 until his murder in 1968.

Southern Manifesto: A document declaring opposition and pledging resistance to the 1954 *Brown v. Board of Education* Supreme Court decision ordering school desegregation. The manifesto was signed by 101 southern members of the U.S. House of Representatives. Future President Lyndon Johnson, the Senate majority leader who was distrusted by his Dixie colleagues as a racial liberal, joined Tennessee Senators Estes Kefauver and Albert Gore, Sr., as the lone southern holdouts in the Senate who did not lend their names to the manifesto.

Southern Strategy: A political plan in which white southern voters would support the Democrats by tapping into their resentment over crime, civil rights laws, school busing and affirmative action.

Spanish Civil War: A civil war in Spain from 1936-1939 resulting in the overthrow of the elected republican government by fascist forces under Francisco Franco with aid from Germany and Italy. Franco established a dictatorship that lasted until his death in 1975.

"Speak softly but carry a big stick": The foreign policy of President Teddy Roosevelt, who served from 1901-1909. Roosevelt believed that the United States should always promote peace in the world but if all such efforts failed, the U.S. should unleash its awesome military power on those it deemed its enemies or the violators of peace.

Sphere of Influence: Diplomatic or foreign policy term used by both U.S. and European imperialists to designate specific regions of the world or regions within a country where a foreign country can exercise political and/or economic dominance. For the United States after 1898, the entire Western Hemisphere became its "sphere of influence," in which no other countries were to have a presence or to politically interfere without first seeking U.S. "permission."

Spock, Benjamin (1903-1998): A physician who wrote the 1946 bestseller *Baby and Child Care* and became a leading voice against the Vietnam War. The Justice Department in 1968-1969 unsuccessfully prosecuted Spock for supposedly aiding and abetting draft dodgers.

Sputnik: A first in a series of Soviet space satellites launched in 1957 that panicked the American political leadership and inspired the start of the U.S.'s *Gemini* manned space program.

Stagflation: An economy marked by both high inflation and high unemployment, first experienced in the 1970s.

Stalwarts: One of three Republican Party factions that emerged by the 1880s who sought dominance within the party. Led by Roscoe Conkling of New York, Stalwarts were strong advocates of the patronage system.

Star Trek: A science fiction series that ran on NBC from 1966 to 1969 and featured a multi-racial cast and address contemporary social issues.

Star Wars: The first in a series of six science fiction films released in 1977 that would eventually earn $1.7 billion and, as of 2011, receive the fourth highest box office in American movie history.

"**Statement on Race**": A document issued in 1950 by the United Nations Educational, Scientific and Cultural Organization that announced that "[s]cientists have reached general agreement that mankind is one; that all men belong to the same species, *Homo sapiens*."

"**status quo**" **in Europe**: After the Berlin crisis in 1948-1949, in which the Soviet Union blockaded West Berlin had passed, the U.S. and the Soviet Union reached a tacit acceptance that Western Europe would be an American sphere of influence and that Eastern Europe would be a Soviet sphere.

Stokely, Carmichael (1941-1998): The civil rights activist who formulated the idea of "Black Power," the idea that the movement should be led by African Americans and that African Americans should embrace their own cultural traditions.

Stonewall Riot: An uprising of young gay men angered by continued homophobic police harassment that began on the night of June 27, 1969 after a police raid on a nightspot, The Stonewall Inn. The event is credited with launching the gay civil rights movement.

Strategic Arms Limitations Treaty (SALT) I: An agreement reached in May 1972 between President Nixon and Leonid Brezhnev that limited the number of intercontinental ballistic missiles the U.S. and the U.S.S.R. could hold

Strategic bombing campaign: A high-altitude bombing campaign against Axis targets in Europe during WW II.

Strategic Defense Initiative (SDI) or "Star Wars": A theoretical weapons system advocated by President Ronald Reagan in which space satellites would use lasers to disable Soviet nuclear missiles.

Strategic hamlets: Villages created by the South Vietnamese government and the American military meant to isolate farmers, forced to move there, from contact with the Vietcong.

Student Non-Violent Coordinating Committee (SNCC): A major civil rights organization of the 1960s that had a younger membership and relied more on direct-action tactics than the Southern Christian Leadership Council. Beginning in the mid-1960s, SNCC's leadership came to admire Malcolm X and pursued a more Black Nationalist direction, expelling its white membership and emphasizing African American political and cultural autonomy.

Students for a Democratic Society (SDS): A student activist group that became a leading force in the anti-war movement during the Vietnam era.

Subtreasury: An idea advanced by the Populist Party. A network of subtreasuries across rural America that would act as government warehouses and creditors.

Summit: Cole War term used to describe a meeting between U.S. president and leader of the Soviet Union to discuss issues resolve tensions.

"**Sun Belters**": Largely white, middle-class Americans who had moved after WWII to the Western states such as California, Arizona, and Texas from the Northeast and Midwest. Another wave of such humanity also inundated these same states and others during the 1970s and 1980s.

Sunday, Billy (1862-1935): A former major-league baseball player who emerged as the most popular fundamentalist preacher of the 1910s and 1920s.

"**Surge**": The 2007 response of President George W. Bush to a continued insurgency in American-occupied Iraq. The White House sent in 30,000 more troops to defeat guerilla forces and to prop up the American-supported regime in Baghdad. Obama decided in early December 2009 to send an additional 30,000 troops to Afghanistan.

Sussex Pledge: Given in 1916 by Germany after its submarines had sunk several civilian merchant ships, causing American casualties and property loss. The Germans declared that their submarines would no longer attack any civilian ships without first securing passenger safety.

Sweatt v. Painter (1950): A United States Supreme Court decision that ruled that the University of Texas's segregated law school violated the Constitution.

Taft, William Howard (1857-1930): The 27th President of the United States (1909-1913) and later the 10th Chief Justice of the United States. Taft was Teddy Roosevelt's chosen successor, but proved a highly conservative chief executive who disappointed his mentor, prompting Roosevelt to run against him in 1912.

Taft-Katsura Agreement (1905): Secret arrangement between the United States and Japan in which both nations agreed to respect each other's spheres of influence in Asia: Philippines for the U.S. and Japanese suzerainty over the Korean peninsula.

Taliban: Afghani Muslim extremists who once controlled most of Afghanistan from 1996 to 2001, imposing one of the most oppressive Islamist regimes anywhere in the world. The Taliban harbored Osama bin Laden, the mastermind of the September 11, 2001 terrorist attacks against the United States, prompting George Bush's decision to invade Afghanistan in December of that year.

Tammany Hall: The name given to a powerful, corrupt New York City political machine. William Marcy Tweed ruled over Tammany Hall, controlling the city's Democratic Party and the municipal government from behind the scenes from 1863 to 1871.

Tampico Affair: The U.S. military occupation of the Mexican port of Tampico came when the United States government became alarmed as one of the armed factions battling in Mexico's post-Revolution civil war in 1914 neared the port city, home to American oil interests. The occupation of Veracruz followed, worsening American-Mexican relations and, ironically, strengthening the hand of Mexican dictator Victoriano Huerta, whose regime the U.S. government opposed.

Taylor, Maxwell (1901-1987): The chairman for the Joint Chiefs of Staff under President Kennedy, and an ambassador to South Vietnam from 1964 to 1965, Taylor recommended at the start of the administration that Kennedy send 8,000 support troops to South Vietnam.

Tea Party Movement: A grass-roots conservative/libertarian backlash movement that emerged in 2009 protesting the government bailouts and alleged general "big-government" policies of both Republican and Democratic administrations and congressional policies as well.

Teapot Dome Scandal: The controversy surrounding the leasing of government-owned petroleum fields to two oil companies found to be authorized by Interior Secretary Albert Fall after receiving gifts valued over $300,000.

"Teflon president": Term used to describe Ronald Reagan, to whom, no matter the setbacks, nothing "stuck;" that is, his popularity with the American people continued despite obvious policy failures and personal shortcomings.

Teller Amendment: Passed by Congress before outbreak of Spanish-American War in 1898, which renounced all U.S. claims on Cuba and any possibility of U.S. acquisition of Cuba as an American colony.

Tennessee Valley Authority (TVA): Begun in 1933, the most massive undertaking by the federal government at rural reclamation; the building of dams, hydroelectric plants, and reservoirs, all of which ended the problem of flooding and the ruining of land and businesses in a four-state area.

Tenure of Office Act of 1867: Bill passed by Radical Republican-controlled Congress designed to further strip President Andrew Johnson of his power by making it illegal for him to remove any cabinet member without Senate approval.

Tet Offensive: A massive communist assault along the length of South Vietnam, particularly targeting cities, that began on January 30, 1968 until March 28.

Texas Rangers: A law-enforcement agency established in the days of the Texas Republic and frequently implicated in violence against Native Americans and Mexican Americans.

Thich Quang Duc (1897-1963): A monk who set himself on fire June 11, 1963 in protest of President Diem's crackdown on Buddhist opponents to the regime. Five more Buddhists would commit suicide through self-immolation before the fall of the Diem dictatorship.

Thieu, Nguyen Van (1923-2001): Dictatorial president of South Vietnam from 1965-1975, Thieu's government became infamous for corruption and military ineffectiveness in the war against the National Liberation Front and the North Vietnamese.

"think tanks": Term used to describe organizations funded by private enterprise to promote and influence the debate on both foreign and domestic issues and influence policy-making.

Thirteenth Amendment: The amendment, ratified in 1865, that abolished slavery and involuntary servitude in the United States.

Three Mile Island: A nuclear power plant near Harrisburg, Pennsylvania that overheated and nearly melted down on March 28, 1979.

Till, Emmett (1941-1955): A 14-year-old Chicago youth beaten to death by two white men in Money, Mississippi August 28, 1955 after supposedly flirting with a white woman. His murder helped galvanize the 1950s civil rights movement

Townsend, Francis (1867–1960): Popular California physician who made concern for the elderly a personal crusade during the Great Depression in the 1930s. In a pamphlet published in 1934 he advocated the payment of $200 monthly to every retired American over the age of 60 provided they spend all of the money within 30 days, which would then open up jobs for younger Americans.

Treaty of Portsmouth (1905): President Theodore Roosevelt's initiative to bring the Russo-Japanese War to a quick conclusion before the Asian balance of power could be undone.

Treaty of Versailles: The treaty ending World War I and creating the League of Nations.

Truman Doctrine: President Harry Truman's 1947 declaration that American isolationism from world affairs was over and that henceforth the U.S. would play an active, decisive role in preserving world peace.

Truman, Harry (1884-1972): Franklin Roosevelt's successor as president in April 1945 who ordered the dropping of the atomic bombs on Hiroshima and Nagasaki in Japan in August of that year and would lead the United States into war in Korea in 1950.

Trust: In the late 19th and early 20th century, a form of horizontal integration where trustees of one company hold stock in various competing firms doing the same business, making for monopolies that eliminated competition.

Turner's "frontier thesis": Historical theory put forth by historian Frederick Jackson Turner that what had molded the unique American character was that the United States had been an ever-open and expanding frontier for most of its history.

Tuskegee Airmen: African American combat pilots who distinguished themselves in Europe during WW II.

Twilight Zone, The: A popular horror and science fiction anthology series that ran on the CBS television network from 1959 to 1964 that dealt with contemporary issues like racism, McCarthyism, and the Holocaust in highly symbolic fashion.

U-Boat: Abbreviated term given to a German submarine, called by the Germans an *unterseeboot*.

Underwood-Simmons Act: The 1913 that reduced tariffs and levied the first federal income tax.

Vertical Integration: A business plan whereby a corporation gained control of every facet of production in an industry.

Vietnam Veterans Against the War: An anti-war group in the 1960s consisting of Vietnam Veterans who held mock war crimes trials and threw away their medals during protests at the Capitol to publicize the human rights abuses and the tragedies ongoing in Southeast Asia through the U.S. military withdrawal in 1973. Future Massachusetts Senator John Kerry, the 2004 Democratic nominee for president, served as spokesman for the group.

Vietnamization: President Richard Nixon's policy of beginning in 1969 of replacing American combat troops with South Vietnamese troops in the war against North Vietnam and heavily supplying the South Vietnamese military.

"voodoo economics": Term used in the 1980s and 1990s to derisively describe President Ronald Reagan's proposal that he could balance the federal budget while cutting taxes and dramatically increasing military spending.

Voting Rights Act of 1965: The act passed by Congress that overturned a variety of practices which denied the right to voter registration by minorities.

***Wabash* Case (1886)**: The United States Supreme Court decision forbidding state regulation of railroads, declaring railroads to be interstate transporters of goods and thus not subject to individual state regulation.

1208 / GLOSSARY

Wade-Davis Bill: The Radical Republicans' counter-proposal to President Abraham Lincoln's "10 percent plan," calling for all southern whites to take an "iron-clad" oath that they had never taken up arms against the United States government before they would be eligible to vote or hold office. The Radicals also proposed requiring 50 percent of a state's white population to swear their allegiance to the United States before that state would be eligible for re-admission.

Wagner Act: In 1935, the United States Supreme Court declared unconstitutional the National Industrial Recovery Act unconstitutional.

Wallace, George C. (1919-1998): An arch-segregationist four-term governor of Alabama who reached national stature when he stood in front of Foster Auditorium at the University of Alabama, to prevent the registration of two African-American students, before stepping aside for accompanying federal marshals.

War on Terror: The term used by President George W. Bush (2001-09) to describe the struggle of the United States against terrorist networks like Al Qaeda, which launched the strikes against the World Trade Center and the Pentagon on September 11, 2001.

War Powers Act: Legislation passed in November 1973 that required the president to notify the Congress within 48 hours of any military deployment where combat is taking place or will likely take place.

Warren Court: The United States Supreme Court under Chief Justice Earl Warren who was appointed by President Dwight Eisenhower. The Warren Court was known for several landmark liberal rulings in the 1950s and 1960s that banned school segregation, expanded the rights of criminal defendants, narrowed the definition of pornography, and overturned laws banning contraceptives and restricting school-directed prayers at public school campuses.

"Wars of National Liberation": Communist military insurgencies which Soviet leader Nikita Khrushchev in 1961 pledged his Moscow regime would support worldwide.

Washington Naval Conference: The world's first international disarmament conference, held from 1921-22, which resulted in limits placed on naval construction and tentative economic agreements among nations trading in China.

WASP: White Anglo-Saxon Protestants. The term was used to describe "old stock" Americans, whose pedigree went back generations from the British Isles and who were intensely nativistic.

Watergate: The scandal enveloping the Nixon White House from 1972-1974 which included charges of domestic spying, tampering with witnesses, abuse of the IRS by the White House to punish political enemies, illegal wiretapping, bribery and burglary.

Watts Riot: A civil disturbance that started in the predominantly African-American neighborhood of Watts in Los Angeles on August 11, 1965 and did not quiet until August 15, by which time 34 people had died and $40 million in property damage had occurred.

"Waving the bloody shirt": The tactic of exploiting emotional memories of the Civil War to win political points came to be known as "waving the bloody shirt."

Weather Underground: A radical group of the late 1960s and early 1970s opposed to the Vietnam War that carried out several violent attacks, including the setting off of a pipe bomb at San Francisco police headquarters in February 1970 and bombings at the Pentagon, the U.S. Capitol and International Telephone and Telegraph's headquarters in New York City between 1971-1973.

Wertham, Fred (1895-1981): A German-born American psychiatrist whose bestselling 1954 book *The Seduction of the Innocent: The Influence of Comic Books on Today's Youth*, argued that comic books promoted anti-social behavior in children, provoked a congressional hearing and led the comic book industry to impose self-censorship.

Whip Inflation Now!: The official name of President Gerald Ford's voluntary anti-inflation program, which encouraged conservation and was promoted with "WIN" buttons and other paraphernalia.

"Whiskey Ring": A network of distillers and revenue agents, exposed in 1875, who refused to pay or collect the federal taxes, instead pocketing the money. Scores of agents amassed personal fortunes by accepting payoffs and bribes.

White Army: The anti-Bolshevik Russians who tried to overthrow, with Allied help, the communist government Vladimir Lenin had established by 1918.

White backlash: The refusal of southern whites during the Reconstruction Era from 1863-1877 to accept the defeat of the Confederacy, the end of slavery, black equality, and federal occupation.

White Citizens Councils: Groups formed across the South beginning in the 1950s made up of lawyers, businessmen and other elites called the "uptown Klan" who organized resistance to desegregation orders.

White House Plumbers: A secret unit created by the Nixon White House given the job of finding out who was leaking secret information such as the *Pentagon Papers* to the press and carried out the Watergate burglary on June 17, 1972.

"Wise Old Men": A group of Johnson advisors who, in the spring of 1968, tried to convince Johnson to end America's involvement in the Vietnam War.

Witcover, Jules (1927--): An American journalist and author who wrote a political column and a book about the 1968 Bobby Kennedy presidential campaign, *85 Days: The Last Campaign of Bobby Kennedy*.

Women Airforce Service Pilots (WASPs): Female civilian pilots during World War II who aided the U.S. military by undertaking a variety of support roles.

Works Progress Administration (WPA): An offshoot of other work project programs during the New Deal in the 1930s, only this particular initiative focused on the visual and performing arts with the purpose of keeping the American creative and aesthetic tradition alive.

Wilson, Woodrow (1856-1924): Democratic governor of New Jersey who became the 28th President of the United States (1913-1921). His administration oversaw the creation of the Federal Reserve Board and the Federal Trade Commission and the American victory in World War I.

Woodstock Music and Art Fair: A rock 'n' roll music festival in upstate New York from August 15-18, 1969 that featured performers, including The Who, Santana, Janis Joplin, Crosby, Stills and Nash, and Jimi Hendrix.

Woodward, Bob (1943-) and **Carl Bernstein (1944-)**: *The Washington Post* reporting team responsible for much of the early coverage and the most important breaks in the Watergate story from 1972-1974.

Workers' compensation: A system providing monetary compensation for workers injured on the job.

Wounded Knee Creek Massacre: The U.S. Army's brutal massacre in 1890 of Sioux men, women and children.

Yalta Conference: Meeting of U.S. President Franklin Roosevelt, British Prime Minister Winston Churchill and Soviet Premier Josef Stalin in February 1945 to plan the final stages of World War II and postwar arrangements.

Yellow journalism: The sensationalistic style of newspapers beginning in the late 1890s that emphasized war, crime and scandal.

"Yellow Peril": Racist term used to describe Chinese and Japanese immigrants on the West Coast in the late 19th and early 20th centuries.

Youth International Party: A loosely organized group of ant-war, anti-capitalist radicals, known as "Yippies," led by Abbie Hoffman and Jerry Rubin, that preferred staging satirical pranks highlighting the absurdity of American politics and played a major role in the protests surrounding the 1968 Democratic National Convention in Chicago.

Yuppies: Shorthand for "Young Urban Professionals," to describe the nouveau riche of the 1980s, born as part of the Baby Boom from 1945 to 1964.

Zimmermann Telegram: A 1917 secret communiqué from the German foreign office to German ambassador to Mexico, Arthur Zimmerman, offering military aid and assistance in taking U.S. territory if Mexico came to war with the United States.

Index

A

Aaron, Hank, 861
Abalone Alliance, 1038
Abernathy, Ralph, 1051
Abington School District v. Schempp, 887
Abortion, 887, 1062
Abramoff, Jack, 1128
Abu Ghraib, 1121
Abzug, Bella, 1040
"A Call to Resist Illegitimate Authority" (Spock), 940
Acheson, Dean, 806, 884
Acuña, Rodolfo, 851
Ad agent, 525
Adams, Eddie, 954
Adamson Act, 639
Addams, Jane, 617, 686
Adenaur, Konrad, 820
Advertising,
  beginning of, 524
Affirmative action, 985, 1062, 1102, 1067
Afghanistan, 1080, 1117
African Americans,
  during World War I, 659–661
  first cavalry units, 568
  in Oklahoma, 570
  Jim Crow laws, 659
  migration to North, 531
  Ninth Cavalry, 569
  strikebreakers, 569
African Queen, The (Bantam edition), 857
Afrika Korps, 763, 776
Agency "capture," 702
Agent Blue, 927
Agent Orange, 928, 1000
Agnew, Spiro, 995, 1003
Agricultural Adjustment Act (AAA), 719, 721, 722
Agricultural Workers Organizing Committee (AWOC), 1034
Aguinaldo, Emilio, 583, 594
Ahmadinejad, Mahmoud, 1149
Aidid, Mohamed Farrah, 1106
AIDS, 1129–1130
AIG, 1140
Ailes, Roger, 976
Alabama (Confederate raider), 501
Alaska, 500, 502

al-Assad, Bashar, 1150
Albright, Madeline, 1095
Alcatraz Island, 1036
Aldrich, Nelson, 540–541
Alfonso XIII, King, 751
Alger, Horatio, 519
Ali, Muhammad, 941
Alito, Samuel, 1126
Allen, Frederick Lewis, 683
All Quiet on the Western Front (Remarque), 752
Alpert, Richard, 1029
Al Qaeda, 1108, 1116
Alsace-Lorraine, 669
Altgeld, John P. 619
Alvarez, Everett Jr., 925
Amalgamated Association of Iron, Steel, and Tin Workers, 538
Amalgamated Clothing, 730
Ambrose, Stephen, 558
Amendment,
  Eighteenth, 691, 692
  Fifteenth, 496, 496–498, 503, 506, 623, 875
  First, 658, 695, 809
  Fourteenth, 485, 487, 493, 497, 503, 526, 534, 875, 887
  Nineteenth, 686
  Ninth, 887
  Seventeenth, 541, 623
  Sixteenth, 637
  Sixth, 888
  Thirteenth, 480
  Twenty-fifth, 672, 677, 1003
  Twenty-first, 692
  Twenty-fourth, 901
  Twenty-sixth, 986
America First Committee, 756
"American Aphrodite," 887
American Bell, 521
American Birth Control League, 687
American Civil Liberties Union (ACLU), 674, 694
American Communist Party, 732
American Enterprise Institute, 1063
American Eugenics Society (AES), 839
American Expeditionary Force (AEF), 663
American Federation of Labor, 537
American Football League, 862
American GI Forum (AGIF), 851
American Hospital Association (AHA), 804
American imperialism, 584–598
American Independent Party, 973
American Indian Movement, 1035
American Legion, 674, 853

American Medical Association (AMA), 525, 566, 804
American Protective Association, 656
American Protective League (APL), 658
American Railway Union, 538
American Recovery and Reinvestment Act, 1141
Americans for Democratic Action (ADA), 802
American Telephone and Telegraph (AT&T), 521
American Tobacco Company, 524, 533, 584, 633
Americorps, 1096
Amnesty International, 1107
Amos 'n' Andy, 861
Anasazi, 555
Anderson, John, 1017
Anderson, Marian, 734
Anderson, Martin, 1067
Anderson, Sherwood, 591
Andrews, John B., 620
Andromeda Strain, The (Crichton), 1024
Andropov, Yuri, 1080
Angelus Temple, 694
Anglo-Iranian Oil Company, 827
Angola, 826
Angus, 560
Anti-Ballistic Missile Treaty, 1115
Anti-Comintern Pact, 752
Anti-Imperialist League, 594
Anti-lynching legislation, 734
Antiquities Act, 632
Anti-Saloon League (ASL), 621, 691
Antiterrorism and Effective Death Penalty Act, 1108
Apaches, 555
Apartheid, 799, 960
Apollo, 1052–1053
Apple Computer, 1137
Apple, Johnny, 968
Arafat, Yasser, 1012, 1074
Arbitration principle, 629
Arctic National Wildlife Refuge, 1115
Ardennes Forest, 781
Argonne Forest, 664
Aristide, Jean Bertrand, 1107
Armour, Philip, 523
Armstrong, Neil, 1051
Army-McCarthy hearings, 814
Army of the Republic of Vietnam (ARVN), 831
Arnett, Peter, 955
Arthur, Chester Alan, 542
Aryan Nation, 1099

Ashcroft, John, 1120
Assad, Hafez, 1073, 1074
Assembly centers, 773
Assembly line, 681
Aswan High Dam, 829
Atchison, Topeka, and Santa Fe Railroad, 517
Atlantic, Battle of the, 764
Atlantic Charter, 757
Atlee, Clement, 789
Atzerodt, George, 478
Auschwitz, 837
Australian ballot system, 622
Austria, 753
Austro-Hungarian empire, 649
Authentic Life of Billy the Kid, The (Garrett and Upson), 562
Autobiography of Malcolm X, The (Malcolm X), 905
Automobile industry, 681–682
Avenger Field (Sweetwater Texas), 768
Axis of Evil, 1122

B

B-29 Super Fortresses, 788
Babcock, Orville, 498, 500
Babe Ruth, 684
Baby Boom generation, 855
Badoglio, Marshal Pietro, 778
Baez, Bonaventura, 500
Baez, Joan, 894, 939, 1052
Baker, Ella, 876
Baker, Howard, 1003
Baker, James, 1093, 1077, 1083, 1067, 1114
Baker, Newton, 661
Balance of power, 990
Balfour, Arthur, 667
Ball, George, 917
Ballinger-Pinchot Affair, 633
Ballinger, Richard, 633
Ballinger, William Pitt, 492
Baltimore and Ohio Railroad, 526, 535
Bandung Conference, 826
Bank of America, 1140
Banks, Dennis, 1035
Banks, Ernie, 861
Bannon, Ann, 858
Bao Dai (Emperor), 916
Barbed wire, 560
Barger, Sonny, 940
Barkan, Elazar, 840
Barker, Bernard, 1001
Barker, Lt. Col. Frank, 957
Barnett, Ross, 890

Barnstormer, 685
Baruch, Bernard, 666
Bataan Death March, 762, 850
Bathing suits, 690
Bayh, Birch, 1063
Beam, Louis, 1000
Beatles, 1027
Beatniks, 863
Bebop artists, 864
Bedford Stuyvesant, 950, 961
Beecher, Henry Ward, 528
Begin, Menachem, 1012
Behr-Stearns, 1140
Beirut massacre, 1074
Belarus, 1083
Belgium, 755
Belknap, William, 498
Bell Aircraft, 766
Bell, Alexander Graham, 521
Bell, Dr. Norman, 880
Belmont, August, 548
Beneš, Eduard, 753
Bennett, Bob, 1097
Benson, Ezra Taft, 976
Bentsen, Lloyd, 1097, 1082, 1068
Berger, Victor, 659, 674
Berle, Adolf, 716
Berlin Crisis, 800, 801, 883
Berlin-Rome "Axis," 753
Berlin Wall, 883
Bernstein, Carl, 987, 988, 1002
Berry, Chuck, 869, 1027
Bessemer, Henry, 518
Bessie, Alvah, 809
Bethlehem Steel, 527
Beveridge, Albert J., 585
Biberman, Herbert, 809
Biden, Joe, 1139
Big Mamma Thornton, 868
Billington, Monroe, 568, 569
Billion Dollar Congress, 545
Billy the Kid, 561–563
bin Laden, Osama, 1015, 1108, 1116, 1134
Birmingham, Alabama, 891
Birth control movement, 687
Birth control pill, 887
Birth of a Nation, The (Griffith), 638, 693, 696
Black Bottom, 688
Black codes, 481
Black is Beautiful movement, 1032
Black Kettle, 556
Black Legion, The, 905
Blacklisted, 809
Blackmun, Harry, 1044
Black Muslim movement, 1102

Black Nationalists, 1032
Black Panther Party, 904, 907, 908, 1006, 1032, 1036
Black Power Movement, 689, 907, 1029–1030
Black Republicans, 474
Black Sox Scandal, 684, 685
Black Star Line, 689
Black Thursday, 705
Black Tuesday, 705
Blaine, James G., 540, 543, 587
Blair, Ezell, 875
Blair, Frank, 495
Blake, J.P., 848
Bland-Allison Act (1878), 546
Bliss, Tasker H., 667
Blitzkrieg, 755
Bloody Sunday, 903
Bloomberg, Michael, 1153
Blue codes, 720
Blue-Dog Democrats, 1145
Blue Eagle, 720
BMW, 1071
"boat people," 1000
Bockscar, 790
Boehner, John, 1141, 1144
Boeing Aircraft, 766
Boesky, Ivan, 1071
Bohemia, 754
Boland Amendment, 1073, 1078
Bolshevik Russia, 668
Bomb shelters, 823
Bonneville Dam, 724
Bonus Army March, 712
Booth, John Wilkes, 478
Bootleg liquor, 692
Borah, William, 671, 747, 753
Borden Condensed Milk, 524
Bork, Robert, 1003
Bosnia, 669
Boulder Dam, 724
Bouncing Bettys, 928
Boutwell, George, 499
Bowers, Samuel, 902
Boxer rebellion, 598–599
Boy Scouts of America, 656
Bracero program, 772, 1034
Bradbury, Ray, 865
Bradley, Bill, 1110
Bradley, General Omar, 817, 837
Brady Bill, 1096, 1098
Brady, James, 1069, 1098
Brady, Nicholas, 1086
Branch Davidian cult, 1099
Branch, Taylor, 894
Brandeis, Louis D., 619, 639
Brando, Marlon, 864

Bremer, Arthur, 987
Brest-Litovsk Treaty, 669
Brezhnev, Leonid, 993
Briand, Aristide, 748
Bridges, Styles, 809
Brigss, A.M., 658
Brinkmanship, 823
Britain, Battle of, 755, 778
British North American Act, 502
British Royal Air Force (RAF), 778
Broder, David, 1066
Brodhead Letter, 495
Brookings Institution, 1063
Brooklyn Bridge 520
Brooklyn Dodgers, 861
Brooks, Gwendolyn, 1032
Broqueville, Charles de, 667
Brotherhood of Sleeping Car Porters, 770
Browder v. Gayle (1956), 848
Brown, Governor Pat, 972
   election of 1966, 909
Brown, H. Rap, 907, 965
Brown, Jesse, 1095
Brown, Michael, 1127
Brown, Minnijean, 850
Brown, Ron, 1095
Brown, Scott, 1146
Brown v. Board of Education (1954), 887
Bruce, Lenny, 864
Bryan-Chamorro Treaty, 646
Bryan, Charles W., 701
Bryant, Anita, 1047
Bryan, William Jennings, 595, 627, 632, 635, 646, 671, 694, 695
Bryce, James, 602
Buchanan, Patrick, 1093
Budget and Accounting Act of 1921, 699
Budweiser, 680
Buffalo, 571–572
Buffalo soldiers, 568–569, 591
Bulge, Battle of the, 771, 781
Bull Moose Party. *See* Progresssive Party
Bunau-Varilla, Philippe, 601
Bundy, McGeorge, 923, 962
Bureau of Corporations, 628, 638
Bureau of Indian Affairs, 735
Bureau of Reclamation, 724
Bureau of the Budget, 699
Burford, Anne, 1067
Burke, Martha Jane, 564
Burleson, Albert, 658
Burma, 761
Burma Road, 758
Burroughs, William, 863

Bush, George H.W.,
   election of 1992, 1093
   Iran-Contra scandal, 1084
   Operation Desert Storm 1084
   presidency of, 1081–1087
Bush, George W., 936
   Axis of Evil speech, 1122
   election of 2000, 1110, 1111–1113
   election of 2004, 1125
   "faith-based" program, 1115
   first term, 1114–1116
   foreign policy after September 11, 1116–1118
   foreign policy pre-September 11, 1115–1116
   Hurricane Katrina, 1126
   Kyoto Protocol, 1116
   National Security Strategy, 1122
   "No Child Left Behind," 1116
   Operation Enduring Freedom, 1122
   Operation Iraqi Freedom, 1124
   preemptive war, 1122
   recession of 2008, 641
   second term, 1125–1127
   social security privatization, 1126
   tax plan, 1115
Busing, 1062
Butterfield, Alexander, 1003
Butternuts, 479
Byrd, Richard, 685
Byrnes, James, 766

C

Cabell, Earle, 895
Caddo, 555
Calles, Plutarco, 647
Calley, Lt. William Laws, 956, 983
Cambodia, 994, 1000
Campbell, Robert A., 570
Campbell Soup, 524
Camp David Accords, 1012, 1106
Camp Logan Riots, 661, 664
Campus Crusade for Christ, 1023
Canada, 502
Cannon, Joseph G., 633
Capone, Al, 692
Capra, Frank, 709, 731
Captain Corelli's Mandolin (De Bernières), 778
Caputo, Philip, 926, 956
Carleton, James H., 557
Carmichael, Stokely, 964, 969, 1030, 1040
Carnegie, Andrew, 518, 840
   anti-imperialist, 595
   philanthropic causes, 528

   plutocrat, 515
   steel industry, 526–527
Carney, Gary O., 570
Carpetbaggers, 489, 493
Carranza, Venustiano, 647, 654
Carson, Rachel, 1037
Carter, Herbert, 957
Carter, Jimmy, 603
   1973 Energy Crisis, 1014
   and human rights, 1012
   as governor, 1008
   Camp David Accords, 1012
   election of 1976, 1008
   election of 1980, 1016
   Haiti negotiations, 1107
   Panama Canal Zone treaty, 1012
   presidency, 1010–1012
Casablanca Conference, 778
Casey, William, 1079
"cash and carry," 752
Cash, Johnny, 868
Castro, Fidel, 596, 878, 881, 883, 895
Castro Village Association, 1048
Catcher in the Rye, The (Salinger), 1025
Catt, Carrie Chapman, 622
Cattle ranching, 559
Caucus, 540
Ceausescu, Nicolae, 1083
Celler, Rep. Emanuel, 900
Central Intelligence Agency (CIA), 827
Central Pacific Railroad, 504, 516
Central Powers, 649
Centralia Massacre, 563
Century of Dishonor, A (Jackson), 571
Ceylon, 841
Chafee, Roger "Bruce," 886
Chamberlain, Neville, 753, 916
Chamberlain, Wilt, 862
Chambers, Whittaker, 809, 972
Chambliss, Robert, 894
Chamorro, Emiliano, 646
Chaney, James, 901
Chapman, J. Wilbur, 693
Charleston, 684, 688
Charlie Company, 956, 983
Chávez, César, 1034–1035
Checkers speech, 819, 972
Cheney, Dick, 1079, 1110, 1123
   Vietnam, 936
Chennault, Colonel Claire, 759
Chernenko, Konstantin, 1080
Cherokee, 555
Chesapeake and Ohio Railroads, 526
Chevron, 1072
Cheyenne, 556
Chiang Kai-shek, 749, 752, 806, 807

Chicago,
  labor radicals in, 536
  meatpacking, 523
  rail hub, 538
Chicago White Sox, 685
Chicanismo, 1034
Chicca, Robert, 952
Chickasaw, 555
Chief Joseph, 552, 578
Chief Victorio, 569
Chile, 990
China, 806
  missionary activity, 584
  open door policy 597–599
Chinese Exclusion Act (1882), 529, 568, 605
Chisholm, Shirley, 1040, 1138
Chisum, John Simpson, 562
Choctaw, 555
Christian Broadcasting Network, 1016
Christian Coalition, 1102, 1103
Christian, Paula, 858
Christie, Chris, 1153
"Christmas Bombing," 998
Chrysler, 1141
Church Committee Hearings, 1006
Church, Frank, 1006, 1063
Churchill, Winston, 755, 820
  Manhattan Project, 789
  postwar view, 796
  Yalta Conference, 781
Church of Scientology, 1048
Cisneros, Henry, 1095
Citibank, 1140
City planning, 618
Civics exams, 623
Civilian Conservation Corps (CCC), 718
Civil Rights Act (1957), 875, 899
Civil Rights Act (1964), 900
Civil Rights Movement, 848
  Freedom Summer, 900
Civil Service Commission, 542, 627
Civil Service Reform, 499–500
Clansman, The (Dixon), 693
Clanton family, 561
Clappe, A.K., 565
Clark, Champ, 634
Clark Memorandum, 747
Clarke, Edward, 696
Clarke, Richard, 1118
Clayton Antitrust Act, 638
Clean Air Act of 1970, 1038
Clemenceau, Georges, 668
Cleveland, Grover,
  anti-imperialist, 594
  as president, 539

election of 1884, 543
Hawaiian affair, 587
immigration, 529
intervention in Cuba, 589
tariffs, 545
Clifford, Clark, 802, 828, 942, 962
Clift, Montgomery, 864
Climo, Lawrence H., 927
Clinton, Bill,
  and Cuba, 1108
  and Haiti, 1107
  and Kosovo, 1107
  and People's Republic of China, 1105
  and Rwanda, 1106
  and Somalia, 1106
  and Vietnam, 1108
  and Yugoslavia, 1107
  Brady Bill, 1098
  Clinton Doctrine, 1104
  deficit reduction 1096
  election of 1992, 1092–1098
  General Agreement on Tariffs and Trade (GATT), 1108
  health-care reform, 1097
  human rights crusade of, 1107
  Monica Lewinsky affair, 1109–1111
  NAFTA, 1098
  presidency of, 1095–1097
  terrorism escalation during, 1108
  Vietnam, 936
  Vietnam protest, 995
  World Trade Organization (WTO), 1108
Clinton, Hillary, 1054, 1093
  election of 2008, 1138
Cloning, 1129
Cloture vote, 900
Coca Cola, 525, 631
Cocaine, 631
Cochran, Jacqueline, 768
Cochran, Johnny, 1101
Code talkers, 773
Cody, William "Buffalo Bill," 571, 578
Coffee, Linda, 1044
Coffin, William Sloane, 940
Cohen, Ben, 717, 737
Cohen, Warren, 746
Cohen, William, 1118
Cohn, Roy, 814, 858
COINTELPRO (Counter Intelligence Program), 942, 966, 1006
Coit, Stanton, 617
Cold War,
  beginning of, 807–808
  defense spending in, 822–823
  espionage during, 809–810

Iron Curtain and, 801, 834
Korean War and, 814–818
McCarthyism in, 810–812
mutual assured destruction (MAD) in, 823
nuclear arms race during, 824
Vietnam War and, 829–831
Cole, Lester, 809
Coleman, Henry, 951
Colfax Massacre, 503
Colfax, Schuyler, 498
College Settlement (New York City), 617
Collier, John, 735
Collins, General Lawton, 830
Collins, Judy, 939
Collins, Susan, 1146
Colorado, 560
Colorado Volunteers, 556
Colson, Charles, 998, 1004
Columbia Broadcasting System (CBS), 681
Columbia University, 950–951
Comanche, 555
Combined Bomber Offensive, 778
Comic books, 864–865
Comics Code Authority, 865
Comics Magazine Association of America, 865
Comiskey, Charles, 685
Committee for a Sane Nuclear Policy, 940
Committee for Industrial Organization, 730
Committee for the Survival of a Free Congress, 1063
Committee of 14, 877
Committee on Public Information (CPI), 655
Committee to Defend America by Aiding the Allies, 756
Committee to Re-elect the President (CREEP), 987
Communications Decency Act, 1131
Communist Party (CP), 732
Communist Party of Kampuchea (CPK), 1001
Comprehensive Environmental Response Compensation and Liability Act, 1039
Comprehensive Nuclear Test Ban Treaty, 1115
Compromise of 1877, 540
Computer revolution, 1131–1132
Comstock Lode, 560
Coney Island, 531
Congo, 585

Congress of Industrial Organizations, 730
Congress of Racial Equality (CORE), 772, 888, 894
Conkling, Roscoe, 540, 541, 542
Connally, Gov. John, 894
Connor, Eugene "Bull," 889–890, 891
Conscience Whig, 499
Conservative Caucus, 1063
Consolidated Vultee, 766
Consolidation, 523
Containment, 797
Containment Culture: American Narrative, Postmodernism and the Atomic Age (Nadel), 870
Conti, Dennis, 957
Contraceptives, 887
"Contract With America," 1099
Conveyor belts, 679, 681
Cooke, Jay, 504
Coolidge, Calvin, 698–700, 701, 713
  as governor, 673
  election of 1920, 698
Coontz, Stephanie, 854, 855, 857
Cooper, Gary, 809
Coors, Joseph, 1063
Copperheads, 495
Copper wire, 560
Coral Sea, Battle of the, 762–763
Corbin, Abel R., 497
Corcoran, Tom, 717, 737
Cornejo, Juan, 1033
Corning Glass v. Brennan (1974), 1041
Corona, Bert, 1033
Corporations, beginning of, 526
Corpus Christi, Texas, 852
Corsica, 776
Corso, Gregory, 863
Coughlin, Father Charles, 726
Counterculture, 1026
Cow Island, 476
Cowling, Eli, 888
Cox, Archibald, 1003
Cox, Edward, 1004
Coxey, Jacob, 547
Cox, James M., 698
Cox, Samuel D., 499
Cox, Sgt. George, 957
Crane, Philip, 1063
Crawford, James, 965
Crazy Horse, 573
Creek, 555
Creel, George, 655, 657
Crete, 763
Criswell, W.A., 880
Crocker, Richard, 517

Croly, Herbert, 635, 641
Cronkite, Walter, 955, 975
Crook, George, 564
Crusade for Justice, 1035
Crystal City, Texas, 1033
Cuba, 1108
Cuban Revolutionary Party, 589
Cultural pluralism, 736
Culver, John, 1063
Curry, Izola Ware, 964
Curtis, Benjamin R., 491
Curtis, George William, 499
Custer, George Armstrong, 564, 573, 1036
Czechoslovakia, 669, 753, 829

D

Dahl, Steve, 1018
Dai, Bao, 830
Daley, Mayor Richard, 881, 974
Dallek, Robert, 897
Danang, Vietnam, 926
Dana, Richard, 568
Dancing,
  religious bans, 690
Darlan, Jean François, 776
Darrow, Clarence, 695
Darwin, Charles, 694
Daugherty, Harry, 700
Daughters of the American Revolution, 734
Davis, Chester, 717
Davis, Henry Winter, 478
Davis, John W., 701
Davis, Sr., Benjamin O., 770
Dawes, Charles G., 746
Dawes Plan, 746
Dawes Severalty Act, 574
"Days of Rage," 1037
Dayton (Ohio) Accords, 1107
Dean, Howard, 1125
Dean, James, 864
Dean, John, 1002
Death of a Salesman (Miller), 1024
Deaver, Michael, 1066, 1067
Debayle, Anastasio Somoza, 1012
Debs, Eugene, 538, 635, 658, 699, 700
Deere, John, 544
de Gaulle, Charles, 755, 820
De La Beckwith, Byron, 845
Delaware, 555
DeLay, Tom, 1128
  Vietnam, 936
Delgado v. Bastrop ISD (1948), 852
Del Monte, 1033

de Lôme, Enrique Dupuy, 589
D'Emilio, John, 856
Demilitarized Zone (DMZ), 953
Democratic Leadership Council (DLC), 1092
Democratic National Convention of 1964, 902
Dempsey, Jack, 684
Denmark, 755
Dennis, David, 902
Department of Agriculture,
  growth of during the New Deal, 722
Department of Commerce, 628
Depression of 1893, 547
Desert Storm, 1093
Détente, 992
Deutsch, Sarah, 558
Devolution, 985
Dewey, Commodore George, 583, 590
Dewey, Thomas, 781, 801, 818, 865
Dharma Bums, The (Kerouac), 863
Diamond Match Company, 620
Dianetics: The Modern Science of Mental Health (Hubbard), 1049
Diaz, Adolfo, 608
Diaz, Porfirio, 647
Diem, Ngo Dinh, 830
Dienbienphu, Battle of, 830
Dies, Martin, 808
DiMaggio, Joe, 862
Dinnerstein, Leonard, 838
Direct primary, 623
Dirksen, Everett, 900
Dirty tricks, 987
Disco Demolition Night, 1018
Disney, Walt, 809
Divine, Robert A., 749, 751
Dixiecrats, 801, 834
Dixon, A. C., 693
Dmytryk, Edward, 809
Doar, John, 890
Dobrynin, Anatoly, 884
Dodd, Christopher, 1146
Dodd-Frank Wall Street Reform and Consumer Protection Act, 1146
Doenitz, Admiral Karl, 764
Dolan, John, 562
Dole, Robert, 1009
  election of 1996, 1099, 1103
  Senate minority leader, 1096
Dole, Sanford B., 588
Dollar diplomacy, 607
Dominican Republic, 499, 600, 646, 746
Domino, Fats, 869
Domino theory, 798, 806, 918

Donahue, Phil, 1093
"Don't Ask, Don't Tell," 1096
Double V campaign, 772, 842
Doughboys, 663
Douglas Aviation, 766
Douglas, Helen Gahagan, 972
Douglas, Lewis, 717
Douglass, Frederick, 479
Dow Chemical, 939, 950, 1000
Dowell, Denzill, 1032
Doyle,, Henry, 844
Draft, peacetime, 756
Drake, Edwin, 520
Dred Scott, 491
Drew, Daniel, 517
Drew, Elizabeth, 1075
Duarte, Jose Napoleon, 1072
Du Bois, W.E.B., 661, 689, 842
Dukakis, Michael, 1082
Duke, James B., 533, 584, 633
Dulles, Allen, 827
Dulles, John Foster, 814, 821, 827, 1066
Dunkirk, 755
Duong Van Minh, 921
Durbin, Senator Dick, 1098
Durham,, W.J., 843
Dust Bowl, 560, 721
Dutch East Indies, 760
Dyer, Gwynne, 915
Dylan, Bob, 870, 894, 979, 1026-1028

E

Eagleton, Thomas, 987
Earhart, Amelia, 686
Earth Day, 1038
Earth First, 1038
Easter Offensive, 998
Eastland, James, 890
Eastman, Crystal, 620
Eastman Kodak Company, 682
Economic Opportunity Act, 961
Ederle, Gertrude, 684
Edison, Thomas Alva, 521
Edwards, John, 1125
Egypt, 827
Ehrenreich, Barbara, 858
Ehrlichman, John, 984, 998, 1003
Einstein, Albert, 789
Eisenhower, Dwight,
    Eisenhower Doctrine, 829
    atomic bomb usage, 789
    election of 1952, 818
    election of 1956, 849
    Farewell Address, 832

    gay purge, 858
    Interstate Highway Act, 859
    Little Rock, Arkansas crisis, 849
    McCarthyism and, 813
    military-industrial complex, 823, 832
    National Defense Education Act, 832, 885
    Operation TORCH, 776
    Supreme Commander, 837
    Vietnam and, 829
Eisenstein, Serge, 1081
Eizenstat, Stuart, 1010
El Alamein, 776
Election,
    of 1860, 557; of 1866, 486;
    of 1868, 494; of 1872, 500, 503;
    of 1874, 505; of 1876, 507;
    of 1880, 542; of 1884, 543;
    of 1888, 545; of 1890, 545;
    of 1892, 546; of 1894, 548;
    of 1896, 548; of 1900, 595;
    of 1904, 629; of 1908, 632;
    of 1910, 634; of 1912, 623, 634;
    of 1914, 639; of 1916, 639–640;
    of 1920, 698; of 1924, 701;
    of 1934, 731; of 1936, 726;
    of 1938, 740; of 1940, 756;
    of 1942, 767; of 1948, 801;
    of 1952, 818, 972; of 1956, 849;
    of 1958, 877; of 1960, 877, 888;
    of 1964, 902, 923, 959;
    of 1968, 962, 970; of 1972, 988;
    of 1974, 1006; of 1980, 1016;
    of 1982, 1071; of 1984, 1075;
    of 1992, 1092; of 1994, 1095;
    of 1996, 1103; of 2000, 1110;
    of 2004, 1125; of 2006, 1128;
    of 2008, 909, 1128-1130;
    of 2010, 1144; of 2012, 1151-1152;
Electric guitar, 868
Electricity, 522–524
Electric Kool-Aid Acid Test, The (Wolfe), 1029
Electric light bulb, 522
Elgin Watch Company, 682
Elkins Act, 629
Ellington, Duke, 689
Elloree Training School, 846
Ellsberg, Daniel, 998
El Salvador, 1072
Emancipation Proclamation, 476
Emergence of a Republican Majority, The (Phillips) 1061
Emergency Banking Act, 718
Emergency Quota Act of 1921, 692

Emergency Relief and Construction Act, 712
Emergency Relief Appropriation Act, 727
Emerson, Ralph Waldo, 939
Emmanuel, King Victor, 778
Endangered Species Act, 1038
End Poverty in California (EPIC), 732
Energy Crisis, 1973, 989
Energy Crisis, 1979, 1014
Eniwetok, 785
Enlai, Premier Zhou, 992
Enola Gay (bomber), 789
Environmental Protection Agency (EPA), 985, 1038, 1148
Epperson v. Arkansas (1968), 695
Equal Employment Opportunity Commission (EEOC), 1039
Equal Pay Act of 1963, 1039
Equal Rights Amendment (ERA), 686, 1015, 1041, 1062
Erhard Sensitivity Training (EST), 1050
Erie Railroad, 497, 517, 526
Ervin, Sam, 1002
Espionage Act, 658
Espy, Mike, 1095
Essex coach, 681
Establishment clause, 695, 887
Estelle v. Griswold (1965), 887
Estonia, 669, 1083
Eugenics movement, 839
European Economic Community (ECC), 800
European Union, 800
Evangelical Right, 1062
Evans, Hiram Wesley, 697
Evans, John, 556
Evarts, William M., 491
Evers, Medgar, 846, 893, 1026
Exchange Stabilization Fund, 1108
Executive Order (2679A), 665
Executive Order 8802, 770
Executive Order 9066, 773, 840
Executive Order 9835, 808
Executive Order 9981, 842
Exner, Judith, 966
Explorer I, 885
Exxon-Mobil Corporation, 520

F

Fairbanks, Charles W., 629, 632
Fair Deal, 818
Fair Employment Practices Commission (FEPC), 770
Fair Labor Standards Act (1938), 737

Fall, Bernard, 917
Falwell, Jerry, 1015, 1042, 1046, 1054, 1062
Family life,
  after WW II, 855
  double standard, 856
  premarital pregnancy, 856
  women discontent, 855
Farley, Jim, 737
Farmer, James, 888
Farmer-Labor Party, 732
Farm Security Administration, 767, 736
Farrakhan, Louis, 1102
Fascism, 749
Fast food, 860
Fats Domino, 868
Faubus, ov. Orval, 849
Fechner, Robert, 719
Federal Communications Commission, 861
Federal Deposit Insurance Corporation (FDIC), 718
Federal Election Campaign Act of 1971, 1006
Federal Election Campaign Act of 1974, 1006
Federal Election Commission, 1006
Federal Emergency Management Agency (FEMA), 1127
Federal Emergency Relief Administration (FERA), 718
Federal Employee Loyalty Program, 808
Federal Extension Service, 698
Federal Farm Loan Act, 639
Federal Highways Act, 639
Federal Reserve, 740
Federal Reserve Act, 637
Federal Reserve Board, 1070
Federal Reserve System, 634
Federal Trade Commission Act, 638
Federal Trade Commission (FTC), 638, 702
Feingold, Russell, 1146
Feminine Mystique, The (Friedan), 856, 1039
Feminism, 1062
Ferber, Michael, 941
Ferdinand, Franz, 650
Ferraro, Geraldine, 1076
Field Foundations, 900
Field, James G., 575
Fields, Jason, 690
Filipino-American War, 584
Final Days, The, (Woodward and Bernstein), 1005

Financial capitalism, 526
Finkbine, Sherri Chessen, 1043
Finland, 755
Fish, Hamilton, 502
Fiske, John., 586
Fisk, Jim, 497–499, 517
Fitzgerald, F. Scott, 683, 688
Five Civilized Tribes, 555, 570
Five-Power Treaty, 748
Flagpole sitting, 684
Flappers, 687
Fleischer, Ari, 1121
Flowers, Gennifer, 1093
Flying Fortresses, 777, 778
Flynn, Helen Gurley, 674
Foch, Ferdinand, 663
Foley, Mark, 1128
Foley, Neil, 854
Folsom, Jim, 843
Food Administration, 711
Food and Drug Administration, 631
Foraker Act (1900), 596
Forbes, Charles, 700
Ford Foundation, 1063
Ford, Gerald,
  as vice president, 1003, 1005
  background of, 1005
  election of 1974, 1006
  election of 1976, 1007
  member of Warren Commission, 896
  Vietnam, 1000
Ford, Henry, 679, 680, 766, 763, 729
Ford, John, 731
Ford, Robert, 564
Forest Rangers, 632
Formosa, 806
Forrestal, James, 828
Fortas, Abe, 962
Fort Sumner, 557
Foster, Vince, 1098
Fountain of Age, (Friedan), 1128
Four Freedoms, 796
Four-Minute Men, 656
Four-Power Treaty, 748
Fourteen Points (Wilson), 651, 667
Fox Trot, 684, 688
Fox, Yolanda Betzbeze, 876
Fragging, 996
Franco, General Francisco, 751
Frankfort, Illinois, 692
Freberg, Stan, 865
Freedman, Estelle B., 856
Freedmen's Bureau, 482–485, 492
Freedom of Access to Clinic Entrance Act, 1101
Freedom riders, 888–889

Freedom Schools, 901
Freedom Summer, 900
Freud, Sigmund, 688, 855
Frick, Henry Clay, 538
Friedan, Betty, 856, 1039, 1128
Friedman, Lawrence M., 888
Friendly, Fred, 814
Fromm, General Friedrich, 781
Frye, Marquette, 907
Fuel and Food Control Act, 665
Fujita, Frank, 774–775
Fulbright, J. William, 801, 923
Fundamentalists, 693
Fundamentals, The (Bible Institute), 693
F.W. Woolworth Company, 876

G

Gabrielson, Guy, 858
Gaddafi, Muammar, 1012, 1150
Gagarin, Yuri, 886
Gaines, William, 864, 865
Galleani, Luigi, 693
Galt, Edith, 672
Galveston Plan, 618
Gamble, Clarence J., 840
Gandhi, Mahatma, 1034
Garcia, Dr. Hector, 852, 898
García, Macario, 745
Garfield, Harry A., 665
Garfield, James A., 542
Garrett, Pat, 562
Garvey, Marcus, 689, 905
Gates, Bill, 1131
Gatling gun, 649
Gaye, Marvin, 1038
Gay Liberation Movement, 1046
Gay Rights movement,
  beginning of, 857
  gay communities, 857
  Gay Scare, 858
  media views, 858
Gelb, Leslie, 1118
Gender gap, 1076
General Accounting Office, 699
General Agreement on Tariffs and Trade (GATT), 1108
General Electric Company, 523, 526, 1072
General Manager's Association, 538
General Motors, 681, 730, 732, 1141, 739
Generation Gap, 1030
Geneva Accords, 830, 1120
Geneva Convention, 1120
Geneva Peace Accords, 916

Gentleman's agreement, 605, 861
George, David Lloyd, 668
George V, 649
Gephardt, Richard, 1125
German Democratic Republic, 801
Germany,
    colonial expansion, 649
Geronimo, 573
Ghana, 826
Ghost Dances, 553–554
Giancana, Sam, 883
G.I. Bill, 850
Gideon v. Wainwright (1963), 888
GI Forum, 1034
Gilded Age,
    advertising in, 524
    labor strife, 535
    laissez-faire policy, 534
    literary works in, 537
    machine politics, 539
    plutocrats in, 515
    politicians of, 539
Gilded Age, The (Twain and Warner), 499
Gillespie, Dizzy, 864
Gillette, Michael, 844
Gingrich, Newt, 936, 1098
Ginsberg, Allen, 838, 863, 940, 1026
Ginsburg, Ruth Bader, 1095
Giovanni, Nikki, 1032
Gitlin, Todd, 877, 896, 937, 1024
Glasshow, Samuel, 837
Glass-Steagall Act (1933), 718
Glenn, John, 886, 1128
Global warming, 1147
Glynn, Martin, 639
Godkin, E. L., 543, 588
Goering, Hermann, 755
Goldman, Emma, 674
Goldman, Ronald, 1101
Goldstein, Robert, 658
Goldwater, Barry, 902, 973, 1004
    election of 1964, 923
Gompers, Samuel, 595
    American Federation of Labor, 537
    anti-imperialist, 595
Gonzales, Alberto, 1120
Gonzalez, Henry B., 854
Gonzalez, Rodolfo "Corky," 1035
Goodman, Andrew, 901
Goodman, Mitchell, 941
Good Neighbor Policy, 746–747
Goodwin, Doris Kearns, 922
Gorbachev, Mikhail, 1079
Gore, Al,
    election 1996, 1093
    election of 2000, 1110

Gore, Albert Sr., 898
Gospel of wealth, 527, 528
Gossens, Allende, 990
Gould, Jay, 497–499, 515, 516
Grady, Henry, 533
Graham, Billy, 824, 880
Graham, Bob, 1125
Gramm, Phil, 1098
Grand Canyon, 632
Grand Coulee Dam, 724
Grange, 545
Grange, Harold "Red," 684
Grant, Madison, 838
Grant Park riot, 974
Grant, Ulysses S., 491, 495–497, 541
    and civil service reform, 499
    at Appomattox, 478
    election of 1868, 494
    election of 1872, 503
    first administration, 497–499
    foreign policy issues of, 499–501
    Panic of 1873, 504
Grape pickers' strike, 1034
Grapes of Wrath, The (Steinbeck), 722, 731
Grasso, Ella, 1041
Grateful Dead, 1029
Great American Desert, 558
Greater Houston Ministerial Association, 880
Great Gatsby, The (Fitzgerald), 683
"Great Man" theory, 978
Great Northern Railroad, 517, 526, 628
Great Railroad Strike of 1877, 535
Great Recession, 641
Great Sioux War, 572
Great Society, 899, 1067
Greece, 763
Greeley, Horace, 475, 504
Greenback Labor Party, 546
Greenbacks, 494, 575
Greenberg, Hank, 838
Greenglass, David, 810
Gregory, Thomas, 658
Grenada, 1075
Grey, Zane, 690
Griffith, D. W., 638, 693
Grissom, Virgil "Gus," 886
Gruening, Ernest, 925
Guadalcanal, 762
Guam, 592, 593, 761
Guantanamo Bay, 884, 1120
Guatemala, 827
Guiteau, Charles, 542
Gulags, 824
Gulf of Tonkin Resolution, 925

Gulf Oil, 1072
Gunskirchen camp, 838
Guthrie, Woody, 938
Guzman, Colonel Jacobo Arben, 827

H

Haber, Al, 938
Habsburgs, 649
Haiti, 476, 646, 1107
Halberstam, David, 862, 921, 934
Haldeman, Earl, 1003
Haley, Bill, 868
Half-Breeds, 541
Halsey, Admiral William "Bull," 786
Hamer, Fannie Lou, 1040
Hamilton, Alexander,
    industrialization vision, 534
Hamilton, Alice, 620
Hamlets, 918
Hammond, Robert, 952
Hampton, Fred, 1032
Hancock, Winfield Scott, 495, 542
Hanoi Hilton, 933
Harding, Warren G.,
    election of 1920, 698, 711
    presidency of, 699, 713
    Supreme Court appointees, 633
Hard-money advocate, 494
Harlem Globetrotters, 862
Harlem Hell Fighters, 660
Harlem Renaissance, 688
Harriman, E. H., 628
Harris, C.L., 876
Harrison, Benjamin, 545, 570
Harrison, George, 1027
Hart, Gary, 1076, 1081
Hartsfield, William B., 843
Hastings, Lansford, 568
Hawaii, 593
Hawaiian Revolution, 588
Hawley-Smoot Tariff, 712
Hay-Bunau-Varilla Treaty (1903), 601
Hayden, Sterling, 809
Hayden, Tom, 938
Hayes, Ira, 772
Hayes, Rutherford B., 507, 539, 541, 587
Hay, Henry, 858
Hay-Herrán Treaty, 601
Hay, John, 590, 597–599
Haymarket Square, 536
Haynes, Abner, 862
Hay-Pauncefote Treaty (1901) 601
Hays, William H., 691, 699
Hayward, William, 660
Head Start, 899

1218 / INDEX

Health care, 1128–1130
Hearst, George, 540
Hearst, William Randolph, 588, 602, 647
Hefner, Hugh, 857, 1040
Heinz, Henry John, 523
Heinz, Teresa, 1125
Hell's Angels, 940
Helsinki Accords, 1009
Henderson, Elmer W., 844
Henderson v. the United States (1950), 844
Hendricks, Thomas, 495
Henry Street Settlement, 619
Hepburn Act, 630
Hepburn, William, 630
Hereford cattle, 560
Heritage Foundation, The, 1063
Hernandez v. Driscoll CISD (1957), 852
Heroin, 631
Herrán, Tomás, 601
Herrick, John J., 924
Hersh, Seymour, 1006
Herzegovina, 669
Hester Street, 530
Hetch Hetchy Valley, 632
Hezbollah, 1078
Hickok, James Butler "Wild Bill," 564
Hill-Burton Act, 804
Hill, James J., 517, 584, 628
Hillman, Sidney, 730
Hilsman, Roger, 919
Hinckley, John, 1069
Hiroshima, 789
Hiss, Alger, 809, 972
History of the Standard Oil Company, The (Tarbell), 521, 616
Hitler, Adolf,
  rise to power, 750–751
Hoar, Rockwood, 499
Hobby, Oveta Culp, 768
Ho Chi Minh, 817, 916, 924, 953
Hoffa, Jimmy, 896
Hoffman, Abbie, 974
Hoffman, Albert, 1028
Holding Company Act (1935), 727, 733
Holly, Buddy, 869
Hollywood Ten, 809
Holmes, John Clelon, 863
Holmes, Oliver Wendell, 659
Holocaust, 837
Home Loan Bank Board, 712
Homeowner's Loan Corporation (1933), 719
Homestead Act of 1862, 484, 558

Homestead Steel Strike, 538
Homeward Bound: American Families in the Cold War Era (May), 855
Hong Kong, 761
Hood, James A., 892
Hooker Chemical & Plastics Corporation, 1038
Hoover, Herbert, 710
  as Commerce Secretary, 700
  election of 703
  Neutrality Acts, 755
  presidency of, 710–715
  repatriation, 735
Hoover, J. Edgar, 689, 858, 889, 902, 965
Hopkins, Harry, 716, 717, 718, 728
Hopkins, Mark, 517
Horizontal integration, 520
Horton, Willie, 1082
Hotchkiss machine gun, 554
House, Edmund, 668
House on Un-American Activities Committee (HUAC), 808
House Rules Committee, 633
Housing market collapse, 1141
Howard, O.O., 482
Howells, William Dean, 595
Howl (Ginsberg), 863
How the Other Half Lives (Riis), 616
Hubbard, L. Ron, 1048
Huckabee, Mike, 1139
Hudson cars, 681
Huerta, Victoriano, 647
Hughes, Charles Evans, 639, 747
  as Secretary of State, 700
Hughes, Howard, 1001
Hughes, Langston, 689, 911
Hull, Cordell, 747, 759
Hull House, (Chicago), 617
Human Rights Watch, 1107
Humphrey, Hubert, 803, 878, 900, 903, 959
  election of 1968, 974, 975
Humphrey, William E., 702
"Hundred Days," 717
Hungarian Revolution, 824
Hunt, E. Howard, 998
Huntington, Collis P., 517
Hurricane Katrina, 1126
Hurricane Sandy, 1153
Hussein, Saddam, 1084, 1107, 1124
  eight-year war with Iraq, 1073
Hutu militias, 1106
Hyde Amendment, 1045
Hydraulic mining, 560
Hydroelectric generators, 723
Hydrogen bomb, 807, 938

I

Ia Drang Valley, Battle of, 929
Ickes, Harold, , 716, 734, 717
"I Have a Dream" speech, 894
Illinois Occupational Disease Commission, 620
Immigration,
  Chinese, 567–568, 605
  Japanese, 605
  late nineteenth century, 529
  Mexican American, 568, 850
  restriction before WW II, 839–840
Immigration Reform and Control Act (1986), 1078
India, 826, 841
Indian Arts and Crafts Board, 736
Indian Reorganization Act of 1934, 736
Indonesia, 826, 1105
Industrial Workers of the World (IWW), 658
Influence of Sea Power on History, The 1660-1783 (Mahan), 586
"In God We Trust," 887
Initiative, 623
Inquiry, 667
Institute for Defense Analyses (IDA), 950
Intermediate Nuclear Forces Treaty (INF), 1081
International Business Systems (IBM), 840
International Church of the Foursquare Gospel, 694
International Convention against Torture, 1120
International Criminal Court, 1115
International Harvester, 544
International Ladies Garment Workers Union, 731
International Telephone and Telegraph, 990
International Treaty Council, 1036
Interstate Commerce Act (1887), 545
Interstate Commerce Commission (ICC), 534, 545, 630
Interstate Highway Act, 859
Iran, 827, 990
Iran-Contra affair, 1077, 1085
Ireland,
  during WW I, 651
Irish American Fenian Brotherhood, 502
Iron clad oath, 478
Irreconcilables, 672
Isolationism, 751

INDEX / 1219

Israel, 827, 1073, 1147
Issei, 692, 773
It's a Wonderful Life (Capra), 709
Ivory Soap, 525
Iwo Jima, Battle of, 772, 786

J

Jackson, Helen Hunt, 571
Jackson, Henry, 987
Jackson, Jesse, 968, 1076, 1081
Jackson, Mahalia, 894
Jacobson, Matthew Frye, 840
Jagger, Mick, 1053
James, Jesse Woodson, 563
James, William, 595
Jameson, Elizabeth, 566
James-Younger Gang, 563
Japanese-American internment, 740
Jara, Victor, 991
Jarvis, Howard, 1016
Javits, Jacob, 961
Jaworski, Leon, 1004
Jazz Age, 688
Jim Crow laws, 659
Jingoists, 588
Job Corps, 728, 899
Jobs, Steven, 1137
Johnson, Andrew,
  as president, 478–479
  impeachment proceedings of, 490–492
  presidential pardons of, 480
  Reconstruction policy, 480–481
  views toward slavery, 479
Johnson, Hiram, 640, 672, 698
Johnson, Hugh, 717, 720, 729
Johnson, Lyndon,
  as president, 899–901
  Civil rights, 896
  Civil Rights Act (1964), 900
  election of 1948, 898
  election of 1960, 877, 899
  election of 1964, 923
  Longoria funeral service, 853
  National Aeronautics and Space Agency (NASA), 832
  National Youth Administration, 728
  Senate majority leader, 898
Johnson-O'Malley Act (1934), 736
Johnson, Paul, 902
Johns, Ralph, 875
Jones, Bobby, 684
Jones, Jesse, 717
Jones, Jim, 1049
Jones, Judge Walter B., 846
Jones, Leroi, 1032
Jones, Paula, 1098, 1109

Jones, Samuel L. "Golden Rule," 617
Jonestown, Guyana, 1049
Joplin, Janis, 1052
J.P. Morgan and Company, 752
Juarez, Benito, 501
Jungle, The (Sinclair), 630

K

Kaiser, Charles, 949–951
Kaiser, Henry J., 766
Kalakaua, King, 588
Kamikaze attacks, 786
Kansas City Monarchs, 861
Kansas-Pacific Line, 559
Karnow, Stanley, 917, 922, 998
Kasserine Pass, 777
Katyn Forest Massacre, 755
Kaufman, Irving, 810
Kazakhstan, 1083
KDKA in Pittsburgh, 681
Kearney, Denis, 568
Keating-Owen Child Labor Act, 639, 642
Kefauver, Estes, 803, 818, 898
Keith, Minor, 608
Kelley, Florence, 619, 686
Kellogg-Briand Pact, 748
Kellogg, Frank, 748
Kelly, Alvin "Shipwreck," 683
Kelly, William, 518
Kemp, Jack, 1103
Kennan, George, 797, 808
Kennedy, Edward,
  Chappaquiddick, 1009
Kennedy, John F.,
  Catholic issue, 880
  inaugural address of, 882
  in Bay of Pigs, 883
  in Cuban missile crisis, 884
  in election of 1960, 877
  Kennedy-Khrushchev Clash, 883
  "March on Washington," 893
  McCarthyism and, 811
  New Frontier, 882
  Nixon debates, 880
  Vienna Summit, 883
  Vietnam views, 916
Kennedy, Joseph P., 878
Kennedy, Robert, 878, 879, 884, 923, 958–959
  and Freedom Riders, 889
  election of 1964, 959
  election of 1968, 961, 970
  McCarthyism and, 811
  Ole Miss admitance of Farmer, 890
  voter registration, 900

Kent State riots, 995
Kentucky Fried Chicken, 860
Kenya, 826, 1108, 1117
Kerensky, Alexander, 668
Kerner, Otto, 907
Kerouac, Jack, 1026
Kerry, John, 944, 1125, 1063
  Vietnam protest, 997
Kesey, Ken, 940
Kesselring, Field Marshall Albert, 778
Key, David, 509
Keynesian, 727, 740
Keynes, John Maynard, 767, 1068, 727
Khe Sanh, Battle of, 953
Khmer Rouge, 994, 1000
Khomeini, Ayatollah Ruhollah, 1013
Khrushchev, Nikita, 824, 883
Killen, Edgar Ray, 902
Kilpatrick, James J., 876
Kim Il-Sung, 815, 952
Kim Phúc, 998
King, B.B, 868
King, Martin Luther Jr., 848, 879
  Atlanta arrest, 879
  non-violent techniques, 876
King, Rodney, 1086, 1101
Kinsey, Alfred, 856, 1043
Kiowa, 555
Kirk, Grayson L., 950
Kissinger, Henry, 984, 988, 998
Kitchin, Claude, 655
Kleagles, 696
Klondike Gold Rush, 502
K Model Chevrolet, 681
Knights of Labor, 535, 537
Knox, Philander C., 607, 628
Konoye, Prime Minister Prince Fumimaro, 760
Kopechne, Mary Jo, 1009
Koppel, Ted, 1015
Korean War, 814–816
  Project BLUEBIRD, 1007
Korematsu, Fred, 775
Korematsu v. United States (1944), 775
Koresh, David, 1099
Kosovo, 1107
Kovacs, Ernie, 865
Kruger, Richard, 845
Krupsak, Mary Anne, 1041
Kucinich, Dennis, 1125
Ku Klux Klan, 502
  beginning of, 493
  Ku Klux Klan Act, 503
  organization of, 489
  second, 696–697
  Women of the Ku Klux Klan, 697

Kurds, 1085
Kwajalein Atoll, 785
Kyoto Protocol, 1116, 1147
Kyushu, 788

L

Laboratory of democracy, 623
Laffer, Arthur, 1068
La Follete, Philip, 731
La Follette, Robert, 623, 630, 632, 634, 659, 672, 701
Laissez-faire, 534
Lakota, 571
Lame duck president, 629
Landon, Alfred, 733, 1085
Lan Guttmacher Institute, 1044
Lansing, Robert, 652, 672
Laos, 935, 994
Lardner, Ring Jr., 809
Late, Great Planet Earth, The (Lindsey), 1023
Latvia, 669, 1083
Lawrence, William (Bishop), 528
Lawson, John Howard, 809
Laxatives, 631
League of Nations, 670, 699, 747
League of United Latin American Citizens (LULAC), 745, 851
League of Women Voters, 687
Leahy, Admiral William, 789
Leary, Timothy, 1029
Lebanon, 829, 1074
Lebensraum, 750
Le Duc Tho, 998
Lehman Brothers, 1140
Lehrer, Tom, 865, 999
LeMay, Curtis, 788, 884, 926, 976
Lend-Lease Act (1941), 757
Lenin, V. I., 668
Leningrad, 755
Lerner, Mitchell B., 952
"Letter From a Birmingham Jail" (King), 891
Levinson, Salmon, 748
Levitt, William, 860
Levittown, 863
Lewinsky, Monica, 1109
Lewis and Clark expedition, 578
Lewis, Carl, 1076
Lewis, Jerry Lee, 868
Lewis, John L., 888, 767, 720, 730
Leyte Gulf, Battle of, 786
Libby, I. Lewis "Scooter," 1128
Liberal Republicans, 504
Liberty Bonds, 656
Libya, 776

Liddy, G. Gordon, 998
Lieberman, Joseph, 1110
Lifton, Robert J., 855
Liliuokalani, Queen, 588
Limbaugh, Rush, 1098
Limerick, Patricia Nelson, 560
Limited war, 814
Lincoln, Abraham,
  colonization of blacks, 476
  Emancipation Proclamation, 476
  expanding presidential power, 490
  preserving the Union, 475
  Proclamation of Reconstruction, 477
  racial views of, 475–476
  Ten Percent Plan, 477
  views toward southern whites, 476
Lincoln County War, 562
Lindbergh, Charles, 685, 755, 840
Lindsay, John, 996
Lindsey, Hal, 1023
Lippman, Walter, 667
Lipsitz, George, 910
Literacy Corps, 1014
Literacy tests, 623
Lithuania, 669, 1083
Little Big Horn, Battle of, 564, 571
Little Richard, 869
Little Rock, Arkansas, crisis, 849–850
Little Rock Nine, 849
Liuzzo, Viola, 904
Lloyd, Henry Demarest, 541
Lochner v. New York (1905), 619
Lodge, Henry Cabot, 529, 587, 632, 669, 671, 747, 818, 920
Loewen, James, 936
Lomax, John and Alan, 868
London, Jack, 938
Long, Huey P., 725
Longoria, Felix, 853, 898
Lon Nol, 1000
Looking Backward (Bellamy), 537
Lorraine Motel, 967
Los Angeles race riots, 1086
Lost Cause, 489
Love Canal, 1038
Lovelady, Commander William, 837
Lovett, Robert, 828
Lowden, Frank, 698
Lowell, Abbott, 693
Lowell, Robert, 941
Loyalty Review Board, 809
Ludlow Amendment, 752
Lusitania, 653
Luzon Island, 785
Lysergic acid diethylamide (LSD), 1006
Lytle, Mark, 888

M

MacArthur, Douglas, 761, 783, 790, 814, 815, 1063
  Bonus Army, 713
MacFarlane, Robert, 1073
Machine politics, 539
Madero, Francisco, 647
Mae Collins, Addie, 894
Magaziner, Ira, 1097
Maginot Line, 753, 755
Mahan, Alfred Thayer, 586
Mahdi, 1118
Maine (U.S. battleship), 589
Makin Atoll, 785
Malaria, 557
Malaysia, 826
Malcolm X, 905, 932, 941, 1029
Malenkov, Georgi, 824
Malone, Vivian, 892
Maltz, Albert, 809
Manchuria, 607
  Japanese invasion of, 749
Manhattan Project, 789, 795, 797
Manifest Destiny, 499, 584–587
Manila Bay, 761
  (Wilson and Franzen), 1024
Mann-Elkins Act, 633
Mansfield, Mike, 923
Manson, Charles, 1024
Mao Zedong, 752, 806, 992
Marathon dancing, 684
March on the Pentagon, 941
March on Washington, 893
Margin buying, 703
Marianas, 785
Marijuana, 1028
Mark the Matchboy (Alger), 519
Marlboro Men, 860
Marne, Battle of, 650
Marne, Second Battle of, 663
Marshall, George C., 776, 789, 799, 807, 813, 915
Marshall Islands, 785
Marshall Plan, 799
Marshall, Thurgood, 845
Marshall, William, 1031
Marti, Jose, 589
Martin, Ralph G., 880, 884
Masaryk, Jan, 803
Mattachine Society, 858
Mattson, Kevin, 1014
Matusow, Allen J., 878
Mays, Willie, 861
Maximilian, 501
May, Elaine Tyler, 855
Maytag, 1119

Mazo, Earl, 881
McAdoo, William Gibbs, 666, 698, 701
McCabe, E.P., 570
McCain, Franklin, 875
McCain, John, 933, 1110, 1138, 1139
McCarthy, Eugene, 961
McCarthyism, 674, 809, 810
McCarthy, Joseph, 809, 810, 858, 861, 878, 1062
McConnell, Mitch, 1144, 1146
McCord, James W., 1001
McCormick Plant, 536
McCulloch, Hugh, 494
McDonald's, 860
McFarlane, Robert, 1078
McGovern, George, 986, 1063
 election of 1972, 987
McGrath, J. Howard, 809
McGuffey Readers, 528
McKinley Tariff, 545, 546
McKinley, William,
 intervention in Cuba, 589
McLaughlin, James, 554
McLaurin v. Oklahoma State Regents (1950), 844
McLaury brothers, 561
McLean, Don, 870
McManes, James, 539
McNair, Denise, 894
McNamara, Robert, 942, 955, 997
McNary-Haugen Bills, 702
McNeil, Joseph, 875
McPherson, Aimee Semple, 693
McSween, Alexander, 562
McVeigh, Timothy, 1101
Means, Russell, 1036
Meat Inspection Act, 630
Meatpacking, 523
Medicaid, 899
Medicare, 899
Medicine Lodge Treaty, 571
Meese, Edwin, 1067
Megachurch, 694
Meir, Golda, 988
Mellon, Andrew W., 700
Memoirs v. Massachusetts (1966), 887
Memphis race riots, 486
Memphis Sanitation Workers' Strike, 967
Méndez v. Westminster School District (1946), 852
Mensheviks, 668
Merck, Frederick, 561
Meredith, James, 890
Merriam, Frank, 732

Merrill-Lynch, 1140
Merry Pranksters, 1029
Mescalero Apache, 556
Meuse-Argonne Forest campaign, 663
Mexican American Political Organization (MAPA), 1033
Mexican Farm Labor Program Agreement, 772
Mexican Revolution, 647–648
Meyerson, Bess, 838
Microsoft, 1131
Midway, Battle of, 762
Midwives, 566
Mieczkowski, Yanek, 1007
Miers, Harriet, 1126
Miles, Nelson A., 578
Military-industrial complex, 823, 832
Milk, Harvey, 1048
Miller, 680
"Million Man March," 1102
Milosevic, Slobodan, 1107, 1108
Minikus, Lee, 907
Minow, Newton, 861
Miranda v. Arizona (1966), 888
Mississippi appendectomies, 840
Mississippi Freedom Democratic Party (MFDP), 901
Mississippi Plan, 507, 507–508
Missouri Pacific Railroad, 536
Mitchell, George, 1035
Mitchell, John, 628, 985, 1004
Model A, 681
Model T, 681
Mohr, James C., 567
Moley, Raymond, 716
Moline Plow Company, 702
Mondale, Walter, 1009, 1076, 1085
Monroe Doctrine, 501, 600
Montenegro, 669
Montgomery, General Bernard, 763, 777, 781
Montgomery Improvement Association (MIA), 848
Montgomery Industrial School for Girls, 847
Moore, Michael, 1151
Moore, Robert B., 924
Moral Majority, 1015, 1062
Moratorium, 995
Moravia, 754
Morgan, J. P., 515, 522, 526, 628, 634
Morgenthau, Henry, 716
Morningside Park, 950
Morrill Act, 559
Morrison, Norman, 940
Morris, Stephen, 932

Morse, Samuel F. B., 517
Morse, Wayne, 923, 925
Morton, Jelly Roll, 689
Moses, Robert, 900, 939
Mossadegh, Mohammad, 827, 1013
Motion picture camera, 522
Motion Pictures Association of America (MPAA), 691
Mountain States Legal Foundation, 1067
Movie Ratings System, 691
Mozambique, 826
Mubarak, Hosni, 1150
Muckrakers, 616
Mugwumps, 541, 542
Muir, John, 631, 632
Mulford, Don, 1032
Muller v. Oregon (1908), 619
Multiculturalism, 1093
Mundt, Karl, 814
Munich Conference, 754
Municipal housekeeping, 686
Munn v. Illinois (1877), 545
Murphy, Frank, 730
Murphy, Lawrence J., 561
Murray, Madalyn, 887
Murray, Phillip, 809
Murray v. Curlett (1963), 887
Murrow, Edward R., 813, 860
Muskie, Edmund, 986, 1078
Muslims, 1147
Mussolini, Benito, , 726, 782
Mutual assured destruction (MAD), 823
My Lai Massacre, 956–957, 983

N
Nadel, Alan, 870
Nader, Ralph, 1112
Nagasaki, 790
Nakamura, Norman, 932
Naked Lunch (Burroughs), 863
Namath, Joe, 998
Napalm-B, 788, 928, 950, 998
Napoleon III, 501
NASCAR, 692
Nash, Diane, 889
Nash, Jay Robert, 563
Nasser, Gamal Abdel, 827
Nast, Thomas, 504
National Aeronautics and Space Administration (NASA), 832, 885
National American Woman Suffrage Association (NAWSA), 622, 656, 686

National Association for the Advancement of Colored People (NAACP), 626
  cancellation of Amos 'n' Andy, 861
National Association of Manufacturers, 674
National Broadcasting Company (NBC), 681
National Child Labor Committee, 618
National Conference of Citizens for Religious Freedom, 880
National Conservative Political Action Committee (NCPAC), 1006
National Consumers' League, 619
National Defense Education Act, 832, 885
National Endowment for the Arts, 985
National Farm Workers Association, 1034
National Football League, 862
National Guard, 936
National Indian Youth Council (NIYC), 1035
National Industrial Recovery Act (NIRA), 719
Nationalist Party (South Africa), 799
National Labor Relations Act, 733, 735
National Labor Relations Board (NLRB), 730
National Liberation Front (Vietnam), 830, 916
National maximum highway speed limit, 989
National Mobilization Committee Against the War, 941
National Organization for Women (NOW), 1040
National Origins Act, 692
National Reclamation Act, 631
National Recovery Administration, 720
National Right to Life Committee, 1063
National Security Council document 68 (NSC-68), 807
National Security Council (NSC), 1073, 1078
National Security Strategy, 1122
National Union of Social Justice, 726
National Union Party, 486
National War Labor Board, 666, 767
National Woman's Party (NWP), 686
National Women's Political Caucus, 1040
National Youth Administration (NYA), 728, 767

Nation of Islam (NOI), 689, 906, 1032
Nation, The (Godkin), 588
Native Americans, 1035–1036
Nativism,
  definition of, 692
Navajos, 556, 736
Nazi Party, 750
Nazi-Soviet Non-Aggression Pact, 754
Neff, Pat, 690
Negro Infantry Regiments, 592
Negro Leagues, 861
Negro Nationalism movement, 689
Negro Project, 840
Neibuhr, Reinhold, 1008
Nelson, Donald, 766
Nelson, Gaylord, 1038, 1063
Nepotism, 499
Nervous Generation, The (Nash), 690
Netherlands, 755
Neutrality Acts, 752, 755
Nevada, 560
New Dealers, 710
New Deal Glass-Steagall Act, 1146
New Deal, The Second, 727
New Departure, 492–495
New Freedom, 635
New Frontier, 882–883
New Guinea, 762
Newlands, Francis G., 631
"New Left," 937
New Look, 822
Newman, Paul, 864
New Nationalism, 635
New Orleans, 1126
  race riots, 486
New Right,
  direct mail, 1062
  mobilization of, 1062–1063
  think tanks, 1063
New South, 533–534
Newspapers,
  advertising, 524
Newton, Huey P., 908
New York Central Railroad, 518
New York City,
  advertising industry, 525
  Stock Exchange, 705
Nez Percé Indians, 578
Ngo Dinh Nhu, 917
Ngo Dinh Nhu, Madame, 920
Ngo Dinh Tuc, 920
Nguyen Luan, 998
Nguyen Ngoc Loan, 953
Nguyen Van Thieu 922
Niagara Movement, 626
Nicaragua, 608, 747, 1072

Nicaraguan Canal Treaty, 646
Nicholas II, 668
Nichols, Terry, 1101
Niebuhr, Reinhold, 802
Nigeria, 826
Nimitz, Admiral Chester, 762, 783
Nimoy, Leonard, 1031
Nine-Power Treaty, 748
Nisei, 773
Nitze, Paul, 807
Nixon, E.D., 848
Nixonland: The Rise of a President and the Fracturing of America (Perlstein), 983
Nixon, Richard, 810
  1973 energy crisis, 989
  affirmative action of, 985
  as congressman, 971
  background of, 984
  balance of power, 990
  Checkers speech, 972
  Chile, 990
  Clean Air Act of 1970, 1038
  détente, 992
  dirty tricks of, 987
  election of 1952, 819, 972
  election of 1960, 877
  election of 1962, 972
  election of 1972, 988
  foreign policy of, 989–994
  Hiss case, 972
  House Un-American Activities Committee, 972
  Kennedy debates, 880
  Nixon Doctrine, 989
  Operation Menu, 994
  Pentagon Papers, 997
  "Southern Strategy" of, 984
  stagflation, 985, 988
  Vietnamization, 994
  Watergate Scandal, 987, 1001
Noble Experiment, 692
"No Child Left Behind," 1116
Nol, General Lon, 995
Nolting, Frederick, 920
Nomura, Admiral Kichisaburo, 759
Non-Aggression Pact, 755
Nordhausen, 837
Nordics, 839
Noriega, Manuel, 1073, 1084
Norris, Frank, 616
Norris, George W., 633
North American Free Trade Agreement (NAFTA), 1098, 1108
North Atlantic Treaty Organization (NATO), 805
North, Colonel Oliver, 1073, 1078

Northern Pacific Railroad, 504, 517, 526, 628
Northern Securities Company, 526, 628
North Vietnamese Army (NVA), 918
Northwestern Farmers Alliance, 575
Norway, 755
Novak, Robert, 987
Nuclear arms race, 824
Nye, Gerald, 752

O

Obama, Barack,
  Afghanistan surge, 1149
  American Recovery and Reinvestment Act, 1141
  auto industry, 1141
  Dodd-Frank Wall Street Reform and Consumer Protection Act, 1146
  election of 2008, 909, 1128–1130
  financial crisis for, 1140
  foreign policy of, 1147
  housing market colllapse, 1141
  job creation of, 1141
  Nobel Peace Prize of 2009, 1147
Obregón, General Alvaro, 647, 746
O'Brien, Lawrence, 1001
Obscenity laws, 887
Occupational Safety and Health Administration (OSHA), 985
Occupy Wall Street, 1150
O'Connor, Sandra Day, 1075, 1078, 1126
Octopus, The (Norris), 616
Odett, Clifford, 731
Office of Management and Budget, 1068
Office of Price Administration (OPA), 768
Office of War Mobilization (OWM), 766
Ohrdruf Concentration Camp, 837
Oil embargo, 988
O'Leary, Hazel, 1095
Oligopoly, 527
Olney, Attorney General Richard, 538
Olson, Dr. Frank, 1007
Olson, Floyd, 732
Omaha Beach, 780
One Flew Over the Cuckoo's Nest (Kesey), 1029
O'Neill, John, 1125
O'Neill, Tip, 1070
Only Yesterday: An Informal History of the 1920s (Allen), 683
On the Road (Kerouac), 863

Open Door Policy, 597, 748
Operation Barbarossa, 755
Operation Breadbasket, 968
Operation Desert Storm 1084–1085
Operation Enduring Freedom, 1122
Operation Frequent Wind, 1000
Operation Iraqi Freedom, 1124
Operation Linebacker, 998
Operation Market-Garden 781
Operation Menu, 994, 1000
Operation Mongoose, 883
Operation OVERLORD, 780
Operation Paperclip, 886
Operation Ranch Hand, 1000
Operation Rescue, 1101
Operation Rolling Thunder, 925
Operation TORCH, 776
Operation Wetback, 850
Orbison, Roy, 868
Oregon Improvement Company, 569
Organization of Petroleum Exporting Countries (OPEC), 988
Orlando, Vittorio, 668
Ornitz, Samuel, 809
Osage, 555
Oslo (Norway) Accords, 1105
Oswald, Lee Harvey, 895
Our Country (Strong), 586
Outsourcing, 1126
Office of Strategic Services (OSS), 827

P

P-51 Mustang, 779
Pabst, 680
Pago Pago, 587, 588
Pahlavi, Mohammad Reza Shah, 827, 1013
Pakistan, 826, 1149
Palestine, 828
Palestine Liberation Organization (PLO), 1105
Palestinian Authority, 1106
Palestinian Liberation Organization (PLO), 1012, 1074
Palin, Sarah, 1139
Palmer, A. Mitchell, 673
Palmer, General Bruce Jr., 929
Palmer, Robert, 868
Panama Canal Zone, 600, 746, 1012
Pan-American Conference, 747
Panay, 753
Panic in 1873, 504–505
Panic of 1893, 547
Paramilitary units,
  Confederate, 480, 495
Park Chung Hee, 952

Parker, Alton B., 629
Parker, Charlie, 864
Parker, "Colonel" Tom, 869
Parks, Rosa, 847
Passing of the Great Race: or The Racial Basis of European History, The (Grant) 838
Patriot Act, 1120
Patronage, 499, 539
Patterson, John, 877, 888
Pattillo, Melba, 850
Patton, General George, 713, 771, 777, 781, 837
Paul, Alice, 686, 1041
Paulus, Field Marshal Freidric, 764
Pax Americana, 1072
Peace Corps, 939
Peale, Norman Vincent, 880
Pearl Harbor, 588, 760–762
Peck, Gregory, 998
Peek, George N., 702, 717
Pelosi, Nancy, 1145
Pena, Federico, 1095
Pendleton Act (1883), 499, 542
Pendleton, George H., 495
Pennsylvania Railroad, 517–518
Pentagon Papers, 997
People's Republic of China (PRC), 1105
Peoples Temple Christian Church Full Gospel, 1049
Perkins, Carl, 868
Perkins, Frances, 716, 729, 737
Permanent Subcommittee on Investigations, 813
Perot, Ross, 924
  election of 1992, 1092, 1093
  election of 1996, 1103
Pershing, John "Black Jack," 648, 660, 663
Pétain, Philippe, 755
Peter, Paul, and Mary, 894
Pfeifer, Michael J., 561
Phan Khac Suu, 922
Philippines, 784
Philippine Sea, Battle of the, 785
Phillips, Howard, 1063
Phillips, Kevin, 1061
Phillips Records, 868
Phillips, Sam, 868
Phonograph, 522
Phossy jaw, 620
Pikes Peak, 560
Pilgrim's Progress (Bunyan), 616
Pillsbury, 524
Pinchot, Gifford, 631, 633
Pine Ridge Indian Reservation, 1036

Pingree, Hazen S., 617
Pinkerton Detective Agency, 538, 563
Pinkham, Lydia, 525
Pinochet, Augusto, 991, 1108
Plains Indians, 555
Plame, Valerie, 1128
Planet of the Apes, The 1024
Planned Parenthood, 688, 1043, 1046
Platt Amendment, 596, 747
Platt, Tom, 540
Playboy (magazine), 857
Plessy v. Ferguson (1896), 660, 844, 887
Pletcher, Captain J.D., 838
Pluck and Luck (Alger), 519
Plumbers Unit, 1001
Plutocrats, 515
Pocket veto, 478
Pogroms, 530
Poindexter, Admiral John, 1078
Poison gas, 663
Poitier, Sidney, 1030
Poland, 669, 754
Poles, Spotswood, 660
Political action committees (PACs), 1006
Political Association of Spanish-Speaking Organizations (PASO), 1033
Pollack, Jackson, 864
Poll taxes, 623
Pol Pot, 994
Poor People's March, 966
Population Bomb, The (Ehrlich), 1024
Populist Party, 624
Pork-barrel, 545
Pornography, 856, 1062
Port Huron Statement, 938
Posse Comitatus, 1099
Postwar economic boom, 681
  advertising, 682
  automobile industry, 680
  electrical household appliances, 681
  installment buying, 682
  radio, 681
Postwar economic problems, 680
  agriculture, 680
  sick industries, 680
Potsdam Declaration, 789
Powderly, Terence, 529, 535
Powell, Colin, 1085, 1114, 1123, 1128
Powell, Lewis, 478
Powers, Francis Gary, 825, 878
Prager, Robert, 656
Prairie View A&M, 844
Predatory lending, 1141

Preemptive war, 1122
Premarital pregnancy, 856
President,
  lame duck, 629
  term limits, 629
President's Commission on the Status of Women, 1039
President's Committee on Civil Rights, 842
Presley, Elvis, 869
Price, Cecil, 901
Processed food industry, 523
Proclamation of Amnesty, 477
Proclamation of Reconstruction, 477
Procter & Gamble, 524
Production Code Administration (PCA), 691
Professional Air Traffic Controller's Organization 1070
Profiles in Courage (Kennedy), 878
Progressive Party (1912), 635
Progressive Party (1948), 801
Progressivism,
  definition of, 614
  influences upon, 615
  nature of, 614
  strands or categories of, 615
  urban reform, 616
Prohibition, 566, 621, 674, 691–692, 716
Prohibition Amendment, 680
Project BLUEBIRD, 1007
Project Phoenix, 930
Pro-life, 1062
Promontory Point, 504
Proposition, 623
Proposition 13, 1016
Proposition 14, 908, 973
Proposition 187, 1101
Protest movement,
  students in, 876–877
Public Credit Act, 497
Public Works Administration (PWA), 722
Pueblo Relief Act, 736
Puerto Rico, 592, 596
Pulitzer, Joseph, 589
Pullman, George, 538
Pullman Strike, 538
Pumpkin Papers, 972
Pure Food and Drug Act, 631
Pu Yi, 749

Q

Quaker Oats, 524
Quakers, 939

Quang Duc, 920
Quantrill's Raiders, 563
Quantrill, William Clarke, 563
Quapaw, 555
Quarantine, 884
Quarantine Speech, 752
Quayle, Dan, 936, 1081
Quay, Matt, 540
Quevedo, Edward, 1033

R

Race-baiting, 495
Racism,
  after World War II, 842, 850
  and the cold war, 841
  before World War II, 838
Radar, 755
Radical Republicans, 477
Radio, 681
Ragged Dick (Alger), 519
Railroad Administration, 666
Railroads,
  business practices, 516–518
  consolidation of, 517
  rise of, 516
  stock speculation, 516
Rainbow coalition, 1076
Randolph, A. Phillip, 770
Rankin, Jeannette, 655, 761
Raskin, Marcus, 941
Rather, Dan, 975
Rationing, 768
Rauschenbush, Walter, 615
Rayburn, Sam, 893, 898
Ray, Dixie Lee, 1041
Ray, James Earl, 967
Raymond Orteig Prize, 685
Reading Railroad, 526
Reaganomics, 1068–1072, 1077
Reagan, Ronald,
  1980 election, 1060–1063
  air traffic controllers strike, 1070
  and abortion, 1044
  as governor, 908
  assassination attempt, 1069–1070
  contras, 1073
  deregultion, 1067
  domestic policy of, 1067–1071
  election of 1966, 909
  election of 1968, 974
  election of 1976, 1008
  election of 1980, 1012, 1016
  foreign policy of, 1066
  gun owners rights, 1032
  Iran Contra Affair 1078–1079
  Middle East conflict, 1073

Moral majority, 1062
pre-presidency, 809
Reagan Democrats, 1081, 1092
Reaganomics, 1068–1072
Reagan Revolution, 1070
Teflon President, 1070
voodoo economics, 1068
Rebels, 495
Rebel Without a Cause, 854
Recall, 623
Recession of 1937-38, 740
Reconstruction,
 Andrew Johnson and, 478–480
 issues of, 474
 presidential, 475–477
 Radical Republicans and, 477, 485–489
 retreat from, 505–507
 white backlash, 502
Reconstruction Acts of 1867, 487–488, 493
 southern response, 492–493
Reconstruction Finance Corporation (RFC), 712
Red Army, 668, 796
Red-baiting, 674, 820
Red Cloud, 572
Red Cross, 656
Redeemers, 493, 505, 540
"Red Power" movement, 1035
Red River War, 573
Red Scare, 673
Red Shirts, 506
Red Tails, 771
Reed, Jim, 564, 903
Reed, Ralph, 1102
Reeves, Richard, 984
Referendum, 623
Reform,
 labor, 618–620
  workers' compensation laws, 620
 political, 622
  initiative, 623
  proposition, 623
  recall, 623
  referendum, 623
 prohibition, 621
 state, 618–625
 urban, 616
 woman suffrage movement, 621–622
Refrigerated railcars, 523, 560
Regan, Donald, 1077
Rehnquist, William, 1126
Reichstag, 750
Reid, Harry, 1145
Religious Right, 1099

"rendition" of suspects, 1121
Reno, Janet, 1095, 1099
Repatriation, 735
Reservationists, 671
Reserve Officer Training Corps (ROTC), 939
Reuther, Walter, 802
Revenue Act of 1916, 639
Revenue Act of 1942, 767
Revisionists, 796
Rhee, Syngman, 817
Rhineland, 669, 750
Rhodes, James, 995
Richardson, Elliott, 984, 1003
Richardson, J.P., 869
Richardson, Seth, 809
Richberg, Donald, 717
Richmond, J.R. David, 875
Rich's Department Store, 879
Rifle Clubs, 506
Right to life, 1062
Right to work, 1007
Riis, Jacob, 616
Rising Tide of Color Against White World-supremacy, The (Stoddard), 839
Rivera, Geraldo, 1093
Roberts, John, 1126
Robertson, Carole, 894
Robertson, Pat, 1016, 1046, 1093, 1062
Roberts, Steve, 1023
Robinson, A.G., 656
Robinson, Jackie, 861
Robinson, Joseph, 703
Rockefeller Foundation, 1063
Rockefeller, John D., 515, 520, 633, 840
Rockefeller, Nelson, 879, 973, 1008
"Rocket 88," 868
Rock 'n' roll, 868
Roddenberry, Gene, 1031
Roe v. Wade (1973), 887, 1044–1045, 1062, 1068
Romania, 1083
Rometsch, Ellen, 966
Rommel, Erwin, 763
Romney, George, 907, 973
Romney, Mitt, 1139
Roosevelt, Eleanor, 739, 770, 802, 1039
 Native Americans, 735
 racial equality, 734
 WPA committment, 728
Roosevelt, Franklin Delano,
 1936 election, 733
 advisors of, 716

anti-lynching laws, 740
as vice presidential candidate, 698
Atlantic Charter, 757
background of, 714
Bank Holiday, 717
differences from Hoover, 716
Executive Order 9066, 773
Good Neighbor Policy 747
leadership of, 710
Lend-Lease Act, 757
liberalism of, 715
Neutrality Acts, 752
New Deal,
 Native American rights, 736
 women's rights, 737
 working class and middle class conditions, 734
recession of 1937, 740
Second New Deal, 727
third term of, 757
TVA project, 723
Roosevelt, Theodore,
 arbitration principle use of, 629
 conservation efforts, 631
 corollary, 600
 Department of Commerce, 628
 foreign policy of, 598–600
 Hepburn Act, 630
 muckrakers coined, 616
 Northern Securities Company and, 628
 Panama Canal, 600
 presidency, 539
 Progressive Party, 635
 railroad regulation, 629–630
 regulation of the nation's food and medicine, 630
 Rough Riders, 591
 Spanish-American War, 626
 Square Deal of, 629
 views toward McKinley, 589
 views toward Spanish-American War, 590
 views toward World War I, 639
Root, Elihu, 602, 632
Roots (Haley), 1033
Root-Takahira Agreement (1908), 604
Roselli, Johnny, 883
Rosenberg, Jack, 1050
Rosenberg, Julius and Ethel, 810
Rosenman, Samuel, 737
Rosenthal, Joe, 772
Rosine, Louise, 690
Ross, John, 555
Roth v. United States (1957), 887
Rough Riders, 591, 627
Rove, Karl, 1125

Rowe, Gary Thomas, 904
Rubin, Jerry, 974
Ruby, Jack, 896
Ruckelshaus, William D., 1003
Rudd, Mark, 950, 1037
Rumor of War, A (Caputo), 926
Rumsfeld, Donald, 1114, 1123, 1128
Rural Electrification Administration, 727
Rusk, Dean, 884
Russell, Bill, 862
Russell, Richard, 900
Rwanda, 1106
Ryan, Leo, 1049
Ryan, Paul, 1152

S

Saar, 669
Sacco, Nicola, 693
"Sacrifice for Dignity," 876
Sadat, Anwar, 1012
Safe Drinking Water Act, 1038
Safer, Morley, 934
Saga of Billy the Kid, The (Burns), 562
Sagarin, Edward, 859
Sagebrush Rebellion, 1067
Saipan, Battle of, 785
Salisbury, Harrison, 934
Samoa, 587
Samuels, Zerelda, 563
Sandbrook, Dominic, 1033
Sand Creek Reserve, 556
Sanders, Harlan, 976
Sandinistas, 1012
Sanger, Margaret, 687, 840
San Juan Islands, 502
Santo Domingo Affair, 499
Saturated markets, 704
"Saturday Night Massacre," 1004
Saturn V, 886
Saudi Arabia, 1105
Save Our Children, 1047
Saving Private Ryan (Spielberg), 780
Scalawags, 489, 493
Scalia, Antonin, 1126
Schenck, Charles, 659
Schenck v. the United States (1919), 659
Schine, G. David, 814
Schlafly, Phyllis, 1016, 1042, 1046
Schlesinger, Arthur, 918
Schlesinger, James, 1010
Schlieffen Plan, 650
Schlitz, 680
Schlosser, Eric, 860
Schofield, John M., 492

School Book Depository, 895
School prayer, 887, 1062
Schorr, Daniel, 998
Schultz, George, 1078
Schultz v. Wheaton Glass Co. (1970), 1041
Schurz, Carl, 500, 507
Schuschnigg, Kurt, 753
Schwarzkopf, General H. Norman, 1085
Schwerner, Michael, 901
Scopes, John T., 695
Scott, Adrian, 809
Scott, Emmett J., 661
Scott, Hugh, 1004
Scott, Rick, 1112
Scott, Tom, 519
Scowcroft, Brent, 1124
Screen Actor's Guild, 1070
Scrowcroft, Brent, 1078
Seale, Bobby, 908
"search and destroy," 929
Securities Act (1933), 718
Securities and Exchange Commission, 718
Securities Exchange Act (1934), 718
Sedition Act, 658, 660
Seduction of the Innocent: The Influence of Comic Books on Today's Youth (Wertham), 865
Seigenthaler, John, 889, 890
Selassie, Haile, 749
Select Committee on Intelligence, 1007
Selective Service Act, 656, 941
Selective Training and Service Act, 766
Selma, Alabama, 903
Seminole, 555
Serbia, 669
Serling, Rod, 861
Settlement houses, 617
Seward, William, 478, 500
Sexual Behavior in the Human Male (Kinsey), 856
Sexual freedom, 1062
Seymour, Horatio, 495
Shalala, Donna, 1095, 1097
Sharecropping, 484
Share-Our-Wealth Plan, 726
Sharon, Ariel, 1074
Sharpton, Al, 1125
Shatner, William, 1031
Shawnee, 555
Shepard, Alan, 886
Sheppard-Towner Maternity and Infancy Protection Act, 698
Shepperd, John Ben, 846

Sheridan, General Philip, 570
Sherman Antitrust Act (1890), 538, 545, 628
Sherman Silver Purchase Act (1890), 546
Sherman, William T., 484, 491, 573
Shifting coalitions, 614
Shiite Muslims, 1085, 1124
Shipping Board, 666
Shirley, Myra Belle, 564
Shivers, Governor Allan, 849
S.H. Kress, 876
Shopping mall, 860
Shriver, Sargent, 987
Shultz, George, 1084
Sicily, 777
Sick industries, 680
Sierra Club, 631, 1038, 1068
Sigma Reproductive Health Services Clinic, 1046
"Significance of the Frontier in American History, The" (Turner), 585
Sihanouk, Prince Norodom, 994
Silent Majority, 984, 996
Silent Spring (Carson), 1037
Silicon Valley, 1062
Silver,
  western mines, 560
Silverites, 546
Simmons, William J., 696
Simple Justice: The History of Brown v. Board of Education and Black America's Struggle for Equality (Kruger), 845
Simpson, O.J., 1101
Sinatra, Frank, 840
Sinclair, Upton, 630, 938, 732
Singapore, 761
Sirhan Sirhan, 970
Sirica, John, 1003
Sit-down strike, 730, 739
Sit-in movement (1960), 876
Sitting Bull, 554, 573, 578
Six-Day War, 970, 988
Sixteenth Street Baptist Church, 892
Sixties: Years of Hope, Days of Rage, The (Gitlin), 877
Slaveocracy, 473
Smith Act, 808
Smith, Adam, 534
Smith, Al, 698, 701, 878
  election of 703
  ethnic vote, 734
Smith-Connally War Labor Disputes Act, 767
Smith, Howard, 900
Smith, Jesse, 701

Smith-Lever Act, 638
Smith, Margaret Chase, 1138
Smith v. Allwright (1944), 772, 843
Smith, William French, 1067
Snowe, Olympia, 1146
Snyder, Gary, 1038
Sobell, Morton, 810
Social Darwinism,
   expansionist ideology, 586
   ideology, 527
Social Gospel Movement, 537, 615
Socialist Labor Party, 536
Socialist Party of America, 635
Social Security Act (1935), 729, 733, 735, 740
   pension fund, 737, 740
   workers' compensation, 620
Soil Conservation and Domestic Allotment Act (SCDAA), 722
Soil Conservation Service, 721
Solidarity, 1083
Solomon Islands, 784
Somalia, 1106
Sometimes a Great Notion (Kesey), 1029
Somoza, Anastasio, 747, 1073
Sorenson, Ted, 878, 892
South Africa, 799
Southern Christian Leadership Council (SCLC), 876, 894
Southern Farmers Alliance, 575
Southern Homestead Act, 484
Southern Manifesto, 898
Southern Pacific Railroad, 517
Southern Railway, 844
"Southern Strategy," 984
South Manchuria Railway, 607, 749
Soviet-American Friendship Society, 809
Spanish-American War, 588–593
   American Army's capacities 590
   American naval superiority, 590
   newspaper sensationalism, 588
   Philippines, 590
   yellow journalism, 589
Spanish Civil War, 751
Spanish flu, 679–680
Sparkman, John, 818
Sparks, Lee, 662
Speakeasies, 679, 691
Spencer, Herbert, 528
Spheres of influence, 796
Spirit of '76, The (movie), 658
Spirit of St. Louis, The (monoplane), 685
Spock, Dr. Benjamin, 940
Spoils system, 499

Sprague, Rear Admiral Clifton, 786
Springsteen, Bruce, 1019
Sputnik I, 885
Sputnik II, 831, 885
Square Deal, 629
Stagflation, 986, 988
Stalingrad, Battle of, 764
Stalin, Joseph, 824
   Nazi-Soviet Non-Aggression Pact, 754
   Yalta Conference, 781
Stalwarts, 541, 542
Stanbery, Henry, 491
Standard Oil Company, 520, 545, 633
Stanford-Binet IQ tests, 839
Stanford, Leland, 517
Stanton, Edwin, 490
Stanton, Frank, 934
Starr, Ellen Gates, 617
Starr, Kenneth, 1098, 1109
Statement on Race (UNESCO), 840
States' Rights Party. *See* Dixiecrats
Steel,
   birth of industry, 518
Steffens, Lincoln, 616
Stephens, Alexander H., 481
Stephenson, David, 697
Stern Family Fund, 900
Stevenson, Adlai, 877, 878, 884, 895
Stevenson, Governor Coke, 898
Stevens, Thaddeus, 477, 484
Stewart, Lyman, 693
Stimson Doctrine, 749
Stimson, Henry, 749, 766, 795
Stockdale, James, 924
Stockett, Joseph, 1046
Stockman, David, 1068, 1071
Stock market crash (1929), 704, 710
Stoddard, Lothrop, 838
Stokely Carmichael, 907
Stonewall Riot (New York City), 859
Storer, Horatio, 567
Strangers in the Land: Patterns of American Nativism, 1860-1925 (Higham), 530
Strategic Arms Limitation Treaty (SALT I), 993
Strategic Defense Initiative (SDI), 1080
Strong, Josiah, 586
Strong, William L., 617
Stuckey, Sterling, 868
Student Nonviolent Coordinating Committee (SNCC), 875, 876, 900, 906, 939, 964, 1036
Student Peace Union, 939
Students' Afro-American Society, 950

Students for a Democratic Society (SDS), 937, 950, 1028
Submarine warfare, 649, 652
Subterraneans, The (Kerouac), 863
Suburb, 860
Sudetenland, 669, 753
Suez Canal, 603
Suez Crisis, 827–828
Suffragettes, 497
Sullivan, Anne, 861
Sumner, Charles, 477, 500
Sumner, William Graham, 528
Sun Belt, 1061
Sunday, Billy, 693
Sunni Muslims, 1124
Sunnunu, John, 1086
Sun Records, 868
Superdome, 1127
Superfund law, 1039
Superman, 737
Supply and demand, 534
Sussex Pledge, 653
Sweatt, Heman Marion, 843
Swift Boat Veterans for the Truth, 1125, 1063
Swift, Gustavus, 523
Swiveling truck, 558
Syria, 827, 1073, 1085

T

Taber, John, 809
Taconic Foundation, 900
Taft-Hartley Act, 802
Taft-Katsura Agreement, 604–606, 607
Taft, Robert, 757, 806, 818
Taft, William Howard, 604–605
   as Chief Justice, 699
   election of 908, 632
   Philippines, 595
   presidency of, 607–608, 632–634
   Roosevelt (T) and, 607
   Taft-Katsura Agreement, 607
Taiwan, 806
Taliban, 1080, 1117, 1149
Tammany Hall, 498, 543
Tampico, 647
Tango, 690
Tanzania, 826, 1108, 1117
Tarawa's Betio Island, 785
Tarbell, Ida, 521, 616
Task Force Barker, 957
Tavibo, 553
Taylor, Glen, 841
Taylor, Maxwell, 917, 921
Teach-in, 939

Teamsters Union, 1034
Tea Party movement, 1143–1144
Teapot Dome affair, 701
Teddy Bears, 627
Teflon President, 1070
Tehran Conference, 780
Telegraph, 517
Telephone, 521
Television, 820, 860
Teller Amendment, 590, 596
Telstar TV satellite, 886
Temperance, 541
Tenant farming, 484
Tennessee, 486
Tennessee Coal and Iron Company, 634
Tennessee Valley Authority Act (1933), 723
Ten Percent Plan, 477
Tenure of Office Act, 490
Term limits, 629
Terrorists, 1091
Tesla, Nikola, 523
Tet Offensive, 953–955
Texas Rangers, 568
Thayer, Webster, 693
Third Parties, rise of radical, 731
Third World, 826
This Side of Paradise (Fitzgerals), 683
Thomas, Clarence, 1126
Thomas, Norman, 755, 756
Thompson, Hugh Clowers, 958
Thompson, Robert, 918
Thoreau, Henry David, 939
Three Mile Island, 1010
Thurmond, Sen. Strom, 801
Tiananmen Square massacres, 1105
Tijerina, Felix, 852
Tilden, Bill, 684
Tilden, Samuel J., 507
Till, Emmett, 846
Tilman, Ben, 548
Title IX, 1041
Title VII, 1040
Tito, Marshal Josip Broz, 798
Tojo, General Hideki, 760
Tombstone, 560
Toms, Coons, Mulattoes, Mammies & Bucks: An Interpretive History of Blacks in American Films (Bogle), 1030
Torrijos, Omar, 1012, 1015
"To Secure These Rights," 842
Totalitarianism,
 Italy rise of, 749
 Japan rise of, 748–750
 Spain, rise of, 751

Tower Commission, 1078
Tower, John, 1078
Townsend, Francis, 726
Toynbee Hall, 617
Tracy, Spencer, 737
Trade associations, 700
Trade deficits, 986
Trafficante, Santos, 883
Transcontinental rail system, 516
Treaty of Fort Laramie, 572
Treaty of Paris (1898), 583, 592
Treaty of Washington (1871), 502
Triangle Shirtwaist Company, 613
Tribulation, 1023
Tripartite Pact, 759
Triple Entente, 649
Tripp, Linda, 1109
Trotsky, Leon, 668
Trotter, William Monroe, 624
Trujillo, General Rafael, 747
Truman, Harry,
 atomic bomb and, 797
 Berlin Crisis, 800
 Churchill and, 796
 containment, 797
 domino theory of, 798
 election of 1948, 801
 election of 1952, 818
 hydrogen bomb and, 807
 Marshall Plan, 799
 North Atlantic Treaty Organization (NATO), 805
 Soviet Union and, 795–796
 Truman Doctrine, 797–800
 vice presidency of, 795
Trumbo, Dalton, 809
Trumbull, Lyman, 485
Trump, Donald, 1071
Trust, 520
Tsongas, Paul, 1063
Tugwell, Rexford G., 716, 723
Tunisia, 776, 1150
Tunstall, John Henry, 562
Turkey, 1105
Turner, Frederick Jackson, 585
Tuskegee Airmen, 771
Twain, Mark, 595
Tweed, William Marcy, 498, 539
Twenties record breaking events,
 athletic events, 684
 flag pole sitting, 683
 marathon dancing, 683
Twilight Zone, The, 861
Twining, Nathan, 830
Tyler, Elizabeth, 696

U

U-boat, 652
Ukraine, 1083
ULTRA, 764
Underwood, Oscar, 634, 637
Underwood-Simmons Tariff Act, 637
Unilateralism, 1116
Unionists, 474, 480
Union League, 489, 492
Union Pacific Railroad, 498, 504, 516, 536
Unitarians, 939
Unitas, Johnny, 862
United Arab Republic, 829
United Auto Workers, 730
United Fruit Company, 608, 827
United Klans of America, 894
United Latin American Citizens (LULAC), 1033
United Mine Workers, 628, 720, 767, 730
United Nations Educational, Scientific and Cultural Organization (UNESCO), 840
United Negro Improvement Association (UNIA), 689
United Service Organizations (USO), 768
United States Forest Service, 632
United States Holocaust Memorial Museum, 840
United States Steel, 526, 527, 634, 730
United States v. Nixon (1974), 1004
Unlawful combatants, 1120
Uptown Klan, 845
U.S. Bureau of Alcohol, Tobacco, and Firearms (ATF), 1099
U.S.S. Cole, 1117
U.S.S. Maddox, 924
Utley, Robert, 561
Ut, Nick, 998

V

Vagrancy laws, 481
Vail, Theodore N., 521
Valens, Ritchie, 869
Vallandigham, Clement, 756
Van Allen Radiation Belts, 885
Vandenberg, Arthur, 757, 808
Vanderbilt, Cornelius, 497, 518
Van Winkle, Peter G., 492
Vanzetti, Bartolomeo, 693
Veeck, Bill, 1018
Venezuela, 600
Veracruz, Mexico, 647

Verdun, Battle of, 664
Versailles Treaty, 669, 746
Vertical integration, 519
Veteran's Bureau, 700
Vichy France, 755
Vienna Summit, 883
Vietcong, 830, 916, 917–918, 927–930, 934, 940–942, 941
Vietminh, 830
Vietnam, 817, 1108
  Agent Orange, 1000
  Battle at Ban Tre, 956
  Battle of Khe Sanh, 953
  Battle of Pleiku, 925
  Battle of the Battangan Peninsula, 929
  Battle of the Ia Drang Valley, 929
  "boat people," 1000
  Buddhists in, 919–920
  casualties, 927
  Charlie Company, 956, 983
  "Christmas Bombing," 998
  coup d'etat, 921
  defoliants, 927
    Agent Orange, 928
  Diem regime, 916
  Easter Offensive, 998
  Gulf of Tonkin Resolution, 925
  Hanoi Hilton, 933
  U.S.S. Maddox, 924
  My Lai Massacre, 983
  Napalm-B, 928
  Operation Frequent Wind, 1000
  "Operation Homecoming," 932
  Operation Linebacker, 998
  "Operation Ranch Hand," 1000
  Operation Rolling Thunder, 925
  quarantine of peasants, 918
  "search and destroy" missions, 957
  television coverage of, 934–935
  Tet Offensive, 953–956
Vietnam Veterans Against the War (VVAW), 997
Vigilantes, 561
Viguerie, Richard, 1062, 1063
Vilas, William, 540
Villa, Pancho, 647
Virgin Islands, 500, 647
Viva Kennedy!, 1033
Volcker, Paul, 1070
Volstead Act, 691
Von Braun, Dr. Werner, 886
von Eckardt, Heinrich, 654
Vo Nguyen Giap, 830, 955
von Stauffenberg, Colonel Claus, 780
Voorhis, Jerry, 972
Vostok I, 886

Voter Education Project, 900
Voting Rights Act (1965), 904, 909

W

Wabash, St. Louis, and Pacific Railway Co. v. Illinois, 545
Wade, Benjamin, 478, 489, 491
Wade-Davis Bill, 478
Wade, Henry, 1044
Wagner Act, 730
Wagner, Robert, 734
Waiting For Lefty (Odett), 731
Wake Island, 761
Walgreen's, 876
Walker, John Jr., 952
Walker, T-Bone, 868
Wallace, George, 923, 987
  civil rights, 894
  election of 1964, 902, 908
  University of Alabama desegregation, 892
  views toward boycott, 892
Wallace, Henry, 716, 801
Wallace, Lew, 562
Walter-McCarran Act, 841
War bonds, 767
War Industries Board (WIB), 666
Warlocks, 1029
War Manpower Commission (WMC), 767
Warner, Charles Dudley, 499
War Powers Act, 999
War Production Board (WPB), 766
War relocation centers, 773
Warren, Chief Justice Earl, 844, 887
Warren Commission, 896
Warren Court,
  Abington School District v. Schempp, 887
  Baker v. Carr, 887
  Brown v. Board of Education, 887
  Estelle v. Griswold, 887
  Gideon v. Wainwright, 888
  Loving v. Virginia, 887
  Memoirs v. Massachusetts, 887
  Miranda v. Arizona, 888
  Murray v. Curlett, 887
  Plessy v. Ferguson, 887
  Reynolds v. Sims, 887
  Roe v. Wade, 887
  Roth v. United States, 887
Washington, Booker T., 625, 627
Washington Conference, 748
Water-boarding, 1120
Watergate, 987, 1001–1002
"watering stock," 516

Watt, James, 1067
Watts riots, 907
Wealth Against Commonwealth (Lloyd), 541
Weather Underground, 951, 1036
Weaver, James B., 546
Weber, Ron, 957
Weddington, Sarah, 1044
Weimar Republic, 746
Weinberger, Caspar, 1078, 1084
Weisbrot, Robert, 891
Weiss, Carl, 726
Welfare capitalism, 729
Werthem, Dr. Frederic, 865
Wesler, Cynthia, 894
West, Elliott, 565
Western Electric, 522
Western swing music, 868
Western Union, 517
Westinghouse, George, 523
Westmoreland, General William, 923, 942, 953, 955, 956
Wetbacks, 850
Weyler, General Valeriano, 588
Whalen, Robert, 1039
Wheeler Dam, 723
Whigs,
  post Civil War, 492
Whip Inflation Now! (WIN), 1007
Whiskey Ring, 498
White Bird Canyon, 578
White Citizens Council, 845
White, Ed, 886
White flight, 860
Whitehead, Mathew J., 843
White House Plumbers, 998
White Leagues, 506
White primary, 843
White Revolution, 1014
Whites (the anti-Bolshevik forces), 796
White supremacy, 540, 1099
White, Walter, 770
Whitewater, 1109
White, William Allen, 756
Why We Can't Wait (King), 891
Wichita, 555
Wilderness Society, 1068
Wilhelm II, 649
Wilkins, Roy, 1030
Williamson, Joel, 841
Willkie, Wendell, 757, 767
Willow Run, 766
Wilson, Cicero, 950
Wilson, M. L., 716
Wilson, Woodrow,
  acceptance of social reform, 639
  Adamson Act, 639

Allies' war debt, 746
background of, 636
election of 1912, 634
Federal Highways Act, 639
first term of,
  banking and currency reforms, 637
  Clayton Antitrust Act, 638
  Federal Reserve Act, 637
  Federal Trade Commission Act, 638
  tariff reform, 637
foreign policy of, 646–648
Fourteen Points, 651
Keating-Owen Child Labor Act, 639, 642
New Freedom, 635
presidency of, 636–639
Revenue Act of 1916, 639
State of the Union Address, 637
Winfrey, Oprah, 1093
"Winter Soldier Investigation," 997
Wisconsin Idea, 623
Wisconsin Loyalty League, 659
Wisconsin Progressive Party, 731
Witcover, Jules, 970
Withholding tax deduction system, 767
Wobblies. *See* International Workers of the World
Woebbelin camp, 837
Wofford, Harris, 879, 889
Wolfe, Tom, 1019
Wolfowitz, Paul, 936, 1123
Woman of the Year, 737
Woman's Christian Temperance Union, 621
Women,
  abortion, 566
  after WW II, 854
  during WW II, 854
  family life, 855
  Ku Klux Klan and, 697
  portrayal in movies, 855
  suffrage,
    in the West, 566
    Progressive era crusade of the, 621
Women Accepted for Volunteer Emergency Service (WAVES), 768
Women Airforce Service Pilots (WASPs), 768
Women's Army Corps (WACs), 768
Women's Christian Temperance Union, 566, 691
Women's National Basketball Association, 1054
Wood, Leonard, 591, 655, 698
Woods, Rosemary, 985
Woodstock Music and Art Fair, 1050, 1052
Woodward, Bob, 987, 1001
Woolworth's, 876
Work Accidents and the Law (Eastman), 620
Workers' compensation laws, 620
Workingman's Party, 568
Works Progress Administration (WPA), 728
World Court, 70, 747
World Trade Center, 1108, 1118
World Trade Organization (WTO), 1108
World War I,
  African Americans in, 659
  American neutrality in, 650–651
  causes of, 648–651
  declaration of war, 655
  dissenters in, 658
  home front, 665–668
  League of Nations, 670
  naval and submarine warfare, 652
  postwar racism, 672
  propaganda in, 655
  suppression of civil liberties in, 658
  women in. 656
World War II,
  African Americans in, 770–771
  Attack on Pearl Harbor, 759–761
  Battle of Britain, 778
  Battle of Midway, 762
  Battle of Saipan, 785
  Battle of Stalingrad, 764
  Battle of the Atlantic, 764
  Battle of the Bulge, 771, 781
  Battle of the Coral Sea, 762
  Battle of the Philippine Sea 785
  Casablanca Conference, 778
  civilian sacrifice in, 768
  "Double V" campaign, 772
  end of the war, 782–783
  Enola Gay, 789
  financing of, 767–768
  Hispanics in, 772
  industrialization in, 765
  "island hopping" strategy 784
  Japanese American internment, 773
  Manhattan Project, 789
  mobilization of forces, 766
  Native American contributions, 772
  Operation Market-Garden, 781
  Operation OVERLORD, 780
  Operation TORCH, 776
  Pacific theater, 783
  Philippines fight, 785–786
  Potsdam Declaration, 789
  second front, 776
  Sicily, 777
  strategic bombing campaign of,, 778
  strategies of, 775
  Tehran Conference, 780
  women during, 768
  Yalta Conference, 781
Wounded Knee Massacre, 574
Wounded Knee, South Dakota, 1036
Wovoka, 553
Wozniak, Stephen, 1137
Wrath of Angels: The American Abortion War (Risen and Thomas), 1043
Wright, Herbert, 660
Wright, Jim, 1010

Y

Yalta Conference, 781
Yalu River, 816
Yarborough, Ralph, 895
Yellow journalism, 589
Yellow Peril, 605
Yeltsin, Boris, 1083
Yemen, 1150
Yosemite Valley, 632
Young, Charles, 660
Younger, Cole, 563
Young, Marilyn B., 920
Young, Neil, 996
Young Plan, 746
Youth International Party (Yippies), 974
Ypres, Battle of, 664
Yugoslavia, 669, 798, 1107
Yuppies, 1018

Z

Zapata, Emiliano, 647
Zeigler, Ron, 1002
Zelaya, Jose Santos, 608
Zimmermann, Arthur, 654
Zionists, 828
Zoning, 618
Zoot Suit Riots, 772